INTERNATIONAL LAW

INTERNATIONAL LAW

Third Edition

EDITED BY

MALCOLM D. EVANS

Professor of Public International Law, University of Bristol

OXFORD
UNIVERSITY PRESS

OXFORD

UNIVERSITY PRESS

Great Clarendon Street, Oxford OX2 6DP

Oxford University Press is a department of the University of Oxford.
It furthers the University's objective of excellence in research, scholarship,
and education by publishing worldwide in

Oxford New York

Auckland Cape Town Dar es Salaam Hong Kong Karachi
Kuala Lumpur Madrid Melbourne Mexico City Nairobi
New Delhi Shanghai Taipei Toronto

With offices in

Argentina Austria Brazil Chile Czech Republic France Greece
Guatemala Hungary Italy Japan Poland Portugal Singapore
South Korea Switzerland Thailand Turkey Ukraine Vietnam

Oxford is a registered trade mark of Oxford University Press
in the UK and in certain other countries

Published in the United States
by Oxford University Press Inc., New York

First published 2003
This edition 2010

British Library Cataloguing in Publication Data
Data available

Library of Congress Cataloging in Publication Data
International law / edited by Malcolm D. Evans.—3rd ed.
p. cm.
Includes bibliographical references and index.
ISBN 978-0-19-956566-5 (pbk.)
1. International law. I. Evans, Malcolm D. (Malcolm David), 1959-
KZ1242.I573 2010
341—dc22   2010014851

Typeset by Newgen Imaging Systems (P) Ltd., Chennai, India
Printed in Great Britain
on acid-free paper by
Ashford Colour Press Ltd, Gosport, Hampshire

ISBN 978-0-19-956566-5

3 5 7 9 10 8 6 4 2

OUTLINE CONTENTS

PART IV   THE SCOPE OF SOVEREIGNTY

PART V   RESPONSIBILITY

PART VI   RESPONDING TO BREACHES OF
INTERNATIONAL OBLIGATIONS

CONTENTS

PART II THE STRUCTURE OF INTERNATIONAL LEGAL OBLIGATION

PART III   THE SUBJECTS OF THE INTERNATIONAL
LEGAL ORDER

PART IV   THE SCOPE OF SOVEREIGNTY

11 JURISDICTION   313
Vaughan Lowe and Christopher Staker

12 INTERNATIONAL LAW AND RESTRAINTS ON THE
EXERCISE OF JURISDICTION BY NATIONAL COURTS OF STATES   340
Hazel Fox

PART V RESPONSIBILITY

PART VI   RESPONDING TO BREACHES OF INTERNATIONAL OBLIGATIONS

PART VII   THE APPLICATION OF INTERNATIONAL LAW

PREFACE TO THE THIRD EDITION

The second edition of International Law appeared in print only three years after the first edition and so changes were, by and large, incremental. This third edition appears four years on from then, and some seven years since the first edition. As a result, the time has come for a degree of change as well as for more general updating.

The aims and objectives, and the basic approach to their realization, are set out in the Editor's Introduction and remain unaltered. All chapters have been thoroughly updated to reflect the many developments in international law which have taken place over the last four years. The chief structural alteration is the addition of a new chapter by Spencer Zifcak on the newly emerging concept of 'the responsibility to protect', or the 'R2P', which is considered within the context of State responsibility rather than of the use of force (as is so often the case) since it is, perhaps, best seen as a means of broadening of the scope of international obligations than merely as a vehicle for intervention. Another structural change is the removal of the opening series of reflections on international law—a regrettable necessity given the need to prevent the book expanding too much in size. It is a fact of editorial life that revisions to chapters tends to make them longer rather than shorter, as new material supplements rather than supplants the old. I am therefore very grateful to all the contributors for updating and developing their chapters in ways which are both concise and comprehensive—and, of course, comprehensible!

A final development is the inclusion of entirely new chapters on a number of topics—by Matthew Craven on the Statehood, Self-determination, and Recognition, by Robert Cryer on International Criminal Law, and by David Turns on International Humanitarian Law (all topics which have come under close scrutiny and undergone significant development in recent times). In addition, Chris Staker has joined Vaughan Lowe in exploring and expounding the central issue of jurisdiction. I am immensely grateful to them all for their willingness to 'join the team'. Another 'new member of the team' is Jennifer Courage of OUP who has been tireless in ensuring that the text was submitted more or less on time and in keeping us all in order. Her work—along with that of all her colleagues at the Press—has been essential to the successful production of this edition.

It remains for me to hope that this new edition finds favour with its readers and continues to provide a means of furthering the education and understanding of students, scholars, and practitioners of international law.

Malcolm D Evans
April 2010

FROM THE EDITOR'S INTRODUCTION
TO THE FIRST EDITION

International law is a rich and varied subject, bearing upon most of the great issues facing individuals and communities. This work aims to capture something of that breadth and diversity by drawing on the knowledge and experience of a broad range of contributors who are intimately engaged in its teaching and practice. It is designed to present the essential elements of the international legal system in a clear and accessible fashion, but seeks to go further, addressing a number of key questions which challenge many of the assumptions upon which the international legal system is founded. It also seeks to provide a succinct introduction to a range of topics that are subject to increasingly detailed international regulation.

Parts I–VI consider the key building blocks of the subject whilst Part VII provides a series of introductory overviews of particular areas of contemporary interest. The structure, coverage, and level of the book are intended to reflect the requirements of undergraduate courses in public international law, although it will also be of use on general courses at the masters' levels as well as being of interest to academics and practitioners.

Although structured to form a coherent presentation of international law, each chapter can be read as a self-contained unit, balancing exposition with argument and reflecting the distinct perspective of its author(s). No attempt has been made to harmonize the views expressed or to produce a single 'voice'. Even if this had been possible, it would have been undesirable. As any teacher—as any lawyer—knows, opinions are best formed through exposure to competing argument. The chapters in this volume combine to address international law from a variety of perspectives: rather than one voice there is a range of voices and a range of opinions. It is to be hoped that this will be a source of stimulation, since the work as a whole aims to be more than just a compendium of knowledge. It aims to be a resource of value to all those interested in probing and testing the international legal enterprise.

NOTES ON CONTRIBUTORS

Ademola Abass LLM, PhD, is Professor of International Law and International Organization at Brunel University, West London and Associate of the Conflict, Security and Development Group (CSDG), King's College, University of London. He specializes in Public International Law, Collective Security Law, and International Criminal Law. His publications include *Regional Organisations and the Development of Collective Security: Beyond Chapter VIII of the UN Charter* (Oxford: Hart Publishing, 2004); *Protecting Human Security in Africa* (ed) (OUP, 2010, forthcoming), and *Complete International Law: Text, Cases and Materials* (OUP, 2011, forthcoming). He advises international organizations on matters of peace and security and served as the African Union's Expert on Regional Mechanisms. He is a member of the Academic Council on the United Nations Systems and a Fellow of the Cambridge Commonwealth Society.

Dapo Akande is University Lecturer in Public International Law at the University of Oxford and Yamani Fellow at St Peter's College, Oxford. He is also Co-Director of the Oxford Institute for Ethics, Law and Armed Conflict and has recently been Visiting Professor of Law at Yale Law School. He has published articles on international organizations, international criminal law, the law of armed conflict and international dispute settlement. He has acted as consultant to the African Union on the International Criminal Court and on Terrorism. He has also advised and assisted counsel in a number of international law cases before national and international courts.

Alan Boyle is Professor of Public International Law at the University of Edinburgh School of Law. His publications include *International Law and the Environment* (with PW Birnie and C Redgwell) and *The Making of International Law* (with C Chinkin). He is a barrister at Essex Court Chambers in London and has appeared before the ICJ, ITLOS and PCA.

Matthew Craven is Professor of Public International Law at the School of Oriental and African Studies, University of London. His publications include *The Decolonization of International Law: State Succession and the Law of Treaties* (2007) and *The International Covenant on Economic, Social and Cultural Rights: A Perspective on its Development* (1997).

James Crawford, SC, FBA is Whewell Professor of International Law, University of Cambridge. He was a member of the International Law Commission from 1992–2001 and in that capacity directed the ILC work on a Draft Statute for an International Criminal Court (1994) and was its Special Rapporteur on State Responsibility (1997–2001). He is a member of Matrix Chambers and has an extensive practice before international courts and tribunals.

Robert Cryer is Professor of International and Criminal Law at the University of Birmingham. His teaching and research interests are in international law, criminal law and legal theory. He is the author of, *inter alia*, *Prosecuting International Crimes: Selectivity and the International Criminal Law Regime* (Cambridge: CUP, 2005), and (with Neil Boister) *The Tokyo International Military Tribunal: A Reappraisal* (Oxford: OUP, 2008).

Eileen Denza was formerly Assistant Lecturer in Law, Bristol University, a Legal Counsellor to the Foreign and Commonwealth Office, Counsel to the EC Committee of the House of Lords and Visiting Professor of Law at University College London. Her publications include *Diplomatic Law* (3rd edn, 2008) and *The Intergovernmental Pillars of the European Union* (2002).

Malcolm D Evans, OBE, is Professor of Public International Law at the University of Bristol and a former Dean of its Faculty of Social Sciences and Law. His areas of special interest are the law of the sea and the international protection of human rights, and in particular the freedom of religion and the prevention of torture. His principal publications include *Religion and International Law in Europe* (1997) and (with Professor Rod Morgan) *Preventing Torture* (1998) and *Combating Torture in Europe* (2001). He is also a member of the United Nations Subcommittee for Prevention of Torture.

Professor Malgosia Fitzmaurice holds a chair of public international law at the Department of Law, Queen Mary, University of London. Her main interests include international environmental law, the law of treaties, the international water law and indigenous peoples. She has published widely on these subjects. She is a former secretary of the International Water Resources Committee and at present is a Co-Rapporteur of the Committee on Non-State Actors of the International Law Association. In 2001 she delivered The Hague Academy of International Law lecture on the topic of international environmental law. She participated in many international conferences and taught in many law schools abroad, the most recently at the University of Berkeley School of Law.

Hazel Fox CMG QC (Lady), Member of the Institut de Droit International, Bencher of Lincoln's Inn and Hon Fellow of Somerville College, University of Oxford; formerly Director of the British Institute of International and Comparative Law and General Editor of the *International and Comparative Quarterly*, author of the *Law of State Immunity* (2nd edn 2008).

Christine Gray, MA, PhD, is Professor in International Law at the University of Cambridge. She is author of *International Law and the Use of Force* (2008) and of *Judicial Remedies in International Law* (1990) as well as of many articles on the use of force.

Martti Koskenniemi, Professor of International Law, University of Helsinki, Hauser Global Visiting Professor of Law, New York University School of Law and a former member of the International Law Commission. His principal publications include *The Gentle Civilizer of Nations: The Rise and Fall of International Law 1870–1960* (Cambridge University Press, 2001) and *From Apology to Utopia: The Structure of International Legal Argument* (Reissue with a New Epilogue, Cambridge University Press, 2005).

Gerhard Loibl, Dr iur, LLB, Professor, Chair of International and European Law at the Diplomatic Academy of Vienna and Associate Professor at the University of Vienna. He has published widely on subjects of public international and European law, in particular in the area of international environmental and economic law and has participated in numerous international negotiations on behalf of Austria. In 2005 he delivered The Hague

Academy of International Law lecture on access to international justice with regard to environmental matters.

Vaughan Lowe QC is Chichele Professor of Public International Law and a Fellow of All Souls College, Oxford. He is an associé of the *Institut de Droit International* and a barrister practising from Essex Court Chambers, London.

Robert McCorquodale is the Director of the British Institute of International and Comparative Law, and Professor of International Law and Human Rights at the University of Nottingham. He is co-author of one of the leading texts in international law, *Cases and Materials on International Law* (Oxford University Press, 5th edn, 2010), and is on the editorial board of a number of respected academic journals. He has published widely about international law, especially on international human rights law and on the impact of non-state actors on international law.

John G Merrills, BCL, MA, is Professor of International Law (Emeritus) at the University of Sheffield, a former Dean of the Faculty of Law, and an Associate Member of the *Institut de Droit International*. He is the author of *International Dispute Settlement, Human Rights in Europe, Judge Sir Gerald Fitzmaurice and the Discipline of International Law* and several other books, as well as numerous articles in law reviews.

Stephen C Neff is a Reader in International Law at the University of Edinburgh, specializing in the history of international law. His publications include *Friends But No Allies: Economic Liberalism and the Law of Nations* (1990), *The Rights and Duties of Neutrals: A General History* (2000), and *War and the Law of Nations: A General History* (2005).

Phoebe N Okowa is Reader in Public International Law at Queen Mary, University of London. She has written extensively in many areas of Public International Law. Her most recent publication is *Environmental Law and Justice in Context* with Jonas Ebbesson (Cambridge University Press). She is also the co-editor of *Foundations of Public International Law* (Oxford University Press) and author of *State Responsibility for Transboundary Air Pollution in International Law* (Oxford University Press, 2000).

Simon Olleson, MA (Cantab), LLM (NYU), Dip Int Law (Cantab) is a barrister at 13 Old Square Chambers, Lincoln's Inn, London, specializing in public international law.

Catherine Redgwell, BA (Hons), LLB, MSc, is Professor of International Law at University College London and General Editor of the *International and Comparative Law Quarterly*. She has published extensively in the international law field within the areas of environmental law, energy law, and treaty law.

Iain Scobbie LLB (Hons) (Edin), LLB (Cantab), GDIL (ANU), PhD (Cantab), Sir Joseph Hotung Research Professor in Law, Human Rights and Peace Building in the Middle East at the School of Oriental and African Studies, University of London. He has written on diverse matters such as the jurisprudence and practice of the International Court, legal aspects of the Israel-Palestine question, and the law of armed conflict, as well as the theory of international law.

Dinah Shelton is the Mantt/Ahn Professor of Law at The George Washington University Law School, USA. She is a member of the Board of Editors of the *American Journal of International Law*, counsellor to the American Society of International Law, and a consultant to various international organizations. She has authored three prize-winning books on international human rights law and published numerous articles in journals throughout the world. In June 2009 she was elected to the Inter-American Commission on Human Rights for a four year term.

Christopher Staker, BA LLB (Hons) (Adelaide), DPhil (Oxford) is a barrister at 39 Essex Street Chambers in London. Positions that he has previously held include Deputy (Chief) Prosecutor of the Special Court for Sierra Leone (Freetown, Sierra Leone), Principal Legal Secretary at the International Court of Justice (The Hague, Netherlands), Senior Appeals Counsel at the International Criminal Tribunal for the Former Yugoslavia (The Hague), Counsel Assisting the Solicitor-General of Australia, and Counsel in the Office of International Law of the Australian Attorney-General's Department (Canberra, Australia). He has appeared as counsel before international and national courts, including the International Court of Justice, International Tribunal for the Law of the Sea, international criminal courts, and the High Court of Australia. He has authored various publications on international law and related areas.

Henry J Steiner, Jermiah Smith, Jr Professor of Law Emeritus at Harvard University, is founder and was director (1984–2005) of the Harvard Law School Human Rights Program, and was co-organizer and chair of the University Committee on Human Rights Studies. He has published articles on a broad range of human rights topics and is co-author of a leading coursebook, *International Human Rights in Context* (Oxford University Press, 3rd edn, 2008). He has lectured on human rights subjects in over 30 countries.

Hugh Thirlway, MA, LLB, Dr. en droit, spent most of his career in the legal department of the Registry of the International Court of Justice, including many years as Principal Legal Secretary and Head of Department, but he served also as Professor of International Law at the Graduate Institute of International Studies in Geneva; having now retired from the service of the ICJ he remains Visiting Professor at a number of European universities. Plans are well advanced for his long series of detailed and authoritative studies of the Court's case-law in the *British Yearbook of International Law* to be issued in a single publication, revised and updated.

David Turns is Senior Lecturer in International Laws of Armed Conflict at the Defence Academy of the United Kingdom (Cranfield University). From 1994 to 2007 he was Lecturer in Law at the University of Liverpool, and he taught previously at the London School of Economics. In 2002 he was a Visiting Professor at the Institute for International Law and International Relations, University of Vienna. Since 2008 he has been the Chairman of the UK National Group of the International Society for Military Law and the Law of War, and a Member of the Society's Board of Directors. He is on the Visiting Faculty of the International Institute of Humanitarian Law (San Remo) and the NATO School (Oberammergau), has taught on military staff and legal advisers' courses in several countries and has published widely in the field of international law.

Nigel D White is Professor of Public International Law at the University of Nottingham, formerly Professor of International Law at the University of Sheffield. In addition to publishing numerous articles and essays, he is author of several books including *Keeping the Peace: The United Nations and the Maintenance of International Peace and Security*

(Manchester University Press, 2nd edn, 1997), *The Law of International Organisations* (Manchester University Press, 2nd edn, 2005), *The UN System: Toward International Justice* (Lynne Rienner, 2002), and *Democracy Goes to War: British Military Deployments under International Law* (Oxford University Press, 2009). He is also editor of a number of leading collections, primarily *Collective Security Law* (Ashgate, 2004), and co-editor of *The UN, Human Rights and Post Conflict Situations* (Manchester University Press, 2005), *International Conflict and Security Law* (Cambridge University Press, 2005), *European Security Law* (Oxford University Press, 2007), and *International Law and Dispute Settlement* (Hart, 2010). He is co-editor-in-chief of the *Journal of Conflict and Security Law* published by Oxford University Press; and is co-editor of the UK's contribution to *International Law in Domestic Courts* also published on-line by Oxford University Press.

Chanaka Wickremasinghe is an Assistant Legal Adviser to the Foreign and Commonwealth Office. He was formerly a lecturer in law at Bristol University and a research officer at the British Institute of International and Comparative Law.

Spencer Zifcak is Allan Myers Professor of Law and Director of the Institute of Legal Studies at the Australian Catholic University. He is also Benjamin Meaker Visiting Professor in the Institute of Advanced Studies at the University of Bristol. His principal interests are in public international law, international organizations and international human rights law. His most recent books are *United Nations Reform: Heading North or South* and *Globalisation and the Rule of Law*, both published by Routledge.

ABBREVIATIONS

AALCC	African Asian Legal Consultative Committee
ACHR	American Convention on Human Rights
AFP	Australian Federal Police
AIA	Advanced Informed Agreement
AJIL	*American Journal of International Law*
ARSIWA	Articles on the Responsibility of States for Internationally Wrongful Acts
ASCOBANS	Agreement on the Conservation of Small Cetaceans of the Baltic and North Seas
ASEAN	Association of Southeast Asian Nations
ATCA	Alien Tort Claims Act (US)
AU	African Union
BCN	biological, chemical, nuclear (weapon)
BITs	Bilateral Investment Treaties
BverfGE	*Die Entscheidungen des Bundesverfassungsgerichts*
BYIL	*British Yearbook of International Law*
CAFTA	Central American Free Trade Agreement
CBD	Convention on Conservation of Biological Diversity
CCAMLR	Convention on the Conservation of Antarctic Marine Living Resources
CCSBT	Commission for the Conservation of Southern Bluefin Tuna
CEDAW	Convention on the Elimination of All Forms of Discrimination Against Women
CERD	International Convention on the Elimination of All Forms of Racial Discrimination
CESCR	Committee on Economic, Social and Cultural Rights
CFC	Convention on Fisheries and Conservation of the Living Resources of the High Seas
CFCs	chlorofluorocarbons
CFI	Court of First Instance
CIS	Commonwealth of Independent States
CITES	Convention on International Trade in Endangered Species
CLC	Convention on Civil Liability for Oil Pollution Damage
CMLR	*Common Market Law Review*
COP	Conference of the Parties
CSC	Continental Shelf Convention
CSCE	Conference on Security and Cooperation in Europe
DARIO	Draft Articles on the Responsibility of International Organizations
DEA	Drugs Enforcement Agency
DRC	Democratic Republic of the Congo
DSB	Dispute Settlement Body

DSU	Dispute Settlement Understanding
EAC	East African Community
EBRD	European Bank for Reconstruction and Development
EC	European Community
ECE	(United Nations) Economic Commission for Europe
ECHR	European Convention on Human Rights
ECJ	European Court of Justice
ECOMOG	Economic Community of West African States Monitoring Group
ECOSOC	Economic and Social Council
ECOWAS	Economic Community of West African States
ECSI	European Convention on State Immunity
ECtHR	European Court of Human Rights
EEC	European Economic Community
EEZ	Exclusive Economic Zone
EFZ	Exclusive Fishing Zone
EHRR	*European Human Rights Review*
EJIL	*European Journal of International Law*
EU	European Union
EUROFIMA	European Company for the Financing of Railroad Rolling Stock
FAO	Food and Agriculture Organization
FATF	Financial Action Task Force
FCCC	Framework Convention on Climate Change
FCN	Friendship, Commerce and Navigation (Treaties)
FCO	Foreign and Commonwealth Office
FGM	Female Genital Mutilation
FRY	Federal Republic of Yugoslavia
FSIA	Foreign Sovereign Immunities Act (US)
GA	General Assembly
GAB	General Agreements to Borrow
GATS	General Agreement on Trade in Services
GATT	General Agreement on Tariffs and Trade
GEF	Global Environmental Facility
HCHR	High Commissioner for Human Rights
HIPC	Heavily Indebted Poor Countries
HRC	Human Rights Committee
HRLJ	*Human Rights Law Journal*
HSC	High Seas Convention
IAC	Iraqi Airways Company
IACHR	Inter-American Commission on Human Rights
IAEA	International Atomic Energy Authority
IBRD	International Bank for Reconstruction and Development (World Bank)
ICAO	International Civil Aviation Organization
ICBP	International Council for Bird Preservation
ICC	International Criminal Court
ICCPR	International Covenant on Civil and Political Rights
ICESCR	International Covenant on Economic, Social and Cultural Rights

ICISS	International Commission on Intervention and State Sovereignty
ICJ	International Court of Justice
ICLQ	*International and Comparative Law Quarterly*
ICOMOS	International Council on Monuments and Sites
ICRC	International Committee of the Red Cross
ICSID	International Centre for the Settlement of Investment Disputes
ICTR	International Criminal Tribunal for Rwanda
ICTY	International Criminal Tribunal for the Former Yugoslavia
IDA	International Development Agency
IFAD	International Fund for Agricultural Development
IFC	International Finance Corporation
IGAD	Intergovernmental Authority on Development
IGO	Inter-Governmental Organization
IHL	International Humanitarian Law
IHRR	*International Human Rights Reports*
ILA	International Law Association
ILC	International Law Commission
ILM	International Legal Materials
ILO	International Labour Organization
ILR	International Law Reports
IMF	International Monetary Fund
IMO	International Maritime Organization
IMT	International Military Tribunal
IPCC	Intergovernmental Panel on Climate Change
Iran-USCTR	Iran-US Claims Tribunal Reports
ISA	International Seabed Authority
ITC	International Tin Council
ITLOS	International Tribunal for the Law of the Sea
ITO	International Trade Organization
ITTA	International Tropical Timber Agreement
ITU	International Telecommunications Union
IUCN	International Union for the Conservation of Nature
IWRB	International Waterfowl and Wetlands Research Bureau
KAC	Kuwait Airways Corporation
LMO	Living Modified Organism
LNTS	League of Nations Treaty Series
LOAC	Law of Armed Conflict
LOSC	Law of the Sea Convention
LRTAP	Long-Range Transboundary Air Pollution
MAI	Multilateral Agreement on Investment
MARPOL	International Convention for the Prevention of Pollution from Ships
MERCOSUR	Mercado Común del Sur or Mercado Común del Cono Sur
MIGA	Multilateral Investment Guarantee Agency
NAB	New Arrangements to Borrow
NAFO	North Atlantic Fisheries Organization
NAFTA	North American Free Trade Agreement

NAM	Non-Aligned Movement
NATO	North Atlantic Treaty Organization
NGOs	Non-Governmental Organizations
NLM	National Liberation Movement
NYBIL	*Netherlands Yearbook of International Law*
nyr	not yet reported
OAPEC	Organization of Arab Petroleum Exporting Countries
OAS	Organization of American States
OASTS	Organization of American States Treaty Series
OAU	Organization of African Unity
ODIL	*Ocean Development and International Law*
OECD	Organization for Economic Cooperation and Development
OECS	Organization of East Caribbean States
OEEC	Organization for European Economic Cooperation
ONUC	United Nations Operation in the Congo (Organisation des Nations Unies au Congo)
ONUCA	United Nations Observer Group in Central America
OPEC	Organization of Petroleum Exporting Countries
OSCE	Organization for Security and Cooperation in Europe
OSPAR	Convention for the Protection of the Marine Environment of the North-East Atlantic
PCIJ	Permanent Court of International Justice
PLO	Palestine Liberation Organization
PMSC	Private Military Security Company
POPs	Persistent Organic Pollutants
POW	Prisoner of War
PSI	Proliferation Security Initiative
R2P	Responsibility to Protect
Recueil des Cours	*Recueil des cours de l'Académie de droit international*
RFB	Regional Fisheries Body
RFMO	Regional Fisheries Management Organisation
RGDIP	*Revue General de Droit International Public*
RIAA	*Reports of International Arbitral Awards*
RSC	Rules of the Supreme Court (UK)
SADC	South African Development Community
SBDC	Sea-Bed Disputes Chamber
SC	Security Council
SCSL	Special Court for Sierra Leone
SDR	Special Drawing Rights
SFRY	Socialist Federal Republic of Yugoslavia
SIA	State Immunity Act 1978 (UK)
SPS	Sanitary and Phytosanitary Measures
SSC	UN Agreement on Straddling Stocks and Highly Migratory Species
STL	Special Tribunal for Lebanon
SUA Convention	Rome Convention on the Suppression of Unlawful Acts Against the Safety of Maritime Navigation

TAC	Total Allowable Catch
TNCs	Transnational Corporations
TPRM	Trade Policy Review Mechanism
TRAFFIC	Trade Records Analysis of Flora and Fauna in Commerce
TRIMs	Trade-Related Investment Measures
TRIPS	Agreement on Trade-Related Aspects of Intellectual Property Rights
TSC	Territorial Sea and Contiguous Zone Convention
UAE	United Arab Emirates
UEMO	Union Economique de Monétaire Ouest-Africaine
UKTS	United Kingdom Treaty Series
UN	United Nations
UNAMIR	United Nations Assistance Mission for Rwanda
UNCC	United Nations Compensation Commission
UNCITRAL	United Nations Commission on International Trade Law
UNCLOS	United Nations Conference on the Law of the Sea
UNCTAD	United Nations Conference on Trade and Development
UNDP	United Nations Development Programme
UNEF	United Nations Emergency Force
UNEP	United Nations Environment Programme
UNESCO	United Nations Educational, Scientific and Cultural Organization
UNGA	United Nations General Assembly
UNHCR	United Nations High Commissioner for Refugees
UNICEF	United Nations International Children's Economic Foundation
UNIDO	United Nations Industrial Development Organization
UNITA	União Nacional para a Independência Total de Angola
UNMIK	United Nations Mission in Kosovo
UNOSOM	United Nations Operation in Somalia
UNPROFOR	United Nations Protection Force
UNSCR	UN Security Council Resolution
UNTAET	United Nations Transitional Administration in East Timor
UNTS	United Nations Treaty Series
UNYB	*United Nations Yearbook*
UPU	Universal Postal Union
VCCR	Vienna Convention on Consular Relations
VCDR	Vienna Convention on Diplomatic Relations
VCLT	Vienna Convention on the Law of Treaties
WEOG	Western Europe and Others Group (Nations)
WHC	World Heritage Convention
WHO	World Health Organization
WIPO	World Intellectual Property Organization
WMO	World Meteorological Organization
WTO	World Trade Organization
WWF	World Wildlife Fund
YBIEL	*Yearbook of International Environmental Law*
YBILC	*Yearbook of the International Law Commission*
YIHL	*Yearbook of International Humanitarian Law*

TABLE OF INTERNATIONAL INSTRUMENTS AND OTHER DOCUMENTS

TABLE OF DOMESTIC INSTRUMENTS BY COUNTRY

TABLE OF INTERNATIONAL CASES

TABLE OF DOMESTIC CASES
BY COUNTRY

PART I
THE HISTORY
AND THEORY OF
INTERNATIONAL LAW

1

A SHORT HISTORY OF INTERNATIONAL LAW

Stephen C Neff

SUMMARY

This history will emphasize broad trends in international law, in both the conceptual sphere and in State practice. The discussion will move chronologically, beginning with a cursory look at the ancient world, followed by a rather fuller discussion of the great era of natural law in the European Middle Ages. The classical period (1600–1815) witnessed the emergence of a dualistic view of international law, with the law of nature and the law of nations co-existing (more or less amicably). In the nineteenth century—the least known part of international law—doctrinaire positivism was the prevailing viewpoint, though not the exclusive one. Regarding the inter-war years, developments both inside and outside the League of Nations will be considered. Since the post-1945 period will occupy most of the remainder of this book, this discussion will confine itself to a few historically-oriented comments on some of its most general features.

I. INTRODUCTION

No area of international law has been so little explored by scholars as the history of the subject. This is a remarkable state of affairs, probably without parallel in any other academic discipline (including other branches of law). Although this intellectual scandal (as it well deserves to be called) is now being remedied, we are still only in the earliest stages of the serious study of international legal history. Many blank spots exist, some of which will be identified in passing in the discussion below.

This short history—inevitably *very* short history—can give only the most general flavour of the major periods of development of international law. It will accordingly not be possible to give more than the most token attention to developments outside the Western mainstream. Both ideas and State practice will be covered. The ideas chiefly concern what international law was thought to consist of in past times. State practice is concerned with what States actually *did*. It was the two in combination—if not always in close harmony—that made international law what it became.

II. ANCIENT WORLDS

For a vivid indication of how persons from even the most diverse cultures can relate to one another in a peaceful, predictable, and mutually beneficial fashion, it is difficult to top Herodotus's description of 'silent trading' between the Carthaginians and an unnamed North African tribe in about the sixth century BC. When the Carthaginians arrived in the tribe's area by ship, they would unload a pile of goods from their vessels, leave them on the beach and then return to their boats and send a smoke signal. The natives would then come and inspect the goods on their own, leave a pile of gold, and retire. Then the Carthaginians would return; and, if satisfied that the gold represented a fair price, they would take it and depart. If not satisfied, they would again retire to their ships; and the natives would return to leave more gold. The process would continue until both sides were content, at which point the Carthaginians would sail away with their gold, without a word exchanged between the two groups. 'There is perfect honesty on both sides', Herodotus assures us, with no problems of theft or conflict (Herodotus, *Histories*, p 336).

This silent trading arrangement may have been successful in its way, but a process of interaction so inflexibly ritualistic and so narrow in subject matter could hardly suffice for political interactions between States, even in ancient times. Most people probably have the feeling that something rather more elaborate is required to merit the grand name of 'international law'. Indeed, the ambiguity of the term 'international law' leads to various different answers to the question of when international law 'began'. If by 'international law' is meant merely the ensemble of methods or devices which give an element of pre-dictability to international relations (as in the silent-trading illustration), then the origin may be placed virtually as far back as recorded history itself. If by 'international law' is meant a more or less comprehensive substantive code of conduct applying to nations, then the late classical period and Middle Ages was the time of its birth. If 'international law' is taken to mean a set of substantive principles applying *uniquely* to States as such, then the seventeenth century would be the starting time. If 'international law' is defined as the integration of the world at large into something like a single community under a rule of law, then the nineteenth century would be the earliest date (perhaps a trifle optimistically). If, finally, 'international law' is understood to mean the enactments and judicial decisions of a world government, then its birth lies (if at all) somewhere in the future—and, in all likelihood, the distant future at that.

If we take the most restricted of these definitions, then we could expect to find the best evidence for a nascent international law in the three areas of ancient Eurasia that were characterized by dense networks of small, independent States sharing a more or less common religious and cultural value system: Mesopotamia (by, say, the fourth or third millennium BC), northern India (in the Vedic period after about 1600 BC), and classical Greece. Each of these three State systems was characterized by a combination of political fragmentation and cultural unity. This enabled a number of fairly standard practices to emerge, which helped to place inter-State relations on at least a somewhat stable and pre-dictable footing. Three particular areas provide evidence of this development: diplomatic relations, treaty-making, and the conduct of war.[1] A major additional contribution of the Greek city-States was the practice of arbitration of disputes, of which there came to be a very impressive body of practice (see Ager, 1996).

It was not inordinately difficult for some of these practices to extend across deeper cultural lines as well. One of the earliest surviving treaty texts is between Egypt and the Hittite Empire, from the thirteenth century BC. The agreement concerned an imperial division of spheres of influence, but it also dealt with the extradition of fugitives. The problem of good faith and binding force was ensured by enlisting the gods of both nations (two thousand strong in all) to act as guardians (Bederman, 2001, pp 147–150).

With the advent of the great universal religions, far more broadly-based systems of world order became possible. One outstanding example was the Islamic empire of the seventh century AD and afterwards. Significantly, the body of law on relations between States within the Muslim world (the *Dar al-Islam*, or 'House of Islam') was much richer than that regarding relations with the outside world (the *Dar al-Harb*, or 'House of war'). But even with infidel States and nationals, a number of pragmatic devices evolved to permit relations to occur in predictable ways—such as 'temporary' truces (in lieu of treaties) or safe-conducts issued to individuals (sometimes on a very large scale).[2]

In Western history, the supreme exemplar of the multinational empire was Rome. But the Roman Empire was, in its formative period, a somewhat tentative and ramshackle affair, without an over-arching ethical or religious basis comparable to the Islamic religion in the later Arab empire. That began to change, however, when certain philosophical concepts were imported from Greece (from about the second century BC). The most important of these was the idea of a set of universal principles of justice: the belief that, amidst the welter of varying laws of different States, certain substantive rules of conduct were present in *all* human societies. This idea first surfaced in the writings of Aristotle (*Rhetoric*, p 1370). But it was taken much further by the philosophers of the Stoic school, who envisaged the entire world as a single 'world city-State' (or *kosmopolis*) governed by the law of nature. Cicero, writing under Stoic influence, characterized this law of nature as being 'spread through the whole human community, unchanging and eternal' (Cicero, *Republic*, pp 68–69).

This concept of a universal and eternal natural law was later adopted by two other groups, the Roman lawyers and the Christian Church, and then bequeathed by them to medieval Europe. The lawyers in particular made a distinction that would have a very long life ahead of it: between a *jus naturale* (or natural law properly speaking) and a *jus gentium* (or law of peoples). The two were distinct, but at the same time so closely interconnected that the differences between them were often very easily ignored. Natural law was the broader concept. It was something like what we would now call a body of scientific laws, applicable not just to human beings but to the whole animal kingdom as well. The *jus gentium* was the human component, or sub-category, of it. Just as the law of nature was universal in the natural world, so was the *jus gentium* universal in the *human* world.

---

[1] On the Middle Eastern and Greek practice, see generally Bederman, 2001. On ancient India, see Bhatia, 1977.

[2] On Islamic views of international law, see generally Khadduri, 1955.

III. THE MIDDLE AGES: THE NATURAL LAW ERA

The European Middle Ages offers an intriguing picture of dizzying variety and complexity, combined—not always very coherently—with the most sweeping universality. The variety was most apparent in the de-centralized world of feudalism, with its complex and interlocking layers of rights and duties, and its diffusion of governmental powers and jurisdictions. The universality was evident in two major spheres: philosophically and jurisprudentially, in the continued stress on natural law; and politically, in the Holy Roman Empire and in the revival of Roman law which underpinned it.

A. THE UNIVERSALIST OUTLOOK: MEDIEVAL NATURAL LAW

The European Middle Ages became the great age of natural-law thought. During this period, natural-law conceptions developed under the umbrella of the Catholic Church. But it must be remembered that the idea was not specifically Christian in its inception, but rather was a legacy of the classical Stoic and Roman legal traditions. The dominant tradition—represented outstandingly by Thomas Aquinas—was rationalist in outlook, holding the content of the natural law to be susceptible of discovery and application by means of human reason rather than of revelation.

Natural law is one of the many parts of international law that have never received the systematic study that they merit. In the present context, only a few of its most salient features can be noted.[3] Perhaps its single most outstanding feature was its all-embracing character. It encompassed and regulated the natural and social life of the universe in all its infinite variety—from the movements of the stars in their courses to the gurgling of the four humours through the veins and arteries of the human body, from the thoughts and deeds of all of the creatures of land, sea, and air, to those of human beings and the angels in the heavens. Its strictures applied universally to all cultures and civilizations, past, present, and future.

There continued to be, as in the ancient period, a distinction between the *jus naturale* and the *jus gentium*, though still without any very sharp line between the two. The *jus gentium* was much the lesser of the two, being seen largely as an application of the broader natural law to specifically human affairs. Sometimes it was regarded as comprising universal customs of purely human creation—and therefore as a sort of supplement to natural law properly speaking. These *jus gentium* rules were sometimes referred to as 'secondary' natural-law rules. It must be stressed that this original *jus gentium* did not consist entirely, or even primarily, of what would now be called rules of international law. Instead, it was a collection of laws common to all nations, affecting individuals in all walks of life, from the highest to the lowest, and dealing with all aspects of human social affairs—contract, property, crime, and the like. It was more in the nature of an ethical system of universal or trans-cultural scope, setting out general norms of conduct, as opposed to a legal code with a list of prohibitions and punishments. One aspect of this grand intellectual scheme should be particularly stressed: the fact that there was no strong tendency to think that any body of law existed that was applicable *uniquely* to international relations as such. States,

---

[3] For a good short account of medieval natural-law theory, see generally Gierke, 1938.

like private persons, were permitted lawfully to wage war for such purposes as the punishment of wickedness or, generally, for the enforcement of the law—but not for vainglory or conquest or oppression.[4] This in fact was the conceptual kernel of natural law's most outstanding contribution to international law: the doctrine of the just war.

B. THE PLURALIST OUTLOOK: THE ITALIAN CITY-STATES

Even if (as the natural-law writers maintained) the whole of human society formed a single moral and ethical community, there was no denying that the world also consisted of a welter of different polities, of a bewildering variety of sorts, and of varying degrees of independence from one another—extending all the way from the great empire of Rome itself (ie, of Byzantium) to the patchwork of feudal jurisdictions which carpeted Western Europe.

Nowhere was the tension between the universalistic and the pluralistic tendencies of the period more evident, in practice, than in the debates over the legal status of the various 'independent' city-states of northern Italy. These obtained substantial *de facto* independence from the Holy Roman Empire in the late twelfth century, when the cities of the Lombard League defeated the forces of Emperor Frederick I. There was, however, considerable debate over what this 'independence' really meant. To this matter, two of the most prominent medieval lawyers—Bartolus of Sassoferato and his student Baldus of Ubaldis, who both wrote in the fourteenth century—turned their attention. Broadly speaking, the conclusion of Bartolus (largely echoed by Baldus) was that the cities were independent in the sense of being wholly self-governing and independent of *one another*, but that, in their relations *inter se*, they continued to be subject to rules of the Empire. Here we see the first glimmer, in European society, of the concept of independence of States operating in conjunction—sometimes very uneasily—with subjection to a larger set of norms governing inter-State relations (Hinsley, 1986, pp 81–82, 88–90, 167–174). For this reason, Bartolus has been called, with some justice, the first theorist of international law (Sereni, 1943, pp 58–63).

C. DEVELOPMENTS IN STATE PRACTICE

It is from the pluralist rather than the universalist side of the great medieval conceptual divide that we must look for innovations in State practice. The reason is easily seen: it is in the day-to-day relation of different States and peoples with one another that the practical problems of law are most likely to arise.

Much of the State practice in the Middle Ages consisted of traditional ways inherited from ancient times. The area of diplomatic relations is an example, with diplomats increasingly being accorded a broad (but not absolute) degree of immunity from judicial process in host States. Beginning in about the eleventh century, European (chiefly Italian) States began to conclude bilateral treaties that spelled out various reciprocal guarantees of fair treatment. These agreements, sometimes concluded with Muslim States, granted a range of privileges to the foreign merchants based in the contracting States, such as the right

---

[4] For a thorough exposition of medieval just-war theory, see Russell, 1975. For a shorter account, see Neff, 2005, pp 44–68.

to use their own law and courts when dealing with one another. The same process was at work in the sphere of maritime trading. The seafaring community made use of the laws of Oléron (which were actually a series of court decisions from the small island of that name in the Bay of Biscay), and also of a code of rules called the *Consolato del Mare*, compiled in about the thirteenth century for the maritime community of Barcelona. These codes governed the broad range of maritime activities, including the earliest rules on the rights of neutral traders in wartime.

Certain aspects of the conduct of war witnessed a high level of refinement in the Middle Ages—most notably the law on the ransoming of prisoners of war (a welcome step forward from the alternatives of enslavement and summary killing). 'The law of arms' (as it was known) was expounded in the fourteenth century, first by John of Legnano and later by a monk named Honoré de Bonet (or Bouvet), whose book entitled *The Tree of Battles*, of the 1380s, became very influential.[5] Accounts of medieval warfare, however, incline observers to harbour grave doubts as to whether even these practical rules exerted much real influence.

With the European explorations of Africa and, particularly, the New World from the fourteenth century onward, questions of relations with non-European societies assumed an urgent importance—while, at the same time, posing an immense practical test for the universality of natural law. The Spanish conquest of the Indian kingdoms in the New World sparked especially vigorous legal and moral debates (even if only after the fact). The Dominican scholar, Francisco de Vitoria, in a series of lectures at the University of Salamanca, concluded that the Spanish conquest was justified, on the ground that the Indians had unlawfully attempted to exclude Spanish traders from their kingdoms, contrary to natural-law rules. But he also confessed that his blood froze in his veins at the thought of the terrible atrocities committed by the Spanish in the process.[6] In 1550–51, there occurred one of the major legal confrontations of history, when two prominent figures—Juan Inés de Sepúlveda and Barolomé de las Casas—debated, at length, the lawfulness and legal bases of the Spanish conquest of the New World, under the judgeship of the theologian and philosopher Domingo de Soto. The result, alas, was inconclusive, as Soto declined to render a judgment (Pagden, 2001, pp 77–79).

In short, medieval international law was a jumble of different beliefs and practices—from the rarefied conceptions of the law of nature, to the more serviceable rules by which various communities conducted their actual day-to-day business, from warfare and diplomacy, to buying and selling.

IV. THE CLASSICAL AGE (1600–1815)

In the seventeenth and eighteenth centuries, a new spirit entered into doctrinal thought on international law. This is sometimes put in terms of a secularization of natural-law thought. That, however, is a very misleading characterization, since natural-law itself was (and had always been) primarily secular in nature. What was new in the seventeenth

---

[5] On medieval law on the conduct of war, see Keen, 1965.
[6] Vitoria, 'On the American Indians', in *Political Writings*, pp 231–292; Letter to Miguel de Arcos, ibid, pp 331–333.

century was a willingness to give a degree of formal recognition to State practice as a true source of law, rather than regarding it as merely illustrative of natural-law principles. The result was a kind of dualistic outlook, with natural law and State practice maintaining a wary, and rather uneasy, form of co-existence—a state of affairs much in evidence to the present day.

A. GROTIUS AND HOBBES

The principal harbinger of this new outlook was the Dutch writer Hugo Grotius, whose major work *On the Law of War and Peace* was published in Paris in 1625—a work so dense and rich that one could easily spend a lifetime studying it (as a number of scholars have).[7] As a natural-law writer, he was a conservative, writing squarely in the rationalist tradition inherited from the Middle Ages. In international law specifically, he had important forerunners, most notably the Italian writer, Alberico Gentili, who produced the first truly systematic study of the law of war at the end of the sixteenth century.[8]

Where Grotius did break important new ground—and where he fully earned the renown that still attaches to his name—was in his transformation of the old *jus gentium* into something importantly different, called the *law of nations*. The distinctive feature of this law of nations was that it was regarded as something distinct from the law of *nature*, rather than as a sub-category or means of application of natural law. Furthermore, and most significantly, this law of nations was not regarded (like the old *jus gentium*) as a body of law governing human social affairs in general. Instead, it was a set rules applying specifically to one particular and distinctive category of human beings: rulers of States. Now, for the first time in history, there was a clear conception of a systematic body of law applicable specifically to the relationship between nations. Eventually, although not until the late eighteenth century, the label 'international law' would be applied to this corpus of rules—with Jeremy Bentham as the coiner of the term (Nussbaum, 1947, pp 135–136).

It should be appreciated that Grotius's law of nations, or 'voluntary law' as it was sometimes known, was not designed to supplant or undermine traditional natural law. Far from it. The function of this law of nations was basically an interstitial one—of filling gaps where the natural-law principles were too general, or devising workable rules as pragmatic substitutes where the application of the strict natural law was, for some reason, unfeasible. The law of nature and the law of nations, in short, were seen as partners rather than as rivals. For this reason, the earliest academic chairs in the field were commonly designated as being devoted to 'the law of nature and nations', in (presumably) happy partnership. The first such chair was occupied by Samuel Pufendorf, at the University of Heidelberg in 1661. In the English-speaking world, the first one was created at the University of Edinburgh in 1707.

There were some, however, who contended that the partnership between the law of nature and the law of nations was anything but a happy one. Foremost amongst these

---

[7] Much of the study of Grotius has been by political scientists rather than specifically by international lawyers. Remarkably, there is no comprehensive and accessible survey of his international legal thought and influence in English. For an older work that is still of value, see Knight, 1925. For a brief overview of his legal thought, see Tuck, 1999, pp 78–108. For a more thorough study, see Haggenmacher, 1983.

[8] On Gentili, see generally Van der Molen, 1968.

dissidents was the English writer Thomas Hobbes, whose master work *Leviathan* was written in 1651, shortly after Grotius's death. In sharp contrast to Grotius, Hobbes denied that the pre-political condition of human society had been orderly and law-governed. He maintained, instead, that it was a chaotic, even violent, world, with self-preservation as the only true natural right (Hobbes, *Leviathan*, pp 80–84). Security could only be attained by the radical step of having all of the persons in a state of nature surrender their natural rights to a sovereign power of their own creation—with the result that, henceforth, the *only* law which they would live under would be the law promulgated by that sovereign. Natural law was not rejected in its entirety, but it was radically stripped-down, to the point of being reduced, in essence to two fundamental tenets: a right of self-preservation, and a duty to perform contracts or promises. It was this stripped-down version of natural law which, in the opinion of Hobbes, constituted the sole body of law between independent nation-states.

On this thesis, the only possible way in which States could construct a stable international system was through the painstaking process of entering into agreements whenever this proved feasible. The natural-law duty to perform promises was the fundamental basis of this system, with the detailed substantive rules being provided by the various agreements that were actually concluded. These agreements could take either of two forms: written or unwritten. The written form, of course, comprised treaties, of the sort of that States had been concluding for many centuries. The unwritten form was customary law, which in this period was seen predominantly as simply a tacit or unwritten treaty.

It is hardly surprising that, amongst traditional natural lawyers (ie, followers of Grotius), Hobbes's conclusions were unwelcome in the extreme, since they entailed the ruthless discarding of so much of the content of traditional natural law. But they were also not easily refuted. Some writers, such as Pufendorf, attempted to take at least some of Hobbes's ideas into account, while still adhering to the older idea of a detailed, substantive natural law. Others basically ignored the Hobbesian challenge as best they could and continued to expound natural law in a systematic manner. In fact, the seventeenth and eighteenth centuries were the great age of systematic jurisprudence, in which natural law was re-housed (it might be said) in grand logical edifices of a hypothetico-deductive nature, modelled on that most magnificent of all intellectual constructions, mathematics.

The culmination of this systematic natural-law movement came in the mid-eighteenth century, at the hands of the German philosopher Christian Wolff, who fittingly had been trained as a mathematician. Wolff's massive eight-volume encyclopaedia of natural law contained detailed discussions of practically everything under the sun and even beyond (including a discourse on the characteristics of the inhabitants of other planets)—while paying virtually no heed to State practice. It holds an honourable place on the list of the world's great unread masterpieces.[9]

The most famous and influential writer in the Grotian tradition was the Swiss diplomat Emmerich de Vattel, whose famous exposition of *The Law of Nations* was published in London in 1758. As the first systematic international-law treatise of the modern kind, it would not

---

[9] On Wolff's cosmological views, see Wolff, *Cosmologia*. Only the final volume of the main work on natural law concerned international law. For an English translation, see Wolff, *Law of Nations Treated According to a Scientific Method*.

look drastically out of place on a twenty-first century bookshelf, as the works of Grotius or Wolff certainly would. Instead of setting out a grand philosophical scheme, Vattel's intention was to provide a sort of handbook for lawyers and statesmen. Moreover, its graceful style ensured it a wider usage by lawyers, judges, and lay persons than any other international-law writing had previously had. It can make a good claim to being the greatest international-law textbook ever written. With it, we stand at the threshold of modern international-law writing.[10]

In a number of ways, Vattel's treatise was a popularization of Wolff's ideas, but it was written in a very different spirit. Where Wolff had been disdainful of the voluntary law, Vattel fully embraced it, cheerfully and candidly expounding it alongside the natural law whenever appropriate. He has been accused of inconsistency—of constantly being on both sides of issues—but that charge is unfair. The fact is that he had two bodies of law to expound, which sometimes provided differing solutions to practical problems. He was generally very forthright about which law he was treating at any given time. It is we who tend to misunderstand the nature of his task because the dualistic mentality of that era is so foreign to us.

The best example of the dualistic 'method' concerned war. The natural law on just wars allowed a State to resort to force in self-help to vindicate a legal right that had actually been violated (or was threatened with violation)—so that, in a given conflict, one side would be fighting justly, and the other one not. The voluntary law, however, was not concerned over which party had the stronger legal claim to use force (ie, it did not deal with the *jus ad bellum*, in legal terminology). Instead, it simply treated each side *as if* it had lawfully resorted to war. It then contented itself with regulating the conduct of wars, fixing rules for both parties to apply, on an even-handed basis, in their contention against one another (the *jus in bello*, in the common legal parlance). In effect, then, the natural law saw war in terms of law enforcement and as a sanction for wrongdoing. The voluntary law, in contrast, saw war more in terms of a duel.

B. THE LAWS OF NATURE AND NATIONS IN ACTION

The writing of Grotius and Hobbes and their followers was not done in a vacuum. Various forces were at work in this period, which served to give this new law of nations a concrete reality. One of the most important of these trends was the emergence (gradual to be sure) of strong central governments, at least in Western Europe, which increasingly gained the upper hand over the older, diffused jurisdictions of the feudal age. Particularly important for this trend was the innovation of standing armies in place of the older temporary feudal levies. In addition, these centralizing Nation-States were coming to be seen as permanently existing, corporate entities in their own right, separate from the rulers who governed them at any given time—with long-term interests and political agendas of their own.

At least some of the flavour of the medieval natural law survived, however, chiefly in the form of the idea of the existence of something that has come to be called the 'community of States'. The clearest symbol of this—if that is the right word for it—was the peace settlement arrived at in Westphalia in 1648, at the conclusion of the Thirty Years War in Germany. It is curious that something called the 'Westphalian system' is sometimes spoken of as a

---

[10] On Vattel, see generally Jouannet, 1998.

synonym of anarchy or of radical views of absolute State sovereignty—conceptions which actually belong (as will be seen) to the nineteenth century and not to the seventeenth.[11] In reality, the Westphalian settlement was an arrangement reached *within* the framework of the Holy Roman Empire, with certain prerogatives of the imperial government carefully preserved—ie, with the older medieval idea of 'independent' States being subject, at the same time, to certain higher norms. The Peace of Westphalia did, however, provide a sort of template for later times in the way in which it marked out a division of labour (so to speak) between national and international spheres, placing religion carefully in the realm of domestic law.

The idea of a community of a community States—distinct from, but also analogous to, a community of individual persons—was apparent in sundry other ways in the seventeenth and eighteenth centuries. One of these was in the concept of a balance of power. This was hardly an altogether new idea, but in this period it attained a formal articulation and recognition that it had never had before (most notably in the Peace of Utrecht in 1713, at the conclusion of the War of the Spanish Succession). In conjunction with this concept, the period was one of limited—though also of frequent—warfare. At least in Western Europe, war was largely conducted with trained professional forces, and for limited ends. As a result, European diplomacy bore more resemblance to a meticulous game of chess than to a lurid Hobbesian inferno of mayhem and turmoil. Even warfare often had a ritualistic air, with its emphasis on manoeuvre and siege rather than on pitched battle.

Economic relations manifested much this same combination of cooperation and competitiveness. On the competitive side, this period marked the high tide of mercantilism, with its intense rivalry for trade advantage. But there was also a high degree of cooperation, under an ever-strengthening rule of law, chiefly in the form of a network of treaties of friendship, commerce, and navigation ('FCN treaties' in the standard legal parlance), which provided a range of safeguards for merchants operating in and trading with foreign countries.

V. THE NINETEENTH CENTURY (1815–1919)

The nineteenth century, extraordinarily, is the least explored area of the history of international law. Its outstanding feature was the rise, and dominance, of the legal philosophy known as positivism. This conferred onto international law a scientific gloss—or alternatively, in the opinion of some, tied it into a narrow strait-jacket. But positivism did not, or not quite, have the century to itself. A new tendency known as the historical school of law made some important contributions; and natural law, against heavy odds, managed to survive, although in new and unexpected ways.

A. 'THE PUBLIC LAW AND SYSTEM OF EUROPE'

With the definitive defeat of revolutionary and imperial France in 1815, the victorious European powers (Britain, Prussia, Russia and Austria) crafted a new kind of peace settlement, based not merely on the balance of material power between the major States but

---

[11] See, for example, the discussion of the 'logic of Westphalia' in Falk, 1975, pp 59–69.

also on a set of general principles of a more substantive character. These general principles were, to be sure, of a decidedly conservative character. The goal was to craft a continent-wide set of political arrangements that would (it was hoped) keep the scourge of revolution from breaking out again.

The peace settlement was to be policed by the major powers—who were, of course, self-appointed to the task—by way of military intervention where necessary. The powers even had a grand name for their enterprise: the 'public law and system of Europe'. This legal order was based on faithful adherence to treaty commitments, together with respect for established laws and legitimate governments and property rights *within* the States of Europe. But it also included a duty on the part of rulers to 'earn' their legitimacy by providing responsible and efficient government to their peoples and also by cooperating with movements for orderly and peaceful change.

A few of these interventions by the Concert of Europe may be noted briefly. The first ones were in the cause of 'legitimacy' in the 1820s, when there were military interventions to subdue revolutions in Naples and Sardinia (by Austria) and in Spain (by France). Also in the 1820s, the intervention of Britain, France, and Russia in the Greek independence struggle led to independence for the Kingdom of Greece. Great-power involvement similarly led to Belgian independence in the 1830s. Sometimes the powers intervened diplomatically in post-war peace settlements, if the terms imposed on the losing side looked to be too destabilizing for the continent as a whole. This occurred in 1878, when the major powers stepped in to prevent Russia from exacting too harsh a peace against Turkey after a victorious war.

On at least some of these occasions, humanitarian considerations played a part, alongside the more usual political jockeying. The most common cause for concern on this front was the relief of Christian populations that were held to be victims of oppression in the Ottoman Empire. This was certainly one of the motivations for the Greek intervention in the 1820s. In 1860, the powers intervened in a communal-violence crisis in the Mount Lebanon area. The most forceful of these great-power humanitarian actions was probably the one in Crete in 1897, when the powers stepped in to stop atrocities and counter-atrocities between Greeks and Turks. In virtually none of these cases was there a pure humanitarian motive, untouched by any other consideration. But some (arguable) precedents were established for later advocates of the lawfulness of humanitarian intervention.

The Concert of Europe 'system' (if it could really be called that) was overtly hegemonic, in modern parlance. There was little sign of any principle of equality of States. Still, the Concert of Europe did at least provide an ideal—if not always the reality—of collective, orchestrated State action for the preservation of international peace. To that extent, it foreshadowed the post-1945 United Nations. International lawyers, however, never gave it much attention.[12] Instead, their ambitions were directed to another end: to unshackling international law from its natural-law heritage and making it something like a science in the modern sense of that term.

---

[12] For one of the few legal texts to treat this subject, see Dupuis, *Principe d'équilibre*, 1909. See also Simpson, 2004, which devotes considerable attention to policing practices of the major powers in the nineteenth century.

B. THE POSITIVIST REVOLUTION

On the conceptual front, the major feature of the nineteenth century was the dominant role of positivism. By 'positivism' is meant such a wealth of things that it may be best to avoid using the term altogether. The expression 'positive law' had been in use since the Middle Ages (since at least the fourteenth century) to refer to the man-made law of particular States, in contrast to divine law (ie, the commands of God) or natural law. What was new in the nineteenth century, however, was something called a 'positive *philosophy*,' the chief propounder of which was the French social philosopher Auguste Comte. By 'positive', Comte meant something like 'scientific' or 'objective' or 'empirical', in contrast to speculative or religious modes of thought. He maintained that the human race had gone through three great historical stages: the theological, the metaphysical, and (now) the 'positive'. In the theological stage, religious ideas had been dominant. In the metaphysical stage, legalistic and jurisprudential thinking had prevailed—meaning, in essence, natural law. But the third age—the 'positive' era (as Comte called it)—was now dawning, promising the true and final liberation of the human mind from the superstitions and dogmas of the past.

In its original form, positivism envisaged the emergence of a sort of technocratic utopia, in which the world would be governed not by clerics or politicians or lawyers (as in the past benighted ages of theology and metaphysics), but rather by engineers and industrialists and financiers. This vision had first been put forward by the eccentric French nobleman, the Comte de St-Simon, in the early nineteenth century.[13] (Auguste Comte's early career, incidentally, had been spent as St-Simon's secretary.) This early vision, taken to its logical conclusion, envisaged the obsolescence of the nation-state.

This original positivism of St-Simon and Comte was a strange amalgam of technocracy and evangelism. Indeed, positivism actually did become a religion, with the most influence, as it happened, in Brazil (whose national flag is emblazoned with the positivist motto 'Order and Progress'). Not surprisingly, lawyers turned the positive philosophy in a somewhat different direction.

1. The positive philosophy applied to international law

As noted above, there was nothing the least bit new in the nineteenth century about the idea of positive law. What was distinctive about positiv*ism* as a school of jurisprudential thought was the doctrinaire insistence that positive law is the *only* true law, ie, the wholesale and principled rejection of natural law as a valid or binding guide to conduct. On this point, nineteenth-century positivism went even further than Hobbes, who was its major progenitor. The doctrinaire positivists (as they could fairly be termed), that is to say, held fast to the voluntary law, while at the same time breaking the link between it and the natural law—that link which had been so central a feature of the Grotian tradition. The partnership between the law of nations and the law of nature, in short, was now regarded as irredeemably dissolved.

One of the most central aspects of positivism was its close attention to questions of the sources of international law—and, in particular, to the proposition that international law was, fundamentally, an outgrowth or feature of the will of the States of the world. Rules of

---

[13] On St-Simonism, see Manuel, 1956.

law were created by the States themselves, by consent, whether express (in written treaties) or tacit (in the form of custom). International law was therefore now seen as the sum total, or aggregation, of agreements which the States of the world happen to have arrived at, at any given time. In a phrase that became proverbial amongst positivists, international law must now be seen as a law *between* States and not as a law *above* States. International law, in other words, was now regarded as a corpus of rules arising from, as it were, the bottom up, as the conscious creation of the States themselves, rather than as a pre-existing, eternal, all-enveloping framework, in the manner of the old natural law. As a consequence, the notion of a systematic, all encompassing body of law—so striking a feature of natural law—was now discarded. International law was now seen as, so to speak, a world of fragments, an accumulation of specific, agreed rules, rather than as a single coherent picture. In any area where agreement between States happened to be lacking, international law was, perforce, silent.

Another important effect of positivism was to replace the older, medieval, teleological picture with what might be termed an instrumentalist outlook. That is to say, the law was no longer seen as having any innate goal of its own, or as reflecting any universal master plan. Instead, the law was now regarded, in technocratic terms, as a means for the attainment of goals which were decided on by political processes. Law, in short, was now seen as a servant and not as a master. It was to be a tool for practical workmen rather than a roadmap to eternal salvation.

Closely allied to the consent-based view of international law was the firm insistence of most positivists on the centrality of the State as the principal (or even the sole) subject of international law, ie, as the exclusive bearer of rights and duties on the international plane. States were now perceived as possessing what came to be called 'international personality'—and, crucially, as also possessing a set of fundamental rights that must be protected at all times. Foremost of these fundamental rights was the right of survival or self-preservation. This meant that, in emergency situations, States are entitled to take action that would otherwise be contrary to law. The most dramatic illustration of this point in the nineteenth century occurred in 1837, when the British government, faced with an insurgency in Canada, sent troops into the United States, in pursuit of insurgents who were using that country's territory as a safe haven. They succeeded in capturing the miscreants, killing several persons in the process and destroying a boat named the *Caroline*. The United States vigorously objected to this armed incursion into its territory. Britain justified its action as self-defence. The diplomatic correspondence between the two countries in this dispute produced the classic exposition of the principle of self-defence: action in the face of a crisis that is 'instant, overwhelming, leaving no choice of means, and no moment for deliberation'.[14] This remains today as the canonical statement of the criteria for the exercise by States of self-defence (although it really was a statement of the general principle of necessity rather than of self-defence *per se*).

The stress on the basic rights of States also gave to positivism a strongly pluralistic cast. Each nation-State possessed its own distinctive set of national interests, which it was striving to achieve in an inherently competitive, even hostile, environment. Each State was sovereign within its territory. And each State's domestic law could reflect that country's own particular history, values, aspirations, traditions, and so forth. It was in this period that

---

[14] 29 *British and Foreign State Papers* pp 1137–1138.

the principle of 'the sovereign equality of States' became the fundamental cornerstone—or even the central dogma—of international law, along with the concomitant rule of non-intervention of States into the internal affairs of one another.

A final point is in order concerning the technocratic outlook of positivism. This had the important effect of de-politicizing international law, at least in principle. International lawyers in the nineteenth century became increasingly reluctant to trespass into areas of political controversy. In this regard, they presented a sharp contrast to their natural-law forbears, who had proudly worn the mantle of the social critic. The positivist lawyers were more inclined to see themselves instead as the juridical counterparts of Comte's engineers. In particular, it came to be widely agreed that fundamental national-security interests were questions of politics and not of law—a distinction that Grotius and Vattel would have found difficult to grasp. By the same token, positivism had a strongly non-moralistic flavour. Nowhere were these features more important than on the subject of war. Positivists tended to view the rights and wrongs of a State's decision to resort to war (the *jus ad bellum*) as a political rather than a legal issue. Therefore, war was now seen as an inevitable and permanent feature of the inter-State system, in the way that friction was an inevitable and permanent feature of a mechanical system.

2. The professionalization of international law

The scientific and technocratic and a-political ethos of positivism brought a new sense of precision, a business-like character to the study and practice of international law. One consequence of this was an increasing sense of professionalism and, to a certain extent, of corporate solidarity. An important sign of this was the founding, in 1873, of two major professional bodies in the field, the International Law Association and the Institut de Droit International. This was also the period in which international law became a subject of university studies in its own right, separate from general jurisprudence—and, in particular, from the study of natural law. (This is also a subject which still awaits detailed treatment.)

The nineteenth century was also the period in which major systematic treatises began to be written in the various European languages. Where Vattel had led, many followed. In 1785, Georg Friedrich de Martens wrote an important treatise, which departed from earlier writing in being based primarily on State practice rather than on natural-law doctrine. In English, the most notable early exposition was by Henry Wheaton, an American diplomat and legal scholar, whose *Elements of International Law* was first published in 1836. Its popularity is indicated by the fact that it was translated into French, Spanish, and Italian, with new editions produced for fully a century after the first one. Wheaton was followed in Britain by Robert Phillimore, whose treatise of 1854–61 ran to four volumes (with two further editions). The first major German-language exposition was by Auguste Wilhelm Heffter in 1844 (which ran to eight editions by 1888). The first treatise to be a conscious embodiment of the positive philosophy was by an Argentinian diplomat, Carlos Calvo, in 1868.[15] This text expanded from two to six volumes over the course of five editions to 1896. The French were slightly later in the field, with a *Précis du droit des gens*, by Théophile Funck-Brentano and Albert Sorel in 1877. More influential was the *Manuel de droit international public* by Henry Bonfils in 1894 (with eight editions by the 1920s). One of the most

---

[15] Calvo, 1880–81. For the first edition, in Spanish, see Carlos Calvo, *Derecho internacional teórico y práctico de Europa y América* (2 vols, Paris: D'Amyot, 1868).

popular texts was that of the Swiss writer Johann Kaspar Bluntschli, whose exposition in 1870 (in French) took the form of a systematic 'code'.

A pronounced difference of style, if not of substance, emerged between the Anglo-American writers and their continental European counterparts. Doctrinaire positivism, as a systematic philosophy, was primarily the product of continental writing, the two most outstanding figures being the Italian Dionisio Anzilotti (later to be a notable World Court judge) and the German Heinrich Triepel. English-language writers, for the most part, were more empirical in outlook, concentrating more heavily on State practice, court decisions, and the like, treating international law as a sort of transnational version of English common law. This intellectual division of labour (so to speak) between the pragmatic and the doctrinal remains in evidence to the present day.

C. THE HISTORICAL AND NATURAL-LAW SCHOOLS

If positivism was by far the dominant trend in nineteenth century international law, it did fall short of having a complete monopoly. Two other schools of thought in particular should be noted. The first was a new arrival: the historical school, which was intimately connected with the romantic movement of the period. Its impact in international law has received, as yet, hardly any serious attention. The other alternative to positivism was natural law, severely reduced in prestige to be sure, but surviving rather better than has generally been appreciated.

1. The historical school

At the core of the historical school's philosophy was the thesis that each culture, or cultural unit, or nation possessed a distinctive group consciousness or ethos, which marked it off from other cultures or nations. Each of these cultural units, as a consequence, could only really be understood in its own terms. The historical school therefore rejected the universalist outlook of natural law. This opposition to universal natural law was one of the most important features that the historical school shared with the positivists.

In international law, the impact of the historical school is evident in three principal areas. The first was with regard to customary law, where its distinctive contribution was the insistence that this law was not a matter merely of consistent practice, however widespread or venerable it might be. A rule of customary law required, in addition, a mental element—a kind of group consciousness, or collective decision on the part of the actors to enact that practice into a rule of law (albeit an unwritten one). In fact, this collective mental element was seen as the most important component of custom, with material practice relegated to a clear second place. Customary law was therefore seen, on this view, as a kind of informal legislation rather than as an unwritten treaty (as the positivists tended to hold). This thesis marked the origin of the modern concept of *opinio juris* as a key component of customary international law.[16]

The second major contribution of the historical school to international law was its theory that the fundamental unit of social and historical existence was not—or not quite—the State, as it was for the positivists, but rather the *nation*-state. In this vision, the State, when properly constituted, comprised the organization of a particular culture into a political

---

[16] See Tasioulas, 2007. See also Thirlway, below, Ch 4.

unit. It was but a short step from this thesis to the proposition that a 'people' (ie, a cultural collectivity or nation or, in the German term, *Volk*) had a moral right to organize itself politically as a State. And it was no large step from there to the assertion that such a collectivity possesses a *legal* right so to organize itself. This 'nationality school' (as it was sometimes called) had the most impact in Italy, where its leading spokesman was Pasquale Mancini, who was a professor at the University of Turin (as well as an office-holder in the government of unified Italy). Although the nationality thesis did not attract significant support amongst international lawyers generally at the time, it did prefigure the later law of self-determination of peoples.[17]

The third area where the influence of the historical school was felt was regarding imperialism—a subject that has attracted strangely little attention from international lawyers. It need only be mentioned here that the historical school inherited from the eighteenth century a fascination with 'stages' of history. Under the impact of nineteenth-century anthropological thought, there came to be wide agreement on a three-fold categorization of States: as civilized, barbarian, and savage.[18] The Scottish lawyer James Lorimer was the most prominent international-law writer in this category. The implication was all too clear that there was a kind of entitlement—moral and historical, if not strictly legal—for the 'civilized' countries to take their 'savage' counterparts in hand and to bring them at least into contact with the blessings of modern scientific life.

2. The survival of natural law

The dominance of positivism, with its stern and forthright opposition to the very concept of natural law, brought that venerable body of thought to its lowest ebb so far in the history of international law. Virtually the only important legal figure explicitly to claim allegiance to that tradition was Lorimer. It should not be thought, though, that the natural-law ideals of old died out altogether. That was far from the case. If they lost the central position that they had previously held, they nevertheless maintained their hold in many ways that were not altogether obvious.

One reason that natural-law ideas were not always recognizable was that, to some extent, they were re-clothed into a materialistic and scientific garb. This was particularly so with the new science of liberal political economy. Underlying this new science was a belief, directly imported from traditional natural-law thought, in a natural harmony of interests amongst human beings across the globe. This was first enunciated in a systematic way by the French physician François Quesnay in the 1750s, and then developed into its modern form in Britain by Adam Smith, David Ricardo, and John Stuart Mill. The centrepiece of their programme was support for free trade—and, more generally, for a breaking down of barriers between individual economic actors the world over. They were, in short, the pioneers of what came to called 'globalization' (Neff, 1990, pp 28–44).

In more traditional areas of international law, the legacy of natural law is most readily discerned in the area of armed conflict—specifically concerning what came to be called measures short of war. It has been observed that positivism basically accepted the outbreak of war as an unavoidable fact of international life, and contented itself with regulating

---

[17] On the nationality (or Italian) School, see Sereni, 1943, pp 155–178. On the modern law of self-determination, see Craven, below, Ch 8.

[18] See Kuper, 1988, pp 76–78.

the conduct of hostilities. But that approach applied to war properly speaking. Regarding lesser measures of coercion, the legacy of just-war thought lingered on. This was the thesis that a resort to armed self-help was permissible to obtain respect for legal rights, if peaceful means proved unavailing. The most important of these forcible self-help measures were armed reprisals. These were far from an unusual occurrence. Indeed, the nineteenth century was a golden age (if that is the right word for it) of armed reprisals. The most common cause of such actions was injury to nationals that had gone unredressed by the target country. A famous illustration was Britain's action against Greece in the 'Don Pacifico' incident of 1850, in which Britain blockaded Greek ports to compel that country to pay compensation for injury inflicted by mob action against a British subject. One of the largest scale operations was a blockade of Venezuelan ports in 1902–03 by a coalition of major European powers, to induce that State to pay various debts that were owing to foreign nationals. Reprisals sometimes also included occupations of territory and even bombardments of civilian areas.

It could hardly escape the attention of observers that reprisal actions were, for obvious practical reasons, a prerogative of the major powers—and that they accordingly gave rise to some strong feelings of resentment in the developing world. In the wake of the Venezuelan incident of 1902–03, the Foreign Minister of Argentina, Luis Drago, proposed an outright ban against the use of force in cases of contract debts. That was not forthcoming. But a milder restriction was agreed, in the so-called Porter Convention of 1907 (named for the American diplomat who was its chief sponsor), adopted by the Second Hague Peace Conference. This convention merely required certain procedural steps to be taken before armed reprisals could be resorted to in debt-default cases.

It is one of history's great ironies that the natural-law tradition, which had once been so grand an expression of idealism and world brotherhood, should come to such an ignominiously blood-spattered pass. A philosophy that had once insisted so strongly on the protection of the weak against the strong was now used as a weapon of the strong against the weak. It is, of course, unfair to condemn a whole system of justice on the basis of abuses. But the abuses were many, and the power relations too naked and too ugly for the tastes of many from the developing world. Along with imperialism, forcible self-help actions left a long-lasting stain on relations between the developed and the developing worlds.

D. THE ACHIEVEMENTS OF THE NINETEENTH CENTURY

One explanation for the remarkable lack of attention by international lawyers to the nineteenth century lies perhaps in the pervasive dominance of doctrinaire positivism over international legal writing generally. There was much, admittedly, that was unattractive about nineteenth-century positivism, particularly to modern eyes—its doctrinaire quality, its narrow horizons, its lack of high ideals, the aura of superficiality raised to the pitch of dogma, its narrowly technocratic character, its ready subservience to power. But it would be wrong to judge it on these points alone because its solid achievements were many. If it lacked the breadth and idealism of natural-law thought, it also discarded the vagueness and unreality that often characterized natural-law thought at its worst. In many ways, positivism was a breath (or even a blast) of fresh air, countering the speculative excesses of natural-law thought. Even if positivism sometimes went too far in the opposite direction, we should nonetheless appreciate the valuable services that it performed in its time.

It is clear from even a cursory survey of the nineteenth century that, when the wills of States were coordinated, impressive results could follow (see generally Lyons, 1963). In the spirit of the St-Simonians, there were various forms of what would come to be called the functional cooperation of States. Progress on this front was most notable in the areas of international communication and transportation: from the international river commissions that were set up to ensure freedom of navigation on the Rhine and Danube Rivers (which had been commercial backwaters since the Middle Ages), to special arrangements for the Suez and Panama Canals, to the founding of the International Telegraphic and Universal Postal Unions (1865 and 1874 respectively). In the spirit of the liberal economists, policies of tariff reduction gathered momentum (with conclusion of the Cobden-Chevalier Treaty in 1860 between France and Britain being the seminal event). Barriers between States were assiduously broken down in other ways as well. The late nineteenth century became an age of remarkable freedom of movement of peoples, with migration on a massive scale (passports were unnecessary for much of international travel in the nineteenth century). Capital too moved with great freedom, thanks to the linking of currencies through the gold standard. The period was, in short, a great age of globalization, with the world more closely integrated economically than it would be for many decades thereafter (and in some ways more so than today) (see Neff, 1990, pp 38–71).

The positivist era was also the period in which we first see the international community 'legislating' by way of multilateral treaties, for the most part in areas relating to armed conflict. The first major example of this was the Declaration of Paris of 1856. It restricted the capture of private property at sea, by providing that 'free ships make free goods' (ie, that enemy private property could not be captured on a neutral ship). It also announced the abolition of privateering. Within five years, it attracted over 40 ratifications. In 1868, the Declaration of St Petersburg contained a ban on exploding bullets. More importantly, it denounced total-war practices, by stating that the *only* permissible objective of war is the defeat of the enemy's armed forces. Alongside the law of war—and in some ways in close partnership to it— was the full flowering of the law of neutrality, which, for the first time, emerged in the full light of juridical respectability as a sort of counterpart to the unrestricted right of States to resort to war on purely political grounds.[19]

There was 'legislation' in other fields too. On the humanitarian front, the period witnessed a concerted effort by the nations of the world to put an end to slave trading. The culmination of this effort occurred in 1890, when the General Act of the Brussels Conference established an International Maritime Office (at Zanzibar) to act against slave trading. In the less-than-humanitarian sphere of imperialism, the major powers established, by multilateral treaty, the 'rules of the game' for the imperial partitioning of Africa. This took place at the Berlin Conference of 1884–85. (Contrary to the belief of some, that conference did not actually allocate any territories; it established the criteria by which the powers would recognize one another's claims.)

The culmination of nineteenth-century international legislation—and the arrival of parliamentary-style diplomacy and treaty-drafting—came with the two Hague Peace Conferences of 1899 and 1907. The first Conference drafted two major conventions: one on the laws of war and one on the establishment of a Permanent Court of Arbitration (which was actually a roster of experts prepared to act as judges on an ad hoc basis, and not a

---

[19] For the most magisterial exposition of this subject, see Kleen, 1898–1900.

standing court). The Second Hague Peace Conference, in 1907, was a much larger gathering than the earlier one (and hence less Europe-dominated). It produced 13 conventions on various topics, mostly on aspects of war and neutrality.[20]

Yet another major achievement of the nineteenth century was in the area of the peaceful settlement of disputes. Although it was widely agreed that fundamental security issues were not justiciable, the nineteenth century marked a great step forward in the practice of inter-State arbitration. The trend began with the Jay Treaty of 1794, in which the United States and Britain agreed to set up two arbitration commissions (comprising nationals of each country) to resolve a range of neutrality and property-seizure issues that had arisen in the preceding years. These were followed by a number of ad hoc inter-State arbitrations in the nineteenth century, of which the most famous, again between Britain and the United States, took place in 1871–72, for the settlement of a host of neutrality-related issues arising from the American Civil War.[21]

For all the impressiveness of these achievements, though, the state of the world was well short of utopian. Economic inequality grew steadily even as growth accelerated. The subjection of much of the world to the European imperial powers, together with the 'gunboat diplomacy' that sometimes followed in the wake of legal claims, stored up a strong reservoir of ill-will between the developed and the developing worlds. Nor did the Concert of Europe prove adequate, in the longer term, to the maintenance of international peace. The Franco-Prussian War of 1870–71 proved, all too dramatically, that war between major powers, on the continent of Europe, was far from unthinkable—and the steady advance in weapons technology and armaments stockpiles promised that future wars could be far more deadly than any in the past. In due course, the Great War of 1914–18 delivered—spectacularly—on that menacing promise.

VI. THE TWENTIETH AND TWENTY-FIRST CENTURIES (1919–   )

Since much of this book will cover twentieth-century developments, no attempt will be made at comprehensive coverage here, particularly of the post-1945 period. But certain aspects of both the inter-war and the post-1945 periods which have received comparatively little attention so far will be emphasized.

A. THE INTER-WAR PERIOD

The carnage of the Great War of 1914–18 concentrated many minds, in addition to squandering many lives. Many persons now held that nothing short of a permanently existing organization dedicated to the maintenance of peace would suffice to prevent future ghastly wars. Their most prominent spokesman was American President Woodrow Wilson. The fruit of their labours was the establishment of the League of Nations, whose Covenant was set out in the Versailles Treaty of 1919. This new system of public order would be of an

---

[20] For an informative and lively account of these conferences, see Tuchman, 1966, pp 265–338.
[21] For a detailed and informative account, see Crook, 1975.

open, parliamentary, democratic character, in contrast to the discreet great-power dealings of the Concert of Europe. The League was, however, tainted from the outset by its
close association with the Versailles peace settlement, an incubus which it never managed
to shake off.

1. The League and its supplements

The League was a complex combination of conservatism and boldness. On the side of conservatism was the decision to make no fundamental change in the sovereign prerogatives
of nation-States as these had developed up to that time. No attempt was made to establish
the League as a world government, with sovereign powers *over* its member States. Nor did
the Covenant of the League prohibit war. Instead, the resort to war was hedged about with
procedural requirements—specifically that either a judicial or political dispute-settlement
process must be exhausted before there could be war between League member States. On
the side of boldness was the Covenant's provision for automatic enforcement action against
any League member State resorting to war without observing the peaceful-settlement
rules. This enforcement took the form of economic sanctions by all other League member
States, a tactic inspired by the Allied blockade of Germany during the Great War. There
was, however, no provision for military action against delinquent States.

In due course, two major initiatives supplemented the League's efforts to maintain
peace. In 1928, the Pact of Paris was concluded, in which the States parties forswore
any resort to war as a means of national policy. The practical effects of this initiative,
however, were not impressive. For one thing, no sanctions were provided. It was also
carefully understood by the signatories that self-defence action would be permitted—a
potentially large loophole. The second initiative was the Stimson Doctrine of 1932,
announced by the United States (and named for its Secretary of State at the time) in
the wake of Japan's occupation of Manchuria. It held that any situation brought about
by aggression would not be accorded legal recognition by the United States. Here too,
the immediate material impact was not great; but it had some precedential value, since
the UN General Assembly endorsed it as a general principle of international relations
in 1970.

Only on one occasion was the sanctions provision of the Covenant invoked: against Italy
for its invasion of Ethiopia in 1935–36. The sanctions failed to save Ethiopia, since the conquest was completed before they could have any serious effect. This failure led to a period
of profound soul-searching amongst international lawyers as to what the role of law in the
world should be.[22] It similarly led States into desperate searches for alternative sources of
security to the League Covenant. A number of countries, such as Switzerland, Belgium,
and the Scandinavian States, reverted to traditional neutrality policies. But there were
also a number of imaginative proposals for informal, but coordinated, action by States
against aggressors (eg, Cohn, 1939; Jessup, 1936). There was even a sort of return to ad hoc
great-power management, in the form of a collective and coordinated non-intervention
policy organized by the major powers at the outbreak of the Spanish Civil War in 1936.
Unfortunately, this effort too was largely unsuccessful because of inadequate implementation and great-power rivalry (see Watters, 1970).

---

[22] See, notably, Niemeyer, 1940.

2. The achievements of the inter-war period

Although the League failed as a protector against aggressors, it would be far wrong to suppose that the inter-war period was a sterile time in international law generally. Precisely the opposite was the case. It was a time of ferment, experiment, and excitement unprecedented in the history of the discipline. A World Court (known formally, if optimistically, as the Permanent Court of International Justice) was established as a standing body, with its seat at the Hague in the Netherlands. It did not have compulsory jurisdiction over all disputes. But it decided several dozen cases, building up, for the first time, a substantial body of international judicial practice. These cases were supplemented by a large number of claims commissions and arbitrations, whose outpourings gave international lawyers a volume of case law far richer than anything that had ever existed before.

The codification of international law was one of the ambitious projects of the period. A conference was convened for that purpose by the League of Nations in 1930, but its fruits were decidedly modest (consisting mainly of clarifications of various issues relating to nationality). But there were further initiatives by the American States in a variety of fields. These included a convention on the rights and duties of States in 1933, which included what many lawyers regard as the canonical definition of a 'State' for legal purposes.[23] The American States also concluded conventions on maritime neutrality, civil wars, asylum, and extradition.

The inter-war period also witnessed the first multilateral initiatives on human rights. A number of bilateral conventions for the protection of minorities were concluded between various newly created States and the League of Nations. In the event, these proved not to be very effective; but they set the stage for later efforts to protect minority rights after 1945, as well as human rights generally. The principle of trusteeship of dependent territories was embodied in the mandates system, in which the ex-colonies of the defeated countries were to be administered by member States of the League. But this was to be a mission of stewardship—'a sacred trust of civilization'—under the oversight of the League. Finally, the League performed heroic labours for the relief of refugees, in the face of very great obstacles—in the process virtually creating what would become one of the most important components of the law of human rights.

It was a period also of innovative thinking about international law. That the doctrinaire positivism of the nineteenth century was far from dead was made apparent by the World Court in 1927, when it reaffirmed the consensual basis of international law, in the famous (or infamous) *Lotus* case.[24] But positivism also came under attack during this period, from several quarters. One set of attackers were the enthusiasts for collective security, as embodied in the League of Nations. The American scholar Quincy Wright was a notable exemplar. This group were sympathetic to the return of just-war ideas, with the Covenant's restrictions on the resort to war and the provision for collective aid to victims of unlawful war. Their single most notable contention was that neutrality must now be regarded as obsolete.

Within the positivist camp itself, a sweeping revision of nineteenth-century thought was advanced by writers of the Vienna School, led by Hans Kelsen. They discarded the State-centred, consent-based, pluralistic elements of nineteenth-century positivism, while

---

[23] See Craven, below, Ch 8.   [24] *'Lotus', Judgment No 9, 1927, PCIJ, Ser A, No 10.*

retaining its general scientific outlook. The Vienna School then reconceived international law—and indeed the whole of law—as a grand, rationalistic, normative system.[25] The French lawyer Georges Scelle advanced a broadly similar vision, though with a sociological flavour, in contrast to the austere formalism of Kelsen.[26] There was even something of a revival of natural-law thought, most notably in the writing of the Austrian Alfred Verdross (who was something of a maverick member of the Vienna School).[27]

In short, the inter-war period did not bring an end to war or aggression. But it was the most vibrant and exciting era in the history of the discipline up to that time (and perhaps since).

B. AFTER 1945

In the immediate aftermath of the Second World War, international law entered upon a period of unprecedented confidence and prestige, for which 'euphoria' might not be too strong a word. International lawyers even found themselves in the (unaccustomed) role of heroic crusaders, with the dramatic prosecutions of German and Japanese leaders for crimes under international law at Nuremberg and Tokyo in the late 1940s (see generally Taylor, 1992; and Cryer and Boister, 2008). At the same time, great plans for the future were being laid.

1. Building a new world

The founding of the United Nations in 1945, to replace the defunct League of Nations, was a critical step in the creation of a new world order. With the UN came a new World Court (the International Court of Justice, or ICJ), though still without compulsory jurisdiction over States. The heart of the organization was the Security Council, where (it was hoped) the victorious powers from the Second World War would continue their wartime alliance in perpetuity as a collective bulwark against future aggressors. (It may be noted that 'United Nations' had been the official name for the wartime alliance.) The UN therefore marked something of a return to the old Concert of Europe approach. The special status of the five major powers (the principal victors in the Second World War, of course) was formally reflected in their possession of permanent seats on the Security Council, together with the power of veto over its decisions.

The UN Charter went further than the League Covenant in restricting violence. It did this by prohibiting not only war as such, but also 'the use of force' in general—thereby encompassing measures short of war, such as armed reprisals. An express exception was made for self-defence. Regarding action against aggressors, the UN was both bolder and more timid than the League had been. It was bolder in that the Charter provided not only for economic sanctions but also for armed action against aggressors. The UN Charter was more timid than the League, however, in that sanctions (whether economic or military) were not mandatory and automatic, as in the League Covenant. The Security Council— dominated by the major powers—was to decide on an ad hoc basis when, or whether, to

---

[25] On the Vienna School, see Kunz, 1934. For a clear and succinct account, see Friedmann, 1949, pp 105–117. See also Nijman, 2004, pp 149–192.

[26] See Scelle, 1932–34. See also Dupuy, 1990; Nijman, 2004, pp 192–242.

[27] See Verdross, 1927.

impose sanctions. The result was to make the UN a more overtly political body than the League had been.

Parallel to this security programme was another one for the promotion of global economic prosperity. The economic-integration effort of the nineteenth century, shattered by the Great War and by the Great Depression of the 1930s, was to be restructured and given institutional embodiments. The International Monetary Fund was founded to ensure currency stability, and the World Bank to protect and promote foreign investment and (in due course) economic development. Trade liberalization would be overseen by a body to be called the International Trade Organization (ITO).

In a host of other areas as well, the aftermath of World War II witnessed a huge increase in international cooperation. There scarcely seemed any walk of life that was not being energetically 'internationalized' after 1945—from monetary policy to civil aviation, from human rights to environmental protection, from atomic energy to economic development, from deep sea-bed mining to the exploration of outer space, from democracy and governance to transnational crime-fighting. The cumulative effect was to weld the States of the world in general—and international lawyers in particular—into a tighter global community than ever before. It is easy to understand that, amidst all this hubbub of activity, a certain triumphalist spirit could pervade the ranks of international lawyers.

The euphoric atmosphere proved, alas, to be very short-lived. Scarcely had the UN begun to function than it became paralysed by Cold-War rivalry between the major power blocs—with the notable exception of the action in Korea in 1950–53 (only made possible by an ill-advised Soviet boycott of the Security Council at the relevant time). Nor did the new World Court find much effective use in its early decades. The ITO never came into being (because of a loss of interest by the United States). Plans for the establishment of a permanent international criminal court were also quietly dropped. Nor did the UN Charter's general ban against force have much apparent effect, beyond a cruelly ironic one: of propelling self-defence from a comparative legal backwater into the very forefront of international legal consciousness. Since self-defence was now the only clearly lawful category of unilateral use of force, the UN era became littered with self-defence claims of varying degrees of credibility, from the obvious to the risible. In particular, actions that previously would have been unashamedly presented as reprisals now tended to be deftly re-labelled as self-defence.[28]

All was not gloom, though, by any stretch of the imagination. In non-political spheres, lawyers fared a great deal better, very much in the technocratic spirit of nineteenth-century positivism. The codification of international law, for example, made some major strides, in large part from the activity of a UN body of technical experts called the International Law Commission. The principal areas of law that received a high degree of codification included the law of the sea (with four related conventions on the subject in 1958, replaced in 1982 by a single, broader convention), diplomatic and consular relations (in the early 1960s), human rights (with two international covenants in 1966), and the law of treaties (in 1969).

At the same time, though, it was not so clear that the fundamentals of the subject had changed very much. The basic positivist outlook continued to have great staying power. Some of the most important political and intellectual upheavals of the twentieth century

---

[28] See Gray, below, Ch 21.

left strangely little mark on international law. Socialism, for example, far from being a major challenge to lawyers, was actually a conservative force. Socialist theorists tended to write more dogmatically in the positivist vein than their Western counterparts did, insisting with particular strength on the upholding of respect for State sovereignty (see Tunkin, 1974). Nor did the massive influx of developing States onto the world scene bring about any fundamental conceptual upheaval. For the most part, the developing countries readily accepted established ways, although they made some concrete contributions in specific areas. One was the establishment of self-determination as a fundamental, collective human right. Another was in the area of succession to treaties by newly independent States, with the States being given an option of choosing which colonial treaties to retain.

2. New challenges

Around the 1980s, a certain change of atmosphere in international law became evident, as something like the idealism of the early post-war years began, very cautiously, to return. There were a number of signs of this. One was a sharp upturn in the judicial business of the World Court. This included a number of cases of high political profile, from American policy in Central America to the Tehran hostages crisis to the Yugoslavian conflicts of the 1990s.[29] In the 1990s, the ITO project was revived, this time with success, in the form of the creation of the World Trade Organization (WTO), which gave a significant impetus to what soon became widely, if controversially, known as 'globalization'.[30] Human rights began to assume a higher profile, as a result of several factors, such as the global campaign against South African apartheid and the huge increase in activity of non-governmental organizations.[31] The end of the Cold War led to tangible hopes that the original vision of the UN as an effective collective-security agency might, at last, be realized. The expulsion of Iraq from Kuwait in 1991 lent strong support to this hope. Perhaps most remarkable of all was the rebirth of plans for an international criminal court, after a half-century of dormancy. A statute for a permanent International Criminal Court was drafted in 1998, entering into force in 2002 (with the first trial commencing in 2009).[32]

In this second round of optimism, there was less in the way of euphoria than there had been in the first one, and more of a feeling that international law might be entering an age of new—and dangerous—challenge. International lawyers were now promising, or threatening, to bring international norms to bear upon States in an increasingly intrusive manner. A striking demonstration of this occurred in 1994, when the UN Security Council authorized the use of force to overthrow an unconstitutional government in Haiti. In 1999, the UN Security Council acquiesced in (although it did not actually authorize) a humanitarian intervention in Kosovo by a coalition of Western powers. It was far from clear how the world would respond to this new-found activism—in particular, whether the world would really be content to entrust its security, in perpetuity, to a Concert-of-Europe style directorate of major powers.

International legal claims were being asserted on a wide range of other fronts as well, and frequently in controversial ways and generally with results that were unwelcome to some. For example, lawyers who pressed for self-determination rights for various minority groups and indigenous peoples were accused of encouraging secession

---

[29] See Thirlway, below, Ch 20.   [30] See Loibl, below, Ch 24.
[31] See Steiner, below, Ch 26.   [32] See Cryer, below, Ch 25.

movements. Some human-rights lawyers were loudly demanding changes in the traditional practices of non-Western peoples. And newly found (or newly rejuvenated) concerns over democracy, governance, and corruption posed, potentially, a large threat to governments all over the world. Some environmental lawyers were insisting that, in the interest of protecting a fragile planet, countries should deliberately curb economic growth. (But which countries? And by how much?) Economic globalization also became intensely controversial, as the IMF's policy of 'surveillance' (a somewhat ominous term to some) became increasingly detailed and intrusive, and as 'structural adjustment' was seen to have potentially far-reaching consequences in volatile societies. Fears were also increasingly voiced that the globalization process was bringing an increase in economic inequality.

VII. CONCLUSION

How well these new challenges will be met remains to be seen. At the beginning of the twenty-first century, it is hard to see the UN 'failing' in the way that the League of Nations did and being completely wound up. No one foresees a reversion to the rudimentary ways of Herodotus's silent traders. But it is not impossible to foresee nationalist or populist backlashes within various countries against what is seen to be excessive international activism and against the élitist, technocratic culture of international law and organization. If there is one lesson that the history of international law teaches, it is that the world at large—the 'outside world' if you will—has done far more to mould international law than *vice versa*. By the beginning of the twenty-first century, international lawyers were changing the world to a greater extent than they ever had before. But it is (or should be) sobering to think that the great forces of history—religious, economic, political, psychological, scientific—have never before been successfully 'managed' or tamed. And only a rash gambler would wager that success was now at hand. Perhaps the most interesting chapters of our history remain to be written.

REFERENCES

AGER, SL (1996), *Interstate Arbitrations in the Greek World, 337–90 B.C.* (Berkeley, Calif.: University of California Press).

ARISTOTLE, 'Rhetoric', in *The Basic Works of Aristotle* (McKeon, R (ed) 1941), (New York: Random House), pp 1325–1451.

BEDERMAN, DJ (2001), *International Law in Antiquity* (Cambridge: Cambridge University Press).

BHATIA, HS (ed) (1977), *International Law and Practice in Ancient India* (New Delhi: Deep and Deep Publications).

BLUNTSCHLI, JC (1870), *Le droit international codifié* (Lardy, MC (trans.)) (Paris: Guillaumin).

BONET, H (1949), *The Tree of Battles* (Coopland, GW (trans.)) (Liverpool: Liverpool University Press).

BONFILS, H (1894), *Manuel de droit international public* (Paris: A Rousseau).

CALVO, C (1880–81), *Le droit international théorique et pratique précédé d'un exposé historique des progrès de la science du droit des gens,* 3rd edn, 4 vols, (Paris: Pedone-Lauriel).

CICERO, MT (1998), *Republic* (Rudd, N (trans.)) (Oxford: Oxford University Press).

COHN, G (1939), *Neo-neutrality* (Kellar, AS and Jensen, E (trans.)) (New York: Columbia University Press).

CROOK, A (1975), *The Alabama Claims: American Politics and Anglo-American Relations, 1865–1872* (Ithaca, NY: Cornell University Press).

CRYER, R and BOISTER, N (2008), *The Tokyo International Military Tribunal* (Oxford: Oxford University Press).

DE MARTENS, GF (1785), *Primae lineae iuris gentium Europaearum practici in usum auditorum adumbratae* (Göttingen: Johann Christian Dieterich).

DE VATTEL, E (1916), *The Law of Nations* (Fenwick, CG (trans.)) (Washington, DC: Carnegie Institution of Washington).

DE VITORIA, F (1991), *Political Writings* (Pagden, A and Lawrance, J (eds)) (Cambridge: Cambridge University Press).

DUPUIS, C (1909), *Le principe d'équilibre et le concert européen de la Paix de Westphalie à l'Acte d'Algésiras* (Paris: Perrin).

DUPUY, R-J (1990), 'Images de Georges Scelle', 1 *EJIL* 235.

FALK, RA (1975), *A Study of Future Worlds* (New York: Free Press).

FRIEDMANN, W (1949), *Legal Theory* 2nd edn (London: Stevens and Sons).

FUNCK-BRENTANO, T and SOREL, A (1877) *Précis du droit des gens* (Paris: E. Plon).

GENTILI, A (1933), *On the Law of War* (Rolfe, JC (trans.)) (Oxford: Clarendon Press).

GIERKE, O (1938), *Political Theories of the Middle Age* (Maitland, FW (trans.)) (Cambridge: Cambridge University Press).

GROTIUS, H (1925), *The Law of War and Peace* (Kelsey, FW (trans.)) (Oxford: Clarendon Press).

HAGGENMACHER, P (1983), *Grotius et la doctrine de la guerre juste* (Paris: Presses Universitaires de France).

HEFFTER, AW (1844), *Das europäische Völkerrecht der Gegenwart, auf den bisherigen Grundlagen* (Berlin: EH Schroeder).

HERODOTUS (1954), *Histories* (De Sélincourt, A (trans.)) (Harmondsworth: Penguin).

HINSLEY, FH (1986), *Sovereignty*, 2nd edn (Cambridge: Cambridge University Press).

HOBBES, T (1957), *Leviathan; or The Matter, Forme and Power of a Commonwealth Ecclesiastical and Civil* (Oakeshott, M (ed)) (Oxford: Blackwell).

JESSUP, PC (1936), *Today and Tomorrow*, vol 4 of Jessup, PC and Deák, F, *Neutrality: Its History, Economics and Law* (4 vols, 1935–37) (New York: Columbia University Press).

JOHN OF LEGNANO (1917), *Tractatus de Bello, de Represaliis et de Duello* (Holland, TE (ed), Brierly, JL (trans.)) (Oxford: Oxford University Press).

JOUANNET, E (1998), *Emer de Vattel et l'émergence doctrinale du droit international classique* (Paris: Pedone).

KADDURI, M (1955), *War and Peace in the Law of Islam* (Baltimore, Md.: Johns Hopkins University Press).

KEEN, M (1965), *The Laws of War in the Late Middle Ages* (London: Routledge and Kegan Paul).

KLEEN, R (1898–1900), *Lois et usages de la neutralité d'après le droit international conventionnel et coutûmier des États civilises*, 2 vols (Paris: Marescq).

KNIGHT, WSM (1925), *Life and Works of Hugo Grotius* (London: Sweet & Maxwell).

KUNZ, J (1934), 'The 'Vienna School' and International Law', 11 *New York University Law Quarterly Review* 370–421.

KUPER, A (1988), *The Invention of Primitive Society: Transformations of an Illusion* (London: Routledge, 1988).

LORIMER, J (1883–84), *The Institutes of the Law of Nations: A Treatise of the Jural Relations of Separate Political Communities*, 2 vols (Edinburgh: W Blackwood).

LYONS, FSL (1963), *Internationalism in Europe, 1815–1914* (Leyden: AW Sythoff).

MANCINI, PS (1851), *Della Nazionalità come fondamento del diritto delle genti* (Turin: Eredi Botta).

MANUEL, FE (1956), *The New World of Henri St-Simon* (Notre Dame, Ind.: University of Notre Dame Press).

NEFF, SC (1990), *Friends But No Allies: Economic Liberalism and the Law of Nations* (New York: Columbia University Press).

——(2005), *War and the Law of Nations: A General History* (Cambridge: Cambridge University Press).

NIEMEYER, G (1940), *Law Without Force: The Function of Politics in International Law* (New Brunswick, NJ: Transaction Publications).

NIJMAN, JE (2004), *The Concept of International Legal Personality: An Inquiry into the History and Theory of International Law* (The Hague: TMC Asser Press).

NUSSBAUM, A (1947), *A Concise History of the Law of Nations* (New York: Macmillan).

PAGDEN, A (2001), *Peoples and Empires: Europeans and the Rest of the World, from Antiquity to the Present* (London: Phoenix Press).

PHILLIMORE, R (1854–61), *Commentaries upon International Law*, 4 vols (London: WG Benning).

PUFENDORF, S (1934), *On the Law of Nature and Nations* (Oldfather, CH and Oldfather, WA (trans.)) (Oxford: Clarendon Press).

RUSSELL, FH (1975), *The Just War in the Middle Ages* (Cambridge: Cambridge University Press).

SCELLE, G (1932–34), *Précis de droit des gens*, 2 vols (Paris: Sirey).

SERENI, AP (1943), *The Italian Conception of International Law* (New York: Columbia University Press).

SIMPSON, G (2004), *Great Powers and Outlaw States: Unequal Sovereigns in the International Legal Order* (Cambridge: Cambridge University Press).

TASIOULAS, J (2007), 'Customary International Law and the Quest for Global Justice', in Perreau-Saussine, A and Murphy, JB (eds), *The Nature of Customary Law: Legal, Historical and Philosophical Perspectives* (Cambridge: Cambridge University Press), p 307–335.

TAYLOR, T (1992), *The Anatomy of the Nuremberg Trials: A Personal Memoir* (Boston: Little, Brown).

TUCHMAN, B (1966), The Proud Tower: A Portrait of the World Before the War (Dobbs Ferry, NY: Ballantine).

TUCK, R (1999), *The Rights of War and Peace: Political Thought and the International Order from Grotius to Kant* (Oxford: Oxford University Press).

TUNKIN, GI (1974), *Theory of International Law* (Butler, WE (trans.)) (Cambridge, Mass.: Harvard University Press).

VAN DER MOLEN, G (1968), *Alberico Gentili and the Development of International Law* (Leiden: Sijhoff).

VERDROSS, A (1927), 'Le fondement du droit international', 16 *Recueil des Cours* 247–323.

WATTERS, WE (1970), *An International Affair: Non-intervention in the Spanish Civil War* (New York: Simon and Schuster).

WHEATON, H (1866), *Elements of International Law*, 8th edn (Dana, RH (ed) 1936) (Oxford: Oxford University Press).

WOLFF, C (1737), *Cosmologia Generalis*, 2nd edn (Frankfurt: Officini Libraria Rengeriana).

—— (1934), *The Law of Nations Treated According to a Scientific Method* (Drake, JH (trans.)) (Oxford: Clarendon Press).

FURTHER READING

BEDERMAN, DJ (2001), *International Law in Antiquity* (Cambridge: Cambridge University Press), very ably covers the ancient Near East, together with classical Greece and Rome.

DE VISSCHER, C (1968), *Theory and Reality in Public International Law*, 2nd edn (Princeton: Princeton University Press), has a section at the beginning which provides an excellent survey of the history of international law, focusing on doctrine and ideas.

EHRLICH, L (1962), 'The Development of International Law as a Science', 105 *Recueil des Cours* 173–265, provides a very good overview of the intellectual history of the field.

GREWE, WG (2000), *The Epochs of International Law* (Byers, M (trans.)) (Berlin: Walter de Gruyter), is a general historical survey of international law, focusing on State practice and having a generally political slant.

GUGGENHEIM, P (1958), 'Contributions à l'histoire des sources du droit des gens', 94 *Recueil des Cours* 1–84, is very enlightening on the key debates, and rival schools of thought, concerning the sources of international law through history.

HINSLEY, FH (1986), *Sovereignty*, 2nd edn (Cambridge: Cambridge University Press), is an excellent survey of the evolution of ideas and conceptions of sovereignty over the centuries. It is particularly strong on the medieval period.

KOSKENNIEMI, M (2001), *The Gentle Civilizer of Nations: The Rise and Fall of International Law 1870–1960* (Cambridge: Cambridge University Press) contains a vast wealth of information on continental European (particularly French and German) thought in the nineteenth and early twentieth centuries.

NUSSBAUM, A (1947), *A Concise History of the Law of Nations* (New York: Macmillan) is a very broad-brush general historical survey of international law, concentrating largely on doctrine.

PAGDEN, A (2001), *Peoples and Empires: Europeans and the Rest of the World, from Antiquity to the Present* (London: Phoenix Press), is a sweeping survey of the historical (including the legal) evolution of imperialism, with careful attention to legal issues.

TASIOULAS, J (2007), 'Customary International Law and the Quest for Global Justice', in Perreau-Saussine, A and Murphy, JB (eds), *The Nature of Customary Law: Legal, Historical and Philosophical Perspectives*, (Cambridge: Cambridge University Press), pp 097–335 is a stimulating analysis of the historical and intellectual roots of our modern ideas of customary international law.

TUCK, R (1999), *The Rights of War and Peace: Political Thought and the International Order from Grotius to Kant* (Oxford: Oxford University Press), examines international law in the seventeenth and eighteenth centuries, concentrating on the doctrines of the major thinkers rather than on State practice.

The following works trace the history of certain topics:

DHOKALIA, RP (1970), *The Codification of Public International Law* (Manchester: Manchester University Press).

FREY, LS and FREY, ML (1999), *The History of Diplomatic Immunity* (Columbus, OH: Ohio University Press).

NEFF, STEPHEN C (1990), *Friends But No Allies: Economic Liberalism and the Law of Nations* (New York: Columbia University Press).

—— (2000), *The Rights and Duties of Neutrals: A General History* (Manchester: Manchester University Press).

—— (2005), *War and the Law of Nations: A General History* (Cambridge: Cambridge University Press).

NIJMAN, JE (2004), *The Concept of International Legal Personality: An Inquiry into the History and Theory of International Law* (The Hague: TMC Asser Press).

RALSTON, JH (1929), *International Arbitration from Athens to Locarno* (London: Oxford University Press).

2

WHAT IS INTERNATIONAL LAW FOR?

Martti Koskenniemi

SUMMARY

The objectives of international law appear differently depending on one's standpoint. International law certainly seeks to realize the political values, interests, and preferences of various international actors. But it also appears as a standard of criticism and means of controlling those in powerful positions. Instrumentalism and formalism connote two opposite sensibilities of what it means to be an international lawyer, and two cultures of professional practice, the stereotypes of 'the advisor' to a powerful actor with many policy-alternatives and 'the judge' scrutinizing the legality of a particular international behaviour. Beyond pointing to the oscillation between instrumentalism and formalism as styles of legal thought and practice, however, the question 'what is international law for?' also invokes popular aspirations about peace, justice, and human rights, and thus acts as a platform for an international political community. Whatever its shortcomings, international law also exists as a promise of justice, and thus as encouragement for political transformation.

I. THE PARADOX OF OBJECTIVES

Attempting to answer the question in the title one first meets with a familiar paradox. On the one hand, it seems indisputable that international law 'has a general function to fulfil, namely to safeguard international peace, security and justice in relations between States' (Tomuschat, 1999, p 23). Or as Article 1 of the UN Charter puts it, the organization has the purpose to 'be a centre for harmonizing the actions of nations in the attainment of...common ends' such as international peace and security, friendly relations among nations, and international cooperation. Such objectives seem self-evident and have never been seriously challenged. On the other hand, it is hard to see how or why they could be challenged—or indeed why one should be enthusiastic about them—because they exist at such high level of abstraction as to fail to indicate concrete preferences for action. What do 'peace', 'security', or 'justice' really mean? As soon as such words are defined more closely, disagreement emerges. To say that international law aims at peace *between States* is perhaps already to have narrowed down its scope unacceptably. Surely it must also seek to advance 'human rights as well as the rule of law domestically inside States for the benefit of human beings...' (Tomuschat, 1999, p 23). But what if advancing human rights would call for the destruction of an unjust peace?

In the end, very little seems to depend on any general response to the question 'what is international law for?' The real problem seems always to be less about whether international law should aim for 'peace', 'security', or 'human rights' than about how to resolve interpretative controversies over or conflicts between such notions that emerge when defending or attacking particular policies. There is no disagreement about the objective of peace in the Middle East between Israel and the Palestinian people. But if asked what 'peace' might mean for them, the protagonists would immediately give mutually exclusive answers. Nor is the 'Asian values' debate about being 'for' or 'against' human rights but about what such rights might be and how they should be translated into social practices in the relevant societies. Therefore, to inquire about the objectives of international law is to study the political preferences of international actors—what it is that *they* wish to attain by international law. And because those preferences differ, the answer to the question in the title can only either remain controversial or be formulated in such broad terms as to contain the controversy within itself—in which case it is hard to see how it could be used to resolve it.

It would thus be wrong to think of the paradox of objectives as a technical problem that could be disposed of by reflecting more closely on the meaning of words such as 'peace', 'security', or 'justice' or by carrying out more sophisticated social or economic analyses about the way the international world is or indeed by drafting definitions of such words in legal instruments. Such notions provide an acceptable response to the question 'what is international law for?' precisely because of their ability to gloss over existing disagreement about political choices and distributional priorities. If they did not work in this way, and instead permanently preferred some choices over other choices, they would no longer provide the neutral platform for peaceful political argument that we expect of them. In accordance with the founding myth of the system, the Peace of Westphalia in 1648 laid the basis for an agnostic, procedural international law whose merit consisted in its refraining from imposing any external normative ideal on the international society. The objectives of that society would now arise from itself and not from any religious, moral or political notions of the good given externally to it. If there is an 'international community', it is a practical association not designed to realize ultimate ends but to coordinate action to further the objectives of existing communities.[1] Sovereign equality builds on this: because there are no natural ends, every member of the international society is free to decide on its own ends, and to that extent, they are all equal. The law that governs them is not natural but artificial, created by the sovereigns through the processes that are acceptable because neutral (see eg, Nardin, 1983). To say that international law is for 'peace', 'security', and 'justice' is to say that it is for peace, security, and justice *as agreed and understood between the members of the system*.[2]

---

[1] This is why it is so easy to discuss it in terms of the ethics of Immanuel Kant, an ethics of universalizable principles of *right action* rather than as instrumental guidelines for attaining the Good. Cf, eg, O'Neill, 2000.

[2] Henkin writes that instead of 'human values', the system is centred upon 'State values' (Henkin, 1989, p 109). This polemical contrast undermines the degree to which States—including principles of sovereignty and non-interference—find their moral justification in late-eighteenth century liberal individualism and

What this means for international legal argument can be gleaned, for instance, from the opinion of the International Court of Justice in the *Reservations* case (1951). Here the Court was called upon to examine the admissibility of reservations to the 1948 Convention on the Prevention and Punishment of the Crime of Genocide. The Court first outlined what seemed a natural consequence of the principles of neutrality and sovereignty, namely that no reservation should be effective against a State that has not agreed to it. To stay with this understanding, however, might have undermined the Convention by creating a system in which some reservations were in force in regard to some States (namely those accepting them) but not against others, while each non-accepting State would be free to regard the reservation-making State as not a party to the Convention at all. This would have gone against the universal nature of the Convention. Thus, the Court continued, a State having made a reservation that has been objected to by some of the parties, may still be held a party to the Convention if the reservation is compatible with the 'object and purpose' of the Convention. At this point, then, the Court moved to think of the law expressly in terms of its objectives. However, there were no objectives to the Convention that were independent from the objectives of the *parties* to the Convention. Thus, it was up to each party to make the determination 'individually and from its own standpoint'.[3]

Such an argument defines the objectives of international law in terms of the objectives of the (sovereign) members of the international society—in this case the society formed by the parties to the Genocide Convention—bringing to the fore two types of problems: what will happen in cases where States disagree about the objectives? And why would only State objectives count?

II. CONVERGING INTERESTS?

If no antecedent order establishes a firm priority between what States want, then any controversy about them either will have to remain open or we shall have to assume that the procedure in which the disagreement is revealed will somehow be able to dispose of it to the satisfaction of all. The latter suggestion embodies the idea of the 'harmony of interests', the presence of an underlying convergence between apparently conflicting State preferences. Under this view, any actual dispute would always be only superficial. At a deeper level, State interests would coalesce and the objective of international law would then be to lead from the former level to the latter.[4]

---

the ideal of national self-rule: 'State values' persist because they channel 'human values' within a political community. See also Paulus, 2001, pp 69–97.

[3] *Reservations to the Convention on the Prevention and Punishment of the Crime of Genocide, Advisory Opinion, ICJ Reports 1951*, p 15 at p 26.

[4] This argument, always implicit in moral objectivism and theories of natural law, was made in a dramatic way by Hersch Lauterpacht, speaking at Chatham House in 1941, as bombs were falling over Coventry and his family was being destroyed by the Nazis in Poland: 'The disunity of the modern world is a fact; but so, in a truer sense, is its unity. Th[e] essential and manifold solidarity, coupled with the necessity of securing the rule of law and the elimination of war, constitutes a harmony of interests which has a basis more real and tangible than the illusions of the sentimentalist or the hypocrisy of those satisfied with the existing *status quo*. The ultimate harmony of interests which within the State finds expression in the elimination of private violence is not a misleading invention of nineteenth century liberalism' (Lauterpacht, 1975, p 26).

It is difficult to defend this view against realist criticisms. Why would harmony, instead of conflict, be the true nature of international politics? What evidence is there that, rightly understood, the interests of States are compatible? Might the harmony not rather seem a form of wishful thinking that prevents people from clearly seeing where their interests lie, and acting accordingly? Hans Morgenthau, one of the fathers of realist thought in international affairs, attacked the inter-war legalism precisely for having made this mistake. To believe in harmony under the League of Nations had left the world unprepared for Hitler's aggression in 1939 (Morgenthau, 1940, pp 261–284). EH Carr, another powerful realist thinker, described the harmony as an ideological smokescreen: 'Biologically and economically, the doctrine of the harmony of interests was tenable only if you left out of account the interest of the weak who must be driven to the wall, or called in the next world to redress the balance of the present' (Carr, 1946, p 50).

International lawyers have responded to such criticisms in two ways. Some have accepted that only a marginal scope is left by power to law and defined any existing legal regimes as variables dependent on a central power (Schmitt, 1988; Grewe, 2001), or have developed purely instrumental accounts of the use of law in the defence of particular interests or preferences (McDougal, 1953, pp 137–259; Goldsmith and Posner, 2004). Others have sought to articulate the harmony under a more elaborate theory of interdependence or globalization: 'International trade and commerce, international finance, international communication—all are essential to the survival of States, and all require an international legal system to provide a stable framework within which they may function' (Watts, 2000, p 7). Institutional, procedural, and even linguistic theories have been used to argue that even the articulation of State interests is based on legal notions such as 'sovereignty', 'treaty', and 'binding force' that delimit and define what may count as State interests or even State identity in the first place.[5] In other words, many lawyers have in fact accepted the political realists' premise (that international law is completely determined by power) but seek to show either that power cannot have its way without international law or that it is in fact useful for everyone that some issues are left to be settled in a predetermined procedural framework.

A first thing to be said about this is that it does highlight that the opposition between 'realism' and 'idealism' is only of limited usefulness. The labels invoke contrasting political sensibilities and different jurisprudential techniques that often merge into each other. Even the hardest 'realism' reveals itself as a moral position (for example by highlighting the priority of the national interest) inasmuch as, 'philosophically speaking, realism is unthinkable without the background of a prior idealistic position deeply committed to the universalism of the Enlightenment and democratic political theory' (Guzzini, 1998, p 16). On the other hand, any serious idealism is able to point to aspects of international reality that support it, and needs such reference in order to seem professionally credible. Much of the realism-idealism controversy is in fact about what element of a many-faceted 'reality' should be chosen as the starting point of one's analysis. Progress in the discipline of international law has then occurred by a new generation of lawyers rejecting the previous one as either 'utopian' because excessively idealist or as 'apologist' because too impressed

---

[5] This is the 'constructivist' explanation of international law's impact on States, much used today in international relations studies. See, eg, Finnemore, 1996. For a discussion, see Brunnee and Toope, 2000, pp 19–74; Kratochwil, 2000, pp 55–59.

by sovereign power. These critiques are as available today as they were a century ago. Care must be taken not to associate any position or doctrine permanently with either: 'idealism' and 'realism' are best understood as forms of critique and channels for institutional reform in accordance with particular political sensibilities. They are crudely simplifying disciplinary labels, more useful for polemical than analytic purposes.

The second noteworthy aspect of this strategy is that in approving the realist premises it may in fact concede too much—namely that there are definable (political) interests or objectives that legal rules should only seek to realize. But this may often in fact not be the case (as will be discussed below). In such cases, there is no 'prior' realm of the political to which the law should always pay deference. In fact the determination of the political objective or interest is not independent from seeking to find the legally plausible way of dealing with a matter.[6]

Many lawyers—and increasingly often political theorists—have, however, made a more ambitious defence of international law. They have argued that, however neutral in regard to political principles, the structure of international law is not devoid of an autonomous normative direction. In their view, international law is accompanied by a cunning logic that slowly socializes initially egoistic States into the law's internationalist spirit.[7] It is possible (though not necessary) to picture this ethic as the 'inner morality of law' that accompanies any serious commitment to work in a legal system.[8] An alternative but parallel approach would be to characterize the system in terms of a 'culture of civility' shared by its administrators and excluding certain types of secrecy, dishonesty, fraud, or manipulation. Such an explanation resonates with international law's emergence in the late nineteenth century as an aspect of optimistic evolutionism among the liberal élites of Europe and North America. It is to assume that by entering into the processes it provides, States come to define not only their objectives but perhaps even their identity by principles offered by international law (Koskenniemi, 2001a).

III. THE SIGNIFICANCE OF STATEHOOD

But the Westphalian myth leaves also unexplained why only *State objectives* count. Ever since Immanuel Kant published his essay on the *Perpetual Peace* (1795), philosophers, political theorists, and lawyers have routinely challenged the State-centrism of the international system, arguing that whatever instrumental value States may have for the coordination of affairs of particular communities, the 'ultimate' members of those communities are individuals and that many other human groups apart from States ('peoples', 'nations', 'minorities', 'international organizations', 'corporations') also play important roles (Westlake, 1910, p 16). Globalization and the crisis of sovereignty have intensified

---

[6] This is one of the central arguments in Koskenniemi, 2005.

[7] A defence of the view that law socializes States not by constraint but by 'compliance strategies [that] seek to remove obstacles, clarify issues, and convince parties to change their behavior', as well as by 'various manifestations of disapproval: exposure, shaming, and diffuse impacts on the reputations and international relationships of a resisting party', is found in Chayes and Chayes, 1995, pp 109, 110. A more recent, proceduralist defence, insisting on the moral core of the international legal process is Habermas, 2004.

[8] The point about law necessarily containing certain 'aspirations of excellence' without which an order would not be recognized as 'law' in the first place, is made, of course, in Fuller, 1969, especially pp 41–94.

the criticisms of international law as State law from sociological, functional, and ethical standpoints. These critiques have often sought to project a material value or an idea of social justice outside of statehood that they suggest should be enforced by international law (Koskenniemi, 1994, pp 22–29).

The universalizing vocabularies of human rights, liberalism, economic and ecological interdependence have no doubt complicated inter-sovereign law by the insertion of public law notions such as *jus cogens* and 'obligations owed to the international community as a whole' and by 'fragmenting' the international system into functional institutions (see Section VIII below). But no alternative to statehood has emerged. None of the normative directions—human rights, economic or environmental values, religious ideals—has been able to establish itself in a dominating position. On the contrary, what these values may mean and how conflicts between them should be resolved is decided largely through 'Westphalian' institutions. This is not to say that new institutions would not enjoy a degree of autonomy from their members. Human rights and many economic and environmental regimes provide examples of such. The European Union has developed into an autonomous system that functions largely outside the frame of international law. How far these other regimes are from that of the EU can, however, be gleaned from the characterization of the WTO system by the Appellate Body in the *Alcoholic Beverages* case (1996):

The *WTO Agreement* is a treaty—the international equivalent of a contract. It is self-evident that in an exercise of their sovereignty, and in pursuit of their own respective national interests, the Members of the WTO have made a bargain. In exchange for the benefits they expect to derive as members of the WTO they have agreed to exercise their sovereignty according to commitments they have made in the *WTO Agreement*.[9]

This outlook was reaffirmed by the International Court of Justice in the *Nuclear Weapons* Advisory Opinion in 1996. In response to the question about the lawfulness of the threat or use of such weapons, the Court concluded that whatever the consequences, it could not exclude that such use would be lawful 'in an extreme circumstance of self-defence, when the very survival of a State would be at stake'.[10] 'Benefits' to the States and State survival remain the highest objectives of the system. Bodies such as the European Court of Human Rights or the UN Human Rights Committee recognize that the treaties they administer function in a State-centred world: the margin of appreciation and the wide scope of derogations allow for national security reasons if 'necessary in a democratic society' to operate with notions of 'security' and 'democracy' that are embedded in a world of States.[11]

The defence of international law's State-centredness is thoroughly practical. 'Stated quite simply', James Brierly once wrote, 'what [international law] tries to do is to define or delimit the respective spheres within which each of the . . . States into which the world

---

[9] *Japan—Taxes on Alcoholic Beverages*, Appellate Body Report (AB–1996–2) DSR 1996: I p 108 (4 October 1996).

[10] *Legality of the Threat or Use of Nuclear Weapons, Advisory Opinion, ICJ Reports 1996*, p 226, paras 96, 101(E).

[11] Or in other words, these mechanisms are only subsidiary: 'The [European Convention on Human Rights] leaves to each contracting State . . . the task of securing the rights and freedoms it enshrines', *Handyside* v *UK*, Judgment of 7 December 1976, Ser A, no 24, 1 *EHRR* 737, para 48. As Susan Marks points out, liberal reformers conceive of 'democratization' in terms of reform of *domestic* (and not international) institutions (Marks, 2000, pp 76–100).

is divided for political purposes is entitled to exercise its authority' (Brierly, 1944, p 3). Little of this justification has changed. A form and a process is needed that channels interpretative conflicts into peaceful avenues. This is not to say that non-State values such as 'human rights', 'efficient economies', 'clean environment', or 'democracy' would be unworthy objectives of political action. Disagreement about them provides the life and blood of international politics. The defenders of the State-system would only add that such values conflict and that 'States alone have provided the structures of authority needed to cope with the incessant claims of competing social groups and to provide public justice essential to social order and responsibility' (Schachter, 1997, p 22). States may be set aside, of course, by consent or revolution but there are dangers in such transformations, some of which are well known, and something about those dangers results from the single-mindedness of the teleologies pursued by the institutions seeking to replace statehood.

On the other hand, there is no doubt that international politics is far from the Westphalian ideal. The informal networks and epistemic communities that influence international developments beyond the rigid forms of sovereign equality are populated by experts from the developed West. It is hard to justify the attention given and the resources allocated to the 'fight against terrorism' in the aftermath of the attacks on New York and Washington in September 2001 in which nearly 3,000 people lost their lives, while simultaneously six million children under five years old die annually of malnutrition by causes that could be prevented by existing economic and technical resources.[12] What becomes a 'crisis' in the world and will involve the political energy and resources of the international system is determined in a thoroughly Western-dominated process (Charlesworth, 2002; Orford, 2003).

It is widely believed that the informal and fluid economic, technological, and cultural processes often termed 'governance' rather than 'government' strengthen the political position of the most powerful actors—transnational networks, large corporations, Western developed States—and marginalize public international law (eg, Hurrell and Woods, 1999; Arnaud, 2003). Weak States despair over their inability to hold on to achieved positions and privileges by the antiquated rhetoric of sovereignty. But the latter's awkward defence of the conservative system of sovereign equality undermines the extent to which globalization may also open avenues for contestatory transgovernmental action within international civil society, or by what Hardt and Negri call the 'multitude' (Hardt and Negri, 1999, pp 393–413). There is room for conflict and consensus both *within* and *beyond* the Westphalian system and little political worth lies in deciding *a priori* in favour of either. Formal rules as well as anti-formal objectives and standards may each be used for progressive or conservative causes.[13] The choice of technique must reflect a historically informed assessment of the effect of particular institutional alternatives.

In the following sections I will try respond to the question 'what is international law for?' by describing its role in a world that is not one of pre-established harmony or struggle but of both cooperation *and* conflict simultaneously. I will argue that international law operates—and should operate—as an instrument for advancing particular claims

---

[12] 'The State of Food Insecurity in the World 2002', http://www.fao.org/DOCREP/005/Y7352e/ Y7352e00.HTM (last visited 24 October 2002).

[13] For the varying use of the rule/principle, opposition in self-determination arguments about change, participation, and community, see Knop, 2002, pp 29–49.

and agendas *as well as* a relatively autonomous formal technique. This is not to claim political neutrality. Much instrumental thinking about international law today adopts the point of view of the decision-maker in a relatively prosperous State or transnational network, in possession of resources and policy-options and seeking guidance on how to fit their objectives within international legality—or to overrule legality with minimal cost. Clearly, international law exists 'for' such decision-makers. But it should not exist exclusively for them. My argument is that there is often a reason to adopt a 'formalist' view on international law that refuses to engage with the question of its objectives precisely in order to constrain those in powerful positions. The question 'what is international law for?' needs to be rescued from the context of legal routines and re-instated in the political arenas where it can be used to articulate claims by those who are sidelined from formal diplomacy and informal networks and feel that something about the routines of both is responsible for the deprivations they suffer. In other words, there is reason to defend a legal 'formalism' against a 'pragmatism' that views international law only in terms of the immediate objectives it serves. In order to do that, however, it is necessary first to outline the power of pragmatism.

IV. INTO PRAGMATISM?

The paradox of objectives shows that the formal law of Westphalia cannot be replaced by social objectives or ethical principles without invoking controversies that exist in regard to the latter. 'Whoever invokes humanity wants to cheat', Carl Schmitt once wrote (Schmitt, 1996, p 54), citing the nineteenth century French socialist Pierre Joseph Proudhon and making a useful point about the use of abstract humanitarianism to label one's political adversary as an enemy of humanity so as to justify extreme measures against him—a point that applied in today's context 'lacks neither lucidity nor relevance' (Kervégan, 1999, p 61). One need not think only of the extreme case of the 'war against terrorism' to canvass the slippery slope from anti-formal reasoning to human rights violation. Quite everyday legal argument assumes the analytical priority of the reasons for the law over the form of the law in a fashion that underwrites Stanley Fish's perceptive dictum: 'once you start down the anti-formalist road, there is no place to stop' (Fish, 1989, p 2).

For example, the right of self-defence under Article 51 of the Charter is formally conditioned by the presence of an 'armed attack'. But what about the case of a *threat* of attack by mass destruction weapons? Here we are tempted to look for guidance from the objective of Article 51. The rationale for allowing self-defence lies, presumably, in the objective of protecting the State. Surely we cannot expect a State to wait for an attack if this would bring about precisely the consequence—the destruction of the State—that the rule was intended to prevent. Because the rule itself is no more valuable than the reason for its existence, we erase the condition of prior armed attack and entitle the State to act in an anticipatory way.[14] Or the other way around: surely formal sovereignty should not be a bar for humanitarian intervention against a tyrannical regime; in oppressing its own population,

---

[14] This is the argument for the 'Bush doctrine' of pre-emptive self-defence, as made in the United States security strategy, published on 20 September 2002. Cf the text in, eg, *Financial Times*, 21 September 2002, p 4.

the State undermines its sovereignty. We honour 'sovereignty' as an expression of a people's self-rule. If instead of self-rule there is oppression, then it would seem nonsensical to allow formal sovereignty to constitute a bar to intervention in support of the people.[15]

Such arguments are based on a thoroughly pragmatic-instrumentalist view of the law, a view that highlights that we do not honour the law because of the sacred aura of its text or its origin but because it enables us to reach valuable human purposes. We follow the emission reduction schedule of chlorofluorocarbons (CFCs) in Article 2 of the 1987 Montreal Protocol on the Protection of the Ozone Layer because we assume that it will reduce the depletion of the ozone layer and the incidence of skin cancer. We honour the domestic jurisdiction clause in Article 2(7) of the UN Charter because we assume it upholds the ability of self-determining communities to lead the kinds of life they choose. But what if it were shown that ozone depletion or skin cancer bears no relationship to the emissions of CFCs, or that domestic jurisdiction merely shields the arbitrary reign of tyrants? In such cases we would immediately look for an equitable exception or a counter-rule so as to avoid the—now unnecessary—costs that would be incurred by bowing to the empty form of the original rule. Article 10(1) of the European Convention on Human Rights provides for freedom of speech. If applying the right would enable the distribution of fascist propaganda, it is always possible to interfere and prohibit it by the counter-rule in Article 10(2) that enables the 'prevention of disorder or crime' and to ensure 'the protection of morals', with a margin of appreciation lying with State authorities. Enabling those authorities to protect 'national security' is indispensable if they are to secure the liberal rights-regime. Yet, because setting the 'balance' between security and rights lies with the authorities against whom the rights-regime was established, the door to abuse remains open (see Cameron, 2000, pp 62–68).

We often allow the reason for the rule to override the rule. We do this because we believe the rule itself has no intrinsic worth. If it fails to support the purpose for which it was enacted—or worse, prevents its attainment—why should it be honoured? In domestic society, abstract law-obedience can be defended in view of the routine nature of the cases that arise, and the dangers attached to entitling citizens to think for themselves. Such arguments are weak in the international realm where situations of law-application are few, and disadvantages of obedience often significant. Few States that were economically or politically dependent on Iraq fully implemented the sanctions set up in 1990. Though they were in formal breach of Articles 25 and 48 of the Charter, the UN preferred to look the other way. The European Union is not going to give up the prohibition of importation of hormone-treated meat merely because a WTO dispute settlement organ may have decided it should do so. The importance of the interest in living peacefully with a powerful neighbour and of deciding on national health standards vastly outweighs any consideration about the importance of abstract law-obedience (see Koskenniemi, 2001b).

And yet, there is a dark side to such pragmatic instrumentalism. A legal technique that reaches directly to law's purposes is either compelled to think that it can access the right purpose in some politics-independent fashion—in which case it would stand to defend its implicit moral naturalism—or it transforms itself to a licence for those powers in a position to realize their own purposes to do precisely that. In this way, pragmatism inculcates

---

[15] This position is often combined with the argument for pro-democratic intervention. For useful analysis, see Chesterman, 2001, pp 88–111.

a heroic mindset: we *can* do it! It is the mindset of well-placed, powerful actors, confident in their possessing the 'right' purpose, the mindset that drove Stalin to collectivization, or Israel to destroy the Osiraq nuclear power plant in 1981. It is the mindset of the civilizing mission and of 'regime change' by force if necessary.

Instrumental action may or may not be acceptable in view of the circumstances and its advisability is typically the object of political controversy. But the instrumentalist mindset—the readiness to act as soon as that seems what one believes useful or good— creates a consistent bias in favour of dominant actors with many policy-alternatives from which to choose and sufficient resources to carry out their objectives.[16] To always look for reasons, instead of rules, liberates public authorities to follow their reasoning, and their purposes—hence their frequent aversion against rules in the first place: the International Criminal Court, disarmament or human rights treaties, environmental or law of the sea regimes, and so on (see Byers and Nolte, 2003).

The difficulty with the instrumentalist mindset is that there never are simple, well-identified objectives behind formal rules. Rules are legislative compromises, open-ended and bound in clusters expressing conflicting considerations. To refer to objectives is to tell the law-applier: 'please choose'. There is no doubt that Article 2(4) of the UN Charter aims towards 'peace'. Yet it is equally certain that most people disagree on what 'peace' might mean in a particular case. This is not only about semantic uncertainty. Even apparently unobjectionable objectives such as 'peace' contain a paradox. To be in favour of 'peace' cannot, for example, mean that nobody can ever take up arms. 'Perhaps the most serious problem with outlawing force is that sometimes it is both necessary and desirable' (Watts, 2000, p 10). The UN Charter expressly allows for the use of military force under the authority of the Security Council or in pursuance of the right of self-defence. The positive law of the Charter is both pacifist and militarist—and receives its acceptability by such schizophrenia. Without something like a right to use force in self-defence, aggression would always be rewarded. The European Convention on Human Rights seeks to protect individuals' rights to both freedom and security. But one person's freedom often conflicts with another's security. Whether or not authorities should be entitled to censor prisoners' letters or prohibit the publication of obscene materials, for instance, cannot be reached through instrumental reasoning that would be independent from a political choice (see Koskenniemi, 2000, pp 99–106). The will of the drafters *is* the language of the instrument. Beyond that, there is only speculation about what might be a good (acceptable, workable, realistic, or fair) way to apply it.

Practitioners usually understand international law as being more about routine application of standard solutions, ad hoc accommodation, and compromise than discourse about large objectives. Providing advice to a non-governmental organization or drafting judgments at the International Court of Justice are usually held to require pragmatic reconciliation of conflicting considerations, balancing between 'equitable principles', conflicting rights, or other *prima facie* relevant aspects of the case at hand. Settlement of the conflicts during the dissolution of the Former Yugoslavia in the early 1990s was understood to involve the balancing of conflicting considerations about stability of frontiers and expectations of just change, managing the *uti possidetis* principle together with

---

[16] For a description of instrumentalism as a culture, see Binder, 1988, pp 906–909.

minority rights for populations left on the wrong side of the boundary.[17] The balance struck between these considerations was in no way dictated by the law but reflected the negotiators' pragmatic assessment of what might work (Lâm, 2000, pp 141–151). At the European Court of Human Rights, individual freedoms are constantly weighted against the need for interference by public authorities. It is established case-law that 'an interference must achieve a "fair balance" between the demands of the general interests of the community and the requirements of the protection of the individual's fundamental rights'.[18] In a like manner, the law concerning the delimitation of frontier areas or the sharing of natural resources resolves itself into a more or less flexible cluster of considerations about distributive justice—sometimes described in an altogether open-ended fashion in terms of 'equitable principles' or 'equitable use'—in view of attaining a pragmatically acceptable end-result.[19] And hard cases within the laws of war invariably turn into a contextual assessment of what number of non-combatant casualties might still be within the limits of proportionality by reference to the military objective (military experts and humanitarian lawyers agreeing on the need to 'calculate' (see Kennedy, 2004)).

Few international lawyers think of their craft as the application of pre-existing formal rules or great objectives. What rules are applied, and how, which interpretative principles are used and whether to invoke the rule or the exception—including many other techniques—all point to pragmatic weighing of conflicting considerations in particular cases (Corten, 1997). What is sought is something practical, perhaps the 'fairness' of the outcome, as Thomas M Franck has suggested. Under this image, law is not about peace *or* justice, freedom *or* security, stability *or* change, but always about both one *and* the other simultaneously. 'The tension between stability and change, if not managed, can disorder the system. Fairness is the rubric under which the tension is discursively managed' (Franck, 1995, p 7). The lawyer's task is now seen in terms of contextual 'wisdom', or 'prudence', rather than the employment of formal techniques.[20] In a fluid, fragmented world, everything hinges on the sensitivity of the practising lawyer to the pull of contextually relevant considerations.

V. A TRADITION OF ANTI-FORMALISM

The move to pragmatism emerges from a series of recurrent criticisms of international law's alleged 'formalism'. Pragmatism was supported in the last third of the nineteenth century by the use of a flexible notion of 'civilization' that enabled liberal lawyers to look beyond diplomatic protocol and an outdated natural law. The inter-war lawyers attacked the formalism of sovereignty they projected on pre-war doctrines and advocated (as

---

[17] See Opinions 2 and 3 of the Arbitration Commission of the Peace Conference on the Former Yugoslavia (1992) 31 ILM 1497–1500.

[18] *Fredin v Sweden*, Judgment of 18 February 1991, Ser A, no 192, 13 *EHRR* 784, para 51; *Lopez Ostra v Spain*, Judgment of 9 December 1994, Ser A, no 303–C, 20 *EHRR* 277, para 51.

[19] See eg, Separate Opinion of Judge Jiménez de Aréchaga, *Continental Shelf (Tunisia/Libyan Arab Jamahiriya), Judgment, ICJ Reports 1982*, p 18, pp 103–108 (paras 11–31) and, eg, the International Convention on the Non-Navigational Uses of International Watercourses, A/RES/51/229 (8 July 1997). I have analysed this 'turn to equity' in, among other places, Koskenniemi, 1999b, pp 27–50.

[20] For a celebration of judicial creativity in this regard, see Lauterpacht, 1958.

conservatives) 'tradition' and (as progressives) 'interdependence' as bases for their pragmatic commitment. After the next war, reformist lawyers indicted what they described as
the legalistic formalism of the League basing their 'realism' on Cold War themes, either
expressly in favour of the West or in a more social-democratic way to support international
institutions (see Kennedy, 2000, pp 380–387). Legal realism always had its Hawks and its
Doves but for both, it seemed useful to criticize old law for its 'formalism' in order to support 'dynamic' political change.

Interdisciplinary studies in the 1990s highlighted the extent to which the formal
validity of a standard was independent from its compliance pull (see, eg, Shelton, 2000).
As the law was seen instrumentally, its formality seemed to bear no particular merit:
'hard law' was just one choice among other possible regulative techniques, including
soft standards or the absence of any standards at all in cases where the imposition of
one's preference seemed within the limits of the possible and preferable given that it
might 'minimise transaction and sovereignty costs'.[21] In such debates formal law has
nobody speaking in its favour and is indicted as a utopianism supporting conservative causes. Anti-formalism is always a call for transformation: to overrule existing law
either because it does not really exist at all, or if it does, because it should not. The debate
on soft law and *jus cogens* in the 1980s and 1990s manifested both of these criticisms and
Prosper Weil's famous analysis of the pathological problems (the 'dilution' and 'gradu-
ation' of normativity) introduced in international law by such notions were unpersua-
sive to anti-formalist critics who wanted to realize the good society *now* and had no
doubt that they knew how to go about this (see Weil, 1983; Tasioulas, 1996). Avant-garde
instrumentalism at the beginning of a new century reads like German public law conservatism a hundred years earlier: over every international rule hangs the sword of *clausula rebus sic stantibus* (see Kaufmann, 1911).

What makes the formalism/anti-formalism debate suspect is the extent to which *anything* may be and has been attacked as 'formalism' (see Kennedy, 2001). The following
views, at least, have been so targeted:

(a) rationalistic natural-law theories;

(b) views emphasizing the importance of (formal) sovereignty;

(c) views limiting international law's scope to treaties or other (formal) expressions of
consent;

(d) views highlighting the importance of international institutions;

(e) views emphasizing 'rigour' in law-application;

(f) views stressing the significance of formal dispute-settlement;

(g) views insisting on a clear boundary between law and politics.

---

[21] For a particularly straightforward instrumental approach, see Posner, 2003. An interdisciplinary
research on the recent 'move to law' uses a method of assessing 'legalization' by reference to the standards'
obligatory nature, precision, and the presence of a centralized authority. The project examines 'legalization'
instrumentally, by concentrating on the conditions under which it constitutes a rational choice. See, eg,
Abbott and Snidal, 2001, pp 37–72. Such instrumentalism is not neutral: to assess law from the perspective
of rational choice is to occupy the perspective of a small number of actors that actually may choose their
options by agendas they set. It celebrates the managerial culture of Western experts at work to advance
Western interests.

The list is by no means exhaustive. In fact, anything can be labelled 'formalism' because the term is purely relational. When a speaker advocates something (a norm, a practice) by its material fullness, the opposite view will inevitably appear to be holding fast to the dead weight of some 'form'. The almost uniformly pejorative use of the term 'formalism' in international law reflects the predominance of the instrumentalist mindset in diplomacy and international politics. The way the legal idiom constructs and upholds the structures of diplomacy and politics is left invisible.

The contrast between instrumentalism and formalism is quite fundamental when seeking to answer the question 'what is international law for?' From the instrumental perspective, international law exists to realize objectives of some dominant part of the community; from the formalist perspective, it provides a platform to evaluate behaviour, including the behaviour of those in dominant positions. The instrumental perspective highlights the role of law as social engineering; formalism views it as an interpretative scheme. The instrumental perspective is typically that of an active and powerful actor in possession of alternative choices; formalism is often the perspective of the weak actor relying on law for protection.

If instrumentalism today needs no particular defence, it may be useful to highlight the twin virtues of formalism. First, it is indispensable. Every standard is always substantive and formal at the same time. The very ideas of treaty and codification make sense only if one assumes that at some point there emerges an agreement, an understanding, a standard that is separate from its legislative background. When States enter an agreement, or when some behaviour is understood to turn from habit into custom, the assumption is that something that was loose and disputed crystallizes into something that is fixed and no longer negotiable. The point of law is to give rise to standards that are no longer merely 'proposed' or 'useful' or 'good', and which therefore can be deviated from if one happens to share a deviating notion of what in fact is useful or good. This is what it means to say that in addition to their acceptability and effectiveness, legal rules are should also possess 'validity'. To accept that positive law enjoys that property is not to say anything about how it is recognized in individual rules or standards, nor indeed of whether any actual standard so recognized would possess any particular meaning as against some other putative meaning. Validity indicates a formal property that leaves the norm so characterized a flat, substanceless surface—but a surface without which no 'law' could exist at all.

Secondly, the fact that the legal form is a 'flat substanceless surface' is not politically insignificant. It does something to those it accepts as legal subjects. In a world without or 'before' international law, the acting persons or entities exist as subjects of interests and preferences, both liberated and weighed down by their irreducible particularity. The logic of a social structure between them is a logic of instrumentalism, each subject a *homo economicus*, poised to perpetuate the realization of its idiosyncratic preference. Such actors are completely controlled by the environmental conditions that make interest-fulfilment possible. For them, the external world—including other actors—has no meaning beyond interest-fulfilment: on its own, it is chaotic, incomprehensible. Paradoxically, however, a single-minded instrumentalism is bound to be frustrated in the end: at the mercy of a dangerous and incomprehensible world where every action creates unforeseen consequences, and always falls short of satisfying the ever intensifying interests (eg, Foucault, 2005, pp 280–281). This is one of the tragedies of the continuing war in Afghanistan.

By contrast, as legal subjects, actors, as it were, give up their particularity in order to participate in what is general. By recourse to the medium of law that claims 'validity', they are lifted from the tyranny of subjective interests and preferences. The *homo juridicus* in a way decentralizes its own perspective, opening itself to the world at large. In other words, and as thinkers as diverse as Kant, Foucault, and Habermas have pointed out, the political significance of formal law—that is, of law irrespective of what interests or preferences particular legislation might seek to advance—is that it expresses the universalist principle of inclusion at the outset, making possible the regulative ideal of a pluralistic international world. (See Kant, 1999, pp 24–25; Foucault, 2005, pp 280–281; Habermas, 2004. See also Supiot, 2005.) '[O]nly a regime of noninstrumental rules, understood to be authoritative independent of particular beliefs or purposes is compatible with the freedom of its subjects to be different' (Nardin, 1998, p 31). The form of law constructs political adversaries as equals, entitled to express their subjectively felt injustices in terms of breaches of the rules of the community to which they belong no less than their adversaries—thus affirming both that inclusion and the principle that the conditions applying to the treatment of any one member of the community must apply to every other member as well. In the end, competent lawyers may disagree about what this means in practice. But the legal idiom itself reaffirms the political pluralism that underlies the Rule of Law, however inefficiently it has been put into effect. In fact, the failures in the international legal system are always recognized and constructive projects formulated by a prior (though often undisclosed) acceptance of the idea of the rule of formal law. Without that idea, much of the criticisms we all make of the international political world would no longer make sense.

Of course, formal law does not apply itself. Between that form and any decision to project on it meaning 'x' instead of 'y', is a professional technique that may be more or less successful in expressing these regulative ideals. In particular, there is a constant push and pull in the professional world between a *culture of instrumentalism* and a *culture of formalism*. It would be wrong to associate this dialectic with fixed positions representing particular interests or preferences. Instrumental action by lawyers is a necessary part of the search for good rules or institutions beyond the *status quo*. And any present rules are always also mechanisms to support particular interests and privileges. 'Power' and 'law' are entangled in such complex ways that it is often pointless to interpret particular events as manifesting either one or the other: power works through 'formal rules'—just like instead of 'naked power', we see everywhere power defined, delimited, and directed by rules.

But the two cultures do play distinct political roles in particular historical situations. As the debates around the fluid dynamism of globalization have demonstrated, formal standards and institutions are often called upon to provide protection for weak actors, and to pose demands on powerful ones.[22] Irrespective of its philosophical justification, there is no magic about formalism as a legal practice, however. It may also come to buttress privilege, apathy, or both. Hence it is important also to focus on instrumentalism and formalism as 'cultures', sensibilities, traditions and frameworks, sets of rituals and self-understandings among institutional actors. As pointed out above, the 'heroic' mindset of the *homo economicus* that sees law only as an instrument for *my objectives* often leads to collateral damage, frustration and tragedy. Against it, I would invoke a practice of formalism, with its associated tropes about valid law, rights, and

---

[22] Out of a burgeoning literature, see, eg, Tsagourias, 2000; Koskenniemi, 2009.

constitutionalism, less as definite institutional models than as regulative ideals for a profession without which no community could rule itself by standards it recognizes as its own (instead of those of some influential faction). The idea of a universal law needs servants that define themselves administrators (instead of inventors) of universal standards—the class of lawyers. The traditions and practices of this class are significant only to the extent they remain attached to the 'flat, substanceless surface' of the law.

VI. INSTRUMENTALISM, FORMALISM, AND THE PRODUCTION OF AN INTERNATIONAL POLITICAL COMMUNITY

Modern international law puts the international lawyer at the heart of the legal system. It is possible to represent that position schematically by reference to the two types of logic at play in the international rule of law. Here is the international relations theorist Hedley Bull:

The special interests of the dominant elements in a society are reflected in the way in which the rules are defined. Thus the particular kinds of limitations that are imposed on resort to violence, the kinds of agreements whose binding character is upheld, or the kinds of right to property that are enforced, will have the stamp of those dominant elements. But that there should be limits of some kind to violence, and an expectation in general that agreements should be carried out, and rules or property of some kind, is not a special interest of some members of a society but a general interest of all of them. (Bull, 1977, p 55)

So described, law unites an *instrumentalist logic*, one that looks for the realization of objectives through law, with a *formalist logic*, one that establishes standards of behaviour. Now it is obvious that neither logic is fully constraining. The instrumental logic is indeterminate as the objectives always leave a number of possible choices: what does 'peace and security' mean and how should it be realized in the Middle East, for example? Nor is the formalist logic ever fully formal, but always in practice somehow partial and biased. However general the rules of law are, their equal application may appear unjust because the reality to which they are applied is profoundly unequal: should large and small States, democracies, and dictatorships really be treated alike? The form of law is realized in particular rules or decisions that are no longer formal but that always institute a bias in favour of some substantive preferences.

In the *Nuclear Weapons* case (1996), the ICJ was requested by the UN General Assembly to give an advisory opinion on the legal status of nuclear weapons. From the perspective of the instrumentalist logic, the relevant regulation (human rights law, environmental law, humanitarian law, and the law concerning the use of force) sought to accomplish several types of objectives: above all protection of human life and the environment, as well as the survival of States. These objectives proved indeterminate, however, and both opponents and supporters of nuclear weapons argued by reference to them: are people better protected with or without nuclear weapons? The instrumental logic did set some limits to what the Court could say, but it did not—indeed could not—fully constrain it. A decision by the Court was needed to bring the instrumental logic into a conclusion.

The formalist logic was equally under-determined. To decide that nuclear weapons were *illegal* would have created a consistent material bias in favour of States in possession of conventional weapons or in de facto possession of undisclosed nuclear weapons. To require the dismantling of disclosed nuclear arsenals would have revolutionized the existing military-political relationships in unforeseen ways. But to decide that nuclear weapons were *lawful* would have maintained the systemic bias in security policy in favour of the Great Powers and gone against the deep-rooted popular sense that the existence of such weapons constitutes a permanent hostage-taking by nuclear weapons States of most of the world's population. Neither illegality nor legality could remain fully within the formalist logic. Both broke through pure form and created one or another type of material preference. Indeed, it was impossible to decide either way without the decision seeming 'biased' from the opposed standpoints. And because the political choice in this case seemed too important for the Court to take, it chose the path of recognizing the insufficiency of both logics: 'the Court considers it does not have sufficient elements to enable it to decide with certainty that the use of nuclear weapons would be necessarily at variance with the principles and rules applicable in armed conflict in any circumstance'.[23]

I have defended elsewhere the Court's silence inasmuch as it protected the need for a sustained *political* condemnation of the killing of the innocent, lifting it from the banal instrumentalism and formalism of modern law (Koskenniemi, 1999a). Irrespective of that position, however, the case illustrates the indeterminacy of both of the two types of logic behind the Rule of Law, as outlined by Bull above. Neither instrumental calculation nor a purely formal analysis could grasp the status of such weapons: a *decision* was needed that was irreducible to the two logics. Here the decision was silence. In other cases, the Court may have recourse to literalism, balancing, contextualization, and bilateralization, among a host of other techniques, to complete the instrumental and formal structures within which it works (Koskenniemi, 1989, pp 410–421). Each of such techniques is, again, indeterminate. None of them explain why *this* argument was held relevant, why *that* interpretation was chosen. The decision always comes about, as the political theorist Ernesto Laclau has put it, as a kind of 'regulated madness', never reducible to any structure outside it (Laclau, 1996, p 58).

A court's decision or a lawyer's opinion is always a genuinely political act, a choice between alternatives not fully dictated by external criteria. It is even a *hegemonic* act in the precise sense that though it is partial and subjective, it claims to be universal and objective (see further Koskenniemi, 2004a). But it is this very partiality and political nature of the decision that ensures that it is an aspect of, or even a creative moment of, a political community. Here finally is the significance of the under-determination of the two logics behind the Rule of Law. The society upheld by international law is not an effect of instrumental reason, nor even of (some conception) of formal reason *tout court*. It is an effect of decisions that invoke as their justification, and thus offer as valid points of criticism, an idea of (international) community beyond sectorial interests or preferences. An idea of solidarity informs that practice. Of course, such decisions are made under conditions of uncertainty and conflict. They are amenable for criticism from alternative standpoints: there is the solidarity of the lion and that of the antelope. But that this decision-making practice is not the passive reproduction of some globalizing (economic, environmental,

---

[23] *Legality of the Threat or Use of Nuclear Weapons, Advisory Opinion, ICJ Reports 1996*, p 226, para 95.

humanitarian) structure, projects the international society as a *political community* that seeks to decide for itself what rules govern it. The practice of international law, as Bull suggested, seeks a union of 'dominant elements' with 'general interest'. As such, it remains a terrain in which the never-ending struggle between the two is being waged: hegemony, and critique of hegemony at the same time.

VII. BEYOND INSTRUMENTALISM AND FORMALISM

In other words, although notions such as 'peace', 'justice', or 'human rights' do not fit well within the techniques of legal formalism, and are quite disappointing as behavioural directives, they give voice to individuals and groups struggling for spiritual or material well-being, fighting against oppression, and seeking to express their claims in the language of something greater than merely their personal interests. Law—including international law—has a 'utopian, aspirational face' (Cotterell, 1995, p 17) expressed in large notions such as 'peace', 'justice', or 'human rights' that in countless international law texts appeal to solidarity within community. They do this in three distinct, but related ways.

First, they redescribe individuals and groups as claimants of rights or beneficiaries of entitlements and in so doing provide them with an identity that they may assert against the homogenizing pull of society's dominant elements. As Karen Knop has pointed out, the treatment of claims of self-determination by marginalized groups such as indigenous peoples in legal institutions has sometimes enabled those groups to be represented by an identity 'that might resonate with those represented' and thus to 'equalize cultures in international law' (Knop, 2002, p 210). Secondly, legal principles give an international voice to communities by allowing them to read their particular grievances as claims of universal entitlement, at the same level as claims made by other members of the community. To be able to say that some act is an 'aggression' or that the deprivation of a benefit is a 'human rights violation' is to lift a private grievance to the level of a public law violation, of concern not only to the victim but to the community. Such notions—and the whole debate about the objectives of international law—act in the political realm to challenge what Norman Geras has termed the 'contract of mutual indifference'—the tendency to regard violations as a private matter between the victim and the perpetrator, and therefore not of concern to others (Geras, 1998). They challenge the way claims are blocked in the international realm as matters of 'security', 'economics', or, for example, 'private law', thus helping to contest dominant discourses and practices that seek to justify themselves by their a-political self-evidence. And thirdly, to make those claims as *legal* claims (instead of moral aspirations or political programmes) is to imagine—and thus to create—the international world as a set of public institutions within which public authorities should use their power in roughly predictable ways and with public accountability to the community at large.

The fact that public law notions such as *jus cogens* or of obligations *erga omnes* tend to be formulated in such large terms as to restate the paradox of objectives has made them seem quite useless from an instrumental perspective. But, we may now assume, their role may be precisely to counteract the ideological effects of instrumentalism. Again, the *form* of those ideas—of an 'international legal community'—is important in allowing the articulation of the most varied types of claims as more than claims about personal preference, thus integrating the claimants as members of a pluralistic community. 'Self-determination', typically, may be constructed analytically to mean anything one wants it to mean, and many studies have invoked its extreme flexibility. Examined in the light of history, however, it has given form and strength to claims for national liberation and self-rule from the French Revolution to decolonization in 1960s, the fall of the Berlin Wall, and the political transitions that have passed from Latin America through Eastern Europe and South Africa. 'Peace', too may be an empty notion, perfectly capable of coexisting with economic deprivation and suppression of human rights. On the other hand, peace movements have been an invaluable aspect of political contestation inasmuch as they 'mobilise support and highlight the inconsistencies in international concepts of peace and security' (Charlesworth and Chinkin, 2000, p 272). Even if 'justice' does lie in the eye of the beholder, without a language of justice, the international struggles for resources, recognition, democracy, or, for instance, 'ending the culture of impunity', would have seemed like so many meaningless games played by diplomats.

In other words, though the question 'what is international law for?' is seldom useful as an aspect of the deliberations over particular problems among international lawyers, it is absolutely crucial as a focus for international law's emancipatory potential. This is why it was significant that the demonstrations against the war in Iraq in 2003 focused on the war's 'illegality'. In this way, the special scandal of Western military action could be articulated as not just the violation of the private interests of Iraqi citizens but as directed against the (legal) community, and thus everyone. The fabricated character of the justifications invoked for the war further highlighted the significance of the claim of the war's formal illegality: behind the contrast between a morality of 'freedom' and a morality of 'law', there was a deeper question about who should be entitled to rule us and what can we take on trust.

None of this deviates from the need to recognize that while the culture of formalism is a necessary though often misunderstood aspect of the legal craft, as a historical matter, it has often provided a recipe for indifference and needs to be accompanied by a live sense of its political justification. To lift the debate about objectives from diplomatic instruments or academic treatises to the level of political debates is a necessary counterweight to the bureaucratic spirit often associated with formalism. This will enable the reconstruction of international law as a political project. As modern international law arose in the last decades of the nineteenth century, it did so as a part of the élitist politics of European liberal internationalism that expected public opinion and democracy to pave the way for a rationally administered world (see Koskenniemi, 2001a; Pemberton, 2001). The last articulations of that spirit date from the first decade following the Second World War (see, eg, Lauterpacht, 1946). Since then, a gap has been created between the utopian and the pragmatic parts of international law, the former becoming a rather grandiose justification over the latter. But when formalism loses political direction, formalism itself is lost.[24] Hence the turn to pragmatism and instrumentalism surveyed above.

The question 'what is international law for?' needs to be resuscitated from the paralysis that it is infected with because of the indeterminacy of the responses given to it. But this

---

[24] For a useful reconstruction of Hans Kelsen's formalism in terms of the political project that inspired it, see von Bernstorff, 2001.

necessitates a reformulation of the relationship of international law to politics, in either of its two guises, as principles and doctrines on the one hand, and as institutional practices on the other. Both political realism and institutional pragmatism arose as reactions to failed expectations about international law's autonomy: realists rejected legal institutions as a sham and told politicians to aim directly at their objectives. Institutionalists were wary of such objectives and instead relied on techniques of adjustment and compromise.

VIII. BETWEEN HEGEMONY AND FRAGMENTATION: A MINI-HISTORY

These reaction formations are intellectually disappointing and politically dubious. Neither provides space for anything but a most formal debate about 'what is international law for?' and no space at all for responding to that question by reference to popular aspirations about peace, order, and justice. A first step in trying to account for such aspirations is to accept that these notions are subject to political controversy and that even as they are formulated in universal terms, they are constantly appropriated by particular agents and interests so as to support their agendas and causes. They are aspects of *hegemonic struggle*, that is to say, part of an argumentative practice in which particular subjects and values claim to represent that which is universal (see Mouffe and Laclau, 2001; Koskenniemi, 2004a). That the question 'what is international law for?' is a terrain of such controversy is a natural aspect of a pluralistic society and a precondition for conceiving its government in democratic terms.

The hegemonic nature of the debate about international law's objectives may be illustrated in terms of its history (see also Koskenniemi, 2004b; Supiot, 2005, pp 275–305). When Spain and Portugal at the end of the fifteenth century divided the non-European world between themselves by reference to a Papal directive, they claimed to be speaking as Christian powers on behalf of humankind as a whole. When the Spanish theologians, Vitoria or Las Casas later were claiming that God had given the Indians a soul just as He had given it to the Spanish, a particular form of Christian scholasticism—Dominican theology—came to speak in terms of universal principles, equally constraining on the Princes and the Indians. And when Hugo Grotius in 1608 challenged the Iberian claims, he was redefining the objectives of international law within a hegemonic struggle that opposed a Reformation-inspired commercial universalism against the *ancien régime* of (Catholic) Christianity. The narrative of international law from those days to the nineteenth century may be depicted as a succession of natural law arguments that were united by their always emerging from some European intelligentsia that claimed it was speaking on behalf of the world as a whole. When de Emmerich Vattel in 1758 formulated his 'necessary law of nations' in terms of the commands of natural reason, and found that it consecrated a balance of power between European sovereigns, he already filled the category of the 'universal' with a profoundly particular understanding that was a part of the (European) Enlightenment.

Since the first appearance of the (modern) international law profession in Europe in the late nineteenth century, that profession imagined itself as, in the words of the Statute of the *Institut de droit international* (1873), the 'juridical conscience of the civilised world'.

This understanding, too, was born in a cultural environment that imagined its own experience—which it labelled 'civilization'—as universal and postulated it as the end-result of the development of societies everywhere. The civilizing mission enthusiastically propagated by late nineteenth-century international lawyers was a hegemonic technique, embedded in an understanding of the law as not simply a technical craft or a set of formal instruments and institutions. It was a spontaneous aspect of 'civilization' which had the natural tendency to become universal.

If the First World War destroyed whatever was left of the civilizing mission, it also gave rise to a series of efforts to articulate anew the universal basis of international law, sometimes in terms of a law-like movement of societies to ever more complex forms of division of labour and interdependence (eg, Huber, 1910), sometimes through a reinstatement of the hierarchical principles that were a natural part of legal systems (eg, Verdross, 1923). Most of the reconstructive scholarship of the inter-war period, however, simply generalized the legal experience of European societies into the international level, bringing into existence a universal international law through private law analogies, conceiving the Covenant of the League of Nations as a constitution of the world and by allocating to the juristic class the function of 'filling the gaps' in an otherwise primitive-looking legal system (see Lauterpacht, 1933; Koskenniemi, 1997). The particular European experience with the Rule of Law became the placeholder for the aspirations of peace and justice that lawyers saw were demanded by populations struggling with industrialism and social conflict.

In the more recent post-war era, much of that kind of language—like the political liberalism with which it was associated—has lost credibility. When somebody today claims to be acting on behalf on the 'international community', we immediately recognize the hegemonic technique at work (see Klein, 2001; Feher, 2000; Koskenniemi, 2004a). As against the diplomatic antics of public international law, new specializations today often carry the ideals of universalism and progress. Recently, this has occasioned a lively debate about the 'fragmentation of international law'—the emergence and consolidation of special regimes and technical sub-disciplines: human rights law, environmental law, trade law, humanitarian law, and so on, each field projecting its preferences as universal ones. The result has been increasing normative and jurisdictional conflicts. In its *Tadić* judgment of 1999, the International Criminal Tribunal for the Former Yugoslavia (ICTY) expressly deviated from the practice of the International Court of Justice, as laid out in its *Nicaragua* case in 1986 concerning the attribution of conduct by military irregulars to a State. To move from a standard of 'effective control' to one of 'overall control' significantly enhanced the accountability of foreign States indirectly involved in internal conflicts, constituting a shift of normative preference with respect to one set of international problems.[25] The continuing debate about the relevance of environmental, human rights, or labour standards within the WTO system reflects a search for the relative priority of political objectives within WTO institutions as those priorities have not been set at the level of the relevant agreements themselves. The autonomy invoked by human rights regimes constitutes a subtle manoeuvre by human rights implementation organs to universalize their jurisdiction. 'Dynamic' arguments and the object and purpose test allow

---

[25] *Prosecutor v Dusko Tadic*, Judgment, Case No. IT-94-1-A, Appeals Chamber, 15 July 1999, 38 ILM 1518, para 137.

the creation of a systemic bias in favour of the protected individuals that could be difficult to justify under traditional law.

Such 'fragmentation' is not a technical problem resulting from lack of coordination. The normative preferences of environmental and trade bodies differ, as do preferences of human rights lawyers and international law 'generalists', and each organ is determined to follow its own preference and make it prevail over contrasting ones. The result is, sometimes, deviating interpretations of the general law, such preferences reflecting the priorities of the deciding organ, at other times the creation of firm exceptions in the law, applicable in a special field (Koskenniemi and Leino, 2002). Such fragmentation is also an aspect of hegemonic struggle where each institution, though partial, tries to occupy the space of the whole. Far from being a problem to resolve, the proliferation of autonomous or semi-autonomous normative regimes is an unavoidable reflection of a 'postmodern' social condition and a, perhaps at least to some extent, beneficial prologue to a pluralistic community in which the degrees of homogeneity and fragmentation reflect shifts of political preference (Stark, 2002).

IX. LEGAL FORMALISM AND INTERNATIONAL JUSTICE

Let me close by four responses to the question 'what is international law for?' Two are rather straightforward. First, international law exists to advance the values, interests and preferences that those in dominant positions seek to realize in the world. It is an instrument of power. Secondly, it also gives voice to those who have been excluded from powerful positions and are regularly treated as the objects of other peoples' policies; it provides a platform on which claims about violence, injustice, and social deprivation may be made even against the dominant elements. It is an instrument for the critique of power. To bring these two aspects of international law together means that there is no fixed set of objectives, purposes, or principles that would exist somewhere 'outside' or beyond international law itself, that they are always the objectives of particular actors involved in polemical confrontations. The law is instrumental, but what it is an instrument for cannot be fixed outside the political process of which it is an inextricable part.

This is why, thirdly, international law's objective is always also international law itself. For, as I have tried to argue above, it is international law's formalism that brings political antagonists together as they invoke contrasting understandings of its rules and institutions. In the absence of agreement over, or knowledge of, the 'true' objectives of political community—that is to say, in an agnostic world—the pure form of international law provides the shared surface—the *only* such surface—on which political adversaries recognize each other as such and pursue their adversity in terms of something shared, instead of seeking to attain full exclusion—'outlawry'—of the other. In this sense, international law's value and its misery lie in its being the fragile surface of political community among social agents—States, other communities, individuals—who disagree about their preferences but do this within a structure that invites them to argue in terms of an assumed universality.

But there is a fourth response as well: international law exists as a promise of justice. The agnosticism of political modernity has made the articulation of this teleological view extremely difficult. For the justice towards which international law points cannot be enumerated in substantive values, interests, or objectives. It has no predetermined institutional form. The lawyer's political advocacy and institutional reform-proposals express inadequate and reified images, (partial) points of view. Even when acceptable in their general formulation, as soon as they are translated into particular policies, and start to prefer some interests or values over others, they become vulnerable to the critique of 'false universalism'. For the *homo economicus*, none of this is too important. All that count are the external objectives projected upon the law. If law fails in realizing them, then it loses its authority. The image of law embodied in the metaphor of the *homo juridicus* is quite different. Now law itself—independently of the objectives projected upon it—has authority. This authority comes from the way it describes the international world as a (legal) community where questions of just distribution and entitlement are constantly on the agenda, where claims of legal subjects receive an equal hearing and where the acts of public officials are assessed by a language of community standards. For the instrumental view, the constraint received from law is justified only in view of the authority of the law's (external) objectives. In the formalist view, law is used to compel because the violations cannot coexist with the aspirations of universality embedded in the legal form. Such violations are singular until the law lifts them from the purely subjective into public illegality:

Law is the name of the semblance of order—the assembling, the ordering, the establishing of commonality—that is made of our otherwise (subjective) differences when we take, or interpret them to be a world that can be judged, rather than mere subjective experiences. (Constable, 2000, p 95)

But the justice that animates political community is not one that may be fully attained. Not only is law never justice itself, the two cannot exist side by side. If there is justice, then no law is needed—and if there is law, then there is only a (more or less well-founded) *expectation* of justice. Here is the truth in instrumentalism about positive law being a pointer beyond itself. There is a Messianic structure to international law, the announcement of something that remains eternally postponed. It is this 'to-come' that enables the criticism of the law's own violence, its biases and exclusions. No doubt, law and justice are linked in the activity of lawyers, paradigmatically in the legal judgment. This is the wisdom grasped by legal pragmatism. But the judgment is always insufficiently grounded in law, just like positive law is always insufficiently expressive of justice. In the gap between positive law and justice lies the necessary (and impossible) realm of the politics of law. Without it, law becomes pure positivity, its violence a mere fact of power.

REFERENCES

ABBOTT, K and SNIDAL, D (2001), 'Hard and Soft Law in International Governance', in Goldstein, JL, Kahler, M, Keohane, RO, and Slaughter, A-M, *Legalization and World Politics* (Cambridge, Mass.: MIT Press), pp 37–72.

ARNAUD, A-J (2003), *Critique de la raison juridique 2: Gouvernants sans frontiers. Entre mondialisation et post-mondialisation* (Paris: LGDJ).

BINDER, G (1988), 'Beyond Criticism', 55 *U Chi LR* 688–915.

BRIERLY, J (1944), *The Outlook for International Law* (Oxford: Oxford University Press).

BRUNNEE, J and Toope, SJ (2000), 'International Law and Constructivism: Elements of an Interactional Theory of International Law', 39 *Col J Transnat'l L* 19–74.

BULL, H (1977), *The Anarchic Society. A Study of Order in World Politics* (London: Macmillan).

BYERS, M and NOLTE, G (2003), *United States Hegemony and the Foundations of International Law* (Cambridge: Cambridge University Press).

CAMERON, I (2000), *National Security and the European Convention on Human Rights* (Stockholm: Iustus).

CARR, EH (1946), *The Twenty-years' Crisis 1919–1939* (London: Macmillan).

CHARLESWORTH, H (2002), 'International Law: A Discipline of Crisis', 65 *MLR* 377–392.

—— and Chinkin, C (2000), *The Boundaries of International Law. A Feminist Analysis* (Manchester: Manchester University Press).

CHAYES, A and CHAYES, AH (1995), *The New Sovereignty. Compliance with International Regulatory Agreements* (Cambridge, Mass.: Harvard University Press).

CHESTERMAN, S (2001), *Just War or Just Peace? Humanitarian Intervention and International Law* (Oxford: Oxford University Press).

CONSTABLE, M (2000), 'The Silence of the Law: Justice in Cover's "Field of Pain and Death"', in Sarat, A (ed), *Law, Violence and the Possibility of Justice* (Princetown, NJ: Princeton University Press).

CORTEN, O (1997), *L'utilisation du 'raisonnable' par le juge international. Discours juridique, raison et contradictions* (Brussels: Bruylant).

COTTERELL, R (1995), *Law's Community. Legal Theory in Sociological Perspective* (Oxford: Clarendon Press).

FEHER, M (2000), *Powerless by Design. The Age of the International Community* (Durham, NC: Duke University Press).

FINNEMORE, M (1996), *National Interests in International Society* (Ithaca, NY: Cornell University Press).

FISH, S (1989), *Doing What Comes Naturally. Change, Rhetoric, and the Practice of Theory in Literary and Legal Studies* (Oxford: Oxford University Press).

FOUCAULT, M (2005), *Naissance de la biopolitique. Cours au Collège de France 1978–79* (Paris: Gallimard/Seuil).

FRANCK, TM (1995), *Fairness in International Law and Institutions* (Oxford: Oxford University Press).

FULLER, LL (1969), *The Morality of Law*, 2nd rev edn (New Haven, Conn.: Yale University Press).

GERAS, N (1998), *The Contract of Mutual Indifference. Political Philosophy after the Holocaust* (London: Verso).

GOLDSMITH, J and POSNER, E (2005), *The Limits of International Law* (Oxford: Oxford University Press).

GREWE, W (2001), *The Epochs of International Law* (Byers, M (trans.)) (Berlin: De Gruyter).

GUZZINI, G (1998), *Realism in International Relations and International Political Economy* (London: Routledge).

HABERMAS, J (2004), *Der gespaltene Westen* (Frankfurt: Suhrkamp).

HARDT, M and NEGRI, A (1999), *Empire* (Cambridge, Mass.: Harvard University Press).

HENKIN, L (1989), 'International Law: Politics, Values and Functions', 216 *Recueil des Cours* 9–416.

HUBER, M (1910/1928), *Die soziologischen Grundlagen des Völkerrechts* (Berlin: Rothschild).

HURRELL, A and WOODS, N (1999), *Inequality, Globalization and World Politics* (Oxford: Oxford University Press).

KANT, I (1999), *Critique of Practical Reason* (Gregor, M (ed), Introduction by Reath, A) (Cambridge: Cambridge University Press).

KAUFMANN, E (1911), *Das Wesen des Völkerrechts und die Clausula rebus sic stantibus* (Tübingen: Mohr).

KENNEDY, DAVID (2000), 'When Renewal Repeats: Thinking Against the Box', 32 *NYU JILP* 335–500.

—— (2004), *The Darker Side of Virtue. Reassessing International Humanitarianism* (Princeton, NJ: Princeton University Press).

KENNEDY, DUNCAN (2001), 'Formalism', in *The International Encyclopedia of Social & Behavioral Sciences* (The Hague: Kluwer).

KERVÉGAN, J-F (1999), 'Carl Schmitt and "World Unity"', in Mouffe, C (ed), *The Challenge of Carl Schmitt* (London: Verso), pp 54–74.

KLEIN, P (2001), 'Les problèmes soulevés par la référence à la communauté internationale comme facteur de legitimite', in Corten, O and Delcourt, B (eds), *Droit légitimation et politique exterieure: L'Europe et la guerre du Kosovo* (Brussels: Bruylant), pp 261–297.

KNOP, K (2002), *Diversity and Self-Determination in International Law* (Cambridge: Cambridge University Press).

KOSKENNIEMI, M (1989), *From Apology to Utopia. The Structure of International Legal Argument*, 2005 reissue with new Epilogue (Cambridge: Cambridge University Press).

—— (1994), 'The Wonderful Artificiality of States', 88 *ASIL Proc* 22–29.

—— (1997), 'Lauterpacht, The Victorian Tradition in International Law', 8 *EJIL* 215–263.

—— (1999a), 'The Silence of Law/The Voice of Justice', in Boisson de Chazournes, L and Sands, P (eds), *International Law, the International Court of Justice and Nuclear Weapons* (Cambridge: Cambridge University Press), pp 488–510.

—— (1999b) 'The Limits of International Law: Are There Such?', XXVIII *Thesaurus Acroasiarum: Might and Right in International Relations*, pp 27–50.

—— (2000), 'The Effect of Rights on Political Culture', in Alston, P (ed), *The EU and Human Rights* (Oxford: Oxford University Press), pp 99–116.

—— (2001a), *The Gentle Civilizer of Nations. The Rise and Fall of International Law 1870–1960* (Cambridge: Cambridge University Press).

—— (2001b), 'Solidarity Measures: State Responsibility as a New International Order?', 72 *BYIL* 339–356.

—— (2004a), 'International Law and Hegemony: A Reconfiguration', 17 *Cambridge Review of International Affairs*, 197–218.

—— (2004b), 'Legal Universalism: Between Morality and Power in a World of States', in Cheng, S (ed), *Law, Justice and Power: Between Reason and Will* (Stanford, NJ: Stanford University Press) 46–69.

—— (2005), 'International Law in Europe: Between Tradition and Renewal', 16 *EJIL* 113–124.

—— (2009), 'Miserable Comforters. International Relations as New Natural law', 15 *EJIR*, 395–422.

—— and Leino, P (2002), 'The Fragmentation of International Law: Postmodern Anxieties', 16 *LJIL* 533–579.

KRATOCHWIL, F (2000), 'How Do Norms Matter?', in Byer, M (ed), *The Role of Law in International Politics. Essays in International Relations and International Law* (Oxford: Oxford University Press), pp 35–68.

LACLAU, E (1996), 'Deconstruction, Pragmatism, Hegemony', in Mouffe, C (ed),

Deconstruction and Pragmatism (London: Verso).

LÂM, MC (2000), *At the Edge of the State: Indigenous Peoples and Self-Determination* (Dobbs Ferry, NY: Transnational).

LAUTERPACHT, H (1933), *The Function of Law in the International Community* (Oxford: Oxford University Press).

—— (1946), 'The Grotian Tradition in International Law', 23 *BYIL* 1–53.

—— (1958), *The Development of International Law by the International Court* (London: Stevens).

—— (1975), 'The Reality of the Law of Nations', in *International Law, being the Collected Papers of Hersch Lauterpacht*, vol 2, pp 22–51.

McDOUGAL, MS (1953), 'International Law, Power and Policy. A Contemporary Conception', 82 *Recueil des Cours* 137–259.

MARKS, S (2000), *The Riddle of All Constitutions. International Law, Democracy and the Critique of Ideology* (Oxford: Oxford University Press).

MORGENTHAU, H (1940), 'Positivism, Functionalism, and International Law', 34 *AJIL* 261–284.

MOUFFE, C and LACLAU, E (2001), *Hegemony and Socialist Strategy*, 2nd edn (London: Verso).

NARDIN, T (1983), *Law, Morality and the Relations between States* (Princeton, NJ: Princeton University Press).

—— (1998), 'Legal Positivism as a Theory of International Society', in Mapel, DR and Nardin, T, *International Society. Diverse Ethical Perspectives* (Princeton, NJ: Princeton University Press), pp 17–35.

O'NEILL, O (2000), *Bounds of Justice* (Cambridge: Cambridge University Press).

ORFORD, A (2003), *Reading Humanitarian Intervention. Human Rights and the Use of Force in International Law* (Cambridge: Cambridge University Press).

PAULUS, A (2001), *Die internatinale Gemeinschaft im Völkerrecht. Eine Untersuchung zur Entwicklung des Völkerrechts im Zeitalter der Globalisierung* (Munich: Beck).

PEMBERTON, J-A (2001), *Global Metaphors. Modernity and the Quest for One World* (London: Pluto Press).

POSNER, R (2003), 'Do States have a Moral Obligation to Obey International Law?', 55 *Stanford Law Journal* 1901–1920.

SCHACHTER, O (1997), 'The Decline of the Nation-state and its Implications for International Law', *Col J of Transnat'l L* 7–23.

SCHMITT, C (1988), *Der Nomos der Erde im Völkerrecht des Jus Publicum Europaeum*, 3rd edn (Berlin: Duncker & Humblot).

—— (1996), *The Concept of the Political* (trans. and intr. by Schwab, G) (Chicago: University of Chicago Press).

SHELTON, D (ed) (2000), *Commitment and Compliance. The Role of Non-Binding Norms in the International Legal System* (Oxford: Oxford University Press).

STARK, B (2002), 'After/Word(s): Violation of Human Dignity and Postmodernism in Law', 27 *Yale JIL* 336–347.

SUPIOT, A (2005), *Homo juridicus. Essai sur la fonction anthropologique de droit* (Paris: Seuil).

TASIOULAS, J (1996), 'In Defence of Relative Normativity: Communitarian Values and the Nicaragua Case', 16 *OJLS* 85–128.

TOMUSCHAT, C (1999), 'International Law: Ensuring the Survival of Mankind on the Eve of New Century', 23 *Recueil des Cours* 1–281.

TSAGOURIAS, N (2000), 'Globalization, Order and the Rule of Law', XI *FYBIL* 247–264.

VERDROSS, A (1923), *Die Einheit des rechtlichen Weltbildes* (Tübingen: Mohr).

VON BERNSTORFF, J (2001), *Der Glaube an das Universale Recht. Zur Völkerrechstheorie Hans Kelsens und seiner Schüler* (Baden-Baden: Nomos).

WATTS, SIR A (2000), 'The Importance of International Law', in Byers, M (ed), *The Role of Law in International Politics. Essays in International Relations and International Law* (Oxford: Oxford University Press), pp 5–16.

WEIL, P (1983), 'Towards Relative Normativity in International Law?', 77 *AJIL* 413–442.

WESTLAKE, J (1910), *International Law*, 2nd edn, vol 2 (Cambridge: Cambridge University Press).

3

WICKED HERESIES OR LEGITIMATE PERSPECTIVES? THEORY AND INTERNATIONAL LAW

Iain Scobbie

Legal theory is always more or less closely connected with philosophical thinking, political conditions, and ideological currents.

Karl Olivecrona, *Law as Fact*
(1971), p 27

[T]heories of law...are one of the principal causes of low morale among students of international law.

Ian Brownlie, *International Law at the Fiftieth Anniversary of the United Nations* (1995), p 22

SUMMARY

International law does not exist in an intellectual vacuum. Our understanding of the nature of international law—of what it is and what it can and should do—is ultimately dependent on theoretical assumptions and presuppositions. These can be latent and unexamined, in which case they are likely to foster only an acritical complacency. As all law has a political dimension, because law attempts to provide authoritative models of how people should behave, it is not surprising that theoretical models of international law encode specific views of the world and of relations between States. These assumptions and presuppositions influence the analysis of substantive issues, thus active engagement with theory is a matter which should neither be ignored nor be simply left behind in the academy.

I. THE PROLOGUE: MAPPING THE DISCIPLINE—DIFFERING PERSPECTIVES OR WICKED HERESIES?

Geography has always been a presence in international law as anyone who has ever had to read a complete case report (as opposed to a pre-packaged extract in a casebook) of a terrestrial or maritime boundary dispute knows to their cost. Even worse if you have to read more than one. These cases demonstrate, in often excruciating detail, that the material delineation of the physical area within which States, the principal actors in the international legal system, exist and act is geographical. Some theorists argue that geography is a neglected factor in the theoretical analysis of international law (see, for instance, Borgen, 2007; Landauer, forthcoming; and Osofsky, 2007). One would suspect that with geography comes maps, but Landauer suggests that much legal scholarship 'seems more interested in "mapping" than maps'.

The notion of maps and mapping is a useful metaphor to describe international legal theory. We use different maps for different purposes, and in mapping different maps we encode different information. An atlas may be useful to plan a journey, but is likely to be of little use to navigate an unknown city, and a tourist guide to the city's sites gives a different picture than an A-Z street map. All maps suppress some information in order that they may highlight others and, in that sense, all maps are incomplete—but the selection of the information relevant to a map is always a more or less conscious choice on the part of cartographer. The perceived purpose of the map determines its content. Legal theories are like this: their authors decide the aspects of law they want to discuss and in highlighting some, they downplay or ignore others. In rhetorical theory, this is known as 'presence':

choice is…a dominant factor in scientific debates: choice of the facts deemed relevant, choice of hypotheses, choice of the theories that should be confronted with the facts, choice of the actual elements that constitute facts. The method of each science implies such a choice, which is relatively stable in the natural sciences, but is much more variable in the social sciences.

By the very fact of selecting certain elements and presenting them to the audience, their importance and pertinency to the discussion are implied. Indeed, such a choice endows those elements with a *presence*, which is an essential factor in argumentation (Perelman and Olbrechts-Tyteca, 1969, p 116; see generally pp 115–120).

Like maps, all theoretical discussions of international law are incomplete in one way or another because different theorists emphasize—give presence to—different aspects of this ever-changing discipline. Some contemporary—and not so contemporary—theorists argue that these differences are inevitable, because one's whole personality is inextricably involved in one's approach to and understanding of (international) law.[1] Accordingly, there can be no objectivity, no intellectual space beyond the individual analyst—'there is

---

[1] See, eg, Kennedy, 2004 and Koskenniemi, 1999; compare Frank, 1949, pp 146–156 and Lasswell and McDougal, 1943, p 236: see also Duxbury, 1995, pp 125–135.

no there there' (Stein, 1938, p 251). Thus, Professor Charlesworth has claimed that the 'most intriguing aspect' of Professor Kennedy's views on the international human rights system 'is the self-portrait of its author' (Charlesworth, 2002a, p 127 in response to Kennedy, 2002 (reprinted in Kennedy, 2004)). Different analysts bring to bear different concerns, different aims and different presuppositions—in short, different perspectives—to their thinking about international law. To criticize someone for perceived omissions or improper agendas, whether hidden or evident, in their analysis is perhaps simply to affirm that they have some other concerns which they think interesting and important—and thus ultimately to acknowledge (whether consciously or not) that they are not you. Should we acknowledge and embrace this diversity or should we burn those with whom we disagree because they are heretics, wilfully blind to the truth to which we adhere?

Although, in recent years, international legal theory has started to examine the implications of globalization, global governance, and the constitutionalization of the international legal order (see, for instance, works as diverse as Allott, 2002; Berman, 2005; Dunoff and Trachtman, 2009; and Slaughter, 2004), the focus of international law remains on the State. Geography bites: the very fact of the possession of territory gives legal primacy to the State. All law has a political dimension as it aims to provide authoritative models of how those subject to it should behave. Law inevitably privileges some values and interests while ignoring or prejudicing others. In the case of international law, the privileged entities are States, as the world has long been characterized by the primacy of States as the principal actors on its political stage, making international law in pursuit of their policies. The substantive content of international law is asymmetric: it privileges States' interests above all else, relegating those of non-State entities to, at best, a secondary consideration. So embedded is this expectation of State privilege that some complain when non-State actors attempt to make States and State officials live up to their obligations imposed by international law. A US military lawyer, Charles Dunlap, coined the term 'lawfare' initially to describe the way that law has been deployed as a weapon during war, for instance, by those seeking to gain a moral or propaganda advantage by claiming that war crimes have been committed by a stronger adversary (see Dunlap, 2001 and 2007). The notion has since been extended, and can be summarized as the employment of the power of legal accountability, generally by a non-State actor such as a non-governmental organization (NGO), in opposition to official State action (see, eg, Herzberg, 2008). Lawfare thus employs international law against the State, whether in domestic or international fora—for example, in courts or before human rights treaty bodies. It could be described as the use of soft normative power against the more naked coercion of the State. As such, it may be seen as a strategy of resistance to the political desires of States, which seeks to disrupt the principal asymmetry or structural bias of international law which lies in its State-centric nature.

On the other hand, lawfare might be seen as an attempt to guard against a tendency which Professor Carty terms 'the decadence of international lawyers':

The decadence of the profession shows itself in it willingness to turn a blind eye to the deficiencies... The profession consists of those who realize that functioning authoritative institutions provide a framework within which legal argumentation can take place as structured dialogue... [A] profession is decadent when it closes its own practices off against the sufferings of the humanity it should endeavour to serve. The profession debates with itself and shuns direct contact with non-professionals, ie with the world outside its own meetings and journals. (Carty, 1997, pp 188–189)

The practice of lawfare is, of course, not without normative danger. In seeking to attack a practice, it may end up legitimating it in whole or in part. For example, the attempt by human rights NGOs to employ international law to have Israel's policy of targeted killings declared unlawful extra-judicial killings resulted in an equivocal judgment from Israel's High Court which ruled that targeted killings were at times lawful, depending on the circumstances.[2]

The asymmetry of the international legal system is reflected in theoretical discussions of international law. While it should not be surprising that a great deal of international legal theory has been instrumental, directed at elucidating and explaining the role and conduct of States in the international sphere, another tendency has been more idealistic and critical of the international system that we have.

On the one hand, international legal theory has frequently been employed to provide instrumental methodologies which aim at embedding States' political programmes into the substance of international law—'Legal doctrines dissolve far too easily into thin disguises for assertions of national interests' (Kennedy, 1985, p 371). I shall demonstrate this by examining two dominant schools of international legal thought, that are principally associated with the antagonistic world views of the United States and the Soviet Union as they each vied for power during the Cold War—the New Haven School and Marxist-Leninist theory. It might be thought that these approaches to international law have now, essentially, been consigned to history: if nothing else, Soviet theory changed radically after perestroika.[3] Instrumentalist approaches, however, did not die with the Cold War, but remain alive and well in contemporary legal theory. Not only has there been a resurgence in interest in the New Haven School (see, eg, Borgen, 2007; Dickinson, 2007; Hathaway, 2007; Koh, 2007; Levit, 2007; Osofsky, 2007; and Reisman, Wiessner, and Willard, 2007), but instrumentalism is also located in arguments that international law should, for instance, be liberal (see, eg, Kennedy, 2003 and Slaughter, 1995; compare Alvarez, 2001), be hegemonic (eg, Bolton, 2000; Goldsmith and Posner, 2005; and Rabkin, 2005; compare Carty, 2004 and Vagts, 2001), or be Marxist in one way or another (eg, Chimni, 2004; Marks, 2008; and Miéville, 2004).

On the other hand, the concentration on the concerns of States has stimulated a counter-reaction which argues, in effect, that international law is something far too important to be left to States. Indeed for some theorists, particularly those associated with the New Stream, or New Approaches to International Law group, this appears to amount to a manifesto: 'students of international law should reformulate their sense of cause and effect in international affairs: rejecting reliance upon visions both of State interests that we too often take to propel doctrine and of the law that we take to restrain statesmen' (Kennedy, 1985, p 381).[4]

For scholars such as Professor Allott, the leading exponent of idealist theory in the United Kingdom[5] what matters is humanity rather than a collection of States, the pursuit of whose interests has all too often harmed humans. The edifice of the State does not have

---

[2] See *Public Committee against Torture in Israel* v *Government of Israel*, HCJ 769/02, (2006) 46 ILM 375.

[3] See, eg, McWhinney, 1990, and Vereshchetin and Müllerson, 1990; also Tunkin, 2003.

[4] See also Kennedy, 1999 and 2000. Good overviews of New Stream, or New Approaches to International Law work are Cass, 1996; Paulus, 2001; and Purvis, 1991.

[5] For what might be his manifesto, see Allott, 1998, although the *Preface* to Allott, 2001 might give an easier understanding of his enterprise; but compare Prager, 1998.

its agenda set by the people of the society it encompasses, but rather by the much narrower class of politicians and officials:

The state (public realm under the authority of a government) having developed as a way of internally organizing a certain sort of society…came to be conceived also as the external manifestation of the given societies. The state was turned inside out, like a glove. The governments of the statally organizing societies recognize in each other that which is *state*, not that which is *society*. (Allott, 2001, p 243, para 13.105(1))

The pursuit of State concerns in the international arena has given rise to the perception that domestic and international affairs are 'intrinsically and radically separate' (p 244, para 13.105(6)): morality is discontinuous between the domestic and international spheres. Citizens can only participate in international affairs through the mediation of their governments. This allows State concerns to trump a demotic humanitarian impulse, as 'governments, and the human beings who compose them, are able to will and act internationally in ways that they would be morally restrained from willing and acting internally, murdering human beings by the million in wars, tolerating oppression and starvation and disease and poverty, human cruelty and suffering, human misery and human indignity' (p 248, para 13.105(16)). What we are left with is 'a world fit for governments' (p 249, para 13.109) in which 'international law is left speaking to governments the words that governments want to hear' (p 296, para 16.1). The State-centric nature of international *unsociety* (to use Allott's term) and the conduct of international relations thus greatly attenuates, if not eliminates, individual moral responsibility for the content and operation of international law.

Given these fundamentally different approaches and concerns, the burden of my argument is that an understanding of legal theory is not only crucial to the whole enterprise of international law, but also in the instrumental concerns of the practical application of international law. It is undeniably true that individual theorists, or groups of theorists who share common concerns and intellectual and/or methodological approaches, can exert an influence on the way that international law is understood and used and criticized. Doubtless some would deny this; for instance Professor Brownlie has claimed that '[t]here is no doubt room for a whole treatise on the harm caused to the business of legal investigation by theory' (Brownlie, 1983, p 627).[6] He could have a point. For instance, it is apparent that hegemonic theory influenced the advice given to President George W Bush that resulted in the denial of prisoner of war status to those detained in Guantanamo Bay, and in the authorization of interrogation techniques which led to the scandalous maltreatment of prisoners in Abu Ghraib (see below, Section V).

An example is not, however, an argument and Brownlie's argument begs the question: 'How can one know what there is "legal" to investigate unless one subscribes to some abstract conception of law?' That is a matter for legal theory. It need not provide a water-tight definition of what law is and what it is about, but it can at least give basic criteria which enables the identification of what counts as 'legal investigation' in the first place. A disavowal of theory can also simply denote a conservative commitment to a hidden or latent theory that rests content with the status quo and seeks neither to question nor justify either the substance or practice of international law (Warbrick,

---

[6] For Brownlie's antipathy to theory, see also Brownlie, 1981, pp 5–8, and Brownlie, 1995, pp 22ff.

1991, pp 69–70).[7] If so, this disinterest simply amounts to a conscious refusal to think about what one is doing. It constitutes an intellectual self-censorship which suppresses analysis and critical evaluation at least as much as an external authoritarian enforcement of conformity to some 'official' or received model of the nature and function of international law—such as the Soviet theory of international law.

Despite, in some quarters (eg, Bolton, 2000, pp 2, 4–5, and 48), a lingering attachment to the classical Austinian positivist claim that, because there is no determinate sovereign superior to States capable of promulgating and enforcing its commands, international law is not law but merely amounts to positive morality, this view is no longer generally accepted (see Austin, 1832 (1995), Lecture V, pp 123–125). With the posthumous publication of the works of Jeremy Bentham, it is clear that Austin owed much to Bentham's more sophisticated analysis of law. Further, '[a]lthough there is no question that Bentham had doubts about the law-like character of international law, he was by no means the skeptic that Austin was' (Janis, 2004, p 16, see pp 16–18 generally). It seems somewhat bizarre to rely on a discredited nineteenth century legal philosophy which speaks of the 'sovereign' and is essentially pre-democratic (at least in terms of universal suffrage) as the foundation for a contemporary understanding of law, or as the expression of a hostility to—or even a fear of—the very notion of international law. As Professor Franck (1995, p 6) affirms: 'international law has entered its post-ontological era. Its lawyers need no longer defend the very existence of international law. Thus emancipated from the constraints of defensive ontology, international lawyers are now free to undertake a critical assessment of its content'.[8]

Some contemporary theorists, however, on grounds far divorced from the crudities of Austinian analysis, deny the very existence of a discipline we can identify as 'international law', as something distinct from other disciplines, particularly politics:

Our inherited ideal of a World Order based on the Rule of Law thinly hides from sight the fact that social conflict must still be solved by political means and that even though there may exist a common legal rhetoric among international lawyers, that rhetoric must, *for reasons internal to the ideal itself*, rely on essentially contested—political—principles to justify outcomes to international disputes. (Koskenniemi, 1990, p 7)[9]

This effacement of international law as an entity distinct from politics is, of course, a critique of other theories which see international law as something separate, something distinctly 'legal': it has itself been challenged (see, eg, Beckett, 2005 and, more generally, MacCormick, 1990). To understand the critique, we must first understand the orthodoxy which engendered it. I do not propose here to offer anything like a comprehensive account of the diverse theories of international law, or to offer some 'master' theory which trumps all others. My aim is much more modest: to offer an outline of some theoretical perspectives, or heresies, which should provide a basis for thinking about the nature and

---

[7] See also Warbrick, 2000, p 621 passim, but especially at pp 633–636; and Lasswell and McDougal, 1943, p 207. This was their first co-authored work, and is reprinted as an appendix in Lasswell and McDougal, 1992, vol II at p 1265.

[8] On the ontological argument of whether international law is really law, see, for instance, Arend, 1999, Ch 1, especially at pp 28ff; and Franck, 1990, Ch 2.

[9] See also, for instance, Kratochwil, 1989; and Koskenniemi, 1989: for a commentary on both, see Scobbie, 1990.

function(s) of international law. But this presupposes an initial question: what is a 'theory', and what does it do?

II. WHAT IS A 'THEORY' AND WHAT DOES IT DO?

Kant provides a useful notion of a theory for our purposes. He defined a theory as:

A collection of rules, even of practical rules, is termed a *theory* if the rules concerned are envisaged as principles of a fairly general nature, and if they are abstracted from numerous conditions which, nonetheless, necessarily influence their practical application. Conversely, not all activities are called *practice*, but only those realizations of a particular purpose which are considered to comply with certain generally conceived principles of procedure... [N]o-one can pretend to be practically versed in a branch of knowledge and yet treat theory with scorn, without exposing the fact that he is an ignoramus in his subject. He no doubt imagines that he can get further than he could through theory if he gropes around in experiments and experiences, without collecting certain principles (which in fact amount to what we term theory) and without relating his activities to an integral whole (which, if treated methodically, is what we call a system). (Kant, 1793 (1970), pp 61–62)

But what does this mean? It means that the function of a theory is to formulate or guide practice; to provide a relatively abstract framework for the understanding and determination of action. A theory is necessary because it provides us with the intellectual blueprint which enables us to understand the world, or some specific aspect of human affairs. Kant's notion of a system, which comprises an integrated body of knowledge rather than simply a collection of essentially unrelated general rules, underlines the constitutive function of theory. Theory makes data comprehensible by providing a structure for the organization of a given discipline or body of knowledge.

Contrast this with Hart's analysis of international law. He argued that it formed a set, but not a system, as the rules of international law were 'not unified by or deriv[ed] their validity from any more basic rule' (Hart, 1994, p 234). Rather he claimed (p 214) that:

international law not only lacks the secondary rules of change and adjudication which provide for legislature and courts, but also a unifying rule of recognition specifying 'sources' of law and providing general criteria for the identification of its rules.

This view was wrong when Hart first expressed it in 1961. Despite criticism, whether on grounds of inadequacy or inept drafting,[10] it is generally accepted that Article 38 of the Statute of the International Court of Justice provides at least a starting place for the enumeration of the sources of international law and thus functions as a 'rule of recognition' for the international legal system, should one wish to adopt a Hartian analysis. Hart defines the rule of recognition as 'a public, common standard of correct judicial decision' (Hart, 1994, p 116).[11] Article 38 falls squarely within this notion, particularly as

---

[10] For instance, see Carty, 1986, pp 13ff; Charlesworth and Chinkin, 2000, pp 67ff; Jennings, 1982, p 9; Higgins, 1994, pp 18–19; Tunkin, 1974, pp 118, 123–124.

[11] For a commentary on the rule of recognition, see MacCormick, 1981, pp 108ff.

one of the criticisms made of it is that it was constructed precisely to specify the sources which the judges of the Permanent Court of International Justice, and subsequently the International Court, should apply in their decision-making, rather than specify sources for the non-judicial identification and application of international law (see, eg, Higgins, 1994, p 18).

Indeed, much contemporary theoretical analysis of international law is precisely concerned with the investigation of the sources of international law—the identification of what counts, or should count, as international law, which is, for instance, exemplified in the contemporary debate about relative normativity[12]—as opposed to the conceptual exegesis of distinct substantive themes or fields. The latter type of analysis, however, is not lacking, finding expression in works such as Franck's account of the emergence of individualism as a core concept in international law (Franck, 1999); in the numerous applications of New Haven analysis to such diverse topics as the law of the sea, (McDougal and Burke, 1962) human rights (McDougal, Lasswell, and Chen, 1969 and 1980), and armed conflict (McDougal and Feliciano, 1994); in Ragazzi's exegesis of obligations *erga omnes* as rooted ultimately in natural law (Ragazzi, 1997, pp 183–185); and in Charlesworth and Chinkin's scrutiny of international law through the lens of feminism (Charlesworth and Chinkin, 2000).

Ultimately, however, all conceptual issues of sources—the identification of what counts as international law—is a question of theory in the sense just indicated: 'There is no separating legal philosophy from substantive norms when it comes to problem solving in particular cases' (Higgins, 1994, p 267). The identification of sources is the determination of general principles which classify phenomena such as documents, the statements and behaviour of international actors and so on, as relevant or irrelevant to the enterprise of international law. On this, the former President of the International Court of Justice, Professor Higgins has commented:

As international lawyers, we have perhaps ceased to notice how very strange it is that we spend so much time talking about the provenance of the norms that bind the participants in the international legal system. In domestic legal systems the sources of legal obligation are treated in a much more matter-of-fact way...But we have become so preoccupied with jurisprudential debate about the sources of international law that we have, I think, lost sight of the fact that it is an admission of an uncertainty at the heart of the international legal system. I do not mean that there are uncertainties about what particular norms provide (which there may be), but about how we identify norms. (Higgins, 1994, p 17)

These uncertainties should not be overstated. There is a general consensus on core sources doctrine, with doctrinal disagreement attaching to specific, but nonetheless important, issues—such as the inter-relationship and relative importance of *opinio iuris* and State practice, and the very existence and potential effects of the doctrine of persistent objection, in the formation of customary international law.

Doctrinal divergences and disagreements are inevitable because all theoretical positions are, to some degree, subjective. They reflect the author's own predispositions and concerns, some of which can be quite transient. Consider, for instance, the discussion of the doctrine of persistent objection in the formation of customary

---

[12]   See, eg, Weil, 1983; Tasioulas, 1996; Beckett, 2001; and Roberts, 2001.

international law in articles written by Charney and Stein in the mid-1980s. To an extent, this was informed or influenced by the then-recent conclusion of the 1982 Law of the Sea Convention and its initial repudiation by various developed States which objected to the regime it created for deep seabed mining, which both Charney and Stein used to illustrate their different views on the question of persistent objection (see Charney, 1985, p 4, n 12, and Stein, 1985, pp 462, 474–475). Charney and Stein took diametrically opposed views on whether non-signatory States, despite their protests, could or should be bound by any customary regime on deep seabed mining that the Convention might generate. This specific substantive issue masked more deeply held views about the nature of international law, and in particular the roles of sovereignty and State consent in the formation of customary international law. Charney saw the doctrine of persistent objection as one that held only a temporary or strategic utility, which a State could employ 'to force an accommodation of interests in the international community with respect to the evolution of new rules of law' (Charney, 1985, p 23). He stressed consensus and a contextual approach which downplayed the need for State consent to individual rules. Stein, on the other hand, argued in favour of the persistent objection doctrine by emphasizing State sovereignty and claiming that 'the central premise of international law theory' is:

that the international legal order lacks a hierarchically superior sovereign authorized to prescribe rules for the subjects of the order. In the absence of such a sovereign, law must result from the concurrent wills of states and, at the very least, cannot bind a state that has manifestly and continuously refused to accept it. (Stein, 1985, pp 458–459)

Accordingly, because writers start from different, and often inarticulate, premises about the nature and function of international law, it is not surprising that adhesion to different theoretical presuppositions results in different conclusions about what counts as international law in the first place (Lauterpacht, 1933, p 57).

Encoded within expositions of substantive international law—within general textbooks, specialized monographs, and articles in scholarly journals—are preconceptions about and expectations of international law. For instance, consider computer network attacks, which are hostile operations aimed at degrading or destroying information held on computers and computer networks, or the computers or networks themselves. There have been attempts to analyse the legal implications of computer network attacks; in particular, to determine whether they would amount to a use of force prohibited under of Article 2(4) of the UN Charter. Professor Schmitt's views on this issue undoubtedly inform, if not structure, much of the current debate (see, eg, Schmitt, 1998; 1999a; 1999b; and 2002). He makes clear his theoretical assumptions. In discussing the interpretation of Article 2(4), he notes that the dominant interpretation is 'positivist'. It starts from the premise that the text of the Charter must authorize a use of force for it to be lawful, rather than 'from the postulate that force is permissible unless a specific Charter prohibition thereon applies' (Schmitt, 1999a, p 901). Although conceding that this is 'textually sound', Schmitt argues that it is detached from reality, because it is wedded to disappointed expectations that the Charter's collective security system would dispense with the need for the unilateral use of force. Adherence to a strict textual interpretation could frustrate 'the Charter's world order aspirations' (Schmitt, 1999a, p 902). Rather, he argues that the tenets of the New Haven School, as exemplified in the writings of Reisman, should be adopted. This emphasizes the context in which force is used, and the values it seeks to advance or protect (see Reisman, 1985). Accordingly:

every threat or use of force is evaluated on its own merits based upon the context in which it occurs...the operational code is contextual. Moreover, the categories in which uses of force are sometimes considered appropriate evolve...Ultimately...extra-Charter uses of force will fall outside the operational code if they fail to advance shared world order values. (Schmitt, 1999a, p 903)

To determine whether a use of force, and perhaps derivatively a computer network attack, is lawful by applying the theoretical presuppositions of the New Haven School can only be controversial: it has few adherents outside the United States, and yet its tenets underpin this body of influential doctrine on an emerging topic.

An author's theoretical presuppositions are, however, frequently inarticulate, if not invisible, in works of substantive exposition; nevertheless they mould tacit under-standings of and approaches to the rules of international law and their content. For example, consider the current debate about the proper relationship between the law of armed conflict and human rights law. As Professor Koskenniemi observes, one of the characteristics of contemporary international legal practice is specialization, where dis-crete sets of substantive issues are packaged into categories such as trade law or envir-onmental law. These specializations 'cater for special audiences with special interests and special ethos'. Each contains structural biases in the form of dominant expecta-tions about the values, actors, and solutions appropriate to that specialization, which thus affect practical outcomes. The actors in these different fields conceptualize issues in ways which pull upon the biases encoded within that specialization (Koskenniemi, 2009: see also Beckett, 2009 and Scobbie, 2009). Human rights law and the law of armed conflict are obviously two such specialist areas of international law with their own par-ticular structural biases.

Professor Kretzmer points out that the doctrine of proportionality employed by the law of armed conflict differs from that employed by human rights law. Proportionality in the law of armed conflict concerns collateral damage, and thus permits civilian death and injury, an advance calculation which is an anathema to human rights law. He observes that Additional Protocol II, which regulates non-international armed conflict, makes no reference to proportionality, but that the ICRC customary international law study claims it is an accepted principle in non-international armed conflict (see Henckaerts and Doswald-Beck, 2005, Vol I, pp 46–50). Kretzmer comments that this appears to assume that proportionality protects potential victims of an armed conflict, but its introduc-tion could rather weaken the protection they enjoy under a human rights regime (see Kretzmer, 2009, pp 17–22). This example underlines a point made, amongst others, by Professors Allott and Koskenniemi, namely that as lawyers we must be conscious of what we are doing and why we are doing it and, above all, take responsibility for our argu-ments. This must include the duty to scrutinize the presuppositions we bring with us to our work.

Identifying authorial predispositions is simply crucial to evaluating the weight to be given to an argument. Indeed, identifying the very author of a text can be decisive in law, in a way alien to other disciplines. For instance, in literature, Foucault argues in favour of the death of the author—the idea that the identity and personality of the author of a work of fiction is irrelevant to the authority and interpretation of the text. He acknowledges:

I seem to call for a form of culture in which fiction would not be limited by the figure of the author…All discourses, whatever their status, form, value, and whatever the treatment to which they will be subjected, would then develop in the anonymity of a murmur. We would no longer hear the questions that have been rehashed for so long: Who really spoke? Is it really he and not someone else? With what authenticity or originality? And what part of his deepest self did he express in his discourse… [W]e would hear hardly anything but the stirring of an indifference: What difference does it make who is speaking? (Foucault, 1998, p 222)

Foucault claims that the ascription of an author to a text entails that it 'is not ordinary everyday speech that merely comes and goes…On the contrary, it is a speech that must be received in a certain mode and that, in a given culture, must receive a certain status' (p 211). Yet the identity of the person or body promulgating some types of legal texts has precisely this function. A document's legal significance can depend on its author; because its author is a judge; because its author is a legislature; because its author is a foreign ministry; and so on. Legal texts, and their authors, only make sense within the context of the system that gives them authority and meaning.

Literary, artistic, even philosophical texts, on the other hand, are a great deal more autonomous. Does it *really* matter who wrote *Pride and Prejudice* (Austen, 1813) or, for that matter, *Pride and Prejudice and Zombies* (Austen and Grahame-Smith, 2009)? At the extreme, as in the case of the fictitious Australian poet Ern Malley whose works were fabricated to satirize modernist poetry, but which now form part of the Australian literary canon, the 'author' need not exist (see Heyward, 1993). Or consider Socrates: he left no writings, and we are dependent on contemporary authors such as Aristophanes, Plato, and Xenophon for accounts of his life (but especially his death) and thought. As Vlastos, 1994, demonstrates, the precise ideas ascribed to him are still disputed. Would it matter if 'Socrates', like Ern Malley, never existed?

In some circumstances, authorial dispositions and concerns are important to gain a full understanding of a text, or to locate it within a framework where it might be properly understood. Some, however, argue that all readings of a text are partial, and that a search for authorial intent, even in law, cannot generate a 'correct' interpretation (eg Balkin, 1986, p 772). There is a degree of truth in this, but it is equally true that legal texts, unlike literary texts, form part of an inter-locking system of meaning and are not free radicals that bear the meaning anyone chooses to put upon them. There is a difference between a legal text such as Article 51 of the UN Charter, whose interpretation is admittedly contested in regard to matters such as whether it would allow a kinetic (bullets, bombs, and things that go bang) response in self-defence to a non-kinetic (computer network) attack, and a literary text which can bear any meaning one chooses, such as these lines from Gertrude Stein's poem *Lifting belly* (Stein, 1998b, p 410 at 435):

I say lifting belly and then I say lifting belly and Caesars. I say lifting belly gently and Caesars gently. I say lifting belly again and Caesars again. I say lifting belly and I say Caesars and I say lifting belly Caesars and cow come out. I say lifting belly and Caesars and cow come out.

While some literary critics interpret passages such as this as lesbian eroticism written by Stein for her lover Alice B Toklas (but see Turner, 1999, pp 24–31), reading early

Stein, such as *Lifting belly*, generally involves a fruitless search for meaning, because it is an attempt to unlock the sense which she took pains consciously to erase (see Dydo, 2003):

most of what Miss Stein publishes nowadays must apparently remain absolutely unintelligible even to a sympathetic reader. She has outdistanced any of the Symbolists in using words for pure purposes of suggestion—she has gone so far that she no longer even suggests. We see the ripples expanding in her consciousness, but we are no longer supplied with any [clue] as to what kind of object has sunk there. (Wilson, 1996, p 276)

Does this matter? Stein's purpose in writing was to make manifest her genius: her work did, and does, not need to 'mean' anything. It exists in, and for, itself—as well as for the Greater Glory of Gertrude.

Legal texts, on the other hand, do need to have an identifiable meaning, or range of acceptable meanings, because the practice of law is an instrumental activity aimed at practical outcomes. Accordingly, the more overtly a writer uncovers his or her theoretical assumptions, perhaps the more honest the writing, as his or her model of international law is exposed on the page for all to see. This should give us cause to pause and reflect; for instance, if we do not share Ragazzi's religious commitments, can we still accept his exposition of obligations *erga omnes*? If we reject Schmitt's New Haven inspired interpretation of Article 2(4) of the Charter, should we also jettison his analysis of computer network attacks?

Law and legal theory do not exist in a value-free vacuum but are inevitably concerned with political concerns and conditions.[13] Often an issue emerges that is perceived to require regulation, and the contours of its legal analysis are determined by recourse to broadly political values. An early example is Vitoria's *De Indis (On the American Indians)* (1537) which applied Scholastic natural law reasoning to undermine the legitimacy of Spanish claims to sovereignty over its American possessions:

Vitoria's writings on power and the rights of conquest effectively set the agenda for most subsequent discussions on those subjects in Catholic Europe until the late seventeenth century... [A]lthough it is clearly false to speak of Vitoria as the father of anything so generalized and modern as 'International Law', it is the case that his writings became an integral part of later attempts to introduce some regulative principle into international relations.[14]

Or, to take a more contemporary example; assuming that non-kinetic hostile acts attributable to a State and directed against another do not clearly breach Article 2(4) of the UN Charter, what political factors and value choices should be considered to decide whether a computer network attack should allow the targeted State to avail itself of Article 51 of the UN Charter and take forcible measures in self-defence? This does not entail an inevitable collapse of law into politics. These factors may be evaluated to decide what the law should be, and this solution then incorporated into law.[15]

---

[13] For instance, for an overview of the political context of the development of jurisprudential ideas, see Olivecrona, 1971, Ch 1; and also Tuck, 1999.

[14] Editor's Introduction to Vitoria, 1991, p xxviii: *De Indis* is at pp 231ff. See also Tuck, 1999, pp 72–75.

[15] Compare Raz on the deliberative and executive stages of legal reasoning: Raz, 1980, pp 213–214.

III. THE LEGAL STRUCTURE OF THE COLD WAR: LIBERAL DEMOCRACY VERSUS MARXIST-LENINISM

To illustrate the formative power of theory, it is useful to contrast two very different accounts of international law, namely the New Haven School which was elaborated principally by Myres McDougal and Harold Lasswell in Yale Law School, and the pre-perestroika Soviet theory of international law propounded by GI Tunkin. Products of the Cold War, these were distinctive theories of international law which set out to bolster and justify the external projection of the political values of the United States and Soviet Union. Although they thus shared a similar purpose, they embodied profoundly different political aims and objectives: this is abundantly clear in their approach to sources and methodology.

It could be argued that the chasm between the two theories runs deeper, that there is an architectonic difference between the two, as the New Haven School sees law as facilitative whereas Soviet theory amounts to a constitutive theory. Posner explains the facilitative approach as claiming that law provides, 'a service to lay communities in the achievement of those communities' self-chosen ends rather than as a norm imposed on those communities in the service of a higher end' (Posner, 1990, p 94).

McDougal and Lasswell (1981, p 24) defined 'human dignity' as 'a social process in which values are widely and not narrowly shared, and in which private choice, rather than coercion, is emphasized as the predominant modality of power'. Accordingly, the New Haven goal of clarifying and implementing a world order of human dignity could be seen as falling squarely within Posner's notion of a facilitative theory. This is not the case. The *raison d'être* of the New Haven School is the pursuit of an imposed 'higher end', namely, the defence and maintenance of (American) liberal democracy as a bulwark against the spread of communism. In itself, this is ideological, the attempted globalization of the claim that the United States is morally exceptional and 'endowed by its creator with a special mission, a "manifest destiny", to "overspread" the North American continent and perhaps the world, so as to evangelize it with the twin gospels of American democracy and American capitalism' (Hodgson, 2005, p 20). As Falk observes, New Haven analysis is constructed around an:

ideological bipolarity of a world order that pits totalitarian versus free societies as the essential struggle of our time, a view that anchors the McDougal and Lasswell jurisprudence in the history of the Cold War era. (Falk, 1995, p 2004)

For McDougal and Lasswell the choice was one between nuclear annihilation and the global promotion of US democratic values (Falk, 1995, p 2002; Duxbury, 1995, pp 195–198). They, in an act of 'ideological partisanship' (Falk, 1995, p 2003), chose the latter.

A. THE NEW HAVEN SCHOOL

The genesis of New Haven lay in the Second World War and the emergence of communism as an international political force. McDougal and Lasswell argued that, when US law schools reopened after the war, they should be 'a place where people who have risked their lives can wisely risk their minds' (Lasswell and McDougal, 1943, p 292). The aim of legal education was to provide systematic training for policy-makers attuned to 'the needs of a free and productive commonwealth':

The proper function of our law schools is, in short, to contribute to the training of policy-makers for the ever more complete achievement of the democratic values that constitute the professed ends of American polity. (Lasswell and McDougal, 1943, p 206; see also Falk, 1995, p 1993)

These values should be so reinforced that the student applies them automatically to 'every conceivable practical and theoretical situation' (Lasswell and McDougal, 1943, p 244). As lawyers influence or create policy when indicating whether a proposed course of action is or is not lawful (p 209), the law school curriculum should aim towards the implementation of 'clearly defined democratic values in all the areas of social life where lawyers have or can assert responsibility' (p 207). Policy and value permeate law; there are no autonomous or neutral theories of law which can ignore the policy consequences of rules (McDougal and Reisman, 1983, p 122). Therefore:

In a democratic society it should not, of course, be an aim of legal education to *impose* a single standard of morals upon every student. But a legitimate aim of education is to seek to promote the major values of a democratic society and to reduce the number of moral mavericks who do not share democratic preferences. The student may be allowed to reject the morals of democracy and embrace those of despotism; but his education should be such that, if he does so, he does it by deliberate choice, with awareness of the consequences for himself and others, and not by sluggish self-deception. (Lasswell and McDougal, 1943, p 212)

Although Lasswell and McDougal initially (1943, passim) envisioned the comprehensive application of their theory to reform the entire law school curriculum, it rapidly focused specifically on international law (Duxbury, 1995, p 191). The practical aim of the New Haven School is to advance 'a universal world order of human dignity' which secures the widespread enjoyment of values by individuals. A value is simply 'a preferred event' or, in other words, whatever an individual or decision-maker desires. A full enumeration of values is impossible—'if we were to begin to list all the specific items of food and drink, of dress, of housing, and of other enjoyments, we should quickly recognize the unwieldiness of the task'. McDougal and Lasswell claim that any given value will fall within one or more of the categories that they identify as enlightenment, respect, power, well-being, wealth, skill, affection, and rectitude (McDougal and Lasswell, 1981, p 20).[16] Human dignity, however, is not foundational, 'We postulate this goal, deliberately leaving everyone free to justify it in terms of his preferred theological or philosophical tradition' (McDougal and Lasswell, 1981, p 24).[17]

This goal reflects the New Haven School's basis in, and intended refinement of, the American Legal Realist school of jurisprudence and its inter-twining of law and the social sciences, especially economics.[18] Realism rejected formalist accounts of law that claimed

---

[16] See also Lasswell and McDougal, 1943, pp 217–232; McDougal and Reisman, 1983, p 118; Arend, 1999, p 72; and Duxbury, 1995, p 178.

[17] See also Lasswell and McDougal, 1943, p 213.

[18] On American Legal Realism, see Duxbury, 1995, Chs 1 and 2; and Feldman, 2000, pp 105–115. More elementary accounts of this school may be found in standard textbooks on jurisprudence, such as Freeman, 2001, Ch 9.

to be value-neutral and relied on the logical exegesis of legal principle to explain the operation of the courts and legal system. One of the principal strands of realism—rule scepticism—argued that uncertainty lay in the very formulation of rules, and thus judicial decisions could not lay claim to be simply the inexorable application of the law to the issue in question. This is reflected in Lasswell and McDougal's admonition that:

From any relatively specific statements of social goal (necessarily described in a statement of low-level abstraction) can be elaborated an infinite series of normative propositions of ever increasing generality; conversely, normative statements of high-level abstraction can be manipulated to support any specific social goal. (Lasswell and McDougal, 1943, p 213)

Realism, contrary to formalism, laid stress on the social consequences of the law which should be taken into account in judicial decisions, and thus emphasized empiricism. This aimed at determining the real factors involved in judgments beyond the formal appeal to rules, and also at demonstrating the social impact that alternative judicial choices might have. Law was seen as a form of social engineering that could be used as a tool to attain desired societal goals. The New Haven School built on this tradition in American jurisprudence by rejecting the notion that law is merely a system of rules, by trying to achieve a more empirical account of the operation of law in society, and by postulating the instrumental aim of achieving human dignity.[19]

The New Haven School displaces the conception of law as a system of rules in favour of one where law is a normative social system which revolves around trends of authoritative decisions taken by authorized decision-makers including, but not restricted to, judges. There is, after all, more to law than what happens in court rooms—'If a legal system works well, then disputes are in large part *avoided*' (Higgins, 1994, p 1 (emphasis in original)). International lawyers, giving legal advice that moulds policy and action, are more likely to be in foreign ministries than appearing before the International Court of Justice. Contemporary New Haven doctrine is more radical: it claims that its methodology 'can be especially empowering for individuals not associated with the state, a class that classical international law all but disenfranchised'. Applying its techniques, either alone or as part of an interest group, individuals can be involved in influencing the decisions that affect their lives (see Reisman, Wiessner, and Willard, 2007, pp 576–578), and law is a continuing process of decisions involving choices aimed at realizing the common value of human dignity:

the major systems of public order are in many fundamental respects rhetorically unified. All systems proclaim the dignity of the human individual and the ideal of a worldwide public order in which this ideal is authoritatively pursued and effectively approximated. (McDougal and Lasswell, 1981, p 19)

The New Haven process of decisions has been likened to the Heraclitan aphorism that one never steps into the same river twice, because the river moves on. For New Haven adherents, because the social context of decisions change, and because the trends and implications of past decisions can be unclear, the quest for human dignity necessitates the rejection of a model of law that comprises simply the neutral or impartial application of rules. Rules are:

inconsistent, ambiguous, and full of omissions. It was Mr. Justice Cardozo who aptly remarked that legal principles have, unfortunately, the habit of travelling in pairs of opposites. A judge

---

[19] See Morison, 1982, pp 178–188 for an exposition and defence of New Haven as an empirical theory of law.

who must choose between such principles can only offer as justification for his choice a proliferation of other such principles in infinite regress or else arbitrarily take a stand and state his preference; and what he prefers or what he regards as 'authoritative' is likely to be a product of his whole biography. (Lasswell and McDougal, 1943, p 236)

This, in itself, appears to be a New Haven refinement of the realist notion of the intuitive nature of judicial decision-making. Hutcheson had argued that, in hard cases, the judge does not decide by an abstract application of the relevant rules, but decides intuitively which way the decision should go before searching for a legal category into which the decision will fit—'No reasoning applied to practical matters is ever really effective unless motivated by some impulse' (Hutcheson, 1928–29, p 285). The New Haven School conceded that the application of its method could not overcome discretion or bias on the part of the decision-maker. As a bulwark against this, and thus the tendency to intuitive reductionism advanced by Hutcheson, it counselled that decision-makers should be as self-conscious as possible about their predispositions, and undertake as systematic and comprehensive assessment of policy choices relevant to their decisions as the state of available knowledge allowed (Falk, 1995, p 1999).

Rules are only 'shorthand expressions of community expectations' and thus, like any shorthand, are inadequate as a method of communication (Duxbury, 1995, p 194). Rules simply cannot be applied automatically to reach a decision because that decision involves a policy choice:

Reference to 'the correct legal view' or 'rules' can never avoid the element of choice (though it can seek to disguise it), nor can it provide guidance to the preferable decision. In making this choice one must inevitably have consideration for the humanitarian, moral, and social purposes of the law. (Higgins, 1994, p 5)

Higgins continues that the New Haven School's articulation of relevant policy factors, and their systematic assessment in decision-making, precludes the decision-maker unconsciously giving preference to a desired policy objective under the guise of it being 'the correct legal rule'.

The realization of preferred values is not, however, the sole factor in decision-making: law does constrain. Recourse must be made to trends of past decisions; and how these relate to the goals the decision-maker wishes to achieve; and how these decisions may be deployed to realize these goals—'the task is to think creatively about how to alter, deter, or accelerate probable trends in order to shape the future closer to his desire' (Lasswell and McDougal, 1943, p 214). Further, these goals can only be achieved if the decision taken is both authoritative and controlling:

Authority is the structure of expectation concerning who, with what qualifications and mode of selection, is competent to make which decisions by what criteria and what procedures. By control we refer to an effective voice in decision, whether authorized or not. The conjunction of common expectations concerning authority with a high degree of corroboration in actual operation is what we understand by law. (McDougal and Lasswell, 1981, p 22)

More succinctly, Higgins describes law as 'the interlocking of authority with power' (Higgins, 1994, p 5).[20]

---

[20] See also Arend, 1999, pp 77–79.

Thus the New Haven School aims at providing a framework of values and matrix of effective and authoritative decision-making in pursuit of the democratic ideal it favours. In this matrix, the actual and desired distribution of values affects every authoritative decision. In turn, the future distribution of values which stems from these decisions aims to mould and secure community public order to maximize the realization of human dignity (McDougal and Reisman, 1983, p 118).

B. SOVIET THEORY

The other principal Cold War doctrine—the theory of international law sponsored by the Soviet Union, rooted in Marxism-Leninism, and reaching its apogee in the pre-perestroika works of Tunkin[21]—was a diametrical opposite to the New Haven School, both in its professed structure and envisaged political outcome. This orthodoxy, enforced by the Soviet bloc, relied not on the values encompassed in human dignity to explain international law, but on the 'objective' rules of societal development and the historical inevitability of socialism:

The foreign policy and diplomacy of socialist states is armed with the theory of Marxism-Leninism and a knowledge of the laws of societal development. Proceeding on the basis of a new and higher social system replacing capitalism, they adduce and defend progressive international legal principles which correspond to the laws of societal development and which are aimed at ensuring peace and friendly cooperation between states and the free development of peoples. (Tunkin, 1974, p 277)[22]

Under Soviet theory, international law was 'under the decisive influence of the socialist states, the developing countries, and the other forces of peace and socialism', and was aimed at 'ensuring peace and peaceful coexistence, at the freedom and independence of peoples, against colonialism in all of its manifestations, and at the development of peaceful international cooperation in the interests of all peoples' (Tunkin, 1974, p 251). The role of international law was to promote human progress, which necessarily led to socialism. Indeed, Soviet writers argued that socialism was the inevitable outcome of social processes and, with its triumph, the State and law (including international law) would be eradicated as these are the products of class division, although there would still be rules of conduct (eg, Tunkin, 1974, pp 42, 238: see pp 232ff generally). Until then, international law was 'immortalize[d]...as an instrument of struggle between states belonging to opposed social systems' (Damrosch and Müllerson, 1995, p 4) in which the most that could be achieved was peaceful co-existence between capitalist and socialist States.

Soviet theory is firmly rooted in Marxist-Leninist theory to the extent that, at times, it seems simply to amount to taking the dogma for a walk. Perhaps paradoxically, Soviet theory is much more traditional, more conservative, than New Haven, placing its emphasis

---

[21] See Bowring, 2008 for a more nuanced account of Soviet legal theory.
[22] For an overview of Marxist theory of law, see Freeman, 2001, Ch 12. For a clear, succinct, and critical introduction, see Collins, 1984. For an account of the early formation of Soviet concepts of international law, see Macdonald, 1998.

on rules and State consent to rules, rather than the New Haven realization of values by authorized decision-makers:

both the Soviet government and Soviet doctrine consistently treated the existing corpus of international law as a system of sufficiently determinate principles and norms which all states are obliged to observe in their mutual relations, in contrast to some Western scholars who find international law to be more or less adaptable and argue that law should fit behaviour rather than the other way around. The Soviet preference for a relatively rigid rule-bound approach was not merely an outgrowth of traditional jurisprudential conventions, but also served political and polemical functions. (Damrosch and Müllerson, 1995, p 9 (footnotes omitted))

Soviet theory was rooted in the class struggle, and the Marxist-Leninist tenet that the mode of production within a society (the economic base) is the principal influence on the will of the ruling class, and thus on the social institutions (the superstructure) of that society. Only with the emergence of private property and social classes does the State emerge 'as an organ of the economically dominant class', along with law which constitutes the will of this ruling class in defence of its interests (Kartashkin, 1983, p 81).[23]

Capitalist and socialist States have different interests, and thus wills, given the difference in their socio-economic organization—'the influence of the economic structure of society and its societal laws affects the process of creating norms of international law through the will of a state, since the content of this will basically is determined by the economic conditions of the existence of the ruling class in a given state' (Tunkin, 1974, p 237). While the dominant economic class determines the will of a capitalist State, in a socialist State, this comprises 'the will of the entire Soviet people led by the working class' (p 249 and, eg, p 36). One clear consequence of this divergence in interest is Soviet theory's rejection of 'general principles of law recognized by civilised nations' (Article 38(1)(c) of the Statute of the International Court of Justice) as an independent source of international law. Because of the opposed nature of their socio-economic systems, Tunkin denied the possibility that there could exist normative principles common to socialist and bourgeois legal systems. Even if principles superficially appeared to be common to the two types of system, they were 'fundamentally distinct by virtue of their class nature, role in society, and purposes' (p 199).

A common ideology, however, is unnecessary for the development of international law, but the existence of two opposed social systems places limits on the content of the norms of international law. Because these must be agreed by States on the basis of equality—'only those international legal norms which embrace the agreement of all states are norms of contemporary general international law'—they can be neither socialist nor capitalist (pp 250–251; see also 1974, Ch 2, passim, and Kartashkin, 1983, pp 96ff).

Consent between States, albeit reflecting the interests of their ruling classes (Tunkin, 1974, pp 36, 291), to specific rules is the keystone of Soviet theory which, furthermore, recognizes only treaties and custom as sources of international law. There is no room for

---

23 See also pp 79–83 generally; and Tunkin, 1974, pp 27, 36, 232ff. Kartashkin (1983, p 81) notes that according to Marxist-Leninist theory, there are five socio-economic formations of society—primitive communal, slave, feudal, capitalist, and communist. Compare Smith's notion of the four stages of society found, for instance, in Smith (1978, pp 4ff): 'in these several ages of society, the laws and regulations with regard to property must be very different' (p 16).

some authoritative decision-maker to determine or influence the content of international law—for instance, 'The [International] Court does not create international law; it applies it' (p 191). Norm creation necessarily requires State consent, whether express or tacit (p 124 and Ch 4, passim):

the majority of states in international relations cannot create norms binding upon other states and do not have the right to attempt to impose given norms on other states. This proposition is especially important for contemporary international law, which regulates relations of states belonging to different and even opposed social systems. (p 128)

One consequence of this strict requirement of consent is that Soviet theory endorses the doctrine of persistent objection to the formation of customary international law (p 130).

Tunkin stresses that international law, as it exists between socialist and capitalist States, rests on democratic principles of peaceful co-existence which include the principles of the sovereign equality of States and non-interference in their domestic affairs (pp 29 and 251). Tunkin's strict requirement of State consent underpins these principles—for example, he claims (p 210) that because natural law theorists of international law undermine its consensual basis, this creates a climate which increases the 'possibilities for an international legal justification of the imperialist policy of *diktat*, coercion, and military adventurism'.

The application and implications of the principles of peaceful co-existence, however, differ in the international relations between States from opposed socio-economic systems and the relations between socialist States *inter se*. Relations between socialist States are not predicated on the notion of peaceful co-existence but on the principle of socialist or proletarian internationalism (p 47: this doctrine is expounded at length at pp 427ff). Thus Kartashkin maintains that:

principles of general international law, when applied in relations among socialist countries, expand their shape and acquire new socialist content. They go beyond general principles of international law. For example, the general principle of international law—the equality of states—acquires a new content when applied in relations among socialist states. Parallel to the respect for legal equality, its implementation presupposes the achievement of factual equality of all socialist states and the equalization of their economic level. The principles of socialist internationalism are used by socialist states to strengthen their relations, to protect them from anti-socialist forces, and to ensure the construction of socialism. Thus, in relations among socialist states two types of norms function—the socialist and general principles and the norms of international law. (Kartashkin, 1983, pp 82–83)

The principle of proletarian internationalism is that of 'fraternal friendship, close cooperation, and mutual assistance of the working class of various countries in the struggle for their liberation' (Tunkin, 1974, p 4).[24] This manifests itself in principles of socialist legality which, in the relations between socialist States, are *lex specialis* to the norms of general international law (Tunkin, 1974, pp 445–456).[25] These principles are, 'first and foremost', those of 'fraternal friendship, close cooperation, and comradely mutual assistance' (Tunkin, 1974, pp 434–435).[26] Their implementation requires close cooperation between

---

[24] See also Butler, 1971, pp 796–797; cf Hazard, 1971.
[25] See also Osakwe, 1972, p 597.   [26] See also Butler, 1971, p 797; Osakwe, 1972, p 598.

Socialist States in foreign and defence policy to secure 'the gains of socialism from possible feeble imperialist swoops' (Tunkin, 1974, p 430).

At its most stark, this aim was expressed in the Brezhnev doctrine, the claim that socialist States could, if necessary, use force to ensure that another socialist State did not divert from socialism and revert to capitalism. This doctrine asserted that a threat to socialism in one State was 'a threat to the security of the socialist community as a whole'[27] and thus a common problem. It therefore constituted 'the joint defense of the socialist system from any attempts of forces of the old world to destroy or subvert any socialist state of this system' (Tunkin, 1974, p 434). Although the Brezhnev doctrine was promulgated following the forcible suppression of moves towards democratization in Czechoslovakia in 1968 (see, eg, Butler, 1971, p 797; Franck, 1970, p 833; and Schwebel, 1972, p 816), this principle of socialist internationalism was employed to justify the Soviet intervention in Hungary in 1956 (Tunkin, 1974, pp 435–436) and its 1980 invasion of Afghanistan (see Brezhnev, 1980, pp 6–9).

C. NEW HAVEN AND SOVIET APPROACHES COMPARED

Accordingly, just as New Haven has the teleological aim of achieving human dignity, and thus the external projection of democratic liberal values, so Soviet theory has the aim of realizing proletarian internationalism, and thus the global triumph of socialism. While New Haven rejects any foundational basis for human dignity, in that it is indifferent to the philosophical positions which individuals may use to justify human dignity, Soviet theory maintains that, by way of objective rules of societal development, the goal of proletarian internationalism is historically inevitable. In the meantime, according to Tunkin (1974, p 48) common ground must be sought in which competing social systems may peacefully co-exist: despite opposed theories regarding the nature and function of international law, agreement on specific international legal norms was not impossible. For instance, the international regulation of human rights occurred despite the absence of a common ideology:

Marxist-Leninist theory proceeds from the premise that human rights and freedoms are not inherent in the nature of man and do not constitute some sort of natural attributes. Rights and freedoms of individuals in any state are materially stipulated and depend on socio-economic, political and other conditions of the development of society, its achievements and progress. Their fundamental source is the material conditions of society's life. (Kartashkin, 1983, p 95)

McDougal and Lasswell would undoubtedly see this as an example where 'allegedly universal doctrines' such as sovereignty, domestic jurisdiction, and non-intervention are used 'to resist the institutional reconstructions which are indispensable to security'. In this case, the Soviet claim was that the content of internationally agreed human rights fell within the domestic jurisdiction of the implementing State (Tunkin, 1974, pp 82–83). McDougal and Lasswell (1981, p 18) resisted such 'false conceptions of the universality of

---

[27] Brezhnev doctrine as quoted in Schwebel, 1972, pp 816–817; see also Franck, 1970, pp 832–833. Franck argues that the United States foreshadowed the Brezhnev doctrine in its policy towards the Americas—see ibid, pp 833–835, and pp 822–835 generally.

international law', and argued that the discrediting of such false claims was necessary in order to clarify 'the common goals, interpretations, and procedures essential to achieving an effective international order'.

On the other hand, the policy science approach of New Haven was an anathema to Soviet thinking:

Even though states may use international law as a support for foreign policy, this does not mean that international law is merged with policy. Mixing international law with policy inevitably leads to a denial of the normative character of international law, that is to say, to a denial of international law, which becomes buried in policy and vanishes as law.

Professor McDougal's concept of the policy approach to international law is an example of this kind of mixing or blending of foreign policy and international law.

...McDougal, while not denying the importance of international law in so many words and sometimes also stressing it, in fact drowns international law in policy. In consequence thereof, international law in McDougal's concept is devoid of independent significance as a means of regulating international relations; it disappears into policy and, moreover, is transformed in to a means of justifying policies which violate international law. (Tunkin, 1974, p 297)

This criticism that New Haven analysis results in the eradication of international law is commonplace (see, eg, Arend, 1996, p 290; Bull, 2002, pp 153–154; and Kratochwil, 1989, pp 193–200). Falk notes that, although not inevitable, the outcome of the application of New Haven analysis to a given issue 'had an uncomfortable tendency to coincide with the outlook of the US government and to seem more polemically driven than scientific-ally demonstrated' (Falk, 1995, p 2001, see also p 1997, and Koh, 2007, p 563). It cannot be doubted that the same was true of Soviet international law, despite its reliance on 'norms'. As Damrosch and Müllerson (1995, pp 8–9) comment:

The political climate of the Cold War undoubtedly contributed to the sense that the inter-national legal order was far from approaching an optimal or perhaps even minimal level of determinacy. Especially in highly politicized areas such as the use of force or intervention, as well as in many aspects of human rights law, the content and clarity of principles and norms suffered from the fact that states proceeded from opposed interests; while they wanted to delineate parameters for the behaviour of the other side, they were wary of tying their own hands. The positions of the two sides were not only different but often irreconcilable; yet those positions were sometimes dictated more by ideological considerations than by real national interests.

The New Haven tendency to make law malleable in its pursuit of human dignity, McDougal and Lasswell's 'penchant for applying their theory in justification of U.S. foreign policy' (Falk, 1995, p 1997), undoubtedly gives an impression of normative indeterminacy. Could it be argued, however, that this mistakes the anomaly for the paradigm? One of the criticisms of formalism made by realist scholars was that it focused on the judgments of appellate courts which concentrate on contestable points of law (Duxbury, 1995, pp 57, 135–137). Is this not also true of the common impression gained of the New Haven School (and equally of Soviet theory for that matter)? As Higgins (1994, pp 6–7) notes, New Haven does not require:

one to find every means possible if the end is desirable. Trends of past decisions still have an important role to play in the choices to be made, notwithstanding the importance of both context and desired outcome. Where there is ambiguity or uncertainty, the policy-directed choice can properly be made.

Koskenniemi has observed that when he worked for the Finnish foreign ministry, politicians seeking international legal advice saw every situation as 'new, exceptional, [a] crisis'. The legal adviser's function was to link this back to precedents, to 'tell it as part of a history', and thus to present it as meshed in 'narratives in which it received a generalizable meaning' in order that the politician 'could see what to do with it' (Koskenniemi, 2005, p 120).[28]

The application of most international law is not problematic: standardized rules are applied to standardized situations otherwise, as Franck (1990, p 20) points out, 'for example, no mail would go from one state to another, no currency or commercial transactions could take place ... [V]iolence, fortunately, is a one-in-a-million deviance from the pacific norm'. Higgins' point appears to be that if ambiguity exists, then the decision-maker can make a choice which implements or is justified by existing legal material. Choice is inevitable in legal decision-making because rules are not fully determined—for instance, is or is not a computer network attack a prohibited use of force under Article 2(4) of the UN Charter, or an event which could justify a forcible response taken in self-defence under Article 51? If not, should the interpretation of the Charter be extended to encompass network attacks? In these circumstances, Higgins (1994, p 5) thinks it:

desirable that the policy factors are dealt with systematically and openly. Dealing with them systematically means that all factors are properly considered and weighed, instead of the decision-maker unconsciously narrowing or selecting what he will take into account in order to reach a decision that he has instinctively predetermined is desirable. Dealing with policy factors openly means that the decision-maker himself is subjected to the discipline of facing them squarely.

While one can disagree with the policy factors Higgins thinks relevant, at least this approach has the virtue of making these factors candid. Analysis and evaluation are easier because one knows the factors in play.

IV. BEYOND STATE INSTRUMENTALISM?

Despite their differences, the New Haven and Soviet schools share a common approach: both are instrumental theories of law, aimed at guiding and informing practice. Not all legal philosophy has this focus, despite the fact that this might cause disappointment:

Lawyers and law teachers ... think (rightly) that legal practice is a practical business, and they expect the philosophy of law to be the backroom activity of telling front-line practitioners how to do it well, with their heads held high. When a philosopher of law asserts a proposition that neither endorses nor criticizes what they do, lawyers and law teachers are often frustrated ... They cannot accept that legal philosophy is not wholly (or even mainly) the backroom activity of identifying what is good or bad about legal practice, and hence of laying on practical proposals for its improvement (or failing that, abandonment). (Gardner, 2001, p 204)

---

[28] Compare Charlesworth, 2002b.

Much contemporary theory is non-instrumental, and thus detached from the practice of international law. This tendency towards detachment, a perceived disinclination to making clear commitments to anything but being 'critical', has caused adverse comment. For instance, Higgins (1994, p 9) argues that this approach 'leads to the pessimistic conclusion that what international law can do is to point out the problems but not assist in the achievement of goals'. This is precisely the criticism made of Kennedy by Charlesworth (Charlesworth, 2002b). Others have taken a more extreme view, denouncing critical scholars as engendering legal nihilism (eg, Carrington, 1984).

Although these criticisms of the critics contain a degree of truth, they fail to give due weight to the idea that reason and knowledge are contextually embedded, that different discourses have different aims and functions. Consider Balkin's epistemologist who engages in a discussion with her colleagues in the philosophy department about the reliability of our knowledge of the passage of time. When, as a result of this discussion, she gets home later than she should and is upbraided by her husband because they are late for a dinner engagement, Balkin observes that it would be beside the point for her to respond using her philosophical arguments to question his knowledge of the passage of time—'in the context of dinner engagements, these speculations are irrelevant and philosophical scepticism is quite out of bounds' (Balkin, 1992, p 752).

Non-instrumental theories of international law are more akin to epistemological arguments regarding the passage of time than the more prosaic knowledge necessary to be prompt for dinner dates. Kennedy, for instance, is much more concerned with the critique of the practice and consequences of the practice of international law than in guiding that practice. As such, he could be seen as falling into an American intellectual tradition:

Artists and writers began to conceive of themselves as refugees from the American mainstream, the specially endowed inhabitants of a transcendental region sealed off from the hurly-burly of the marketplace, the banality of popular opinion, and the grime of industrialized society. Alienation became the customary and most comfortable posture for American intellectuals; criticism rather than celebration of the dominant American institutions and attitudes became the accepted norm ... [T]he voluntary withdrawal of American artists and intellectuals into a separate sphere was not peculiar; it was merely part of a major fragmentation that occurred as American society modernized. (Ellis, 1979, p 221)

Nevertheless, an important theme in Kennedy's work (eg, 2004) is that individuals should shoulder responsibility for their actions in the international arena, eg, in human rights activism. Unfortunately, he also seems to indicate that we can never know the full consequences of our action, which would suggest that we cannot even 'point out the problems'. This could lead to paralysis; a reluctance or refusal to act because we cannot assess the effects of any planned intervention. From Higgins' perspective as a New Haven lawyer, this is indeed a fatal flaw: decisions must be made on the basis of available knowledge with a view to action.

In contrast, Philip Allott, whose work is avowedly iconoclastic (for a range of views, see Allott et al, 2005), is essentially a non-instrumentalist critical theorist who demands action. Unlike some tendencies within the New Stream, Allott is imbued with a regenerative idealism, and places his faith in the power of the human mind to reform the future by imagining what that future should be, and then use reason to implement this idea. Human consciousness thus provides the template for human action and human reality,

'We make the human world, including human institutions, through the power of the human mind. What we have made by thinking we can make new by new thinking' (Allott, 2001, p xxvii).

Thus at the heart of Allott's project lies an elemental conviction in the power of ideas, of human consciousness, both to structure and to change—to restructure—the world. Allott seeks a 'revolution, not in the streets but in the mind' (p 257, para 14.9) in order to achieve 'a social international society [where] the ideal of all ideals is *eunomia*, the good order of a self-ordering society' (p 404, para 18.77).

Allott argues for the rejection of the State as the primary unit of authority, and thus for the reconstruction of world affairs. The emphasis in international relations on the centrality of the State is at least a mistake, if not a tragedy, because it encapsulates a fundamental misconception about what matters: it authorizes the pursuit of specifically State interests to the detriment of those of humanity. This structure of international relations, derived from Vattel:

is not merely a tradition of international law. It implies a pure theory of the whole nature of international society and hence of the whole nature of the human social condition; and it generates practical theories which rule the lives of all societies, of the whole human race. It is nothing but mere words, mere ideas, mere theory, mere values—and yet war and peace, human happiness and human misery, human wealth and human want, human lives and human life have depended on them for two centuries and more. (p 243, para 13.105)

Just as the State is not co-extensive with society, international unsociety, where States dominate, is markedly less representative of humanity.

This was the inevitable outcome of the reception of Vattellian thought in international affairs (pp 248–249, para 13.106), which played into the hands of ruling élites. The conduct of international affairs through the conduit of the State made sovereignty, which projects 'an authority-based view of society', the structural premise of international affairs. This:

tend[s] to make all society seem to be essentially a system of authority, and...to make societies incorporating systems of authority seem to be the most significant forms of society, at the expense of all other forms of society, including non-patriarchal families, at one extreme, and international society, at the other. (p 200, para 12.54)

Thus the notion of the State, organized as sovereign authority over specified territory, trumps membership of other possible societies which are not as exclusive, and whose consciousness and ideals may differ from those of the State (see also Franck, 1999). Moreover, the consciousness of the State is impoverished, concentrating on State rather than human interests. At least in some States, however, the notion of sovereignty has been surpassed by that of democracy which relocates power in society rather than in the simple fiat of authority. This introduces a profound shift in social consciousness as democracy 'seeks to make the individual society-member seek well-being in seeking the well-being of society. Democracy seeks to make society seek well-being in seeking the well-being of each individual society-member' (Allott, 2001, p 217, para 13.31).

International unsociety, on the other hand, has chosen 'to regard itself as the state externalized, undemocratized, and unsocialized' (p 240, para 13.98). The purposes pursued in the world of States are those of States: 'purposes related to the survival and prospering of each of those state-societies rather than the survival and prospering of an international society of the whole human race' (p 247, para 13.105(13)). Morality thus becomes discontinuous between the domestic and international spheres (p 244, para 13.105(6)), and governments are able to act internationally free from the moral restraints that constraint them in domestic affairs, 'murdering human beings by the million in wars, tolerating oppression and starvation and disease and poverty, human cruelty and suffering, human misery and human indignity' (p 248, para 13.105(16)). *This cannot be how the world was meant to be.* Allott's fundamental belief is that international society has the capacity to enable all societies to promote the ever-increasing well-being of themselves and their members:

It is in international society that humanity's capacity to harm itself can achieve its most spectacular effects. And it is in international society that the ever-increasing well-being of the whole human race can, must, and will be promoted. (p 180, para 12.5)

The State system, and consequent discontinuity between international and domestic affairs, alienates people from international law which 'seems to be the business of a foreign realm, another world, in which they play no personal part' (pp 298–299, para 16.8). It is something, at best, imposed upon them and not something in which they participate, nor forge through the force of their consciousness. International law has not been integrated into the social process of humanity and is 'doomed to be what it has been— marginal, residual, and intermittent' (p 304, para 16.17). As things stand, international law cannot play its proper part in the realization of *eunomia*—'the good order of a self-ordering society'.

When *Eunomia* first appeared, Allott's vision was criticized as utopian. It assumes that a fully socialized international society will be benevolent and eschew conflict, as conflict arises from the competing interests of States. Allott (p xxxii) denies that the criticism of utopianism has any force:

In response to this criticism, it is surely only necessary to say that our experience of the revolutionary transformation of national societies has been that the past conditions the future but that it does not finally and inescapably determine it. We have shown that we can think ourselves out of the social jungle.

It is equally true that we can think ourselves into that jungle: the betrayal of the idealism of the 1917 Russian revolution by subsequent reigns of terror sometimes aimed, although often not, at the realization of socialism is only one case in point. Allott's presupposition that humanity would develop a more just, loving, and peaceful consciousness— and choose to implement this in its social reality were it allowed to do so—is difficult to accept without hesitation. His argument is predicated on the belief that bad or wicked choices have been made which have caused human misery. It might be that Allott does not believe in the possibility of 'pure' evil, of wicked acts done in and for themselves. For Allott, human evil might simply be a contingent possibility, the product of a perverted consciousness arising, for instance, from the asocial conduct of international affairs. Accordingly, for Allott, evil might not be a necessary part of the human condition and may be banished through the transformation of human consciousness in the strive for *eunomia*. This belief, nevertheless, appears to be more an act of faith than a demonstrable proposition.

On the other hand, one consequence of Allott's vision must surely be that of taking responsibility for international society and thus for international law. If Allott's inclusive international society were to be realized, international law would become a matter directly within individual consciousness. Accordingly, individuals (ultimately) rather than the State would determine and thus be responsible for the substantive content of international law. With that responsibility, Allott's hope is that morality would no longer be discontinuous between domestic and international society.

V. THE DECADENCE OF HEGEMONIC INSTRUMENTALISM

There are, however, countervailing tendencies which seek to reinforce this discontinuity, to privilege domestic concerns to the prejudice of the international, and to exalt the State. For instance, hegemonic theory is predicated on the allegedly unique international status of the United States, whose continued existence is apparently threatened by European tendencies aimed at the elimination of the nation State and on the supremacy of its constitutional and democratic practices over international engagements (Bolton, 2000, pp 15ff; see also Rabkin, 2005, pp 130ff).[29] Accordingly Bolton castigated then-Secretary of State Madeleine Albright's attempt, pending the outcome of the proceedings before the International Court of Justice in the *Vienna Convention on Consular Relations (Paraguay v United States)* case (1998), to stay the execution of Angel Bréard:

Albright's real failure, and those who supported the intrusion of 'international law' into the Breard case, was ignoring the legitimate, indeed overwhelming, national interest in honoring our own laws and our own Constitution. (Bolton, 2000, p 34)

The late Professor Franck claims that the change in the United States' attitude to international law started with the Clinton, and not the Bush, administration when Albright was Secretary of State. While acknowledging that there were significant differences in the policies these administrations pursued:

Albright managed to obscure them much more than necessary. It's the opportunities Dr Albright *missed* at a moment when history might have swung on its hinge were missed in the name of American policy-science hubris: a nicer, gentler hubris than that which led, later, but inexorably, into the invasion of Iraq and the demolition of the whole construct of post World War II multilateralism. But still: naked hubris all the same. This is the American century. You're either with us or against us, quoth La Madeleine. (Franck, 2009)

Hegemonic theory views international law through the prism of a variant of United States constitutional theory that is rooted in a conservative, if not libertarian, democratic doctrine. This is utilized to determine whether an international obligation may be imposed on the United States:

We should be unashamed, unapologetic, uncompromising American constitutional hegemonists. International law is *not* superior to, and does not trump the Constitution. The rest of the world may not like that approach, but abandoning it is the first step to abandoning the United States of America. (Bolton, 2000, p 48 (emphasis in original))

---

[29] On hegemony generally, see Byers and Nolte, 2003 and Murphy, 2004.

The aim is to retain a radical freedom of action for the United States which isolates 'a constitution-based decision-making structure' from 'the vagaries of world opinion' (p 37; see also pp 26–27). Accordingly, Bolton (pp 6–7) dismisses customary international law as a legitimate form of creating international obligations because it does not amount to law enacted by Congress through a defined constitutional process. Municipal law thus becomes the determinant of a State's international engagements. This is the apotheosis of Allott's image of international relations as a glove turned inside out: indeed, this is a glove that grasps at nothing. It is the effacement of the international in favour of the national.

This hegemonic theory underpinned the legal memoranda that structured the Bush administration's treatment of those detained in Guantanamo Bay and Abu Ghraib, by denying the applicability of the Geneva Conventions and international prohibitions on torture and inhumane treatment. Although some within the administration opposed this approach, arguing for adherence to an orthodox understanding of relevant customary and treaty commitments (see Greenberg and Dratel, 2005, p 122 (Powell) and p 129 (Taft)), this did not prevail when faced with the hegemonic tendencies of, for instance, Bybee, Gonzales, and Yoo. Arguing from their outlook on United States constitutional doctrine, it was claimed that customary international law could not bind the President because it was not 'an independent source of federal law or ... a constraint on the political branches of government' (p 112 (Bybee, 22 January 2002 memorandum on *Application of Treaties and Laws to al Qaeda and Taliban Detainees*): see pp 111ff). The draft version of this memorandum, dated 9 January 2002 and written by Yoo and Delabunty, made clear the hegemonic underpinnings of the apparent irrelevance of customary international law, which would otherwise circumscribe the President's discretion as Commander in Chief and Chief Executive under the Constitution to conduct military affairs:

Allowing international law to interfere with the President's war power in this way, however, would expand the federal judiciary's authority into areas where it has little competence, where the Constitution does not textually call for its intervention, and where it risks defiance by the political branches ... This position makes sense even at the level of democratic theory, because conceiving of international law as a restraint on warmaking would allow norms of questionable democratic origin to constrain actions validly taken under the U.S. Constitution by popularly accountable national representatives. (p 75; see pp 70–76 generally, and Bolton, 2000, pp 37ff)

The consequences of these memoranda perfectly illustrate Allott's observation that reasons of State all too often displace humanitarian concerns. Absent from these memoranda is any sense of responsibility for the implications of the policy they advocate. If—or when—a captured US serviceman is tortured by his captors, will Bybee *et al* accept that they helped create a climate which encouraged this? Are they, in Carty's terms, not simply decadent but rather wilfully decadent? They consciously sought to create deficiencies in the fabric of US foreign policy, disregarding the humanity of the individuals who would ultimately bear the brunt of their vision of US constitutional theory writ large and international. Should we also wonder whether hegemonic theory collapses into the internationalization of Aleister Crowley's dictum, 'Do what thou wilt shall be the whole of the law'? Allott may be a utopian idealist, but there is a practical edge in his, and indeed in Kennedy's, argument for an accountability which encompasses international affairs as much as domestic polity.

Lawyers' responsibility for law and legal practice also constitutes the burden of Professor Franck's final paper which, to return to the mapping theme with which I started this chapter, I shall call Tom Franck's 'moral compass'. This envisages a new role for lawyers:

the role of the lawyer is not simply to maximize his client's advantages vis-a-viz its adversary. Rather, it is to ensure that each party to the specific dispute is fully aware of the precise cost *to that party* of succeeding at that cost... [T]hat means preparing your own client to alter his sense of what is in his own self-interest. It may mean having to prepare your client to do battle with the very people who have been providing the essential political means by which he has been pursuing, heedlessly, ends that were never in his interest, or that were only in his narrowest short-term interest. The lawyer may need to change his client's whole sense of identity of interest: between himself, as the leader, with those he purports to lead... I don't mean anything like a revolution. I mean a redefinition of the national interest in which nothing America does will ever be justified again except as the reciprocal of how we would be willing to be treated by other states... Well, the **other** thing didn't work, did it? (Franck, 2009)

VI. AND IN THE END

Tom Franck's moral compass ties in nicely with the thesis presented in Allott's *Eunomia*. It is a fundamental critique of the contemporary conduct of international affairs and is, at the very least, a useful and profound corrective to the notion that international law is ultimately about States. States are neither conscious nor sentient. States neither bleed nor starve nor are forced to flee for their lives. This might seem to be simply a self-evident and perhaps mundane corrective, but Allott exposes the intellectual foundations of the centrality accorded to States and proposes a reformative alternative. The realist, allegedly, tells us as it is, but as Gertrude Stein—this time intelligibly—cautions us, 'If you do write as you have heard it said then you have to change it' (Stein, 1936 (1998a), p 411). This is precisely the point of Allott's *Eunomia*. Having looked at the world and found it sadly wanting, *Eunomia* provides a blueprint for making it better. Its idealism is not about thinking the unthinkable, it is about thinking the unthought, and then grasping the challenge to put these thoughts into practice. Thinking, after all, is what theory is all about.

REFERENCES

ALLOTT, PJ (1998), 'Out of the Looking Glass', 24 *Review of International Studies* 573.

—— (2001), *Eunomia: New Order For a New World* (Oxford: Oxford University Press) (first printed in 1990, reprinted 2001 with an extensive new preface).

—— (2002), *The Health of Nations: Society and Law Beyond the State* (Cambridge: Cambridge University Press).

ALLOTT, PJ *et al* (2005), 'Thinking Another World: "This Cannot Be How the World was Meant to Be"', 16 *EJIL* 255, including the following essays:

FRANCK, TM, 'The Fervent Imagination and the School of Hard Knocks', p 343;

HIGGINS, R, 'Final Remarks', p 347;

KNOP, K, '*Eunomia* is a Woman: Philip Allott and Feminism', p 315;

KOSKENNIEMI, M, 'International Law as Therapy: Reading *The Health of Nations*', p 329; and

SCOBBIE, I, 'Slouching Towards the Holy City: Some Weeds for Philip Allott', p 299.

ALVAREZ, JE (2001), 'Do Liberal States Behave Better? A Critique of Slaughter's Liberal Theory', 12 *EJIL* 183.

AREND, AC (1996), 'Toward an Understanding of International Legal Rules', in Beck, RJ, Arend, AC, and Lugt, RDV (eds), *International Rules: Approaches From International Law and International Relations* (New York: Oxford University Press), p 289.

—— (1999), *Legal Rules and International Society* (New York: Oxford University Press).

AUSTEN, J (1813), *Pride and Prejudice* (London: Egerton, and myriad editions since).

AUSTEN, J and Grahame-Smith, S (2009), *Pride and* PREJUDICE *and* ZOMBIES (Philadelphia: Quirk).

AUSTIN, J (1832), *The Province of Jurisprudence Determined* (Rumble, WE (ed) (1995)) (Cambridge: Cambridge University Press).

BALKIN, JM (1986), 'Deconstructive Practice and Legal Theory', 96 *Yale LJ* 743.

—— (1992), 'Just Rhetoric?', 55 *MLR* 746.

BECKETT, J (2001), 'Behind Relative Normativity: Rules and Process as Prerequisites of Law', 12 *EJIL* 627.

—— (2005), 'Countering Uncertainty and Ending Up/Down Arguments: *Prolegomena* to a Response to NAIL', 16 *EJIL* 213.

—— (2009), 'The Politics of International Law—Twenty Years Later: A Reply', **http://www.ejiltalk.org/author/jason-beckett**.

BERMAN, PS (2005), 'From International Law to Law and Globalization', 43 *Columbia Journal of Transnational Law* 485.

BOLTON, JR (2000), 'Is There Really "Law" in International Affairs?', 10 *Transnational Law and Contemporary Problems* 1.

BORGEN, CJ (2007), 'Whose Public, Whose Order? Imperium, Region, and Normative Friction', 32 *Yale Journal of International Law* 331.

BOWRING, B (2008), 'Positivism Versus Self-determination: the Contradictions of Soviet International Law', in Marks, S (ed), *International Law on the Left: Re-examining Marxist Legacies* (Cambridge: Cambridge University Press) p 133.

BREZHNEV, L (1980), *On Events in Afghanistan: Leonid Brezhnev's Replies to a Pravda Correspondent* (Moscow: Novosti Press).

BROWNLIE, I (1981), 'The Reality and Efficacy of International Law', 52 *BYIL* 1.

—— (1983), 'Recognition in Theory and Practice', in Macdonald, RStJ and Johnston, DM (eds), *The Structure and Process of International Law: Essays in Legal Philosophy Doctrine and Theory* (Dordrecht: Martinus Nijhoff), p 627.

—— (1995), 'International Law at the Fiftieth Anniversary of the United Nations: General Course on Public International Law', 255 *Recueil des Cours* 9.

BULL, H (2002), *The Anarchical Society: a Study of Order in World Politics*, 3rd edn (Basingstoke: Palgrave).

BUTLER, WE (1971), ' "Socialist International Law" or "Socialist Principles of International Relations"?', 65 *AJIL* 796.

BYERS, M and NOLTE, G (eds) (2003), *United States Hegemony and the Foundations of International Law* (Cambridge: Cambridge University Press).

CARRINGTON, PD (1984), 'Of Law and the River', 34 *J of Legal Education* 222.

CARTY, A (1986), *The Decay of International Law? A Reappraisal of the Limits of Legal Imagination in International Affairs*

(Manchester: Manchester University Press).

—— (1997), 'Theory of/or Theory Instead of/International Law', 8 *EJIL* 181.

—— (2004), 'Marxism and International Law: Perspectives for the American (Twenty-First) Century', 17 *Leiden JIL* 247.

CASS, D (1996), 'Navigating the Newstream: Recent Critical Scholarship in International Law', 65 *Nordic JIL* 341.

CHARLESWORTH, H (2002a), 'Author! Author!: A Response to David Kennedy', 15 *Harvard HRJ* 127.

—— (2002b), 'International Law: A Discipline of Crisis', 63 *MLR* 377.

——and CHINKIN, C (2000), *The Boundaries of International Law: A Feminist Analysis* (Manchester: Manchester University Press).

CHARNEY, J (1985), 'The Persistent Objector Rule and the Development of Customary International Law', 56 *BYIL* 1.

CHIMNI, BS (2004), 'An Outline of a Marxist Course on Public International Law', 17 *Leiden JIL* 1.

COLLINS, H (1984), *Marxism and Law* (Oxford: Oxford University Press).

DAMROSCH, LF and MÜLLERSON, R (1995), 'The Role of International Law in the Contemporary World', in Damrosch, LF, Danilenko, GM, and Müllerson, R (eds), *Beyond Confrontation: International Law for the Post-Cold War Era* (Boulder, Colo.: Westview Press), p 1.

DICKINSON, LA (2007), 'Toward A "New" New Haven School of International Law', 32 *Yale Journal of International Law* 547.

DUNLAP, CJ (2001), 'Law and Military Interventions: Preserving Humanitarian Values in 21st Century Conflicts', available at **http://www.duke.edu/~pfeaver/dunlap.pdf**.

——(2007) 'Lawfare Amid Warfare', *Washington Times*, 3 August 2007, available at **http://www.washingtontimes.com/news/2007/aug/03/lawfare-amid-warfare**.

DUNOFF, JL and TRACHTMAN, JP (eds) (2009), *Ruling the World? Constitutionalism, International Law and Global Governance* (New York: Cambridge University Press).

DUXBURY, N (1995), *Patterns of American Jurisprudence* (Oxford: Clarendon Press).

DYDO, UE (2003), *Gertrude Stein: The Language that Rises* (Evanston, Ill.: Northwestern University Press).

ELLIS, JJ (1979), *After the Revolution: Profiles of Early American Culture* (New York: Norton).

FALK, RA (1995), 'Casting the Spell: The New Haven School of International Law', 104 *Yale LJ* 1991.

FELDMAN, SM (2000), *American Legal Thought from Premodernism to Postmodernism: An Intellectual Voyage* (New York: Oxford University Press).

FOUCAULT, M (1998), 'What is an Author?', in Faubian, JD (ed), *Essential Works 1954–84*, vol 2, *Aesthetics* (New York: New Press), p 203.

FRANCK, TM (1970), 'Who Killed Article 2(4)? or: Changing Norms Governing the Use of Force by States', 64 *AJIL* 809.

——(1990), *The Power of Legitimacy Among Nations* (Oxford: Oxford University Press).

—— (1995), *Fairness in International Law and Institutions* (Oxford: Clarendon Press).

—— (1999), *The Empowered Self: Law and Society in the Age of Individualism* (Oxford: Clarendon Press).

—— (2009) 'The New Clientage (Andy and Me At Vanderbilt Hall)', unpublished: quoted with the kind permission of Martin Daly.

FRANK, J (1949), *Courts on Trial: Myth and Reality in American Justice* (Princeton, NJ: Princeton University Press).

FREEMAN, MDA (2001), *Lloyd's Introduction to Jurisprudence*, 7th edn (London: Sweet & Maxwell).

GARDNER, J (2001), 'Legal Positivism: 5½ Myths', 46 *American J of Jurisprudence* 199.

GOLDSMITH, JL and POSNER, EA (2005), *The Limits of International Law* (New York: Oxford University Press).

GREENBERG, KJ and DRATEL, JL (2005), *The Torture Papers: The Road to Abu Ghraib* (New York: Cambridge University Press).

HART, HLA (1994), *The Concept of Law*, 2nd edn (Oxford: Clarendon Press).

HATHAWAY, OA (2007), 'The Continuing Influence of the New Haven School', 32 *Yale Journal of International Law* 553.

HAZARD, J (1971), 'Renewed Emphasis Upon a Socialist International Law', 65 *AJIL* 142.

HENCKAERTS, J-M and DOSWALD-BECK, L (2005), *Customary International Humanitarian Law* (Cambridge: Cambridge University Press).

HERZBERG, A (2008), 'NGO "Lawfare": Exploitation of Courts in the Arab-israeli Conflict' (Jerusalem: NGO Monitor), available at http://www.ngo-monitor.org/data/images/File/lawfare-monograph.pdf.

HEYWARD, M (1993), *The Ern Malley Affair* (London: Faber and Faber).

HIGGINS, R (1994), *Problems and Process: International Law and How We Use It* (Oxford: Clarendon Press).

HODGSON, G (2005), 'The *Other* American Presidential Election: Choosing A President and Psychoanalyzing A Nation', (Oxford: Europaeum) available at http://www.europaeum.org/files/publications/pamphlets/GodfreyHodgson.pdf.

HUTCHESON, JC (1928–29), 'The Judgment Intuitive: The Function of the "Hunch" in Judicial Decision', 14 *Cornell LQ* 274.

JANIS, MW (2004), *The American Tradition of International Law: Great Expectations 1789–1914* (Oxford: Clarendon Press).

JENNINGS, RY (1982), 'The Identification of International Law', in Cheng, B (ed), *International Law: Teaching and Practice* (London: Stevens), p 3.

KANT, I (1793), 'On the Common Saying: "This May be True in Theory, But it Does Not Apply in Practice" ', in Reiss, H (ed) (1970), *Kant's Political Writings* (Cambridge: Cambridge University Press), p 61.

KARTASHKIN, V (1983), 'The Marxist-Leninist Approach: The Theory of Class Struggle and Contemporary International Law', in Macdonald, RStJ and Johnston, DM (eds), *The Structure and Process of International Law: Essays in Legal Philosophy Doctrine and Theory* (Dordrecht: Martinus Nijhoff), p 79.

KENNEDY, D (1985), 'International Legal Education', 26 *Harvard ILJ* 361.

—— (1999), 'The Disciplines of International Law and Policy', 12 *Leiden JIL* 9.

—— (2000), 'When Renewal Repeats: Thinking Against the Box', 32 *NYU JILP* 335.

—— (2002), 'The International Human Rights Movement: Part of the Problem?', 15 *Harvard HRJ* 101.

—— (2003), 'Tom Franck and the Manhattan School', 35 *NYU JILP* 397.

—— (2004), *The Dark Sides of Virtue: Reassessing International Humanitarianism* (Princeton, NJ: Princeton University Press).

KRETZMER, D (2009), 'Rethinking Application of IHL in Non-International Armed Conflict', 42 *Israel Law Review* 1.

KOH, HH (2007), 'Is There a "New" New Haven School of International Law?', 32 *Yale Journal of International Law* 559.

KOSKENNIEMI, M (1989), *From Apology to Utopia: The Structure of International Legal Argument*, 2005 reissue (Cambridge: Cambridge University Press).

—— (1990), 'The Politics of International Law', 1 *EJIL* 4.

—— (1999), 'Letter to the Editors of the Symposium', 93 *AJIL* 351.

—— (2005), 'International Law in Europe: Between Tradition and Renewal', 16 *EJIL* 113.

—— (2009) 'The Politics of International Law—Twenty Years Later', 20 *EJIL* 7, and in summary form, **http://www.ejiltalk.org/author/martti-koskenniemi**.

KRATOCHWIL, FV (1989), *Rules, Norms and Decisions: On the Conditions of Practical and Legal Reasoning in International Relations and Domestic Affairs* (Cambridge: Cambridge University Press).

LANDAUER, C (forthcoming), 'Regionalism, Geography, and the International Legal Imagination', in Sellers M (ed), *Parochialism, Cosmopolitanism, and the Foundations of International Law* (Cambridge: Cambridge University Press).

LASSWELL, HD and McDOUGAL, MS (1943), 'Legal Education and Public Policy: Professional Training in the Public Interest', 52 *Yale LJ* 203.

—— and —— (1992), *Jurisprudence For a Free Society: Studies in Law, Science and Policy* (Dordrecht: Martinus Nijhoff).

LAUTERPACHT, H (1933), *The Function of Law in the International Community* (Oxford: Clarendon Press).

LEVIT, JK (2007), 'Bottom-Up Lawmaking: Reflections on the New Haven School of International Law', 32 *Yale Journal of International Law* 393.

MacCORMICK, N (1981), *HLA Hart* (London: Edward Arnold).

—— (1990), 'Reconstruction after Deconstruction: A Response to CLS', 10 *Ox JLS* 539.

MACDONALD, RStJ (1998), 'Rummaging in the Ruins. Soviet International Law and Policy in the Early Years: Is Anything Left?', in Wellens, K (ed), *International Law: Theory and Practice. Essays in Honour of Eric Suy* (The Hague: Martinus Nijhoff), p 61.

—— and JOHNSTON, DM (eds) (1983), *The Structure and Process of International Law: Essays in Legal Philosophy Doctrine and Theory* (Dordrecht: Martinus Nijhoff).

McDOUGAL, MS and BURKE, WT (1962), *The Public Order of the Oceans: A Contemporary International Law of the Sea* (New Haven, Conn.: Yale University Press).

—— and FELICIANO, FP (1994), *The International Law of War: Transnational Coercion and World Public Order* (Dordrecht: Martinus Nijhoff).

—— and LASSWELL, HD (1981), 'The Identification and Appraisal of Diverse Systems of Public Order', in McDougal, MS and Reisman, WM (eds), *International Law Essays* (Mineola, NY: Foundation Press), p 15; first published (1959) 53 *AJ* 1.

——, ——, and CHEN, LC (1969), 'Human Rights and World Public Order: A Framework for Policy-oriented Inquiry', 63 *AJIL* 237.

——, ——, and —— (1980), *Human Rights and World Public Order: The Basic Policies of an International Law of Human Dignity* (New Haven, Conn.: Yale University Press).

—— and REISMAN, WM (1983), 'International Law in Policy-oriented Perspective', in Macdonald, RStJ and Johnston, DM (eds), *The Structure and Process of International Law: Essays in Legal Philosophy Doctrine and Theory* (Dordrecht: Martinus Nijhoff), p 103.

McWHINNEY, E (1990), 'The "New Thinking" in Soviet International Law: Soviet Doctrine and Practice in the Post-Tunkin Era', 28 *Canadian YIL* 309.

MARKS, S (ed) (2008), *International Law on the Left: Re-examining Marxist Legacies* (Cambridge: Cambridge University Press).

MIÉVILLE, C (2004), 'The Commodity-Form Theory of International Law: An Introduction', 17 *Leiden JIL* 271.

MORISON, WL (1982), *John Austin* (London: Edward Arnold).

MURPHY, JF (2004), *The United States and the Rule of Law in International Affairs* (Cambridge: Cambridge University Press).

OLIVECRONA, K (1971), *Law as Fact*, 2nd edn (London: Stevens).

OSAKWE, C (1972), 'Socialist International Law Revisited', 66 *AJIL* 596.

OSOFSKY, HM (2007), 'A Law and Geography Perspective on the New Haven School', 32 *Yale Journal of International Law* 421.

PAULUS, AL (2001), 'International Law After Postmodernism: Towards Renewal or Decline of International Law?', 14 *Leiden JIL* 727.

PERELMAN, C and OLBRECHTS-TYTECA, L (1969), *The New Rhetoric: a Treatise on Argumentation* (Notre Dame, Indiana: University of Notre Dame Press: translation of *La nouvelle rhétorique: traité de l'argumentation*, 1958).

PRAGER, CAL (1998), 'Allott in Wonderland', 24 *Review of International Studies* 563.

POSNER, RA (1990), *Cardozo: A Study in Reputation* (Chicago: University of Chicago Press).

PURVIS, N (1991), 'Critical Legal Studies in Public International Law', 32 *Harvard JIL* 81.

RABKIN, JA (2005), *Law Without Nations? Why Constitutional Government Requires Sovereign States* (Princeton, NJ: Princeton University Press).

RAGAZZI, M (1997), *The Concept of International Obligations Erga Omnes*, (Oxford: Clarendon Press).

RAZ, J (1980), *The Concept of a Legal System: An Introduction to the Theory of Legal System*, 2nd edn (Oxford: Clarendon Press).

REISMAN, WM (1985), 'Criteria for the Lawful Use of Force in International Law', 10 *Yale JIL* 279.

—— WIESSNER, S, and WILLARD, AR (2007), 'The New Haven School: a Brief Introduction', 32 *Yale Journal of International Law* 575.

ROBERTS, AE (2001), 'Traditional and Modern Approaches to Customary International Law: A Reconciliation', 95 *AJIL* 757.

SCHMITT, MN (1998), 'Bellum Americanum: The US View of Twenty-first Century War and its Possible Implications for the Law of Armed Conflict', 19 *Michigan JIL* 1051.

—— (1999a), 'Computer Network Attack and the Use of Force in International Law: Thoughts on a Normative Framework', 37 *Columbia J of Transnat'l L* 885.

—— (1999b), 'The Principle of Discrimination in 21st Century Warfare', 2 *Yale Human Rights and Development LJ* 143.

—— (2002), 'Wired Warfare: Computer Network Attack and Jus in Bello', 84/846 *International Review of the Red Cross* 365.

SCHWEBEL, SM (1972), 'The Brezhnev Doctrine Repealed and Peaceful Co-existence Enacted', 66 *AJIL* 816.

SCOBBIE, I (1990), 'Towards the Elimination of International Law: Some Radical Scepticism about Sceptical Radicalism', 61 *BYIL* 339.

—— (2009) 'On the Road to Avila?: a Response to Koskenniemi', http://www.ejiltalk.org/author/iscobbie/.

SLAUGHTER, AM (1995), 'International Law in a World of Liberal States', 6 *EJIL* 1.

—— (2004), *A New World Order* (Princeton: Princeton University Press).

SMITH, A (1978), *Lectures on Jurisprudence*, (Meek, RL, Raphael, DD, and Stein, P (eds)) (Oxford: Clarendon Press).

STEIN, G (1936), 'The Geographical History of America or The Relation of Human

Nature to the Human Mind', in Stein, G (1998a), *Gertrude Stein: Writings 1932–1946* (Stimpson, CR and Chessman, H (eds)) (New York: Library of America), p 365.

—— (1938), *Everybody's Autobiography* (London: Heinemann).

—— (1998b), *Gertrude Stein: Writings 1903–1932* (Stimpson, CR and Chessman, H (eds)) (New York: Library of America).

STEIN, T (1985), 'The Approach of a Different Drummer: The Principle of the Persistent Objector in International Law', 26 *Harvard ILJ* 457.

TASIOULAS, J (1996), 'In Defence of Relative Normativity: Communitarian Values and the *Nicaragua* Case', 16 *Ox JLS* 84.

TUCK, R (1999), *The Rights of War and Peace: Political Thought and the International Order from Grotius to Kant* (Oxford: Oxford University Press).

TUNKIN, GI (1974), *Theory of International Law* (Butler, WE (trans.)) (London: Allen & Unwin).

—— (2003), *Theory of International Law* (Butler, WE (trans.)), 2nd edn (London: Wildy, Simmonds and Hill).

TURNER, K (ed) (1999), *Baby Precious Always Shines: Selected Love Notes Between Gertrude Stein and Alice B. Toklas* (New York: St Martin's Press).

VAGTS, D (2001), 'Hegemonic International Law', 95 *AJIL* 843.

VERESHCHETIN, VS and MÜLLERSON, R (1990), 'The Primacy of International Law in World Politics', in Carty, A and Danilenko, G (eds), *Perestroika and International Law: Current Anglo-Soviet Approaches to International Law* (Edinburgh: Edinburgh University Press), p 6.

VITORIA, F De (1991), *Political Writings* (Pagden, A and Lawrance, J (eds)) (Cambridge: Cambridge University Press).

VLASTOS, G (1994), 'The Historical Socrates and Athenian Democracy', in Vlastos (Burnyeat, M (ed)), *Socratic Studies* (Cambridge: Cambridge University Press), p 87.

WARBRICK, C (1991), 'The Theory of International Law: Is there an English contribution?', in Allott, P *et al*, *Theory and International Law: an Introduction* (London: BIICL), p 49.

—— (2000), 'Brownlie's *Principles of Public International Law*: An Assessment', 11 *EJIL* 621.

WEIL, P (1983), 'Towards Relative Normativity?', 77 *AJIL* 413.

WILSON, E (1996), *Axel's Castle: A Study of the Imaginative Literature of 1870–1930*, first published 1931 (New York: Modern Library)

FURTHER READING

In addition to the works cited in the bibliography, the following are useful in providing a variety of theoretical perspectives on international law, although this is an enormous and expanding field.

BECK, RJ, AREND, AC, and LUGT, RD (eds) (1996), *International Rules: Approaches From International Law and International Relations* (New York: Oxford University Press) is an excellent introductory collection of readings and commentary which covers the principal contemporary schools of international legal thought.

BYERS, M (ed) (2000), *The Role of International Law in International Politics: Essays in International Relations and International Law* (Oxford: Oxford University Press) is a collection of essays by distinguished authors which examines the interface between international law and politics. This is for a more advanced audience than Beck although it remains fairly accessible.

DALLMEYER, DG (ed) (1993), *Reconceiving Reality: Women and International Law* (Washington, DC: American Society of International Law) is a fairly early and important group of essays on feminist approaches to international law.

KOSKENNIEMI, M (2001), *The Gentle Civilizer of Nations: the Rise and Fall of International Law 1870–1960* (Cambridge: Cambridge University Press) is an extensive scholarly analysis of the intellectual history of modern international law.

RUBIN, AP (1997), *Ethics and Authority in International Law* (Cambridge: Cambridge University Press) is a readable and slightly idiosyncratic account of the influence of the naturalist and positivist schools of legal theory on our understanding of international law.

TESÓN, FR (1998), *A Philosophy of International Law* (Boulder, Colo.: Westview Press) expounds an essentially Kantian notion of international law.

Finally, the *European Journal of International Law* frequently publishes articles that discuss diverse aspects of the theory of international law, and periodically symposia on specific figures such as Kelsen (vol 9, 1998), Lauterpacht (vol 8, 1997), and Franck (vol 13, 2002).

PART II

THE STRUCTURE OF INTERNATIONAL LEGAL OBLIGATION

4

THE SOURCES OF INTERNATIONAL LAW

Hugh Thirlway

SUMMARY

A rule of international law must derive from one of the recognized sources, namely:
(1) treaties and conventions; (2) international custom; (3) general principles of law; and (4)
the 'subsidiary sources' of judicial decisions and legal teachings. Treaties are binding only on
the parties to them; custom (which pre-supposes an established practice and a psychological
element known as the *opinio juris*) is in principle binding on all States, unless it is a 'special'
or 'local' custom, and save for the exceptional case of the 'persistent objector'. The general
principles of law (as evidenced by national legal systems) may be appealed to if a point is
not settled either by treaty or custom. Other sources, or alternative conceptions of how law
comes into being, have from time to time been suggested, but the traditional analysis continues to be used in practice, in particular by the International Court.

I. INTRODUCTION: WHAT ARE SOURCES OF LAW?

The essence of every legal system is a body of principles and rules that lay down the rights
and obligations of the subjects of that system.[1] These may for convenience be called the
'primary rules' of the system. However, each system also contains rules which can be
applied to determine what are the primary rules, how they come into existence and how
they can be changed; these we may term 'secondary rules'.[2] In municipal legal systems, ie,

---

[1] The question whether international law is *solely* a set of principles and rules is controversial, but no-one
denies that such principles and rules are comprised in it, and for present purposes it will be sufficient to limit
our attention to those principles and rules. Cf the discussion of 'formalism' and 'anti-formalism' in Ch 2,
Section V, above. The concept of 'sources' is in itself essentially formalist.

[2] The terminology is that employed by Hart, 1994 in the context of municipal systems; it is less commonly used in this context in international law, but makes for clarity. The distinction primary/secondary
was also used by the International Law Commission in its study of State responsibility: the primary roles are

the legal systems applicable within individual States, the presence of these secondary rules is easy to overlook in the actual practice of the law. The landowner suing his neighbour for trespass, or the prosecution in a criminal case, normally do not need to stop and ask themselves, 'Why does encroachment on someone else's land invite legal consequences?', or 'Why is it an offence to do what the defendant has done?'—the law so provides, and that is all. The primary legal rules being applied in these cases did not however spring up from nowhere: they exist because the legislature passed particular legislation, or because a long line of judicial decisions has established that the common law is to this or that effect. Thus there exist secondary rules, to the effect that a Parliament, or other legislative body, has the power to make law; and that the common law as expressed in judicial precedents, constitutes the law of the land—the body of primary rules.

In international law, there exist similar secondary rules, but they are less clearly defined, for a number of reasons. There is, for example, at the international level neither a universal legislative body corresponding to a national Parliament, nor a system of universal judicial jurisdiction which has built up a wide-ranging body of precedent. At the municipal level, legal disputes are usually over the precise application or interpretation of rules, the existence of which is generally recognized: do the circumstances of the case fall within the rule enunciated by the judges in a particular line of cases, or within the purview of a particular statute, as correctly interpreted? At the international level, disputes may frequently turn on whether the legal rule relied on by one State exists at all as a legal rule,[3] since there are controversial aspects of the workings of the secondary rules. There may also be recognition of a rule, but dispute whether it is a rule binding on one or the other party to the dispute (since, as we shall see, not all rules of international law are binding on all States).

These secondary rules are referred to in international law as the *sources* of international law. This terminology highlights the idea that a rule must come *from* somewhere, as well as the idea that there is a flow, a process, which may take time: a rule may exist conceptually, as a proposal or a draft, and later come to be accepted as binding. The problem may then be to determine at what moment the rule acquired the status of a rule of existing, binding, law. Prior to that moment, it forms part of what is called *lex ferenda* (law which ought to be made, ie, developing or embryonic law); thereafter it is part of the *lex lata* (law which has been made, positive law).

It is traditional to distinguish between what are called the *material sources* of international law, and the *formal sources*. In relation to a particular rule which is alleged to be a rule of international law, the material source is simply the place—normally a document of some kind—in which the terms of the rule are set out. This may be a treaty, a resolution of the UN General Assembly, a proposal of the UN International Law Commission, a judicial decision, a 'restatement' by a learned body, or even a statement in a textbook. In identifying a material source, no account need be taken of the legal authority of the textual instrument: for example, a treaty which has never come into force at all, and is thus not binding

those imposing specific obligations on States; the secondary rules determine how those obligations are to be implemented, or what consequences flow from their breach.

[3] For example, the dispute between Hungary and Slovakia whether there exists in customary law a rule of automatic succession to a treaty by a successor State in case of dissolution of a State party to the treaty: *Gabčíkovo-Nagymaros Project (Hungary/Slovakia), Judgment, ICJ Reports 1997*, p 7, paras 116–121; and in a more narrow context, the *Dispute regarding Navigational and Related Rights between Costa Rica and Nicaragua*, Judgment of 13 July 2009, paras 34–36.

on anyone as a treaty, may still be the material source for a rule which has acquired the force of binding law by another route.[4]

The question of the authority for the rule as a rule of law, binding on States, is determined by the *formal* source of the rule. The generally recognized formal sources are identified in Article 38 of the Statute of the International Court of Justice (ICJ), to be examined in more detail below, but the two most important sources in practice are treaties and international custom. If a rule is laid down in a treaty, then it is binding on the States parties to that treaty, and the treaty is at once the material source and the formal source of the rule. The rule may however be taken over and applied in the practice of other States, not parties to the treaty, in such a way, and to such an extent, that it takes on the character of a customary rule. For these States, the material source of the rule will still be the original treaty, but the formal source will be international custom.

If the secondary rule defining the recognized sources of international law operates to make it possible to determine what are the primary rules, governing the actual conduct of States, what rule—presumably a tertiary rule—determines the identification of the secondary rules? If the question is asked, 'Why should I comply with this primary rule?', the answer may be, 'Because it is a rule of treaty-law, laid down in a treaty to which you are a party'; but what then is the answer to the question, 'Why must I comply with treaty-law?' The classic answer is that there is a principle *pacta sunt servanda*, that what has been agreed to must be respected; this is an example of a secondary rule, one which defines treaties and agreements as formal sources of international law. Theoretically one may then ask, 'But why should I respect the principle *pacta sunt servanda*? Is there a higher principle still requiring me to respect it?' Article 38 of the ICJ Statute, already referred to, provides that the Court, in deciding disputes in accordance with international law, is to apply international treaties and conventions in force; but that is no more than a recognition of treaties as one of the formal sources of primary rules. The Statute is in fact a material source of the secondary rule that treaties make law, but not a formal source of that rule.

Much legal ingenuity has been deployed to discuss this problem, to avoid an infinite regression of secondary, tertiary, quaternary, etc, rules, by establishing, for example, a 'fundamental norm' on which all international law is based. None of the theories advanced commands universal assent; but nor are any of them actually essential to international legal relations in practice. The issue is fortunately one of purely academic interest. The realistic answer to the conundrum can probably only be that this is the way international society operates, and has operated for centuries, and probably the only way in which anything that can claim to be a society or community could possibly operate. This is particularly evident in the case of the principle *pacta sunt servanda*: if an agreement does not have to be respected, is there any point in making it?[5]

The doctrine of sources has attracted an enormous amount of discussion and criticism among international lawyers, and various proposals have been made for re-thinking the subject, or for getting rid of the idea of 'sources' altogether. While the traditional view presents some anomalies and difficulties, it has so far proved the most workable method

---

[4] For example, the 1933 Montevideo Convention on the Rights and Duties of States is regularly referred to as containing a convenient legal definition of a 'State', and of the conditions which must be met for that status to be acquired, despite the fact that for want of ratifications it never came into force as a treaty.

[5] There does of course exist a class of agreements not intended to be strictly legally binding: the obligations so created are known as 'soft law'. (See Ch 5 and Ch 6 Section IV, below.)

of analysing the way in which rules and principles develop that States in practice accept as governing their actions. The reasoning in the decisions of the International Court of Justice has used the traditional terminology and structure of source-based law, consistently with the requirements of Article 38 of the Court's Statute (which is commonly treated as an enumeration of 'sources' although the text does not use the term). At the present time, it seems unlikely that any other system will be able to replace the traditional approach. It is striking that such a comparatively recent development as international environmental law rests on the application of the traditional sources (see Ch 23, Section V, below).

II. ARTICLE 38 OF THE STATUTE OF THE INTERNATIONAL COURT OF JUSTICE

When the Permanent Court of International Justice was to be established in 1922, a Commission of Jurists was appointed to draw up its Statute, the legal instrument to govern its workings. The Permanent Court was to be the first standing international tribunal to decide disputes between States; if States were to be willing to accept it, one of the matters that had to be defined in advance was the nature of the law that the Court would apply. There was at the time an established tradition of referring inter-State disputes to binding arbitration, on an ad hoc basis, or of submitting groups of related disputes to a temporary standing body, usually called a Claims Commission; but the terms of reference of arbitral bodies or claims commissions were almost always defined in the international agreement (known as the *compromis*) by which they were established.

The text which was adopted as Article 38 of the Permanent Court Statute was re-adopted after the Second World War, when the Permanent Court was wound up and replaced by the International Court of Justice, with one change in the wording. The present text is as follows:

(1) The Court, whose function is to decide in accordance with international law such disputes as are submitted to it, shall apply:

(a) international conventions, whether general or particular, establishing rules expressly recognized by the contesting states;

(b) international custom, as evidence of a general practice accepted as law;

(c) the general principles of law recognized by civilized nations;

(d) subject to the provisions of Article 59,[6] judicial decisions and the teachings of the most highly qualified publicists of the various nations, as subsidiary means for the determination of rules of law.

(2) This provision shall not prejudice the power of the Court to decide a case *ex aequo et bono*, if the parties agree thereto.

The clause in the first paragraph 'whose function is to decide in accordance with international law such disputes as are submitted to it' was added in 1946; its effect is to emphasize that, by applying what is mentioned in sub-paragraphs a to d, the Court will be

---

[6] Article 59 provides that 'The decision of the Court has no binding force except between the parties and in respect of that particular case'.

applying international law, ie, that the sources mentioned in those sub-paragraphs constitute recognized sources of international law, and (presumably) the sole sources of that law. That this was already the intention of the text is clear from the records of its drafting; but it also follows from the inclusion of paragraph 2. To decide a case *ex aequo et bono* is by definition to decide otherwise than in accordance with the applicable law: to decide simply what seems to the judge or arbitrator the fairest solution in the circumstances.[7] Since the Court only possesses the power to decide in this way when the parties agree to it, all other decisions must be in accordance with law—and law as derived from the sources mentioned in paragraph 1.

Article 38 has been much criticized as a definition of the sources of international law, and it has often been suggested that it is inadequate, out of date, or ill-adapted to the conditions of modern international intercourse. As already noted, there have been suggestions that the whole concept of 'sources' should be thrown overboard, to be replaced by, for example, the 'recognized manifestations of international law'; it has also been suggested that the existence of additional sources should be accepted. Some of these latter suggestions will be addressed in Section IV below; but the fact is that no new approach has acquired any endorsement in the practice of States, or in the language of their claims against each other; and the International Court has in its decisions consistently analysed international law in the terms of Article 38. It may of course be objected that this is not necessarily significant, because whether or not Article 38 is obsolete as a general statement, the Court remains bound by it; but if there had really been a substantive change in international legal thinking on the question of sources, the Court might have been expected at the least to have taken note of it, while drawing attention to its inability to go beyond the terms of its own Statute.

A. TREATIES AND CONVENTIONS IN FORCE

The principle *pacta sunt servanda* has already been mentioned as the basis for the binding nature of treaties. The whole point of making a binding agreement is that each of the parties should be able to rely on performance of the treaty by the other party or parties, even when such performance may have become onerous or unwelcome to such other party or parties. Thus a treaty is one of the most evident ways in which rules binding on two or more States may come into existence, and thus an evident formal source of law. The 1969 Vienna Convention on the Law of Treaties,[8] which is to a very large extent the codification of pre-existing general law on the subject, states the principle in Article 26, under the heading '*Pacta sunt servanda*': 'Every treaty is binding upon the parties to it and must be performed by them in good faith'.

It has been argued that a treaty is better understood as a source of *obligation*, and that the only rule of *law* in the matter is the basic principle that treaties must be observed

---

[7] The Court has never been asked by the parties to a dispute to decide it in this way; but it has been suggested (by Judge Oda) that maritime delimitation cases, in view of the difficulty of basing any specified delimitation line on a framework of logically compelling legal argument, have in fact been decided on an unavowed *ex aequo et bono* basis, with the tacit consent of the parties.

[8] A multilateral convention adopted in 1969, on the basis of a draft prepared by the UN International Law Commission, and accepted by a large number of States. It codifies practically the whole of the law of treaties (see further Ch 7 below).

(Fitzmaurice, 1958). Certainly the content of, let us say, a bilateral customs treaty, setting rates of duties and tariffs on various goods, does not look much like 'law'. At the other extreme, there are more and more examples in modern law of so-called 'law-making' treaties: multilateral conventions that lay down for the parties to them a whole regime, as for example the Geneva Conventions in the field of humanitarian law, the Genocide Convention, or the Vienna Convention on the Law of Treaties itself. The principle in each case is however the same: that the States parties accept a commitment to certain behaviour that would not be legally required of them in the absence of the treaty. They may indeed by treaty vary or set aside the rules that general international law imposes on all States, though such variation or exclusion is only effective between the parties; and this power is subject to the limits imposed by *jus cogens*.[9] The traditional doctrine that treaties are sources of law is therefore recommended by logic and convenience.

If it is axiomatic that a party to a treaty is committed to what has been agreed in the treaty, it is equally axiomatic that a State which is not a party to a treaty is under no such obligation. The principle *res inter alios acta nec nocet nec prodest* (a transaction between others effects neither disadvantage nor benefit) is as valid as *pacta sunt servanda* and can in fact be regarded as a corollary of that principle. As the Vienna Convention on the Law of Treaties (Article 34) expresses the point: 'A treaty does not create either obligations or rights for a third State without its consent'. The Vienna Convention being itself a treaty, its codifying provisions are thus themselves only applicable *as treaty-law* to the States which have ratified it.

There are two apparent exceptions to this principle—but they are only apparent. First, the situation in which an obligation stated in a treaty is or becomes an obligation of general customary law (a process to be examined below), in which case the non-party State may be bound by the same substantive obligation, but as a matter of customary law, and not by the effect of the treaty. This is in fact the case of the Vienna Convention on the Law of Treaties itself; its provisions have frequently been applied by the International Court, on the basis that such provisions state rules which apply to all States as customary law, to a State not party to the Convention. Secondly, it is possible for a State not a party to a treaty to accept an obligation stated in the treaty, or to derive a benefit from the treaty, if all States concerned—the parties to the treaty and the outsider State—are so agreed. In effect a new treaty is concluded extending the scope of the original treaty to the third State.[10]

The normal way in which a State becomes bound by the obligations provided for in a treaty is by becoming a party to it, through the processes to be described in Chapter 7, Section III. Where the treaty is a multilateral convention of the 'law-making' type, it is possible that a State could, simply by conduct, indicate its acceptance of the regime of the convention as applicable to itself. In the *North Sea Continental Shelf* case before the International Court, it was argued by Denmark and the Netherlands that the Federal

---

[9] This concept is examined in Section IV B below, and will be dealt with more fully in Ch 6: briefly, international law is regarded as divided into *jus dispositivum*, the rules of law from which States may freely contract out, by treaty; and *jus cogens*, a category composed of a limited number of norms which, because of their importance in and to the international community, remain binding notwithstanding any agreement to the contrary (see Articles 53 and 64 of the Vienna Convention on the Law of Treaties). The concept is generally accepted, but there remains considerable controversy as to its application, as to how rules of *jus cogens* acquire that status, and which rules have in fact acquired it.

[10] See Articles 35 and 36 of the Vienna Convention on the Law of Treaties.

Republic of Germany, which had signed but not ratified the 1958 Geneva Convention on the Continental Shelf, had 'by conduct, by public statements and proclamations, and in other ways,... unilaterally assumed the obligations of the Convention; or... manifested its acceptance of the conventional régime.'[11] The Court rejected this contention on the facts of the case, but did not absolutely rule out any possibility of such a process; it did however make it clear, first that 'only a very definite, very consistent course of conduct on the part of [the] State' could have the effect suggested, and secondly that there could be no question of a State being permitted to claim rights or benefits under a treaty 'on the basis of a declared willingness to be bound by it, or of conduct evincing acceptance of the conventional regime'.[12]

Article 38 of the ICJ Statute refers to 'treaties and conventions in force', thus excluding treaties which have not, or not yet, come into force, or which have ceased to be binding on the parties.[13] The question whether a particular treaty is 'in force' between a particular pair of States is however not an absolute one, to be answered simply by checking that each of them has ratified it. A new State may be bound by certain treaties concluded by its predecessor, without a formal Act of Accession thereto. A further complication is due to the possibility of reservations made by parties when signing or ratifying the treaty: in the case of a complex multilateral treaty, there may in effect be a number of parallel regimes operating between different pairs of States, depending on the extent to which a State may have excluded certain provisions of the treaty by reservation, and the extent to which the reservation has been accepted (or more precisely, not objected to) by other States parties. The operation of the rules as to reservations will be explained more fully in Chapter 7, Section VI.

B. CUSTOM

1. Introduction

It is probably a universal characteristic of human societies that many practices which have grown up to regulate day-to-day relationships imperceptibly acquire a status of inexorability: the way things have always been done becomes the way things *must* be done. In treating custom as a source of legal rules, international law does not deviate from the pattern discernible in municipal legal systems. Historically, at the international level, once the authority of natural law, in the sense of what was given by God or imposed by the nature of an international society made up of independent princes, had weakened, it was natural to derive legal obligations from the legitimate expectations created in others by conduct. The precise nature and operation of the process have, however, always presented obscurities.

---

[11] *North Sea Continental Shelf, Judgment, ICJ Reports 1969*, p 3, para 27.

[12] Ibid, para 28. Underlying the distinction is of course the question of the consent of the original parties: they may be presumed to have no objection to other States accepting the *obligations* of the Convention, but if other States are to enjoy *benefits* under it there must be positive consent of the original parties, as indeed the Vienna Convention requires. This point was made by the ICJ in the *North Sea Continental Shelf* case, ibid, para 28.

[13] The question whether neglected treaties cease to be binding through 'desuetude' was raised, but not answered, before the ICJ in the *Nuclear Tests* and *Aegean Sea Continental Shelf* cases; it remains controversial.

One approach is to regard all custom as a form of tacit agreement: States behave towards each other in given circumstances in certain ways, which are found acceptable, and thus tacitly assented to, first as a guide to future conduct and then, little by little, as legally determining future conduct. The difficulty of this analysis is that if agreement makes customary law, absence of agreement justifies exemption from customary law. On that basis, a given rule would only be binding on those States that had participated in its development, and so shown their assent to the rule. Yet it is generally recognized that, subject to two exceptions, to be indicated below, a rule of general customary international law is binding on all States, whether or not they have participated in the practice from which it sprang. The problem is particularly acute in the case of new States: during the period of decolonization after the Second World War, some attempt was made by the newly independent States to argue that they began life with a clean slate, so far as rules of customary law were concerned. They claimed to be able to pick and choose which established rules of law they would accept, and which they would reject. This view was not accepted by other States, and later quietly abandoned by its adherents. It was probably realized that it could have been a two-edged sword; that most rules of general custom are such that a State which rejects one of them today in one dispute, may find it needs to invoke the same rule in its favour tomorrow in a different dispute.[14]

2. The two-element theory

The traditional doctrine is that the mere fact of consistent international practice in a particular sense is not enough, in itself, to create a rule of law in the sense of the practice; an additional element is required. Classical international law sees customary rules as resulting from the combination of two elements: an established, widespread, and consistent practice on the part of States; and a psychological element known as the *opinio juris sive necessitatis* (opinion as to law or necessity), usually abbreviated to *opinio juris*. The judicial *locus classicus* on the point is the ICJ judgment in the *North Sea Continental Shelf* case; the Court was discussing the process by which a treaty provision might generate a rule of customary law, but its analysis is applicable to custom-creation generally:

Not only must the acts concerned amount to a settled practice, but they must also be such, or be carried out in such a way, as to be evidence of a belief that this practice is rendered obligatory by the existence of a rule of law requiring it. The need for such a belief, ie, the existence of a subjective element, is implicit in the very notion of the *opinio juris sive necessitatis*.[15]

The idea that State practice, to be significant, must be accompanied by a conviction of adhering to an *existing* rule of law, is here merely re-stated; it had long been recognized in international law. It has however been frequently pointed out that it is paradoxical in its implications: for how can a practice ever develop into a customary rule if States have to believe the rule already exists before their acts of practice can be significant for the

---

[14] The question of the application to a new State of treaties concluded by its predecessor, where each treaty could be considered independently, continued to cause controversy.

[15] *North Sea Continental Shelf, Judgment, ICJ Reports 1969*, p 3, para 77. See also *Continental Shelf (Libyan Arab Jamahiriya/Malta), Judgment, ICJ Reports 1985*, p 13, para 27; *Military and Paramilitary Activities in and against Nicaragua (Nicaragua v United States of America), Merits, Judgment, ICJ Reports 1986*, p 14, paras 183 and 207.

creation of the rule? Or is it sufficient if initially States act in the *mistaken* belief that a rule already exists, a case of *communis error facit jus* (a shared mistake produces law)?

The problem has been argued over endlessly by legal writers,[16] some of whom have sought to escape the dilemma by denying the two-element theory itself. It is clear that the elements of practice and *opinio* are closely intertwined: the Court spoke of the practice as 'evidence' of the existence of the *opinio juris*, and for some authors only the psychological element is essential, the role of State practice being merely to prove the existence of that element. This makes it possible to see a rule of international customary law where there is insufficient practice, or none, but there is other evidence that States believe in the existence of a rule of law; this is particularly relied on by those who see General Assembly resolutions as law-creating. An alternative approach is to see custom as essentially practice, the only relevance of the beliefs or intention of the States involved in the practice being to exclude practices rendered legally binding by a treaty obligation, or regarded by all concerned as dictated merely by courtesy or comity, without any legal commitment to continued observance.

Since the *opinio juris* is a state of mind, there is an evident difficulty in attributing it to an entity like a State; and in any event it has to be deduced from the State's pronouncements and actions, particularly the actions alleged to constitute the 'practice' element of the custom. It should not be overlooked that State practice is two-sided; one State asserts a right, either explicitly or by acting in a way that impliedly constitutes such an assertion, and the State or States affected by the claim then react either by objecting or by refraining from objection. The practice on the two sides adds up to imply a customary rule, supporting the claim if no protest is made, or excluding the claim if there is a protest. The accumulation of instances of the one kind or the other constitutes the overall practice required for establishment of a customary rule.

It also follows from the psychological requirement of *opinio juris*, the consciousness of conforming to a rule, that if the acts of practice are to be attributed to a motive other than such consciousness, they cannot show *opinio juris*. This point also arose in the *North Sea Continental Shelf* case: the Court, when considering whether a rule of maritime delimitation laid down in the 1958 Geneva Convention on the Continental Shelf had become a customary rule, noted that a number of instances of delimitation complying with the rule were delimitations effected by States parties to the Convention. Those States 'were therefore presumably...acting...in the application of the Convention', and thus 'From their action no inference could legitimately be drawn as to the existence of a rule of customary law...'[17]

Similar reasoning may be applied to the situation of States which, for one reason or another, cannot participate in a practice giving rise to a customary rule: an obvious example is that of land-locked States in relation to a rule concerning the delimitation of maritime areas off the coasts of coastal States. Such States may have a view as to the existence of such a rule, but one which cannot be demonstrated by acts of practice, and thus not a true *opinio juris*. It was probably this consideration that led the International Court, in the *North Sea Continental Shelf* case, to refer to the importance, in assessing the law-creative effect of State practice, of the participation in it of 'States whose interests are

---

[16] For an idiosyncratic modern re-statement of the difficulties, see Kammerhofer, 2004.

[17] *North Sea Continental Shelf, Judgment, ICJ Reports 1969*, p 3, para 76.

specially affected'.[18] More controversial was the question that arose in the case concerning the *Legality of the Threat or Use of Nuclear Weapons*:[19] was the practice of the States that actually possessed such weapons more significant than that of the States which did not? The Court did not, in its advisory opinion, comment directly on the point.

A further problem of a similar nature is the determination of customary law in a field in which there is no practice at all, because the subject matter is new. This was the case when the first satellites were launched into space, and the idea of a landing on the moon or other celestial bodies began to look like something more than an impractical dream. Did a satellite, in orbiting the earth, infringe the sovereignty of the States whose territory it overflew? Were celestial bodies open to appropriation and sovereignty in the same way as unoccupied territories on earth? On the first point, the only practice at the time of the Russian *Sputnik* was the launching of that object itself, and the reaction, or lack of reaction, of other States: on the second point, there was no practice, and unlikely to be any for a number of years. The problem was solved by international treaty;[20] but it was in this context that the suggestion was made that there had come into existence a new form of customary law, usually known as 'instant custom'. According to this view, first advanced in 1965 (Cheng, 1965), custom could be deduced from declarations in General Assembly resolutions, such resolutions constituting at once elements of State practice and evidence of the necessary *opinio juris*. This theory, though influential for a time, never gained full acceptance, and eventually it was implicitly rejected by the International Court in the cases of *Military and Paramilitary Activities in and against Nicaragua*[21] and *Legality of the Threat or Use of Nuclear Weapons*,[22] in which General Assembly resolutions were treated as evidence of *opinio juris*, but not as acts of State practice. The position appears to be that in a field of activity in which there has not yet been any opportunity for State practice, there is no customary law in existence.

3. Practice

Since international law, including custom, regulates the relationships between States, the practice that is relevant for establishing a rule of customary law is essentially the practice (action or inaction) of States in relation to each other, or in relation to other recognized international actors, such as international organizations. This follows from the nature of the process whereby custom grows from action by one subject of law which is either accepted, rejected, or tolerated by the other subjects of law. Consequently, the practice of a State in relation to its own citizens, a matter of 'domestic jurisdiction' within the meaning of Article 2 (7) of the United Nations Charter, is in principle without significance for the establishment of a customary rule.[23] This may appear to be in contradiction with the

---

[18] Ibid, para 74.

[19] *Legality of the Threat or Use of Nuclear Weapons, Advisory Opinion, ICJ Reports 1996*, p 226.

[20] Treaty on Principles Governing the Activities of States in the Exploration and Use of Outer Space, including the Moon and Other Celestial Bodies (1967), 610 UNTS, p 205.

[21] *Military and Paramilitary Activities in and against Nicaragua (Nicaragua v United States of America), Merits, Judgment, ICJ Reports 1986*, p 14, paras 184 and 188.

[22] *Legality of the Threat or Use of Nuclear Weapons, Advisory Opinion, ICJ Reports 1996*, p 226, para 73.

[23] The treatment of foreign nationals, in particular those resident or present in the State's territory, may give rise to a claim of diplomatic protection by the national State, and is thus very relevant to the development of customary law in this field.

corpus of the modern law of human rights, which prescribes numerous limitations on the freedom of states in this domain. Human rights law has however grown very largely through the adoption of wide-ranging international conventions, precisely because of the difficulty in establishing a practice-based customary law.[24] Since many of these conventions have been ratified by almost all States, and in the view of the moral authority of the principles which they embody, it is widely argued that the conventional provisions, or some of those principles, are binding also on non-parties, and one of the grounds for this contention is that there is, despite the theoretical problem just noted, a customary law of human rights. The question remains controversial, though there are signs that many States recognize a compromise approach which is workable, even if it may be difficult to define legally.[25]

The controversy over customary human rights law also involves the problem whether non-binding resolutions of international bodies, particularly the United Nations General Assembly, rank as State practice: on this see Section IV B 3 below.

The settled practice required to establish a rule of customary law does not need to be the practice of every single State of the world, as long as it is widespread and consistent. A special problem is that of the divergence between States' assertion of the existence of a particular rule of customary law, and their practice inconsistent with it. In the field of human rights law, for example, it is probably the case that the municipal law of practically every State of the world prohibits torture, and States are generally agreed, in theory, that there is a rule of international law forbidding it; yet there is no doubt that torture continues to be widely practised. Can a rule which flies in the face of consistent practice still be said to have existence as one of customary law? An observation of the International Court in the case of *Military and Paramilitary Activities in and against Nicaragua*, in connection with the question of the existence of customary rules forbidding the use of force or intervention, is in point here:

It is not to be expected that in the practice of States the application of the rules in question should have been perfect, in the sense that States should have refrained, with complete consistency, from the use of force or from intervention in each other's internal affairs. The Court does not consider that, for a rule to be established as customary, the corresponding practice must be in absolutely rigorous conformity with the rule. In order to deduce the existence of customary rules, the Court deems it sufficient that the conduct of States should, in general, be consistent with such rules, and that instances of State conduct inconsistent with a given rule should generally have been treated as breaches of that rule, not as indications of recognition of a new rule. If a State acts in a way prima facie inconsistent with a recognized rule, but defends its conduct by appealing to exceptions or justifications contained within the rule itself, then whether or not the State's conduct is in fact justifiable on that basis, the significance of that attitude is to confirm rather than to weaken the rule.[26]

---

[24] The problem is not merely whether other States *may* legally object to actions by a State regarded as contrary to human rights, but also whether they will have any interest in doing so, and thus in carrying out acts creative of State practice; the situation is very different in the field of, for example, international trade.

[25] See Byers, 1999, pp 43–35.

[26] *Military and Paramilitary Activities in and against Nicaragua (Nicaragua v United States of America), Merits, Judgment, ICJ Reports 1986*, p 14, para 186.

The Court here rules that conduct inconsistent with an existing rule is not necessarily an indication of the recognition, or even the emergence, of a new rule; but it does at the same time recognize that this is a way in which a new rule may be discerned. Later in the same decision, discussing the principle of non-intervention, it observed that 'Reliance by a State on a novel right or an unprecedented exception to the principle might, if shared in principle by other States, tend toward a modification of customary international law'.[27] The paradox of *opinio juris* is of course here emphasized: if a State decides to act in a way inconsistent with a recognized rule of custom, it will no doubt have good and sufficient reason for doing so, and perhaps even for thinking that its approach should be generalized—that the rule needs to be modified consistently with its action. It will however, almost by definition, not be acting because it is convinced that there is already a new rule. The process by which customary rules change and develop thus presents theoretical difficulties; but it is a process which does occur. Customary law, in the traditional conception of it, is not a rigid and unchangeable system, though it is sometimes criticized as being such.

An important difference between customary law and law derived from treaties is that, as already observed, in principle customary law is applicable to all States without exception, while treaty-law is applicable as such only to the parties to the particular treaty. A State which relies in a dispute on a rule of treaty-law has to establish that the other party to the dispute is bound by the treaty; whereas if a claim is based on general customary law, it is sufficient to establish that the rule exists in customary law, and there is no need to show that the other party has accepted it, or participated in the practice from which the rule derives.[28] There are two exceptions to this principle: alongside general customary law there exist rules of *special* or *local* customary law, which are applicable only within a defined group of States; and it is in principle possible for a State which does not accept a rule which is in the process of becoming standard international practice to make clear its opposition to it, in which case it will be exempted from the rule when it does become a rule of law, having the status of what is generally called a *persistent objector*.

As regards *local customary law*, perhaps the only clear and well-known example is that relating to the practice of diplomatic asylum in Latin America, whereby the States of the region recognize the right of the embassies of other States of the region to give asylum to political fugitives.[29] The rule is purely local in that it is not asserted in favour of, or against, States outside the region: for example, neither the British Embassy in Buenos Aires, nor the Argentine Embassy in London, would be regarded as entitled to offer asylum. The International Court had to consider the detailed application of the rule in the *Asylum* and *Haya de la Torre* cases, in which Colombia relied, against Peru, on 'an alleged regional or local custom peculiar to Latin-American States'. In the *Asylum* case the Court observed that:

---

[27] Ibid, para 207.

[28] If the dispute is subjected to arbitration or judicial settlement, there is theoretically no need even to establish the existence of the rule; according to the principle *jura novit curia* (the court knows the law), no proof of general rules of law is required. However, in practice litigant States do endeavour to prove the existence of the rules of law on which they base their claims.

[29] Another alleged rule of regional customary law was pleaded in the *Dispute regarding Navigational and Related Rights between Costa Rica and Nicaragua*, but the ICJ found it unnecessary to decide whether such a rule existed: Judgment of 13 July 2009, paras 34–36.

The Party which relies on a custom of this kind must prove that this custom is established in such a manner that it has become binding on the other Party. The Colombian Government must prove that the rule invoked by it is in accordance with a constant and uniform usage practised by the States in question, and that this usage is the expression of a right appertaining to the State granting asylum and a duty incumbent on the territorial State.[30]

Further on in its judgment, the Court held that 'even if such a custom existed between certain Latin-American States only, it could not be invoked against Peru which, far from having by its attitude adhered to it, has on the contrary repudiated it...'.[31] This has been held by some commentators to constitute a finding that Peru had the status of 'persistent objector', to be discussed in a moment; but it can also be understood as a finding that the regional custom, at least on the specific point in dispute, applied to a group of States which did not include Peru.

It has even been held that a special custom may exist between two States only: in the *Right of Passage over Indian Territory* case, Portugal relied on such a custom as regulating the relationship between itself and India concerning access to certain Portuguese enclaves in Indian territory. The Court held that:

It is difficult to see why the number of States between which a local custom may be established on the basis of long practice must necessarily be larger than two. The Court sees no reason why long continued practice between two States accepted by them as regulating their relations should not form the basis of mutual rights and obligations between the two States.[32]

It would seem evident that two must be the minimum number of States to be subject to a special custom: if a single State claimed (otherwise than as a 'persistent objector'—see below) to be entitled in certain respects to rely on rules different from those generally in force, such a claim could only be maintained as the result of a general acceptance making it a matter of general customary law. Thus the suggestion that has from time to time been made that the USA, by reason of its position as sole remaining superpower, and self-appointed global policeman,[33] is not necessarily bound by such rules as that of non-intervention, cannot rest on the assertion of a special custom.

The notion of the *'persistent objector'* has been identified in the reasoning in the *Asylum* case; but the idea is usually traced back to the earlier *Fisheries* case between the UK and Norway, which concerned the legality of the baselines drawn by Norway around its coasts in order to calculate the breadth of its territorial sea. The UK argued that the Norwegian baselines were inconsistent with a rule of customary law referred to as the 'ten-mile rule', but the Court was not satisfied that any such general rule of customary law existed. However it then added, 'In any event the ten-mile rule would appear to be inapplicable

---

[30] *Asylum, Judgment, ICJ Reports 1950*, p 266 at p 276.   [31] Ibid, pp 277–278.

[32] *Right of Passage over Indian Territory, Merits, Judgment, ICJ Reports 1960*, p 6 at p 39. Cases of this kind are likely to be rare, since it would normally be more appropriate to analyse such a situation as one of tacit agreement, ie, in effect governed by treaty-law. In the *Right of Passage* case this interpretation would have raised problems of succession, the arrangement dating back to the Mughal period, and left undisturbed by the successive British and independent Indian governments.

[33] Cf the views of McDougal on hydrogen bomb testing, and (more recently) Murswiek, 2002, pp 195ff, rejecting the US approach as contrary to the principle of the sovereign equality of States.

as against Norway inasmuch as she has always opposed any attempt to apply it to the Norwegian coast'.[34]

As a result of, in particular, a very influential article by Sir Gerald Fitzmaurice (Fitzmaurice, 1953), it became accepted by most scholars that a State which objected consistently to the application of a rule of law while it was still in the process of becoming such a rule—in other words, while practice consistent with the possible rule was still accumulating, but before the rule could be regarded as established—could continue to 'opt out' of the application of the rule even after it had acquired the status of a rule of general customary law.

This is an attractive theory, since if there were no possibility of dissent from a nascent rule, customary law would be created by the majority of States and imposed willy-nilly on the minority; but there is little State practice to support it (and if it exists, it is itself a rule of customary law established by practice), and its very existence has been questioned by commentators (Charney, 1993). What is certain is that customary law is not made simply by majority: in the case of *Legality of the Threat or Use of Nuclear Weapons*, the Court accepted that the opposition of the handful of nuclear States to any customary rule prohibiting such weapons blocked the creation of such a rule, even though it was favoured by a substantial majority of the States of the world.[35]

C. THE GENERAL PRINCIPLES OF LAW

When Article 38 of the Statute of the Permanent Court was being drafted, the Commission of Jurists was concerned that in some cases the future Court might find that the issues in dispute before it were not governed by any treaty, and that no established rule of customary law either could be found to determine them. It was thought undesirable, and possibly inappropriate in principle, that the Court should be obliged to declare what is known as a *non liquet*—a finding that a particular claim could neither be upheld nor rejected, for lack of any existing applicable rule of law. This is to be distinguished from a finding that a particular claim is not supported by a positive rule of law, which is tantamount to a finding that there exists a negative rule of law. For example, in the *Barcelona Traction, Light and Power Co* case,[36] Belgium claimed that it could demand reparation from Spain for the economic loss suffered by Belgian shareholders in a Canadian company as a result of the bankruptcy of the company in Spain—allegedly brought about by unlawful action attributable to Spain. The Belgian claim was dismissed, on the ground that in customary law, only the national State of the company (Canada) could seek reparation; this was not a *non liquet*, a finding that there was no law on the point, but a finding as to the content of customary law.

The extent to which international legal relations were governed in the 1920s, at the time of the Commission's work, by anything beyond treaties and custom, was obscure, but the Commission was able to agree that, failing one of those sources, the Court should apply 'the general principles of law recognized by civilized nations'. Up to the present, neither the Permanent Court nor the ICJ has based a decision on such principles, though there are

---

[34] *Fisheries, Judgment, ICJ Reports 1951*, p 116 at p 131.

[35] *Legality of the Threat or Use of Nuclear Weapons, ICJ Reports 1996*, p 226, para 73.

[36] *Barcelona Traction, Light and Power Company, Limited, Second Phase, Judgment, ICJ Reports 1970*, p 3.

decisions by arbitral bodies (to whom, of course, Article 38 of the ICJ Statute has no direct application) which have relied on the concept. There is however no unanimity among scholars as to the nature of the principles which may be invoked under this head. There are broadly two possible interpretations.

According to one interpretation, the principles in question are those which can be derived from a comparison of the various systems of municipal law, and the extraction of such principles as appear to be shared by all, or a majority, of them.[37] This interpretation gives force to the reference to the principles being those 'recognized by civilized nations'; the term 'civilized' is now out of place, but at the time it was apparently included inasmuch as some legal systems were then regarded as insufficiently developed to serve as a standard of comparison.[38] In line with this interpretation, parties to cases before the ICJ have at times invoked comparative studies of municipal law.[39] An alternative interpretation is to the effect that, while the Commission of Jurists may have had primarily in view the legal principles shared by municipal legal orders, the principles to be applied by the Court also include general principles applicable directly to international legal relations, and general principles applicable to legal relations generally. Many of these find expression in customary law, and therefore exist as rules derived from that source; others are in effect assertions of secondary rules (of the kind defined in the Introduction to this chapter), eg, the principle *pacta sunt servanda*. Some are applied unquestioningly as self-evident: for example the principles already mentioned for determining the relationship between successive treaties (and possibly successive legal rules generally)—the principles that the special prevails over the general, and that the later prevails over the earlier.

There is however a striking lack of evidence in international practice and jurisprudence of claims to a specific right of a concrete nature being asserted or upheld on the basis simply of the general principles of law.[40] It may be that such a phenomenon is inconsistent with the nature of such principles; in any event, this particular source of law is of less practical importance in determining the rights and obligations of States in their regular relations.

---

[37] A pioneering and influential work on this subject was Lauterpacht, 1927. A clearer statement of the derivation of general principles from national systems is to be found in the Rome Statute of the International Criminal Court: 'general principles of law derived by the Court from national laws of legal systems of the world' (Article 21(1)(c)). On the dangers of analogy from municipal systems, see Thirlway, 2002.

[38] In the *Abu Dhabi* arbitration in 1951, 18 ILR 144, the arbitrator found that the law of Abu Dhabi contained no legal principles that could be applied to modern commercial instruments, and could not therefore be applied to an oil concession.

[39] In the case of *Right of Passage over Indian Territory*, Portugal argued that general principles of law supported its right to passage from the coast to its enclaves of territory, and adduced a comparative study of the provisions in various legal systems for what may be called 'rights of way of necessity'. When for the first time an application was made by a State (Malta) to intervene in a case between two other States (Tunisia and Libya) on the basis of having an interest which might be affected by the decision in the case (a possibility referred to in Article 62 of the Court's Statute), Malta similarly relied on a comparative law study showing the conditions and modalities of intervention in judicial proceedings in various national courts.

[40] One field in which the existence of a general principle of law has been asserted is on the controversial question of the binding effect of provisional measures (see below, Ch 20, Section VI A). When the question was examined by the ICJ in the *LaGrand* case, the Court dealt with it purely as a question of interpretation of the Statute, without recourse to 'general principles', *LaGrand (Germany v United States of America), Merits, Judgment, ICJ Reports 2001*, p 466, para 99.

D. SUBSIDIARY SOURCES: JUDICIAL DECISIONS AND TEACHINGS

Paragraph 1(d) of Article 38 makes a clear distinction between, on the one hand, the sources mentioned in the preceding paragraphs, and on the other, judicial decisions and teachings, inasmuch as it refers to the latter as being merely 'subsidiary means for the determination of rules of law'. The reason for this is evident: if a rule of international law is stated in a judicial decision, or in a textbook, it will be stated as a rule deriving either from treaty, custom, or the general principles of law. The judge, or the author of the textbook, will not assert that the rule stated is law *because* he has stated it; he will state it because he considers that it derives from one of the three principal sources indicated in paragraphs (a) to (c) of Article 38. The first three sources of Article 38 are formal sources; those of paragraph (d) are material rather than formal sources, but material sources having a special degree of authority.

This was so even in the early days of the development of international law, when the opinions of eminent legal writers such as Vattel, Grotius, Bynkershoek, or Vitoria carried much more weight than do the authors of even the most respected textbooks of today. Those eminent classical authors based their views much more on natural law than on State practice or judicial decisions.[41] Natural law, by definition, as it were, is only visible in the form stated by legal authors; and the greater the authority of the author, the more trust is to be placed in his definition of what natural law prescribes. Nevertheless, the authority of the law stated as natural law rested on what would now be called the general principles of law, and not on the say-so of the writer, whatever his eminence.

Now that there exists a much greater body of judicial and arbitral decisions enunciating rules of law, the emphasis in practice has shifted to the contribution made by such decisions, and away from the views of 'the most highly qualified publicists of the various nations'. Furthermore, the judges and arbitrators are more often than not themselves eminent scholars and practitioners, so that the distinction between judicial precedent and teachings is not a sharp one. It remains the case, however, that States involved in a dispute, or their counsel, will cite the leading textbooks and monographs in support of their claims, as will arbitrators and individual judges of the ICJ in separate or dissenting opinions. The Court itself does not quote teachings, and only rarely refers to arbitral decisions; it does however habitually cite its own previous decisions when deciding a point of customary law, to such an extent that it has been accused of paying these more attention than the actual State practice creative of the rules it is called upon to state.

The judicial decisions referred to in Article 38 of course include the decisions of the ICJ, as being of the highest authority. The Court has however made clear that, even for the Court itself, they are not in the nature of binding precedents. In a recent case in which one of the points in issue was directly covered by an earlier decision, the Court said in relation to that decision: 'It is not a question of holding [the parties to the current case] to decisions reached by the Court in previous cases. The real question is whether, in this case, there is cause not to follow the reasoning and conclusions of earlier cases'.[42]

---

[41] See above, Ch I, Section III.

[42] *Land and Maritime Boundary between Cameroon and Nigeria, Preliminary Objections, Judgment, ICJ Reports 1998*, p 275, para 28.

The scope of Article 38(1)(d) is however not limited to the decisions of international courts and tribunals; they include the decisions of municipal courts also. Such decisions may play a dual role: on the one hand they may contain a useful statement of international law on a particular point (thus constituting a material source); on the other, the courts of a State are organs of the State and their decisions may also rank as State practice on a question of customary law. In the ICJ case concerning the *Arrest Warrant*, the question was whether Heads of State and Foreign Ministers enjoy absolute immunity from prosecution for crimes allegedly committed during their period of office, and whether there is an exception to this rule in the case of war crimes or crimes against humanity. The parties (Belgium and the Democratic Republic of the Congo) both relied on decisions on the point by the UK House of Lords in the *Pinochet* case[43] and the French *Cour de cassation* in the *Qadaffi* case.[44] The statements of international law in those decisions could have been regarded as 'subsidiary means' for the determination of the customary law on the subject; they were however presented as evidence of State practice, and the Court dealt with them as such.[45] The Court referred to the 'few' decisions of national courts on the question; the paucity of practice was obviously relevant to the question whether a customary rule had become established (as explained in Section II B above). But if the decisions had been classified as 'subsidiary means' under Article 38(1)(d), the only question would have been whether they correctly stated the law, not whether they represented a widespread practice of national judicial bodies.[46]

III. THE RELATIONSHIPS BETWEEN THE SOURCES OF INTERNATIONAL LAW

A. RELATIONSHIP BETWEEN TREATY AND CUSTOM

The State practice which is required for the establishment of a rule of customary law has to take the form of action by a State on the international level, that is to say, in relation to one or more other States. An act of a State that has no impact outside its territory, or in relation to any but its own subjects, is irrelevant as State practice.[47] One of the most normal and essential acts of a State in relation to another State or States is however the conclusion of a treaty or agreement; and consequently treaties may well serve as acts of practice significant for the development of custom. The treaty in itself creates certain rights and obligations which are not of a customary nature; but if a number of States make a habit of concluding treaties containing certain standard provisions, then this may, in suitable circumstances,

---

[43] *R v Bow Street Metropolitan Stipendiary, ex parte Pinochet Ugarte (Amnesty International Intervening), (No 3)* [1999] UKHL 17; [2000] AC 147; [1999] 2 All ER 97.

[44] *SOS Attentat and Castelnau d'Esnault v Qadaffi, Head of State of the State of Libya*, France, Court of Cassation, criminal chamber, 13 March 2000, No 1414.

[45] *Arrest Warrant of 11 April 2000 (Democratic Republic of Congo v Belgium), Preliminary Objections and Merits, Judgment, ICJ Reports 2002*, p 3, paras 57, 58.

[46] However, since they would only be subsidiary means of proving the law, it would have been necessary to show that there was *other* State practice supporting a customary rule.

[47] This statement should perhaps be qualified as regards human rights law: see Ch 26, Section III A, below.

be taken to show that they recognize the existence of a custom requiring them to do so. The difficulty is of course that it can also be argued that the very fact that States have recourse to treaties to establish certain rules shows that they consider that those rules would not be applicable if no treaty were concluded, ie, that there is *no* customary rule of that nature. This is a difficulty that has caused controversy, for example, over the question whether there is a customary rule to the effect that a State is not bound to extradite persons accused of political offences. A provision to that effect is almost always included in extradition treaties; does that signify the existence of a custom, or of a need which has to be met on each and every occasion by a special clause?

As observed above, as a result of the parallel existence of treaties and custom as sources of international law, the same question may be governed simultaneously by a treaty, as regards the relationships between the parties to the treaty, and by customary rules, as regards the relationship between non-parties, or between a party to the treaty and a non-party. It has even been held, by the International Court in the case of *Military and Paramilitary Activities in and against Nicaragua*, that where a customary rule has been replaced by a multilateral treaty, the customary rule continues to exist, not only for non-parties to the treaty, but also for the parties to it, 'behind' the treaty, as it were. Such continued existence will normally be of purely theoretical importance, so long as the treaty continues to bind, but in the case referred to, the customary rule rather than the treaty rule fell to be applied by the Court (for special reasons connected with the nature of the Court's jurisdiction in the case).

The relationship between treaty and customary rules is not necessarily static, however. In the *North Sea Continental Shelf* case, the International Court identified three situations in which the existence or creation of a customary rule might be related to treaty provisions. In the first place, as already observed, a treaty may embody already established rules of customary law, so that it is, to that extent, simply declaratory of existing rules. There are probably very few multilateral treaties of which every provision does no more than state existing customary law (since such a treaty would have little raison d'être).[48] Most such treaties contain a mixture of re-statement and new conventional rules, the problem being to determine to which category a given clause belongs. This is certainly the case of, for example, the Vienna Convention on Diplomatic Relations, or the Vienna Convention on the Law of Treaties, and the 1982 Montego Bay Convention on the Law of the Sea; as regards the convention in issue in the *North Sea* cases, the 1958 Geneva Convention on the Continental Shelf, the Court recognized that some provisions represented existing customary law, though not the delimitation Article (Article 6).

Secondly, it is possible that a multilateral treaty states rules and principles which can be found reflected in the practice of States prior to the adoption of the treaty, so that they can be regarded as *lex ferenda* which is ripe for transition to *lex lata*;[49] in such case, the processes of negotiation and adoption of the treaty may be regarded as having what the Court referred to as a 'crystallizing' effect on the nascent customary rules. This is probably particularly likely if the treaty results from the labours of the International Law Commission,

---

[48] In the *Asylum* case, it was argued that the 1933 Montevideo Convention 'has merely codified principles which were already recognised by Latin-American custom' but the Court rejected this view: *ICJ Reports 1950*, p 266 at p 277.

[49] For these concepts, see Section I (Introduction) above.

whose methods of work allow for considerable input from governments, which is taken into account in the drafting of texts presented for incorporation in a convention.

Finally, it may be that, after the convention has come into force, States other than the parties to it find it convenient to apply the convention rules in their mutual relations, and this may constitute State practice leading to the development of a customary rule. The contention that this had occurred in relation to Article 6 of the 1958 Geneva Convention signified, in the view of the Court:

treating that Article as a norm-creating provision which has constituted the foundation of, or has generated a rule which, while only conventional or contractual in its origin, has since passed into the general *corpus* of international law, and is now accepted as such by the *opinio juris*, so as to have become binding even for countries which have never, and do not, become parties to the Convention. There is no doubt that this process is a perfectly possible one and does from time to time occur; it constitutes indeed one of the recognized methods by which new rules of customary international law may be formed. At the same time this result is not lightly to be regarded as having been attained.[50]

The Court pointed out that the rule in question would have to be 'of a fundamentally norm-creating character such as could be regarded as forming the basis of a general rule of law';[51] not every rule which finds a place in a multilateral convention is appropriate for general adoption. For a suitable rule to pass into customary law, 'it might be that, even without the passage of any considerable period of time, a very widespread and representative participation in the convention might suffice of itself', and it was in this respect that the Court emphasized, as already mentioned, the role of 'States whose interests were specially affected'.[52] What the Court regarded as 'indispensable' was that:

within the period in question, short though it might be, State practice, including that of States whose interests are specially affected, should have been extensive and virtually uniform in the sense of the provision invoked;—and should moreover have occurred in such a way as to show a general recognition that a rule of law or legal obligation is involved.[53]

B. THE HIERARCHY OF SOURCES

In general, when there exists more than one rule that is prima facie applicable to a given situation, the choice between them can be made by the application of one or other of two principles: *lex specialis derogat generali* and *lex posterior derogat priori*: that is to say, the special rule overrides the general rule and the later rule overrides the earlier rule. However, when these principles are applied to the acts of a legislator, they may be regarded as ways of interpreting legislative intention: normally a new law is intended to replace or modify an older law, and legislation providing for a special case or regime is intended to constitute an exception to any general regime. There is normally no difficulty in applying these principles to treaties, which represent the shared intentions of the parties,[54] but it is less clear that they can operate in relation to custom.

---

[50] *North Sea Continental Shelf, Judgment, ICJ Reports 1969,* p 3, para 71.
[51] Ibid, para 72.   [52] Ibid, para 73.   [53] Ibid, para 74.
[54] Article 30 of the Vienna Convention on the Law of Treaties, dealing with 'Application of successive treaties relating to the same subject-matter', in effect applies first the criterion of the actual intention of the parties, and then a combination of the two principles here discussed.

Since, as explained above, it was the intention of the draftsmen of the PCIJ Statute that the 'general principles of law' should provide a fall-back source of law in the event that no treaty and no customary rule could be found to apply to a given situation, it is clear that to this extent there exists a hierarchy of sources. If a treaty rule or a customary rule exists, then there is no possibility of appealing to the general principles of law to exclude or modify it. The text of Article 38 does not however indicate whether there was a hierarchy of application between custom and treaty; a proposed provision, indicating specifically that the Court should apply the sources named in the order in which they were mentioned in that Article, was rejected during the drafting.

It will normally be the case that a treaty is *lex specialis*, and as such prevails over any inconsistent rules of customary law, or at least such as existed at the time of the conclusion of the treaty. It is to be presumed that the parties to the treaty were aware of the existing customary rule, and decided to provide otherwise in their treaty precisely in order to exclude the customary rule.[55] More difficult is the question whether a custom which arises subsequently to the conclusion of a treaty, and which might be regarded as *lex specialis* in relation to the regime established by the treaty, has the effect of overriding the treaty, or such part of it as is inconsistent with the customary rule, as between the parties. If the new customary norm is one accepted as *jus cogens*, then according to the Vienna Convention on the Law of Treaties, not merely is any inconsistent provision in the treaty overridden, but 'any existing treaty which is in conflict with that norm becomes void and terminates' (Article 64).

Assuming however that the new norm is not of that nature, what is the position? If the parties to the treaty have themselves contributed to the development of the new customary rule by acting inconsistently with the treaty, or have adopted the customary practice in their relations after the rule has become established, then the situation may be analysed as in effect a modification (or even perhaps an interpretation) of the treaty. There is a well-settled practice of the Security Council, treating as valid a resolution adopted over the abstention of one of the permanent members, despite the requirement in Article 27(3) of the Charter for the 'concurring votes' of the permanent members. This practice was upheld by the Court in the *Namibia* case,[56] in terms which left it obscure whether this was an agreed 'interpretation' of the Article, or an agreed amendment; no reference was made to any subsequently developed rule of custom.

The real problem arises when none of the parties, or only some of them, have participated in the new customary rule. Article 41 of the Vienna Convention on the Law of Treaties lays down a defined procedure for amendment of a multilateral treaty between certain of the parties only, thereby excluding a tacit amendment of this kind; but it is not certain that customary law is so exigent. At all events, the real question is whether the new customary rule can be asserted against those of the parties to the treaty that have not participated in it, or assented to it. One view of the matter is that the very existence of the distinction between *jus cogens* and *jus dispositivum* implies that a newly developed customary rule

---

[55] In the *Dispute regarding Navigational and Related Rights between Costa Rica and Nicaragua*, the Court found it unnecessary to examine rules of customary law in the presence of a treaty that 'completely define[d] the rules applicable' to the matter: Judgment of 13 July 2009, para 36.

[56] *Legal Consequences for States of the Continued Presence of South Africa in Namibia (South West Africa) notwithstanding Security Council Resolution 276 (1970), Advisory Opinion, ICJ Reports 1971*, p 16, paras 21–22.

which is not *jus cogens* does not affect the operation of a pre-existing treaty; but the point must probably be regarded as unsettled.

IV. IS THE ENUMERATION OF ARTICLE 38 EXHAUSTIVE? POSSIBLE NEW OR ADDITIONAL SOURCES

A. HOW CAN NEW SOURCES COME INTO EXISTENCE?

On the basis that the enumeration of sources of international law indicated in Article 38 of the PCIJ Statute was complete and exhaustive at the time of its drafting, there is a certain difficulty in postulating that a new source has come into existence subsequently. The enumeration of sources is, as we have seen, a secondary rule of law, one of those that lays down how the primary rules, those that directly govern conduct, may be created or modified. As was explained in the Introduction to this chapter, the quest for what might be called a 'tertiary' rule, one that lays down how the secondary rules might be created or modified, for a 'fundamental norm' underlying all international law has proved to be vain. We must, it seems, be content to say that international society has established certain secondary rules that correspond to the nature of that society and are universally accepted.

Does it then follow that if the nature of international society changes, there may be a modification of the secondary rules, that is to say of the list of recognized sources of law? It is certain that the nature of international society has changed radically since, for example, the date of the preparation of the PCIJ Statute, in particular in view of the great increase in number of sovereign States, and in the complexity of their relations with each other. One cannot exclude *a priori* the possibility of a modification of the secondary rules.

But by what process is such modification to occur? In the absence of what we have called tertiary rules, it is difficult to imagine any process that does not in effect involve invoking a secondary rule to effect a modification of a secondary rule. For example, let us suppose that it is contended that the resolutions of the UN General Assembly have become a new independent source of international law. How would one set about proving that this was so? Presumably, by showing that in their relations with each other States asserted rules stated in such resolutions, and accepted such rules as binding when asserted against them. This would however amount to saying that an international custom had arisen whereby such resolutions created binding international law. It would follow, either that a new source (resolutions) had arisen through the operation of an existing source (custom); or, perhaps more accurately, that the scope of custom as a source had become widened to include resolutions. On the latter view, a resolution would be (as it is now) a material source of law, but the formal source would be custom.

B. SOME ADDITIONAL SOURCES OR QUASI-SOURCES THAT HAVE BEEN SUGGESTED

1. Unilateral acts

Unilateral acts relevant in international law may be of two kinds. There are acts, unilateral in the sense that the State performing such an act chooses of its own will to do so, but the consequences of which are governed by general international law. In this category fall, for example, the ratification of a treaty, or protest at the action of another State. The question here to be considered is whether there exists a category of unilateral acts not directed to a specified addressee, and the effects of which are defined, not by pre-existing legal rules, but by the simple intention of the State performing them.

The place of unilateral acts of States of this kind in the structure of international law had been regarded as doubtful or somewhat marginal until the decision of the International Court in 1974 in the *Nuclear Tests* cases. In those cases, the Court held that France had assumed legally binding obligations through unilateral declarations, made to the world at large, to the effect that it would not hold any further atmospheric nuclear tests in the Pacific. The Court laid down a general rule in the following terms:

It is well recognized that declarations made by way of unilateral acts, concerning legal or factual situations, may have the effect of creating legal obligations... When it is the intention of the State making the declaration that it should become bound according to its terms, that intention confers on the declaration the character of a legal undertaking.[57]

The Court recognized that 'Of course, not all unilateral acts imply obligation...'[58] but found on the facts that France had intended to enter into a binding commitment. As a result, the Court was able to hold that the purpose of the proceedings brought by Australia and New Zealand against France, namely a cessation of the atmospheric tests in the Pacific, had been achieved, and the case had therefore become 'without object' or moot.

The application of the traditional doctrine of sources to this decision posed problems. What was the formal source of France's obligation? It was not a treaty; neither of the other two States had indicated any acceptance of France's olive branch, so as to give rise to a contractual or conventional obligation. The Court had also made it clear that it was not ruling on the vexed question whether France had any obligation under customary law to stop its tests; if France was bound to do so, it was only because it had declared that it would do so. Was a unilateral act then to be treated as a new source of law?

This conclusion has been drawn by some scholars; but it does not seem to be an ineluctable one. Notwithstanding the Court's sweeping general statement, quoted above, the normal consequence of a unilateral declaration is either that it is accepted by the State or States to which it is addressed, and it will then become in effect part of a treaty settlement; or it will be ignored and rejected, and the other State or States will not seek to enforce it, so that it will become a dead letter. Even without any explicit acceptance, the moment that one of the addressees of the unilateral declaration seeks to rely on the legal obligation indicated in it, this will itself constitute the acceptance needed to convert it into a bilateral, conventional, relationship. The *Nuclear Tests* cases were exceptional in that, for reasons not relevant to the present discussion, the Court was seeking to impose on Australia and New Zealand a settlement of their claims on terms which they had not themselves accepted. Whatever view one may take of the specific *Nuclear Tests* decisions, to base a theory of sources on a decision in a case the special facts of which are very unlikely to be repeated, does not appear a sound approach.

---

[57] *Nuclear Tests (Australia v France), Judgment, ICJ Reports 1974*, p 253, para 43.
[58] Ibid, para 44.

2. Equity

Invocations of equity have played an increasing part in international legal discourse of recent years, but the exact nature of the concept is elusive. It has been said that 'Whatever the legal reasoning of a court of justice, its decision must by definition be just, and therefore in that sense equitable',[59] which however does not carry matters much further. The idea of 'equitable principles' or an 'equitable result' plays an important part in the specialized field of maritime delimitation, both in judicial and arbitral decisions and in Articles 74 and 83 of the 1982 United Nations Convention on the Law of the Sea.[60] Equity in many legal systems may play a moderating role in the sense that when the rigorous application of accepted rules of law leads to a result which appears unjust, equity may step in to adjust the outcome. This is in fact the way in which the concept has developed historically, from Aristotle to the distinction between common law and equity which still survives in the English legal system. Whether this is its role in international law, and if so whether it is its only role, is a controversial issue.

We are here concerned only with the question whether something bearing the label 'equity' can be considered to be a formal source of law: that is to say, whether a legal right or obligation can be asserted, which does not derive from any treaty or any rule of customary law, simply on the basis of being 'equitable'. There is little support for such a view either in State practice or in judicial decisions. In the *Barcelona Traction, Light and Power Co* case, the Court, having dismissed the Belgian legal claim against Spain (for injury to Belgian shareholders in the Canadian company), considered the possibility that 'considerations of equity might call for the possibility of protection of the shareholders in question by their own national State'; it took the view however that that hypothesis did not correspond to the circumstances of the case.[61] This might be read as implying that in different circumstances a claim based on equity alone might have succeeded; but in fact it seems that the real point was that customary law on the point is equitable in its effects, so that the point does not arise.

Equity is probably best regarded, in words applied by the International Court to the comparable principle of good faith, as one of the basic principles governing the creation and performance of legal obligations, but 'not in itself a source of obligation where none would otherwise exist'.[62]

3. Resolutions of the UN General Assembly

The decisions of the UN Security Council are binding upon the member States, but this does not mean that they constitute an independent source of law: under Article 25 of the Charter the members agree to accept and carry out such decisions, so that their legal force derives from the Charter as a treaty. Resolutions of the UN General Assembly are not attributed such force by the Charter. Many Assembly resolutions are however convenient material sources of law, inasmuch as they state, with apparent

---

[59] *North Sea Continental Shelf, Judgment, ICJ Reports 1969*, p 3, para 88.

[60] See below, Ch 22, Section VI A.

[61] *Barcelona Traction, Light and Power Company, Limited, Second Phase, Judgment, ICJ Reports 1970*, p 3, para 93.

[62] *Border and Transborder Armed Actions (Nicaragua v Honduras), Jurisdiction and Admissibility, Judgment, ICJ Reports 1988*, p 12, para 94.

authority, propositions of general law, and are often assented to by a very large majority of the Members, and thus of the States of the world.[63] It is therefore tempting to
confer on them also the authority of a formal source of law, to look no further than
the resolution itself in order to assert the binding quality of the rules enunciated. This
is particularly so when the resolution in question is of a declaratory or 'law-making'
type, and when it is difficult to discern a consistent practice of States in application of
those rules, adequate to permit the conclusion that a customary rule exists, one may
seek to equate the votes in favour of the resolution with *opinio juris*. This is however a
too simplistic approach.[64] States vote as they do in the General Assembly (in particular)
for a variety of reasons, only some of which may be declared or otherwise visible to the
observer. Custom is also traditionally regarded as composed of two elements, practice
and *opinio juris*; even if the voting may exhibit *opinio juris*, can it simultaneously be
treated as an act of practice?[65]

The theoretical difficulties involved in seeing resolutions as an independent source of
law have already been adverted to. When rules declared in resolutions have been relied on
in international litigation, the resolutions have been judicially assessed as no more than
declaratory of customary law, or at most as evidence of the existence of the *opinio juris*. In
the case of *Military and Paramilitary Activities in and against Nicaragua*, the International
Court declared that:

The mere fact that States declare their recognition of certain rules is not sufficient for the
Court to consider these as part of customary international law, and as applicable as such to
those States.[66]

Had it considered that, independently of customary law, declarations in General Assembly
resolutions were creative of law as a formal source, it would surely have so found. In the
case concerning *Legality of the Threat or Use of Nuclear Weapons*, the Court interpreted
the numerous General Assembly resolutions on the question of nuclear weapons as doing
no more than revealing 'the desire of a very large section of the international community'
to take steps toward nuclear disarmament.[67]

---

[63] For example, the Declaration on Principles of International Law Concerning Friendly Relations and
Cooperation among States in Accordance with the Charter of the United Nations, GA Res 2625 (XXV);
Declaration of Principles Governing the Sea-Bed and the Ocean Floor, and the Subsoil Thereof, Beyond the
Limits of National Jurisdiction, GA Res 2749 (XXV); Declaration on the Establishment of a new International
Economic Order, GA Res 3202 (S–VI).

[64] As was pointed out by an informed observer many years ago: see Higgins, 1970.

[65] For an interesting analysis whereby the legal significance of States' attitudes to resolutions of international bodies may be assessed in terms of each State's ability to manifest its practical interest in the question, defined as the 'cost' of such manifestation, see Byers, 1999, 151–153, 156–167.

[66] *Military and Paramilitary Activities in and against Nicaragua (Nicaragua v United States of America),
Merits, Judgment, ICJ Reports 1986*, p 14, para 184. Similarly in the case concerning *Legal Consequences of
the Construction of a Wall in the Occupied Palestinian Territory, ICJ Reports 2004*, p 136, para 87, the Court
referred to the principle excluding the acquisition of territory by the use of force, laid down in the 'Friendly
Relations Declaration' (GA Res 2625 (XXV)) as a reflection of customary law.

[67] *Legality of the Threat or Use of Nuclear Weapons, ICJ Reports 1996*, p 226, para 73. See also the dissenting opinion of Judge Schwebel, ibid, p 319: 'The General Assembly has no authority to enact international law'.

4. The problem of 'superior norms'

In the classical theory of international law, any priority of conflicting rules or norms was resolved simply according to the de facto hierarchy of the sources from which they derived, coupled with the principles of the overriding effect of *lex posterior* and *lex specialis* (see Section III B above). For this purpose, the content of the rules in issue was irrelevant, except insofar as it was taken into account to judge whether there was in fact a conflict at all (the scope of each rule), and whether one rule was *specialis* in relation to the other, and if so, which was which.

In more recent years, however, more and more attention has been paid to the concept of *jus cogens*—the category of 'peremptory' legal norms, norms from which no derogation by agreement is permitted. Exactly which norms can be so designated in modern international law is still subject to some controversy[68] but it is accepted that the status of peremptory norm derives from the importance of the *content* of the norm to the international community: an example is the prohibition of genocide. A further development is the attempt to assimilate such norms to those creating 'obligations *erga omnes*'[69]—obligations which are regarded as being owed to the whole international community, with the practical consequence that the right to react to any violation of the norm is not confined to the State or States directly injured or affected by the violation, but appertains to every State.[70] Another linked concept was that of the 'international crime' introduced by the International Law Commission into its draft Articles on State Responsibility, but deleted again at a later stage of the Commission's work.

All these concepts will be examined more fully in Chapter 6; they are mentioned here simply to draw attention to the theoretical and practical difficulties of analysing their development in terms of the classical theory of sources. A rule of *jus cogens* is normally (perhaps necessarily) a rule of customary law,[71] as is implied by the reference in Article 63 of the Vienna Convention of the Law of Treaties to the development of a new rule of this type after the conclusion of a treaty. To be such a rule at all, it has to be based upon the consistent practice of States, backed by the *opinio juris*. One would therefore expect that, for a rule to be one of *jus cogens*, or to give rise to obligations *erga omnes*, there would have been practice of such a kind as to show a conviction that the developing rule was of that specific nature, ie, a sort of superior *opinio juris*. If a State endeavoured to rely on a treaty as justifying conduct otherwise flagrantly in conflict with a rule of international law, and

---

[68] For a light-hearted, but well-reasoned, debunking of the whole concept, see d'Amato, 1991.

[69] The Latin phrase '*erga omnes*' means 'towards all' or 'in relation to all'. Consequently, a right *erga omnes* is not necessarily the counterpart of an obligation *erga omnes*: the one is a right which has to be respected by all States; the other an obligation which can be enforced by every State, whether or not it has suffered from the breach of the obligation. A number of writers have made this confusion, which seems also to have touched the ICJ: see the advisory opinion on *Legal Consequences of the Construction of a Wall in the Occupied Palestine Territory, Advisory Opinion, ICJ Reports 2004*, p 136, paras 154–159, and the critical comments of Judges Higgins, ibid, pp 216–217, paras 37–39, and Kooijmans, ibid, pp 231–234, paras 40–50. The counterpart of an obligation *erga omnes* is a right *omnium* (of all), as is recognized (for example) by Villalpando, 2005, pp 265ff.

[70] See the judgment in the *Barcelona Traction, Light and Power Company, Limited, Second Phase, Judgment, ICJ Reports 1970*, p 3, paras 33–35 and para 91. This assimilation is by no means self-evident; the Commentary to the ICL Articles on State Responsibility suggests that there is at least 'a difference in emphasis' (Commentary to Article 40, Part I, para (7)).

[71] For an alternative view, that *jus cogens* is a matter of consensus, see the combative article by Kolb, 1998.

the universal reaction of States was to assert that that rule was such that no derogation by treaty was permitted, this could be read as practice showing an *opinio* that the rule was one of *jus cogens*. Similarly, if a State not directly affected by a breach of international law took counter-measures against the offending State, and that State conceded its right to do so, this would show an *opinio* that an obligation *erga omnes* was involved. In fact however, that has not been at all the way in which norms of *jus cogens* and obligations *erga omnes* have come to be identified; and the first hypothesis, of assertion of a treaty as justifying conduct universally condemned, is *a priori* somewhat unlikely to be realized.

V. CONCLUSION

Ubi societas, ibi jus: wherever there is a social structure, you will find law. This is ultimately the only explanation for the development of international law, for the respect generally shown for it by States as international actors, and for the general recognition of the 'secondary rules' whereby law acquires binding effect. Historically, the more individual States found it necessary to relate to each other, the greater the need for generally respected rules and guidelines. Even the concept of 'natural law' related to what was fitting and necessary for the good ordering of society; and the positivist approach, which sees all law as established by the express or tacit agreement of those subject to it, is in effect a prolongation of the 'social contract'.

The establishment of the Permanent Court of International Justice brought to a focus the ideas as to the sources of law that had, over the years, made their appearance in State practice, arbitral decisions, and the views of scholars. The definition given in Article 38 of the Statute of the Court has proved to embody a workable structure of recognized law-making processes, and despite the criticisms made of it, and the multiplicity of new approaches to international law,[72] that definition seems likely to continue to guide the international community and the international judge.

REFERENCES

BYERS, M (1999), *Custom, Power and the Power of Rules* (Cambridge: Cambridge University Press).

CHARNEY, R (1993), 'Universal International Law', 87 *AJIL* 529.

CHENG, B (1965), 'United Nations Resolutions on Outer Space: "Instant" Customary Law?', *Ind JIL* 23.

D'AMATO, A (1990), 'It's a Bird, it's a Plane, it's *Jus Cogens*', 9 *Conn JIL* 1; reprinted

in D'AMATO, A (2004), *International Law Sources, Collected Papers*, vol III (The Hague: Nijhoff).

FITZMAURICE, G (1953), 'The Law and Procedure of the International Court, 1951–1954', 30 *BYIL* 21.

—— (1958), 'Some Problems Regarding the Formal Sources of International Law', *Symbolae Verzijl* (The Hague: Nijhoff).

---

[72] A useful panoramic view of a number of modern methodologies will be found in a Symposium published in (1999) 93 *AJIL* 293.

HART, H (1994), *The Concept of Law*, revised edn (Oxford: Oxford University Press).

HIGGINS, R (1970), 'The UN and Law-Making: the Political Organs', *Proceedings, American Society of International Law*, Vol 64, p 37.

KAMMERHOFER, J (2004), 'Uncertainty in the Formal Sources of International Law: Customary International Law and Some of its Problems', 15 *EJIL* 523–553.

KOLB, R (1998), 'The Formal Source of *Ius Cogens* in Public International Law', 53 *Zeitschrift für öffentliches Recht*, p 69.

LAUTERPACHT, H (1927), *Private Law Sources and Analogies of International Law* (London: Longmans, Green & Co).

MURSWIEK, D (2002), 'The American Strategy of Pre-emptive War and International Law', XIII *FYBIL* 195.

THIRLWAY, HWA (2002), 'Concepts, Principles, Rules and Analogies: International and Municipal Legal Reasoning', 294 *Recueil des Cours* 268–405.

VILLALPANDO, S (2005), *L'émergence de la communauté internationale dans la responsabilité des États* (IUHEI, Geneva: Presses universitaires de France).

FURTHER READING

D'AMATO, A (2004), International Law Sources, Collected Papers, vol III (The Hague: Nijhoff): a collection of papers from various dates, written in a vigorous and accessible style.

HIGGINS, R (1994), *Problems and Process: International Law and How We Use It* (Oxford: Clarendon Press) (particularly Chs 1 and 2): for a study from a more 'policy-oriented' perspective.

KOLB, R (2006), 'Principles as Sources of International Law (with Special Reference to Good Faith)', 53 *Netherlands International Law Review* 1

KOSKENNIEMI, M (1989), *From Apology to Utopia: the Structure of International Legal Argument*, 2005 reissue (Cambridge: Cambridge University Press): a highly original approach to international law, not easy reading, but still relevant after 20 years.

MENDELSON, M (1995), 'The Subjective Element in Customary International Law', 66 *BYIL* 177: an eloquent plea for the abandonment of the concept of *opinio juris*.

SCHACHTER, O (1989), 'Entangled Treaty and Custom', in Dinstein, Y (ed), *International Law at a Time of Perplexity: Essays in Honour of Shabtai Rosenne*, p 717: on the inter-relationship of the two sources in modern law.

SHELTON, D (2006) 'Normative Hierarchy in International Law', 100 *AJIL* 291.

THIRLWAY, HWA (1990), 'The Law and Procedure of the International Court of Justice, 1960–1989 (Part Two)', 61 *BYIL* 1: a survey of problems that have arisen before the ICJ concerning the various sources of international law.

5

SOFT LAW IN INTERNATIONAL LAW-MAKING

Alan Boyle

SUMMARY

From a law-making perspective the term 'soft law' is simply a convenient description for a variety of non-legally binding instruments used in contemporary international relations by States and international organizations. Soft law in this sense can be contrasted with hard law, which is always binding. Non-binding soft law instruments are not law *per se*, but they may be evidence of existing law, or formative of the *opinio juris* or State practice that generates new customary law. They may additionally acquire binding legal character as elements of a treaty-based regulatory regime, or constitute a subsequent agreement between the parties regarding the interpretation of a treaty or the application of its provisions. Thus the effect of non-binding soft law instruments may not be fundamentally different from those multilateral treaties which serve much the same law-making purposes. Both treaties and soft law instruments can thus become vehicles for focusing consensus on rules and principles, and for mobilizing a consistent, general response on the part of States. Other non-binding soft-law instruments are significant mainly because they are the first step in a process eventually leading to conclusion of a multilateral treaty, or because they provide the detailed rules and technical standards required for the implementation of a treaty. An alternative view of soft law focuses on the contrast between 'rules', involving clear and reasonably specific commitments which are in this sense hard law, and 'norms' or 'principles', which, being more open-textured or general in their content and wording, can thus be seen as soft even when contained in a binding treaty. Nevertheless, this form of soft law is also not without legal significance. For all these reasons it is a fallacy to dismiss soft law, properly understood: it can and does contribute to the corpus of international law.

I. THE SIGNIFICANCE OF SOFT LAW

Soft law is often misunderstood, although evidence of its importance as an element in modern international law-making is abundant, most notably in the declarations or resolutions adopted by States in international conferences or in the United Nations or other international organizations. Certainly, the concept has had its critics. Prosper Weil famously argued in his classic article 'Towards Relative Normativity in International Law?' that there is only law and non-law.[1] For him, soft law is a non-sequitur. More recently, Jan Klabbers has also dismissed the concept of soft law as redundant.[2] It is true that soft law may appear to some as another example of the preference for 'informal regimes' which Martti Koskenniemi identifies with a 'managerialist' approach to international affairs, resulting in a dilution of their legal force.[3] But as Koskenniemi rightly observes, 'To believe that a commitment to 'law' would be an automatically progressive choice is no less crude a directive to policy than the belief that all needs to be streamlined for the attainment of imperial preference.'[4] However, it is not necessary to indulge in high theory in order to make sense of soft law. As Rosalyn Higgins has observed in the context of UN General Assembly (UNGA) resolutions, '…the passing of binding decisions is not the only way in which law development occurs. Legal consequences can also flow from acts which are not, in the formal sense, "binding". And, further, law is developed by a variety of non-legislative acts which do not seek to secure, in any direct sense, "compliance" from Assembly members…'.[5]

Perhaps the most important point to make at the outset therefore is simply that some of the forms of 'soft law' under consideration here are potentially law-making in much the same way that multilateral treaties are potentially law-making. The proposition is not that non-binding declarations or resolutions of the General Assembly or any other soft law instrument are law *per se*, but that in appropriate cases such instruments may be evidence of existing law, or formative of the *opinio juris* or State practice that generates new customary law. Widespread acceptance of soft law instruments will tend to legitimize conduct, and make the legality of opposing positions harder to sustain. They may additionally acquire binding legal character as elements of a treaty-based regulatory regime,[6] or constitute a 'subsequent agreement between the parties regarding the interpretation of the treaty or the application of its provisions',[7] or influence the development and application of treaties or general international law.[8]

It is certainly a fallacy to dismiss these forms of soft law as not law and therefore of no importance: they can and do contribute to the corpus of international law, as the examples considered below will show. Nor is reliance on soft law to be confused with the application of *lex ferenda* or 'evolving law'.[9] If it is true that some soft law instruments are—like treaties—part of the process by which customary law evolves, then it is equally true that in the evolutionary stage they have not yet generated actual law, and we should not pretend otherwise. Identifying when law in the making has become law is of course precisely the point on which States and international lawyers will often disagree, but it is precisely at that point that 'soft law' is in reality no longer soft. The focus in this chapter is on soft law as

---

[1] Weil, 1983, p 411.   [2] Klabbers, 1996, pp 167–182.

[3] Koskenniemi, 2009, p 15. See also Koskenniemi, 1992, p 123.

[4] Koskenniemi, 2009, p 17.   [5] Higgins, 1995, p 24.

[6] Eg under the 1982 UN Convention on the Law of the Sea, Articles 210–211, or the 1994 Nuclear Safety Convention, on which see below.

[7] See 1969 Vienna Convention on the Law of Treaties, Article 31(3)(a).

[8] See *Gabčíkovo-Nagymaros Project (Hungary/Slovakia), Judgment, ICJ Reports 1997*, p 7, para 140.

[9] *OSPAR Arbitration* (2003) PCA, 42 ILM 330, paras 101–104. On the applicability of evolving law see the very sensible comments by McDorman, 2004.

one element in the law-making process precisely because it leads to law, not to something less than law.

II. WHAT IS SOFT LAW?

'Soft law' has a range of possible meanings.[10] From a law-making perspective the term 'soft law' is simply a convenient description for a variety of non-legally binding instruments used in contemporary international relations by States and international organizations. It encompasses *inter alia* inter-State conference declarations such as the 1992 Rio Declaration on Environment and Development; UNGA instruments such as the 1948 Universal Declaration of Human Rights, the 1970 Declaration on the Principles of Friendly Relations Among States, the 2007 Declaration on the Rights of Indigenous Peoples, or other resolutions dealing with outer space, the deep seabed, decolonization, or natural resources; or codes of conduct, guidelines and recommendations of international organizations, such as the United Nations Environment Programme (UNEP)'s 1987 Guidelines on Environmental Impact Assessment, the Food and Agriculture Organization (FAO)'s Code of Conduct on Responsible Fisheries, or many others adopted by the International Maritime Organization (IMO), International Atomic Energy Agency (IAEA), FAO and so on.

Soft law in this sense can be contrasted with hard law, which is always binding. Seen from this angle, the legal form is decisive: treaties which have entered into force are by definition hard law, at least for the parties. So, in principle, are UN Security Council Resolutions adopted under Chapter VII of the UN Charter, because all UN member States have agreed to accept and carry out these decisions.[11] If the form is that of a non-binding agreement, such as the Helsinki Accords (Schachter, 1977), or a UNGA resolution or declaration,[12] it will not be a treaty for precisely that reason and we will have what is in effect a 'soft' agreement. Of course, the question whether an agreement is a binding treaty is not necessarily easy to answer, as we can observe in the *Qatar-Bahrain Maritime Delimitation* case.[13] The test is one of substance and intent; the label attached to the instrument is not decisive. Moreover, an agreement involving a State and another entity may be binding, even if it is not a treaty,[14] so the distinction between hard and soft agreements is not simply synonymous with the distinction between treaties and other instruments. Furthermore, once soft law begins to interact with binding instruments, its non-binding character may be lost or altered.

As we have seen, reliance on soft law as part of the law-making process takes a number of different forms. While the legal effect of declarations, resolutions, guidelines, and other soft law instruments is not necessarily the same, it is characteristic of nearly all of them that they are carefully negotiated, and often carefully drafted statements, which are in

[10] See generally Baxter, 1980; Chinkin, 1989; Dupuy, 1991; Sztucki, 1990; Hillgenberg, 1999.

[11] UN Charter, Article 25.

[12] In UN practice a 'declaration' is used in preference to a 'resolution' when 'principles of great and lasting importance are being enunciated'. See UN Doc. E/CN.4/L.610 (1962), cited in Cheng, 1965, at p 32.

[13] *Maritime Delimitation and Territorial Questions between Qatar and Bahrain, Jurisdiction and Admissibility, Judgment, ICJ Reports 1994*, p 112.

[14] *See Anglo-Iranian Oil Co, Preliminary Objections, Judgment, ICJ Reports 1952*, p 93.

some cases intended to have some normative significance despite their non-binding, non-treaty form. There is at least an element of good faith commitment,[15] evidencing in some cases a desire to influence State practice or expressing some measure of law-making intention and progressive development. In this sense non-binding soft law instruments are in some cases not fundamentally different from those multilateral treaties which serve much the same law-making purposes. They may also be both an alternative to and part of the process of multilateral treaty-making. In the following sections we will explore the uses of soft law and consider what legal effect it may have.

III. TREATIES OR SOFT LAW?

There are several reasons why soft law instruments may represent an attractive alternative to law-making by treaty. First, it may be easier to reach agreement when the form is non-binding. Use of soft law instruments enables States to agree to more detailed and precise provisions because their legal commitment and the consequences of any non-compliance are more limited. Secondly, it may be easier for some States to agree to non-binding instruments because they can avoid the domestic treaty ratification process, and perhaps escape democratic accountability for the policy to which they have agreed. Of course this may also make it comparably harder to implement such policies if funding, legislation, or public support, are necessary. Thirdly, soft law instruments are flexible. They will normally be easier to supplement, amend, or replace than treaties, particularly when all that is required is the adoption of a new resolution by an international institution. Two good examples are the nuclear safety standards adopted by the IAEA,[16] which amplify and interpret the basic obligations contained in the Nuclear Safety Convention, and FAO's Code of Conduct on Responsible Fisheries, which has itself been further developed by non-binding 'Plans of Action' adopted by the FAO Conference.[17] Treaties take time to replace or amend, and the attempt to do so can result in an awkward and overlapping network of old and new obligations between different sets of parties. One of the better examples of the confused state of the law which sometimes results from repeated treaty revisions is the 1929 Warsaw Convention Relating to International Carriage by Air (Gardiner, 1998). Lastly, soft law instruments may provide more immediate evidence of international support and consensus than a treaty whose impact is heavily qualified by reservations and the need to wait for ratification and entry into force. All of these points are well illustrated by some of the examples discussed in later sections of this chapter.

Given the relative advantages of soft law over treaties, it is perhaps surprising that the multilateral treaty has until now been the International Law Commission (ILC)'s preferred instrument for the codification of international law.[18] One important advantage of the treaty as an instrument of codification is that States have significant input into

---

[15] On the role of good faith in relation to unilateral undertakings see in particular the *Nuclear Tests (Australia v France), Judgment, ICJ Reports 1974*, p 253; *(New Zealand v France), Judgment, ICJ Reports 1974*, p 457. A soft law declaration *may* result in binding unilateral obligations: see *OSPAR Arbitration* (2003) PCA, 42 ILM 330, para 90.

[16] See note 35 below.   [17] See Section IV.

[18] Articles 17 and 23 of the Statute of the Commission do refer expressly to the conclusion of conventions, but other possibilities are left open.

the negotiations and they have sometimes made substantial changes to ILC drafts.[19] This renegotiation does not necessarily happen when the UN General Assembly simply adopts or takes note of a declaration of principles drafted by the Commission. A treaty basis may also be required when creating new international organizations or institutions, or for dispute settlement provisions. Nevertheless, in some situations soft law instruments appear to be just as useful a means of codifying international law as treaties. The Commission's draft articles on the law of State responsibility could equally well be codified using either a GA resolution or a treaty.[20] Indeed a GA resolution may in this case be more effective than a treaty, which, like the Vienna Convention on the Law of Treaties, runs the risk of securing only a relatively small number of parties and taking many years to enter into force. The Vienna Convention is among the ILC's most successful and authoritative codifications, but it is difficult to suggest that this owes much to its treaty status, or to the number of States parties, currently standing at 111.

The argument for using a treaty rather than a soft law instrument is stronger in the case of new law-making or the revision of existing law, such as the re-negotiation of the law of the sea or the elaboration of human rights law, although in many of these cases institutions with extensive powers were also established at the same time and a treaty was thus desirable in any event. But even for new law, non-binding instruments may still be useful if they can help generate widespread and consistent State practice and/or provide evidence of *opinio juris* in support of a customary rule. There are good examples of UNGA resolutions and intergovernmental declarations having this effect in the *Nicaragua* case,[21] the *Nuclear Weapons Advisory Opinion*,[22] and the *Western Sahara Advisory Opinion*.[23]

What all of this suggests is that the non-binding form of an instrument is of relatively limited relevance in the context of customary international law-making. Treaties do not generate or codify customary law because of their binding form but because they either influence State practice and provide evidence of *opinio juris* for new or emerging rules, or because they are good evidence of what the existing law is. In many cases this is no different from the potential effect of non-binding soft law instruments. Both treaties and soft law instruments can be vehicles for focusing consensus on rules and principles, and for mobilizing a consistent, general response on the part of States. Depending upon what is involved, treaties may be more effective than soft law instruments for this purpose because they indicate a stronger commitment to the principles in question and to that extent they may carry greater weight than a soft law instrument, but the assumption that they are necessarily more authoritative is misplaced. To take only one example, the 1992 Rio Declaration on Environment and Development both codifies existing international law and seeks to develop new law.[24] It is not obvious that a treaty with the same provisions

---

[19] Eg the 1969 Vienna Convention on the Law of Treaties and the 1997 International Convention on the Non-navigational Uses of International Watercourses. On the comparative advantages of different forms see Crawford, 2002, pp 58–60.

[20] The ILC recommended that the UN General Assembly simply 'take note' of the draft articles.

[21] *Military and Paramilitary Activities in and against Nicaragua (Nicaragua v United States of America)*, *Merits, Judgment, ICJ Reports 1986*, p 14.

[22] *Legality of the Threat or Use of Nuclear Weapons, ICJ Reports 1996*, p 226.

[23] *Western Sahara, Advisory Opinion, ICJ Reports 1975*, p 12.

[24] See *Legality of the Threat or Use of Nuclear Weapons, ICJ Reports 1996*, p 226, paras 29–30 and Boyle and Freestone, 1999, Ch 1; Sands, 1993, Chs 1 and 3.

would carry greater weight or achieve its objectives any more successfully. On the contrary, it is quite possible that such a treaty would, several years later, still have far from universal participation, whereas the 1992 Declaration secured immediate consensus support, with such authority as that implies. At the same time, it seems clear that agreements such as those on climate change and biological diversity adopted in 1992 could only be in treaty form, because of the combination of their status as new law, their more detailed terms, and their institutional provisions. For rather different reasons the ILC articles on State immunity were adopted as a treaty in order to facilitate giving effect to the necessary changes in the national law of those States with a monist view of the relationship between treaties and national law.[25] In these cases, because of the content and objective of the agreement, incorporation in a treaty was the right option and does carry a greater sense of commitment than a soft law instrument.

IV. SOFT LAW AS PART OF THE MULTILATERAL TREATY-MAKING PROCESS

Some non-binding soft-law instruments are significant because they are the first step in a process eventually leading to the conclusion of a multilateral treaty. Thus the non-binding Universal Declaration of Human Rights was adopted long before agreement on the 1966 Covenants became possible, but it was always intended by the Human Rights Commission that further binding agreements would follow. Examples are numerous, but they include UNGA resolutions on outer space, the deep seabed, and climate change;[26] the IAEA Guidelines[27] which formed the basis for the rapid adoption of the 1986 Convention on Early Notification of a Nuclear Accident following the Chernobyl accident; UNEP's Guidelines on Environmental Impact Assessment[28] which were subsequently substantially incorporated in the 1991 ECE Convention on Environmental Impact Assessment in a Transboundary Context; and UNEP's Guidelines on Land-based Sources of Marine Pollution,[29] which provided a model for regional treaties.[30]

Other soft law instruments are used as mechanisms for authoritative interpretation or amplification of the terms of a treaty, and to that extent must be taken into account. The ILC Commentary to what is now Article 31(3)(a) of the Vienna Convention on the Law of Treaties notes simply that '...an agreement as to the interpretation of a provision reached after the conclusion of the treaty represents an authentic interpretation by the parties which must be read into the treaty for purposes of its interpretation'.[31] There are well-known instances of UNGA resolutions interpreting and applying the UN Charter,

---

[25] See 2004 UN Convention on Jurisdictional Immunities of States and their Property.

[26] 1963 Declaration of Legal Principles Governing the Activities of States in the Exploration and Use of Outer Space, UNGA Res.1962 (XVIII); 1970 Declaration of Principles Governing the Sea Bed and Ocean Floor and Subsoil Thereof Beyond the Limits of National Jurisdiction, UNGA Res.2749 (XXV); 1988 Resolution on Protection of Global Climate for Present and Future Generations of Mankind, UNGA Res.43/53.

[27] IAEA/INFCIRC/321 (1985). [28] UNEP/GC14/25 (1987).

[29] UNEP/WG.120/3 (1985).

[30] See eg 1990 Kuwait Protocol for the Protection of the Marine Environment Against Marine Pollution from Land-based Sources.

[31] ILC, 'The Law of Treaties,' commentary to Article 27, at para (14), in Watts, 2000, p 689.

including the Universal Declaration of Human Rights and others dealing with decolonization or the use of force.[32]

The same task of giving guidance on or amplifying the terms of a treaty is performed
more frequently by resolutions, recommendations and decisions of other international
organizations, and by the conferences of parties to treaties. Thus it was a resolution of
the parties to the Montreal Protocol to the Ozone Convention which first set out the
terms of the non-compliance procedure provided for in the protocol.[33] The procedure was
subsequently revised and then incorporated by amendment as an annex in the protocol,
showing again how non-binding soft law can be transformed into binding form. Similarly,
UNEP's Cairo Guidelines on the Transport of Hazardous Wastes[34] can be regarded as an
amplification of the obligation of 'environmentally sound management' provided for in
Article 4 of the 1989 Basel Convention on the Control of Transboundary Movements of
Hazardous Wastes.

A related role for soft law instruments is to provide the detailed rules and technical
standards required for implementation of some treaties. Environmental soft law is quite
often important for this reason, setting standards of best practice or due diligence to be
achieved by the parties in implementing their obligations. These 'ecostandards' are essential in giving hard content to the overly-general and open-textured terms of framework
environmental treaties (Contini and Sand, 1972). The advantages of regulating environmental risks in this way are that the detailed rules can easily be changed or strengthened
as scientific understanding develops or as political priorities change. Such standards could
of course be adopted in binding form, using easily amended annexes to provide flexibility,
but this is not always what parties want.

The IAEA has made particular use of formally non-binding standards, through its nuclear safety codes and principles. These generally represent an authoritative technical and
political consensus, approved by the Board of Governors or General Conference of the
Agency. Despite their soft law status it is relatively easy to see them as minimum internationally endorsed standards of conduct, and to regard failure to comply as presumptively a failure to fulfil the customary obligation of due diligence in the regulation and
control of nuclear activities.[35] However, because of the uncertainty posed by this very soft
approach to the regulation of nuclear safety, the 1994 Convention on Nuclear Safety and
the 1997 Joint Convention on the Safety of Spent Fuel and Radioactive Waste Management
have now incorporated in binding treaty articles the main elements of IAEA's fundamental safety standards for nuclear installations, radioactive waste management and
radiation protection, and most of its Code of Practice on the Transboundary Movement

---

[32] 1960 Declaration on the Granting of Independence to Colonial Countries and Peoples, UNGA
Res.1514 (XV); 1970 Declaration on Principles of International law Concerning Friendly Relations and
Co-operation Among States in Accordance with the Charter of the United Nations, UNGA Res.2625 (XXV).
See *Western Sahara, Advisory Opinion, ICJ Reports 1975*, p 12; *Military and Paramilitary Activities in and
against Nicaragua (Nicaragua v United States of America), Merits, Judgment, ICJ Reports 1986*, p 14.

[33] Decision II/5, UNEP/OzL.Pro/WG.3/2/2, Annex III (1990).

[34] UNEP/WG.122/3.

[35] The preamble to the Nuclear Safety Convention recognizes that internationally formulated safety
guidelines 'can provide guidance on contemporary means of achieving a high level of safety'. IAEA guidelines would be the obvious starting point for determining what constituted the 'appropriate steps' with
regard to safety controls required by Articles 10–19 of the Convention.

of Radioactive Waste (Birnie, Boyle and Redgwell, 2009, Ch 9). Those remaining IAEA standards which retain a soft law status will still be relevant when determining how the basic obligations of States parties to these agreements are to be implemented. Moreover, under the Joint Convention there is also an obligation on States parties to take account of relevant IAEA standards in adopting national law. These various agreements have significantly strengthened the legal force of IAEA standards and, in conjunction with non-binding soft-law safety standards, have created a more convincing legal framework for the international regulation of nuclear risks. They exemplify once again how soft-law and treaties can interact in a complex regulatory framework.

Nor is IAEA unique in this respect. FAO has made use of a mixture of hard and soft law instruments to promote implementation of the fisheries provisions of the 1982 United Nations Conference on the Law of the Sea (UNCLOS). The 1993 Agreement to Promote Compliance with Conservation Measures on the High Seas is a binding treaty, but it forms an integral part of the non-binding 1995 Code of Conduct on Responsible Fishing, which is itself further implemented by other measures including the 2001 Plan of Action on Illegal, Unreported and Unregulated Fishing, also a soft-law instrument. Negotiated in the same manner as treaties, and adopted by consensus in FAO,[36] these non-binding 'voluntary instruments' are aimed at regional fisheries organizations and the fishing industry as well as States, but in part they also reiterate, interpret and amplify relevant provisions of UNCLOS and the 1995 Fish Stocks Agreement. The scope of the Code is much broader than either of these treaties, however. It contains some elements which are unlikely to find their way into a binding agreement, and others which could not be agreed on as part of the UN Fish Stocks Agreement. The 1993 Agreement and the 1995 Code were negotiated in parallel with the Fish Stocks Agreement, and all three 'can be viewed as a package of measures that reinforce and complement each other' (Moore, 1999, pp 91–92). Reviewing the effect of all these inter-related measures, a former FAO Legal Adviser concludes that 'There can be little doubt that the sum total of the changes introduced has substantially strengthened the regime of the 1982 UN Convention, leaving aside the question whether there has been a *de facto* amendment of it in some respect.' (Edeson, 1999, p 165; see also Edeson, 2003, p 165)

Sometimes binding force is conferred on soft-law instruments by incorporating them into the terms of a treaty by implied reference. The 1982 UNCLOS makes use of this technique, impliedly incorporating recommendations and resolutions of IMO, as well as regulatory annexes to treaties such as the 1973/78 MARPOL Convention, under provisions variously requiring or permitting States to apply 'generally accepted rules and standards established through the competent international organization or general diplomatic conference'.[37] Thus although IMO has no general power under its constitution to adopt binding resolutions, UNCLOS may indirectly render some of these resolutions obligatory.

Lastly, soft law instruments may operate in conjunction with a treaty to provide evidence of *opinio juris* for the possible emergence of a rule of customary international law.

---

[36] However some States expressed significant reservations when adopting the Plan of Action: see FAO, *Report of the Committee on Fisheries*, 24th Session (2001).
[37] 1982 UNCLOS, Articles 207–212.

ICJ case law, including the *Nicaragua* case,[38] shows how the interplay between the UN Charter and resolutions of the General Assembly can have this effect.

These examples all point to the conclusion that the non-binding force of soft-law can be over-stated. In many of the above examples States are not necessarily free to disregard applicable soft-law instruments: even when not incorporated directly into a treaty, they may represent an agreed understanding of its terms. Thus, although of themselves these instruments may not be legally binding, their interaction with related treaties may transform their legal status into something more.

V. TREATIES AS SOFT LAW

An alternative view of soft law focuses on the contrast between 'rules', involving clear and reasonably specific commitments which are in this sense hard law (eg 'No State may validly purport to subject any part of the high seas to its sovereignty'), and 'norms' or 'principles', which, being more open-textured or general in their content and wording, can thus be seen as soft.

The point was made many years ago by the late Judge Baxter that some treaties are soft in the sense that they impose no real obligations on the parties (Baxter, 1980). Though formally binding, the vagueness, indeterminacy, or generality of their provisions may deprive them of the character of 'hard law' in any meaningful sense. The 1992 Framework Convention on Climate Change provides another example. Adopted by consensus at the Rio Conference, this treaty does impose some commitments on the parties, but its core articles, dealing with policies and measures to tackle greenhouse gas emissions, are so cautiously and obscurely worded and so weak that it is doubtful whether any real obligations are created.[39] Moreover, whatever commitments have been undertaken by developing States are also conditional on performance of solidarity commitments by developed State parties to provide funding and transfer of technology.[40]

Such treaty provisions are almost impossible to breach and in that limited sense Judge Baxter is justified in calling them soft law. More of a political bargain than a legal one, these are 'soft' undertakings of a very fragile kind. They are not normative and cannot be described as creating 'rules' in any meaningful sense. This is probably true of very many treaties, a point recognized by the International Court in the *North Sea Continental Shelf* case when it specified that one of the conditions to be met before a treaty could be regarded as law-making is that it should be so drafted as to be 'potentially normative' in character.[41]

There is, however, a second and more significant sense in which a treaty may be 'soft' in character because it articulates 'principles' rather than 'rules' or 'obligations' but is

---

[38] *Military and Paramilitary Activities in and against Nicaragua (Nicaragua v United States of America), Merits, Judgment, ICJ Reports 1986*, p 14; *Western Sahara, Advisory Opinion, ICJ Reports 1975*, p 12.

[39] Especially Articles 4(1) and (2). The United States' interpretation of these articles was that 'there is nothing in any of the language which constitutes a commitment to any specific level of emissions at any time...'. The parties determined at their first meeting in 1995 that the commitments were inadequate and they agreed to commence negotiation of the much more specific commitments now contained in the 1997 Kyoto Protocol.

[40] Article 4(7).   [41] *North Sea Continental Shelf, Judgment, ICJ Reports 1969*, p 3, para 72.

nevertheless potentially normative. Here it is the *formulation* of the provision which is decisive in determining whether it is hard or soft, not its form as a treaty or binding instrument. An example of a soft formulation, which nevertheless has binding form, is Article 87(2) of the 1982 UNCLOS, which provides that high seas freedoms 'shall be exercised by all States with due regard for the interests of other states in their exercise of the freedoms of the highs seas...'. What is meant by 'due regard' for the interests of other States will necessarily depend on the particular circumstances of each case and in that sense the provision is more of a 'principle' than a rule.[42] The rule of customary law providing for equitable delimitation of maritime boundaries is another example of a comparably 'soft' formulation.[43]

The Convention on Climate Change once again provides other good examples of such principles explicitly included in a major treaty. Indeed, given how weak the rest of the treaty is, the principles found in Article 3 are arguably the most important 'law' in the whole agreement because they prescribe how the regime for regulating climate change is to be developed by the parties. It is worth quoting the main elements of this provision:

Article 3: Principles
In their actions to achieve the objective of the Convention and to implement its provisions, the parties shall be guided, inter alia, by the following:

1. The Parties should protect the climate system for the benefit of present and future generations of humankind, on the basis of equity an in accordance with their common but differentiated responsibilities...
3. The Parties should take precautionary measures to anticipate, prevent, or minimise the causes of climate change and mitigate its adverse effects...
4. The Parties have a right to, and should, promote sustainable development...

These elements of Article 3 are all drawn directly from the non-binding Rio Declaration on Environment and Development; they reflect principles which are not simply part of the Climate Change Convention, but which are also emerging at the level of general international law, even if it is as yet premature to accord them the status of custom. They are not expressed in obligatory terms: the use of 'should' qualifies their application, despite the obligatory wording of the chapeau sentence. All of these principles are open-textured in the sense that there is considerable uncertainty concerning their specific content and they leave much room for interpretation and elaboration. They are not at all like rules requiring States to conduct an environmental impact assessment, or to prevent harm to other States.

Given their explicit role as guidance and their softer formulation, the 'principles' in Article 3 are not necessarily binding rules which must be complied with or which entail responsibility for breach if not complied with; yet, despite all these limitations they are not legally irrelevant.[44] At the very least Article 3 is relevant to interpretation and

---

[42] See *Fisheries Jurisdiction (United Kingdom v Iceland), Merits, Judgments, ICJ Reports 1974*, p 3; *(Federal Republic of Germany v Iceland), Merits, Judgment, ICJ Reports*, 1974, p 175; *Nuclear Tests (Australia v France), Judgment, ICJ Reports 1974*, p 253; *(New Zealand v France), Judgment, ICJ Reports 1974*, p 457.

[43] 1982 UNCLOS, Articles 74 and 83; *North Sea Continental Shelf, Judgment, ICJ Reports 1969*, p 3; *Delimitation of the Maritime Boundary in the Gulf of Maine Area, Judgment, ICJ Reports 1984*, p 246; *Maritime Delimitation in the Area between Greenland and Jan Mayen, Judgment, ICJ Reports 1993*, p 38.

[44] See the debate between Sands and Mann in Lang, 1995, pp 53–74.

implementation of the Convention as well as creating expectations concerning matters which must be taken into account in good faith in the negotiation of further instruments.

Article 3 takes a novel approach to environmental protection, but in the context of a dynamic and evolutionary regulatory regime such as the Climate Change Convention it has the important merit of providing some predictability regarding the parameters within which the parties are required to work towards the objective of the Convention. In particular, they are not faced with a completely blank sheet of paper when entering subsequent protocol negotiations or when the Conference of the Parties takes decisions under the various articles empowering it to do so. Thus it is significant that the relevance of Article 3 was reiterated in the mandate for negotiation of the Kyoto Protocol[45] and is referred to in the preamble to the Protocol. It is a nice question whether the parties collectively are entitled to disregard the principles contained in Article 3, or what the legal effect of decisions which do so may be, but however weak it may seem, parties whose interests are affected do have a right to insist on having the principles of Article 3 taken into account. As we shall see in the following section, sustainable development, intergenerational equity, or the precautionary principle, are all more convincingly seen in this sense: not as binding obligations which must be complied with, but as principles, considerations or objectives to be taken account of—they may be soft, but they are still law.

VI. SOFT LAW GENERAL PRINCIPLES

The idea that general norms or principles can affect the way courts decide cases or the exercise of discretionary powers by an international organization is not confined to treaty regimes. Indeed in modern international relations such general norms or principles are probably more often found in the form of non-binding declarations or resolutions of international organizations than in the provisions of multilateral treaties. The Universal Declaration of Human Rights remains one of the most influential examples of soft law of this kind. International courts have of course always had the power under Article 38(1)(c) of the ICJ Statute to refer to general principles of law. In most cases this entails borrowing by analogy from common elements of national law, such as non-discrimination or the right to a fair hearing.[46] In essence, resort to general principles of this kind is judge-made law.

However, it is also possible for States to adopt general principles not derived from national law, with the intention that courts and States should apply them when relevant. Such general principles do not have to create rules of customary law to have legal effect. Rather, their importance derives principally from the influence they can exert on the interpretation, application, and development of other rules of law. Article 31(3) of the 1969 Vienna Convention on the Law of Treaties requires subsequent agreements, practices and rules of international law to be taken into account when interpreting a treaty

---

[45] The so-called 'Berlin mandate': Decision 1/CP.1, in *Report of the Conference of the Parties on its 1st Session,* UN Doc.FCCC/CP/1995/7/Add.1.

[46] See *South West Africa, Second Phase, Judgment, ICJ Reports 1966,* p 6, Dissenting Opinion of Judge Tanaka, p 250 at 294–301; *Golder* v *UK,* Judgment of 21 February 1975, ECtHR, Ser A, No 18, paras 10–36, 1 *EHRR* 524, but cf dissenting opinion of Judge Fitzmaurice, paras 18–46 and 48 and see generally Cassese, 1986, pp 170–174; Cheng, 1953; Friedmann, 1963.

(McLachlan, 2005; Boyle, 2005, at 572–574). This provision appears to include reference to general principles as an aid to treaty interpretation.[47] If that is correct, soft law declarations such as the 1992 Rio Declaration on Environment and Development or the 1948 Universal Declaration of Human Rights will have to be taken into account insofar as they articulate general principles agreed by consensus. The point is not confined to treaty interpretation, however. A general principle of this kind may also influence the interpretation and application of customary law.

The precautionary approach (or principle), endorsed by consensus in Principle 15 of the 1992 Rio Declaration on Environment and Development, is a case in point. The precautionary approach is a common feature of almost all the Rio and post-Rio global environmental agreements. Principle 15 of the Rio Declaration provides as follows:

Principle 15: In order to protect the environment, the precautionary approach shall be widely applied by states according to their capabilities. Where there are threats of serious or irreversible damage, lack of full scientific certainty shall not be used as a reason for postponing cost-effective measures to prevent environmental degradation.

Its purpose is thus to make greater allowance for uncertainty in the regulation of environmental risks and the sustainable use of natural resources.

Some writers and governments have argued that the precautionary principle or approach is a rule of customary international law, but international courts and most governments have been noticeably hesitant to accept this characterization.[48] If, alternatively, the precautionary principle is viewed as a general principle of law, on which decision-makers and courts may rely when deciding cases and interpreting treaties, then its subsequent use by national and international courts, and by international organizations, is easier to explain. As the *Southern Bluefin Tuna* cases show, the interpretation and application of treaties may be affected.[49] Moreover, so may the interpretation and application of customary international law. Thus in the law relating to transboundary harm, as Brownlie observes, 'The point which stands out is that some applications of the principle, which is based on the concept of foreseeable risk to other states, are encompassed within existing concepts of state responsibility' (Brownlie, 2008, p 278). The ILC special rapporteur on transboundary harm has taken the same view, concluding that the precautionary principle is already a component of customary rules on prevention of harm and environmental impact assessment, 'and could not be divorced therefrom'.[50]

Much the same could be said of sustainable development. Lowe (1999, at p 31) makes the essential point with great clarity:

Sustainable development can properly claim a normative status as an element of the process of judicial reasoning. It is a meta-principle, acting upon other rules and principles—a legal

---

[47] Thus in the *Golder* case the ECHR referred to access to a court as a 'general principle of law' when interpreting Article 6 of the European Convention on Human Rights. Note, however, that general principles cannot override or amend the express terms of a treaty: see *Beef Hormone Case*, Appellate Body Report, WT/DS26/AB/R, WT/DS48/AB/R (16 January 1998), paras 124–125.

[48] See eg ibid, paras 120–125; *Southern Bluefin Tuna cases (Provisional Measures)* (1999) ITLOS Nos 3 and 4, paras 77–79.

[49] *Southern Bluefin Tuna cases*, ibid, and see also Judges Laing at paras 16–19; Treves at para 9, and Shearer.

[50] Report of the International Law Commission, Fifty-Second Session, A/55/10, para 716.

concept exercising a kind of interstitial normativity, pushing and pulling the boundaries of true primary norms when they threaten to overlap or conflict with each other.

Sustainable development thus becomes a mediating principle between the right to development and the duty to control sources of environmental harm. Modifying norms or principles need not impose obligations or regulate conduct, they do not depend on State practice, and they do not need the same clarity or precision as rules.

What gives general principles of this kind their authority and legitimacy is simply the endorsement of States—*opinio juris* in other words.[51] Such principles have legal significance in much the same way that Dworkin (1977) uses the idea of constitutional principles.[52] They lay down parameters which affect the way courts decide cases or how an international institution exercises its discretionary powers. They can set limits, or provide guidance, or determine how conflicts between other rules or principles will be resolved. They may lack the supposedly harder edge of a 'rule' or 'obligation', but they should not be confused with 'non-binding' or emerging law. That is perhaps the most important lesson to be drawn from the ICJ's references to sustainable development in the *Case Concerning the Gabcikovo-Nagymaros Dam*.[53] Even if sustainable development is not in the nature of a legal obligation, it does represent a policy goal or principle that can influence the outcome of litigation and the practice of States and international organizations, and it may lead to significant changes and developments in the existing law.[54] In that important sense, international law appears to require States and international bodies to take account of the objective of sustainable development, and to establish appropriate processes for doing so.

These examples show that subtle changes in the existing law and in existing treaties may come about through reliance on such general principles. In any system of law the ability to make changes on a systemic basis is important. How else could this be done in international law? New *rules* of customary law are not necessarily appropriate to the elaboration of general principles and could not be created quickly enough; moreover, a treaty endorsing the precautionary principle or sustainable development would only bind the parties. A binding resolution of the UN Security Council may be a possible option, but only where questions of international peace and security are at stake. Thus, the consensus endorsement by States of a general principle enshrined in a soft law declaration is an entirely sensible solution to such law-making challenges.

VII. SOFT LAW AND CUSTOMARY LAW

Resolutions of international organizations and multilateral declarations by States may be soft in the sense that they are usually not legally binding on States, but as we saw earlier this does not mean that they have no legal effect on customary law. Whether they do provide

---

[51] Lowe, 1999, p 33, dispenses even with *opinio juris*, but unless such norms emerge from thin air at the whim of judges the endorsement of States must be a necessary element. All the norms Lowe relies on do in fact have such endorsement.

[52] This argument is developed further by Sands, 1995, Ch 5.

[53] *Gabčíkovo-Nagymaros Project (Hungary/Slovakia), Judgment, ICJ Reports 1997*, p 7, para 140.

[54] See for example the inclusion of provisions on sustainable use or sustainable development in the 1994 WTO Agreement, the 1995 UN Fish Stocks Agreement, and the 1997 UN Convention on International Watercourses.

evidence of existing law, or of the *opinio juris* necessary for new law, or of the practice of States, will depend on various factors which must be assessed in each case.

A potentially law-making resolution or declaration need not necessarily proclaim rights or principles *as law*, but as with treaties, the wording must be 'of a fundamentally norm-creating character such as could be regarded as forming the basis of a general rule of law.'[55] The context within which soft law instruments are negotiated and the accompanying statements of delegations will also be relevant if assessing the *opinio juris* of States. Lastly, the degree of support is significant. A resolution adopted by consensus or by unanimous vote will necessarily carry more weight than one supported only by a two-thirds majority of States. Resolutions opposed by even a small number of States may have no law-making effect if those States are the ones most immediately affected.[56] The attempt by the General Assembly in the 1970s to change the law on expropriation of foreign investments is a well-known example of the inability of majorities of States to legislate for minorities in this fashion.[57] The General Assembly's ban on deep seabed mining outside the framework of UNCLOS is another. In this case, the minority of objecting States established their own parallel regime, until eventually a compromise agreement was reached.[58]

In an international system where the consent or acquiescence of States is still an essential precondition for the development of new law or changes to existing law, these examples show that opposing votes matter. Even if such resolutions do change the law for States which vote in favour, it is clear that they do not do so for the dissenting minority. Moreover, even consensus adoption will not be as significant as it may at first appear if accompanied by statements which seriously qualify what has been agreed, or if it simply papers over an agreement to disagree without pressing matters to a vote. For all these reasons, the adoption of resolutions by international organizations or of declarations by States should not be confused with law-making *per se*.

Professor Cheng has argued that, if appropriately worded, General Assembly resolutions can create 'instant' customary law (Cheng, 1965). In his view the clearly articulated expression of *opinio juris* through the medium of a non-binding resolution or declaration may be enough, without further State practice, to afford evidence of a new rule of customary or general international law. For anyone seeking to use the UN General Assembly as a law-making instrument this is an attractive but generally unsustainable argument. Cheng himself rightly cautions against the facile assumption that UNGA resolutions make law, and his view of instant law-making is limited to very specific

---

[55] *North Sea Continental Shelf, Judgment, ICJ Reports 1969*, p 3, para 72 and see Lowe, 1999; Brownlie, 1979, pp 260–262.

[56] See on this point the cautionary dissent of Schwebel in the *Legality of the Threat or Use of Nuclear Weapons, ICJ Reports 1996*, p 226, noting that: 'If a resolution purports to be declaratory of international law, if it is adopted unanimously (or virtually so, qualitatively as well as quantitatively) or by consensus, and if it corresponds to State practice, it may be declaratory of international law.'

[57] See 1974 Charter of Economic Rights and Duties of States, UNGA Res.3281 (XXX) and *Texaco Overseas Petroleum Co v Libyan Arab Republic* (1977) 53 ILR 422 at paras 80–91; 120 States voted for the resolution, 6 voted against, 10 abstained.

[58] The 1970 Declaration of Principles Governing the Seabed and Ocean Floor etc, UNGA Res.2749 (XXV), was adopted by 108 votes in favour with 14 abstentions. For an account of the subsequent disagreements over the legal status of the deep seabed and the Reciprocating States regime established by Western States see Churchill and Lowe, 1999, pp 224–235.

circumstances. Firstly, it depends on a strong consensus in favour of such a resolution.[59] Secondly, it requires appropriate wording. In his view, the principal UNGA resolutions on outer space fail this test, because they merely articulate principles by which States 'should be guided',[60] rather than potentially normative rules. In this respect they compare unfavourably with, for example, the rights proclaimed in the Universal Declaration of Human Rights or the Declaration on the Granting of Independence to Colonial Territories and Peoples. However, neither of these resolutions was adopted by consensus and it is very doubtful that their impact has ever been instantaneous. Cheng was also writing before any of the leading modern ICJ cases on the creation of customary law were decided, and even his cautious formulation may now be too generous. The jurisprudence is not favourable, it must be said, to notions of instant law-making, but stresses instead the need for subsequent confirmatory practice, or at least the absence of contrary practice.[61]

If the resolutions on outer space did not make instant law, and were designed to be replaced by treaties,[62] why adopt them at all? Apart from important practical considerations of simplicity and speed of adoption compared to treaties, the importance of resort to the UNGA lies in the collective affirmation which is thereby provided for general principles otherwise only impliedly asserted by the space States. The resolutions provided both a record of what all States believed the relevant rules should be, and evidence of *opinio juris* demonstrating the law-making significance of their earlier practice. As Brownlie (1991, p 204) observes, 'In the face of a relatively novel situation the General Assembly provides an efficient index to the quickly growing practice of States.' Elsewhere he refers to the 'decisive catalytic effect' which such resolutions may have on State practice (Brownlie, 1979, p 261).

In those circumstances it would be safe for space States to proceed on the assumption that there would be no opposition to activities conducted in conformity with the principles endorsed by the resolutions. That these principles were subsequently reaffirmed in treaty form shows both the value of soft law precedents as a prelude to later agreement on a more detailed international regime, and the preference for treaties as a means of stabilizing the law within an appropriate institutional framework once the views and practice of States are settled. This may suggest a perception that soft law is too fragile an instrument to sustain the long-term regulation of common areas such as space or the deep seabed,[63] but it is certainly an effective starting point when States need reassurance before commencing novel and previously unregulated activities.

---

[59] Resolutions 1721 (XVI)(1961) and 1962 (XVIII)(1963) were agreed first by the USA and USSR (the only space States at that time), then adopted unanimously by the Outer Space Committee, the 1st Committee and the UNGA.

[60] UNGA Res.1962 (XVIII) (1963). The wording of Resolution 1721 (XVI) is even weaker: 'The General Assembly...commends to States for their guidance...the following principles.'

[61] See especially *North Sea Continental Shelf, Judgment, ICJ Reports 1969*, p 3 and *Military and Paramilitary Activities in and against Nicaragua (Nicaragua v United States of America), Merits, Judgment, ICJ Reports 1986*, p 14. But the *Gabčíkovo-Nagymaros Project (Hungary/Slovakia), Judgment, ICJ Reports 1997*, p 7 may be more favourably inclined to instant law-making.

[62] See now the 1967 Outer Space Treaty and the 1979 Moon Treaty.

[63] The USSR had from the start argued in favour of a treaty; Cheng, 1965, at p 31 surmises that it agreed to the adoption of a resolution out of concern that any treaty might be vetoed by the US Senate.

The adoption of non-binding resolutions or declarations can also lead to changes in the existing law, in some cases quite quickly. The termination of driftnet fishing on the high seas is a good example of the successful use of UNGA resolutions in this way.[64] Although the resolutions themselves have no legal force, and do not make 'instant' law, the widespread opposition to such fishing has been effective in pressuring the small number of States involved to comply with the resolutions and phase out the use of driftnets. Such changes in the law can of course only come about as a result of changes in practice by those States most closely involved. Moreover, even States which initially voted against such resolutions may eventually conform to the general will. The initial opposition of colonial powers to UN resolutions on self-determination soon faded, and as the *Western Sahara* and *East Timor* cases show,[65] former colonial States have become the principal advocates of self-determination for their former colonies.

Why use non-binding resolutions for such purposes? Negotiating a global treaty on driftnets would have taken as long or longer; it would not have entered into force until there were enough ratifications, and if the relevant States failed to become parties they would not be bound anyway. In the latter case the law would not change unless these States changed their practice, which is no less true of the non-binding resolutions adopted by UNGA. In such cases, if the consensus for a change in practice is strong enough, a treaty is not necessary. If it is not strong enough a treaty will not necessarily strengthen it.

Banning a specific form of fishing is a relatively simple change in the law. Soft law instruments may not be as useful when more complex changes are needed. When it became apparent that the provisions of the 1982 UNCLOS relating to the high seas would not be sufficient to ensure sustainable fishing, an additional treaty was negotiated. The 1995 Agreement on Straddling and Highly Migratory Fish Stocks in effect elaborates and amends the 1982 UNCLOS. It is an important and far-reaching instrument which makes notable changes in the law of high seas fishing. *Inter alia*, freedom of fishing is confined to States which operate within the rules of regional fisheries organizations; fisheries law is given a newly environmental focus, emphasizing sustainability and conservation of biological diversity and ecosystems; the enforcement powers of other States are extended, and regional agreements are brought within the UNCLOS dispute settlement system (see Freestone and Makuch, 1996; Davies and Redgwell, 1996). However strong the consensus in favour of these changes, given their far-reaching nature and impact on other treaties, a treaty was clearly the only possible instrument in this situation. In reality, some of these measures have been controversial, and some fishing States remain non-parties to the 1995 Agreement, but resort to soft law would not have been any more effective in such circumstances. But if the weakness of soft law is that States are not obliged to comply, the same is no less true of an unratified or poorly ratified treaty. Whether the 1995 Agreement changes the law will still depend on how far it influences the practice of States, rather than on its binding force.

---

[64] UNGA Res.44/225, 22 December 1989 and UNGA Res.46/215, 20 December 1991 on Large Scale Pelagic Driftnet Fishing, and other instruments collected in FAO, *Legislative Study 47: The Regulation of Driftnet Fishing on the High Seas* (Rome, 1991). See Kaye, 2000, pp 188–194.

[65] *Western Sahara, Advisory Opinion, ICJ Reports 1975*, p 12; *East Timor (Portugal v Australia) Judgment, ICJ Reports 1995*, p 90.

VIII. CONCLUSIONS

Soft law is manifestly a multi-faceted concept, whose relationship to treaties, custom, and general principles of law is both subtle and diverse. It is further explored in the following chapter by Dinah Shelton. At its simplest, soft law facilitates progressive evolution of customary international law. It presents alternatives to law-making by treaty in certain circumstances, at other times it complements treaties, while also providing different ways of understanding the legal effect of different kinds of treaty. Those who maintain that soft law is simply not law have perhaps missed some of the points made here; moreover those who see a treaty as necessarily having greater legal effect than soft law have perhaps not looked hard enough at the 'infinite variety' of treaties, to quote Baxter once more. Soft law in its various forms can of course be abused, but so can most legal forms, and it has generally been more helpful to the process of international law-making than it has been objectionable. It is simply another tool in the professional lawyer's armoury.

REFERENCES

BAXTER, RR (1980), 'International Law in "Her Infinite Variety"', 29 *ICLQ* 549.

BIRNIE, P, BOYLE, AE and REDGWELL, C (2009), *International Law and the Environment*, 3rd edn (Oxford: Oxford University Press).

BOYLE, AE (2005), 'Further Development of the Law of the Sea Convention: Mechanisms for Change', 54 *ICLQ* 563.

—— and FREESTONE, D (eds) (1999), International Law and Sustainable Development: Past Achievements and Future Prospects (Oxford: Oxford University Press).

BROWNLIE, I (1979), 'The Legal Status of Natural Resources', 162 *Recueil des Cours* 245.

—— (1991), *Basic Documents on International Law*, 3rd edn (Oxford: Oxford University Press).

—— (2008), *Principles of Public International Law*, 7th edn (Oxford: Oxford University Press).

CASSESE, A (1986), *International Law in a Divided World* (Oxford: Oxford University Press).

CHENG, B (1953) (1987 reprint), *General Principles of Law as Applied by International Courts and Tribunals* (Cambridge: Grotius).

—— (1965), 'United Nations Resolutions on Outer Space: "Instant" Customary Law?', 5 *Indian J Int L* 23–48 (reprinted in Cheng, B (ed) (1982), *International Law Teaching and Practice* (London: Stephens and Sons), p 237).

CHINKIN, CM (1989), 'The Challenge of Soft Law: Development and Change in International Law', 38 *ICLQ* 850.

CHURCHILL, RR and LOWE, AV (1999), *The Law of the Sea*, 3rd edn (Manchester: Manchester University Press).

CONTINI, P and SAND, P (1972), 'Methods to Expedite Environment Protection: International Ecostandards', 66 *AJIL* 37.

CRAWFORD, J (2002), *The International Law Commission's Articles on State Responsibility* (Cambridge: Cambridge University Press).

DAVIES, P and REDGWELL, C (1996), 'International Legal Regulation of Straddling Fish Stocks' 67 *BYIL* 199.

DUPUY, P-M (1991), 'Soft Law and the International Law of the Environment', 12 *Michigan JIL* 420.

DWORKIN, R (1977), *Taking Rights Seriously* (London: Duckworth).

EDESON, W (1999), in BOYLE, AE and FREESTONE, D (eds) (1999), *International Law and Sustainable Development: Past Achievements and Future Prospects* (Oxford: Oxford University Press), p 165.

—— (2003), 'Soft and Hard Law Aspects of Fisheries Issues', in NORDQUIST, M, MOORE, G and MAHMOUDI, S (eds.), *The Stockholm Declaration and Law of the Marine Environment* (The Hague: Nijhoff), p 165.

FAO (1991), *The Regulation of Driftnet Fishing on the High Seas: Legal Issues* (Rome: FAO).

FREESTONE, D and MAKUCH, Z (1996), 'The New International Environmental Law of Fisheries', 7 *YbIEL* 3.

FRIEDMANN, W (1963), 'The Uses of General Principles in the Development of International Law', 57 *AJIL* 279.

GARDINER, R (1998), 'Revising the Law of Carriage by Air: Mechanisms in Treaties and Contract', 47 *ICLQ* 278.

HIGGINS, R (1995), *Problems and Process: International Law and How We Use It* (Oxford: Oxford University Press, 1995).

HILLGENBERG, H (1999), 'A Fresh Look at Soft Law', 10 *EJIL* 499.

KAYE, S (2000) *International Fisheries Management* (The Hague: Kluwer Law International).

KLABBERS, J (1996), 'The Redundancy of Soft Law', 65 *Nordic JIL* 167.

KOSKENNIEMI, M (1992), 'Breach of Treaty or Non-Compliance? Reflections on the Enforcement of the Montreal Protocol', 3 *YbIEL* 123.

—— (2009), 'The Politics of International Law', 20 *EJIL* 7.

LANG, W (ed) (1995), *Sustainable Development and International Law* (The Hague: Kluwer Law International).

LOWE, AV (1999), 'Sustainable Development and Unsustainable Arguments' in BOYLE, AE and FREESTONE, D (eds) (1999), *International Law and Sustainable Development: Past Achievements and Future Prospects* (Oxford: Oxford University Press), p 24.

MANN, H (1995), Comment, in LANG, W (ed) (1995), *Sustainable Development and International Law* (The Hague: Kluwer Law International), p 67.

MCDORMAN, T (2004), 'Access to Information under Article 9 of the OSPAR Convention', 98 *AJIL* 330.

MCLACHLAN, C (2005), 'The Principle of Systemic Integration and Article 31(3)(c) of the Vienna Convention', 54 *ICLQ* 279.

MOORE, G (1999) 'The Code of Conduct for Responsible Fisheries', in Hey, E (ed), *Developments in International Fisheries Law* (The Hague: Nijhoff), at p 85.

SANDS, P (ed) (1993), *Greening International Law* (London: Earthscan).

—— (1995), 'International Law in the Field of Sustainable Development', in LANG, W (ed) (1995), *Sustainable Development and International Law* (The Hague: Kluwer Law International), p 53.

SCHACHTER, O (1977), 'The Twilight Existence of Non-Binding International Agreements', 71 *AJIL* 296.

SZTUCKI, J (1990), 'Reflections on International "Soft Law"', in Ramberg, J and others (eds), *Festskrift till Lars Hjerner: Studies in International Law*, (Stockholm: Norstedts), p 549.

WATTS, A (ed) (2000), The International Law Commission, Vol II (Oxford: Oxford University Press).

WEIL, P (1983), 'Towards Relative Normativity in International Law', 77 *AJIL* 411.

FURTHER READING

BAXTER, RR (1980), 'International Law in "Her Infinite Variety"', 29 *ICLQ* 549: A classic account of the diversity of treaties and their legal effect.

CHARNEY, J (1993), 'Universal International Law', 87 *AJIL* 529: One of the best analyses of the evolution of general international law through soft law, although it does not use the term.

CHENG, B (1983), 'Custom: The Future of General State Practice in a Divided World', in Macdonald, R St J and Johnston, DM (eds), *The Structure and Process of International Law* (Dordrecht: Martinus

Nijhoff) at pp 513–554. A sceptical treatment of idea that General Assembly resolutions can be instant customary international law.

CHINKIN, CM (1989), 'The Challenge of Soft Law: Development and Change in International Law', 38 *ICLQ* 850: This remains one of the best discussions of the subject.

SLOAN, B (1987), 'General Assembly Resolutions Revisited', 58 *BYBIL* 39: The classic account of the legal effect of UN General Assembly resolutions, but now dated.

6

INTERNATIONAL LAW AND 'RELATIVE NORMATIVITY'

Dinah Shelton

SUMMARY

'Relative normativity' concerns the nature and structure of international law. It involves issues of hierarchy and implicates the rules of recognition by which law is distinguished from norms that are not legally binding. There is general agreement that the main sources of international law do not imply a hierarchical relationship *inter se*, and debates have centred instead on three other topics. The first among these topics involves questions about the existence, content, and impact of superior or peremptory norms that override other norms and bind all States. State practice and judicial opinion now generally recognize their theoretical existence and have identified a few such norms, but the legal consequences of identifying a peremptory norm remain unclear and controversial. Secondly, the expansion or 'fragmentation' of international law into many new subject areas, with a corresponding proliferation of international treaties and institutions, can produce conflicts in substantive norms or procedures within a given subject area or across legal regimes, necessitating the development and application of interpretive rules to reconcile or prioritize the competing norms. Thirdly, States and international institutions frequently adopt texts that contain norms or statements of obligation, but which are not in a legally-binding form. Such 'soft law' texts are political commitments that can lead to law (custom, treaty, or general principle) and they are sometimes used to interpret or fill gaps in the law, but they are not legally binding on their own.

I. INTRODUCTION: THE CONCEPT OF RELATIVE NORMATIVITY

'Relative normativity' is a question of hierarchy of norms and the definition of law. As such, it concerns the nature, structure, and content of the international legal system. In practice issues of relative normativity arise in determining whether a legal rule exists to govern a problem, and in deciding whether priority must be given to a specific rule among several that may be applicable to a legal matter or dispute.

Systems of law usually establish a hierarchy of norms based on the particular source from which the norms derive. In national legal systems, it is commonplace for the fundamental values of society to be given constitutional status and afforded precedence in the event of a conflict with norms enacted by legislation or adopted by administrative regulation; administrative rules themselves must conform to legislative mandates, while written law usually takes precedence over unwritten law and legal norms prevail over non-legal (political or moral) rules. The mode of legal reasoning applied in practice is thus naturally hierarchical, establishing relationships and order among normative statements and levels of authority (Koskenniemi, 1997).

Since a seminal article highly critical of the concept appeared in 1983, the question of hierarchy or relative normativity in international law has been widely discussed (Weil, 1983). In practice, conflicts among norms and their interpretation are probably inevitable in the present, largely decentralized international legal system where each State is entitled initially and equally to interpret for itself the scope of its obligations and the means of implementation such obligations require. The interpretations or determinations of applicable rules may vary considerably, making all international law somewhat relative, in the absence of institutions competent to render authoritative interpretations binding on all States.

Conceptual problems abound in determining relative normativity, in part because almost every purported principle of precedence (eg, *lex specialis derogate lex generali*) has exceptions and no rule establishes when to apply the principle and when to apply the exception.[1] There appears to be supremacy of process over content, however, because the identification of legal norms and their relative normativity occurs only through consideration of the procedural norms that allow recognition of substantive rules. Some scholars argue from the International Court of Justice (ICJ) Statute and from the sovereign equality of States that no hierarchy exists and logically there can be none: international rules are equivalent, sources are equivalent, and procedures are equivalent (Dupuy, 1995, pp 14–16) all deriving from the will of States. Others point to the concept of the community of States as a whole, expressed in Article 53 of the Vienna Convention on the Law of Treaties (VCLT) as an emerging limit on unilateral relativism (Salcedo, 1997, p 588).

Even identifying law can be problematic in a decentralized system like the international society of States. It is not always clear where law ends and non-law begins, or, to use the common terminology, where 'soft' law should be placed. The consequences can be significant. The jurisdiction of the ICJ in the dispute between Quatar and Bahrain,[2] for example, turned on whether or not 'minutes' taken 25 December 1990 constituted a legally binding agreement or a simple record of negotiations. On the merits, effective application of the principle *pacta sunt servanda*—that legal agreements should be carried out in good faith—necessitated some basic consensus about existence of a '*pacta*' or legal agreement. Is it necessary for a norm to be contained in a legally binding instrument in order for it to be

---

[1] Compare for example the different approaches of the ICJ in *Legal Consequences for States of the Continued Presence of South Africa in Namibia (South West Africa) notwithstanding Security Council Resolution 276 (1970), Advisory Opinion, ICJ Reports 1971*, p 16 and *South West Africa, Second Phase, Judgment, ICJ Reports 1966*, p 6.

[2] *Maritime Delimitation and Territorial Questions between Qatar and Bahrain, Jurisdiction and Admissibility, Judgment, ICJ Reports 1994*, p 112.

accepted as binding (*pacta*)? Traditional international law clearly distinguished between binding and non-binding instruments, and this distinction seems to remain, despite the growing body and variety of 'soft law' instruments.

States have agreed on the means (or 'sources') to identify binding international obligations for the purpose of resolving their disputes, but they have not determined a hierarchy of norms. As formulated initially in the Statute of the Permanent Court of International Justice (PCIJ) and iterated in the ICJ Statute, the Court should decide an international dispute primarily through application of international conventions, international custom, and general principles of law.[3] The Statute makes no reference to hierarchy, except by listing doctrine and judicial decisions as 'subsidiary' and evidentiary sources of law. Although the Statute is directed at the Court, it is the only general text in which States have acknowledged the authoritative procedures by which they agree to be legally bound to an international norm. No mention is made of *jus cogens* as a source of obligation nor do non-binding instruments figure in the Statute.

Much recent debate has centered on whether or not State behaviour in adopting and complying with non-binding instruments evidences acceptance of new modes of law-making not reflected in the Statute of the Court. Of course, efforts to resolve social problems are not invariably in the form of law in any community. Societies strive to maintain order, prevent and resolve conflicts, and assure justice in the distribution and use of resources not only through law, but through other means of action. Issues of justice may be addressed through market mechanisms and private charity, while conflict resolution can be promoted through education and information, as well as negotiations outside legal institutions. Maintenance of order and societal values can occur through moral sanctions, exclusions, and granting or withholding of benefits, as well as by use of legal penalties and incentives. In the international arena, just as at other levels of governance, law is one form of social control or normative claim, but basic requirements of behaviour also emerge from morality, courtesy, and social custom reflecting the values of society. They form part of the expectations of social discourse and compliance with such norms may be expected and violations sanctioned.

Legal regulation, however, has become perhaps the most prevalent response to social problems during the last century. Laws reflect the current needs and recognize the present values of society. Law is often deemed a necessary, if usually insufficient, basis for ordering behaviour. The language of law, especially written language, most precisely communicates expectations and produces reliance, despite inevitable ambiguities and gaps. It exercises a pull toward compliance by its very nature. Its enhanced value and the more serious consequences of non-conformity lead to the generally accepted notion that fundamental fairness requires some identification of what is meant by 'law', some degree of transparency and understanding of the authoritative means of creating binding norms and the relative importance among them. A law perceived as legitimate and fair is more likely to be observed. This alone makes the issue of relative normativity an important topic, but recent evolution in the international legal system has fostered a burgeoning interest in the issue. Three developments appear particularly important.

---

[3] See ICJ Statute, Article 38 and Ch 4 above.

The first development centres on the role of consent in determining legal obligation. Classical writers[4] claimed the existence of necessary law natural to and binding all States, overriding contrary treaties and custom. A distinction thus was made between consent-based law and universal, overriding norms which could not be amended or altered by the will of States. This theory is not widely accepted today. Instead, international law has been defined as a system of equal and sovereign States whose actions are limited only by rules freely accepted as legally binding.[5] Even *jus cogens*, or peremptory norms are seen as defined and recognized in positive international law by the international community of States as a whole.[6]

A problem remains for many, however: are there substantive limits on law-making or only procedural constraints? The emergence of global resource crises such as the widespread depletion of commercial fish stocks, destruction of the stratospheric ozone layer, and anthropogenic climate change, has produced growing concern about the 'free rider', the holdout State that benefits from legal regulation accepted by others while enhancing its own profits through continued utilization of the resource or by on-going production and sale of banned substances. The traditional consent-based international legal regime lacks a legislature to override the will of dissenting States,[7] but efforts to affect their behaviour are being made, first through the doctrine of peremptory norms applicable to all States, and, secondly, through expanding the concept of international law to include 'soft law'. The same approach may be taken towards States seeking to denounce or acting to violate multilateral agreements that reflect widely and deeply held values, such as human rights or humanitarian law.

To press free riders or dissenting States into behaviour conforming to the needs of international society, States inside and outside international organizations may find it particularly useful to adopt normative statements in the form of non-legally binding instruments such as declarations, resolutions, and programmes of action. International law permits States to use political pressure to induce others to change their practices. In contrast, States generally cannot demand that others conform to legal norms the latter have not accepted. Non-binding commitments may be entered into precisely to reflect the will of the international community to resolve a pressing global problem over the objections of the one or few States causing the problem, while avoiding the doctrinal barrier of their lack of consent to be bound by the norm.[8]

The second development that spurs consideration of relative normativity is the substantial expansion of international law. Until the twentieth century, treaties were nearly

---

[4] H Grotius, *De Jure Belli Ac Pacis Libri Tres* (1625), 1, Ch. 1, X, 5; E de Vattel, *Le Droit des Gens ou Principes de la Loi Naturelle* (1758), para 9; C Wolff, *Jus Gentium* (1764), para 5.

[5] See 'Lotus', *Judgment No 9, 1927, PCIJ, Ser A, No 10* at p 18.

[6] The voluntarist approach to *jus cogens* is reflected in the report of the International Law Commission to the Vienna Conference on the Law of Treaties. It noted that 'it would clearly be wrong to regard even rules of *jus cogens* as immutable and incapable of modification in the light of future developments', a notion inconsistent with the natural law approach of classic writers. See *YBILC* (1966) Vol II (part two), pp 247 *et seq*.

[7] Thus Salcedo argues that 'In principle...most rules of international law are only authoritative for those subjects that have accepted them' (Salcedo, 1997, p 584).

[8] The UN General Assembly actions on driftnet fishing were directed at members and non-members of the United Nations whose fishing fleets decimated dwindling fish resources through use of the driftnet 'walls of death'. The international community made clear its resolve to outlaw driftnet fishing and enforce the ban, albeit it was not contained in a legally binding instrument.

all bilateral and the subject matter of international legal regulation mostly concerned diplomatic relations, the seas and other international waterways, trade, and extradition. Today, the number of international instruments has grown substantially, multilateral regulatory treaties are common, the topics governed by international law have proliferated, and non-State actors are increasingly part of the system. This complexity demands consideration and development of means to reconcile conflicts of norms within a treaty or given subject area, as well as across competing regimes, such as free trade and environmental protection.

New topics of regulation also require innovative means of rule-making with respect to non-State actors. Apart from some international organizations, non-State actors generally are not parties to treaties or involved in the creation of customary international law. The emergence of codes of conduct and other 'soft law' reflects this development.

Third, the emergence of international criminal law has led to considering the nature of international crimes and the relationship of this body of law to doctrines of obligations *jus cogens*, discussed below, and obligations *erga omnes*. The ICJ was the first to identify the category of obligations *erga omnes* in *dicta* in the *Barcelona Traction* case.[9] Unlike obligations arising in respect to specific injured States (eg, in the field of diplomatic protection), obligations *erga omnes* are owed to the international community as a whole. The broad nature of the obligation could be based upon the fact that such obligations generally aim at regulating the internal behaviour of a State, such as in the field of human rights, and thus there are likely to be no States materially affected by a breach. The principle of effectiveness thus supports broad standing, because without it violations could not be challenged. However, the rationale stated by the ICJ for recognizing this category of obligations appears more substantive: that 'in view of the importance of the rights involved, all States can be held to have a legal interest in their protection'.[10] This statement suggests that obligations *erga omnes* have specific and broad procedural consequences *because of* the substantive importance of the norms they enunciate. In addition, the fact that all States can complain of a breach may make it more likely that a complaint will be made following commission of a wrongful act, suggesting a higher priority accorded to these norms even if they are not considered substantively superior. The ICJ's examples of such obligations included the outlawing of aggression and genocide and the protection from slavery and racial discrimination. Nonetheless, the ILC has concluded that obligations *erga omnes* do not implicate normative hierarchy; while all *jus cogens* obligations have an *erga omnes* character, the reverse is not necessarily true.[11]

Similar to obligations *erga omnes*, international crimes are so designated because the acts they sanction are deemed of such importance to the international community that

[9] *Barcelona Traction, Light and Power Company, Limited, Second Phase, Judgment, ICJ Reports 1970*, p 3, para 33.

[10] Idem. See also *East Timor (Portugal v Australia), Judgment, ICJ Reports 1995, p 90, para 29; Application of the Convention on the Prevention and Punishment of the Crime of Genocide, Preliminary Objections, Judgment, ICJ Reports 1996*, p 595, para 31.

[11] International Law Commission, Report of the Study Group on Fragmentation of International Law: Difficulties arising from the Diversification and Expansion of International Law, A/CN.4/l.676, 29 July 2005, paras 48, 50.

individual criminal responsibility should result from their commission.[12] Unlike obligations *erga omnes*, international criminal norms can raise problems of relative normativity. First, the question has been posed as to whether there is a hierarchy among the crimes. Secondly, it has been clear since the Nuremburg Trials that conforming to or carrying out domestic law is no excuse for breach of international criminal law; it would seem plausible as well, if unlikely to arise in practice, that a defence would fail based on carrying out norms of international law, such as those contained in a bilateral treaty, if those norms contradict the requirements of criminal law.[13] In this respect, norms of criminal law could be given supremacy over other international law in practice.

Other aspects of the inter-relationship of these categories of norms and the sources that create them should be noted. First, neither the designation of international crimes or obligations *erga omnes* involves a purported new source of law: crimes are created and defined through the conclusion of treaties; obligations *erga omnes* through treaty and customary international law. Secondly, it appears logical that all international crimes are obligations *erga omnes* because the international community as a whole identifies and may prosecute and punish the commission of such crimes. The reverse is not the case, however. Not all obligations *erga omnes* have been designated as international crimes. Racial discrimination, for example, is cited as an obligation *erga omnes*, but is not included among international crimes. Among those acts designated as international crimes, there appears to be no hierarchy. The International Criminal Tribunal for the Former Yugoslavia (ICTY) has rejected the notion of hierarchy, declaring in the *Tadić* judgment that 'there is in law no distinction between the seriousness of a crime against humanity and that of a war crime'.[14]

II. PEREMPTORY NORMS

Jus cogens or peremptory norms[15] are defined as rules from which no derogation is permitted and which can be amended only by a new general norm of international law of the same value. The only references to peremptory norms in positive law are found in the Vienna conventions on the law of treaties. Article 53 of the 1969 Vienna Convention on the Law of Treaties (VCLT), concerning treaties between States, provides that a treaty will be void 'if, at the time of its conclusion, it conflicts with a peremptory norm of general international law'. Such a norm is defined by the VCLT as one 'accepted and recognized by the international community of states as a whole as a norm from which no derogation is permitted and which can be modified only by a subsequent norm having the same character'. Article 64 adds that the emergence of a new peremptory norm of general

---

[12] The collective nature of the State as subject of international law makes imposition of State criminal responsibility problematic. Although the International Law Commission included a provision on State crimes in early versions of its Articles on State Responsibility, the provision was eventually excluded.

[13] The treaty itself might be considered void as a violation of peremptory norms if it required or authorized the commission of an international crime.

[14] *Prosecutor v Dusko Tadić*, Case No IT-94-1-A, Judgment in Sentencing Appeals, Appeals Chamber (26 January 2000), para 69. For a criticism of this view and discussion of the conflicting practice of the ICTY, see Danner, 2000.

[15] The terms *jus cogens* and peremptory norms are used interchangeably. VCLT Article 53 is entitled 'treaties conflicting with a peremptory norm of general international law (*jus cogens*)'.

international law will render void any existing treaty in conflict with the norm. No clear agreement was reached during the VCLT negotiations, nor has one emerged since then about the content of *jus cogens*.

In national legal systems, it is a general principle of law that individual freedom of contract is limited by the general interest, generally expressed in public law and policy.[16] Agreements that have an illegal objective are void and those against public policy will not be enforced.[17] Private agreements, therefore, cannot derogate from public policy of the community. The international community remains divided over the extent to which the same rules apply to the international legal system.

A strictly voluntarist view of international law rejects the notion that a State may be bound to an international legal rule without its consent and thus does not recognize a collective interest that is capable of overriding the will of an individual member of the society. States are deemed to construct the corpus of international law either through agreements or through repeated practice out of a sense of legal obligation (see Henkin, 1989, p 45; Weil, 1983; Danilenko, 1991, p 42; Lukashuk, 1989). The PCIJ, in one of its first decisions, stated that '[t]he rules of law binding upon States ... emanate from their own free will as expressed in conventions or by usages generally accepted as expressing principles of law'.[18] As recently as 1986, the ICJ reaffirmed this approach in respect to the acquisition of weaponry by States. In the *Nicaragua* judgment the Court stated:

In international law there are no rules, other than such rules as may be accepted by the State concerned, by treaty or otherwise, whereby the level of armaments of a sovereign State can be limited, and this principle is valid for all States without exception.[19]

Some legal theorists have long objected that the source of international obligation cannot lie in consent, but must be based on a prior, fundamental norm that imposes a duty to comply with obligations freely accepted (Kelsen, 1935). Without a source of this norm outside consent there is an unavoidable circularity of reasoning. A natural law origin of international obligation was dominant among scholars until the nineteenth century, when positivism and an emphasis on the sovereignty of States emerged in theory and practice.[20]

Others object that positivism fails to describe adequately the reality of the current international order. According to Tomuschat: '[t]he fact is that the cohesive legal bonds tying States to one another have considerably strengthened since the coming into force of the United Nations Charter; ... a community model of international society would seem to come closer to reality than at any time before in history' (Tomuschat, 1993, pp 210–211). The community consists of States that live within a legal framework of a few basic rules that nonetheless allow them considerable freedom of action. Such a framework has become necessary in the light of global problems threatening human survival in an unprecedented fashion. Recalcitrant States not only profit by rejecting regulatory regimes adopted by the

[16] In Roman law, the maxim 'ius publicum privatorum pactis mutari non potest' (D.2.14.38) made absolute the non-derogation from norms which were defined as *ius publicum*.

[17] Article 6 of the Code Napoléon is illustrative: 'On ne peut déroger, par des conventions particulières, aux lois qui intéressent l'ordre public et les bonnes moeurs'.

[18] *'Lotus', Judgment No 9, 1927, PCIJ, Ser A, No 10 at p 18.*

[19] *Military and Paramilitary Activities in and against Nicaragua (Nicaragua v United States of America), Merits, Judgment, ICJ Reports 1986,* p 14, para 269.

[20] See Ch 1 above.

overwhelming majority of States, they threaten the effectiveness of such regimes and pose risks to all humanity.

The extent to which the system has moved and may still move toward the imposition of global public policy on non-consenting States remains highly debated, but the need for limits on State freedom of action seems to be increasingly recognized. International legal instruments and doctrine now often refer to the 'common interest of humanity'[21] or 'common concern of mankind' to identify fundamental issues that could form part of international public policy. References also are more frequent to 'the international community' as an entity or authority of collective action.[22] In addition, multilateral international agreements increasingly contain provisions that affect non-party States, either providing incentives to adhere to the norms, or allowing parties to take coercive measures that in practice require conforming behaviour of States not adhering to the treaty. The UN Charter itself contains a list of fundamental principles and in Article 2(6) asserts that these may be imposed on non-parties if necessary to ensure international peace and security.

It should be noted that the problem of dissenting States is not as widespread as might be assumed. First, the obligations deemed basic to the international community—to refrain from the use of force against another State, to settle disputes peacefully, and to respect human rights, fundamental freedoms, and self-determination—are conventional obligations contained in the UN Charter, to which all member States have consented. All States have accepted the humanitarian conventions on the laws of war which express customary international law. The multilateral regimes for the oceans, outer space, and key components of the environment (climate change, protection of the ozone layer, and biological diversity) are also widely accepted. Thus in most cases the problem is one of ensuring compliance by States with obligations they have freely accepted and not one of imposing obligations on dissenting States.

The notion of *jus cogens* or peremptory norms as a limitation on international freedom of contract arose in the UN International Law Commission (ILC) during its work on the law of treaties. An early ILC rapporteur on the subject proposed that the ILC draft convention on the law of treaties include a provision voiding treaties contrary to fundamental principles of international law.[23] This proposal clearly constituted a challenge to the consensual basis of international law, which viewed States as having the right *inter se* to opt out of any norm of general international law. It also represented 'progressive development' of international law and not a codification of existing State practice.[24]

In addition to potentially invalidating treaties, the proposal raised difficulties for some in respect to the determination of norms *jus cogens*. If such norms could be created by general treaties, a treaty norm could become binding on non-parties. Even without peremptory norms, this could happen, however, because the VCLT provides that States can

---

[21] See UN Conference on the Law of the Sea (UNCLOS), Article 137(2); Treaty on Principles Governing the Activities of States in the Exploration and Use of Outer Space, Including the Moon and Other Celestial Bodies (1967), pmbl, para 2.

[22] See, eg, VCLT Article 53; UNCLOS Articles 136–137.

[23] Sir Humphry Waldock proposed the concept and three categories of *jus cogens*: (1) illegal use of force; (2) international crimes; and (3) acts or omissions whose suppression is required by international law. The categories were dropped by the ILC, because each garnered opposition from at least two-thirds of the Commission. See Kearney and Dalton, 1970, p 535.

[24] Robledo, 1982, p 17 called it 'une innovation profonde et un grand pas franchi'.

become bound by treaty norms if those norms are already or subsequently become rules of customary international law. Some scholars have suggested that it is only through the evolution of a treaty norm to custom that it can eventually emerge as *jus cogens*; for others the 'international community of states as a whole' could designate such a norm directly by treaty.

The proposal to include peremptory norms in the VCLT was controversial from the start and divided the Vienna Conference on the Law of Treaties. Strong support came from the Soviet bloc and from newly independent States, who saw it as a means of escaping colonial-era agreements. Western countries were less positive and several expressed opposition to the notion of peremptory norms, voting against the provision and withholding ratification of the treaty because of persisting objections to the concept. To date, the VCLT has been accepted by 109 States, a little more than half the countries of the world.

The drafting of the second treaty on treaties, the 1986 Vienna Convention on the Law of Treaties between States and International Organizations, indicated continued controversy over the concept of norms *jus cogens*. The text proposed by the ILC included provisions on *jus cogens* modelled after the 1969 VCLT. The commentary called the prohibition of the illegal use of armed force embodied in the UN Charter 'the most reliable known example of a per-emptory norm' and also claimed that the notion of peremptory norms, as embodied in VCLT Article 53, 'had been recognized in public international law before the Convention existed, but that instrument gave it both a precision and a substance which made the notion one of its essential provisions'.[25] The representative of France disagreed during the plenary drafting session, expressing his government's opposition to VCLT Article 53 'because it did not agree with the recognition that article gave to *jus cogens*' whilst another government called *jus cogens* 'still a highly controversial concept which raised the fundamental question of how to recognize the scope and content of a peremptory norm of general international law', noting that time had revealed 'a divergence of views since 1969 regarding the nature of norms of *jus cogens*, which it had not been possible to define'.[26] The text of the Convention was adopted by 67 to one, with 23 States abstaining; it has yet to enter into force. Several States explained their abstention by referring to the Articles concerning *jus cogens*, including the dispute settlement provisions on the topic.[27] Even some of those that favored *jus cogens* expressed uncertainty. The representative of Brazil called *jus cogens* 'a concept in evolution'.[28]

In practice, the concept has been invoked largely outside its original context in the law of treaties. At the ICJ the term initially appeared in separate or dissenting opinions;[29] States still rarely raise the issue,[30] and until recently the Court seemed to take pains to

---

[25] According to the Commentary, 'it is apparent from the draft articles that peremptory norms of interna-tional law apply to international organizations as well as to states, and this is not surprising' (A/Conf.129/16/ Add.1 (vol II), pp 39, 44).

[26] United Nations Conference on the Law of Treaties between States and International Organizations or Between International Organizations, Vienna, 18 February–21 March 1986, A/Conf.129/16 (vol I), 17. See also the concerns expressed by Germany, and similar objections raised to Article 64 which concerns the emergence of a new peremptory norm of general international law (p 18).

[27] Ibid, pp 186–194.   [28] Ibid, p 188.

[29] See, eg, *Right of Passage over Indian Territory, Merits, Judgment, ICJ Reports 1960*, p 6 at pp 135, 139–140 (Judge ad hoc Renandes dissenting); *South West Africa, Second Phase, Judgment, ICJ Reports 1966*, p 6 at p 298 (Judge Tanaka dissenting).

[30] *Gabčíkovo-Nagymaros Project (Hungary/Slovakia), Judgment, ICJ Reports 1997*, p 7, para 112, noting that neither side had argued that new peremptory norms of environmental law had emerged.

avoid any pronouncement on it.[31] The 1986 *Nicaragua* decision, most often cited for the Court's approval of *jus cogens*, does not in fact recognize either the concept or the content of such norms.[32] In a subsequent advisory opinion on nuclear weapons, the ICJ utilized descriptive phrases that could be taken to refer to peremptory norms, although the language is unclear. The ICJ called some rules of international humanitarian law so fundamental to respect for the human person and 'elementary considerations of humanity' that 'they constitute intransgressible principles of international customary law'.[33] Whether 'intransgressible' means the rules are peremptory or only that they are general customary international law legally binding on States not party to the conventions that contain them is uncertain.

The Court again avoided adjudicating the existence or impact of *jus cogens* in the *Arrest Warrant* judgment of 14 February 2002. Belgium issued an international arrest warrant charging the Congolese foreign minister with grave breaches of the Geneva Conventions of 1949 and with crimes against humanity.[34] Congo claimed that in issuing the warrant Belgium violated 'the rule of customary international law concerning the absolute inviolability and immunity from criminal process of incumbent foreign ministers'.[35] The Congo contended that immunity from criminal process is absolute or complete and thus subject to no exception, even for international crimes. The Court failed to mention *jus cogens* in deciding that 'certain holders of high-ranking office' enjoy immunity from civil and criminal process and concluded that no customary international law restricts diplomatic immunity when accused are suspected of having committed war crimes or crimes against humanity.[36]

In 2006, in its *Congo v Rwanda*[37] judgment, the Court affirmed both the existence of peremptory norms in international law, and asserted that the prohibition of genocide is 'assuredly' such a norm. Nonetheless, the Court emphasized that the *jus cogens* status of the prohibition of genocide did not have an impact on its jurisdiction, which remained governed by consent. A dissenting opinion questioned whether the *jus cogens* prohibition of genocide meant that a reservation to the Court's jurisdiction might be incompatible with the object and purpose of the Genocide Convention, but the 'novelty and far-reaching implications' of declaring that *jus cogens* trumps reservations restrained the other judges.

---

[31] See *North Sea Continental Shelf, Judgment, ICJ Reports 1969*, p 3, para 72, declining to enter into or pronounce upon any issue concerning *jus cogens*.

[32] *Military and Paramilitary Activities in and against Nicaragua (Nicaragua v United States of America), Merits, Judgment, ICJ Reports 1986*, p 14 at para 190, citing the ILC assertion that the norm against aggression is a peremptory norm as evidence that it is an obligation under customary international law.

[33] *Legality of the Threat or Use of Nuclear Weapons, Advisory Opinion, ICJ Reports 1996*, p 226, para 79.

[34] Belgium specifically argued that immunities cannot apply to war crimes or crimes against humanity, citing treaties, international and national tribunals, and national legislation.

[35] The Vienna Convention on Diplomatic Relations and Vienna Convention on Consular Relations were said to reflect customary international law.

[36] Only one of the 10 opinions in the *Arrest Warrant* case mentions the concept of *jus cogens* norms despite its obvious relevance to the issues in the case. The dissenting opinion of Judge Al-Khasawneh refers to *jus cogens*, linking immunity and impunity. *Arrest Warrant of 11 April 2000 (Democratic Republic of Congo/Belgium), Preliminary Objections and Merits, Judgment, ICJ Reports 2002*, p 3, Dissenting Opinion of Judge Al-Khasawneh, para 7.

[37] *Armed Activities on the Territory of the Congo (New Application: 2002) (Democratic Republic of the Congo v Rwanda), Jurisdiction and Admissibility, Judgment, ICJ Reports 2006*, p 6, para 64.

After its 2006 judgment, the Court has increasingly been confronted with issues that touch on assertions of peremptory norms and the potential hierarchical impact of such norms. In December 2008, the Federal Republic of Germany filed an application against Italy at the ICJ, asserting that the Italian courts' exercise of jurisdiction over Germany in relation to claims of World War II forced labour and other war crimes constituted a wrongful denial of sovereign immunity.[38] The application does not refer to peremptory norms or *jus cogens*, but instead cites to the Italian 'doctrine of non-invocability of sovereign immunity in cases of grave violations of human rights and humanitarian law'. The application adds that the Italian Corte di Cassazione itself acknowledged that it was not applying international law in force, but that it wished to develop the law based on a rule 'in formation.' By not explicitly invoking *jus cogens*, the German government may have intended to suggest a broader claim of jurisdiction by the Italian courts.

Neither *jus cogens* nor peremptory norms have been mentioned in decisions of the UN Tribunal for the Law of the Sea, nor have they been referred to by the Iran or Iraq Claims Tribunals. Human rights tribunals until recently also avoided pronouncing on *jus cogens*. In its first human rights judgment to discuss *jus cogens*, decided in 2002, a Grand Chamber of the European Court of Human Rights, by a 9:8 majority, called the prohibition of torture a peremptory norm, but denied that a violation of the norm could act to deprive a State of sovereign immunity.[39] The court found that it was 'unable to discern' any basis for overriding State immunity from civil suit where acts of torture are alleged. More recently, the Court followed the ICJ, but without citing its judgments, in calling the prohibition of genocide a peremptory norm.[40]

In the Inter-American Court of Human Rights, *jus cogens* has been increasingly referred to since its first mention in a 2003 advisory opinion on the juridical condition and rights of undocumented migrants.[41] Mexico requested the opinion largely to indicate its concern with domestic labour laws and practices in the United States. Perhaps in an effort to anticipate possible US arguments that it has not consented to relevant international norms, Mexico's fourth question to the court asked: 'What is the nature today of the principle of non-discrimination and the right to equal and effective protection of the law in the hierarchy of norms established by general international law and, in this context, can they be considered to be the expression of norms *jus cogens*.' Mexico also asked the court to indicate the legal effect of a finding that these norms are *jus cogens*? In addition to citing unnamed publicists and the views of the International Law Commission, Mexico argued that 'international morality' is a source of law and provides a basis for establishing norms *jus cogens*. It called for the 'transfer' of the Martens clause from humanitarian law to the field of human rights to imply new norms and obligations, even those characterized as *jus cogens*. The Inter-American Commission's position simply asserted that the international community is unanimous in considering the prohibition of racial

---

[38] *Jurisdictional Immunities of the State (Germany v Italy)*, Application of 22 December 2008.

[39] *Al-Adsani* v *UK*, [GC], no 35763/97, ECHR 2001-XI, 34 *EHRR* 11. See also *Fogarty* v *UK* [GC], no 37112/97, ECHR 2001-XI, 34 *EHRR* 12 and *McElhinney* v *Ireland and UK* [GC], no 31253/96, ECHR 2001-XI, 34 *EHRR* 13 decided the same day as *Al-Adsani*. For a critique of the case, see Clapham, 2007.

[40] *Jorgic* v *Germany*, no 74613/01, ECHR 2007-XI, para 68.

[41] *Juridical Condition and Rights of the Undocumented Migrants*, Advisory Opinion, OC-18/03 Ser A, No 18 (Sept 17, 2003).

discrimination as an obligation *erga omnes*, then leaps to the conclusion that the principle of non-discrimination is a norm *jus cogens*.

The court's opinion, which it expressly stated applies to all OAS member States whether or not they are party to the American Convention on Human Rights, appears clearly to view natural law as a source of obligation. According to the court, 'All persons have attributes inherent to their human dignity that may not be harmed; these attributes make them possessors of fundamental rights that may not be disregarded and which are, consequently, superior to the power of the State, whatever its political structure.' The court nonetheless cited 19 treaties and 14 soft law instruments on the principle of non-discrimination, finding that taken together they evidence a universal obligation to respect and guarantee human rights without discrimination. On whether this principle amounts to *jus cogens*, the court asserted that 'by its definition' and its development, *jus cogens* is not limited to treaty law.[42] The court concluded that non-discrimination is *jus cogens*, being 'intrinsically related to the right to equal protection before the law, which, in turn, derives "directly from the oneness of the human family and is linked to the essential dignity of the individual."' The court added that the principle belongs to *jus cogens* because the whole legal structure of national and international public order rests on it and it is a fundamental principle that permeates all laws. The effect of this declaration, according to the court, is that all States are bound by the norm *erga omnes*. The court's opinion considerably shifts law-making from States to international tribunals, as the latter assess the demands of human dignity and international public order.

The court has subsequently affirmed *jus cogens* norms in contentious cases, broadening the list to include the prohibition of torture,[43] access to justice,[44] the prohibition of forced disappearance, and the duty to prosecute violations of *jus cogens* norms.[45] In 2009, the

[42] In stating that *jus cogens* has been developed by international case law, the court wrongly cited the ICJ judgments in the *Application of the Convention on the Prevention and Punishment of the Crime of Genocide, Preliminary Objections (Bosnia-Herzegovina v Yugoslavia, ICJ Reports 1996*, p 595 and the *Barcelona Traction, Light and Power Company, Limited, Second Phase, Judgment, ICJ Reports 1970*, p 3, neither of which discusses the subject.

[43] See the Inter-American Court of Human Rights cases *Bayarri v Argentina, Preliminary Objection, Merits, Reparations and Costs*, Judgment of 30 October 2008, Ser C, no 187, para 81; *Martiza Urrutia v Guatemala, Merits, Reparations and Costs*, Judgment of 27 November 2003, Ser C, no 103, para 92; *Tibi v Ecuador, Preliminary Objections, Merits, Reparations and Costs*, Judgment of 7 September 2004, Ser C, no 114, para 143; *Bueno-Alves v Argentina, Merits, Reparations and Costs*, Judgment of 11 May 2007, Ser C, no 164, para 76; *Case of the Rochela Massacre v Colombia, Merits, Reparations and Costs*, Judgment of 11 May 2007, Ser C, no 163, para 132; *Case of the Miguel Castro-Castro Prison v Peru, Merits, Reparations and Costs*, Judgment of 25 November 2006, Ser C, no 160, para 271.

[44] Inter-American Court of Human Rights, case of *La Cantuta v Peru, Merits, Reparations and Costs*, Judgment of 29 November 2006, Ser C, no 162, para 160 ('... Access to justice constitutes a peremptory norm of International Law and, as such, it gives rise to the States' *erga omnes* obligation to adopt all such measures as are necessary to prevent such violations from going unpunished, whether exercising their judicial power to apply their domestic law and International Law to judge and eventually punish those responsible for such events, or collaborating with other States aiming in that direction...').

[45] Ibid, para 157; also *Ríos et al v Venezuela, Preliminary Objections, Merits, Reparations, and Costs*, Judgment of 28 January 2009, Ser C, no 194; *Tiu-Tojín v Guatemala, Merits, Reparations and Costs*, Judgment of 26 November 2008, Ser C, no 190, para 91 ('... [W]e should reiterate to the State that the prohibition of the forced disappearance of persons and the related duty to investigate them and, if it were the case, punish those responsible has the nature of jus cogens. As such, the forced disappearance of persons cannot be considered a political crime or related to political crimes under any circumstance, to the effect of preventing the criminal persecution of this type of crimes or suppressing the effects of a conviction. Additionally, pursuant with the

court explained: 'The duty to investigate becomes particularly compelling and important in view of the seriousness of the crimes committed and the nature of the rights wronged, since the corresponding duty to investigate and punish those responsible has become *jus cogens*'.[46] In its own jurisprudence, the Inter-American Commission on Human Rights has declared the right to life to be a norm *jus cogens*:

derived from a higher order of norms established in ancient times and which cannot be contravened by the laws of man or nations. The norms of *jus cogens* have been described by public law specialists as those which encompass public international order...accepted...as necessary to protect the public interest of the society of nations or to maintain levels of public morality recognized by them.[47]

The International Criminal Tribunal for the Former Yugoslavia (ICTY), was the first tribunal to discuss *jus cogens* and declare the prohibition of torture as one such norm:

Because of the importance of the values it protects, [the prohibition against torture] has evolved into a peremptory norm or *jus cogens*, that is, a norm that enjoys a higher rank in the international hierarchy than treaty law and even 'ordinary' customary rules. The most conspicuous consequence of this higher rank is that the principle at issue cannot be derogated from by states through international treaties or local or special customs or even general customary rules not endowed with the same normative force....Clearly, the *jus cogens* nature of the prohibition against torture articulates the notion that the prohibition has now become one of the most fundamental standards of the international community.[48]

The discussion had no bearing on the guilt or innocence of the person on trial, nor on the binding nature of the law violated. It was not asserted that any treaty or local custom was in conflict with the customary and treaty prohibition of torture. The reference served a rhetorical purpose only. Similarly, an International Labor Organization (ILO) report on a 1996 complaint against Myanmar for forced labour referred to *jus cogens* although the State had long been a party to ILO Convention (No 29) concerning Forced or Compulsory Labour.[49] The Report's statement that the practice of forced labour violates a *jus cogens* norm appears intended to invite the criminal prosecution of individuals using forced labour, labelling the systematic practice of forced labour a 'crime against humanity'.[50]

Expert bodies have been willing to develop illustrative lists of *jus cogens* norms. The ILC's Commentary on its articles on State responsibility claims that peremptory norms 'that are clearly accepted and recognized' include the prohibitions of aggression,

preamble of the Inter-American Convention on Forced Disappearance, the systematic practice of the forced disappearance of persons constitutes a crime against humanity and, as such, entails the consequences established in the applicable international law.')

[46] *Perozo et al* v *Venezuela, Preliminary Objections, Merits, Reparations, and Costs*, Judgment of 28 January 2009, Ser C, no 195, citing *La Cantuta* v *Perú*, ibid, para 157.

[47] OAS, Inter-American Commission on Human Rights, 81st Sess, Annual Report of the Inter-American Commission on Human Rights, *Victims of the Tugboat '13 de Marzo'* v *Cuba*, Rep No 47/96, OR OEA/Ser.L/V/II.95/Doc.7, rev (1997) at 146–147.

[48] *Prosecutor* v *Furundzija*, Judgment, Case No IT-95–17/1-T, Trial Chamber (10 December 1998), para 153.

[49] 28 June 1930, 39 UNTS 55.

[50] Report of the Commission of Inquiry on Forced Labour in Myanmar (Burma), ILO Official Bulletin, 1998, Special Supp, vol LXXXI, Ser B, para 538.

genocide, slavery, racial discrimination, crimes against humanity and torture, and the right to self-determination.[51] The Human Rights Committee addressed *jus cogens* in its General Comment No 29 on States of Emergency, issued 31 August 2001. According to the Committee, the list of non-derogable rights in Article 4(2) of the Covenant on Civil and Political Rights is related to, but not identical with the content of peremptory human rights norms. While some non-derogable rights are included 'partly as recognition of the[ir] peremptory nature', other rights not included in Article 4(2) figure among peremptory norms. The Committee emphatically insists that 'States parties may in no circumstances invoke article 4 of the Covenant as justification for acting in violation of humanitarian law or peremptory norms of international law, for instance by taking hostages, by imposing collective punishments, through arbitrary deprivations of liberty or by deviating from fundamental principles of fair trial, including the presumption of innocence' (General Comment No 29, para. 11). While this may appear to be adding new conditions to Article 4, in fact paragraph 1 explicitly provides that any measures taken by states in derogation of Covenant rights must not be 'inconsistent with their other obligations under international law'. In terms of consequences of this extension, the Committee asserts that one test of the legitimacy of measures in derogation of Covenant rights can be found in the definition of certain violations as crimes against humanity.

The concept of norms *jus cogens* has been asserted most strongly in domestic courts. In the United States, lawyers initially sought to avoid US constitutional doctrine that considers treaties and custom equivalent to other federal law, allowing the President and Congress to enact US law inconsistent with international law. Obligations *jus cogens* thus were asserted in an effort to enforce the 1986 ICJ judgment against the United States in the *Nicaragua* case.[52] Lawyers argued that the constitutional precedents do not apply to norms *jus cogens*, which have a higher status that bind even the President and Congress. The Court accepted *arguendo* the theory, but held that compliance with a decision of the ICJ is not a *jus cogens* requirement.

Other domestic court cases involving *jus cogens* fall into one of two categories. First are cases in which sovereign immunity has acted to shield defendants from civil lawsuits for damages. The issue has arisen most often in courts of the United States and the United Kingdom.[53] In both fora lawyers argued that the foreign sovereign immunity must be interpreted to include an implied exception to sovereign immunity for violations of *jus cogens* norms. The argument relies on the idea of implied waiver, positing that State agreement to elevate a norm to *jus cogens* status inherently results in an implied waiver of sovereign immunity. Every court thus far has rejected the argument and upheld immunity, although some judicial panels have split on the issue.[54]

In the case of former Chilean leader, Augusto Pinochet Ugarte, the issue of *jus cogens* was pressed in response to his claim of immunity from criminal prosecution. Among the many opinions in the case, Lord Millett stated that '[i]nternational law cannot be supposed to have established a crime having the character of a *jus cogens* and at the same time to have

---

[51] Commentary to Article 26, para 5, Report of the ILC, GAOR, Supp No 10 (A/56/10) p 208.

[52] *Committee of US Citizens Living in Nicaragua* v *Reagan*, 859 F.2d 929, 940 (DC Cir 1988).

[53] *Al-Adsani* v *Kuwait* was litigated in English courts before it was submitted to the European Court of Human Rights.

[54] See, eg, *Siderman de Blake* v *Republic of Argentina*, 965 F.2d 699 (9th Cir 1992), cert denied, 113 S Ct 1812 (1993).

provided an immunity which is co-extensive with the obligation it seeks to impose.'[55] The judgment ultimately did not rely on *jus cogens* to determine the issue, however, because the situation was controlled by the relevant treaty.

Four recent cases from different national courts demonstrate the confusion over *jus cogens* and its relationship to issues of immunity. In all of the cases the courts held that the underlying violations constituted breaches of norms *jus cogens*—two cases involved war crimes and two concerned torture—but the courts split evenly on whether a finding of *jus cogens* violations results in overriding traditional immunity. In a case from Greece and one from Italy, the respective highest national courts held that German crimes committed during World War II were not protected by sovereign immunity.[56] In contrast, an Ontario, Canada Court of Appeal and a English appellate tribunals have held that the *jus cogens* prohibition of torture does not override sovereign immunity.[57] The Italian decision has given rise to a German application to the International Court of Justice.

A second category of domestic law cases in which the nature of norms as *jus cogens* has been asserted are cases filed pursuant to the US Alien Tort Claim Act (ATCA).[58] Some of the plaintiffs assert violations of norms *jus cogens*, often wrongly claiming that the landmark decision *Filartiga* v *Peña-Irala* held torture to be a violation of international *jus cogens*. In fact, the federal appellate court in that case held that official torture constitutes a violation of the law of nations and never mentioned the doctrine of *jus cogens* norms.[59] No ATCA case has turned on the character of the norm as *jus cogens* or 'ordinary' custom.

The ILC Articles on State Responsibility and accompanying Commentary acknowledge that the issue of hierarchy of norms has been much debated, but find support for *jus cogens* in the notion of *erga omnes* obligations, the inclusion of the concept of peremptory norms in the Vienna Convention on the Law of Treaties, in international practice and in the jurisprudence of international and national courts and tribunals.[60] Article 41 sets forth the particular consequences said to result from the commission of a serious breach of a peremptory norm. To a large extent Article 41 seems to be based on United Nations practice, especially actions of the Security Council in response to breaches of the UN Charter

---

[55] *R v Bow Street Metropolitan Stipendiary Magistrate and others, ex parte Pinochet Ugarte* [1999] 2 All ER 97 (HL) at 179.

[56] See *Prefecture of Voiotia* v *Federal Republic of Germany*, Case No 11/2000 (Areios Pagos, Supreme Court of Greece, 4 May 2000) and *Ferrini* v *Federal Republic of Germany*, Italian Court of Cassation, Judgment No. 5044 of 11 March 2004, 128 ILR 659; (2005) 99 *AJIL* 242. See De Sena & De Vittor, 2005. In the subsequent *Lozano* case, decided in July 2008, the Italian Court of Cassation gave preference to the functional immunity of a State agent over allegations that he had committed a war crime, on the ground that only grave breaches constitute of humanitarian law constitute war crimes such as to override immunity. Such breaches require large-scale, odious, and inhuman intentional acts; lesser acts do not constitute an international crime. The court referred to the peremptory nature of international humanitarian law in respect to grave breaches. For a summary and critique of the judgment, see Cassese, 2008.

[57] See *Bouzari* v *Iran*, Ontario Court of Appeal, OJ No 2800 (2004), 1991–1 Feuille fédérale, pp 440–442 and *Jones* v *Ministry of Interior for the Kingdom of Saudi Arabia and Ors* [2006] UKHL 26, [2007] 1 AC 270.

[58] 28 USC §1350 ('The [federal] district courts shall have original jurisdiction of any civil action by an alien for a tort only, committed in violation of the law of nations or a treaty of the United States'). Judiciary Act of 1789, ch 20, §9(b) (1789), codified at 28 USC §1350.

[59] *Filartiga* v *Peña-Irala*, 630 F.2d 876 (2nd Cir 1980). The only United States Supreme Court decision to consider issues arising under the ATCA, *Sosa* v *Alvarez-Machain*, 542 US 692 (2004), reprinted in (2004) 43 ILM 1390, also failed to mention *jus cogens*.

[60] Article 40, Commentaries, para 2.

in Southern Africa and by Iraq.[61] The text imposes positive and negative obligations upon all States. In respect to the first, '[w]hat is called for in the face of serious breaches is a joint and coordinated effort by all states to counteract the effect of these breaches'.[62] The Commentary concedes that the proposal 'may reflect the progressive development of international law' as it aims to strengthen existing mechanisms of cooperation. The core requirement, to abstain from recognizing consequences of the illegal acts, finds support in State practice, with precedents including rejection of the unilateral declaration of independence by Rhodesia,[63] the annexation of Kuwait by Iraq,[64] and the South African presence in Namibia.[65] Article 41 extends the duty to combat and not condone, aid, or recognize certain illegal acts beyond those acts that breach the UN Charter.

The primary purpose of asserting that a norm is *jus cogens* seems to be to override the will of persistent objectors to a norm of customary international law.[66] If *jus cogens* is 'a norm from which no derogation is possible' and its creation by 'the international community as a whole' means anything less than unanimity, then the problem arises of imposing the norm on dissenting States. It is not clear that the international community as a whole is willing to accept the enforcement of widely-accepted norms against dissenters. In reality, the problem is likely to arise only rarely because those norms most often identified as *jus cogens* are clearly accepted as customary international law and there are no persistent objectors. Even if States violate the norms in practice, no State claims the right to acquire territory by the illegal use of force, to commit genocide, or to torture.

The question of dissenters could arise in the future if the number of purported norms *jus cogens* expands in an effort to further the common interests of humanity. The literature is replete with claims that particular international norms form part of the *jus cogens*. Proponents have argued for inclusion of all human rights, all humanitarian norms (human rights and the laws of war), the duty not to cause transboundary environmental harm, the duty to assassinate dictators, the right to life of animals, self-determination, and territorial sovereignty (despite legions of treaties transferring territory from one State to another).

The concerns raised are serious ones, for the most part, and the rationale that emerges from the literature is one of necessity: the international community cannot afford a consensual regime to address many modern international problems. Thus, *jus cogens* is a necessary development in international law, required because the modern independence of

---

[61] Eg, UN SC Res 662 (9 August 1990), saying that the annexation of Kuwait had 'no legal validity and is considered null and void' and calling on the international community not to recognize the annexation and to refrain from any action or dealing that might be interpreted as a recognition of it. See also *Legal Consequences for States of the Continued Presence of South Africa in Namibia (South West Africa) notwithstanding Security Council Resolution 276 (1970), Advisory Opinion, ICJ Reports 1971*, p 16, para 126, declaring the illegality of South Africa's presence in Namibia as having *erga omnes* effects.

[62] Article 41, Commentaries, para 3.   [63] UN SC Res 216 (12 November 1965).

[64] UN SC Res 662 (9 August 1990).

[65] *Legal Consequences for States of the Continued Presence of South Africa in Namibia (South West Africa) notwithstanding Security Council Resolution 276 (1970), Advisory Opinion, ICJ Reports 1971*, p 16, para 126.

[66] Theoretically, of course, the concept would be applicable if two or more States actually decided to enter into an agreement to commit genocide or territorial acquisition by aggression and one of them later changed its mind. According to the VCLT, only a party to an illegal agreement can invoke the illegality to escape its treaty obligations. The ILC Articles on State Responsibility go further and impose obligations on all States to repress breaches of *jus cogens* norms.

States demands an international *ordre public* containing rules that require strict compliance. The ILC Commentary on the Articles on State responsibility favours this position, asserting that peremptory rules exist to 'prohibit what has come to be seen as intolerable because of the threat it presents to the survival of states and their peoples and the most basic human values'.[67] The urgent need to act that is suggested fundamentally challenges the consensual framework of the international system by seeking to impose on dissenting States obligations that the 'international community' deems fundamental. State practice has yet to catch up with this plea of necessity and it has been international and national courts which have pushed the concept forward.

III. HIERARCHY AMONG CONFLICTING NORMS AND PROCEDURES

The expansion of international law in the past half century has led to wide discussions of fragmentation as a problem or challenge to unity and coherence in the law. Certainly the 'transposition of functional differentiations of governance from the national to international plane' has resulted 'in the creation of more or less complete regulatory regimes which may at times compete with each other' (Simma, 2009). There are potentially numerous problems of hierarchy posed by the need to apply or balance different rights and obligations contained within a single treaty, reconcile norms and procedures in multiple treaties governing the same topic, or resolve conflicts across regimes. International texts sometimes include terms that imply a hierarchy, for example, distinguishing 'fundamental' from other rights or 'grave' from ordinary breaches of law. Treaties also may contain 'savings clauses' that give express preference to other agreements or rules of customary international law. General rules of interpretation help resolve some problems of conflict but difficult issues remain of determining international priorities among areas of regulation that have developed independently of each other.[68]

The ILC decided in 2000 to include the topic of fragmentation in its long-term program of work.[69] The topic included discussion of hierarchy of norms, including *jus cogens* and *erga omnes* obligations, as well as the conflict of law rules applicable when competing norms may govern the same issue, and the impact of Article 103 of the United Nations Charter. After an initial discussion, the 2002 ILC Report cautioned that there is neither a well-developed and authoritative hierarchy of values in international law nor an institutional system to resolve conflicts (para 506). The lack of international institutional hierarchy alluded to has resulted in one well-known conflicting view of international law when the ICJ and the ICTY adopted different standards on State responsibility for the activities of an armed military or paramilitary group.[70]

---

[67] Article 40, Commentaries, para 3.

[68] See *Continental Shelf (Tunisia/Libyan Arab Jamahiriya), Judgment, ICJ Reports 1982*, p 18, para 38; *Military and Paramilitary Activities in and against Nicaragua (Nicaragua v United States of America), Merits, Judgment, ICJ Reports 1986*, p 14, para 274.

[69] See Report of the International Law Commission on its Fifty-Second Session, GAOR Fifty-fifth Session, Supp No 10, UN Doc.A/55/10 (2000), ch IX.a. 1, para 729.

[70] Compare the 'effective control' test of the ICJ in the *Case concerning Military and Paramilitary Activities in and against Nicaragua (Nicaragua v United States of America), Merits, Judgment, ICJ Reports*

A. HIERARCHY WITHIN A SINGLE TREATY

The question of hierarchy and the need to balance or resolve conflicts of norms within a single treaty has arisen in a variety of contexts, from arbitral awards such as the *Beagle Channel Arbitration*[71] to the application of human rights treaties, where the exercise of one right may be deemed to conflict with another. Human rights tribunals attempt to resolve such conflicts by developing rules of interpretation. The European Court of Human Rights starts from the premise that the Convention 'must be read as a whole, and interpreted in such a way as to promote internal consistency and harmony between its various provisions'.[72] The court also utilizes the doctrine of *lex specialis*. It thus, in considering the relationship between Article 13 on the right an effective remedy before a national court and Article 5(4) that specifies that anyone deprived of liberty shall 'be entitled to take proceedings by which the lawfulness of his detention shall be decided speedily by a court and his release ordered if the detention is not lawful', held that the stricter requirements of Article 5 must be considered *lex specialis*.[73] It has similarly held with respect to the relationship between Article 13 and the fair trial requirements of Article 6.[74]

Human rights texts are sometimes seen as establishing a hierarchy of human rights norms through the use of non-derogation provisions, limitation clauses, and restrictions on reservations to core rights. In respect to derogations, the International Covenant on Civil and Political Rights (ICCPR), Article 4, the American Convention on Human Rights, Article 27, and the European Convention for the Protection of Human Rights and Fundamental Freedoms, Article 15, permit States parties to take measures suspending certain rights 'to the extent strictly required by the exigencies of the situation provided that such measures are not inconsistent with their other obligations under international law and do not involve discrimination solely on the ground of race, color, sex, language, religion or social origin' (ICCPR, Article 4(1)). The African Charter on Human and Peoples Rights contains no derogation provision and the African Commission has interpreted the omission to mean that the Charter as a whole remains in force even during periods of armed conflict, suggesting a superior status for the entire instrument.[75]

Non-derogable rights common to the three instruments that discuss the matter are the right to life, the right not to be subjected to torture or to cruel, inhuman or degrading treatment or punishment, the right to be free from slavery, the right to be free from *ex post facto* criminal laws, and the right to be free from discriminatory treatment in respect to derogations. These non-derogable rights provide the starting point for a hierarchy of positive norms, particularly when added to the provisions of the slavery conventions, the Genocide Convention, and the Torture Conventions, none of which contain

---

1986, p 14 at paras 106–116 with the ICTY's 'overall control' test in *Prosecutor v Dusko Tadić*, Judgment, Case No IT-94-1-A, Appeals Chamber, 15 July 1999, 38 ILM 1518, paras 115–145.

[71] *Case concerning a dispute between Argentina and Chile concerning the Beagle Channel*, UNRIAA, vol XXI (1997).

[72] *Demir and Baykara v Turkey* [GC], no 34503/97, Judgment of 12 November 2008, para 66.

[73] *Brannigan and McBride v UK*, Judgment of 26 May 1993, ECHR Ser A, no 258-B, para 76; see also *Nikolova v Bulgaria* [GC], no 31195/96, ECHR 1999-II, para 69.

[74] *Yankov v Bulgaria*, no 39084/97, ECHR 2003-XII, para 150.

[75] See *Commission Nationale des Droits de l'homme et des Libertés v Chad*, Comm 74/92, Ninth Annual Activity Report of the African Commission on Human and Peoples' Rights 1995/96, AGH/207 (XXXII), Annex VIII no 3; Murray and Evans, 2001, p 449.

derogations provisions. International humanitarian instruments further reinforce this thesis. In addition to the protections applicable during international armed conflicts, Common Article 3 to the four 1949 Geneva Conventions demands that in case of armed conflict not of an international character, all non-combatants must be treated humanely and without discrimination by race, colour, religion, sex, birth, wealth, or any similar criteria. Specifically protected are life and freedom from torture, humiliating and degrading treatment, hostage-taking, and fundamental due process.

The issue of derogations is linked to that of reservations. Many human rights treaties have no provisions on the topic, leaving the question to be regulated by the provisions of the VCLT. States thus may attach reservations that are compatible with the object and purpose of the agreement. The UN Human Rights Committee, in its General Comment No 24 on the ICCPR, has expressed doubt that reservations to non-derogable rights are permissible and also has stated that a reservation to the Article on derogations would be incompatible with the object and purpose of the agreement. The Inter-American Court has gone further, stating that 'a reservation which was designed to enable a state to suspend any of the non-derogable fundamental rights must be deemed to be incompatible with the object and purpose of the Convention and, consequently, not permitted by it'.[76]

In respect to economic, social, and cultural rights, global and regional bodies have through General Comments and other normative statements cautiously implied a hierarchy of norms. The International Committee on Economic, Social and Cultural Rights, General Comment No 3 (1990), expresses the view 'that a minimum core obligation to ensure the satisfaction of, at the very least, minimum essential levels of each of the rights is incumbent upon every State party. Thus, for example, a State party in which any significant number of individuals is deprived of essential foodstuffs, of essential primary health care, of basic shelter and housing, or of the most basic forms of education is, prima facie, failing to discharge its obligations under the Covenant'. In a separate General Comment (No 12) on the right to adequate food, the Committee established a core minimum obligation to ensure freedom from hunger, as distinguished from the more general right to adequate food.[77]

The Inter-American Commission on Human Rights (IACHR) also has adopted a 'basic needs' approach to economic, social, and cultural rights. According to the Commission, the obligation of member States to observe and defend human rights, set forth in the American Declaration and the American Convention, obligates them, 'regardless of the level of economic development, to guarantee a minimum threshold of these rights'.[78] States are obligated to immediately ensure 'a minimum level of material well-being which is able to guarantee respect of their rights to personal security, dignity, equality of opportunity and freedom from discrimination'. Finally, the European Social Charter and the

---

[76] 'Merely to restrict certain aspects of a non-derogable right without depriving the right as a whole of its basic purpose' is, however, permissible. See Inter-American Court of Human Rights, *Restrictions to the Death Penalty, Articles 4(2) and 4(4) American Convention on Human Rights,* Advisory Opinion OC–3/83, Ser A, No 3 (8 September 2003), para 61.

[77] The International Covenant on Economic, Social and Cultural Rights (ICESCR) itself makes this distinction, speaking in Article 11(1) of the right of everyone to adequate food and in Article 11(2) of the 'fundamental right of everyone to be free from hunger'.

[78] IACHR, The Realization of Economic, Social and Cultural Rights in the Region, Annual Report of the Inter-American Commission on Human Rights, 1993, OEA/Ser.L/V.II.85, doc 9, rev 11 February 1994, pp 519–534.

ILO Declaration of Fundamental Rights of Workers also indicate that certain core rights are deemed of particular significance in the economic and social field.

In some instances, the reference to a single right in a general treaty or repeated references in several agreements may be deemed to imply a hierarchy. The United Nations Charter mentions a single human right, non-discrimination, as it adds the phrase 'without distinction on the basis of race, sex, language or religion' to every reference to human rights and fundamental freedoms in the body of the Charter. The 1993 Declaration adopted at the conclusion of the Vienna Conference on Human Rights called non-discrimination 'a fundamental rule of international human rights law'. A possible preferred status for non-discrimination is supported by the Convention on the Suppression and Punishment of the Crime of Apartheid, the only international instrument apart from the Convention on the Prevention and Punishment of the Crime of Genocide to designate the acts covered by the treaty as a 'crime under international law'.[79]

The identification of certain human rights violations as crimes may also imply a hierarchy supremacy. In addition to genocide and apartheid, global and regional treaties against torture call upon each State party to 'ensure that all acts of torture are offences under its criminal law'.[80] Similarly, the Geneva Conventions of 1949 and the Protocols of 1977 require States parties to suppress and punish 'grave breaches' of the Conventions. In the Inter-American system, forced disappearances can be added to this category.[81] The establishment of ad hoc international tribunals for the former Yugoslavia and for Rwanda, as well as the conclusion of the Rome Statute for a permanent International Criminal Court reinforce the understanding that the international community places the commission of certain acts in a higher category for which individual criminal responsibility will be imposed in addition to State responsibility.

To a large extent, these provisions of positive law reflect theoretical approaches that posit maximum claims for equality, personal security, and subsistence rights. While there is some variety from one region to another in the number of rights deemed non-derogable, a minimum core does exist and supports the idea of a hierarchy of rights contained in each legal instrument.

B. HIERARCHY AMONG TREATIES GOVERNING THE SAME TOPIC

The proliferation of international law includes multilateral global and regional treaties, bilateral treaties, general and regional custom. The co-existence of these various forms of law results in multiple agreements and sources of law governing the same topic. Conflicts among treaties governing the same topic increase as global framework instruments are supplemented by regional arrangements or competing regimes within the same region apply to the same subject matter.[82]

---

[79] Convention on the Prevention and Punishment of the Crime of Genocide (1948), Article 1; International Convention on the Suppression and Punishment of the Crime of Apartheid (1973), Article 1. Earlier, the 1968 Proclamation of Teheran, para 7, called the policy of apartheid a 'crime against humanity'.

[80] Convention against Torture and Other Cruel, Inhuman and Degrading Treatment or Punishment (1984), Article 4(1); Inter-American Convention to Prevent and Punish Torture, Article 6.

[81] Inter-American Convention on Forced Disappearance of Persons (1994), Article 3.

[82] In Europe, three regional institutions address issues of human rights, sometimes with different interpretations of the same rights. See Shelton, 2003.

The proliferation of treaties governing the same subject matter can raise particular difficulties for dispute settlement mechanisms. When global treaties comprehensively regulate a topic, such as the law of the sea, they usually establish a long-term regime and sometimes provide compulsory dispute settlement mechanisms. The problem of escaping jurisdiction through recourse to another, regional, treaty can arise. Usually the treaties do not expressly resolve the matter. In the first arbitration under the LOS Convention, the arbitral tribunal decided that it lacked jurisdiction to adjudicate the claims because of an intervening regional agreement concluded by the three parties to the arbitration.[83]

Interpretive rules are sometimes suggested to reconcile the conflicts that emerge (Akehurst, 1974–75). The VCLT provides that generally the treaty later in time should prevail when the two instruments concluded by the same parties relate to the 'same subject-matter', subject to the primacy of the UN Charter. Determining when two or more instruments relate to the same subject matter can be problematic. The European Court of Human Rights made clear in 2008 that it 'has never considered the provisions of the Convention as the sole framework of reference for the interpretation of the rights and freedoms enshrined therein.' Instead, citing VCLT Article 31(3)(c), the Court indicated that it 'must also take into account any relevant rules and principles of international law applicable in relations between the Contracting Parties.'[84] This means it will determine the precise obligations imposed on the parties in the light of relevant international treaties on the same subject, in order to avoid inconsistencies with other international instruments and to make the Convention effective. Relevant rules also include 'general principles of law' which can be found in texts of universal scope and case law of human rights bodies. 'Intrinsically non-binding instruments' and the common practices or standards adopted by 'the vast majority of states' also are useful in interpreting the Convention consistent with other norms. This accumulation and comparison of normative instruments, if done on a consistent basis by the European Court and similar human rights tribunals, can solidify jurisprudence around progressive development of the law.

C. HIERARCHY AMONG REGIMES

As a general rule, the VCLT promotes a certain coherence and unity of international law by providing that treaties should be interpreted in the light of 'relevant rules of international law applicable in the relations between the parties' (VCLT, Article 31(3)(c)). These rules can derive either from treaty or from custom. The European Court of Human Rights has referenced VCLT Article 31(3)(c) in considering how to reconcile other norms of international law with those of the European Convention on Human Rights. Other tribunals, including the World Trade Organization (WTO),[85] the ICJ,[86] and the North American

---

[83] Convention for the Conservation of Southern Bluefin Tuna (1993); Oxman, 2002.

[84] *Demir and Baykara* v *Turkey* [GC], no 34503/97, Judgment of 12 November 2008, para 67.

[85] WTO United States: Import Prohibition of Certain Shrimp and Shrimp Products—Report of the Appellate Body (12 October 1998) WT/DS58/AB/R, (1999) 38 ILM 118. See also Korea—Measures Affecting Government Procurement, 1 May 2000, WT/DS163/R, para 7.96: 'customary international law applies generally to the economic relations between the WTO Members. Such international law applies to the extent that the WTO treaty agreements do not "contract out" from it'.

[86] *Oil Platforms (Islamic Republic of Iran v USA), Judgment, ICJ Report 2003*, p 161.

Free Trade Agreement (NAFTA) Tribunal[87] have also applied the VCLT to read treaty provisions in the light of customary norms. UNCLOS Article 293(1) indeed requires that the LOS Tribunal 'shall apply this Convention and other rules of international law not incompatible with this Convention'. It would appear that although a written agreement expresses concretely the will of the parties, there is a presumption that the parties do not intend to derogate from general international law.

Despite the general conciliatory approach of the VCLT, some institutions or treaties assert a hierarchical supremacy of one area of regulation over another or one treaty over others. The primacy of the United Nations Charter is set forth in Article 103 which provides that 'in the event of a conflict between the obligations of the members of the United Nations under the present Charter and their obligations under any other international agreement, their obligations under the present Charter shall prevail'. This 'supremacy clause' has been taken to suggest that the aims and purposes of the United Nations—maintenance of peace and security and promotion and protection of human rights—constitute an international public order to which other treaty regimes and the international organizations giving effect to them must conform. In addition, the VCLT Article 30(1) reiterates the priority of obligations under the UN Charter.

At the same time, the actions of UN organs themselves have come under increasing scrutiny from the perspective of hierarchy of norms. Judge Lauterpacht, in his separate opinion in *Application of the Convention on the Prevention and Punishment of the Crime of Genocide*, was the first jurist to suggest that a Security Council resolution will be void if it conflicts with a *jus cogens* norm, 'as a matter of simple hierarchy of norms'.[88] The courts of the European Union have taken up this issue and provoked considerable controversy in doing so. In the *Yusuf* and *Kadi* cases,[89] the Court of First Instance (CFI) decided on an action for annulment of EU legislative acts implementing some UN Security Council actions for the suppression of international terrorism. The CFI declined to review these acts on the basis of EU law because the EC, it found, is bound by the obligations of the UN Charter, Article 103, in the same way as EC member States and cannot review the lawfulness of the Security Council resolutions indirectly. However, the CFI held that it could review the resolutions for compatibility with *jus cogens* because Security Council resolutions themselves must respect the fundamental peremptory norms of *jus cogens*.

On appeal, the European Court of Justice took a different tack, declaring that the CFI had no competence to engage in a review of the kind it did, but had to decide cases before it on the basis of EU law.[90] It held that the Community judicial organs must ensure the full

[87] Eg *Award on the Merits*, 10 April 2001; *Award in Respect of Damages*, 31 May 2002, (2002) 41 ILM 1347.

[88] *Application of the Convention on the Prevention and Punishment of the Crime of Genocide, Provisional Measures, Order of 13 September 1993, ICJ Reports 1993*, p 325 at p 440.

[89] Case T-306/91, *Yusuf* v *Council* [2005] ECR II-3533; Case T-315/01, *Kadi* v *Council* [2005] ECR II-3649. The court found the contents of *jus cogens* to be the 'mandatory provisions concerning the universal protection of human rights…intransgressible principles of international customary law', ibid at para 231.

[90] *Kadi and Al Barakaat International Foundation* v *Council*, Joined Cases 402/05 and 415/05, Judgment of 3 September 2008, nyr. See also the decisions of the European Court of Human Rights in *Behrami and Behrami* v *France and Saramati* v *France, Germany and Norway* (Dec) [GC], nos 71412/01 and 78166/01, 2 May 2007 and *Beric and Others* v *Bosnia and Herzegovina* (Dec), no 36357/04 and others, ECHR 2007-XII. In the former cases, the European Court of Human Rights declared itself incompetent to judge the existence of human rights violations in Kosovo allegedly committed by forces whose presence was authorized by the

review of the lawfulness of all Community acts, including those giving effect to Security Council resolutions under Chapter VII.

At the national level a decision by the Swiss Federal Supreme Court held that member States could annul Security Council resolutions in conflict with *jus cogens* norms.[91] Notably, both the CFI and the Swiss court found no *jus cogens* violations.

Perhaps the most oft-cited regime conflict is that between trade and the environment, especially between WTO rules on free trade and the trade-restricting measures mandated or permitted under multilateral environmental agreements (Pauwelyn, 2001). Trade restrictions are imposed by the Convention on International Trade in Endangered Species, the Montreal Protocol on Ozone-Depleting Substances, and the Biosafety Protocol to the Convention on Biological Diversity (Safrin, 2002). While no dispute settlement body of the WTO has addressed the issue, various panels have found unilateral trade measures taken for environmental purposes to be contrary to WTO obligations.[92] The World Summit on Sustainable Development, held in Johannesburg, South Africa in 2002, seemed to lean towards favouring the free trade regime over environmental protection; it suggested that means to balance or reconcile conflicts between the two areas of international regulation should be decided within the WTO bodies rather than by the United Nations Environment Program or a general forum like the UN General Assembly.[93]

Treaties sometimes contain specific choice of law provisions preserving rights and obligations under other treaties or regimes. The NAFTA contains obligations generally similar and additional to those imposed by the World Trade Organization 'Uruguay Round'. NAFTA Article 103 reaffirms the parties' 'existing rights and obligations with respect to each other under the General Agreement on Tariffs and Trade [GATT] and other agreements to which such Parties are party', but the Article also states that the NAFTA prevails over those agreements in the event of an inconsistency. The 'Objectives' Chapter (Chapter 1) similarly provides that in the event of an inconsistency, certain listed international environmental agreements take precedence over the NAFTA (Article 104), but parties must choose the actions least inconsistent with NAFTA obligations. The NAFTA also includes a preference for NAFTA dispute resolution procedures when disputes concern measures adopted or maintained to protect human, animal, or plant life or health, or the environment, and raise factual issues concerning the environment, health, safety, or conservation (NAFTA, Article 2005(4)).

Other regimes more aggressively assert their primacy. Some human rights bodies have asserted the priority of human rights guarantees over other international law. The UN Committee on Economic, Social and Cultural Rights in a 1998 statement on globalization and economic, social, and cultural rights,[94] declared that the realms of trade, finance, and

Security Council. The latter case involved actions of the High Representative, a post established by Security Council Res 1031 (1995).

[91] *Nada* v *SECO*, Bundesgericht, Nov 14, 2007, 133 Entscheidungen des Schweizerischen Bundesgerickts II 450 (Switz).

[92] See eg, *EC Measures Concerning Meat and Meat Products (Hormones)*, Panel Report, WT/DS26/R/USA, WT/DS48/R/CAN (18 August 1997) and *Beef Hormone Case*, Appellate Body Report, WT/DS26/AB/R, WT/DS48/AB/R (16 January 1998); *United States—Import Prohibition of Certain Shrimp and Shrimp Products*, Appellate Body Report, WT/DS58/AB/R (12 October 1998); *United States—Standards for Reformulated and Conventional Gasoline*, Appellate Body Report, WT/DS2/AB/R (29 April 1996); *United States—Restriction on the Imports of Tuna*, GATT Panel Report, (1991) 30 ILM 1594.

[93] See World Summit on Sustainable Development, Plan of Implementation (2002) para 91.

[94] Statement on Globalization (May 1998) (1999) 6 *IHRR* 1176.

investment are in no way exempt from human rights obligations. The Committee's concerns were raised a second time in a statement urging WTO members to adopt a human rights approach to trade matters, recognizing the fact that 'promotion and protection of human rights is the first responsibility of Governments'.[95]

The former Sub-Commission on Promotion and Protection of Human Rights similarly affirmed the 'centrality and primacy' of human rights obligations in all areas of governance and development, including international and regional trade, investment and financial policies, agreements, and practices.[96] The Commission on Human Rights has asserted that 'the exercise of the basic rights of the people of debtor countries to food, housing, clothing, employment, education, health services and a healthy environment cannot be subordinated to the implementation of structural adjustment policies and economic reforms arising from the debt'.[97] The UN Special Rapporteurs on Globalization and Its Impact on the Full Enjoyment of Human Rights forthrightly assert that 'the primacy of human rights law over all other regimes of international law is a basic and fundamental principle that should not be departed from'.[98]

The assertion of the primacy of human rights law has not been reflected in State practice. If eventually accepted, it means that there is no *lex specialis* for trade or other fields where States can claim to be free from human rights obligations. It could also profoundly impact the work of all international organizations, which commonly claim to be governed only by their constituting legal instruments and the mandate therein conferred.

Other treaties contain specific provisions establishing priorities of application or hierarchies. For example, UNCLOS Article 311 establishes the agreement of the parties to maintain the basic principle of the common heritage of mankind 'and that they shall not be party to any agreement in derogation thereof'. Article 311(3) further holds that States parties may not conclude agreements that would derogate from a provision if the agreement would impact the effective execution of the object and purpose of the Convention or affect the application of its basic principles. The Convention on Biological Diversity, Article 22, establishes its relationship with other international conventions in force, providing that rights and duties under them shall not be affected, 'except where the exercise of those rights and obligations would cause a serious damage or threat to biological diversity'. Specific reference is made to implementing the Convention consistent with rights and obligations of States under the law of the sea.

IV. 'SOFT LAW'

The use of non-binding normative instruments in several fields of international law is widespread (Shelton, 2000). There is no accepted definition of 'soft law' but it usually refers to any international instrument other than a treaty containing principles, norms,

---

[95] Statement to the Third Ministerial Conference of the World Trade Organization (1999), UN Doc E/C.12/1999/9 of 26 November 1999, para 6.

[96] *Human rights as the primary objective of trade, investment and financial policy*, E/CN.4/Sub.2/RES/1998/12, 20 August 1998.

[97] Effects of structural adjustment policies and foreign debt on the full enjoyment of all human rights, particularly economic, social and cultural rights, E/CN.4/RES/2000/821, 27 April 2000.

[98] 'Globalization and its impact on the full enjoyment of human rights', preliminary report submitted by J Oloka-Onyango and Deepika Udagama, E/CN.4/Sub.2/2000/13, 15 June 2000.

standards, or other statements of expected behaviour. The term 'soft law' is also sometimes employed to refer to the content of a binding instrument. Some recent multilateral treaties contain weak commitments that may be considered 'soft law' if the term is applied to the content of the obligation.[99] In fact, the term 'soft law' seems more appropriate for use when referring to the more hortatory or promotional language of certain treaty provisions than when applied to instruments concluded in non-binding form, because treaties are legally binding even if specific commitments are drafted in general or weak terms.

In many cases, hard law instruments can be distinguished from soft law by internal provisions and final clauses, although the characteristics of each are increasingly difficult to identify. Recently, supervisory organs have been created to oversee compliance with non-binding norms. The Commission on Sustainable Development, for example, supervises implementation of Agenda 21, the plan of action adopted in 1992 at the Rio Conference on Environment and Development. In other instances, States have been asked to submit reports on compliance with declarations and programmes of action, in a manner that mimics if it does not duplicate the mechanisms utilized in treaties.

Some scholars have distinguished hard law and soft law by stating that breach of law gives rise to legal consequences while breach of a political norm gives rise to political consequences. Such a distinction is not always easy to make. Testing normativity based on consequences can be confusing since breaches of law may give rise to consequences that may be politically motivated. A government that recalls its ambassador can either be expressing political disapproval of another State's policy on an issue, or sanctioning non-compliance with a legal norm. Terminating foreign assistance also may be characterized either way. Even binding UN Security Council resolutions based on a threat to the peace do not necessarily depend upon a violation of international law.

Assertions that States are bound by law require identifying the process by which legal rules and principles are authoritatively created. If States expect compliance and in fact comply with rules and principles contained in soft law instruments as well as they do with norms contained in treaties and custom, then perhaps the concept of international law, or the list of sources of international law, requires expansion. Alternatively, it may have to be conceded that legal obligation is not as significant a factor in State behaviour as some would think. A further possibility is that law remains important and States choose a soft law form for specific reasons related to the requirements of the problem being addressed and unrelated to the expectation of compliance.

In respect to 'relative normativity', scholars debate whether binding instruments and non-binding ones are strictly alternative or whether they are two ends on a continuum from legal obligation to complete freedom of action, making some such instruments more binding than others. If and how the term 'soft law' should be used depends in large part on whether one adopts the binary or continuum view of international law. To many, the line between law and not-law may appear blurred. Treaty mechanisms are including more 'soft' obligations, such as undertakings to endeavour to strive to cooperate. Non-binding instruments in turn are incorporating supervisory mechanisms traditionally found in

---

[99] Eg, ICESCR (1966), Article 2(1): each State party 'undertakes to take steps, individually and through international assistance and co-operation, especially economic and technical, to the maximum of its available resources, with a view to achieving progressively the full realization of the rights recognized...by all appropriate means, including particularly the adoption of legislative measures'.

hard law texts. Both types of instrument may have compliance procedures that range from soft to hard. Some case law refers to UN resolutions as having 'a certain legal value' but one that 'differs considerably' from one resolution to another.[100]

Non-binding norms have complex and potentially large impact on the development of international law. Customary law, for example, one of the two main sources of international legal obligation, requires compliance (State practice) not only as a result of the obligation, but as a constitutive, essential part of the process by which the law is formed. In recent years, non-binding instruments sometimes have provided the necessary statement of legal obligation (*opinio juris*) to evidence the emergent custom and have assisted to establish the content of the norm. The process of drafting and voting for non-binding normative instruments also may be considered a form of State practice.

The reality seems to be a dynamic interplay between soft and hard obligations similar to that which exists between international and national law. In fact, it is rare to find soft law standing in isolation; instead, it is used most frequently either as a precursor to hard law or as a supplement to a hard law instrument. Soft law instruments often serve to allow treaty parties to authoritatively resolve ambiguities in a binding text or fill in gaps. This is part of an increasingly complex international system with variations in forms of instruments, means, and standards of measurement that interact intensely and frequently, with the common purpose of regulating behaviour within a rule of law framework. The development of complex regimes is particularly evident in international management of commons areas, such as the high seas and Antarctica, and in ongoing intergovernmental cooperative arrangements. For the latter, the memorandum of understanding has become a common form of undertaking, perhaps 'motivated by the need to circumvent the political constraints, economic costs, and legal rigidities that often are associated with formal and legally binding treaties' (Johnston, 1997, p xxiv).

From the perspective of State practice, it seems clear that resolutions, codes of conduct, conference declarations, and similar instruments are not law, soft or hard, albeit they may be related to or lead to law in one manner or another. States and other actors generally draft and agree to legally non-binding instruments advertently, knowingly. They make a conscious decision to have a text that is legally binding or not. In other words, for practitioners, governments, and intergovernmental organizations, there is not a continuum of instruments from soft to hard, but a binary system in which an instrument is entered into as law or as not-law. The not-law can be politically binding, morally binding, and expectations can be extremely strong of compliance with the norms contained in the instrument, but the difference between a legally binding instrument and one that is not appears well understood and acted upon by government negotiators. Although a vast amount of resolutions and other non-binding texts includes normative declarations, so-called soft law is not law or a formal source of norms. Such instruments may express trends or a stage in the formulation of treaty or custom, but law does not have a sliding scale of bindingness nor does desired law become law by stating its desirability, even repeatedly.

Despite their limited juridical effect, non-binding instruments have an essential and growing role in international relations and in the development of international law. Such instruments may (1) precede and help form international customary and treaty law;

---

[100] *Texaco Overseas Petroleum Co v Libyan Arab Republic, Arbitral Award* (1977) 53 ILR 422; (1978) 17 ILM 28–29.

(2) fill in gaps in international legal instruments and further define existing custom; (3) form part of the subsequent State practice that can be utilized to interpret treaties; and (4) substitute for legal obligation when on-going relations make formal treaties too costly and time-consuming or otherwise unnecessary. In the first three categories, non-binding instruments are often linked in one way or another to binding ones. The last category is perhaps the most interesting, because the extent to which members of the international community are willing to accept informal commitments and non-binding expressions of expected behaviour in their relations with others may reflect a maturing of the legal system and international society.

The first category posits that non-binding norms precede binding ones. It is evident that compliance with non-binding norms can lead to the formation of customary international law. In recent years, non-binding instruments sometimes have provided the necessary statement of legal obligation (*opinio juris*) to precede or accompany State practice, assisting in establishing the content of the norm.[101]

The adoption of non-binding normative instruments also can and often does lead to similar or virtually identical norms being codified in subsequent binding agreements. Indeed, the process of negotiating and drafting non-binding instruments can greatly facilitate the achievement of the consensus necessary to produce a binding multilateral agreement. In the human rights field, nearly all recent multilateral conventions have been preceded by adoption of a non-binding declaration. In environmental law, this has been the case with the Rotterdam Convention on Prior Informed Consent (1998).

The second category considers that non-binding instruments act interstitially to complete or supplement binding agreements. Sometimes this is foreseen in the agreement itself, eg, the Bonn Convention on Migratory Species of Wild Animals (1979), the Antarctic Treaty (1959) regime, and agreements of the International Atomic Energy Agency (IAEA) concerning non-proliferation of nuclear weapons.[102] In other instances, the non-binding accords may appear relatively independent and free-standing, but upon examination make reference to existing treaty obligations, as is the case for example, with the Helsinki Accords that led to the Organization for Security and Cooperation in Europe (still lacking a treaty basis) and the Zangger Committee for multilateral weapons control.

In the third category are those non-binding instruments that are adopted by States parties to 'authoritatively interpret' broad and undefined treaty obligations. The examples of the Inter-American and Universal Declarations of Human Rights, as they relate to the human rights provisions of the OAS and UN Charters, and the more recent ILO Declaration on Fundamental Principles and Rights at Work can be cited here. One could add the General Comments[103] of various human rights treaty bodies, albeit the interpretation is accomplished by an independent treaty body conferred that authority and not by the States parties directly. While they are not legally-binding, General Comments are 'today one of the potentially most significant and influential tools available to each of the

---

101   Eg, the UN General Assembly ban on Driftnet Fishing in UNGA Res.46/215 (20 December 1991).

102   IAEA, The Structure and Content of Agreements Between the Agency and States Required in Connection with the Treaty on the Non-Proliferation of Nuclear Weapons, IAEA Doc INFCIRC/153 (May 1971).

103   A General Comment is 'a formal statement of [a Committee's] understanding on an issue which arises out of the provisions of a treaty whose implementation it supervises', an understanding 'to which it attaches major importance.' See Alston, 2001, p 764.

six United Nations human rights treaty bodies in their endeavours to deepen the understanding and strengthen the influence of international human rights norms.'[104] Some
States have criticized particular General Comments, but national courts have looked to
them in some cases[105] to understand and apply vague and broadly-worded human rights
norms. The World Bank Operational Standards also seem intended to give guidance to
employees in furthering the mandate of the World Bank.

Non-binding instruments are used by courts as well. The International Court of Justice
often refers to texts adopted by the International Law Commission, especially the articles
on State responsibility. The European Court of Human Rights cites to resolutions and
declarations adopted by the Council of Europe and other international organizations.
National courts invoke the Universal Declaration of Human Rights and the Stockholm
Declaration on the Human Environment, among other normative non-binding texts.

Finally, there are some instances of free-standing normative instruments that are neither
related to nor intended to develop into binding agreements. The proliferating Memoranda
of Understanding generally can be included here, along with non-binding export control
guidelines developed by international weapons suppliers and the guidelines concerning
money laundering adopted by the Financial Action Task Force (FATF).

States and other actors adopt non-binding normative instruments for a variety of reasons. In some cases that is all they can do in the given setting. International organizations
in which much of the modern standard-setting takes place generally do not have the power
to adopt binding texts. In addition, non-State actors can sign on, participate, and be targets
of regulation, which is much more difficult to do with treaties. Non-binding instruments
are faster to adopt, easier to change, and more useful for technical matters that may need
rapid or repeated revision. This is particularly important when the subject matter may not
be ripe for treaty action because of scientific uncertainty or lack of political consensus.
Finally, non-binding texts serve to avoid domestic political battles because they do not
need ratification.

In some instances, compliance with non-binding norms and instruments is extremely
good and probably would not have been better if the norms were contained in a binding
text. In fact, in many cases the choice would not have been between a binding and a non-
binding text, but between a non-binding text and no text at all. In instances where the
choice is presented, there is some evidence that there may be less compliance with non-
binding norms, but that the content of the instrument is likely to be more ambitious and
far-reaching than would be the product of treaty negotiations, so the overall impact may
still be more positive with a non-binding than a binding instrument.

The considerable recourse to and compliance with non-binding norms may represent a
maturing of the international system. The on-going relationships among States and other
actors, deepening and changing with globalization, create a climate that may diminish
the felt need to include all expectations between States in formal legal instruments. Not
all arrangements in business, neighbourhoods, or in families are formalized, but are often
governed by informal social norms and voluntary, non-contractual arrangements. Non-
binding norms or informal social norms can be effective and offer a flexible and efficient

---

[104] Ibid, at p 773.
[105] Eg *Government of the Republic of South Africa et al* v *Grootboom*, Constitutional Court of South
Africa Case 11/00 (4 October 2000).

way to order responses to common problems. They are not law and they do not need to be in order to influence conduct in the desired manner.

V. CONCLUSION

The growing complexity of the international legal system is reflected in the increasing variety of forms of commitment adopted to regulate State and non-State behaviour in regard to an ever-growing number of transnational problems. The various international actors create and implement a range of international commitments, some of which are in legal form, others of which are contained in non-binding instruments. The lack of a binding form may reduce the options for enforcement in the short term (ie, no litigation), but this does not deny that there can exist sincere and deeply held expectations of compliance with the norms contained in the non-binding form.

What has been striking in recent years has been the growing role of international courts and quasi-judicial tribunals in aggregating to themselves a strong role in normative development and the creation of hierarchy among norms. International tribunals have begun identifying norms *jus cogens*, usually without pointing to or supplying evidence on which they have based their conclusion that the norm in question has been accepted as peremptory by the international community of States as a whole. It thus appears to be a rather subjective determination. For the most part States have not objected, although extreme efforts on the part of some in the Bush administration to re-define narrowly what constitutes torture challenged the very prohibition of the practice, whether or not it is prohibited by *jus cogens*. The Inter-American Court has been the most forceful in pressing its competence to identify peremptory norms and to add other norms to the prohibitions of genocide and torture accepted by other courts. International tribunals have also been willing to assess the extent to which norms contained in non-binding instruments have a juridical status as custom or general principles of law. The latter function seems more in keeping with the traditional role of international courts. In contrast, declaring *jus cogens* by judicial fiat seems to draw the courts into legislating unnecessarily, but thus far no consequences have followed from any of the declarations that have been made.

REFERENCES

AKEHURST, M (1974–75), 'The Hierarchy of the Sources of International Law', 47 *BYIL* 273.

ALSTON, P (2001), 'The Historical Origins of the Concept of 'General Comments' in Human Rights Law' in Boisson de Chazournes, L and Gowlland-Debbas, V (eds), *The International Legal System in Quest of Equity and Universality, Liber Amicorum Georges Abi-Saab* (Leiden: Brill Publishers), p 763.

CASSESE, A (2008) 'The Italian Court of Cassation Misapprehends the Notion of War Crimes', 6 *J Int Crim Justice* 1077.

CLAPHAM, A (2007), 'The *Jus Cogens* Prohibition of Torture and the Importance Sovereign State Immunity', in Kohen, MG (ed), *Promoting Justice, Human Rights and Conflict Resolution through International Law, Liber Amicorum Lucius Caflisch* (The Hague: Martinus Nijhoff), p 151.

DANILENKO, G (1991), 'International *Jus cogens*: Issues of Law-Making', 2 *EJIL* 42.

DANNER, AM (2000), 'Constructing a Hierarchy of Crimes in International Criminal Law Sentencing', 87 *Va L Rev* 415.

DE SENA, P and DE VITTOR, F (2005), 'State Immunity and Human Rights: The Italian Supreme Court Decision on the Ferrini Case', 16 *EJIL* 89.

DUPUY, P-M (1995), *Droit international public*, 3rd edn (Paris: Dalloz).

HENKIN, L (1989-IV), 'International Law: Politics, Values and Functions', 216 *Recueil des Cours* 9.

JOHNSTON, DM (1997), *Consent and Commitment in the World Community* (Irvington-on-Hudson, NY: Transnational).

KEARNEY, RD and DALTON, RE (1970), 'The Treaty on Treaties', 64 *AJIL* 495.

KELSEN, H (1935), 'The Pure Theory of Law', 51 *LQR* 517.

KOSKENNIEMI, M (1997), 'Hierarchy in International Law: A Sketch', 8 *EJIL* 566.

LUKASHUK, II (1989), 'The Principle Pacta Sunt Servanda and the Nature of Obligation under International Law', 83 *AJIL* 513.

MURRAY, R and EVANS, MD (2001), *Documents of the African Commission on Human and Peoples Rights* (Oxford: Hart Publishing).

OXMAN, B (2002), 'Complementary Agreements and Compulsory Jurisdiction', 95 *AJIL* 277.

PAUWELYN, J (2001), 'The Role of Public International Law in the WTO: How Far Can We Go', 95 *AJIL* 535.

ROBLEDO, AG (1982–III), 'Le Ius Cogens International: Sa Genese, Sa Nature, Ses Fonctions', 172 *Recueil des Cours* 17.

SAFRIN, S (2002), 'Treaties in Collision? The Biosafety Protocol and the World Trade Organization Agreements', 96 *AJIL* 606.

SALCEDO, JAC (1997), 'Reflections on the Hierarchy of Norms in International Law', 8 *EJIL* 583.

SHELTON, D (2003) 'Boundaries of Human Rights Jurisdiction in Europe', 13 *Duke JI & CL* 95.

—— (ed) (2000), *Commitment and Compliance: The Role of Non-Binding Norms in the International Legal System* (Oxford: Oxford University Press).

SIMMA, B (2009), 'Universality of International Law from the Perspective of a Practitioner', 20 *EJIL* 265.

TOMUSCHAT, C (1993), 'Obligations Arising for States Without or Against Their Will' (1993–IV) 241 *Recueil des Cours* 191.

WEIL, P (1983), 'Towards Relative Normativity in International Law?', 77 *AJIL* 413.

WEISS, EB and JACOBSON, H (eds) (1998), *Engaging Countries: Strengthening Compliance with International Environmental Accords* (Cambridge, Mass.: MIT Press).

FURTHER READING

The following works provide useful amplification of the topics surveyed in this chapter:

D'AMATO, A (1990), 'It's a Bird, It's a Plane, It's Jus Cogens', 9 *Conn JIL* 1.

DE HOOGH, A (1996), *Obligations Erga Omnes and International Crimes* (The Hague: Kluwer Law International).

HANNIKAINEN, L (1988), *Peremptory Norms (Jus cogens) in International Law*

(Lakimiesliiton Kustannus: Finnish Lawyer's Publishing Co).

RAGAZZI, M (1997), *The Concept of International Obligations Erga Omnes* (Oxford: Clarendon Press).

SZTUCKI, J (1974), *Jus Cogens and the Vienna Convention on the Law of Treaties* (Vienna: Springer).

THOMUSCHAT, C and THOUVENIN, J-M (eds) (2006), The Fundamental Rules of the International Legal Order: Jus Cogens and Obligations Erga Omnes (The Hague: Martinus Nijhoff).

7

THE PRACTICAL WORKING OF THE LAW OF TREATIES

Malgosia Fitzmaurice

SUMMARY

This chapter considers key structural questions and fundamental problems relating to the law of treaties. The structural matters considered include: the concept of a treaty; the anatomy of treaties (including the making of treaties; authority to conclude treaties; expression of consent to be bound; invalidity of treaties (non-absolute grounds for invalidity of treaties, absolute grounds for invalidity of treaties, amendment and modification); suspension and termination.

The key issues addressed include the scope of legal obligation (the principle *pacta sunt servanda*, treaties, and third States); interpretation and reservation to treaties (including interpretative declarations); and finally, problems concerning the grounds for termination (supervening impossibility and material breach). The chapter takes into consideration the theory and practice of the law of treaties, with broad analysis of the case law of various international courts and tribunals, with special emphasis on jurisprudence of the International Court of Justice.

I. INTRODUCTION

Treaties are one of the means through which States deal with each other and a precise method of regulating relations between States. Treaties almost exclusively regulate some areas of international law, such as environmental law, whilst they are of the utmost importance in others, such as international economic relations, and play a decisive role in the field of human rights. International trade and international investments as well as international communication are unimaginable without treaties. Thus knowledge of the law of treaties is essential to an understanding of how international relations and international law work. That law is codified in the 1969 Vienna Convention on the Law of Treaties (the VCLT), the provisions of which will be presented and analysed in this chapter.

II. BASIC CONCEPTS AND STRUCTURES

A. WHAT IS A TREATY?

VCLT Article 2(2) defines a treaty as '[a]n international agreement concluded between States in written form and governed by international law, whether embodied in a single instrument or in two or more related instruments and whatever its particular designation'.

The term 'treaty' is used generically (Aust, 2007, p 17) and a treaty may be described in a multitude of ways. The International Law Commission (ILC) said:

In addition to a 'treaty', 'convention', and 'protocol,' one not infrequently finds titles such as 'declaration,' 'charter,' 'covenant,' 'pact,' 'act,' *statute,* 'agreement,' 'concordat,' whilst names like 'declaration,' 'agreement', and *modus vivendi* may well be found given both to formal and less formal types of agreements. As to the latter, their nomenclature is almost illimitable, even if some names such as 'agreement,' 'exchange of notes,' 'exchange of letters,' 'memorandum of agreement,' or 'agreed minute', may be more common than others...there is no exclusive or systematic use of nomenclature for particular types of transaction.[1]

The Vienna Convention does not require that a treaty be in any particular form or comprise any particular elements so if there is a dispute concerning the status of a document—eg, a joint communiqué—as a treaty, an objective test is used to determine the question, taking into account its actual terms and the particular circumstances in which it was made. For example, minutes of a meeting can comprise a treaty. In the *Qatar v Bahrain* case the International Court of Justice (ICJ) said:

The Court does not find it necessary to consider what might have been the intentions of the Foreign Minister of Bahrain or, for that matter those of the Foreign Minister of Qatar. The two ministers signed a text recording commitment accepted by their Governments, some of which were to be given an immediate application. Having signed such a text, the Foreign Minister of Bahrain, is not in the position subsequently to say that he intended to subscribe only to a 'statement recording political understanding', and not to an 'international agreement'.[2]

Since a treaty is a method of creating binding legal obligations, there must be an intention to create legal relations. The Rapporteur of the ILC stated that the element is implicitly present in the phrase 'governed by international law'.[3] There are some international acts that may assume the form of international agreements but which were never intended

---

[1] *YBILC* (1966), vol II (part two), p 188.

[2] *Maritime Delimitation and Territorial Questions between Qatar and Bahrain, Jurisdiction and Admissibility, Judgment, ICJ Reports 1994*, p 112, para 27. See also *Land and Maritime Boundary between Cameroon and Nigeria (Cameroon v Nigeria; Equatorial Guinea Intervening), Judgment, ICJ Reports 2002*, p 303 in which the Court analysed two documents: 1975 Maroua Declaration and the 1971 Youndé II Declaration. On the basis of the manner in which these Declarations were concluded (signed by the Heads Cameroon and Nigeria), the Court stated as follows: '[t]he Court considers that the Maroua Declaration constitutes an international agreement concluded between States in written form and tracing a boundary; it is thus governed by international law and constitutes a treaty in the sense of the Vienna Convention on the Law of Treaties...and which in any case reflects customary international law in this respect' (para 263).

[3] Fourth Report on the Law Treaties, *YBILC* (1965), vol II, p 12.

to create legal obligations, such as the 1975 Final Act of the Conference on Security and Cooperation in Europe.[4]

Such Acts are sometimes called 'soft law'[5] and their legal status is not clear. However, as they are not legally binding, they are not enforceable in courts. However, they cannot be ignored since soft law may 'harden' into a treaty[6] or become a norm of international customary law. Some authors see 'soft law' as a more flexible alternative to treaty-making (Boyle, 2000) though others consider the whole concept misconceived, both in that if it is not binding, it is not law, and that it creates an expectation of compliance whilst simultaneously undermining the authority of law (Weil, 1983).

Finally, in the *Nuclear Test* cases,[7] the ICJ made it clear that unilateral statements of States can have binding effect if the intention that they be legally binding is clear; that there is clear evidence regarding the circumstances in which they are made; and that the question is approached with due caution. However, it has been argued that there is little evidence to support the Court's view and, in any case, there was insufficient evidence of intent on the facts of the case.

B. THE VIENNA CONVENTIONS

The 1969 Vienna Convention on the Law of Treaties was opened for signature on 23 April 1969 and entered into force on 27 January 1980. It was the product of the International Law Commission[8] and the UN Conference on the Law of Treaties that met at Vienna from 26 March to 24 May 1968, and from 9 April to 22 May 1969. The subsequent 1986 Vienna Convention between States and International Organizations or Between Organizations adapts these rules to its subject matter and although not in force is considered to be applicable as law. Finally, the 1978 Vienna Convention on Succession of States in Respect of Treaties is in force but not all of its rules are considered to represent customary international law. The present chapter is based mainly on the provisions of the 1969 Vienna Convention.

1. The scope of the Vienna Convention

The Vienna Convention regulates treaties concluded between States (Article 1) and in written form (Article 2(1)(a)). This does not mean that oral agreements have no effect under international law or that principles found in the VCLT do not apply to such agreements, merely that they are not governed by the VCLT itself. Questions of succession of treaties, State responsibility, and the effect of the outbreak of hostilities on treaties are also excluded from its scope (Article 73). Furthermore, the Convention is not retroactive and

---

[4] The Act stated that it was not eligible for registration under UN Charter Article 102 and was generally understood not to have binding force. The failure to register a treaty under UN Charter Article 102 does not mean that the instrument in question is not a treaty, whilst the act of registration does not mean that it is. For example, the 1957 Declaration by Egypt concerning the nationalization of the Suez Canal was registered by the Egyptian Government but was not a treaty.

[5] Other examples include the 1972 Stockholm Declaration on Human Environment and the 1992 Rio Declaration on Environment and Development. On soft law generally, see Ch 5, above.

[6] Eg, the 1988 Baltic Sea Ministerial Declaration and the 1992 Baltic Sea Declaration hardened into the 1992 Convention on the Protection of the Baltic Sea and the Baltic Sea Area ('The Helsinki Convention').

[7] *Nuclear Tests (Australia v France), Judgment, ICJ Reports 1974*, p 253, paras 42–43. The need for intention was reiterated by the Court in *Frontier Dispute, Judgment, ICJ Reports 1986*, p 554, para 39.

[8] The Special Rapporteurs of the Commission were Professors Briely and Lauterpacht, Sir G Fitzmaurice and Sir H Waldock.

only applies to treaties concluded after its entry into force (Article 4). It acts as a residual rule, ie, it is applicable unless a particular treaty provides otherwise; or unless the parties agree otherwise; or if a different intention is otherwise established. Although the VCLT does not apply to treaties between States and international organizations *per se*, those of its provisions that reflect rules of international customary law do apply to such treaties (Article 3(b)). Moreover, the provisions of the VCLT apply as between States parties to the VCLT as regards treaties to which other forms of subjects of international law (such as international organizations) are also parties (Article 3(c)).

2. The Vienna Convention and customary law

There are two problems concerning the relationship between the Vienna Convention and international customary law: (i) which provisions of the Vienna Convention codified customary law and which constituted progressive development and (ii) how does customary law relating to treaties operate?

It is difficult, if not impossible, to answer the first of these questions. Certain provisions of the Convention that represented progressive development at the time of its signing—such as reservations and modification of treaties—were probably already within the body of international customary law by the time of its entry into force (Sinclair, 1984, pp 10–21). In the *Gabčíkovo-Nagymaros Project* case the ICJ identified the rules concerning termination and suspension of treaties as codificatory[9] and in the *Kasikili/Sedudu Island* case said that the rules of interpretation reflected customary international law.[10]

As to the second problem, Articles 3(b), 4, 38, and 43 combine to provide that when the provisions of the Convention are inapplicable the rules of international customary law (or in some instances general principles of law) with the same legal content may be applicable. The most significant is Article 4 concerning the non-retroactive effect of provisions of the VCLT that were not reflective of customary law.

III. THE ANATOMY OF A TREATY

A. THE MAKING OF TREATIES

Treaties are by far the most important tools of regulating international relations. They may be concluded between States, States and international organizations, and between international organizations. International organizations, in particular the United Nations, play a most important role in international law-making as initiators of treaties and as a source of expertise.

B. AUTHORITY TO CONCLUDE TREATIES

VCLT Articles 7 and 8 concern the making of treaties. A most important issue is that of full powers,[11] the holder of which is authorized to adopt and authenticate the text of a treaty and

---

[9] *Gabčíkovo-Nagymaros Project (Hungary/Slovakia), Judgment, ICJ Reports 1997*, p 7, para 46.

[10] *Kasikili/Sedudu Island (Botswana/Namibia), Judgment, ICJ Reports 1999*, p 1045, para 18.

[11] Defined in Article 2(1)(c) as a 'Document emanating from the competent authority of a State designating a person or persons to represent a State for negotiating, adopting or authenticating the text of a treaty, for expressing consent of the State by a treaty, or for accomplishing any other acts with respect to a treaty'.

to express the consent of the State to be bound by a treaty, although there are a growing number of treaties, particularly bilateral treaties, which are concluded in a simplified form that does not require the production of full powers (for example exchange of notes). The general rule expressed in the VCLT (Article 7 paragraph 1(a) and (b)) is that a person is considered as representing a State for the purpose of expressing the consent of the State to be bound by it if he or she produces appropriate full powers or it appears from the practice of the States concerned or from other circumstances that their intention was to consider that person as representing the State for such purposes and to dispense with full powers. There is, however, a group of persons who by virtue of their functions and without having to produce full powers, are considered to have such authority, these being: Heads of State, Heads of Government, and Ministers for Foreign Affairs; heads of diplomatic missions, for the purpose of adoption of the text of a treaty between the accrediting State and the State to which they are accredited; representatives accredited by States to an international organization or one of its organs, for the purpose of adopting the text of a treaty in that conference, organization, or organ (Article 7(2)). The ICJ in the *Cameroon* v *Nigeria* case confirmed this rule.[12] In 2006 in the *Democratic Republic of Congo* v *Rwanda* the Court examined the powers of the 'Big Three' (The Head of State, Head of Government and Minister for Foreign Affairs) to bind the States and, after having again confirmed the 'well established rule', went on to say that: 'The Court notes, however, that with increasing frequency in modern international relations other persons representing a State in specific fields may be authorised by that State to bind it by their statements in respect to matters falling within their purview. This may be true, for example, of holders of technical ministerial portfolio exercising powers in their field of competence in the area of foreign relations, and even of certain officials.'[13]

Full powers have to be distinguished from credentials, which are submitted to an international organization or a government hosting an international conference by a delegate attending to negotiate a multilateral treaty. Credentials only authorize the delegate to adopt the text of a treaty and to sign a Final Act. Signing the treaty itself requires full powers or specific instructions from government. Full powers and credentials may be combined in one document.

Where an unauthorized person purports to conclude a treaty Article 8 provides that the action is without legal effect, unless subsequently confirmed by the State. On the other hand, Article 47 provides that where an authorized representative of a State expresses consent to be bound although instructed by their State not to do so, this does not invalidate that consent, unless the limitation on their authority was notified to other negotiating States beforehand.

C. EXPRESSION OF CONSENT TO BE BOUND

The role of the expression of consent by States to be bound by a treaty is to constitute a mechanism by which the treaty becomes a juridical act. According to Article 11, 'The

---

See also *Case Concerning the Land and Maritime Boundary between Cameroon and Nigeria (Cameroon* v *Nigeria; Equatorial Guinea Intervening), Judgment, ICJ Reports 2002,* p 303.

[12] *Land and Maritime Boundary between Cameroon and Nigeria (Cameroon* v *Nigeria; Equatorial Guinea Intervening), Judgment, ICJ Reports 2002,* p 303, para 265.

[13] *Armed Activities on the Territory of the Congo (New Application: 2002) (Democratic Republic of Congo* v *Rwanda) Jurisdiction of the Court and Admissibility of the Application, ICJ Reports 2006,* p 6, para 47.

consent of a state to be bound by a treaty may be expressed by signature, exchange of instruments constituting a treaty, ratification, acceptance, approval or accession, or by any other means if so agreed'. Article 11 lists a number of particular means of expressing consent to be bound, whilst also allowing parties to adopt any other means on which they agree. The precise method is, therefore, for the parties to a treaty to decide amongst themselves.

The legal effect of signature of a treaty depends upon whether or not it is subject to ratification, acceptance, or approval. If it is, then signature constitutes an intermediate step, indicating that the delegates have agreed upon the text and are willing to accept it. Signature under these circumstances does not express the final consent to be bound and the signing of a treaty does not impose any obligation on a State to ratify it or even, in the absence of an express term to this effect, to submit it to the national legislator for consideration. However, the initial signature also constitutes a juridical act in the sense that by its signature each State accepts certain legal consequences, for example under VCLT Articles 18, 24(4), and 25. The intermediate stage between signature and ratification enables States to promulgate necessary legislation or obtain necessary parliamentary approval. Ratification conforms to the democratic principle that the government should consult public opinion either in parliament or elsewhere before finally approving a treaty (Shearer, 1994, p 414).

1. Signature

Signature only expresses consent to be bound when it constitutes the final stage of a treaty-making process. Article 12 lists a variety of possible means to express consent to be bound by signature, including signature *ad referendum*. This commonly indicates either that the signatory State is currently unable to accept the terms of the treaty, or that the plenipotentiary concerned had no definitive instructions in the matter. Signature *ad referendum* becomes a full signature if subsequently confirmed by the State concerned. Article 12 also provides that initialling a treaty constitutes signature when it is established that the negotiating State so agreed.

2. Ratification

Ratification is understood as a formal, solemn act on the part of a Head of State through which approval is given and a commitment to fulfil its obligations is undertaken, although the significance of the act at the international level has changed over time. As Judge Moore said in 1924, the older view that treaties might be regarded as binding before they had been ratified was now 'obsolete, and lingers only as an echo from the past'.[14]

VCLT Article 2(1)(b) provides that: '"ratification", "acceptance", "approval" and "accession" mean in each case the international act so named whereby a state establishes on the international plane its consent to be bound by a treaty'. Despite the use of the word 'means', this does not define ratification, but indicates its effect. Article 14 provides that consent to be bound is expressed by ratification if (a) the treaty expressly so provides; (b) the negotiating States otherwise agree that ratification is necessary; (c) the treaty has been signed subject to ratification; or (d) an intention to sign subject to ratification appears from the full powers or was expressed during negotiations.

---

[14] *Mavrommatis Palestine Concessions, Judgment No 2, 1924, PCIJ, Ser A, No 2*, at p 57.

Ratification is unconditional and, unless the treaty in question provides otherwise, is not dependent on the receipt or deposit of instruments of ratification by other States. Some support for a relatively relaxed approach to the formalities of ratification can be gleaned from the attitude of the ICJ in the *Nicaragua* case where Nicaragua's failure to ratify the Statute of the former Permanent Court of International Justice and convert 'potential commitment to effective commitment' was seen as being rectified by its ratification of the ICJ Statute.[15]

3. Accession

This means of consent to be bound is regulated by VCLT Article 15 and refers to the means by which a State expresses its consent to become a party to a treaty that it was not in a position to sign.[16] A State can only accede to a treaty if the treaty so provides or the parties agree. Treaties setting up regional regimes may often permit accession by invitation.[17]

Can a State accede to a treaty that is not yet in force? The International Law Commission has pointed out that:

An examination of the most recent treaty practice shows that in practically all modern treaties which contain accession clauses the right to accede is made independent of the entry into force of a treaty, either expressly, by allowing accession to take place before the date fixed for the entry into force of the treaty, or impliedly, by making the entry into force of the treaty conditional on the deposit, *inter alia*, of instruments of Accession.[18]

4. Acceptance and approval

These are recognized and widely used methods of expressing consent to be bound and are regulated by VCLT Article 14(2). There are no great differences between signature subject to acceptance or approval and signature subject to ratification. The use of these methods of consent to be bound was intended to simplify procedures by, for example, avoiding constitutional conditions that might require obtaining Parliamentary authority prior to ratification. The rules applicable to ratification apply to acceptance and approval (Aust, 2007, p 110) and, unless provided otherwise, acceptance and approval have the same legal effect as ratification. Expressing consent to be bound by acceptance or approval without prior signature is analogous to accession. In many of the more recent conventions concluded under the auspices of the United Nations, such as the 1997 UN Convention on the Law of the Non-Navigational Uses of International Watercourses,[19] all means of consent to be bound are listed as available options.

D. INVALIDITY OF TREATIES

The grounds for invalidity of treaties within the VCLT can be divided into two groups: relative grounds in Articles 46–50 and absolute grounds in Articles 51–53.[20] The main

---

[15] *Military and Paramilitary Activities in and against Nicaragua (Nicaragua v United States of America), Jurisdiction and Admissibility, Judgment, ICJ Reports 1984*, p 392.

[16] Very rarely it can be the principal means of expressing consent to be bound, as in the often cited yet isolated example of the 1928 General Act for the Pacific Settlement of International Disputes.

[17] Eg, 1992 Convention on the Protection of the Marine Environment of the Baltic Sea Area.

[18] *YBILC* (1966), vol II (part two), p 199.   [19] (1997) 36 ILM 700.

[20] Sinclair divides cases of invalidity into three groups, concerning: the capacity of the parties (Articles 46–47); the validity of consent to be bound (Articles 48–50); and the lawfulness of the object of the treaty (Articles 51–53) (Sinclair, 1984, p 160).

difference between these grounds is that the relative grounds render a treaty voidable at the insistence of an affected State whereas the absolute grounds means that the treaty is rendered void *ab initio* and without legal effect. The Vienna Convention does not differentiate between bilateral and multilateral treaties. However, in the case of bilateral treaties the legal effect of establishing a relative ground of invalidity has the same legal effect as establishing absolute invalidity: the treaty falls (Sinclair, 1984). In the case of multilateral treaties, however, establishing an absolute ground means that the treaty has no legal force at all whereas establishing a relative ground—meaning that the consent of a particular State to a multilateral treaty is vitiated—does not affect the validity of the treaty as a whole as between the other remaining parties (Article 69(4)).

Article 46 concerns the failure to comply with internal law regarding competence to conclude a treaty, and provides that this may only be a ground for invalidating consent to be bound if that failure was 'manifest'. In the *Cameroon* v *Nigeria* case, Nigeria argued that '...it should have been 'objectively evident' to Cameroon, within the meaning of Article 46, paragraph 2 of the VCLT that the Nigerian Head of State did not have unlimited powers'[21] but the Court, whilst accepting that '[t]he rules concerning the authority to sign treaties are constitutional rules of fundamental importance', took the view that '...a limitation of a Head of State's capacity in this respect is not manifest in the sense of Article 46, paragraph 2, unless at least properly publicized. This is particularly so because Heads of States belong to the group of persons who, in accordance with Article 7, paragraph 2, of the Convention...are considered as representing the State'.[22]

Article 47 is similar, concerning cases in which the representatives purporting to conclude a treaty were acting beyond the scope of their instructions.[23] Article 48 concerns error as a vitiating ground, and follows the approach of the ICJ in the *Temple* case. In that case, Thailand argued that the boundary line indicated on a map annexed to a treaty was in error since it did not follow the watershed line that was prescribed by the treaty text. The Court rejected this argument, saying:

It is an established rule of law that the plea of error cannot be allowed as a vitiating consent if the party advancing it contributed by its conduct or error, or could have avoided it, or the circumstances were such as to put party on notice of a possible error. The Court considers that the character and qualifications of persons who saw Annex I map on the Siamese side would alone made it difficult for Thailand to plead error in law...[24]

Articles 49 and 50 concern fraud and corruption. There is a paucity of materials relating to these Articles, though as far as corruption is concerned, the ILC observed that only an act calculated to exercise a substantial influence on the disposition of a representative to conclude a treaty could be invoked as a reason to invalidate an expression of consent that had subsequently been given.[25]

---

[21] *Land and Maritime Boundary between Cameroon and Nigeria (Cameroon* v *Nigeria; Equatorial Guinea Intervening), Judgment, ICJ Reports 2002*, p 303, para 258.

[22] *Land and Maritime Boundary between Cameroon and Nigeria (Cameroon* v *Nigeria; Equatorial Guinea Intervening), Judgment, ICJ Reports 2002*, p 303, para 265.

[23] *YBILC* (1966), vol II (part two), p 243.

[24] *Temple of Preah Vihear, Merits, Judgment, ICJ Reports 1962*, p 6 at p 26.

[25] *YBILC* (1966), vol II (part two), p 244.

Turning from the relative to the absolute grounds for invalidity, Article 51 deals with the coercion of a representative, Article 52 the coercion of a State, and Article 53 the conflict with norms of *jus cogens*. In all these cases a treaty is void *ab initio*, in the latter case by virtue of its conflicting with international public policy (the consequences of which are addressed in Article 71). Practice in relation to all these Articles is limited. The classic example relating to Article 51, the coercion of a representative, concerns the pressure exerted by Göring and Ribbentrop upon President Hacha of Czechoslovakia to sign a treaty with Germany establishing a German protectorate over Bohemia and Moravia in 1939. There is a clear link between Article 52—the coercion of a State—and the prohibition of the use of force under international law. Iceland advanced a claim of this nature in the 1973 *Fisheries Jurisdiction* case and the ICJ stated that:

There can be little doubt, as implied in the Charter of the United Nations and recognised in Article 52 of the Vienna Convention on the Law of Treaties, that under contemporary international law an agreement concluded under the threat or use of force is void . . . [26]

E. AMENDMENT AND MODIFICATION

The growth in number of multilateral treaties resulted in the necessity of devising amendment procedures and, in order to make amendment procedures more flexible, modification procedures. These are addressed in VCLT Articles 39–41. The ILC explained that amendment is a formal matter introducing changes into the treaty text whereas modification is a less formal procedure which affects only certain parties to a treaty.[27] However, in practice it is often difficult to distinguish between these two procedures (Sinclair, 1984, p 107).

Amendments to treaties should be distinguished from the revision of a treaty. Revision is a more comprehensive process resulting in changes to a treaty. However, a diplomatic conference is often needed both to revise and to amend a treaty, as, for example, in the case of the 1992 Convention on the Protection of the Marine Environment of the Baltic Sea (the '1992 Helsinki Convention').[28] Amendments are subject to approval by the parties to the treaty. However, some treaties—such as the Helsinki Convention—contain technical annexes, which may, if the treaty so provides, be amended by a simplified system whereby an amendment to an annex is deemed to have been accepted at the end of a specified period unless in the meanwhile any State party has submitted a written objection to the Depositary.

F. TERMINATION AND SUSPENSION OF THE OPERATION OF TREATIES

The general provisions on suspension and termination of treaties are set out in VCLT Articles 54–59. Termination of a treaty may result from the grounds of termination that

---

[26] *Fisheries Jurisdiction (United Kingdom v Iceland), Jurisdiction of the Court, Judgment, ICJ Reports 1973*, p 3, para 24. However, on the facts of the case the Court concluded that 'The history of negotiations which led up to the 1961 Exchange of Notes reveals that these instruments were freely negotiated by the interested parties on the basis of the perfect equality and freedom of decision on both sides'.

[27] *YBILC* (1966), vol II (part two), p 232.

[28] 'A conference for the purpose of a general revision of or an amendment to this Convention may be convened with the consent of the Contracting Parties or the request of the Commission' (Article 30).

are internal to the treaty as well as from grounds external to the treaty. The 'internal' grounds will be considered here. The 'external grounds', concerning breach of obligations, will be considered later. As regards the 'internal' grounds for termination or suspension, the general rule in Article 54 is that a treaty may be terminated or a party may withdraw from a treaty in accordance with the provisions of the treaty itself or at any time by consent of all parties following consultations. Article 57 provides that the operation of a treaty with regard to all parties or to a particular party may be suspended in accordance with the provisions of the treaty in question.

Some treaties provide that they will remain in force only for a specific period of time whereas others provide for termination by a resolution of the contracting parties. As to withdrawal from a treaty, some treaties provide for a period of notice whilst others do not. For example, the 1992 Helsinki Convention provides that at any time after the expiry of five years from the date of its entry into force any party may, by giving written notification to the depositary, withdraw from the Convention. Withdrawal takes effect on the thirtieth day of June of the year following the year in which the depositary was notified of the withdrawal.

VCLT Article 58 provides for suspension of the operation of a multilateral treaty by agreement between certain parties only. This Article must be read in conjunction with Article 41 which provides for the modification of treaty provisions between certain parties only. Article 59 covers the case of tacit termination of a treaty. There is a particular problem concerning the relationship between tacit termination in accordance with Article 59 and Article 30, which concerns the effect of successive treaties relating to the same subject matter and which relates to cases in which the parties clearly intended the earlier treaty to be abrogated or its operation wholly suspended by the conclusion of the subsequent treaty.

IV. THE SCOPE OF LEGAL OBLIGATIONS

A. THE PRINCIPLE *PACTA SUNT SERVANDA*

The principle *pacta sunt servanda* is enshrined in Article 26 of the VCLT which provides that '[e]very treaty in force is binding upon the parties to it and must be performed by them in good faith'. Good faith is itself a legal principle and forms an integral part of the *pacta sunt servanda* principle.[29]

The fundamental importance of *pacta sunt servanda* was confirmed by the ICJ in the 1997 *Gabčíkovo-Nagymaros* case, which, generally speaking, advocated its strict observance. The case concerned the implementation of a 1977 treaty providing for the construction of a hydro-electric scheme along stretches of the Danube in Hungary and Slovakia. Hungary argued that the conduct of both parties indicated that they had repudiated this bilateral treaty, which, therefore, had come to an end. The Court, however, took the view that the reciprocal wrongful conduct of both parties 'did not bring the Treaty to an end nor justify its termination'.[30] The effect of breaching treaty obligations will be considered later, but at this point it should be noted that, despite both parties being in fundamental

---

[29] *YBILC* (1966), vol II (part two), p 211.
[30] *Gabčíkovo-Nagymaros Project (Hungary/Slovakia), Judgment, ICJ Reports 1997*, p 7, para 114.

breach of important elements of their treaty obligations, the Court though the 1977 Treaty 'cannot be treated as voided by unlawful conduct'.[31]

The Court made a direct reference to the principle *pacta sunt servanda*, saying that 'What is required in the present case by the rule *pacta sunt servanda*, as reflected in Article 26 of Vienna Convention of 1969 on the Law of Treaties, is that the parties find solution within the co-operative context of the Treaty'.[32] The Court observed that the two elements in Article 26—the binding force of treaties and the performance of them in good faith— were of equal importance and that good faith implied that, 'in this case, it is the purpose of the Treaty, and the intentions of the parties in concluding it, which should prevail over its literal application. The principle of good faith obliges parties to apply it in a reasonable way in such a manner that its purpose can be realised'.[33]

These are far-reaching statements and, whilst they may have been particularly suited to the issues in the *Gabčíkovo-Nagymaros* case itself, it is still impossible to determine the extent to which they bear upon the application of the principle *pacta sunt servanda* in the law of treaties in general.

B. TREATIES AND THIRD STATES

The issue of treaties and non-State parties—third States—are addressed in VCLT Articles 34–38. The fundamental rule concerning the relationship between treaties and third States is expressed by the maxim *pacta tertiis nec nocent nec prosunt*, enshrined in Article 34. The Convention then deals with an obligation (Article 35) and a right (Article 36—often referred to as stipulations *in favorem tertii*) arising from a treaty for a third State. As to the obligation, the requirements are so strict that, when fulfilled, they in fact amount to the existence of a collateral agreement between the parties to the treaty and the third State and it is this collateral agreement, rather than the original treaty, which is the legal basis for the third State's obligation.

There are procedural differences in the establishment of an obligation and of a right. The third State must accept an obligation in writing, whereas in a case of the right, the assent of the third State(s) is presumed, unless the treaty provides otherwise or there are indications to the contrary. Any obligation arising for a third State can be revoked or modified only with the consent of the parties to the treaty and of the third State, unless it is established that they agreed otherwise. Any right arising for a third State can be revoked or modified only by the parties if it is established that the right was intended to be revocable or subject to modification without the consent of the third State. Caution is usually recommended when considering whether a treaty has given rise to stipulations *in favorem tertii*. As the PCIJ said:

It cannot be lightly presumed that stipulations favourable to a third State have been adopted with the object of creating an actual right in its favour. There is however nothing to prevent the will of sovereign States from having this object and this effect. The question of the existence of a right acquired under an instrument drawn between other States is therefore one to be decided in each particular case: it must be ascertained whether the States which have stipulated in favour of the third State meant to create for that State an actual right which the latter has accepted as such.[34]

---

[31] Ibid, para 133.   [32] Ibid, para 142.   [33] Idem.
[34] *Free Zones of Upper Savoy and the District of Gex, Judgment, 1932, PCIJ, Ser A/B, No 46*, p 96 at pp 147–148.

Nothing in the VCLT prevents a rule set out in a treaty from becoming binding upon third States as a customary rule of international law if recognized as such (Article 37). However, the VCLT does not deal specifically with the question of whether the objective regimes created by treaties are binding only on States parties to those instruments or whether they are valid as against the entire international community—are valid *erga omnes*. Examples of such treaties would include those providing for the neutrality or demilitarization of a certain territory or area, or establishing freedom of navigation in international waterways such as the Suez Canal, Kiel Canal, and the Turkish Straits.[35]

V. GENERAL PRINCIPLES OF INTERPRETATION

A. GENERAL ISSUES

'There is no part of the law of treaties which the text writer approaches with more trepidation than the question of interpretation' (McNair, 1961). The complex issue of treaty interpretation will be discussed in the light of the work of the ILC during its codification of the law of treaties, the principles of interpretation included in the Vienna Convention, and the jurisprudence of the international and national courts and tribunals, with special regard to the case law of the ICJ. The purpose of interpretation is to establish the meaning of the text that the parties intended it to have 'in relation to circumstances with reference to which the question of interpretation has arisen' (*Oppenheim's International Law*, 1992).

Basing himself on the jurisprudence of the World Court,[36] the ILC's Rapporteur, Fitzmaurice (Fitzmaurice, 1951) drew up the following comprehensive set of principles of interpretation:

Principle I: *actuality of textuality*—that treaties are to be interpreted as they stand, on the basis of their actual texts.

Principle II: *the natural and ordinary meaning*—that, subject to principle of contemporaneity (where applicable), particular words and phrases are to be given their normal, natural, and unstrained meaning in the context in which they occur. This principle can only be displaced by direct evidence that the terms used are to be understood in manner different to their natural and ordinary meaning, or if such an interpretation would lead to an unreasonable or absurd result.

Principle III: *integration*—that treaties are to be interpreted as a whole. This principle is of fundamental importance and means that individual parts, chapters or sections of a treaty are not to be interpreted out of their overall context.

The remaining principles take effect subject to the three principles outlined above. There are:

Principle IV: *effectiveness (ut magis valeat quam pereat)*—that treaties are to be interpreted with reference to their declared or apparent objects and purposes; and particular

---

[35] The ILC took the view that Article 36(1) provided sufficient basis for rights to be accorded to all States and Article 38 a sufficient basis for the establishment of treaty rights and obligations *erga omnes*. For criticism see Chinkin, 1993.

[36] *YBILC* (1966), vol II (part two), p 220.

provisions are to be interpreted so as to give them the fullest effect consistent with the normal sense of the words and with the text as a whole in such a way that a reason and meaning can be attributed to every part of the text.

Principle V: subsequent practice—that recourse may be had to subsequent practice of parties relating to the treaty.

Principle VI: contemporaneity—that the terms of a treaty must be interpreted in the light of linguistic usage current at the time when the treaty was concluded.

In general, there are three main schools of interpretation: the subjective (the 'intention' of parties) approach; the objective (the 'textual') approach, and the teleological (or 'object and purpose') approach. These schools of interpretation are not mutually exclusive (Sinclair, 1984) and the VCLT draws on all three. It is the reconciliation of the objective and the subjective approaches that is the most difficult, controversial and, some would say, impossible, task (Koskenniemi, 1989). For the ILC, the starting point was the text rather than the intention of the parties,[37] since it presumed that the text represented a real expression of what the parties did in fact intend. It also appears that the ICJ's preferred method of interpretation is reliance on the text of a treaty.

B. PRACTICE

VCLT Article 31(1) provides:

A treaty shall be interpreted in good faith in accordance with the ordinary meaning to be given to the terms of the treaty in their context and in the light of its object and purpose.

The ICJ has acknowledged this to constitute international customary law.[38] The underlying principle is that a treaty will be interpreted in good faith. The 'rule' (in the singular) of interpretation is a procedure consisting of three elements: the text, the context, and the object and purpose. The context of a treaty is set out in some detail in Article 31(2) and embraces any instrument of relevance to the conclusion of a treaty, as well as a treaty's preamble and annexes. There is no hierarchy between the various elements of Article 31; rather, they reflect a logical progression, 'nothing more' (Aust, 2007, p 234).

The Court has consistently adhered to the textual interpretation as being the most important. In the *Libya/Chad* case, the Court stated that:

Interpretation must be based above all upon the text of a treaty. As a supplementary measure recourse may be had to means of interpretation such as the preparatory work of the treaty.[39]

Article 31 reflects the principle that a treaty has to be interpreted in good faith that is the embodiment of the principle *pacta sunt servanda*. The determination of that ordinary meaning of term is undertaken in the context of a treaty and in the light of its object and

---

[37] Idem.

[38] *Territorial Dispute (Libyan Arab Jamahiririya/Chad), Judgment, ICJ Reports 1994*, p 6, para 41; *Oil Platforms (Islamic Republic of Iran v United States of America), Preliminary Objections, Judgment, ICJ Reports 1996*, p 803, para 23; *Kasikili/Sedudu Island (Botswana/Namibia), Judgment, ICJ Reports 1999*, p 1045, para 18.

[39] *Territorial Dispute*, idem. The use of supplementary material is considered below.

purpose. A good example is the Advisory Opinion *On the Interpretation of the Convention of 1919 Concerning Employment of Women During the Night*. Article 3 of that Convention ('women without distinction of age shall not be employed during the night in any public or private industrial undertaking, or in any branch thereof, other than an undertaking in which members of the same family are employed') left unclear its application to certain categories of women other than manual workers. The Court said:

The wording of Article 3, considered by itself, gives rise to no difficulty; it is general in its terms and free from ambiguity or obscurity. It prohibits the employment during the night in industrial establishments of women without distinction of age. Taken by itself, it necessarily applies to the categories of women contemplated by the question submitted to the Court. If, therefore, Article 3 ... is to be interpreted in such a way as not to apply to women holding posts of supervision and management and not ordinarily engaged in manual work, it is necessary to find some valid ground for interpreting the provision otherwise than in accordance with the natural sense of words. The terms of Article 3 ... are in no respect inconsistent either with the title, or with the Preamble, or with any other provision of the Convention. The title refers to 'employment of women during the night'. The Preamble speaks of 'women's employment during the night'. Article 1 gives a definition of 'an industrial undertaking.' Article 2 states what is meant by the term 'night.' These provisions, therefore, do not affect the scope of Article 3, which provides that 'women shall not be employed during the night either in any public or private industrial undertaking, or in any branch thereof.[40]

This might be compared with the views of the Judge Anzilloti who argued that 'If article 3, according to the natural meaning of its terms, were really perfectly clear, it would be hardly admissible to endeavour to find an interpretation other than that which flows from the natural meaning of its terms'.[41] He thought that only the intention of the parties should have been used to determine the correct interpretation.

Another problem concerns what is to count as subsequent practice for the purposes of interpretation, the use of which is sanctioned as forming a part of the context of the treaty by Article 31(3). In the *Kasikili/Sedudu Island* case the Court adhered to the ILC's view that the subsequent practice of parties to a treaty constitutes an element to be taken into account when determining its meaning,[42] but it took a narrow approach to what comprises subsequent practice and did not take account of unilateral acts of the previous authorities of Botswana on the grounds that these were for internal purposes only and unknown to the Namibian authorities. The Court also considered the relevance of an alleged 'subsequent agreement' between the previous authorities in Namibia and Botswana as only amounting to 'collaboration' over matters concerning the border and not having any effect on the interpretation of the treaty in question.[43] However, the Court was prepared to accord such material some role, noting them as facts which supported the interpretation of the 1890 Treaty in accordance with the ordinary meaning of its terms.[44] This is a usage not explicitly foreseen by the VCLT.

[40] *Interpretation of the Convention of 1919 Concerning Employment of Women During the Night, Advisory Opinion, 1932, PCIJ, Ser A/B, No 50*, p 365 at p 373.

[41] Dissenting Opinion of Anzilloti, ibid, p 383.

[42] *Kasikili/Sedudu Island (Botswana/Namibia), Judgment, ICJ Reports 1999*, p 1075, para 49.

[43] See generally ibid, paras 52–79.   [44] Ibid, para 80.

The issue of the importance of subsequent practice of States arose in connection with the interpretation of the term '*comercio*' (commerce) in the 2009 *Costa Rica* v *Nicaragua* case. The Court said:

This does not, however signify that, where a term's meaning is no longer the same as it was at the date of conclusion, no account should ever be taken of its meaning at the time when the treaty is to be interpreted for purposes of applying it.

On the one hand, the subsequent practice of the parties, within the meaning of Article 31(3)(*b*) of the Vienna Convention, can result in a departure from the original intent on the basis of a tacit agreement between the parties. On the other hand, there are situations in which the parties' intent upon conclusion of the treaty was, or may be presumed to have been, to give the terms used—or some of them—a meaning or content capable of evolving, not one fixed once and for all, so as to make allowance for, among other things, developments in international law. In such instances it is indeed in order to respect the parties' common intention at the time the treaty was concluded, not to depart from it, that account should be taken of the meaning acquired by the terms in question upon each occasion on which the treaty is to be applied.[45]

C. *TRAVAUX PRÉPARATOIRES*

VCLT Article 32 makes it clear that supplementary means of interpretation—including *travaux préparatiores*, preparatory work—may be used either to confirm the meaning of the treaty or as an aid to interpretation where, following the application of Article 31, the meaning is ambiguous or obscure or leads to a result which is manifestly absurd or unreasonable. Both the *Employment of Women During the Night* Advisory Opinion and the *Kasikili/Sedudu* case, considered above, illustrate the use of supplementary means to confirm an interpretation arrived at on the basis of Article 31. It is the use of preparatory work as a supplementary means of interpretation that gives rise to most difficulties, as is illustrated by the jurisdictional phases of the *Qatar* v *Bahrain* case.

The problem in this case centred on whether Qatar and Bahrain had ever entered into an agreement that would permit one of them to bring their case before the ICJ without the express approval of the other. The ICJ first decided that the fragmentary nature of the preparatory work meant that it could only be used with caution but noted that:

…the initial…draft expressly authorised a seisin by one or other of the parties and that that formulation was not accepted. But the text finally adopted did not provide that the seisin of the Court could only be brought about by the two parties acting in concert, whether jointly or separately. The Court is unable to see why abandonment of a form of words corresponding to the interpretation given by Qatar…should imply that they must be interpreted in accordance with Bahrain's thesis. As a result, it does not consider the *travaux préparatoires*, in the form in which they have been submitted to it—i.e., limited to the various drafts…—can provide it with conclusive supplementary elements for the interpretation of the text adopted; whatever may have been the motives of each of the parties, the Court can only confine itself

---

[45] *Dispute regarding Navigational and Related Rights between Costa Rica and Nicaragua*, Judgment of 13 July 2009, para 64.

to the actual terms of the Minutes as the expression of their common intention, and to the interpretation of them which it has already given.[46]

The Court concluded that a unilateral application was legitimate. Judge Schwebel criticized this, arguing that the Court's interpretation did not reflect the common intention of the parties. He argued that the Court's view that the preparatory work did not provide conclusive supplementary elements was unconvincing, observing that:

since deletion of the specification, 'either of the two parties may submit the matter to the International Court of Justice' in favour of the adopted provision 'the two parties may submit the matter…' surely manifested Bahrain's intention that 'either of the two parties' may *not* submit the matter, the Court's inability to see so plain a point suggests to me an unwillingness to do so.[47]

He considered that 'the requisite common, ascertainable intention of the parties to authorize unilateral reference to the Court is absent. Its absence is—or should be have been—determinative'[48] and concluded that:

What the text and context of the Doha Minutes leaves unclear is, however, crystal clear when those Minutes are analysed with the assistance of the *travaux préparatoires*… the preparatory work of itself is not ambiguous; on the contrary, a reasonable evaluation of it sustains only the position of Bahrain.[49]

D. THE OBJECT AND PURPOSE OF A TREATY

Article 31 of the Vienna Convention stipulates that a treaty should be interpreted 'in the light of its object and purpose' but this is a vague and ill-defined term, making it an unreliable tool for interpretation. Indeed, the ILC itself voiced certain doubts as to the usefulness of this criterion, particularly as regards reservations[50] (a topic considered below). A further problem concerns the relationship between the 'object and purpose' of a treaty and the principle of effectiveness which is considered in the following section.

E. THE PRINCIPLE OF EFFECTIVENESS

The principle of effectiveness, enshrined in the maxim *magis valeat quam pereat*, was acknowledged by the ILC, which observed that '[w]hen a treaty is open to two interpretations one of which does and the other does not enable the treaty to have appropriate effects, good faith and the objects and purposes of the treaty demand that the former interpretation should be adopted'.[51]

Although the principle of effectiveness can operate as an element within the 'object and purposes' test, it is not limited to this role and, as Thirlway notes, the ICJ has used it to

---

[46] *Maritime Delimitation and Territorial Questions between Qatar and Bahrain, Jurisdiction and Admissibility, Judgment, ICJ Reports 1995*, p 6, para 41.

[47] Ibid, Dissenting Opinion of Judge Schwebel, p 27 at p 36.

[48] Ibid, at p 37.

[49] Ibid, at pp 38–39. For similar analyses see the Dissenting Opinions of Judges Shahabuddeen, ibid, p 51 and Koroma, ibid, p 67.

[50] First Report on the Law of Treaties, *YBILC* (1962), vol II, pp 65–66.

[51] *YBILC* (1966), vol II (part two), p 219.

ascertain the intention underlying the treaty and as a starting point for a broader discussion. It also operates in the broader context of giving effect to the terms of a text.

The principle of effectiveness has two meanings. The first is that all provisions of the treaty or other instrument must be supposed to have been intended to have significance and to be necessary to express the intended meaning. Thus an interpretation that renders a text ineffective and meaningless is incorrect. The second operates as an aspect of the 'object and purposes' test, and it means that the instrument as a whole and each of its provisions must be taken to have been intended to achieve some end, and that an interpretation that would make the text ineffective to achieve that object is also incorrect. Thirlway observes that this latter approach is similar to the 'object and purpose' criterion, and 'has therefore, like this criterion, to be employed with discretion' (Thirlway, 1992).

F. THE DYNAMIC (EVOLUTIVE) INTERPRETATION OF TREATIES AND THE EUROPEAN COURT OF HUMAN RIGHTS (ECtHR)

One of the most contentious, disputed and discussed issues in treaty interpretation is so-called the dynamic (evolutive) interpretation of treaties, which in particular has been developed in the jurisprudence of the European Court of Human Rights. The basis for such as an interpretative method is predicated upon the principle that the treaty is a living instrument. There are several cases (such as 1975 *Tryer*, 1978 *Golder*, and 1979 *Marckx*) in which the Court decided to override the consent of the Parties in the name of 'the interests served by the protection of the human rights and fundamental freedoms guaranteed by the Convention', which 'extend beyond individual interests of the parties concerned'. This resulted in the establishment by the Parties to the Convention of the 'standards forming part of the public law of Europe'. First of all, the interpretative method of the ECtHR derives from the special legal nature of this Convention and the obligations, which doctrinal basis was enunciated in the 1965 *Austria v Italy*. The Court also stressed the 'essentially objective character' of the 'obligations undertaken by the High Contracting Parties'. The 'objective legal order' 'benefits from the 'collective enforcement'. However, such an interpretative method was a subject of much criticism (eg by Sinclair and Fitzmaurice) as overriding intention and the consent to be bound of the Parties to the Convention and introducing the element of uncertainty for the Parties due to much more extensive interpretation of the provisions of the Convention. There are other international judicial bodies, which to a certain degree adopted such a method, such as eg within the World Trade Organization (WTO).

G. PLURILINGUAL TREATIES

A further problem concerns the interpretation of treaties drawn up in more than one language. The ILC observed that:

...the majority of more formal treaties contain an express provision determining the status of the different language versions. If there is no such provision, it seems generally accepted that each of the versions in which the text of the treaty was 'drawn' up is to be considered authentic, and therefore authoritative for the purpose of interpretation. Few plurilingual treaties containing more than one or two articles are without some discrepancy between the texts ... the plurality of texts may be a serious additional source of ambiguity or obscurity in the terms of the treaty. On the other hand, when meaning of terms is ambiguous or obscure in one language, but it is clear and convincing as to the intentions of the parties in another, the plurilingual character of the treaty facilitates interpretations of the text the meaning of which is doubtful.[52]

In the *Mavrommatis Palestine Concession* case, the ICJ had to interpret the phrases 'public control' and 'contrôle public' in the French and English authentic languages texts of the Palestine Mandate. The Court said:

... Where two versions possessing equal authority exist one of which appears to have a wider bearing than the other, it is bound to adopt the more limited interpretation which can be made to harmonise with both versions and which, as far as it goes, is doubtless in accordance with the common intention of the parties.[53]

The matter is covered by VCLT Article 33, which reflects these general approaches to the problem.

In conclusion it may be said that there are numerous examples of the difficulties concerning the treaty interpretation. Such an example is the interpretation of Article 18 of the 1929 Geneva Convention on the Treatment of Prisoners of War, which provides that prisoners were to salute the officers of the captor country. In 1944, this clause was a subject of an interpretative dispute. In the period between 1939 and 1944, allied prisoners of war in Germany saluted their German captors in a classical manner, by touching their hands to the visors of their caps. Articles 18 of the Convention is silent as to whether the salute be returned, which is a universal military tradition: 'a salute unreturned is like the sound of one hand clapping' (Vagts, 1993, at p 490). After the failed attempt at Hitler's assassination (20 July 1944), regular German army troops were ordered to salute prisoners of war in a Nazi style, which resulted in the protest of the British. Eventually, due to the services of the International Committee of the Red Cross, the issue was resolved and prisoners permitted to the salute prevalent in their own army.[54]

VI. RESERVATIONS TO TREATIES

A. THE GENOCIDE CONVENTION CASE

Reservations to multilateral treaties are one of the most problematic issues in the law of treaties. According to VCLT Article 2(d) 'Reservation means a unilateral statement, however phrased or named, made by a State, when signing, ratifying, accepting, approving or

---

[52] *YBILC* (1966), vol II (part two), pp 224–225.

[53] *Mavrommatis Palestine Concessions, Judgment No 2, 1924, PCIJ, Ser A, No 2*, p 19.

[54] Example from Vagts (1993, at p 490) who comments, 'Thus we find interpretation of the Convention being presented and considered by persons far away from the original negotiating process. Most of them were not lawyers and they had no access to *travaux préparatoires* (which, as so often happens, would not have been helpful). There was no-decision-maker to force a solution upon the parties. Yet it is apparent that the parties in dispute, although coming from different and at the time violently hostile states, did share assumptions about what a "salute" was, and when and how one should be rendered. Indeed, it seems likely the professional and traditional German officers had more in common on this point with their British counterparts than with their Nazi colleagues'.

acceding to a treaty, where, it purports to exclude or to modify the legal effect of certain provisions of the treaty in their application to that State'.

In its role as a treaty depository, the League of Nations had only allowed reservations that were accepted by all contracting parties to a treaty, otherwise it treated both the reservations and the signatures or ratifications to which they were attached as null and void. The Pan-American Union adopted a different, more flexible approach, the gist of which was that a treaty was considered to be in force as between a reserving State and States that accepted the reservation but not in force as between a reserving State and States that did not accepted the reservation.

The modern approach is derived from the 1951 Advisory Opinion of the ICJ in the *Reservation to the Convention on Genocide* case, the principal features of which were that:

A State which has made and maintained a reservation which has been objected to by one or more of the parties to the Convention but not by others, can be regarded as being a party to the Convention if the reservation is compatible with the object and purpose of the Convention; otherwise, that State cannot be regarded as being a party to the Convention.[55]

The Court added that:

If a party to the Convention objects to a reservation which it considers to be incompatible with the object and purpose of the Convention, it can in fact consider that the reserving State is not a party to the Convention...if on the other hand, a party accepts the reservation as being compatible with the object and purpose of the Convention, it can in fact consider that the reserving State is a party to the Convention.[56]

It has to be said that although the Court's approach was subsequently reflected in the VCLT, the Court had made it clear that it was expressing its views on the operation of reservations only in relation to the Genocide Convention, noting that:

In such a Convention the contracting States do not have any interests of their own; they merely have, one and all, a common interest, namely the accomplishment of those high purposes which are the *raison d'être* of the convention. Consequently in a convention of this type one cannot speak of individual advantages or disadvantages to States, or of the maintenance of a perfect contractual balance between rights and duties.[57]

And that:

The object and purpose of the Genocide Convention imply that it was the intention of the General Assembly and of States which adopted it that as many States as possible should participate. The complete exclusion from the Convention of one or more States would not only restrict the scope of its application, but would detract from the authority of the moral and humanitarian principles which are its basis.[58]

It was for these reasons that the Court departed from the more rigid system operated by the League of Nations, which some judges had considered to reflect international

---

[55] *Reservations to the Convention on the Prevention and Punishment of the Crime of Genocide, Advisory Opinion, ICJ Reports 1951*, p 15 at p 29. See also *Armed Activities on the Territory of the Congo (New Application: 2002), (Democratic Republic of the Congo v Rwanda), Jurisdiction of the Court and Admissibility of the Application*; see also Joint Separate Opinion of Judges Higgins, Kooijmans, Elaraby, Owada, and Simma, *ICJ Reports 2006*.

[56] Idem.   [57] Ibid, p 23.   [58] Ibid, p 24.

customary law.[59] However, it was the General Assembly itself which requested that the UN Secretary-General adopt this new approach when acting in his capacity as depositary of multilateral treaties.[60]

The question of a reservation to Article IX of the Genocide Convention was a subject-matter of the *Democratic Republic of Congo v Rwanda* case. The DRC argued that the reservation made by Rwanda to Article IX of the Genocide Convention (ie to the submission of disputes arising from the interpretation of this Convention to the ICJ), was against the spirit of Article 53 of the 1969 VCLT as it prevented 'the . . . Court from fulfilling its noble mission of safeguarding peremptory norms'.[61] The Court, however, decided that 'the prohibition of genocide, cannot of itself provide a basis for jurisdiction of the Court to entertain that dispute. Under the Court's Statute that jurisdiction is always based on the consent of the parties'.[62] This prompted a powerful Joint Separate Opinion by Judges Higgins, Koojimans, Elaraby, Owada, and Simma who, in light of recent developments in relations to reservation in general and to human rights treaties, were of the view that '[i]t is thus not self-evident that a reservation to Article IX could not be regarded as incompatible with the object and purpose of the Convention and we believe that this is a matter that the Court should revisit for further consideration'. [63]

B. THE REGIME OF THE 1969 VIENNA CONVENTION

The Court's approach is reflected in VCLT Article 19 and so attempts to strike a balance between ensuring the integrity of a treaty whilst encouraging universal participation. Article 20(4) tips the balance towards widening participation by providing that even if a State party objects to a reservation attached to the signature or ratification of another State, the treaty will nevertheless enter into force and the reservation be effective between them unless 'a contrary intention is definitely expressed by an objecting State'. Moreover, the idea that the approach in the *Genocide Convention* case should be limited to those treaties where there was no particular advantage or disadvantage for an individual State was abandoned and Article 20(5) provides that, a reservation is considered to have been accepted by a State if it has not objected to it within 12 months of being notified of it, unless the reservation concerns the constituent instrument of an international organization, or the treaty in question provides otherwise.

Again following the *Genocide Convention* case, VCLT Article 19(c) provides that a State may not submit a reservation, which is 'incompatible with the object and purpose of the treaty'. This criterion is vague and difficult to grasp. However, reservations of general character are considered to be incompatible with the 'object and purpose' of a treaty.[64] Whilst reservations to treaty provisions which codify international customary law are

---

[59] See Joint Dissenting Opinion of Judges Guerrero, Sir Arnold McNair, Read, and Hsu Mo, ibid, p 31.

[60] GA Res 598 (VI), 12 January 1952.

[61] *Armed Activities on the Territory of the Congo (New Application: 2002) (Democratic Republic of Congo v Rwanda) Jurisdiction of the Court and Admissibility of the Application*, ICJ Reports 2006, p 6, para 56.

[62] Ibid, para 64.

[63] Ibid, Joint Separate Opinion of Judges Higgins, Koojimans, Elaraby, Owada and Simma, para 29.

[64] See, before the European Court of Human Rights, *Belilos v Switzerland*, Judgment of 29 April 1988, Ser A, No 132, para 55.

possible,[65] there is no doubt that reservations to provisions reflecting norms of *jus cogens* are not.

How are those reservations, which are incompatible with the object and purpose of a treaty, distinguished from those which are not? There are two schools of thought: the permissibility school and the opposability school. The permissibility school is based on a two-stage assessment procedure: first, the reservation must be objectively assessed for compatibility with the object and purpose of the treaty. If it is not compatible, acceptance by other States cannot validate it.[66] If, however, the reservation is compatible with the object and purpose of the treaty, the parties may decide whether to accept or object to the reservation on whatever other grounds they wish, such as for political reasons. The opposability school bases the validity of the reservation entirely upon whether it has been accepted by other parties and sees the compatibility test as merely a guiding principle for the parties to contemplate when considering whether to accept or object to the reservation.[67]

Some treaties attempt to deal with this question on a treaty-by-treaty basis. For example, the 1965 International Convention on Elimination of All Forms of Racial Discrimination, Article 20 uses a mathematical test, providing that a reservation is incompatible with the 'object and purpose' of the treaty if at least two-thirds of the contracting parties object to it.

The *Restrictions to the Death Penalty* Advisory Opinion concerned a reservation made by Guatemala to the prohibition of the infliction of capital punishment 'for political offenses or related common crimes' found in Article 4(4) of the 1969 American Convention on Human Rights, which is a non-derogable provision. Faced with the question whether a reservation was permissible in the light of the object and purpose of the Convention, the Inter-American Court of Human Rights said that:

...a reservation which was designed to enable a State to suspend any of the non-derogable fundamental rights must be deemed incompatible with the object and purpose of the Convention and, consequently, not permitted by it. The situation would be different if the reservation sought merely to restrict certain aspects of a non-derogable right without depriving the right as a whole of its basic purpose. Since the reservation...does not appear to be of a type that is designed to deny the right to life as such, the Court concludes that to that extent it can be considered, in principle, as being not incompatible with the object and purpose of the Convention.[68]

One unresolved question concerns the legal effect of having attached an impermissible reservation to a signature or ratification. There are two possible solutions: the first is that unless it is withdrawn, a State making an impermissible reservation will not be considered

---

[65] See, eg, *North Sea Continental Shelf, Judgment, ICJ Reports 1969*, p 3, paras 29 and 72 which seem to accept the possibility. But cf UN HRC General Comment No 24(52) on issues relating to Reservations made upon ratification or accession to the Covenant or Optional Protocols thereto, or in relation to declarations under Article 41 of the Covenant, 11 November 1994 (for text see (1995) 15 *HRLJ* 262) which argues that reservations to provisions in human rights treaties which represent customary international law are not permissible. This is considered further below.

[66] UN Doc A/CN.4/470 (30 May 1995) (First Report on Reservations), p 49, para 102. See also *YBILC* (1995), vol II (part two), p 101.

[67] Idem.

[68] *Restrictions to the Death Penalty*, Advisory Opinion, Inter-American Court of Human Rights, AO OC-3/83, 8 September 1983, para 61, (1984) 23 ILM 320 at p 341.

a party to a treaty. The second is that the impermissible reservation may be severed and the State be bound by the treaty in its entirety. Although, as will be seen below, there is some practice supporting the severability approach in the human rights sphere, it is difficult to see how the reservation can legitimately be severed if the consent to be bound is made expressly subject to such a reservation, albeit an impermissible one.

C. THE PROBLEM OF RESERVATIONS TO HUMAN RIGHTS TREATIES

The system of reservations found in the Vienna Convention was supposed to be comprehensive but it became clear in the 1980s that the system was difficult to apply particularly as regards the compatibility of reservations to human rights treaties with their 'object and purpose' and in 1993 the topic of the Law and Practice Relating to Reservations to Treaties was added to the ILC's agenda. Human rights treaties are not contractual in nature and do not create rights and obligations between States on the traditional basis of reciprocity; they establish relationships between States and individuals. Several undecided issues had to be solved: were all reservations made by States permissible? If not, who decides on their permissibility? What are the legal effects of accepting or rejecting a reservation or of having made an impermissible reservation? Broadly speaking there are two main approaches: one illustrated by the approach of the UN Human Rights Committee (the HRC) that stresses the inadequacies of the VCLT regime and the other that considers that regime absolutely satisfactory.

There are very few international bodies, other than the European Court of Human Rights and the Inter-American Court of Human Rights, that have an institutionalized procedure to decide upon the permissibility of reservations. In the *Belilos* case the European Court of Human Rights decided that a declaration made by Switzerland when ratifying the ECHR was in fact a reservation of a general character and therefore impermissible under the terms of ECHR Article 64. The Court severed the reservation and decided that Switzerland was bound by the Convention in its entirety.[69] Similarly, in the *Lozidou* case the European Court of Human Rights considered that Turkish reservations to the jurisdiction of the Commission and Court to consider applications relating to activities in Northern Cyprus were invalid and severable, meaning that such applications could be considered by the Strasbourg organs, notwithstanding the intention of Turkey to prevent this.[70]

The question of reservations to human rights treaties was considered by the UN HRC in a controversial General Comment.[71] The HRC is the body established under the 1966 ICCPR and has the task of overseeing compliance by States parties with their obligations under the Covenant. In its General Comment, the Committee took the view that the Vienna Convention provisions, which give a role to State objections in relation to reservations, are inappropriate in the context of human rights treaties, which do not comprise a web of inter-State reciprocal exchanges of mutual obligations but are concerned with endowing

---

[69] *Belilos* v *Switzerland*, Judgment of 29 April 1988, Ser A, No 132, paras 52–55, 60.

[70] *Lozidou* v *Turkey (Preliminary Objections)*, Judgment of 23 March 1995, Ser A, No 310, paras 15, 27, 89, 90, 95.

[71] See above, n 65.

individuals with rights. The HRC took the view that reservations offending peremptory norms would not be compatible with the object and purpose of the Covenant and raised the question of whether reservations to non-derogable provisions of the Covenant were compatible with its object and purpose. It expressed the view that reservations to the system of individual communications to the Committee established under the first Optional Protocol to the Covenant would not be compatible with its object and purpose. The HRC also took the view that it was the Committee itself, which should determine whether a specific reservation was compatible with the object and purpose of the Covenant.

The General Comment provoked strong reaction, including from the UK and US who considered VCLT Article 19(c) both adequate and applicable to reservations to human rights treaties and considered it for States parties to determine whether a reservation is compatible with the object and purpose of that treaty rather than the Committee. Moreover, the United States stressed that reservations formed an integral part of the consent to be bound and are not severable. The Committee, however, affirmed its General Comment in the *Rawle Kennedy* case, though it was questioned by a number of members who in a dissenting opinion observed that:

The normal assumption will be that the ratification or accession is not dependent on the acceptability of the reservation and the unacceptability of the reservation will not vitiate the reserving State's agreement to be party to the Covenant. However, this assumption cannot apply when it is abundantly clear that the reserving State's agreement to becoming party to the Covenant is *dependent* on the acceptability of the reservation. The same applies with reservations to the Optional Protocol.[72]

However, in his Second Report as ILC Special Rapporteur Alain Pellet, argued that the system of the Vienna Convention is adequate to address reservations in human rights treaties[73] and has recently noted that the practice of human rights bodies not in uniform and eg, the Committees of the Conventions on Elimination of Discrimination against Woman and International Convention on the Elimination of All Forms of Racial Discrimination attempt to persuade States to withdraw offending reservations rather than to decide on impermissibility.[74] It is, then, clear that there is a significant on-going controversy surrounding this question.

This was confirmed by the 2007 meeting between the ILC and human rights regarding reservations to human rights treaties. During this meeting the representatives of several human rights bodies as well as the members of the Commission presented their views on this issue. During the discussion several issues were raised, the most important being the invalidity of reservation to treaties. Although the special character of human rights treaties was noted, a view was expressed that there were other areas such as environmental protection which also had special characteristics. However, a distinctive feature of human rights treaties was the presence of the human rights bodies. It was observed, nevertheless,

---

[72] *Rawle Kennedy* v *Trinidad and Tobago*, Comm. No 845/1999, Decision, 2 November 1999, UN Doc A/55/40, vol II, Annex XI, A, Individual Dissenting Opinion of Ando, Bhagwati, Klein, and Kretzmer, para 16.

[73] For a summary see *YBILC* (1997), vol II, pp 53–54, 57.

[74] A Pellet, *Eighth Report on Reservations to Treaties*, ILC, Fifty-fifth Session (2003), A/CN.4/535, paras 17–27.

that the law of treaties generally and the regime set up under Article 19 of the VCLT were applicable and adequate to deal with reservations to human rights treaties but should be applied in 'an appropriate and suitably adopted manner'. The heart of the discussion was the issue of the delicate balance between the integrity and universality of treaties in respect of reservations. All participants were in agreement as to the competence of the human rights bodies to assess the validity of reservations. The most important issue was so-called 'reservation dialogue' between the reserving State and the human rights body. Such an approach was the best the understanding of the political situation underlying reservations and giving the opportunity for the human rights body to exercise pragmatism (which is a particular feature of these bodies' policy towards reservations) and discretion. However, the question of the severance of an offending reservation from consent to be bound by a treaty, remains an unresolved problem in cases of the impossibility of ascertaining intention of the States parties in this respect. On one hand, there were views of the human rights bodies which supported the right of such bodies to severe reservations; on the other hand, some participants adhered to the view that the principle of sovereignty must prevail. [75]

D. INTERPRETATIVE DECLARATIONS

Interpretative declarations are not addressed by the VCLT. They are appended to treaties by governments at the time of signature, ratification, or acceptance and are explanatory in character, setting out how a State understands its treaty obligation when expressing its consent to be bound. However, such declarations must be subject to close scrutiny. If they change the scope of the obligation, they cease to be declarations and become reservations. The legal effect of interpretative declarations depends upon whether they aim to offer an interpretation of the treaty that may subsequently be proved incorrect (a 'mere interpretative declaration') or whether they offer an interpretation that is to be accepted by others (a 'qualified interpretative declaration'). In practice, distinguishing between reservations and forms of interpretative declarations can be a very daunting task.

According to the ILC, this task should be undertaken in good faith in accordance with the ordinary meaning to be given to its terms, in light of the treaty to which it refers. Due regard should be given to the intention of the State or the international organization concerned at the time the statement was formulated.

VII. PROBLEMS CONCERNING THE GROUNDS FOR TERMINATION

This section will consider some specific issues concerning the external grounds for terminating or suspending a treaty, these being material breach, supervening impossibility of performance, and fundamental change of circumstances.

---

[75] A Pellet, *Fourteenth Report on Reservation to Treaties*, ILC, Sixty-first Session (2009), A/CN.4/6/14, 1–37, pp 27–34.

A. MATERIAL BREACH

VCLT Article 60 regulates the consequences of a breach of a treaty obligation deriving from the law of treaties, rather than from the law of State responsibility. The guiding principle is that of reciprocity. The ILC took a cautious approach to material breach, considering that a breach of a treaty, however serious, did not *ipso facto* put an end to a treaty but that within certain limits and subject to certain safeguards the right of a party to invoke the breach of a treaty as a ground for terminating it or suspending its operation must be recognized and Article 60 takes the same approach.

Taking a strict approach to the effect of a material breach aims at striking a balance between the need to uphold the stability of treaties and the need to ensure reasonable protection for the innocent victim of a breach, though it may appear that the stability of treaties is the first priority. It is certainly true that the ICJ takes a restrictive approach to the application of Article 60. For example, in the *Gabčíkovo-Nagymaros* case it responding to Hungary's claim that Slovakia's actions in relation to other treaties had a bearing upon the assessment of Hungary's own actions by saying that 'It is only material breach of the treaty itself, by a State party to that treaty, which entitles the other party to rely on it as a ground for terminating the treaty'.[76] The Court explained that, whilst the violation of any other treaty or rules of general international law might justify an injured State taking other measures, such as countermeasures, it did not constitute a ground for termination of the treaty under the law of treaties.

This case is also illustrative of what comprises a material breach. Hungary relied on the construction of a bypass canal in pursuance of a plan known as 'Variant C' by Czechoslovakia, and which was unauthorized by the original 1977 Treaty between the parties, as the basis for invoking material breach of that treaty. Czechoslovakia claimed that its plans were justified as a legitimate response to prior breaches of the treaty by Hungary. The Court found that Czechoslovakia had indeed violated the 1977 Treaty when it diverted the waters of the Danube into the bypass canal in October 1992 but that the construction of the works prior to this had not been unlawful. Thus the notification by Hungary in May 1992 that it was terminating the 1977 Treaty for material breach was premature, as no breach had yet occurred. Moreover, the Court took the view that by attempting to terminate the 1977 Treaty by means of a declaration issued on 6 May 1992 with effect as of some 19 days later on 25 May 1992, Hungary had not acted in accordance with the principle of good faith and therefore had by its own conduct prejudiced its right to terminate the 1977 Treaty. The Court stated that:

This would still have been the case even if Czechoslovakia, by the time of the purported termination, had violated a provision essential to the accomplishment of the object or purpose of the Treaty.[77]

The relationship between the material breach of a treaty and the law of State responsibility, and particularly with countermeasures, is extremely problematic. Although not resolved by the ILC in its work on the law of treaties it appears that its intention was that the two regimes should co-exist and the ILC's Commentary to its Articles on State Responsibility

---

[76] *Gabčíkovo-Nagymaros Project (Hungary/Slovakia), Judgment, ICJ Reports 1997*, p 7, para 106.
[77] Ibid, para 110.

reflect this, indicating that State responsibility does not deal with the 'consequences of breach for the continual or binding effect of the primary rule (eg, the right of an injured State to terminate or suspend a treaty for material breach, as reflected in Article 60 of the Vienna Convention on the Law of Treaties)'. The Special Rapporteur, James Crawford, explained that:

There is thus a clear distinction between action taken within the framework of the law of treaties (as codified in the Vienna Convention) and conduct raising questions of State responsibility (which are excluded from the Vienna Convention). The law of treaties is concerned essentially with the content of primary rules and with the validity of attempts to alter them; the law of State responsibility takes as given the existence of primary rules (whether based on a treaty or otherwise) and is concerned with the question whether the conduct inconsistent with those rules can be excused and, if not, what consequences of such conduct are. Thus it is coherent to apply the Vienna Convention rules as to the materiality of breach and the severability of provisions of a treaty in dealing with issues of suspension, and the rules proposed in the Draft articles as to proportionality etc, in dealing with countermeasures.[78]

B. SUPERVENING IMPOSSIBILITY OF PERFORMANCE

This ground for termination is well established and uncontested. VCLT Article 61 limits this ground to the 'permanent disappearance or destruction of an object indispensable for the execution of a treaty' and it cannot be invoked by a party that was itself instrumental in causing these circumstances to come about by the breach of its treaty obligations. Once again, the ICJ has taken a strict approach. In the *Gabčíkovo-Nagymaros* case Hungary argued that the essential object of the 1977 Treaty was a joint economic investment, which was inconsistent with environmental considerations and had ceased to exist, rendering the 1977 Treaty impossible to perform. The Court observed that if the joint exploitation of the investment was no longer possible, this was because of Hungary's failure to perform most of the works for which it was responsible under the 1977 Treaty and, as indicated above, impossibility of performance cannot be invoked by a party as a ground for terminating a treaty when it is the result of that party's own failure to perform its treaty obligations.

C. FUNDAMENTAL CHANGE OF CIRCUMSTANCES

Fundamental change of circumstances as a ground for the termination of a treaty is controversial. The principle of stability of contractual obligations and the conviction that 'it is a function of the law to enforce contracts or treaties even if they become burdensome for the party bound by them' militates against it (*Oppenheim's International Law*, 1992) but this needs to be balanced against the view that 'One could not insist upon petrifying a state of affairs which had become anachronistic because it is based on a treaty which either does not contain any specific clause as to its possible termination or which even proclaimed itself to be concluded for all times to come' (Nahlik, 1971). VCLT Article 62 takes a particularly cautious approach. It accepts that termination on these grounds is possible, but it is of limited scope. It may not be invoked in relation to a treaty, which establishes

---

[78] Third Report on State Responsibility, A/CN.4507/Add.3.

a boundary; and, as with Article 61, a State may not invoke Article 62 if the change was caused by a breach of its own international obligations, either under the treaty in question or any other international agreement.

The ICJ has taken a very cautious approach to this principle. In the *Fisheries Jurisdiction* case it said:

International law admits that a fundamental change of circumstances which determined the parties to accept a treaty, if it has resulted in a radical transformation of the extent of obligation imposed by it, may, under certain conditions, afford the party affected a ground for invoking the termination or suspension of a treaty. This principle, and the conditions and exceptions to which it is subject, have been embodied in Article 62 of the Vienna Convention on the Law of Treaties, which may in many respects be considered as a codification of existing customary law on the subject of termination of a treaty relationship on account of changed circumstances.[79]

The *Gabčíkovo-Nagymaros* case again illustrates the Court's approach. Hungary identified several 'substantive elements' that had been present when the 1977 Treaty had been concluded but which it claimed had changed fundamentally when it issued its notice of termination in May 1992, these being: the whole notion of socialist economic integration which underpinned the 1977 Treaty; the replacement of a joint and unified operational system with separate unilateral schemes; the emergence of market economies in both States; the Czechoslovakian approach that had turned a framework treaty into an immutable norm; and, finally, the transformation of a treaty inconsistent with environmental protection into a prescription for environmental disaster.[80]

The Court concluded that whilst the political situation was relevant to the conclusion of the 1977 Treaty, its object and purpose—the joint investment programme for the production of energy, the control of floods, and the improvement of navigation on the River Danube—were not so closely linked to political conditions that the political changes in central Europe had radically altered the extent of obligations still to be performed.[81] The Court drew the same conclusion regarding the changes in economic systems concluding that even if by 1992 the projected profitability of the scheme had declined, it had not done so to an extent that would transform the nature of the parties' obligations. Likewise, developments in environmental knowledge and environmental law were not completely unforeseen. Having analysed the parties' arguments the Court concluded that 'the changed circumstances advanced by Hungary are, in the Court's view, not of such nature, either individually or collectively, that their effect would radically transform the extent of the obligation still to be performed in order to accomplish the Project'.[82] The Court therefore interpreted VCLT Article 62 strictly, believing that a 'fundamental change of circumstances must have been unforeseen; the existence of the circumstances at the time of the Treaty's conclusion must have constituted an essential basis of consent of the parties to be bound by the Treaty,' believing that 'the stability of treaty relations requires that the plea of fundamental change of circumstances be applied only in exceptional cases'.[83]

---

[79] *Fisheries Jurisdiction (United Kingdom v Iceland), Jurisdiction of the Court, Judgment, ICJ Reports 1973*, p 3, para 36.

[80] *Gabčíkovo-Nagymaros Project (Hungary/Slovakia), Judgment, ICJ Reports 1997*, p 7, para 95.

[81] Idem.   [82] Ibid, para 104.   [83] Ibid.

VIII. CONCLUSION

This chapter has presented the main issues of treaty law found in the 1969 Vienna Convention on the Law of Treaties. It has attempted to illustrate the application and interpretation of the Convention in practice through the case law, in particular that of the International Court of Justice. Although rightly considered as one of the greatest accomplishments of the ILC, the Vienna Convention does not cover all possible areas and issues, particularly the question of reservation to human rights treaties and the relationship between State responsibility and material breach. The law of treaties is a classical yet constantly developing branch of international law. Treaties are the main tool of relations between States and therefore it is only to be expected that the rules that govern their application are not static but constantly evolve and reflect the development of other branches of international law.

REFERENCES

Aust, A (2007), *Modern Treaty Law and Practice*, 2nd edn (Cambridge: Cambridge University Press).

Boyle, A (2000), 'Some Reflections on the Relationship of Treaties and Soft Law', in Gowlland-Debbas, V (ed), *Multilateral Treaty Making* (The Hague: Martinus Nijhoff), p 25.

Chinkin, C (1993), *Third Parties in International Law* (Oxford: Oxford University Press).

Fitzmaurice, Sir G (1951), 'Treaty Interpretation and Certain Other Treaty Points, 1947–1951', 22 *BYIL* 1.

Koskenniemi, M (1989), *From Apology to Utopia; The Structure of International Legal Argument*, 2005 reissue (Cambridge: Cambridge University Press).

McNair, AD (1961), *The Law of Treaties*, 2nd edn (Oxford: Clarendon Press).

Nahlik, SE (1971), 'The Grounds of Invalidity of and Termination of Treaties', 65 *AJIL* 747.

Oppenheim, L (1992), Jennings, Sir R and Watts, Sir A (eds), *Oppenheim's International Law*, 9th edn (Harlow: Longman) (2008 reprint, Oxford: Oxford University Press).

Shearer, IA (1994), *Starke's International Law*, 11th edn (London: Butterworths).

Sinclair, Sir I (1984), *The Vienna Convention on the Law of Treaties*, 2nd edn (Oxford: Oxford University Press).

Thirlway, H (1992), 'The Law and Procedure of the International Court of Justice, 1960–1989', Part Three, 63 *BYIL* 1.

Vagts, D (1993), 'Treaty interpretation and the New American Ways of Law Reading', 4 *EJIL* 472.

Weil, P (1993), 'Towards Relative Normativity in International Law', 77 *AJIL* 413.

FURTHER READING

Aust, A (2007), *Modern Treaty Law and Practice*, 2nd edn (Cambridge: Cambridge University Press). This book is a comprehensive study of the modern law of treaties written from the point of view of an experienced practitioner.

Fitzmaurice, M and Elias, O (2005), *Contemporary Issues in the Law of Treaties* (Utrecht: Eleven International Publishing). This is a collection of essays dealing with some pertinent and often unresolved issues of the law of treaties.

Gardiner, R (2008), *Treaty Interpretation* (Oxford: The Oxford International Law Library). This book is an in-depth study of treaty interpretation, based on meticulous analysis of Article 31 of the 1969 Vienna Convention on the Law of Treaties, including the historical development of treaty interpretation; the work of the International Law Commission; relevant case law and the views of doctrine.

Klabbers, J (1996), *The Concept of Treaty in International Law* (The Hague: Kluwer Law International). This book is a highly original study of the law of treaties, often controversial but very thought-provoking. It includes an overview of relevant jurisprudence of the International Court of Justice.

Lestsas, G (2007), *A Theory Interpretation of the European Convention on Human Rights* (Oxford: Oxford University Press).

McNair, AD (1961), *The Law of Treaties*, 2nd edn (Oxford: Clarendon Press). The classical treatise on the law of treaties.

Reuter, P (1995), *Introduction to the Law of Treaties* (Moco, J and Haggenmacher, P (trans.)) (London: Kegan Paul International). This book presents an in-depth study of the 1986 Convention on the Law of Treaties between States and International Organizations or Between International Organizations.

Sinclair, Sir I (1984), The Vienna Convention on the Law of Treaties, 2nd edn (Manchester: Manchester University Press). This is a classical book on the 1969 Vienna Convention on the Law of Treaties that also includes practice of States and the overview of the ILC's work on the codification of the Convention.

Villiger, M (1997), *Customary Law and Treaties, A Manual on the Theory and Practice of the Interrelation of Sources*, 2nd edn (Zurich: Schulthess Polygraphisher Verlag and The Hague: Kluwer Law International). This book is a systematic and erudite study on written and unwritten international law.

Ziemele, I (ed) (2004), *Reservations to Human Rights Treaties and the Vienna Convention Regime, Conflict, Harmony or Reconciliation* (The Hague: Martinus Nijhoff). This book gives a comprehensive overview of the practice of human rights bodies in relation to reservations, as well a theoretical background.

PART III

THE SUBJECTS OF THE INTERNATIONAL LEGAL ORDER

8

STATEHOOD, SELF-DETERMINATION, AND RECOGNITION

Matthew Craven

SUMMARY

The proposition that international law is largely concerned with States—what they do and how they behave in relation to one another—has long been one of the most axiomatic features of international legal thought. Yet the actual place occupied by the State in such thought and practice has always been equally elusive. In one direction, the existence of a society of independent States appears to be a necessary presupposition for the discipline— something that has to precede the identification of those rules or principles that might be regarded as forming the substance of international law. In another direction, however, statehood is also something that appears to be produced through international law follow- ing from a need to determine which political communities can rightfully claim to enjoy the prerogatives of sovereignty. Whereas in the past, this relationship between law and sover- eignty could be mediated through an imperial 'standard of civilization' that differentiated between 'new' and 'old' States, or European and non-European forms of sovereignty, by the middle of the twentieth century such forms of discrimination were no longer tenable. The contradictions implicit in the idea of statehood (that it be both antecedent and a product of international law) were then to come to the fore demarcating debates as to the implications of self-determination (whether determining or determined) and of recognition (whether declaratory or constitutive). Intertwined within in such debates are an array of political commitments—to democracy and self-government, human rights, and the combating of violence—all of which relate thoroughly ambiguously to the role assigned to States within international legal thought in the sense that they remain both the source of the problem and the mode of emancipation.

I. INTRODUCTION

It is a remarkable feature of our contemporary understanding of the world that if forced to describe it, we would normally do so in one of two ways. One would be in terms of its physical and biological geography (a description of continents, oceans, climate, and plant or animal lifeforms); the other in terms of its political geography, as being a world divided systematically and uniformly by reference to the territorial parameters of States (as may be represented cartographically by the coloured segments within an atlas). That the second form of representation appears significant, is to mark the extraordinary power that the idea of the State has come to play in the formation of our social, political, economic and cultural world view. Not only is it now an apparently universal institution, but it is one that assumes for itself the same kind of permanence and solidity in descriptions of our social and political environment that one would normally associate with geological formations in the physical world.

Of course, the world has not always existed as we know it today, and States (if we like to trace their origins to early forms of political society) have changed much over time (Tilly, 1992; Morris, 1998, chapter 2). At one stage political authority around the globe could largely be described in terms of its relative intensity: those exercising the prerogatives of rule generally enjoying high levels of loyalty and allegiance amongst the community in more densely populated urban sites, shading off in the more remote frontier zones that characterized the outer edges of the realm. In place of this disparate and localized form of social organization has emerged a global order framed in terms of a European model of the nation state marked by the possession of determinate and increasingly non-porous boundaries, centralized bureaucratic structures, categorical modes of membership, and a singular uniform system of law (Weber, 1978; Giddens, 1985). The purchase of this institution upon the political imagination has been such as to ensure not only that the daily routine of 'politics' remains firmly embedded within its frame (institutionalized, for example, in parliamentary debates, elections and campaigns for office), but that even the movements of resistance adopt it as their primary mode of emancipation. The secessionist movements active in places as diverse as Bougainville, Chechnya, Nagorno-Karabakh, Southern Sudan, Somaliland, or West Irian almost invariably seek, as their objective, the establishment of an independent State. In some ways, it is hard to think what the alternative might be.

As much as movements for independence seem, in some respects, to affirm the singularity of the state as the primary mode of political organization, they also undeniably lay down a challenge before it. Not only do they place in question the authority of the State against which they assert their independence, they also put in question the capacity of the broader international order to protect or guarantee the integrity of those States which, in some respects, constitute its rationale. Not all such initiatives turn out in the same way in practice of course. In some, claims to independence are given the definitive seal of Statehood by membership in the United Nations (eg Eritrea 1993), in others effective self-government continues yet the claim to independent statehood goes decisively unrecognized (eg Somaliland 1996–). Some, furthermore, survive in an apparent twilight zone of partial recognition (eg Kosovo 2009–, Palestine 1988–). At such moments, international lawyers are often asked for advice: is it right or proper for other States to recognize such claims? What are the implications for doing so, or indeed for refusing such recognition? How far does institutional membership go to determine the outcome in such cases? What consideration should be given to the democratic credentials of the new State or the role played by human rights? International lawyers seem to have some kind of expertise here, and one that is sought not only by those concerned with the distributional consequences of any political change, but by the public at large.

The answers, for the most part, are often hesitant: 'it depends' is usually a stock phrase. It 'depends' because as much as a community might be able to ground its claims to independence in a sense of ethnic, cultural, or historic sense of self-identity, or in terms of its abuse at the hands of an 'alien' authoritarian elite, there are still broader matters of stability or security to be addressed. It depends because as much as one or two States may have seen fit to recognize the new entity, this is not usually sufficient (albeit the case that it is hard to say quite what is sufficient). It depends because whilst we used to be quite clear about the conditions under which new States might come into being, things seem to be changing and practice coalescing around new potential rules or principles. It depends because rule and practice rarely neatly align and because the law and the politics of recognition appear difficult to separate. These, and many other common concerns, are such as to make definitive pronouncement a seemingly precarious business. Yet the fact remains that the creation or disappearance of States is not something about which international lawyers are, or indeed can be, entirely neutral. There are always legal consequences attendant to forms of political change that involve the alteration of borders (see generally Craven, 2007). More than this, however, international lawyers also have an important linguistic and conceptual toolbox (which includes notions of sovereignty, territory, recognition, personality, and self-determination) that provides a language for both projecting and evaluating claims made in respect of those processes of political and social change.

In some respects, however, the place assumed by the 'State' in international law is almost too self-evident. If international law is defined, as it has traditionally, as being the law that applies as between sovereign States, then some engagement with States, what they are, how they come into being, and how they change has to be part of the disciplinary orientation. Yet, the central position assumed by States in legal doctrine is also problematic. In the introduction to his *Principles of International Law* of 1895 Lawrence suggested that '[t]he meagre proposition that the Subjects of International Law are Sovereign States is often put forward as if it contained all the information that need be given about the matter.' (Lawrence, 1895, p 55) Of course, it wasn't all the information needed in his view, and he then proceeded to set out why that was the case, and why one needed to differentiate, for example, between different kinds of States and different forms of sovereignty. But at the same time he was aware that the figure of the sovereign State occupied such a central position within the discipline of international law that its presence or absence was not something that could be adequately conceptualized internally within that same framework. Since in absence of sovereign States there was no possibility of international law, their existence or demise could only be presupposed, or appreciated at some distance from the everyday discourse of an otherwise relational conception of law. One needed, in other words, to either postulate the existence of an international society prior to the legal relations that are generated within it (in which case regulation only reflects back on the pre-existent 'fact' of a State's existence) or to conceive of the place occupied by States as being part of a much broader and diverse cosmopolitan universe that somehow attributes legal competences to designated actors (which would include States or governments but would not necessarily be confined to them). In the event, Lawrence wanted to have it both ways—States were, for him, a presupposition in the sense that they existed as factual orders of power quite independently of their legal relations, but whose emergence and entry into the international family of nations could also be regulated.

For all the difficulties that Lawrence and other international lawyers had in grasping or conceptualizing the place of the sovereign State within their discipline, they were in no doubt as to its importance, or of the central role assumed by it in international relations. A hundred years later, however, talk of both the exclusivity of States as subjects of international law and of States as primary actors in international relations is largely regarded as an antiquated, if not wholly, misleading proposition. Within international law itself, the recognition given to the rights and responsibilities of international organizations, to the rights and duties of individuals and a variety of different groups or communities of one form or another (minorities, indigenous peoples, corporations), has made the language of exclusive 'subjects' or 'objects' of international law largely redundant. Non-State actors (whether non-governmental organizations or international organizations) are playing an increasingly important role in treaty making, and the figure of the 'international community' is repeatedly invoked (in the context, for example, of the elaboration of *erga omnes* obligations) as an entity having some, albeit still rather vague, legal status.[1] Increasingly frequently, furthermore, the notion of 'sovereignty' has become seen as either redundant or as a dangerous fiction, and 'Statism' a derogatory label attached to any approach to international law that is seen to prioritize what States do or say at the expense of individuals and communities over whom they hold authority (see Marks, 2006).

Several considerations have informed this change in disciplinary orientation—some of which may be attributed to the somewhat elusive phenomenon of 'globalization', some to the dynamics of the post-cold war world. In an article written sometime before the attack on the World Trade Center (which, of course, spawned several new reflections upon the role of non-State actors of one kind or another), Oscar Schachter (1998) was to reflect upon the 'decline of the Nation state' which he observed as being evidenced in four related developments:

(i)   The growth, and increased mobility, of capital and technology (enhanced by global communications networks), coupled with a decreasing capacity to regulate foreign direct investment or protect national producers through tariff or non-tariff barriers, has undermined the centrality of the State in the organization of the economy. The age of capital-exporting imperialism or defensive mercantilism is over, and 'the superiority of markets over state control is almost universally accepted' (Schachter, 1998, p 10).

(ii) The phenomenal growth of organized non-governmental movements operating across national borders in fields such as human rights, the environment and disarmament (but also including scientific and technical bodies) have become a force for mobilization and political change 'in areas long seen as domestic' and have fostered 'new social identities that cross national lines' (Schachter, 1998, p 13).

---

[1] See eg ILC Articles on the Responsibility of States for Internationally Wrongful Acts (2001), Articles 33, 42, 48.

The enhanced role of this nascent international 'civil society' has also been paralleled in the emergence of a new transnational 'uncivil society' of drug traffickers, arms traders, terrorists, and money launderers whose power has vastly increased as a consequence of the emergence of new communication networks and the deregulation of financial markets. All of these activities underscore 'the weakness of nation-states and of the international legal system' (Schachter, 1998, p 15).

(iii) The (re)emergence of a range of sub-state 'identities' that have increasingly challenged the central authority of the juridical State. On one side, the old anti-colonial policy of self-determination has led to the emergence of a much broader array of secessionist movements demanding forms of autonomy or self-government the claims of which are located in a sense of historical, cultural, linguistic, or religious difference (Schachter, 1998, p 16). On the other side, as Franck argued, globalization has led to the emergence of new modes of loyalty and community that are neither 'genetic nor territorial', but rather focused upon a range of increasingly transnational agendas such as human rights, the environment, or feminism (Franck, 1996). This 'modern type of cosmopolitanism', in Schachter's view can again be seen to be an indication of the 'decline in the authority of the State' (Schachter, 1998, p 18).

(iv) Finally, and for Schachter the 'most dramatic' example, of the decline in State authority, is identified with the emergence of a new phenomenon of 'failed States' (examples of which he cites as being Liberia, Somalia, and Afghanistan) in which government and civil order have virtually disappeared, and in which the survival of the State depends upon concerted international action. Thus in Cambodia a costly and elaborate 'rescue effort' was put in place involving UN oversight of a process of internal reconstruction that included elections, the creation of a reconciliation process and the establishment of constitutional government. For a period of two years, although Cambodia formally remained a State for international purposes, its government 'did not have full freedom to direct the internal affairs of the country' (Schachter, 1998, p 18).

All of these, in Schachter's view, posed challenges to a global order of States regulated by rules of international law, but were not in themselves sufficient to warrant fundamentally changing either our ideas about international society or of the way in which international law itself was conceptualized. Despite the trends, he concludes that 'it is most unlikely that the state will disappear in the foreseeable future'. Not only has the State provided the structures of authority needed to cope with the 'incessant claims of competing societal groups', it still promises dignity and protection for the individual with access to common institutions and the equal protection of the law (Schachter, 1998, p 22). For Schachter, then, the key question was not so much whether the State as such would survive, but whether international law could adjust to such phenomena and respond to the changing demands of the environment in which it operated.

Whether or not one accepts Schachter's confidence in this respect, it is evident that there are broadly two themes that are interwoven here: one is a sociological reflection on the changing character of international society and the declining power or authority of the nation state, which has given rise to the elaboration of new schemes of legal responsibility and control for purposes of buttressing or replacing those exercised by States themselves.[2] The other is an ethical variant which regards the tradition of state 'sovereignty' to be an archaic impediment to the pursuit of humanitarian or other cosmopolitan agendas (human rights, environmental protection, etc) and which has recommended various interventionist policies of a unilateral or multilateral character. In some ways, of course, these two forms of reflection work against each other: the first believing States to be increasingly marginalized by social forces that escape their regulative or coercive capabilities; the second believing that States retain an authority that needs to be dismantled before emancipatory agendas may be put in place. Where they meet, however, is in an alarming vision of global order in which the State as political agent instructed with the task of 'mediating' between the individual and the general interest (as Hegel would put it) has neither the ability nor competence to resist a global civil society that claims both power and justice on its own side.[3]

II. HISTORY

At the beginning of the Fourth Edition of his influential *Treatise on International Law* prepared for publication in 1895 shortly before his death, Hall was to start (much as he had in his earlier editions) with a succinct definition:

International law consists in certain rules of conduct which modern civilised states regard as being binding on them in their relations with one another with a force comparable in nature and degree to that binding the conscientious person to obey the laws of his country, and which they also regard as being enforceable by appropriate means in case of infringement. (Hall, 1895, p 1)

This statement was remarkable in several respects. To begin with, there is the question of tone: this is not the beginning of an enquiry, or a speculation that has to be situated in some historical context. There is no attempt to locate his subject in contemporary debate or practice. This is international law written as science, beginning (as indeed seemed necessary) with a definition. International law it is not merely a language, or a way of describing certain activities or practices. It is already a thing with definite content and there to be described. The description itself, of course, is significant. The content of international law is to be found, as far as Hall is concerned, in rules of conduct which States regard as binding upon them. This demands no access to a world of natural law (whether religious or rational), or engagement with the complex of social and political relations that constitute the authority of each of the States involved. Still less is there any requirement to speak about that complex idea—sovereignty—which John Austin had placed at the heart of his description of law. International law was simply to be located in an empirical practice of consent and obligation. At the heart of it, of course, was the 'modern civilised State' whose actions were both the object and measure of this science. One needed a community of

---

[2] See, for example, proposals relating to the development of 'Global Administrative Law' (Kingsbury, Krisch, and Stewart, 2005) or other initiatives directed towards the development of the accountability of non-State actors more generally (Clapham, 2006).

[3] See Hardt and Negri, 2000, p 15: 'Empire is formed not on the basis of force itself but on the basis of the capacity to present force as being in the service of right and peace'.

civilized States for there to be rules of conduct. One needed also for those States to have a will, or consciousness, as to the binding force of their commitments (*opinio iuris*). One needed, furthermore, for those States to understand that they had committed themselves to a system of law warranting the enforcement 'by appropriate means'. The figure of the State thus stood at centre stage around which an elaborate architecture of legal rules was to be described and generated.

At the time at which Hall was writing, nearly all treatises on international law began in similar manner and would be followed by one or more chapters containing an extemporized discussion of the State as the primary subject of international law (See Westlake, 1904; Twiss, 1884; Lawrence, 1895; Wheaton, 1866; Phillimore, 1871). Typically this section or chapter would seek to define what was meant by a State for purposes of international law, determine who or what would count for such purposes, and address matters of classification (distinguishing perhaps between 'sovereign' or 'semi sovereign' States, and identifying vassals, protectorates, and unions as particular classes) and passing comment on difficulties of nomenclature (whether everything called a State could be treated as a State and whether States differed from 'nations'). In the process there would usually also be some associated reflections upon the notion of 'sovereignty' and what that might mean in the context of international relations and of the putative role that 'recognition' might play.

This format was not merely a haphazard aesthetic choice, but reflected in large measure a desire to lay down in an ordered manner the principle axioms or presuppositions of the discipline that might thereafter be deployed in a variety of different particular contexts. Once, in other words, one had established who the subjects of law were, and the framework for determining the extent and scope of their rights and obligations (ie sources), one could go on to apply those principles to a range of more concrete matters such as the law of the sea, the protection of nationals abroad or belligerent relations. The fact that this discussion of States and their character was always the starting point—almost a professional *a priori* as Koskenniemi has put it—was significant in more ways than one. In one respect, it bespoke of a changing attitude towards the sources of international law reflecting the determination to identify international law so far as possible with the specific determinants of state practice and consent rather than with the inherited tradition of natural rights. In another respect however it also spoke of the central position that had come to be assumed by 'the State' understood as an idea quite distinct from many of its earlier designations—whether that be the people, the nation, civil society, the sovereign, the monarch, or the multitude. Whilst Hall, like many others, continued to use Bentham's terminology in describing his subject matter (international law), he no longer attributed any significance to the 'nation' as such.

As much as Hall and others were to mark themselves out from their intellectual predecessors, they nevertheless uniformly saw themselves as working in a well-established tradition. This was a tradition understood to have its roots in the Roman Law notion of the *jus gentium* as subsequently received and modified through the work of those such as Suarez, Ayala, Gentili, Grotius, Bynkershoek, Pufendorf, Wolff, and de Vattel. In many respects what seemed to tie these classic works together as a tradition was not simply their espousal of the existence of a law that transcended the sovereign, but in the fact that the adumbrated *jus gentium* (or, in some works, the *jus inter gentes*) necessarily presupposed the existence of a plurality of sovereign subjects (whatever the particular terminology) all of which had 'external' relations that would be regulated by its terms. A key moment in this story, thus, was the development of a secular international society within Europe the inauguration of which was marked by the Peace of Westphalia of 1648, in which that community finally emerged from the shadow of the Holy Roman Empire and the coercive authority of the Catholic Church (Hall, 1895, pp 55–60).

This emphasis given to the Peace of Westphalia was significant at a systemic level since it sufficed for such purposes to think of international society as a society of independent sovereigns. But this of course said very little about the State itself as an idea, the meaning and significance of which certainly did not stay stable over the ensuing centuries. As Machiavelli's account in *The Prince* suggested the archetypal sixteenth century sovereign existed, 'in a relationship of singularity and externality', or of 'transcendence', to his or her principality (Foucault, 2007, p 91). Since the Prince could receive his principality by inheritance, acquisition, conveyance, or conquest, it was clear there was nothing but a synthetic link between the two. The principality, including both its territory and population, thus stood in a quasi-feudal relation to the Prince's authority, and international relations proceeded on the assumption that what was in issue was the rights, possessions, entitlements and obligations of the person of the sovereign.

By the time at which Grotius and Pufendorf were writing in the following century, however, two new traditions of thought had started to emerge. One of these, marked by an invocation of the idea of the social contract (partially present in the work of Grotius, but later given much more concrete form in the work of Hobbes and Locke), sought to forge a definitive link between the people (understood as a community of individuals or as a 'multitude') and the sovereign (the individual or group of people who were endowed with the right to rule). The other tradition, which was associated with the emergence of mercantilist thought in the seventeenth century, began conceptualizing the territory and people in terms of a unit of economic activity (Foucault, 2007). Since sovereignty, as Locke in particular was to aver, was underpinned by the appropriation and use of land,[4] the idea developed that the exercise of sovereign rights ought to be oriented in that direction: the people should be governed and not merely ruled. Alongside, therefore, the emergence of a new 'art of government' defined in terms of some innate purpose (*raison d'état* as it was to become known), there also emerged the notion of the 'State' as an idea that framed the respective component elements of territory, population and government but yet was reducible to none of them. Both of these traditions of thought were important in the developing idea of the State. On the one hand the State internalized the idea of government (which, in Pufendorf's terms, could be Democratic, Aristocratic, or Monarchical) and set it in relation to the people and its territory. Governments might come and go yet the State, so long as it retained the core elements, would remain the same. On the other hand, the State was not to be defined merely in terms of a relationship between its component parts, but in the idea that it also had some immanent end— whether that be simply to maintain common peace and security or further the cause of society. The State was thus to be described both in terms of its composition and its purpose.

---

[4] Locke, *Second Treatise of Government*, 1690, pp 18–30. See also Vattel, *The Law of Nations*, pp 37–8: 'The whole earth is designed to furnish sustenance for its inhabitants; but it cannot do this unless it be cultivated. Every Nation is therefore bound by the natural law to cultivate the land which has fallen to its share'.

Both of these strands of thought come to be neatly expressed in Pufendorf's definition of the State as a 'compound Moral Person, whose will being united and tied together by those covenants which before passed amongst the multitude, is deemed the will of all, to the end that it may use and apply the strength and riches of private persons towards maintaining the common peace and security'. (Pufendorf, *On the Law of Nature and Nations*, Bk VII, c. 2, s. 13). A key feature of this definition, which itself had been anticipated in Hobbes' description of the Leviathan, was the personification of the State as a moral entity in its own right. To describe the State as a 'person', a moral or legal entity, had several obvious consequences. One was that it allowed jurists to differentiate between the interior and exterior of the State as Bodin had suggested (Bodin, *Six Books of the Commonwealth*, pp 51–77), and accordingly treat differences in the internal order or structure of states as largely irrelevant to their character as homogenous subjects of the law of nations. Another was that it allowed a separation between the location of sovereignty and the incidental exercise of sovereign powers—a distinction which later cemented itself in a firm differentiation that survives today between the idea of the State on the one hand and that of government on the other.

All of this was to pave the way for the subsequent work of Wolff and Vattel, who had, perhaps, the most profound influence on the character of international law as it was to develop in the nineteenth and twentieth centuries. Both Wolff and Vattel, whilst differing in many important respects, insisted upon the pertinence of the 'domestic analogy' for understanding international law. They re-appropriated the earlier conception of the 'state of nature' that had been deployed as a heuristic device in the work of Hobbes and Locke for purposes of elaborating their contractarian schemes of political authority, and posited it as being a principal characteristic of international society. For Wolff and Vattel, States were in a position analogous to individuals prior to the establishment of civil society seeking security and community in their relations with others. The principal objective of the State was to preserve and protect itself and be given the opportunity to promote its own ends. They thus enjoyed the same rights 'as nature gives to men for the fulfilment of their duties' (Vattel, *The Law of Nations*, p 4) and enjoyed such natural liberties as befitted their character. The law of nations provided the structure by which that freedom and equality was to be preserved and promoted within the frame of a wider international society.

In many respects it is difficult to underestimate the enduring significance of Vattel's appealingly simplistic account of the State in international relations. However far international thought may have moved away from the idea of States enjoying certain natural prerogatives, or of sovereignty being sharply demarcated between internal and external domains, the idea that the world could be described in terms of States as a sociological category, possessing a distinct 'will', 'mentality', or 'motivation' that may encourage them to interact with one another in certain determinate ways is one that endures to this day. Its social purchase is nothing short of astonishing. Nevertheless, for those receiving this tradition in the nineteenth century there were always evident complexities that had to be negotiated. To begin with, it was not exactly easy to translate this monadic description of international society as a society of 'free and independent' nations into practice at the time. Writing in the middle of the century, for example, Phillimore was to identify eleven different categories of State, four of which were 'peculiar' cases (Poland, Belgium, Greece, and Egypt), the rest of which included, in addition to States under one sovereign, two categories of Unions, States that took the form of Free Towns or Republics, Tribute-paying States (Vassals), and two further categories of States under different forms of protection. Further to this, there was the complex phenomenon of the German Confederation (a loose alliance of 70 independent 'States') to be explained (Phillimore, 1871, p 101). This was, on no account, a uniform scheme of political organization.

By the end of that century, the picture had become still more complex, primarily as a consequence of a reflection upon the extent to which international law could be applied with equal ease in relation to the non-European world (a concern which had been explicitly taken up by the newly-formed Institut de Droit International in 1879[5]). The problem was this: in their desire to avoid the abstract rationalism of natural law and locate international rights and obligations instead in the empiricism of practice and custom, international lawyers had come to speak about international law in specifically European terms. At a time at which the idea of the nation as a cultural and linguistic community was emerging in a specifically political form (demanding an alignment between nation and State), it seemed obvious that the international relations of such a community of nation-States would be imbued with, or built upon, the same consciousness of history and tradition. Custom seemed to imply some kind of social consensus, and consensus a commonality of understanding and outlook (what Westlake referred to as a 'juridical consciousness') that could only readily be supposed in relation to 'civilized' communities in Europe (or those communities of 'European origin' elsewhere). For some, in fact, international law was actually more properly described as the Public Law of Europe, as the work of those such as Martens (1864) and Klüber (1851) attests.

Yet for all this, international lawyers were also aware of the long history of treaty-making with all manner of local sovereigns in Asia, Africa and elsewhere the form of which seemed to suppose that those relations were to be governed by the terms of international law (see Alexandrowicz, 1967; Anghie 2005). Indeed the fact that from the early 1880s onwards European exploration of the interior of Africa was to be marked, amongst other things, by the systematic and widespread conclusion of treaties with local kings and chiefs providing for 'Protection' or for the 'cession' of sovereignty was only to make the issue more pressing. How might an exclusively European system of public law conceive of such arrangements? And what might this imply as regards the status of those communities?

In one sense the answer was obvious. Although few international lawyers at the time were to explicitly introduce into their definitions of the State an explicit requirement that they be 'civilized',[6] the existence of an implicit 'standard of civilization' ran through most of their work in relation to recognition or territorial title, or when describing the character of international law (Gong, 1984; Anghie, 2005). Thus, whilst Hall spoke in quite abstract terms about the 'marks of an independent state' (being permanently established for a political end, possessing a defined territory and being independent of external control) he was still to make clear that international law consisted of those rules of conduct which 'modern *civilised* states' regarded as being binding upon them (Hall, 1895, p 1). One could not, in other words, assume that simply because there existed treaty relations with

---

[5] Twiss, 1879–1880, p 301. See generally Koskenniemi, 2001, pp 98–178.
[6] See eg Phillimore, 1871, p 94. Occasionally, the point was made more explicit. See Westlake, 1894, pp 102–103; Lawrence, 1895, p 58.

non-European States such as China or Japan, that those latter States were to be regarded as having the same rights and privileges as other European States. As Lawrence was to note:

there are many communities outside the sphere of International Law, though they are independent states. They neither grant to others, nor claim from themselves the strict observance of its rules. Justice and humanity should be scrupulously adhered to in all dealings with them, but they are not fit subjects for the application of legal technicalities. It would, for instance, be absurd to expect the king of Dahomey to establish a Prize Court, or to require the dwarfs of the central African forest to receive a permanent diplomatic mission. (Lawrence, 1895, p 58)

By and large, thus, international lawyers began to differentiate in their accounts between those 'normal' relations that pertained between European States and those that characterized relations with other political communities on the outside. Beyond Europe, the treaties that put in place regimes of Protection or for consular jurisdiction and extraterritoriality, or those that purported to 'cede' territory, took the *form* of agreements between sovereign States, the substance of which however was to deny any such pretension.

Yet there was also a paradoxical difficulty here. Even if such non-European States did not possess a sovereignty equivalent to that of European States, it was not convenient to deny them status of any kind, as to do so would have put in question the validity of the agreements upon which European privileges seemed to depend (Koskenniemi, 1989, pp 136–143). Some position within the broader frame of international law had to be found for them. They had to be simultaneously included yet excluded from the realm of international law.[7] In the event, there were several different ways in which this matter was approached. Some differentiated between legal relations as might exist between European States and non-legal, moral, or ethical, propositions that governed relations with the non-civilized world (Westlake, 1894, pp 137–140), some differentiated between States enjoying full membership and those enjoying merely partial membership in the family of nations (Wheaton, 1866; Oppenheim, 1905), some differentiated between plenary and partial recognition (Lorimer, 1883, pp 101–123). One point was clear, however, namely that in order to be admitted into the European family of nations, those aspirant States had to demonstrate their 'civilized' credentials. To be 'civilized' furthermore, largely meant the creation of institutions of government, law, and administration modelled upon those found in Western Europe (Westlake, 1894, pp 141–143). This was a message fully understood in Japan whose rapid process of 'Westernization' in the latter half of the nineteenth century eventually allowed it to rid itself of the regimes of consular jurisdiction that had been put in place in order to insulate Western merchants and traders from the application of local law. Only once this 'badge of imperfect membership' had been removed could it be said to have become a full member of international society (Westlake, 1894, p 46).[8]

---

[7] Schmitt. 1974, p 233, examining Rivier's *Lehrbuch des Volkerrechts* (1889), notes that his overview of 'current sovereign states' included 25 States in Europe, 19 in the Americas, then 'States in Africa' including the Congo Free State, the Free State of Liberia, the Orange Free State, the Sultanate of Morocco, and the Sultanate of Zanzibar. Schmitt notes that in respect of the latter category these were called States but the word sovereign was avoided and in case of Morocco and Zanzibar, Rivier had noted that 'obviously' they did 'not belong to the community of international law'. Schmitt asks pithily: 'Why were they even included in the enumeration?'

[8] A contrast might be drawn here with the rather slower progress made in the case of China. The Nine Power Treaty of 1922 sought to guarantee the 'Open Door' policy in China (by which was meant 'equality of

These ideas, it has to be said, by no means disappeared overnight. Indeed many of them were remodelled and given institutional form in the League of Nations. Article 38(1)(c) of the statute of the Permanent Court of International Justice still referred to 'the general principles of law recognized by *civilised* nations', and the theme was maintained in the institutions of the Mandate system designed to deal with the situation of the colonies and territories extracted from Germany and the Ottoman empire under the terms of the various Peace Treaties. Under article 22 of the Covenant on the League, 'advanced nations' (viz Britain, France, Belgium, Australia, New Zealand, South Africa, and Japan) were entrusted with the task of exercising 'tutelage' on behalf of the League over those colonies and territories which were 'inhabited by peoples not yet able to stand by themselves under the strenuous conditions of the modern world'. The purpose of this 'sacred trust' was to advance the 'well-being and development of such peoples' the precise implications of which depended upon a classification set out within that same article. Certain territories (designated as Class A Mandates) were regarded as having 'reached a stage of development where their existence as independent nations can be provisionally recognized' in which case the Mandatory power was to provide administrative advice and assistance 'until such time as they are able to stand alone'. This category included those territories in the Middle East separated from the Ottoman Empire (Iraq, Palestine and Transjordan, Syria, and Lebanon). Class B territories (those in Africa with the exception of South-West Africa) were to be subject to significantly more intensive degrees of administrative control without any explicit expectation of independence, and Class C territories (Pacific Islands and South West Africa) were those declared to be 'best administered under the laws of the Mandatory as integral portions of its territory', subject to certain safeguards 'in the interests of the indigenous population' (see Anghie, 2005, pp 115–195).

Whilst, as Schwarzenberger suggested, the Mandate system came very close to being a mechanism for the continuation of colonialism 'by other means' (Schwarzenberger, 1950, p 134), the very decision to employ 'other means' was significant. To begin with, the institution of an international trusteeship seemed to make clear that Mandate powers were not acquiring such territories as 'colonies', and therefore could not be taken to enjoy the normal rights of sovereignty in relation to such territories. But if that was the case, it posed the obvious question as to where sovereignty lay (Wright, 1930). The territories themselves, could barely be described as sovereign in their own right, as otherwise the restrictions on their independence would have been intolerable. Some other status had to be devised for them, or at least some language that avoided the problematic implications of the notion of 'sovereignty'. This, of course, was not a problem solely related to the institution of the Mandate, but was equally relevant to the authority exercised by the League of Nations itself—how might its powers be described within an international order comprising of sovereign States?

Whether or not as a consequence of reflecting upon such problems, international lawyers began to regard the notion of sovereignty and its correlates (sovereign equality and

opportunity in China for the trade and industry of all nations') to be secured by barring any agreement that might secure special commercial privileges for any one State. A special Commission was set up to examine the question as to whether the continuation of extraterritorial privileges was justified. It reported back in 1926 concluding that although progress had been made, more was needed before such regimes could be suspended. See Summary and Recommendations of the Report of the Commission on Extraterritoriality in China, 1926 in (1927) 21 *AJIL*, Supplement 58.

domestic jurisdiction) not as something integral to their understanding of international law, but as an obstacle to be overcome. For many, a fixation with the idea of sovereignty as both indicative of the absence of any higher authority, and as the source of law (understood, perhaps, as the will or command of the sovereign) had not only left the discipline in a condition of internal contradiction,[9] but ill-equipped to deal with a world of new international institutions and novel forms of governance. Writing in 1924, for example, Brierly joined the emerging chorus, dismissing the idea of sovereignty as an 'idolon theatre' (theatrical artifice) that bore little relation to the way in which States actually related to one another in practice (Brierly, 1924, p 13). If 'sovereignty' was to be retained as an idea it had, at the very least, to be re-packaged or re-shaped in some significant way.

One can turn to Hall's Treatise of 1895 as an early illustration of this change. One of the most significant features of the Treatise is its almost total avoidance of the term 'sovereignty' except in relation to those matters which were presumptively 'internal' such as might engage the relationship between the State and its subjects. In place of the word 'sovereignty' when describing the existence or authority of the State, he used the term 'personality'. Legal personality, of course, was a term that had already acquired a prominence in municipal law with the development of the limited liability corporation, but was not a term that had been extensively employed (at that time) in the context of international law. Its significance, however, lay in the fact that the idea of 'personality' assumed the existence of a systemic order that attributed a range of competences to certain designated actors. Just as a corporation, if duly brought into being, would then have the legal capacity to sue and be sued, so also one might think that States could similarly be understood to have been 'accorded' a certain capacity in international law. Statehood in that context, was no longer something intrinsic, carrying with it certain natural rights or prerogatives (and one may think here, for example, of the idea of an 'inherent' right to self-defence), but descriptive of a capacity attributed or accorded to certain entities fulfilling the requisite criteria.[10] In contrast to the Vattelian idea of States enjoying a natural liberty in a state of nature, for Hall this liberty of action was one 'subject to law' (Hall, 1895, p 24).

This semantic turn was one that may be appreciated not merely in a shift in linguistic usage from sovereignty to personality (as by no means everyone took that step), but also in an active reconceptualization of the idea of sovereignty itself.[11] Thus, in the *Wimbledon case*, when presented with the claim by Germany that the granting of an unfettered right of passage to vessels of all nationalities through the Kiel canal would 'imply the abandonment by Germany of a personal and imprescriptible right, which forms an essential part

---

[9] Kennedy, 1997, p 114 associates a scepticism of sovereignty with positivism: 'To fulfil their polemical mission, to render plausible a legal order among sovereigns, the philosophy which sets this question, which makes sovereigns absolute or requires a sovereign for legal order, must be tempered, if not rejected. As a result, to inherit positivism is also to inherit a tradition of response to the scepticism and deference to absolute State authority, which renders legal order among sovereigns *implausible* in the first place'.

[10] See O'Connell, 1970, Vol I, p 80: 'It is clear that the word "person" is used to refer to one who is a legal actor, but that it is of no assistance in ascertaining who or what is competent to act. Only the rules of international law may do this, and they may select different entities and endow them with different legal functions, so it is a mistake to suppose that merely by describing an entity as a "person" one is formulating its capacities in law'.

[11] For a more recent account of the transformation of sovereignty into a new global form of Empire see Hardt and Negri, 2000.

of her sovereignty' the Permanent Court of International Justice responded by stating that it:

declines to see in the conclusion of any Treaty by which a State undertakes to perform or refrain from performing a particular act an abandonment of its sovereignty. No doubt any convention creating an obligation of this kind places a restriction on the exercise of sovereign rights of the State, in the sense that it requires them to be exercised in a certain way. But the right of entering into international engagements is an attribute of State sovereignty.[12]

Sovereignty, in other words, was not to be understood as an unfettered freedom from external constraint, but rather as a way of describing a capacity for binding others to, and being bound by, international law. It was no longer something that had any innate content (such as describing certain natural rights or prerogatives), nor something that could be raised as an objection to legal obligations once entered into.[13] It was merely a way of describing those remaining powers and liberties afforded to the State under international law.

This new way of thinking was undoubtedly helpful in several respects. To begin with, it allowed a dissociation between the possession of 'sovereign rights' on the one hand and the actual order of power on the other: territories under belligerent occupation,[14] subject to a treaty of Protection or placed under the administration of a Mandatory power could be conceived as being subject to the governmental authority of another yet not part of its territorial sovereignty. Sovereignty in such cases survived in suspended form. It also disposed of the problem of sovereign equality and domestic jurisdiction: States could regard themselves as equal, so long as it was clear that 'equality' meant an equal capacity to enjoy rights and bear obligations. They also retained a right of domestic jurisdiction so far as this described a residual domain of freedom left untrammelled by the constraints of external obligation.[15] It was only a short move from here to the position adopted by Kelsen, amongst others, that States were nothing but legal orders, described fully and completely in terms of propositions of law.[16] It was also only a short step to admitting that States were not the only legal subjects contemplated under the terms of the international legal order—there was nothing to exclude the possibility of other agents, whether that be international organizations, individuals, or other groups, from being described as having some measure of international personality even if not on a par with that enjoyed by States.

---

[12] S. S. 'Wimbledon', Judgments, 1923, PCIJ, Series A, No 1, at p 25.

[13] See also Military and Paramilitary Activities in and against Nicaragua (Nicaragua v United States of America), Merits, Judgment, ICJ Reports 1986, p 14, para 259: 'A State...is sovereign for purposes of accepting a limitation of its sovereignty'.

[14] See Article 43 of the Hague Regulations (1907).

[15] One may note, in that respect, the same reconceptualization occurring in relation to the notion of 'domestic jurisdiction'. See eg, Nationality Decrees Issued in Tunis and Morocco, Advisory Opinion, 1923, PCIJ, Series B, No 4, p 24: 'The question whether a certain matter is or is not solely within the jurisdiction of a state is an essentially relative question; it depends upon the development of international relations.'

[16] Kelsen, 1942, pp 64–65: 'The State is not its individuals; it is the specific union of individuals, and this union is the function of the order which regulates their mutual behaviour...One of the distinctive results of the pure theory of law is its recognition that the coercive order which constitutes the political community we call a state, is a legal order. What is usually called the legal order of the state, or the legal order set up by the state, is the state itself.'

Yet for all the determination to formalize Statehood and oppose an inherited tradition that associated sovereignty with the possession of certain determinate rights and obligations, there was a strongly resistant current in the shape of the principle of national self-determination. National self-determination, in the form advanced by President Wilson in 1918 (see below) implied a substantive conception of the State rooted in ideas of community and cultural homogeneity, determined perhaps by religious or linguistic markers. The sovereignty that this idea demanded was not one that would be regulated from outside, but that inhered in a determinate people with values and interests that required protection and advancement. To the extent that the promotion of national self-determination seemed to go hand in hand with the simultaneous juridification of sovereignty meant that legal doctrine was systematically cut through by an opposition between two ideas of Statehood (one formal, the other substantive) and two ideas of sovereignty (one innate, the other attributed or delegated) of which neither could ultimately attain ascendancy (Koskenniemi, 1989, pp 59–60, 224–233). This opposition, indeed, was to continue to infect the discourse on statehood through the period of decolonization and on into the new millennium—its presence being felt in debates as to the relationship between self-determination and *uti possidetis* (whether 'people' determined the territory, or the territory the people) and in discussions over the implications of recognition (whether it was 'constitutive' or 'declaratory').

III. DEFINING THE STATE

The shift in legal thought described above from the idea of States existing in a Vattelian state of nature between whom a thin architecture of legal relations came to be established, to one in which States were understood to exist as legal entities endowed with a certain competences under international law, was one that could be described in terms of an increasing concern to identify those 'marks' or 'criteria' by which statehood could be measured. For Vattel, describing or defining the State was primarily a matter of trying to capture, in as neutral as possible terms, the plurality of different kinds of political communities existing in Europe in the middle of the eighteenth century, but for those doing the same 100 or 200 years later, the project of description had taken on a different character.

For a period of time, it wasn't entirely clear whether what was being described in the process was a sociological fact or a legal category (one could construe a definition that merely outlined the 'marks' of a State in either way), but the terms of description became more explicitly exclusionary in nature as time went by. Thus when Wheaton in 1866 endorsed Cicero's classic definition of the State as 'a body political, or society of men, united together for the purpose of promoting their mutual safety or advantage by their combined strength' he was constrained to point out, at the same time, its limitations. It did not include, as far as Wheaton was concerned, corporations created by the State itself, nor 'voluntary associations of robbers or pirates', nor 'unsettled horde[s] of wandering savages', nor indeed nations since the State 'may be composed of different races of men' (Wheaton, 1866, s 17). The definition of the State thus became a vehicle not merely for purposes of description (providing an analytical framework for understanding the character of international society for purposes of law) but also for distinguishing between those political communities that might properly be regarded as subjects of international law and those that would not. For some, this shift in orientation was decisive. As O'Connell was later to suggest (1970, p 81): 'the proposition "France is a State" is not a description or a definition but merely a conclusion to a train of legal reasoning'.

Yet there was clearly a difficulty associated with this move from fact to law (or, if you prefer, from description to prescription). How, and in what way, might one conceive of international law participating in the establishment of territorial political communities? The title of Crawford's influential book on the subject—*The Creation of States in International Law*—would appear to attribute to international law an excessively grandiose role. States are surely not 'created' by international law in the same sense that a cabinet maker might craft a piece of furniture; rather they typically emerge through spontaneous or organized political action on the part of a community who articulate their common destiny in terms of political independence. Indeed, to the extent to which there is reliance upon the notion of 'effectiveness' for purposes of determining the existence or otherwise of a State would suggest that the role of law is almost entirely *ex post facto*. 'Sovereignty', after all, as Wade was to claim seemed to be 'a political fact for which no purely legal authority can be constituted' (Wade, 1955, p 196). But Crawford was not naïve in this sense. What he was arguing against was an exclusively 'empirical' notion of statehood. A State is not, as he puts it, 'a fact in the sense that a chair is a fact' it is rather 'a legal status attaching to a certain state of affairs by virtue of certain rules or practices' (Crawford, 2006, p 5). A closer analogy therefore might be the idea of the status of 'criminality' being generated through the institutions and structures of the criminal law, or of 'insanity' through the discipline of psychiatry (Foucault, 2006). Just as 'a thief' is a designation appropriate only once it has been determined that the person concerned has unlawfully appropriated the property of another, so also to call something a 'State' is to draw attention to the legal framework within which the powers and competences of a State may properly be acquired (Kelsen, 1942).

Whilst this usefully directs our attention both to the relational aspect of statehood and the idea that it's meaning is constituted in a range of ideas about authority and responsibility, it still doesn't quite deal with the problem. Crawford's assumption that the legal order accords 'statehood' to those entities that possess the requisite characteristics might work so far as one may conceive of States emerging through an essentially consensual process. The emergence of new Republics out of the defunct Soviet Union in the early 1990s, for example, posed relatively few problems on this score for the simple reason that Russia had effectively renounced, in the Alma Ata Declaration and Minsk Accord,[17] any legal interest or claims to sovereignty over those regions (Mullerson, 1993). Here, one could conceive of the parent State either 'delegating' sovereign authority to the nascent regime (much in the same way as Czechoslovakia, Poland or the Serb-Croat-Slovene State were 'created' at the Peace Conferences in the aftermath of the 1914–18 war), or perhaps as creating the necessary legal 'space' for the new State to then assert its rights over the territory and population concerned.[18] By and large, in fact, this has been the predominant means by

---

[17] Agreement Establishing the Commonwealth of Independent States (Minsk Accord), 8 December 1991, 31 ILM (1992) 143; Alma Ata Declaration, 21 December 1991, ibid, p 148.

[18] One may note here, that the answer often depends upon the stance adopted in relation to the role of recognition. See eg Hall, 1895, p 88: 'Of course recognition by a parent state, by implying an abandonment of all pretensions over the insurgent community, is more conclusive evidence of independence than recognition by a third power, and it removes all doubt from the minds of other governments as to the propriety of

which new States have emerged since 1945 even if many have done so under the rubric of 'self-determination'.

Yet it is also evident that in many cases the issue is not one of the consensual devolution of sovereign authority but of the emergence of a new State out of a condition of dispute or conflict. Here the question remains as to how one might conceive of a moment in which sovereign authority is created out of the mere fact of the forcible or violent seizure of power? In a lecture entitled 'Force of Law: the Mystical Foundation of Authority' Jacques Derrida (1989–90, p 927) posed the following question:

How are we to distinguish between the force of law of a legitimate power and the supposedly originary violence that must have established this authority and that could not itself have been authorized by any anterior legitimacy, so that, in this initial moment, it is neither legal nor illegal—or, others would quickly say, neither just nor unjust?

Taking as his starting point Walter Benjamin's distinction between 'constituted' and 'constitutive' force (between force authorized by law and force that originally establishes legal authority), Derrida's essay was concerned with highlighting how these two ideas converged and to point out the continued presence within all schemes of law and legal thought of an originary (extra-legal) violence that necessarily accompanied the establishment of that legal authority. Of course, even if the authority of an original constitution can never be thought to depend upon the law which it brings into effect, one might nevertheless look to international law for purposes of validating such authority 'from the outside' so to speak. Yet there are two remaining difficulties. The first is that in order to sustain the argument that other States may authorize or validate the existence of a new State, one would still have to move back to determine the basis upon which those authorities claimed that ability. How might existing States bring into existence another State with 'law creating capacity' without the latter being seen, in some respects, a subordinate authority? And in that respect the image of an international legal community as a closed 'club' of European States both territorially incomplete and politically imperial is never far in the background. The second difficulty is that, as mentioned above, in a world already fully demarcated in terms of sovereign jurisdiction (in which there is no effective space for the emergence of an entirely new State like that of Liberia in 1847 or the Congo Free State in 1885) the process of 'creation' can only be achieved by way of displacing in some manner or other the prior claims to sovereignty of an existing State. Unless existing claims to territorial sovereignty are lifted or suspended in some way (such as by consent), the emergence of a new State could not be achieved without some measure of illegality.

Whatever the problems associated with this move from description to prescription, it was always evident that if States were to be regarded as actors endowed with personality by a superordinating legal order, it was necessary to set out somewhere the terms under which this 'attribution' of authority might take place and the consequences of it. Strange as it may seem, although the United Nations and the League of Nations before it were committed to a process of the codification of international law, they managed to accomplish neither of these tasks. In 1949 the International Law Commission did produce a Draft Declaration

recognition by themselves; but it is not a gift of independence; it is only an acknowledgement that the claim made by the community to have definitively established its independence'.

on the Rights and Duties of States,[19] which went in some direction towards summarizing what the implications of Statehood might be, albeit the case that this draft was not adopted by the General Assembly. Alongside a list of ten duties the Draft Declaration included four rights: 'the right to independence and hence to exercise freely, without dictation by any other States, all its legal powers, including the choice of its own form of government (Article 1), 'the right to exercise jurisdiction over its territory and over all persons and things therein, subject to the immunities recognized by international law' (Article 2), the right to 'equality in law with every other State' (Article 5), and the 'right of individual and collective self-defence against armed attack' (Article 12). Each of these, with some qualification, seems to describe those powers possessed only by States to which may be added, perhaps, a plenary competence to perform legal acts such as conclude treaties, a right not to be subject to compulsory international process or dispute settlement without consent, and the benefit of a presumption that they enjoy an 'unlimited freedom' subject only to those constraints determined by law (the *Lotus* principle) (Crawford, 2006, pp 40–41). These, in some respects at least, might suggest why Statehood remains an attractive proposition.

Whilst drafting the Declaration, the International Law Commission also briefly discussed the merits of seeking to define the State for purposes of international law. The general reaction, at that time, was that such a project was unnecessary because it was either too self-evident, or too controversial (the concern being that it would only have salience as regards 'new' rather than 'old' States). In some respects at least, this caution was probably informed by the fact that the Pan American Union (the predecessor of the Organization of American States) had already drafted the Montevideo Convention on the Rights and Duties of States 1933, Article 1 of which set out a basic definition which, if not definitive, could be taken as the starting point for most discussions of territorial status. Article 1 provides as follows:

The State as a person of international law should possess the following qualifications:

(a) a permanent population;

(b) a defined territory;

(c) government; and

(d) capacity to enter into relations with other states.

For all its significance Article 1 is still treated with a certain degree of circumspection. The 'capacity to enter into relations with other states' seems to be a conclusion rather a starting point, and there is no mention of other putatively relevant matters such as independence, legitimacy, democracy or self-determination. Precisely what Article 1 'declares', furthermore, is a little unclear. As a legal prescription, the terms of the Montevideo convention appear to be either too abstract or too strict. They are too abstract in the sense that to say that an entity claiming to be a State needs to be able to declare itself as having people, territory and a form of government is really to say very little, and certainly does nothing to guide responses to claims by aspirant states such as Chechnya, Kosovo, Northern Cyprus, Palestine, or Quebec. Certainly it may exclude Wheaton's private corporation or his nomadic society, but one may ask what else? And to what end?

---

[19] GA Res 375(VI), 6 December 1949, Annex.

What appears to be needed here is one of two things. One possibility is that it requires a quantitative measure of intensity: so instead of merely necessitating the existence of a people, a territory and something that describes itself as a government, it requires that these qualities are possessed in sufficient degree. It must be large enough and effective enough to warrant being regarded as both self sufficient and, as the final qualification suggests, have the capacity to enter into relations with other States. Another possibility is that it requires some qualitative evaluation—so rather than merely expecting a claim to be made in respect of a people or a territory, it expects those claims to be justified in some way for example on the basis that they respond to a principle of self-determination or are capable of substantiation without impinging upon the rights and duties of other sovereign States.

But both of these measures—of intensity and justification—seem then to demand too much. The measure of intensity seems to require the articulation of a 'threshold' evaluation the establishment of which would be virtually impossible in the abstract—who could say in advance how much territory or how many people are required in order to create a State? Surely what would matter is whether it is capable of surviving as an independent State, and that, presumably, is something to be determined after the fact so to speak. The measure of justification has a similar problem; it seems to rely upon the prior establishment of internationally recognized regimes of entitlement and responsibility (recognized claims over territory or in relation to nationals) the validity of which would assume that the State as a legal subject is already in existence. In either case, the problem is how one moves from fact to law, or from cognition of the existence of a State to its legal recognition without, in a sense, assuming that the thing being offered the imprimatur of 'legality' is not somehow already legally existent.

A. POPULATION

As suggested above, one of the critical ideas accompanying the development of the idea of the State was that the people were not merely the accidental objects of a sovereign's authority, but that they also partook of that sovereignty and were the immediate object of an emergent art of government (for which Lincoln's phrase 'government by the people, for the people, and of the people' was an obvious cumulative expression). A population was not merely a means of demonstrating the wealth and power of the sovereign, or a means by which the State could ultimately secure itself in competition with others (through the drafting of troops and the cooption of labour for the production of wealth). It also provided the rationality for government itself: the purpose of government (and hence of the State) was, amongst other things, the promotion of the prosperity and happiness of the populace.

That the State was to have this immanent end was to encourage the idea that, to be politically and economically viable, it needed to be of sufficient size (Hobsbawm, 1992, pp 29–39). The smaller, more backward, nationalities, as Mill was to aver, were much better off being absorbed into larger nations, rather than 'sulk on [their] own rocks ... cut off from the general movement of the World' (Mill, *Considerations on Representative Government*, pp 363–364). Unification thus became the dominant theme of nation-building in the nineteeth century and the claims of those such as the Fenians in Ireland or the Bretons in France routinely disparaged. This was an idea not entirely shaken off in the early part of the twentieth century as doubt continued to be expressed as to whether small States such as Luxembourg or Liechtenstein, for example, could properly be regarded as independent States. Liechtenstein, indeed, was denied membership of the League of Nations in 1920—the formal reason for which was its lack of independence from Austria (to whom it had 'delegated' certain customs and postal duties under Agreement). Underlying that, however, was an evident concern over its size and the political implications of allowing micro-States the same voting rights as other States in the organs of the League (Duursma, 1996, pp 173–174). Later practice in the context of the United Nations, however, has suggested that such a consideration is no longer quite what it used to be. Alongside Liechtenstein as members of the United Nations (for which, as article 4 of the UN Charter makes clear, being a State is a prerequisite) sit States such as Andorra, Monaco, Brunei, Kiribati, Nauru, Palau, Vanuatu, and the Marshall Islands, all of which have populations of under 1 million. As most conclude, whatever the Montevideo Convention says, there seems to be no minimum threshold population necessary in order to obtain statehood.

If the criterion of population seems not to relate to the notion of a threshold, then perhaps it refers instead to the idea that there must exist a population enjoying exclusive relations of nationality with the nascent State. Whilst it is certainly true that in the early years of the twentieth century nationality did enjoy this aura of exclusivity—and hence, in some respects, represented a way of demarcating the populations of different States—this was merely an expectation rather than an obligation. The competence to confer and withhold nationality was still regarded as a matter falling within the domain of domestic jurisdiction in the sense that international law neither required such conferral in any particular case nor prohibited its withdrawal.[20] The only context in which international law seemed to be relevant was where one state sought to rely upon the bond of nationality when bringing a claim against another State alleging harm to one of its nationals and in which the reality of that 'bond' was open to dispute.[21] Not only did the conferral of nationality thus seem to be a competence that ensued from having legal capacity as a State (a consequence, that is, not a precondition), but as the toleration of multiple nationality has increased (see Franck, 1999, pp 61–75) even the theoretical possibility of it being regarded as an effective condition for statehood has similarly disappeared. In fact the almost total conceptual separation between statehood and the idea of a constitutive population was marked in the second opinion of the Badinter Commission in 1992 in which the Commission suggested, in the context of the collapse of the Socialist Federal Republic of Yugoslavia, that one of the possible implications of the principle of self-determination was that the individuals concerned should have a right to choose their own nationality.[22] That this offered the possibility that a majority of the population of a new State might 'opt' for the nationality of a neighbouring State was treated as largely irrelevant for purposes of determining whether the new State met the conditions necessary for its own legal existence. Rather than being a condition of statehood, thus, the existence of a 'population' seems to be cast in metaphorical terms—they must be exist 'as if' in relationship to an order of government over territory, in which their presence as objects of coercion is necessary, but their identity as participants in that political community remains indeterminate.

[20] *Nationality Decrees issued in Tunis and Morocco, Advisory Opinion, 1923, PCIJ, Series B, No 4,* p 24.

[21] *Nottebohm, Second Phase, Judgment, ICJ Reports 1955,* p 4.

[22] See also, Articles 1 and 11, ILC Draft Articles on Nationality of Natural Persons in Relation to the Succession of States (1999).

B. TERRITORY

Much of the above also applies in relation to the criterion of territory. Just as there appears to be no threshold requirement for purposes of population, so also it is hard to discern any specific condition concerning possession of sufficient portions of land. Monaco has a territory of less than 1.95 km² and the Vatican City (a 'non-member State' at the UN) less than 0.5 km² (Duursma, 1996, p 117). At the same time, it is clear that the real issue in most cases is not the issue of size, nor indeed the mere factual possession or control over territory (as, of course, possession may always be 'adverse' as in cases of belligerent occupation), but rather the ability to rightfully claim the territory as a domain of exclusive authority. If, as Arbitrator Huber put it in the *Island of Palmas Case*, sovereignty signifies independence, and independence 'in regard to a portion of the globe…the right to exercise therein, to the exclusion of any other State, the function of a State',[23] then the existence or absence of competing claims to sovereignty would appear to be key.

There is, however, an obvious difficulty here. If what is required of new States is the possession of territory that is otherwise 'unclaimed' or 'undisputed' then, unless one were to be able to identify the territory in question as *terra nullius* (unoccupied territory),[24] or territory which has been explicitly or tacitly 'ceded' to it, then it remains very difficult to see how any such nascent State might establish the requisite authority over territory. This indeed, seems to be the condition of most secessionist enterprises and the extent cause for most to go unfulfilled. Yet the position is not quite as straightforward as this might suggest. It is classically maintained that the absence of clearly delimited boundaries is not a prerequisite for statehood. Albania, for example, was admitted to the League of Nations in 1920 despite the fact that its frontiers had yet to be finally fixed, the subsequent delimitation of which came to be the subject of an Advisory Opinion of the PCIJ in the *Monastery of Saint Naoum* case of 1924.[25] Reflecting upon this practice, the International Court of Justice subsequently affirmed in the *North Sea Continental Shelf* case that:

The appurtenance of a given area, considered as an entity, in no way governs the precise delimitation of its boundaries, any more than uncertainty as to boundaries can affect territorial rights. There is for instance no rule that the land frontiers of a State must be fully delimited and defined, and often in various places and for long periods they are not…[26]

Of course, one can rationalize this practice to the extent that one treats the border and the territory of the State as two different things. Borders seem to be the consequence of the possession of territory—their delimitation proceeding on the basis that there are legitimate entitlements on either side. Territory, in the context of statehood, however, seems incapable of being framed purely in terms of ownership or possession for the simple reason that it concerns the prior question as to the very existence of the legal person rather than merely its spatial parameters.

This distinction between territory and its boundaries is an appealing one in the sense that it allows for the disposal of ongoing disputes over the location of borders (often by

---

[23] *Island of Palmas Case* (1928) 2 *RIAA* 829.
[24] For a discussion of this notion in the context of Western Sahara, see *Western Sahara, Advisory Opinion, ICJ Reports 1975*, p 12, paras 79–81.
[25] *Monastery of Saint-Naoum, Advisory Opinion, 1924, PCIJ, Series B, No 9*.
[26] *North Sea Continental Shelf, Judgment, ICJ Reports 1969*, p 3, para 46.

reference to the classical 'modes' by which territory might be acquired such as discovery, cession, annexation, occupation or prescription[27]) without, at the same time, continually calling into question the identity of the States whose borders are the subject of dispute. It would be almost absurd to argue, for example, that the alteration of the UK's jurisdiction that occurred as a consequence of its assertion of sovereignty over the Island of Rockall in 1972 was such as to affect its legal identity and therefore required it to apply afresh for membership in the UN or EU. At the same time, it is clear that radical changes to borders can have that function—as was demonstrated, in particular, in the case of Yugoslavia/ Serbia (see Blum, 1992). Borders, after all, are not merely lines on the ground, or ways of delimiting spheres of public jurisdiction, but serve also to delimit the existence of a political order by means of its separation from others. The supposition, thus, that a lack of delimited borders is of no consequence is hard to maintain. Perhaps the most difficult example is that of the emergence of Israel in 1948, for example, it was not merely the case that *some* of its borders were in question, but the entirety of its territory which had been carved out of the defunct Mandate for Palestine. In that context, however, no small significance can be attributed to the general atmosphere of uncertainty generated, amongst other things, by the Security Council's failure to endorse the General Assembly's plan for partition outlined in Resolution 181(II) of 1947 and the apparent termination of the Mandate occasioned by the withdrawal of the British administration. The lack of an effective interlocutor able to claim that recognition of the new State constituted a violation of its own territorial sovereignty (even though there were clearly arguments to be made on the part of the Palestinian population generally) was such as to allow a critical space for recognition of the State of Israel without the kinds of qualms associated with premature recognition that would naturally arise in other contexts. Once again, thus, the criterion of territory assumes a highly indeterminate form in the legal conception of statehood—it being a simultaneously indispensable quality, but yet one incapable of being articulated in anything other than an abstract, and once again metaphorical, way.

C. INDEPENDENT GOVERNMENT

To a large extent, those addressing the criteria for statehood are unified on one matter above all else: that the criteria are ultimately aimed towards the recognition of 'effective' governmental entities. Governmental effectiveness understood as its power to assert a monopoly over the exercise of legitimate physical violence within a territory (to paraphrase Weber, 1994, pp 310–311) is taken to be central.[28] In a sense, the Weberian definition is somewhat tautological—to say whether an entity enjoys a monopoly over the exercise of legitimate violence assumes the prior establishment of a distinction between legitimate and illegitimate violence (between the violence of the police and that of the insurgent), and that kind of distinction as Derrida pointed out was ultimately unavailable. But what is clearly meant, here, is that the government concerned must demonstrate unrivalled possession and control of public power (whatever the specificities of that might be in any

---

[27] For a classical account of the modes of acquisition of territory see Jennings, 1963.

[28] See Lauterpacht, 1947, pp 340–341: 'The principal and probably the only essential condition of recognition of States and governments is effectiveness of power within the State and of actual independence of other States. Other conditions are irrelevant to the true purposes and nature of recognition.'

particular setting), and that once that unrivalled possession is established with a degree of permanence recognition of statehood may follow. This emphasis upon governmental effectiveness forms a key part of Crawford's thesis. Given that 'nationality is dependent upon statehood, not vice versa' and that territory is defined 'by reference to the extent of governmental power exercised', 'there is a good case' he suggests 'for regarding government as the most important single criterion of statehood, since all the others depend upon it' (Crawford, 2006, p 56).

Crawford's argument doesn't stop here though. His purpose is not simply to point out that, as the Commission of Jurists maintained in the *Aaland Islands* case, a new State only comes into existence once it is 'strong enough to assert [itself] throughout the territories of the state without the assistance of foreign troops.'[29] Rather, it is to suggest that this criterion of effectiveness operates as a legal principle the effect of which is conditioned by other relevant principles such as that of self-determination or the prohibition on the use of force. He is thus able to maintain that, in some contexts, relatively effective political entities such as the Turkish Republic of Northern Cyprus or Southern Rhodesia have not come to be recognized as independent States for the reason that to offer such recognition would have violated other relevant norms of international law having the status of *jus cogens*. In the same sense, but to different effect, he also maintains that the criterion of effectiveness is, in practice, of relatively less significance if the State in question is one that enjoys a right of self-determination.

Crawford cites, by way of illustration, the case of the Belgian Congo which was granted a hurried independence in 1960 as the Republic of the Congo in circumstances in which little preparation had been made for independence and in which public order broke down shortly after (with secessionist factions seeking their own independence in Katanga and elsewhere). Belgian troops were reintroduced into the territory under the guise of humanitarian intervention and the United Nations responded by establishing ONUC for purposes of restoring order whose mission continued until 1964. As Crawford puts it '[a]nything less like effective government it would be hard to imagine. Yet despite this there can be little doubt that in 1960 the Congo was a State in the full sense of the term' (Crawford, 2006, p 57). Its admission to the United Nations for membership had already been approved and UN action had been taken on the basis of preserving the 'sovereign rights of the Republic of the Congo'. Crawford suggests ultimately that there were three possible ways of interpreting this practice: (i) that the international recognition of the Congo was simply premature because it did not possess an effective government; (ii) that international recognition of the Congo had the effect of creating a State despite the fact that it was not properly qualified (ie, that recognition was thereby 'constitutive'); or (iii) that the requirement of 'government' was, in certain particular contexts, less stringent than might otherwise be thought.

Crawford's clear preference is for the third of these three options and he explains the position as follows:

by withdrawing its own administration and conferring independence on local authorities, Belgium was precluded from denying the consequences of its own conduct. Thereafter there was no international person as against whom recognition of the Congo could be unlawful.

[29] LNOJ, Sp Supp 4 (1920) pp 8–9.

It is to be presumed that a new State granted full and formal independence by a former sovereign has the international right to govern its territory... On the other hand, in the secessionary situation the position is different. A seceding entity seeks statehood by way of an adverse claim, and in general statehood can only be obtained by effective and stable exercise of governmental powers. (Crawford, 2006, pp 57–58)

It is important to understand the role assigned to the idea of effectiveness here. To begin with, it is presented as a general principle of international law—it is not, in that sense, a 'law creating fact' (as might be expressed in the phrase *ex factis jus oritur*), but simply a circumstantial trigger that produces certain legal consequences. Effectiveness, furthermore, is not sufficient on its own: just as some effective entities have not been recognized as States (such as Taiwan whose recognition as an independent State has been almost permanently deferred as a consequence of the claims made by China over its territory), so also other non-effective entities have continued to be regarded as States despite that condition (and one may mention here both States under a condition of belligerent occupation such as the Baltic Republics between 1940 and 1990 or Kuwait in 1990–91, and States which, like Lebanon and Burma in the 1970s, have experienced extended periods of internal turmoil). Effectiveness, in other words, operates as a principle the parameters of which are legally determined and may interact with other relevant principles such as those of self-determination or the prohibition on the use of force, and those that putatively govern the 'extinction' of States.

Yet it is equally clear that the further one goes in seeking to juridify the condition of 'effective government', the more clearly one exposes the inevitable tension between a legal principle that seeks to allow the recognition of new aspirant entities once they have become legal 'facts' so to speak, and one that prohibits any such recognition as being a violation of the territorial sovereignty of the State from which that entity is to emerge. In the nineteenth century, the criterion of effectiveness was intimately linked with the idea of premature recognition. If a third State were to recognize an insurgent movement as an independent State before the moment at which it had fully established itself, that recognition would constitute 'a wrong done to the parent state' and, indeed, 'an act of intervention' (Hall, 1895, p 89).[30] European powers were, thus, very cautious when addressing the recognition of the new States in South America, frequently modulating their response by reference to what seemed to be happening on the ground. Usually the insurgent communities were initially recognized *de facto*, *de iure* recognition coming once it was clear that Spain had effectively given up the fight. The importance of effectiveness, in such a context, was found in the way in which it served to definitively mark the moment at which the rights of the parent State gave way in face of those of the secessionist movement, much in the same was as it served to mark the point at which territory was acquired by way of annexation or occupation. This also meant that effectiveness was something of a movable feast: it never really meant quite the same thing in every place.[31] What was required in

---

[30] In practice, even the intermediary step of recognizing insurgents as belligerents, as Britain and France did in relation to the secessionist States in the American Civil War of 1861–5, was frequently treated as an unjustified intervention.

[31] *Island of Palmas Case* (1928) 2 *RIAA* 829 per Huber: 'Manifestations of territorial sovereignty assume... different forms according to conditions of time and place. Although continuous in principle, sovereignty cannot be exercised in fact at every moment on every point of a territory. The intermittence and discontinuity compatible with the maintenance of the right necessarily differ according as inhabited or

order to establish territorial sovereignty depended upon the nature and strength of rival claims such that a relatively ineffective Congo Free State could garner recognition in 1885 simply because of the apparent absence of any other recognized sovereign whose rights would be impeded in the process, yet considerably more was required for the recognition of the new Republics in Latin America. For all the subtle modulations of this early practice, however, such arguments clearly became more problematic in the course of the twentieth century once it came to be accepted that the use of force was no longer a legitimate means of acquiring title to territory.[32]

If the general prohibition on the use of force implies the illegality of the annexation of territory, it is very hard to see how one might legitimate the establishment of a State on the territory of another by that means (*ex inuria jus non oritur*). The now classic case of Manchukuo—cited mainly as an exemplar of the doctrine of non-recognition—is perhaps an example. When Japan engineered the establishment of the State of Manchukuo in China in 1931, the Lytton Commission, which had been dispatched by the League of Nations on a fact-finding mission, concluded that the Japanese action was inconsistent with both the Covenant and the Kellogg-Briand Pact and that Manchukuo itself remained largely under Japanese control. Its report underpinned the subsequent articulation of the 'Stimson doctrine' the substance of which affirmed the refusal of the United States (and those States which followed it) to 'admit the legality of any situation *de facto*...which may impair...the sovereignty, the independence, or of the territorial and administrative integrity of the Republic of China' that had been brought about by means contrary to the Pact of Paris.[33] Several League of Nations resolutions were adopted on this basis calling for non-recognition and the 'State' was finally dismantled in 1945. More recently than this, the establishment of the Turkish Republic in Northern Cyprus following the Turkish intervention in 1974 was denied recognition, principally again on the basis that its creation was the product of an unlawful military intervention.[34] Similar arguments were also put forward by Bosnia in its memorial in the *Genocide Case* which maintained that the Republica Srpska was not a State in part at least because its creation was associated with a violation of the prohibition on the use of force on the part of Serbian forces.[35]

It is worth noting, in this context, that the prohibition on the use of force has also been an idea instrumental not merely in resisting the establishment of puppet regimes, but in preserving the formal 'continuity' of States during periods of occupation. The Baltic Republics (Estonia, Latvia and Lithuania), for example, were occupied by the Soviet Union in 1940 and incorporated within the Union. A good many States refused to recognize the legality of the incorporation (Ziemele, 2005, pp 22–27) and when in 1990 the Supreme Councils of the three Baltic States resolved to 're-establish' their independence (which involved the re-invocation of laws pre-dating the occupation and the rejection of obligations assumed on their behalf by the Soviet Union) the EC adopted a Declaration

uninhabited regions are involved, or regions enclosed within territories in which sovereignty is incontestably displayed or again regions accessible from, for instance, the high seas.'

[32] See Article 2(4) UN Charter; Declaration of Principles of International Law Concerning Friendly Relations and Co-operation among States in Accordance with the Charter of the UN, GA Res. 2625(XXV), (24 October 1970), Principle 1. See generally Korman, 1996.

[33] 1 Hackworth 334.

[34] See *Cyprus* v *Turkey* [GC], no 2571/94, ECHR 2001-IV, 120 ILR 10.

[35] *Memorial of the Government of the Republic of Bosnia and Herzegovina*, 15 April 1994, p 264.

welcoming 'the restoration of sovereignty and independence of the Baltic States which they had lost in 1940' and resolving to re-establish diplomatic relations with them.[36] The prohibition on the use of force, in other words, seems to work not only as a way of denying the recognition of what might otherwise be regarded as effective entities, but as a way of keeping alive (as a formal idea at least) States which have been the subject of occupation and annexation and which are, to all intents and purposes, therefore 'ineffective'. In some respects at least, this seems to be unavoidable: one may recall the first Gulf War of 1990 was authorized by the Security Council in Resolution 678 (29 November 1990) on the basis of seeking to protect and secure the territorial integrity and political independence of Kuwait the continued existence of which had to be presupposed for purposes of authorizing international action despite the fact that its government had been effectively displaced by that of Iraq.

If this analysis is accurate, however, it does pose the question as to whether the principle of governmental effectiveness has any real meaning other than as a form of historical retrospection. If it is an idea that is systematically displaced by rules relating to the use of force or otherwise modulated by the principle of self-determination, its significance as a way of marking out the moment at which a State may be said to have come into legal existence seems to have significantly diminished. On one side, one may note an increased willingness to recognize as States (for one reason or another) entities that are in some respects ineffective—one may recall in recent years for example, that both Bosnia-Herzegovina and Croatia were recognized by the EC as independent States in 1992 at a time at which the governments concerned had effective control over only a portion of the territory in question (Rich, 1993). On the other side, it is also hard to think of many examples of new States being recognized simply because they have managed to secure their independence as a matter of fact. There are clearly several that have not (Katanga, Abkhazia, and the Republika Srpska for example) and for those that seem to be plausible cases, some other explanatory framework is usually deployed (such as consent, self-determination or disintegration) as a means of displacing the claims of the territorial sovereign. The most problematic cases are those of Bangladesh and Eritrea, the recognition of which could not easily be framed in terms of the standard understanding self-determination. Yet even here, commentators have tended to seek some other interpretive framework for explaining such practice: relying, for example, on the idea that Eritrea had been unlawfully seized by Ethiopia and that Bangladesh had been effectively governed as a non-self-governing territory by Pakistan (a case 'approximating' colonial rule).

This tendency towards the promotion of an exclusively 'juridical' idea of statehood in which questions of effectiveness are routinely subordinated by reference to other legal principles has been noted in the work of those such as Jackson and Kreijen. For Jackson (1990, pp 21–31), decolonization marked the moment at which the notion of sovereignty increasingly took on a negative cast (as implying merely freedom from external interference as opposed to a positive capacity to act), leading to the recognition of what he calls 'quasi-states': States which, because of their precipitous independence, were given the imprimatur of statehood before developing the necessary internal capacity for political self-government and economic independence. Rather than be developed prior to

---

[36] 7/8 Bull EC (1991) 1423.

independence, such States (mainly those in Africa it seems) have had to develop themselves after it. A similar stance is adopted by Kreijen who speaks of this change in terms of the 'transformation of the notion of independence from an inherently material concept based on internal sovereignty to a mere formal legal condition primarily depending on external recognition' (Kreijen, 2002, p 92). For Kreijen, this 'juridification of statehood' was a situation that demanded ameliorative action such as through the recognition of a right to development or the reintroduction of the notion of trusteeship into international law.

Such reflections draw upon themes that are common to recent debates over 'failed' or 'fragile' States, the significance of which goes someway beyond the narrow confines of a discussion as to the conditions under which a new State should be recognized, but nevertheless have resonance for an understanding of what the implications of statehood might be. In an influential article, Helman and Ratner (1992) commented upon what they saw to be a new phenomenon in international relations: the emergence of 'failed' or 'failing States'. Failed States were those such as Somalia, Sudan, Liberia, and Cambodia in which civil conflict, government breakdown and economic privation imperilled their own citizens and threatened their neighbours 'through refugee flows, political instability, and random warfare' (Helman and Ratner, 1992, p 3). The designation of such States as 'failed', of course, was not simply a neutral exercise in description or diagnosis, but formed a necessary prelude for the adumbration of a series of policy recommendations the central feature of which was the proposed introduction of a system of 'United Nations Conservatorship' along the lines subsequently established in East Timor, Bosnia-Herzegovina, and Kosovo for purposes of national, post-conflict, reconstruction. Whilst for Helman and Ratner, the notion was one that recommended reconstructive activity, in other hands, State failure has formed the basis for advocacy of a 'preventive' system including the imposition of sanctions upon such States and their exclusion from membership in international organizations (Rotberg, 2002). In some even, the notion has been employed as the basis for a refusal to recognize or implement treaty obligations.[37] As Simpson points out, such ideas are redolent of those abounding at the end of the nineteenth century in which critical differentiations were made between different kinds of State (such as, between civilized and uncivilized States) for purposes of legitimating a range of different kinds of intervention (Simpson, 2004, pp 240–242) On such a view the re-emergence of this 'liberal anti-pluralist' theme within international legal doctrine (in which the principles of territorial sovereignty and sovereign equality are routinely downplayed or excised) recalls the intellectual structures of nineteenth century imperialism (Gordon, 1997). Yet it is also run through with many of the same kinds of contradictions. Just as nineteenth century international lawyers struggled with the problem of having to both recognize and deny the status of political communities in the extra-European world, so also those invoking the notion of State failure seem to maintain the idea that these are indeed still States for purposes of attributing responsibility for their condition, but yet not entitled to the normal prerogatives of sovereignty that the intervening States would expect for themselves. As Crawford succinctly concludes, '[t]o talk of States as "failed" sounds suspiciously like blaming the victims' (Crawford, 2006, p 722).

---

[37] See Yoo, Memorandum, 9 January 2002 explaining that the Geneva Conventions did not apply because Afghanistan was a failed State.

IV. SELF-DETERMINATION

As observed above, one of the key characteristics of the idea of the State as it was to emerge in social and political thought from the time of Grotius onwards was that it was never solely reducible to the authority of the ruler or government of the time. The State embraced, simultaneously, the idea of a nation or a society in relation to which governmental authority was related. It is no accident, thus, that international law acquired the designation attributed to it by Bentham—it was always seen as the law between nations or societies as much as that between sovereigns, and the term *civitas* or *respublica* more often than not merely denoted the internal relationship between one thing and the other. Nevertheless, there were two immanent traditions of thought which informed this relationship between nation and State as they were to develop—one being what might be termed a tradition of civic republicanism that conceived of sovereign authority as being a product of relations between individuals existing within the frame of a pre-conceived society (exemplified most clearly in the theory of the social contract), the other a 'communitarian' tradition that emphasized the corporate character of the society or nation the institutional expression of which would be the State (exemplified in Pufendorf's characterization of the State as a 'moral person'). In both cases, the 'nation' remained an important idea—on one side as the social frame within which the contract of sovereignty would be formed, on the other side as a natural community endowed with certain innate ends and prerogatives (and, indeed, perhaps an independent 'will')—but in either case, the nation was never entirely reducible to the State itself.

In the course of the nineteenth century these two themes came to be summarized in a single verbal expression—that of 'national self-determination'—but which nevertheless merely internalized the two traditions within a single frame. One form of self-determination, associated with emergent 'nationalist' thought in Germany and Italy (sustained in the work of Herder, Fichte, and Mazzini amongst others), conceived of the idea that nation and State should be made congruent. It was the perfection of national society (understood variously as a society determined by reference to racial, ethnic, religious, linguistic or historic homogeneity) that was to be sought in the promotion of its self-determination. Another form of self-determination, associated with the tradition of civic republicanism (with roots in the work of those such as Kant), conceived of the idea of self-determination in terms of representative self-governance: it being the promotion of individual liberty through the technique of self-rule that was to be sought. Here, as Mill was to suggest, the frame of the 'nation' remained important if only because social uniformity and national homogeneity were necessary productive conditions for self-governance.[38] These two concepts of self-determination presented very different challenges to the existing order of sovereign States—the first as an 'external' challenge to the spatial ordering of a dynastic European society and its failure to map itself congruously with the geography of 'nations' as they were to perceive themselves; the second presenting a challenge to the authority of governments to represent externally the will of a people to whom they were not internally

---

[38] Mill, *Considerations on Representative Government*, Chapter XVI: 'it is in general a necessary condition of the institutions, that the boundaries of governments should coincide in the main with those of nationalities'.

responsible. These were not identical claims by any means: the latter appeared to confront the sovereign's authority with a criterion of legitimacy founded upon a rationalistic conception of representation, whereas the former appeared to challenge authority (even representative authority) with a claim to power based upon group identity (Berman, 1987–88, p 58). In either sense, however, national self-determination was clearly the language of change and reform (see Cobban, 1945).

It was in the reconstruction of Europe in the aftermath of the 1914–18 War, however, that the principle of national self-determination was to obtain its most concrete institutional expression. The agenda had been set by President Wilson in his speech to Congress in 1918 in which he famously set out the 'Fourteen Points' which he believed should inform the peace process. None of these points referred explicitly to the principle of national self-determination, but it was nevertheless made clear that boundaries in the new Europe should be configured so far as possible by reference to 'historically established' relations of nationality and allegiance. The Polish State was resurrected, Czechoslovakia and a Serb-Croat-Slovene State created out of the former Austro-Hungarian Empire and various other border adjustments made with provision for plebiscites in various locations. In many respects, however, it was an imperfect plan. On the one hand, it was always evident that the task of aligning political boundaries around the various 'nations' of Europe would be impossible, not simply because of the difficulties of determining which 'nation' deserved a State, but also because of their dispersed character. This recommended two expedients—one being the forcible transfer of certain populations (such as between Greece and Turkey[39]), the other being the institution of minority agreements within the Peace Treaties in order to protect those residual national communities cut adrift from the 'kin State' to which they were naturally thought to belong (Claude, 1955, pp 12–30). On the other hand, it was also evident that the Wilsonian project of self-determination was destined to be geographically limited—national self-determination was not something that was envisaged as being applicable in relation to the victorious powers themselves (eg for the Flemish, Irish, or Basques), nor was it regarded as applicable to territories outside Europe which, in the terms of the time, had yet to discover their national consciousness (Hobsbawm, 1992, pp 131–141).

If national self-determination was merely the implicit premise behind the reorganization of Europe after the First World War, it became a very much more explicit part of the settlement after the Second World War, but in some ways on quite different terms. The UN Charter identified respect for the principle of equal rights and self-determination of peoples as being one of the purposes of the Organization (Article 1), Chapter XI of which made clear that the primary concern was to foster self-government, development and the political, economic, social and educational advancement of those peoples which had 'not yet attained a full measure of self-government'. That this was to be interpreted as meaning 'decolonization' was later made clear by the General Assembly in a series of Resolutions beginning with the Declaration on the Granting of Independence to Colonial Territories of 1960.[40] Over the course of the next 30 years most of those territories identified as 'non-self-governing' by the United Nations were to acquire their independence and become, as an important marker of their new status, members of the Organization.

---

[39] Convention Concerning the Exchange of Greek and Turkish Populations, Lausanne, 30 January 1923.
[40] GA Res 1514 (14 December 1960). See also GA Res 1541 (15 December 1960).

Whilst decolonization was obviously to transform the membership of the UN, and radically re-shape the character and nature of its activities, its implications as an instance of the application of the principle of self-determination were somewhat less clear. In one direction, of course, it posed the question whether self-determination was a principle applicable only the context of decolonization, or whether it might also legitimate secession in other cases. UN practice seemed limited in that sense (Bangladesh remaining a problematic exception), but limited in a way that seemed to speak of pragmatism rather than principle. If what was in contemplation was the 'self-determination of 'all peoples' as Article 1(1) of the two UN Covenants on Human Rights affirmed,[41] then on what grounds might one want to restrict it only to those overseas territories that formed part of the maritime Empires of European States? Was it only in that context that one could speak of peoples being non-self-governing or subject to oppression or alien rule? But of course the practice was not one of 'national' self-determination in the sense that President Wilson had understood it at all. It was self-determination for those 'selves' that had been specifically designated as being entitled to determine their own political future through the plebiscite and ballot box. It did not extend to those other, self-selecting communities, such as the Ibo in Biafra or the Katangese in the Congo who demanded independence on their own initiative and whose claims to independence largely fell on deaf ears.

It was soon to become apparent that the primary means for this process of designation, or prior determination, was worked out through the medium of colonial administration. In some instances, the external boundaries of the colony defined the presumptive unit of self-determination—as, for example, in the case of Ghana or the Belgian Congo. In other cases, it was determined by reference to the internal boundaries that demarcated the different administrative units of a single colonial power (such as the boundary between Uganda and Tanganyika). The principle, in this second case, came to be expressed in the phrase *uti possidetis*—which referred to a concept having its origins in the somewhat hazy practice of boundary delimitation in South America, but which subsequently came to be affirmed as 'a general principle...logically connected with the phenomenon of obtaining independence, wherever it occurs'[42] (see generally Shaw, 1986). Precisely what 'logic' strictly required obeisance to the inherited parameters of colonial administration was not clear, but there did at least seem to be a need to determine who the people were before they were asked to decide upon their political future.

All of this, however, seems to be a long way away from the radical notion of self-determination as an idea which, as Berman puts it, challenges legal thought 'by posing the problem of law's relationship to sources of normative authority lying beyond the normal rules of a functioning legal system' (Berman, 1988–89, p 56). The more the principle could be described in terms of a prosaic institutional practice, or as a pragmatic obeisance to the determined character of existing boundaries, the less dangerous (and indeed less emancipatory) it seemed. Yet, fundamentally, there was still an inevitable tension between, on the one hand, the lofty proclamation of self-determination with its open-ended demand for self-government, and the simultaneous commitment to the principle of territorial integrity (which was almost invariably mentioned in General Assembly resolutions in the same

---

[41] International Covenant on Civil and Political Rights (1966) Article 1(1); International Covenant on Economic, Social and Cultural Rights (1966), Article 1(1).

[42] *Frontier Dispute, Judgment, ICJ Reports 1986*, p 554, para 20.

breath as that of self-determination). Of course, preserving intact all external and internal administrative boundaries nodded in the direction of this idea of territorial integrity, and certainly served to secure the political integrity of the newly emergent States once they had become established. It is no great surprise, in that sense, that the member States of the Organization of African Unity pledged in Resolution 16(1) of 1964 to respect colonial frontiers as they existed at the moment of independence (Shaw, 1996, pp 97–105). But at the same time, it still evaded the larger question as to how, and on what basis, the colonies may have enjoyed a right of self-determination, rather than the different peoples that comprised those colonies or, as Belgium cynically insisted, other non-self-governing communities elsewhere in the world. Part of the answer must be found in the gradual prioritization during this period of the idea of self-determination as a principle associated with the republican notion of self-governance rather than as a vehicle for aligning the boundaries of the polis with that of the nation. In one direction, for example, one may note that the principle of self-determination had, by this stage, lost its prefix; 'peoples' had replaced 'nations' as the relevant subjects of the right, and the identification of a community as ethnically or linguistically homogenous increasingly became a marker of its status as a minority rather than as a people entitled to political independence. In another direction, this new alignment was also evident in the increased emphasis placed upon the intrinsic relationship between 'internal' self-determination and the protection of individual and collective human rights (Cassese, 1995, pp 101–140; McCorquodale, 1994).

Nevertheless, this still only answers half of the question: it may explain, for example, why self-determination took the shape it did, and why it was a right denied to other 'minority' communities, but still doesn't answer how it was that decolonization could be squared with the principle of territorial integrity. For some colonial powers, after all, the colony was still largely regarded as part of the Metropolitan State (very much more so for Portugal and France than for Britain) the separation of which necessarily implied some diminution of the sovereign claims of the colonial powers. The right of self-determination, furthermore, seemed to speak of a process of determining future status, rather than a status in its own right. This, as Berman was puts it, posed the question as to how international law was able to 'recognize a right accruing to an entity which, by its own admission, lacks international legal existence?' (Berman, 1988–89, p 52). The answer to both questions seemed to be that self-determination had a suspensive capacity the effect of which was to displace claims to sovereignty on the part of the parent State, and affirm, somewhat obscurely, the nascent claims to sovereignty on the part of the people whose future had yet to be determined. There was, in fact, a model for this idea already in place and which had already informed some of the practice of the ICJ in its deliberations on the question of sovereignty in case of Protectorates (such as Morocco)[43] and Mandate territories. In the latter context, as McNair was to suggest, the question of sovereignty seemed to lie in 'abeyance'.[44] The rights of the colonial power were not those of a sovereign, but rather those enjoyed in virtue of agreement, to be exercised by way of sacred trust. Independence thus in no way implied a loss of sovereignty, or a violation of the principle of territorial integrity, rather

[43] *Rights of Nationals of the United States of America in Morocco, Judgment, ICJ Reports 1952*, p 176 at p 188 where, despite the French Protectorate, Morocco was declared to be 'a sovereign State'.
[44] *International Status of South West Africa, Advisory Opinion, ICJ Reports 1950*, p 128, Separate Opinion of Judge Mc Nair, p 150.

the fruition of a status temporarily subordinated by the fact of colonial administration. In that respect, the most remarkable feature of process of decolonization was the generalized, and quasi-legislative, statement found in the General Assembly's Declaration on Friendly Relations[45] which declared that 'the territory of a colony or other non-self-governing territory has, under the Charter of the United Nations, a status separate and distinct from the territory of the State administering it'. In virtue of this, any apparent tension that existed between its espousal of the principle of self-determination and simultaneous reaffirmation of the principle of territorial integrity largely evaporated.

If the principle of self-determination seemed to imply a suspension of claims to sovereignty on the part of the Metropolitan State and a commitment to the positive promotion of self-government on the part of 'dependent' peoples, it also seemed to imply the non-recognition of attempts to subvert that process. Thus, for example, when a minority white regime in what was then Southern Rhodesia declared its independence from Britain in 1965 its unilateral declaration of independence was immediately condemned by both the UN General Assembly[46] and the Security Council which called upon States not to recognize the 'illegal racist minority regime', and provided for a regime of sanctions to be imposed.[47] Similarly, but in a different context, when the South African government, in pursuit of its policy of apartheid, established the Bantusans of Transkei, Ciskei, Venda, and Bophuthatswana in the years 1976–1981 under the pretext that this constituted an implementation of the principle of 'self-government', those claims were again rejected with the General Assembly and Security Council condemning their establishment and calling for non-recognition.[48] Only in cases in which the subversion of self-determination came at the hands of another 'newly independent State' (Goa, West Irian, East Timor, and Western Sahara) was the reaction somewhat more muted or equivocal, and one may sense that this was probably informed by the idea that the rubric of colonialism had somewhat less purchase in such cases.

Yet, for all its continuing associations with the process of decolonization, the story of self-determination does not end there. After the fall of the Berlin Wall in 1989 and the collapse of the Soviet rule, the principle of national self-determination was once again to acquire a prominence in international legal thought and practice. Of the new States that were to emerge in the 1990s, most did so on a platform of national self-determination, most also held plebiscites or national polls by way of authorization, some also sought to make as a determinant of subsequent citizenship a facility with the national language (Cassese, 1995, pp 257–277). Not all such cases, however, posed problems as far as the question of statehood was concerned. In some cases the change could be conceived as little more than a change of government (Hungary, Romania, Ukraine, Poland, Belarus, and Bulgaria for example), in some as the emergence from a condition of unlawful annexation (the Baltic Republics), in some as a basis for consensual re-unification (Germany), or of separation (the Czech and Slovak Republics). In the cases of the former USSR and Socialist Federal Republic of Yugoslavia, however, the role to be played by the principle of self-determination was to assume considerably more significance.

---

[45] GA Res 2625 (XXV) (24 October 1970).
[46] GA Res 2379 (SSVI) (28 October 1968).
[47] SC Res 232 (16 December 1966); SC Res 253 (29 May 1968).
[48] GA Res 31/6A (26 October 1976); SC Res 402 (22 December 1976).

In the case of the Soviet Union, the problem was effectively resolved at two meetings in Minsk and Alma Ata (see above) which, whilst by no means wholly consistently, put in place the idea that the independence of the new Republics in Central Asia and elsewhere had come about through the consensual secession of the administrative units of the Union leaving Russia as the rump State. If the language of national self-determination was relevant, here, it was not such as to challenge or disrupt the principle of sovereignty or territorial integrity in any profound way. The case of Yugoslavia, by contrast, was far more difficult (see Radan, 2002). Prior to 1989, Yugoslavia had been a Federal State comprising of six Republics representing the major 'nationalities' and two autonomous enclaves (Kosovo and Vojdvodina) each of which had representation in the administration of the Federation. The death of President Tito in 1980 was followed by a power-struggle within the Federation culminating in declarations of independence being announced on the part of Slovenia and Croatia in 1991 recalling, in their terms, the principle of national self-determination (which itself had some recognition in the Federal Constitution). These initiatives, however, were forcibly resisted and the subsequent outbreak of violence was then to engulf Bosnia-Herzegovina, the severity of which led ultimately to the dispatch of peacekeeping forces (UNPROFOR), the establishment of the International Criminal Tribunal for the Former Yugoslavia and the later submission of claims of genocide to the International Court of Justice.

One of the key questions here for other European States was whether or not to recognize the Statehood of the entities emerging from the conflict. Doing so had several important implications as regards the characterization of the ongoing conflict (as international rather than merely internal (see Gray, 1996)) and as to the justification for the arms embargo. It also, and more significantly for present purposes, would seem to bring into play the possibility that there might exist a 'post-colonial' right of secessionary self-determination, the implications of which would extend far beyond the confines of the conflict itself. Sensing that there were a number of delicate issues involved, the States participating in the Conference on Yugoslavia in 1991 established what became known as the 'Badinter Commission' (so named, after its Chairman Robert Badinter, President of the French Constitutional Court) to provide advice on the legal issues arising (see Craven, 1995; Terrett, 2000). In the Autumn of 1991 the Badinter Commission issued two significant Opinions that set the stage for the subsequent recognition of Croatia, Slovenia, Bosnia-Herzegovina and, somewhat later, that of Macedonia. The key advice given by the Badinter Commission, having specifically been asked about the implications of the principle of self-determination, was to declare that the former SFRY was 'in the process of disintegration' on the basis that the Federal organs could no longer wield effective power (it being hinted that those Federal organs such as the Yugoslav National Army that continued to operate had been effectively co-opted by the Serbian government). The significance of this should not be lost. What the Commission signally refused to say was that the 'nationalities' within the federation had a right of secessionary self-determination. They could plausibly have linked such a claim to the provisions of the Constitution that spoke of self-determination, to the emerging idea that self-determination is legitimate in cases of abusive or totalitarian exercises of power, or indeed, more simply to the proclamations of independence on the part of the various Republics. Doing the latter would obviously have been a little awkward given the claims to independence on the part of the Serbian community in Bosnia,[49] but its general reluctance here, no doubt, was informed by the sense that the recrudescent ethnic nationalism that underpinned the claims to independence were a throwback to a pre-modern primitivism the function of which had merely been to exacerbate the conflict in the first place. Caught thus in a position of neither wanting to ally itself with the Milosevic regime whose campaign of violence had been pursued under the banner of the preservation of the territorial integrity of Yugoslavia (in whose name the government of Serbia and Montenegro continued to act), nor wanting to provide continuing justification for inter-ethnic violence in the name of national self-determination, the Commission's determination that the Federation was in the process of dissolution was an extraordinarily dextrous act. Its effect was to provide a necessary analytical space for the recognition of the emergent Republics (whether or not on the basis of the principle of self-determination[50]) without running the risk of undermining respect for the principle of territorial integrity. Indeed, on the latter score, the Badinter Commission reaffirmed, in its second Opinion, the principle of *uti possidetis*, making clear in the process that the entities emerging from the former Yugoslavia were to be those that already had enjoyed administrative recognition within the Federation. That this was always to leave a certain ambiguity as to the status of Kosovo, which of course had a degree of administrative independence within the Federal structure albeit not as a constitutive nationality, perhaps goes some way to explain the ease by which the UN administration over the territory was established (the question always being in the air as to whether this was, indeed, 'Serbian' territory). Nevertheless, what appears from this, yet again, is the idea that the principle of self-determination is not something that rubs directly against the grain of statehood, nor that it necessarily stands in competition with the principle of territorial integrity. Rather it is an idea that has been allowed to flourish in the interstices of the existing order, occupying those spaces which have been opened up for it through the prior displacement of arguments about territorial sovereignty—whether that be through the idea that colonial territories had a status distinct from that of the metropolitan States, that independence was 'granted' rather than acquired, or that conflict had led to the dissolution of State from which the republics were to emerge.

V. DEMOCRACY AND HUMAN RIGHTS

For all the normalizing characteristics of much of this practice, there has remained a stand in much international legal thought that has resisted the implication that self-determination is nothing other than a process of describing how new States emerge. If 'national' self-determination understood in its ethnic, cultural, religious, or linguistic sense has been carefully avoided (or perhaps subsumed within the discourse of minority rights), self-determination in its civic republican sense has not. Indeed events in the 1990s have, if nothing else, given considerable impetus to the idea that there exists an emerging right to democratic governance in international law (Franck, 1996; Fox and Roth, 2000) the

---

[49] In Opinion No 2, the Commission addressed the claim to self-determination on the part of the Serbs in Bosnia and decided that, as a minority, they were not entitled to independence. It did suggest, however, that self-determination might be reinterpreted as implying a right of each individual to the nationality of their choice.

[50] See on this Koskenniemi, 1994a.

source of which is often traced to the linkage between the principle of self-determination and the individual rights of political participation (Article 25 International Covenant on Civil and Political Rights) and evidenced in the emerging practice of multilateral election monitoring and other initiatives designed to promote democracy and human rights. At first glance of course, the idea of a right to democratic governance has little obvious resonance for questions of statehood. Since it is concerned primarily with the issue of governmental rather than State legitimacy it may thus be thought to have salience in relation to a range of discretionary relations (diplomatic, financial and trade relations for example), but not so in relation to the qualities of statehood itself. Yet it is clear that those advocates of the 'emerging' right to democratic government do not see it as so confined.

There are two plausible ways in which a concern for democracy and human rights may impinge upon the question of statehood: one as an additional 'condition' that needs to be met before independence may be recognized (one of the earliest examples being Fawcett's interpretation of the Southern Rhodesian crisis in 1965 (Fawcett, 1965–66)); the other as a basis for the exercise of self-determination on the part of a community suffering oppression or systematically excluded from access to government. In respect of the first issue, as Murphy points out, elements of recent State practice seem to point towards a development in that direction. Shortly after the beginning of the conflict in Yugoslavia in 1991 the EC member States convened at an extraordinary EPC ministerial meeting to adopt a common policy on the recognition of States emerging from the Soviet Union and Yugoslavia. In the guidelines they were to produce, they affirmed 'their readiness to recognise, subject to the normal standards of international practice and political realities in each case, those new states which . . . have constituted themselves on a democratic basis'.[51] Further to this, they set out several conditions including: (1) respect for the provisions of the UN Charter and the Helsinki Final Act 'especially with regard to the rule of law, democracy and human rights'; (2) to guarantee the rights of ethnic and national groups and minorities; (3) to respect the inviolability of existing borders; (4) to accept all relevant arms control commitments; and (5) to commit to settle all questions of State succession and regional disputes by agreement. Whilst clearly evidence of a potential shift in practice, these guidelines were nevertheless very loosely applied in the subsequent process by which the EC member States came to recognize the new Yugoslav Republics. The recognition of Croatia proceeded in early 1992 despite the fact that the Badinter Commission had found that it had not fully complied with the relevant conditions, whereas the recognition of Macedonia was held up as a consequence of an ongoing dispute with Greece over its name. The guidelines, it seems, were simply what they declared themselves to be: merely guidelines. Commentators were thus doubtful as to whether such criteria had yet been definitively established (Murphy, 2000, p 139) even if there was considerable enthusiasm for the idea that the new States acquiring their independence would remain bound by all pre-existent human rights treaty commitments that were formally applicable to that territory (Kamminga, 1996; Craven, 2007, pp 244–256).

To some extent, however, this idea has been given a further lease of life in the form of the recent regimes for international territorial administration (East Timor, Bosnia-Herzegovina, and Kosovo) put in place, amongst other things, for purposes of securing the

---

[51] Declaration on the 'Guidelines on the Recognition of New States in Eastern Europe and in the Soviet Union' (1992) 31 ILM 1486.

rule of law and the protection of human rights (Wilde, 2008). As some have argued, such regimes have seemed to function as institutional precursors to independence in such a way as to be evidence of a new emerging doctrine of 'earned sovereignty'—'earned' in the sense that independence will often be phased, conditional and perhaps constrained (Williams, Scharf, and Hooper, 2002–3). On the face of it, such arguments seem to promote a radical revision of the standard approach to statehood—forefronting the requirement of compliance with human rights and democratic conditions, and relativizing the notion of sovereignty. Yet, whatever the intrinsic merits of such an agenda, and however far this may be thought to open out a new realm of policy alternatives, it is hard to shake off the sense that this is anything other than a highly selective reinstitution, under UN auspices, of the old Mandate/Trusteeship arrangement in which territories were 'prepared' for independence under the tutelage of colonial masters.

Just as there might be hesitancy about the role that considerations of democracy and human rights might play in the recognition of new States, so also there is equivocation over the extent to which those considerations might serve as a basis for legitimating secession. In its advisory opinion concerning the secessionist claims of Quebec, the Canadian Supreme Court summarized what it saw to be the contemporary position:

the international law right to self-determination [gives rise to]…a right to external self-determination in situations of former colonies; where a people is oppressed, as for example under foreign military occupation; or where a definable group is denied meaningful access to government to pursue their political, economic, social and cultural development. In all three situations, the people in question are entitled to a right to external self-determination because they have been denied the ability to exert internally their right to self-determination.[52]

Since Quebec 'did not meet the threshold of a colonial people or an oppressed people' and since the Quebecers had not been denied 'meaningful access to government' the Court concluded that they did not enjoy the right to effect the secession of Quebec from Canada unilaterally. Rather, they enjoyed a (Constitutional) right to negotiate the terms of a separation.

The most interesting feature of this opinion, however, was the attempt by the Court to run a thread through the three instances of secessionary self-determination outlined in its Opinion by linking each one to a violation of 'internal self-determination'. There are two ideas in play here: one is a three-fold association being forged between the fact of alien rule, the denial of human rights (oppression) and the lack of access to government, each of which is taken as expressive of the same denial of self-determination. The other, associated, idea is one that effectively makes conditional any claim to sovereignty (or territorial integrity) upon the preservation and promotion of individual and collective rights and the maintenance of a system of government by consent. One might conclude from this that in cases where a determinate people have been oppressed, abused, or routinely denied their rights (treated, in some respects, as a non-self-governing territory), a claim for secessionary self-determination might be sustained simply by reason of the fact that the parent state is no longer in the position of being able to justify its claim to

---

[52] *Reference Re Secession of Quebec*, Canadian Supreme Court (1998) 37 ILM 1340, para 138.

sovereignty. This 'remedial' notion of self-determination, on some accounts at least, goes some way to explain practice in the case of Eritrea, Bangladesh, and perhaps even Kosovo (Crawford, 2006, p 126).

In the case of Kosovo, one may certainly appreciate that, in some instances, recognition of its independence has been explicitly linked to the violence and abuse directed against the Kosovo Albanian population prior to the establishment of UNMIK, and to the consequential impossibility of it being 'returned' to Serbia. Yet one may also note that many other of the recognizing States (of which there are 62) were deeply equivocal on this score, making great play of the *sui generis* character of the situation, the 'suspensory' character of SC Resolution 1244 (1999) which authorized the establishment of an international civil administration in the territory, and the 'special role' played by the UN Special Envoy within the political process that had culminated in the development of the Comprehensive Proposal for the Kosovo Status Settlement (the Ahtisaari Plan). The apparently exceptional character of the position of Kosovo had two obvious implications. The first was that it spoke of a determination to make clear that, whatever the outcome, the case of Kosovo should not set any kind of precedent for other aspirant communities. Far from reinforcing, therefore, the idea of a right to remedial secession, it appears to do the opposite. The second implication is that the asserted non-exemplary character of the Kosovan situation was such as to allow recognition to proceed unimpeded. Its apparent 'uniqueness' made it perfectly feasible for recognizing States to take a completely independent view on the matter, attuning their policies not to generic concerns about sovereignty or territorial integrity, but to an appreciation as to what might seem politically viable.

Needless to say, it is evident that the kind of reasoning that tends to underpin this idea of remedial secession is not confined to that particular discourse. Precisely the same structure of argument is to be found in the debates over humanitarian intervention (and, more recently, the Responsibility to Protect[53]). In the view of those such as Reisman, for example, the abusive, totalitarian government is one that should no longer be allowed to enjoy the privilege of sovereignty as a defence against external intervention. Sovereignty, for him, is a relic of an absolutist past that has been profoundly reconfigured by the emergent law of human rights. And recent State practice—such as that exemplified in the interventions in Haiti (1994), Panama (1989), and Sierra Leone (1997)—were evidence of a beneficial shift in thought and practice (Reisman, 1990). Others, following this theme, have been cautious of its unilateralist bent, recommending in contrast, collective intervention under auspices of the United Nations in such circumstances (Franck, 2000). Yet for all the well-intentioned bravura associated with such 'muscular humanitarianism' (Orford, 2003), it poses all too many questions regarding the opacity of the conditions warranting intervention, the selective character of practice that underpins it and, if nothing else, its evidently imperial (and gendered) overtones. One may recall, after all, that the nineteenth century Scramble for Africa was justified, in part at least, upon the basis that it was necessary in order to combat the slave trade—a claim that was almost immediately shown to be the merest figment given the subsequent violence that accompanied colonial rule in the Congo Free State and South West Africa.

---

[53] See 2005 World Summit Outcome, GA doc. A/60/L.1, (2005) paras 138–139. See also Ch 17 below.

VI. STATEHOOD AND RECOGNITION

As has been suggested above, a key feature of the development of international law at the end of the nineteenth century was a certain critical ambivalence as to the process by which new states might come to acquire rights and obligations under international law. The Vattelian image of States existing in a state of nature in their relations with one another, subject only to such obligations as might have been voluntary accepted (through treaty or adherence to custom) seemed to place States in some respect prior to law. This, of course, had some enduring resonance: international law itself did not create States by way of some legislative fiat, rather they emerged through the spontaneous and concerted action of a community or society organizing itself internally as a sovereign political community. International law merely had a role in acknowledging the reality of something which already been put in place. A State 'is a State', as Wheaton put it, simply 'because it exists' (Wheaton, 1866, p 28).

In so far as the society of States remained entirely stable this might have sufficed, yet by the beginning of the nineteenth century the emergence of new States in South America and the establishment of Belgium and Greece within Europe, brought to prominence the practice of recognition, which had previously been employed largely for purposes of identifying a condition of belligerency or insurgency. This immediately posed a question as to the relationship between that practice of diplomatic recognition and the general status of the communities being thereby recognized. Even if the existence of States was merely a question of fact, their claims to sovereignty often had to be judged by reference to the competing claims of other States. In case of secession, for example, it was understood that to recognize a new State before the moment at which it had fully established its independence was not merely to offend the sensibilities of the State attempting to suppress the rebellion, but also constituted an act of unlawful intervention. This was to subtly change, even if not to radically transform, the initial hypothesis. One could still think of the existence of States primarily in terms of their internal effectiveness, but the function of recognition came to determine the question of participation or membership in the wider international community. Wheaton (1866, s 21, p 28) thus distinguished between internal and external sovereignty for such purposes:

So long, indeed, as the new State confines its action to its own citizens, and to the limits of its own territory, it may well dispense with such recognition. But if it desires to enter into that great society of nations, all the members of which recognize rights to which they are mutually entitled, and duties which they may be called upon reciprocally to fulfil, such recognition becomes essentially necessary to the complete participation of the new State in all the advantages of this society.

What this immediately put on the table was a distinction between the existence of States on the one hand, and their participation in the international community on the other. Questions of status and relations thus seemed separable: diplomatic recognition being relevant to the latter not the former. Of course, this only really made sense in a context in which international law was understood as occupying a specific geographical space. The hypothesis that there might be States possessing 'internal sovereignty' yet not participating in the 'great society of nations' had its concrete expression in the postulated divide between the European and non-European worlds at the time. This was precisely the way in which one could rationalize, in some degree at least, knowledge of the existence of the Ottoman Empire, China, and Japan as independent political communities yet not assume they were, as a consequence, subjects of international law in the fullest sense.

Nevertheless, the division between internal and external sovereignty, or between the existence of States and their participation in the international community was cause for a certain amount of ambivalence. To begin with, there were two possible constructions of the position. One was that the State existed for legal purposes from the moment of its existence *de facto*, and that recognition and 'participation' were merely complementary benefits (see eg Heffter, 1857, p 43). Another was that its existence for purposes of international law was determined by the moment of participation since it was only through recognition that legal relations with other members of the international community would be definitively established.[54] In some respects it seemed to be necessary to maintain both of these positions. On the one hand, in order for the society of nations to have determinate content, there needed to be a proximate relation between the subjects of law and the boundaries of that society understood as a legal order. On the other hand, it seemed equally necessary to admit the legal existence of unrecognized States in order to give legal effect to treaty relations with non-European States and societies. Colonization of the non-European world thus depended upon a simultaneous process of exclusion and inclusion: the native sovereign being excluded from the European legal order in order to justify the claims of the latter to be a society of civilized sovereigns, yet simultaneously included within the legal order in order to rationalize the treaty relations upon which colonization depended. The maintenance of an ambivalent relationship between recognition and statehood was the means by which that could be achieved.

Although by the beginning of the twentieth century, the project of 'land appropriation' in Africa had largely run its course, international lawyers were no clearer as to the nature or character of the process of recognition. In a remarkably obtuse passage Hall (1895, p 87) summarizes the position as follows:

Theoretically a politically organized community enters of right...into the family of states and must be treated in accordance with law, so soon as it is able to show that it possesses the marks of a state. The commencement of a state dates nevertheless from its recognition by other powers; that is to say from the time at which they accredit ministers to it, or conclude treaties with it, or in some other way enter into such relations with it as exist between states alone. For though no state has a right to withhold recognition when it has been earned, states must be allowed to judge for themselves whether a community claiming to be recognised does really possess all the necessary marks, and especially whether it is likely to live. Thus although the right to be treated as a state is independent of recognition, recognition is the necessary evidence that the right has been acquired.

Whilst overtly assuming what was to become known as a 'declaratory' approach to recognition (the essence of which insists that a state exists as a subject of international law at the

---

[54] Wheaton, 1866, s 21: 'until such recognition becomes universal on the part of the other States, the new State becomes entitled to the exercise of its external sovereignty as to those States only by whom that sovereignty has been recognized'; Lorimer, 1883, p 106: 'Though recognition is often spoken of as admission into the family of nations, it leaves the State which has claimed and obtained it from one State only, in the same position in which it formerly stood to every other State'.

moment at which it 'possesses the marks of a state' as defined by international law), this is immediately qualified in two ways. First, since international law is fundamentally relational, the 'theoretical' existence of the State remains precisely that—theoretical—until placed in a social context, and recognition thus marks the commencement of the State for practical purposes. Secondly, the fulfilment of the criteria for statehood (which, of course, included such notions as to whether the State was sufficiently civilized) was in no circumstances either self-evident or self-expressive but something that that had to be subject to critical judgment and appreciation. In absence of any other determining mechanism, furthermore, the judgment and appreciation had to be that of existing States. Hall veers, at this point, towards the idea that recognition is, in fact, 'constitutive' in the sense that the legal existence of a State is thus dependent upon its recognition by others. But appreciating perhaps that this would fatally cut the ground from underneath his first assertion, Hall finally tries to regain his initial standpoint by insisting that this recognition is ultimately merely 'evidential' and that the 'right to be treated as a state' is independent of, such recognition. In a single paragraph, Hall thus seems to occupy all conceivable positions: recognition is both declaratory and constitutive; States exist prior to recognition but commence on recognition; recognition is a duty but also a privilege.

Hall's equivocation here summarizes in short form much of the ensuing debate over the character of recognition in the following century. For the most part those adopting a constitutive approach to recognition point to the speciousness of Hall's theoretical position—however confidently a political community might believe itself to have fulfilled the criteria for statehood, it is only through acceptance of that fact by other States, that one can say with any assurance that it has. It is meaningless to assert that Abkhazia, North Ossetia, or Taiwan *are* States if no one is prepared to accept them as such. Those, by contrast, adopting a declaratory approach point to the political and discretionary character of recognition—to the fact that, as in the *Tinoco Arbitration*, a State like the UK may refuse to recognize another (government in that case) not because of any perceived defect in origin or competence, but simply because it does not wish to have diplomatic relations with it.[55] The determinants of statehood must, therefore, must be posited as anterior to the practice of recognition even if the latter may be thought to provide evidence for the former.

To a large extent the respective positions on the question of recognition turn, not so much on the question as to whether the existence of a State is a self-expressive fact, or upon the fulfilment or lack thereof of the requisite criteria, but upon the analytical relationship between the two elements of 'status' and 'relations'. In one (the declaratory approach) these are kept distinct: the question of status has to be determined prior to the creation of relations with others. Only those entities fulfilling the requisite criteria can be said to have the capacity to enter into legal relations with others as States. In the other, the two issues are merged such that the existence or otherwise of such relations becomes the mode by which status is determined. Only those entities having relations with other States can be assumed to have the legal capacity to do so. The difficulty with the declaratory position is that it seeks to maintain both the idea that the creation of States is rule-governed, and that the conferral or withholding of recognition is an essentially political and discretionary act. To postulate the existence of a rule, but then deny it any ground for being applied is to rely rather heavily upon the self-executory character of formal rule. The difficulty with the

---

[55] *Tinoco Arbitration (Costa Rica v Great Britain)* (1923) 1 RIAA 369; (1924) 18 *AJIL* 147 at p 154.

constitutive position, by contrast, is that it seeks to maintain that the conferral or with-holding of recognition is a legal act (or at least one with legal effects) but that in the absence of either a 'duty to recognize' (as asserted by Lauterpacht, 1947) or of the existence of an agency competent to adjudicate (as asserted by Dugard, 1987), then allows the question of status to become entirely dependent upon the individual position of the recognizing States. The best one could say, in any particular context, was that a political community was 'more or less' a State.

For the most part, although many profess to prefer the 'declaratory approach' (support for which is found, once again, in the Montevideo Convention),[56] doctrine on recogni-tion remains fundamentally ambivalent on most of these key questions.[57] There are two particular difficulties. To begin with, it is clear that recognition of another State will have certain legal implications: it implies, at the very least, a commitment to respect the sover-eignty and territorial integrity of the State it has recognized and will also have a range of domestic legal consequences as might concern the recognition of its law and legal transac-tions occurring within its jurisdiction. By the same token, it is almost universally held that recognition will not necessarily imply a willingness to enter into diplomatic relations with that other State nor indeed, a recognition of its government (prior to 2001, for example, only three States recognized the Taliban as the government of Afghanistan, yet there was no doubt that all recognized the State of Afghanistan). The difficulty, however, is that it is frequently impossible to entirely dissociate the fact of recognition from the idea of political approval. This was typically a problem of particular acuteness in the context of govern-mental recognition (relevant primarily in case of those governments establishing their authority by unconstitutional means) and led to the enunciation by the Mexican Secretary of Foreign Relations of what became known as the 'Estrada Doctrine' the effect of which was to recommend the recognition of all effective governments irrespective of the means by which they came to power (Jessup, 1931). That this never quite avoided the problem (given that there would still be questions of interpretation in cases in which there were two rival governments competing for power) recommended a general abandonment of the pol-icy of formally recognizing any governments at all (a policy which the British Government belatedly adopted in 1980) (for a critique of this position see Talmon, 1998, pp 3–14).

The difficulty of separating law from policy, however, was not confined to govern-mental recognition, but also influenced practice in relation to the recognition of States. Whilst non-recognition, as observed above, has been employed as a way of signalling the international community's condemnation of attempts to subvert processes of self-determination or to establish new States by recourse to force, the fact that it is also still seen to be an essentially 'discretionary act that other States may perform when they choose and in the manner of their own choosing',[58] is such as to make it a somewhat hap-hazard semeiotic device. In an enlightening typology, Warbrick (1997, pp 10–11) explains

---

[56] Article 3: 'The political existence of the State is independent of recognition by the other States' and Article 6: 'The recognition of a State merely signifies that the state which recognizes it accepts the personality of the other with all the rights and duties determined by international law'). See also, Badinter Commission, Opinions 8 and 10, 92 ILR 201, 206 (1992).

[57] See Brownlie, 1982: 'in the case of "recognition", theory has not only failed to enhance the subject but has created a *tertium quid* which stands, like a bank of fog on a still day, between the observer and the con-tours of the ground which calls for investigation'.

[58] Badinter Commission, Opinion No 10 of 1992, 92 ILR 206, p 208.

that the mere statement 'We (State A) do not recognize entity X as a State' has at least five possible meanings:

(1) We take no decision, one way or another, about recognizing X [in A's eyes, X may or may not be a State];

(2) We have chosen not to recognize X (although we could do) for political reasons not related to X's status [by implication, A does consider X to be a State];

(3) We do not recognize X because it would be unlawful/premature for us to do so [A does not regard X as legally a State];

(4) We do not recognize X, although it might (appear to) be a State, because there are customary law obligations or specific treaty obligations which prohibit us from doing so;

(5) We do not recognize X, although it might (appear to) be a State, because there is a specific obligation imposed by the Security Council not to do so.

Much would seem to depend, thus, upon how the recognizing State would characterize or understand its own actions. Only by looking behind the refusal to recognize might one determine a difference in stance, for example, between the refusal to recognize the Turkish Republic of Northern Cyprus (informed, it seems, by a reflection upon the illegality of the Turkish intervention in Cyprus) and the similar refusal to recognize the former Yugoslav Republic of Macedonia in early 1992 (informed, it seems, by an unwillingness to prejudice diplomatic relations with Greece). In some cases, however, the position is simply opaque. It was never entirely clear, for example, as to whether those Arab States which refused to recognize the State of Israel before 1993, really believed that Israel did not exist as a State (and hence was not bound by the various treaty obligations to which it was a party), or merely desired to make clear that it *should* not exist even if it did so in fact. This poses a particular problem since just as it seems necessary to read recognition policy symptomatically (as being fundamentally an expression of something else), so also the result of such an enquiry might actually make it more, rather than less, difficult to disentangle those considerations that bear upon the question of legal status and those that apparently do not.

This relates to a second difficulty with the practice of recognition namely that even in cases in which States have taken a firm position in seeking to avoid recognition of a State (and hence avoid any sense of condoning its existence) they are not infrequently unable or unwilling to live with the consequences. As pointed out, it seemed unlikely that the Arab States, in refusing to recognize Israel, also believed that Israel was not therefore bound by the Geneva Conventions of 1949 in relation to its occupation *of* the West Bank and Gaza, or that it was otherwise free to ignore general principles of international law governing the use of force. Once again, their position was one of simultaneous inclusion and exclusion. In a more explicit sense, however, domestic courts have also frequently sought to avoid the consequences of non-recognition policies, and have resorted to a variety of different expedients to allow judicial cognition of the laws of what are formally unrecognized States. In the *Carl Zeiss* case, for example, the House of Lords avoided the obvious consequences of the British government's refusal to recognize the German Democratic Republic by treating the legislative acts of the GDR as essentially those of the USSR.[59] Similarly, in *Hesperides Hotels*, Lord Denning adopted a policy, already well established in the United States, to allow recognition of the laws of unrecognized States (in that case the Turkish Republic of Northern Cyprus) insofar as they related to 'the day to day affairs of the people, such as their marriages, their divorces, their leases, their occupations and so forth'.[60] In the UK, in fact, this latter policy has come to find formal expression in the Foreign Corporations Act of 1991 which states that foreign corporations having status under the laws of an unrecognized State may nevertheless be treated as a legal person if those laws are 'applied by a settled court system in that territory'. In each of these cases, an important consideration seems to have been a concern to insulate the 'innocent' population from the 'illegalities' associated with the claims to authority on the part of their governments; but they also illustrate in some ways a continued prevarication between the need, on the one hand, to recognize 'effective' entities whilst, on the other, to ensure at least the semblance of some commitment to the legal values that a refusal to recognize might have embodied.

More often than not, this dual commitment to admitting the reality of a situation whilst not accepting its 'legality' is spoken of in terms of 'pragmatism'. A pragmatist, in this sense, seems to be one who is not willing to commit to legal principle to the point at which it is disadvantageous either to the recognizing State or, as suggested above, to the population concerned. It bespeaks either of an opposition to either a rigid commitment to the formal rule, or of the necessity of accepting, in an imperfect world, imperfect solutions. Yet what this characterization of the situation misses is that the counterpoint is not between 'law' and 'reality' (or indeed any other alternative to 'law') but a counterpoint that has always existed within international law itself. Just as, in the past, the distinction between recognition *de jure* and recognition *de facto*, allowed States the opportunity to have dealings with insurgent governments without, at the same time, being seen to implicate themselves to overtly in an act of intervention (see Baty, 1936, p 378), so also the practice of recognizing the acts of certain governments whilst not recognizing their claims to statehood itself is one that really just goes to the point that legal doctrine has consistently sought to embed both law and fact within itself (however contradictory that might seem).

If doctrine on statehood and recognition seems to admit the necessity of a constructive ambiguity, perhaps the most obviously anomalous (or is that representative?) case is that of Taiwan (Crawford, 2006, pp 198–221). Having formerly been recognized as the government of China until 1971, Taiwan then was removed from the United Nations and replaced by the Government of the People's Republic of China. Since then, it has never entirely renounced its claim to be the government of China, nor unequivocally asserted its existence as an independent State. Taiwan nevertheless has many dealings with other States largely on the same basis as any other State (but without the same diplomatic privileges). Taiwanese government agencies are often regarded as having legal status in other countries and a capacity to sue and be sued. It is a party to a number of treaties and has membership in the WTO (as a 'Separate Customs Territory' under the name 'Chinese Taipei'). In the UK, Taiwanese corporations are allowed to do business under the terms of the 1991

[59] *Carl-Zeiss-Stiftung* v *Rayner & Keeler Ltd (No 2)* [1967] 1 AC 853.
[60] *Hesperides Hotels Ltd* v *Aegean Turkish Holidays Ltd* [1978] QB 205 at p 218.

Foreign Corporations Act 'as if' Taiwan was a recognized State, and in the US relations have largely been 'normalized' under the terms of the Taiwan Relations Act 1979 which seeks to implement the policy of maintaining 'unofficial relations'. As Crawford observes '[i]t is surprising it does not suffer from schizophrenia' (Crawford, 2006, p 220). The same might be said of international lawyers more generally.

VII. CONCLUSION

In an article written in the early 1990s, Martti Koskenniemi reflected upon the contemporary resonance of Engel's notion of the 'withering away' of the State. In his view, there were two versions of this thesis in circulation. One was a 'sociological' version that, on observing the recent globalization of politics, argues that 'states are no longer able to handle problems such as massive poverty, pollution of the atmosphere, or even their own security' without entering into forms of cooperation that entail the 'gradual dissolution of sovereignty' (Koskenniemi, 1994b, p 22). The other was an 'ethical' version that regards statehood as a form of 'morally indefensible egotism' that either serves to create and perpetuate 'artificial distinctions among members of the human community' or to justify the use of State apparatus for oppression. Each of these critiques stresses the artificiality of the State as an idea or institution; each also sees its withering away as essentially beneficial.

The point of Koskenniemi's article was not so much to defend the State as an institution as against these two critiques, but rather to defend the *idea* of the State as a place (or a language) in which various conceptions of justice, right or economic efficiency might be worked out on an ongoing basis. What informs his argument here is that both versions of the thesis tend to take as 'given' that which they are using as the point of critique:

The problem with the critiques of the state is their inability to reach into what is authentic and agree on what it requires in terms of political action. In suggesting that we must realize something that is already there—and in consequently de-emphasizing the decision processes needed to get there—the critiques function as political ideologies, and their claim to spontaneity, following Adorno, is 'a jargon of authenticity' instead of an expression of some hidden truth.' [footnotes omitted] (Koskenniemi, 1994b, p 22)

To posit, in other words, the withering away of the State on the basis that it is either a sociological necessity or ethically desirable omits to reflect upon the unstable, or at the very least contestable, character of either the sociology or ethics that underpin them. The 'fact' of globalization or the 'justice' of certain rights claims may, after all, look very different in different parts of the world.

The resonance of Koskenniemi's observations here, however, relate to more than merely a reflection upon the debates over globalization, human rights or the survival of the State as an institution, but more generally to the question surrounding the relationship between international law and the condition of statehood. The two key standpoints that Koskenniemi highlights—the ethical and the sociological—operate not merely as standpoints external to the State, but rather run through the discourses on sovereignty, self-determination, legitimacy, and recognition that constitute the very idea of the State in the first place. There is a constant equivocation, in all such discussions, as to whether the world is to be taken 'as it is' (in which we might be inclined to treat statehood as a question of fact, effectiveness as the primary condition, recognition as declaratory and sovereignty as innate), or as something which must be engineered to correspond to those values which we take to be universal and necessary (in which case, we might treat statehood as being a matter of law, self-determination or democratic legitimacy as primary conditions, recognition as quasi-constitutive, and sovereignty as delegated and conditional). To note the equivocation, here, however is to advert to the untenable character of either position. We can no more rely upon the assumption that States simply exist independently of the relations they have with others (the supposed 'authenticity of the real') than we can upon the assumption that justice always lies in the hands of those who have the capacity to speak its name (the supposed 'authenticity of the ethical').

One of the purposes of this chapter, however, has been to explain how many of these seemingly abstract theoretical arguments about recognition, statehood or sovereignty had a definitive context, namely that which arose as a consequence of the European engagement with the non-European world in the late nineteenth century. The difficulties associated with both seeking to delimit, in a descriptive sense, the geographical orientation of international law by reference to the pre-existence of European nation states, but simultaneously employ a prescriptive of notion of statehood as a way of supervising the 'entry' of new States into the family of nations, have largely conditioned many of the theoretical puzzles that subsequently emerged. Statehood is both presumed and regulated, recognition both constitutive and declaratory, sovereignty both a source of right and a product of law, self-determination both an expression of autonomy and a product of prior-regulation. Running through those debates has always been a dynamic of inclusion and exclusion which, in the past, served as a way of negotiating in a complex way the relationship with the non-European world, but in more recent times has come to mark the various projects and proposals associated with the identification of new categories: failed States, rogue States, illiberal or illegitimate States. In many cases such projects have been initiated on the premise that they are seeking to avoid or cast aside the authoritarian characteristics of what they take to be a nineteenth century 'positivist' international law, but have strangely re-appropriated precisely the same structures of thought or argument.

In all of this, however, what may be remarked upon is the relative strength within international legal thought of what might be called a civic republican tradition that, recalling Kant's project of perpetual peace, forges a rough alignment between the idea of the State as a civic enterprise the object of which is to guarantee individual human rights and freedoms, of sovereignty as a set of entitlements conditioned by the government's democratic credentials (or ability to fulfil its mandate), of international law as a cosmopolitan order that supervises and regulates the relationship between those largely arbitrary collections of individuals and agencies, and of international organizations as the nascent institutional expression of the values and interests of the international community writ large. In this account, the place of community, culture or tradition is assigned no direct role and may merely occupy the spaces left available to it within that framework—as that which marks participation within a minority or indigenous community, or as that which is engendered by the State through the institutional apparatus of government (nationalism as a political agenda). In the same sense, the State as an institution becomes ultimately vulnerable to an essentially instrumental critique: either it does its job and can be justified on that basis, or it doesn't and can't. This, in many ways, does seem to represent the key shift in legal thought that has occurred over the course of the last century, but it is one that is strangely quiet on the key questions Koskenniemi poses for it: how does it claim authenticity for the values that it proclaims and what kind of political action does it entail?

REFERENCES

ALEXANDROWICZ, C (1967), *An Introduction to the History of the Law of Nations in the East Indies* (Oxford: Clarendon Press).

ANGHIE, A (2005), *Imperialism, Sovereignty and the Making of International Law* (Cambridge: Cambridge University Press).

BATY, T (1936), 'Abuse of Terms: "Recognition", "War"', 30 *AJIL* 377.

BERMAN, N (1988–89), 'Sovereignty in Abeyance: Self-Determination and International Law', 7 *Wisc ILJ* 51.

BLUM, Y (1992), 'UN Membership of the "New" Yugoslavia: Continuity or Break?', 86 *AJIL* 830.

BODIN, J, *Six Books of the Commonwealth* (1967, first published 1578), (Tooley, M (trans.)) (Oxford, Blackwell).

BROWNLIE, I (1982), 'Recognition in Theory and Practice', 53 *BYIL* 197.

BRIERLY, J (1924), 'The Shortcomings of International Law', 5 *BYIL* 13.

CASSESE, A (1995), *Self-Determination of Peoples: A Legal Reappraisal* (Cambridge: Cambridge University Press).

CLAPHAM, A (2006), *Human Rights Obligations of Non-State Actors* (Oxford: Oxford University Press).

CLAUDE, I (1955), *National Minorities; an International Problem* (Cambridge, Mass: Harvard University Press).

COBBAN, A (1945), *National Self-Determination* (Oxford: Oxford University Press).

CRAVEN, M (1995), 'The European Community Arbitration Commission on Yugoslavia', 67 *BYIL* 333.

—— (2007), *The Decolonization of International Law: State Succession and the Law of Treaties* (Oxford: Oxford University Press).

CRAWFORD, J (2006), *The Creation of States in International Law*, 2nd edn (Oxford: Oxford University Press).

DERRIDA, J (1989–90), 'Force of Law: The Mystical Foundations of Authority', 11 *Cardozo Law Review* 921.

DUGARD, J (1987), *Recognition and the United Nations* (Cambridge: Cambridge University Press).

DUURSMA, JC (1996), *Fragmentation and the International Relations of MicroStates* (Cambridge: Cambridge University Press).

FAWCETT, JES (1965–66), 'Security Council Resolutions on Rhodesia', 41 *BYIL* 103.

FRANCK, T (1996), 'Clan and Superclan: Loyalty, Identity and Community in Law and Practice', 90 *AJIL* 359.

—— (1999) *The Empowered Self: Law and Society in an Age of Individualism* (Oxford: Oxford University Press).

—— (2000), 'Legitimacy and the Democratic Entitlement', in Fox, GH and Roth, BR (eds) *Democratic Governance and International Law* (Cambridge: Cambridge University Press), p 25.

FOUCAULT, M (2006), *Psychiatric Power: Lectures at the College De France, 1973–1974* (Davidson, A (ed)) (London: Palgrave Macmillan).

——(2007), *Security, Territory, Population: Lectures at the College de France 1977–1978* (Senellart, M (ed)) (London: Palgrave Macmillan).

Fox, GH and ROTH, BR (2000) (eds) *Democratic Governance and International Law* (Cambridge: Cambridge University Press)

GIDDENS, A (1985), *The Nation-State and Violence* (Cambridge: Polity Press).

GONG, G (1984), *The Standard of 'Civilization' in International Society* (Oxford: Clarendon Press).

GORDON, R (1997), 'Saving Failed States: Sometimes a Neo-colonialist Notion', 12 *American ULILP* 904.

GRAY, C (1996), 'Bosnia and Herzegovina: Civil War or Inter-State Conflict?' 67 *BYIL* 155.

HALL, WE (1895), *A Treatise on International Law*, 4th edn (Oxford: Clarendon Press).

HARDT, M and NEGRI, A (2000), *Empire* (Cambridge, Mass.: Harvard University Press)

HEFFTER, A-G (1857), *Le droit international publique de l'Europe* (Paris: Cotillon)

HELMAN, G and RATNER, S (1992–93), 'Saving Failed States' 89 *Foreign Policy* 3.

HOBBES, T (1957, first published 1651), *Leviathan; or The Matter, Forme and Power or a Commonwealth Ecclesiastical and Civil* (Oakeshott, M (ed)) (Oxford: Blackwell)

HOBSBAWM, E (1992), *Nations and Nationalism since 1780*, 2nd edn (Cambridge: Cambridge University Press).

JACKSON, R (1990), *Quasi-States: Sovereignty, International Relations and the Third World* (Cambridge: Cambridge University Press).

JENNINGS, R (1963), *The Acquisition of Territory in International Law* (Manchester: Manchester University).

JESSUP, P (1931), 'The Estrada Doctrine' 25 *AJIL* 719.

KAMMINGA, M (1996), 'State Succession in Respect of Human Rights Treaties' 7 *EJIL* 469.

KELSEN, H (1941–42), 'The Pure Theory of Law and Analytical Jurisprudence', 55 *Harv LR* 44.

KENNEDY, D (1997), 'International Law and the Nineteenth Century: History of an Illusion', 17 *Quinnipiac Law Review* 99.

KINGSBURY, B, KRISCH, N and STEWART, R (2005), 'The Emergence of Global Administrative Law', 68 *Law and Contemporary Problems* 15.

KLÜBER, J (1851), *Europaishes Völkerrecht*, 2nd edn (Schotthausen: Hurter).

KORMAN, S (1996), *The Right of Conquest: The Acquisition of Territory by Force in International Law and Practice* (Oxford: Oxford University Press).

KOSKENNIEMI, M (1989), *From Apology to Utopia: The Structure of International Legal Argument*, 2005 reissue (Cambridge: Cambridge University Press).

——— (1994a), 'National Self-Determination Today: Problems of Legal Theory and Practice' 43 *ICLQ* 241.

——— (1994b), 'The *Wonderful Artificiality* of States', 88 *ASIL Proceedings* 22

——— (2001) *The Gentle Civiliser of Nations: The Rise and Fall of International Law 1870–1960* (Cambridge: Cambridge University Press).

KREIJEN, G (2002) 'The Transformation of Sovereignty and African Independence: No Shortcuts to Statehood', in Kreijen, G (ed), *State Sovereignty and International Governance* (Oxford: Oxford University Press), p 45.

LAWRENCE, TJ (1895), *The Principles of International Law* (Boston: D C Heath and Co).

LAUTERPACHT, H (1947), *Recognition in International Law* (Cambridge: Cambridge University Press).

LOCKE, J, *Second Treatise of Government* (1980, first published 1690) (McPherson, CB (ed)) (Indianapolis: Hackett Publishing Co).

LORIMER, J (1883), *The Institutes of the Law of Nations* (Edinburgh: W Blackwood).

McCORQUODALE, R (1994), 'Self-Determination: A Human Rights Approach', 43 *ICLQ* 857.

MARKS, S (2006), 'State-Centrism, International Law, and the Anxieties of Influence', 19 *Leiden JIL* 339.

MARTENS, G DE (1864), *Précis du droit des gens moderne de l'Europe*, 2nd edn (Paris: Guillaume).

MILL, JS (1890) *Considerations on Representative Government* (London: Holt & Co).

MORRIS, C (1998), *An Essay on the Modern State* (Cambridge: Cambridge University Press).

MULLERSON, R (1993) 'The Continuity and Succession of States by Reference to the Former USSR and Yugoslavia', 42 *ICLQ* 473.

MURPHY, S (2000), 'Democratic Legitimacy and the Recognition of States and Governments', in Fox, G and Roth, B (eds) *Democratic Governance and International Law* (Cambridge: Cambridge University Press, 2000), p 123.

O'CONNELL, D (1970), *International Law*, 2nd edn (London: Stevens).

OPPENHEIM, L (1905), *International Law: A Treatise* (London: Longmans).

ORFORD, A (2003), *Reading Humanitarian Intervention: Human Rights and the Use of Force in International Law* (Cambridge: Cambridge University Press).

PHILLIMORE, R (1871), *Commentaries on International Law* (London: Butterworths).

PUFENDORF, S (1934), *On the Law of Nature and Nations* (1934, first published 1698), (Oldfather, CH and Oldfather, WA (trans.)) (Oxford: Clarendon Press).

RADAN, P (2002), *The Breakup of Yugoslavia and International Law* (London: Routledge).

REISMAN, W (1990), 'Sovereignty and Human Rights in Contemporary International Law', 84 *AJIL* 866.

RICH, R (1993), 'Recognition of States: The Collapse of Yugoslavia and the Soviet Union', 4 *EJIL* 36.

ROTBERG, R (2002), 'Failed States in a World of Terror', 81 *Foreign Affairs* 127.

SCHACHTER, O (1998), 'The Decline of the Nation-State and its Implications for International Law', 36 *Col JTL* 7.

SCHMITT, C (1974), *The Nomos of the Earth* (trans Ulmen, G, (2003)) (New York: Telos).

SCHWARZENBERGER, G (1950), *A Manual of International Law*, 2nd edn (London: Stevens).

SHAW, M (1986), *Title to Territory in Africa: International Legal Issues* (Oxford: Oxford University Press).

—— (1996), 'The Heritage of States: The Principle of *Uti Possidetis Juris* Today', 67 *BYIL* 75.

SIMPSON, G (2004), *Great Powers and Outlaw States: Unequal Sovereigns in the International Legal Order* (Cambridge: Cambridge University Press).

TALMON, S (1998), *Recognition of Governments in International Law* (Oxford: Clarendon Press).

TERRETT, S (2000), *The Dissolution of Yugoslavia and the Badinter Arbitration Commission* (Aldershot: Ashgate).

TILLY, C (1992), *Coercion, Capital and European States: AD 990–1992* (Oxford: Blackwell).

TWISS, T (1879–1880), 'Rapport', 3–4 *Annuaire Institut de Droit International*.

—— (1884), *Law of Nations Considered as Independent Political Communities* (Oxford: Clarendon Press).

WADE, H (1955), 'The Basis of Legal Sovereignty' [1955] *Cam LJ* 172.

WARBRICK, D (1997) 'Recognition of States: Recent European Practice', in Evans MD (ed) *Aspects of Statehood and Institutionalism in Contemporary Europe* (Aldershot: Dartmouth Publishers), p 9.

WEBER, M (1978), *Economy and Society* (Berkeley: University of California Press).

——(1994), 'The Profession and Vocation of Politics', in Lassman, P and Speirs, R (eds) *Weber: Political Writings* (Cambridge: Cambridge University Press), p 309.

WESTLAKE, J (1894), *Chapters on the Principles of International Law* (Cambridge: Cambridge University Press).

——(1904), *International Law* (Cambridge: Cambridge University Press).

WHEATON, H (1866), *Elements of International Law,* 8th edn (Dana, RH (ed), 1936) (Oxford Clarendon Press).

WILDE, R (2008), *International Territorial Administration: How Trusteeship and the Civilising Mission Never Went Away* (Oxford: Oxford University Press).

WILLIAMS, P, SCHARF, M, and HOOPER, J (2002–03), 'Resolving Sovereignty-Based Conflicts: the Emerging Approach of Earned Sovereignty', 31 *Denv JILP* 349.

WRIGHT, Q (1930), *Mandates under the League of Nations* (Chicago: The University of Chicago Press).

VATTEL, E DE, *The Law of Nations or the Principles of Natural Law* (1916, first published 1758) (Fenwick, G (trans.)), (Washington DC: Carnegie Institute).

ZIEMELE, I (2005), *State Continuity and Nationality: The Baltic States and Russia* (Leiden: Martinus Nijhoff).

FURTHER READING

ANGHIE, A (2005), *Imperialism, Sovereignty and the Making of International Law* (Cambridge, Cambridge University Press). An important corrective for all accounts of international law that fail to engage with the non-European world.

BERMAN, N (1988–89), 'Sovereignty in Abeyance: Self-Determination and International Law', 7 *Wisc ILJ* 51. The foremost author on the subject of nationalism and international law—here turning to the subject of self-determination.

CRAWFORD, J (2006), *The Creation of States in International Law* (Oxford: Clarendon Press). A monumental, encyclopaedic, work that remains the key reference point on the subject of statehood.

KOSKENNIEMI, M (2005), 2nd edn, *From Apology to Utopia: The Structure of International Legal Argument* (Cambridge: Cambridge University Press). A challenging, structuralist, critique that lays out the indeterminacy of legal argumentation on the question of sovereignty (especially chapter 4).

LAUTERPACHT, H (1947), *Recognition in International Law* (Cambridge, Cambridge University Press) Dated, and inevitably stamped with his own idiosyncrasies, yet still the best account of the doctrinal debate over recognition.

SIMPSON, G (2004), *Great Powers and Outlaw States: Unequal Sovereigns in the International Legal Order* (Cambridge: Cambridge University Press). Traces the persistence of the idea of sovereign inequality and imperialism in international law.

WILDE, R (2008), *International Territorial Administration: How Trusteeship and the Civilising Mission Never Went Away* (Oxford: Oxford University Press). The most comprehensive and effective account of the historic and contemporary practice of international territorial administration.

9

INTERNATIONAL ORGANIZATIONS

Dapo Akande

SUMMARY

This chapter examines the legal framework governing international organizations. It begins with an examination of the history, role and nature of international organizations. It is argued in the chapter that although the constituent instruments and practices of each organization differ, there are common legal principles which apply to international organizations. The chapter focuses on the identification and exploration of those common legal principles. There is an examination of the manner in which international organizations acquire legal personality in international and domestic law and the consequences of that legal personality. There is also discussion of the manner in which treaties establishing international organizations are interpreted and how this differs from ordinary treaty interpretation. The legal and decision-making competences of international organizations are considered as are the legal responsibility, privileges and immunities of international organizations. Finally, the chapter examines the structure and powers of what is probably the leading international organization—the United Nations.

I. INTRODUCTION

A distinctive feature of modern international affairs is the large number of international organizations through which States seek to achieve cooperation. This chapter looks at the place occupied by international organizations within the international legal system and sketches the legal framework governing their activities. It also describes the structure and activities of the leading global international organization—the United Nations (UN).

A. HISTORY AND ROLE OF INTERNATIONAL ORGANIZATIONS

International organizations were first created in the nineteenth century as a means of conducting international relations and fostering cooperation between States. They evolved from the ad hoc multilateral conferences convened by States to deal with particular situations—such as the Congress of Vienna (1815) which settled issues arising from the end of the Napoleonic wars—into institutions in which member States not only met regularly but which also possessed organs that functioned on a permanent basis. The early international organizations dealt with technical, non-political matters and included Commissions regulating European rivers such as the Rhine, the International Telegraphic Union (1865), and the Universal Postal Union (1874). The League of Nations, created in 1919 after the First World War, was the forerunner of the United Nations and was the first international organization established to deal with general political and other relations between States and which aspired to universal membership.

International organizations now play a significant role in international affairs generally and in the development of international law specifically. They exist in practically all fields of endeavour ranging from general political cooperation to protection of the environment, defence, provision of humanitarian and development assistance, promotion of trade, etc. It is a reflection of the significant role that international organizations play in international affairs and in the exercise of public power that attention is now being paid to the question of what the limits of their powers are and the principles relating to when and how these organizations may be held accountable or responsible for the exercise of such powers.[1]

Within their diverse fields of operation, international organizations perform a number of functions. These include:

- Providing a forum for identifying and deliberating upon matters of common interests.
- Acting as vehicles for taking action on international or transnational problems.
- Providing a forum for developing rules on matters of common interest.
- Providing mechanisms for promoting, monitoring and supervising State compliance with agreed rules and policies as well as for gathering information regarding the conditions in and practices of States.
- Providing a forum for the resolution of international disputes.

B. DEFINITION, DISTINCTIONS, AND DIFFERENCES

Given the variety of organizations that are international in character, it is difficult to lay down a satisfactory and all-encompassing definition which distinguishes those organizations considered as 'international organizations' under international law from other types of organizations (Klabbers, 2009, p 6). Article 2(a) of the International Law Commission's 2009 Draft Articles on the Responsibility of International Organizations provides that:

'international organization' means an organization established by treaty or other instrument governed by international law and possessing its own international legal personality. International organizations may include as members, in addition to States, other entities.[2]

---

[1] See generally, Reinisch, 2001; ILA Committee Reports, 1996–2000; and ILC Reports, 2009, Ch 4 'Responsibility of International Organizations'.

[2] ILC Reports, 2009, p 43.

This definition embodies the key criteria for identifying whether an entity is an international organization. First, such an entity must be composed predominantly of States and/or other international organizations, though the membership may extend to other entities as well. Secondly, the entity must be established under international law. Although international organizations are usually created by treaty, they can also be created by other means, such as the resolution of another international organization, the resolution of a conference of States or by joint unilateral acts of States. Examples of organizations created other than by treaty include the Organization for Security and Cooperation in Europe (OSCE) and the Organization of the Petroleum Exporting Countries (OPEC). Thirdly, for an entity to be an international organization it must possess autonomous organs having a will which is separate from that of the members. In practice this means that an organization must have a separate legal personality and be able to act on a majority basis.

The criteria set out above distinguish intergovernmental organizations which are the subject of this chapter from other types of international associations such as international non-governmental organizations and international public corporations. The key factor distinguishing international or intergovernmental organizations, such as the UN or the World Trade Organization (WTO), from international non-governmental organizations, such as Amnesty International or Greenpeace, is that the former are composed predominantly of States (and other intergovernmental organizations) whilst the latter are composed of private entities though they operate in more than one country. International public corporations or joint inter-State enterprises are entities jointly created by a number of States for the performance of commercial functions. Examples include the European Company for the Financing of Railway Rolling Stock (EUROFIMA) or Air Afrique (an airline established by eleven West African States). Whilst international organizations are entities created under international law and have international legal personality, joint inter-State enterprises are formally established under the corporate law of one of the member States, even though the enterprise may have its roots in a treaty.

Despite sharing a common definition, there are many differences between international organizations. The most obvious differences concern membership and functions. Membership may either be universal (open) or closed. Universal organizations are open to all States and examples include the UN and its specialized agencies (see Section VII A.2 below). Closed organizations limit membership to those States fulfilling certain criteria. Examples based on geographic criteria include regional organizations such as the Organization of American States (OAS) and the African Union (AU). Other examples based on economic criteria include OPEC and the Organization for Economic Cooperation and Development (OECD). Some international organizations, such as the UN, have general functions within broad areas whereas the functions of others are restricted to particular fields, such as telecommunications, labour, health or trade. Membership and function can be combined in various ways: some closed regional organizations exercise general functions (eg, the OAS and the Council of Europe), whilst some universal organizations only have competence in limited field (eg, the UN specialized agencies and the International Labour Organization (ILO)).

In considering whether or not a body or institutional structure qualifies as an international organization, one must consider the substance of the structure established by States rather than whether it is formally designated as an international organization. The key is whether the above criteria are fulfilled rather the designation of the organization.

Therefore, the more informal institutional arrangements established by some multilateral environmental treaties[3] and which are comprised simply of (i) a conference of the parties to the relevant treaty (COP) which meet regularly; (ii) one or more subsidiary bodies of the COP; and (iii) a secretariat which services the work of the COP and subsidiary bodies, may qualify as international organizations when they have a will distinct from those of the members. In some cases, these 'institutions' have even entered into treaties with States or other international organizations (Churchill and Ulfstein, 2000; Sands, 2003, pp 108–109).

C. IS THERE A COMMON LAW OF INTERNATIONAL ORGANIZATIONS?

Given their great diversity, the existence of a common law applicable to international organizations has been questioned. On one view, since the law governing each organization derives from its own constituent instrument and practices (its 'constitution'), each will be governed by different legal principles which can only be applied by analogy to other organizations. It is true that these 'constitutions' regulate many matters, such as membership, competences and financing, in differing ways. However, it is equally true that customary international law and, to a much lesser degree, treaties have generated principles of general application to international organizations. These common principles concern matters such as the legal personality of international organizations, implied competences, interpretation of constituent instruments, employment relations, immunities and privileges and the liability and responsibility of the organization and its member States (see ILC Report, 2009, Ch 4). These common principles apply in the absence of any contrary principle provided for in the law of the particular organization, and as regards liability and responsibility may even apply despite contrary provisions in the internal law of the organization. It is also accepted that the solutions adopted by one organization to a problem have a relevance to the approach to be taken to an analogous problem in another. The following sections outline the most important elements of this common law applicable to international organizations.

II. LEGAL PERSONALITY

In considering the legal position of international organizations it is useful to start by considering whether such entities possess legal personality and, if so, what the consequences of that legal personality are. Because international organizations usually operate on both the international plane and in national territories, one must consider whether these organizations possess international legal personality and legal personality in domestic law. Section II A examines the meaning of international legal personality and the sources of that personality for international organizations especially in cases in which it is not expressly provided for in the constituent instrument of that organization. It also examines the consequences for international organizations of the possession of international legal personality. Section II B considers whether non-member States of an international

---

[3] Eg, the London Convention on the Prevention of Marine Pollution by Dumping of Wastes and other Matter (1972); the United Nations Framework Convention on Climate Change (1992), and the Kyoto Protocol (1997). See further, Churchill and Ulfstein, 2000, pp 623–625.

organization are bound to recognize its legal personality. Section II C examines the obligation of member States to confer personality in domestic law and the various techniques used by States to confer such personality.

A. PERSONALITY IN INTERNATIONAL LAW

1. The meaning of international legal personality

To say that an entity has international legal personality is to say that the entity is a bearer of rights and duties derived from international law. Although it was often asserted in the nineteenth and early twentieth centuries that States were the only subjects of international law it was decisively established in the *Reparations for Injuries* Advisory Opinion that other entities, particularly international organizations, also possess international legal personality. The case arose out of the murder of a UN mediator in Jerusalem by a Jewish group. The UN General Assembly requested an opinion from the International Court of Justice on whether the UN had the capacity to bring an international claim (against Israel) for the purpose of obtaining reparation for injuries done to the organization and its agents. While Article 104 of the Charter imposes an obligation on UN Member States to confer legal personality on the Organization within their domestic legal systems, there is nothing in the Charter which expressly grants international personality to the UN. Nevertheless, the Court found that the UN possesses international legal personality, arguing that this was necessary for the fulfilment of its functions. The Court also deduced legal personality from the powers and rights that had been given to the UN (the power of decision-making, domestic legal personality, immunities, and privileges and treaty-making powers) under the Charter. The Court also noted that the Organization 'occupies a position in certain respects in detachment from its Members' and that:

> ... the Organization was intended to exercise and enjoy, and is in fact exercising and enjoying, functions and rights which can only be explained on the basis of the possession of a large measure of international personality and the capacity to operate on the international plane.[4]

To say that international organizations possess international legal personality tells us that they are capable of possessing international rights, capacities or duties. However, apart from a few specific capacities indicated below (Section II A.3), possession of international legal personality does not define the particular capacities, rights or duties that any particular organization possesses nor does it indicate that they possess the same capacities, rights or duties.

2. The sources of international legal personality for international organizations

Although treaties establishing universal international organizations do not usually provide expressly that they possess international legal personality, there are treaties dealing with closed international organizations which do so.[5] Where there is no express treaty basis, international personality may be deduced by other means.

---

[4] *Reparation for Injuries Suffered in the Service of the United Nations, Advisory Opinion, ICJ Reports 1949*, p 174 at p 179.

[5] Examples include Treaty of European Union (as amended by Lisbon Treaty), Article 47; EC Treaty, Article 210; European Coal and Steel Community Treaty, Article 6; Agreement Establishing the African Development Bank, Article 50.

There are two basic schools of thought regarding the method by which the personality is to be established in the absence of an express treaty provision. The first school—the inductive approach—asserts that the personality of an international organization is to be implied from the capacities, powers, rights and duties conferred on that organization in its constituent instrument and developed in practice (Schermers and Blokker, 1995, §1565; Reinisch, 2000, pp 54–59; Bowett, 2009, para 15–006). According to this school of thought, an international organization will only have personality if its members intended it to have such personality or if it can be asserted that such personality is necessary for the fulfilment of the functions ascribed to it by its members. The second school—the objective approach—asserts that an international organization has international legal personality as long as certain objective criteria set out by law are fulfilled (Seyersted, 1964; Rama Montaldo, 1970). Thus personality is not derived from the will of the members but from the presence of the criteria stated above in the definition of an international organization.[6]

There has been much debate regarding which of these two approaches was taken by the Court in the *Reparation for Injuries* Advisory Opinion. It that case, the Court made reference on more than occasion to the intention of the parties in ascribing legal personality to the UN. However, this does not necessarily mean that the Court took the inductive approach. What the Court seemed to be saying was that the intention of the members to ascribe certain rights, functions and characteristics to the UN, could only be given effect if the organization possessed its own legal personality. This is not inconsistent with saying that the members had ascribed characteristics to the organization which satisfied the criteria required for conferring international personality. While the key factor is the possession of those characteristics, they necessarily arise out of the will of the members. Thus, there is no radical difference between the two schools if one accepts that the characteristics which confer international legal personality on international organizations must necessarily be conferred on it by its members. Once those characteristics are conferred (by the will of the members through its constituent instrument or subsequent practice), the rules of international law confer international personality on the organization with all the consequences that this entails. Arguably, all that the Court did in the *Reparation for Injuries* Advisory Opinion was to search to see if the characteristics necessary for international personality (and which are predetermined by international law) had been conferred on the UN by its members.[7]

3. The consequences of the possession of international legal personality by international organizations

Possessing international legal personality means that an organization possesses rights and duties in international law but this does not usually tell us the particular rights and capacities possessed by a particular organization. However, there are certain consequences

---

[6] Amerasinghe, 2005, p 83 tries to merge both schools by arguing that the intention required is not subjective but objective and to be found in the circumstances surrounding the creation of the organization.

[7] See quote at n 4 above. In the sentences following that quote the Court states that the UN 'could not carry out the intention of its founders if it were devoid of legal personality. It must be acknowledged that its Members, by entrusting certain functions to it, with attendant duties and responsibilities, have clothed it with the compliance required to enable those functions to be effectively discharged'.

which flow from the possession of international legal personality by an international organization.

(i) Personality distinguishes the collective entity (the organization) from the members. In particular, legal personality, separates out the rights and obligations of the organization from those of the members (Lauterpacht, 1986, p 407).

(ii) Personality entitles the organization to bring a claim in international law for the purpose of maintaining its own rights.[8] Such claims by international organizations will be brought through the mechanisms which exist in international law for the settlement of international disputes and can only be made in an international tribunal if that the tribunal has jurisdiction to deal with the case.

(iii) Personality entails the consequence that an international organization is responsible or liable for the non-fulfilment of its obligations (Article 3, ILC Articles on Responsibility of International Organizations, 2009). Personality also gives rise to a presumption that members of the organization are not liable with respect to the obligations of the organization, although this presumption can be displaced (see Section V below).[9]

These first three consequences are inherent in the very notion of international legal personality and apply to any international legal person. However, there are other consequences of the personality of international organizations which do not apply to all international legal persons but result from the nature of personality possessed by international organizations.

(iv) Customary international law confers, at least within the host State, certain privileges and immunities on international organizations that are necessary for the efficient and independent functioning of the organization (see further Section VI below). As Higgins (1994, p 91) puts it, 'members—and a fortiori the headquarters State—may not at one and the same time establish an organization and fail to provide it with those immunities that ensure its role as distinct from that of the host State.'

(v) International organizations possess a power to conclude agreements which are subject to the law of treaties.[10] Although the question whether a particular type of treaty is within the competence of any particular organization depends on its implied powers, every organization at least has the competence (where not expressly denied) to enter into certain types of treaties. These include host State agreements and treaties for the purpose of settling claims by and against the organization.[11]

---

[8] Schermers and Blokker, 2004, §1856 argue that this capacity is an implied power but one possessed by all international organizations.

[9] See ILC's commentary to Article 61, ILC Draft Articles on Responsibility of International Organizations, ILC Report, 2009, 167.

[10] Vienna Convention on the Law of Treaties between States and International Organizations or between International Organizations (1986), preambular para 11.

[11] See *Reparation for Injuries Suffered in the Service of the United Nations, Advisory Opinion, ICJ Reports 1949*, p 174 at p 181.

B. OBJECTIVE LEGAL PERSONALITY AND RELATIONS WITH NON-MEMBER STATES

Given that international organizations are created by treaties—which do not bind non-parties without their consent[12]—it might be argued that the personality of an international organization is only binding on members.[13] This would mean that non-members would only be bound to accept that personality where they have 'recognized' the organization as a legal person. However, the better view is that the personality of international organizations is in fact objective, which means that it is opposable to non-members and that non-members are bound to accept that organization as a separate legal person.[14]

In the *Reparation for Injuries* opinion, the Court had to consider whether the UN could bring a claim against a State (Israel) which was not a member of the Organization. It took the view that:

> ...fifty States, representing the vast majority of the members of the international community, had the power, in conformity with international law, to bring into being an entity possessing objective international personality and not merely personality recognised by them alone....[15]

Clearly then international organizations with a membership consisting of the vast majority of the international community possess objective international personality. However, it is important to note that the Court did not say that *only* such organizations possess objective personality and there are good reasons of practice and principle for concluding that the personality possessed by any international organization is objective and opposable to non-members. In practice, 'no recent instances are known of a non-member State refusing to acknowledge the personality of an organization on the ground that it was not a member State and had not given the organization specific recognition' (Amerasinghe, 2005, p 87). Furthermore domestic courts of non-member States do acknowledge the international personality of international organizations.[16] As a matter of principle, the personality of international organizations derives from the effect that customary international law (which is binding on all States) ascribes to their characteristics. Thus, once international law ascribes personality to an organization, a subject of international law is created with its own rights and its own duties.

C. PERSONALITY IN DOMESTIC LAW

1. The obligation to confer domestic legal personality

Since international organizations also operate within the territory of States, they usually need to possess domestic legal personality, including the capacity to perform legal acts in domestic law. For example, international organizations will need to be able to enter

---

[12] Vienna Convention on the Law of Treaties (1969), Article 34.

[13] See *Third Restatement*, 1987, §223.

[14] See ILC's commentary to Article 2, ILC Draft Articles on Responsibility of International Organizations, ILC Reports, 2009, p 47.

[15] *Reparation for Injuries Suffered in the Service of the United Nations, Advisory Opinion, ICJ Reports 1949*, p 174 at p 185.

[16] Eg, *International Tin Council* v *Amalgamet* (1988), 80 ILR 31; 524 NYS 2d 971.

into contracts, own property and institute legal proceedings. Many treaties establishing international organizations provide that they are to have the necessary legal capacities in domestic law, for example, UN Charter, Article 104. Even where there is no express treaty obligation, there may be an implied obligation for members to provide the organization with such domestic capacities as are necessary to allow it to function effectively (Reinisch, 2000, p 44).

2. The manner in which domestic legal personality is recognized

States confer domestic legal personality on international organizations in various ways. The technique used depends in part on the relationship between international law and the national law of the State concerned. The technique also varies between member States of an organization and non-members. In member States which adopt a more monist tradition of the relationship between international law and national law, the domestic personality is often taken to flow directly from the treaty provision requiring the conferment of such personality. This position has been taken in (i) the United States and Belgium[17] with respect to the UN; (ii) the Netherlands with respect to the United Nations Relief and Rehabilitation Administration;[18] and (iii) Italy with respect to the North Atlantic Treaty Organization (NATO).[19]

In member States in which treaties do not form part of domestic law such treaty obligations will usually need to be transformed into national law by a national instrument. This is the technique adopted in common law countries like the UK where the International Organizations Act 1968 provides that the Executive may by Order in Council confer the legal capacities of a body corporate on any international organization of which the UK is a member.[20]

Thus in the UK, the House of Lords in *JH Rayner (Mincing Lane) Ltd* v *Department of Trade and Industry* stressed that the legal persona of the ITC in English law was created not by the constituent agreement of the organization but by the domestic legislation. According to Lord Oliver:

Without the Order in Council the I.T.C. had no legal existence in the law of the United Kingdom.... What brought it into being in English law was the Order in Council and it is the Order in Council, a purely domestic measure, in which the constitution of the legal persona is to be found and in which there has to be sought the liability of the members which the appellants seek to establish, for that is the act of the I.T.C.'s creation in the United Kingdom.[21]

The consequence of this was that the liability of members for the organization's debts depended on domestic legislation rather than on the position in international law.

The legal personality of international organizations will also be recognized by the courts of non-member States. Under private international law domestic courts will recognize the legal status and capacities of an organization created by foreign law. Since an international

---

[17] *Manderlier* v *Organisation des Nations Unies & Etat Belge (Ministre des Affairs Etrangères)* (1972), 45 ILR 446; *UN* v *B* (1952), 19 ILR 490.

[18] *UNRRA* v *Daan* (1949), 16 ILR 337.   [19] *Branno* v *Ministry of War* (1955), 22 ILR 756.

[20] International Organizations Act 1968, s 2(a). Similar legislation exists in the United States, Australia, Canada, and New Zealand.

[21] [1989] 3 WLR 969, 1012c.

organization has personality under the law of its creation—international law—that personality will be recognized by domestic courts.[22]

In the UK, the legal personality of an international organization of which the UK is not a member will be recognized where the organization has been accorded legal personality under the law of the host State or of another member State[23] rather than by virtue of international law and the relevant constituent treaty. Taken to its logical conclusion, this approach would have the unfortunate consequence that the law governing the status and capacities of the organization would be the foreign domestic law. Happily, the High Court in *Westland Helicopters Ltd v Arab Organization for Industralization*[24] held that while the personality of an international organization of which the UK was not a member would only be recognized in the UK if a foreign State had accorded that organization personality in its domestic law, the law governing the status and capacities of the organization is international law, including the relevant treaties.

III. INTERPRETATION OF CONSTITUENT INSTRUMENTS

Treaties which establish international organizations set out both the purposes, structure and competences of the organization as a whole and the particular functions and powers granted to its individual organs. These treaties, therefore define the position of the organization towards its members as well as the relationship between the individual organs. In many cases, they also create rights and impose obligations between the members. Finally, they may to some degree define the relationship between the organization and third parties. Consequently, the manner in which they are interpreted is of considerable importance. The following subsections consider (i) who is empowered to interpret constituent treaties of international organizations and (ii) the relevant principles of treaty interpretation.

A. WHO IS EMPOWERED TO INTERPRET?

Since the organs of international organization will need to have some appreciation of the scope of their functions and powers in order to carry them out, these organs will necessarily and routinely have to interpret the treaty setting up the international organization. In the *Certain Expenses* Advisory Opinion, the ICJ accepted that 'each organ [of the UN] must, in the first place at least, determine its own jurisdiction.'[25] Interpretations by organs will take place either formally and explicitly (eg, in a legal act of the organ)—particularly in cases where dispute arises as to the meaning of particular provisions—or impliedly as a result of the practice of the organ in question. Some constituent treaties provide for formal and definitive interpretations by a particular organ. This is particularly common

---

[22] See *International Tin Council v Amalgamet* (1988), 80 ILR 31; 524 NYS 2d 971; *Arab Organization for Industrialisation and others v Westland Helicopters Ltd and others* (1987), 80 ILR 622.

[23] *Arab Monetary Fund v Hashim* [1990] 1 All ER 685. A similar approach was taken in the US case *In Re Jawa Mahmoud Hashim* (1995), 107 ILR 405.

[24] *Westland Helicopters Ltd v Arab Organization for Industralization* [1995] 2 All ER 387; 108 ILR 564.

[25] *Certain Expenses of the United Nations, Advisory Opinion, ICJ Reports 1962*, p 151 at p 168.

with respect to international financial institutions where there is often an obligation to submit questions of interpretation to the Executive Board, Board of Directors, or the Board of Governors of the institution for decision.[26] In such circumstances, the interpretations given by these organs are binding, at least on the parties to the dispute, if not on all members and other organs. Where there is no formal power of interpretation given, and interpretation arises simply in the course of the work of the organization, such interpretations are not binding on member States. In the same way that organs will have to interpret constituent treaties in the course of their functions, members will similarly have to do so.

Judicial or arbitral tribunals may also have occasion to interpret constituent instruments. Such bodies may be created to deal with legal issues which arise within the system of the international organization in question. Examples include the Court of Justice of the European Communities and the International Tribunal for the Law of the Sea. International organizations do not have standing to be parties in contentious cases before the ICJ although UN organs and UN specialized agencies may request Advisory Opinions from the ICJ on legal questions arising within the scope of their competence, including the interpretation of their constituent instruments.[27] In the case of specialized agencies, this competence to request Advisory Opinions will be contained in agreements concluded with the UN or in their constituent instruments.[28] The ICJ may also have to interpret the constituent instrument of international organizations in contentious cases between States, where such a case raises questions relating to the rights and obligations of States arising from such treaties.

The constituent treaties may also provide for disputes arising thereunder to be referred to international arbitration.[29] Alternatively, an arbitral tribunal established under a treaty or contract between an international organization and a third party may have to interpret the constitution of that organization.[30] As has already been seen, national courts may also have to construe the constituent instruments of international organizations.

B. WHAT ARE THE RELEVANT PRINCIPLES OF INTERPRETATION TO BE APPLIED?

Since the constituent instruments establishing international organizations are usually treaties, interpretation is governed by Articles 31 and 32 of the Vienna Convention on the Law of Treaties (see above, Chapter 7). Article 5 of that Convention expressly states that the Convention applies to such treaties and in the *Nuclear Weapons Advisory Opinion (Request by WHO)* the ICJ stated that:

From a formal standpoint, the constituent instruments of international organizations are multilateral treaties, to which the well-established rules of treaty interpretation apply.[31]

---

[26] Eg, IMF Articles of Agreement, Article XXIX(a); IBRD Articles of Agreement, Article IX(a); Agreement Establishing the Asian Development Bank, Article 59.

[27] Although there are implications to the contrary in the *Legality of the Use by a State of Nuclear Weapons in Armed Conflict), Advisory Opinion, ICJ Reports 1996*, p 66, para 28, the better view is that an authorized UN specialized agency is always entitled to request an Advisory Opinion on the interpretation of its constituent instrument. See Akande, 1998, pp 452–457.

[28] Eg, WHO Constitution, Article 76; IMO Constitution, Article 66.

[29] Eg, Universal Postal Union Constitution, Article 39.

[30] See *Westland Helicopters v Arab Organization for Industrialization et al* (1989), 80 ILR 595.

[31] *Legality of the Use by a State of Nuclear Weapons in Armed Conflict (Request by WHO), Advisory Opinion, ICJ Reports 1996*, p 66, para 19.

However, the ICJ has noted that constituent instruments have 'certain special characteristics'[32] and that:

...the constituent instruments are also treaties of a particular character; their object is to create new subjects of law endowed with a certain autonomy, to which the parties entrust the task of realizing common goals. Such treaties can raise specific problems of interpretation, owing, *inter alia*, to their character which is conventional and at the same time institutional; the very nature of the organization created, the objectives which have been assigned to it by its founders, the imperatives associated with the effective performance of its functions, as well as its own practice, are all elements which may deserve special attention when the time comes to interpret these constituent treaties.[33]

To the extent that constituent instruments are in some senses 'constitutions', the general rules of treaty interpretation have to be applied differently when such treaties are under consideration (Lauterpacht, 1976, p 416; Amerasinghe, 2005, p 59). It is these differences that are focused on below.

1. The role of objects and purposes—the principle of effectiveness

Article 31 of the Vienna Convention provides that:

A treaty shall be interpreted in good faith, in accordance with the ordinary meaning to be given to the terms of the treaty in their context and in the light of its object and purpose.

The ICJ has stated that 'interpretation must be based above all upon the text of the treaty'[34] and generally speaking, the objects and purpose of a treaty are subsidiary to the text (Aust, 2007, p 235). However, when interpreting constituent instruments of international organizations special prominence is given to the objects and purposes of the instrument and of the organization. In the *Nuclear Weapons* Advisory Opinion the Court spoke of 'the very nature of the organization created, the objectives which have been assigned to it by its founders, the imperatives associated with the effective performance of its functions' as elements which may 'deserve special attention' in interpreting the constituent instruments of international organizations. Likewise in the *Reparation for Injuries* Advisory Opinion, the Court stated that 'the rights and duties of an entity such as the Organization must depend on its purposes and functions as specified or implied in its constituent documents or developed in practice.'[35] Frequently, the Court 'will seek to determine what are the purposes and objectives of the organization and will give to the words in question an interpretation which will be most conducive to the achievement of those ends' (Lauterpacht, 1976, p 420). This is known as the principle of effectiveness. The primary example of this principle is the doctrine of implied powers, by which an organization is deemed to have those powers that are necessary for achieving its purposes even in the absence of words in the text which indicate that the organization is to have such a power (Section IV A).

---

[32] *Certain Expenses of the United Nations, Advisory Opinion, ICJ Reports 1962,* p 151 at p 157.

[33] *Legality of the Use by a State of Nuclear Weapons in Armed Conflict, Advisory Opinion, ICJ Reports 1996,* p 66, para 19.

[34] *Territorial Dispute (Libya/Chad), Judgment, ICJ Reports 1994,* p 21, para 41.

[35] *Reparation for Injuries Suffered in the Service of the United Nations, Advisory Opinion, ICJ Reports 1949,* p 174 at p 180.

2. The role of subsequent practice

The practice of the organization is often given a special role, and is used not only in cases where the text of the agreement is ambiguous but also in cases of silence and to graft new rules on to the constituent instrument. The justification for this is that such treaties must be regarded as living instruments and be interpreted in an evolutionary manner, permitting the organization to fulfil its purposes in changing circumstances (Ress, 2002, pp 35–37). A well-known example of this is the *Namibia* Advisory Opinion,[36] where the Court, relying on the consistent practice of the Security Council and its members, held that abstentions by a permanent member of the Security Council was a 'concurring vote' within the meaning of Article 27(3) of the United Nations Charter and not a veto. Similarly, in the *Reparation for Injuries* Advisory Opinion the Court referred to the practice of the UN and the fact that it had entered into treaties as confirming the legal personality of the organization.[37]

Reference to the practice of parties as a means of treaty interpretation is permitted by the Vienna Convention, Article 31(3)(b). However, the Court has also drawn on the practice of the organs of the organization. This is significant since some organs are not composed of all the organization's members and, even if they are, many operate on a majority basis. Thus such practice may not reflect the position of all parties to the treaty. Where some members object to the practice of an organ, allowing that practice to influence interpretation or development of new rules amounts to imposing new obligations on the minority without their consent. This is contrary to the general principle of international law that obligations can only arise from express or implied consent and some judges of the ICJ have counselled against this approach.[38] Some authors claim there is an independent rule permitting the use of the practice of organs which members of organizations must be deemed to have accepted (Lauterpacht, 1976, p 460; Ress, 1995, pp 39–42). However, subsequent practice of a majority within an organ must not be used as a means of constitutional amendment (Amerasinghe, 2005, p 54; Lauterpacht, 1976, p 465). It is noteworthy that in practically all cases where the ICJ has referred to subsequent practice of organs it has simply been used as a means of confirming an interpretation already arrived at using other methods of interpretation. Subsequent practice of organs should therefore be confined to cases where it establishes the agreement of the parties, confirms a result already reached or to cases where other methods of interpretation lead to an ambiguity or an unreasonable result.

IV. POWERS OF INTERNATIONAL ORGANIZATIONS

In addition to the powers expressly conferred on international organizations by their constituent treaties these organizations also possess powers which are implied. This section examines the basis for those implied powers. It then surveys the kinds of decision-making

[36] *Legal Consequences for States of the Continued Presence of South Africa in Namibia (South West Africa) notwithstanding Security Council Resolution 276 (1970), Advisory Opinion, ICJ Reports 1971*, p 16, paras 20–22.

[37] *Reparation for Injuries Suffered in the Service of the United Nations, Advisory Opinion, ICJ Reports 1949*, p 174 at p 179.

[38] See the Separate Opinion of Judge Spender in *Certain Expenses of the United Nations, Advisory Opinion, ICJ Reports 1962*, p 151 at p 197.

powers possessed by international organizations and finally examines the legal consequences when organizations act beyond their powers.

A. IMPLIED POWERS

In the *Reparation for Injuries* Advisory Opinion, the ICJ stated that:

Under international law, an Organization must be deemed to have those powers which, though not expressly provided in the Charter, are conferred upon it by necessary implication as being essential to the performance of its duties.[39]

This doctrine of implied powers has been applied by the ICJ in a number of cases. In the *Reparation for Injuries* Advisory Opinion, the Court held that the UN was entitled to present an international claim on behalf of its agents even though such a power is not stated in the Charter. Likewise, in the *Certain Expenses* Advisory Opinion,[40] the Court held that the UN Security Council and the General Assembly were competent to establish peace-keeping operations although that concept is not mentioned in the Charter.

Implied powers are not restricted to those powers necessary for carrying out of express powers or functions. On the contrary, ICJ practice shows that powers can be implied whenever they are 'essential' for the fulfilment of the organization's objects and purposes. Furthermore, 'essentiality' does not mean that the power to be implied must be 'indispensably required' (Lauterpacht, 1976, pp 430–432). The Court has been rather liberal in its approach and has been willing to imply a power where it would 'promote the efficiency of the Organization'.[41] The main limitation is that the power must be directed at achieving the aims and purposes of the organization. As the ICJ stated in *Certain Expenses* Advisory Opinion:

When the Organization takes action which warrants the assertion that it was appropriate for the fulfilment of one of the stated purposes of the United Nations, the presumption is that such action is not *ultra vires* the Organization.[42]

B. DECISION-MAKING POWERS

International organizations are often given the power to take decisions relating to their spheres of activity. Some decisions relate to the internal workings of the organization itself and are directed at the organs of the organization—for example, decisions approving the budget, staff regulations, rules of procedure or decisions establishing subsidiary organs. Other decisions are taken in the course of carrying out the tasks entrusted to the organization and are directed at the members of the organization or, exceptionally, at third parties such as individuals and other non-State entities. Examples include decisions of the WHO setting standards with respect to pharmaceutical and other products; decisions of the UN

---

[39] *Reparation for Injuries Suffered in the Service of the United Nations, Advisory Opinion, ICJ Reports 1949*, p 174 at p 182.

[40] *Certain Expenses of the United Nations, Advisory Opinion, ICJ Reports 1962*, p 151 at p 177.

[41] Akande, 1998, p 444.

[42] *Certain Expenses of the United Nations, Advisory Opinion, ICJ Reports 1962*, p 151 at p 168.

Security Council imposing sanctions on a State; decisions of the ICAO Council relating to safety standards for international aviation.

In determining whether or not a particular decision of an international organization is legally binding on its addressee one must consider, first, whether that organ or organization is empowered by its constitution (expressly or impliedly) to take binding decisions and secondly, whether the language of the decision reveals an intention on the part of the organ to issue a binding decision.

Some constituent treaties expressly confer on organizations the power to issue decisions binding on their members. For example, Article 25 of the UN Charter obliges members to carry out decisions of the Security Council and under Article 22 of the WHO Constitution regulations adopted by the World Health Assembly are binding, unless a member opts out of the regulation *ab initio*.

Since international organizations do not generally have law-making powers, they are usually given power to take non-binding decisions which may take a number of forms. The most common is the power to make *recommendations* to members concerning matters within the scope of the organization (eg, UN General Assembly under Articles 10–14 of the UN Charter). Other decisions may be *determinations* consisting of findings of facts or characterizations or formal *declarations* of principles which the organ considers applicable in a particular area. Since these decisions are not binding, they do not, of themselves, create obligations for member States.

However, the non-binding nature of decisions does not mean that a particular decision is devoid of legal effect for members. Some constituent instruments oblige members to consider recommendations in good faith. For example, the International Labour Organization (ILO) and UN Educational, Scientific and Cultural Organization (UNESCO) Constitutions (Articles 19(6) and Articles 4(4) and 8 respectively) require member States to submit recommendations to their competent national authorities for consideration and are to report back to the organization on action taken. Furthermore, a separate international treaty may contain an obligation to have regard to (and possibly to comply with) non-binding decisions of an international organization. For example, the WTO Agreement on Sanitary and Phytosanitary Measures (SPS), Article 3 encourages members to base their SPS measures on standards adopted by other international organizations. Although members are not required to confirm these standards, measures in conformity are presumed to comply with the relevant WTO provisions.[43] Likewise a number of provisions of the United Nations Convention on the Law of the Sea require States to comply with standards adopted by the 'competent international organization' (usually the IMO). Additionally, it is arguable that there is a presumption that members acting in accordance with a relevant decision of an international organization are acting lawfully at least as between the members of that organization.

Finally, non-binding decisions of international organizations may contain rules of law which are or become binding through other processes of international law. Resolutions of the UN General Assembly which are couched in declaratory terms are a good example.[44] Where such declarations elaborate on rules contained in the constituent treaty of the organization or other treaties adopted within the organization they

---

[43] *Beef Hormone Case*, Appellate Body Report, WT/DS26/AB/R, WT/DS48/AB/R (16 January 1998).

[44] Eg, Universal Declaration of Human Rights, GA Res 217A (1948); Declaration of Principles of International Law Concerning Friendly Relations Among States, GA Res 2625 (1970).

may be regarded as authoritative interpretations of the treaty in question or, alternatively, as subsequent practice establishing the agreement of the parties to the treaty.[45] Furthermore, such resolutions may be declaratory of pre-existing rules of customary international law. Alternatively, such resolutions may play a role in the formation of *new* customary rules so that the rules contained therein may come to be regarded as binding. As the ICJ noted in the *Nuclear Weapons* Advisory Opinion:

... General Assembly resolutions, even if they are not binding, may sometimes have normative value. They can, in certain circumstances, provide evidence important for establishing the existence of a rule or the emergence of an *opinio juris*. To establish whether this is true of a given General Assembly resolution, it is necessary to look at its content and the conditions of its adoption; it is also necessary to see whether an *opinio juris* exists as to its normative character. Or a series of resolutions may show the gradual evolution of the *opinio juris* required for the establishment of a new rule.[46]

Thus whilst some international organizations have the competence to adopt decisions which are binding on member States and others, most do not possess this power. However, non-binding decisions of international organizations are not without legal effect and the rules contained in those decisions may be binding through a link with other treaties or under customary international law.

C. *ULTRA VIRES* DECISIONS OF INTERNATIONAL ORGANIZATIONS

What is the effect of a decision that is beyond the powers (*ultra vires*) of the organ or the organization? Are such decisions nullities and therefore of no effect at all (void *ab initio*)? Or are they only voidable, meaning that they are effective until they are set aside by a competent body? And whatever view is taken, how is one to determine whether a particular decision is *ultra vires* or not? Very few international organizations have, like the EC, a judicial system competent to compulsorily adjudicate on the legality of acts of the organs of the organization. There is, for example, no general procedure by which the ICJ can consider the legality of decisions of the UN or its specialized agencies. However, such questions may be raised in Advisory Opinions requested by the organ or organization or may arise incidentally in a contentious case between States (Akande, 1997).

An example of such opportunities for judicial review arose in the *Certain Expenses* Advisory Opinion,[47] where the General Assembly requested an opinion from the Court on whether expenditures related to peace-keeping missions set up by the Security Council and the General Assembly were expenses of the UN within the meaning of Article 17 of the Charter. In considering that question, the Court felt it necessary to consider whether the peace-keeping operations in question had been lawfully established by the Security Council and the General Assembly. In the *Namibia* Advisory Opinion,[48] the Court was asked to consider the legal consequences for States of the continued presence of South

---

45 Article 31(3)(c), Vienna Convention on the Law of Treaties.

46 *Legality of the Use by a State of Nuclear Weapons in Armed Conflict, Advisory Opinion, ICJ Reports 1996*, p 66, para 70. See also *Military and Paramilitary Activities in and Against Nicaragua (Nicaragua v United States), Merits, Judgment, ICJ Reports 1986*, p 14 at pp 99ff.

47 *Certain Expenses of the United Nations, Advisory Opinion, ICJ Reports 1962*, p 151 at pp 156–168.

48 *Legal Consequences for States of the Continued Presence of South Africa in Namibia (South West Africa) notwithstanding Security Council Resolution 276 (1970), Advisory Opinion, ICJ Reports 1971*, p 16, paras 45–53.

Africa in Namibia following the termination of South Africa's mandate for the territory by the General Assembly and the decision by the Security Council in Res 276 that States had an obligation to refrain from dealing with South Africa in regard to that territory. In that case, the Court stated that whilst there was no established procedure of judicial review within the UN system, the Court was competent and would review the legality of the relevant decisions of the General Assembly and the Security Council. In both cases just referred to the Court found the relevant decisions to be lawful.

The dearth of procedures for reviewing the legality of decisions makes the view that illegal decisions are voidable (Osieke, 1983, p 255) problematic. In effect, it would mean that illegal decisions stand unless, by accident, there is the possibility of review. This is clearly unsatisfactory and the better view is that *ultra vires* decisions—but not those merely suffering some minor procedural defect—are a nullity.[49] As Judge Morelli said in the *Certain Expenses* case:

In the case of acts of international organizations…there is nothing comparable to the remedies existing in domestic law in connection with administrative acts. The consequence of this is that there is no possibility of applying the concept of voidability to the acts of the United Nations. If an act of an organ of the United Nations had to be considered as an invalid act, such invalidity could constitute only the *absolute nullity* of the act. In other words, there are only two alternatives for the acts of the Organization: either the act is fully valid, or it is an absolute nullity, because absolute nullity is the only form in which invalidity of an act of the Organization can occur.[50]

Thus, where a decision is illegal, a State is free to depart from it.[51] However there is always the risk that the decision might later be found to be lawful and the non-compliant State in breach of its obligations.

It must be noted that given the limited opportunities for judicial review, the principle that *ultra vires* acts are void *ab initio* might undermine the certainty of decisions of international organizations and permit States to seek to evade their treaty obligations. However, this danger is reduced by the presumption, already referred to, that acts of international organizations directed at the fulfilment of the purposes of the organization are valid, meaning that the burden of proof is on the State arguing otherwise. Additionally, mere procedural defects do not render decisions invalid. The combination of these principles is sufficient to ensure stability.

V. RESPONSIBILITY OF INTERNATIONAL ORGANIZATIONS

As was pointed out above, one of the consequences of the separate legal personality possessed by international organizations is that these organizations are responsible under international law for breaches of their international obligations. As a result of the separate

---

[49] The constitution of the organization might provide that wrongful decisions become void only following the determination of a competent body. See Osieke, 1983, pp 244–245.

[50] *Certain Expenses of the United Nations Advisory Opinion, ICJ Reports 1962*, p 151 at p 222.

[51] See Separate Opinion of Judge Gros, *Interpretation of the Agreement of 25 March 1951 between the WHO and Egypt, Advisory Opinion, ICJ Reports 1980*, p 73 at p 104.

legal personality of international organizations, there is a presumption that members of the organization are not liable with respect to the obligations of the organization, although this presumption can be displaced.[52] The principle that members of the organization are not liable for its obligations is illustrated by the *International Tin Council* (ITC) cases. These cases arose out the failure of the ITC—an international organization established to control the price of tin on the world markets—to meet its commercial obligations. The ITC operated a buffer stock of tin and bought tin when prices were low (thus creating a demand) and sold when prices were high. The organization was empowered to borrow money to finance these transactions. As a result of a persistent drop in the price of tin, the organization was no longer in a position to carry out trading and defaulted on a number of contracts with tin brokers and commercial bankers. These parties brought an action in England (and elsewhere) seeking, amongst other things, to hold the members of the ITC liable for its debts. These actions were dismissed at all levels of the English courts on the ground that the personality of the organization precluded holding the members liable. The House of Lords relied primarily on English domestic law[53] whilst the majority in the Court of Appeal reached the same conclusion on the basis of international law.[54]

In 2002, the ILC commenced work on a set of Draft Articles on the Responsibility of International Organizations (DARIO). The ILC provisionally adopted a complete set of Draft Articles in 2009 (the so called first reading of the articles),[55] following which it will proceed to a final consideration (the second) and adoption of the articles. The ILC's Draft Articles on the Responsibility of International Organizations is modelled after the ILC's Articles on State Responsibility (see Ch 15). In most areas, the ILC has taken the same approach that it took with regard to State responsibility, even using similar wording in many of the corresponding articles. Article 3 of the ILC's Draft Articles states that 'Every internationally wrongful act of an international organization entails the international responsibility of the international organization.' As is the case with State responsibility, an international organization commits an internationally wrongfully act when (i) conduct is attributable to that organization under international law and (ii) that conduct constitutes a breach of an international obligation of that international organization (Article 4, DARIO). The ILC has adopted similar rules (when compared with State responsibility) with regard to attribution, breaches of international obligations, circumstances precluding wrongfulness, the content of international responsibility and the implementation of the international responsibility of international organization. In some of these areas (for example, circumstances precluding wrongfulness like countermeasures and necessity), there is very little practice with regard to the responsibility of international organizations and the ILC has simply proceeded by analogy with State responsibility.

Despite the similarity with State responsibility, there are notable differences between States and international organizations that have warranted a different approach in

---

[52] See ILC's commentary to Article 61, ILC Draft Articles on Responsibility of International Organizations, *ILC Reports*, 2009, 167.

[53] *JH Rayner v Department of Trade and Industry* [1988] 3 All ER 257; [1989] 3 WLR 969 (HL).

[54] [1988] 3 All ER 257 (CA), particularly Ralph Gibson LJ at 353. Likewise in the *Arab Organization for Industrialisation and others v Westland Helicopters Ltd and others* (80 ILR 622 Court of Justice, Geneva (1987); Swiss Federal Supreme Court (1988)), the Swiss courts held the member States of the organization were not bound by the obligations undertaken by the organization towards a private entity.

[55] ILC Reports, 2009, Chapter IV.

some parts of the regime of responsibility of international organizations or which have required special attention. One area which has required special attention is the division of responsibility between international organizations and their member States. Often, international organizations act through their members and this raises the question whether the acts of the members (or the organs of the members) when acting within the context of the organization will create responsibility for the State or for the organization. The general rule with regard to attribution of acts to international organization is that the conduct of organs or agents of the organization are to be regarded as that of the organization when the organ or agent acts in the performance of their functions (Article 5, DARIO). However, there are circumstances when States lend their organs to an international organization, with the result that those organs become organs of the international organization, but they also remain organs of the lending State because they still act, in part, on behalf of the State. The question that arises in such a case is whether the act of the organ is to be attributed to the international organization or to the lending State. This question is of importance in the context of peacekeeping because, although UN peacekeeping forces are subsidiary organs of the UN, the troops are contributed by States and these States retain jurisdiction and some degree of control over their troops. Article 6 of the ILC's DARIO provides that:

The conduct of an organ of a State or an organ of or agent of an international organization that is placed at the disposal of another international organization shall be considered under international law an act of the latter organization if the organization exercises effective control over that conduct.

Therefore, whether the UN is legally responsible for the acts of peacekeeping forces will depend on the factual control exercised by the UN over the troops in question and over the conduct. Usually UN peacekeeping forces, as opposed to forces engaged in enforcement action authorized by the UN, are placed under the operational command and control of the United Nations. This command and control is exercised by a UN Force Commander who is responsible to a civilian Head of Mission who is in turn responsible to the Security General who acts under authority given by the Security Council. Where this chain of command is able to effectively control the forces, the acts of those forces will be attributable to the UN. However, contrary to what the European Court of Human Rights has stated in *Behrami v France and Saramati v France, Germany and Norway*[56] the key test is not whether the organization has ultimate authority or control over the forces but rather whether it has actual operational control of the activity in question. Since UN peacekeepers often to continue to act within their national chain of command as well, it is only the troop contributing State that will be responsible in cases where it is that State that has directed the activities of the forces in question. To assert otherwise, as the European Court of Human Rights did, is to suggest that States 'can retain actual control over their forces [assigned to UN action] and at the same time have absolutely no liability for anything that these forces do, since their actions are supposedly attributable solely to the UN.'[57] This is an untenable position.

---

[56] *Behrami and Behrami v France and Saramati v France, Germany and Norway* (Dec) [GC], nos 71412/01 and 78166/01, 2 May 2007; 45 *EHRR* 85.

[57] See Milanović and Papić, 2009. See also *R (Al Jedda) v Secretary of State* [2007] UKHL 58, paras 22–25.

Although, as discussed above in the section on personality, members of an international organization are not ordinarily responsible for the acts of the organization, member States may not escape responsibility for breaches of their own (ie the members') obligations simply by causing the organization to perform an act, which if performed by the member State would be a breach of the member's obligation (Article 60, DARIO). Thus, the European Court of Human Rights has held that States parties to the European Convention on Human Rights cannot free themselves from obligations under the Convention by transferring functions to an international organization.[58] In such cases, 'the State is considered to retain Convention liability in respect of treaty commitments subsequent to the entry into force of the Convention.'[59] This principle is important as it prevents States circumventing their international obligations through the creation of an international organization which is then conferred with competence to act in the area in question.

Where an international organization is responsible for an internationally wrongful act it has an obligation to make reparation for the injury caused by the wrong (Article 30, DARIO). However, the mechanisms by which such responsibility can be established and through which injured parties can obtain redress against international organizations remain undeveloped. As will be seen in the following section, such organizations are usually immune from the jurisdiction of domestic courts. Furthermore, international organizations cannot be parties to contentious cases before the International Court of Justice and there are few standing tribunals with competence to decide cases involving international organizations. Therefore the quest for enhancing the accountability of these organizations must not only involve an elucidation of the relevant principles of responsibility but also the development of mechanisms through which that responsibility can be determined.

VI. PRIVILEGES AND IMMUNITIES

International organizations require certain privileges and immunities for the effective performance of their tasks. These immunities are granted to preserve the independence of the organization from its member States and to secure the international character of the organization. They ensure that no member State is able to unilaterally interfere through its legislative, executive or judicial branches with the workings of an international organization set up to act in the common interests of members. This section considers the sources and content of the privileges and immunities of international organizations.

A. SOURCES OF PRIVILEGES AND IMMUNITIES

The privileges and immunities of international organizations may be derived from a number of sources.

---

[58] *Waite and Kennedy v Germany* [GC], no 26083/94, ECHR 1999-I; *Bosphorus Hava Yollary Turizm v Ticaret Anonim Sirketi v Ireland* [GC], no 45036/98 ECHR, 2005-VI, pp 157–158.
[59] *Bosphorus Hava Yollary Turizm v Ticaret Anonim Sirketi v Ireland* [GC], no 45036/98 ECHR, 2005-VI, pp 157–158.

1. Treaties

There are three types of treaties which deal with the privileges and immunities of inter-national organizations. First, the constituent instrument of the organization often includes provisions requiring member States to grant the organization immunities. Such provi-sions are usually very basic and, like Article 105 of the UN Charter, only contain a general statement that the organization, its officials and representatives of members are to enjoy such privileges and immunities as are necessary for the exercise of their functions.[60]

Second, there are general multilateral agreements dealing with the immunities of par-ticular international organizations or groups of organizations. These types of agreements are regarded as a necessary supplement to the more basic provisions in the constituent instruments. The leading examples include the 1946 General Convention on the Privileges and Immunities of the United Nations and the 1947 Convention on the Privileges and Immunities of the Specialised Agencies.[61]

The third type of treaty is bilateral agreements between international organizations and individual States which set out specific privileges and immunities. They are most commonly concluded between the organization and a State in which the former (or an organ of the organization) is situated (eg headquarters agreements) or with States in which the organization is to perform a particular mission, such as a peace-keeping or fact-finding activity (eg Status of Forces Agreements). Such States need not be members of the organization.[62]

2. Customary international law

In the absence of a treaty obligation, customary international law requires States to grant privileges and immunities to international organizations.[63] This has been recognized both by the domestic courts of member States of an organization and those of non-member States which have consented to the organization functioning in their territory.[64] The obli-gation is one of good faith and only requires the 'provision of what is necessary for an organization to perform its functions' (Higgins, 1994, p 91).

---

[60] See also ILO Constitution, Article 40; WHO Constitution, Article 12; Council of Europe Statute, Article 4(a); OAS Charter, Articles 133 and 134. However, the constitutional texts of international finan-cial institutions contain fairly elaborate provisions. See, eg, IBRD Articles of Agreement, Article VII; IMF Articles of Agreement, Article IX; EBRD Constitution, Articles 46–55.

[61] Similar treaties exist within the OAS, Council of Europe, European Communities, League of Arab States, and the OECD.

[62] For a long time Switzerland was not a member of the UN but had an agreement with the UN regarding the UN's office in Geneva.

[63] See Reinisch, 2000, pp 145ff; Higgins, 1994, pp 90–94; *Third Restatement*, 1987, §467(1); Amerasinghe, 2005, pp 344–348; Szasz, 1995, p 1328. But see Bowett, 2009, §15–039 who only accepts such a customary obligation in some cases.

[64] See *X et al* v *European School Munich II* (Bavarian Administrative Court, Germany, 1995), referred to by Reinisch, 2000, pp 150–151; *Iran-United States Claims Tribunal* v *AS*, 96 ILR 321, 329 (Dutch Supreme Court, 1985); *ESOC Official Immunity Case* 73 ILR 683 (Federal Labour Court, FR Germany, 1973); *Branno* v *Ministry of War*, 22 ILR 756 (Court of Cassation, Italy, 1954); *International Institute of Agriculture* v *Profili*, 5 ILR 413 (Court of Appeal, Italy, 1930). Courts of States other than the host State have held that they are not obliged to grant immunities to international organizations in the absence of a treaty. See *Bank Bumiputra Malaysia BHD* v *International Tin Council*, 80 ILR 24 (High Court, Malaysia, 1987); *International Tin Council* v *Amalgamet*, 80 ILR 31 (New York Supreme Court, 1988); *ECOWAS* v *BCCI*, 113 ILR 473 (Court of Appeal of Paris, France, 1993).

3. National law

Since privileges and immunities are to be enjoyed within the national legal order, many States have enacted domestic legislation governing their being granted. The relevant legislation in the UK is the International Organizations Act 1968 which provides that the Executive may by subsidiary legislation (Order in Council) grant the stated privileges and immunities to international organizations of which the UK is a member.

B. SCOPE OF PRIVILEGES AND IMMUNITIES

The particular privileges and immunities which a State is to grant an international organization flow from the source of the obligation which will most commonly be a treaty. Despite the impressive number of treaties providing for the privileges and immunities, there are remarkable similarities in their contents. This has permitted rules of customary international law to develop. However, these similarities relate to general matters and details vary from treaty to treaty.

Who is entitled to the immunity? Most treaties accord privileges and immunities to three categories of person: first, to the organization itself; secondly, to officials of the organization (including experts on mission for the organization); thirdly, to representatives of member States (or exceptionally of other bodies) to the organization. This chapter considers only the privileges and immunities of the organization itself since the personal immunities of international officials and State representatives are considered in Chapter 13. The five main privileges and immunities conferred on international organizations are considered in the following sections.

1. Immunity from jurisdiction

International organizations are usually granted absolute immunity from the judicial jurisdiction of States. For example, Article II, Section 2 of the 1946 Convention on the Privileges and Immunities of the United Nations provides that:

The United Nations, its property and assets wherever located and by whomsoever held, shall enjoy immunity from every form of legal process except insofar as in any particular case it has expressly waived its immunity. It is, however, understood that no waiver of immunity shall extend to any measure of execution.

Similar provisions exist in many treaties setting out the immunities of international organizations.

This immunity from jurisdiction prevents law suits against organizations before domestic courts unless they have waived their immunity by consenting to the proceedings. As has been the case with State immunity, there has been pressure to restrict the absolute nature of the immunity granted to international organizations. It has been argued that according such immunity may cause injustice where individuals have no other means of obtaining redress or may even lead to a violation of the human rights of individuals.[65] For these reasons, a number of domestic courts have applied to international organizations the concept

---

[65] See the arguments advanced by the applicants in *Waite and Kennedy v Germany* [GC], no 26083/94, ECHR 1999-I and in *Association of Citizens 'Mothers of Srebrenica' v Netherlands & United Nations*, Rechtbank 's-Graveenhage [the Hague, District Court], 10 July 2008, 295247/HA ZA 07-2973.

of restrictive immunity, granting them jurisdictional immunity only in relation to acts *jure imperii* (in the exercise of sovereign authority) rather than acts *jure gestionis* (done privately).[66] Alternatively, it has been argued that the grant of immunity should be conditional on the presence of alternative methods of resolving disputes involving international organizations (Gaillard and Pingel-Lenuzza, 2002). The first approach, which relies on an analogy with State immunity is based on the misapprehension that since international organizations are composed of States they are to be placed in the same position as foreign States. This approach is incorrect for at least two reasons. First, it is contrary to the express provisions of the relevant treaties. Secondly, international organizations are not sovereign entities and do not exercise sovereign authority. Their immunity is not granted to protect sovereign or public acts but is functional and granted in respect of acts done in the exercise of their functions. Such functions and acts may well be commercial and so classified as private if done by a State. Thus immunity may arise for an international organization in cases where a foreign State will be denied immunity. For example, employment disputes fall within the immunity of an international organization even if the relations with the particular employee might be classified as *jure gestionis*. The second approach, which conditions immunity on the existence of alternative dispute resolution mechanisms, is not in accordance with the treaties providing immunity. Although such treaties may provide an obligation for the organization to make provision for alternative modes of dispute settlement (eg Article 29, UN Convention discussed below) that obligation is not expressed as limiting the immunity of the organization before domestic courts. The two obligations (that of the organization to find alternative methods of dispute settlement and that of the State to accord immunity) are independent of each other.[67] However, the European Court of Human Rights has held that where member States create an international organization and accord such organization immunity from domestic legal process without creating alternative methods of dispute settlement, this may amount to a violation, on the part of the members, of their obligation to provide access to a court.[68] The invocation of this obligation is likely to lead to pressure on the member States to ensure that the organization provides adequate dispute settlement obligations.

It should be noted that some international organizations are not granted absolute immunity by the relevant treaties. In particular, constituent instruments of a number of international financial institutions such as the World Bank (IBRD) do not extend immunity to certain kinds of actions. This is because these organizations operate in the commercial world where it is felt necessary to permit creditors to institute actions in some instances.

2. Immunity from execution

International organizations also enjoy immunity from measures of execution. This prevents the seizure or even the pre-judgment attachment of its property or other assets. It is important to note that a waiver of jurisdictional immunity does not include a waiver of the enforcement jurisdiction which must be given expressly and separately. In some cases,

---

[66] See Reinisch, 2000, pp 185–205 who notes that this trend is most common in Italy.

[67] *Association of Citizens 'Mothers of Srebrenica' v Netherlands & United Nations*, Rechtbank 's-Gravenhage, July 10, 2008, 295247/HA ZA 07–2973, para 5.15.

[68] *Waite and Kennedy v Germany* [GC], no 26083/94, ECHR 1999-I.

particularly as regards international financial institutions, the immunity from execution granted by the relevant treaty only applies before the delivery of final judgment.

3. Inviolability of premises, property, and archives

Practically all relevant treaties provide that the premises of an international organization are to be inviolable and that its property and assets are to be immune from search, requisition, confiscation or other forms of interference by State authorities.[69] Thus, national authorities may not enter such premises without the consent of the international organization, even when a crime has been committed on the premises or a criminal is sheltering there. The treaties also impose an obligation on the national authorities to exercise due diligence in protecting those premises from acts of third parties.

The archives (documents) of an international organization are usually inviolable wherever located.[70] This ensures the confidentiality of communications within and with the international organization, enabling it to function effectively and independently. Consequently, international organizations are not obliged to produce their official documents, or other documents held by them, in proceedings before national courts. In one of the Tin Council cases—*Shearson Lehman Bros* v *Maclaine Watson & Co*[71]—the House of Lords held that documents issued by an international organization but which had been communicated to third parties by officials of the organization did not benefit from these principles. This decision has been criticized because the documents were sent by the organization to the States in their capacity as members—not as third parties—and in relation to the work of the organization. Plainly, the confidentiality of such documents requires protection.

4. Currency and fiscal privileges

Since many international organizations exercise their functions in a number of countries they will need to transfer funds. Several treaties provide that such transactions are to be free from financial restrictions. For example, the UN Convention provides that the organizations (a) 'may hold funds, gold or currency of any kind and operate accounts in any currency' and (b) may freely transfer their 'funds, gold or currency from one country to another or within any country and to convert any currency held by them into any other currency.'[72] International organizations are usually exempt from direct taxation of their assets, income and property as well as from custom duties and other import and export restrictions in respect of articles for official use.[73] However, this does not extend to charges for public utility services or excise duties or sales taxes.

5. Freedom of communication

It is commonly provided that official communications by international organizations shall be accorded treatment at least as favourable as that accorded to foreign

---

[69] UN Convention 1946, Article II, Section 3; Specialized Agencies Convention 1947, Article III, Section 5.

[70] UN Convention 1946, Article II, Section 4; Specialized Agencies Convention 1947, Article III, Section 6.

[71] *Shearson Lehman Bros* v *Maclaine Watson & Co*, 77 ILR 107 (1987).

[72] UN Convention, Article II, Section 5; Specialized Agencies Convention, Article III, Section 7.

[73] UN Convention, Article II, Section 7; Specialized Agencies Convention, Article III, Section 9.

governments.[74] In addition it is sometimes provided that no censorship shall be applied to official communications of the organization and that the organization shall have the power to use codes as well as couriers and bags having the same status as diplomatic couriers and bags.[75]

International organizations should not use their privileges and immunities to circumvent either the domestic laws of States or their responsibility towards third parties. In order to prevent immunity being used to avoid legal responsibility, Article 29 of the UN Convention provides that 'The United Nations shall make provisions for appropriate modes of settlement of (a) disputes arising out of contracts or other disputes of a private law character to which the United Nations is a party...' In practice international organizations will often include arbitration clauses in contracts that they enter into. Furthermore, most organizations have a system for the settlement of employment disputes which includes recourse to an international administrative tribunal.

Finally, it must be remembered that international organizations remain responsible in international law for breaches of their obligations even if they are immune from process before domestic courts. As the ICJ has stated 'the question of immunity from legal process is distinct from the issue of compensation for any damages incurred as a result of acts performed by the United Nations or by its agents acting in their official capacity.'[76]

VII. THE UNITED NATIONS SYSTEM

The remainder of this chapter will look at the structure and powers of what is perhaps the leading family of international organizations—the United Nations system. The United Nations was established after the Second World War with very broad aims, including: (i) the maintenance of international peace and security; (ii) the development of friendly relations among nations; (iii) international cooperation in solving international problems of an economic, social, cultural or humanitarian character; and (iv) the promotion of human rights (Article 1, UN Charter). The work of the UN and its specialized agencies touches on practically every area of human life and endeavour.

A. THE STRUCTURE OF THE UNITED NATIONS

Like all international organizations, the UN is composed of a number of organs. In addition, the UN system comprises a family of international organizations which share certain common institutions and practices.

1. The United Nations organs

Article 7 of the UN Charter identifies two types of organs within the United Nations: principal organs and subsidiary organs. Article 7(1) lists the six principal organs of the United

---

[74] UN Convention, Article III, Section 9; Specialized Agencies Convention, Article IV, Section 11; IBRD Articles of Agreement, Article VII(7).

[75] UN Convention, Article III, Sections 9 and 10; Specialized Agencies Convention, Article IV, Section 12.

[76] *Difference Relating to Immunity from Legal Process, Advisory Opinion, ICJ Reports 1999*, p 62, para 66.

Nations: (i) the General Assembly; (ii) the Security Council; (iii) the Economic and Social Council (ECOSOC); (iv) the Trusteeship Council; (v) the International Court of Justice; and (vi) the Secretariat. The structure and powers of each of these organs shall be discussed below. Article 7(2) provides that 'such subsidiary organs as may be found necessary may be established in accordance with the present Charter'. Whilst the list of principal organs is exhaustive and no additional organs may be established or wound up except by amendment of the Charter, subsidiary organs can always be created by the principal organs. Their lifespan is determined by the principal organ that has established them.

The powers, functions and composition of the principal organs are determined by the Charter, whilst those of subsidiary organs are determined by the principal organ that establishes them. Subsidiary organs established by the General Assembly include the Human Rights Council, International Law Commission, the United Nations Environment Programme (UNEP), the Office of the UN High Commissioner for Refugees (UNHCR), UNICEF, and the United Nations Development Programme (UNDP). Subsidiary organs set up by the Security Council include peace-keeping missions, Sanctions Committees, the International Criminal Tribunals for the Former Yugoslavia and Rwanda, and the United Nations Compensation Commission (UNCC).

In most cases, a principal organ will confer some of its powers on a subsidiary organ that it creates. However, a principal organ may be entitled to confer on the subsidiary organ powers which it does not itself possess where the power to establish such a subsidiary organ is necessary for the performance of the functions of the principal organ (Sarooshi, 1996, pp 426–431). Thus, both the General Assembly and the Security Council have established subsidiary organs that have judicial powers even though they themselves do not have such powers. The legality of their doing so was confirmed by the ICJ in the *Administrative Tribunal* Advisory Opinion[77] and by the Appeals Chamber of the International Criminal Tribunal for the Former Yugoslavia.[78] Moreover, in the *Administrative Tribunal* case it was held that the General Assembly was bound to give effect to the awards of the Administrative Tribunal thus confirming that a principal organ can establish a subsidiary organ with powers to bind the principal organ.

2. The specialized agencies

The Charter also refers to another type of body known as specialized agencies. Unlike the subsidiary organs, these are international organizations in their own right. They are established by separate treaties and brought into relationship with the UN by agreement (Articles 57 and 63). They operate in particular technical fields and, like the UN, are open organizations with worldwide membership and responsibilities. There are currently 17 specialized agencies.[79]

---

[77] *Effects of Awards of Compensation made by the United Nations Administrative Tribunal, Advisory Opinion, ICJ Reports 1954*, p 47.

[78] *Prosecutor v Tadić*, Decision on the Defence Motion for Interlocutory Appeal on Jurisdiction (Interlocutory Appeal), Case No IT–94–1–AR72 (2 October 1995); 105 ILR 419 at pp 470–1.

[79] These are: (1) The International Labour Organization (ILO); (2) The Food and Agriculture Organization (FAO); (3) The United Nations Educational, Scientific and Cultural Organization (UNESCO); (4) The World Health Organization (WHO); (5) The International Bank for Reconstruction and Development (IBRD or World Bank)—within the World Bank group are three agencies which are also specialized agencies but are run together with World Bank; (6) The International Development Association (IDA); (7) The International

Although they are independent international organizations, the UN Charter provides that the UN may coordinate their activities (Articles 57–60), principally through ECOSOC. In practice, coordination and cooperation are achieved through the United Nations System Chief Executives Board for Coordination (CEB), composed of the executive heads of the organizations within the UN, and its High Level Committees. Development assistance is coordinated by UNDP.

In the *Nuclear Weapons Advisory Opinion (WHO Request)*,[80] the ICJ, relying on what it termed the 'logic of the overall system contemplated by the Charter', appeared to suggest that overlap within the UN system should be avoided. According to the Court, the Charter 'laid the basis of a "system" designed to organize international co-operation in a coherent fashion by bringing the United Nations, invested with powers of a general scope, into relationship with various autonomous and complementary organizations, invested with sectorial powers.' The Court stated that the WHO 'cannot encroach on the responsibilities of other parts of the United Nations system'. Thus, since questions of disarmaments and arms regulations are within the competence of the UN itself they were held to be outside the competence of the specialized agencies.

However, the constitutions of the specialized agencies and their practice show that legitimate overlap can and does exist in the work of the specialized agencies. For example, both the WHO and the ILO are competent to deal with health of workers. Likewise IMO, UNEP and the International Atomic Energy Agency cooperate regarding transportation of nuclear fuel by sea (Akande, 1998).

3. Treaty bodies

A variety of treaties concluded under the auspices of the UN establish bodies which maintain very close relations with the UN and are considered as UN bodies. Examples include the various committees set up by human rights treaties to monitor compliance with the obligations they contain, such as the Human Rights Committee and the Committee Against Torture. These bodies only act in relation to those States which are parties to these treaties. They meet in the UN, are serviced by the UN Secretariat and submit reports to the General Assembly.

B. PRINCIPAL ORGANS OF THE UNITED NATIONS

1. The General Assembly

The General Assembly is the plenary organ of the United Nations and is the only principal organ composed of all member States (Article 9). It is a deliberative not a legislative body and unlike the Security Council, is not in permanent session but meets annually in regular

---

Finance Corporation (IFC); (8) The Multilateral Investment Guarantee Agency (MIGA); (9) The International Monetary Fund (IMF)—the IMF is separate from the World Bank but closely related as another 'Bretton Woods' Institution; (10) The International Civil Aviation Organisation (ICAO); (11) The Universal Postal Union (UPU); (12) The International Telecommunications Union (ITU); (13) The World Meteorological Organization (WMO); (14) The International Maritime Organisation (IMO); (15) The World Intellectual Property Organisation (WIPO); (16) The International Fund for Agricultural Development (IFAD); (17) The United Nations Industrial Development Organization (UNIDO).

[80] *Legality of the Use of Nuclear Weapons in Armed Conflict, Advisory Opinion, ICJ Reports 1996*, p 66, para 26.

session which usually takes place between September and December (Article 20). It may also meet in special session outside its regular sessions. At its regular sessions, agenda items are allocated to one of the six main committees (eg, Disarmament and International Security; Economic and Financial; and Legal), where substantive discussion and decision-taking occurs.

There are also two procedural and two standing committees. The procedural committees, which unlike the main committee are not composed of all UN members, are the General Committee (responsible for organizing the work of the session and for deciding on the agenda) and the Credentials Committee (which examines the credentials of representatives of member States). The standing committees—the Advisory Committee on Administrative and Budgetary Questions and the Committee on Contributions—assist the Fifth Committee with financial matters and are composed of experts rather than representatives of member States.

The Assembly has competence to discuss and make recommendations upon the very broad range of matters falling within the scope of Charter (Article 10). However, it can only make binding decisions on internal administrative matters. Articles 11–17 of the Charter specifically provide that General Assembly has competence with regard to peace and security, promoting human rights, and international cooperation in political, economic, social, cultural, educational, and health fields. However, the Assembly may not make recommendations concerning disputes or situations in respect of which the Security Council is exercising its functions unless requested to do so by the Council (Article 12) and, together with UN as a whole, it may not intervene 'in matters which are essentially within the domestic jurisdiction of any State' (Article 2(7)). Voting in the Assembly is on the basis of one member one vote. Decisions on important questions must be adopted by two thirds of members present and voting. There is a non-exhaustive list of such important questions. Other decisions are to be taken by simple majority (Article 18).

2. The Security Council

The Security Council is composed of 15 member States of the UN. There are five permanent members of the Council (USA, Russia, UK, France, China) and 10 which are elected by the Assembly for two-year terms (Article 23). Its competence is mainly (though not exclusively) limited to issues concerning the maintenance of international peace and security, for which it bears primary responsibility within the UN system (Article 24). Although each member has one vote, decisions on non-procedural matters must be adopted by the affirmative vote of nine members and include the concurring vote of the permanent members who therefore possess a veto with respect to substantive decisions. Abstentions, however, are not deemed to be vetos.[81] The powers of the Security Council in the areas of peace and security dispute settlement are explored in Chs 19 and 21. It suffices here to note that the Council has the power to adopt decisions which are binding on members of the UN (Articles 24 and 25).

3. The Economic and Social Council (ECOSOC)

ECOSOC is the primary organ responsible for economic and social matters within the UN. It is composed of 54 members who serve for three years; each member has one vote.

---

[81] *Legal Consequences for States of the Continued Presence of South Africa in Namibia (South West Africa) notwithstanding Security Council Resolution 276 (1970), Advisory Opinion, ICJ Reports 1971*, p 16, paras 20–22.

ECOSOC can make or initiate studies in the area of its competence and make recommendations to the General Assembly, the member States or the specialized agencies on such matters (Article 62). ECOSOC has special responsibility for the promotion of human rights. It has been active in preparing treaties in the human rights areas (eg, the International Covenant on Civil and Political Rights). It also has responsibilities regarding the specialized agencies, concerning their relations with the UN and the coordination of their activities.

   ECOSOC has created a number of subsidiary organs: five regional commissions—for Africa, Asia Pacific, Europe, Latin America and the Caribbean, and Western Asia—and nine functional Commissions dealing with particular topics, including the Commission on Sustainable Development and the Commission on the Status of Women. ECOSOC also has a few standing committees (eg, the Commission on Human Settlements and the Commission on Transnational Corporations) and a number of standing bodies of experts.

4. The International Court of Justice

This is the principal judicial organ of the United Nations and is considered in Chapter 20 below.

5. The Secretariat

The secretariat consists of the staff of the UN and is headed by the Secretary General. It services the work of the UN organs, except the ICJ, and carries out other functions that they assign to it. In addition, the Secretary General may bring to the attention of the Security Council any matter which he considers may threaten international peace and security (Article 99). Members of the secretariat are to be independent of governments and may not seek or receive instructions from them (Article 100).

6. Trusteeship Council

The Trusteeship Council was set up to administer the trusteeship system established by Chapter XII of the Charter. This concerned the administration of territories that had been League of Nations mandates (ie, territories taken from Germany and Turkey following the First World War) and territories 'detached from enemy States as a result of the Second World War' (Article 77) with the objective of promoting the advancement of the inhabitants and their progressive development towards self-government and independence. The work of the Council was suspended in 1994 when the last of the Trust territories, Palau, achieved independence.

VIII. CONCLUSION

Despite the diversity in the nature and tasks of international organizations, it has proved possible to identify some common legal principles which govern these organizations. However, it cannot be forgotten that the structure, functions and powers of each organization are primarily to be derived from the treaty setting up the organization and the practice which has built up regarding that organization.

The fact that States continue to create new international organizations to deal with emerging problems in international affairs is principally the result of three factors. First, there is the realization that a number of problems faced by States and their populations can only be resolved or can best be resolved through international cooperation. Secondly, there is the realization that such cooperation often needs to be multilateral. Thirdly, it is clear that such cooperation needs to be permanent. The heightened awareness by States of these points and the increasing emergence of 'global problems', means that there is likely to be an increase not only in the number of international organizations but also in the powers and functions accorded to those organizations. However, together with this increasing delegation of public powers by States to international organizations it is likely that greater attention will be paid to developing means to hold these organizations accountable for the exercise of such powers.[82] This is a process that has already generated much interest and will involve careful analysis of the limits of the powers of international organizations.

REFERENCES

AKANDE, D (1997), 'The International Court of Justice and the Security Council: Is there Room for Judicial Control of Decisions of the Political Organs of the United Nations?', 46 *ICLQ* 309.

—— (1998), 'The Competence of International Organizations and the Advisory Jurisdiction of the International Court of Justice', 9 *EJIL* 437.

AMERASINGHE, CF (2005), *Principles of the Institutional Law of International Organizations*, 2nd edn (Cambridge: Cambridge University Press).

AUST, A (2007), *Modern Treaty Law and Practice*, 2nd edn (Cambridge: Cambridge University Press).

BOWETT's *Law of International Institutions* (2001), Sands, P and Klein, P (eds), 5th edn (London: Sweet & Maxwell).

CHURCHILL, RR and ULFSTEIN, G (2000), 'Autonomous Institutional Arrangements in Multilateral Environmental Agreements: A Little-Noticed Phenomenon in International Law', 94 *AJIL* 623.

GAILLARD, E and PINGEL-LENUZZA, I (2002), 'International Organizations and Immu-

nity from Jurisdiction: To Restrict or to Bypass', 51 *ICLQ* 1.

HIGGINS, R (1994), *Problems and Process: International Law and How We Use It* (Oxford: Oxford University Press).

ILA Committee Reports (1996–2000), International Law Association Committee on Accountability of International Organization, *Report of the 68th Conference of the ILA held at Taipei*, p 584 (First Report); (Second and Third Reports) (available via **http://www.ila-hq.org**).

ILC Reports (2009), *Report of the International Law Commission on the Work of its 57th Session* (UN Doc A/64/10).

KLABBERS, J (2009), *An Introduction to International Institutional Law*, 2nd edn (Cambridge: Cambridge University Press).

LAUTERPACHT, H (1976), *The Development of the Law of International the Decisions of International Tribunals*, 52 *Recueil des Cours* 377.

MILANOVIĆ, M and PAPIĆ, T (2009), 'As Bad As It Gets: The European Court Of Human Rights's *Behrami And Saramati*

---

[82] See generally, Reinisch, 2001; ILA Committee Reports, 1996–2000; and ILC Reports 2009.

Decision And General International Law',
58 *ICLQ* 267.

Osieke, E (1983), 'The Legal Validity of
Ultra Vires Decisions of International
Organizations', 77 *AJIL* 239.

Rama Montaldo, M (1970), 'International
Legal Personality and Implied Powers of
International Organizations', 44 *BYIL* 111.

Reinisch, A (2000), *International Organizations in Domestic Courts* (Cambridge:
Cambridge University Press).

—— (2001), 'Securing the Accountability
of International Organizations', 7 *Global
Governance* 131.

Ress, G (2002), 'The Interpretation of the
Charter', in Simma, B (ed), *The Charter
of the United Nations: A Commentary*
(Oxford: Oxford University Press), p 13.

Sands, P (2003), *Principles of International
Environmental Law*, 2nd edn (Cambridge,
Cambridge University Press).

Sarooshi, D (1996), 'The Legal Framework
Governing United Nations Subsidiary
Organs', 67 *BYIL* 413.

Schermers, HG and Blokker, N (1995),
International Institutional Law, 3rd rev
edn (The Hague: Martinus Nijhoff).

Seyersted, F (1964), 'International Personality of Intergovernmental Organizations:
Do their Capacities Really Depend upon
their Constitutions?', 4 *IJIL* 1.

Szasz, P (1995), 'International Organizations,
Privileges and Immunities', in Bernhardt,
R (ed), *Encyclopaedia of Public
International Law*, 2nd edn (Amsterdan:
North Holland), p 1325.

Third Restatement (1987), *Third Restate-
ment of the Law: The Law of Foreign
Relations of the United States*, vol 1 (St
Pauls, Minn.: American Law Institute
Publishers).

FURTHER READING

Alvarez, JE (2005), *International
Organizations as Law-makers* (Oxford:
Oxford University Press): this considers
the law-making and dispute-settlement
functions of international organizations.

Amerasinghe, CF (2005), *Principles of
the Institutional Law of International
Organizations*, 2nd edn (Cambridge:
Cambridge University Press): provides an
excellent overview of the law relating to
international organizations.

Bekker, PHF (1994), *The Legal Position
of Intergovernmental Organizations: A
Functional Necessity Analysis of Their
Legal Status and Immunities* (Dordrecht:
Martinus Nijhoff): a good introduction to
the legal status, privileges, and immunities of international organizations.

Bowett's *Law of International Institutions*
(2009), Sands, P and Klein, P (eds), 6th edn
(London: Sweet & Maxwell): this provides

an excellent overview of the structure of
the leading international organizations as
well as of the common legal issues relating
to these organizations.

Reinisch, A (2000), *International
Organizations in Domestic Courts*
(Cambridge: Cambridge University
Press): an excellent consideration of
the legal issues which arise when international organizations sue and are sued
in domestic courts.

Schachter, O and Joyner, J (eds) (1995),
United Nations Legal Order, 2 vols
(Cambridge: Cambridge University
Press): a detailed examination of the
structure of the United Nations and its
specialized agencies, considering the
competence of these organizations in a
variety of areas.

Schermers, HG and Blokker, N (2004),
International Institutional Law, 4th rev

edn (The Hague: Martinus Nijhoff): a detailed examination of the law relating to international organizations.

SIMMA, B (ed) (2002), *The Charter of the United Nations: A Commentary*, 2nd edn (Oxford: Oxford University Press): an article by article analysis of the Charter of the United Nations.

SLOAN, B (1991), *United Nations General Assembly Resolutions in Our Changing World* (Ardsley, NY: Transnational Publishers): a very good consideration of the status of UN General Assembly resolutions.

WELLENS, K (2002), *Remedies Against International Organizations* (Cambridge: Cambridge University Press): an overview of the law relating to responsibility of international organizations.

WHITE, N (1996), *The Law of International Organizations* (Manchester: Manchester University Press): this provides an excellent overview of the law relating to international organizations.

10

THE INDIVIDUAL AND THE INTERNATIONAL LEGAL SYSTEM

Robert McCorquodale

SUMMARY

This chapter explores the role of the individual in the international legal system today. It considers the extent to which the individual, including groups of individuals, is an independent participant in this system. This participation is explored by reference to the direct rights and responsibilities of individuals under the international legal system, their capacity to bring international claims and their ability to participate in the creation, development, and enforcement of international law. Particular examples from a wide range of areas of international law, including international human rights law, international criminal law, and international economic law, will be used to show the conceptual and practical participation of individuals in the international legal system. The conclusion reached is that individuals are participants in that system, and are not solely objects that are subject to States' consent, though their degree of participation varies depending on the changing nature of the international legal system.

I. INTRODUCTION

The issue of the role of the individual in international law has been a part of the debate over the nature of the international legal system for centuries. In 1532 Francisco de Vitoria considered that the indigenous peoples of South America had some claim to protection under international law (Anaya, 2004) and, in the twenty-first century, the entry into force of the International Criminal Court confirmed the customary international law position of the direct responsibility of individuals under international law for certain actions (see Cryer, Ch 25, below).

However, for much of this time the dominant view has been that individuals had no effective independent role in the international legal system. Their role was wholly determined by States and was entirely subject to States' consent (Remec, 1960; Tornaritis, 1972). The development of international law, particularly of international human rights law, in the second half of the twentieth century has been the main reason why the issue of the role of individuals in the international legal system has again come to prominence.

A. THE INDIVIDUAL

'The individual' is defined and conceived in a number of different ways in the international legal system. It clearly includes each human being. When human beings (usually known in law as 'natural persons') have any involvement in the international legal system, it is often as part of a group of natural persons acting together. For example, groups of indigenous people and groups who have the right of self-determination are natural persons who act together in regard to some international legal issues. As such, they should be considered to be 'individuals' within the international legal system. Natural persons do form groups due to common interests, such as non-governmental organizations (eg, Amnesty International, Oxfam), although these groups are legally separate entities from natural persons. Corporations are also separate entities that are formed to further the common interests of natural persons and all legal systems recognize the existence and activities of corporations and acknowledge them as non-natural legal persons (Dine, 2000; Muchlinski, 2007). Therefore, the notion of 'individuals' could include all these types of legal person, natural and non-natural.

This chapter takes the concept of 'the individual' within the international legal system to include all those natural and non-natural persons acting separately and as groups.[1] The justification for taking such a view is that the international legal system is primarily a State-based system. The roles of any natural and non-natural persons (what may be termed 'non-State actors') in this system is compared with that of the State. Consequently, excluded from this concept of 'the individual' are States and also those entities who have authority and power that is State-like, such as intergovernmental organizations (eg, the United Nations), armed opposition groups who control territory (see an example in *Elmi v Australia*),[2] or sub-State units in a federal State. In order to clarify as comprehensively as possible the role of the individual in the international legal system, this chapter considers as wide and as diverse a range of 'individuals' acting within that system as possible.

B. INDIVIDUALS IN THE INTERNATIONAL LEGAL SYSTEM

The international legal system is traditionally constructed as a State-based system with State sovereignty being supreme. The dominant positivist theories of international law confirm that construction, as their view is that '[s]ince the Law of Nations is a law between States only and exclusively, States only and exclusively are subjects of the Law of Nations' (Oppenheim, 1905, p 341). A 'subject' of the international legal system has direct rights and responsibilities under that system, can bring international claims and, it is argued, is able to participate in the creation, development, and enforcement of international law.

---

[1] This definition is similar to that adopted under the European Convention on Human Rights, see Committee of Ministers, 2001.

[2] *Elmi* v *Australia*, UN Committee Against Torture, No 120/1998, 7 *IHRR* 603.

Historically, under this dominant view, any role of the individual in the international legal system is purely as an 'object' of that system and not as a 'subject' (cf Anaya, 2004).[3] In their view, individuals are objects, either in the same sense as territory or rivers are objects of the system because there are (State created) legal rules about them, or in the sense that they are beneficiaries under the system, so that treaties on, for example, diplomatic persons or commerce, indirectly benefit individuals.

This creation of a binary opposition of 'subject' v 'object' has become part of the definition of international legal personality. An entity has international legal personality if it has direct international rights and responsibilities, can bring international claims, and is able to participate in the creation, development, and enforcement of international law, ie, if it is a subject of the international legal system. The International Court of Justice (ICJ) clarified the issues of international personality, and what is a 'subject' of the international legal system, in its *Reparations for Injuries* Opinion:

The subjects of law in any legal system are not necessarily identical in their nature or in the extent of their rights, and their nature depends on the needs of the community. Throughout its history, the development of international law has been influenced by the requirements of international life, and the progressive increase in the collective activities of States has already given rise to instances of action upon the international plane by certain entities which are not States…In the opinion of the Court, the [UN] Organisation was intended to exercise and enjoy, and is in fact exercising and enjoying, functions and rights which can only be explained on the basis of the possession of a large measure of international personality and the capacity to operate upon an international plane…That is not the same thing as saying that it is a State, which it certainly is not, or that its legal personality and rights and duties are the same as those of a State…It does not even imply that all its rights and duties must be upon the international plane, any more than all the rights and duties of a State must be upon that plane. What it does mean is that it is a subject of international law and capable of possessing international rights and duties, and that it has capacity to maintain its rights by bringing international claims.[4]

This is an important statement of international legal principles. It directly links being a subject of international law with international legal personality. It clarifies that there can be subjects of the international legal system that are not States. These subjects do not all possess the same rights and duties, and not all of these rights and duties need to be on the international plane alone. It also explains how the international legal system has developed, and continues to develop, in ways that allow non-States to have international legal personality and so to act independently in the international legal system (see Nijman, 2004). In this Opinion the ICJ applied these principles to the position of the UN itself to decide that it did have international legal personality. A later ICJ decision[5] has applied these principles to other international (intergovernmental) organizations.

---

[3] It was argued by the Chinese delegate (Mr Hsu) to the UN General Assembly's Sixth Committee in October 1954 that 'An individual who had no State to protect him was entitled to a direct international remedy. Moreover, while international delinquents, such as pirates or offenders against the peace and security of mankind, had been accepted as subjects of international law, it would be strange if stateless persons in need of protection would be regarded as outside its scope' (my thanks to Professor Sir Eli Lauterpacht for this material).

[4] *Reparation for Injuries Suffered in the Service of the United Nations, Advisory Opinion, ICJ Reports 1949,* p 174 at pp 178–179.

[5] *Legality of the Use of Nuclear Weapons in Armed Conflict, Advisory Opinion, ICJ Reports 1996,* p 66.

While some writers argue that the *Reparations for Injuries* Opinion only applies to State-created bodies such as the UN (Orakhelashvili, 2001), this Opinion clearly sets out broad principles that could be applied to any non-State actor on the international plane. It recognizes that, while the State is the primary subject of the international legal system, the subjects of that system can change and expand depending on the 'needs of the [international] community' and 'the requirements of international life'. It does not say whether these 'needs' and 'requirements' are solely determined by States (as the dominant theories of international law would suggest) or by other means. After all, the term 'the international community' is here expressly not limited to an international community of States alone (in comparison to the Vienna Convention on the Law of Treaties, Article 53) and so should include States and non-States. So it certainly indicates that there can be subjects of the international legal system that are not States.

Some writers have argued that, rather than the State being the primary 'subject' of the international legal system, the primary 'subject' is the individual (Scelle, 1932). They argue, for example, that individuals are the real actors beneath the State, as the State itself does not exist without individuals. A variation on these ideas is that of Hersch Lauterpacht, one of the most influential British international lawyers of last century, who argued that individuals could become subjects of the international legal system. He considered that the claim of the State to unqualified exclusiveness in the field of international relations was not tenable, especially as:

Fundamental human rights are rights superior to the law of the sovereign State... [and must lead to the] consequent recognition of the individual human being as a subject of international law. (Lauterpacht, 1950, p 72)

Philip Allott adopts an even broader view in which he sees international society as not being comprised of States but as arising from the 'self-creating' of all human beings (Allott, 1992). So these writers would argue that the nature of the international legal system and the 'needs' of the international community have meant that individuals are subjects—the primary or only subjects—of the international legal system.

Of course, individuals are necessary for an entity to be recognized as a State, in the sense that an entity must have 'a population' to be a State (see Craven, Ch 8, above). In any event, the State is a legal fiction and so it cannot act by itself. Instead individuals and groups act on behalf of the State and in the State's name.[6] Thus individuals are at the very core of the international legal system, no matter how that system is defined. Yet this does not necessarily make them 'subjects' or 'objects' of this system.

The 'subject' v 'object' dichotomy has been criticized by a number of writers, not least because it privileges certain voices and silences others (eg, Koskenniemi, 1989; Charlesworth and Chinkin, 2000). Rosalyn Higgins, a President of the ICJ, offers an alternative approach, arguing that:

the whole notion of 'subjects' and 'objects' has no credible reality, and, in my view, no functional purpose. We have erected an intellectual prison of our own choosing and then declared it to be an unalterable constraint. (Higgins, 1994, p 49; see also Higgins, 1979)

---

[6] Though the individual, in his private capacity, remains distinct from the actions he takes on behalf of the State (Geuss, 2007).

Rather she prefers the idea of the 'participant' in the international legal decision-making process. She explains this by use of an example:

The topics of minimum standard of treatment of aliens, requirements as to the conduct of hostilities and human rights, are not simply exceptions conceded by historical chance within a system that operates as between States. Rather, they are simply part and parcel of the fabric of international law, representing the claims that are naturally made by individual participants in contradistinction to state-participants. (Higgins, 1994, p 50)

Under this view, there are many participants in the international legal system, in the sense that there are many different entities, from States and international organizations to transnational corporations and natural persons, who engage in international activity (or 'upon an international plane' to use the ICJ's words set out above in the *Reparations for Injuries* Opinion). Participation may be extensive and over a wide range of international matters or it can be limited to a few issues. Participation will depend on the particular area of the international legal system concerned and the activity and involvement of entities in that area, rather than on the determination by States (and only States) as to whether any non-States are 'subjects' for a specific purpose. Acknowledging these different degrees of participation in the international legal system is consistent with the position in most national legal systems, where different areas of law will involve different participants, from company law to family law. As the international community changes and the 'needs' or areas governed by international law develop, then so will participation in the international legal system.

This argument for considering individuals as 'participants' in the international legal system, rather than as 'objects' or 'subjects', is a compelling and practical one, and does not require an adoption of Higgins' broader conception of the international legal system (Meijknecht, 2001). Indeed, the notion of participation as a valuable framework to explore involvement in the international legal system (and thus as a means to determine if individuals have a voice in the system) has been applied effectively by Karen Knop from a different conceptual standpoint to that of Higgins (Knop, 2002). At the same time, it is still consistent with the dominant State-based concept of the international legal system, as participation in the system could be viewed as largely dependent on State consent. Participation, as an appropriate way to examine activity in the international legal system, falls within the broad legal principles expressed by the ICJ in its *Reparations for Injuries* Opinion. Therefore, participation as a framework for considering the role of individuals in the international legal system is flexible and open enough to deal with developments in that system over the centuries and is not constricted to a State-based concept of that system or to appearances before international bodies. Accordingly, if it can be shown that individuals are exercising and enjoying 'in fact' (to use the ICJ's words) certain rights, privileges, powers, or immunities in the international legal system then they can be presumed to be acting as international legal persons (Meron, 2006; Boyle and Chinkin, 2007).

Of course, these individuals do not all share the same aims or values across the international community. Many individuals are criticized for their lack of legitimacy, few democratic processes and limited representativeness (Cullen and Morrow, 2001). They can also reflect the hierarchies and political agendas within States, and can be captive to States and to power. Yet the decision to participate on the international plane is made by the particular individual and is not dictated by States' views, though it may be prompted by State action (eg, to seek investment in a national industry) or State inaction (eg, to fill the need for a secretariat of a treaty body). The degree of participation by an individual will vary, often depending on its own resources, its functions and on the attitude of other participants, including States (Puvimanasinghe, 2007).

It is the extent of that participation in the international legal system by individuals, and the State's role in determining the degree of participation, that will be considered in this chapter. This will be examined by reference to the direct rights and responsibilities of individuals under the international legal system, their capacity to bring international claims and their ability to participate in the creation, development, and enforcement of international law as independent participants.

II. INTERNATIONAL RIGHTS AND RESPONSIBILITIES

A. INDIVIDUAL RIGHTS

The Permanent Court of International Justice (PCIJ) had to consider in *Jurisdiction of the Courts of Danzig* whether it was possible for individuals to have rights under international law. They held:

[I]t cannot be disputed that the very object of an international agreement, according to the intention of the contracting parties, may be the adoption by the parties of some definite rules creating individual rights and obligations and enforceable by the national courts.[7]

While this Opinion confirmed that individuals can have rights in the international legal system, these rights will not all be of the same nature. As Wesley Hohfeld (1913) demonstrated, a 'right' can mean a claim-right, a privilege, a power, or an immunity (or a number of these at once). In some instances, the right of the individual within the international legal system is of the nature of the ability to bring a claim (a claim-right) against the State (see further below). However, many of the rights of individuals in the international legal system are more in the nature of an immunity from action against them, such as those that arise due to their status as prisoners of war, or a privilege, such as the liberty to travel on the high seas without interference. In the same way, States have a variety of rights within the international legal system, not all of which enable claims to be brought (eg, International Law Commission, 2001). The rights of individuals and the rights of States in the international legal system are not identical but, whilst they may overlap or interact (such as under international humanitarian law in relation to use of force on a territory affecting combatants and non-combatants), they are distinct rights.

The area where individual rights are most developed is in relation to human rights, which include both rights of individuals and of groups, and which are now a matter of international law. At one time governments dealt with those within their jurisdiction as they wished and resisted all criticisms of their actions by claiming that human rights were matters of 'domestic jurisdiction' (under Article 2(7) UN Charter) and the responsibility of each State alone. However, human rights are now an established part of the international

---

[7] *Jurisdiction of the Courts of Danzig, Advisory Opinion, 1928, PCIJ, Ser B, No 15*, pp 17–18.

legal system with an institutional structure, including supervisory mechanisms to check compliance with legal obligations, and with a defined content of human rights (see Steiner, Ch 26, below). Every single State has ratified at least one treaty containing legal obligations to protect human rights. Human rights issues are raised in political, economic, social, and cultural interactions across the world, in a global way (Falk, 1993). Human rights, as law, are part of the discourse of the international community as it speaks to the élites and to the oppressed, to institutions and to communities. Importantly, all States have acknowledged that 'the promotion and protection of all human rights is a legitimate concern of the international community'.[8]

This acknowledgement that human rights are a legitimate concern of the international community has a direct effect on State sovereignty (Reisman, 1990), in that one aspect of each State's control and authority over its activities on its territory and within its jurisdiction is now subject to international legal review. This applies when a State has expressly agreed to this review by ratifying a treaty protecting human rights. It also applies when the protection of a human right has become a matter of customary international law or *jus cogens*, which can happen without a State having any express practice on the issue. Some human rights create legal obligations on States that the State cannot evade by contrary practice. For example, the ICJ took the view that South Africa was bound by international obligations in relation to racial discrimination despite its clear contrary practice[9] and also that all States must comply with the right of self-determination.[10]

States have, by treaty and other practice, placed human rights for individuals (including groups of individuals) within the international legal system. There are problems with the way international human rights law has been created, such as the conception that rights are only held in relation to a centralized State (Otto, 1997) and the exclusion of non-State actors from direct responsibility for human rights violations (Clapham, 1993; Addo, 1999; McCorquodale and La Forgia, 2001). Nevertheless, international human rights law is significant in terms of demonstrating that individuals have rights within the international legal system.

Individuals also have rights in the international legal system outside the specific context of international human rights law. For example, within international humanitarian law, individuals have certain rights depending on their status as, for example, prisoners of war or non-combatants (Dinstein, 1984; Provost, 2002; Lopes and Quénivet, 2008). Many of these individual rights are now considered to be customary international law or even *jus cogens*. Yet the rights of individuals within the international legal system were all initially determined and placed within that system by States. States decided and agreed that these rights were rights within that system and not solely rights within a national legal system. Martti Koskenniemi concludes from this that the creation of these rights of individuals by

---

[8] Vienna Declaration (1993), para 4 (1993) 32 ILM 1661. Similar statements are found in the Concluding Document from the Moscow Conference on the Human Dimension of the Conference on Security and Co-Operation in Europe (CSCE) (now OSCE) (1991) 30 ILM 1670.

[9] *Legal Consequences for States of the Continued Presence of South Africa in Namibia (South West Africa) notwithstanding Security Council Resolution 276 (1970), Advisory Opinion, ICJ Reports 1971*, p 16, paras 21–22.

[10] *East Timor Case (Portugal v Australia), Judgment, ICJ Reports 1995*, p 90, *Legal Consequences of the Construction of a Wall in the Occupied Palestine Territory, Advisory Opinion, ICJ Reports 2004*, p 136, paras 118 and 122.

States, particularly within international human rights law, affirms the position of States as the sole rights-holder in the international legal system:

> By establishing and consenting to human rights limitations on their own sovereignty, states actually define, delimit, and contain those rights, thereby domesticating their use and affirming the authority of the state as the source from which such rights spring. (Koskenniemi, 1991, p 406)

This is a powerful argument. However, as demonstrated above, each State no longer has complete control over the continuance, development, and interpretation of individuals' rights, and the rights of individuals are distinct from the rights of States. Thus a number of the rights of individuals in the international system are now, to some extent, separate from the specific control and direction of States, at least as they are protected by customary international law (or by *jus cogens*), and are independent rights within the international legal system. It can be concluded, therefore, that, although originally based on the agreement of States, individuals now have some distinct rights in the international legal system.

B. INDIVIDUAL RESPONSIBILITY

Responsibility in the international legal system is generally considered to mean a legal obligation that, if breached, can give rise to international consequences (see Crawford and Olleson, Ch 15, below). Even though individuals have been a part of international activity for centuries, from trading to colonizing, generally the actions of individuals did not give rise to any international responsibility on them; it only arose when those actions were attributed to the State and then the State was internationally responsible.[11]

The development of individual responsibility for certain crimes under both international criminal law and international humanitarian law illustrate the lineage of individual responsibility in the international legal system, with both piracy and slavery also widely seen as offences against the whole international community, for which individuals were directly responsible (Ratner and Abrams, 2009). The justification for this was that 'the pirate and the slave trader... [are each] *hostis humani generis*, an enemy of all mankind'.[12] Individuals, even when acting as part of the organs of the State and under orders from the State, are independently responsible within the international legal system for certain actions. This was neatly summarized by the Nuremberg International Military Tribunal:

> Crimes against international law are committed by men, not by abstract entities [of States], and only by punishing individuals who commit such crimes can the provisions of international law be enforced.[13]

This individual responsibility has recently begun to be enforced through international tribunals and will be in the future by international criminal courts (see Cryer, Ch 25, below). Prior to this, the individual responsibility still existed, and was occasionally enforced in

---

[11] See *United States Diplomatic and Consular Staff in Tehran, Judgment, ICJ Reports 1980*, p 3.

[12] *Filartiga* v *Peña-Irala*, 630 F.2d 876 (2nd Cir 1980).

[13] *Nuremberg Judgment*, 22 Trial of the Major War Criminals before the International Military Tribunal 466 (1948).

national courts,[14] even though no international judicial body enforced it. In the same way, State responsibility exists even where no other State takes action to enforce it (such as seen in the lack of any legal action after the Chernobyl nuclear power plant explosion). Thus, even though it was necessary for States to agree to the decisions or treaties that created these recent international criminal tribunals and courts, the individual responsibility under international law still existed independently of these agreements. The responsibility arose through customary international law and no one State now has the ability to limit this responsibility, at least with regard to acts such as piracy and genocide.

There has also been a development in international law in relation to the responsibilities of corporations for breaches of international law. Despite the significant impact of these corporations, any international legal responsibility currently remains with the State, though there are sound arguments that there may be some areas, such as international criminal law, where there could be direct responsibility on corporations (Clapham, 2008).

There are limits to the responsibility of individuals under international law. This has been seen most dramatically after major international terrorist acts, most notably those in the USA in 2001, Bali in 2002, Madrid in 2004, and London in 2005 (McGoldrick, 2004; Sands, 2005). These acts do not necessarily fall within the parameters of existing individual responsibility under international law generally or under international human rights law specifically (Warbrick, 2004; Lowe, 2005). Yet a possibility of extending this responsibility of individuals under international law is seen in Security Council Resolution 1373 (2001), where the Security Council declared that:

[A]cts, methods, and practices of terrorism are contrary to the purposes and principles of the United Nations and that knowingly financing, planning and inciting terrorist acts are also contrary to the purposes and principles of the United Nations.

As this paragraph (also repeated in later Resolutions) does not refer to crimes against humanity or other acknowledged areas of individual responsibility under international law, it must be asserting that terrorist actions *per se* give rise to individual responsibility. There is no requirement here to link those activities to a State for there to be international responsibility. Whilst Security Council Resolutions are not automatically international law, they can indicate the direction that international law may be headed (perhaps to apply international humanitarian legal obligations on non-State actors under occupation).[15] It appears, therefore, that certain actions by individuals (being terrorist actions) could be in breach of international law and so give rise to international responsibility by those individuals.

The importance of establishing responsibility of individuals for international crimes is that it demonstrates that there are some actions by individuals that lead to direct international responsibility on an individual. The individual is responsible without any need to link the individual with the State. This draws a clear distinction between the individual and the State in terms of international responsibility.

---

[14] Eg, *Attorney-General of the Government of Israel* v *Eichmann* (1961), 36 ILR 5.
[15] Report of the UN Fact-Finding Mission on the Gaza Conflict to the UN Human Rights Council, 15 September 2009 ('Goldstone Report'), (http://www2.ohchr.org/english/bodies/hrcouncil/specialsession/9/docs/UNFFMGC_Report.pdf).

III. INTERNATIONAL CLAIMS

A. BRINGING INTERNATIONAL CLAIMS

The conceptual understanding that individuals have rights and responsibilities in the international legal system does not automatically mean that they have the ability to bring international claims to assert their rights or are able to claim an immunity to prevent their responsibilities being enforced (Hohfeld, above). Thus the PCIJ declared that 'it is scarcely necessary to point out that the capacity to possess civil rights does not necessarily imply the capacity to exercise those rights oneself'.[16] Instead, the conclusion reached by most writers is that 'individuals are extremely handicapped in international law from the procedural point of view' (Higgins, 1994, p 51). Many of the international institutions that determine claims, such as the ICJ, are barred to individuals, even though a significant number of their cases arise from actions by, or against, individuals. This was seen most starkly in the *East Timor* case[17] where the claims of the East Timorese themselves could not be brought to, or directly considered by, the ICJ.

Traditionally, the only means available for individuals to bring a claim within the international legal system has been when the individual is able to persuade a government to bring a claim on the individual's behalf. Even then, it is not the individual's international rights that are being asserted but the State's own rights, as the PCIJ noted:

[I]n taking up the case of one of its nationals, by resorting to diplomatic action or international judicial proceedings on his behalf, a State is in reality asserting its own right, the right to ensure in the person of its nationals respect for the rules of international law.[18]

The justification that a State has to assert this type of claim is through the linkage of nationality.[19] The international legal system has developed intricate rules regarding the nationality of people in terms of their relationship to States, as determined by the degree of connection individuals have to the territory of a State. Even then, this nationality connection may be insufficient if there are other international rules that override it or if the State chooses not to take action. Indeed, the ICJ has stated that:

[t]he State must be viewed as the sole judge to decide whether its protection will be granted, to what extent it is granted, and when it will cease [and...] [s]hould the natural or legal persons on whose behalf it is acting consider that their rights are not adequately protected, they have no remedy in international law.[20]

This position was been challenged in the UK in a case arising from the clearly internationally unlawful detention by the US of prisoners in Guantanamo Bay from the time of the

---

[16] *Appeal from a Judgment of the Hungaro/Czechoslovak Mixed Arbitral Tribunal, Judgment, 1933, PCIJ, Ser A/B, No 61,* p 208 at p 231.

[17] *East Timor Case (Portugal v Australia), Judgment, ICJ Reports 1995,* p 90.

[18] *Panevezys-Saldutiskis Railway, Judgment, PCIJ, Ser A/B, No 76,* p 4. Cf *LaGrand (Germany v United States of America), Merits, Judgment, ICJ Reports 2001,* p 466, para 42.

[19] There are some instances where a State might be able to bring a claim on behalf of the international community (of States and non-States): see International Law Commission (2001), Article 48.

[20] *Barcelona Traction, Light and Power Company, Limited, Second Phase, Judgment, ICJ Reports 1970,* p 3, paras 78–79.

Afghanistan conflict in 2001. In *Abbasi v Secretary of State for Foreign and Commonwealth Affairs*[21] the applicant (a British national) sought judicial review of the adequacy of the diplomatic actions of the British government with the US government. The UK Court of Appeal found that there was a legitimate expectation (though a limited one) by nationals that their government would make representations to another government to assist them and the courts could thus consider the diplomatic activity of the UK government. In this instance, the Court found that the UK government's actions were sufficient, yet it also expressed its very deep concern about the violation of international law that was occurring in Guantanamo Bay.

This position, by which the individual could not assert claims directly to international bodies, began to change during the twentieth century. A series of international bodies were established in the early part of that century as a means to settle conflicts between States and included in their powers was the ability to consider claims by individuals. These bodies included the Central American Court of Justice, the Mixed Arbitral Tribunals in Europe, the minority protections offered by the League of Nations, and the dispute mechanisms of the International Labour Organization (Menon, 1992; Butler, 2007). In the second half of that century, the vast growth of international human rights supervisory bodies and international commercial arbitral bodies has taken the issue of individuals bringing international claims to a higher level.[22]

Rather than set out the detailed provisions of the large number of treaties or other documents that enable individuals to bring claims in an international context, the rest of this section will summarize the main aspects of the key areas of international law in which individuals can bring claims: international human rights law and international economic law. However, it should be noted that individuals can also bring international claims in other areas: thus victims of violations of international criminal law may seek reparations under Article 75 of the Statute of the International Criminal Court (Schabas, 2007), and employees of some international organizations may bring claims against that organization to an international body (Gray, 1987).

B. INTERNATIONAL HUMAN RIGHTS LAW

Within international human rights law, a number of treaties permit individuals to bring claims against a State, alleging violations of their human rights, before both international and regional bodies. This is an extraordinary development in the international legal system away from a position in which a State's actions on its own territory were not subject to international review. Claims can be brought by individuals against the State of which they are a national and against a State in whose jurisdiction they happen to be, even if temporarily, irrespective of whether they are a national of that State (Paust, 2003).[23] In most instances, the individual is a direct party to the proceedings before the international

---

[21] *Abbasi v Secretary of State for Foreign and Commonwealth Affairs* [2002] EWCA Civ 1316, 19 September 2002; (2003) 42 ILM 358.

[22] See the International Law Commission Reports on Diplomatic Protection and its changes over time: UN Doc A/CN.4/484 (1998) and UN Doc A/CN.4/506 (2000). See also the international arbitration of a dispute between the Government of Sudan and the Southern Sudan People's Liberation Movement by the Permanent Court of Arbitration in 2009.

[23] Eg, *Soering v United Kingdom*, Judgment of 7 July 1989, Ser A, no 161, 11 *EHRR* 439.

body (with most proceedings being conducted by written submissions). Decisions can be made, or 'views' given, by international bodies in which States are found to be in violation of their human rights obligations and remedies are indicated. These remedies range from monetary compensation to ordering the State to conduct investigations into the violations (Shelton, 2005).

Despite all of this, the State is still an intermediary, or directly involved in, these international claims by individuals. Such claims cannot be brought unless the relevant State has ratified the relevant treaty (whether a human rights treaty or a treaty establishing an international organization, such as the United Nations Charter, which facilitates claims by individuals), or the State has accepted the relevant Article of the treaty that allows individuals to bring the claim. In addition, no international claim can be brought by an individual unless he or she has exhausted domestic remedies in the relevant State. The reason for the latter is to enable States to resolve the issues at national level first, with the international bodies only being involved after all proceedings or other action at the State level have been effectively exhausted. Thus, in principle, there is no independent ability for individuals to bring claims before international human rights bodies.

Nevertheless, there are some aspects to these individual claims that show, in practice, some independent ability for individuals to bring international claims in this area. First, under the European Convention on Human Rights (ECHR) and the American Convention on Human Rights (ACHR) individuals can appear and bring their claims direct to the relevant Court. In addition, under the pre-Lisbon Treaty on European Union Article 6, ratification of the ECHR was required before a State could be party to the European Union (Nowak, 1999). Thus, in practice, European States are no longer able to prevent individual claims under that regional human rights system, which means that there are now about 800 million individuals who have the right to bring international claims under that treaty. Further, even if a State is not party to a particular human rights treaty, some international bodies, such as the Inter-American Commission on Human Rights and the UN Human Rights Council, can still, on the basis of individuals' claims revealing a consistent pattern of gross and reliably attested violations of human rights, make public conclusions about that State's human rights record.

Second, the link between nationality and the ability to bring claims is no longer essential. The link is now jurisdiction. If a State has jurisdiction over an individual, which power can include where that individual is not a national of that State and even where that State's jurisdiction over the individual is unlawful,[24] then an individual can bring a claim against that State if that State has ratified a relevant human rights treaty. The State of which that individual is a national does not have to be a party to the treaty and the individual could be a stateless person. This has meant that, in practice, States are now subject to a wider number of claims by individuals before international bodies. This represents 'a momentous advance in the world community' (Cassese, 1986, p 102).

Third, these treaties give individuals the procedural capacity to bring international claims. While this is a restricted capacity as it is dependent on State consent (as seen above), it does have significant practical effects. States rarely ignore the individual's claim to an international body. Rather they often respond to the claim at some length (though the practice is by no means universal) especially as, if they do not respond,

---

[24] *Loizidou* v *Turkey (Preliminary Objections)*, Judgment of 23 March 1995, Ser A, no 310, 20 *EHRR* 99.

the international body will still consider the matter, as there is some onus on the State to prove that there has been no violation.[25] When an international human rights body reaches a conclusion in relation to an individual's claim then States usually treat this conclusion as a serious matter that requires some response. If the conclusion is that there is no violation of a human right then the State will ensure that the media is aware of this. If the conclusion is that there has been a violation, then the State will respond in some way, from amending the relevant law or practice[26] to making a derogation from the relevant provision (should this be possible)[27] or offering a justification for their actions. Sometimes a State will even seek to denounce the treaty and criticize the international body: Peru, for example, withdrew its acceptance of the jurisdiction of the Inter-American Court of Human Rights before later re-accepting it. Very rarely will the State not respond at all. So these individual claims are treated seriously by States, in the same way as a claim brought against a State by another State before an international body is treated seriously.

Finally, the conclusions reached by international human rights bodies about individual claims can have practical effects on a State through the adoption of those conclusions by national courts[28] and by other international bodies whose decisions are legally binding on a State. The latter is seen in the approach taken by the European Court of Justice, which decided that 'respect for fundamental [human] rights forms an integral part of the general principles of [European] Community law protected by the Court of Justice'.[29] Thus the practical effects of individuals being able to bring claims before international human rights bodies are such as to place effective limits upon a State's ability to control or restrict those claims. The State's role as an intermediary, or barrier, between the individual and an international human rights body, whilst still crucial for an individual to be able to bring a claim is, in practice, permeable.

C. INTERNATIONAL ECONOMIC LAW

One of the areas of significant growth in the international legal system since the latter part of the twentieth century has been international economic law. Part of this growth has included the creation and development of mechanisms by which individuals, usually corporations, can bring claims against States. These mechanisms were initially ad hoc arbitration bodies and inter-State bodies to which individuals have access, for example, the Iran-US Claims Tribunal and the United Nations Compensation Commission. They now include institutional bodies (both treaty-based and non-treaty based) with established procedures, such as under the International Chamber of Commerce and the International Centre for the Settlement of Investment Disputes and through the model law of the United Nations Commission on International Trade Law (see Loibl, Ch 24, below).

---

[25] Bleier v Uruguay, decision of 29 March 1982 1 Selected Decisions of the Human Rights Committee 109.

[26] Eg, Sunday Times v UK, Judgment of 29 April 1979, ECtHR, Ser A, No 30, 2 EHRR 245.

[27] Eg, Brogan v United Kingdom, Judgment of 29 November 1988, ECtHR, Ser A, No 135–B, 11 EHRR 117.

[28] As in R v Bow Street Metropolitan Stipendiary, ex parte Pinochet Ugarte (Amnesty International Intervening) (No 3) [2000] 1 AC 147; [1999] 2 All ER 97.

[29] Internationale Handelsgesellschaft v Einfur und Voratsstelle Getreide, Case 11/70 [1970] ECR Reports 1125, para 4.

Each of these mechanisms allows individuals to bring claims against a State to an international body, which makes a decision, usually legally binding and enforceable, in relation to the claim (Redfern et al, 2004). The ability of an individual to bring an international claim against a State was considered by Arbitrator Dupuy in *Texaco* v *Libya* to show the international legal personality of an individual:

[S]tating that a contract between a State and a private person falls within the international legal order means that for the purposes of interpretation and performance of the contract, it should be recognized that a private contracting party has specific international capacities. But, unlike a State, the private person has only a limited capacity and his quality as a subject of international law does enable him only to invoke, in the field of international law, the rights which he derives from the contract.[30]

While Dupuy's reasoning is consistent with that of the ICJ in the *Reparations for Injuries* Opinion in relation to the ability of non-State actors to have international legal capacity for specific purposes and functions, it does not completely reflect the position today. Most of the disputes between individuals and States in this area are now resolved by a combination of public and private international law (Sornarajah, 1997), with decisions of international bodies enforced through national law, often as a consequence of a treaty obligation (such as the New York Convention on the Recognition and Enforcement of Foreign Arbitral Awards 1958).

In international economic law, as with international human rights law, it is the State that enables the individual to bring a claim either by ratifying the relevant treaty and/or through a contract agreed specifically by the State with the individual. However, in this area of law the ability of the State to refuse to allow individuals to bring international claims is often quite limited. In many instances the State, particularly a developing State, has little ability to resist an individual's (usually a transnational corporation) request to be able to bring an international claim (or to ratify the relevant treaty to enable such a claim to be made). This is because the economic power of such individuals is far greater than that of many States (McCorquodale, 2002). In addition, many economically powerful States will place pressure on other States to allow (eg, by ratifying the relevant treaty) individuals to bring these claims due to the power of the individual in that economically powerful State. For example, in a case between a company (Santa Elena) with a majority of US shareholders and Costa Rica before an ICSID Arbitral Tribunal, it was stated that 'a $US175,000,000 loan by the Inter-American Development Bank to Costa Rica was delayed at the behest of the US until Costa Rica consented to refer the Santa Elena case to international arbitration'.[31]

In addition, many of the claims brought by States to international economic legal bodies, such as under the dispute settlement procedures of the World Trade Organization (WTO), are initiated, sponsored, and prosecuted in effect by the individual corporations that are affected by the trade action that is the subject of the claim (Croley and Jackson, 1996; Charnovitz, 2001). Examples of the driving role of corporations in directing litigation under the WTO, include Kodak and Fuji representatives being on the US and Japanese delegations on a case affecting them, and the large banana corporations convincing the

---

30 *Texaco Overseas Petroleum Company* v *Libyan Arab Republic* (1977) 53 ILR 389.
31 *Santa Elena* v *Costa Rica* (ICSID Case No ARB/96/1), Final Award of 17 February 2000, para 25.

US and the EU to litigate about the trade in bananas from the Caribbean, despite the very few bananas produced in the US and the EU (Tietje and Nowrot, 2004; Brown and Hoekman, 2005). Indeed, the drafting of key international economic treaties is often done at either the instigation of, or with the direct involvement of, transnational corporations, as seen in the Agreement on Trade-Related Aspects of Intellectual Property Rights 1994. Further, the World Bank has created an Inspection Panel, which allows individuals who believe that they will be affected detrimentally by a project in a State that is to be funded by the World Bank to ask the Panel to investigate their claim (Resolution No 93–6, 1993). The Bank can do this even if the State is opposed to such investigation. A similar system is operated by the Asian Development Bank and the Inter-American Development Bank. This pressure from individuals for more control over international activity in the economic area will increase with globalization.

The major economic region of Europe provides the opportunity for individuals to bring claims to an international body. In *Van Gend en Loos* the European Court of Justice held:

The European Economic Community [now European Community] constitutes a new legal order of international law for the benefit of which the States have limited their sovereign rights, albeit within limited fields, and the subjects of which comprise not only Member States but also their nationals. Independently of the legislation of Member States, Community law therefore not only imposes obligations on individuals but is also intended to confer upon them rights which become part of their legal heritage. These rights arise not only where they are expressly granted by the Treaty, but also by reason of obligations which the Treaty imposes in a clearly defined way upon individuals as well as upon the Member States and institutions of the Community.[32]

This decision highlights the limitations on the ability of States to prevent claims by individuals under European law. Though there are some situations in which the individual can bring a claim directly to the Court, in fact the main avenue for individuals to bring claims under the European Union treaties is in their national courts (De Witte, 1999). There is also indirect access to the European Court of Justice, as most cases are brought to the Court by national courts seeking an interpretation from the Court in relation to European Community Treaty issues arising in the individual claim before that national court (Treaty Establishing the European Community, Article 234). Whilst States can withdraw from these European treaties, the practical consequences of withdrawal from these foundational elements of the European Union are such that a State's ability to do this has effectively now disappeared.

The ability of individuals (mainly corporations) to bring international claims in international economic law is now considerable. The main participants in a number of areas of international economic law are primarily States and corporations and they are often acting on equal terms. In negotiation of contracts where a transnational corporation is involved, an agreement on a dispute settlement mechanism is vital. Invariably this will be an international body to which the corporation can bring a claim and obtain an enforceable judgment. For most States that seek to encourage foreign investment, such an agreement allowing international dispute settlement is necessary and is not able to be rejected. Thus, to all intents and purposes, individuals now have an independent

---

[32] *Van Gend en Loos*, Case 26/69 [1969] ECR 419.

capacity to ensure that they can bring an international claim in some areas of international economic law.

D. IMMUNITIES

It is generally considered that, under the international legal system, only States have immunities from claims. These immunities can arise through non-acceptance of an international or a national legal mechanism. In addition, diplomats, Heads of State, representatives of international organizations, and others may have personal immunities arising from their relationship with the State or State-based bodies, even when acting outside their official roles. Even former Heads of State[33] and former Foreign Ministers[34] can have some personal immunity. These latter types of immunity are personal to the individual concerned and cannot be easily revoked by the State (though they are revocable). So it is possible to see an increasing recognition of the development of an immunity for individuals separate to that of the immunity of States.

Overall, the development of international law, particularly in the areas of human rights and economic law, has provided individuals with the ability of make claims to international bodies and have some personal immunities. In principle this ability is determined by States and their agreement to certain treaties that provide for individuals to make claims. But in practice many States are becoming less able to restrict, or to prevent, individuals having the ability to make international claims. There are at least some aspects of the international legal system that allow individuals an effective independent capacity to bring an international claim.

IV. CREATION, DEVELOPMENT, AND ENFORCEMENT OF INTERNATIONAL LAW

One of the essential aspects of an international legal person is 'the capacity to participate in international lawmaking and to enforce rules of international law' (Orakhelashvili, 2001, p 256). From the classical definition of the sources of international law found in Article 38 of the Statute of the ICJ, where State practice and State treaty-making are pre-eminent, to the laws on territory and jurisdiction being about State boundaries, it is the State that appears to decide exclusively on the creation, development, and enforcement of international law. Even the definition of which entity is a State is decided (through the process of recognition) by other States. It is necessary to see the extent to which individuals have been involved in the creation, development, and enforcement of international law.

A. RIGHT OF SELF-DETERMINATION

One area where the role of the individual can be seen as a challenge to the State-based system and where individuals have been involved in the creation, development, and enforcement

---

[33] *R v Bow Street Metropolitan Stipendiary, ex parte Pinochet Ugarte (Amnesty International Intervening) (No 3)* [2000] 1 AC 147; [1999] 2 All ER 97.

[34] *Arrest Warrant of 11 April 2000 (Democratic Republic of Congo/Belgium), Preliminary Objections and Merits, Judgment, ICJ Reports 2002*, p 3.

of international law is with respect to the right of self-determination. Article 1 of both the International Covenant on Economic, Social and Cultural Rights and the International Covenant on Civil and Political Rights provides that 'all peoples have the right of self-determination. By virtue of that right they freely determine their political status and freely pursue their economic, social and cultural development'. This right is a collective right, that is, a right of a group of individuals as a group. Its importance in relation to this chapter is that it is a part of the international legal system where the priority is given to groups of individuals and not to States. Whilst the definition of the right of self-determination, including its limitations, have been drafted by States and a number of decisions about its exercise, such as whether to recognize a self-determining entity as a State, are decided by States, much of its development has been by individuals acting as a group.

This can be shown in a number of ways: from its original focus in the early part of the twentieth century on minorities within and across States; its development beyond a legal justification for decolonization (which operated largely within a State-based structure) to its application outside the colonial context to independent States and internal self-determination; and its emphasis on the right of the people to decide their own destiny (McCorquodale, 1994). Some of these aspects were explained by Judge Nagendra Singh in the *Western Sahara* Opinion, when he said that:

[T]he consultation of the people of a territory awaiting decolonization is an inescapable imperative... Thus even if integration of territory was demanded by an interested State, as in this case, it could not be had without ascertaining the freely expressed will of the people— the very *sine qua non* of all decolonization.[35]

Indeed, the British government, one of the largest colonizers, went further when it stated: '[A]s the [United Nations] Charter and the two International Covenants expressly declare, [it is] a right of peoples. Not States. Not countries. Not governments. Peoples.'[36] It can be seen that 'the peoples in whom [the] right is vested are not inherently or necessarily represented by States or by governments of States' (Crawford, 1988, p 166).

In fact, so successful have groups of individuals been in relation to the right of self-determination that new States have arisen despite the expressed wish of some very powerful States that this should not happen (eg, in the early stages of the break-up of the former Yugoslavia) and States are now forced to accept that self-determination applies to groups within States.[37] Indeed, it could be considered that the right of self-determination has changed the international legal system significantly as even the elements taken into consideration as to whether an entity is a State now include whether that entity complies with the right of self-determination. With all the restrictions that States can bring to the exercise of the right of self-determination, its development has been beyond the control of States and its enforcement has frequently been due to the persistence of individuals and not of States, which largely remain unwilling participants in this area. Whilst there remain concerns about the abuse of the right and the unequal impact of the right, especially on women (Charlesworth and Chinkin, 2000), the participation of peoples in this area opens the possibility of a less State-based and territorial idea of the right of self-determination

---

[35] *Western Sahara, Advisory Opinion, ICJ Reports 1975*, p 12 at p 81.

[36] Statement by the United Kingdom representative to the United Nations Commission on Human Rights (Mr H Steel), 9 February 1988 (1988) 59 *BYIL* 441.

[37] *Reference Re Secession of Quebec*, Canadian Supreme Court (1998) 37 ILM 1340.

(Marks, 2000; Young, 2000; Knop, 2002). The power of the people is expressed by Judge Ammoun in the *Namibia* Opinion:

Indeed one is bound to recognize that the right of peoples to self-determination, before being written into charters that were not granted but won in bitter struggle, had first been written painfully, with the blood of the peoples, in the finally awakened conscience of humanity.[38]

B. INDIGENOUS PEOPLES

Another area of international law where the 'conscience of humanity' has been awakened is in relation to indigenous peoples. Although their international legal status had been acknowledged in the sixteenth century and some national courts considered them as communities distinct from States, it was not until late in the twentieth century that substantial renewed consideration was given to their position in the international legal system (Anaya, 2004). Most significantly, the Sub-Commission of the then UN Human Rights Commission (now the Human Rights Council) established a Working Group in Indigenous Populations in 1982. This Working Group comprised many representatives of indigenous peoples, who could participate fully in the drafting of (what became) the UN Declaration on the Rights of Indigenous Peoples 2007. This Declaration was adopted, after many years of delay, by the UN General Assembly with only four votes against (Australia, Canada, New Zealand, and the United States—though the governments of each of those States have since changed). Its importance also lies in the fact that the process of the creation and development of this Declaration was largely outside the sole control of States. It was drafted with a significant degree of participation by indigenous peoples, who were, in the drafting process, acting on almost equal terms to State representatives. This process was revolutionary in the United Nations system (Lâm, 2000; Xanthaki, 2007).

Process and procedure, as discussed in relation to human rights, are significant aspects of the international legal system in terms of clarification of the participants in that system. In addition, the Declaration (even when it was a draft) assisted courts and other bodies in upholding the rights and separate status of indigenous peoples.[39]

C. NON-GOVERNMENTAL ORGANIZATIONS

The participation of individuals, usually as groups or peoples, in the creation, development, and enforcement of international law in the areas of self-determination and indigenous peoples has been fostered by the growing role of non-governmental organizations (NGOs). These organizations, which are part of international civil society, have had an increasingly crucial effect on the creation, development, and enforcement of many parts of the international legal system Even in earlier centuries their role was relevant, as seen in the activities of the Anti-Slavery Society being crucial to the abolition of slavery

---

[38] *Legal Consequences for States of the Continued Presence of South Africa in Namibia (South West Africa) notwithstanding Security Council Resolution 276 (1970), Advisory Opinion, ICJ Reports 1971*, p 16 at p 74.

[39] See *Cal v Attorney-General* (Claim 121/ 2007), Supreme Court of Belize, 18 October 2007, and Inter-American Court of Human Rights, *Case of the Saramanka People v Suriname*, Preliminary Objections, Merits, reparations and Costs, Judgment of 28 November 2007, Ser C no 173.

and the role of women's groups (Bianchi, 1997). In more recent times NGOs have been important in the creation of international law, with, for example, NGOs assisting in the drafting of the Convention on the Rights of the Child (as acknowledged in the *travaux préparatoires* of that treaty, Detrick, 1992) and the Convention on the Conservation of Migratory Species of Wild Animals 1979 (Bowman, 1999), organizing a systematic campaign towards the adoption of the Convention Against Torture and other related documents (Van Boven, 1990), the creation of the International Criminal Court (Pace and Thieroff, 1999), and the banning of landmines (Anderson, 2000), as well as fostering proposals for the establishment of a UN High Commissioner for Human Rights (Clapham, 1994).

There are two areas of the international legal system where the law has developed primarily as a response to the activities of NGOs. These are international humanitarian law, where the role of the International Committee of the Red Cross (ICRC) has been crucial, and issues relating to labour conditions, where trade unions and employer organizations have played a significant role. The ICRC has the unusual express acknowledgement of its role in the Geneva Conventions 1949 and the 1977 Protocols. For example, States can entrust the fulfilment of their duties to the ICRC (common Article 10 (or 11) of the Conventions), they must cooperate with the ICRC during conflicts (Article 81 Geneva Prisoner of War Convention) and before any proposed amendment by a State to the Protocols can be acted upon, the ICRC must be consulted (Article 97 Protocol I and Article 24 Protocol II). Similarly, trade unions and employer organizations are institutionally part of the International Labour Organization, which has adopted many treaties and other international documents. Of similar power, but with a less institutional role, have been the activities of environmental NGOs, who are a vital element in the creation and sustenance of international environmental law (Cullen and Morrow, 2001).

The roles that NGOs play in relation to the development of international law are numerous. They include 'elaborating further interpretative rules in connection with already existing international instruments...[which have come to be] referred to as...authoritative sources' (Van Boven, 1990, p 357). They are involved in international decision-making, usually indirectly, by their participation in international fora, from the UN itself to its agencies and as a distinct part of international conferences. Indeed, NGOs can be 'sought-after participants in a political process...that allow NGOs to move from the corridors to the sessions' (Knop, 1993). Sometimes this participation can be important as a balance against States' views, as seen in the Bangkok NGO Declaration on Human Rights that appeared successfully to reduce the impact of the Asian States' Declaration in relation to cultural relativism (Steiner and Alston, 2000, p 549), and sometimes NGOs act in opposing ways due to their different objectives (eg, during the Beijing Conference on Women—Otto, 1999). Sometimes NGOs are essential to the continuing operation of some international bodies, as the African Commission on Human Rights has acknowledged (Motala, 2008), due to their provision of information, people, and resources. In the area of international environmental law the role of NGOs has been particularly crucial, for example, in relation to the protection of birds:

[T]he role of [NGOs] has proved to be of vital importance. Not only have they regularly pressed for the adoption of agreements...they have frequently shown a willingness to undertake much of the preliminary drafting work necessary to make such projects a reality.

Insofar as these agreements, once concluded, have required to be sustained by technical resources and expertise, NGOs have been prominent in the provision of such support... [In relation to one treaty,] one such [NGO] has also provided the administrative infrastructure for the establishment of a secretariat. (Bowman, 1999, p 298)

Thus the terms of the treaties that are eventually ratified are often drafted and negotiated by NGOs. The participation of NGOs in the treaty process itself also ensures greater transparency and accountability of States for their negotiating positions. To look solely at the end process (ie, the ratified treaty) without any examination of the process by which that law is made, ignores the discursive context, power structures and interests involved in international law-making. This powerful role has been recognized at times, with NGOs being parties, with States, to Memoranda of Understanding (which are international agreements, though are not treaties) concerning conservation measures about particular species, with responsibilities being placed on both States and NGOs under these Memoranda (Bowman, 1999).

NGOs are also active participants in the enforcement of international law. In many instances they assist individuals to bring international claims, or bring claims themselves, and they provide information to international bodies that will often not be provided by States (Charnovitz, 2006). These roles of NGOs are accepted now in practice by States, by the rules of procedure of the international bodies, and are even specifically referred to in some treaties (eg, Article 45 of the Convention on the Rights of the Child). NGOs have regularly brought *amicus curiae* information to international bodies, whereby they have sought to assist the international bodies in making decisions in cases brought by others against a State. This role is important and could be extended to the ICJ as:

[ICJ] judgments affect not only the rights and obligations of states parties to the dispute, but also increasingly the rights and obligations of individuals, justice requires that [NGOs] representing the public interest have the opportunity to submit information and arguments to the Court. Such participation reinforces the concept of obligations *erga omnes* and can lead to enhancing the role of the Court and the long-term development of international law. (Shelton, 1994, p 642)

At the same time, NGOs and individuals have used national legal systems to enforce international legal obligations of States (Vazquez, 1992). In addition, NGOs operate as fact-finding bodies, lobbyists, and advocates in a way that generates publicity about violations of international law. These can be most effective means of enforcing compliance with international law by States in an international legal system where other forms of enforcement are often lacking or rarely operate. NGOs can also have such a powerful effect on States that some States will act directly against them, even if this is in breach of international law. For example, the persistent activities of Greenpeace, an environmental NGO, against French nuclear testing in the South Pacific led to the French government ordering some of its agents to sink the Greenpeace ship 'Rainbow Warrior' in a New Zealand harbour. As a consequence of this breach of international law, France had to pay compensation to New Zealand for interference in its sovereignty (but not to Greenpeace) and send its agents to a remote Pacific island.[40]

---

[40] *Rainbow Warrior (France/New Zealand)* (1990) 20 *RIAA* 217; 82 ILR 499.

It is beyond doubt that NGOs have participated in the creation, development, and enforcement of international law. They have brought new ideas, sustained focus and pressure, and effective means of action in the international legal system (Rajagopal, 2003; Lindblom 2005). They offer an alternative voice to States, though they share the problems of lack of legitimacy, few democratic processes, and limited representativeness of many States (Cullen and Morrow, 2001). They provide a means to hold States and State-based organizations to account and they seek to increase the transparency of international decision-making (Charnovitz, 2006). The importance of their roles has been acknowledged in the European Convention on the Recognition of the Legal Personality of International NGOs 1991 and the UN Declaration on the Rights of Human Rights Defenders 1998. Much of NGOs' activity is only possible because States allow it to happen, such as participation in international fora, but not all of it is controlled by, or controllable by, States. As a consequence a 'peculiar process of interaction between traditional law mechanisms and transnational social processes with the mediation of non-State actors has become a novel method of law-making and law enforcement' (Bianchi, 1997, p 201). NGO participation may be a novel method of international law-making but it is now an accepted method.

D. JURISTS

The role of jurists, or individual writers on international law, has had a long-term effect on international law. Jurists have been given a special position in the creation, development, and enforcement of international law with Article 38(d) of the ICJ Statute authorizing the ICJ to apply 'the teachings of the most highly qualified publicists of the various nations as [a] subsidiary means for the determination of rules of [international] law'. Their influence can be specific, such as their influence on the inclusion of persecutions on the basis of gender being considered as crimes against humanity (Bianchi, 1997), the drafting of the Siracusa Principles on derogations and the Limburg Principles on economic, social, and cultural rights, and on decisions of international bodies (Brownlie, 2008). It can also be general, such as the role of individual jurists on the various Draft Articles of the International Law Commission. The roles of jurists as experts on international law, from membership of international bodies, such as the ICJ and international human rights bodies, to advising States and being members of expert panels in international organizations (from the World Health Organization to the Atomic Energy Agency), is also important.

From the earliest philosophers, the understanding of what is the nature of international law has been a crucial part of the development of rules and principles in the international legal system. Allott has shown how the ideas of Vattel 'determined the course of history' (Allott, 1989, p 14) as Vattel propounded a sovereignty theory of the State (in contrast to the more inclusive 'all humanity' idea that had been expounded earlier), which now forms the basis of much of the dominant understanding of international law.

Indeed, much of our understanding of what is the international legal system, and the role of individuals in it, is affected by the writings of jurists. For example, jurists who adopt a positivist approach to the international legal system, although generally considering that the individual has no independent role from that of the State, have been important in identifying rules of customary international law and persuading States that these rules legally bind them (Oppenheim, 1905). Yet it has been argued that the positivist concept of international law as a State-based process 'is incapable of serving as the normative

framework for present or future political realities...new times call for a fresh conceptual
and ethical language' (Tesón, 1992, pp 53–54). Some of the fresh conceptual and ethical
language that has been suggested includes the application of feminist theory to the international legal system, which shows the limitations of the State as a framework for engagement in gender issues (Charlesworth, Chinkin, and Wright, 1991) and a recognition that
relying on constant binary oppositions, such as State v non-State, cannot produce a coherent international legal system (Koskenniemi, 1989). Others consider that 'the burgeoning
canon of individual rights has begun to crack open the previously encrusted [positivist]
Vatellian system' (Franck, 1999, p 281) or that the notion of State sovereignty has always
been indeterminate and fluctuating (Kostakopoulou, 2002) so that 'we should adjust our
intellectual framework to a multi-layered reality consisting of a variety of authoritative
structures...[in which] what matters is not the formal status of a participant...but its
actual or preferable exercise of functions' (Schreuer, 1993, p 453). Others reject the current
conceptual parameters and argue for a new understanding of international society (Allott,
2001). Each of these conceptual approaches seeks to explain the law-making processes of
the international legal system and, in so doing, offers reflections on the role of the individual in that system. These approaches have occasionally been taken up by States and others
in ways that have affected the development of international law (eg, in ICJ decisions and
UN resolutions). A specific example is found in the speech of the UN Secretary-General,
Kofi Annan, on the award of the Nobel Peace Prize 2001 to him and to the UN:

Over the past five years, I have often recalled that the United Nations' Charter begins with
the words: 'We the peoples'. What is not always recognized is that 'We the peoples' are made
up of individuals whose claims to the most fundamental rights have too often been sacrificed
in the supposed interests of the State or the nation...In this new century, we must start from
the understanding that peace belongs not only to States or peoples, but to each and every
member of those communities. The sovereignty of States must no longer be used as a shield
for gross violations of human rights. Peace must be made real and tangible in the daily existence of every individual in need. Peace must be sought, above all, because it is the condition
for every member of the human family to live a life of dignity and security...Throughout my
term as Secretary-General, I have sought to place human beings at the centre of everything
we do—from conflict prevention to development to human rights. Securing real and lasting
improvement in the lives of individual men and women is the measure of all we do at the
United Nations. (Annan, 2001, pp 2–3)

Therefore, it can be seen that, in various ways, individuals have had, and continue to have,
an important part in the creation, development, and enforcement of international law.
This has been by groups of individuals, from peoples with the right of self-determination
and indigenous peoples, to NGOs, as well as the influence of jurists. It can also be seen in
the contribution of women and men throughout the centuries, who offer new ideas and
practical applications in relation to international law.

V. CONCLUSION

The role of the individual in the international legal system remains a contentious one.
It can depend on how the nature of the system is conceptualized and applied, as well as
an understanding of diverse areas of international law. In most cases the crucial issue is

whether the individual has an independent role in the system or whether the individual's role is solely dependent on State consent.

In approaching these issues, a broad definition of the 'individual' has been adopted, with the understanding that 'participation' in the international legal system (as against the 'subject' v 'object' stricture) is the relevant context for considering the role of the individual. This has opened up more possibilities to discover the conceptual and practical role of the individual in the system. It has been shown that individuals do have considerable international rights and responsibilities in the system, a number of which are independent from a State's ability to control or determine them. The vast array of international claims available to individuals are largely still within the control of States in principle, but not in practice. It is clear that the individual has been a crucial factor in the creation, development, and enforcement of international law. As the ICJ noted, the 'needs of the [international] community' and 'the requirements of international life' (see above) have ensured that the individual has a continuing role in the international legal system. In addition, individuals, by their actions, influence not only the concept and content of international law but also the way it is applied by States and the extent and manner by which a State consents to rules of international law (see further McCorquodale, 2004). Individuals can begin to contribute to the development of customary international as their participation affects the practice of international law, including the possibility that an agreement between a State and a non-State actor (such as an armed opposition group) may be considered to be an international agreement or a treaty.[41] Indeed, 'the proposal that individuals ought to included in the process of customary international law formation is both theoretically grounded and technically feasible' (Ochoa, 2007, p 169; Müller, 2008) Yet this conclusion is a challenge to much of the current dominant view as Judge Cançado Trindade, then President of the Inter-American Court of Human Rights noted:

The doctrinal trend which still insists in denying to individuals the condition of subjects of international law is...unsustainable [and] that conception appears contaminated by an ominous ideological dogmatism, which had as the main consequence to alienate the individual from the international legal order. It is surprising—if not astonishing—besides regrettable, to see that conception repeated mechanically and ad nauseam by a part of the doctrine, apparently trying to make believe that the intermediary of the State, between the individuals and the international legal order, would be something inevitable and permanent. Nothing could be more fallacious.[42]

Individuals may not yet be participating in the international legal system to the same extent as States. But the trend is clear: the role of the individual in this system is continuing to expand, often despite the wishes of States. If, as Annan asserts, the ultimate foundation of the international legal system is 'We, the Peoples', then the role of each State is not to ensure and perpetuate its own power but to enable every individual to live a life of dignity and security and so to ensure human flourishing. The interests of individuals must count for more than the interests of States.

---

[41] For example, France includes its agreements with Palestine under the categoery of 'bi-lateral treaties', though cf *Prosectuor* v *Kallon: Amnesty Decision*, Appeals Chamber of the Special Court of Sierra Leone, 13 March 2004, paras 36–50.

[42] *Juridical Status and Human Rights of the Child*, Advisory Opinion OC-17/02 Ser A, No 17 (28 August 2002), (2004) 11 IHRR 510, Concurring Opinion of Judge Cançado Trindade, at paras 26–27.

REFERENCES

ADDO, M (ed) (1999), *Human Rights Standards and the Responsibility of Transnational Corporations* (The Hague: Kluwer).

ALLOTT, P (1989), *International Law and International Revolution: Reconceiving the World* (Hull: Hull University Press).

—— (1992), 'Reconstituting Humanity— New International Law', 3 *EJIL* 219.

—— (2001), *Eunomia: New Order for a New World*, rev edn (Oxford: Oxford University Press).

ANAYA, J (2004), *Indigenous Peoples in International Law*, 2nd edn (Oxford: Oxford University Press).

ANDERSON, K (2000), 'The Ottawa Convention Banning Landmines, The Role of International Non-Governmental Organisations and the Idea of International Civil Society', 11 *EJIL* 91.

ANNAN, K (2001), 'We can love what we are without hating what—and who—we are not', Nobel Peace Prize Lecture, 10 December 2001, http://www.un.org/News/Press/docs/2001/sgsm8071.doc.htm.

BIANCHI, A (1997), 'Globalization of Human Rights: The Role of Non-State Actors', in Teubner, G (ed), *Global Law Without a State* (Aldershot: Dartmouth).

BOWMAN, M (1999) 'The Global Protection of Birds', 11 *Journal of International Environmental Law* 87.

BOYLE, A and CHINKIN, C (2007), *The Making of International Law* (Oxford: Oxford University Press).

BROWN, C and HOEKMAN, B (2005), 'WTO Dispute Settlement and the Missing Developing Country Case: Engaging the Private Sector', 8 *J Int'l Econ. L* 861.

BROWNLIE, I (2008), *Principles of Public International Law*, 7th edn (Oxford: Oxford University Press).

BUTLER, I (2007), *Unravelling Sovereignty: Human Rights and the Structure of International Law* (Groningen: Intersentia).

CASSESE, A (1986), *International Law in a Divided World* (Oxford: Clarendon Press).

CHARLESWORTH, H and CHINKIN, C (2000), *The Boundaries of International Law: A Feminist Analysis* (Manchester: Manchester University Press).

——, ——, and WRIGHT, S (1991), 'Feminist Approaches to International Law,' 85 *AJIL* 631.

CHARNOVITZ, S (2001), 'Economic and Social Actors in the World Trade Organization', 7 *ILSA J of International and Comparative Law* 259.

—— (2006), 'Non-Governmental Organizations and International Law', 100 *AJIL* 348.

CLAPHAM, A (1993), *Human Rights in the Private Sphere* (Oxford: Oxford University Press).

—— (1994), 'Creating the High Commissioner for Human Rights: The Outside Story', 5 *EJIL* 556.

—— (2008), 'Extending International Criminal Law beyond the Individual to Corporations and Armed Opposition Groups' 6 *J Intl Criminal Justice* 899.

COMMITTEE of MINISTERS (2001), Report of the Evaluation Group on the European Court of Human Rights, 22 *HRLJ* 308.

CRAWFORD, J (ed) (1988), *The Rights of Peoples* (Oxford: Oxford University Press).

CROLEY, S and JACKSON, J (1996), 'WTO Dispute Procedures, Standard of Review and Deference to National Governments', 90 *AJIL* 193.

CULLEN, H and MORROW, K (2001), 'International Civil Society in International Law: The Growth of NGO Participation', 1 *Non-State Actors in International Law* 7.

DETRICK, S (ed) (1992), *The United Nations Convention on the Rights of the Child: A Guide to the 'Travaux Préparatoires'* (Dordrecht: Martinus Nijhoff).

DE WITTE, B (1999), 'The Past and Future of the Role of the European Court of Justice in the Protection of Human Rights', in Alston, P, Bustelo, M, and Heenan, S (eds), *The EU and Human Rights* (Oxford: Oxford University Press).

DINE, J (2000), *The Governance of Corporate Groups* (Cambridge: Cambridge University Press).

DINSTEIN, Y (1984), 'Human Rights in Armed Conflict', in Meron, T (ed), *Human Rights in International Law: Legal and Policy Issues* (Oxford: Oxford University Press).

FALK, R (1993), 'The Making of Global Citizenship', in Brecher, J, Childs, J, and Cutler, J (eds), *Global Visions: Beyond the New World Order* (Cambridge, Mass.: South End Press).

FRANCK, T (1999), *The Empowered Self: Law and Society in the Age of Individualism* (Oxford: Oxford University Press).

GEUSS, R (2007), *History and Illusion in Politics* (Cambridge: Cambridge University Press).

GRAY, C (1987), *Judicial Remedies in International Law* (Oxford: Clarendon Press).

HIGGINS, R (1979), 'Conceptual Thinking about the Individual in International Law', 11 *New York Law School Law Review* 11.

—— (1994), *Problems and Process: International Law and How We Use It* (Oxford: Oxford University Press).

HOHFELD, W (1913), 'Fundamental Legal Conceptions as Applied to Judicial Reasoning', 23 *Yale LJ* 16.

International Law Commission (2001), *Articles on Responsibility of States for Internationally Wrongful Acts*, 53rd Session, UN Doc A/CN.4/L.602/Rev.1, 26 July 2001, available at **www.un.org/law/ilc**.

KNOP, K (1993), 'Re/statements: Feminism and State Sovereignty in International Law', 3 *Transnational and Contemporary Legal Problems* 293.

—— (2002), *Diversity and Self-Determination in International Law* (Cambridge: Cambridge University Press).

KOSKENNIEMI, M (1989), *From Apology to Utopia: The Structure of International Legal Argument*, 2005 reissue (Cambridge: Cambridge University Press).

—— (1991), 'The Future of Statehood', 32 *Harvard ILJ* 397.

KOSTAKOPOULOU, D (2002), 'Floating Sovereignty: A Pathology or Necessary Means of State Evolution', 22 *Ox JLS* 135.

LÂM, MC (2000), *At the Edge of the State: Indigenous Peoples and Self-Determination* (Ardsley, NY: Transnational Publishers).

LAUTERPACHT, H (1950), *International Law and Human Rights* (London: Stevens).

LINDBLOM, A-K (2005), *Non-Governmental Organisations in International Law* (Cambridge: Cambridge University Press).

LOPES, C and QUÉNIVET, N (2008), 'Individuals as Subjects of International Humanitarian Law and Human Rights Law', in Arnold, R and Quénivet, N (eds), *International Humanitarian Law and Human Rights Law—Towards a New Merger in International Law* (Boston, Brill Academic).

LOWE, V (2005), ' "Clear and Present Danger": Responses to Terrorism', 54 *ICLQ* 185.

McCORQUODALE, R (1994), 'Self-Determination: A Human Rights Approach', 43 *ICLQ* 857.

—— (2002), 'Human Rights and Global Business', in Bottomley, S and Kinley, D (eds), *Commercial Law and Human Rights* (Aldershot: Ashgate).

—— (2004), 'An Inclusive International Legal System', 17 *Leiden JIL* 477.

—— and LA FORGIA, R (2001), 'Taking off the Blindfolds: Torture by Non-State Actors', 1 *HRLR* 189.

McGOLDRICK, D (2004), *From '9–11' to the 'Iraq War 2003': International Law in an Age of Complexity* (Oxford: Hart Publishing).

MARKS, S (2000), *The Riddle of all Constitutions: International Law, Democracy and the Critique of Ideology* (Oxford: Oxford University Press).

MEIJKNECHT, A (2001), *Towards International Personality: The Position of Minorities and Indigenous Peoples in International Law* (Groningen: Intersentia).

MENON, PK (1992), 'The International Personality of Individuals in International Law: A Broadening of the Traditional Doctrine', 1 *J of Transnt'l Law and Policy* 151.

MERON, T (2006), *The Humanization of International Law* (Boston: Brill Academic).

MOTALA, A (2008), 'Non-Governmental Organisations in the African System', in Evans, M and Murray, R (eds), *The African Charter on Human and Peoples' Rights*, 2nd edn (Cambridge: Cambridge University Press).

MUCHLINSKI, P (2007), *Multinational Enterprises and the Law*, 2nd edn (Oxford: Oxford University Press).

MÜLLER, T (2008), 'Customary Transnational Law: Attacking the Last Resort of State Sovereignty', 15 *Ind J of Global Legal Studies* 19.

NIJMAN, J (2004), *The Concept of International Legal Personality* (The Hague: TMC Asser Press).

NOWAK, M (1999), 'Human Rights "Conditionality" in Relation to Entry to, and Full Participation in, the EU', in Alston, P (ed), *The EU and Human Rights* (Oxford: Oxford University Press).

OCHOA, C (2007), 'The Individual and Customary International Law Formation', 48 Va J Int'l L 119.

OPPENHEIM, L (1905), *International Law*, vol 1 (London: Longmans).

ORAKHELASHVILI, A (2001), 'The Position of the Individual in International Law', 31 *California Western ILJ* 241.

OTTO, D (1997), 'Rethinking Universals: Opening Transformative Possibilities in International Human Rights Law', 18 *Aust YBIL* 1.

—— (1999), 'A Post-Beijing Reflection on the Limitations and Potential of Human Rights Discourse for Women', in Askin, K and Koenig, D (eds), *Women and International Human Rights Law*, vol 1 (Ardsley, NY: Transnational Publishers).

PACE, W and THIEROFF, M (1999), 'Participation of Non-Governmental Organisations', in Lee, R (ed), *The International Criminal Court* (The Hague: Kluwer).

PAUST, J (2003), 'The Reality of Private Rights, Duties and Participation in the International Legal Process', 25 *Mich J Int'l L* 1229.

PROVOST, R (2002), *International Human Rights and Humanitarian Law* (Cambridge: Cambridge University Press).

PUVIMANASINGHE, S (2007), *Foreign Investment, Human Rights and the Environment* (Leiden: Brill Academic).

RATNER, S and ABRAMS, J (2009), *Accountability for Human Rights Atrocities in International Law*, 3rd edn (Oxford: Oxford University Press).

REDFERN, A, HUNTER, M, BLACKABY, N, and PARTASIDES, C (2004), *Law and Practice of International Commercial Arbitration*, 4th edn (London: Sweet & Maxwell).

RAJAGOPAL, B (2003), *International Law from Below* (Cambridge: Cambridge University Press).

REISMAN, M (1990), 'Sovereignty and Human Rights in Contemporary International Law', 84 *AJIL* 866.

REMEC, P (1960), *The Position of the Individual in International Law According to Grotius and Vattel* (The Hague: Martinus Nijhoff).

SANDS, P (2005), *Lawless World: America and the Making and Breaking of Global Rules* (London: Penguin).

SCELLE, G (1932), *Précis de droit des gens* (Paris: Recueil Sirey).

SCHABAS, W (2007), *Introduction to the International Criminal Court*, 3rd edn (Cambridge: Cambridge University Press).

SCHREUER, C (1993), 'The Waning of the Sovereign State: Towards a New Paradigm for International Law', 4 *EJIL* 447.

SHELTON, D (1994), 'The Participation of Nongovernmental Organizations in International Judicial Proceedings', 88 *AJIL* 611.

—— (2005), *Remedies in International Human Rights Law*, 2nd edn (Oxford: Oxford University Press).

SORNARAJAH, M (1997), 'Power and Justice in Foreign Investment Arbitration', 14 *J of Internt'l Arbitration* 103.

STEINER, H and ALSTON, P (2000), *International Human Rights in Context*, 2nd edn (Oxford: Oxford University Press).

TESÓN, F (1992), 'The Kantian Theory of International Law', 92 *Col LR* 53.

TIETJE, C and NOWROT, K (2004), 'Forming the Centre of a Transnational Economic Legal Order? Thoughts on the Current and Future Position of Non-State Actors in WTO Law', 5 *European Business Organization LR* 321.

TORNARITIS, C (1972), *The Individual as a Subject of International Law* (Nicosia: Public Information Office).

VAN BOVEN, T (1990), 'The Role of Non-Governmental Organizations in International Human Rights Standard-Setting: A Prerequisite for Democracy', 20 *California Western ILJ* 207.

VAZQUEZ, C (1992), 'Treaty-Based Rights and Remedies of Individuals', 92 *Col LR* 1082.

WARBRICK, C (2004), 'The European Response to Terrorism in an Age of Human Rights', 15 *EJIL* 989.

YOUNG, IM (2000), *Inclusion and Democracy* (Oxford: Oxford University Press).

FURTHER READING

It is in the nature of the topic that the vast amount of relevant literature in this area is found in articles and book chapters many of which are referred to in the text and listed above. The only publications of particular note are:

ALSTON, P (2005), *Non-State Actors and Human Rights* (Oxford: Oxford University Press).

CLAPHAM, A (2006), *Human Rights Obligations of Non-State Actors* (Oxford: Oxford University Press).

DUPUY, P-M and VIERUCCI, L (2008), *NGOs in International Law* (Cheltenham, Edward Elgar).

NØRGAARD, C (1962), *The Position of the Individual in International Law* (Copenhagen: Munksgaard).

Non-State Actors and International Law (a journal published since 2001 by Brill Publishers).

PART IV

THE SCOPE OF SOVEREIGNTY

11

JURISDICTION

Vaughan Lowe and Christopher Staker

SUMMARY

Each State has the right to regulate its own public order, and to that end it is entitled to legislate for everyone within its territory. But States are also entitled to legislate for their nationals, and some actions extend over national boundaries; and there are accordingly situations in which two or more States may seek to apply their laws to the same conduct. This chapter is concerned with the principles of international law that regulate the right of States to apply their laws to conduct, and with the resolution of disputes arising from overlapping jurisdictional claims, and also with the problems of enforcing national laws.

I. INTRODUCTION

A. THE MEANING OF 'JURISDICTION'

'Jurisdiction' is the term that describes the limits of the legal competence of a State or other regulatory authority (such as the European Community) to make, apply, and enforce rules of conduct upon persons. It 'concerns essentially the extent of each state's right to regulate conduct or the consequences of events'.[1]

States regulate conduct in this sense in various ways, which may involve any of the branches of government. Thus, the Legislature may lay down rules by statute, or the Executive may do so by order. Laws on the provocation of religious hatred, and statutory instruments forbidding the export of certain goods to certain countries, are obvious examples. Some laws are less obviously prescriptive, but are nonetheless equally part of the structure of the social order: for example, laws regarding the qualifications for the acquisition of a State's nationality or determining the circumstances in which contractual obligations may be avoided, or describing the conditions upon which a person will be liable to pay taxes to the State. States also regulate conduct by means of the decisions of their courts, which may order litigating parties to do or abstain from doing certain things. So, too, may the State's administrative bodies, which may apply rules concerning,

---

[1] *Oppenheim's International Law*, 1992, p 456.

for example, the issuance of licences to export goods to certain countries. The police, and other law-enforcement agencies, are also involved, in the arrest and detention of persons, and the seizure of goods. All of these activities are in principle regulated by the rules of international law concerning jurisdiction.

The term 'jurisdiction' is also commonly used in international law to describe the scope of the right of an international tribunal, such as the International Court of Justice or the International Criminal Court, to adjudicate upon cases and to make orders in respect of the parties to them. In abstract terms, the jurisdiction of States and the jurisdiction of tribunals are both instances of the concept of the scope of the powers of a legal institution; but it is traditional, and practically useful, to distinguish between them and to treat them separately. The jurisdiction of international tribunals is, accordingly, not treated in this chapter.

B. THE SIGNIFICANCE OF THE PRINCIPLES OF JURISDICTION

The legal rules and principles governing jurisdiction have a fundamental importance in international relations, because they are concerned with the allocation between States, and other entities such as the European Union, of competence to regulate daily life—that is, the competence to secure the *differences* that make each State a distinct society. Inasmuch as they determine the reach of a State's laws, they may be said to determine what the boundaries of that State's particular public order are. For instance, the rejection by western States of the *fatwah* issued against Salman Rushdie was, in essence, a denial that the jurisdiction of the Iranian authorities extended so far as to regulate conduct in the United Kingdom.[2] There are many other examples of contested jurisdictional claims, perhaps less spectacular but affecting a much wider range of interests. For example, the United States has at various times enacted laws that purport to forbid foreign businesses, based outside the United States, to trade with certain States such as the former Soviet Union, Iran, and Cuba. Those laws have imposed significant economic costs and disadvantages on non-US companies; and they raise the question of the propriety—indeed, the legality—of one State purporting to forbid persons in another State to do things that are perfectly lawful in the State where those persons are located.

Similarly, as the principles governing jurisdiction define the limits of the State's coercive powers, they effect one of the most important delineations of the different societies into which the world is divided. It is these principles that dictate, for example, that the British authorities have no right to operate in French territory in order to regulate the conduct of asylum-seekers at Sangatte, and that the Scottish courts have no right to sit in the Netherlands. It was necessary for France and the United Kingdom to conclude an agreement allowing the customs and immigration officers of each to operate in the territory of the other in relation to the Channel Tunnel,[3] and for the Netherlands and the United Kingdom to conclude an agreement to permit the Scottish court to sit at Camp Zeist in

---

[2] It appears that it was technically a religious authority, rather than what in western terms would be thought of as a typically 'governmental' authority, that issued the *fatwah*. This raises the interesting question of the limits of the notion of 'the State' for the purposes of State responsibility. On this question see Part V of this book and see *United States Diplomatic and Consular Staff in Tehran, Judgment, ICJ Reports 1980*, p 3.

[3] See the Sangatte Protocol, 25 November 1991, Cm 1802; 62 *BYIL* 623–625 (1991).

the Netherlands to hear the cases against the Libyan nationals accused of blowing up a US aeroplane in the skies above Lockerbie in Scotland.[4]

In view of their significance, it is not surprising that the principles governing jurisdiction have attracted considerable attention from jurists over the years. In fact, however, international controversy over the limits of jurisdiction, which was intense in the four or five decades after 1945, seems to have abated somewhat during recent years.

Before turning to the examination of those principles in more detail, it is necessary to say a word about the framework within which jurisdictional principles are analysed by international lawyers.

C. THE DOCTRINAL ANALYSIS OF JURISDICTION

Jurisdiction, as a topic of international law, has a less solid and universal basis than is often supposed. English-language monographs typically devote a chapter to the topic,[5] as they have done since the late nineteenth century:[6] continental monographs, on the other hand, have tended to adopt a rather different approach, regarding jurisdiction as an aspect of statehood or territory or the law of the sea or of some other aspect of international law. There is, on this continental approach, no comprehensive, consolidated statement of all of the principles of jurisdiction.[7] It is notable that there is, for example, no volume devoted to jurisdiction in Verzijl's great treatise, *International Law in Historical Perspective*. That pattern appears to be changing. In 1968 the Council of Europe produced a *Model Plan for the Classification of Documents concerning State Practice in the Field of Public International Law*,[8] which distributed the treatment of jurisdiction under a number of different headings, including 'Personal Jurisdiction', 'State Territory and Territorial Jurisdiction', and 'Seas, Waterways, Ships', in line with the continental approach. In 1997, that plan was revised, and jurisdiction now has its own separate chapter in the Model Plan, divided up as follows:

Part Eight: Jurisdiction of the State

I. *Bases of jurisdiction*

    A. Territorial principle

    B. Personal principle

    C. Protective principle

    D. Universality principle

    E. Other bases

II. *Types of jurisdiction*

    A. Jurisdiction to prescribe

---

[4] See the Agreement concerning a Scottish Trial in the Netherlands, 18 September 1998, UKTS No 43 (1999); 117 ILR 664, 666, 673. See also Aust, 2000.

[5] See, eg, the texts by Oppenheim, 1992; Brownlie, 2008; O'Connell, 1970.

[6] See, eg, the texts by Twiss, 1884 and Hall, 1895.

[7] See, eg, Verhoeven, 2000.

[8] Council of Europe Res (68) 17 of 28 June 1968. This scheme is used to arrange the survey of United Kingdom Materials on International Law, in each year's *British Yearbook of International Law (BYIL)*.

    B. Jurisdiction to adjudicate

    C. Jurisdiction to enforce

  III. *Extra-territorial exercise of jurisdiction*

    A. General

    B. Consular jurisdiction

    C. Jurisdiction over military personnel abroad

    D. Others (artificial islands, *terrae nullius,* etc)

  IV. *Limitations upon jurisdiction (servitudes, leases, etc)*

   V. *Concurrent jurisdiction*

While European doctrine thus seems to be moving towards the traditional 'English' approach, there are signs of a different development in the United States. The great *Digests* of US practice, edited by Marjorie Whiteman, Marian Nash and others, had until 1988 separate chapters on jurisdiction, in accordance with the traditional approach. The more recent volumes, published (after a gap in publication) from 2001 onwards, do not. These volumes distribute material on jurisdiction under headings such as 'taxation', and 'international criminal court'. The shift may appear insignificant; and it may prove to be so. It may, however, signal a change in attitude to the very nature of jurisdiction. Whereas in the past jurisdiction was seen, both in the 'English' and the continental views, as a matter of the reach of the authority of a State, this development in US doctrine appears to treat jurisdiction as an aspect of the substantive topic that is regulated. If this trend persists the principles of jurisdiction may fragment, so that States may assert a more extensive jurisdiction over, say, tax matters and 'terrorist' offences than they do over unlawful arms sales and other crimes.

    Should that happen, and should the assertions of jurisdiction be recognized in international law, the near-inevitable result is that jurisdictional claims will steadily expand, and that the States most interested in regulating particular areas of conduct will increasingly apply their laws to activities outside their own borders and within the borders of other States—much in the manner of the Rushdie *fatwah.* For purposes of this chapter, however, the approach of the Council of Europe scheme will be adopted.

1. Types of jurisdiction

The first section of the Council of Europe Model Plan, 'Bases of jurisdiction', is concerned with the ambit of a State's laws: that is, with its jurisdiction to prescribe rules, or its 'legislative' or 'prescriptive' jurisdiction, as it is sometimes called. The second section, 'Types of jurisdiction', somewhat illogically steps up to a higher level of abstraction and distinguishes between, on the one hand, the jurisdiction to prescribe rules and, on the other hand, the jurisdiction to enforce them, or 'enforcement jurisdiction' as it is commonly known. Thus, the United Kingdom may enact a law forbidding, say, murder and make that law applicable to all British citizens wherever in the world they might be. That would fall within the United Kingdom's prescriptive jurisdiction, in accordance with what is called the 'nationality' or 'personal' principle (Section I B in the Council of Europe scheme). But if a British citizen were to commit murder in, say, Argentina, the United Kingdom authorities would have no right to enter Argentina and arrest the murderer; and if they did so they would violate Argentinean sovereignty.[9] The United Kingdom's enforcement jurisdiction, like that of every other State, is in principle limited to its own territory. That is why States need to seek the extradition of persons accused of committing crimes within their jurisdiction, in circumstances where the accused is living in another State.

There is another 'Type of jurisdiction' identified in the Council of Europe scheme, and in similar frameworks adopted elsewhere:[10] that is the 'jurisdiction to adjudicate', or 'adjudicative jurisdiction' or 'curial jurisdiction'. This refers to the right of courts to receive, try, and determine cases referred to them. It is doubtful whether it is necessary to separate out this type of jurisdiction. Insofar as parties choose to submit to the jurisdiction of a national court, there can be no cause for complaint unless one or more of the parties is subject to an order made under the law of another State, obliging them not to submit to the foreign court. If such an antisuit order is made, there is a clash of prescriptive jurisdictions, as there is if two or more courts hear the same case and issue conflicting orders.[11] But all of this can be analysed in terms of prescriptive and enforcement jurisdiction. It seems unnecessary to introduce a separate category of 'jurisdiction to adjudicate', and that category is not employed in this chapter.

2. Other jurisdictional issues

The third category in the Council of Europe scheme, 'Extra-territorial exercise of jurisdiction', is concerned with the exceptional circumstances in which a State is entitled to exercise its enforcement jurisdiction (and with it, by necessary implication its legislative jurisdiction) in the territory of another State. A common example in NATO States is the network of arrangements under which troops of one NATO State are stationed in another, but subject to the control of their home State authorities, so that, for instance, United States military police will have the right to arrest and imprison members of US forces on military bases in the United Kingdom.

The fourth and fifth of the Council of Europe 'Types' are of a rather different kind. The 'Limitations upon jurisdiction' instanced by servitudes and leases are limitations that arise when a particular piece of territory is 'leased' to another State (as part of Hong Kong was leased by China to the United Kingdom from 1898 to 1997, as the Panama Canal Zone was leased by Panama to the United States from 1903 to 1977, and as Guantanamo Bay has since 1903 been, and still is, leased by Cuba to the United States), and under the terms of the lease the territorial sovereign permits the lessee to exercise exclusive jurisdiction over the area. This is not so much a 'type' of jurisdiction as a particular consequence of the temporary transfer or alienation of rights of sovereignty over areas of State territory, and it will not be further discussed here.[12] The final category, 'Concurrent jurisdiction', concerns the issues that arise when two or more States are entitled to exercise legislative (or, rarely, enforcement) jurisdiction in relation to the same factual circumstances.

---

[9] For an example of such a violation see *Attorney-General of the Government of Israel* v *Adolf Eichmann* (1961), 36 ILR 5.

[10] See, eg, the American Law Institute's *Restatement of the Law: the Foreign Relations Law of the United States*, 3rd edn, 1987; Akehurst, 1972–73, pp 145–217.

[11] See 'The Principles for Determining When the Use of the Doctrine of *forum non conveniens* and Antisuit Injunctions is Appropriate', Institut de Droit International, *Annuaire*, vol 70–I (2002–2003), p 14.

[12] See further Ch 8, above.

II. PRESCRIPTIVE JURISDICTION

To whom may a State extend its laws? Whom may the State order to do this, or not to do that? Or, to ask a question of a slightly different kind, who may be deemed by a State to be, say, a citizen, or 'married', or 'an infant'; or how far may a State rule that a particular ceremony counts as a valid wedding, or divorce; what, in other words, are the limits of the right of a State to impose legal characterizations upon persons or events? These are all questions about the reach, the ambit or scope, of a State's laws; that is, about the limits of its prescriptive or legislative jurisdiction.

Before turning to the principles that explain the bases upon which States are entitled to exercise prescriptive jurisdiction, it is necessary to refer to a tiresome and oddly persistent fallacy that arose from an early case in the Permanent Court of International Justice (PCIJ). The case concerned a collision on the high seas (ie, that part of the sea that is beyond the territorial jurisdiction of every State), between the French steamer, the *Lotus*, and the Turkish steamer, the *Boz-Kourt*, which resulted in eight deaths. When the *Lotus* entered Constantinople, the Turkish authorities prosecuted M Demons, the officer of the watch on the *Lotus*. Proceedings were also instituted against the captain of the Turkish ship. France objected to the proceedings against M Demons on the ground that no State is entitled to extend its law to foreign ships on the high seas, and that Turkey, accordingly, was not entitled to prosecute M Demons. The PCIJ held that Turkey was entitled to prosecute. The passage in question is so often quoted, and so much misunderstood, that it is worthwhile reproducing it here. The Court said:[13]

the first and foremost restriction imposed by international law upon a State is that—failing the existence of a permissive rule to the contrary—it may not exercise its power in any form in the territory of another State. In this sense jurisdiction is certainly territorial; it cannot be exercised by a State outside its territory except by virtue of a permissive rule derived from international custom or from a convention.

That proposition is not controversial. It asserts that a State's *enforcement* jurisdiction is in principle confined to the State's territory (a point considered further below). In the *Lotus* case, this was not an issue. Turkish authorities had not gone out on to the high seas to arrest M Demons: they had waited until the *Lotus* entered a Turkish port and so came within Turkish territory and thus within Turkish enforcement jurisdiction. The question was whether having arrested M Demons in Turkey he, as a French citizen, could then be prosecuted by the Turkish authorities for his acts outside Turkish territory, on the high seas. The Court continued, addressing itself to this question, as follows:[14]

It does not, however, follow that international law prohibits a State from exercising jurisdiction in its own territory, in respect of any case which relates to acts which have taken place abroad, and in which it cannot rely on some permissive rule of international law. Such a view would only be tenable if international law contained a general prohibition to States to extend the application of their laws and the jurisdiction of their courts to persons, property and acts outside their territory, and if, as an exception to this general prohibition, it allowed States to do so in certain specific cases. But this is certainly not the case under international law as it

---

[13] *'Lotus', Judgment No 9, 1927, PCIJ, Ser A, No 10*, pp 18–19.   [14] Ibid, p 19.

stands at present. Far from laying down a general prohibition to the effect that States may not extend the application of their laws and the jurisdiction of their courts to persons, property and acts outside their territory, it leaves them in this respect a wide measure of discretion which is only limited in certain cases by prohibitive rules...

That passage has been read as indicating that a State may extend the reach of its prescriptive jurisdiction as it chooses, except in circumstances where it can be shown that some rule of international law specifically prohibits it from doing so. A moment's thought will indicate that it is extremely improbable that this is what the Court meant to say. Suppose, for example, that Zimbabwe were to enact a law that made it an offence for anyone, of whatever nationality and wherever in the world they might be, to make a complaint to a UN body alleging that any State had violated its international human rights obligations; and suppose that a British citizen, on holiday in Zimbabwe, was arrested and charged with breaking that law by writing to the UN Human Rights Committee from his home in Birmingham with a complaint that, say, Iraq had violated its obligations.[15] Could it really be supposed that the onus would be upon the United Kingdom to prove that some prohibitive rule of international law forbade such exercises of legislative jurisdiction by Zimbabwe?

There are many reasons for thinking that international law does not impose the burden of proof upon those objecting to egregious assertions of jurisdiction over foreigners outside the territory of the legislating State. Two are of particular relevance here. First, in more than a century of objections to exercises of extraterritorial jurisdiction, from the *Cutting* case[16] onwards, there seems to be not a single instance of an objecting State either seeking to prove that there existed a prohibitive rule forbidding the contested exercise of extraterritorial jurisdiction, or indicating that it might consider itself to be under any legal obligation to do so. When States object to exercises of jurisdiction, they simply assert that the other State has 'no right' to exercise jurisdiction in the way that it claims. State practice is consistently based upon the premiss that it is for the State asserting some novel extraterritorial jurisdiction to prove that it is entitled to do so. Secondly, the argument in favour of the alleged presumption of freedom is fallacious. In the *Lotus* case the Court argued that:

International law governs relations between independent States. The rules of law binding upon States therefore emanate from their own free will as expressed in conventions or by usages generally accepted as expressing principles of law and established in order to regulate the relations between these co-existing independent communities or with a view to the achievement of common aims. Restrictions upon the independence of States cannot therefore be presumed.[17]

Even if the characterization of international law as fundamentally consensual is accepted, it does not follow that a sovereign State is free to do what it wishes. The sovereign equality of States is equally a fundamental principle of international law. Claims by one State to prescribe rules for persons in another State encroach upon the right of the State where those persons are based to exercise jurisdiction itself over those persons within its territory.

---

[15] An extreme example: Zimbabwe has not, as far as I know, enacted any such law. The United States, however, has enacted a law in somewhat similar terms: see below, n 48.

[16] *Foreign Relations of the United States*, 1887, p 751; idem, 1888, II, pp 1114, 1180.

[17] 'Lotus', *Judgment No 9, 1927, PCIJ, Ser A, No 10*, p 18.

There are two States—two 'co-existing independent communities'—involved, and there plainly can be no presumption that the one asserting extraterritorial jurisdiction is entitled to prevail in the event of a conflict, and to impose its laws on persons within the territory of another State.

The best view is that it is necessary for there to be some clear connecting factor, of a kind whose use is approved by international law, between the legislating State and the conduct that it seeks to regulate. This notion of the need for a linking point, which has been adopted by some prominent jurists,[18] accords closely with the actual practice of States. If there exists such a linking point, one may presume that the State is entitled to legislate; if there does not, the State must show why it is entitled to legislate for anyone other than persons in its territory and for its nationals abroad (who are covered by the territorial and the national principles respectively).

There are two of these linking points, or 'Bases of Jurisdiction', or 'principles of jurisdiction' (the terms mean the same thing) that are firmly established in international law: territoriality, and nationality.

A. THE TERRITORIAL PRINCIPLE

The territorial principle is a corollary of the sovereignty of a State over its territory. That sovereignty entails the right of the State to prescribe the laws that set the boundaries of the public order of the State. It is taken for granted that foreign visitors to a State are bound by the State's criminal law in the same way as everyone else in the State. It may be less obvious, but it is no less true, that States may impose the entirety of their laws—economic, social, cultural, or whatever—upon everyone within their territories. In practice, States generally exercise this power with moderation. While the basic principle is that everyone within the territory is equally obliged to obey the law, those laws may be drafted so as to exempt people who are merely visiting the State from certain obligations, such as obligations to pay income tax or to perform compulsory military service (and equally, so as to exclude them from certain rights, such as the right to vote, or to social security payments). Exactly how and where these lines are drawn is a matter for each State to decide, subject to its treaty commitments and its duty to respect basic human rights.

The 'territory' of the State includes not only its land territory but also both its territorial sea, which extends 12 miles from its coast, and the airspace above its land and sea territory. States may thus legislate for ships off their coasts, and for aircraft in their skies. It was the latter right that entitled the United Kingdom to prosecute the Libyan nationals accused of blowing up a US aircraft in the skies above Lockerbie, Scotland, in 1988. Again, in practice States usually leave the prescription of rules applicable on board ships or aircraft to the State of registry of the craft,[19] asserting jurisdiction only in exceptional cases. The routine application of the customs and excise laws of the territorial State is a common exception to this pattern, which is one reason why duty-free sales cease shortly before the craft arrives at its destination.

States enjoy 'plenary' jurisdiction over their territory. That is to say, subject to their duties under human rights laws and similar constraints, they may legislate as they please, on any matter whatsoever. At sea, States enjoy an additional but functionally limited jurisdiction.

---

[18] See the discussion in *Attorney-General of the Government of Israel* v *Adolf Eichmann* (1961), 36 ILR 5.
[19] See, for example, the handling of the problem of drunks on aircraft: 74 *BYIL* 681 (2003).

Beyond the 12-mile territorial sea they may claim a 12-mile contiguous zone, in which they can exercise jurisdiction in relation to customs, fiscal, sanitary, and immigration matters, and also in order to safeguard submarine archaeological sites. Subject to certain limitations, they may also assert jurisdiction over the exploration for and exploitation of living and non-living resources (such as fish and oil) and energy, over the establishment of artificial islands and structures, and over pollution and scientific research, in an Exclusive Economic Zone (EEZ) that extends 200 miles from the coast. And they may assert full civil and criminal jurisdiction over installations, such as oil rigs, set up on their continental shelves or in their EEZs in order to exploit seabed resources. These zones that lie beyond the territorial sea are not part of the territory of the State; but the coastal State is permitted to exercise limited jurisdiction in them, in contrast to the position on the high seas (and in outer space) where, in principle, craft and those on board them are subject to the jurisdiction only of the State of registry (the 'flag' State).[20]

Most acts, most bank robberies, weddings, and daily struggles to earn a living, take place squarely within the territory of a single State. The territorial principle is entirely adequate to sustain jurisdiction over such acts. Indeed, in the domestic law of many States there is a presumption that the State's laws, in particular its statutes, apply throughout the State's territory but not outside that territory, unless there is clear indication that the law is intended to apply outside the territory. Some acts, however, straddle more than one jurisdiction. The Lockerbie bomb is said to have been loaded aboard the aircraft in Malta, before it entered the United Kingdom; the September 11th attacks are said to have been planned and prepared by people in a number of different countries. Which State has jurisdiction? One solution would be to allow each State to exercise jurisdiction over the particular fragment of the greater scheme that was located within its territory: one State might prosecute the offence of loading a bomb on board an aircraft, another the offence of causing an explosion on board an aircraft, another, murder, and so on. Whatever theoretical tidiness might be preserved by such an approach, it has no practical merits to commend it. It is more efficient if the investigation and prosecution of an offence is concentrated largely in the hands of a single State. That is what States in fact do. Territorial jurisdiction has spawned two variants to cope with such situations. They are commonly known as subjective territorial jurisdiction and objective territorial jurisdiction.

1. Subjective territorial jurisdiction

'Subjective territorial jurisdiction' is the name given to the exercise of prescriptive jurisdiction by a State in circumstances where it applies its law to an incident which is initiated within its territory but completed outside its territory. The prosecution for murder of bombers by the State in which they put the bomb on board an aircraft, even though the bomb exploded in the airspace of another State, is an example.

2. Objective territorial jurisdiction

'Objective territorial jurisdiction' is the name given to the exercise of prescriptive jurisdiction by a State in circumstances where it applies its law to an incident that is completed

---

[20] See the UN Convention on the Law of the Sea, 1982, Articles 2, 33, 56, 60, 92, 303. For the case of ships having no nationality, see for instance *United States* v *Bravo*, 480 F.3d 88 (2007). Developments have been anticipated in relation to jurisdiction over activities in outer space with the emergence of private travel in that realm. See Hobe, 2007; Blount, 2007.

within its territory, even though it was initiated outside its territory. The prosecution for murder of bombers by the State in whose airspace a bomb on board an aircraft exploded, even though the bomb had been loaded onto the aircraft in another State, is an example. The *Lotus* case is another example. Ships (and aircraft) are treated for jurisdictional purposes much as if they are pieces of floating territory of the State of registration, although they are, in law, quite clearly not parts of the State's territory. The act of the *Lotus* in colliding with the Turkish ship was, therefore, an act completed within Turkish territorial jurisdiction—literally, within the Turkish ship—and accordingly liable to be prosecuted by the Turkish authorities.

Both subjective and objective territorial jurisdiction are routinely asserted by States, in order to secure the application of their laws to all elements of offences that they wish to prosecute. In English law, examples include *DPP* v *Doot*,[21] *DPP* v *Stonehouse*,[22] and *Liangsiriprasert* v *Government of the United States of America*.[23]

3. The 'effects' doctrine

Exercises of subjective territorial jurisdiction have not proved problematic; but the same cannot be said for exercises of objective territorial jurisdiction. There is little difficulty with cases where distinct physical elements of the overall crime take place within the jurisdiction of different States. But some States, notably the United States of America, have sought to extend the concept much further. The clearest example of this is the so-called 'effects' doctrine, developed first in the context of US antitrust law. In the *Alcoa* case, *US* v *Aluminium Co of America*,[24] the United States asserted jurisdiction over the conduct of a non-US company that was a member of a cartel whose activities were intended to affect imports to or exports from the United States, and actually did so. The significance of the decision was that it did not depend upon the commission of physical acts within US territory: the intentional production of economic 'effects' within the United States was sufficient.

This idea reached what is perhaps its fullest expression in the *Uranium Antitrust* litigation, which surfaced in the English courts in *Rio Tinto Zinc Corp* v *Westinghouse Electric Corp*.[25] There, uranium producers in a number of States, including the United Kingdom, formed, with the knowledge or encouragement of their national governments, a cartel, primarily in order to maintain the world market price of uranium. This was in response to a protectionist US law that had effectively shut them out of the United States market, which amounted to more than two-thirds of the world market. Meanwhile, Westinghouse, a US company, had contracted to sell uranium to a public utility in the United States, at a price set some years earlier, but needed to buy the uranium on the world market. The cartel's success in maintaining the market price of uranium was such that Westinghouse could not afford to fulfil the contract. Westinghouse was sued for $2bn; and it in turn sued some members of the cartel for $6bn, under a provision of US antitrust law that allows those injured by cartels to recover treble damages. Here, US law was to be applied to non-US

---

[21] *DPP* v *Doot* [1973] AC 807; [1973] 1 All ER 940 (HL).

[22] *DPP* v *Stonehouse* [1978] AC 55; [1977] 2 All ER 909 (HL).

[23] *Liangsiriprasert* v *Government of the United States of America* [1991] 1 AC 225; [1990] 2 All ER 866 (PC).

[24] *United States* v *Aluminium Co of America*, 148 F.2d 416 (1945).

[25] *Rio Tinto Zinc Corp* v *Westinghouse Electric Corp* [1978] 1 All ER 434 (HL); and see Lowe, 1983.

companies, in respect of their acts outside the United States, at a time when they were forbidden by US law to trade in the United States. The only jurisdictional link was the 'effect' of the cartel upon the United States: there was no intraterritorial conduct in the United States at all. It is the reliance upon economic repercussions within the territory, rather than upon some element of intraterritorial conduct, that distinguishes the 'effects' doctrine in its pure form from objective territorial jurisdiction, which does require some intraterritorial conduct. The assertion of extraterritorial jurisdiction by the United States in this case was met with strong protests from many other States.

It is sometimes said that other States also assert jurisdiction on the basis of the 'effects' doctrine. There is some truth in this. States such as France and Germany, and the EC in cases such as *Woodpulp*,[26] have adopted laws or decisions that appear to involve such an assertion; but on a closer inspection it is clear that such laws are usually applied only in circumstances where there is some element of intraterritorial conduct.

B. THE NATIONAL PRINCIPLE

States have an undisputed right to extend the application of their laws to their citizens (that is, those who have the nationality of the State), wherever they may be. This type of jurisdiction has a longer history than jurisdiction based upon the territorial principle. Rulers asserted jurisdiction over those who owed allegiance to them even before the rulers' control over their land territory was consolidated to the point where they could be said to assert territorial jurisdiction. Nonetheless, the advent of the European territorial State as the paradigmatic unit of the international legal order has long since given territorial jurisdiction pre-eminence. Jurisdiction based on nationality is used relatively infrequently.

States are in principle left free to decide who are their nationals, and to lay down the conditions for the grant of nationality in their own laws. It is usual to accord nationality to anyone born in the territory; except, perhaps, in cases where the mother's presence is merely transient—for example, as a passenger on a ship or aircraft transiting the State's territory. This basis of nationality is sometimes known as the *jus soli*. It is common also to accord nationality to children one or both of whose parents are themselves nationals of the State. This is sometimes known as the *jus sanguinis*. States also commonly provide for the conferral of nationality by naturalization, the process in which those who fill whatever residential and other requirements the State may lay down apply to become nationals of the State. Naturalization usually involves the renunciation of any other nationalities the person might have; but it is not uncommon for people to have two nationalities, one derived from the nationality of their parents, the other from the place where they were born. Such people are known as 'dual nationals'. Some people may have three, or even more, nationalities.

The nationality of companies is also a matter for each State to determine under its own laws; but here the practice is more complex. As the International Court noted in the *Barcelona Traction* case,[27] there is a divergence in State practice. Broadly speaking, there is a tendency for common law States to accord nationality to companies on the basis of their incorporation in the territory of the State, regardless of where the actual business

---

[26] *Ahlström Osakeyhtiö v Commission*, Cases 89/85 [1988] ECR 5193.

[27] *Barcelona Traction, Light and Power Company, Limited, Second Phase, Judgment, ICJ Reports 1970*, p 3.

or management of the company is carried out. In contrast, at least some civil law States confer their nationality not on the basis of the place of incorporation but rather on the basis of the place where the company has the seat of its management. As companies may be formally incorporated in one State for tax reasons, but maintain their actual business or management elsewhere, this is a significant point. In contrast to individuals it seems that companies cannot change their nationality, for example by naturalization. They can only achieve a comparable result, by dissolving the company and transferring all of its assets and responsibilities to a new company in another State. This is, however, more a matter of corporate succession than of a change of nationality.

The freedom of States to fix the conditions for the grant of nationality extends also to ships and aircraft. The same is true of comparable structures, such as offshore oil rigs (which appear to be regarded as having the nationality of the State of registry while they are in transit, even though they fall under the jurisdiction of the coastal State while they are actually operating on the continental shelf). Typical conditions might include a require-ment that the vessel operates from a home port in the State, or has a certain proportion of the owners, or perhaps of the crew, having the nationality of the State. In this respect, many States tend to be more restrictive in granting nationality to ships and aircraft than they are in granting nationality to companies.

This freedom to determine nationality is not absolute. The existence of limitations upon the international effectiveness of grants of nationality was discussed by the International Court in the *Nottebohm* case,[28] which is sometimes supposed to be authority for the proposition that a genuine and close link between the individual and the national State is necessary if nationality is to be effective: ie, if other States are to be obliged to accept it as an adequate basis for the State to treat the individual as its national. The Court did not say that. It did hold that nationality should, in principle, be the juridical expression of a close factual link between the individual and the national State. But the Court was not concerned with the effectiveness of nationality in general, but only with the much narrower issue of its effectiveness as the basis for diplomatic protection. The Court was not even concerned with the general question of the right of a national State to exercise diplomatic protection. The Court limited itself to the particular question whether a State with which a naturalized citizen has no real links can exercise diplomatic protection on behalf of the citizen against another State with which the citizen, while not a national of that State (Nottebohm was not a dual national), does have close and real links. The deci-sion was, accordingly, of no relevance whatever to the question of the efficacy of nation-ality for jurisdictional purposes. Indeed, as Nottebohm had himself chosen to become a naturalized citizen of a State, Liechtenstein, with which he had no real links, it is difficult to see any ground on which Liechtenstein could be denied the right to impose its laws upon Nottebohm in accordance with the nationality principle.

One may also note that on the one occasion, post-*Nottebohm*, when the International Court was invited to rule that grants of nationality not underpinned by some close factual connection with the putative national State were ineffective, it did not do so, but instead reaffirmed that it is for each State to fix the conditions for the grant of its nationality.[29] There

---

[28] *Nottebohm, Second Phase, Judgment, ICJ Reports 1955*, p 4.

[29] See the *Constitution of the Maritime Safety Committee of the Inter-Governmental Maritime Consultative Organization, Advisory Opinion, ICJ Reports 1969*, p 150.

are, no doubt, limits to this freedom. The mass imposition of nationality upon unwilling people, or nationality obtained by fraud or corruption, or a nationality acquired for vessels in order to circumvent legal regulations based upon the nationality of ships, for example, might in certain circumstances be held not to be effective. For practical purposes, however, States remain free to decide who are their nationals. (It should also be noted that it is arguable that the exercise of legislative jurisdiction based upon nationality is not a matter for international law at all. The way that a State treats its nationals is—questions of human rights apart—in general not a matter for international law. If a State were to legislate for persons who were indisputably its nationals, who could complain?)

In practice, States now rarely exercise legislative jurisdiction over their nationals.[30] They tend to do so in order to prohibit serious offences which not only disturb the peace of the place where they are committed, but also signal a characteristic of the offender in which the national State has an interest. For example, a State would plainly have an interest in forbidding its nationals to engage in bigamous marriages abroad, and forbidding them to commit murder abroad. Another motive for asserting jurisdiction over nationals is beginning to appear in State practice, too. The emergence of bodies such as the International Criminal Court (Cassese, Gaeta, and Jones, 2002), and of obligations under international treaties to surrender to another State persons accused of various specified crimes, if they are not tried by the State in which they are found, is increasing the chances of a national of a State being tried by a foreign court. Some States are fearful of this; and some have principled objections to the surrender of their nationals to foreign tribunals. There are signs that States are taking steps to ensure that they can themselves prosecute their nationals for offences for which the surrender of the national might otherwise be sought. Whether this is a sign of the seriousness with which States intend to prosecute nationals accused of such offences, or rather of the determination of States to keep their nationals as far as possible out of the hands of foreign courts, is not entirely clear.

There is an increasing tendency for States to extend the extraterritorial application of their laws not only to nationals but to residents, in order to make the repression of serious crimes more effective. The UK's Crime (International Co-operation) Act 2003 introduced such provisions into ss 63B and 63C of the Terrorism Act 2000.[31] States may also apply their own laws (including human rights law) to extraterritorial acts of their own governmental authorities, or persons contracted by or under the authority of their own governmental authorities.[32]

C. THE PROTECTIVE PRINCIPLE

It has long been recognized that when essential interests of the State are at stake States need to, and will, act in order to preserve themselves. Accordingly, when vital issues are

---

[30] But see, for instance, *United States v Clark*, 435 F.3d 1100 (2006). For an argument that nationality jurisdiction should be used more frequently see Arnell, 2001.

[31] See also Ratner, 2003. Cf Arnell, 2001 at p 984. See also, for instance, *XYZ v The Commonwealth* [2006] HCA 25 (High Court of Australia).

[32] See for instance *R (Al-Skeini and others) v Secretary of State for Defence* [2007] UKHL 26; [2008] 1 AC 153; cf *R (Al-Jedda) v Secretary of State for Defence* [2007] UKHL 58; [2008] 1 AC 332; *R v Hape* 2007 SCC 26, [2008] 1 LRC 551; *Munaf v Geren* 553 US (2008); *United States v Passaro*, 577 F.3d 207 (2009). See also Ryngaert, 2008.

threatened, even if by non-nationals acting outside the territory of the State, the State's interests are engaged and it may exercise its legislative jurisdiction over them. The counterfeiting of a State's currency is a typical example, as is an extraterritorial conspiracy to evade the State's immigration laws.

The category of vital interests is not closed. The United States has asserted jurisdiction over foreigners on the high seas on the basis of the protective principle, in cases such as *US v Gonzalez*,[33] and in statutes such as the 1986 Maritime Drug Law Enforcement Act (see Murphy, 2003).[34] It argues that the illegal trade in narcotics constitutes so severe a threat to United States' society that the protective principle allows this extension of its jurisdiction. Other States have acquiesced in this United States' move; but they have tended not to follow it but rather to extend their jurisdiction by means of treaty arrangements concerning the suppression of unlawful drug trafficking.

The rationale of the protective principle is clearly linked to the protection of vital State interests. Accordingly, while the category is not closed, the potential for its expansion is limited. Whereas States could, in principle, apply any law that they might choose to their nationals, by no means every law could be given extraterritorial scope under the protective principle. That is why offences against, for example, a State's competition laws are not prosecuted on the basis of this principle but are instead explained as applications of the territorial principle or the 'effects' doctrine. That said, the overblown rhetoric with which governments from time to time describe their attempts to combat various 'threats' to the State, or to civilized values or to the world order or whatever, must take their toll. The pressure to expand the use of this principle, and the danger of unshackling it from the protection of truly *vital* interests and of permitting its use for the convenient advancement of important interests, is clear.

D. THE UNIVERSAL PRINCIPLE

Some crimes are regarded as so heinous that every State has a legitimate interest in their repression. That is the traditional explanation of universal jurisdiction.[35] But given that the first, and one of the most firmly established, of the instances of crimes covered by the universal principle is piracy, one may wonder if the traditional explanation is entirely satisfactory.

It is probably more accurate to say that there are two strands running together to make up the universal principle. One is the strand that is indeed made up of heinous crimes, such as genocide, crimes against humanity, and serious war crimes,[36] all of which are subject to universal jurisdiction.[37] The second is crimes that are serious, and which might otherwise go unpunished. Piracy—which means simply an unauthorized act of violence

---

[33] *US v Gonzalez* 776 F.2d 931 (1985).

[34] See also for instance *US v Reumayr*, 530 F.Supp.2d 1210 (2008), at 1221–1222 and the cases there cited; *US v Yousef*, 327 F.3d 56 (2003) at 110–111.

[35] See, eg, *US v Yunis*, 681 F.Supp 896 (1988); *Arrest Warrant of 11 April 2000 (Democratic Republic of the Congo v Belgium), ICJ Reports 2002*, p 3; (2002) 41 ILM 563.

[36] The catalogue of crimes subject to universal jurisdiction is not yet definitively enumerated: for the view that it does not include terrorism, see *US v Yousef*, 327 F.3d 56 (2003) at 108.

[37] The extent to which crimes are subject to universal civil jurisdiction, in addition to universal criminal jurisdiction, may be an emerging issue: see, for instance, Donovan and Roberts, 2006.

or depredation committed by a private vessel on the high seas against another vessel, for private ends—may involve relatively minor uses of force; and not every act of piracy can properly be described as heinous. Yet for centuries, piracy was covered by universal jurisdiction, but murder, armed robbery, rape, and arson on land, which could surely be equally heinous, were (and are) not. The justification for universal jurisdiction over pirates is not so much that piracy is inherently heinous, and on a par with genocide and war crimes, as the fact that because pirates operate on the high seas it is very easy for them to evade the jurisdiction of any State that might have jurisdiction over them on some other basis (for example, the flag State of their ship, or their national State), unless any State that happens to have them within its jurisdiction is entitled to try them.[38]

This point is not trivial. One might argue that the principle could be extended to justify assertions of jurisdiction over others who commit serious crimes in places beyond the territorial jurisdiction of the State. Crimes committed in Antarctica would be one example (which the United States has in fact addressed by making certain acts, such as murder, committed by or against US nationals in Antarctica, subject to US jurisdiction).

Universal jurisdiction has undergone something of a renaissance in recent years.[39] Belgium is one of a number of States that have enacted laws providing for universal jurisdiction over particularly serious offences such as war crimes (see Reydams, 2003a). In the *Arrest Warrant* case[40] the Democratic Republic of the Congo complained that Belgium had issued a warrant for the arrest of the DRC's acting Minister of Foreign Affairs, Mr Yerodia, charging him with provoking massacres of Tutsi civilians, contrary to the Belgian War Crimes Act. There were no links between Belgium and the alleged offence or offender. The case was decided on grounds of the Foreign Minister's immunity, but some of the Separate and Dissenting Opinions discuss the validity of Belgium's claim to universal jurisdiction. The Opinions differ, but are mostly supportive of Belgium's claim. However, in 2003 the Belgian legislation was amended so that, as is presently the case in certain other countries, prosecutions of serious violations of international humanitarian law committed extraterritorially require a link connecting the violations with Belgium, as the State exercising jurisdiction.[41]

E. TREATY-BASED EXTENSIONS OF JURISDICTION

If the territorial principle, in all its variants, is overwhelmingly the most important principle in the day-to-day application of a State's laws, much the most important basis for the assertion of extraterritorial jurisdiction is now the large, and constantly growing, network

---

[38] See again the *Yunis* case, idem. See further Goodwin, 2006. For a recent practical example of jurisdictional issues relating to piracy, see for instance Treves, 2009. The same argument might apply to any ship on the high seas that is without any nationality: compare *United States* v *Bravo* 480 F.3d 88 (2007).

[39] See *The Princeton Principles on Universal Jurisdiction* (2001), and the *Cairo-Arusha Principles on Universal Jurisdiction in Respect of Gross Human Rights Offences* (2002).

[40] *Arrest Warrant of 11 April 2000 (Democratic Republic of the Congo v Belgium), ICJ Reports 2002*, p 3.

[41] See Reydams, 2003b. See also *Jiménez Sánchez and ors* v *Gibson and ors*, Appeal Judgment, No 1240/2006; ILDC 993 (ES 2006) (Spain, Supreme Court, Criminal Chamber) (but compare the earlier decision of the Spanish Constitutional Tribunal in the *Guatemala Genocide* case (2006) 100 *AJIL* 207). Such a link might be the nationality or residence of the victim or the presence of the accused person in the territory of the State exercising jurisdiction.

of treaties in which States cooperate to secure the effective and efficient subjection to the law of offences of common concern.

Most of these treaties follow the same broad pattern. A particular offence or range of offences is defined. For example, Article 1 of the 1971 Montreal Convention for the Suppression of Unlawful Acts against the Safety of Civil Aviation (which was at the centre of the *Lockerbie* case in the International Court of Justice),[42] states that a person commits an offence if he unlawfully and intentionally performs an act of violence against a person on board an aircraft in flight if that act is likely to endanger the safety of that aircraft, or if he commits certain other specified acts. The Convention then goes on to require all States Parties to make such acts punishable by severe penalties and to assert their jurisdiction over such offences if they are committed in certain specific circumstances, including offences committed in the territory of the State or on board an aircraft registered in the State, and offences committed in cases where the aircraft lands in the State's territory with the alleged offender still on board. Most significant of all is the obligation to provide for jurisdiction over offences in every case where the alleged offender is *found* within the State's territory, regardless of the offender's nationality or of the place where the offence was committed. This is a crucial element in what is often known as the *aut dedere, aut iudicare* provision, which stipulates that in every case where an alleged offender is found within the State's territory the State must either extradite him to face trial in another State that seeks him for the purposes of prosecution (and for this purpose, the Convention offences are deemed by the Convention to be included in the lists of extraditable crimes that appear in any extradition treaties that may be in force between the two States), or if it does not extradite him, it must submit the case to its competent authorities for the purpose of prosecution.

Thus, the aim is to ensure that alleged offenders do not escape prosecution; and the Convention does this in part by creating what is in essence a form of universal jurisdiction as between the parties (O'Keefe, 2004). (It is, strictly speaking, only applicable between the parties. In theory, if an alleged offender was prosecuted for an offence outside the territory of, and not on an aircraft registered in, the prosecuting State, and the national State of the alleged offender was not a party to the Convention, it could object to the assertion of jurisdiction over its citizen. There do not appear to have been any such protests, however.)

There are many conventions that follow a similar pattern, most of them designed to counter various forms of terrorist activity or internationally organized crime. Some, such as the 1979 International Convention Against the Taking of Hostages, have introduced a different, wider range of circumstances in which States parties must establish their jurisdiction over offences defined in the convention. The 1979 Hostages Convention stipulates that States Parties must establish their jurisdiction over convention offences committed: in the State's territory, or on board a ship or aircraft registered in the State; or by any of its nationals (and, if the State considers it 'appropriate' also by any stateless persons who have their habitual residence in its territory); or 'in order to compel that State to do or abstain from doing any act'; or with respect to a hostage who is a national of that State, 'if that State considers it appropriate'. The last two circumstances are particularly interesting.

---

[42] See *Questions of Interpretation and Application of the 1971 Montreal Convention arising from the Aerial Incident at Lockerbie, Provisional Measures, Orders of 14 April 1993, ICJ Reports 1992*, pp 3, 114; 94 ILR 478; *Preliminary Objections, Judgment, ICJ Reports 1998*, pp 9, 115; 117 ILR 1.

In the last circumstance, jurisdiction is based on the nationality of the victim, a ground often known as the 'passive personality' principle, which will be discussed below. It would allow, for example, the United States to prosecute someone who took a US citizen hostage in a foreign State. The other extension of jurisdiction, to States which are the target of the hostage-taker's pressure, would allow, for example, Israel to prosecute someone who took a non-Israeli Jew hostage in order to bring pressure upon Israel—a scenario similar to the hijacking of the *Achille Lauro* in 1985,[43] in which a Jewish US citizen was killed as part of a campaign to pressurize Israel. Novel and striking as such bases of jurisdiction might be, in the context of the treaty their effect is less dramatic. The general *aut dedere, aut judicare* principle requires the State to prosecute *every* alleged offender found within its territory, if it does not extradite him. The law of States Parties must therefore provide for jurisdiction over offenders whether or not the offence was committed within the State's territory or ships or aircraft, or by or against a national of the State, or in order to compel the State to do something. The broad grounds of treaty jurisdiction are all in effect swallowed up within the quasi-universal jurisdiction that the *aut dedere, aut judicare* principle requires. What the treaty regime does add, however, is a clear entitlement of States whose links with the offence fall within one of the specified grounds to seek the extradition of the alleged offender.[44] The treaty provisions have the important practical effect of extending the range of States acknowledged as having a legitimate interest in the prosecution of the alleged offender.

These extensions of jurisdiction treaty grounds have induced some parallel developments in the unilateral practice of States. For example, after the 1985 *Achille Lauro* incident, the United States followed the broad approach of these international treaties by enacting the 1986 Omnibus Diplomatic Security and Anti-Terrorism Act, which asserted jurisdiction over physical attacks on US citizens outside the United States. (It is interesting to note that this development was recorded in the *Cumulative Digest of United State Practice in International Law 1981–88* under the heading 'Jurisdiction Based on Universal and Other State Interests'—an indication of an increasingly robust approach to extraterritorial jurisdiction over terrorists.) Similarly, in United Kingdom law universal jurisdiction is asserted in ss 47 and 51 of the Anti-Terrorism, Crime and Security Act 2001, in respect of the offence of knowingly causing a nuclear explosion without authorization. The Rule of Law is a wondrous thing.

F. CONTROVERSIAL BASES OF PRESCRIPTIVE JURISDICTION

The bases of jurisdiction described above are generally accepted in State practice. There are certain other bases that have been advanced by States from time to time, which have not found general acceptance. These are instances of States considering that the link between them and the conduct that they seek to regulate is sufficient to warrant the exercise of prescriptive jurisdiction. The objections of other States, however, operate to preclude the

---

[43] See (1985) 24 ILM 1509. See also Cassese, 1989.

[44] In the case of an *aut dedere aut judicare* provision in a human rights treaty for alleged violations of which there is a right of individual complaint, a victim of an alleged human rights violation may also be able to complain that the State in which the alleged perpetrator is present has failed to extradite or prosecute: see for example *Guengueng et al* v *Senegal*, Committee Against Torture, Communication No 181/2001, decision of 19 May 2006, CAT/C/36/D/181/2001.

emergence of a 'general practice accepted as law' and the consequent establishment of the claimed basis of jurisdiction in customary international law.

1. Passive personality

One of the oldest controversial bases of prescriptive jurisdiction is the so-called 'passive personality' principle: that is, the principle that would allow the national State of the victim of an offence to assert prescriptive jurisdiction. That principle lay behind the controversy that arose in 1885 when Mr AK Cutting, a citizen of the United States, was imprisoned in Mexico and charged with having libelled a Mexican citizen in a paper published in the United States. In his annual address to Congress in 1886, President Grover Cleveland recalled that the incident 'disclosed a claim of jurisdiction by Mexico novel in our history, whereby any offense committed anywhere by a foreigner, penal in the place of its commission, and of which a Mexican is the object, may, if the offender be found in Mexico, be there tried and punished in conformity with Mexican laws'. He went on to say that '[t]he admission of such a pretension would be attended with serious results, invasive of the jurisdiction of this Government and highly dangerous to our citizens in foreign lands. Therefore I have denied it and protested against its attempted exercise as unwarranted by the principles of law and international usages.' It is a perfect example of a protest against an excessive jurisdictional claim. It will be noted that the United States assumed that the burden lay upon Mexico to prove its entitlement to exercise jurisdiction in this way; no attempt was made by the United States to establish a 'prohibitive rule' of the kind that is sometimes said to be required by the *Lotus* case.

Claims to jurisdiction based upon the passive personality principle have continued to be made. For example, in 1975 the United States again had cause to protest against assertions of passive personality jurisdiction, on that occasion by Greece.[45] There is, however, a trend in favour of accepting it. As one of the Separate Opinions in the *Arrest Warrant* case noted, '[p]assive personality jurisdiction, for so long regarded as controversial...today meets with relatively little opposition, at least so far as a particular category of offences is concerned.'[46] The qualification is important. Passive personality jurisdiction is indeed widely tolerated when used to prosecute terrorists. Whether it would be as acceptable if used to prosecute, for example, adulterers and defamers is another matter.

2. National technology

One of the most imaginative, and least successful, attempts to extend the scope of legislative jurisdiction was made by the United States in the 1980s. In the course of its attempts to prohibit trade with the Soviet Union, following the imposition of martial law in Poland, the United States made it a criminal offence for anyone, regardless of their nationality or State of residence, to export to the Soviet Union goods that contained more than a certain proportion of components of US origin or which had been created using US technology. This was an attempt to assert jurisdiction on the basis of the 'nationality' of technology (a concept unknown in international law); and it was vigorously resisted by the European

---

[45] See the *Digest of United States Practice in International Law 1975*, p 339.

[46] *Arrest Warrant of 11 April 2000 (Democratic Republic of the Congo v Belgium)*, ICJ Reports 2002, p 3, Joint Separate Opinion of Judges Higgins, Kooijmans, and Buergenthal, at p 11; *Lozano v Italy*, Appeal Judgment, Case No 31171/2008; ILDC 1085 (IT 2008) 24 July 2008.

States whose nationals bore the brunt of the prohibition. The main European protest appears in the Comments of the European Community dated 12 August 1982.[47] Again, however, the refusal of other States to accept the right of the United States unilaterally to impose its law on anyone who handles US technology has not prevented the acceptance of that basis of jurisdiction on an agreed basis in international treaties. For example, States appear to have been willing to conclude agreements relating to transfers of nuclear materials, under which the consent of the supplying State is required in the event of subsequent transfers of the material.

3. Unprincipled assertions of jurisdiction

From time to time, States are tempted to assert an extended extraterritorial jurisdiction in a manner that appears to be almost totally unprincipled. One of the most startling examples is to be found in the US Military Order of 13 November 2001, concerning the detention at a US base, Guantanamo Bay in Cuba, of 'international terrorists' seized by the United States in Afghanistan. Section 7 of that Order stipulates, in relation to detained individuals, that:

the individual shall not be privileged to seek any remedy or maintain any proceeding, directly or indirectly, or to have any such remedy or proceeding sought on the individual's behalf, in (i) any court of the United States, or any State thereof, (ii) any court of any foreign nation, or (iii) any international tribunal.[48]

It is not clear whether this curiously drafted Order was intended to prevent the making of applications to bodies such as the Inter-American Commission of Human Rights;[49] but insofar as it is intended to forbid non-US citizens to make such applications, it is difficult to see that even the protective principle could be stretched so far as to justify this provision, even if it were otherwise compatible with the United States' international obligations.

G. INADEQUACIES OF THE TRADITIONAL APPROACH

The traditional approach to the bases of jurisdiction is beset by considerable difficulty in practice. Two problems stand out. First, the problem of locating acts; and second, the problem of reconciling conflicts when two or more States have concurrent jurisdiction.

1. The difficulty of locating acts

The territorial principle, both in its plain form and its objective and subjective variants, presupposes that it is clear *where* an act is committed; but that is far from always the case. Take, for example, the case of the hijacking of an aircraft. If control over an aircraft registered in State A is seized while the aircraft is in the airspace of State B, is the hijack 'committed' (or, rather, *still being* committed) when the aircraft lands in State C? And, to take another example, suppose that individuals in States L and M conspire by fax, telephone, and e-mail to import narcotics into State K, but that only one of them ever sets

---

[47] (1982) 21 ILM 891.

[48] http://georgewbush-whitehouse.archives.gov/news/releases/2001/11/20011113–27.html.

[49] To its credit the Inter-American Commission acted anyway: see (2002) 41 ILM 532. So did the US Supreme Court: see *Rasul* v *Bush*, 542 US 466 (2004).

foot in State K. Could each of States K, L, and M assert jurisdiction over the entire conspiracy and all of the participants?[50]

As a matter of domestic law (the law under which the accused will, of course, be tried), it is evident that much will depend upon the particular way in which the crime with which they are charged is defined. The English courts have distinguished between 'conduct' crimes and 'result' crimes, the former focusing upon what is actually done and the latter upon the consequences of what is done, in a manner that lends itself respectively to the application of the subjective and objective variants of territorial jurisdiction.[51]

While such approaches may be sufficient to enable national courts to overcome any difficulties that they may have in determining the reach of the laws that they have to apply, it does not answer the question whether the jurisdictional reach asserted in those laws is in conformity with international law. Indeed, the drafting of national laws may aggravate the problem. It is quite possible to redraft every offence so as to make it a crime to enter the State having done x, y, or z before entry. For example, the customs laws of some Commonwealth States made it an offence for ships to enter the territorial sea *having broken* a bulk cargo into smaller parcels on the high seas (such breaking being almost invariably the prelude to smuggling of goods ashore). Was that an extension of the State's jurisdiction onto the high seas? Or was it an assertion of jurisdiction over acts that took place within the State's territory? A slightly different issue was raised in the 1920s by the US Prohibition Law, which sought to forbid the importation of alcohol into the United States. That law was applicable to foreign cruise ships entering US ports from the high seas. Did that therefore mean that the US was forbidding those ships to carry alcohol on the high seas? That was certainly the practical effect of the enforcement of the Prohibition Law; but was it the proper juridical characterization of that law?

There is no clear theoretical answer to this problem. As usual, however, there is much to be said for falling back on common sense. Where other States consider that the jurisdictional claim has gone too far—as they did in relation to the application of the Prohibition Law to foreign cruise ships,[52] but not in relation to the laws on the breaking of bulk cargo—they will protest. Those protests generally hold jurisdictional claims within reasonable bounds. If other States choose to acquiesce in the claim, it will become established in customary law.[53]

There was much speculation that the internet would lead to near-unimaginable difficulties concerning jurisdiction. In fact international law appears to have accommodated crimes in cyberspace with barely the flicker of a monitor: the regime under the 2001 Council of Europe Convention on Cybercrime[54] is based upon the traditional territorial and national principles of jurisdiction. However, issues remain.[55]

---

[50] See further Blackmore, 2006.

[51] See *DPP* v *Doot* [1973] AC 807; [1973] 1 All ER 940 (HL); *DPP* v *Stonehouse* [1978] AC 55; [1977] 2 All ER 909 (HL); *Liangsiriprasert* v *Government of the United States of America* [1991] 1 AC 225; [1990] 2 All ER 866 (PC). And see Hirst, 2003.

[52] The dispute was largely settled by an accommodation in the series of bilateral 'Liquor treaties' made with the United States.

[53] For an application of acquiescence as a basis for jurisdiction see *US* v *Suerte*, 291 F.3d 36 (2002), *Digest of United States Practice in International Law 2002*, p 133.

[54] ETS No 185; 41 ILM 282 (2002). See Article 22.1.d.

[55] See, for instance, Bigos, 2005; Schultz, 2008.

2. The difficulty of overlapping jurisdiction

All of the examples cited in the previous section in fact involve overlapping jurisdiction: that is, more than one State can make out a claim on the basis of established principles of international law to apply its laws to the conduct in question. That is why the cases are problematic: it is unlikely that a State will complain about the assertion of jurisdiction over an individual unless there is some other State that might more appropriately assert jurisdiction. In the 'Prohibition' cases, for example, the protesting European States thought it right that the flag State, and not the State of each port at which a cruise ship might call, should decide whether or not the ship could carry alcohol on board.[56]

Instances of 'overlapping', or 'concurrent', jurisdiction give rise to the question of priority. If the applicable laws diverge, which is to prevail? In some cases it may appear clear which law is to yield. There is a considerable body of practice supporting the view that a State may not require anyone outside its territory to do an act that would violate the criminal law of the place where the act would be done. Thus, courts in the United States allow what is sometimes known as the 'foreign sovereign compulsion' defence. For example, the court may excuse a failure to produce documents in pursuance of an order of the court, if the failure results from a prohibition on disclosure under the criminal law of the State where the documents are located.[57] (This defence is not available in circumstances where the duty of non-disclosure arises under the civil, rather than the criminal, law of the territorial State.)[58]

Some States have sought to utilize the foreign sovereign compulsion defence by enacting laws that oblige persons in their territory to do or not to do certain things. For instance, the United Kingdom enacted the Protection of Trading Interests Act 1980 (a more powerful successor to the Shipping Contracts and Commercial Documents Act 1964), under which the Secretary of State may order any person in the United Kingdom not to comply with orders from a foreign court for the production of evidence or, indeed, with substantive orders made on the basis of extraterritorial jurisdiction by a foreign State. The powers under the Act were invoked in 1982 in order to forbid British businesses to comply with US orders not to supply goods to the Soviet Union for use in connection with the construction of the Siberian gas pipeline, during the so-called 'pipeline' dispute[59]—an unusual example of one NATO State making it a criminal offence to comply with the law of another NATO State in respect of dealings with the Soviet Union during the Cold War. Similar laws, often known as 'blocking' statutes, have been adopted by a number of other States including Australia, Belgium, Canada, Denmark, Finland, France, Germany, Italy, Japan, the Netherlands, New Zealand, Norway, the Philippines, South Africa, Switzerland, and—the most dramatic measure of all—the European Community.[60]

Blocking statutes are no solution to jurisdictional conflicts. Quite apart from the fact that they represent a degree of friction in the international system that inevitably impairs its efficiency, they do nothing to overcome the problem of what might be called 'prudential

---

[56] Compare that situation with the case of *US v Neil*, 312 F.3d 419 (2002), *Digest of United States Practice in International Law 2002*, p 131.

[57] See, eg, *Société Internationale v Rogers*, 357 US 197 (1958).

[58] See, eg, *US v First National City Bank*, 396 F.2d 897 (1968).

[59] See the symposium in (1984) 27 *German Yearbook of International Law* 11–142. Cf Killman, 2004.

[60] See European Community Council Regulation (EC) 2271/96, published in (1996) OJ L309. For other measures, see Lowe, 1983.

compliance'. Even though an extraterritorial measure may be patently unlawful as matter of international law, and though it is possible that a person may at some point be ordered not to comply with it, the risk of the legislating State imposing sanctions for non-compliance is so great that anyone caught by the extraterritorial claim must, if they are prudent, organize their affairs so as to comply with the law. European businesses, for example, often organize transactions so as to comply with US law, even though the United States may have no legitimate claim to jurisdiction over them; and the converse is increasingly true of US companies in relation to EU law.

Jurisdictional disputes continue to arise, though their forms change. Thus, in 1996 the United States enacted laws providing for sanctions against Cuba (the Helms-Burton Act) and against Iran and Libya (the D'Amato Act). Those laws contained a range of extraterritorial measures, including the imposition of sanctions upon non-US businesses which purchased, in good faith and for full value, property in Cuba that had been confiscated in the 1960s from US owners who had not been compensated for the takings. These measures provoked a strong response from the European Community, resulting in an uneasy stand-off when the full implementation of the American laws was suspended.[61]

The States that claim extraterritorial jurisdiction are by no means always and wholly insensitive to the views of other States. US courts, in particular, have developed what they call the 'balancing of interests' approach to jurisdiction of conflicts. This approach has a number of variants, which may be seen in the leading cases such as *Timberlane*, *Mannington Mills*, and *Hartford Fire Insurance*.[62] Broadly speaking, under this approach the court considers the nature and extent of the United States' interest in having its law applied, and the interests of the other State in not having US law applied, and also factors such as the nationalities of the parties involved and the nature of their links with the United States. It then decides whether, on balance, it is right to apply United States law or to exercise judicial restraint. Not surprisingly, it is practically invariably decided to apply United States law. Nonetheless, there is no doubt that judges in United States courts are now more sensitive to the constraints of international law and the demands of international comity than they were in the 1960s and 70s.[63]

There are more satisfactory approaches to a solution to jurisdictional conflicts than unilateral restraint and blocking statutes. Sometimes States may be able to harmonize their policies[64] so that even though their jurisdictional claims may overlap, individuals affected by those laws are not subjected to conflicting demands. Sometimes, States may be able to establish consultation procedures in order to seek to eliminate on a case-by-case basis extraterritorial applications of laws which would cause difficulty for the State in whose territory the regulated conduct occurs. A good example of this is the antitrust cooperation procedure established by the European Community and United States.[65] Such steps have,

---

[61] See Lowe, 1997.

[62] The cases are discussed in *Hartford Fire Insurance Co v California*, 509 US 764;113 S Ct 2891 (1993); and Lowenfeld, 1995.

[63] See the decision of the Supreme Court in *F Hoffman–La Roche Ltd v Empagran SA*, 542 US 155; 124 S Ct 2359 (2004).

[64] For instance, through international treaties, or measures adopted in the context of regional organizations such as the European Union: see for instance, Mitsilegas, 2009.

[65] EC-US Agreement on the Application of Positive Comity Principles in the Enforcement of their Competition Laws, OJ L173 of 18 June 1998.

in recent years, done much to defuse disputes over jurisdiction, which are now somewhat less common and less acute than they were in the 1980s—though whether this trend is anything more than temporary remains to be seen. Ultimately, however, it must be recognized that jurisdictional conflicts are conflicts over the right to prescribe the rules that make up the public order of the State. Whatever solution is adopted, it must be a solution that ensures the right of every State, as an equal sovereign, to decide for itself upon the precise nature of that public order, to the extent that it can do so without invading and subverting the right of other States to do likewise.

III. THE FUNDAMENTAL PRINCIPLE GOVERNING ENFORCEMENT JURISDICTION

In contrast to the principles governing the exercise of prescriptive jurisdiction, the international law governing the exercise of enforcement jurisdiction is clear and simple. There is one basic principle: enforcement jurisdiction may not be exercised in the territory of any other State without the consent of that State. In other words, enforcement jurisdiction is in principle limited to the territory of the State concerned. (In fact, those two propositions are not precisely the same: there are areas outside the territory of a State that do not fall within the territory of another State—for example, the high seas, and the exclusive economic zones of other States).

One particular application of this principle is that the courts of one State will generally not enforce the public laws of another. 'Public laws', in this context, means not only criminal laws but also laws relating to matters such as taxation, that are quintessentially manifestations of the State's sovereign power, rather than laws that lay down the ground rules for the creation of rights and duties between individuals, in the way that, say, contract, family, and land law do. The most difficult laws to classify on this basis are tort laws. These are in some respects private, but may also be viewed as laws by which the State prescribes rules of conduct for society, in the same way that it does in its criminal law, but leaving the enforcement of those rules up to private parties. This dual nature of tort law is most evident in US antitrust laws, where those injured by unlawful anticompetitive practices are enabled to recover treble damages, as an incentive to act as 'private attorneys general' in the enforcement of the laws. For that reason, English courts have refused to enforce US antitrust laws.[66]

It is unusual, but not unknown, for one State to give another permission to exercise enforcement jurisdiction in its territory. Perhaps the most significant agreements of this kind in recent years are the so-called 'ship rider' agreements made, for example, by the United States with a number of Caribbean States, under which US navy vessels may in certain circumstances enter the territorial seas of the other party in order to pursue and arrest vessels suspected of being engaged in the illicit traffic in narcotic drugs. Similar agreements have been prepared on a multilateral basis in order to facilitate international action against narcotics traffic and (in the 2005 amendments to the 1988 Convention for the Suppression of Unlawful Acts Against the Safety of Maritime Navigation) against terrorism.

---

[66] See the submissions of the Attorney-General in *Rio Tinto Zinc v Westinghouse Corp* [1978] AC 547 (HL). Cf *Lewis v Eliades* [2003] EWCA Civ 1758.

Ordinarily, where an alleged offender who is sought for the purposes of prosecution is within the territory of another State, the State that seeks him must request the State where he is found to surrender him. Many States are, under their own domestic law, bound not to surrender individuals except in accordance with an extradition agreement that is in force with the requesting State. In addition, some States are bound under their own law not to surrender their nationals to foreign States under any circumstances. There is a rich body of international law and practice concerning the interpretation and application of extradition treaties, but shortage of space precludes its discussion here.

It is not unknown for States to attempt to obtain custody of alleged offenders without going through the formalities of extradition procedures—or, indeed, any other formalities. For example, individuals are sometimes simply transported over national borders into the hands of law enforcement officers on the other side. This appears, for example, to have been the way in which many members of the European terrorist organizations such as the Red Brigades and the Baader-Meinhof Gang were moved around Europe in the 1970s. On occasion, States have gone further, and themselves seized wanted persons from the territory of another State.[67] Such actions patently violate the territorial sovereignty of the State from which the persons are seized. If that State should retrospectively 'consent' to the seizure, that may cure the illegality; alternatively, the State may declare that it does not intend to pursue the question of the violation, and will regard the matter as closed. This seems to have happened, for instance, in relation to the seizure, apparently by agents of the government of Israel, of Adolf Eichmann from Argentina. Initially unaware of Eichmann's abduction, the government of Argentina subsequently agreed to abandon its claim for reparation for the violation of its territorial sovereignty.

What is the position if a State seizes an accused person, in violation of territorial sovereignty of another State, and then puts that person on trial in its own courts? As a matter of international law, one might say that the subsequent trial compounds the violation of the other State's territorial sovereignty; and even if that State acquiesces, as Argentina did in the trial of Eichmann, there is at least the possibility that the national State of the abducted individual might complain that its rights, too, have been violated. As far as the individual is concerned, the position is less clear. In some States the illegality of the abduction may, as a matter of the domestic law of the State, preclude the trial of the individual. In most States, however, it is likely that the illegality of the abduction will be regarded as a matter to be handled by the Executive, if and when the State from which the defendant is taken complains, but not a matter that the trial court needs to take into account. So, for example, in the United States the most egregious violation of international law appears to be insufficient to constitute a bar to the trial of the abducted defendant: even the sand-bagging of suspects and the smuggling of their comatose bodies back to the United States was held to be no obstacle to their trial before a US court, on the curious ground that the individuals did not enjoy the protection of US Constitutional safeguards while they were outside US territory.[68] The English courts adopt a somewhat different approach. Having long taken the view that it was no concern of the court how the defendant happened to have arrived before it, in more recent years the courts have moved towards the view that the forcible

---

[67] Or tried to ship them abroad in wooden crates: see the two episodes noted in Harris, 2004, at p 369.
[68] See *US v Toscanino*, 500 F.2d 267 (1974); *US v Verdugo-Urquidez*, 494 US 259 (1990); *US v Alvarez-Machain*, 504 US 655,112 S Ct 2188 (1992). Cf *Sosa v Alvarez-Machain*, 542 US 692 (2004).

abduction of defendants in violation of agreed procedures may be so serious as to amount to an abuse of process, in which case their trial should not proceed.[69] Such a finding will, however, be unusual, and be made only where the British police or prosecuting authorities have themselves acted illegally or colluded in unlawful procedures in order to secure the presence of the defendant in the United Kingdom, or have violated international law or the law of a foreign State or otherwise abused their powers.[70]

IV. CONCLUSION

This chapter has surveyed, albeit briefly, the principles of international law governing exercises of legislative and enforcement jurisdiction. These are truly principles, and not rules. The difficulties of applying the principles rigidly have been noted, and are implicit in the nature of jurisdiction. It is not possible to devise strict rules that would divide jurisdiction between sovereign States in any practical manner. The solution to jurisdictional problems has to be found by increasing the sensitivity of States to the constraints imposed by international law, and also to the fact that the interests of other States demand respect. It should be clear that if in any case the exercise by one State of its jurisdiction threatens to subvert the laws that another State has enacted to regulate life in its own territory, in the exercise of its sovereign right to choose how to organize life within its borders, the boundaries of lawful jurisdiction have been over-stepped. If States wish to do more than they are able to do within the limits of the jurisdiction allowed to them, they must first seek the agreement and cooperation of other States.

REFERENCES

AKEHURST, M (1972–73), 'Jurisdiction in International Law', 46 *BYIL* 145–217.

ARNELL, P (2001), 'The Case for Nationality-Based Jurisdiction', 50 *ICLQ* 955.

AUST, AI (2000), 'Lockerbie: The Other Case', 49 *ICLQ* 278.

BIGOS, O (2005), 'Jurisdiction over cross-boundary wrongs on the internet', 54 *ICLQ* 585.

BLACKMORE, JDA (2006), 'The jurisdictional problem of the extraterritorial conspiracy', 17 *Criminal Law Forum* 71.

BLOUNT, P *et al* (2007), 'Jurisdiction in Outer Space: Challenge of Private Individuals in Space', 33 *Journal of Space Law* 299.

BROWNLIE, I (2008), *Principles of Public International Law*, 7th edn (Oxford: Oxford University Press).

CASSESE, A (1989), *Terrorism, Politics and The Law* (Cambridge: Polity Press).

——, GAETA, P, and JONES, JRWD (2002), *The Rome Statute of the International Criminal Court: A Commentary* (Oxford: Oxford University Press).

DONOVAN, D and ROBERTS, A (2006), 'The Emerging Recognition of Universal Civil Jurisdiction', 100 *AJIL* 142.

GOODWIN, J (2006), 'Universal Jurisdiction and the Pirate: Time for an Old Couple to Part', (2006) 39 *Vand J Transnat'l L* 973.

---

[69] *Bennett v Horseferry Road Magistrates' Court* [1994] 1 AC 42; [1993] 3 All ER 138 (HL). And see the South African case of *State v Ebrahim* (1992), 31 ILM 888.

[70] *R v Staines Magistrates Court, ex parte Westfallen* [1998] 4 All ER 210.

HALL, W (1895), *A Treatise on International Law*, 5th edn (Oxford: Clarendon Press).

HARRIS, DJ (2004), *Cases and Materials on International Law*, 6th edn (London: Sweet & Maxwell).

HIRST, M (2003), *Jurisdiction and the Ambit of the Criminal Law* (Oxford: Oxford University Press).

HOBE, S *et al* (2007), 'Space Tourism Activities: Emerging Challenges to Air and Space Law' 33 *Journal of Space Law* 359.

KILLMAN, E (2004), 'Enforcement of Judgments and Blocking Statues', 53 *ICLQ* 1025.

LOWE, V (1983), *Extraterritorial Jurisdiction* (Cambridge: Grotius).

—— (1997), 'US Extraterritorial Jurisdiction: the Helms-Burton and D'Amato Acts', 46 *ICLQ* 378–390.

LOWENFELD, A (1995), 'Conflict, Balancing of Interests, and the Exercise of Jurisdiction to Prescribe: Reflections on the *Insurance Antitrust Case*', 89 *AJIL* 42.

MITSILEGAS, V (2009), 'The third wave of third pillar law. Which direction for EU criminal justice?', 34 *European Law Review* 523.

MURPHY, S (2003), 'Extraterritorial Application of US Laws to Crimes on Foreign Vessels', 97 *AJIL* 183.

O'CONNELL, DP (1970), *International Law*, 2nd edn (London: Stevens).

O'KEEFE, R (2004), 'Universal Jurisdiction: Clarifying the Basic Concept', 2 *Jo Int Crim Justice* 735.

OPPENHEIM, L (1992), JENNINGS, Sir R and WATTS, SIR A (eds), *Oppenheim's International Law*, 9th edn (Harlow: Longman).

RATNER, S (2003), 'Belgium's War Crimes Statute. A Postmortem', 97 *AJIL* 888.

REYDAMS, L (2003a), *Universal Jurisdiction: International and Municipal Legal Perspectives* (Oxford: Oxford University Press).

—— (2003b), 'Belgium Reneges on Universality: The 5 August 2003 Act on Grave Breaches of International Humanitarian Law', 1 *Journal of International Criminal Justice* 679.

RYNGAERT, C (2008) 'Litigating abuses committed by private military companies', 19 *EJIL* 1035

TREVES, T (2009), 'Piracy, law of the sea, and use of force: developments off the coast of Somalia', 20 *EJIL* 399.

TWISS, SIR T (1884), *On the Rights and Duties of Nations in Times of Peace* (Oxford: Clarendon Press).

SCHULTZ, T (2008) 'Carving up the internet: jurisdiction, legal orders, and the private/public international law interface', 19 *EJIL* 799.

VERHOEVEN, J (2000), *Droit international public* (Brussels: Larcier).

FURTHER READING

Curiously, there is no satisfactory modern monograph on jurisdiction. There are, however, some good articles that discuss the basic principles of jurisdiction in international law in the light of the various disputes that have arisen over the years:

AKEHURST, M (1972–73), 'Jurisdiction in International Law', 46 *BYIL* 145.

BOWETT, DW (1982), 'Jurisdiction: Changing Patterns of Authority over Activities and Resources', 53 *BYIL* 1.

LOWE, V (1981), 'Blocking Extraterritorial Jurisdiction: the British Protection of Trading Interests Act, 1980', 75 *AJIL* 257.

—— (1985), 'The Problems of Extraterritorial Jurisdiction: Economic

Sovereignty and the Search for a Solution', 34 *ICLQ* 724.

MANN, FA (1964–I), 'The Doctrine of Jurisdiction in International Law', 111 *Recueil des Cours* 1.

—— (1984–III), 'The Doctrine of International Jurisdiction Revisited after Twenty Years', 186 *Recueil des Cours* 9.

SCHLOSSER, P (2000), 'Jurisdiction and International Judicial and Administrative Co-operation', 284 *Recueil des Cours* 9.

12

INTERNATIONAL LAW AND RESTRAINTS ON THE EXERCISE OF JURISDICTION BY NATIONAL COURTS OF STATES

Hazel Fox

SUMMARY

This chapter examines the methods, which we may call avoidance techniques, by which States prevent their national courts from deciding disputes which relate to the internal affairs of another State. Three main avoidance techniques are used: immunity, act of State, and non-justiciability. This chapter will examine all three doctrines, and examine in some detail the operation of the restrictive doctrine of State immunity. The chapter will end with a discussion of the arguments for and against the current prohibition on the determination of one State's disputes in the national courts of another State and identify the challenges today which the rule of law, an individual's right of access to court, and the implementation of *jus cogens* norms present to the maintenance of these avoidance techniques.

I. INTRODUCTION

A. INTRODUCTION

The three restraints—State immunity, act of State, and non-justiciability—with which this chapter is concerned are consequences of the independence and equality which States enjoy under international law.

Long before any system of international law was established by international convention or decision of an international tribunal, law and justice were enforced within the territory of a State and administered by national courts. Inevitably, therefore, when claims were brought in the national court against another State in respect of its acts or agents, the question arose and enquiry was made of international law how such a litigant should be treated. Was a warship operated by one State, forced by bad weather to enter the port of another State to undergo repairs, to be detained by a claim of an individual that the ship had been expropriated without proper compensation? Could a State be sued in the court of another State for failure to pay rent for premises which it had requisitioned to accommodate staff to implement emergency relief work following a war? Could an individual who had been refused a visa or import permit sue a foreign State for the consequent expense incurred or the loss to his business?

The immediate solution to issues of this sort, as with the practice in the UK with regard to claims against the Crown until the Crown Proceedings Act 1947, was to separate the settlement of claims arising from the conduct of States from the determination by the national courts of disputes between private persons. To keep lines of communication open and to preserve friendly relations with other States, agents of the State, including Heads of State themselves, were accorded a privileged position when present within the territory of another State. One method of conferring such privileges, was to grant them immunity from criminal or civil proceedings in national courts (see Ch 13, below). Similarly activities of governments and their departments were accorded immunity by the courts of other States, even though the conduct complained of might be categorized as breach of contract, defamation or expropriation.

Such a plea of immunity is similar to that granted by national law to the legislature and its members; to ensure, when it is in session, that neither the legislative body nor a member of parliament when it is in session is prevented by threat of litigation or criminal prosecution from conducting their legislative functions and the proper representation of the electorate. The unhindered function of the MP and the legislature is held in law to be preferred to the immediate right of a creditor or prosecutor to seek justice in the national court. Of course the reasons for the conferment of immunity on a State or its official differ. In the case of the legislature, the justification derives from the constitution of the country, the balance of powers between legislature, courts and the executive and the requirement that no attempt by the executive to use the power of the courts should prevent the proper exercise of the legislative function. In the case of diplomatic and State immunity the underlying purpose is the maintenance of peaceful relations between States and the settlement of disputes by consent rather than the diktat of one State; to that end international law recognizes the independence and equality of States and accordingly requires restraint from subjecting one State to adjudication of its disputes in the national courts of another State. The best known example of such a restraint is the prohibition of the threat or use of force by one State in Article 2(4) of the UN Charter against the territorial integrity or political independence of another State.

Similarly, by the plea of Act of State national common law courts of other States respect the legislation and public acts of other States; and, when a question relating to an international boundary, or State succession or State responsibility arises, national courts treat such international transactions between States as non-justiciable by municipal law and by accepting a plea of non-justiciability, refer any dispute to settlement by international law.

However, disputes relating to contract and trade are generally recognized as matters to be determined by a court of law and with the State's increasing engagement in commercial activities, State practice came to recognize that the immunities afforded to the State and its agents by international law need not be extended to commercial transactions into which the State entered in a manner similar to a private person. Thus, if a State failed to pay for goods or service ordered, immunity increasingly was held to provide no bar, though to enable the State to operate unhindered, special treatment continued to be afforded to the head and members of its diplomatic mission and to certain contracts of employment which it might make.

But, if national courts were recognized by international law to have jurisdiction to adjudicate claims brought against States in respect of matters coming properly within private commercial law, surely, with the development of international law of human rights and recognition of international crimes, (it came to be asked) international law should equally permit national courts to exercise jurisdiction and disregard immunity where the defendant State had committed a breach of 'established rules of international law of fundamental importance'. In plain terms, why should a claim that a State or its official had tortured an individual or in the course of armed conflict had caused loss of life or property be barred by a claim of immunity from adjudication in the national court of another State, if it could be shown that the alleged acts were in breach of international law?

This chapter aims to show the complex issues which are involved in answering that question. But it is useful to point out at once some of the difficulties which arise. First, can a national court be relied on to determine a breach of international law, when that court is established by one State without any participation or consent of the defendant State? Second, acts of torture tend to be committed by the police or armed forces of a State—agencies which are closely concerned with defence and internal security of the State. To allow the national court of another State to review judicially the propriety of the conduct of such agencies would constitute a major intrusion into the internal administration of another State with consequent loss of independence.

How best to accommodate the claims of individuals for protection of human rights and for the enforcement of democratic rule with the responsibility of a State for the maintenance of internal law and order and of peaceful external relations with other States is still being worked out in the law relating to international immunities. The reader should be aware that this area of the law is undergoing rapid change, as evidenced by the considerable revisions which have had to be made to this chapter in this third edition.

Let us now look more closely at the techniques which international law has evolved to deal with these problems.

B. STATE IMMUNITY, ACT OF STATE, AND NON-JUSTICIABILITY AS AVOIDANCE TECHNIQUES

International law limits the independence of any one over-powerful State by making legal equality a consequence of statehood with an accompanying obligation on all States to respect each other's independence and equality. That respect is given expression in an obligation of non-intervention in the internal affairs of another State and a prohibition on the settlement of disputes without the consent of all the States to whom such disputes relate. The obligation of non-intervention is given effect by the recognition accorded by other States to the validity of the legislative, adjudicative, and administrative acts of a State within its permitted area of jurisdiction. The consent requirement in dispute settlement is given effect by a rule of exhaustion of local remedies which provides an opportunity for a State to settle the claim in its own manner or by the removal of the dispute to the international plane, for diplomatic settlement. To honour this obligation of non-intervention in international law one State (known as the forum State by reason of the fact that the court before whom the proceedings are instituted is located in its territory) employs various methods to prevent its courts from deciding disputes which relate to the internal affairs of another State.

Some methods or avoidance techniques exist by virtue of the constitutional or municipal law of a State so as to restrict a particular court's competence or direct the case to a more appropriate forum; thus certain matters, such as the recognition of the existence of another State or government may be reserved to the executive branch of government; or a court of competence in civil and commercial matters may have no power to hear a matter relating to public administration; or a common law court may refuse to hear a case, exercising a discretion on a plea of *forum non conveniens* to rule that another forum, having competent jurisdiction is the appropriate forum for the trial of the case more suitably for the interest of the parties and the ends of justice.[1]

But the three avoidance techniques with which this chapter is concerned are more directly related to a State's obligation to respect the independence and equality of other States by not requiring them to submit to adjudication in a national court or to settlement of their disputes without their consent. These three avoidance techniques are immunity, act of State, and non-justiciability.

Immunity by reason of the sovereign independent status of a State is only available where proceedings are brought against a foreign State and is a preliminary plea taken at the commencement of the proceedings. It serves two purposes: first, it debars the court of the State where proceedings are brought (the forum court or national court) from exercising jurisdiction to inquire further into the claim; and second, it removes the claim to another process of settlement, most frequently to settlement through diplomatic channels, though proceedings in the foreign State's own court are also a possibility. Because it brings a halt to proceedings it is, from a potential defendant's position, the most effective plea.

The other two pleas may be raised in proceedings where private persons or a foreign State is a party. Act of State is a defence to the substantive law requiring the forum court to exercise restraint in the adjudication of disputes relating to legislative or other governmental acts which a foreign State has performed within its territorial limits. Non-justiciability bars a national court from adjudicating certain issues, particularly international relations between States, by reason of their lacking any judicial or manageable standards by which to determine them.

In studying the subject it is important to keep a proper historical perspective. All three doctrines are based on a concept of the State and have developed to reflect the changing conception of the role of the State in the international community and its increasing subjection to the rule of law in both its internal and external dealings. The doctrine of immunity in particular, has moved from an absolute to an increasingly restrictive phase, that is from total immunity to the recognition of exceptions to immunity permitting the institution of certain proceedings in a national court against a foreign State. The dualist approach of common law which treated international and municipal law as two separate systems has

---

[1] *Spiliada Martime Corporation* v *Cansulex Ltd* [1987] AC 460; [1986] 3 All ER 843 (HL) at 854; and see Collins (*Dicey, Morris and Collins*), 2006, ch 12 and Fawcett, Carruthers and North (*Cheshire, North and Fawcett*), 2008, Ch 13, 15, and 16.

been considerably modified by the reception of international standards into common law, without express legislative enactment.

A description of the three avoidance techniques will now be given followed by a comparison of their scope.

II. STATE IMMUNITY

A. ORIGINS OF THE PLEA OF STATE IMMUNITY

Following the Treaty of Westphalia 1648 the modern State emerged with its centralization of legislative, judicial, and enforcement powers. The need for protection of representatives of foreign States led to the development of diplomatic immunity for the Ambassador and members of a foreign embassy. The visits of personal sovereigns required development of a principle of inviolability of their person and immediate possessions and entourage as well as immunity from suit in the local court. The visits of warships of friendly States to national ports required the recognition of the ships' immunity from local jurisdiction. From these separate regimes, a parallel concept of State immunity developed to provide protection from national courts' powers for the legal entity of the State itself.

B. DEVELOPMENT OF THE COMMON LAW RELATING TO STATE IMMUNITY

Indeed, for the common law it was in the course of formulating an immunity from the jurisdiction of the national court for warships that the general principle of State immunity was first established in the leading case of *The Schooner Exchange* v *McFaddon*.[2] The US Supreme Court rejected a creditor's claim for attachment and ordered the release of a vessel which by reason of bad weather was present undergoing repairs in the port of Philadelphia, having been seized under a decree of the French Emperor Napoleon and converted into a public armed ship. The court thereby established the immunity in common law courts of a ship of war of a State from arrest and process in the courts of another State. Marshall CJ stated the immunity to be based upon the consent of the territorial State to waive its exclusive jurisdiction but did so by reference to an implicit obligation so to do in the law of nations. His subtle reconciliation of the territorial State's jurisdiction and the foreign State's independence has been the source of much subsequent comment and was expressed as follows:

This perfect equality and absolute independence of sovereigns and this common interest impelling them to mutual intercourse and an interchange of good offices with each other, have given rise to a class of case in which every sovereign is understood to waive the exercise of a part of that complete exclusive territorial jurisdiction, which has been stated to be the attribute of every nation.

The English Court of Appeal in *The Parlement Belge*[3] applied the ruling in the *Schooner Exchange* more widely to cover all ships of a foreign State regardless of whether they were

---

[2] *The Schooner Exchange* v *McFaddon* (1812) Cranch 116 (US).
[3] *The Parlement Belge* (1879–90) 5 Prob Div 197 (CA).

engaged in public service or trade. It held immune a packet boat owned by the King of the Belgians involved in a collision in the port of Dover, and which at the time was carrying both royal mail and passengers and merchandise for hire.

Despite growing disquiet, the absolute rule, declared in *The Parlement Belge*, treating all acts of a foreign State as immune continued to be observed in English law and applied by English courts[4] until the 1970s. An interdepartmental committee appointed in 1950 failed to offer any satisfactory reform[5] and attempts to confine immunity to the central government of the State, and to exclude departments or agencies which enjoyed separate legal personality,[6] or to treat consent of the State given in an agreement prior to the dispute as constituting waiver of immunity,[7] were unsuccessful in the English courts.

By the 1970s developments elsewhere, however, encouraged a bolder approach. In 1977, the Privy Council in *The Philippine Admiral*[8] reinterpreted *The Parlement Belge*, declaring that it had not laid down the wide proposition that 'a sovereign can claim immunity for vessels owned by him even if they are admittedly being used wholly or substantially for trading purposes'. It accordingly rejected a plea of immunity in respect of *in rem* proceedings (that is proceedings for attachment and sale directed against the vessel itself) brought for goods supplied to a vessel operated as an ordinary trading ship in which the Philippine government retained an interest. The next year the Court of Appeal in *Trendtex v Central Bank of Nigeria*[9] refused to allow a plea of immunity as a bar to proceedings against the Central Bank of Nigeria for failure to honour a commercial letter of credit;[10] the court, unanimously, held that the bank by the terms of its establishment was an independent entity and not to be treated as part of the State of Nigeria; and, by a majority, that English law recognized no immunity in respect of proceedings brought for a commercial activity such as the issue of a letter of credit. In accepting a restrictive doctrine of immunity in the common law—a move which was confirmed by the House of Lords in *I Congreso del Partido*,[11] the English courts were much influenced by legal developments elsewhere and these developments finally led to the enactment in 1978 of the State Immunity Act (SIA) providing for a restrictive scheme of immunity.

C. DEVELOPMENT IN CIVIL COURTS AND THE USA

With increased participation of States in trading activities following the First World War there was much dissatisfaction with the denial of legal redress against States for their commercial activities. Certain civil countries, notably in Italy, Belgium, and the Egyptian mixed courts, led the way in adopting a restrictive doctrine construing international law

---

[4] *The Cristina* [1938] AC 485 (HL) per Lord Atkin at 491.

[5] Interim Report of Interdepartmental Committee on State Immunities dated 13 July 1951.

[6] *Baccus SRL v Servicio Nacional del Trigo* [1957] 1 QB 438; 28 ILR 160 (CA).

[7] *Kahan v Pakistan Federation* [1951] 2 KB 1003; 18 ILR 210 (CA).

[8] *The Philippine Admiral* [1977] AC 373; [1976] 1 All ER 78; 64 ILR 90 (PC).

[9] *Trendtex Trading Corporation v Central Bank of Nigeria* [1977] 1 QB 529; [1977] 1 All ER 881; 64 ILR 111 (CA).

[10] A letter of credit is an undertaking given by a bank to pay a certain sum of money on receipt of documents of title and transport relating to a particular consignment of goods; it may be enforced against the bank independently of the solvency or any refusal to pay on the part of the consignor.

[11] *I Congreso del Partido* [1983] 1 AC 244; [1981] 2 All ER 1064 at 1074; 64 ILR 307 (HL).

as requiring immunity for proceedings relating to acts committed in exercise of sovereign authority (*acta jure imperii*) and not for trading activities or acts which a private person may perform (*acta jure gestionis*); in 1963, in a magisterial decision surveying State practice, bilateral and multilateral treaties, and legal writing, the German Federal Constitutional Court declared that international law permits a restrictive doctrine of State immunity and that the proper criterion for the distinction between sovereign and private acts is the nature of the act, not its purpose. It allowed proceedings by a builder to recover the cost of repair carried out to the Iranian Embassy, holding the repair contract to relate to a non-sovereign act of the foreign State and hence not to be immune.[12]

Further support for the restrictive doctrine was given in the adoption in 1926 of the Brussels Convention for the Unification of Certain Rules concerning the Immunities of Government Vessels and later its 1934 protocol, providing that State-owned or operated ships used exclusively for non-governmental commercial purposes should enjoy no immunity and be subject to the same substantive legal rights and obligations as ships owned or operated by private persons for the purposes of trade; and in 1972 by the signature of the European Convention on State Immunity (ECSI) which introduced a number of exceptions to immunity from adjudication which were broadly based on the commercial or private law distinction and modified the absolute rule against coercive measures by an optional scheme. In 1952 the State Department of the United States announced in the Tate letter that in future US policy would be to follow the restrictive theory of sovereign immunity and in 1976, in part responding to the need of commercial banks financing sovereign States' debt to have legal recourse, Congress enacted the Foreign Sovereign Immunities Act (FSIA), being the first legislation to introduce the restrictive doctrine into the common law.

D. PRESENT DAY SOURCES OF THE INTERNATIONAL LAW OF STATE IMMUNITY

Until 2004 no universal international convention on State immunity had been adopted. The 1926 Brussels Convention, referred to above, and ratified by 29 States, merely removed immunity in respect of State-owned or operated ships and their cargoes engaged in trade. Only eight States (Austria, Belgium, Cyprus, Germany, Luxembourg, Netherlands, Switzerland, and UK) are parties to the 1972 European Convention. In the absence of direct authority at the international level, resort was made to State practice in the form of national legislation and decisions of national courts, to provide evidence of international custom and 'general principles of law', the sources of law referred to in Article 38(1)(b) and (c) of the ICJ Statute (Crawford, 1983, p 77; Higgins, 1982, p 268). From 1976 onwards, a considerable number of common law countries enacted legislation on State immunity[13]

---

[12] *Empire of Iran Case*, 45 ILR 57 at 80 (German Federal Constitutional Court, 30 April 1963).

[13] Foreign Sovereign Immunities Act 1976 (USA) (cited as FSIA); State Immunity Act 1978 (UK) (cited as SIA); Foreign States Immunities Act 1985 (Australia); Canadian State Immunity Act 1982; Immunities and Privileges Act 1984 (Malaysia); The Pakistan State Immunity Ordinance 1981; Singapore State Immunity Act 1979; The South African Foreign States Immunities Act 1981; Malawi Immunities and Privileges Act 1984 (No 16 of 1984). Other small common law jurisdictions have enacted similar legislation, eg, St Kitts 1979.

and they and other common law jurisdictions[14] along with the civil law systems of France and other western or central European countries now apply a restrictive doctrine in their courts.[15] The position as to countries which have enacted no legislation and have had no or few proceedings before their courts is more difficult to ascertain; but some have indicated tentative signs of moving to a restrictive position.[16] Thus the Russian Article 127 of the 1994 Civil Code of Procedure made provision for reform of the absolute rule of State immunity, but to date no such law has been enacted.[17] China in 2005 enacted a national law providing for judicial immunity from execution of central banks of foreign States similar to the restrictive rule provided in the UN convention[18] and as a member of the WTO and signatory of other international conventions indicated a willingness to consent to applying a restrictive rule in its courts (Dahai Qi, 2008).

Since 2004, however, the position has changed. In 2004, the UN General Assembly adopted and opened for signature an International Convention on Jurisdictional Immunities of States and their Property (the UN Convention on State Immunity).This convention adopts the restrictive doctrine of State immunity with regard to civil and administrative proceedings in national courts. As at the end of March 2010, 28 States including China, India, Japan, Iran, the Russian Federation, Switzerland and many of the members of the European Community including France, Sweden, and the UK had signed, and eight States (Austria, Iran, Kazakhstan Lebanon, Norway, Romania, Portugal, and Sweden) had ratified the convention. Arguably China and Russia as signatory States, who are also parties to the 1969 Vienna Convention on Treaties, are, by Article 18 of the 1969 Treaty, obliged to refrain from acts which would defeat the object and purpose of the 2004 Convention on State Immunity which they have signed; and hence are obliged to

14 Kenya, *Ministry of Defence of Government of UK v Ndegna*, Kenya Court of Appeal, 17 March 1983, 103 ILR 235; Ireland, *Government of Canada v Employment Appeals Tribunal and Burke* [1992] ILRM 325, 95 ILR 467, Irish Supreme Court; New Zealand, *Governor of Pitcairn v Sutton* [1995] INZLR 426,104 ILR 508; *Fang and Others v Jiang and Others* [2007] NZAR 420 (HC); Zimbabwe, *Barker McCormac (Private) Ltd v Government of Kenya* [1986] CR Comm (Const) 21, 84 ILR 18; Nigeria, *Kramer v Government of Kingdom of Belgium; Embassy of Belgium* [1989] 1 CLRQ 126, 103 ILR 299.

15 See Hafner, Kohen, Breau, 2006 (hereafter referred to as Hafner). This is a collection of the practice of all the member States of the Council of Europe as regards national legislation and judicial decisions relating to State immunity conducted under the supervision of its Committee of Legal Advisers on public international law (CAHDI).

16 Documentation of the practice of other governments, particularly of China, Russia, and developing States relating to State immunity is largely derived from the research instituted by the ILC in support of its work on State immunity. It is to be found in the *Collection of Materials on Jurisdictional Immunities of States and their Properties* prepared by the Codification Section of the UN Office of Legal Affairs in 1982, ST/Leg/Ser.B/20, and the answers of governments to the questionnaire of Mr Ogiso, 2nd ILC Special Rapporteur in 1988, provide some further information.

17 Thus the Russian Article 127 of the 1994 Civil Code of Procedure makes provision for enactment of a federal law on State immunity and the First and Second Draft Laws indicate the likelihood of a restrictive rule, but as at 2009 no such law has been enacted See Byhovskaya, 2008, p 154 ff. In 2001 the Russian High Arbitration Court rejected a claim relating to a construction contract brought against a foreign Embassy see Hafner, 2006, p 526; the Constitutional Court of the Russian Federation, however, stated that article 435 of the Civil Procedural Code providing for the immunity of an Embassy of a foreign State was subsidiary to provisions of the Labour Code in disputes arising from employment contracts and returned the case for reconsideration to the High Arbitration Court. See *Kalashnikova v United States,* Constitutional Court of the Russian Federation, 2 Nov 2000, Hafner, 2006, p 528.

18 Law of the People's Republic of China on Judicial Immunity from Measures of constraint for the property of foreign central Banks, adopted on 25 October 2005. See *FG Hemisphere Assoc v Congo*, HK App. Ct. (10.02.2010).

refrain from continuing activity to support an absolute rule contrary to the provisions of the 2004 convention. In addition there have been a succession of cases relating to State immunity in the International Court of Justice: four of these relate to the eluci- dation of the scope of immunity from criminal jurisdiction of the State and its serv- ing head of State and other high-ranking officials. Beginning with the *Arrest Warrant* case, which declared the issue and international circulation of an arrest warrant by the Belgian court in respect of a serving minister for foreign affairs of another State to be a breach of international law,[19] two further applications have followed challenging the legality of national procedures instituting criminal proceedings against serving heads of State and ministers;[20] and one application by Belgium alleging Senegal's breach of its obligation under the 1984 UN Torture Convention and international customary law either to prosecute or extradite a former head of State alleged to have committed torture and crimes against humanity.[21] A fifth outstanding application relates to State immun- ity from civil jurisdiction and concerns an application by Germany claiming violation of its immunity by Italy by reason of its national court's exercise of jurisdiction over the commission by Germany of war crimes during the Second World War.[22] Further, the International Law Commission with RA Kolodkin as its Special Rapporteur has undertaken a study of the immunity of State officials from foreign criminal jurisdiction (Kolodkin, 2008).[23]

The 2004 UN convention is based on Articles prepared by the International Law Commission, finalized in 1991, and amended in the course of 10 years' consideration in the Sixth (Legal) Committee of the United Nations and its working groups. It provides a comprehensive code based on the restrictive doctrine of immunity, further elaborated in the commentaries which accompanied the ILC draft Articles in 1991, for the immunity of a State and its property from the civil and administrative jurisdiction of the courts of another State. (As the UNGA resolution adopting the convention makes plain, there is a general understanding that the convention does not cover criminal proceedings.) The restrictive rule of immunity and the exceptions, which the convention sets out as regards both the adjudication and the enforcement of judgments in national courts against a for- eign State, are broadly recognized in State practice and reflect a balance between the legit- imate interests of States as to the exercise of governmental powers and of private parties as regards commercial undertakings; the convention thus provides 'a solid foundation on which States can base their domestic law' either by direct incorporation or harmonization (Stewart, 2005, p 206).

The ratification of 30 States is required to bring the convention into force. At the present time, therefore, it remains necessary when ascertaining the current law relating to State immunity to construe the provisions of the convention by reference to the extent to which

---

[19] *Arrest Warrant of 11 April 2000 (Democratic Republic of Congo v Belgium), Preliminary Objections and Merits, Judgment, ICJ Reports 2002*, p 3.

[20] *Certain Criminal Proceedings in France (Republic of the Congo v France), Provisional Measure, Order of 17 June 2003, ICJ Reports 2003*, p 102; *Certain Questions of Mutual Assistance in Criminal Matters (Djibouti v France) Judgment of 4 June 2008*.

[21] *Questions relating to the Obligation to Prosecute or Extradite (Belgium v Senegal), Provisional Measures, Order of 28 May 2009*.

[22] *Jurisdictional Immunities of the State (Germany v Italy)*, Application filed 23 December 2008.

[23] See also Memorandum by the Secretariat A/CN.4/596.

they are supported by State practice as evidenced in the legislation and case law of the principal municipal jurisdictions.

E. THE ELEMENTS CONSTITUTING THE PLEA OF STATE IMMUNITY

1. The plea as a bar to proceedings before a court

The plea concerns immunity from the judicial power of another State, though the enforcement of that power may also involve the executive power and the administrative authorities of that other State. It does not relate to the legislative power of the State—the State's jurisdiction to prescribe—which goes more to the plea of non-justiciability, act of State, and substantive liability (see below). A State may claim and enjoy other privileges and immunities from the forum State such as immunity for its nationals from military conscription or the privilege of payment of no import duties or preferential rates on petroleum fuel or alcoholic drinks, but these are not the direct concern of the plea of State immunity before a court.

International tribunals State immunity primarily constitutes a bar to proceedings brought in national courts. It is not generally a bar to proceedings before an international tribunal where States enjoy equal standing and which is not operated within one State's legal system. Where the authority of the international tribunal derives from a Resolution of the UN Security Council made under Chapter VII which imposes binding obligations on all States, State immunity is no bar to prosecution of a State official. Thus the serving heads Milosevic of the former Yugoslavia, and Jean Kambanda, the former Prime Minister of Rwanda, were prosecuted in the International Criminal Tribunals for the former Yugoslavia (ICTY) and the International Criminal Tribunal for Rwanda (ICTR) respectively for international crimes and the International Criminal Court acting under UN SC Resolution 1593 (2005) has indicted a serving Head of State, President Bashir of Sudan, in respect of the Darfur situation. On somewhat similar grounds Charles Taylor, the serving Head of State of Liberia, was held to enjoy no immunity from the jurisdiction of the Sierra Leone Special Court in respect of criminal proceedings, because that court ruled that it was not a national court but an international tribunal established by agreement between the United Nations and Sierra Leone pursuant to Security Council Resolution 1315 (2000) for the sole purpose of prosecuting persons who bear the greatest responsibility for serious violations of international humanitarian law and Sierra Leonean law committed in the territory of Sierra Leone. The Special Court, citing its Statute, Article 6(2) which provides the official position of any accused person shall not relieve such person of criminal responsibility, and referring to the *Arrest Warrant* case, held that: 'the principle of State immunity derives from the equality of States and therefore has no relevance to international criminal tribunals which are not organs of a State but derive their mandate from the international community'.[24] But it should be noted that Liberia challenged this conclusion and filed an application against Sierra Leone before the International Court of Justice asserting that the Special Court was not a UN organ,

---

[24] *Prosecutor v Charles Taylor*, Appeals Chamber, No SCSL–2003–01–I, Judgment of 31 May 2004; 128 ILR 239.

nor established as an international criminal court, and that the Special Court 'cannot impose legal obligations on States that are not parties to the Agreement between Sierra Leone and the United Nations'.[25]

It may indeed, be necessary to make a distinction between the accused State official whose claim to immunity will have no force before an international tribunal and the position of the State to which such official belongs where questions of enforcement of the tribunal's orders are concerned. Such distinctions may be particularly relevant in respect of 'mixed' or 'hybrid' courts which have been set up, that is courts whose constitution and powers are in some respects of an international character and in others of the character of the national law of a particular State; these include the Extra Chamber of Cambodia, East Timor Special Panels for Serious Crimes, the Bosnian and Serbian War Crimes Chambers, and the Special Tribunal for Lebanon (STL) (see below Ch 25, Section IV D). This last tribunal, the STL, well illustrates the mixed international and national character of its constitution: although set up by a Chapter VII Security Council Resolution, the jurisdiction of the tribunal conferred is over 'the persons responsible for the attack of 14 February 2005 resulting in the death of former Lebanese Prime Minister Rafiq Hariri and in the death or injury of other persons' and 'the provisions of the Lebanese Criminal Code relating to the prosecution and punishment of acts of terrorism, crimes and offences against life and personal integrity...' are made applicable to the prosecution of such persons for the attack.[26] It would seem that immunity is no bar to the prosecution of a crime under Lebanese law of any individual present in Lebanon and charged before the STL but enforcement against a State other than Lebanon may require its consent or a Chapter VII SC resolution.

Whether or not one characterizes the situation as one of immunity or not, that the effective operation of international tribunals remains dependent on the cooperation of States, a fact clearly recognized in the principle of complementarity and the need for an express provision relating to diplomatic and State immunity in the Rome Statute which established the International Criminal Court (ICC). Whilst providing that official status should in no case exempt a person from criminal responsibility, and that immunity based on such status should be no bar to the jurisdiction of the court (Article 27), the Rome Statute also provides that an immunity recognized by international law may continue to constitute a valid bar in a national court. By Article 98(1) of the Rome Statute, the ICC may not proceed with a request for surrender which would require the requested State to act inconsistently with its obligations with respect to the State or diplomatic immunity of a person or property of a third State unless that State agrees to cooperate. Immunity may therefore continue as a bar to surrender to the ICC in respect of States not parties to the Statute, unless, as in the proceedings relating to President Bashir of Sudan, the UN Security Council has expressly referred the issue to the ICC Prosecutor.[27] States parties

---

[25] International Court of Justice Press Release 2003/26 (5 August 2003). However, on 3 April 2006 Taylor, who had sought asylum in Nigeria, was, on the request of the new Liberian President, detained and his trial before the Special Court of Sierra Leone for crimes against humanity and war crimes is now proceeding in The Hague.

[26] UN SC Res 1757 (30 May 2007) and Agreement for the Special Tribunal for Lebanon annexed thereto.

[27] UN SC Res 1593 (31 March 2005). On 4 March 2009 the ICC issued an arrest warrant against President al-Bashir. See *Prosecutor v Omar Hassan Ahmad Al Bashir*, Pre Trial Chamber 1, 4 March 2009, Case No ICC-02/05–01/09.

to the Statute are deemed by their ratification to have waived such immunity (see further Ch 13, below, p 405).

National courts   The main significance of a plea of State immunity relates to its effect upon the jurisdiction of a national court.

2. Procedural plea not an exemption from liability

The plea is one of immunity from suit, not of exemption from law. Hence if immunity is waived the case can be decided by the application of the law in the ordinary way.[28] The underlying liability or State responsibility of the defendant State is unaffected though, as will be seen where no remedy is available in a court of the defendant State, the immunity from suit may enable liability to be avoided.

3. Adjudication and enforcement jurisdiction

A distinction is made in the plea of immunity between 'adjudication jurisdiction' and 'enforcement jurisdiction'. The application of coercive measures to a State and its property involves different and more directly intrusive mechanisms than the ruling of a municipal court as to liability. Adjudication jurisdiction relates to the court's inquiry into the claim and its adjudication by means of a judgment or declaration of the rights and obligations of the parties; it extends to interlocutory proceedings and appeal. Enforcement jurisdiction relates to the making and execution of mandatory orders or injunctions against the State in respect of, for example, attachment of property, restitution, damages, penalties, production of documents or witnesses, and accounts.

4. A plea available before all judicial and quasi-judicial tribunals

Immunity can be pleaded in any tribunal exercising judicial or quasi-judicial powers, whether in criminal, civil, family, or other matters, including administrative tribunals. The position regarding arbitration tribunals is different since they derive their authority directly from the consent of the parties. Without that consent the arbitration tribunal has no competence to determine the dispute; however, insofar as the tribunal looks to the forum State and its courts to enforce an arbitral award, the plea of State immunity may have relevance (see 'waiver', below).

5. The scope of the plea

The plea affords to a varying degree immunity to one State in respect of criminal and civil proceedings in the court of another State.

Immunity from civil proceedings   A general rule of immunity from civil jurisdiction subject to exceptions for acts of a private law or commercial nature—the restrictive doctrine—is applied in the UN Convention on State Immunity and by the United States, common law countries, and Western European States, and is considered further in Section II G. Exceptions to adjudication jurisdiction. For the current position as

---

[28] This is well illustrated by the analogous case of diplomatic immunity where in *Dickinson v Del Solar* [1930] KB 376, the court held the company who insured the driver involved in a motor accident liable under the policy to pay damages for injuries caused, notwithstanding that the driver as secretary of the Peruvian legation enjoyed diplomatic immunity.

to immunity from civil proceedings for acts in contravention of international law, see Section VI below.

Immunity from criminal proceedings   The immunity of a foreign State in respect of criminal proceedings brought in another State remains generally absolute. However, the growing consensus that perpetrators of international crimes should not go unpunished has encouraged national courts to prosecute high ranking State officials for such crimes. In 1999, in *Pinochet No 3*,[29] the Judicial Committee of the House of Lords declared that a former Head of State present in England had no immunity from extradition proceedings, brought at the request of the State of the nationality of some of the victims, relating to the alleged offence of State torture under the 1984 UN Torture Convention, that is proceedings relating to an international crime involving violation of a fundamental human right, even though committed while in office and for the purposes of the State. Following this decision, which marks a significant change in the law, proceedings have been initiated in the national courts of other countries against many high ranking officials, including serving[30] as well as former Heads of State.[31] In 2002 the International Court of Justice reaffirmed the former position by holding in the *Arrest Warrant* case that a Minister for Foreign Affairs, whether in office or no longer serving, enjoys complete immunity from criminal proceedings in a court of another State save for 'acts committed in a private capacity'. The Court emphasized that immunity does not translate into impunity and spelt out four circumstances where the immunities enjoyed by an incumbent or former Minister for Foreign Affairs (and by analogy Heads of State or Government) would not bar criminal prosecution (see further Ch 13, below, Section V). The International Court of Justice's ruling has subsequently been applied by national courts who have dismissed criminal proceedings brought against serving heads of State or government in Belgium, Spain, and the UK.[32]

6. Waiver

Since the plea of immunity acts as a personal bar *ratione personae* it may be removed by consent of the defendant State. Accordingly, if the beneficiary State waives the immunity, the national courts of the other State will have jurisdiction to proceed against it. Modern law has broadened the occasions on which consent may be given; but three conditions remain—(a) that consent to waive the immunity must be given by the State itself not by the agency or individual performing the sovereign act on the State's behalf; (b) its expression be unequivocal and certain; (c) that waiver of immunity from execution requires a separate waiver from immunity from adjudication. US law interprets these requirements to permit implied as well as express consent to waive both immunity from jurisdiction

---

[29] *R v Bow Street Metropolitan Stipendiary, ex parte Pinochet Ugarte (Amnesty International Intervening) (No 3)* [1999] UKHL 17; [2000] 1 AC 147; 119 ILR 135. See Fox, 1999.

[30] *SOS Attentat and Castelnau d'Esnault v Qadaffi, Head of State of the State of Libya*, France, Court of Cassation, criminal chamber, 13 March 2000, No 141, 124 ILR 508; the court quashed a ruling of the Paris court of appeal that absolute criminal immunity of a serving Head of State was subject to an exception in respect of a terrorist offence of use of explosives causing the destruction of an aircraft in flight and loss of life to French nationals.

[31] *Habré*, Senegal Court of Cassation, Dakar, 20 March 2001, 125 ILR 659; the Court annulled a prosecution initiated against the former President of the State of Chad for alleged complicity in acts of torture.

[32] *HAS v Ariel Sharon*, Belgian Court of Cassation, 12 February 2003, 42 ILM 596; *Application for extradition warrant for Robert Mugabe*, District Judge—Bow Street, 14 January 2004 (see Warbrick, 2004).

and from execution, but waiver of immunity from pre-judgment attachment of a State's property must be by express consent.[33] English law is narrower; it has abandoned the strict requirement that submission be made in the face of the court (to the judge hearing the case), but still requires that separate consents to both jurisdiction and execution be given in writing.[34] A general waiver of immunity is not of itself to be construed as amounting to a submission to the jurisdiction of the English courts as required by the State Immunity Act 1978 (SIA) s 2(1).[35]

Implied consent to local proceedings has been used to develop the restrictive doctrine—if the State consents to trade then it is deemed to consent to adjudication of disputes with private parties relating to such trade by the courts and law of the place where that trade is conducted. Similarly, reliance has been placed on the consent of a State contained in an arbitration agreement to support the supervision of an arbitral process by the national courts of the State where the arbitration takes place or whose law is applicable.[36] More controversial is whether consent to arbitration can be construed as consent to the execution of the award either by the courts of the State where the arbitration is held or by courts elsewhere. To avoid such fictional extensions of consent, SIA, s 9, along with other common law legislation, has enacted an express exception to immunity for proceedings which relate to an arbitration. Another argument has been put forward that implied consent justifies the removal of immunity for claims arising from the commission of war crimes and crimes against humanity, the argument being that if the State consents to acts which contravene international obligations voluntarily assumed by treaty then it must be deemed to consent to the removal of immunity for such crimes.[37] However, this line of argument has been rejected. US courts have held that the provision in the FSIA relating to implied waiver is subject to an intentionality requirement. 'Implied waiver depends upon the foreign government's having at some point indicated its amenability to suit'.[38]

F. DEFINITION OF THE FOREIGN STATE FOR THE PURPOSE OF STATE IMMUNITY

Application of a restrictive doctrine has brought about a change in focus from the person of the State to the acts performed by the State or its agents, from status to function; the question is less whether an entity established, managed, or funded by the State is immune *ratione personae* and more whether the act performed by whosoever is of governmental nature and hence immune *ratione materiae* (see also Ch 13, below, Section VI). Nonetheless the relationship between an agency and the foreign State remains important

---

[33] See US FSIA ss 1605(a)(1), 1610(a)(1) and (d)(1).

[34] Consent that UK law shall apply is not to be regarded as submission to jurisdiction (SIA s 2(2)).

[35] *Svenska Petroleum Exploration AB v Government of the Republic of Lithuania & Anor* [2006] EWCA Civ 1529 [2007] 2 WLR 876, confirming [2005] EWHC 2437 (Comm), [2006] 1 All ER 731 (Gloster J).

[36] *Creighton v Qatar*, France Court of Cassation, ch civ.1, 6 July 2000 (see Pingel, 2000). In *Orascom Telecom Holding SAE v Republic of Chad & Ors* [2008] EWHC 1841 (Comm), 2 Lll Rep [2008] 397, para 49 Stanley Burnton J refused to construe a foreign State's submission to arbitration and the signing of terms of reference containing express reference to ICC Rules Article 28(6) to constitute waiver so as to expand the waiver of immunity beyond the commercial purposes exception in SIA s 13(4).

[37] *Siderman de Blake v Republic of Argentina*, 965 F.2d 688 (9th Cir 1992); 103 ILR 454; *Princz v Federal Republic of Germany*, 26 F.3d 1166 (DC Cir 1994); 103 ILR 594.

[38] *Princz, op cit* at 1174.

in determining the extent to which immunity, and its special procedural requirements of notice of proceedings and judgments and delayed time limits, apply to State agencies. The US Act goes so far as to treat all instrumentalities and agencies as coming within the definition of a foreign State for the purposes of immunity. Other jurisdictions distinguish between the central organs or departments of government which come within the protection of State immunity and other State agencies; the UK SIA s 14(2) only confers immunity where such 'a separate entity' acts in exercise of sovereign authority and the circumstances are such that the foreign State itself would be immune. Whether the entitlement to immunity depends on the act of the agency being authorized by the State or performed in exercise of sovereign authority remains controversial; these criteria are made cumulative in the UN Convention on State Immunity which in Article 2.1(b)(iii) defines 'State' as including 'agencies or instrumentalities of the State or other entities, to the extent that they are entitled to perform and are actually performing acts in the exercise of sovereign authority'. In the English Act the central bank of a State, whether or not a department or separate entity, is treated as the State for purposes of enforcement (see SIA s 14(4)).[39]

The UN Convention's inclusion within its definition of 'State' 'representatives of the State acting in that capacity', Article 2.1(b)(iv), is likely to cause confusion, given that Article 3 states that the convention is without prejudice to the privileges of diplomatic missions, consular missions, special missions and missions to international organizations and the privileges and immunities accorded under international law to heads of State *ratione personae*. The object would seem to bring within the convention official acts performed by officials of the State on behalf of the State, and to grant immunity *ratione materiae* for such acts,[40] but to exclude, as governed by other international conventions or international customary law, the immunity *ratione personae* enjoyed by such high ranking officials by virtue of their office. The confusion may be compounded in that no exclusion is contained in the UN Convention or the accompanying Understandings relating to acts performed by the armed forces of a State, although on introducing the convention for adoption by the UNGA 6th (Legal) Committee, the Chairman of the ad hoc committee, Professor Gerhard Hafner, stated his belief that a general understanding had always prevailed that military activities were not covered by the convention and referred to the 1991 ILC Commentary on draft Article 12 (the exception relating to personal injuries and damage to property) stating it did not apply to situations of armed conflict.[41]

G. EXCEPTIONS TO ADJUDICATION JURISDICTION

In this section the exceptions to immunity from civil jurisdiction will first be outlined, followed by a discussion whether a special jurisdictional connection to the forum State

[39] See below as to immunity conferred on the property of a central bank.

[40] Cf *Propend Finance Pty* v *Sing* (1997), 111 ILR 611, 2 May 1997 the Court of Appeal held the word 'government' in SIA, s 14(1) had to be construed as affording to individual employees or officers of a foreign State protection under the same cloak as protected the State itself. The protection afforded to States by SIA would be undermined if employees or officers of the State could be sued as individuals for matters of State conduct in respect of which the State they were serving had immunity. This was affirmed in *Jones* v *Ministry of Interior for the of Kingdom of Saudi Arabia and Ors* [2006] UKHL 26, [2007] 1 AC 270, paras 30, 78.

[41] The ratifications of Norway and Sweden contain a similar declaration which excludes military activities both during an armed conflict and activities performed in the course of official duties.

is required for the exercise of jurisdiction over such non-immune activities of the foreign State.

1. The exceptions to immunity from civil jurisdiction of a foreign State

Today there is widespread acceptance that the immunity of the foreign State from adjudication jurisdiction may properly be restricted by exceptions, whereas immunity from enforcement jurisdiction remains largely absolute.

Exceptions from State immunity which are widely recognized include proceedings relating to contracts which a private party may enter or which are of a commercial nature, contracts of employment other than those with nationals of the sending State engaged in public service, immoveable property, personal injuries, or damage or loss to property of a tangible nature, and proceedings relating to the operation of sea-going ships and their cargo. The US Act stands alone in removing immunity for claims in respect of expropriation of property contrary to international law. As explained in the *Empire of Iran* case, 'the generally recognized sphere of sovereign activity' which remains immune 'includes the activities of the authorities responsible for foreign and military affairs, legislation, the exercise of police power and the administration of justice'. The main exception in the restrictive doctrine relates to commercial transactions between a private party and the foreign State (immunity is preserved where the sole parties to an agreement are States and in respect of contracts made in the territory and governed by the administrative law of the foreign State).

It has proved difficult to find a workable criterion, particularly for borderline cases, by which to distinguish a commercial transaction from one in exercise of sovereign authority. The competence of civil courts as in France is restricted to civil and commercial matters, and does not extend to public and administrative matters; it is, therefore, not too difficult to apply the civil court's criterion of an act or transaction in which an individual may engage, as opposed to 'un acte de puissance publique ou un acte qui a été accompli dans l'intérêt d'un service public' to proceedings brought against a foreign State. A reflection of this approach is to be found in Article 4 of ECSI which allows an exception for proceedings relating to an obligation of a State by virtue of a *contract*—a contract being a legal transaction in which a private person may engage. Applying the same approach to non-contractual claims, immunity was refused by the Austrian Supreme Court when sought by the United States in respect of a claim for damages arising out of a road accident due to the negligence of an embassy driver when collecting the mail of the US air attaché.[42] The court distinguished a sovereign act from a private one, such as the operation of a motor car and the use of public roads, where the relationship between the parties was on the basis of equality with no question of supremacy, rather than subordination; in applying the distinction the court looked to the nature of the act of driving as opposed to its purpose, being the collection of mail between government departments.

Common law courts are generally not of limited competence and consequently have no national practice as to what constitutes an act performable by a private person as opposed to a State. But mindful of the underlying rationale of the restrictive doctrine—that States which engage in trade should be amenable to jurisdiction—they have applied a test of commerciality in determining the non-immune nature of the proceedings. Questions

---

[42] *Holubek v The Government of United States*, Austrian Supreme Court, 10 February 1961, 40 ILR 73.

concerning contracts made in the territory of the foreign State and governed by its administrative law are expressly excluded from the commercial transaction exception in the UK SIA s 3(2).

Section 1605(a)(2) of the US FSIA removes immunity where claims are based upon a commercial activity and s 1603(d) provides that, 'The commercial character of an activity shall be determined by reference to the nature of the course of conduct or particular transaction or act, rather than by any reference to its purpose'. Commerciality is not defined by the US Act and conflicting and inconsistent decisions have been given in proceedings relating to development of natural resources, foreign assistance programmes, and government exchange control. Thus US courts have held immune the cancellation of an agreement licensing the export of rhesus monkeys,[43] and mistreatment by police resulting from a whistle-blowing complaint made in the course of employment under contract in a hospital;[44] and held non-immune a technical assistance contract under which the contractor enjoyed diplomatic immunities and tax exemption,[45] a foreign government's undertaking to reimburse doctors and the organ bank for kidney transplants performed on its nationals in US hospitals,[46] and a restriction on the payment of government-issued bonds due to a shortage of foreign reserves;[47] and evaded determining the issue whether the leasing of prisoners of war as slave labour by the Nazi regime to German industrial concerns constituted a commercial activity.[48]

To avoid such difficulties, the European Convention, the UK Act, and similar legislation of other Commonwealth States, have adopted a listing method by which proceedings relating to specific categories of commercial transactions are listed as non-immune; thus s 3 of the UK SIA lists as non-immune commercial transactions 'sale of goods or supply of services', and 'loans or other transaction for the provision of finance, guarantee or indemnity of any such transaction or of other financial obligation' (s 3(3)(a) and (b)) (such transactions are not qualified by the condition 'otherwise than in the exercise of sovereign activities)[49]; and both that Act and the 1972 European Convention also make non-immune proceedings relating to certain contracts of employment, to participation in companies or associations, and to claims relating to patents, trademarks, and other intellectual property rights (ECSI Articles 5, 6, and 8; SIA ss 4, 7, and 8). Even with this method provision has to be made for a residuary category which turns on the application of the public/private act distinction, and the cases of *I Congreso del Partido* (whether disposal of a cargo by a State agency contrary to terms of the contract of carriage on orders of the State for political reasons was immune)[50] and *Kuwait Airways Corp v Iraqi Airways Co* (whether seizure and transfer of Kuwaiti aircraft to Iraq after the invasion of Kuwait with a view to incorporation in the Iraqi civil airfleet was immune),[51] demonstrate the

---

[43] *Mol Inc v Peoples Rep of Bangladesh*, 736 F.2d 1326 (9th Cir 1994) cert denied 105 S Ct 513.

[44] *Saudi Arabia v Nelson*, 123 L Ed 2d 47 (Sup Ct 1993); 100 ILR 544.

[45] *Practical Concepts v Republic of Bolivia*, 811 F.2d 1543 (DC Cir 1987); 92 ILR 420.

[46] *Rush-Presbyterian-St Luke's Medical Center v the Hellenic Republic*, 877 F.2d 574 (7th Cir 1989) cert denied 493 US 937; 101 ILR 509.

[47] *Republic of Argentina v Weltover*, 504 US 607(1992); 100 ILR 509.

[48] *Princz v Federal Republic of Germany*, 26 F.3d 1166; (DC Cir 1994); 33 ILM 1483.

[49] *Orascom Telecom Holding SAE v Republic of Chad & Ors* [2008] EWHC 1841 (Comm) 2 Lll Rep [2008] 397, citing Lord Diplock in *Alcom Ltd v Republic of Colombia* [1984] 1 AC 580 at 603.

[50] *I Congreso del Partido* [1983] 1 AC 244; [1981] 2 All ER 1064; 64 ILR 307 (HL).

[51] *Kuwait Airways Corp v Iraqi Airways Co* [1995] 3 All ER 694; 103 ILR 340 (HL).

difficulty of distinguishing a commercial transaction from an act in exercise of sovereign authority. The accepted solution applied by English courts is to determine the nature and not the purpose of the activity. But when applied to determine the nature of use of funds in a bank account of a diplomatic embassy this test proved arbitrary; such funds could be treated as deployed on purchases of goods and services, clearly commercial acts, or more broadly for the discharge of diplomatic functions which was clearly activity in exercise of sovereign authority.[52]

Faced with these difficulties, Lord Wilberforce reformulated the test in a much cited passage:

...in considering, under the restrictive theory, whether State immunity should be granted or not, the court must consider the whole context in which the claim against the State is made, with a view to deciding whether the relevant act(s) on which the claim is based should, in that context, be considered as fairly within an area of activity, trading or commercial or otherwise of a private law character, in which the State has chosen to engage or whether the relevant activity should be considered as having been done outside the area and within the sphere of governmental or sovereign activity.[53]

Courts have relied on the passages from the *Empire of Iran* case and Lord Wilberforce's words in *I Congreso del Partido* in deciding cases both under the statute[54] and under the common law, to apply a purposive construction of the public/private criterion, referring to the whole context and the place where, the persons by whom the acts were alleged to be committed, and those who were designed to benefit from the conduct complained of. Thus, a complaint of libel contained in a report of a supervising officer of a civilian lecturer engaged to give a course to visiting US forces,[55] and a claim of medical negligence against a service doctor treating an airman on a US base in the UK,[56] although the acts by their nature were ones which a private person might commit, were held to be immune as performed in the exercise of sovereign authority by reason of the service personnel involved and the commission of the acts in pursuance of the purpose of maintaining an efficient fighting force.

The International Law Commission engaged in lengthy debate as to the extent, if at all, account should be taken, in providing a commercial transaction exception to State immunity, of its purpose as well as its nature. The final formulation appears in Article 2.2 of the UN Convention on State Immunity and reads as follows:

In determining whether a contract or transaction is a 'commercial transaction' under paragraph 1 (c), reference should be made to the nature of the contract or transaction, but its purpose should also be taken into account if the parties to the contract or transaction have so agreed, or, if in the practice of the State of the forum, that purpose is relevant to determining the non-commercial character of the contract or transaction.

---

[52] In *Alcom Ltd* v *Republic of Colombia* the Court of Appeal adopted the first view [1983] 3 WLR 906; [1984] 1 All ER 1 and the House of Lords the second [1984] AC 580; [1984] 2 WLR 750; [1984] 2 All ER 6 (HL).

[53] *I Congreso del Partido* [1983]1 AC 244; [1981] 2 All ER 1064 at 1074; 64 ILR 307 (HL).

[54] *Propend Finance Pty Ltd* v *Sing*, 111 ILR 611, 2 May 1997 (CA).

[55] *Holland* v *Lampen-Wolfe* [2000] 1 WLR 1573; [2000] 3 All ER 833; 119 ILR 367 (HL).

[56] *Littrell* v *USA (No 2)* [1994] 4 All ER 203; [1995] 1 WLR 82; 100 ILR 438 (CA).

The reference to purpose is in part designed to accommodate the concerns of certain developing States to retain immunity for contractual transactions vital to their economy or to disaster prevention or relief but it has resulted in a complex piece of drafting strengthening the defendant's immunity by which the national court may be required to engage in a four-stage exercise in determining whether it has jurisdiction in a commercial transaction under Article 2.1(c)(iii).[57] The Annex of Understandings contains nothing specific with regard to this Article and it would seem that the ambiguities present in the Article constitute an open invitation for reservation or interpretative declaration to any State proposing to give effect to the convention in its law by ratification. However it should not be forgotten that the Working Group of the ILC itself in 1999, after an exhaustive review of the whole subject, concluded that 'the distinction between the so-called nature and purpose tests might be less significant in practice than the long debate about it might imply'.[58]

In addition to the various exceptions which remove immunity for specified commercial activities, the UN Convention and State practice in legislation and court decisions allow an exception for certain non-contractual delictual activities of a foreign State. Thus, Article 12 of the 2004 UN Convention on State Immunity contains an exception from immunity in civil proceedings which 'relates to pecuniary compensation for death or injury to the person, or damage to or loss of tangible property, caused by an act or omission which is alleged to be attributable to the State, if the act or omission occurred in whole or in part in the territory of that other State, and if the author of the act or omission was present in that territory at the time of the act or omission.' Three comments are relevant to understanding the scope of this exception for delictual or tortious conduct of a foreign State. First, its scope is narrow, being confined to physical infliction of damage to the person or property; proceedings relating to false, defamatory, or negligent statements are not included and this exclusion ensures that much delictual conduct arising from complaints as to the information or publications of a foreign State remains immune. Secondly, the exception only relates to wrongful conduct of a foreign State committed in the territory of the forum State: the UK SIA s 5 merely refers to '(a) the death or personal injury; or (b) damage to or loss of tangible property, caused by act or omission in the United Kingdom'; the US FSIA s 1605(a) (5) is similar with the personal injury, death or damage to or loss of property occurring in the United States (but excludes any claim based on failure of any State official or employee to exercise or perform a discretionary function); the UN Convention Article 12, following the 1977 European Convention on State Immunity, Article 11, is even stricter, limiting proceedings to where the author is present in the forum State at the time when the facts occurred. This territorial requirement present in all conventional or legislative formulations of the exception prevents the exception's application to personal injuries inflicted abroad and restricts the exercise of extraterritorial jurisdiction over a foreign State in respect of such claims. Thirdly, the exception

---

[57] These stages being to consider the nature of the transaction, first in the absence and second in the presence of evidence of the purpose of the transaction; third, to take account of such purpose where an agreement of the parties so as to take such purpose into account is proved; and fourth to have regard to purpose if it is relevant in the practice of the forum State, *not* of its law, in determining the non-commercial character of the transaction.

[58] See A/CN.4/L.576, para 60.

in the UN Convention and common law legislation contains no requirement that the personal injury or damage to property be caused in the course of commercial activity; injury or damage resulting from an act in exercise of sovereign authority is recoverable, as for example proceedings for State-ordered assassination of a political opponent which has been held non-immune under a similar tort exception in the US FSIA. However, not all jurisdictions accept such a wide removal of State immunity for non-contractual claims; in a case relating to immunity in respect of an assault by a soldier of the foreign State while within the territory of the forum State, the European Court of Human Rights after a survey of State practice, concluded that a 'trend in international and comparative law towards limiting State immunity in respect of personal injury caused by an act or omission within the forum State' refers primarily 'to "insurable" personal injury, that is incidents arising out of ordinary traffic accidents, rather than matters relating to the core area of State sovereignty such as the acts of a soldier on foreign territory which, of their very nature may involve sensitive issues affecting diplomatic relations between States and national security.'[59]

Recently Greek and Italian courts in the *Voiotia* and *Ferrini* cases respectively have applied this exception to claims relating to war damage. These decisions have given rise to controversy resulting in an application by Germany to the ICJ that Italy has violated international law by its highest court taking jurisdiction and developing 'the contested doctrine of non-inviolability of sovereign immunity in cases of grave violation of human rights and humanitarian law'. In *Voiotia* v *Germany*, decided in 2000, the Greek Supreme Court applied a restrictive doctrine of State immunity and accepted as customary law the exception for personal injuries and damage to property set out in Article 11 of the European Convention on State Immunity, and accordingly awarded some $30 million in damages to Greek nationals for personal injuries and loss of property suffered at Distomo by reason of acts of the German occupying forces in 1944.[60] No enforcement of the Greek judgment in Greece has been obtained: the Greek Minister of Justice refused to authorize enforcement and when the matter was referred to Strasbourg the European Court of Human Rights held that Greece, in refusing to authorize enforcement, enjoyed a wide margin of appreciation, particularly in matters of foreign relations, and had acted in accordance with international law, and 'in the public interest', '*à éviter des troubles dans les relations entre la Grèce et l'Allemagne*'; and that Germany's responsibility was in no way engaged for lack of enforcement of the judgment.[61]

In 2004, in *Ferrini* the Italian Supreme Court held that the national courts had jurisdiction to permit inquiry into a claim against Germany for forcible deportation and forced labour of an Italian national by German military authorities during the Second

[59] *McElhinney* v *Ireland and the UK* [GC], no 31253/96, para 38, ECHR 2001-XI, 34 *EHRR* 13.

[60] *Prefecture of Voiotia* v *Federal Republic of Germany*, Case No 11/2000, Supreme Court, 4 May 2000, 123 ILR 513. Subsequently somewhat undermining the authority of the earlier proceedings a specially convened Constitutional Greek court competent to decide issues of international law, in a judgment of 17 September 2002 ruled that international law continues to vest foreign States with immunity when sued for acts which take place in the territory of the forum and in which its armed forces were implicated, whether or not these acts violated *jus cogens*, *Margellos* v *Federal Republic of Germany*, Case No 6/2002, Supreme Court, 17 September 2002, 129 ILR 526.

[61] *Kalogeropoulou* v *Greece and Germany* (dec), no 59021/00, ECHR 2002-X, 129 ILR 537. The German courts also held the Greek judgment unenforceable against Germany: see *Distomo Massacre Case*, Germany Federal Constitutional Court, 15 February 2006, 135 ILR 185.

World War.[62] The court relied on the *jus cogens* nature of fundamental human rights in the Italian constitution to override the defendant State's plea of immunity; it concluded that violations of fundamental human rights 'offend universal values which transcend the interests of individual national communities' and provide 'legal parameters' not solely to determine an individual's criminal liability but the State's obligation not to recognize or to lend its aid to the wrongful situation.

Whilst the application of the modern restrictive law of State immunity to events which took place 70 years ago, during an armed conflict and as conferring direct rights on individuals remains controversial,[63] the occurrence of the alleged acts in *Voiotia* and *Ferrini* within the forum State territory at least provides a jurisdictional connection on which to base the jurisdiction of the forum State's court and bring the proceedings within the exception to State immunity for personal injuries and tangible loss. That, however is not the case where the alleged acts are performed wholly within the defendant State's own territory, and in particular where such acts are in exercise of sovereign authority such as acts of the police or security forces of a State.

2. Jurisdictional connection of non-immune proceedings with the forum State

The limitation of the personal injuries exception to acts committed in the forum territory highlights the general question whether the jurisdiction of national courts over foreign States is conditional on some close link with the territory of the forum State, and whether such a link is the same or stricter than that which principles of private international law provide for civil litigation between private parties. Both the European Convention on State Immunity and the US FSIA require as regards the removal of State immunity that there be a nexus or jurisdictional connection with the forum State in respect of every exception to State immunity that they provide for. That jurisdictional connection for some exceptions, as with employment contracts and personal injuries, is stricter than those recognized in private international law for private party litigation. The UK and other common law jurisdictions which follow the SIA are alone in stipulating no additional jurisdictional link for the commercial transaction exception other than those required in ordinary litigation for the exercise of extraterritorial personal jurisdiction under Civil Procedure Rules, r 6.26 (formerly RSC Order 11, r 1) or like common law procedures. The UN Convention adopts a neutral position, referring the determination of jurisdiction over the commercial transaction exception to 'the applicable rules of private international law' of the forum State, Article 10.1, ILC Commentary to that article, paragraphs (3) and (4).

For proceedings which are clearly identical to those brought in private litigation, there may be no need to require any special additional jurisdictional link where the defendant is a foreign State. But for proceedings which relate to conflicts of jurisdiction between States, as further discussed below in Part VI, the plea of immunity at the present time serves to demarcate the limits of State jurisdiction exercisable over the public acts of another State. Until agreed rules for the allocation of jurisdiction replace the present exclusive

---

[62] *Ferrini* v *Federal Republic of Germany*, Italian Court of Cassation, Judgment No 5044 of 11 March 2004, 128 ILR 659.

[63] See Iovane, 2005; Gattini, 2005; Bianchi, 2005. Cf *FILT-CGIL Trento* v *USA*, Italian Court of Cassation, 3 August 2000, 128 ILR 644 where the fundamental rights in the Italian Constitution concerning the right to an effective remedy were held not to restrict or exclude the application of the principle of jurisdictional immunity in relation to acts performed *jure imperii*.

jurisdiction of the State over acts in exercise of sovereignty performed within its own territory, the restriction of the exception to immunity for non-contractual delictual acts to the performance of those within the territory of the forum State and indeed the general bar of State immunity is likely to remain.

H. IMMUNITY FROM EXECUTION

Unlike the restricted immunity from adjudication which it enjoys today, a foreign continues largely immune from forcible measures of execution against its person or property. Professor Sucharitkul, the ILC's Special Rapporteur has even gone so far as to describe immunity from execution as 'the last fortress...the last bastion of State immunity'.[64]

1. Immunity of the person of the State or representatives from coercive measures

Immunity from measures against the person of the State remains absolute. As recently confirmed by the International Court of Justice in the *Arrest Warrant* case, no head of State, head of government, or Minister for Foreign Affairs whilst in office may be arrested by order of the national court of another State or preliminary measures such as the issue or international circulation of an arrest warrant taken against such persons.[65] The personal immunity enjoyed by such persons while in office is an important element of the State's own immunity enabling it to function effectively. In the *Djibouti v France* case the Court laid down a requirement that 'the State which seeks to claim immunity for one of its organs is expected to notify the authorities of the other State concerned, whether through diplomatic exchanges or before a French judicial organ,' and explained that 'this would allow the court of the forum State to ensure that it does not fail to respect any entitlement to immunity and might thereby engage the responsibility of that State. Further the State notifying a foreign court that judicial process should not proceed, for reasons of immunity against its State organs, is assuming responsibility for any internationally wrongful act at issue committed by such organs'.[66] It would thereby effect a warning that any failure to respect immunity might engage the international responsibility of the forum State and further inform that State that the notifying State assumes its own responsibility for any internationally wrongful act committed by such organs.

No injunction or order for specific performance may be directed by a national court against a foreign State on pain of penalty if not obeyed. Thus the Netherlands Supreme Court has ruled that it has no jurisdiction to declare a foreign State bankrupt:

Acceptance of this jurisdiction would imply that a trustee in bankruptcy with farreaching powers could take over the administration and the winding up of the assets of a foreign power under the supervision of a Dutch public official. This would constitute an

---

[64] *YBILC* (1991), vol II (part two), p 13, Commentary to ILC Draft Articles, Article 18, para 1.

[65] *Arrest Warrant of 11 April 2000 (Democratic Republic of Congo v Belgium), Preliminary Objections and Merits, Judgment, ICJ Reports 2002,* p 3, paras 62–71; 128 ILR 1. In the *case concerning Certain Criminal Proceedings in France (Republic of Congo v France)* brought in 2003 the applicant State claims the initiation of a criminal investigation by the French court without service on the foreign State constitutes a violation of a serving Head of State's immunity.

[66] *Certain Questions of Mutual Assistance in Criminal Matters (Djibouti v France),* Judgment of 4 June 2008, para 196.

unacceptable infringement under international law of the sovereignty of the foreign State concerned.[67]

For this same reason the UK SIA s 13(1) prohibits the imposition of any penalty by way of committal or fine in respect of any failure or refusal by the State to disclose information or produce any document, and s 13(2) the giving of any relief against a State by way of injunction or order for specific performance or recovery of land or other property.

2. Immunity of State property from coercive measures

Some relaxation of immunity would seem appropriate where a judgment is rendered in respect of a non-immune commercial or private law transaction; one might expect that the restrictive doctrine would permit the local court to have jurisdiction to execute such a judgment against the property of the foreign State, by forcible means if necessary. The practice of the Swiss courts in fact endorses such an approach stressing 'the overall unity of substantive law', and that 'a judgment imports enforceability'. The Swiss Federal Tribunal has held that to refuse execution would mean that the judgment would lack its most essential attribute, namely that it will be executed even against the will of the party against which it is rendered.[68]

The practice of other States, however, remains more cautious and reflects underlying political realities that there is no international law of insolvency to resolve a State's general inability to meet its financial commitments. Rescheduling of State debt continues today as largely a political process.[69] Short of resort to war there is, therefore, little alternative where property in the control of the debtor State is concerned but to reach a settlement of judgment debts with its cooperation and by diplomatic means.

In consequence, as declared in another decision of the German Federal Constitutional Court in *The Philippine Embasssy* case '…Whilst the general rules of international law imposed no outright prohibition on execution by the State of the forum against a foreign State they do impose material limits on execution'.[70] Such limits prevent a State from levying execution on property located in its territory of the foreign State which is in use for sovereign purposes. In accordance with this decision, State practice and the UN Convention on State Immunity now recognize an exception to the general rule of immunity from execution in respect of State property in use for commercial purposes. English law now permits the recognition and enforcement of a foreign judgment given against a State, (other than the United Kingdom or the State to which that court belongs) provided the foreign court would have had jurisdiction if it had applied the United Kingdom rules on sovereign immunity set out in SIA ss 2 to 11, but execution without the consent of the State remains

---

[67] *WL Oltmans* v *The Republic of Surinam*, Netherlands Supreme Court, 28 September 1990 (1992) 23 *NYIL* 442 at 447.

[68] *Kingdom of Greece* v *Julius Bar and Co*, Swiss Federal Tribunal, 6 June 1956, 23 ILR 195. See also *United Arab Republic* v *Mrs X*, Swiss Federal Tribunal, 10 February 1960, 65 ILR 384.

[69] Following the insolvency of the Republic of Argentine creditor, States showed little enthusiasm to adopt the proposal of Gordon Brown, UK Chancellor of the Exchequer for a plan for an international bankruptcy procedure (the Jubilee Framework 2000).

[70] *The Philippine Embassy Bank Account* case, German Federal Constitutional Court, 13 December 1977, 46 *BverfGE*, 342; 65 ILR 146 at 184.

solely in respect of State property shown to be in use for commercial purposes.[71] The UN Convention on State Immunity draws a distinction, also generally recognized, between measures of enforcement against the property of a State prior to adjudication from those taken post judgment; whilst as regards both prior and post judgment the rule of immunity is absolute unless the State has consented, or allocated or earmarked the property for the satisfaction of the claim. An additional exception to immunity is permitted in respect of post judgment measures for State property which satisfies the stipulated conditions of being in commercial use, Article 19(c) (and see Section II H.6 below).

3. State property generally recognized as immune

The categories of State property which are generally recognized as in use for sovereign purposes and consequently enjoy immunity from seizure, even in the event of a general waiver by the State of its immunity from enforcement, include diplomatic and military property, and property of central banks. The UN Convention on State Immunity adds two relatively new categories, property forming part of the cultural heritage of a State or of its archives, and property forming part of an exhibition of objects of scientific, cultural, or historical interest (Articles 21(1)(d) and (e)).[72]

Property of the diplomatic mission   In *The Philippine Embasssy* case (referred to above) attachment was sought of the account of the Philippine diplomatic mission in Bonn to satisfy a judgment for unpaid rent of an office. The Vienna Convention on Diplomatic Relations Article 22.3 explicitly provides:

The premises of the mission, their furnishings and other property thereon and the means of transport of the mission shall be immune from search, requisition, attachment or execution.

Although the bank account of the mission is not expressly mentioned in this convention, State practice, confirmed by Article 21.1(a) of the UN Convention which expressly refers to 'any bank account', overwhelmingly recognizes that an account of a diplomatic mission held in a bank in the forum State enjoys immunity unless it can be affirmatively shown that the sums deposited have been specifically allocated to meet commercial commitments.

Military property   Ships of war were recognized to be immune from local jurisdiction from the eighteenth century or earlier, but the modern category of military property, as defined in the UN Convention on State Immunity as 'property of a military character or used or intended for use in the performance of military functions' (Article 21(1)(b)), is capable of a wider meaning.[73] The US Act adopts a similar definition of property used

---

[71] Civil Jurisdiction and Judgments Act 1982 s.31, *NML Capital Ltd* v *The Republic of Argentina* [2009] 1 Lloyd's Rep 378, reversed [2010] EWCA Civ 41. For registration of a judgment against the UK see SIA Part II ss 18–19; no procedure is available for registration of a judgment given by a court against a State to which that court belongs *AIC Ltd* v *Federal Government of Nigeria and Attorney-General of Federation of Nigeria* [2003] EWHC 1357 (QB), 129 ILR 871.

[72] The immune categories may lose their immunity by express consent or specific allocation.

[73] The UNGA Ad Hoc Committee decided in view of the uncertainty of the law to exclude aircraft and space objects by stating in article 3 that the 2004 UN Convention is without prejudice to the immunities enjoyed by a State under international law with respect to aircraft and space objects owned or operated by a State. This would seem to exclude this type of State property from the category of military property declared immune in article 19.(1)(c).

or intended to be used 'in connection with a military activity', which, the House Report explains, includes not only all types of armaments and their means of delivery but also basic commodities such as food, clothing and fuel to keep a fighting force operative.[74] The existence of such an immune category exposes sales of military equipment to a plea of immunity from jurisdiction. Such a possibility would seem to be avoided in English law and come within the s 3 definition of a commercial transaction provided the sale is in ordinary private law form and not pursuant to an agreement between States.

Central bank property   As regards the property of a central bank, the practice under US and UK legislation and some other States, though some countries have no specific rules on the matter, supports immunity from execution of property of a central bank where that bank performs the functions of a central as opposed to commercial bank; China recently has adopted legislation conferring similar immunity from 'measures of constraint such as attachment and execution' on the property of foreign central banks unless there has been express waiver in writing or allocation of the property.[75] Article 19(1)(c) of the UN Convention on State Immunity is in line with this practice when it provides that property of the central bank or other monetary authority of the State shall be immune and not treated as property in use or intended commercial use unless the State has expressly consented in writing or specifically allocated or earmarked such property to satisfy the judgment. In a case relating to the of State property held by a private corporation in the name of the State's central bank the English court construed the term 'property of the State' in the SIA 'include all real and personal property and will embrace any right, interest, legal, equitable or contractual in assets that might be held by a State or any 'emanation of the State' or central bank or other monetary authority that comes within sections 13 and 14 of the Act.'[76] Recently the placing of excess foreign exchange reserves in Sovereign Wealth Funds by certain States, often with a declared purpose of their 'use for future generations', has raised issues relevant to their enjoyment of immunity from execution, particularly where invested in equities, derivatives or short term commercial assets (Truman, 2007). Such Funds whether held in the name of the State or its central Bank currently enjoy, under US, UK, and Chinese legislation and the UN Convention, complete immunity from enforcement measures. Where, however, such a fund is deployed for the purpose of wealth enhancement by 'playing the markets', it would seem, at least as regards the fees of brokers, banks and other third parties which such transactions generate, that for the purposes of attachment these credits in the funds might be treated as for commercial purposes despite the overall long term intention of the fund to serve as a reserve for the State and its people.

Cultural heritage of the State   The two new categories in the UN Convention relating to protection of property forming part of the cultural heritage of a State not intended for sale and State property on loan for exhibition purposes would seem desirable to encourage exchange solely for purposes of exhibition, and to deter pillage and illegal export of a

---

[74] FSIA s 1611(b)(2); Legislative History of the Foreign Sovereign Immunities Act 1976, House Report No 94–1487, 94th Cong, 2nd Sess 12 reproduced in (1976) 15 ILM 1398 at 30–31.

[75] Law of the People's Republic of China on Judicial Immunity from Measures of Constraint for the property of foreign central banks adopted on 25 October 2005.

[76] *AIG Capital Partners Inc & Anor* v *Kazakhstan (National Bank of Kazakhstan intervening)* [2006] 1 WLR 1420; 129 ILR 589.

country's scientific, cultural or historical treasures. As to the first category, the subject is complicated by applicable laws of ownership, State regulation of privately owned national treasures, and claims of individuals to property expropriated in time of armed conflict.[77] Where the presence of cultural objects is restricted to their temporary public exhibition State practice seems more favourable to conferment of immunity; in 2004 the Swiss Ministry of External Affairs declared that cultural property of a State on exhibition was immune and overruled a court order on the application of a creditor of Russia, the Swiss trading company NOGA for the seizure of paintings from the Moscow's Pushkin Museum on exhibition in Switzerland and ordered their return to Russia.[78] The US Immunity Seizure Act of 1966 and the UK Tribunals and Courts Act 2007 Part 6 confer protection from seizure or attachment on objects in possession of a foreign State sent for exhibition subject to prior notification of their intended exhibition, though the UK Act does not bar museums in the UK or lenders being subject to proceedings, other than specific restitution, in respect of exhibited works of art.

Apart from these accepted categories of immune property State practice in determining when a foreign State's property is in commercial use and subject to execution remains diverse. Whereas it is relatively easy to determine that a seagoing vessel equipped with guns and manned by personnel of a State's navy is not to be treated as property in commercial use, it is much more difficult to ascertain the character of funds held in the name of a State. Three particular problems arise—what evidence is available to establish intended commercial use of State property? How are mixed funds held both for commercial and sovereign purposes to be treated? And is the property to be attached to have a connection with the subject matter of the claim which it is sought to satisfy?

4. Proof of use for sovereign purposes

In answer to the first question, the evidence and burden of proof, in the *Philippine Embassy* case the German court considered that it would constitute interference contrary to international law in matters within the exclusive competence of the sending State for any inquiry, beyond obtaining the Ambassador's certificate, to be instituted as to the intended use of funds held in a mission's bank account. A similar position prevails in English law. By s 13(4) of the UK SIA, property in use or intended use for commercial purposes is made subject to attachment; s 17 defines 'commercial purposes' to mean 'purposes of such transactions or activities as are mentioned in section 3(3)', that is, use in relation to a sale of goods or supply of services, a transaction for provision of finance or a commercial, industrial, professional, or industrial activity. In a case seeking attachment of a diplomatic mission's account for unpaid surveillance equipment, the English Court of Appeal construed the statutory words 'intended use for commercial purposes' as covering commercial transactions entered into by the Ambassador; but the House of Lords declared the current account of a foreign diplomatic mission was held for the sovereign purpose of meeting the expenses of the mission and was not susceptible of anticipatory dissection into the various

---

[77] The ruling by the US Supreme Court in *Republic of Austria* v *Altmann* (2004) 541 US 677 that there was no limitation on the retroactive operation of the FSIA, renders applicable the restrictive doctrine including the expropriation exception to State immunity in s 1605(a)(3) to such claims for war damage. In that case Austria sought to rely on the rule of absolute immunity in force prior to 1952 as a bar to a claim by the owner of several Klimt paintings confiscated by the Nazis and exhibited by the Austrian national gallery.

[78] RSDIE 14 (2004) 674.

uses, commercial as well as sovereign, to which monies drawn on it might be used in the future. Only specific earmarking of a fund for present or future commercial use, the House of Lords held, would meet the exception to immunity from execution provided in the SIA for commercial property in use or intended use for commercial purposes (SIA s 13(4)).[79] A modification of this strict requirement was permitted in *Orascom*; a London bank account (not of the diplomatic mission) into which the oil revenues of a foreign State were paid for the purpose of discharging a commercial debt owed to World Bank with the surplus, if any, to be held for general use including sovereign purposes, was treated as an account for commercial purposes and non-immune.[80]

5. Mixed bank accounts

This English decision also provides the answer to the second question relating to mixed accounts: funds held for both sovereign and commercial purposes in a mission's bank account remain immune unless a specific account is opened or specific allocation made for a commercial purpose. This ruling has had its critics. A US District Court allowed attachment of a mixed diplomatic bank account; exemption of mixed accounts would in the court's view create a loophole, for any property could be made immune by using it, at one time or other, for some minor public purpose.[81] A later court however refused attachment of a mixed bank account holding that such attachment would be contrary to the United States' obligation under Article 25 of the Vienna Convention on Diplomatic Relations to afford full facilities to the diplomatic mission of a sending State; and the US President, even in the face of federal legislation removing immunity from execution of property where judgment was obtained against commercial property of a foreign State designated as a State sponsor of terrorism, has by exercise of his waiver, preserved the immunity of mixed accounts of diplomatic missions in the United States.[82]

6. The requirement of a connection between the State property to be attached and the subject matter of the proceedings

On the third issue, there is a division in State practice. In addition to being located within the United States and used for commercial activity, the US FSIA requires that the State property 'is or was used for the commercial activity upon which the claim was based' (s 1610(a)(2)). This restriction, which is not one the UK SIA requires, serves two purposes; it ensures that execution of State property only takes place in respect of commercial activity which pursuant to an earlier section in the FSIA is within an exception to immunity and for which consequently the US courts have jurisdiction. Secondly it limits the property to satisfy the judgment to resources of the State already committed to the non-immune transaction. This requirement of a connection between the property and the claim restricts considerably the scope of the execution permitted against the property of a foreign State. It is to be noted that the US FSIA only imposes the connection condition when execution is sought against a State, but not as against a State agency or instrumentality. In this

---

[79] *Alcom v Republic of Colombia* [1984] AC 580; [1984] 2 WLR 750; [1984] 2 All ER 6 (HL).

[80] *Orascom Telecom Holding SAE v Republic of Chad & Ors* [2008] EWHC 1841 (Comm); 2 Lll Rep [2008] 397. To the same effect, *EM Ltd v Republic of Argentina* 473 F 3d 463 (2d Cir 2007).

[81] *Birch Shipping Corp v Embassy of United Republic of Tanzania*, 507 F.Supp 311 (DDC 1990); 63 ILR 524.

[82] *Flatow v Republic of Iran*, 74 F.2d Supp 18 (DDC 19 December 1999). See Murphy, 2002, pp 70–77 and Murphy, 2005, pp 66–81.

event all property used for commercial activity is permitted.[83] Where, however, the acts are of a tortious nature as in the exception for personal injuries, there is unlikely to be any prior commitment of resources of the State to those acts, with the consequence that, as the Second Circuit Appeals Court held, the connection requirement in the FSIA 'create[s] a right without a remedy'.[84]

In respect of State property but not the property of a State agency, French law imposes a similar requirement of a connection between the property to be attached and the subject matter of the claim, but enlarges it to include prejudgment by '*saisie conservatoire*'.[85] As confirmed in *Sonatrach* 'the assets of a foreign State are in principle not liable (subject to) seizure, subject to exceptions in particular where they have been allocated for an economic or commercial activity under private law which is at the origin of the title of the attaching debtor'.[86] The UN Convention on State immunity's provision dealing with this issue was much debated and Article 19(c) makes post-judgment measures against the property of the State subject to three requirements: the property is to be (i) in use or intended use by the State for other than governmental non-commercial purposes; (ii) in the territory of the forum State; and (iii) to have a connection with the entity against which the proceeding was directed. This article is accompanied by three annexed understandings defining 'entity' as one enjoying independent legal personality, 'property' as 'broader than ownership or possession' and in order to prevent evasion of the State of its liability to meet its judgments, reserves the position under national laws as to 'piercing the veil'.

Thus, to sum up, the original absolute rule relating to immunity from execution for State property has been replaced, at any rate in the practice of western industrialized States, by three rules—the general rule is now confined to the exempt categories and other property in public use; there is a second rule providing no immunity for State property in commercial use; and the property of separate entities of the State in general enjoys no immunity from execution.

III. THE OTHER TWO AVOIDANCE TECHNIQUES

A. ACT OF STATE

In accordance with the principles of private international law the applicable law will generally be the law of the State in whose territory the act takes place and the defence of act of State broadly provides an application of those principles to legislative or governmental acts affecting title to private property, moveable or immoveable, located within the territory of another State.

The principle enunciated in *Underhill* v *Hernandez*[87] that the courts of one State will not sit in judgment on the acts of the government of another done within its territory provides a further ground for imposing restraint on the English court. Thus in the leading case of

---

[83] US FSIA s 1610(b)(2).

[84] *Letelier* v *Republic of Chile*, 748 F.2d 790 (2nd Cir 1984) at 798; 63 ILR 378.

[85] *Islamic Republic of Iran* v *Eurodif*, Court of Appeal, Paris, 21 April 1982, 65 ILR 93, Court of Cassation, 14 March 1984, JDI 1984 598; 77 ILR 513.

[86] *Societe Sonatrach* v *Migeon*, France, Court of Cassation, 1 October 1985 rev crit 1986, 526, (1987) 26 ILM 998; 77 ILR 525.

[87] *Underhill* v *Hernandez* 168 US 250 (1897).

Luthor v *Sagor* the English court upheld the validity of an expropriatory decree relating to timber situated in Russia of the newly established Soviet government. The governmental nature of the act performed by a foreign sovereign State was clearly a factor deterring the court from inquiry into the validity of the expropriation, with Scrutton LJ considering it would be 'a serious breach of international comity' to postulate that its legislation is 'contrary to essential principles of justice and morality'.[88] Later cases held the rule of recognition of foreign decrees applied to aliens as well as to nationals of the foreign State.[89] The act of State defence is subject to exceptions, which are comprehensively covered by the general statement that the English court will not enforce a foreign government act if it is contrary to public policy. It is established that public policy prevents the court from enforcing the penal or fiscal laws of another country[90] or discriminatory legislation directed against particular individuals or a particular class of individuals. In *Oppenheimer* v *Cattermole*[91] a Nazi decree of 1941 which deprived all Jews outside Germany of their German nationality, was declared *obiter dicta* to be contrary to public policy as legislation in contravention of fundamental human rights. At this point questions of non-justiciability impinge; whether an exception to the act of State rule is permitted depends not merely on the issue being contrary to public policy but also a justiciable issue. Recently in *Kuwait Airways Corp* v *Iraqi Airways Co (No 2)* to be discussed below, the House of Lords have confirmed that the exception to the act of State rule as contravening public policy is not confined to a foreign State's acts in contravention of fundamental human rights but also extends to legislation of a foreign State contrary to fundamental and well-established principles of international law. In doing so the Lords narrowed the scope of non-justiciability.

B. NON-JUSTICIABILITY

Non-justiciability remains today a doctrine of uncertain scope. It may be raised as a plea in proceedings whether or not a foreign State is itself made a party to them, and may be dealt with as a preliminary issue, but being highly fact specific it may not be possible to decide such issues until after disclosure or even until trial. In origin it operated in a manner similar to a plea of immunity barring further inquiry into matters falling within another State's jurisdiction or for international settlement. In the *Buttes Gas* case Lord Wilberforce sought to formulate non-justiciability into a distinct doctrine.[92]

The *Buttes Gas* case concerned a defamation action between companies in which, if it were to proceed, in the House of Lords' view, the English court would have to make a determination on a disputed maritime boundary between foreign States, involving a series of inter-State transactions from 1969 to 1973, of States' motives and the lawfulness of actions taken by Sharjah, and possibly Iran and the United Kingdom. Lord Wilberforce in the single judgment of the court declared:

They have only to be stated to compel the conclusion that these are not issues on which a municipal court can pass. Leaving aside all possibility of embarrassment in our foreign

---

88 *Luther* v *Sagor* [1921] 3 KB 532 (CA).
89 *In re the Claim of Helbert Wagg & Co Ltd* [1956] 1 Ch 323; [1956] 1 All ER 129.
90 *Government of India, Ministry of Defence (Revenue) Division* v *Taylor* [1955] 1 All ER 292.
91 *Oppenheimer* v *Cattermole* [1976] AC 249; [1975] 1 All ER 538.
92 *Buttes Gas and Oil Company* v *Hammer* [1982] AC 888 at 938; [1981] 3 All ER 616 at 628 (HL).

relations... there are, to follow the Fifth Circuit Court of Appeals [in litigation on the same matter brought in the US courts], no judicial or manageable standards by which to judge these issues or to adopt another phrase,... the court would be in judicial no man's land: the court would be asked to review transactions in which four foreign States were involved, which they had brought to a precarious settlement, after diplomacy, and the use of force, and that at least part of these were 'unlawful' under international law. I would just add, in answer to one of the respondents' arguments, that it is not to be assumed that these matters have now passed into history so that they now can be examined with safe detachment.[93]

Lord Wilberforce in *Buttes* brought together a number of separate strands of legal authority relating to the English court's treatment of 'the transactions of foreign States' which contributed to his general principle of judicial restraint or abstention. These strands of authority are very diverse; some authorities relate to constitutional division of powers between the branches of central government, with the courts having no competence where the legislature enacts laws to give effect to treaty provisions and the executive negotiates and ratifies treaties, declares war, and recognizes States and the diplomats who represent them. These constitutional limits on the competence of the judicial branch of government continue in effect today but the other strand of authority supporting the proposition that 'transactions of independent States are governed by other laws than those which municipal courts administer'[94] has undergone considerable modification with the reception of European Community and human rights law. Whilst Lord Wilberforce's ruling that courts must declare non-justiciable matters continues to apply to international relations which depend on diplomacy, countermeasures, and sanctions, and the use of force for their resolution, in situations where State practice has been reduced to a generally accepted and certain rule, though of international rather than municipal law, English courts may find sufficient judicial and manageable standards to determine the issues. In the words of Lord Nicholls, the principle of non-justiciability does not 'mean that the judiciary must shut their eyes to a breach of an established principle of international law committed by one State against another when the breach is plain and indeed acknowledged.' As Lord Hope in the same case stated 'restraint is what is needed, not abstention'.[95]

Thus where the issues relate purely to transactions between foreign States operating solely on the international plane, as they did in *Buttes* case the court will declare the issues as non justiciable: so in the *Petrotimor* case the Australian High Court rejected a claim of expropriation on the ground that the alleged concession granted by Portugal required examination of the international law relating to the legality of Indonesia's acquisition of East Timor and the sovereign right of Australia over the seabed.[96] Similarly where a declaration was sought from the English court that military action in Iraq would be in breach of international law unless expressly authorized by a second UN resolution Simon Brown LJ refused to entertain the application saying that in the case 'there is... no point of reference in domestic law to which the international law issue can be said to go; there is nothing here susceptible of challenge in the way of the determination of rights, interests

93 *Op cit* [1982] AC 888 at 893; [1981] 3 All ER 616 at 633.
94 *Cook* v *Sprigg* [1899] AC 572 (PC); *Sec of State in Council of India* v *Kamachee Boye Sahaba* (1859) 7 Moo Ind App 476.
95 *Kuwait Airways Corp* v *Iraqi Airways Co* [2002] UKHL 19, 16 May 2002, paras 26 and 141.
96 *Petrotimor Petroleos Companhia de Petroleos SARL* v *Commonwealth of Australia* [2003] 126 FCR 354.

of duties under domestic law to draw the court into the field of international law'. He later expressed the point thus: 'Here there is simply no foothold in domestic law for any ruling to be given on international law'.[97] But where the determination of rights, interests or duties under domestic law requires the court to consider issues of international law non-justiciability may provide no bar to the court's exercise of jurisdiction, as in the case of the *AY Bank* where the issue was the correct valuation according to principles of English banking law of a debt in an English bank, the sharing of which between the successors to Yugoslavia had been determined by an international treaty.[98] A further illustration is provided by *Occidental Exploration & Production Company* v *Republic of Ecuador* where objection to the English court's jurisdiction to interpret an arbitration award was made on the ground that it required the English court to interpret provisions of the bilateral investment treaty between the USA and Ecuador; rejecting the objection based on non justiciability, Mance LJ said:

The case is not concerned with an attempt to invoke at a national legal level a Treaty which operates only at the international level. It concerns a Treaty intended by its signatories to give rise to rights in favour of private investors capable of enforcement, to an extent specified by the Treaty wording, in consensual arbitration against one or other of its signatory States.[99]

The operation of the rule of non-justiciability is well illustrated by a request to the UK government for diplomatic protection by a British national captured in Afghanistan, and detained as an illegal combatant at Guantanamo Bay in Cuba without charge or legal representation by the United States. In *Abbasi* the Court of Appeal held that the legitimate expectation of a citizen that, if subjected abroad to a violation of a human right, his government would exercise measures of diplomatic protection was a justiciable issue; the duty to provide diplomatic protection was justiciable but the government enjoyed wide discretion, by reference to the gravity of the violation and to foreign policy considerations, in deciding whether and in what manner to grant such protection.[100]

IV. THE THREE AVOIDANCE TECHNIQUES COMPARED

The pleas are related one to the other. Respect for the independence and equality of a foreign State when it is a party to proceedings is achieved by a plea of State immunity which brings the case to a halt. Where the proceeding is between private parties such an immediate halt will only take place if by reason of the non-justiciability of the issues to be determined the court decides that it had no competence to decide them. In cases where

---

[97] *R* v *Prime Minister of the United Kingdom, ex parte Campaign for Nuclear Disarmament* [2002] EWHC 2777, paras 36 and 40. See also *Gentle & Anor, R (on the application of)* v *Prime Minister & Ors* [2006] EWCA Civ 1689, paras 26–34; *Al-Haq* [2009] EWHC 1910 (Admin).

[98] *AY Bank Ltd (in liquidation)* v *Bosnia and Herzegovina & Ors* [2006] EWHC 830; [2006] 2 All ER Comm 463.

[99] *Occidental Exploration and Production Co* v *Republic of Ecuador* [2005] EWCA Civ 1116, [2006] QB 432, [2006] 2 WLR 70, para 37.

[100] *R (on the application of Abbasi)* v *Sec of Foreign and Commonwealth Affairs and Sec of Home Office* [2002] EWCA Civ 1598, [2003] UKHRR 76, 6 November 2002.

the proceedings between private parties progresses to examination of the substantive law, the court may also conclude that it has no judicial or manageable standards by which to decide the issues and declare them non-justiciable; alternatively it may accept a plea of act of State and decide that the recognition of the validity of a foreign State's governmental act deprives the claim of any basis for its assertion. Thus by accepting a plea of act of State the English court goes some way to endorsing the validity of the act of the foreign State whereas in immunity the court remains neutral, merely deciding that it is not the appropriate forum. In exceptional cases, as illustrated by the case now to be discussed, where the foreign State's acts constitute a gross violation of a fundamental principle of international law, the forum court assumes jurisdiction over matters normally within the territorial jurisdiction of the other State; exceptionally it will then determine the issues by reference to international law.

The case of *Kuwait Airways* illustrates the operation of the three pleas, but also in allowing an exception to the doctrines of act of State and non-justiciability where a clear and generally accepted violation of international law is established, raises the question whether the plea of immunity should also allow an exception for acts constituting a gross violation of a fundamental rule of international law. In that case Kuwait Airways (KAC) brought proceedings in the English court against Iraq and Iraqi Airways (IAC) for their removal and detention of 10 Kuwaiti civilian aircraft following the invasion and occupation of Kuwait by Iraq in 1990. In the first phase of the litigation the defendants, the Republic of Iraq and the State agency, IAC pleaded immunity. The plea was successful against Iraq by reason of procedural inability to serve the process; it was also successful against IAC in respect of the initial seizure and removal of the 10 civilian aircraft to Iraq on the grounds that these acts were performed in exercise of governmental authority *jure imperii*, namely the prosecution of aggression, and by SIA s 14(2) a State entity enjoys the same immunity as the State where it performs acts in exercise of sovereign authority.[101] But a majority of the Lords held IAC not entitled to immunity once Iraq enacted expropriatory legislation transferring title from KAC to IAC; it considered IAC was then acting on its own account conducting the ordinary commercial operation of a civilian airline. Accordingly, a second set of proceedings was brought by KAC claiming against IAC damages for conversion of the ten Kuwaiti aircraft by their incorporation into the Iraqi commercial fleet; IAC pleaded act of State and non-justiciability. IAC claimed that the applicable law to govern title in the expropriated aircraft was the law of the State in whose territory they were located and by legislation of that State, Resolution 369 enacted by the Iraqi Revolutionary Command Council, title had been vested in IAC. Whilst accepting that the situation fell within the scope of the act of State doctrine given that the validity of Iraqi legislation within the territory of Iraq was at issue, the Lords took the view that public policy required an exception to be made because Resolution 369, along with Iraq's seizure of the planes, constituted 'a gross violation of established rules of international law of fundamental importance'; there was universal consensus as to its illegality and clear evidence that recognition of its

---

[101] *Kuwait Airways Corp v Iraqi Airways Co*, 3 July 1992, Evans J [1995] 1 Lloyd's Rep 25 (CA); [1995] 3 All ER 694; 103 ILR 340 (HL). See Staker, 1995; O'Keefe, 2002. Following dismissal of a petition to the House of Lords to vary this judgment on the ground that evidence of IAC witnesses was perjured, *Kuwait Airways Corp v Iraqi Airways (No 2)* [2001] 1 WLR 439, in new proceedings IAC's dealings with the Kuwaiti aircraft have been held to have been at all times of a commercial nature *Kuwait Airways Corp v Iraqi Airways Co* [2003] EWHC 31 (Comm), 24 January 2003.

validity would be contrary to the UK's international obligations. Accordingly the Lords determined that IAC's acts incorporating the aircraft into its civil airline constituted conversion of assets belonging to KAC.[102]

The judgment breaks new ground being 'the first decision to hold that acts of a foreign State within its territory may be refused recognition because they are contrary to international law'.[103] The consequences of that refusal of recognition go beyond a mere declaration of invalidity; the Lords refused to recognize the law which private international law rules identified as the proper law to determine both the tortious nature of the act and the ownership of the aircraft, being the law where the act was committed and the *lex situs*, the law where the title was transferred.

The judgment in *Kuwait Airways*, in its application to expropriation in time of armed conflict, raises difficult issues of applicable law relating to property. Whilst there were strong grounds of public policy to give effect to the international condemnation of Iraq's action in looting the aircraft, the application of public international law, unlike private international law rules, provides little guidance as to the detailed consequences in municipal law on acts held contrary to international law. It may be that the proper law of the whole transaction, once the Iraqi legislation was struck down, was the law of Kuwait. But the Lords' decision made no reference to the law of Kuwait. The English court, which itself had no substantive connection with the claim—the original taking was from Kuwait, the alleged conversion in Iraq—it would seem, by reference to English law, construed the conduct of IAC as tortious and a deprivation of property although Iraqi law held it to be lawful and IAC to be the owner.

As regards fundamental human rights violations, the choice of an applicable municipal law may be less acute in that for States which have ratified them international human conventions provide a set of rules for the consequences of such violations but, as shown by the rejection by the House of Lords of a claim for reparation by the victims of alleged torture committed in a State prison, problems still remain as to the jurisdiction and cause of action exercisable by a national court in respect of such violations committed within the territory of another State, as seen in the case of *Jones v Minister of Interior of Kingdom of Saudi Arabia* considered further below.

V. THE ARGUMENTS FOR AND AGAINST THE USE OF AVOIDANCE TECHNIQUES

Three main grounds are given for the grant of immunity to foreign States: first, that the national court has no power of enforcement of its judgments against a foreign State; secondly, that the independence and equality of States prevents the exercise of jurisdiction by the courts of one State over the person, acts, and property of another State; and thirdly, that foreign States ought properly to enjoy a like immunity to that accorded by national courts to their own forum State. Additional grounds are found in the territoriality of the jurisdiction of the courts of the receiving State and on reciprocity and international comity.

---

[102] *Kuwait Airways Corp v Iraqi Airways Co* [2002] UKHL 19, 16 May 2002.
[103] *Op cit* per Lord Steyn at para 114.

As shown above, the first ground is in part contradicted by modern State practice whereby the forum State authorities execute validly obtained judgments against State property in commercial use. Whilst the third ground provides support for a general application of the rule of law, to impose on another State without its consent the constitutional restraints of municipal law which the forum State accepts smacks of a new sort of paternal imperialism.

This leaves as the main justification the second ground, the independence and equality of States. These attributes of the State were a foundation of the Westphalian system of international law which was built on the recognition and equal status of countries with defined territorial boundaries exercising State power. Whilst the competing interests of States, who differ sharply as to their internal policies, religion or culture, may be met by the use of the avoidance techniques which we have been discussing, such techniques arguably take little account of the interests of the individual or the larger concerns of the international community as a whole. International immunities of States and the pleas of State immunity and non-justiciability based on them have consequently come under attack both as contrary to the administration of justice of national courts and as conferring impunity from violations of international law.

VI. CHALLENGES TO IMMUNITY AND JUDICIAL RESTRAINT

A. AS AN OBSTACLE TO THE ADMINISTRATION OF JUSTICE

Before assessing whether the independence and equality of States continues today as a justification for international immunities of States, let us consider the strength of these challenges. As an obstacle to the administration of justice in national courts, objection may be based on the formulation and operation of the rule itself; the unsatisfactory nature of the restrictive doctrine may be criticized as one based on a distinction lacking objective content and provoking conflicting decisions even among courts of the same country. In particular the commercial transaction exception is attacked as logically unsound, strait-jacketing all State activity into a two-fold distinction of public and private acts— how should a State grant of a scholarship to a student be categorized?—and as one which penalizes a State for using private-law forms for its activities. But such criticism may be too facile; many rules of law are difficult to apply in borderline cases but work perfectly satisfactorily for the ordinary run of cases.

A second attack on the rule of State immunity as an obstacle to the administration of justice is based on the procedural right of access to justice granted by Article 14 of the International Convention on Civil and Political Rights 1966 which, in the determination of a criminal charge, confers a right to 'a fair and public hearing by a competent, independent and impartial tribunal established by law,' and by Article 6 of the European Convention on Human Rights 1950 which, 'in the determination of his civil rights and obligations and of any criminal charge against him' confers on everyone a right to 'a fair and public hearing within a reasonable time by an independent and impartial tribunal'. On this ground the procedural right of access to court State immunity has been challenged in the European Court of Human Rights in regard to three separate types of claim: alleged torture committed abroad in a prison of the foreign State (*Al-Adsani v UK*); assault by a soldier of the foreign State while within the territory of the forum State (*McElhinney v Ireland*); and discrimination on the basis of sex for appointment to a post in a foreign embassy (*Fogarty v UK*). In all three cases it was contended that the national courts had wrongly applied immunity to bar access to a national court and its exercise of jurisdiction. Relying on Article 6(1) of the European Convention of Human Rights, the Court in all three cases confirmed its previous ruling that 'a State could not, without restraint or control by the convention enforcement bodies, remove from the jurisdiction of the courts a whole range of civil claims or confer immunities from civil liability on large groups or categories of persons'. But it distinguished State immunity from immunities imposed by a single municipal law: in *Al-Adsani v UK* it held that State immunity was a part of the body of relevant rules of international law which the Convention as a human rights treaty must take into account; the Convention 'cannot be interpreted in a vacuum' and must 'so far as possible be construed in harmony with other rules of international law of which it forms part including those relating to the grant of State immunity'. The Court declared:

Sovereign immunity is a concept of international law, developed out of the principle *par in parem non habet imperium*, by virtue of which one State shall not be subject to the jurisdiction of another State. The court considers that the grant of immunity to a State in civil proceedings pursues the legitimate aim of complying with international law to promote comity and good relations between States through the respect of another State's sovereignty.[104]

However, whilst holding that State immunity could not be struck down as contrary to the right of access to a court, the European Court held it to be always necessary to ensure that the barring of a civil right was not disproportionate to the legitimate aim which State immunity pursues. The Court held that none of the individual claims came within recognized exceptions to State immunity and that the plea on the facts in each case was legitimate and proportionate: the exception for proceedings for personal injuries was generally intended to cover 'insurable' business acts of a State such as traffic accidents occurring within the forum State's territory, and did not include torture in a foreign prison; an act of a visiting member of the armed forces of another country was clearly an act *jure imperii*; and a claim for discrimination in recruitment of staff to an embassy, as opposed to a claim for compensation for wrongful dismissal, equally fell within a State's exercise of authority. Nonetheless the majority of nine to eight judges in favour in *Al-Adsani* was very slim; to satisfy the Court in future that a ban on civil proceedings against a foreign State for torture pursues a legitimate aim in a proportionate manner it may be necessary for the forum State to identify some alternative means available to the victim or the relatives for investigation of the alleged human rights violations. A number of cases in the English court have challenged a plea of immunity by a State as disproportionate but none to date so far have been successful.[105]

---

[104] *Al-Adsani v UK* [GC] no 35763/97, ECHR 2001-XI, 34 *EHRR* 11, paras 54–55. The other two decisions are *Fogarty v UK* [GC], no 37112/97, ECHR 2001-XI, 34 *EHRR* 12 and *McElhinney v Ireland and the UK* [GC], no 31253/96, ECHR 2001-XI, 34 *EHRR* 13.

[105] *Grovit v De Nederlandsche Bank NV* [2005] EWHC 2994 (QB) [2006] 1 WLR 3323; [2007] EWCA Civ; *AIG Capital Partners Inc & Anor v Kazakhstan* [2005] EWHC 2239 (Comm); [2006] 1 All ER (Comm) 1.

B. AS CONFERRING IMPUNITY FOR VIOLATION OF INTERNATIONAL LAW

Challenge to the rule of State immunity has also been made on the ground that it confers impunity from violation of international law. The English court's greater willingness to apply international law as demonstrated by the *Kuwait Airways* case provides support for a challenge now emerging which maintains that the avoidance techniques described above should provide no bar to adjudication by the national courts of the forum State of activities of a foreign State which are contrary to international law. One way of formulating this challenge is in terms of *jus cogens*, or peremptory norms of international law which by reason of their superior status override the bar of immunity so as to permit the adjudication of their violation by national courts. The extent of such primacy or overriding effect remains uncertain. A distinction was drawn by the Strasbourg Court in the three cases referred to above between substantive and procedural norms, and applied as regards the procedural right of access to justice derived from human rights conventions. This distinction was applied by the English court in refusing to set aside a plea of State immunity in a claim brought by British nationals for alleged acts of torture committed in a Saudi prison and on the orders of the Minister of Saudi Arabia. In *Jones v Ministry of Interior of the Kingdom of Saudi Arabia*, Lord Hoffman explained the distinction: 'To produce a conflict with state immunity, it is therefore necessary to show that the prohibition on torture has generated an ancillary procedural rule which, by way of exception to state immunity entitles or perhaps requires states to assume civil jurisdiction over other states in cases in which torture is alleged. Such a rule may be desirable... [b]ut contrary to the assertion of the minority in *Al-Adsani*, it is not *entailed* by the prohibition of torture'.[106] As Lord Bingham in the same case succinctly stated: 'The International Court of Justice has made plain that breach of a jus cogens norm of international law does not suffice to confer jurisdiction (*Democratic Republic of the Congo v Rwanda*, ICJ, 3 February 2006, para 64)'.[107] In general, on this view the overriding effect of a *jus cogens* norms has been restricted; provided local remedies are available and effective, the doctrine of State immunity is held compatible with obligations under international law relating to the implementation of *jus cogens* norms.

Another argument for removal of immunity and judicial restraint in respect of acts contrary to international law is based on the concept of universal jurisdiction. Whilst the exercise of universal criminal jurisdiction in pursuance of an obligation in a convention to which both forum and defendant State are parties is now recognised, its exercise on the basis of customary international law remains uncertain and has been challenged by the Republic of the Congo in pending proceedings against France in the ICJ.[108] Where an international convention such as the 1974 UN Torture Convention or the 1979 International Convention against the Taking of Hostages imposes an obligation to prosecute

---

[106] *Jones v Ministry of Interior for the Kingdom of Saudi Arabia and Ors* [2006] UKHL 26; [2007] 1 AC 270, para 45.

[107] Ibid, para 24.

[108] *Case concerning Certain Criminal Proceedings in France (Republic of the Congo v France)* ICJ Oral Proceedings, 28 April 2003 am, Case for Congo, M Verges, para 10; M DeCocq, paras 11 et seq. See also *Questions relating to the Obligation to Prosecute or Extradite (Belgium v Senegal)*, Application to the ICJ, 19 Feb 2009.

or extradite, national courts of States parties to these conventions may exercise criminal jurisdiction where the accused is present within the country. Where an accused is not present within the country, national legislation usually requires some connecting factor such as nationality, or long-term residence before initiating criminal proceedings. But as discussed above in Section II E.2 and E.5, no such criminal proceedings may be instituted against persons enjoying State or diplomatic immunities. In the *Arrest Warrant* case the International Court of Justice declared that, despite the general irrelevancy of official status as regards persons prosecuted for international crimes, a national court may not exercise universal jurisdiction for war crimes or crimes against humanity against a Minister for Foreign Affairs, (and by analogy against a serving Head of State or government) either when serving or when he has left office in respect of acts which he has performed in the course of official functions.[109] It is argued that these limitations on the exercise of universal criminal jurisdiction are also to be applied to universal civil jurisdiction. Thus, it follows from the limitations which State immunity imposes on the exercise of universal criminal jurisdiction that State practice does not permit the exclusive domestic jurisdiction of a State to be circumvented by bringing civil proceedings for reparation for the same acts either against the State itself or against a Head of State or Minister of Foreign Affairs, whether serving or out of office.[110] In the case referred to above, the House of Lords adopted this approach in rejecting as barred by immunity a claim for reparation brought by the victims in respect of alleged torture committed in a State prison by the Minister of the Interior, police officials and by the State of Saudi Arabia itself.

On the other hand whilst the perpetrator's criminal intent (*mens rea*) and the inapplicability of criminal jurisdiction of one State over another State may explain how logically it is possible to remove immunity from criminal proceedings in respect of the State official who perpetrates the international crime but not the State which orders it, by reason of the perpetrator's criminal intent (*mens rea*), no such difference operates in respect of universal civil jurisdiction. It may well be argued that the State who supplies the means and gives the orders for the violation of international law is equally or more liable than the individual perpetrator for the injury to the victim and for reparation, reparation by the responsible State being the international remedy for violation of international law. Thus, it would seem much less sound where reparation is claimed to distinguish between the State and the individual perpetrator. The US has partially resolved this dilemma, though at the expense of universality, by enacting legislation which selectively removes the bar of State immunity from civil jurisdiction for such States as are designated by the State Department as sponsors of terrorism. The Anti-terrorism and Death Penalty Act 1996 deprives such designated State of immunity from claims for money damages for personal injury or death cause by an act of torture, extrajudicial killing, aircraft sabotage, hostage taking or the provision of material support or resources to terrorists. Cuba, Iran, North Korea, Syria, and Sudan have been designated as sponsors of terrorism, as were Iraq and Libya, for whom the designation has now been lifted. So far as individuals are concerned the Alien Tort Act

---

[109] *Arrest Warrant of 11 April 2000 (Democratic Republic of Congo v Belgium), Preliminary Objections and Merits, Judgment, ICJ Reports 2002*, p 3, paras 54–61; see also *Case concerning Certain Criminal Proceedings in France (Republic of the Congo v France) Provisional Measure, Order of 17 June 2003, ICJ Reports 2003*, p 102. See Cassese, 2002.

[110] *Tachiona v United States*, 386 F.3d 205, (2d Cir 6 Oct 2004) (*Tachiona II*); *Wei Ye v Jiang Zemin*, 383 F.3d 620, (7th Cir 8 Sept 2004).

1789, extended by the Torture Victim Protection Act 1991 to US citizens who are victims, provides a civil remedy in damages against any individual who, under actual or apparent authority or under colour of law of any foreign State, subjects any individual to torture or extrajudicial killing; two recent attempts to apply this legislation to corporations who have aided and abetted such torture or extrajudicial killings have resulted in out of court settlement and payment of damages.[111] The statute permits the court to decline jurisdiction if it appears that local remedies have not been exhausted. The Seventh Circuit Appeal Court dismissed for lack of proof that local remedies had been exhausted, a claim brought against a former general in the Nigerian governing military regime by the dependents of a political opponent seeking election for torture and unlawful detention in prison resulting in his death.[112]

VII. CONCLUSION

At the present day the three avoidance techniques, immunity, act of State, and non-justiciability, by application of the restrictive doctrine of State immunity as now set out in the UN Convention, have maintained in large measure a reasonable balance between the regulatory powers of States and the commercial rights of private parties. The techniques are now undergoing close scrutiny so as to conform to the standards set by human rights and international humanitarian law.

Much is written about the replacement of the club of sovereign States by an international community representing the interests of all, particularly individuals, yet States remain the main source of authority and implementation of the law in international relations. In consequence their qualities of independence and equality encapsulate three principles which are given effect in the plea of immunity: the principle of domestic jurisdiction by which the organization and legal relations of the State are exclusively or primarily matters for that State to determine; the principle that certain disputes involving States are to be settled on the international plane, not subjecting the State to the compulsory jurisdiction of a municipal court of another State; and the rule of exhaustion of the local remedies which provides an opportunity for the foreign State to settle the dispute in accordance with its own laws. Reduced to its simplest, the justification for use of avoidance techniques, particularly of the plea of immunity, is to allocate in the most appropriate manner suitable to all interests and the ends of justice jurisdiction between the forum and the foreign States.

The value of the techniques described in this chapter as a restraint on any abuse of jurisdiction by States should not be overlooked. As the strong separate opinion of Judges Buergenthal, Higgins, and Kooijmans in the *Arrest Warrant* case emphasized, a balance has to be struck between two sets of functions both of which are valued by the international community. One is the rejection of impunity and the punishment of the perpetrators of

---

[111] In 2005 UNOCAL Corporation made an out of court settlement with 15 Burmese villagers in respect of a claim for human rights violations while carrying out the construction of gas project in Myanmar. See *Wiwa v Shell Petroleum Development Company of Nigeria Limited*, Summary Order, Settlement and other documents (2d. Cir. June 3, 2009) 12 June 2009, ILIB.

[112] *Enahoro v Abubakar* (Interlocutory Appeal), United States Court of Appeals for the Seventh Circuit (23 May 2005); *Sarei et al v Rio Tinto, PLC & Rio Tinto Limited* (9th Cir. Dec. 16, 2008).

international crimes; the other relates to the law of privileges and immunities. The international law of privileges and immunities 'retains its importance since immunities are granted to high State officials to guarantee the proper functioning of the network of mutual inter-State relations which is of paramount importance for a well-ordered and harmonious international system'.[113]

REFERENCES

BIANCHI, A (2005), 'International Decision: Ferrini v Federal Republic of Germany', 99 *AJIL* 242.

BYHOVSKAYA, E (2008), *State Immunity in Russian Perspective 2008* (London: Wildy, Simmonds and Hill).

CASSESE, A (2002), 'When may senior State officials be tried for international crimes? Some comments on the *Congo v Belgium* Case' 13 *EJIL* 853.

COLLINS, L (Gen ed) (2006), *Dicey, Morris and Collins on Conflicts of Laws*, 14th edn (London: Thomson Sweet & Maxwell).

CRAWFORD, J (1983), 'A Foreign State Immunities Act for Australia?', 8 *Aust YBIL* 71.

DAHAI, QI (2008), 'State Immunity, China and its shifting position', 7 *Chinese J Int Law* 307.

FAWCETT, J, CARRUTHERS, J and NORTH, P, (2008), *Cheshire, North and Fawcett: Private International Law*, 14th edn (Oxford: Oxford University Press).

FOX, H (1999), 'The *Pinochet Case No 3*', 48 *ICLQ* 687.

GATTINI, A (2005), 'War Crimes and State Immunity in the *Ferrini* Decision', 3 *J Int Crim Justice* 224.

HAFNER, G, KOHEN, M, and BREAU, S (eds) (2006), *State practice regarding State Immunities: La pratique des Etats concernant les immunités des Etats in English and French* (Strasbourg: Council of Europe).

HIGGINS, R (1982), 'Certain Unresolved Aspects of the Law of State Immunity', 29 *Netherlands ILR* 265.

INTERNATIONAL LAW ASSOCIATION (2005), Committee on Reparation for Victims of Armed Conflict, Furuya 'Procedural aspects'.

INTERNATIONAL LAW COMMISSION (1991), Draft Articles on Jurisdictional Immunities of States and their Property, and Commentary, *YBILC* [1991] vol II, part 2.

IOVANE, M (2005), 'The *Ferrini* Judgement of the Italian Supreme Court: opening up domestic courts to claims of reparation for victims of serious violations of fundamental human rights', 14 *It YBIL*165.

KOLODKIN, R (2008), *Preliminary report of State officials from foreign criminal jurisdiction prepared by the Special Rapporteur Mr. Roman Anatolevich Kolodkin*, UN Doc ILC A/CN.4/601 (see also Memorandum by the Secretariat A/CN.4/596).

MURPHY, SD (2003), *United States Practice in International Law, Vol I 1999–2001* (Cambridge: Cambridge Oxford University Press).

—— (2005) *United States Practice in International Law, Vol II, 2002–2004* (Cambridge: Cambridge University Press).

O'KEEFE, R (2002), 'Decisions of British Courts in 2001 Involving Questions of Public or Private International Law', 73 *BYIL* 400.

---

[113] Ibid, Joint Separate Opinion of Judges, Higgins, Kooijmans, and Buergenthal, para 75.

PINGEL, N (2000), 'Creighton v Qatar', (2000) JDI 1054.

STAKER, C (1995), 'Decisions of British Courts in 1994 Involving Questions of Public or Private International Law' 66 BYIL 496.

STEWART, DP (2005), 'The UN Convention on Jurisdictional Immunities of States and their Property', 99 AJIL 194.

TRUMAN, EM (2007), 'Sovereign Wealth Funds: the Need for Greater Transparency and Accountability', Peterson Institute Policy Brief BP 07-6.

WARBRICK, C (2004), 'Immunity and International Crimes in English Law', 53 ICLQ 769.

FURTHER READING

ALEBEEK, R VAN (2008), The Immunities of States and Their Officials in International Criminal Law and International Human Rights Law (Oxford: Oxford University Press).

AKANDE, D (2004), 'International Law Immunities and the International Criminal Court', 98 AJIL 407.

DELLAPENNA, JW (2003), Suing Foreign Governments and their Corporations, 2nd edn (Dobbs Ferry, NY: Transnational Publishers Ltd).

CASSESE, A (2003), International Criminal Law, 2nd edn (Oxford: Oxford University Press), ch 14.

CRYER, B, FRIMAN, H, ROBINSON, D and WILMSHURST, E (2007) An Introduction to International Criminal Law and Procedure (Cambridge: Cambridge University Press), ch 20.

DICKINSON, A, LINDSAY, R, and LOONAM, JP (2004), State Immunity: Selected Materials and Commentary (Oxford: Oxford University Press).

FOX, H (2008), The Law of State Immunity, 2nd Edn (Oxford: Oxford University Press). A survey of the entire field of law covered by State immunity including an analysis of the 1991 Draft Articles on Jurisdictional Immunities of States and their Property as proposed by the International Law Commission and debated in the United Nations Sixth Committee and its working parties.

LAUTERPACHT, H (1951), 'The Problem of Jurisdictional Immunities of Foreign States', 28 BYIL 220: the seminal article which greatly influenced US and UK lawyers in the adoption of a restrictive doctrine of State immunity.

ORAKHELASHVILI, A (2006), Peremptory Norms of International Law (Oxford: Oxford University Press).

SINCLAIR, I (1980), 'Law of Sovereign Immunity—Recent Developments', 167 Recueil des Cours 113: this provides an historical account of the adoption of the restrictive doctrine of State immunity in both common law and civil jurisdictions.

SYNVET, H (1984), 'Quelques reflexions sur l'immunite d'execution de l'Etat etranger', (1984) JDI 22: this article in French gives an excellent summary of the operation of the law of State immunity as understood by a civil lawyer.

WOLFRUM, R (Gen ed) (2008), Encyclopaedia of Public International Law 3rd edn, 'Acts of State'. This short piece provides a convenient summary and comparison of the scope of the US and English act of State.

13

IMMUNITIES ENJOYED BY OFFICIALS OF STATES AND INTERNATIONAL ORGANIZATIONS

Chanaka Wickremasinghe[1]

SUMMARY

This chapter seeks to explain the immunities enjoyed by various categories of officials of States and international organizations involved in the conduct of international relations. It sets out the broad rationale underlying these immunities as being to facilitate the processes of communication between States on which international relations and cooperation rely. The law relating to the various categories of officials is then considered in turn, noting in particular the extent of the immunities from jurisdiction which they enjoy.

Finally the question of the inter-relation of the law on immunities (which developed largely as a 'self-contained regime') with recent developments in the field of international criminal law is considered. The discussion focuses on the challenges to immunities which are presented by measures to end the impunity of those who commit the most serious international crimes including, the development of extraterritorial jurisdiction and the establishment of international criminal tribunals. A range of judicial decisions, such as the House of Lords decision in the *Pinochet No 3* case, the judgment of the International Court of Justice in the *Arrest Warrant* case, and most recently the decision of the International Criminal Court relating to the arrest warrant in the *Al Bashir* case are reviewed in order to consider how international law has sought to reconcile these apparently conflicting priorities.

[1] The views expressed here are purely personal. I am grateful to Sir Michael Wood, Daniel Bethlehem, Chris Whomersley, Diana Brooks, Doug Wilson, and Malcolm Evans for helpful suggestions and improvements to earlier drafts.

I. INTRODUCTION

The primary focus of this chapter is on the immunities which officials of States and international organizations enjoy from the jurisdiction of other States, since it is in this area that many of the most difficult problems of diplomatic law lie.[2] For these purposes diplomatic law means the law by which international relations are conducted, and the processes of communication at the public international level are facilitated. Such communication can occur by a variety of means and in a number of settings. It includes both eye-catching, single events such as State visits and summits between Heads of States, as well as the more everyday work of foreign ministries, diplomatic missions, consular posts, and international organizations (James, 1991). The setting for such international communication ranges from simple ad hoc bilateral meetings of State officials, to the permanent institutionalized cooperation in large international organizations such as the UN and its specialized agencies.

Diplomatic law has ancient roots, and today comprises a large and, in many respects, highly developed body of law, from a variety of sources. These include the 1961 Vienna Convention on Diplomatic Relations (VCDR), the 1963 Vienna Convention on Consular Relations (VCCR), and the 1969 UN Convention on Special Missions. Additionally, in relation to international organizations there is a large number of treaties which deal with both the privileges and immunities of representatives of States to international organizations and the privileges and immunities of the officials employed by those organizations. The best known examples are the 1946 Convention on the Privileges and Immunities of the United Nations, and the 1947 Convention on the Privileges and Immunities of the Specialized Agencies. A further important component of diplomatic law is the Convention on the Prevention and Punishment of Crimes against Internationally Protected Persons, including Diplomatic Agents 1973.[3]

However diplomatic law is not fully codified, and certain categories of those engaged in the conduct of international relations therefore enjoy immunity only by virtue of customary international law. For example, as we shall see, the law governing the privileges and immunities of foreign Heads of State and other senior government officials remains largely uncodified at the international level. To the body of treaties and custom which comprise diplomatic law, we can also add a number of important judicial decisions of both international and national courts and tribunals in which its rules have been interpreted and applied.

In earlier eras, when the range of diplomatic communication was less developed, its governing law was less sophisticated and the rationales on which that law rested were broad approximations. In the modern era, however, the legal fiction of extraterritoriality of foreign missions has now been discredited (Brownlie, 2008, p 343) and

---

[2] Whilst the primary focus will be on diplomatic law, its interaction with other more recent developments in international law, including in human rights law and international criminal law will be considered in a number of the subsequent sections of this chapter.

[3] For text see (1974) 13 ILM 41. This Convention comprises an important aspect of the duty of protection States owe to officials of States and international organizations engaged on international business, providing for broad extraterritorial jurisdiction in respect of crimes relating to attacks on these persons. For a commentary on its drafting and negotiation see Wood, 1974.

the identification of representatives of a State with the State itself (the 'representative theory') has been subjected to more rigorous rationalization.[4] Accordingly it is now the 'functional necessity' theory which provides the most convincing explanation of the modern law of diplomacy.[5] This theory recognizes that international cooperation between States, from which political, economic, social, and cultural benefits flow, is entirely dependent on effective processes of communication. It is therefore essential that international law should protect and facilitate those processes of communication, and it is to that end that modern diplomatic law seeks to ensure an appropriate balance between the interests of the sending and receiving States. Professor Denza (2008, p 2) observes:

Diplomatic law in a sense constitutes the procedural framework for the construction of international law and international relations. It guarantees the efficacy and security of the machinery through which States conduct diplomacy, and without this machinery States cannot construct law whether by custom or by agreement on matters of substance.

The primary aspect of diplomatic law on which this chapter will concentrate is the grant of immunity from local jurisdiction. In this respect it is important to note that international law recognizes two basic types of immunity from jurisdiction in relation to officials of States and international organizations.

The first is immunity *ratione personae*, ie, immunities enjoyed by certain categories of State officials by virtue of their office. The functions of certain key offices of State are so important to the maintenance of international relations that they require immunity for their protection and facilitation.[6] These immunities are often wide enough to cover both the official and the private acts of such office-holders, since interference with the performance of the official functions of such a person can result from the subjection of either type of act to the jurisdiction of the receiving State (eg, if a diplomat is arrested it will interfere with his ability to perform his official functions whatever the reason for his arrest). This often means that these categories of official enjoy complete personal inviolability (including freedom from arrest and/or detention) and absolute immunity from criminal jurisdiction. Immunity from civil jurisdiction may also be recognized (though given the less coercive nature of civil jurisdiction, this immunity may be limited in respect of certain purely private actions of members of certain categories of official).[7] However because immunities *ratione personae* attach only to enable the proper functioning of particular offices of State, rather than to benefit the office-holder individually, they lapse when he leaves office.

---

[4] The representative theory suggests that diplomats, as representatives of the sending State should enjoy the same immunities as the State does itself. The preamble of the VCDR states that: '...the purpose of such privileges and immunities is not to benefit individuals but to ensure the efficient performance of the functions of diplomatic missions as representing States...' In any event it might also be noted that the immunities of States themselves are now more limited and are increasingly based on function rather than simply on status.

[5] See introductory comments to Section II, of the ILC Commentary on its final draft Articles, 1958 *YBILC* vol II, pp 94–95; see also comments of Sir Gerald Fitzmaurice, *YBILC* (1957), vol I (part two), at para 10.

[6] See, eg, the preamble to the VCDR and the judgment of the ICJ in *Arrest Warrant of 11 April 2000 (Democratic Republic of Congo v Belgium), Preliminary Objections and Merits, Judgment, ICJ Reports 2002,* p 3.

[7] Denza, 2008, pp 280–283 notes how, historically, the immunities of diplomats from civil jurisdiction were less readily accepted than immunities from criminal jurisdiction.

The second type of immunity is immunity *ratione materiae*—these immunities attach to the official acts of State officials. They are determined by reference to the nature of the acts in question rather than by reference to the particular office of the official who performed them. As such they cover a narrower range of acts than immunities *ratione personae*, but cover a wider range of actors—indeed they potentially apply to the official acts of all State officials. Furthermore because they relate to the nature of the act in question, a former State official can claim the benefit of such immunity for his official acts performed whilst in office, even after he has left office.

It might be noted that both of these types of immunity operate simply as procedural bars to jurisdiction, and can be waived by appropriate authorities of the sending State, thus enabling the courts of the receiving State to assert jurisdiction.

The related, but conceptually distinct, doctrines of non-justiciability and/or act of State are not dealt with here. Non-justiciability is sometimes confusingly described as 'subject-matter immunity', but is in fact distinct from procedural immunity, since it essentially asserts that the subject matter of the claim is in fact governed by international law (or, in some cases, foreign public law) and therefore falls outside the competence of national courts of other States to determine.[8] The plea of non-justiciability requires the court to give closer examination to the basis of the proceedings than when it deals with a procedural immunity. However further confusion may arise from the fact that these various forms of objection to jurisdiction are not mutually exclusive, but can in fact exist simultaneously (see Barker, 1998). Cases where different grounds for objection to jurisdiction coexist will usually be dismissed on the basis of a procedural immunity, since that question must be decided at the outset of proceedings, and will often be the simplest means of bringing the proceedings to an end.[9]

Despite the considerable constraint which procedural immunities (and other privileges of foreign diplomatic missions) place on the territorial jurisdiction of the receiving State, States generally observe them scrupulously. Perhaps more surprisingly, despite certain notorious cases of their abuse, there is no substantial body of opinion which advocates their abolition or restriction. For example, in response to the *St James's Square Incident* of 1984 (in which a police officer was killed by a shot fired from within the Libyan People's Bureau in London, whilst she was patrolling a political demonstration outside the Bureau), both the Foreign Affairs Committee of the UK Parliament and the UK government considered whether amendment of the VCDR should be sought, but rejected this on the grounds that it was neither practicable nor desirable.[10]

The generally high level of compliance with diplomatic law is usually ascribed to the reciprocal nature of diplomatic exchange (see, eg, Higgins, 1985). Since each State is both a sending State and a receiving State, each State has an interest in maintaining the proper

---

[8] See *Buttes Gas and Oil Co v Hammer* [1982] AC 888 (HL). For the limits of this doctrine see the recent case of *Kuwait Airways Corp v Iraqi Airways Co (No 2)* [2002] UKHL 19, 16 May 2002. For the application of the doctrine of non-justiciability alongside questions of the immunity of a former State official see the dissenting speech of Lord Lloyd in the *Pinochet (No 1)* case [1998] 3 WLR 1456 at pp 194–196 and discussed by Denza, 1999, pp 956–958.

[9] Procedurally non-justiciability/act of State is considered more as a substantive defence rather than simply a procedural bar to the jurisdiction of the court, and is therefore considered at a later stage of proceedings—eg, the judgment of Lord Goff in *Kuwait Airways Corp v Iraqi Airways Co (No 1)* [1995] 1 WLR 1147 (HL).

[10] See *Abuse of Diplomatic Privileges and Immunities*, FAC First Report 1984–5 (HC 127), at paras 53–57, and the Government's Reply (Misc No 5 (1985), Cmnd 9497), at paras 9–11.

equilibrium between the rights of sending and receiving States. This explains the restraint shown both by receiving States in respecting the privileges and immunities of foreign missions, and by members of diplomatic missions in their conduct while abroad.

It should be noted that diplomatic law has grown up largely as a 'self-contained regime', setting out the rights and obligations of receiving States and sending States, and with its own remedies available in cases of abuse. This has been observed by the ICJ[11] and is also reflected in the ILC Articles on State Responsibility, Article 50 of which provides that States are not permitted to infringe the inviolability of diplomatic and consular agents, premises, archives, and documents when taking countermeasures (Crawford, 2002, pp 50 and 288–293). However, as shall be seen in Section VII below, the interaction of diplomatic law with recent developments in other areas of international law, and particularly in international criminal law, has raised difficult problems which have yet to be fully answered.

II. DIPLOMATIC RELATIONS

The primary, though not exclusive, means of communication between governments is through the establishment of diplomatic relations, usually involving the exchange of permanent diplomatic missions. A diplomatic mission is of course in a position of considerable vulnerability, being located in territory over which another State exercises jurisdiction, and thus having limited means available to it for ensuring its own security. From the earliest times international society has therefore recognized the need to protect diplomatic agents so as to enable diplomatic exchange (Young, 1964; Barker, 1996, pp 32–55). The rules of international law which govern the establishment and maintenance of such diplomatic relations are now codified in the 1961 Vienna Convention on Diplomatic Relations (VCDR). With over 180 parties, the VCDR is amongst the most widely ratified of all international conventions, and it is probable that even those of its aspects which were originally progressive development of the law are now considered to reflect customary international law.[12] The VCDR has thus been extraordinarily successful in its aim to create a comprehensive legal framework for the conduct of diplomatic relations.[13]

A. THE SCHEME OF THE VIENNA CONVENTION ON DIPLOMATIC RELATIONS

The VCDR seeks to establish a proper balance of the rights of sending and receiving States. The founding principle set out in Article 2 is that diplomatic relations take place by mutual consent. Article 3 then sets out the primary functions of a diplomatic mission:

(a) to represent the sending State;

(b) to protect the interests of the sending State and its nationals;

---

[11] See *United States Diplomatic and Consular Staff in Tehran, Judgment, ICJ Reports 1980*, p 3, at paras 86–87.

[12] Ibid, paras 45 and 62. For a summary of the main issues on which the VCDR represented progressive development of the law at the time of its negotiation, see Denza, 2008, pp 3–6.

[13] Denza, 2008, pp 2–3 suggests three reasons to explain the success of the VCDR. First, that the law in this area is both long-established and has been relatively stable for a considerable time. Secondly, the important role played by reciprocity in the maintenance of the rules. Thirdly, the careful attention paid in the drafting processes of the ILC and in the Vienna Conference itself to producing a text which could command the general approval of States.

    (c)   to negotiate with the government of the receiving State;

    (d)   to ascertain and report to the government of the sending State the conditions and developments within the receiving State;

    (e)   to promote friendly relations between the sending State and the receiving State, and to develop their relations in economic, cultural and scientific fields.

The next part of the Convention (Articles 4–19) deals with various procedural questions in relation to the establishment of diplomatic relations, and in particular the appointment and accreditation of diplomatic agents. The consent of the receiving State is required in the form of a prior *agrément* for the appointment of the head of mission. Denza (2008) observes:

The justification for the requirement lies in the particular sensitivity of the appointment of a head of mission and the need, if a head of mission is effectively to conduct diplomacy between two States, for him to be personally acceptable to both of them.

In relation to other diplomatic agents (except defence attachés) the sending State does not have to obtain the prior consent of the receiving State (Article 7). Nevertheless the sending State must provide notification (and as far as possible prior notification) to the receiving State of the arrival and final departure (or termination of the functions) of all members of missions (Article 10).[14] Furthermore the receiving State is at any time (including before their arrival in the receiving State), entitled to inform the sending State that the head of the mission or any other member of a mission is *persona non grata*, or unacceptable, without giving reasons for doing so (Article 9).[15] In such cases the sending State must recall the person or terminate his functions. If the sending State fails to respond the receiving State may after a 'reasonable period' treat the person as no longer enjoying diplomatic privileges and immunities.

    Articles 20–28 concern the privileges and facilities which the sending State must grant to the mission itself. Thus under Article 22 the premises of the mission are inviolable, and agents of the receiving State are not entitled to enter them without the consent of the head of the mission. During the drafting work of the ILC and also during the negotiation of the VCDR, it was considered whether there should be any exceptions to this rule in times of extreme emergency. However such proposals were overwhelmingly rejected on the grounds that the power of appreciation as to whether one of the exceptions was applicable to a given situation would belong to the receiving State, and that this might lead to abuse. In 1984 during the *St James's Square Incident* the UK Government scrupulously respected the inviolability of the Libyan Mission throughout, notwithstanding the outrage that had

---

[14] It now appears that the UK courts will not consider that notification is a prerequisite to the entitlement of diplomatic status, *R v Home Secretary, ex parte Bagga* (1990), 88 ILR 404: but see also the earlier cases of *R v Governor of Pentonville Prison, ex parte Teja* (1971), 52 ILR 368, *R v Lambeth Justices, ex parte Yusufu* (1985), 88 ILR 323, and *R v Governor of Pentonville Prison, ex parte Osman (No 2)* (1988), 88 ILR 378—in relation to the latter see also the certificate of the Foreign and Commonwealth Office in (1988) 59 *BYIL* 479.

[15] In its Reply to the Foreign Affairs Committee (above, n 10, at paras 689–690), the Government set out its policy in respect of the kinds of behaviour which would lead to a declaration of *persona non grata*, which included matters such as espionage and incitement to violence, as well as other criminal offences. In addition a serious view would be taken of reliance on diplomatic immunity to evade civil liabilities. Finally the Government also stated a new policy in relation to parking offences, under which persistent failure to pay parking fines would lead to a review of a person's acceptability as a member of a mission. Denza, 2008, p 86 notes how the numbers of parking tickets cancelled on grounds of diplomatic immunity fell from over 100,000 in 1984, to just over 2,300 in 1993.

been perpetrated from there, and the premises were not entered until after the severance of diplomatic relations and the vacation of the premises.[16]

Furthermore under Article 22(2) the receiving State is under a special duty to take all appropriate steps to protect the premises of the mission against all intrusion, and to prevent disturbances to the peace of the mission or impairment of its dignity. Thus in the *Tehran Hostages* case, although those who attacked the US Embassy and Consulates were not acting on behalf of Iran in the initial phase, Iran was nonetheless responsible for having failed to take appropriate steps to protect the premises and their occupants.[17]

In relation to the duty to prevent any disturbance of the peace of the mission or impairment of its dignity in normal times, the question of whether to allow peaceful political demonstrations outside diplomatic missions may require the receiving State to strike a balance between rights of political expression and the maintenance of its obligations towards the sending State.[18]

Similarly under Article 24 the archives of the mission are inviolable.[19] Article 27 provides for the free communication of the mission, including the inviolability of official correspondence, free use of diplomatic bags for diplomatic documents and articles for official use, and the protection from interference of diplomatic couriers.

Articles 29–39 deal with the immunities enjoyed by members of the mission. As well as jurisdictional immunities (considered below), these include other matters such as the inviolability of the private residence of a diplomatic agent, immunity from taxes and customs, and exemption from national service requirements in the receiving State. Thus

---

[16] During the inquiry into the incident by the Foreign Affairs Committee two possible grounds of entry into the mission were examined. First, whether there had been a material breach of treaty by Libya entitling the UK to repudiate it and enter the premises. This was rejected on the basis that the VCDR is a self-contained regime, with its own remedies in case of breach. The second question was whether the UK would have had a right to enter the premises under the doctrine of self-defence. The Legal Adviser to the Foreign and Commonwealth Office told the Committee that self-defence would in principle be available in respect of both action directed against the State and action directed against its nationals. However he believed the circumstances of this case did not justify forcible entry on the grounds of self-defence, as the criteria specified in the *Caroline* case were not met. The Committee accepted the latter conclusion but made no comment on the general point as to the applicability of self-defence as a ground for entering diplomatic premises (n 10, above, at paras 94–95). Mann, 1990, pp 333–337, argued that the inviolability of premises is conditioned by the lawfulness of their use, and so the Government had the right, and the duty, to enter the premises, to search for and remove any weapons held there.

[17] *United States Diplomatic and Consular Staff in Tehran, Judgment, ICJ Reports 1980*, p 3, paras 62–68. During the second period when the Court found that through its support of the hostage-takers, Iran was directly responsible for their actions, it violated, *inter alia*, paras (1) and (3) of Article 22 VCDR (ibid, para 77).

[18] In its Reply to the Foreign Affairs Committee, (above, n 10, para 39(e)) the Government explained that in most cases this was left to the police who tended to manage such situations by, for example, keeping demonstrators on the opposite side of the road to the mission premises.

[19] A violation of Article 24 was found in *United States Diplomatic and Consular Staff in Tehran, Judgment, ICJ Reports 1980*, p 3. For the question of whether inviolability extends to documents which have been removed from the mission and are subsequently used in legal proceedings see *Shearson Lehman Brothers Inc v Maclaine Watson and Co, International Tin Council Intervening* [1988] 1 WLR 16 and Mann, 1990, pp 328–329. See also the Canadian case of *Rose v The King* (1947) 3 DLR 710 in which documentary evidence of espionage against accused persons in criminal proceedings was held to be admissible notwithstanding that it had been stolen from the Russian Embassy and inviolability had not been waived. In the case of *Fayed v Al-Tajir* (CA [1987] 3 WLR 102) an internal memorandum of an Embassy in London was found to be protected by absolute privilege as a diplomatic document, leading to a dismissal of a libel action based on the contents of the document.

members of diplomatic missions enjoy wide protections from interference by the receiving State, which must be given effect in national law, this being done in the UK by the Diplomatic Privileges Act 1964. However it is important to emphasize that the rights and privileges are not granted for the personal benefit of the individuals concerned, but to ensure the efficient performance of the functions of the diplomatic mission.

By way of *quid pro quo* for the enjoyment of privileges and immunities, members of diplomatic missions owe certain duties towards the receiving State. These are:

(a) the duty to respect the laws and regulations of the receiving State (Article 41(1));

(b) the duty not to interfere in the internal affairs of the receiving State (Article 41(1));

(c) all official business of the communication by the mission with the receiving State should be through the Ministry of Foreign Affairs of the receiving State, or with such other ministries as may be agreed (Article 41(2));

(d) the premises of the mission must be not be used in any manner incompatible with the functions of the mission (Article 41(3));

(e) a diplomatic agent must not carry out any professional or commercial activity for personal profit in the receiving State (Article 42).

Finally in Articles 43–46 the convention deals with arrangements on the termination of diplomatic functions and on severance of diplomatic relations.

B. JURISDICTIONAL IMMUNITIES

The VCDR recognizes various categories of staff members of diplomatic missions, each enjoying immunity from jurisdiction to a different extent:

(a) diplomatic agents (ie the head of the mission and other members of the diplomatic staff) and their families (provided that they are not nationals of the receiving State (Article 37(1)) enjoy immunities *ratione personae*, ie by virtue of their office. Thus they are granted personal inviolability, including freedom from arrest and detention (Article 29),[20] and absolute immunity from criminal jurisdiction (Article 31). A diplomatic agent is also immune from civil and administrative jurisdiction,[21] except in three types of case:

   (i) a real action relating to immovable property situated in the territory of the receiving State, unless he holds it on behalf of the sending State for the purposes of the mission;[22]

---

[20] A further aspect of inviolability is the duty to protect diplomatic agents, on which see also the Convention on the Prevention and Punishment of Crimes against Internationally Protected Persons—see n 3, above. For clear breaches of both limbs of Article 29 see *United States Diplomatic and Consular Staff in Tehran, Judgment, ICJ Reports 1980*, p 3, paras 62–63 and 77. Self-defence or an overriding duty to protect human life appears to provide a limited exception. See ibid, para 86 and Denza, 2008, pp 265–269.

[21] This includes civil proceedings concerning private matters. See, eg, the Australian case of *De Andrade v De Andrade* (1984), 118 ILR 299, in which the immunity of a diplomat was upheld in relation to divorce and custody proceedings.

[22] See Denza, 2008, at pp 289–299. On the difficult issue of whether the private residence of a diplomat is included within the exception, see *Intpro Properties v Sauvel* [1983] 2 WLR 908. The private residence of a diplomat is, however, inviolable by virtue of Article 30.

(ii) an action relating to succession in which the diplomatic agent is involved as executor, administrator, heir, or legatee as a private person and not on behalf of the sending State;

(iii) an action relating to any professional or commercial activity exercised by the diplomatic agent in the receiving State outside his official functions.

(b) Administrative and technical staff and their families, who are not nationals or permanent residents of the receiving State, enjoy similar personal inviolability and immunity from criminal jurisdiction to diplomatic agents. However they only enjoy immunity from civil jurisdiction in relation to acts performed in the course of their duties (Article 37(2)).

(c) Service staff who are not nationals or permanent residents of the receiving State enjoy immunity *ratione materiae*, in respect of acts performed in the course of their duties (Article 37(3)).

(d) Diplomatic agents representing the sending State but who are in fact nationals or permanent residents of the receiving State, also enjoy immunity *ratione materiae* in respect of their official acts (Article 38(1)).

(e) All members of diplomatic missions who enjoy immunities whilst in office enjoy a subsisting immunity *ratione materiae* in respect of their official acts even after they have left office (Article 39(2)).[23]

It might be noted that generally immunities under the VCDR operate only in respect of the jurisdiction of the receiving State. However the provisions of Article 40 can be distinguished in that third States must accord diplomatic agents (and their family members) inviolability and such immunities as may be required to ensure their transit or return whilst en route to and from post.[24]

C. REMEDIES IN CASES OF ABUSE

Whilst the immunities set out above impose a considerable derogation from the jurisdiction of receiving States, the VCDR seeks to redress the balance, at least partially, by providing for certain remedies in cases of abuse. Jurisdictional immunities operate purely at the procedural level, by barring the adjudicative powers of the local courts in respect of the holder, but they do not in themselves amount to substantive exemptions from the law itself. Indeed as we have seen members of diplomatic missions are under a duty to respect the law of the receiving State. Therefore where such immunity is waived, the local courts may enjoy jurisdiction within the usual bounds set by international law. Article 32 of the VCDR deals with the question of waiver setting out: (a) that waiver is a prerogative of the sending State (not the diplomatic agent in question) (Article 32(1)); (b) that waiver must always be express (Article 33(2)); and (c) that waiver from jurisdiction in respect of civil or administrative proceedings does not, in itself, imply waiver from execution of the judgment (Article 33(4)).[25]

---

[23] See the German Constitutional Court case of the *Former Syrian Ambassador to the GDR* (1997), 115 ILR 596, see also the *Pinochet* case discussed below. For further explanation see Dinstein, 1966.

[24] See the Netherlands case, *Public Prosecutor v JBC* (1984), 94 ILR 339.

[25] By way of an exception to Article 32(1) and (2), Article 32(3) provides that a waiver will be implied in respect of counterclaims which are directly related to the principal claim in proceedings commenced by the holder of the immunity.

However waivers remain in the discretion of the sending State,[26] and in the event that it refuses, the receiving State must rely on the broader remedy of withdrawing its consent, either in respect of a particular member of the mission by declaring him or her *persona non grata* or, in a particularly egregious case, by breaking off diplomatic relations.

III. CONSULAR RELATIONS

The role of consuls is to represent the sending State, and to promote and/or protect its interests in the receiving State, but with the emphasis of that role on technical and administrative matters rather than political matters (in which diplomatic staff specialize). Consuls often deal with private interests, such as assistance to nationals of the sending State in the receiving State and the promotion of trade, rather than the public interests of the sending State. Nevertheless, generalizations about consular relations must be treated cautiously since the range of consular functions, as set out in VCCR, Article 5, is very broad. It can include:

(a) protecting in the receiving State the interests of the sending State and its nationals;[27]

(b) assisting nationals of the sending State in need of help in the receiving State;

(c) obtaining appropriate legal assistance for nationals of the sending State before tribunals and other authorities of the receiving State;

(d) assistance to vessels and aircraft of the sending State and their crews, as well as exercising rights of supervision and inspection thereof;

(e) promoting trade between the two States;

(f) issuing passports and/or visas and other notarial functions;

(g) promoting cultural exchange.

Though international law on consular relations has ancient roots, the modern law first developed in a vast web of bilateral consular treaties in the nineteenth and twentieth centuries. Yet so varied were these treaty provisions, that it was believed that (unlike the law of diplomatic relations prior to 1961) customary international law played only a very limited role in the establishment and maintenance of consular relations. However, following work by the ILC in the late 1950s and early 1960s, the 1963 Vienna Convention on Consular Relations (VCCR) sought to consolidate and codify a basic body of rules. Whilst the VCCR does establish a widely accepted benchmark for consular relations[28] it expressly states that it shall not affect existing agreements between States, or prevent States from varying its provisions in their future agreements (Article 73).[29]

---

[26] A relatively recent example was the waiver by Colombia to enable the questioning by police of an Embassy official and one of his family members in connection with a murder inquiry—FCO Press Release, 26 September 2002. For this and other examples of practice see also Denza, 2008, p 345–347.

[27] On the VCCR system of consular protection of nationals of the sending State, see *LaGrand (Germany v USA), Merits, Judgment, ICJ Reports 2001*, p 466 at para 74.

[28] For example in *United States Diplomatic and Consular Staff in Tehran, Judgment, ICJ Reports 1980*, p 3, para 62 the ICJ found the protection of consular staff and property under the VCCR also reflected rules of customary international law.

[29] Similarly under the UK implementing legislation, the Consular Relations Act 1968, the relevant provisions of the VCCR are implemented by and scheduled to the Act, but by virtue of s 3 any international

The scheme of the VCCR is not unlike the VCDR, dealing with: the establishment and conduct of consular relations (Articles 2–24); the end of consular functions (Articles 25–27); facilities, privileges, and immunities relating to a consular post (Articles 28–39); facilities, privileges, and immunities relating to consular officers and other members of a consular post (Articles 40–57); the regime relating to honorary consuls (Articles 58–68); and general provisions (Articles 69–73).

The differences in the functions of consuls as compared to diplomats explain the differences in the extent of immunities from jurisdiction that are generally granted to consuls.[30] Consular officers enjoy a more limited personal inviolability—they may not be arrested or detained pending trial, except in the case of a grave crime[31] and pursuant to a decision by the competent judicial authority (Article 41). In relation to immunity from jurisdiction, consular officers enjoy only immunity *ratione materiae*, ie, in respect of acts performed in the exercise of their consular functions (Article 43).[32]

IV. SPECIAL MISSIONS

In addition to the communication between governments that is enabled through the establishment of permanent diplomatic missions, an important means of carrying out particular items of inter-governmental business is through the dispatch of special missions (sometimes called ad hoc diplomacy). Such missions can vary considerably—ranging from missions involving the Head of State in person on matters of great political moment, to missions consisting of relatively junior officials concerned with a purely technical matter between the sending and receiving State.

Similarly the legal status of such missions has been treated somewhat unevenly. There are relatively few decisions from national courts on the point but there is authority for the proposition that some special missions, and in particular high-level missions, enjoy immunities as a matter of customary international law. Thus for example in the 1983 *Tabatabai* case[33] the German Federal Supreme Court found that there was a rule of customary international law that an ad hoc envoy charged with a special political mission by the sending State could be granted immunity with the agreement of the sending State. The court found that given the importance of ad hoc diplomacy, there were functional grounds for granting immunity *ratione personae* to members of special missions. Similarly some

agreement of the UK, under which consular privileges and immunities differ from the VCCR standard, may be given effect by Order in Council.

[30] Though in its practice with certain States, the UK has been willing to agree that the diplomatic standard of privileges and immunities should be extended to consular officers—see, eg, Consular Relations (Privileges and Immunities) (People's Republic of Bulgaria) Order 1970 (SI 1970/1923); Consular Relations (Privileges and Immunities) (People's Republic of China) Order 1984 (SI 1984/1978); Consular Relations (Privileges and Immunities) (Polish People's Republic) Order 1978 (SI 1978/1028); and Consular Relations (Privileges and Immunities) (USSR) Order 1970 (SI 1970/1938). For comparable US practice see Lee and Quigley, 2008, pp 463–469

[31] The term 'grave crime' is not defined under the VCCR. However the UK Consular Relations Act 1968 defines it as any crime punishable by up to a term of five years' imprisonment (s 1(2)).

[32] Determining what constitutes an 'official act' for these purposes can raise difficult questions of characterization. See Lee and Quigley, 2008, pp 440–461.

[33] *Tabatabai* case (1983) 80 ILR 388.

US courts have found there to be a category of special diplomatic envoy which benefit from jurisdictional immunities.[34] However in a recent case a US District Court rejected a plea of immunity from criminal jurisdiction by a visiting government official claiming to be on a special mission and found that the Special Missions Convention does not represent customary international law,[35] though it is perhaps noteworthy that the individual in this case does appear to have been part of a high-level mission. In the UK there have been two recent cases in which a court of first instance has found that visiting Ministers enjoy immunity under customary international law as part of a special mission. The first concerned a visiting Minister of Commerce and International Trade who was a member of a visiting delegation on a State Visit led by the Head of State, and the second concerned a visiting Defence Minister attending high-level meetings with members of the UK Government.[36] Elsewhere, the question of whether immunity can extend to other senior figures in the retinue of a Head of State has also been discussed in the case concerning the arrest in Germany of Rose Kabuye, the Rwandan President's Chief of Protocol, under a European Arrest Warrant issued in connection with proceedings in France.[37]

On other hand the 1969 UN Convention on Special Missions sets out in some detail norms for the conduct of ad hoc diplomacy and the privileges and immunities which attach to special missions. The Convention has not been widely taken up[38] and there is some dispute as to whether all of its provisions reflect customary international law. Whilst the basic principles are not in doubt, Sir Arthur Watts has suggested that the main reason for the limited success of the Convention appears to be its inflexibility, in that it seeks to apply a single standard of treatment to all kinds of missions (see Watts, 1999, pp 344–345). There may also be some concerns arising from the fact that the definition of a special mission is not entirely clear, as well as some practical difficulties arising from the temporary nature of such missions.

[34] See, eg, *Kilroy* v *Windsor, Prince of Wales* (1978), 81 ILR 605 and *HRH Prince Turki Bin Abdulaziz* v *Metropolitan Dade County* (1984), 99 ILR 113.

[35] *USA* v *Sissoko* (US District Court, Florida Southern District, 1997), 121 ILR 599.

[36] See judgment of the Bow Street Magistrates' Court in the case of *Bo Xilai*, 8 November 2005 (128 ILR 713), and that of the Westminster Magistrates' Court in *Re: Ehud Barak*, 29 September 2009, (not yet reported). Other references to special missions in the English courts have been in obiter dicta, where the case has been decided on other grounds; see, eg, *Fenton Textiles Association* v *Krassin et al* (1921) 6 BILC 247; *R* v *Governor of Pentonville Prison, ex parte Teja* [1971] 2 QB 274; and *R* v *Governor of Pentonville Prison, ex parte Osman (No 2)* (1988), 88 ILR 378. See also the contrasting dicta of Lord Millett and Lord Phillips in *R* v *Bow Street Metropolitan Stipendiary, ex parte Pinochet Ugarte (Amnesty International Intervening) (No 3)* (hereafter *Pinochet No 3*) [1999] 2 WLR 827 at 905E and 918E respectively. In France, it is understood that the *Chambre d'Instruction* of the Paris Court of Appeal accepted the plea of immunity by Jean-François N'Dengue in the so-called 'Congo Beach' case, on the ground that he was on a special mission and therefore entitled to immunity in customary international law. The decision was made on 22 November 2004, but is unpublished—see Ryngaert, 2005. It might be noted that the International Court of Justice did not advert to rules of customary international law on special missions when dismissing claims to personal immunities in respect of certain Djiboutian officials, but simply observed that the UN Convention on Special Missions was not applicable to the case (see *Case concerning Certain Questions of Mutual Assistance in Criminal Matters (Djibouti* v *France)* judgment of 4 June 2008, at para 194). However this might be explained by the fact that it was not clear that the officials in question were on a special mission, particularly at the time the alleged breaches of immunity occurred. For discussion see Buzzini, 2009.

[37] See statement of the Rwandan Ministry of Foreign Affairs at **http://www.minaffet.gov.rw/index2 .php?option=com_content&do_pdf=1&id=148**. For discussion see Akande, 2008.

[38] There are currently 38 parties. The UK signed the Convention on 17 December 1970, but has not ratified it.

The Convention broadly follows the familiar scheme of the VCDR and VCCR. It sets out firmly the principle of mutual consent as underlying ad hoc diplomacy (Articles 2 and 3), and then deals with questions of the procedural questions for the sending and conduct of special missions (Articles 2–19). It sets out the facilities, privileges, and immunities of missions (Articles 22–28) and of their staff (Articles 29–48).

Substantive aspects of the Convention also resemble the VCDR; hence for the purposes of jurisdictional immunities the staff are divided into broadly similar categories enjoying immunities to a similar extent.[39] Members of special missions are under an obligation to respect local law (Article 47). Also in cases of abuse the remedies of the receiving States are similar to those under the VCDR, including seeking waiver (Article 41), declaration of *persona non grata* (Article 12), or bringing the mission to an end (Article 20(1)(e)). Finally it might be noted that the Convention provides that such additional privileges and immunities as may be required under international law may be accorded where the mission includes the Head of the sending State, the Head of its Government, its Minister for Foreign Affairs, or other persons of high rank (Article 21).[40]

V. HOLDERS OF HIGH-RANKING OFFICES, SUCH AS HEADS OF STATE, HEADS OF GOVERNMENT, AND MINISTERS FOR FOREIGN AFFAIRS

A. HEADS OF STATE

In previous eras when most States were governed by personal sovereigns such as monarchs or emperors, there was a close identity in international law between such persons and their States. However modern international law tends to consider the rights and competences of Heads of State as attaching to them in their capacity as the highest representatives of their States, rather than inherently in their own right (Watts, 1994, pp 35–37). That said, international law recognizes that the Head of State may exercise a number of important powers in international relations *ex officio*, including the sending and receiving of diplomats and consuls, and the conclusion of treaties.[41]

The immunity from jurisdiction of Heads of State when travelling abroad remains largely uncodified at the international level, but it has undergone some important changes in modern times. During earlier times when international law closely identified a Head

---

[39] Under Articles 29 and 31 'representatives of the sending State in the special mission and members of its diplomatic staff' enjoy personal inviolability and jurisdictional immunities equivalent to those of diplomatic agents under the VCDR (save that in respect of immunity from civil jurisdiction a further exception is made in relation to road traffic accidents outside the official functions of the person concerned). Family members, administrative and technical staff, service staff, and members of the mission who are nationals of the receiving State, all enjoy equivalent immunities to those under the VCDR (see Articles 39, 36, 37, and 40 respectively). Temporally immunities are limited to the duration of the mission, save that immunity *ratione materiae* in relation to official acts continues to subsist even after the mission has come to an end (Article 44(2)).

[40] However it is not clear what additional privileges and immunities this might entail. See *Satow's Diplomatic Practice*, 6th edn, (Roberts, ed) 2009, p 190.

[41] See, eg, 1969 VCLT, Article 7 and *Land and Maritime Boundary between Cameroon and Nigeria (Cameroon v Nigeria: Equitorial Guinea Intervening), ICJ Reports 2002*, paras 263–268.

of State with his or her State, the absolute doctrine of 'sovereign immunity' prevailed. However more recently, as the restrictive doctrine of immunity in relation to States has developed, more distinct rules in relation to Heads of State have also developed (Watts, 1994, pp 52–66).[42]

The International Court of Justice has recently reaffirmed aspects of the law as regards personal inviolability and immunity from criminal jurisdiction, in the following terms:

… A Head of State enjoys in particular 'full immunity from criminal jurisdiction and inviolability' which protects him or her 'against any act of authority of another State which would hinder him or her in the performance of his or her duties'. Thus the determining factor in assessing whether or not there has been an attack on the immunity of the Head of State lies in the subjection of the latter to a constraining act of authority… The Court recalls that the rule of customary international law reflected in Article 29 of the Vienna Convention on Diplomatic Relations, while addressed to diplomatic agents, is necessarily applicable to Heads of State. This provision reads as follows:

'[t]he person of a diplomatic agent shall be inviolable. He shall not be liable to any form of arrest or detention. The receiving State shall treat him with due respect and shall take all appropriate steps to prevent any attack on his person, freedom or dignity.'

This provision translates into positive obligations for the receiving State as regards the actions of its own authorities, and into obligations of prevention as regards possible acts by individuals. In particular, it imposes on receiving States the obligation to protect the honour and dignity of Heads of State, in connection with their inviolability.[43]

Further evidence of the relevant principles of customary international law can also be found in the practice of national courts, as well as in relevant national legislative provisions.

In the UK, s 20 of the State Immunity Act 1978 essentially equates the position of a foreign Head of State with the head of a diplomatic mission. Thus a foreign Head of State (whether on an official or a private visit) will enjoy complete personal inviolability and absolute immunity from criminal jurisdiction *ratione personae*.[44] Immunity from civil jurisdiction is more complex in that it involves determining whether the act in question was performed by the Head of State in his official capacity as an organ of the State, or whether it was performed in his personal capacity. In relation to the acts of a Head of State performed in his public capacity, the provisions in Part I of the Act (relating to the

---

[42] For a US perspective on this development see *Tachiona and others v Mugabe and others* 169 F.Supp. 2d 259 (2001) (although the Court of Appeals (2nd Circuit) did not follow the same line of reasoning in its decision of 6 October 2004, 386F.3d 205). See also *Wei Ye v Jiang Zemin* 383F.3d 620.

[43] *Case concerning Certain Questions of Mutual Assistance in Criminal Matters (Djibouti v France)* judgment of 4 June 2008, at paras 170 and 174. On the facts of the case the Court found that an invitation to a Head of State to testify in the course of criminal proceedings (without any suspicion attaching to him) did not violate his inviolability. However the Court also found that had the French authorities passed confidential information regarding the witness summons to the Press, in the context of an official visit by the Djiboutian Head of State, this could constitute a failure in its obligation to protect his honour and dignity. On the other hand see *Aziz v Aziz and others* [2007] EWCA Civ 712 in which the English Court of Appeal rejected an application by a Head of State for parts of a judgment to which he was not a party to be kept secret, in order to avoid the revelation of personal information about him. In similar vein see *Harb v King Fahd* [2005] EWCA Civ 632, discussed in n 45 below.

[44] See, eg, judgment of the Bow Street Magistrates' Court in *Mugabe* of 14 January 2004 (2004) 53 *ICLQ* 770.

immunity of State itself, and considered in the previous chapter) will be applicable. For all other acts Heads of State will enjoy immunity from civil jurisdiction subject to the three exceptions noted in respect of Article 31(1) VCDR.[45] Finally it should be noted that the immunities of a Head of State can be waived, either by the Head of State himself, or by his State.

On the other hand when a Head of State leaves office, the House of Lords has found that he will enjoy immunities on the same basis as a former diplomat, and in particular subsisting immunity *ratione materiae* for his official acts (as per Article 39(2) VCDR). The extent of this immunity was of course the subject of detailed scrutiny in the *Pinochet* case (examined below).

B. HEADS OF GOVERNMENT AND MINISTERS FOR FOREIGN AFFAIRS

Heads of Government and Ministers for Foreign Affairs enjoy immunity from jurisdiction *ratione personae* under international law to the same extent as Heads of State, since they perform comparable functions in representing their States in international relations.[46] The position in relation to the personal inviolability and immunity from criminal jurisdiction of serving Foreign Ministers was clarified by the International Court of Justice in the *Arrest Warrant* case.[47]

The case concerned the issue by a Belgian magistrate of an international warrant for the arrest of the incumbent Congolese Foreign Minister[48] for his alleged involvement in grave breaches of the Geneva Conventions and the Additional Protocols thereto, and crimes against humanity. The relevant Belgian statute provided for universal jurisdiction in the Belgian courts over these crimes (ie, wherever and by whomsoever they were committed) and provided that 'the immunity attaching to the official capacity of a person shall not prevent the application of the present law'.[49]

---

[45] See, eg, Laddie J in *BCCI v Price Waterhouse* [1997] 4 All ER 108, in which certain acts of Sheikh Zayed of Abu Dhabi were immune from suit under s 20 as he was Head of State of the UAE, notwithstanding that the acts in question were not performed in that capacity. This was so even though Shiekh Zayed was simultaneously head of one of the constituent units of the UAE, and his acts may have been performed in a public capacity in that respect. In the case of *Harb v HM King Fahd bin Abdul Aziz*, [2005] EWCA Civ 632 the President of the Family Division of the High Court upheld a Head of State's assertion of immunity in relation to proceedings for ancillary relief in matrimonial proceedings. The applicant appealed, but King Fahd died before the Court of Appeal could hear the appeal, thus bringing the proceedings to an end (see [2005] EWCA Civ 1324). However the Court of Appeal had already by that stage ruled that the duty of the forum State to protect a Head of State from 'any attack on his person, freedom or dignity' (Article 29 VCDR) did not entail that the proceedings in which King Fahd was asserting immunity must be held in private.

[46] In principle their official acts, like those of other State officials, will also be protected by immunity *ratione materiae* which subsists even after they have left office: see Sections VI and VIII B below.

[47] *Arrest Warrant of 11 April 2000 (Democratic Republic of Congo v Belgium), Preliminary Objections and Merits, Judgment, ICJ Reports 2002*, p 3. For comments see Cassese, 2002; Wirth, 2002; Spinedi, 2002; Sir Robert Jennings, 2002; Stern, 2002; Schreuer and Wittich, 2002; McLachlan, 2002.

[48] In fact whilst he was the incumbent Foreign Minister at the material time, ie at the point the arrest warrant was issued, he subsequently left that office to become the Minister of Education and by the time of the judgment he held no ministerial portfolio at all.

[49] *Act concerning the Punishment of Grave Breaches of International Humanitarian Law* of 10 February 1999 (1999) 38 ILM 921. The Act has since been substantially amended and this provision removing immunity has been repealed.

The ICJ upheld Congo's complaint that the issue of the arrest warrant was a violation of the immunity from criminal jurisdiction and the personal inviolability which an incumbent foreign Minister enjoys under international law. The Court based this conclusion on the functions exercised by a Foreign Minister in international relations. The Court noted that he is in charge of his government's diplomatic activities, and represents it in international negotiations and meetings, as well as his powers under international law to act on behalf of and to bind the State in for example treaty relations, simply by virtue of his office. Such functions required that a Foreign Minister should be able to travel internationally freely and to be able to be in constant communication with his government and its diplomatic missions around the world. Such considerations led the Court to consider that Foreign Ministers enjoy complete personal inviolability and absolute immunity from criminal jurisdiction *ratione personae*, throughout the duration of their office. In that respect it is irrelevant that the acts in question were private or official, or that they were performed prior or subsequently to a Foreign Minister assuming office, or indeed whether that Foreign Minister was in the forum State on a private or an official visit.

Three further points should be noted about the extent of the immunity from jurisdiction of an incumbent Foreign Minster under the judgment.[50] First, it might be noted that Foreign Ministers may rely upon their immunities in any State, whereas for example diplomatic immunity is largely limited to immunity from the courts of the receiving State. Secondly, attention might be drawn to the fact that the Court found specifically that there was no exception to the immunity of a serving Foreign Minister from the criminal jurisdiction of national courts in respect of war crimes or crimes against humanity. Thirdly, the immunity of a Foreign Minister can be waived by his own State.

Though the Court's findings are strictly confined to the immunities enjoyed by Foreign Ministers, it seems clear that similar immunities apply, perhaps *a fortiori*, to Heads of Government.[51] How far such immunities can also be extended to other Ministers or officials may depend on analogous reasoning, based on the involvement of such persons in international relations. Thus, for example in the UK, decisions at first instance have recognized that such immunities extend to a visiting Defence Minister,[52] and to a visiting Minister of Commerce (whose portfolio included responsibility for international trade).[53] Nevertheless it is not yet clear where the lines should properly be drawn, and the task is not made easier by the different ways in which different governments organize themselves internally. In any event it may be that other ministers or senior officials enjoy immunities when on official visits as members of special missions.

---

[50] The Court's comments, strictly speaking obiter dictum, on the extent of the subsisting immunity *ratione materiae* of a Foreign Minister after he has left office are considered below in Section VIII.

[51] See, eg, the US case of *Saltany v Reagan and others* (1988), 80 ILR 19, affirmed (1989), 87 ILR 680.

[52] See judgment of the Bow Street Magistrates' Court in the case of *Mofaz*, 12 February 2004 (2004) 53 *ICLQ* 771–773. See also *Re: Ehud Barak*, 29 September 2009, (not yet reported).

[53] See judgment of the Bow Street Magistrates' Court in the case of *Bo Xilai*, 8 November 2005 (128 ILR 713).

VI. THE IMMUNITIES OF OTHER STATE OFFICIALS

The above appear to be the principal regimes of immunities which international law requires should be granted in respect of particular categories of State official.[54] However under the doctrine of State immunity, all State officials (and, in principle, former State officials[55]) enjoy immunity *ratione materiae* for their official acts from at least the civil jurisdiction of the courts of other States, where the effect of proceedings would be to undermine or render nugatory the immunity of the employer State.[56] In other words it prevents an applicant from seeking to circumvent the impediment of State immunity by adopting the tactic of suing the individual carrying out the business of State. This is reflected in the recently adopted 2004 UN Convention on the Jurisdictional Immunities of States and their Property.[57]

In the UK this proposition finds support in both the common law[58] and in some recent cases under the State Immunity Act 1978. Thus in *Propend Finance v Sing* the Commissioner of the Australian Federal Police (AFP) was permitted to claim State immunity, in connection with contempt proceedings for an alleged breach of an undertaking committed by an AFP officer accredited as a diplomatic agent to the Australian High Commission in London. The Court of Appeal held:

The protection afforded by the Act of 1978 [ie the State Immunity Act 1978] to States would be undermined if employees, officers or (as one authority puts it) 'functionaries' could be sued as individuals for matters of State conduct in respect of which the State they were serving had immunity. Section 14(1) must be read as affording individual employees or officers of a foreign State protection under the same cloak as protects the State itself.[59]

The House of Lords approved this formulation of the principle in the case of *Jones v Ministry of the Interior of the Kingdom of Saudi Arabia*, in the context of civil proceedings relating to allegations of torture against Saudi Arabia and certain of

---

[54] Additional categories would be State officials who staff permanent representations to international organizations. Their status, privileges and immunities will depend on the particular arrangements made under relevant treaties on privileges and immunities as well as the Headquarters Agreement of the organization in question, see for example El-Erian and Scobbie, 1998, pp 857–867.

[55] See for example Article 39(2) VCDR in relation to former members of diplomatic missions, and the treatment of the immunities of former Heads of State in *Pinochet No 3* [1999] 2 WLR 827, discussed below at Section VIII B.

[56] See Lord Browne-Wilkinson in *Pinochet No 3* [1999] 2 WLR 827 at 847F.

[57] Thus in defining the 'State' (the beneficiary of immunity under the convention) it includes in Article 1(b)(iv) 'representatives of the State acting in that capacity'.

[58] See, eg, *Twycross v Dreyfus* (1877) 5 Ch D 605; *Rahimtoola v Nizam of Hyderabad* [1958] AC 379; also *Zoernsch v Waldock* [1964] 2 QB 352. See Whomersley, 1992.

[59] *Propend Finance v Sing* 111 ILR 611 at 669. For criticism see Barker, 1998. But see also the US cases of *Chuidian v Philippine National Bank* (1990), 92 ILR 480 and *Herbage v Meese* (1990), 98 ILR 101. Also the Canadian cases of *Jaffe v Miller* (1993), 95 ILR 446 and *Walker v Baird* (1994) 16 OR (3d) 504. Other cases from the UK include *Re P (No 2)* (1998), 114 ILR 485, and under the common law of State immunity *Holland v Lampen-Wolfe* [2000] 1 WLR 1548.

its officials.[60] Lord Bingham drew the following conclusions as relevant: (1) that the individual defendants were at the material times acting or purporting to act as servants or agents of the State; (2) that their acts were accordingly attributable to the State; (3) that no distinction could be made between the claim against the State and the claim against the individual defendants; and (4) none of the claims fell within any exception to immunity under the State Immunity Act 1978.[61] The Court went on to find that the *jus cogens* nature of the prohibition of torture, did not of itself operate to enable a third State to assert civil jurisdiction in the face of State immunity, and that there was currently no generally accepted exception to State immunity from civil jurisdiction in relation to breaches of international law. Similarly in *Belhas* v *Ya'alon* a US Court of Appeals upheld the immunity of a senior member of the Israeli Defence Force in civil proceedings relating to alleged war crimes.[62]

There have been fewer cases where State officials have invoked State immunity in relation to criminal proceedings. However a recent example is the case of *Italy* v *Lozano*,[63] where the Italian Court of Cassation accepted that a US soldier enjoyed immunity *ratione materiae* in relation to a prosecution brought against him for acts performed in the discharge of his functions. The Court noted that a rule of customary international law was emerging which purported to limit such immunity in relation to serious international crimes. However as the conduct in question did not amount to a war crime, immunity obtained to preclude the jurisdiction of the Italian court. In similar vein, to the extent that the immunities *ratione materiae* of a former Head of State are a manifestation of this more general immunity, it might be noted that in *Pinochet No 3* it was suggested that such immunity could be asserted successfully to bar proceedings in respect of most crimes (with the important exception of certain serious international crimes, such as torture) where these are committed in the performance of the functions of government.[64]

---

[60] *Jones* v *Ministry of Interior for the of Kingdom of Saudi Arabia and Ors* [2006] UKHL 26, [2007] 1 AC 270. The plaintiff has a complaint against the UK pending in the European Court of Human Rights that in upholding the claims to immunity the House of Lords' decision contravened his right of access to a court under Article 6 of the European Convention on Human Rights.

[61] Ibid at para 13.

[62] *Belhas* v *Ya'alon*, US Court of Appeals (DC Circuit), 515 F.3d1279,15 February 2008, However see also the recent decision of *Yousuf* v *Samantar* (552 F.3d 371) in which the Court of Appeals for the Fourth Circuit held that an individual (in this case a former Prime Minister of Somalia) could not benefit from immunity under the Foreign Sovereign Immunities Act. The Supreme Court has subsequently agreed to review the case. However it might be noted that the Court of Appeals for the Fourth Circuit did not address the availability of immunity of State officials under the common law. On this point see the decision of the Court of Appeals for the Second Circuit in *Matar* v *Dichter* (16 April 2009, 563 F.3d 9) and in particular see the *amicus* brief submitted by the Executive Branch available on the website of the Center for Constitutional Rights (http://ccrjustice.org/ourcases/current-cases/matar-v.-dichter).

[63] *Italy* v *Lozano*, Case No 31171/2008; ILDC 1085 (IT 2008), 24 July 2008. For comment see Cassese, 2008 and also Palchetti, 2008.

[64] Thus Lord Hope found that immunity *ratione materiae* of a former Head of State could be relied upon in relation to charges of conspiracy to murder—see [1999] 2 WLR 827 at 881 and 887. See also the speeches of Lords Browne-Wilkinson and Hutton, ibid at 848 and 888 respectively. On the other hand Lord Millett expressly found that immunity *ratione materiae* is not available in respect of an offence committed in the forum State (ibid, at 913). See also *Wei Ye* v *Jiang Zemin* 383F.3d 620.

VII. OFFICIALS OF INTERNATIONAL ORGANIZATIONS

Whilst the immunities of international organizations have been inspired by the immunities granted to State officials, they differ in some respects, reflecting the important differences between international organizations and States. In the normal course of events an international organization will not have its own territory, but rather be based on territory over which a State exercises jurisdiction (special cases of international administration as, for example, the UN administration of Kosovo or in East Timor are not considered here). An international organization will not have its own population, from which its officials are chosen, but instead will employ persons who hold the nationality (with its attendant rights and obligations) of a State. Finally an international organization will not generally perform all the functions of government, with a full legal system of its own. Rather it will have its own institutional law, but will have to rely upon the local law in respect of other matters such as, for example, the maintenance of public order through the exercise of criminal jurisdiction.

Both diplomatic immunities and the immunities of international organizations arise from considerations of functional necessity, and as we shall see the former have inspired the latter in some respects. However it does not follow that they should be identical in extent. Jenks suggests that there are three major differences between diplomatic immunities and those of international officials (Jenks, 1961, p xxxvii). First, it is unusual for a diplomatic agent to have the nationality of the receiving State and in such situations as we have seen the scope of the immunities he enjoys can be restricted by the receiving State to his official activities only. On the other hand for officials of international organizations[65] it may be especially important that they enjoy immunities against their own States of nationality.[66] Secondly, whereas a diplomatic agent may be immune from legal process in the receiving State, he will remain subject to legal process in the sending State. In relation to officials of international organizations there is no sending State as such, and thus appropriate procedures may have to be adopted, either through some international disciplinary procedure established by the organization, or through waiver of immunity. Thirdly, the principle of reciprocity, which plays such an important role in the maintenance of diplomatic law between States, cannot operate in the same way in respect of international organizations. Thus Jenks rejects a simple assimilation of the immunities of international organizations with diplomatic immunities, in favour of looking at the former on their own merits as based upon their particular functional needs.

---

[65] Under relevant instruments additional categories of persons may benefit from similar immunities (though not identical in every respect) see for example the position of 'experts on mission' under the 1946 Convention on the Privileges and Immunities of the United Nations.

[66] Not all States accept that their own nationals when employed by international organizations enjoy the full range of immunities enjoyed by the officials who hold other nationalities. However such limitations often concern fiscal immunities or exemptions from national service rather than immunity from legal process. For examples of the general rule see the ICJ Advisory Opinions in the *Applicability of Article VI, Section 22 of the Convention on the Privileges and Immunities of the United Nations, Advisory Opinion, ICJ Reports 1989*, p 177 ('*Mazilu*') and *Difference Relating to Immunity from Legal Process of a Special Rapporteur of the Commission on Human Rights, Advisory Opinion, ICJ Reports 1999*, p 62 ('*Cumaraswamy*').

It is of course impossible to survey the range of international organizations, and the immunities of each will be governed by their own treaty provisions.[67] Only the immunities of personnel of the United Nations are considered here, as illustrative rather than generally applicable (see further, Michaels, 1971). In broad terms the Convention on the Privileges and Immunities of the United Nations 1946 divides staff members of the UN into three categories:

(a) the Secretary-General and the Assistant Secretaries-General shall be accorded ambassadorial status, and enjoy equivalent immunities *ratione personae* (Article V, s 19);

(b) all other officials of the Organization enjoy immunity from legal process in respect of their official acts, ie immunity *ratione materiae* (Article V, s 18(a)); and

(c) experts on mission (ie, persons who undertake temporary missions for the UN) who enjoy immunity from suit for their official acts (*ratione materiae*), as well as—in view of their need to travel freely in performance of their mission—a specific grant of personal inviolability (Article VI, s 22).

The Convention makes clear that the immunities of officials and experts are granted not for their personal benefit, but for the benefit of the Organization. The Secretary-General thus has the right *and the duty* to waive immunity of any official where the immunity would in his opinion impede the course of justice and can be waived without prejudice to interests of the Organization (Article V, s 20).

However given that most officials and experts of the UN only enjoy immunity *ratione materiae* in respect of their official acts, an interesting question arises as to who should determine whether any particular act is an 'official act'. In many of the cases which might concern the exercise of ordinary criminal jurisdiction it will be possible to say that the offence is not an official act, and so the question of immunity does not arise. Thus for example during the Cold War there were a number of cases in which international officials were accused of espionage in the US, they were unable to claim immunity as the activities in question were not official activities.[68] However in other cases, where there may be some dispute as to the nature of an act, it is necessary to ask whether that issue should be determined by the Secretary-General on behalf of the Organization, or the relevant national court as part of its task in applying the immunity. In the *Cumaraswamy* case, the ICJ gave a rather nuanced answer to the question, stating that:

When national courts are seised of a case in which the immunity of a United Nations agent is in issue, they should immediately be notified of any finding by the Secretary-General concerning that immunity. That finding and its documentary expression creates a presumption

---

[67] Though in relation to most officials of international organizations there is considerable uniformity in the relevant treaty provisions, that they enjoy immunity from jurisdiction *ratione materiae,* ie in relation to their official acts, whilst provision is often made for certain high officials to be granted a wider immunity *ratione personae* whilst in office. In relation to international organizations of which the UK is a member their immunities may be given effect in the UK by Order in Council made under the International Organizations Act 1968.

[68] See, eg, *US v Coplon* 84 F.Supp 472 (1949); *US v Melekh* 190 F.Supp 67 (1960); and *US v Egorov* 222 F.Supp 106 (1963). In another context see also the case of *Westchester County v Ranollo* (1946), 13 ILR 168.

which can only be set aside for the most compelling reasons and is thus to be given the greatest weight by the national courts.[69]

The Court thus sought to balance interests of the organization and the local jurisdiction, though, in the final analysis, it is the local court which must decide whether there are compelling reasons to rebut the presumption established by the Secretary-General's finding.

VIII. THE SCOPE OF IMMUNITIES FOR SERIOUS CRIMES UNDER INTERNATIONAL LAW—IMMUNITY AND IMPUNITY DISTINGUISHED

None of the immunities which have been considered are for the benefit of any particular individual or group of individuals, but rather are for the benefit of the State/international organization which they represent. Thus the sending State/employer international organization can waive any of these immunities, thereby consenting to the jurisdiction of the courts of another State over the official in question. This applies whether the immunity in question is granted *ratione personae* or *ratione materiae*.

However in a parallel development, the scope of international law has now broadened from an almost exclusive concern with the rights and duties of States, so that it now also imposes a considerable body of obligations in respect of individuals. Of particular interest for present purposes is the evolution of individual criminal responsibility under international law for a number of serious international crimes which offend international public order. As Sir Arthur Watts (1994, p 82) points out:

For international conduct which is so serious as to be tainted with criminality to be regarded as attributable only to the impersonal State and not to the individuals who order or perpetrated it is both unrealistic and offensive to common notions of justice.

Furthermore recent years have seen a determination within international society to put an end to the impunity of the perpetrators of such crimes, through the development of extraterritorial jurisdiction and the establishment of international criminal tribunals. In a further development, and in line with the general trend to seek to rationalize all regimes of privilege or immunity (which is observable in other areas of international and national law), the immunities of State officials in respect of international crimes have been subject to particularly keen scrutiny in recent years.[70]

Exactly how these apparently conflicting priorities in the law should be integrated is still being worked out. Simple attempts at seeking to choose between them on the basis of hierarchy by means of the *jus cogens* or *erga omnes* nature of the primary prohibitions of

---

[69] *Advisory Opinion concerning Difference Relating to Immunity from Legal Process of a Special Rapporteur of the Commission on Human Rights, ICJ Reports 1999*, p 62, para 61. For comment see Wickremasinghe, 2000.

[70] In this respect it is to be welcomed that the International Law Commission have adopted the topic of 'Immunity of State officials from foreign criminal jurisdiction'. The Preliminary report of the Special Rapporteur Amb. Kolodkin (UN Doc. A/CN.4/601), and the Memorandum of the Secretariat (UN Doc. A/CN.4/596) contain a wealth of information and insight.

the criminalized conduct appear not to provide answers, particularly in respect of procedural obligations of States.[71] Nevertheless in recent years the law has undergone, and may still be undergoing, considerable re-examination and some significant revisions. What follows therefore does not attempt to prescribe what the law ought to be, but simply seeks to describe the law as it is in its current stage of development.

A. IMMUNITIES *RATIONE PERSONAE*

In the *Arrest Warrant* case the ICJ was concerned with the immunity *ratione personae* of a serving Foreign Minister, and concluded that under customary international law no exception to that immunity exists in respect of war crimes or crimes against humanity. The Court based this upon its review of national legislation[72] and those few decisions of higher courts in national legal systems on the point.[73] One of these was the decision of the French *Cour de Cassation* in the *Qadaffi* case (Zeppala, 2001), in which the immunity of a serving Head of State was found to operate in respect of allegations of his involvement in international terrorism.[74] The other major case referred to is the decision of the House of Lords in the *Pinochet* case, in which in a number of dicta their Lordships suggested that the immunity *ratione personae* of serving Heads of States and serving Ambassadors (unless waived) could be relied upon in proceedings for international crimes.[75]

Thus it seems that based on general principle the immunity *ratione personae* of certain incumbent high State officials, including Heads of State, Heads of Government, Foreign Ministers, certain other senior Ministers, diplomatic agents, and also the members of high-level special missions, are, in the absence of waiver by the sending State, an absolute bar to the criminal jurisdiction of the national courts for the duration of their office/mission,[76] even in relation to these serious international crimes. The reason for this is that the functions which these officials serve in maintaining international relations are such that they should not be endangered by the subjection of such officials (whilst they are in office) to the criminal jurisdiction of another State.

---

[71] See, eg, the ECtHR case of *Al-Adsani* v *UK*, [GC], no 35763/97, ECHR 2001-XI, 34 *EHRR* 11, which dealt with the question of the immunity of the State itself from civil jurisdiction. See also Article 98(1) of the Statute of the International Criminal Court at n 87 below.

[72] In this respect the former Belgian Act of 10 February 1999 under which immunities were not admissible in respect of war crimes, crimes against humanity, and genocide, appeared exceptional and so could not be relied upon as sufficient evidence in itself of an emerging rule of general international law. A point underlined by the fact that this provision was repealed and the Act as whole was substantially amended following the Court's judgment and diplomatic pressure from other States.

[73] Subsequent cases which also support the findings of the ICJ are *Tachiona and others* v *Mugabe and others* 169 F.Supp. 2d 259 (2001) and *Wei Ye* v *Jiang Zemin* 383F.3d 620.; similarly the trio of cases from the Bow Street Magistrates' Court, *Mugabe* of 14 January 2004 (2004) 53 *ICLQ* 770, *Mofaz*, 12 February 2004 (2004) 53 *ICLQ* 771–773 and *Bo Xilai*, 8 November 2005 (128 ILR 713) as well as the case of *Re Ehud Barak* from the Westminster Magistrates' Court (*Re Ehud Barak*, 29 September 2009 (not yet reported).

[74] *Qadaffi* case, 125 ILR 490.

[75] See the speeches of Lord Browne–Wilkinson at 844E–G; Lord Hope at 886G–H; Lord Saville at 903F–G; Lord Millett 913 E–G; and Lord Phillips at 924C–D.

[76] Heads of State, Heads of Government, and Foreign Ministers appear to enjoy immunities in respect of all foreign States (ie, *erga omnes*), whereas the immunities under the VCDR and the Special Missions Convention are primarily enjoyed only in the receiving State (though they also provide for privileges and immunities whilst in transit).

However in the *Arrest Warant* case the ICJ also stressed that immunity was not the same as impunity. In this respect it noted four circumstances in which the availability of immunity *ratione personae* of incumbent office-holders would not prevent their prosecution:

(i)   where the office-holder in question is prosecuted by the courts of his own State;

(ii) where immunity is waived by the office-holder's State;

(iii) when the office-holder leaves office, he may be prosecuted by the court of another State (provided that in other respects it has jurisdiction in accordance with international law) in respect of his acts prior to or subsequent to his period of office, or for his private acts during his period of office; and

(iv) by certain international criminal courts, provided that they have jurisdiction.

The first two of these circumstances are relatively uncontroversial and are well-established in international law, and need little further comment here.[77] However the latter two circumstances form the basis of the consideration of the following subsections.

B. IMMUNITIES *RATIONE MATERIAE*

The prelude to the re-examination of immunities *ratione materiae* in relation to serious crimes under international law was the arrest of the former President of Chile, General Pinochet in 1998. As is well-known Pinochet was arrested whilst temporarily in London for medical treatment, following a request by Spain for his extradition in connection with charges of *inter alia* the widespread use of torture during his period of office as Head of State of Chile. Eventually the House of Lords had to consider whether Pinochet could resist extradition by relying on his subsisting immunity *ratione materiae*, ie, in respect of official acts he performed whilst he was Head of State, notwithstanding that he was no longer in office.

Trying to distil the *ratio* of the judgment of the House of Lords is complicated not only by the nature of the case, but also by the fact the reasoning in each of the judgments of the six judges in the majority differs. A full treatment is therefore beyond the scope of this chapter.[78] The court was faced on the one hand with allegations of the international crime of torture, which by definition requires official involvement,[79] and on the other with Pinochet's claim to immunity *ratione materiae*. By a majority of six to one the House rejected the plea of immunity in respect of the torture allegations.

Put briefly three of their Lordships relied upon an implied waiver of the immunity *ratione materiae*, which it found States parties to the Torture Convention must have

---

[77] It might be noted in respect of (i) that the immunities *ratione personae* of certain high officials of international organizations can be opposed to the jurisdiction of the courts of their own State of nationality.

[78] The case is the subject of a considerable literature, including: Warbrick, Salgado, and Goodwin, 1999; Fox, 1999; Barker, 1999; Denza, 1999; Dupuy, 1999; Dominicé, 1999; Cosnard, 1999; Chinkin, 1999; Van Alebeek, 2000.

[79] See Article 1(1) of the UN Convention Against Torture and other Cruel, Inhuman or Degrading Treatment of Punishment 1984, which defines torture as the international infliction of pain or suffering for various purposes, 'when such pain or suffering is inflicted by or at the instigation of or with the consent or acquiescence of public official or other person acting in an official capacity'.

intended.[80] If this were otherwise the international criminalization of torture under the Convention would have been rendered largely purposeless, as anybody charged with torture would (in the absence of waiver) be able to rely on official act immunity.

However the judgments of the other three of their Lordships who made up the majority appear to have been more broadly based. They suggest that individual responsibility for serious crimes in international law cannot be opposed by reliance upon immunity *ratione materiae* of former Heads of State. That form of immunity only covers official acts in order to ensure that the immunities of the State itself are not undermined by proceedings against its former Head. The purpose of the immunity is therefore to ensure that the national courts of one State do not adjudicate on the responsibility of another State without the consent of the latter. However these judges found that as such immunity is concerned with the responsibility of the State, it cannot be invoked in respect of an individual's own criminal responsibility in international law.[81]

For now what can be said with certainty is that the *Pinochet* case is authority in English law for the proposition that there is an exception to immunity from criminal jurisdiction *ratione materiae* enjoyed by former Heads of State in respect of acts of official torture. It might also be noted that their Lordships found that since the development of individual criminal responsibility in respect of torture represents a distinct basis of responsibility to which official act immunity does not extend, Pinochet's immunity *ratione materiae* from civil process was unaffected. Beyond this it is difficult to draw further conclusions at this stage. Whether the exception to immunity found in this case can be extended in respect of other international crimes and/or in respect of other immunities *ratione materiae* enjoyed by officials or former officials has been much debated, but firm conclusions cannot be drawn.

It should also be recalled that the International Court of Justice in its judgment in the *Arrest Warrant* case also commented on this issue, though these comments are strictly speaking *obiter* since this case was concerned with the immunities *ratione personae* of a serving Foreign Minister. The majority of the Court found that a former Foreign Minister would be liable to prosecution in the courts of another State for the acts he performed during his period of office in his private capacity.[82] If this is taken as a broad statement of the principle that a former Foreign Minister enjoys a subsisting immunity *ratione materiae* for his official acts, it may be unsurprising. However this passage of the judgment has been the subject of criticism for the narrowness of its formulation (McLachlan, 2002) and some

[80]   See the speeches of Lord Browne-Wilkinson at 847; Lord Hope (who found the exception to immunity *ratione materiae* applied only in respect of a systematic or widespread torture) at 882–887; and Lord Saville at 904.

[81]   Lord Hutton accepted the fact that the allegations of torture concerned acts in the performance of public functions, but found that 'certain crimes are so grave and so inhuman that they constitute crimes against international law and that the international community is under a duty to bring to justice a person who commits such crimes'. He then held that individual criminal liability in respect of such crimes was quite distinct from the question of State responsibility which underlay immunities *ratione materiae* (at 887–902). Lord Millett found the existence of immunity *ratione materiae* simply inconsistent with the development of serious crimes of *jus cogens* nature for which extraterritorial jurisdiction was available (at 909–914). Lord Phillips similarly found that the development of international crimes and extraterritorial jurisdiction could not co-exist with immunity *ratione materiae* (at 924).

[82]   *Arrest Warrant of 11 April 2000 (Democratic Republic of Congo v Belgium), Preliminary Objections and Merits, Judgment, ICJ Reports 2002*, p 3, para 61.

have even drawn from it the implication that the subsisting immunity of a former Foreign Minister would be applicable in respect of serious international crimes such as war crimes and crimes against humanity (Wirth, 2002; Spinedi, 2002). If this latter point is what the Court intended then it might suggest that a narrow reading should be given to the decision of the House of Lords in the *Pinochet* case. On other hand, it should be noted that in their Joint Separate Opinion Judges Higgins, Kooijmans, and Buergenthal suggest that the current trend of State practice is that serious international crimes are not covered by the immunities *ratione materiae* of former State officials.[83]

C. IMMUNITIES BEFORE INTERNATIONAL CRIMINAL COURTS

The development of international criminal courts has clearly been a major step in combating impunity for serious international crimes. Whilst a detailed discussion of the question of immunities before such courts is beyond the scope of this chapter, the broad principles will be outlined. As we have noted the ICJ suggested that immunities would not in principle be available before international courts. An apparently similar finding was made by the Appeals Chamber of the Special Court of Sierra Leone.[84] Indeed the Statutes of the Nuremberg and Tokyo Tribunals, the International Criminal Tribunal for the Former Yugoslavia (ICTY), the International Criminal Tribunal for Rwanda (ICTR), the Rome Statute of the International Criminal Court (ICC), and the Statute of the Special Court for Sierra Leone (SCSL) all contain express provisions to the effect that the official capacity of an individual shall in no case exempt him from criminal responsibility.[85] Such provisions would appear to suggest that neither immunity *ratione personae* nor immunity *ratione materiae* would in principle be a bar to the jurisdiction of these international criminal courts.

Nevertheless as Akande has persuasively argued this picture requires some further elaboration in view of the range of different international criminal tribunals which currently exist (Akande, 2004). In particular the question of whether an individual can rely on immunities in international law before an international court will, as a first step, require a consideration of the basis on which the court was established as well as the provisions of its constitutive statute. Moreover, since these international courts will require the assistance of national authorities and national courts in matters such as arresting and transferring suspects, providing evidence and other forms of cooperation, there are also questions as to the availability of immunities before relevant national authorities in these situations.

In this respect the ICTY and ICTR, which were established by the Security Council pursuant to its mandatory powers under Chapter VII of the UN Charter, may be distinguished from tribunals established by treaty. The removal of the immunity of defendants in the Statutes

---

[83] Ibid, Joint Separate Opinion, para 85. See also Akande (2004, p 415) who concludes that 'immunity *ratione materiae* does not exist with respect to domestic criminal proceedings for any of the international crimes set out in the Statute of the ICC'.

[84] See *The Prosecutor v Charles Taylor*, Case No SCSL-2003-01-I (31 May 2004).

[85] See Article 7 of the Charter of the International Criminal Tribunal of Nuremberg and Article 6 of the Charter of the Tokyo Tribunal. See Article 7(2) of the Statute of the ICTY; Article 6(2) of the Statute of the ICTR; Article 27 of the Statute of the ICC; and Article 6(2) of the Statute of the Special Court for Sierra Leone.

of these two Tribunals not only entitles the Tribunals themselves to adjudicate over such individuals, but it also provides a legal basis for all member States of the UN not to afford immunity to such persons when arresting or transferring them pursuant to Orders of the Tribunals. At the same time however it should also be noted that the Appeals Chamber of the ICTY has for example recognized the immunities of State officials *ratione materiae*, exempting them from a requirement to produce documents in evidence which they held by virtue of their official position.[86]

As a body established by treaty, the ICC is in a somewhat different position, since States must consent to be bound by the Rome Statute before they are bound by it. Whilst the Rome Statute appears to limit the immunities available to defendants in proceedings before the ICC itself (Article 27), it is not clear that this provision can restrict the immunities of officials of States that are not parties to the Rome Statute, unless, of course, there is a waiver by the relevant State, or a binding resolution of the Security Council vesting jurisdiction in the ICC. In relation to the availability of immunities to proceedings before national authorities and national courts, relating to requests by the ICC for surrender and assistance, it should be noted that Article 98(1) of the Rome Statute also preserves the State and diplomatic immunities of officials and property of third States.[87] In other words, officials of a State which is not a party to the Rome Statute may be able to claim immunity in respect of their arrest and transfer to the Court, whereas a State party to the Rome Statute has in effect waived such immunities in respect of its own officials both before the ICC itself and in the courts of other States parties in respect of their cooperation with the ICC. However there may be further layer of complexity in cases which are referred to the Court by the Security Council, depending on the terms of such referral.

The first decision of the ICC to deal with these issues, is the recent decision of the Pre-Trial Chamber on the arrest warrant sought by the Prosecutor in the case of *The Prosecutor v Omar Hassan Ahmad Al Bashir*.[88] As is well-known the Prosecutor sought the arrest of President Al Bashir, the serving Head of State of Sudan, for war crimes, crimes against humanity and genocide. In the event the Court decided to issue the warrant in respect of war crimes and crimes against humanity, but not genocide.[89] It dealt with the immunity issue in a short passage that found that the position of Al Bashir, as Head of a State which was not a party to the Rome Statute, had no effect on the jurisdiction of the Court over the case. In support of this finding it considered: (i) that putting an end to impunity was a core goal of the Rome Statute; (ii) Article 27 of the Rome Statute sought to give effect to this goal with specific language limiting exemptions and immunities attaching to persons by reason of their office; (iii) on the basis of the clear language of Article 27, there was no need to examine other sources of law; and (iv) in referring the situation in Darfur to the ICC,

---

[86] See *Prosecutor v Blaskić*, Judgment, Case No IT-95–14-T, Trial Chamber (3 March 2000); 110 ILR 609. However see also the case of *Prosecutor v Krstić*, Judgment, Case No IT-98-33-A, Appeals Chamber (19 April 2004). For comment see Akande, 2004, p 418.

[87] Thus Article 98(1) states: 'The Court may not proceed with a request for surrender or assistance which would require the requested State to act inconsistently with its obligations under international law with respect to the State or diplomatic immunity of a person or property of a third State, unless the Court can first obtain the cooperation of that third State for the waiver of the immunity.'

[88] *The Prosecutor v Omar Hassan Ahmad Al Bashir*, 4 March 2009, Case No ICC-02/05-01/09.

[89] The Prosecutor appealed against the Pre-Trial Chamber's refusal of the warrant in respect of genocide, and that appeal was still pending at the time of writing.

the Security Council accepted that the investigation and any resulting prosecutions would accord with the provisions of the Rome Statute as a whole. Thus it was clear that Al Bashir's position as Head of States was not a bar to the jurisdiction of the Court.

The more complex issue seems to be what steps States may or must take in execution of the warrants.[90] Although the Court did not expressly address the application of Article 98(1), it did consider that Sudan was obliged 'to cooperate fully with and provide any necessary assistance to the Court' by virtue of Security Council resolution 1593(2005), a binding resolution under Chapter VII of the UN Charter and given primacy over other obligations by virtue of Article 103 of the Charter.[91] The Court ordered that the arrest warrant be served on all States parties to the Rome Statute, and all members of the Security Council that are not States parties to the Rome Statute, with a request for the arrest and surrender of Al Bashir. Whilst the reasoning of the Court is concise, it might suggest that the effect of resolution 1593(2005) is to assimilate the position of Sudan with that of a State party, which by virtue of Article 27 cannot assert immunity to oppose arrest proceedings at the national level. If that is the case, then clearly States parties are under an obligation to comply with request for arrest and surrender under Article 89 of the Rome Statute.[92] The effect on non-States parties other than Sudan would depend upon the interpretation of relevant Security Council resolutions.[93]

IX. CONCLUSION

Thus we have seen that in modern diplomatic law there has been considerable movement towards the rationalization of immunities, so that it is now clear that they are not granted for the personal benefit of their holders. Instead they are granted on a functional basis, to facilitate the processes of communication and cooperation in international relations. Carefully considered legal regimes have been created in which the interests of sending and receiving States have been balanced. There is a general acceptance that without these immunities their holders could be impeded from effective performance of these important

[90] Gaeta, 2009 and Akande, 2009.

[91] Paragraph 2 of UNSCR 1593 provides: '*Decides* that the Government of Sudan and all other parties to the conflict in Darfur, shall cooperate fully with and provide any necessary assistance to the Court and the Prosecutor pursuant to this resolution and, while recognizing that States not party to the Rome Statute have no obligation under the Statute, *urges* all States and concerned regional and other international organizations to cooperate fully'.

[92] It might be noted that following the Court's decision, the UK made an Order in Council based on the enabling powers in both s 23(5) of the International Criminal Court Act 2001 and s 1 of the United Nations Act 1946, providing that State or diplomatic immunities will not prevent proceedings in the UK for the arrest and delivery of persons alleged to have committed an ICC Crime as a result of the referral of the situation in Darfur under UNSCR 1593 (see the International Criminal Court (Darfur) Order 2009, SI 699/2009).

[93] A full treatment of all the issues raised (both legal and diplomatic) is beyond the scope of this chapter. It should be noted that the case has resulted in considerable diplomatic activity. President Bashir's ability to travel internationally has been severely curtailed. On the other hand, there is an ongoing process of discussion in the African Union which touches on many of the issues raised here (see most recently 'Recommendations of the Ministerial Meeting on the Rome Statute of the International Criminal Court', 6 November 2009). There have also been calls from some quarters for the Security Council to invoke its powers under Article 16 of the Rome Statute to defer the proceedings, but to date no State has made a formal proposal to the Council in this respect.

functions, the purpose of which serves the international public interest. Following its codification in the 1960s diplomatic law has, for the most part, constituted a well-observed and stable body of rules.

At the same time greater consensus has developed and continues to develop on the standards of governance of those exercising public power, and in particular recently on the criminalization of the gravest excesses in this respect. The wholesale exemption of those who commit such crimes in connection with public purposes would clearly be contradictory. The establishment of the International Criminal Court, in relation to which immunities are not available (except as provided for in Article 98 in respect of non-parties), is clearly a hugely significant step for international law.

However the resolution of these conflicting priorities at the national level is still being worked out, and an authoritative statement of the law is not possible at this point. Nevertheless if the above survey is accepted, international law currently appears to be moving towards compromise. The immunities *ratione personae* attaching to certain offices will render their holders immune from national proceedings, but not necessarily from international proceedings. On the other hand once they have left office, such persons will enjoy a general immunity in respect of their official acts *ratione materiae*, but exceptionally it appears that in respect of certain international crimes they might not be so immune.

REFERENCES

AKANDE, D (2004), 'International Law Immunities and the International Criminal Court', 98 *AJIL* 407.

—— (2008) 'Prosecution of Senior Rwandan Government Official in France: More on Immunity', http://www.ejiltalk. org/prosecution-of-senior-rwandan-government-official-in-france-more-on-immunity/

—— (2009) 'The Legal Nature of Security Council Referrals to the ICC and its Impact on Al Bashir's Immunity', 7 *J Int'l Crim Just* 333.

BARKER, JC (1996), *The Abuse of Diplomatic Privileges and Immunities: A Necessary Evil?* (Aldershot: Dartmouth).

—— (1998), 'State Immunity, Diplomatic Immunity and Act of State: A Triple Protection Against Legal Action', 47 *ICLQ* 950.

—— (1999), 'The Future of Former Head of State Immunity after *ex parte Pinochet*', 48 *ICLQ* 937.

BROWNLIE, I (2008), *Principles of Public International Law*, 8th edn (Oxford: Clarendon Press).

BUZZINI, G (2009) 'Lights and Shadows of Immunities and Inviolability of State Officials in International Law: Some Comments on the *Djibouti* v *France* Case', 22 *Leiden J Int'l Law* 455.

CASSESE, A (2002), 'When may Senior State Officials be Tried for International Crimes? Some Comments on the *Congo* v *Belgium* case', 13 *EJIL* 853.

—— (2008), 'The Italian Court of Cassattion Misapprehends the Notion of War Crimes: the *Lozano* case', 6 *J Int'l Crim Just* 1077.

CHINKIN, C (1999), 'Ex Parte Pinochet Ugarte (No. 3), Casenote', 93 *AJIL* 703.

COSNARD, M (1999), 'Quelques observations sur les décisions de la Chambre des Lords dans l'affaire *Pinochet*', 103 *RGDIP* 309.

CRAWFORD, J (2002), *The International Law Commission's Articles on State Responsibility* (Cambridge: Cambridge University Press).

DENZA, E (1999), '*Ex Parte Pinochet*: Lacuna or Leap?', 48 *ICLQ* 949.

—— (2008), *Diplomatic Law*, 3rd edn (Oxford: Clarendon Press).

DINSTEIN, Y (1966), 'Diplomatic Immunity from Jurisdiction *ratione materiae*', 15 *ICLQ* 76.

DOMINICÉ, C (1999), 'Quelques observations sur l'immunité de jurisdiction pénale de l'ancien Chef d'État', 103 *RGDIP* 297.

DUPUY, P-M (1999), 'Crimes et immunités', 103 *RGDIP* 289.

EL-ERIAN, A and SCOBBIE, I (1998), 'International Organisations and International Relations', in Dupuy, R-J (ed), *A Handbook on International Organisations*, 2nd edn (Dordrecht: Martinus Nijhoff).

FOX, H (1999), 'The *Pinochet No 3* Case', 48 *ICLQ* 687.

GAETA, P (2009) 'Does President Al Bashir Enjoy Immunity from Arrest?' 7 *J Int'l Crim Just* 315.

HIGGINS, R (1985), 'The Abuse of Diplomatic Privileges and Immunities: Recent United Kingdom Experience', 79 *AJIL* 641.

JAMES, A (1991), 'Diplomatic Relations and Contacts', 62 *BYIL* 347.

JENKS, CW (1961), *International Immunities* (London: Stevens).

JENNINGS, SIR ROBERT (2002), 'Jurisdiction and Immunity in the ICJ Decision in the *Yerodia* case', 4 *International Law Forum* 99.

LEE, LT and QUIGLEY, J (2008), *Consular Law and Practice*, 3rd edn (Oxford: Clarendon Press).

MCLACHLAN, C (2002), '*Pinochet* Revisited', 51 *ICLQ* 959.

MANN, FA (1990), ' "Inviolability" and other problems of the Vienna Convention on Diplomatic Relations', in Mann, FA, *Further Studies in International Law* (Oxford: Clarendon Press).

MICHAELS, DB (1971), *International Privileges and Immunities: a Case for a Universal Statute* (The Hague: Martinus Nijhoff).

PALCHETTI, P (2008) '*Lozano v. Italy* – Analysis' ILDC 1085 (IT 2008).

ROBERTS, I (ed) (2009), *Satow's Diplomatic Practice*, 6th edn (Oxford: Oxford University Press).

RYNGAERT, C (2005), 'Universal Criminal Jurisdiction over Torture: a State of Affairs', Working Paper No 66, revised (Institute of International Law, Faculty of Law, Catholic University of Leuven—available on-line at **http://www.internationallaw.be**).

SCHREUER, C and WITTICH, S (2002), 'Immunity v Accountability: the ICJ's Judgment in the *Yerodia* case', 4 *International Law Forum* 117.

SPINEDI, M (2002), 'State Responsibility v Individual Responsibility for International Crimes: *Tertium Non Datur*', 13 *EJIL* 895.

STERN, B (2002), 'Les dits et non dits de la Cour internationale de Justice dans l'affaire RDC contre Belgique', 4 *International Law Forum* 104.

VAN ALEBEEK, R (2000), 'The *Pinochet* case: International Human Rights Law on Trial', 71 *BYIL* 29.

WARBRICK, CJ, SALGADO, EM, and GOODWIN, N (1999), 'The *Pinochet* Cases in the United Kingdom', 2 *YIHL* 1.

WATTS, SIR ARTHUR (1994), 'The Legal Position in International Law of Heads of States, Heads of Governments and Foreign Ministers', 247 *Recueil des Cours* 9.

—— (1999), *The International Law Commission 1949–1998 Vol I* (Oxford: Oxford University Press).

WHOMERSLEY, C (1992), 'Some Reflections on the Immunity of Individuals for Official Acts', 41 *ICLQ* 848.

WICKREMASINGHE, C (2000), 'The Advisory Opinion on the Difference Relating to Immunity from Legal Process of Special Rapporteur of the Commission on Human Rights', 49 *ICLQ* 724.

WIRTH, S (2002), 'Immunity for Core Crimes? The ICJ's Judgment in the *Congo v Belgium* case', 13 *EJIL* 877.

WOOD, M (1974), 'The Convention on the Prevention and Punishment of Crimes against Internationally Protected Persons, including Diplomatic Agents', 23 *ICLQ* 791.

YOUNG, E (1964), 'The Development of the Law of Diplomatic Relations', 40 *BYIL* 141.

ZEPPALA, S (2001), 'Do Heads of State Enjoy Immunity from Jurisdiction for International Crimes? The *Ghaddafi* case before the French *Cour de Cassation*', 12 *EJIL* 595.

FURTHER READING

CONSULS

LEE, LT and QUIGLEY, J (2008), *Consular Law and Practice*, 3rd edn (Oxford: Clarendon Press): the standard guide to consular law.

DIPLOMATS

DENZA, E (2008), *Diplomatic Law*, 3rd edn (Oxford: Clarendon Press): the definitive guide to the Vienna Convention on Diplomatic Relations.

ROBERTS, I (ed) (2009), *Satow's Diplomatic Practice*, 6th edn (Oxford: Oxford University Press): an up to date and very readable edition of a classic work, containing a wealth of information and practice.

HEADS OF STATE, HEADS OF GOVERNMENT, AND FOREIGN MINISTERS

WATTS, SIR ARTHUR (1994), 'The Legal Position in International Law of Heads of State, Heads of Governments and Foreign Ministers', 247 *Recueil des Cours* 9: a very readable survey of the law and its underpinning at that date.

OFFICIALS OF INTERNATIONAL ORGANIZATIONS

ZACKLIN, R (1998), 'Diplomatic Relations: Status Privileges and Immunities' and Scobbie, I (revising El-Erian, A), 'International Organisations and International Relations', both in Dupuy, R-J (ed), *A Handbook on International Organisations*, 2nd edn (Dordrecht: Martinus Nijhoff) at pp 293–313 and 831–867, respectively.

THE INTERPLAY OF INTERNATIONAL CRIMINAL LAW AND THE LAW OF IMMUNITIES

VAN ALEBEEK, R (2008) *The Immunity of States and their Officials in International Criminal Law and International Human Rights Law* (Oxford: Clarendon Press): an interesting attempt to bring coherence to the various legal strands of the issues.

WORK OF THE INTERNATIONAL LAW COMMISSION ON 'IMMUNITY OF STATE OFFICIALS FROM FOREIGN CRIMINAL JURISDICTION'

Preliminary Report of the Special Rapporteur, Amb. Kolodkin (UN Doc. A/CN.4/601): an informed and readable description of the issues.

Memorandum of the Secretariat (UN Doc. A/CN.4/596): a comprehensive survey containing a wealth of practice, information and analysis.

PINOCHET

There is an abundance of literature on this case, a starting point might be:

WARBRICK, CJ, SALGADO, EM, and GOODWIN, N (1999), 'The *Pinochet* cases in the United Kingdom', 2 *YIHL* 1.

For some of the legal policy issues at stake see:

BIANCHI, A (1999), 'Immunity versus Human Rights: the *Pinochet* Case', 10 *EJIL* 237.

DENZA, E (1999), '*Ex parte Pinochet*: Lacuna or Leap', 48 *ICLQ* 949.

IMMUNITIES BEFORE THE ICC

AKANDE, D (2004), 'International Law Immunities and the International Criminal Court', 98 *AJIL* 407.

14

THE RELATIONSHIP BETWEEN INTERNATIONAL AND NATIONAL LAW

Eileen Denza

SUMMARY

Enormous growth in the substance of international law implies that it is now mostly applied and enforced by national authorities and courts. International tribunals are clear that in case of conflict the international rule prevails, but they will not invalidate national law and have traditionally regarded as a domestic matter how the correct international result is achieved. For national legislatures and courts by contrast, their mandate derives from their national constitution. Constitutional provisions are complex and infinitely varied and do not give clear answers to many problems which arise in national courts. There is no prospect of a harmonized approach to the relationship between international and national law, but it is possible to identify factors conducive to the avoidance of conflict. These include close involvement of international lawyers in the treaty-making and ratification process, attention at the time of ratification to implementation questions, teaching of international law as part of professional training of judges, and expert assistance to national courts when international law questions arise.

I. INTRODUCTION

The law of nations was until the twentieth century concerned mainly—though never exclusively—with the conduct of sovereign States and the relations between those States. Now, however, it permeates and radically conditions national legal orders, its rules are applied and enforced by national authorities, and national courts are asked to resolve its most fundamental uncertainties. Yet international law does not itself prescribe how it should be applied or enforced at the national level. It asserts its own primacy over national laws, but without invalidating those laws or intruding into national legal systems, requiring a result rather than a method of implementation. National constitutions are therefore free to choose how they give effect to treaties and to customary international law.

Their choice of methods is extremely varied. Can it be said that certain constitutional approaches are based on greater deference to international law or help to reduce conflict between legal orders? If not, are there other general factors conducive to greater mutual understanding and to resolving the practical problems of co-existence?

II. THE APPROACH OF INTERNATIONAL COURTS AND TRIBUNALS

The jurisdiction given to international courts and tribunals is normally limited to the determination of questions of international law. In theory, there is nothing to prevent two States from referring to international arbitration or even to the International Court of Justice an issue of national law. Given the nature of international relations however, questions of national law usually arise before international tribunals because they are relevant to the construction of an international agreement or to the establishment of breach of an international obligation.

The Permanent Court of International Justice in the cases of *The Serbian Loans*[1] and *The Brazilian Loans*[2] explored the nature of its competence, under a Special Agreement between France and the Kingdom of the Serbs, Croats and Slovenes, to construe the terms of a loan contract between the Kingdom and French bondholders. The Court observed that while its main function was to decide disputes between States on the basis of international law, it also had jurisdiction to determine 'the existence of any fact which, if established, would constitute a breach of an international obligation'. This jurisdiction included questions of municipal law.

The Court made clear however that it was not entitled to undertake its own construction of national laws, with the danger of contradicting rulings of national tribunals. It said that:

It would be a most delicate matter to do so, especially in cases concerning public policy and in cases where no relevant provisions directly relate to the questions at issue. It is French legislation, as applied in France, which really constitutes French law...

In the *Nottebohm* case[3] the International Court of Justice had to determine whether Liechtenstein was entitled to exercise a right of diplomatic protection of Nottebohm—a German national by birth who had become a naturalized citizen of Liechtenstein but without having any real connections with that State. As a general rule, States are entitled to exercise diplomatic protection of their nationals, and international law does not impose limitations on the right of a sovereign State to determine who are its nationals. The Court emphasized, however, that the issue in the case was not the domestic law validity of Nottebohm's naturalization. The question was whether the grant of nationality by Liechtenstein produced international legal effects which must be recognized by Guatemala.[4]

---

[1] *Serbian Loans, Judgment No 14, 1929, PCIJ, Ser A, No 20.*
[2] *Brazilian Loans, Judgment No 15, 1929, PCIJ, Ser A, No 21.*
[3] *Nottebohm, Second Phase, Judgment, ICJ Reports 1955, p 4.*
[4] The *Nottebohm* principle was critically re-examined by an ICSID Tribunal in *Micula v Romania Decision on Jurisdiction and Admissibility, 24 September 2008*, ICSID Case No. ARB/05/20, but without calling into question the approach to national law.

A. WHERE NATIONAL LAW CAUSES BREACH OF INTERNATIONAL LAW

International tribunals have consistently held that in the event of conflict between international obligations and national law, the international rule prevails. The position was set out in the draft Declaration on Rights and Duties of States prepared by the International Law Commission and endorsed in 1949 by the UN General Assembly. Article 13 provided that:

Every state has the duty to carry out in good faith its obligations arising from treaties and other sources of international law, and it may not invoke provisions in its constitution or its laws as an excuse for failure to perform this duty.[5]

The rule was restated in Article 27 of the Vienna Convention on the Law of Treaties[6] as follows:

Internal law and observance of treaties
   A party may not invoke the provisions of its internal law as justification for its failure to perform a treaty. This rule is without prejudice to Article 46.

Article 46 permits a State to argue that its consent to a treaty was invalidated by violation of its internal law only where 'that violation was manifest and concerned a rule of its internal law of fundamental importance'.
   The Permanent Court of International Justice, in the *Exchange of Greek and Turkish Populations* case,[7] stated that it was self-evident that a State which had assumed valid international obligations was bound to make such modifications in its legislation as were necessary to ensure their fulfilment. The need for effective implementation of international human rights obligations in national law so that they can be relied on by individuals is particularly obvious, and the primacy of international obligations over conflicting national law has often been reaffirmed by human rights tribunals. The Inter-American Court of Human Rights, for example, in an Advisory Opinion on *International Responsibility for the Promulgation and Enforcement of Laws in Violation of the Convention* said:

Pursuant to international law, all obligations imposed by it must be fulfilled in good faith; domestic law may not be invoked to justify nonfulfilment. These rules may be deemed to be general principles of law and have been applied by the Permanent Court of International Justice and the International Court of Justice even in cases involving constitutional provisions...[8]

International tribunals will not however declare national laws invalid—merely that these laws or the way in which they have been applied are inconsistent with international law. Thus the Inter-American Court of Human Rights, in the Advisory Opinion just cited made clear that its Opinion related:

...only to the legal effects of the law under international law. It is not appropriate for the Court to rule on its domestic legal effect within the State concerned. That determination is

---

[5] GA Res 375 (IV).   [6] UKTS No 58 (1980), Cmnd 7964.
[7] *Exchange of Greek and Turkish Populations, Advisory Opinion, 1925, PCIJ, Ser B, No 10.*
[8] *Advisory Opinion, OC-14/94, Ser A, No 14* (9 December 1994), para 35, 116 ILR 320.

within the exclusive jurisdiction of the national courts and should be decided in accordance with their laws.[9]

The International Court of Justice in the *LaGrand* case[10] was required to consider the consequences of the admitted failure by the United States to give timely notification to two German nationals of their right to consular protection under Article 36 of the Vienna Convention on Consular Relations. Notwithstanding a provisional order from the ICJ asking the US to 'take all measures at its disposal' to stay execution of Walter LaGrand until the case brought by Germany had been decided,[11] he was executed as scheduled. On the merits Germany later argued, *inter alia*, that the US constitutional rule of 'procedural default' (under which a procedural failing which had not been raised at State level could not be argued at federal level) violated the US obligation under Article 36 of the Vienna Convention. This required the US to give full effect to the purposes for which the rights to notification and consular access are intended. The International Court rejected the suggestion by the US that in pronouncing on the application of Article 36 it was acting as 'a court of appeal of national criminal proceedings'. It further emphasized that:

In itself, the rule does not violate Article 36 of the Vienna Convention. The problem arises when the procedural default rule does not allow the detained individual to challenge a conviction and sentence by claiming, in reliance on Article 36, paragraph 1 of the Convention, that the competent national authorities failed to comply with their obligation to provide the requisite consular information 'without delay', thus preventing the person from seeking and obtaining consular assistance from the sending State.[12]

The Court held that an apology for any future violations of Article 36 would be inadequate reparation, and that the US must allow review and reconsideration of a conviction and sentence in the light of the violation of the rights in the Convention. They stressed however that this obligation could be carried out in various ways, and that 'The choice of means must be left to the United States'.[13]

In the case of *Avena* in 2004 the Court noted that the procedural default rule had not been revised to prevent its application to cases involving breaches of the Vienna Convention on Consular Relations, and it refined its views on adequate reparation, saying:

It follows that the remedy to make good these violations should consist in an obligation on the United States to permit review and reconsideration of these nationals' cases by the United States courts...with a view to ascertaining whether in each case the violation of Article 36 committed by the competent authorities caused actual prejudice to the defendant in the process of administration of criminal justice.[14]

---

[9] Para 34.

[10] *LaGrand (Germany v United States of America), Merits, Judgment, ICJ Reports 2001*, p 466. See Mennecke and Tams, 2002.

[11] *LaGrand (Germany v United States of America), Provisional Measures, Order of 3 March 1999, ICJ Reports 1999*, p 9.

[12] *LaGrand (Germany v United States of America), Merits, Judgment, ICJ Reports 2001*, p 466, paras 79–91.

[13] Ibid, para 125.

[14] *Avena and Other Mexican Nationals (Mexico v United States of America), Judgment, ICJ Reports 2004*, p 12, para 121. See Shelton, 2004.

Responding to the Court's judgment, President Bush ordered courts in the United States to review the cases of 49 Mexicans under sentence of death. But on a further application by one of those covered by the *Avena* decision and again in the face of an order from the International Court calling for a stay of execution, the US Supreme Court in the case of *Medellin* v *Texas*[15] by majority ruled that the ICJ ruling did not constitute enforceable US federal law and that the President had no constitutional authority to alter this position so as to overrule the procedural default rule. Texas executed Medellin in full knowledge that this represented a violation of the international obligations of the United States.[16]

B. INTERNATIONAL LAW LOOKS MAINLY TO THE RESULT

Traditionally, international tribunals and supervisory bodies have concerned themselves only with the result in the specific case where there has been a complaint of breach. The method of national implementation of international obligations has been regarded as an internal affair. There are however signs of a more intrusive approach.

In the European Community law context, the European Court of Justice from the outset, went beyond asserting the primacy of a European Community treaty or secondary obligation. In the case of *Costa* v *ENEL*,[17] the ECJ did not limit itself to saying that Italy was in breach of its Community law obligations because its courts upheld a later national measure which was inconsistent with these obligations. It held that:

By contrast with ordinary international treaties, the EEC Treaty has created its own legal system which, on the entry into force of the Treaty, became an integral part of the legal systems of the Member States...

and that:

...the law stemming from the Treaty, an independent source of law, could not, because of its special and original nature, be overridden by domestic legal provision, however framed, without being deprived of its character as Community law and without the legal basis of the Community itself being called into question.

This formulation of the supremacy of Community law—not self-evident on the face of the European Community Treaties—is among the features distinguishing European Community law from international law (Craig and de Búrca, 2007, Ch 8; Slaughter and Burke-White, 2007). In consequence of the more intrusive nature of the Community legal order Member States may be accountable for the methods by which they implement regulations and directives. The European Commission is charged with ensuring that the provisions of the Treaty are applied, and has vigorously monitored methods of national implementation of Community legal obligations.

---

[15] *Medellin* v *Texas* (2008) 552 US 491, noted in (2008) 102 *AJIL* 859.

[16] For the restrained reaction of the ICJ, see judgment in *Request for Interpretation of the Judgment of 31 March 2004 in the* Case concerning Avena and Other Mexican Nationals *(Mexico* v *United States of America)*, Judgment of 19 January 2009 paras 47–59. It follows that in the US legislation would be required to ensure compliance with the obligations of consular notification and access.

[17] *Costa* v *ENEL* Case 6/64 [1964] ECR 585.

In the field of international criminal law, it is now common for treaties not merely to permit but to require the assumption of criminal jurisdiction at national level, and to set out a uniform definition of certain criminal offences in such a way that detailed changes in national law are required. Under the 1984 United Nations Convention Against Torture and Other Cruel, Inhuman or Degrading Treatment or Punishment,[18] for example, there is first a uniform definition of torture for the purposes of the convention. Secondly, there is a requirement for each party to take effective legislative, administrative, judicial, or other measures to prohibit torture within its own jurisdiction and to ensure that all acts of torture are offences under its criminal law. Thirdly, a party must establish a wider extraterritorial jurisdiction on grounds such as the nationality of the alleged offender and where it does not extradite an alleged offender taken into custody in its territory. The requirements imposed on national laws by successive treaties in the field of international criminal law have become increasingly detailed and specific. Even the 1948 Convention on the Prevention and Punishment of the Crime of Genocide[19] however—which may be regarded as the precursor of these treaties—provided in Article V that:

The Contracting Parties undertake to enact, in accordance with their respective Constitutions, the necessary legislation to give effect to the provisions of the present Convention and, in particular, to provide effective penalties for persons guilty of genocide or any of the other acts enumerated in Article III.

The Statute of the International Criminal Court does not impose express requirements on Parties to incorporate international criminal offences in domestic law, but the principle of complementarity (whereby the ICC assumes jurisdiction only where Parties fail in their primary responsibility to prosecute) ensures that Parties have given close attention to national implementation of substantive rules of criminal law.[20]

The Convention against Torture, like many earlier human rights conventions, establishes a Committee whose functions include monitoring national implementation. Parties are required to report to the Committee against Torture, within one year of becoming legally bound by the convention and subsequently at four-yearly intervals, on the measures they have taken to give effect to their undertakings. The Committee may comment on the effectiveness of national implementing measures, and may make any criticisms public (along with observations by the State concerned) in its own annual report. Governments should therefore give careful thought to implementation at the time of ratification rather than simply leave to their courts the task of giving effect to the convention within the context of national criminal law and procedure. Other modern conventions—on for example non-proliferation of biological or chemical weapons or protection of the environment—may also require for proper implementation administrative supervision or inspection mechanisms at national level for which no international model law can be prescribed.[21]

The need for precise national implementation in criminal matters has been highlighted by the difficulty experienced in controlling piracy off the coast of Somalia. Customary international law permits national arrest and punishment of any pirates apprehended on the high seas—but in addition to problems in arrest of pirates sheltering in a State lacking

---

[18] UKTS No 107 (1991), Cm 1775.   [19] UKTS No 58 (1970), Cmnd 4421; 78 UNTS 277.
[20] See Third Report of ICC Committee of the International Law Association, Rio de Janeiro (2008).
[21] See generally Ulfstein, 2007.

effective participation in the international legal system, it has been found that other States willing to try and to punish pirates lack the necessary national criminal jurisdiction. It has been seen by the international maritime community as urgent that international conventions which plug this gap are widely ratified and effectively enforced at national level.[22]

III. THE APPROACH OF NATIONAL PARLIAMENTS AND NATIONAL COURTS

While the principles applied by international tribunals to the relationship between international and national law are uniform and reasonably straightforward, this is not the case with the approaches taken by national parliaments or by national courts. For each national legislature and court, the starting point for any examination of the relationship is its own constitution. It is not that national bodies dispute as a matter of principle what is said by international tribunals as to the position in international law, or that they dispute the existence or binding character of international law, but rather that they perceive the way in which international law is integrated into and applied within their own legal order as being their own constitutional affair. Other States do not question this autonomy, and even international tribunals—as was illustrated above—regard the detail of national laws and constitutional methods as outside their competence.

Scholars have put forward various theories to explain the relationship between international and national law. Most persistent have been the theories of monism and of dualism. In the view of the monists, there is a single legal system with international law at its apex and all national constitutional and other legal norms below it in the hierarchy. There is no need for international obligations to be 'transformed' into rules of national law, and in case of any apparent conflict, the international rule prevails. The fact that national organs do not behave according to such rules indicates the weakness of international law, but does not invalidate the theory, since the State will incur international responsibility where it permits violations of international legal rules to occur. According to Kelsen, the leading exponent of the monist theory, it could not be based on scientific observation, but was dependent on ethical considerations (Kelsen, 1920).

Under the dualist theory, international law and national law operate on different levels. International law is a horizontal legal order based on and regulating mainly the relations and obligations between independent and theoretically equal sovereign States. To the extent that to be effective it requires to be applied at national level, it is for each State to determine how this is done. If the international rule confers rights or obligations on individuals or entities created under national law, the national legislature may 'transform' it into a rule of national law, and the national judge will then apply it as a rule of national, or domestic law.

There is no indication that either theory has had a significant input into the development or revision of national constitutions, into national debates about the ratification of international agreements, or into decisions of national courts on questions of international law. Except as shorthand indications of the general approach within a particular State to implementation or application of international rules, the theories are not useful in

---

[22] UN SC Res 1846 (2 December 2008) has addressed these problems.

clarifying the relationship between international law and national laws. They suggest—at least to students of international law—that there are only two methods of approach and that one or other theory must be 'correct' or at least preferable. Neither of these impressions is helpful. There are almost as many ways of giving effect to international law as there are national legal systems. To classify a State as 'monist' or 'dualist' does not greatly assist in describing its constitutional approach to international obligations, in determining how its government and parliament will proceed in order to adopt or implement a new treaty, or in predicting how its courts will approach the complex questions which arise in litigation involving international law.

IV. THE SPECTRUM OF CONSTITUTIONAL RULES

Six States have been chosen as spanning the spectrum from monism to dualism and as reflecting constitutions emerging, or undergoing revision, at different historical periods. They are the Netherlands, Germany, France, Russia, the United States of America, and the United Kingdom. In each of these, the approach to international law reflects the historical background to the adoption, or revision of the constitution.[23]

These necessarily brief accounts of constitutional frameworks can give only a partial account of rules which have been extensively interpreted and supplemented by the practice of national legislative, executive, and judicial organs. Only in the light of that practice and jurisprudence can one assess how practical problems are dealt with in each national context.

A. THE NETHERLANDS

The provisions in the Netherlands Constitution, as revised in 1953 and in 1987, are based on two elements—a very strong degree of parliamentary control of the approval of all treaties before the Netherlands becomes bound, and a clear hierarchical superiority of treaties thus ratified over both prior and subsequent laws and statutory regulations. Article 94 of the Constitution provides for the supremacy of treaties binding on all persons in the Netherlands over prior and subsequent national law, but Article 91 makes this supremacy conditional on the treaty having been approved by the States-General and the Council of State. Such approval may be express or tacit. Some categories of treaties are exempted by statute from the requirement of parliamentary approval. Where any provision in a treaty conflicts or may conflict with the Constitution, a two-thirds majority in the States-General is required for approval. Under Article 120, Netherlands courts may not review the compatibility of the treaty with the Constitution, though in other respects they interpret and apply the treaty as national law. Article 93 further provides that treaties and resolutions of international organizations become binding only after they are published.

Article 90 of the Constitution requires the government to promote the development of the international rule of law. This however gives the government no mandate to override careful scrutiny by the States-General, and before approval of treaties, lawyers and other

---

[23] For a wider cross-section of approaches see Nijman and Nollkaemper (eds), 2007 and in particular Peters, 2007, pp 254–270.

negotiators are cross-examined in Parliamentary Committees over the detail of their texts to an extent unparalleled elsewhere in Europe. Van Dijk and Tahzib comment on this system of scrutiny:

Thus a fair balance is achieved between the primary duty of the Government to promote the international legal order and Parliament's control over the way this duty is exercised.[24]

B. GERMANY

The 1949 German Basic Law (Grundgesetz), reflecting the German experience of National Socialism and the Second World War, provides in Article 25 that:

The general rules of public international law shall be an integral part of federal law. They shall take precedence over the laws and shall directly create rights and duties for the inhabitants of the federal territory.

Articles 23 and 24 of the Basic Law permit the Federation by legislation to transfer sovereign powers to intergovernmental institutions, in particular to the European Union established by the Treaty on European Union signed at Maastricht in 1992, and to a system of mutual collective security in order to 'bring about and secure a peaceful and lasting order in Europe and among the nations of the world'. Article 26 makes it unconstitutional to carry out acts with the intention of disturbing peaceful relations between nations, especially preparation of an aggressive war.

Article 59 however provides that:

(2) Treaties which regulate the political relations of the Federation or relate to matters of federal legislation shall require the consent or participation, in the form of a federal law, of the bodies competent in any specific case for such federal legislation...

Under German constitutional practice, Parliament may be involved in treaty negotiations, and policy issues may be discussed in the Foreign Affairs Committee of the Bundestag or in that of the Bundesrat. The treaties regarded as regulating the political relations of the Federation are those which might affect the existence, independence, status, or role of the German State. Ultimate control of new treaties lies with the Federal Constitutional Court (Bundesverfassungsgericht) and its decision in the matter binds all State organs.

The role of the Federal Constitutional Court was of central importance to Germany's position as the last member State to ratify the Maastricht Treaty in 1993. Even following adoption of the new Article 23 of its Basic Law as the basis for participation in the new European Union, Germany was unable to ratify until the Constitutional Court had ruled in the case of *Brunner* v *European Union Treaty*. Brunner argued that the integration to be effected by the Treaty would lead to 'development towards the covert and irrevocable institution of a European federal state'. On this, the court said:[25]

Germany is one of the 'Masters of the Treaties' which have established their adherence to the Union Treaty concluded 'for an unlimited period'...with the intention of long-term

---

[24] Van Dijk and Tahzib, 1994, p 125. See also van Panhuys, 1953; Schermers, 1987; Leigh, Blakeslee, and Ederington (eds), 1999, Peters, 2007, pp 304–305.

[25] *Brunner* v *European Union Treaty*, [1994] 1 CMLR 57, at para 55. See also Schwarze, 1994, 1995, 2001; Treviranus and Beemelmans, 1995.

membership, but could also ultimately revoke that adherence by a contrary act. The validity and application of European law in Germany depend on the application-of-law instruction of the Accession Law. Germany thus preserves the quality of a sovereign State in its own right and the status of sovereign equality with other States...

A similar review of the implications of the 2007 Treaty of Lisbon was carried out by the Constitutional Court, and the Court insisted on further national legislation to elaborate parliamentary rights of control before German ratification.[26]

C. FRANCE

The 1958 Constitution of the Fifth Republic also requires careful control of the ratification of treaties. Article 53 provides that:

Peace treaties, commercial treaties, treaties or agreements concerning international organizations, those which impose a financial burden on the State, those which modify legislative provisions, those concerning personal status, those which effect cession, exchange or addition of territory, may not be ratified or approved except by virtue of a law.

Under Article 54, if the Constitutional Council (*Conseil Constitutionnel*) declares that an international commitment contains provision adverse to the Constitution, authorization to ratify may be given only after amendment of the Constitution. Amendment under the terms of this provision has been made for the ratification of the Treaties of Maastricht and Amsterdam, and more recently for the ratification of the Statute of the International Criminal Court.[27] In 1985 the Constitutional Council concluded that Protocol No 6 to the European Convention on Human Rights and Fundamental Freedoms on the Abolition of the Death Penalty was not in conflict with the Constitution and, in particular, that it was not inconsistent with the essential conditions for national sovereignty (Favoreu, 1985). Article 55 provides that treaties duly ratified have, after publication, an authority superior to legislation. Only in 1989 however did the Conseil d'Etat accept that this superiority applied not only to earlier but also to later national legislation (Eisemann and Kessedijan, 1999). In this context a specific treaty provision must be shown to have direct effect before it may be invoked by a party to litigation in French courts (Errera, 2008).

Under French practice, the Minister for Foreign Affairs may issue an interpretation of a treaty provision to a court, and this interpretation can be relied on in later cases involving the same provision if it is of general application and binding on the court.[28]

D. RUSSIA

In 1993, after a prolonged internal battle between the Constitutional Commission and President Yeltsin, the Russian Federation adopted a new constitution to reflect the newly

---

[26] *BVerfG*, 2 BvR 2/08, 30.6.2009 and Press Release no 72/2009. On the 'cooperative relationship' between German and international courts, particularly on human rights, see Paulus, 2007.

[27] Constitutional Law of 8 July 1999, No 99–568. See Errera in House of Lords EU Committee, 6th Report 2003–04, HL Paper 47 *The Future Role of the European Court of Justice*, QQ 161–168 and Supplementary Notes, 2008; Bell, 2005.

[28] *Affaire Barbie*, 100 ILR 330.

democratic character of Russia and a new acceptance of the international legal order. Article 86 of the Constitution gives the President of Russia the power to negotiate and conclude treaties. Article 106 provides for both Chambers of Parliament (the Duma and the Federal Council) to give consent to treaties by federal law. Some uncertainties as to the meaning of these provisions were later resolved by the 1995 Federal Law on International Treaties which reflected accession by Russia to the Vienna Convention on the Law of Treaties. As with most national constitutions, publication is essential for a treaty to carry binding force in Russian law.

Under Article 15.4 of the 1993 Constitution:

The generally recognized principles and norms of international law and the international treaties of the Russian Federation shall constitute part of the legal system. If an international treaty of the Russian Federation establishes other rules than those stipulated by the law, the rules of the international treaty shall apply.

This provision gives clear priority to both customary international law and treaties in force for Russia over both earlier and later national laws. It marked a radical change from the position under the 1977 Constitution of the Soviet Union which did not permit treaties to be invoked before domestic courts. The numerous treaties on human rights which the Soviet Union had so freely ratified without reservation suddenly became enforceable in Russian courts. Russian courts are increasingly applying principles of international law directly—particularly on human rights—though they have been hampered by the limited experience of judicial independence, the lack of professional training in international law, and the shortage of relevant materials in Russian translation.

Article 15.4 does not however give international law priority over the Russian Constitution. The Constitutional Court may review the compatibility with the Constitution of treaties not yet in force for Russia, and probably also of treaties already in force (Danilenko, 1994; Butler, 1997; Danilenko, 1999).

E. THE UNITED STATES

Under Article II s 2 of the Constitution of the United States, adopted in 1787 when the original confederal system was replaced by a fully federal system, the President:

...shall have Power, by and with the Advice and Consent of the Senate, to make Treaties, provided two thirds of the Senators present concur...

It is clear that the 'advice and consent' was intended to require consultation of the Senate during negotiations, but following one unhappy experience, the first President, George Washington, limited consultation to the approval of treaties before their ratification. The independent power of the Senate to reject or delay approval of treaties submitted by the executive is substantial.

Article VI s 2 further provides that:

This Constitution, and the Laws of the United States which shall be made in Pursuance thereof; and all Treaties made, or which shall be made, under the authority of the United States, shall be the Supreme Law of the Land, and the Judges in every State shall be bound thereby, any Thing in the Constitution or Laws of any State to the Contrary notwithstanding.

International law was accepted as part of the law of the individual States, and following the formation of the United States it was also accepted as part of federal law without the need for incorporation by Congress or by the President. International law is however regarded as subject to the Constitution and thus, at national level, to 'repeal' by later law of the United States. Wherever possible a US statute will be construed in such a way as not to conflict with international law or US treaty obligations. Where no such reconciliation is possible, it is accepted that the change in domestic law does not relieve the United States of its international obligation or the consequences of violation of that obligation.

International law and international agreements binding on the United States may be interpreted and enforced by United States courts. According to the Third Restatement of the Foreign Relations Law of the United States:

> (2) Cases arising under international law or international agreements of the United States are within the Judicial Power of the United States and, subject to Constitutional and statutory limitations and requirements of justiciability, are within the jurisdiction of the federal courts.

> (3) Courts in the United States are bound to give effect to international law and to international agreements of the United States, except that a 'non-self-executing' agreement will not be given effect as law in the absence of necessary implementation.[29]

Determinations of international law by the Supreme Court, including review of State laws on grounds of inconsistency with international law, are binding on the States and on State courts. There are complex rules of constitutional law and practice determining whether an agreement is 'self-executing' in the United States. These were applied by the Supreme Court in the case of *Medellin* v *Texas*, described above, where the majority held that a judgment of the International Court of Justice did not constitute a self-executing obligation in the United States.[30] On ratifying the International Covenant on Civil and Political Rights in 1992, the US Government attached a declaration stating that Articles 1 through 27 of the Covenant were not self-executing, and there has been no implementing legislation. Where an agreement is given effect in United States law, it is the implementing legislation, not the agreement, which is regarded as US law.[31]

Under United States judicial practice, great weight is given to views on questions of international law expressed by the US government, whether by way of *amicus curiae* briefs, interventions as a party or 'executive suggestions'. This is done on the grounds that it is desirable that the United States should speak with one voice on such questions and that the executive branch will have to answer for any alleged breach of international law by the United States.

F. THE UNITED KINGDOM

Under the unwritten constitution of the United Kingdom, Parliament has the supreme power to establish and to change the law of the United Kingdom. The conduct of foreign

---

[29] Chapter 2 Status of International Law and Agreements in United States Law, s 111.

[30] See nn 15 and 16 above.

[31] Third Restatement of the Foreign Relations Law of the US. See also Jackson, 1987; Riesenfeld and Abbott, 1994; Aust, 2007, pp 196–199.

affairs, including the conclusion and termination of treaties, remains under the royal prerogative—which means that it is carried out by the government of the day. The government are broadly accountable to Parliament for their conduct of foreign affairs.

Customary international law has long been regarded as part of the law of England and of Scotland without any need for specific incorporation, and this rule has also applied in Commonwealth States as part of the common law.[32] Treaties however are not regarded as a source of rights or obligations in domestic law. The reason is that otherwise it would be open to the monarch and now to the executive to alter national law by a treaty instead of through the enactment of legislation and thus to bypass the supremacy of Parliament. It is in theory open to the executive to assume international legal commitments, but these will not be given effect within the national legal system if they require changes in the law or the jurisdiction of the United Kingdom or the payment of money (which must be voted by Parliament). The executive may conclude treaties which do not involve changes in domestic law—for example Treaties of Friendship or Investment Promotion and Protection Agreements.

The position was expressed succinctly by Lord Templeman thus in one of the cases which resulted from the collapse in 1985 of the International Tin Council and the attempts of its creditors through UK courts to recover their losses from its member States:

A treaty is a contract between the governments of two or more sovereign states. International law regulates the relations between sovereign states and determines the validity, the interpretation and the enforcement of treaties. A treaty to which Her Majesty's Government is a party does not alter the laws of the United Kingdom. A treaty may be incorporated into or alter the laws of the United Kingdom by means of legislation. Except to the extent that a treaty becomes incorporated into the laws of the United Kingdom by statute, the courts of the United Kingdom have no power to enforce treaty rights and obligations at the behest of a sovereign government or at the behest of a private individual.[33]

By a constitutional convention, known as the Ponsonby rule, all treaties subject to ratification are laid before Parliament for 21 days on which it is sitting.[34] Although in theory this opens the way to a debate, it has almost never happened that for a treaty—even an important one—not requiring any change in UK law, Parliament has pressed for a debate. The Foreign and Commonwealth Office since 1996 accompany the treaty text with an Explanatory Memorandum which enables issues of significance to be identified.[35] Where the treaty will require changes in UK law or payment of money, the government also secure passage of the necessary changes—whether by Act of Parliament or by secondary legislation—before the treaty is brought into force for the UK. The government never deliberately assumes international commitments without being able to give internal effect to them. These constitutional constraints make the United Kingdom a demanding partner in international negotiations, but rigorous scrutiny of national implementation before ratification has meant that it has rarely been found in breach of its commitments.[36]

---

[32] For the position in Canada, for example, see *R v Hape* [2008] 1 LRC 551 at paras [34]–[46].

[33] *JH Rayner v Department of Trade and Industry* [1988] 3 All ER 257; 81 ILR 670.

[34] Under a draft Constitutional Reform and Governance Bill, the Ponsonby rule would become a statutory requirement.

[35] For the new arrangements, see *Hansard*, HC, vol 576 (16 December 1996) WA 1101, 1996 *BYIL* 746 and 753.

[36] See Aust, 2007, pp 187–194.

The UK government does not direct the courts on questions of international law. On request from the court or from a party to litigation however the Foreign and Commonwealth Office issues certificates on points of fact peculiarly within the knowledge of the government. These relate, for example, to whether an entity is recognized as a State or government and to whether an individual has been notified and received as a diplomat. Where a point of international law of interest to the government is in issue in litigation, the Attorney-General may nominate Counsel to assist the court as *amicus curiae*. But although Counsel so nominated may be assisted by government legal advisers, he or she is not directly instructed and remains an independent 'friend of the court'.

These brief and superficial surveys illustrate that at the stage of national acceptance as well as of national judicial application of international law obligations, the methods employed do not turn on any universally applicable theory of the relationship. They turn rather on the relationship between the executive, legislative, and judicial organs of each State, on how a potential new international obligation is to be democratically scrutinized, on how its subsequent application can be effectively guaranteed, and on whether the national courts are judicially independent of the executive in determining issues of international law.

V. SOME PROBLEMS WHICH ARISE IN NATIONAL COURTS

Examination of a few of the cases in national courts where the question of the relationship between international and national law has been raised shows the extreme diversity of the issues which present themselves. In many cases these issues are not capable of easy resolution in terms of national constitutions, far less in terms of general theories.

A. DOES A RULE OF CUSTOMARY INTERNATIONAL LAW PREVAIL OVER CONFLICTING NATIONAL LAW?

It seems that all national legal systems—even those of the United Kingdom and of the Commonwealth States whose constitutions have followed the same approach—accept customary international law as an integral part of national law. Incorporation is specifically provided for in some constitutions, but in others which make no specific provision the result is the same. The nature of customary international law as part of Scots law was examined for the first time in 1999 by the Appeal Court of the High Court of Justiciary in two criminal cases where the defendants, charged with sabotage against Britain's nuclear weapons, argued as 'reasonable excuse' for their conduct the international illegality of the holding of these weapons. The court held, without citing Scottish authority since there was none, that a 'rule of customary international law is a rule of Scots law'. It was not a fact to be established (like foreign law) by expert evidence, but was to be argued by submission and decided by the judge.[37]

---

[37] Cases of *John v Donnelly* and *Lord Advocate's Reference No 1, 2000*, 2001 SLT 507 (*Greenock anti-nuclear activists*), described in Neff, 2002.

English courts however found themselves for many years precluded from applying modern customary international law rules on restricted State immunity because the old rule of absolute State immunity had become embedded, or 'transformed' into English common law by a series of judicial decisions. Under the English rules on precedent, the judges maintained that the old rule could be reversed only by the House of Lords as the supreme appellate body. Eventually Lord Denning, presiding over the Court of Appeal in the case of *Trendtex Trading Corporation Ltd* v *Central Bank of Nigeria* persuaded one of his two judicial colleagues that this attitude was wrong. Customary international law was incorporated into English law so that when its rules changed, English law also changed. Lord Denning said:

International law does change, and the courts have applied the changes without the aid of any Act of Parliament. Thus, when the rules of international law were changed (by the force of public opinion) so as to condemn slavery, the English courts were justified in applying the modern rules of international law...[38]

B. WHAT IS THE MEANING OF AN INTERNATIONAL LAW RULE IN THE CONTEXT OF DOMESTIC LAW?

In most cases, the national court does not merely have to decide whether to apply a rule of international law on its own, but on the meaning and effect of the international rule in the domestic law context where it arises. Thus, in the Scottish nuclear weapons protesters cases described above, holding that international law was part of Scots law was not the end of the matter. The court had then to consider whether the holding of nuclear missiles was lawful under international law—a question which had been carefully avoided by the International Court of Justice[39]—and further whether international law gave individuals a right of forcible intervention to stop international crimes such as would amount to a defence of 'necessity' under Scottish criminal law. The Appeal Court held that the conduct of the UK Government was not illegal and that international law conferred no right of forcible intervention on individuals. The UK House of Lords, dismissing claims by protesters against the impending conflict in Iraq that they were 'preventing crime', held in the case of *R* v *Jones*,[40] that although a crime of aggression existed in international law, it did not follow automatically that 'aggression' was an offence in domestic law. Aggression was a crime committed by a State, not precisely defined under international law, and it would be contrary to modern constitutional practice for English courts to treat it as a crime in English law without specific statutory authority. As to the argument that the crime under international law had been tacitly assimilated into domestic law, Lord Bingham maintained that it was 'very relevant not only that Parliament has so far refrained from taking this step but also that it would draw the courts into an area which, in the past, they have entered, if at all, with reluctance and the utmost circumspection'.

In *Re Al-Fin Corporations's Patent* the Chancery Division of the English High Court had to construe the terms of the Patents Act 1949 which allowed extension of a patent where

---

[38] *Trendtex Trading Corporation Ltd* v *Central Bank of Nigeria* [1977] 1 QB 529; [1977] 1 All ER 881. For critical comment, see Collier, 1989.

[39] *Legality of the Threat or Use of Nuclear Weapons, Advisory Opinion, ICJ Reports 1996*, p 226.

[40] *R* v *Jones* [2006] UKHL 16.

the patentee had suffered loss 'by reason of hostilities between His Majesty and any foreign state'. Al-Fin appealed against a ruling which said that the Korean War of 1950–1953 did not qualify because North Korea had not been recognized by the UK government as a sovereign State. The Foreign Office stated that it did not, in the area of Korea in question, recognize any independent sovereign State either de facto or *de jure*—but made clear that the construction of the Patents Act was a question for the court on the basis of the evidence. The court held:

that the phrase 'any foreign state' although of course it includes a foreign State which has been given Foreign Office recognition, is not limited thereto. It must at any rate include a sufficiently defined area of territory over which a foreign government has effective control.[41]

In 2004 the United States Supreme Court in *Rasul* v *Bush*,[42] in order to determine whether they had jurisdiction to review the legality of the detention of prisoners in the Guantanamo Bay Naval Base in Cuba, applied the terms of the Lease Agreement of 1903 under which Cuba conferred on the United States 'complete jurisdiction and control' over the Base while retaining ultimate sovereignty. The majority inferred from the Agreement that the relevant statute should be construed to give US federal courts jurisdiction.

United States courts were authorized directly to determine questions of international law by the Alien Tort Statute 1789,[43] which confers original jurisdiction on federal district courts to determine 'any civil action by an alien for a tort only, committed in violation of the law of nations or a treaty of the United States'. After the rediscovery of this statute in the celebrated case of *Filartiga* v *Peña-Irala*,[44] where the plaintiff claimed damages for the torture of his son in Paraguay, the courts were invited in many cases to decide whether conduct which had taken place abroad violated modern rules of international law. The Supreme Court however in 2004, in the case of *Sosa* v *Alvarez-Machain*,[45] placed a narrow construction on the statute. They held that it was intended to be a jurisdictional statute covering causes of action where in 1789 the common law imposed personal liability— offences against ambassadors, violation of safe-conducts and piracy. New violations of international law were not entirely excluded, but the courts should be cautious in finding new private rights on the basis of the law of nations.

C. IS THE INTERNATIONAL RULE DIRECTLY APPLICABLE AND DIRECTLY EFFECTIVE?

International courts often have to determine whether an international rule—usually a treaty provision—is directly applicable, so that no further implementing action is required for it to be legally binding at national level. This question is often cast in terms of whether the treaty is 'self-executing'—an expression which may under national law depend solely on construction of the treaty or may also (particularly in the United States) turn on internal constitutional practice. A different question is whether the rule is directly effective—so that an individual may rely on it as a source of rights at national level. The distinction

---

[41] *Re Al-Fin Corporations's Patent* [1970] Ch 160.
[42] *Rasul* v *Bush*, (2004) 542 US 466.   [43] 28 USC §1350.
[44] *Filartiga* v *Peña-Irala*, 630 F.2d 876 (1980); 577 F.Supp 860.
[45] *Sosa* v *Alvarez-Machain* 124 S Ct 2739, 29 June 2004. For a full account and comment see Roth, 2004.

between direct applicability and direct effect has been clarified by the jurisprudence of the European Court of Justice. Contrary to what is sometimes suggested, the ECJ did not invent the doctrine of direct effect, which can be traced back to rulings of the Permanent Court of International Justice and to cases in European jurisdictions, but it did lay down criteria to be uniformly applied throughout the European Community. It is this uniformity which is one of the most striking features distinguishing European Community from public international law.

The cases of *Breard* v *Pruett, Breard* v *Greene* were almost identical to the *LaGrand* case described above.[46] Breard was a national of Paraguay convicted of murder by a Virginia court in the United States. A few days before he was to be executed, Paraguay brought proceedings before the International Court of Justice, on the ground that the authorities had failed to inform him of his rights to consular protection under Article 36 of the Vienna Convention on Consular Relations. The ICJ issued an interim order requesting that the United States should take all measures to suspend the execution pending its final decision.[47] On the day of the execution, the Supreme Court considered petitions seeking a stay. Among the issues was whether Article 36 of the Vienna Convention requiring notification to a person arrested of his rights to consular access and protection, was directly effective in a national court. On this, the Supreme Court held that:

…neither the text nor the history of the Vienna Convention clearly provides a foreign nation a private right of action in United States courts to set aside a criminal conviction and sentence for violation of consular notification provisions.[48]

The Supreme Court denied the petitions by a majority of six to three and Breard was executed in the face of the ICJ's order. The Supreme Court followed the *Breard* ruling in the case of *Sanchez-Llamas* v *Oregon*[49] notwithstanding the intervening decisions of the International Court of Justice casting doubt on the application of domestic procedural rules where Article 36 had been violated. Chief Justice Roberts denied that the interpretation of the International Court was binding on US courts, saying

If treaties are to be given effect as federal law under our legal system, determining their meaning as a matter of federal law 'is emphatically the province and duty of the judicial department' headed by the 'one supreme Court' established by the Constitution.

In *Medellin* v *Texas*, described above,[50] the Supreme Court held further that a judgment by the International Court of Justice in the *Avena* case[51] did not create directly enforceable domestic law.

A similar issue was raised in the case of *US* v *Alvarez-Machain* in 1992. Alvarez-Machain, a national of Mexico, was abducted in an operation for which the US Drugs Enforcement Agency (DEA) was responsible. Charged with kidnap and murder of a DEA agent he argued that his forcible abduction constituted outrageous conduct in violation of customary international law and that US courts therefore lacked jurisdiction to try him. The Supreme Court, reversing by majority the decision of the Court of Appeals, accepted

---

[46] See text above at n 10.

[47] *Vienna Convention on Consular Relations (Paraguay* v *United States of America), Provisional Measures, Order of 9 April 1998, ICJ Reports 1998*, p 248.

[48] 134 F.3d 615 (1998); 118 ILR 23.   [49] *Sanchez-Llamas* v *Oregon* (2006) 548 US 331.

[50] *Medellin* v *Texas* (2008) 552 US 491.   [51] See n 14 above.

that the abduction, against which Mexico had protested, violated general international law principles. This violation did not however give the defendant a free-standing right to contest jurisdiction. Nor could the US-Mexico Extradition Treaty be read as including an implied term prohibiting abduction or prosecution when the defendant's presence was obtained by means outside the Treaty.[52]

In the following year a similar situation arose in the English case of *Bennett v Horseferry Road Magistrates' Court*. There the presence of the accused resulted from abduction by South African police in collusion with English police. The House of Lords by majority held that the courts should decline as a matter of discretion to exercise criminal jurisdiction. Lord Bridge said:

> Where it is shown that the law enforcement agency responsible for bringing a prosecution has only been enabled to do so by participating in violations of international law and of the laws of another state in order to secure the presence of the accused within the territorial jurisdiction of the court, I think that respect for the rule of law demands that the court take cognisance of that circumstance.[53]

D. DOES A TREATY PREVAIL OVER INCONSISTENT NATIONAL LAW?

On the whole, national constitutions give clear directions to their courts on questions of priority, though they differ. For the United Kingdom and for its former dependencies which continued to follow its constitutional approach on becoming independent States within the Commonwealth, an unincorporated treaty cannot prevail over a conflicting statute, whether the statute is earlier or later in time. Under Article 55 of the French Constitution, by contrast, duly ratified and published treaties take precedence over national laws, whether earlier or later. The Constitutional Council in 1988 examined a complaint by candidates in elections to the National Assembly requesting annulment of elections in a particular constituency on the ground that the French Law of 11 July 1986 prescribing the procedure for elections violated Article 3 of the First Additional Protocol to the European Convention on Human Rights and Fundamental Freedoms, signed in 1950. This requires that elections should take place 'under conditions which will ensure the free expression of the opinion of the people in the choice of the legislature'. The Constitutional Council held, however, that taken as a whole, the 1986 Law was not inconsistent with Protocol No 1.

The Russian Constitution of 1993, as explained above, gives priority to customary international law and treaties over inconsistent Russian national laws. Article 17 of the Constitution further guarantees human rights in conformity with generally recognized principles of international law. In the *Case Concerning Certain Normative Acts of the City of Moscow and Some Other Regions*,[54] the Constitutional Court reviewed the legality of local acts reintroducing a residence permit requirement in the light of Article 17. The court held that they were inconsistent with the right to freedom of movement and choice of

---

[52] *US v Alvarez-Machain* (1992) 504 US 655. For the sequel, see *Sosa v Alvarez-Machain*, in the previous Section.

[53] *Bennett v Horseferry Road Magistrates' Court* [1993] 3 All ER 138 at 155.

[54] VKS 1996 No 2, described in Danilenko, 1999, pp 57, 64.

place of residence guaranteed under Article 12 of the International Covenant on Civil and Political Rights, by Protocol No 4 to the European Convention on Human Rights and by general principles of international law.

Under the United States Constitution an act of Congress supersedes an earlier rule of international law if it is clear that this was the intention of the domestic law and the two cannot fairly be reconciled. Thus in the *Breard* case described above, the Supreme Court found that to the extent that Breard had a right to consular assistance on the basis of Article 36 of the Vienna Convention on Consular Relations, it had been superseded in 1996 by the express terms of the Antiterrorism and Effective Death Penalty Act, providing that a petitioner in federal courts alleging that he was held in violation of treaties of the United States would not, as a general rule, be afforded an evidentiary hearing on his claim if he had failed to develop the factual basis of his claim in state courts.[55]

The courts of the US, as well those of other States, will usually go to considerable effort to avoid conflict between national rules and international obligations. The approach of English courts was set out by Lord Denning in *Saloman v Commissioners of Customs and Excise*, where he said of a treaty which could not directly be relied on but which formed part of the background to the statutory provision in issue:

I think we are entitled to look at it because it is an instrument which is binding in international law and we ought always to interpret our statutes so as to be in conformity with international law.[56]

The case of *Alcom v Republic of Colombia and others*[57] in 1984 raised the question whether execution of a judgment could take place against the ordinary bank account of a diplomatic mission. The question had not been expressly regulated by the UK State Immunity Act 1978. The House of Lords accepted, largely on the basis of a 1977 judgment of the German Constitutional Court in proceedings against the Philippine Republic that international law required such immunity from enforcement. Lord Diplock observed that the position in international law at the date of the State Immunity Act did not conclude the question of construction, and said:

It makes it highly unlikely that parliament intended to require United Kingdom courts to act contrary to international law unless the clear language of the statute compels such a conclusion; but it does not do more than that.

A similar approach was taken in 1988 by the Southern District Court of New York in *US v The Palestine Liberation Organization and others*, which held that the US Anti-Terrorism Act 1988 did not supersede the 1946 Headquarters Agreement between the UN and the USA. The District Court emphasized that precedence of a later statute over a treaty occurred only where the two were irreconcilable and Congress had clearly shown an intent to override the treaty in domestic law stating that:

...unless this power is clearly and unequivocally exercised, this court is under a duty to interpret statutes in a manner consonant with existing treaty obligations. This is a rule of

---

[55]   118 ILR 23, at 33–34.

[56]   *Saloman v Commissioners of Customs and Excise* [1967] 2 QB 116. See also Lord Denning in *Corocraft Ltd and another v Pan American Airways Inc* [1969] 1 QB 616.

[57]   *Alcom v Republic of Colombia and others* [1984] 2 All ER 6.

statutory construction sustained by an unbroken line of authority for over a century and a half.[58]

E. CAN A TREATY PREVAIL OVER A NATIONAL CONSTITUTIONAL NORM?

There are many instances where a national constitutional court has reviewed the compatibility with the national constitution of a treaty before its ratification. As mentioned above, both the French and German Constitutions were amended in order to ensure the compatibility of the Treaty on European Union signed at Maastricht with the national constitutional order. It may be argued that in passing the European Communities Act 1972 the United Kingdom also amended its constitution in order to accept features of the Community legal order—in particular direct applicability of Council and Commission regulations and direct effect—which were inconsistent with its own approach to the implementation of international obligations.

With the possible exception of the Netherlands Constitution, there appears on the other hand to be no example of a national legal order requiring the supremacy of international legal obligations over the national constitution. The transparent procedures used before the acceptance of ground-breaking treaties by most States have ensured that direct conflicts between national constitutions and treaties in force have been rare. In 1974 however the German Federal Constitutional Court in the *Internationale Handelsgesellschaft* case[59] considered the possibility that European Community law might infringe the constitutional rights guaranteed under the German Constitution. The court said that so long as [solange] the Community did not have its own catalogue of fundamental rights, the German courts must reserve the right to examine the compatibility of Community law with the fundamental rights in the German Constitution. The judgment (known colloquially as the *Solange* judgment) appeared to challenge the doctrine of the supremacy of European Community law, and it gave rise to the first of successive attempts by the Commission of the European Communities, by Germany and some other Member States to secure accession by the Community to the European Convention on Human Rights. It shows clearly however that for German courts, their own constitution, as amended to provide for acceptance of specific treaties, is their supreme law.

While European law may be compared with international law so far as national legal systems are concerned, in its implementation of its international obligations it is to be compared with national legal systems. The European Court of Justice in its judgment in the *Kadi* case,[60] considering the relationship between the international legal order and the Community legal order, in order to decide whether it could review the legality of Community measures implementing a Security Council resolution on sanctions, also began with its own basic constitutional charter, the European Community

---

[58] *US* v *The Palestine Liberation Organization and others*, 695 F.Supp 1456 (1988); 82 ILR 282.

[59] *Internationale Handelsgesellschaft* v *Einfur und Voratsstelle Getreide*, Case 11/70 [1970] ECR Reports 1125; [1974] 2 CMLR 540.

[60] *Kadi and Al Barakaat International Foundation* v *Council*, Joined Cases 402/05 and 415/05, Judgment of 3 September 2008, nyr, at paras 280–330.

Treaty and fundamental rights as general principles of law guaranteed by the Court. They stressed that:

...the obligations imposed by an international agreement cannot have the effect of prejudicing the constitutional principles of the EC Treaty, which include the principle that all Community acts must respect fundamental rights, that respect constituting a condition of their lawfulness...

Review of a Community implementing instrument would however not entail any challenge to the primacy of the Security Council resolution in international law.

F. SHOULD THE EXECUTIVE DIRECT OR GUIDE THE NATIONAL COURT?

In most States this question is not dealt with in constitutional provisions, but is clear from practice. It cannot be expected that national judges will have up-to-date knowledge of international law, even where it forms part of their legal education. Except where there are practising lawyers with this expertise, or the possibility of international law teachers appearing as advocates, the main source of expert advice will usually be the lawyers working continuously for the government on international law questions. As explained above, national courts seek, consistently with their own constitutional mandate, to avoid conflicts with international obligations which would embarrass their governments. They accept that it is highly desirable that on questions of recognition, jurisdiction, and immunity the State should speak with one voice.

In a surprisingly large number of States—notwithstanding any principle of separation of powers—the executive will direct a national court on questions of international law—particularly on diplomatic and State immunity. In France, for example, the Conseil d'Etat would until recently normally seek guidance from the Ministry of Foreign Affairs on the construction of an international agreement, particularly if it saw a danger of embarrassment to the government. French courts may however decide that a reference is unnecessary because the treaty is clear (*acte clair*) and may dissent from the advice given (de la Rochère, 1987).[61] In the United States, although the courts have general powers to determine questions of international law, it is usual for the executive to give assistance in sensitive cases, either through *amicus curiae* briefs, interventions or 'executive suggestions', though the last of these is no longer in favour. In the legal battles over Concorde's access to Washington and New York, culminating in the case of *Air France and British Airways* v *Port Authority of New York and New Jersey* in the US District Court of New York and the US Court of Appeals, *amicus curiae* briefs from the United States government to the courts on its international obligations under the bilateral air services agreements with the United Kingdom and with France were crucial to the airlines' success and so to Concorde's entry into commercial service (Owen, 1997, Ch 10). In passing the Foreign Sovereign Immunities Act,[62] the US Government sought to delegate to its courts determination of questions of

---

61 See *GISTI* case, Conseil d'Etat, 29 June 1990, 111 ILR 499; *AGYEPONG* case, Conseil d'Etat, 2 December 1994, 111 ILR 531. In the case of *Beaumartin* v *France*, Judgment of 24 November 1994, Ser A, no 296-B; 19 *EHRR* 485 the European Court of Human Rights held that the practice was incompatible with the right, under Article 6 of the ECHR, of access to 'an independent and impartial tribunal established by law'.

62 28 USC § 1603.

decline to give effect to legislative and other acts of foreign states which are in violation of international law...

Although the US and English cases on this form of 'act of state' have developed on parallel tracks, a comparison shows that the US cases are based more closely on deference to the views of the executive, so that the State may speak with a single voice, while the English courts are seeking rather to apply international law themselves.

H. ARE THERE QUESTIONS OF INTERNATIONAL LAW WHICH NATIONAL COURTS SHOULD DECLINE TO ANSWER?

Generally speaking, where questions of international law arise before national courts, they are either (as with immunity) an essential preliminary to assumption of jurisdiction over the claim or criminal charge, or they are incidental to the construction of a national statute or a claim brought under national law. The court, with whatever assistance it can secure from counsel or from its ministry of foreign affairs, must do the best it can. Sometimes, however, where a question of international law is central to the claim, English and US courts have held that they are in effect not competent to answer it. The classic statement of this principle of 'judicial restraint' was the judgment of Lord Wilberforce in the House of Lords in the case of *Buttes Gas and Oil Co v Hammer.*[72] On its face the claim was one of defamation and the defence was justification. But the underlying dispute was over the extent of the territorial waters of Sharjah in the Persian Gulf and the right to exploit natural resources below these waters, and could not be decided without investigation of the conduct of Umm al Qaiwain, Iran, and the United Kingdom as well as Sharjah. Lord Wilberforce, with the support of his judicial colleagues, found that for an English court there were no judicial standards to judge the issues of international law and that:

...the court would be in a judicial no-man's land; the court would be asked to review transactions in which four sovereign states were involved, which they had brought to a precarious settlement, after diplomacy and the use of force, and to say that at least part of these were 'unlawful' under international law.

The principle of judicial restraint was considered in the successive *Pinochet* cases before the House of Lords. In the first case Lord Slynn and Lord Lloyd—both of whom held that General Pinochet was immune as a former Head of State—also maintained that the rule was applicable. Lord Lloyd said assumption of jurisdiction would imperil relations between governments and that:

...we would be entering a field in which we are simply not competent to adjudicate. We apply customary international law as part of the common law, and we give effect to our international obligations so far as they are incorporated in our statute law; but we are not an international court.[73]

Lord Nicholls and Lord Steyn (who with Lord Hoffmann formed the majority in the court) held however that the doctrine did not apply. Lord Steyn maintained that the

---

[72] *Buttes Gas and Oil Co v Hammer* [1982] AC 888; 64 ILR 273 and 331.
[73] *R v Bow Street Metropolitan Stipendiary, ex parte Pinochet Ugarte (No 1)* [1998] UKHL 41; [2000] AC 61; [1998] 4 All ER 897; [1998] 3 WLR 1456 at 1495.

charges against General Pinochet were already in 1973 condemned as high crimes by customary international law and that it would be wrong for English courts to extend the doctrine of judicial restraint in a way which ran counter to customary international law at the relevant time. In the third *Pinochet* case before the House of Lords[74] judicial restraint was given short shrift.

The English High Court also gave a narrow interpretation to non-justiciability in 2005 in *The Republic of Ecuador* v *Occidental Exploration and Production Company*.[75] Aikens J described the doctrine as establishing 'a general principle that the Municipal courts of England and Wales do not have the competence to adjudicate upon rights arising out of transactions entered into independent sovereign states between themselves on the plane of international law.' He held that it did not apply to prevent the court from determining a challenge by Ecuador under the UK Arbitration Act 1996 to an Award made pursuant to a Bilateral Investment Treaty between the USA and Ecuador. The Court of Appeal agreed with his analysis.

In *Mbasogo (President of the State of Equatorial Guinea)* v *Logo*,[76] the English Court of Appeal dismissed a claim for damages arising from an attempted private coup, holding that it was non-justiciable since it involved the exercise or assertion of a sovereign right. English courts had no jurisdiction to enforce the public law of a foreign State.

The *Buttes* case was highly unusual and the doctrine of judicial restraint has been strongly criticized by Rosalyn Higgins (Higgins, 1991, pp 273–274). But the approach is parallel to the restraint shown by the Permanent Court of International Justice in the extract from the *Serbian Loans* and *Brazilian Loans* cases cited at the outset of this chapter. It may also be seen as similar to the rule of *forum non conveniens* in private international law whereby courts abdicate in favour of domestic courts of another State. A solution for some cases would be for the International Court of Justice to be given a jurisdiction similar to that of the European Court of Justice to determine questions of international law referred to it by national courts and thus to ensure the uniform development and application of the law.

VI. CONCLUSION: ELEMENTS OF A HAPPY RELATIONSHIP

Several of the constitutional provisions described in this chapter have been revised in recent years in order more effectively to integrate international law into the national legal order. There is continuous cross-fertilization in attempts to remedy perceived weaknesses. One example not so far mentioned is the UK Human Rights Act 1998 which, without cutting across fundamental principles of parliamentary sovereignty, provided that 'So far as it is possible to do so, primary legislation and subordinate legislation must be read and

---

[74] *R* v *Bow Street Metropolitan Stipendiary, ex parte Pinochet Ugarte (Amnesty International Intervening) (No 3)* [1999] UKHL 17; [2000] 1 AC 147; [1991] 2 All ER 97; [1999] 2 WLR 827; 119 ILR 135. See, on the question of act of State, Denza, 1999. See also *Campaign for Nuclear Disarmament* v *The Prime Minister* [2002] EWHC 2759 (QB) and Note in (2002) 73 *BYIL* 444.

[75] *The Republic of Ecuador* v *Occidental Exploration and Production Company* [2005] EWHC 774 (Comm). See also the judgment of the Court of Appeal at [2007] EWCA Civ 456.

[76] *Mbasogo (President of the State of Equatorial Guinea)* v *Logo* [2006] EWCA Civ 1370, [2007] QB 846.

given effect in a way which is compatible with the [European] Convention rights'.[77] This legislation resulted from a perception that a better system of incorporating the European Convention on Human Rights into UK law would result in more effective enforcement of its provisions, and followed study of entrenchment in other legal systems.[78]

It is however unrealistic to suggest that any fundamental harmonization of national constitutional provisions is practicable. So long as national constitutions reflect the history and identity of independent States, and so long as international law itself remains in general non-intrusive as to how it is applied and enforced at national level, there will be infinite variety in national systems.

It is difficult even to suggest criteria on which a 'scoreboard' of impressive and failing performers could be drawn up. If, for example, the criterion is the production of judgments on general questions of international law which carry weight in other jurisdictions, one would rate Germany at the highest level. The laconic judgments of French courts, however correct, lack wider appeal because there is so little evidence of the legal reasoning behind them. Judgments of the UK House of Lords and the US Supreme Court on key questions probably carry less weight abroad because the courts have so often been openly divided on fundamental questions—*Breard, Alvarez-Machain, Pinochet*, to name only three discussed above. A different constitutional approach would not necessarily have led to more persuasive judgments in these cases. Adverse judgments from international tribunals might be another criterion—and for the UK this was undoubtedly a factor in changing its system of enforcing the European Convention on Human Rights in its domestic legal order. But an objective assessment on this count would also need to take in readiness to accept exposure to international assessment. The UK accepted the right of individual petition under the European Convention at a relatively early stage and is now the only Permanent Member of the Security Council to accept the compulsory jurisdiction of the International Court of Justice.

In the absence of any identification of the ideal relationship between international law and national law, or the best of the alternatives, five factors will be proposed as generally conducive to the avoidance of conflict. They are:

(1) close involvement in the treaty-making process of lawyers with knowledge both of their own legal systems and of international law—in particular the fundamental norms of each;

(2) close attention to questions of national implementation during the treaty-making process and before ratification;

(3) detailed parliamentary scrutiny of treaties before signature wherever possible or at least before national ratification;

(4) teaching of international law as a compulsory element of a law degree and of professional training; and

(5) involvement of specialist international lawyers as counsel and as *amici curiae* whenever difficult questions of international law arise during litigation in national courts.

---

[77] C 42, s 3(1).
[78] See, eg, 'Human Rights Legislation', University College London Constitution Unit, 1996.

Some of these suggestions go to 'the reality of legal culture' (Higgins, 1991, pp 266–268). All of them call for openness to international law, including its imperfections, its uncertainties and its rapid shifts. The motto for national law-makers and judges might well be 'only connect'.

REFERENCES

AUST, A (2007), *Modern Treaty Law and Practice*, 2nd edn (Cambridge: Cambridge University Press).

BELL, J (2005), 'French Constitutional Council and European Law', 54 *ICLQ* 735.

BUTLER, W (1997), *The Russian Law of Treaties* (London: Simmonds and Hill).

CARRUTHERS, JM and CRAWFORD, EB (2003), '*Kuwait Airways Corporation* v *Iraqi Airways Company*', 52 *ICLQ* 761.

COLLIER, J (1989), 'Is International Law Really Part of the Law of England?', 38 *ICLQ* 924.

COLLINS, L (2002), 'Foreign Relations and the Judiciary', 51 *ICLQ* 485.

CRAIG, P and DE BÚRCA, G (2007), *EU Law: Text, Cases and Materials*, 3rd edn (Oxford: Oxford University Press).

DANILENKO, G (1994), 'The New Russian Constitution and International Law', 88 *AJIL* 451.

—— (1999), 'Implementation of International Law in CIS States: Theory and Practice', 10 *EJIL* 51.

DE LA ROCHERE, D (1987), in Jacobs and Roberts (eds), p 39.

DENZA, E (2008), *Diplomatic Law*, 3rd edn (Oxford: Oxford University Press).

—— (1999), 'Ex parte Pinochet: Lacuna or Leap?', 48 *ICLQ* 687.

EISEMANN, P-M and and Kessedijan, C (1995), in Leigh and Blakeslee (eds), p 1.

ERRERA, R (2008), 'Domestic Courts and International Law, the Law and Practice in France', paper given to Colloquium on International Law in Domestic Courts, organized by Amsterdam Center for International Law.

FAVOREU, L (1985), XXXI *Annuaire Français de Droit International* 868.

HIGGINS, R (1991-V), 'International Law and the Avoidance, Containment and Resolution of Disputes', *Recueil des Cours* 273–274.

JACKSON, J (1987), in Jacobs and Roberts (eds), p 141.

JACOBS, F and ROBERTS, S (eds) (1987), *The Effect of Treaties in Domestic Law* (London: Sweet & Maxwell).

KELSEN, H (1920), *Das Problem der Souveränitat und die Theorie des Völkerrechts-Beitrag zu einer reinen Rechtslehre* (Tübingen: JC Mohr).

LEIGH, M and BLAKESLEE, MR (eds) (1995), *National Treaty Law and Practice*, vol 1, (Washington, DC: ASIL).

——, ——, and EDERINGTON, LB (eds) (1999), *National Treaty Law and Practice*, vol 2 (Washington, DC: ASIL).

MENNECKE, M and TAMS, C (2002), 'The LaGrand Case', 51 *ICLQ* 449.

NEFF, S (2002), 'International Law and Nuclear Weapons in Scottish Courts', 51 *ICLQ* 171.

NIJMAN, J and NOLLKAEMPER, A (eds) (2007), *New Perspectives on the Divide Between National and International Law* (Oxford: Oxford University Press).

OWEN, K (1997), *Concorde and the Americans* (Shrewsbury: Airlife Publishing).

PAULUS, A (2007), 'The Emergence of the International Community and the Divide Between International and Domestic Law', in Nijman and Nollkaemper (eds), p 216

PETERS, A (2007), 'The Globalization of State Constitutions', in Nijman and Nollkaemper (eds), p 251.

RIESENFELD, S and ABBOTT, F (eds) (1994), *Parliamentary Participation in the Making and Operation of Treaties* (The Hague: Nijhoff/Kluwer).

ROTH, B (2004), 'Note on *Sosa v Alvarez-Machain*', 98 *AJIL* 798.

SCHERMERS, H (1987), in Jacobs and Roberts (eds), p 109.

SCHWARZE, J (1994), 'La ratification du traité de Maastricht en Allemagne, l'arrêt de la Cour constitutionnelle de Karlsruhe', 1994 *Revue du Marché Commun* 293.

——(1995), 'Towards a Common European Public Law', 1995 *European Public Law* 227.

—— (ed) (2001), *The Birth of a European Constitutional Order* (Baden-Baden: Nomos).

SHELTON, D (2004), 'Note on *Avena and Other Mexican Nationals*', 98 *AJIL* 559.

SLAUGHTER, A-M and BURKE-WHITE, W, (2007), 'The Future of International Law is Domestic (or, The European Way of Law)' in Nijman and Nollkaemper (eds), p 110.

TREVIRANUS, H and BEEMELMANS, H (1995) in Leigh and Blakeslee (eds), p 5.

ULFSTEIN, G (ed, in collaboration with Marauhn, T and Zimmermann, A) (2007), *Making Treaties Work* (Cambridge: Cambridge University Press)

VAN DIJK, P and TAHZIB, BG, in Riesenfeld and Abbott (eds), p 109.

VAN PANHUYS, JHF (1953), 'The Netherlands Constitution and International Law', 47 *AJIL* 537.

FURTHER READING

AUST, A (2007), *Modern Treaty Law and Practice*, 2nd edn (Cambridge, Cambridge University Press), Ch 10, 'Treaties and Domestic Law'. A clear introduction.

CASSESE, A (2005), *International Law*, 2nd edn (Oxford: Oxford University Press), Ch 12, 'The Implementation of International Rules within National Systems'. An up-to-date, thorough account of theory and practice in a large number of States.

CONFORTI, B (1993), *International Law and the Role of Domestic Legal Systems* (The Hague: Nijhoff/Kluwer). Wide-ranging account covering international law-making as well as national implementation.

GARDINER, RK (2003), *International Law* (Harlow: Longman), Ch 4, 'International Law and National Laws'. This focuses particularly on the US and UK and on approaches to treaty interpretation.

JACOBS, F and ROBERTS, S (eds) (1987), *The Effect of Treaties in Domestic Law* (London: Sweet & Maxwell). An excellent comparative study, though on some points now overtaken.

LEIGH, M, BLAKESLEE, MP, and EDERINGTON, LB (eds) (1999), *National Treaty Law and Practice* (Washington, DC: ASIL). The most up-to-date and extensive comparative survey.

NIJMAN, J and NOLLKAEMPER, A (eds) (2007), *New Perspectives on the Divide Between National and International Law* (Oxford: Oxford University Press). A wide variety of critical analyses of theories.

RIESENFELD, S and ABBOTT, F (eds) (1994), *Parliamentary Participation in the Making and Operation of Treaties* (The Hague: Nijhoff/Kluwer).

PART V

RESPONSIBILITY

15

THE NATURE AND FORMS OF INTERNATIONAL RESPONSIBILITY

James Crawford and Simon Olleson

SUMMARY

On the international plane, responsibility is the necessary corollary of obligation: every breach by a subject of international law of its international obligations entails its international responsibility. The chapter starts by giving an overview of different forms of responsibility/liability in international law before examining the general character of State responsibility. Due to the historical primacy of States in the international legal system, the law of State responsibility is the most fully-developed branch of responsibility and is the principal focus of the chapter. Conversely, although the International Law Commission adopted draft Articles on Responsibility of International Organizations on first reading in 2009, the responsibility of international organizations remains an under-developed area; it is considered only briefly, as is the potential responsibility under international law of other international actors.

   The law of State responsibility deals with three general questions: (1) has there been a breach by a State of an international obligation; (2) what are the consequences of the breach in terms of cessation and reparation; (3) who may seek reparation or otherwise respond to the breach as such, and in what ways? As to the first question, this chapter discusses the constituent elements of attribution and breach, as well as the possible justifications or excuses which may preclude responsibility. The second question concerns the various secondary obligations which arise upon the commission of an internationally wrongful act by a State, and in particular the forms of reparation. The third question concerns issues of invocation of responsibility, including the taking of countermeasures.

I. THE SCOPE OF INTERNATIONAL RESPONSIBILITY: INTRODUCTION AND OVERVIEW

Article 1 of the International Law Commission (ILC)'s Articles on the Responsibility of States for Internationally Wrongful Acts ('ARSIWA' or 'the Articles on State Responsibility'),[1] adopted in 2001, provides: 'Every internationally wrongful act of a State entails the international responsibility of that State'.[2] Due to the historical development of international law, its primary subjects are States. It is on States that most obligations rest and on whom the burden of compliance principally falls. For example, the human rights conventions, though they confer rights upon individuals, impose obligations upon States. If other legal persons have obligations in the field of human rights, it is only by derivation or analogy from the human rights obligations accepted by States (see Alston, 2005, Clapham, 2006, and McCorquodale, above, Ch 10). State responsibility is the paradigm form of responsibility on the international plane.

But there can be international legal persons other than States, as the International Court of Justice (ICJ) held in the *Reparation for Injuries* Advisory Opinion.[3] Being a subject of any legal system involves being subject to responsibilities as well as enjoying rights. Thus it would seem unproblematic to substitute the words 'international organization' or 'international legal person' for 'State' in Article 1 of the Articles on State Responsibility; that basic statement of principle would seem equally applicable by definition to all international legal persons.[4]

In relation to international organizations, at least, a corollary of their undoubted capacity to enter into treaties with States or with other international organizations is that they are responsible for breaches of the obligations undertaken; this follows from the principle *pacta sunt servanda*.[5] The same is true for breaches of applicable general international law.

---

[1] Articles on the Responsibility of States for Internationally Wrongful Acts, adopted by the ILC on 10 August 2001: *Report of the International Law Commission, Fifty-third Session*, A/56/10, Chapter IV. The General Assembly took note of the Articles, recommended them to the attention of governments, and annexed them to GA Res 56/83 (10 December 2001), deferring until 2004 any decision on whether the Articles should be adopted in the form of a multilateral Convention; in 2004, the question was again deferred until 2007: see GA Res 59/35 (2 December 2004). In 2007, a decision was again deferred until 2010: see GA Res 62/61 (6 December 2007). For an account of the debate in 2004 see Crawford and Olleson, 2005. The Articles and the Commentaries are reproduced in Crawford, 2002 (the Articles at pp 61–73) and the Articles alone in Evans, 2009, pp 576–584.

[2] See the often quoted dictum of the Permanent Court of International Justice in *Factory at Chorzów, Jurisdiction, Judgment No 8, 1927, PCIJ, Ser A, No 9* at p 21: 'It is a principle of international law that the breach of an engagement involves an obligation to make reparation'.

[3] *Reparation for Injuries Suffered in the Service of the United Nations, Advisory Opinion, ICJ Reports 1949*, p 174 at p 179.

[4] This is the approach adopted by the ILC in its work on Responsibility of International Organizations: see Article 3, draft Articles on Responsibility of International Organizations, as adopted by the ILC on first reading: *Report of the International Law Commission, Sixty-First Session*, A/64/10 (2009), Chapter IV: 'Every internationally wrongful act of an international organization State entails the international responsibility of the international organization'.

[5] See Vienna Convention on the Law of Treaties between States and International Organizations or Between International Organizations (1986), Article 26; cf Morgenstern, 1986, pp 13–16, 32–36, 115.

The potential responsibility of international organizations under general international law was affirmed by the International Court of Justice in the *Cumaraswamy* Advisory Opinion.[6] But there are serious difficulties of implementation, since the jurisdiction of international courts and tribunals has been developed by reference to States and not international organizations.[7]

The ILC has attempted to pull together the sparse international practice in relation to the responsibility of international organizations. In doing so, it has to a large extent based itself upon the model of the Articles on State Responsibility; the draft Articles on Responsibility of International Organizations ('DARIO'), adopted on first reading in 2009, adapt many formulations of the Articles on State Responsibility. But there are also some major differences, reflecting the differences in structure and function as between States and international organizations. The most significant of these concerns attribution.[8] In the law of State responsibility, as will be seen, there are a number of ways in which conduct of organs, instrumentalities and even, in some circumstances, private parties may be attributed to the State (ARSIWA, Articles 4–11). By contrast, given the different structure of international organizations—which are functional entities, not territorial communities—the 'general rule' is that conduct must be that of an organ or agent of the international organization, acting in the performance of its functions (DARIO, Article 5). The 'functional' criteria underlying attribution of conduct to an international organization has parallels in other areas of the law, in particular as concerns the immunity from jurisdiction of agents of international organizations.[9]

The addition of the notion of agents to that of organs substantially widens the rule as compared to the corresponding rule under the law of State responsibility. As a result the rule substantially subsumes the other bases of attribution in the law of State responsibility. For instance, an individual who does not have any official status within an international organization but carries out conduct upon its instructions or under its direction and control will be regarded as its agent and the conduct will be attributable to the organization on that basis.

[6] *Difference Relating to Immunity from Legal Process of a Special Rapporteur of the Commission on Human Rights, Advisory Opinion, ICJ Reports 1999*, p 62, para 66.

[7] Thus the EU, which is not a State, has had to be specifically provided for in order to be a party to contentious proceedings under the 1982 UN Convention on the Law of the Sea (see Article 305 and Annex IX) and under the WTO dispute settlement mechanism. See generally Wellens, 2002; Klabbers, 2009. Similarly, Article 17 of Protocol 14 to the European Convention of Human Rights (2004) provides for the amendment of Article 59 of the Convention so as to permit the European Union to become a party by accession.

[8] Part Five DARIO (Articles 57–61) deals with question of State responsibility in connection with the act of an international organization, and deals with questions paralleling those in Part One, Chapter IV of the Article on State Responsibility as regards aid or assistance, direction and control, and coercion (Articles 57–59). It also attempts to frame rules applicable to the situation in which a member State seeks to avoid compliance with its own international obligations by procuring an act of the international organization to do what it itself is unable to do (Article 60), as well as a provision in relation to the acceptance of responsibility by a State for the internationally wrongful act of an international organization (Article 61). Those provisions undoubtedly constitute progressive development, rather than codification.

[9] Whether the agent was carrying out functions on behalf of an organization is also the criteria on the basis of which is to be determined whether an international organization may bring a claim by way of 'functional protection' in relation to injuries caused to the agent: see *Reparation for Injuries Suffered in the Service of the United Nations, Advisory Opinion, ICJ Reports 1949*, p 174 at pp 177, 180, 181–184.

As a result of the dominant role played by the rule permitting attribution of the conduct of organs and agents of international organizations, the draft Articles on Responsibility of International Organization contain only two alternative bases for the attribution of conduct to an international organization; first, in a similar fashion to the position under the law of State responsibility, conduct will be attributable if it has been acknowledged and adopted by the international organization as its own (DARIO, Article 8). Second, conduct may be attributed to an international organization on the basis that the conduct is that of the organ of a State or the organ or agent of another international organization, which has been placed at the disposal of the international organization and over which the international organization exercises 'effective control'. In contrast to the other provisions dealing with attribution, the purpose of this rule is not to determine *whether* particular conduct is attributable as such, but rather it addresses the question of to which of two entities (the 'borrowing' international organization or the 'lending' State (or international organization)), the conduct is to be attributed.

That provision is of particular relevance in the context of the attribution of the conduct in breach of applicable international obligations of national contingents assigned to United Nations peacekeeping missions. Whether or not the conduct in question is to be attributed to the United Nations or to the contributing State turns on the relative degree of 'effective control' in fact exercised by those entities over the conduct in question. That in turn depends upon a number of factors, including the mandate under which the peacekeeping mission has been set up, any agreements between the United Nations and the contributing State as to the terms on which troops were to be placed at the disposal of the United Nations, the extent to which the troops remain subject to the command and jurisdiction of the contributing State, and whether (operational) United Nations command and control was in fact effective.[10]

The position so far as the international responsibility of individuals, corporations, non-governmental organizations, and other groups are concerned is far less clear. Despite the fact that international law may in certain circumstances, even outside the field of international human rights law, confer rights directly upon individuals,[11] it is doubtful whether they are in any meaningful sense 'subjects' of international law (see McCorquodale, above Ch 10); and so far no general regime of responsibility has developed to cover them.

In relation to individuals, international responsibility has only developed in the criminal field, and then only in comparatively recent times. True, piracy has been recognized as a 'crime against the law of nations' for centuries. But it is better to see this as a jurisdictional rule allowing States to exercise criminal jurisdiction for pirate attacks on ships

---

[10] Cf the decisions of the European Court of Human Rights in *Behrami and Behrami* v *France and Saramati* v *France, Germany and Norway* (Dec) [GC], nos 71412/01 and 78166/01, 2 May 2007, which applied a test of whether the United Nations maintained 'ultimate authority and control' in relation to the question of whether actions of troops forming part of KFOR in Kosovo were attributable to the United Nations. Compare the approach of the House of Lords in *R (Al-Jedda)* v *Secretary of State for Defence* [2007] UKHL 58; [2008] 1 AC 332 as concerns whether the actions of UK troops forming part of the multi-national force in Iraq authorized by SC Res 1546 (8 June 2004) were attributable to the United Nations.

[11] *Jurisdiction of the Courts of Danzig, Advisory Opinion, 1928, PCIJ, Ser B, No 15* at pp 17–21; *LaGrand (Germany* v *United States of America), Merits, Judgment, ICJ Reports 2001,* p 466, para 77; *Avena and Other Mexican Nationals (Mexico* v *United States of America), ICJ Reports 2004,* p 12, para 40.

at sea rather than a rule conferring 'legal personality' on pirates.[12] One does not acquire international legal personality by being hanged at the yardarm.

Since the Second World War, by contrast, real forms of individual criminal responsibility under international law have developed. First steps were taken with the establishment of the Nuremberg and Tokyo war crimes tribunals and the conclusion of the Genocide Convention in the immediate post-war period; after the end of the Cold War there followed, in rapid succession, the creation by Security Council resolution of the International Criminal Tribunal for Yugoslavia (ICTY) (1992) and Rwanda (ICTR) (1994), and the adoption of the Rome Statute of the International Criminal Court (ICC) (1998), which entered into force on 1 July 2002. Further, various 'mixed' or 'hybrid' international criminal tribunals have been set up in, *inter alia*, Bosnia-Herzegovina (2004–), East Timor (2000–2006), Sierra Leone (2002–), Cambodia (2003–), and Lebanon (2007).

By contrast, so far there has been no development of corporate criminal responsibility in international law. Under the two ad hoc Statutes and the Rome Statute only individual persons may be accused. The Security Council often addresses recommendations or demands to opposition, insurgent, or rebel groups—but without implying that these have separate personality in international law. Any international responsibility of members of such groups is probably limited to breaches of applicable international humanitarian law or even of national law, rather than general international law. If rebel groups succeed in becoming the government of the State (whether of the State against which they are fighting or of a new State which they succeed in creating), that State may be responsible for their acts (ARSIWA, Article 10; Commentary, Crawford, 2002, pp 116–120). But if they fail, the State against which they rebelled is in principle not responsible, and any possibility of collective responsibility for their acts fails with them.

It is also very doubtful whether 'multinational corporations' are subjects of international law for the purposes of responsibility, although steps are being taken to develop voluntary adherence to human rights and other norms by corporations.[13] From a legal point of view, the so-called multinational corporation is better regarded as a group of corporations, each created under and amenable to the national law of its place of incorporation as well as to any other national legal system within which it operates.

Thus although Article 58 of the ILC's Articles on State Responsibility reserves in general terms the possibility of 'individual responsibility under international law of any person acting on behalf of a State',[14] a reservation which is not limited to criminal responsibility, so far there has been virtually no development in practice of civil responsibility of individuals or corporations for breaches of international law. Only the United States has legislation dealing (in a very uneven way) with this issue.[15] As the dissenting

---

[12] See the Separate Opinion of Judge Moore in *'Lotus', Judgment No 9, 1927, PCIJ, Ser A, No 10* at p 70; United Nations Convention on the Law of the Sea 1982, Articles 101–107; Rubin, 1998; *Oppenheim's International Law*, 1992, vol 1, pp 746–755.

[13] See, eg, the *ILO Tripartite Declaration of Principles Concerning Multinational Enterprises and Social Policy 1977* (adopted by the Governing Body at its 204th Session), 17 ILM 416; the OECD's *'Guidelines for Multinational Enterprises'* (2000), 40 ILM 237; and the 'Nine Principles' of the UN Global Compact Initiative (2000) (relating to human rights, labour standards, and the environment). See De Schutter, 2006. On the problems of establishing international responsibility of corporations, see Ratner, 2001.

[14] See likewise DARIO, Article 65.

[15] Private parties (US or foreign) can be sued for torts occasioned 'in violation of the law of nations' anywhere committed against aliens, under the unusual jurisdiction created by the Alien Tort Claims Act (28

judges in the *Arrest Warrant* case pointed out, that legislation may be seen as 'the beginnings of a very broad form of extraterritorial jurisdiction'[16] in civil matters. They further commented that although 'this unilateral exercise of the function of guardian of international values has been much commented on, it has not attracted the approbation of States generally'.[17]

The development of international criminal law is considered in Chapter 25 of this book. In this chapter we examine the foundational rules of State responsibility—in particular the bases for and consequences of the responsibility of a State for internationally wrongful acts. Questions of the implementation of such responsibility by an injured State or by other interested parties, as well as possible responses (retorsion, countermeasures, sanctions) are dealt with briefly; they are discussed in greater detail in the following two chapters.

II. STATE RESPONSIBILITY: ISSUES OF CLASSIFICATION AND CHARACTERIZATION

The category 'State responsibility' covers the field of the responsibility of States for internationally wrongful conduct. It amounts, in other words, to a general law of wrongs. But of course, what is a breach of international law by a State depends on what its international obligations are, and especially as far as treaties are concerned, these vary from one State to the next. There are a few treaties (the United Nations Charter, the 1949 Geneva Conventions and some international human rights treaties) to which virtually every State is a party; otherwise each State has its own range of bilateral and multilateral treaty obligations. Even under general international law, which might be expected to be virtually uniform for every State, different States may be differently situated and may have different responsibilities—for example, upstream States rather than downstream States on an international river, capital importing and capital exporting States in respect of the treatment of foreign investment, or States on whose territory a civil war is raging as compared with third parties to the conflict. There is no such thing as a uniform code of international law, reflecting the obligations of all States.

On the other hand, the underlying concepts of State responsibility—attribution, breach, excuses, consequences—seem to be general in character. Particular treaties or rules may

USC §1350). The US cases distinguish between corporate complicity with governmental violations of human rights, and those violations (eg genocide, slavery) which do not require any governmental involvement or State action. See, eg, *Kadić v Karadžić* 70 F.3d 232 (1995) (2nd Cir 1995); 104 ILR 135. Cf also the Torture Victims Protection Act 1992 (PL 102–256, 106 *Stat* 73), under which only designated 'rogue' States can be defendants: the Act on its face contradicts the principle of universality on which it purports to be based. The jurisdiction under the ATCA has survived scrutiny by the Supreme Court in *Sosa v Alvarez-Machain* 124 S Ct 2739; 542 US 692 (2004) although its scope has been somewhat reduced. In *Jones v Ministry of Interior for the of Kingdom of Saudi Arabia and Ors* [2006] UKHL 26, [2007] 1 AC 270, the House of Lords reversed a Court of Appeal decision [2004] EWCA Civ 1394, [2005] QB 699, which had seemed to open the door to claims brought on the basis of the English law of tort against State officials in relation to alleged acts of torture abroad.

[16] *Arrest Warrant of 11 April 2000 (Democratic Republic of Congo v Belgium), Preliminary Objections and Merits, Judgment, ICJ Reports 2002*, p 3, Separate Opinion of Judges Higgins, Kooijmans, and Buergenthal, para 48.

[17] Ibid.

vary these underlying concepts in particular respects, otherwise they are assumed and they apply unless excluded.[18] These background or standard assumptions of responsibility on the basis of which specific obligations of States exist and are applied are set out in the ILC's Articles on State Responsibility. The Articles are the product of more than 40 years' work by the ILC on the topic, and in common with other ILC texts they involve both codification and progressive development (Crawford, 2002, pp 1–60; *Symposium*, 2002, 96 *AJIL* pp 773–890). They are the focus of what follows.

A. RESPONSIBILITY UNDER INTERNATIONAL OR NATIONAL LAW?

Evidently State responsibility can only be engaged for breaches of international law, ie for conduct which is internationally wrongful because it involves some violation of an international obligation applicable to and binding on the State. A dispute between two States concerning the breach of an international obligation, whether customary or deriving from treaty, concerns international responsibility, and this will be true whether the remedy sought is a declaration that conduct is wrongful, cessation of the conduct, or compensation for damage suffered. On the other hand, not all claims against a State involve international responsibility, even if international law may be relevant to the case. For example, if a State is sued on a commercial transaction in a national court, international law helps to determine what is the extent of the defendant State's immunity from jurisdiction and from measures of enforcement, but the underlying claim will derive from the applicable law of the contract. There is thus a distinction between State responsibility for breaches of international law, and State liability for breaches of national law. One does not entail the other.[19]

Responsibility claims were traditionally brought directly between States at the international level, or (much less often) before an international court or tribunal. Both these avenues remain but there is now a further range of possibilities. For example in some cases individuals or corporations are given access to international tribunals and can bring State responsibility claims in their own right, eg for breach of the European Convention on

---

[18] ARSIWA, Article 55 (*lex specialis*). For examples of a *lex specialis* see, eg, the provisions of the WTO Agreements excluding compensation for breach and focusing on cessation, and (perhaps) Article 41 of the European Convention on Human Rights which appears, at least in some circumstances, to give States an option to pay compensation rather than providing restitution in kind; nevertheless they remain bound by Article 46 of the European Convention to abide by the judgments of the European Court, and in that regard, to take, under the supervision of the Committee of Ministers, 'the general and/or, if appropriate, individual measures to be adopted in their domestic legal order to put an end to the violation found by the Court and to redress so far as possible the effects' (*Scozzari and Giunta v Italy* [GC], nos 39221/98 and 41963/98, para 249, ECHR 2000-VIII). After initial hesitations (see eg, *Ireland v UK*, Judgment of 18 January 1978, para 187, Ser A no 25), the recent practice of the European Court of Human Rights appears to be evolving, at least in relation to certain types of breach, towards a requirement of real restitution by way of just satisfaction, rather than merely the payment of compensation: see eg *Assanidze v Georgia* [GC], no 71503/01, paras 202–203 ECHR 2004-II; *Ilaşcu and Others v Moldova and Russia* [GC], no 48787/99, para 490, ECHR 2004-VII; *Sejdovic v Italy* [GC] no 56581/00, paras 125–126, ECHR 2006-II.

[19] ARSIWA, Articles 1, 3, 27; *Elettronica Sicula SpA (ELSI), Judgment, ICJ Reports 1989*, p 15, paras 73 and 124. See also *Compañía de Aguas del Aconquija and Vivendi Universal v Argentine Republic (ICSID Case No ARB/97/3), Decision on Annulment*, 3 July 2002, 41 ILM 1135; *ICSID Reports*, vol 6, p 340, paras 93–103; *SGS Société Générale de Surveillance SA v Islamic Republic of Pakistan (ICSID Case No ARB/01/13), Decision on Objections to Jurisdiction*, 29 January 2004, *ICSID Reports*, vol 8, p 483, paras 146–148.

Human Rights before the European Court of Human Rights, or for breach of a bilateral investment treaty before an arbitral tribunal established under the treaty. Whether such international claims could also be enforced in national courts depends on the approach of the national legal system to international law in general (see Denza, above, Ch 14) as well as on the rules of State immunity (see Fox, above, Ch 12). In certain circumstances it is possible for responsibility claims to be 'domesticated', and the principles of subsidiarity and complementarity indicate an increasing role for national courts in the implementation and enforcement of international standards. But the interaction between rules of jurisdiction and immunity and the relation between national and international law make this a complex area. For the sake of simplicity, this chapter will be confined to claims of State responsibility brought at the international level.

B. THE TYPOLOGY OF STATE RESPONSIBILITY

National legal systems often distinguish types or degrees of liability according to the source of the obligation breached—for example, crime, contract, tort, or delict.[20] In international law it appears that there is no general distinction of this kind. As the arbitral tribunal said in the *Rainbow Warrior* case:

the general principles of International Law concerning State responsibility are equally applicable in the case of breach of treaty obligation, since in the international law field there is no distinction between contractual and tortious responsibility, so that any violation of a State of any obligation, of whatever origin gives rise to State responsibility.[21]

To this extent the rules of State responsibility form the basis for a single system, having no precise equivalent in national legal systems. The reason is that international law has to address a very wide range of needs on the basis of rather few basic tools and techniques. For example, treaties perform a wide range of functions in the international system—from establishing institutions in the public interest and rules of an essentially legislative character to making specific contractual arrangements between two States. Unlike national law, there is no categorical distinction between the legislative and the contractual.

The Tribunal in the *Rainbow Warrior*[22] arbitration and the International Court in the *Gabčíkovo-Nagymaros Project*[23] case both held that in a case involving the breach of a treaty obligation, the general defences available under the law of State responsibility coexist with the rules of treaty law, laid down in the 1969 Vienna Convention on the Law

---

[20] Cf the division of sources of obligation in Roman law into contract, delict, and quasi-contract/unjust enrichment: D.1.1.10.1 (Ulpian): 'Iuris praecepta sunt haec: honeste vivere, alterum non laedere, suum cuique tribuere' ('the principles of law are these: to live honourably, not to harm any other person, and to render to each his own').

[21] *Rainbow Warrior (France/New Zealand)*, (1990) 20 *RIAA* 217, para 75; for the arguments of the parties, see ibid, paras 72–74. See also the ICJ in *Gabčíkovo-Nagymaros Project (Hungary/Slovakia), Judgment, ICJ Reports 1997*, p 7, paras 46–48, especially para 47: 'when a State has committed an internationally wrongful act, its international responsibility is likely to be involved whatever the nature of the obligation it has failed to respect', citing what is now ARSIWA, Article 12: 'There is a breach of an international obligation by a State when an act of that State is not in conformity with what is required of it by that obligation, *regardless of its origin or character*' (emphasis added).

[22] *Rainbow Warrior (France/New Zealand)*, (1990) 20 *RIAA* 217, para 75.

[23] *Gabčíkovo-Nagymaros Project (Hungary/Slovakia), Judgment, ICJ Reports 1997*, p 7, paras 46–48.

of Treaties. But the two sets of rules perform different functions. The rules of treaty law determine when a treaty obligation is in force for a State and what it means, ie, how it is to be interpreted. The rules of State responsibility determine when a breach of such an obligation is to be taken to have occurred and what the legal consequences of that breach are in terms of such matters as reparation. There is some overlap between the two but they are legally and logically distinct. A State faced with a material breach of a treaty obligation can choose to suspend or terminate the treaty in accordance with the applicable rules of treaty law, thus releasing itself from its obligation to perform its obligations under the treaty in the future (VCLT, Article 60). But doing so does not prevent it also from claiming reparation for the breach.[24]

In addition, national legal systems also characteristically distinguish 'civil' from 'criminal' responsibility. By contrast there is little or no State practice allowing for 'punitive' or 'penal' consequences of breaches of international law. In 1976, Chilean agents killed a former Chilean minister, Orlando Letelier, and one of his companions by a car bomb in Washington, DC. The United States courts subsequently awarded both compensatory and punitive damages for the deaths, acting under the local torts exception of the Foreign State Immunity Act.[25] But the local judgment was practically unenforceable.[26] Subsequently, as part of the restoration of relations between the United States and Chile following the latter's return to democracy, it was agreed that a bilateral commission would determine the amount of compensation payable as an *ex gratia* settlement without admission of liability. Under the terms of reference of the Commission, the damages were to be assessed 'in accordance with applicable principles of international law, as though liability were established'.[27] The Commission awarded sums only on a compensatory basis for loss of income and moral damage; the separate opinion of the Chilean member of the Commission made clear that punitive damages were not accepted in international law.[28]

The draft of the ILC's Articles on State Responsibility adopted on first reading in 1996 sought to introduce the notion of 'international crimes' of States.[29] It was not envisaged that States could be fined or otherwise punished—no State has ever been accused of a criminal offence before an international court, even where the conduct involved aggression or genocide (see, eg, Abi-Saab, 1999, p 339; de Hoogh, 1996; Jørgensen, 2000; Pellet, 2001). In 1998, the concept of 'international crimes of States' was set aside, contributing to the unopposed adoption of the Articles on State Responsibility by the ILC in 2001. The episode suggests that State responsibility is an undifferentiated regime, which does not

[24] In other words a State can terminate a treaty for breach while claiming damages for breaches that have already occurred: see VCLT, Articles 70(1)(b), 72(1)(b), 73.

[25] See *Letelier et al v The Republic of Chile et al*: see 488 F.Supp 665 (1980); 19 ILM 409; 63 ILR 378 (District Court, DC) for the decision on State immunity, and see 502 F.Supp 259 (1980); 19 ILM 1418; 88 ILR 747 (District Court, DC) for the decision as to quantum; the Court awarded the plaintiffs approximately $5 million, of which $2 million were punitive damages.

[26] The Court of Appeals for the 2nd Circuit, reversing the District Court, refused to allow enforcement against the Chilean national airline: 748 F.2d 790 (1984); the Supreme Court denied certiorari: 471 US 1125 (1985).

[27] *Re Letelier and Moffitt* (1992), 88 ILR 727 at 731.

[28] Ibid, p 741. The resulting award was paid to the victim's heirs on condition that they waived their rights under the domestic judgment.

[29] For the text of former Article 19 see Crawford, 2002, pp 352–353.

embody such domestic classifications as 'civil' and 'criminal'; and the International Court endorsed this approach in the *Bosnian Genocide* case.[30]

But this does not prevent international law responding in different ways to different kinds of breaches and to their different impacts on other States, on people and on international order. First, individual State officials have no impunity if they commit crimes against international law, even if they may not have been acting for their own individual ends.[31] Secondly, the Articles on State Responsibility make special provision for the consequences of certain serious breaches of peremptory norms of general international law. A breach is serious if it involves a 'gross or systematic failure by the responsible State to fulfil' such an obligation (Article 40(2)). The major consequence of such a breach is the obligation on all other States to refrain from recognizing as lawful the situation thereby created or from rendering aid or assistance in maintaining it (Article 41(2)). In addition, States must cooperate to bring the serious breach to an end 'through any lawful means'; the principal avenues for such cooperation are through the various international organizations, in particular the Security Council, whose powers to take measures to restore international peace and security substantially overlap with these provisions (Koskenniemi, 2001). But they are not the only ones, since the possibility remains of unilateral action by States against other States responsible for such serious breaches as genocide, war crimes, or denial of fundamental human rights.[32]

---

[30] *Application of the Convention on the Prevention and Punishment of the Crime of Genocide (Bosnia and Herzegovina v Serbia and Montenegro), Merits, Judgment,* 26 February 2007 (nyr), paras 65 and 66.

[31] At the international level see the Statute of the ICTY, Articles 7(2), 7(4); the Statute of the ICTR, Articles 6(2), 6(4); Rome Statute of the ICC, Articles 27, 33. At the national level see *R v Bow Street Metropolitan Stipendiary, ex parte Pinochet Ugarte (Amnesty International Intervening) (No 3)* [1997] UKHL 17; [2000] 1 AC 147. However, the ICJ has held that serving foreign ministers (and by implication, serving heads of State and other senior ministers) while in office are inviolable and have absolute jurisdictional immunity from prosecution in the national courts of other States: *Arrest Warrant of 11 April 2000 (Democratic Republic of Congo v Belgium), Preliminary Objections and Merits, Judgment, ICJ Reports 2002,* p 3, paras 51–61. The Court protested that this immunity did not involve impunity, *inter alia* because of the possibility of prosecution at the international level, or prosecution by the national State. The jurisdictional immunity apparently lasts only so long as the individual holds office: cf, however, ibid, paras 60–61, and compare with the Separate Opinion of Judges Higgins, Kooijmans, and Buergenthal, ibid, para 89. As a matter of English law, officials of a foreign State who, in the performance of their functions, commit crimes abroad contrary to international law enjoy immunity before the English courts when faced with *civil* claims in relation to those acts, even if the acts of which they are accused constitute a breach of a peremptory norm of international law (*jus cogens*): *Jones v Ministry of Interior for the of Kingdom of Saudi Arabia and Ors* [2006] UKHL 26, [2007] 1 AC 270; cf the possibility under US law of bringing such a civil claim under the Alien Tort Claims Act and/or the Torture Victim Protection Act (106 Stat. 73 (1992)).

[32] For instance States may adopt measures which are not inconsistent with their international obligations (retorsion). In addition, a right *may* exist allowing States which themselves are not injured to take countermeasures in the case of breach of certain types of obligation. See, for instance, the catalogue of State practice discussed in the commentary to ARSIWA, Article 54, which may be evidence of such a customary international rule. The ILC left the question open in Article 54 for future development. Further, the ILC proposed that in relation to a breach of an obligation 'owed to the international community as a whole', a category that encompasses most, if not all, peremptory norms of international law, any State, in addition to a directly injured State, should be entitled the invoke the responsibility of the wrongdoing State (Article 48(1)(b); given that such States will by definition not normally have suffered any injury save the purely 'legal' injury resulting from the very violation of the norm in question, it was proposed that in invoking the responsibility of the responsible State they should be limited to claiming cessation of continuing wrongful acts and assurances and guarantees of non-repetition, as well as performance of the obligation of reparation 'in the interest of the injured State or the beneficiaries of the obligation breached' (Article 48(2)(a) and (b)). As yet, the ILC's

In the Advisory Opinion on *Legal Consequences of the Construction of a Wall in the Occupied Palestine Territory*, the ICJ discussed the existence of such consequences for third States as a result of the breaches by Israel the right of self-determination and certain obligations of international humanitarian law. The Court made no express reference to Articles 40 and 41 of the Articles; rather it reasoned first that the norms in question constituted rights and obligations *erga omnes* and then held that '[g]iven the character and the importance of the rights and obligations involved', other States were under an obligation not to recognize the illegal situation resulting from the construction of the Wall, and were under an obligation not to render aid and assistance in maintaining the situation thereby created, as well as an obligation 'while respecting the United Nations Charter and international law to see to it that any impediment, resulting from the construction of the wall, to the exercise by the Palestinian people of its right to self-determination is brought to an end.'[33] In addition, the Court was of the view that the 'United Nations, and especially the General Assembly and the Security Council, should consider what further action is required to bring to an end the illegal situation resulting from the construction of the wall...'[34]

III. THE ELEMENTS OF STATE RESPONSIBILITY

As already noted, the international responsibility of a State arises from the commission of an internationally wrongful act. An internationally wrongful act presupposes that there is conduct consisting of an action or omission that (a) is attributable to a State under international law; and (b) constitutes a breach of the international obligations of the State (ARSIWA, Article 2). In principle, the fulfilment of these conditions is a sufficient basis for international responsibility, as has been consistently affirmed by international courts and tribunals.[35] In some cases, however, the respondent State may claim that it is justified in its non-performance, for example, because it was acting in self-defence or was subject to a situation of *force majeure*. In international law such defences or excuses are termed 'circumstances precluding wrongfulness'. They will be a matter for the respondent State to assert and prove, not for the claimant State to negative.

The three elements—attribution, breach, and the absence of any valid justification for non-performance—will be discussed in turn before we consider the consequences of State responsibility, in particular for the injured State or States.

proposal has found no concrete support in State practice (although cf the comments of Judge Simma in *Armed Activities on the Territory of the Congo (Democratic Republic of the Congo v Uganda), Judgment, ICJ Reports 2005*, p 168, Separate Opinion of Judge Simma, paras 32–41.

[33] *Legal Consequences of the Construction of a Wall in the Occupied Palestine Territory, Advisory Opinion, ICJ Reports 2004*, p 136, para 159.

[34] Ibid, para 160.

[35] See the Permanent Court of International Justice in *Phosphates in Morocco, Preliminary Objections, Judgment, PCIJ, Ser A/B, No 74*, p 10, and the International Court of Justice in *United States Diplomatic and Consular Staff in Tehran, Judgment, ICJ Reports 1980*, p 3, para 56; *Military and Paramilitary Activities in and against Nicaragua (Nicaragua v United States of America), Merits, Judgment, ICJ Reports 1986*, p 14, para 226, and *Gabčíkovo-Nagymaros Project (Hungary/Slovakia), Judgment, ICJ Reports 1997*, p 7, para 78. See also the decision of the Mexico-United States General Claims Commission in *Dickson Car Wheel Company* (1931) 4 *RIAA* 669, 678.

A. ATTRIBUTION OF CONDUCT TO THE STATE

Although they seem real enough to their citizens, States are juridical abstractions. Like corporations in national law, they necessarily act through their organs or agents. The rules of attribution specify the actors whose conduct may engage the responsibility of the State, either generally or in specific circumstances. It should be stressed that the issue here is one of responsibility for breaches of international obligations of the State. It does not concern the question which officials can enter into those obligations in the first place. Only senior officials of the State (the head of State or government, the minister of foreign affairs, and diplomats in certain circumstances: see VCLT, Article 7) have inherent authority to bind the State; other officials act upon the basis of express or ostensible authority (VCLT, Article 46).[36] By contrast, any State official, even at a local or municipal level, may commit an internationally wrongful act attributable to the State—the local constabulary or army torturing a prisoner or causing an enforced disappearance,[37] for example, or the local mayor requisitioning a factory.[38]

A clear example of attribution of conduct performed by State agents vis-à-vis another State was the sinking on 10 July 1985 of the Greenpeace ship *Rainbow Warrior* in Auckland harbour. The French Government subsequently admitted that the explosives had been planted on the ship by agents of the Directorate General of External Security, acting on orders received. New Zealand sought and received an apology and compensation for the violation of its sovereignty.[39] This was quite separate from the damage done to Greenpeace, a non-governmental organization, and to the Dutch national who was killed by the explosion; separate arrangements were made to provide compensation for these interests.

On the other hand, a State does not normally guarantee the safety of foreign nationals on its territory or the security of their property or the success of their investments. In terms

---

[36] See also *Maritime Delimitation and Territorial Questions between Qatar and Bahrain, Jurisdiction and Admissibility, ICJ Reports 1994*, p 112, paras 26–27; *Land and Maritime Boundary between Cameroon and Nigeria (Cameroon v Nigeria: Equatorial Guinea Intervening), Merits, Judgment, ICJ Reports 2002*, p 303, paras 264–268. For an analogous question as to whether the position taken by organs of the constituent entities of a federal State are sufficient to give rise to a 'dispute as to the meaning or scope' of a prior judgment in order to form the basis for a request for interpretation of a prior judgment under Article 60 of the Statute of the ICJ, see *Request for Interpretation of the Judgment of 31 March 2004 in the Case concerning Avena and Other Mexican Nationals (Mexico v United States of America) Request for the Indication of Provisional Measures, (Mexico v United States of America), Order of 16 July 2008* (nyr). The Court held that the refusal of the courts of certain constituent states of the United States to give effect to the Court's prior judgment in *Avena*, as well as the decision of the Supreme Court that the judgment was not directly enforceable as a matter of domestic constitutional law, were sufficient *prima facie* to give rise to a 'dispute' as to the meaning of the Court's judgment; this was held to be the case despite the statement of the federal executive authorities that they did not dispute the meaning and effects of the ICJ's judgment in *Avena* to the effect that the United States was under an obligation to allow reconsideration and review of the convictions (ibid, paras 55–56).

[37] See, eg, *Velásquez-Rodríguez v Honduras, Merits, Judgment of 29 July 1988, Ser C no 4*, 95 ILR 259, para 183 ('not all levels of the Government of Honduras were necessarily aware of those acts, nor is there any evidence that such acts were the result of official orders. Nevertheless, those circumstances are irrelevant for the purposes of establishing whether Honduras is responsible under international law'). See also ibid, 296, para 170.

[38] *Elettronica Sicula SpA (ELSI), Judgment, ICJ Reports 1989*, p 15.

[39] *Rainbow Warrior (No 1) (1986)*, 74 ILR 256.

of any injury suffered, there has to be some involvement by the State itself—in effect, by the government of the State, in the conduct which is complained of. A State will generally only be liable for the conduct of its organs or officials, acting as such (ARSIWA, Article 4; Commentary, Crawford, 2002, pp 94–99). Purely private acts will not engage the State's responsibility, although the State may in certain circumstances be liable for its failure to prevent those acts, or to take action to punish the individuals responsible.[40] On the other hand, the scope of State responsibility for official acts is broad, and the definition of 'organ' for this purpose comprehensive and includes 'all the individual or collective entities which make up the organization of the State and act on its behalf'.[41] There is no distinction based on the level of seniority of the relevant officials in the State hierarchy; as long as they are acting in their official capacity, responsibility is engaged. In addition, there is no limitation to the central executive; responsibility may be engaged for acts of federal, provincial or even local government officials. Further, the classification of powers is also irrelevant: in principle, the concept of 'organ' covers legislatures, executive officials and courts at all levels (ARSIWA, Article 4).[42]

Acts or omissions of any State organ or of persons or entities exercising elements of governmental authority, are attributable to the State provided they were acting in that capacity at the time, even if they may have been acting *ultra vires*.[43] Indeed, the State may be responsible for conduct which is clearly in excess of authority if the official has used an official position. For example, in the *Caire* case, a French national in Mexico was shot and killed by members of the Mexican army after he had refused their demands for money. The tribunal held that, for the *ultra vires* acts of officials to be attributable to the State, 'they must have acted at least to all appearances as competent officials or organs, or they must have used powers or methods appropriate to their official capacity'.[44] In the circumstances the responsibility of the State was engaged 'in view of the fact that they acted in their capacity of officers and used the means placed at their disposition by virtue of that capacity'.[45] Similarly, in *Youmans*, United States citizens cornered in a house by a mob were killed after soldiers sent to disperse the crowd, contrary to orders, opened fire on the house, forcing the inhabitants out into the open. The Tribunal held that there was State responsibility given that 'at the time of the commission of these acts the men were on duty under the immediate supervision and in the presence of a commanding officer'. The Tribunal went on to comment that:

Soldiers inflicting personal injuries or committing wanton destruction or looting always act in disobedience of some rules laid down by superior authority. There could be no liability

---

[40] *Janes (US v Mexico)* (1926) 4 *RIAA* 82; cf *Noyes (US v Panama)* (1933) 6 *RIAA* 308.

[41] Commentary to Article 4, paragraph (1). ARSIWA, Article 4 itself and this passage from the Commentary were cited with approval by the ICJ in *Application of the Convention on the Prevention and Punishment of the Crime of Genocide (Bosnia and Herzegovina v Serbia and Montenegro), Merits*, Judgment of 26 February 2007 (nyr), para 388.

[42] ARSIWA, Article 4. See also *LaGrand (Germany v United States of America), Provisional Measures, Order of 3 March 1999, ICJ Reports 1999*, p 9, para 28: 'Whereas the international responsibility of a State is engaged by the action of the competent organs and authorities acting in that State, whatever they may be'.

[43] Article 7 ARSIWA; see also the final words of Article 5 ARSIWA. For an illustration, see *Union Bridge Company (USA v Great Britain)* (1924) 6 *RIAA* 138.

[44] *Caire (France v Mexico)* (1929) 5 *RIAA* 516 at p 530.

[45] Ibid, at p 531.

whatever for such misdeeds if the view were taken that any acts committed by soldier in contravention of instructions must always be considered as personal acts.[46]

By contrast, a State is not responsible for the acts of mobs or of private individuals as such. Their conduct will only be attributable to the State if they were in fact acting under the authority or control of the State (ARSIWA, Article 8), or if the State acknowledges adopts (or in common law terminology 'ratifies') their acts as its own (ARSIWA, Article 11). In the *Tehran Hostages* case, the International Court held that although initially the students who took control of the US embassy in Tehran were not acting as agents of Iran, a subsequent decree of Ayatollah Khomeini endorsing the occupation of the embassy:

translated continuing occupation of the Embassy and detention of the hostages into acts of [Iran]. The militants, authors of the invasion and jailers of the hostages, had now become agents of the Iranian State for whose acts the State itself was internationally responsible.[47]

Similarly, the State will be responsible if the authorities act in collusion with the mob, or participate in the mob violence. However, international tribunals generally require strong evidence of such collusion.[48]

In addition, conduct which is not attributable to a State because it was carried out by persons acting in a purely private capacity may nonetheless be chargeable to the State because the State failed in some obligation to prevent the conduct in question. However, in such a case, responsibility arises as a result of the State's own failings, rather than directly as a result of the conduct of the private individuals. For instance, in the *Tehran Hostages* case, Iran was held to have breached its special obligation of protection of the embassy and consular premises and personnel, even prior to its adoption of the acts of the occupying students.[49] The duty to control a mob is particularly important when the mob is in some way under the control of the authorities.[50]

Like other systems of law, international law does not limit attribution to the conduct of the regular officials or organs of the State; it also extends to conduct carried out by others who are authorized to act by the State or at least who act under its actual direction or control. In the *Nicaragua* case, the International Court stated that:

For this conduct [of the *contra* rebels] to give rise to legal responsibility of the United States, it would in principle have to be proved that that State had *effective control* of the military or paramilitary operations in the course of which the alleged violations were committed.[51]

The Articles on State Responsibility follow this approach: under Article 8, conduct of a person or group of persons is attributable to the State 'if the person or group of persons is in fact acting on the instructions of, or under the direction or control of, that State in carrying out the conduct' (ARSIWA, Article 8; Commentary, Crawford, 2002, pp 110–113); and it was reaffirmed by the International Court in *Bosnian Genocide*, as concerns the

---

[46] *Youmans (USA v Mexico)* (1926) 4 *RIAA* 110; (1927) 21 *AJIL* 571, para 14.
[47] *United States Diplomatic and Consular Staff in Tehran, Judgment, ICJ Reports 1980*, p 3, paras 73–74.
[48] *Janes (USA v Mexico)* (1926) 4 *RIAA* 82.
[49] *United States Diplomatic and Consular Staff in Tehran, Judgment, ICJ Reports 1980*, p 3, para 63.
[50] See, eg, *The Zafiro (Great Britain v USA)* (1925) 6 *RIAA* 160.
[51] *Military and Paramilitary Activities in and against Nicaragua, Merits, Judgment (Nicaragua v United States of America), ICJ Reports 1986*, p 14, para 115 (emphasis added).

attribution to the FRY of the conduct of the Bosnian Serb forces and paramilitary groups.[52] There the Court observed;

the 'overall control' test has the major drawback of broadening the scope of State responsibility well beyond the fundamental principle governing the law of international responsibility: a State is responsible only for its own conduct, that is to say the conduct of persons acting, on whatever basis, on its behalf... [T]he 'overall control' test is unsuitable, for it stretches too far, almost to breaking point, the connection which must exist between the conduct of a State's organs and its international responsibility.[53]

As that last passage illustrates, the governing principle is that of independent responsibility: the State is responsible for its own acts, ie for the acts of its organs and agents, and not for the acts of private parties, unless there are special circumstances warranting attribution to it of such conduct. The same applies where one State is somehow implicated in the conduct of a third State—indeed it applies *a fortiori*, since that third State will ordinarily be responsible for its own acts in breach of its own international responsibilities (ARSIWA, Articles 16–19). But there is another facet to the principle of independent responsibility: a State cannot hide behind the involvement of other States. It is responsible if and to the extent that it contributed to that wrongful conduct by its own acts. Thus in *Nicaragua*, the acts of the *contras* were not as such attributable to the United States, but the United States was responsible for its own conduct (in itself internationally wrongful) in training and financing the *contras* and in carrying out some specific operations, including the mining of a Nicaraguan harbour.[54] Likewise if a number of States act together in administering a territory, each will be responsible for its own conduct as part of the common enterprise.[55]

In another and rather special form of parallelism, the State will be responsible for the conduct of an insurrectional movement which subsequently becomes the government of that State (or, if they are a secessionary movement, of the new State they are struggling to create). The rule is to some extent anomalous, since it determines the attribution of conduct not by events at the time of that conduct but by reference to later contingencies—the success or failure of the revolt or secession. But it is established, and finds expression in Article 10 of the ILC Articles. For instance, in *Yeager*[56] immediately after the revolution in Iran in 1979, the claimant had been detained for several days by 'revolutionary guards' and had then been evacuated from the country. The Tribunal held that, although the guards were not recognized under internal law as part of the State apparatus, they were in fact

---

[52] *Application of the Convention on the Prevention and Punishment of the Crime of Genocide (Bosnia and Herzegovina v Serbia and Montenegro), Merits*, Judgment of 26 February 2007 (nyr), paras 402–407.

[53] Ibid, 406.

[54] *Military and Paramilitary Activities in and against Nicaragua (Nicaragua v United States of America), Merits, Judgment, ICJ Reports 1986*, p 14, in particular paras 75–80, 238, 242, 252, 292(3)–(6).

[55] Cf *Certain Phosphate Lands in Nauru (Nauru v Australia), Preliminary Objections, ICJ Reports 1992*, p 240 where the International Court left the question of possible apportionment of any compensation found to be due between the other implicated States to the merits stage. See also the *Legality of the Use of Force* cases between Yugoslavia and the NATO States (eg, *Legality of the Use of Force (Yugoslavia v Belgium), Provisional Measures, Order of 2 June 1999, ICJ Reports 1999*, p 124); the Court eventually held that it did not have jurisdiction over the claims (eg, *Legality of the Use of Force (Yugoslavia v Belgium), Preliminary Objections, Judgment, ICJ Reports 2004*, p 279).

[56] *Yeager v The Islamic Republic of Iran* (1987), 82 ILR 178.

exercising public functions in the absence of the previous State apparatus: Iran was thus held responsible for their acts.[57]

B. BREACH OF AN INTERNATIONAL OBLIGATION OF THE STATE

The second element of responsibility is breach of an international obligation of the State. Here an initial distinction is drawn between State responsibility arising in the context of direct State-to-State wrongdoing and State responsibility arising in the context of diplomatic protection (injury to aliens or their property). This is so even though the relevant obligations may be contained in a treaty, the breach of which in principle engages direct State-to-State responsibility. The International Court was careful to preserve the distinction in the *ELSI* case, where the United States sought to base its action on breach of a bilateral treaty: nonetheless, the Chamber said, its claim was in the nature of diplomatic protection and was thus subject to such requirements as the exhaustion of local remedies.[58]

Many of the problems which arise in the context of diplomatic protection (nationality of claims, exhaustion of local remedies) do not arise in the context of direct State-to-State disputes. The only issue in these direct State-to-State cases is whether conduct attributable to State B causes legal harm to State A in violation of international law. If so, responsibility is *prima facie* engaged.

On its face, the requirement that there should be a breach of an international obligation of the State seems obvious enough. However, a number of questions arise: for example, causation, the notion of injury, the time factor (rules concerning non-retrospectivity of international law and acts continuing in time), and so on. An important preliminary point should be made: international law is a distinct system, separate from national legal systems. In its own terms it prevails over national law in the event of conflict, and this is so irrespective of the approach taken by the national legal system. Several consequences follow. First, a State cannot invoke its own municipal law as a justification for refusal to comply with its international obligations, whether under treaties or otherwise.[59] The fact that an act or omission is lawful (or unlawful) under national law does not prejudge the question of its lawfulness or otherwise under international law.[60] Secondly, the content of municipal law is a matter of fact for international law;[61] in theory, the two live in distinct spheres, communicating via the rules of evidence. Thirdly, a State cannot seek to invalidate the entry into force of international obligations by reference to municipal law constraints which it failed to observe.[62]

---

[57] Cf however *Short v The Islamic Republic of Iran* (1987), 82 ILR 148 and *Rankin v The Islamic Republic of Iran* (1987), 82 ILR 204 (decided on the basis that the claimants had failed to prove that their departure was caused by actions attributable to Iran, rather than the general turmoil accompanying the revolution).

[58] *Elettronica Sicula SpA (ELSI), Judgment, ICJ Reports 1989*, p 15, para 52.

[59] *Greco-Bulgarian 'Communities', Advisory Opinion, 1930, PCIJ, Ser B, No 17* at p 32; ARSIWA, Articles 3, 32.

[60] *Compañía de Aguas del Aconquija and Vivendi Universal v Argentine Republic (ICSID Case No ARB/97/3), Decision on Annulment*, 3 July 2002, 41 ILM 1135.

[61] *Certain German Interests in Polish Upper Silesia, Merits, Judgment No 7, 1926, PCIJ, Ser A, No 7* at p 19.

[62] *Free Zones of Upper Savoy and the District of Gex, Judgment, 1932, PCIJ, Ser A/B, No 46*, p 96 at p 167 and see ibid, at p 170; *Legal Status of Eastern Greenland, Judgment, 1933, PCIJ, Ser A/B, No 53*, p 22 at p 71, and the Dissenting Opinion of Judge Anzilotti, ibid, pp 91–92. In relation to the law of treaties, see

Of course conduct attributable to a State may consist of both actions and omissions; breach of international obligations by omission is relatively common. For instance in the *Tehran Hostages* case, the International Court held that the responsibility of Iran was due to the 'inaction' of its authorities which 'failed to take appropriate steps' in circumstances where such steps were evidently called for.[63]

1. Fault, injury, and damage

There has been a major debate about whether international law has a general requirement of fault. The debate is between those who maintain that international law requires some fault on the part of the State if it is to incur responsibility and supporters of so-called 'objective responsibility'. The case law tends to support the objective school. Thus in *Caire*, the arbitral tribunal affirmed 'the doctrine of the "objective responsibility" of the State, that is, the responsibility for the acts of its officials or organs, which may devolve upon it despite the absence of any "*faute*" on its part'.[64] However, there are statements which may be seen as going the other way. In the *Corfu Channel* case, the International Court held that:

It is clear that knowledge of the minelaying cannot be imputed to the Albanian Government by reason merely of the fact that a minefield discovered in Albanian territorial waters caused the explosion of which the British warships were victims... [I]t cannot be concluded from the mere fact of the control exercised by a State over its territory and waters that that State necessarily knew, or ought to have known, of any unlawful act perpetrated therein, nor yet that it necessarily knew, or should have known, the authors. This fact, by itself and apart from other circumstances, neither involves *prima facie* responsibility nor shifts the burden of proof.[65]

In that case Albania's responsibility was upheld on the basis that (according to the evidence gathered, including by an expert commission) Albania must have known that the mines had been recently laid and nonetheless, in breach of its international obligations, failed to warn ships passing through the strait of their presence.

When scholarly debate bogs down around some dichotomy such as 'responsibility for fault'/'objective responsibility', something has almost always gone wrong. Here the problem is one of level of analysis: there is neither a rule that responsibility is always based on fault, nor one that it is always independent of it—indeed, there appears to be no presumption either way. This is hardly surprising in a legal system which has to deal with a wide range of problems and disposes of a limited armoury of techniques. But in any

Vienna Convention on the Law of Treaties, Articles 27, 46; and see *Land and Maritime Boundary between Cameroon and Nigeria (Cameroon v Nigeria: Equatorial Guinea Intervening), Judgment, ICJ Reports 2002*, p 303, paras 264–268.

[63] *United States Diplomatic and Consular Staff in Tehran, Judgment, ICJ Reports 1980*, p 3, paras 63, 67. See also *Velásquez-Rodríguez v Honduras, Merits, Judgment of 29 July 1988, Ser C no 4*, 95 ILR 259, para 170: 'under international law a State is responsible for the acts of its agents undertaken in their official capacity and for their omissions...'; *Affaire relative à l'acquisition de la nationalité polonaise (Germany v Poland)* (1924) 1 *RIAA* 425.

[64] *Caire (France v Mexico)* (1929) 5 *RIAA* 516 at p 529.

[65] *Corfu Channel, Merits, Judgment, ICJ Reports 1949*, p 4 at p 18. See also the decision in *Home Missionary Society (USA v Great Britain)* (1920) 6 *RIAA* 42.

event circumstances alter cases, and it is illusory to seek for a single dominant rule. Where responsibility is essentially based on acts of omission (as in *Corfu Channel*), considerations of fault loom large. But if a State deliberately carries out some specific act, there is less room for it to argue that the harmful consequences were unintended and should be disregarded. Everything depends on the specific context and on the content and interpretation of the obligation said to have been breached.

Thus the ILC Articles on State Responsibility endorse a more nuanced view. Under Articles 2 and 12, the international law of State responsibility does not require fault before an act or omission may be characterized as internationally wrongful. However, the interpretation of the relevant primary obligation in a given case may well lead to the conclusion that fault is a necessary condition for responsibility in relation to that obligation, having regard to the conduct alleged (ARSIWA, Articles 2 and 12; Commentary, Crawford, 2002, pp 83–85, 125–130).

Similarly, there has been an intense debate concerning the role of harm or damage in the law of State responsibility. Some authors (and some governments) have claimed that the State must have suffered some form of actual harm or damage before responsibility can be engaged (Bollecker-Stern, 1973). Once more, the ILC Articles leave the question to be determined by the relevant primary obligation: there is no *general* requirement of harm or damage before the consequences of responsibility come into being. In some circumstances, the mere breach of an obligation will be sufficient to give rise to responsibility; for instance, even a minor infringement of the inviolability of an embassy or consular mission. On the other hand, in the context for example of pollution of rivers, it is necessary to show some substantial impact on the environment or on other uses of the watercourse before responsibility will arise.[66]

A corollary of this position is that there may have been a breach of international law but no material harm may have been suffered by another State or person in whose interest the obligation was created. In such cases international courts frequently award merely declaratory relief on the ground that nothing more is required.[67] However, in such circumstances, the main point of asserting responsibility may be for the future, to avoid repetition of the problem, rather than to obtain compensation for the past.

2. Continuing wrongful acts and the time factor

The basic principle is that a State can only be internationally responsible for breach of a treaty obligation if the obligation is in force for that State at the time of the alleged breach. It is therefore necessary to examine closely at what point an obligation entered into force, or at what point the obligation was terminated or ceased to bind the State.

---

[66] Thus the mere risk of future harm was held not to constitute a sufficient basis for responsibility in the *Lac Lanoux Arbitration* (1957), 24 ILR 101. In *Gabčíkovo-Nagymaros Project (Hungary/Slovakia), Judgment, ICJ Reports 1997*, p 7, the ICJ held that preparations for the diversion of the Danube on the territory of one State did not involve a breach of treaty until the diversion went ahead (and caused damage to the other State).

[67] The *'I'm Alone'* (1935) 3 *RIAA* 1609 at p 1618; see also *Corfu Channel, Merits, Judgment, ICJ Reports 1949*, p 4 at pp 35–36, in which the ICJ made such a declaration in relation to Albania's claim of violation of its sovereignty as the result of the mine-sweeping operations carried out within its territorial waters by British warships.

For example in the *Mondev* case,[68] a claim was brought by a Canadian company alleging breach of the NAFTA Chapter 11 investment protection provisions by the United States. The claimant alleged that by various actions of the Boston city authorities the value of the applicant's interests in building and development projects had effectively been expropriated. But all of these actions took place before NAFTA's entry into force on 1 January 1994: the only later events were decisions of United States courts denying Mondev's claims under United States law. The tribunal held that NAFTA could not be applied retrospectively to actions prior to its entry into force. This left open the possibility of a claim of denial of justice in respect of the court decisions after NAFTA came into force, but the courts had not in any way acted improperly, and thus there had been no denial of justice.

The relevant principle is stated in Article 13 of the ILC Articles: 'An act of a State does not constitute a breach of an international obligation unless the State is bound by the obligation in question at the time the act occurs'. The principle is clear enough, but its application may cause problems, in particular regarding changes in customary international law obligations, when it will not be clear precisely when an old customary rule was replaced by a new one.[69] For example, slavery was not always unlawful under international law, yet claims are sometimes made for reparation for persons or groups whose lives are said to have been affected by slavery and the slave trade.[70]

Another problem in applying Article 13 involves determining exactly when, or during what period, a wrongful act occurs. Wrongful acts can continue over a period of time— for instance the continued detention of diplomatic and consular personnel in the *Tehran Hostages* case, or the forced or involuntary disappearance of a person contrary to human rights norms.[71] Other wrongs may be instantaneous, even though their effects may continue after the point of breach. For example, an unlawful killing or a law expropriating property have effect at a specific moment; the breach occurs at the moment the victim is killed or the property passes, and this even though the effects of these breaches are enduring. In general such continuing consequences concern the scope of reparation, not whether there has been a breach in the first place (ARSIWA, Article 14; Commentary, Crawford, 2002, pp 135–140).

These distinctions may also be significant when it comes to issues of the jurisdiction of courts in cases concerning responsibility. For example under the European Convention on Human Rights (ECHR), claims can only be brought against a State party concerning breaches occurring after the Convention entered into force for that State, and previously could only be brought by individuals when the State in question had accepted the right of individual petition.[72] But it may be—depending on how one characterizes

---

[68] *Mondev International Ltd* v *United States of America* (Case No ARB(AF)/99/2), award of 11 October 2002, *ICSID Reports*, vol 6, 192.

[69] See, eg, *Fisheries Jurisdiction (United Kingdom* v *Iceland), Merits, Judgment, ICJ Reports 1974*, p 3.

[70] *Le Louis* (1817) 2 Dodson 210.

[71] See, eg, the judgment of the Inter-American Court of Human Rights in *Blake* v *Guatemala, Merits, Judgment of 24 January 1998, Ser C, no 36* (1998).

[72] Under the ECHR as originally concluded, the jurisdiction of the European Commission on Human Rights and the European Court of Human Rights in relation to claims by individuals was conditional on acceptance of such jurisdiction by the State in question made by way of a declaration (see former Articles 25 and 46). Acceptance of the right of individual petition became compulsory upon entry into force of Protocol No 11 on 1 November 1998 (see now Article 34, ECHR). An analogous provision exists under the American

the conduct—that a breach which was initially committed by a State before it became a party or before it accepted jurisdiction in relation to individual petitions continues thereafter and to that extent falls within the jurisdiction *ratione temporis* of the tribunal in question. For example, the circumstances of the *Loizidou* case before the European Court of Human Rights went back to the Turkish intervention in Cyprus in 1974, after Turkey became a party to the European Convention, but long before it accepted the right of individual petition; but the continuing exclusion of Mrs Loizidou from access to her property in the Turkish-controlled north continued after that date and could be dealt with by the Court.[73]

C. CIRCUMSTANCES PRECLUDING WRONGFULNESS: DEFENCES OR EXCUSES FOR BREACHES OF INTERNATIONAL LAW

As noted above, although conduct may be clearly attributable to a State, and be clearly inconsistent with its international obligations, it is possible that responsibility will not follow. The State may be able to rely on some defence or excuse: in the Articles on State Responsibility these are collected under the heading of 'Circumstances precluding wrongfulness' in Chapter V of Part One. Chapter V is essentially a catalogue or compilation of rules that have been recognized by international law as justifying or excusing non-compliance by a State with its international obligations, and it is not exclusive.[74] It should be noted that none of the circumstances precluding wrongfulness can operate to excuse conduct which violates a peremptory norm (ARSIWA, Article 26): one cannot plead necessity to justify invading Belgium, for example.[75]

1. Consent

Valid consent by a State to action by another State which would otherwise be inconsistent with its international obligations precludes the wrongfulness of that action (ARSIWA, Article 26). This is consistent with the role of consent in international relations generally: thus a State may consent to military action on its territory which (absent its consent) would be unlawful under the United Nations Charter. More mundanely, a State may consent to foreign judicial inquiries or arrest of suspects on its territory.[76] However, the scope of any consent in fact given by a State needs to be carefully examined and

Convention on Human Rights (ACHR) in relation to acceptance by State parties of the jurisdiction of the Inter-American Court of Human Rights (see Article 62).

[73] See *Loizidou v Turkey (Preliminary Objections)*, Judgment of 23 March 1995, Ser A, no 310, 20 *EHRR* 99 and *Merits, RJD 1996–VI*, 23 *EHRR* 513: see also *Papamichalopoulos and others v Greece*, Judgment of 24 June 1993, Ser A, no 260–B (European Court of Human Rights). For cases dealing with similar issues before other human rights bodies, see eg the decision of the Human Rights Committee in *Lovelace v Canada*, decision of 30 July 1981, UN Doc A/36/40, p 166 under the individual petition provisions of the Optional Protocol to the ICCPR; and the judgments of the Inter-American Court of Human Rights in *Blake v Guatemala, Preliminary Objections, Judgment of 2 July 1996, Ser C, no 27 (1996)* and *Blake v Guatemala, Merits, Judgment of 24 January 1998, Ser C, no 36 (1998)*, affirming the continuing character of forced disappearances.

[74] Specific defences or excuses may be recognized for particular obligations: eg, Article 17 of the 1982 Convention on the Law of the Sea. Cf ARSIWA, Article 55.

[75] As Chancellor von Bethmann-Hollweg did before the Reichstag in 1914: see Crawford, 2002, p 178.

[76] See, eg, *Savarkar (Great Britain v France)* (1911) 11 *RIAA* 243.

normally will be strictly construed.[77] Further, consent only goes so far: a State cannot waive the application of what in national law would be called mandatory rules and in international law are called peremptory norms. Thus a State cannot (by treaty or otherwise) consent to or legitimize genocide, a situation expressly provided for in the ILC's formulation of the defence of consent; consent must be 'valid' (ARSIWA Article 20; cf Article 26). Further, consent will only preclude the wrongfulness of conduct with regard to the consenting State; if the obligation breached is owed in parallel to more than one State, the wrongfulness of the act will not be precluded with regard to those States that have not consented.[78]

2. Self-defence

In certain circumstances, a State may permissibly disregard other international obligations whilst acting in self-defence in accordance with the Charter of the United Nations (ARSIWA, Article 21). The point was implicitly recognized by the International Court in the *Nuclear Weapons* Advisory Opinion, when it distinguished between *per se* restrictions on the use of force, whatever the circumstances—in another formulation, 'obligations of total restraint'—and considerations which, even if mandatory in time of peace, might be overridden for a State facing an imminent threat and required to act against it in self-defence.[79]

3. *Force majeure*

In common with most legal systems, international law does not impose responsibility where the non-performance of an obligation is due to circumstances entirely outside the control of the State. This defence obviously needs to be tightly circumscribed, and the language of Article 23(1) of the ILC Articles provides that *force majeure* is a defence only where 'the occurrence of an irresistible force or of an unforeseen event, beyond the control of the State, [makes] it materially impossible in the circumstances to perform the obligation'. The defence of *force majeure* is further circumscribed by the limitations in Article 23(2), which provide that *force majeure* will not apply if either the situation 'is due, either alone or in combination with other factors, to the conduct of the State invoking it', or if, as a result of assessment of the situation, the State seeking to invoke *force majeure* assumed the risk of the situation occurring.

4. Distress and necessity

The two circumstances of distress and necessity have much in common in that they both excuse conduct which would otherwise be wrongful because of extreme circumstances. According to Article 24, distress operates to excuse conduct where the author of the act 'had no other reasonable way...of saving the author's life or the lives of other persons entrusted to the author's care'. By contrast, necessity operates to excuse conduct taken

---

[77] See, eg, the careful consideration given by the ICJ to the scope and extent of the DRC's consent to the presence of Ugandan troops on its territory in *Armed Activities on the Territory of the Congo (Democratic Republic of the Congo v Uganda), Judgment, ICJ Reports 2005*, p 168.

[78] See, eg, *Customs Régime between Germany and Austria, 1931, Advisory Opinion, PCIJ, Ser A/B, No 41*, p 37.

[79] On *per se* restrictions see *Legality of the Threat or Use of Nuclear Weapons, Advisory Opinion, ICJ Reports 1996*, p 226, paras 39, 52; on 'obligations of total restraint', see ibid, para 30.

which 'is the only means for the State to safeguard an essential interest against a grave and imminent peril'. Distress and necessity are to be distinguished from *force majeure* in that violation of the obligation in question is theoretically avoidable, although absolute compliance of the State with its international obligations is not required; a State is not required to sacrifice human life or to suffer inordinate damage to its interests in order to fulfil its international obligations.

The possibilities of abuse are obvious, in particular for invocation of necessity, and in the ILC Articles both circumstances are narrowly confined. Thus reliance on them is precluded if the State has in some way contributed to the situation which it is seeking to invoke to excuse its conduct. Further, the invoking State can only excuse conduct which is not unduly onerous for other States. Reliance on distress is precluded if the act in question 'is likely to create a comparable or greater peril' (Article 24(2)(b)). Likewise, the invocation of a state of necessity is precluded if the action would 'seriously impair an essential interest of the State or States towards which the obligation exists, or of the international community as a whole' (Article 25(1)(b)).

In recent years, Argentina has sought to rely on a state of necessity as justifying the measures it adopted to deal with the Argentine financial crisis between 1999 and 2002; those measures have given rise to a large number of claims by foreign investors under bilateral investment protection treaties. In the majority of cases, the plea of necessity has been rejected on the grounds that the financial crisis and its potential consequences were not sufficiently serious to be regarded as imperilling an 'essential interest' and the situation did not involve a 'grave and imminent peril'; in any case, the measures adopted were not the 'only way' for Argentina to deal with the crisis, there were other lawful means at its disposal in that regard, and Argentina had contributed to the situation.[80]

Although where either distress or a state of necessity is found to have been established the wrongfulness of the act is precluded, other States are not necessarily expected to bear the consequences of another State's misfortune; the invoking State may have to pay compensation for any material loss caused to the State or States to which the obligation breached was owed (Article 27(b)).[81]

5. Countermeasures

As the International Court affirmed in the *Gabčíkovo-Nagymaros Project* case, countermeasures taken by a State in response to an internationally wrongful act of another State

---

[80] See eg *CMS Gas Transmission Company v Argentine Republic (ICSID Case No ARB/01/8)*, Award of 12 May 2005; *Enron Corporation and Ponderosa Assets LP v Argentine Republic (ICSID Case No ARB/01/3)*, Award of 22 May 2007; *Sempra Energy International v Argentine Republic (ICSID Case No ARB/02/16)*, Award of 28 September 2007; *BG Group plc v Republic of Argentina*, Final Award of 24 December 2007. Cf *LG&E Energy Corp, LG&E Capital Corp, LG&E International Inc v Argentine Republic (ICSID Case No ARB/02/1)*, Decision on Liability of 3 October 2006, in which the Tribunal concluded that a state of necessity had existed for at least part of the period in question. The Award in *CMS* was the subject of an application for annulment; the ad hoc Committee, although finding various defects in the reasoning, declined to annul the Award: *CMS Gas Transmission Company v Argentine Republic (ICSID Case No ARB/01/8)*, Decision on Annulment of 25 September 2007.

[81] Cf *LG&E Energy Corp, LG&E Capital Corp, LG&E International Inc v Argentine Republic (ICSID Case No ARB/02/1)*, Decision on Liability of 3 October 2006, in which the Tribunal held that no compensation was payable to the investor in relation to the period during which it held that a state of necessity had existed.

are not wrongful acts, but are recognized as a valid means of self-help as long as certain conditions are respected.[82] Countermeasures as described in the ILC Articles only cover the suspension of performance by a State of one or more of its obligations; they are to be distinguished from acts of retorsion which, since they are by definition not a breach of the obligations of the State, cannot give rise to State responsibility and therefore require no justification. Certain obligations, such as that to refrain from the use of force, those of a humanitarian character prohibiting the taking of reprisals, and those under other peremptory norms may not be suspended by way of countermeasure.

6. Consequences of invoking a circumstance precluding wrongfulness

Despite the fact that the wrongfulness of an act may be precluded by international law, that is not the end of the question. First, the wrongfulness of the act will only be precluded so long as the circumstance precluding wrongfulness continues to exist. For instance, if State A takes countermeasures in response to a breach by State B of obligations owed to State A, if State B recommences performance of its obligations State A must terminate its countermeasures; if it does not, it will incur responsibility for the period from which the countermeasure was no longer justified (Article 27(a) ARSIWA; and see Articles 52(3) (a) and 53 ARSIWA). Secondly, the preclusive effect may be relative rather than general: again, this is obviously true of countermeasures, where conduct which is justified vis-à-vis a wrongdoing State will not or may not be justified *erga omnes*.

IV. THE CONTENT OF INTERNATIONAL RESPONSIBILITY

Upon the commission of an internationally wrongful act, certain secondary obligations arise by operation of law. These are codified in Part Two, Chapter I of the ILC Articles, which identifies two main categories, the obligations of cessation and reparation. The equal emphasis on these involves an important insight. Issues of State responsibility are not only backward-looking, concerned at obtaining compensation for things past. They are at least as much concerned with the restoration of the legal relationship which has been threatened or impaired by the breach—ie with the assurance of continuing performance for the future. This is particularly clear where the individual breach may not have in itself caused any great amount of harm but where the threat of repetition is a source of legal insecurity. It can be seen in matters as diverse as the protection of embassies and protection of the environment. In these and other contexts, the relevant rules exist to protect ongoing relationships or situations of continuing value. The analogy of the bilateral contract, relatively readily terminated and replaceable by a contract with someone else, is not a useful one even in the context of purely inter-State relations, and

---

[82] The conditions required by the ARSIWA, in order for countermeasures to be lawful are: they must be taken to induce compliance with the obligations contained in Part Two of the Articles (reparation, cessation…) (Article 49(1)); they must be as far as possible reversible (Article 49(3)); they must be proportionate (Article 51); and there must have been a request to the State to fulfil its obligations, and notification of the decision to take countermeasures accompanied by an offer to negotiate (Article 52(1)). For the recognition of these conditions as customary see *Gabčíkovo-Nagymaros Project (Hungary/Slovakia), Judgment, ICJ Reports 1997*, p 7.

a fortiori where the legal obligation exists for the protection of a wider range of (non-synallagmatic) interests.

Thus the fact that the responsible State is under an obligation to make reparation for a breach does not mean that it can disregard its obligation for the future, effectively buying its way out of compliance; when an obligation is breached, it does not disappear of its own accord. The obligation continues to bind the responsible State, and the State therefore remains obliged to perform the obligation in question (Article 29). As a corollary, in the case of a continuing wrongful act, the responsible State is under an obligation to bring that act to an end (Article 30(a)). Indeed in certain circumstances it will be appropriate for—and may be incumbent upon—the responsible State to offer appropriate assurances and guarantees of non-repetition of the act in question to the State to which the obligation is owed (Article 30(b)).

The point was made by the International Court in the *LaGrand* case, which concerned the United States' non-observance of obligations of consular notification under Article 36 of the Vienna Convention on Consular Relations. The particular occasion of Germany's complaint was the failure of notification concerning two death row inmates who (notwithstanding their German nationality) had hardly any connection with Germany; but there was a wider concern as to United States' compliance with its continuing obligations of performance under the Consular Relations Convention. Indeed the United States accepted this, and spelled out in detail the measures it had taken to ensure compliance for the future. In consequence the Court held:

that the commitment expressed by the United States to ensure implementation of the specific measures adopted in performance of its obligations under Article 36, paragraph 1(b), must be regarded as meeting Germany's request for a general assurance of non-repetition.[83]

But of course questions of reparation also arise, especially where actual harm or damage has occurred, and under international law the responsible State is obliged to make full reparation for the consequences of its breach, provided that these are not too remote or indirect. The linkage between breach and reparation is made clear, for example, in the Statute of the International Court of Justice, which specifies among the legal disputes which may be recognized as falling within the Court's jurisdiction:

    (c) the existence of any fact which, if established, would constitute a breach of an international obligation;

    (d) the nature or extent of the reparation to be made for the breach of an international obligation.

This link was spelled out by the Permanent Court in the *Factory at Chorzów* case, in a classic passage:

It is a principle of international law that the breach of an engagement involves an obligation to make reparation in an adequate form. Reparation therefore is the indispensable complement of a failure to apply a convention and there is no necessity for this to be stated in the convention itself. Differences relating to reparations, which may be due

---

[83] *LaGrand (Germany v United States of America), Merits, Judgment, ICJ Reports 2001*, p 466, para 124; see also the dispositif, para 128(6).

by reason of failure to apply a convention, are consequently differences relating to its application.[84]

Thus there is no need for a specific mandate to an international court or tribunal to award reparation, if it has jurisdiction as between the parties in the matter: a dispute as to the interpretation or application of a treaty covers a dispute as to the consequences of its breach and thus the form and extent of reparation.

The underlying principle is that reparation must wipe out the consequences of the breach, putting the parties as far as possible in the same position as they would have been if the breach had not occurred. In order to achieve that, reparation may take several forms, including but not limited to monetary compensation. Again, both points were made by the Permanent Court in the *Chorzów* case:

The essential principle contained in the actual notion of an illegal act—a principle which seems to be established by international practice and in particular by the decisions of arbitral tribunals—is that reparation must, so far as possible, wipe out all the consequences of the illegal act and reestablish the situation which would, in all probability, have existed if that act had not been committed. Restitution in kind, or, if this is not possible, payment of a sum corresponding to the value which a restitution in kind would bear; the award, if need be, of damages for loss sustained which would not be covered by restitution in kind or payment in place of it—such are the principles which should serve to determine the amount of compensation due for an act contrary to international law.[85]

As this passage suggests, in theory at least, international law has always placed restitution as the first of the forms of reparation; it is only where restitution is not possible that other forms are substituted. This contrasts with the common law approach, under which money was taken to be the measure of all things and specific performance or restitution in kind were historically somewhat exceptional. In practice the two approaches are tending to converge—on the one hand, it is not infrequently found that specific restitution is not possible or can only be made in an approximate form in international law, while courts in the common law tradition have been expanding the scope of non-pecuniary remedies.

The basic requirement of compensation is that it should cover any 'financially assessable damage' flowing from the breach (ARSIWA, Article 36). In many cases (especially those involving loss of life, loss of opportunity, or psychiatric harm), the process of quantification is approximate and may even appear arbitrary; however, as in domestic legal systems, the difficulty in quantifying intangible loss has never had as a consequence that no compensation is payable.[86] By contrast in cases involving loss of property (including expropriation) a market for the property may exist which will give greater guidance. In addition, issues such as loss of profits may arise and, provided they are clearly established,

---

84   *Factory at Chorzów, Jurisdiction, Judgment No 8, 1927, PCIJ, Ser A, No 9* at p 21.

85   *Factory at Chorzów, Merits, Judgment No 13, 1928, PCIJ, Ser A, No 17* at p 47.

86   See eg the classic statement by Umpire Parker in relation to non-material damage in *The S.S. 'Lusitania'* (*USA* v *Germany*), (1923) 7 *RIAA* 32 at p 40: 'That one injured is, under the rules of international law, entitled to be compensated for an injury inflicted resulting in mental suffering, injury to his feelings, humiliation, shame, degradation, loss of social position or injury to his credit or to his reputation, there can be no doubt, and such compensation should be commensurate to the injury. Such damages are very real, and the mere fact that they are difficult to measure or estimate by money standards makes them none the less real and affords no reason why the injured person should not be compensated therefore as compensatory damages.'

may be compensable. Compensation may be supplemented by interest (including, if this is justified, compound interest); after some prevarication, the ILC decided to treat the issue of interest in a separate article (ARSIWA, Article 38; Commentary, Crawford, 2002, pp 235–239).

Although international tribunals have gradually been moving towards a more realistic appreciation of issues of compensation (Gray, 1987, pp 77–95; Crawford, 2002, pp 218–230)—and of remedies more generally—it remains the case that many international disputes have a distinctly symbolic element. The claimant (whether a State or some other entity) may seek vindication more than compensation, and this is recognized in the international law of reparation by way of the somewhat protean remedy of 'satisfaction'. According to Article 37(2) of the ILC Articles, satisfaction 'may consist in an acknowledgement of the breach, an expression of regret, an apology or another appropriate modality'. In many cases before international courts and tribunals, an authoritative finding of the breach will be held to be sufficient satisfaction: this was the case in terms of Albania's claim that the United Kingdom had violated its sovereignty by conducting certain mine-sweeping operations in its territorial waters in the *Corfu Channel* case,[87] and it has been held to be the situation in innumerable human rights cases, including some where more substantial remedies might have seemed justified (Shelton, 2005, pp 255–268). Similarly, in the *Bosnian Genocide* case, the ICJ held that the FRY had breached its obligation to prevent genocide in relation to the massacre at Srebrenica. Having recognized that restitution was not possible and that compensation was not appropriate given the lack of the necessary 'sufficiently direct and causal nexus' between the breach by the FRY of the obligation and the massacre,[88] it held that a declaration constituted 'in itself appropriate just satisfaction'.[89]

On the other hand, in a situation in which the breach is a continuing one, a declaration of breach and that the responsible State is under a duty to put an end to it may take on some of the characteristics of an injunction, albeit that there are few mechanisms to ensure enforcement or compliance. Thus in *Avena,* the ICJ held that the United States had breached its obligations under the Vienna Convention on Consular Relations in relation to a number of Mexican nationals who had been convicted and sentenced to death by failing to inform them of their right to have the consular authorities notified. The Court made declarations as to the specific violations of the Vienna Convention,[90] and further held that appropriate reparation consisted in a declaration that the United States was 'to provide, by means of its own choosing, review and reconsideration of the: convictions and sentences of the Mexican nationals'.[91] Similarly, in *Bosnian Genocide*, the Court concluded that there had been a failure to comply with the obligation to punish genocide. The Court in that regard made a declaration not only of the fact of the breach, but also ordered that Serbia 'should immediately take effective steps to ensure full compliance' with its obligation to punish, and 'to transfer individuals accused of genocide [...] for trial by the

---

[87] *Corfu Channel, Merits, Judgment, ICJ Reports 1949*, p 4 at p 25 and pp 35–36.

[88] *Application of the Convention on the Prevention and Punishment of the Crime of Genocide (Bosnia and Herzegovina v Serbia and Montenegro), Merits,* Judgment, 26 February 2007 (nyr), paras 460–462.

[89] Ibid, paras 463 and 471(5) and (9).

[90] *Avena and Other Mexican Nationals (Mexico v United States of America), ICJ Reports 2004*, p 12, paras 153(4)–(8).

[91] Ibid, para 153(9).

International Criminal Tribunal for the former Yugoslavia, and to co-operate fully with that Tribunal'.[92]

As was noted above in Section II B, if the breach in question constitutes a serious breach of an obligation arising under a peremptory norm of general international law certain additional consequences arise for all other States under Article 41—in particular, the obligation not to recognize as lawful the situation created and not to render aid or assistance in its maintenance.

V. INVOCATION OF RESPONSIBILITY: RESPONSES BY THE INJURED STATE AND OTHER STATES

Although international responsibility is deemed to arise directly by operation of law on the occurrence of a breach, for practical purposes that responsibility has to be invoked by someone. It may be invoked by the injured State or other party, or possibly by some third State concerned with the 'public order' consequences of the breach. Part Three of the ILC Articles deals with this important issue but in a non-exclusive way. In particular, while it acknowledges that the responsibility of a State may be invoked by an injured party other than a State (eg, by an individual applicant to the European Court of Human Rights), Article 33(2) leaves issues of the rights of persons or entities other than States (including the right of invocation) for treatment elsewhere. The scope of Part Three is thus narrower than that of Parts One and Two of the Articles: these deal with the conditions for and consequences of *all* breaches of international law by a State in the field of responsibility, whereas Part Three only deals with the invocation of the responsibility of a State by another State or States.

Even so, the subject of Part Three is a large and controversial one. To what extent is a State to be considered as injured by a breach of international law on the part of another State? And if not individually injured, to what extent might it demand remedies for the breach—with the inferential consequence of countermeasures if such remedies are not forthcoming? Given that international law includes not only bilateral obligations analogous in national systems to contract and tort (or delict), but also obligations intended to protect vital human interests of a generic kind (peace and security, the environment, sustainable development), the questions dealt with in Part Three could scarcely be more important.

They are primarily addressed through two articles. One (Article 42) defines in relatively narrow and precise terms the concept of the 'injured State', drawing in particular on the analogy of Article 60(2) of the Vienna Convention on the Law of Treaties.[93] The second (Article 48) deals with the invocation of responsibility in the collective interest,

---

[92] *Application of the Convention on the Prevention and Punishment of the Crime of Genocide (Bosnia and Herzegovina v Serbia and Montenegro), Merits*, Judgment, 26 February 2007 (nyr), para 493(8).

[93] Article 60(2) provides as follows:

2. A material breach of a multilateral treaty by one of the parties entitles:

  (a) the other parties by unanimous agreement to suspend the operation of the treaty in whole or in part or to terminate it either:

    (i) in the relations between themselves and the defaulting State; or

    (ii) as between all the parties;

in particular with respect to obligations owed to the international community as a whole, giving effect to the Court's dictum in the *Barcelona Traction* case, set out below. The former category covers the breach of an obligation owed to a State individually. Also treated as 'injured States' are those which are particularly affected by the breach of a multilateral obligation, either because they are 'specially affected' or because the obligation is integral in character, so that a breach affects the enjoyment of the rights or the performance of the obligations of all the States concerned. The contrast is with the 'other States' entitled to invoke responsibility, which are specified in Article 48(1):

Any State other than an injured State is entitled to invoke the responsibility of another State...if:

(a) the obligation breached is owed to a group of States including that State, and is established for the protection of a collective interest of the group; or

(b) the obligation breached is owed to the international community as a whole.

Article 48(1)(b) reflects the distinction drawn by the International Court in *Barcelona Traction* between 'bilaterizable' obligations and obligations owed to the international community as a whole (sometimes called obligations '*erga omnes*'). In the case of the latter:

By their very nature [they] are the concern of all States. In view of the importance of the rights involved, all States can be held to have a legal interest in their protection...[94]

The Court in 1970 gave a number of examples of such obligations, including the prohibition of acts of aggression and genocide and 'the principles and rules concerning the basic rights of the human person, including protection from slavery and discrimination'.[95] Since then, the Court has also recognized the right of self-determination as falling within the category,[96] as well as those obligations of international humanitarian law which it had previously described as 'intransgressible principles of international customary international law'.[97]

Article 48(1)(a) tackles the problem of obligations owed to a group of States and established for the protection of a collective interest, where in the case of a breach there is

---

(b) a party specially affected by the breach to invoke it as a ground for suspending the operation of the treaty in whole or in part in the relations between itself and the defaulting State;

(c) any party other than the defaulting State to invoke the breach as a ground for suspending the operation of the treaty in whole or in part with respect to itself if the treaty is of such a character that a material breach of its provisions by one party radically changes the position of every party with respect to the further performance of its obligations under the treaty.

[94] *Barcelona Traction, Light and Power Company, Limited, Second Phase, Judgment, ICJ Reports 1970*, p 3, para 33.

[95] Ibid, para 34. For reaffirmation of the *erga omnes* nature of the prohibition of genocide, see *Application of the Convention on the Prevention and Punishment of the Crime of Genocide, Preliminary Objections, ICJ Reports 1996*, p 595, para 31; *Armed Activities on the Territory of the Congo (New Application: 2002) (Democratic Republic of the Congo v Rwanda), Provisional Measures, Order of 10 July 2002, ICJ Reports 2002*, p 219, para 71.

[96] See *East Timor (Portugal v Australia), Judgment, ICJ Reports 1995*, p 90, para 29. See also *Legal Consequences of the Construction of a Wall in the Occupied Palestine Territory, Advisory Opinion, ICJ Reports 2004*, p 136, para 155.

[97] Ibid, para 157; the quoted passage is from the *Legality of the Threat or Use of Nuclear Weapons, Advisory Opinion, ICJ Reports 1996*, p 266, para 79.

normally no individual State injured in the sense of Article 42. Examples of such obligations are human rights norms and certain environmental protection norms; the beneficiaries of such obligations are either individuals in the case of the former, or the group of States as a whole in the case of the latter.[98]

In the case of breach of one or other of these categories of obligation, third States can demand cessation and assurances and guarantees of non-repetition, as well as performance of the obligation of reparation on behalf of either the State injured or the beneficiaries of the obligation breached (Article 48(2)).

Part Three of the ILC Articles goes on to consider a number of related questions, for example, the consequences of invocation of responsibility by or against several States, circumstances such as waiver or delay where a State may be considered to have lost the right to invoke responsibility, as well as that ultimate form of invocation, the taking of countermeasures in response to an international wrongful act which remains unredressed and unremedied. Some of these issues are dealt with elsewhere in this volume.

VI. FURTHER DEVELOPMENT OF THE LAW OF INTERNATIONAL RESPONSIBILITY

As we have seen, there has traditionally been a tendency to view international responsibility as, in the first place, essentially a bilateral matter, without wider consequences for others or for the international system as a whole, and, in the second place, as quintessentially an inter-State issue, separated from questions of the relations between States and individuals or corporations, or from the rather unaccountable world of international organizations. This approach works well enough for bilateral treaties between States or for breaches of general international law rules which have an essentially bilateral operation in the field of intergovernmental relations. But international law now contains a range of rules which cannot be broken down into bundles of bilateral relations between States but cover a much broader range. How can these be accommodated within the traditional structure of State responsibility? The attempt to develop the law beyond traditional paradigms was the greatest challenge facing the ILC, and constitutes one of the more fascinating fields of a rapidly developing—and yet precarious—international order.

REFERENCES

ABI-SAAB, G (1999), 'The Uses of Article 19', 10 *EJIL* 339.

ALSTON, P (2005), *Non-State Actors and Human Rights* (Oxford: Oxford University Press).

BOLLECKER-STERN, B (1973), *Le prejudice dans la théorie de la responsabilité internationale* (Paris: Pedone).

CLAPHAM, A (2006), *Human Rights Obligations of Non-State Actors* (Oxford: Oxford University Press).

---

[98] This does not exclude the possibility that one or more States may be injured in the sense of ARSIWA, Article 42 by a breach of an environmental protection norm. In addition, Article 48 seeks to articulate the possible interest of other States in compliance with the obligation.

CRAWFORD, J (2002), *The International Law Commission's Articles on State Responsibility; Introduction, Text and Commentaries* (Cambridge: Cambridge University Press).

—— and OLLESON, S (2005), 'The Continuing Debate on a UN Convention on State Responsibility', 54 *ICLQ* 959.

DE HOOGH, A (1996), *Obligations* Erga Omnes *and International Crimes* (The Hague: Kluwer).

DE SCHUTTER, O (2006), *Transnational Corporations and Human Rights* (Oxford: Hart Publishing).

EVANS, MD (2009), Blackstone's International Law Documents, 9th edn (Oxford: Oxford University Press).

GRAY, C (1987), *Judicial Remedies in International Law* (Oxford: Clarendon Press).

JENNINGS, RY and WATTS, A (1992), *Oppenheim's International Law*, 9th edn (London: Longman).

JØRGENSEN, N (2000), *The Responsibility of States for International Crimes* (Oxford: Oxford University Press).

KLABBERS, J (2009), *An Introduction to International Institutional Law*, 2nd edn (Cambridge: Cambridge University Press).

KOSKENNIEMI, M (2001), 'Solidarity Measures: State Responsibility as a New International Order?', 72 *BYIL* 337.

MORGENSTERN, F (1986), *Legal Problems of International Organizations* (Cambridge: Grotius).

PELLET, A (2001), 'The New Draft Articles of the International Law Commission...A Requiem for States' Crime?', 32 *Netherlands YBIL* 55.

RATNER, SR (2001), 'Corporations and Human Rights: A Theory of Legal Responsibility', 111 *Yale LJ* 443.

RUBIN, AP (1998), *The Law of Piracy*, 2nd edn (Irvington-on-Hudson, NY: Transnational Publishers).

SHELTON, D (2005), *Remedies in International Human Rights Law*, 2nd edn (Oxford: Oxford University Press).

WELLENS, K (2002), *Remedies against International Organizations* (Cambridge: Cambridge University Press).

FURTHER READING

BODANSKY, D, CROOK, J, ROSENSTOCK, R, BROWN WEISS, E, BEDERMAN, DJ, SHELTON, D, CARON, DD, and CRAWFORD, J (2002), 'Symposium: The ILC's State Responsibility Articles', 96 *AJIL* 773–890: a collection of responses to the adoption of the ILC's Articles on State Responsibility.

CRAWFORD, J (2002), *The International Law Commission's Articles on State Responsibility; Introduction, Text and Commentaries* (Cambridge: Cambridge University Press): the ILC's Articles on State Responsibility and authoritative commentaries adopted in 2001, together with an introduction and analytical tools, including an index and table of cases.

—— and OLLESON, S (2005), 'The Continuing Debate on a UN Convention on State Responsibility', 54 *ICLQ* 959: an account of the debate in the Sixth Committee of the General Assembly in late 2004 as to whether the ILC's Articles on State Responsibility should be transformed into a multilateral convention.

CRAWFORD, J, PELLET, A and OLLESON, S (eds) (2010), *The Law of International Responsibility* (Oxford: Oxford University Press).

DUPUY, P-M, NOLTE, G, SPINEDI, M, SICILIANOS, L-A, WYLER, E, TAMS, CJ, GATTINI, A, SCOBBIE, I, ALLAND, D, and KLEIN, P (2002), 'Symposium: Assessing the Work of the International Law Commission on State Responsibility', 13 *EJIL* 1037–1256: a stimulating collection of essays on the ILC's Articles on State Responsibility, with particular emphasis on the 'serious breaches' provisions and the multilateral aspects of invocation.

RAGAZZI, M (2005), *International Responsibility Today. Essays in Memory of Oscar Schachter* (Leiden: Nijhoff): a useful collection of thirty-six essays by specialists covering general and special issues in the field of responsibility.

WEBSITES

http://www.lcil.cam.ac.uk/projects/state_responsibility_project.php: collection of materials on State responsibility, including the reports of the last Special Rapporteur, and various articles.

http://www.un.org/law/ilc: official website of the International Law Commission, maintained by the United Nations Secretariat. Collection of materials on the codification of State responsibility by the Commission.

16

ISSUES OF ADMISSIBILITY AND THE LAW ON INTERNATIONAL RESPONSIBILITY

Phoebe Okowa

SUMMARY

This chapter examines the legal regime governing the admissibility of claims in international adjudication. A central element in the admissibility of claims is the requirement that a litigant should be able to establish a legal interest in respect of the claim brought before an international tribunal. Particular attention is therefore paid to the modalities of establishing a legal interest in respect of claims brought by States in their own right behalf and on behalf of their nationals. The role of nationality is examined and the problems posed by competing claims in relation to multiple nationalities are explored. The unique nature of the problems raised in extending diplomatic protection to corporations and shareholding interests is considered in light of the jurisprudence of international tribunals. The emergence of a large category of obligations designed to protect community values and which do not fit within a private rights model pose particular problems for an international adjudication framework, which is largely bilateral in character. Special consideration is therefore given to the perennial difficulties involved in establishing a legal interest in the case of obligations *erga omnes,* or those designed to protect collective interests and therefore owed to a multiplicity of States. These difficulties, it is suggested are compounded by the fact that the development of obligations *erga omnes* have not been accompanied by any discernible refinement of the mechanisms for their enforcement. The final section considers the extent to which the operation of the rule on exhaustion of local remedies may operate to affect the admissibility of a claim. The parameters of the rule are explored and circumstances when, as a matter of policy, it ought to be regarded as inapplicable are discussed.

I. INTRODUCTION

The legal premises for the imposition of responsibility as well as the excuses that may be available to a State whose responsibility is called into question have already been discussed in the previous chapter. The concern in this chapter is essentially twofold. First, to identify the State or States that could be described as having *locus standi* in relation to a given wrong. Second, to consider the application of other rules of international law that may operate to preclude the admissibility of a claim before an international tribunal even if a cause of action and legal interest are clearly established. Although the basis of responsibility and issues of admissibility generally tend to be treated as discrete topics in much of the literature, there is nevertheless a close relationship between them, and issues of admissibility are closely intertwined with substantive grounds for the imposition of responsibility. For who can sue in respect of a wrong is to a large extent determined by the nature and content of the obligation, manner of breach, and the range of interests the obligation is designed to protect. As a preliminary issue, a litigant State must be able to establish that an obligation owed to it has been breached. In theory, where the obligation breached is designed to protect community values, it should be much easier for a claimant State to establish legal interest by demonstrating that it is within the zone of protection afforded by that obligation (Thirlway, 1995, pp 49–58; Collier and Lowe, 1999).[1] But as will be immediately apparent from the discussion below, the legal regime for protecting community obligations lacks intellectual coherence and the modalities for their implementation are fraught with practical difficulties.

II. LEGAL INTEREST AS A PRE-REQUISITE TO ADMISSIBILITY OF CLAIMS

In general, international law like most other legal systems insists that only those claimants who have a demonstrable interest may bring an action in respect of a wrong. For example in the *South West Africa* cases, the International Court of Justice (ICJ) rejected the applicants' claim principally on the basis that they had no legal right or interest in respect of the subject matter of the dispute brought by them.[2] The obligations in respect of which Ethiopia and Liberia were bringing claims were, in the Court's view, owed to the League of Nations and not to its individual members. Although the correctness of the interpretation of the mandate in question by the Court has been doubted (Dugard, 2004, para 38), there is nevertheless general acceptance that apart from obligations *erga omnes*, only those who are designated as beneficiaries of international obligations have a right to enforce them.[3] In the *Nicaragua* case, the International Court denied that the United States could rely on alleged breaches of obligations owed by Nicaragua to the Organization of American States (OAS) as a basis for imposing countermeasures. The Court pointed out that:

even supposing that such a political pledge had the force of a legal commitment it could not have justified the United States insisting on the fulfilment of a commitment made not

---

[1] The practice of the ICJ unfortunately paints a different picture. In its jurisprudence, the Court has maintained a distinction between the existence of legal interest and the ability to invoke the jurisdictional provisions of the Court. The existence of a legal interest does not necessarily mean that a State will be entitled to bring a claim and other jurisdictional factors may operate to exclude the claim. See *East Timor* case (*Portugal v Australia*), *Judgment, ICJ Reports 1995*, p 90 at para 29.

[2] *South West Africa, Second Phase, Judgment, ICJ Reports 1966*, p 6, para 99; see ILC Commentary to Draft Article 48 (para 7), Official Records of the General Assembly, Fifty-Sixth Session, Supplement No 10 (A/56/10) Chapter V.

[3] *Barcelona Traction, Light and Power Company, Limited, Second Phase, Judgment, ICJ Reports 1970*, p 3, para 35.

directly towards the United States but towards the organisation, the latter alone being empowered to monitor the implementation.[4]

In principle, there is every reason to suppose that the Court would have reached the same conclusion if the obligation in question was not a political commitment but a legal duty owed to the OAS.

A. RATIONALE OF INTERNATIONAL LAW RULES ON *LOCUS STANDI*

Several underlying reasons may be detected in the various rules underpinning *locus standi* in international law. The first and most obvious can in part be explained by the nature of international law as a law primarily between States, and as a consequence only States in general have procedural capacity to bring an action before an international tribunal. Thus in the absence of special treaty arrangements granting individuals, corporations, or other legal entities access to international tribunals, their claims must be channelled through the State of their nationality.[5] In this respect, there is something of an artificiality about international law rules on *locus standi*, for even when it is the individual who has been injured, the traditional view proceeds on the premise that it is the State of which that individual is a national that is wronged and who can therefore bring an action in respect of the wrong (Leigh, 1971, p 453).

Secondly, general international law rules on standing are premised on a particular view of the role of international tribunals, that is, the settlement of disputes between States on a private rights model. They are in large measure concerned with discretely bilateral disputes. Although there has been a fairly consistent jurisprudence recognizing that a large number of obligations do not fit into the private rights model, in particular those designed to protect community values, international law has tended to exclude standing where an applicant State's interest is a general vindication of community values or principles of legality.[6] A related rationale of the rules on *locus standi*, it could be argued, is to provide an orderly framework for the resolution of disputes and to avoid wherever possible overlapping claims or those that are entirely unmeritorious. Nationality in this context provides a convenient tag for channelling claims.

Thirdly, the rules on admissibility attempt to strike a balance between the need for international supervision of obligations and respect for the sovereign power of States to adjudicate on matters within their jurisdiction. Jurisdiction in respect of matters occurring on their territory is an attribute of sovereignty, and in general national courts have a right of first recourse, with international tribunals possessing something akin to a default power, exercisable in large measure where domestic tribunals have failed to grant a remedy. Thus rules on exhaustion of local remedies can in part be explained by reference to the territorial

---

[4] *Military and Paramilitary Activities in and against Nicaragua (Nicaragua v United States of America)*, *Merits, Judgment, ICJ Reports 1986*, p 14, para 262.

[5] The many jurisdictional issues that arise in this context are strictly speaking beyond the scope of the present inquiry and have been extensively dealt with in the literature on jurisdiction of international tribunals. See Fitzmaurice, 1986, pp 427–575; Rosenne, 1997.

[6] See *Barcelona Traction, Light and Power Company, Limited, Second Phase, Judgment, ICJ Reports 1970*, p 3 and *East Timor (Portugal v Australia), Judgment, ICJ Reports 1995*, p 90.

character of jurisdiction. The decisions in the *Nottebohm*[7] and *Barcelona Traction* cases[8] also manifest a particular sensitivity to the right of the territorial State to deal with matters occurring on its territory.

The emergence of a large category of obligations, which do not fit within a bilateral or private rights framework, insofar as they are designed to protect community values and interests, pose a particular challenge for the traditional rules on admissibility of claims. These obligations transcend individual State interests, and protection of the values, which underpin them, can only be realized if expanded notions of standing were adopted so as to permit litigation in the public interest. The obligations principally in the field of human rights, protection of the environment, preservation of peace and security, may affect the interests of the international community at large without affecting the interests of any one particular State.[9] Extended notions of *locus standi* have been proposed *de lege ferenda* in order to make the protection of these values a reality. Thus, there is increasingly a presumption that all States have a general interest in the legality of actions that affect community values, even if the precise implications are yet to be worked out.[10]

B. MODALITIES OF ESTABLISHING LEGAL INTEREST

Given international law's conception of standing as a vindication of primarily private rights, it comes as no surprise that for a claim to be admissible, the applicant State must demonstrate that it has a legal interest in the matter. At a general level, legal interest is defined by reference to the obligation breached; not quite a distinct issue but part of the definition of the cause of action—the party to whom the obligation is owed is the party entitled to claim. However, two broad propositions provide the basic framework for determining legal interest in international litigation. First, in determining the *locus standi* of a State, a distinction is usually maintained between injury to direct interests and those that affect indirect interests (principally injury to nationals whether natural, corporate, or other legal entity recognized by municipal law). There is a presumption that a State as custodian of its sovereign rights must be taken to have a legal interest in respect of those wrongs that affect its direct interests. Although the distinction is well established in the literature, and the jurisprudence of international tribunals, the dividing line between them is not always easy to determine, especially with regard to mixed claims where there are elements of direct injury to a State's own interests as well as injury to its nationals (Meron, 1959, pp 87–88; Wittich, 2001, pp 121–187). Nevertheless, damage to a State's warships, diplomatic missions, members of the armed forces, the executive, including head of State, and damage to State property are, *inter alia*, generally regarded as examples of injury to a State's direct interests.

---

[7] *Nottebohm, Second Phase, Judgment, ICJ Reports 1955*, p 4.

[8] *Barcelona Traction, Light and Power Company, Limited, Second Phase, Judgment, ICJ Reports 1970*, p 3.

[9] Although there has been a general recognition of obligations *erga omnes*, there is not a single case in which an applicant State has successfully brought a claim designed to enforce community values.

[10] See ILC Articles on the Responsibility of States for Internationally Wrongful Acts (ARSIWA), Article 48; Simma, 1994, p 217.

III. THE BASES OF DIPLOMATIC PROTECTION

A. NATIONALITY AS THE BASIS OF LEGAL INTEREST IN INDIRECT CLAIMS

Where injury is suffered by a natural person or other legal entity recognized by municipal law, the general view is that the right to bring a claim in respect of the wrong lies with the State of the victim's nationality. It is the bond of nationality that creates the necessary link between a State and the injury in respect of which a claim is brought.

In the *Mavrommatis* case, the Permanent Court observed that:

It is an elementary principle of international law that a State is entitled to protect its subjects, when injured by acts contrary to international law committed by another State, from which they have been unable to obtain satisfaction through ordinary channels. By taking up the case of one of its subjects and by resorting to diplomatic protection or international judicial proceedings on his behalf, a State is in reality asserting its own rights—rights to ensure, in the person of its subjects, respect for the rules of international law.[11]

Since the exercise of diplomatic protection is generally viewed as the right of the State, the argument has consistently been made that reliance on the right is within the absolute discretion of States (Borchard, 1915, p 29; Oppenheim, 1992, p 934; Malanczuk, 1997, p 257; Dugard, 2000, p 213; ILA, Report of the 96th Conference, 2000). It is further accepted that the decision whether to exercise the discretion or not is invariably influenced by political considerations rather than the legal merits of the particular claim. The international court in the *Barcelona Traction* case succinctly made the point when it noted that:

...within the limits prescribed by international law, a State may exercise diplomatic protection by whatever means and to whatever extent it thinks fit, for it is its own right that the State is asserting. Should the natural or legal person on whose behalf it is acting consider that their rights are not adequately protected, they have no remedy in international law. All they can do is resort to municipal law, if means are available, with a view to furthering their cause or obtaining redress. The municipal legislator may lay upon the State an obligation to protect its citizens abroad, and may also confer upon the national a right to demand the performance of that obligation, and clothe the right with corresponding sanctions. However, all these questions remain within the province of municipal law and do not affect the position internationally.

The State must be viewed as the sole judge to decide whether its protection will be granted, to what extent it is granted, and when it will cease. It retains in this respect a discretionary power the exercise of which may be determined by considerations of a political or other nature, unrelated to the particular case. Since the claim of the State is not identical with that of the individual or corporate person whose cause is espoused, the State enjoys complete freedom of action.[12]

---

[11] *Mavrommatis Palestine Concessions, Judgment No 2, 1924, PCIJ, Ser A, No 2* at p 12.

[12] *Barcelona Traction, Light and Power Company, Limited, Second Phase, Judgment, ICJ Reports 1970,* p 3, paras 78–79.

In *Abbasi* v *Secretary of State for Foreign and Commonwealth Affairs*,[13] the applicant sought judicial review to compel the UK foreign office to make representations on his behalf to the United States Government or to take other appropriate action, or at least give an explanation as to why this had not been done. The English Court of Appeal, after an extended review of authorities came to the conclusion that diplomatic protection did not as such give rise to an enforceable duty under English law. However, the Court emphasized its inherent powers as a matter of English law to review the exercise of this discretion, especially if it could be shown that the decision was irrational or contrary to the rules of natural justice.

As the exercise of diplomatic protection is discretionary, there is in principle no obligation on the part of the State to transmit the damages obtained to any of the individuals concerned. Moreover, insofar as the right of protection is characterized as that of the State, the claiming State may choose to do so even in the face of opposition from the injured individual. It is principally for this reason that tribunals and jurists who considered the issue rejected the so-called *Calvo clause*, by which certain natural and corporate persons entered into contracts with third States under the terms of which they agreed to waive the right of diplomatic protection (Shea, 1955).

The discretionary character of diplomatic protection has in recent years been subjected to trenchant criticism, as being incompatible with an international system committed to human rights. It has therefore been proposed that the right of diplomatic protection should be seen as a legal duty exercisable by the State on behalf of the injured individual.[14] This position already finds some support in national constitutions, which already see diplomatic protection as a right of the individual enforceable even as against the State of which he is a national.[15] However, the right as interpreted in domestic cases still grants to the executive a wide discretion and in many cases the individual is entitled to no more than an expectation that his request for diplomatic representation will treated fairly by the executive. For instance, the South African Constitutional Court in *Kaunda and others* v *President of the Republic of South Africa and others*[16] recognized the right to request diplomatic protection as a constitutional entitlement under the South Africa constitution but went on to hold that its actual exercise was a matter of foreign policy and therefore within the discretion of the executive branch. The decision in Kaunda has been confirmed in two subsequent decisions of the Supreme Court of South Africa. In *Rootman* v *President of the Republic of South Africa*,[17] the Supreme Court refused a request by the applicant that

---

[13] *Abbasi* v *Sec of Foreign and Commonwealth Affairs and Sec of Home Office* [2002] EWCA Civ 1598, 6 November 2002.

[14] Bennouna, *Preliminary Report on Diplomatic Protection*, 1998, paras 34–37, 65–66; Dugard, 2000, paras 17 and 61–74.

[15] Examples include the constitutions of Albania, Belarus, Bosnia and Herzegovina, Bulgaria, Cambodia, China, Croatia, Estonia, Georgia, Guyana, Hungary, Italy, Kazakhstan, Lao People's Democratic Republic, Latvia, Lithuania, Poland, Portugal, Republic of Korea, Romania, Russian Federation, Spain, the Former Yugoslav Republic of Macedonia, Turkey, Ukraine, Vietnam, and Yugoslavia. See Dugard, 2000, para 80.

[16] *Kaunda and others* v *President of the Republic of South Africa and others*, Case CCT 23/04, 2005 (4) SA 235 (CC).

[17] *Rootman* v *President of the Republic of South Africa*, Case 016/06, [2006] SCA 80 (RSA). See also *Van Zyl* v *Government of the Republic of South Africa*, Case 170/06, [2007] SCA 109 (RSA), rejecting the applicant's argument that they had a constitutional right to diplomatic protection and the government a corresponding obligation to provide such protection, including the submission of claims to international

the South African Government should be compelled to take steps to assist him in securing the execution of a money judgment in his favour, granted by the Pretoria High Court,
against the government of the DRC. The applicant had argued that the rule of law requires
the State to assist a citizen to enforce his or her rights. The Court noted that although the
State may engage in diplomatic negotiations with a foreign State to secure the rights of its
citizens, it could not be compelled to do so.

In *Omar Khadr* v *The Prime Minister of Canada*, the applicant argued that the failure of the Canadian Government to make representations to the US government to have
him repatriated to Canada was a violation of his rights under the Canadian Charter
of Rights and Freedoms. This was contested by the Canadian government as respondent, which argued that it had the 'unfettered discretion to decide whether to request the
return of a Canadian citizen detained in a foreign country, this being a matter within
its exclusive authority to conduct foreign affairs'. The Court was therefore called upon
to examine whether Canada had a legal duty to protect Mr Khadr and the ambit of that
duty. The Canadian Supreme Court concluded that in general the right of protection was
not enforceable as it fell within the executive's conduct of foreign policy. However, the
Court would intervene if the government's position is irrational or contrary to a legitimate expectation. The Court concluded that in the specific circumstances of the case,
the failure to exercise diplomatic protection was a violation of the applicant's rights to
life, liberty, and security of the person.[18] The court noted that in Canada, the rule of law
means that all government action is potentially subject to the Charter and the individual
rights it guarantees. The crown prerogative in the conduct of foreign affairs was also subject to the charter.[19]

The decisions of national courts on these constitutional provisions support the thesis
that general international law as it stands does not mandate an enforceable legal duty of
diplomatic protection.[20] Human rights obligations and treaties protecting the economic
interests of individuals have nevertheless substantially qualified the discretionary character of diplomatic protection by creating directly enforceable rights even as against the

---

arbitration or adjudication before the international court. The court, although conceding that the exercise
of diplomatic protection remained the prerogative of state, was prepared to accept that this may in fact entail
a duty to exercise such protection where the fundamental rights of the citizen was involved. In deciding
whether or not to take up the case of one of its nationals, the government was expected to act rationally. The
Court also noted that as the right of diplomatic protection was derived from the constitution as an aspect
of citizenship, the South African government could not be expected to intervene where the wrong had been
done not to South African citizens but to a foreign company in respect of which they had an interest.

[18] *Omar Khadr* v *The Prime Minister of Canada* 2009 FCA 246.

[19] However, in *Ilaşcu and Others v Moldova and Russia* [GC], no 48787/99, ECHR *2004-VII* the European
Court of Human Rights took the view that duty to make representations including judicial claims may be
legally mandatory as a consequence of a State's obligations in Article 1 of the ECHR to 'secure to everyone
within its jurisdiction' the rights guaranteed by the convention. In relation to the detention of the applicants
in the Transdniestrian Republic controlled by the separatists, the Court took the view the Moldova was
under an obligation to make representations to Russia and the separatists to try and secure their release.
Failure to do so was a violation of the obligations in Article 1 of the ECHR.

[20] *Kaunda and others v President of the Republic of South Africa and others*, Case CCT 23/04, 2005 (4)
SA 235 (CC). In the *Hess Decision, BverfGE*, 55, 349, 90 ILR 386, the German Federal Constitutional Court
upheld the existence of a federal constitutional right to diplomatic protection but denied that it was required
by customary international law. See also *Abbasi* v *Sec of Foreign and Commonwealth Affairs and Sec of Home
Office* [2002] EWCA Civ 1598, 6 November 2002. Federal Court of Australia in *Hicks* v *Ruddock* [2007] FCA
299, para 93, did not rule out the possibility that a right of diplomatic protection may in fact be enforceable.

State of which the individual is a national (ILA Reports, 2000, p 634). Unlike its trad-itional role, it is probably more accurate to say that diplomatic protection is today more of a default mechanism for the enforcement claims where there are no direct avenues provided for by international law. A better view, it is suggested is to see diplomatic pro-tection, and enforcement mechanisms in human rights instruments as operating in par-allel, serving related but at times discrete objectives. For example vindication of the rule of law may require that an action be brought on the international plane by a State even in the face of opposition by the wronged individual (Brierly, 1928, p 48; Dugard, 2000, para 73). Secondly, in other instances it must be accepted that States may have wider concerns going beyond the immediate interests of the wronged individual; these interests will at times be better served by exercising the discretion not to bring an action on the inter-national plane. Where the exercise of the discretion in this manner conflicts with funda-mental human rights, the obligation to enforce these rights it is suggested may regarded as paramount.

B. ESTABLISHING NATIONALITY FOR PURPOSES OF DIPLOMATIC PROTECTION

1. Natural persons

It seems to be generally accepted now that the conferment of nationality is *prima facie* within the jurisdiction of States as an attribute of its sovereignty, and in general there is a presumption that nationality granted by a State is valid as long as it complies with the provisions of domestic law. There is nevertheless considerable, if not universal, sup-port for the view that the validity of any nationality so conferred on the international plane is a question of international law, and will only be opposable to other States if it has been granted in a manner that conforms with international law criteria.[21] In particular, for nationality to provide a valid basis for the exercise of diplomatic protection, it must have been granted in a manner consistent with principles of international law. For this reason, nationality may be disregarded on the international plane or treated as a nullity, if it has been granted in excess of jurisdictional limits placed by international law. Dugard has also suggested that international law retains a reserve power to disregard nationality laws that are discriminatory in character, or inconsistent with fundamental principles of human rights.[22] Most authorities also agree that nationality will be invalid if it has been acquired *mala fides*, or on the basis of a tenuous connection such as extending nationality laws to aliens in transit.[23]

The precise role of international law in determining nationality for purposes of dip-lomatic protection is however not free from controversy. In general, two diametrically opposed positions seem to have emerged in the literature. The first proceeds on the premise that questions of nationality must be settled by way of *renvoi* to municipal law, and in prin-ciple the validity of nationality conferred by a State in accordance with the requirements of

[21] See *Nottebohm, Second Phase, Judgment, ICJ Reports 1955*, p 4.

[22] According to Dugard, nationality laws should be disregarded if they discriminate on the basis of race, gender, or religious affiliation. Dugard, 2000, para 104. See also Oppenheim, 1992, pp 856 and 874; Brownlie, 2008, pp 386 and 388.

[23] Dugard, 2000, para 104.

its internal law must be treated as conclusive.[24] The second position denies conclusiveness to municipal law criteria, and takes as its starting point that the validity of nationality on the international plane is a question of international law. In particular, for nationality to be valid on the international plane it must be firmly grounded on the existence of a genuine link between the claimant State and the individual on whose behalf he claims (Brownlie, 2008, p 398; Fitzmaurice, 1957, pp 196–201).

Proponents of the second position argue that although the grant of nationality is a prerogative of States, like most unilateral acts performed on the municipal plane, questions of ultimate validity on the international plane must be determined by reference to international standards if the rule of law is to be maintained.[25] The position received explicit support in Article 1 of the 1930 Hague Convention on certain Questions Relating to the Conflict of Nationality Laws which provided that 'It is for each State to determine under its own law who are its nationals' but with the proviso that:

This law shall be recognized by other States in so far as it is consistent with international conventions, international custom, and the principles of law generally recognized with regard to nationality.[26]

Although most writers agree that international law must retain some quality control in matters of nationality, the precise nature of control is the subject matter of disagreement. As already noted, there is consensus that international law must retain a reserve power to disregard nationality claims that are fraudulent in origin, discriminatory, or in clear violation of generally accepted jurisdictional principles. Beyond that it is controversial whether, at least in the context of diplomatic protection, international law requires that there should exist a genuine or effective link between the State and the national on whose behalf it is claiming.

2. The requirement of the genuine link

In the *Nottebohm* case, the International Court was of the view that for nationality to form a valid basis for diplomatic protection on the international plane, it must be based on a genuine link between the wronged individual and the State on whose behalf it is claiming. It said that:

A State cannot claim that the rules [pertaining to the acquisition of nationality] which it has thus laid down are entitled to recognition by another State unless it has acted in conformity with this general aim of making the legal bond of nationality accord with the individual's genuine connection with the State which assumes the defence of its citizens by means of protection as against other States.

The Court listed the following as indispensable elements of valid nationality for purposes of diplomatic protection:

A legal bond having as its basis a social fact of attachment, a genuine connection of existence and sentiments, together with the existence of reciprocal rights and duties. It may

---

[24] *Nottebohm* case, *Second Phase, Judgment, ICJ Reports 1955*, p 4, Dissenting Opinions of Judges Klaestad (p 30), Reid (p 42), and Guggenheim (p 54).
[25] *Flegenheimer Claim* (1958), 25 ILR 91 at pp 96–112; Oppenheim, 1992, p 855.
[26] 179 LNTS 89.

be said to constitute a juridical expression of the fact that the individual upon whom it is conferred, either directly by the law or as a result of an act of the authorities, is in fact more closely connected with the population of the State conferring nationality than with that of any other State.[27]

In State and arbitral practice, the requirement of genuine link was not without precedent, and had been applied to cases of diplomatic protection involving dual or multiple nationality (Brownlie, 2008, p 407). In the *Nottebohm* case, the Court refused to confine its application to those situations. The majority were of the view that this requirement applied equally to those situations where the national had only one nationality as well as where the national had several.[28]

The decision has been controversial and in the literature and subsequent judicial decisions attempts have been made either to distinguish it, or to limit its application to the facts of the case. In the *Flegenheimer* case, the Italian-United States Commission confined the application of the genuine link requirement to cases involving dual nationals.[29] In the *Barcelona Traction* case, the International Court refused to extend the genuine link requirement to corporations, and further, refrained from expressing an opinion as to correctness of the genuine link requirement as a matter of general international law.[30] A number of reasons have been advanced in support of the view that the *Nottebohm* case must not be taken as laying down general rules of international law applicable to all cases of nationality. First, there was considerable evidence before the Court that the processes of naturalization by which Nottebohm had acquired his citizenship were probably in bad faith. Dugard has therefore suggested that a finding that the links between Nottebohm and Liechtenstein were tenuous provided the Court with a convenient excuse to avoid a nationality claim that was tainted by bad faith without being embroiled in a controversy as to what is legitimate or acceptable in the grant of nationality by sovereign States (Dugard, 2000, para 108).

Secondly, there is no doubt that the Court was influenced by the unique factual context of the dispute. Nottebohm's links with Guatemala were close and long-standing, spanning over a period of some 34 years. On the other hand his connections with Liechtenstein were weak and transitory and, given the circumstances, the Court thought it inequitable to allow Liechtenstein to exercise diplomatic protection as against Guatemala.[31] It is for this reason that in much of the subsequent literature the argument has been made that the Court was not dealing with the question of the validity of Nottebohm's application as against the whole world but more specifically against Guatemala. Indeed many authorities have doubted whether the Court would have reached the same conclusion if the case had been brought by Liechtenstein against some third State with whom Nottebohm had no connection (Harris, 1998, p 594).

It is also possible to argue that although in formal terms the Court was faced with a claim of a person possessing only one nationality, it approached the case as if Nottebohm was a national of both States but with his real and effective nationality being that of

---

[27] *Nottebohm, Second Phase, Judgment, ICJ Reports 1955*, p 4 at p 23.

[28] Ibid.   [29] *Flegenheimer Claim* (1958), 25 ILR at 148–150.

[30] *Barcelona Traction, Light and Power Company, Limited, Second Phase, Judgment, ICJ Reports 1970*, p 3, para 70.

[31] *Nottebohm, Second Phase, Judgment, ICJ Reports 1955*, p 4 at p 26.

Guatemala. If this were so, the *Nottebohm* decision is in keeping with the long-held view that where a person possesses two nationalities, it is the effective nationality that is determinant[32] and the State of second nationality cannot bring a claim against the State of effective first nationality where a genuine link exists.

The Court's formal conclusion that nationality is only valid for purposes of diplomatic protection if it is grounded on a genuine link has also been criticized for two reasons. First, it has been argued that as a matter of policy, it is desirable that the test for nationality be capable of objective determination. The requirement of genuine link introduces into this area of the law a vague and uncertain test, and is therefore open to abuse.[33] Second, that by denying the validity of certain forms of nationality it has the practical effect of severely restricting the scope of diplomatic protection. It has been argued that it is undesirable as a matter of policy that a wrong should go without redress merely because the links between the State and the national on whose behalf he is claiming are weak.[34] In its decision in the *Ahmadou Sadio Diallo* case[35] the Court does not seem to have been particularly troubled by the genuine link requirement, in regarding as admissible Guinea's claims against the Democratic Republic of Congo (DRC). Guinea had instituted proceedings by way of diplomatic protection on behalf of Ahmadou Sadio Diallo, a business man of Guinean nationality who had been resident in the DRC for 32 years. His connections with Guinea were at best tenuous, yet the court's approach to the nationality question was in marked contrast to that taken in the *Nottebohm* case.[36] That Guinea was able to bring this action without any challenge by the respondent State or adverse comment by the Court is further indication of the prevailing uncertainty as to the exact reach of the 'genuine link' requirement. Until his expulsion from the DRC, it appears that all of Mr Diallo's links for a period of 32 years was with that State—a period not dissimilar to the 34-year link between Nottebohm and Guatemala in the *Nottebohm* case. The *Diallo* decision lends some support to the view that the *Nottebohm* decision should be confined to its own facts and not treated as laying down rules of general application (Okowa, 2008).

3. Some conclusions

Notwithstanding the authoritative decision of the majority judgment in the *Nottebohm* case, there is no general support for the genuine link requirement in State practice. This is not to say that there is no role for international law in matters of nationality. A limited reserve power to exclude certain nationality claims is generally accepted in cases of out rightly fraudulent claims or those extended in bad faith, or instances where the grant of nationality is manifestly incompatible with fundamental principles of international law.

[32] *Canevaro* case (Permanent Court of Arbitration) (1912) 11 *RIAA* 397; *Merge* claim (1955), 22 ILR 443; *Esphanian* v *Bank Tejarat* (1983) 2 Iran-USCTR 157.

[33] Dissenting Opinion of Judge Reid, *Nottebohm, Second Phase, Judgment, ICJ Reports 1955*, p 4 at p 46.

[34] See Dissenting Opinion of Judge ad hoc Guggenheim, ibid, at pp 63–64 and see Brownlie, 2008, pp 417–418.

[35] *Ahmadou Sadio Diallo (Republic of Guinea* v *Democratic Republic of Congo), Preliminary Objections*, Judgment of 24 May 2007.

[36] Ibid, para 41. Although it is perhaps significant that Mr Diallo, unlike Nottebohm, was born in Guinea of Guinean parents and lived there for his first 17 years. See application instituting proceedings, p 31.

C. THE NATIONALITY OF CORPORATIONS

Like in the case of individuals, international law proceeds on the premise that it is the State of which the company is a national that may exercise diplomatic protection on its behalf. The general difficulty in this area is in deciding what criteria may be employed to determine the nationality of corporations. The difficulty is not helped by the existence of largely contradictory and incompatible principles both in the literature, and in the jurisprudence of international tribunals.

In the *Barcelona Traction* case, the International Court concluded that the nationality of a company had to be determined by reference to the laws of the State in which it was incorporated or had its registered office. The majority were of the view that the fact of incorporation under the law of a State was conclusive. Moreover, that it was not necessary to lift the corporate veil in order to determine the economic reality of a company, even if this indicated links with a State other than that of incorporation. The Court thus denied that Belgium had a right to bring an action in respect of wrongs done to a Canadian company, in circumstances where the majority of the shareholders were Belgian. In rejecting Belgium's claim, the Court noted that the reality was that a company as an institution of municipal law was an entity distinct from its shareholders. As such, where a wrong was done to the company, the interests of the shareholders may be affected but it was the company alone that had the right to maintain an action in international law. It noted that:

whenever shareholder's interests are harmed by an act done to the company, it is to the latter that he must look to institute appropriate action; for although two separate entities may have suffered from the same wrong, it is only one entity whose rights have been infringed.[37]

The majority went on to list a number of situations where the State of the shareholders' nationality may be entitled to bring a claim on the international plane. Thus the State of the shareholders' nationality would normally have a right to diplomatic protection where the direct rights of shareholders were affected. Examples given by the Court included (a) their rights to dividends; (b) the right to attend and vote at general meetings; and (c) the right to share in the assets of the company after liquidation.[38]

Some judges thought that shareholders may be entitled to diplomatic protection in cases where the company had the nationality of the allegedly wrongdoing State. The Court refrained from expressing an opinion on the correctness of the proposition as a matter of principle, noting that the issue did not arise on the facts of the case since Spain was not the national State of Barcelona.[39] However, the correctness of the proposition is in any event open to challenge. First, it ignores the traditional rule that a State is not guilty of violating international law when it harms one of its own nationals.[40] Secondly, it is difficult to reconcile it with the argument advanced by the majority that, when a wrong is done to a company, the interests of the shareholders may be affected but only the company

---

[37] *Barcelona Traction, Light and Power Company, Limited, Second Phase, Judgment, ICJ Reports 1970*, p 3, para 44.

[38] Ibid, para 47. See also Lowe, 2002, p 275; Watts, 1996, p 435.

[39] Ibid, para 92. There is, however, support for this view in the jurisprudence of the Iran-United States Claims tribunal, eg, *Starrett Housing Corporation, et al v Government of the Islamic Republic of Iran, et al* (1983), 4 Iran-USCTR 122.

[40] See ibid, Separate Opinion of Judge Jessup, p 162 at p 192 (para 52).

has rights which are capable of legal protection. If shareholders are entitled to protection in the situation where the wrong done to the company is by the very State of which it is a national, what is the precise legal basis of the protection? Is there a process here by which mere interests are transformed into rights capable of legal protection?

The Court also thought that shareholders may be entitled to protection where the company has ceased to exist.[41] On the facts the Court took the view that although the Barcelona Traction Company was in receivership, it was formally still in existence, and as such Belgium could not exercise protection on behalf of the shareholders. Other judges were prepared to extend diplomatic protection in those instances where, although a company was still in existence, it had become practically paralysed.[42]

The Court advanced some policy-based justifications to support its conclusions.[43] In rejecting the claims of Belgium, the Court denied that shareholders were vested with any general right of protection. It noted that extension of protection to shareholders, insofar as it exposed the allegedly wrongdoing State to a wide range of claimants, could introduce an element of uncertainty and insecurity into international economic relations. The Court was also concerned with the practical difficulty of ascertaining shareholding interests since such shares frequently change hands, and in many instances it could be difficult to determine which State was entitled to exercise protection, especially where the nominee and beneficiaries were from different States.[44] Moreover, given the fluid character of the shareholding interests, ascertaining the legal interest may be particularly difficult, since for a right of protection to exist nationality must be continuous (a point examined subsequently). In the *Barcelona Traction* case itself, there was some doubt whether the Belgian interest in the shares had been continuous and in particular whether Belgium could have satisfied the test at the time of the injury. The decision is therefore an unequivocal authority, in support of the view, that where the company is injured, it is the national State of the company alone that may bring an action. However, it is clear that some judges were prepared to extend protection to shareholders. Moreover, a number of them favoured a different test for corporations and would have applied the genuine link test as formulated in the *Nottebohm* case, with the result that the State of incorporation did not have an automatic right of protection in the absence of some tangible connection. Furthermore there is evidence that, in practice, States have been prepared to extend diplomatic protection to shareholding interests in foreign corporations, and such a right has been unequivocally advocated for by the ILA in its 2000 report on the law of diplomatic protection. There is also evidence that States have been reluctant to extend protection to companies incorporated in their territory in the absence of substantial link with the national economy. However, the law in this area cannot be stated with certainty. In the *Oil Platforms Case*, Iran denied that the United States had the right as a matter of international law to extend diplomatic protection to US flagged but foreign owned merchant ships, on the basis that there was an absence of a genuine link between the ships and the US government as required by international law.[45] The final judgment of the

---

[41] Ibid, paras 64–68.

[42] See, eg, ibid, Separate Opinion of Judge Fitzmaurice, p 65 at pp 72–75 (paras 14–20).

[43] Ibid, paras 94, 96.

[44] There was some evidence before the Court that the ultimate beneficiaries of the shareholding interest in the *Barcelona Traction* case were themselves non-Belgian.

[45] See *ICJ Pleadings, Oil Platforms (Islamic Republic of Iran v United States of America)*, Reply and Defence to Counter Claim submitted by the Islamic Republic of Iran, vol I, pp 202–214 (10 March 1999).

Court however indicates that the Court was not particularly troubled by the absence of a genuine link on the part of the State exercising diplomatic protection.[46]

The protection of corporations and shareholding interests received extended consideration by the ICJ in the *Case Concerning Ahmadou Diallo*.[47] Mr Diallo, it will be recalled, had settled in Zaire for a period of 32 years. In the intervening period, he had established two companies which were at the centre of the dispute: Africom-Zaire and Africontainers-Zaire. In the course of their business dealings, the DRC, as well as several mining and oil companies operating in the DRC, became indebted to Mr. Diallo's companies. The attempts by Mr Diallo and his companies to sue and recover monies owed was not viewed favourably by the Congolese authorities. According to the pleadings, they had on successive occasions managed to block or set aside judgments obtained, including appeal judgments from Congolese Courts. Guinea argued that the decision of the Congolese authorities to expel Mr Diallo in November 1995 was taken in order to irrevocably frustrate his efforts to enforce a judgment obtained against Zaire Shell for the sum of 60 billion dollars. The DRC raised a number of preliminary objections. It argued that Guinea lacked standing to bring the application, in so far as it related to wrongs allegedly done to Africom-Zaire and Africontainers-Zaire, these being Congolese companies. The DRC relied directly on the *Barcelona Traction* case in maintaining that the rights of the two companies, corporations under Zairean law, were separate from Mr Diallo's rights as shareholder. DRC argued that positive international law at present does not entitle a State to bring an action on behalf of shareholding interests in a registered company. It further denied that international law recognized a process of 'substitution' whereby the rights of a company could be assigned to a shareholder for purposes of enforcement when the State whose responsibility is at issue is also the national State of the company.

The court concluded that Mr Diallo's direct rights as a shareholder in the two companies were affected. It drew a distinction between Mr Diallo's rights and those of the company, and concluded that Guinea as the national State was entitled to exercise diplomatic protection in relation to his rights. The right to protect shareholders' direct interests was explicitly recognized by the majority in the *Barcelona Traction* case.

As noted above the judgment of the ICJ in the *Barcelona Traction* case left unresolved the question whether shareholders were entitled to diplomatic protection if the company had the nationality of the wrong-doing State. In the *Diallo* case, Guinea's third claim rested squarely on the alleged existence of this exception. It claimed a right of diplomatic protection by way of substitution, since the DRC, the national State of Africom-Zaire and Africontainers-Zaire was also the wrong-doing State.

The Court categorically denied the existence of this exception as a matter of customary international law.[48] In support of its claim for a right of diplomatic protection by way of substitution, Guinea had relied on arbitral awards, decisions of the European Commission on Human Rights, ICSID jurisprudence, and bilateral treaties for the promotion and protection of investment disputes, which had recognized protection of shareholding interests,

---

[46] *Oil Platforms (Islamic Republic of Iran v United States of America), Judgment, ICJ Reports 2003*, p 161, passim.

[47] *Ahmadou Sadio Diallo (Republic of Guinea v Democratic Republic of Congo), Preliminary Objections*, Judgment of 24 May 2007.

[48] Ibid, para 89. This aspect of the judgment was followed by the South African Supreme Court in *Van Zyl v Government of the Republic of South Africa*, Case 170/06, [2007] SCA 109 (RSA).

where the respondent State was also the national State of the company. The court treated these arbitral awards and treaty provisions as *lex specialis* and not in anyway supportive of a broad right of diplomatic protection by way of substitution.[49] It distinguished its earlier decision in the *Electtronica Sicula* case, where a chamber of the Court had allowed the United States to bring a claim in respect of a wrong done to an Italian company, the shares of which were held by two American corporations.[50] It noted that this decision was not based general international law but on the applicable treaty which allowed protection of shareholding interests in the circumstances that had arisen.

In its draft articles on diplomatic protection, the ILC had considered a more limited exception, which would only have allowed protection of shareholding interest where a company's incorporation in a respondent State was mandatory as a condition of doing business in that country. The Court noted that on the facts before it there was no evidence that Africom-Zaire and Africontainers-Zaire had been incorporated in Zaire (DRC) as a condition of doing business there. It therefore expressed no opinion on the validity of the ILC's proposed exception as a matter of customary law.

Thus more than 40 years after its landmark decision in the *Barcelona Traction* case, the court has confirmed that judgment in almost all respects. The significance of the Court's judgment should not however be exaggerated. The Court itself noted that the role of diplomatic protection has largely fallen into disuse since most issues relating to diplomatic protection of corporations and shareholding interests are now dealt with comprehensively in international treaties.[51] The significant delays that accompany claims arising by way of diplomatic protection will in practice also account for the lack of interest in this process. The litigation in the *Barcelona Traction* case lasted for almost two decades. Clearly the lessons of that case are yet to be effected; the proceedings in the *Diallo* case were commenced more than 10 years ago and the Court is yet to give a judgment on the merits.

D. APPLYING THE NATIONALITY RULE

1. Nationality must be continuous

To the extent that the State exercising the right of diplomatic protection is acting on its own behalf and not as agent of the injured national, it is generally said to be a requirement that the nationality must be continuous. This is logical, since it is the bond of nationality which establishes the State's interest in the claim. Thus the claim must belong to a person or group of persons, having the nationality of the claimant-State from the time of the injury until the making of the award. Therefore, in cases of subrogation and assignment, it is arguable that the nominee or assignee should have the same nationality as the original holder of the title. Many authorities nevertheless state that the rule should have no application where there has been a forced or involuntary change of nationality, for instance through a process of State succession or changes in a State's frontiers (Brownlie, 2008, p 479). The argument has also been made that rule should be applied flexibly, in the protection of financial interests which frequently change hands and where the ties of nationality are unlikely to be of much significance. It is suggested that the rule should have no

---

[49] Ibid, para 90.
[50] *Elettronica Sicula SpA (ELSI), Judgment, ICJ Reports 1989*, p 15.
[51] Ibid, para 88.

application in those proceedings which have as their object the protection of fundamental human rights.

2. Diplomatic protection and the problem of multiple nationality

Cases of multiple nationalities present particular problems, for they involve a decision as to which of the potentially competing claimants should be entitled to exercise diplomatic protection. They also raise the problem of whether one State of a dual national can maintain a claim against another State of nationality. A number of rules have emerged in State practice to deal specifically with problems posed by dual nationals.

Two broad principles are widely accepted as regulating diplomatic protection in this area. First, diplomatic protection of dual or multiple nationals is governed by the principle of real or dominant nationality, and where there is a conflict of several nationalities, the nationality based on an effective link is to be treated as decisive.[52] The principle has also been explicitly endorsed in the jurisprudence of international tribunals including the Iran-United States Claims Tribunal.[53] It has also been adopted without qualification in claims brought before the United Nations Compensation Commission.[54] In applying the effective nationality test the Commission has been prepared to admit claims by Iraqi nationals provided they also possessed the valid nationality of another State.

Secondly, where the application of the test indicates that the national has equally strong ties with two or more States, neither should be permitted to exercise diplomatic protection on his behalf, against another State of which he is a national, the rule of international law being that one does not have a remedy on the international plane against one's own State.[55] Moreover, to allow protection in these circumstances where the national has strong ties with both States would undermine the sovereign equality of States. In deciding which of the nationalities were to be treated as dominant or effective, tribunals have paid regard to factors such as whether it was the nationality acquired at birth, the residence or domicile of the national, date of naturalization, language, employment and financial interests, whether the nationality was acquired *bona fides*, and whether the national was precluded from denying a nationality that he had in everyday dealings held out as his own.[56]

3. Claims against third States

There is authority for the view that the principle of dominant or effective nationality has no application where any of the national States of a dual national wish to protect him against a third State. In the *Salem* case, the tribunal held that:

the rule of international law [is] that in the case of dual nationality a third power is not entitled to contest the claim of one of the two powers whose national is interested in the case by referring to the nationality of the other power.[57]

---

[52] Eg, *Canevaro* case (1912) 11 *RIAA* 397.

[53] *Esphanian* v *Bank Tejarat* (1983) 2 Iran-USCTR 157 at p 166. The decision in the *Salem* case (1932) 2 *RIAA* 1161 provides an isolated example rejecting the dominant/effective nationality test.

[54] UN Doc S/AC.26/1991/7 Rev1, para 11.

[55] See *Merge* claim (1955), 22 ILR 443 and see Dugard, 2000, p 53; Brownlie, 2008, p 400–402.

[56] See the *Hein* case, *Annual Digest and Reports of Public International Law Cases* 1919–22, Case No 148, p 216; *Canevaro* case (1912) 11 *RIAA* 397.

[57] *Salem* case (1932) 2 *RIAA* 1161 at p 1188.

It is difficult to mount a principled defence of the exclusion of effective nationality rule in these circumstances, unless one takes the view that the rule is no more than a vehicle resolving competing claims in cases involving dual nationals and there is no justification for its application outside those contexts. However it may be taken as another indication that international *lex lata* is not too wedded to the requirement of genuine link.

4. Some issues concerning protection of shareholding interests

In the *Barcelona Traction* case, several judges thought shareholders had an independent right to protection under international law but there were fundamental differences concerning the precise nature of that right. Some thought that shareholders should be regarded as having a secondary right of protection which could be activated if the national State of the company had failed to act on its behalf.[58] The majority, however, rejected this, arguing that a secondary right could only come into existence once the primary right had been extinguished, and the failure of a State to exercise a primary right did not necessarily extinguish it.[59] Furthermore, the Court noted that the national State of the company is perfectly free to decide on the method and extent of protection it should grant to a company having its nationality. It may for instance decide to settle the claim, and to re-open these settlements by granting shareholders either a parallel or subsidiary right would substantially undermine the security of international economic relations.[60]

Another argument in support of extending protection to shareholders is that the genuine link requirement formulated in the *Nottebohm* case also applies to the protection of companies, so that only in cases where there is such a link, can the State of incorporation bring a claim. The existence of a shareholding interest, it is then argued, forms a crucial element in the genuine link requirement, especially in those instances where the shareholders are from the State claiming a right of protection or where the board of directors have ties of nationality with the claimant State. In the *Barcelona Traction* case, for instance, Judge Jessup denied that Canada had a right to exercise diplomatic protection by virtue of the company's incorporation in that State, in the absence of some demonstrable link. He noted that:

If a State extends its diplomatic protection to a corporation to which it has granted a charter of convenience while at the same time similar diplomatic assistance is being extended by another State whose nationals hold 100% of the shares, the situation might be considered analogous to cases of dual nationality of natural persons—Nottebohm principle applies equally here.[61]

In the practice of States and in the jurisprudence of international tribunals there are numerous instances where States have been prepared to intervene and exercise diplomatic protection in respect of shareholding interests in foreign corporations (Oppenheim, 1992, p 322). In the *Barcelona Traction* case the ICJ treated these instances as *lex specialis*, based as it were on the terms of the instruments establishing them. However, in a curious judgment in the 1989 *ELSI* case, and without any reference to the *Barcelona Traction* case,

[58] *Barcelona Traction, Light and Power Company, Limited, Second Phase, Judgment, ICJ Reports 1970*, p 3, Separate Opinion of Judge Fitzmaurice, p 65 at p 96 (para 53).
[59] *Barcelona Traction, Light and Power Company, Limited, Second Phase, Judgment, ICJ Reports 1970*, p 3, para 96.
[60] Ibid, para 97.   [61] Ibid, Separate Opinion of Judge Jessup, p 162 at p 170 (para 19).

the United States was permitted to exercise diplomatic protection in respect of injury to an Italian company, which was wholly owned by two US subsidiaries. Although Italy raised objections, the Court was untroubled by them, and preferred to dispose of the claim on the basis that there had been no violation of the treaty obligations relied on by the United States.[62]

It would therefore seem that notwithstanding the opinion of the majority in the *Barcelona Traction* case, there is a substantial body of international practice and juris-prudence in support of the protection of shareholding interests. However, substantial problems of definition remain as to the precise circumstances when shareholders may be entitled to protection, the range of interests capable of protection and the modalities of reconciling competing claims (Lowe, 2002).

5. Exclusion of the nationality rule

The nexus of nationality is not required in all instances and its application may be waived by treaty or other *ad hoc* arrangements, such as delegation of the right of protection to another sovereign. Treaties may also extend a general right of protection to non-nationals. The most significant development in this respect relates to Article 8C of the Treaty of the European Union which creates a treaty-based right of diplomatic protection for all EU nationals within the jurisdiction of a member State irrespective of nationality (Dugard, 2004, para 8). Other subjects of international law, such as international organizations, may be entitled to exercise such diplomatic protection, as is necessary or incidental to the discharge of their functions. In the *Reparations* case, the ICJ thought nationality irrelevant in cases where the United Nations brings a claim in respect of injuries to agents of the organization incurred in the course of their duties.[63] The claim in these instances could even be addressed to the very State of the victim's nationality, for in these circumstances the bond of nationality is not critical to the admissibility of the claim. Examples of other instances where the rule as to nationality of claims has been regarded as being generally inapplicable include situations where claims have been brought on behalf of aliens in the service of the claiming State;[64] Stateless persons; non-nationals forming a minority in a group of national claimants; refugees and non-nationals with long-term residence in the State espousing diplomatic protection (Oppenheim, 1992, p 515). In *Al-Rawi and Others* v *The Secretary of State for Foreign and Commonwealth Affairs*[65] the English Court of Appeal denied that a sovereign State possessed standing to exercise diplomatic protection on behalf of resident aliens or refugees. It concluded that Article 8 of the ILC draft articles on diplomatic protection[66] which envisaged protection for stateless persons and refugees habitually resident in a claimant

---

62 *Elettronica Sicula SpA (ELSI), Judgment, ICJ Reports 1989*, p 15, para 101. But cf the Dissenting Opinion of Judge Oda, ibid, p 83 who questioned the right of the United States to exercise diplomatic protection on behalf of shareholders in an Italian company when that company had not ceased to exist.

63 *Reparation for Injuries* case (*Advisory Opinion*), *ICJ Reports 1949*, p 174 at pp 179, 181–184.

64 See for example *The M/V Saiga No 2 (Saint Vincent and the Grenadines* v *Guinea)*, ITLOS Case No 2, Judgment of 1 July 1999, in which the International Tribunal for the Law of the Sea accepted that the flag State had the right to protect non-national crew members.

65 *Al-Rawi and Others* v *The Secretary of State for Foreign and Commonwealth Affairs* [2006] EWCA Civ 1279, paras, 63, 64, 89 and 115 ff.

66 See Seventh Report of the ILC Rapporteur on Diplomatic Protection, 7th March 2006, 58th session, A/CN.4/567.

State, was strictly speaking *lex ferenda* and an exercise in the progressive development of the law and not its restatement. *Al-Rawi* is however a decision of a domestic court, and to the extent that it is at odds with the weight of authority in public international law, cannot be regarded as decisive on this point.

IV. ADMISSIBILITY IN CASES CONCERNING OBLIGATIONS OWED TO A PLURALITY OF STATES

A. INTRODUCTION

The obligations forming the basis of claims considered in the previous sections have been in the nature of distinct bilateral duties; they are either owed directly to the State or in the person of its nationals. In both instances, legal interest takes the form of a private law claim; the wronged State must demonstrate either a direct injury to its interests or those of its nationals. Much of the traditional law on State responsibility has been concerned precisely with the enforcement of these bilateral rights and duties. The category of obligations considered in this section takes two forms. The first concerns obligations owed to a State under a treaty instrument, and which have the objective of protecting the collective interests of all the parties. As long as the injury or violation is within the scope of the protected zone of interest, any of the States parties to the treaty instruments has a *prima facie* right to make representations or bring a claim. For instance, States parties to regional human rights treaties invariably have a right to make representations even if the affected individuals are not their nationals. Other treaties creating zones of collective interests include regional nuclear-free zone treaties, regional environmental treaties, and regional instruments for economic integration.[67]

The second variation concerns the so-called *erga omnes* obligations which are owed to the international community as a whole. There has long been a consensus, at least since the Second World War, that international law may have an interest in creating obligations for the benefit of individuals and other non-State entities, such as units of self-determination, international organizations, etc. Other obligations in this category rest on the premise that certain values are fundamental, and are therefore owed to the international community as a whole. The protection of these values may coincide with individual State interests as in the case of aggression, but in most cases they usually transcend such interests. As a result, the international system may recognize a role for third States in their enforcement even if they are not directly injured. An implicit feature of this category of obligations is that the specific requirements of legal interest based either on direct injury or ties of nationality are dispensed with.

In an often cited passage, the International Court of Justice in the *Barcelona Traction* case accepted that there were gradations of obligations in the international system, and

---

[67] For relevant treaties see for instance South Pacific Nuclear Treaty (Raratonga, 1985) (1985) 24 ILM 1442; Treaty of Tlatelolco on the Prohibition of Nuclear Weapons in Latin America (1967) 634 UNTS at 281; Africa Nuclear Free Zone Treaty (1996) 35 ILM 698; ASEAN Nuclear Free Zone Treaty 1996, 35 ILM 635.

that implicitly these qualitative differences, may call for or justify different responses by members of the international community. It observed that:

> An essential distinction should be drawn between obligations of a State towards the international community as a whole and those arising vis-à-vis another State in the field of diplomatic protection. By their very nature the former are the concern of all States in view of the importance of the rights involved, all States can be held to have a legal interest in their protection, they are obligations *erga omnes*. Such obligations derive for example in contemporary international law, from the outlawing of aggression, and of genocide, as also from the principles and rules concerning the basic rights of the human person, including protection from slavery and racial discrimination. Some of the corresponding rights of protection have entered into the body of general international law[68] whilst others are conferred by international instruments of a universal or quasi-universal character.[69]

The Court's pronouncements on the *erga omnes* character of obligations was strictly speaking *obiter*, but the literature accepted that at least at the level of primary rules, international obligations fell into two distinct categories; those in the nature of a civil law right and owed to individual States, and those creating a regulatory framework for dealing with public order concerns, and therefore owed to the international community as a whole (Ragazzi, 1997).

The court's declaration has unfortunately not been matched with practical mechanisms for the enforcement of these collective duties. In particular, there has been a lack of consensus on whether a distinct category of secondary rules has also come into operation; one regulating ordinary breaches, and the other attaching different legal consequences, as well as modalities for the enforcement of *erga omnes* obligations. It remains a moot point whether international law recognizes litigation in the public interest, and in particular whether States have a legal interest to enforce community values.

B. TREATY INSTRUMENTS PROTECTING COLLECTIVE INTERESTS

It has long been recognized that States may have an interest in the observance of treaty instruments to which they are a party even without being directly affected. This interest is reflected for instance in Article 60 of the Vienna Convention on the Law of Treaties which entitles States parties to a treaty to terminate it on account of material breach. Similarly, Article 42 of the ILC's Articles explicitly recognizes the interests of States in ensuring compliance with treaty instruments to which they are a party. The obligations are described as interdependent with the result that non-compliance by any one party automatically affects the interests of all other parties to the treaty instrument. The Commission's approach is to create different degrees of 'affectedness', and the forms of responses that States may be entitled to adopt is determined by the degree to which they are affected by the breach.[70]

---

[68] See *Reservations to the Convention on the Prevention and Punishment of the Crime of Genocide, Advisory Opinion, ICJ Reports 1951*, p 23.

[69] *Barcelona Traction, Light and Power Company, Limited, Second Phase, Judgment, ICJ Reports 1970*, p 3, paras 33–34.

[70] ILC ARSIWA Articles 42 and 48 envisage a distinct role for States in enforcing obligations *erga omnes* including a right to bring an action and obtain compensation on behalf of an injured State.

Arguably in those instances where there is a jurisdictional link between injured States and an international tribunal, there is no reason in principle why a State should not bring an action for the sole purpose that it is interested in enforcing the rule of law as created in the treaty instrument or customary law. It should in principle have the right to do so even if it has suffered no material injury itself, or in the person of its national. Thus, leaving aside the problematic question whether international law recognizes an *actio popularis*, it could be said that at least in respect of those obligations contained in multilateral treaties, to which a large number of States are parties, the public interests concerns are readily met by the recognition that all parties to such instruments may bring an action for their enforcement.

C. LITIGATION IN THE PUBLIC INTEREST AND THE ENFORCEMENT OF *ERGA OMNES* OBLIGATIONS

In Roman law it was always accepted that a plaintiff could bring an action before the court if it was in the public interest, and there was no requirement that the plaintiff should demonstrate a specific injury to its own interests. In the *South West Africa* cases, the international court indirectly considered the question whether general international law recognized the right of States to bring an action in vindication of the public interest. The applicant States, Liberia and Ethiopia had argued that in order to be effective, the mandate for South West Africa should be interpreted in a way that would recognize their own right to bring an action, even though the obligations in question was not owed to them as individuals members of the league but rather to the league itself. The Court rejected this argument and observed that:

Looked at in another way moreover, the argument amounts to a plea that the Court should allow the equivalent of an *actio popularis*, or right resident in any member of a community to take legal action in vindication of public interest. But although a right of this kind may be known to certain municipal systems of law, it is not known to international law as it stands at present: nor is the Court able to regard it as imported by the general principles of law referred to in Article 38, paragraph 1 (c) of its Statute.[71]

Moreover, there are further indications in the *Barcelona Traction* case itself that the Court did not regard the existence of *erga omnes* obligations as necessarily importing recognition of an *actio popularis*. The right of enforcement in the Court's view only existed in those instances when it had been directly granted by a treaty instrument. It observed that:

With regard more particularly to human rights, to which reference has already been made in paragraph 34 of this judgment, it should be noted that these include protection against denial of justice. However, on the universal level, the instruments which embody human rights do not confer on States the capacity to protect the victims of infringements of such rights irrespective of their nationality. It is therefore still on the regional level that a solution to this problem has had to be sought; thus within the Council of Europe, of which Spain is not a member, the problem of admissibility encountered by the claim in the present case has been resolved by the European Convention on Human Rights, which entitles each State

---

[71] *South West Africa, Second Phase, Judgment, ICJ Reports 1966*, p 6, para 88. Judge Jessup who delivered a strong dissent was nevertheless disinclined to accept a general right of *actio popularis*.

which is a party to the convention to lodge a complaint against any other contracting State for the violation of the convention, irrespective of the nationality of the victim.[72]

The conclusion is problematic because it has the effect of depriving the *erga omnes* regime of much practical value. There are few instruments indeed of general application, which provide for the enforcement of *erga omnes* obligations. This lack of realistic mechanisms for enforcement has the unfortunate effect of rendering these obligations largely theoretical.

Even assuming that the case for *actio popularis* as a general rule of international law is defensible as a matter of principle, it will still be subject to the jurisdictional limitations that inhere in international tribunals. Thus, in absence of a jurisdictional connection with the Court on the part of the claimant and respondent State, the Court will invariably be unable to entertain the claim notwithstanding its *erga omnes* basis (Schachter, 1991, p 210; Crawford, 1996, p 605). This much is clear from the ICJ decision in the *East Timor* case.

In this case Portugal brought an action against Australia on the basis that by entering into a treaty with Indonesia regarding the delimitation of the East Timorese continental shelf, Australia had interfered with the right of East Timorese people to self-determination. Yet a substantive judgment on the matter required the Court to rule on the legality of the powers enjoyed by Indonesia over East Timor. Indonesia was not a party to the dispute, nor had it accepted the Court's jurisdiction. It was therefore immediately apparent that the Court was being asked to rule on the rights and obligations of a third party to the dispute contrary to its previous jurisprudence as laid down in the *Monetary Gold* case. Portugal argued that limitations on the Court's jurisdiction under the *Monetary Gold* principle had no application in view of the *erga omnes* character of the obligations involved. The Court rejected the claim and observed that:

…Portugal's assertion that the right of people's to self-determination as it evolved from the Charter and from the UN practice has an *erga omnes* character is irreproachable. The principle of self-determination of peoples has been recognised in the United Nations Charter and in the jurisprudence of the Court. It is one of the essential principles of contemporary international law. However, the Court considers that the *erga omnes* character of a norm and the rule of consent are two different things. Whatever the nature of the obligations invoked, the Court could not rule on the lawfulness of the conduct of a State when its judgment would imply an evaluation of the lawfulness of the conduct of another State which is not a party to the case. Where this is so, the court cannot act even if the right in question is a right *erga omnes*.[73]

In the *Armed Activities in the Territory of the Congo*, the Court confirmed its previous jurisprudence. It noted that the *erga omnes* character of the obligations under the Genocide convention did not give the Court jurisdiction to entertain a dispute in the absence of the parties consent.[74]

---

[72] *Barcelona Traction, Light and Power Company, Limited, Second Phase, Judgment, ICJ Reports 1970,* p 3, para 91.
[73] *East Timor (Portugal v Australia), Judgment, ICJ Reports 1995,* p 90, para 29.
[74] *Armed Activities on the Territory of the Congo (New Application: 2002) (Democratic Republic of the Congo v Rwanda), Jurisdiction and Admissibility, Judgment, ICJ Reports 2006,* p 6, paras 28–70.

Further obstacles in the path of litigation *actio popularis* have been noted. Schachter for instance, has suggested that States are reluctant to set precedents which could be used in future litigation against them, and so they are unlikely to lodge claims even in respect of *erga omnes* obligations unless their direct interests were involved. Moreover, he warns that there is a real risk that an expansive concept of *actio popularis* is likely to deter even further State acceptance of the International Court's compulsory jurisdiction; and those States who accept the compulsory jurisdiction will invariably protect themselves from its consequences by making reservations against *actio popularis* suits (Schachter, 1991, p 212). In any case, it is abundantly clear from the few occasions that the International Court has considered the matter, that it has been particularly reticent to acknowledge public interest litigation as a means of enforcing *erga omnes* obligations.

The Articles finally adopted by the ILC in 2001 explicitly recognize the right of States other than those directly injured to bring an action by way of enforcing the collective interest.[75] The Special Rapporteur in the commentary to Article 48 acknowledged that the Article involved elements of progressive development of the law insofar as it entitled States to bring claims for restitution and reparation on behalf of the beneficiaries of the obligation even when they were not directly affected. The Articles have been commended to States by the UN General Assembly in GA Resolution 56/83 (12 December 2001), but it remains an open question whether this positive endorsement will be reflected in actual State behaviour (Crawford and Olleson, 2005).

V. ADMISSIBILITY OF CLAIMS AND THE RULE ON EXHAUSTION OF LOCAL REMEDIES

A. INTRODUCTION

There is almost universal consensus that in the absence of an agreement to the contrary, a claim is inadmissible on the international plane unless the alien or legal person on whose behalf a claim has been brought has exhausted local remedies in the putative respondent State. The rule has been endorsed in the literature as a rule of customary law and its normative quality has been accepted by international tribunals.[76]

A number of reasons have been put forward in support of the rule. The first is a logical consequence of the sovereignty of States in respect of matters occurring on their territory.

---

[75] Article 48 provides:
  1. Any State other than an injured State is entitled to invoke the responsibility of another in accordance with Para 2 if:
     (a) the obligation breached is owed to a group of States including that State, and is established for the protection of a collective interest of the group; or
     (b) the obligation breached is owed to the international community as a whole.
  2. Any state entitled to invoke responsibility under paragraph 1 may claim from the responsible State:
     (a) cessation of the internationally wrongful act, and assurances and guarantees of non-repetition in accordance with article 30; and
     (b) Performance of the obligation of reparation in accordance with the preceding articles, in the interest of the injured State or of the beneficiaries of the obligation breached.
  3. ...

[76] See for instance *Ahmadou Sadio Diallo (Republic of Guinea v Democratic Republic of Congo), Preliminary Objections,* Judgment of 24 May 2007, paras 42–44.

It is therefore generally accepted that out of respect for sovereignty, a State must be given the first opportunity to exercise jurisdiction in respect of matters occurring in its territory. There is here also a presumption that the wronged national by voluntarily bringing himself within the jurisdiction of the respondent State, must be taken to have assumed the risk, of having local law applied to him.

The second reason rests on considerations of practical convenience. It would be both expensive and futile to bring small claims before an international forum when there is a possibility of expeditious redress before local tribunals. It has also been suggested that in these instances the local courts are better placed to evaluate the facts and the evidence, as well as deciding on the appropriate methods of compensation (Brownlie, 2008, p 492). They are therefore clearly more appropriate fora for the settlement of these disputes than the international arena.

Thirdly, in a number of instances, it is the failure to provide local redress for breach of an international obligation that engages the responsibility of the State. There can be no claim on the basis of denial of justice until local remedies have been exhausted. In this instance failure to exhaust local remedies is not so much a bar to the admissibility of the claim; rather it operates to determine the existence of responsibility, since until such remedies have been exhausted and found to be wanting no case for violation of international law can be made.

B. THE CONTENT OF THE RULE

What are the parameters of the rule requiring exhaustion of local remedies and when and in what circumstances is it discharged? The first general observation is that the rule only applies in those instances where the State brings a claim on behalf of a national. As a matter of principle, a State bringing a claim to protect its direct interests is not obliged to exhaust such remedies. Although there is nothing to preclude it from doing so, and in particular circumstances it may in fact be convenient to explore the availability of remedies in the local courts.

Secondly, there is considerable support for the view that the obligation to exhaust local remedies relates only to legal remedies, and would exclude remedies that are discretionary or that are available as a matter of grace (Brownlie, 2008, p 495; Brierly, 1963, p 281). It also seems to be a general requirement that the national in question must exhaust the remedies available to their fullest extent. In particular they must raise before local courts all the arguments that they may wish to bring before international tribunals,[77] as well as appeal procedures provided for under local law.[78]

It seems perfectly logical that as a corollary there is no obligation to exhaust local remedies where these are unavailable in practice or are unlikely to yield any results. Nevertheless the decision whether legal remedies are unavailable in a particular legal system is a contentious one, and it remains unclear how far the foreign national is expected to test the options under national law before reaching the conclusion that they are bound to be futile. In the *Interhandel* case, brought by Switzerland before the International Court,

---

[77] *Finnish Ships Arbitration*, 1934, 3 *RIAA* 1479; *Elettronica Sicula SpA (ELSI), Judgment, ICJ Reports 1989*, p 15.

[78] *Ambatielos Claim*, 1956, 12 *RIAA* 83.

the Court concluded that as Interhandel's suit was still pending before United States courts, local remedies had not been exhausted.[79] The conclusion on the face of it appeared harsh, since the corporation had been involved in litigation in United States courts for a period of almost 10 years before proceedings were commenced by Switzerland before the International Court.

The jurisprudence of international tribunals indicate that local remedies will generally be regarded as unavailable if the applicant, although granted a right of appeal on a point of law, chooses not to exercise it, because the precise point raised has previously been decided by a higher court to the detriment of a litigant. Similarly, local remedies are treated as unavailable if an appeal would lie on a point of fact, but appellate courts lack the power to review points of fact.[80] In other words, the remedy available must present a reasonable possibility of redressing the personal claim of the litigant (Dugard, 2002, para 45).

C. THE APPLICATION OF THE RULE IN THE CONTEXT OF MIXED CLAIMS

It has been noted that the rule requiring the exhaustion of local remedies only applies in those instances where the State brings forward a claim on behalf of a national as opposed to when it claims on its own behalf. The rule therefore rests on the assumption that it will always be easy to distinguish between claims brought on behalf of a national and instances when the State claims on its own behalf. While the distinction is possible to maintain in a large number of claims, there are many cases where the dividing line is not so clear, especially when the wrong simultaneously results in injury to the State's direct interests as well as those of the national. In these instances, it becomes difficult to decide whether the rule requiring the exhaustion of local remedies applies or not. Moreover, it is not uncommon for the applicant States to simultaneously seek a declaration or interpretation of a treaty involving general rights owed to them, and damages in respect of an injury to their nationals in the same proceedings. Dugard, in his second report on diplomatic protection, has suggested that in respect of mixed claims, the exhaustion of local remedies rule should only apply if the claim is overwhelmingly concerned with injury to the national (Dugard, 2001, paras 19–24).

There is some support in the jurisprudence of international tribunals for the *preponderance* of interests test in the case of mixed claims. In the *Interhandel* case, Switzerland had insisted on the non-applicability of the local remedies rule, insofar as the claim brought by it concerned the failure of the US authorities to apply the terms of an applicable treaty, thus causing it direct injury. In rejecting the claim, the Court noted that the dispute was essentially one in which:

the Swiss Government appears as having adopted the cause of its national Interhandel, for the purpose of securing restitution to that company of assets vested by the government of the United States.

---

[79] *Interhandel, Preliminary Objections, Judgment, ICJ Reports 1959*, p 6.
[80] *Finnish Ships Arbitration*, 1934, 3 *RIAA* 1479; *Panevezys-Saldutiskis Railway, Judgment, 1939, PCIJ, Ser A/B, No 76*, p 4 at p 18.

It further observed that:

...one interest, and one alone of Interhandel has induced the Swiss Government to institute proceedings, and that this interest is the basis for the present claim and should determine the scope of the action brought before the Court by the Swiss Government in its alternative as well as principal form.[81]

In the *ELSI* case, the Chamber of the International Court of Justice rejected the argument of the United States that insofar as the claim was founded on breach of a treaty obligation owed to it, it should be treated as an instance of direct injury to State interests and not as a claim made on behalf of a national for purposes of the local remedies rule. In rejecting the argument the Chamber observed that:

...the matter which colours and pervades the United States Claim as a whole is the alleged damage to Raytheon and Machlett [United States Corporations].[82]

This surely is correct because even claims brought exclusively on behalf of nationals usually originate in some kind of non-compliance with a treaty obligation owed to the applicant State. The fact that a breach of a treaty is at issue cannot therefore be regarded as a reliable test (if at all) for distinguishing between direct injury to a State's interests and those cases where it claims on behalf of a national.

Meron has suggested that in deciding on the nature of the claim it is necessary to have regard to the real interests and goals of the litigant State. Is the State primarily pursuing its own interests or is the action in the nature of a claim brought on behalf of a national? If the claim is primarily concerned with injury to a national, then the rule will operate to exclude the admissibility of the claim including any secondary elements, which strictly speaking are in the nature of inter-State claims (Meron, 1959, p 87). There is also general recognition that claims, which are primarily about treaty interpretation and application, are direct State claims even if they arise in circumstances also affecting the rights of a private person (Oppenheim, 1992, p 523). The subject matter of the dispute may also provide a useful guide as to the true character of the claim. Thus injury to diplomatic or consular staff,[83] or State property[84] will generally be regarded as direct claims and therefore not subject to the operation of the local remedies rule. Although not conclusive, the nature of the remedy sought may also be a useful indicator in claims presenting mixed elements (Adler, 1990, p 652; Dugard, 2001, paras 29–30). There is considerable justification in looking at the essence of the claim and characterizing it by paying regard to its principal objectives. However, a rigid application of the predominance test may preclude valid claims by governments, especially when in the circumstances they are unlikely to obtain any local remedies for breach of their treaty rights (Fitzmaurice, 1961, p 37; Thirlway, 1995, pp 85–90). Moreover the *dominance test* ignores the fact that a State may have a legal interest of its own to protect, such as vindicating the values underpinning the treaty regime, and which are unlikely to be satisfied by any material compensation or restitution of property in national courts.

---

[81] *Interhandel, Preliminary Objections, Judgment, ICJ Reports 1959*, p 6 at p 29.
[82] *Elettronica Sicula SpA (ELSI), Judgment, ICJ Reports 1989*, p 15, para 91.
[83] *United States Diplomatic and Consular Staff in Tehran, Judgment, ICJ Reports 1980*, p 3.
[84] *Corfu Channel, Merits, Judgment, ICJ Reports 1949*, p 4.

D. NATURE OF THE RULE

Is the rule requiring exhaustion of local remedies a rule of procedure or substance? There has been considerable discussion in the literature as to the precise character of the rule requiring exhaustion of local remedies, and in particular whether it is a rule of substance or procedure. This seemingly sterile debate on a closer analysis has important normative consequences, and therefore merits close attention.

A number of different positions have been adopted. The first, which is that it is purely substantive in nature, proceeds from the premise that the exhaustion of local remedies is not so much a condition of admissibility of claims; rather, it determines the very existence of responsibility. On this view until local remedies have been exhausted and found wanting, there can be no international 'delict' to engage the responsibility of the State.[85]

The second position treats the rule as a procedural pre-requisite to the admissibility of a claim. On this view the responsibility of a State is engaged and complete from the time of the wrongful act, but redress on the international plane cannot be effected until local remedies have been effected.

The third position distinguishes between different kinds of wrongs that may cause injury to a national on whose behalf a claim is subsequently brought. On this view, where the national is injured by a violation of a rule of domestic law, no question of international responsibility arises, until local remedies have been exhausted. Only then can a claim be brought on the international plane for denial of justice. Here exhaustion of local remedies is substantive, for until such remedies have failed there can be no question of responsibility on the international plane. Proponents of this third position distinguish the situation where the national is injured by what is clearly a rule of international law. Here, the responsibility of the respondent State is activated from the time of the injury. In this instance, the requirement that local remedies have to be exhausted must be seen as no more than a procedural prerequisite to the admissibility of a claim on the international plane, and does not as such affect the origin of responsibility.

Whether one adopts the procedural or substantive position may have significant consequences for other rules affecting the admissibility of claims such as the requirement of continuous nationality of claims. It has been noted that for a claim to be admissible on the international plane, it must be national in origin. In other words, from the time of the injury until the making of the award, the claim must belong to persons having the nationality of the claimant State. Thus, insofar as the timing of the origin of responsibility differs under the substantive and procedural view, the position adopted has implications for the rule as to the continuous nationality of claim.

Secondly, if the rule determines the origin of responsibility, then it operates as a bar to States wishing to seek declaratory judgments or interpretation of treaties in circumstances where injured nationals have not exhausted local remedies, since, until such remedies have been exhausted, there can be no question of responsibility.

Finally, Dugard has suggested that the rule may also affect the jurisdiction of international tribunals in those instances where States have attached time limits to their acceptances of the court's jurisdiction (Dugard, 2001, para 33). On the procedural view, the effective time for jurisdictional purposes is the occurrence of the injury. On the substantive

---

[85] Ago, R, 'Sixth Report on State Responsibility', *YBILC* (1977), vol II (part one), pp 22–23.

view, the effective time will be after the exhaustion of local remedies. Thus a claim may be admissible or inadmissible depending on which view of the rule one adopts.

E. WHICH VIEW REPRESENTS THE LAW?

The answer to this question must surely be speculative, and has to be approached as a matter of principle rather than on the basis of State and arbitral practice since. No international decision has explicitly addressed the issue, and the positions adopted by governments have been largely partisan, and influenced by the exigencies of litigation. However, the decisions in the *German Interests in Polish Upper Silesia*,[86] *Chorzow Factory*,[87] and *Phosphates in Morocco*[88] cases provide the strongest evidence in support of the procedural position. In both cases the Court reached the conclusion that responsibility was incurred immediately following on the wrongful act, rather than after the exhaustion of local remedies.

As a matter of principle, it is difficult to mount a spirited defence of the substantive position. It means that the determination of whether a breach of international law takes place depends not on the international norm but on the procedures of local tribunals. This potentially undermines the values that underpin international obligations (Dugard, 2001, paras 56 and 63; Amerasinghe, 1990, p 328). Non-compliance with an obligation threatens the values that underpin the applicable norm irrespective of whether local remedies have been exhausted or not. As Judge Lauterpacht noted in the *Norwegian Loans* case:

...the exhaustion of local remedies cannot itself bring within the province of international law a dispute which is otherwise outside its sphere. The failure to exhaust local remedies may constitute a bar to the jurisdiction of the court; it does not affect the intrinsically international character of a dispute.[89]

Secondly, it is generally accepted that States may agree by treaty to exclude the operation of a rule. The validity of such agreements was accepted without qualification in the *ELSI* case. Dugard has suggested that the validity of such waiver is difficult to defend, if one adopts the substantive view, since it is tantamount to saying that States can agree to make something delictual when ordinarily it would not be a breach unless and until it has given rise to subsequent denial of justice (Dugard, 2001, para 33). For this reason most authorities consider the exhaustion of local remedies to be a rule of procedure. The State incurs international responsibility from the moment of the wrongful act but the right to bring an international claim is suspended until the State has had the opportunity to remedy the situation.

F. THE EXCLUSION OF THE LOCAL REMEDIES RULE

There can be no obligation to exhaust local remedies if there are no local remedies to exhaust (Fitzmaurice, 1961, p 59). In order to be considered effective, the local remedy

---

[86] *Certain German Interests in Polish Upper Silesia, Merits, Judgment No 7, 1926, PCIJ, Ser A, No 7.*

[87] *Factory at Chorzow, Merits, Judgment No 13, 1928, PCIJ, Ser A, No 17.*

[88] *Phosphates in Morocco, Judgment, 1937, PCIJ, Ser A/B, No 74, p 10.*

[89] *Certain Norwegian Loans, Judgment, ICJ Reports 1957, p 9, Separate Opinion of Judge Lauterpacht,* p 34 at p 38.

must have the capacity to remedy the complaint. Clearly, when the conduct giving rise to the injury does not violate local law, there will be no local remedies and the matter can immediately be taken up on the international plane. The argument has also been made that there is no obligation to exhaust local remedies in cases where public international law does not permit the respondent State to exercise jurisdiction in the first place (Brownlie, 2008, p 495; O'Connell, 1970, p 951). Thus an attempt to exercise jurisdiction over an alien in circumstances where international law does not grant jurisdiction would clearly be a nullity, and there is considerable merit in the argument that no obligation to exhaust local remedies arises.[90]

Many authorities argue that there is no obligation to exhaust local remedies where there is no voluntary link between the injured individual and the respondent State (Dugard, 2002, para 83). Thus the argument has been made that in principle there should be some degree of connection between the injured individual and the respondent State and that the obligation is therefore dispensed with, where the links are transitory or clearly involuntary. Examples would include air crash victims involuntarily or fortuitously injured by events in the respondent State. On the other hand, it can be argued that it is precisely such cases that local courts are particularly suitable for, given the multiple character of the claims and the clear local interest in the dispute.

Finally, the requirement to exhaust local remedies may be formally dispensed with in a treaty. Many international treaties provide that in the event of a dispute between the State and foreign legal person, the dispute is to be referred to arbitration. Tribunals considering the issue have reached the conclusion that where provision is expressly made for arbitration, then there will clearly be no obligation to exhaust local remedies.

VI. CONCLUSION

The preceding discussion has attempted to isolate the main legal grounds governing the admissibility of claims. These conditions operate across the board irrespective of the particular circumstances of the case. The requirement of legal interest, exhaustion of local remedies, will invariably govern the admissibility of most claims unless on the facts a specific waiver is in operation. Unfortunately the development of *erga omes* obligations has not been accompanied by any discernible refinement of the mechanisms for their enforcement. The work of the International Law Commission, completed in 2001, represents the most significant advance yet, insofar as it provides for a coherent regime for the enforcement of these obligations. Yet even the Commission's proposals especially in Article 48 are clearly stated in *de lege ferenda* terms and their effectiveness will ultimately depend on their reception in State practice.

It is to be regretted though that despite a fairly extensive jurisprudence, the rules governing the nationality of claims, in particular the criteria for nationality, in the context of diplomatic protection cannot be stated with certainty. The decision of the International Commission to undertake a study of the law governing diplomatic protection is a welcome

---

[90] See *Barcelona Traction, Light and Power Company, Limited, Second Phase, Judgment, ICJ Reports 1970,* p 3, Separate Opinion of Judge Fitzmaurice, p 65 at pp 103–110 (paras 66–83).

opportunity to consider some of the uncertainties and conflicting interpretations placed on the law both in the literature and in the practice of States.

This brief survey does not however purport to be a complete account of the infinite variety of circumstances that may legally operate to preclude the admissibility of a claim. Some of these, such as the circumstances when it could be said that a State had waived a claim have received fairly detailed attention in the literature, including the recent work of the International Law Commission (Crawford, 2002, pp 266–269). Other grounds of preclusion—such as a finding that the dispute is without object;[91] that the applicant State has itself indulged in the same wrongful act in respect of which it now complains (the 'clean hands' doctrine);[92] that the applicant has acquiesced in wrongful conduct forming the subject matter of the dispute;[93] or that the chosen forum is inappropriate (especially where the applicant State has instituted proceedings in a forum other than that nominated by the treaty)—are closely intertwined with the merits, and may therefore be treated either as issues of admissibility or as substantive grounds for defeating the claim at the merits stage. Moreover, in certain cases, the operation of estoppel may preclude the examination of a particular issue even in circumstances when the claim itself has been found to be admissible.[94] The survey is also undertaken without prejudice to the *lex specialis* regimes governing the protection of corporations or their shareholders under international economic treaties and protection mechanisms in human rights instruments.

REFERENCES

ADLER, M (1990), 'The Exhaustion of the Local Remedies Rule after the International Court of Justice's Decision in ELSI', 39 *ICLQ* 641.

AMERASINGHE, CF (1990), *Local Remedies in International Law* (Cambridge: Grotius).

BORCHARD, EM (1915), *The Diplomatic Protection of Citizens Abroad* (New York: Banks Law Publishing Co).

BRIERLY, JL (1928), 'The Theory of State Complicity in International Claims', 9 *BYIL* 48.

—— (1963), *The Law of Nations*, 6th edn (Oxford: Clarendon Press).

BROWNLIE, I (2008), *Principles of Public International Law*, 7th edn (Oxford: Clarendon Press).

COLLIER, J and LOWE, AV (1999), *The Settlement of Disputes in International Law* (Oxford: Oxford University Press).

CRAWFORD, J (1996), 'The General Assembly, the International Court and Self-determination', in Lowe and Fitzmaurice (eds), p 585.

---

[91] *Northern Cameroons, Preliminary Objections, Judgment, ICJ Reports 1963*, p 15.

[92] See *ICJ Pleadings, Oil Platforms (Islamic Republic of Iran v United States of America)*, Counter Memorial and Counter Claim Submitted by the United States of America, Part VI, pp 161–179 (23 June 1997) and Reply and Defence to Counter Claim submitted by the Islamic Republic of Iran, vol I, pp 187–198 (10 March 1999); *Gabčíkovo-Nagymaros Project (Hungary/Slovakia), Judgment, ICJ Reports 1997*, p 7, para 133; Dugard, 2005, passim.

[93] *ICJ Pleadings, Passage through the Great Belt (Finland v Denmark)*, Counter-memorial of the Government of the Kingdom of Denmark, Vol I, p 248 (May 1992).

[94] Eg, *Temple of Preah Vihear, Merits, Judgment, ICJ Reports 1962*, p 6 at pp 22–23.

CRAWFORD, J (2002), *The International Law Commission's Articles on State Responsibility* (Cambridge: Cambridge University Press).

—— and OLLESON, S (2005), 'The Continuing Debate on a UN Convention on State Responsibility', 54 *ICLQ* 959

DUGARD, J (2000), *First Report on Diplomatic Protection*, UN Doc A/CN.4/506.

—— (2001), *Second Report on Diplomatic Protection*, UN Doc A/CN.4/514.

—— (2002), *Third Report on Diplomatic Protection*, UN Doc A/CN.4/523.

—— (2004), *Fifth Report on Diplomatic Protection*, UN Doc A/CN.4/538.

—— (2005), *Sixth Report on Diplomatic Protection*, UN Doc A/CN.4/546.

FITZMAURICE, G (1957), 'The General Principles of International Law, Considered from the Standpoint of the Rule of Law', 92 *Recueil des Cours* 1.

—— (1961), 'Hersch Lauterpacht—The Scholar as Judge', 38 *BYIL* 37.

—— (1986), *The Law and Procedure of the International Court of Justice*, vol II (Cambridge: Grotius).

GREIG, D (1976), *International Law*, 2nd edn (London: Butterworths).

HARRIS, DJ (1998), *Cases and Materials on International Law*, 5th edn (London: Sweet & Maxwell).

LEIGH, GIF (1971), 'Nationality and Diplomatic Protection', 20 *ICLQ* 453.

LOWE, AV (2002), 'Shareholders Rights from Barcelona to ELSI', in Ando, N, McWhinney, E, and Wolfrum, R (eds), *Essays in Honor of Judge Oda* (The Hague: Kluwer), p 65.

—— and FITZMAURICE, M (1996), *Fifty Years of the International Court of Justice* (Cambridge: Cambridge University Press).

MALANCZUK, P (1997), *A Modern Introduction to International Law* (London: Routledge).

MERON, Y (1959), 'The Incidence of the Rule of Exhaustion of Local Remedies' 35 *BYIL* 83.

O'CONNELL, DP (1970), *International Law*, 2nd edn (London: Stevens).

OKOWA, P (2008), 'Case Concerning Ahmadou Sadio Diallo (Republic of Guinea v DRC), Preliminary Objections', 57 *ICLQ* 219.

OPPENHEIM, L (1992), *Oppenheim's International Law*, 9th edn (London: Longman).

RAGAZZI, M (1997), *The Concept of International Obligations Erga Omnes* (Oxford: Oxford University Press).

ROSENNE, S (1997), *The Law and Practice of the International Court, 1920–1996*, 3rd edn (The Hague: Nijhoff).

SCHACTER, O (1991), *International Law in Theory and in Practice* (Dordrecht: Martinus Nijhoff).

SHEA, D (1955), *The Calvo Clause* (Minneapolis, Minn.: University of Minnesota Press).

SIMMA, B (1994), 'From Bilateralism to Community Interest in International Law', 250 *Recueil des Cours* 217.

THIRLWAY, H (1995), 'Law and Procedure of the International Court of Justice', 66 *BYIL* 4.

WATTS, A (1996), 'Nationality of Claims: Some Relevant Concepts', in Lowe and Fitzmaurice (eds), p 424.

WITTICH, S (2001), 'Direct Injury and the Incidence of the Local Remedies Rule', 5 *Austrian Rev of Int'l and European L* 121.

FURTHER READING

AMERASINGHE, CF (1990), *Local Remedies in International Law* (Cambridge: Grotius). A comprehensive survey of the law including an in-depth study of the main doctrinal controversies.

CANCADO TRINDADE, AA (1983), *The Application of the Rule of Exhaustion of Local Remedies in International Law* (Cambridge: Cambridge University Press). A useful account of the rule with detailed illustrations from the jurisprudence of human rights tribunals, but rather dated.

DE HOOGH, AJJ (1996), *Obligations Erga Omnes and International Crimes: A Theoretical Inquiry into the Implementation and Enforcement of the International Responsibility of States* (The Hague: Kluwer). A detailed inquiry into the perennial difficulties surrounding the enforcement of *erga omnes* obligations.

INTERNATIONAL LAW ASSOCIATION (2000), *Committee on Diplomatic Protection of Persons and Property, Report of the Sixty-Ninth Conference* (London). A comprehensive and interesting examination of a wide range of issues relating to diplomatic protection.

PARRY, C (1956), 'Some Considerations Upon the Protection of Individuals in International Law', 90 *Recueil des Cours* 657. A good analysis of the law on diplomatic protection and includes some consideration of claims brought by international organizations.

WARBRICK, C (1988), 'Protection of Nationals Abroad: Current Legal Problems', 37 *ICLQ* 1002. A useful analysis of some of the problematic aspects of diplomatic protection.

17

THE RESPONSIBILITY
TO PROTECT

Spencer Zifcak

SUMMARY

The responsibility to protect has succeeded humanitarian intervention as the primary conceptual framework within which to consider international intervention to prevent the commission of mass atrocity crimes. First conceived in 2001, the doctrine has obtained international recognition in a remarkably short time. Its acceptance by the UN World Summit of political leaders in 2005, and later by the UN Security Council, provided the foundation for its further elaboration in international relations theory and political practice. This chapter provides the background to the new doctrine's appearance with a survey of the existing law and practice with respect to humanitarian intervention. It traces the responsibility to protect's subsequent intellectual and political development both before and after the adoption of the World Summit resolutions that embodied it. This analysis discloses that debate about the doctrine has been characterized by significant differences of opinion and interpretation between nations of the North and the South. In that context, the chapter concludes with a detailed consideration of the contemporary standing of the doctrine in international law.

I. INTRODUCTION

The genocide in Rwanda and ethnic cleansing in the Balkans left the international community's political leadership with a formidable dilemma. Plainly, the international community could no longer stand by while mass atrocities were committed. The cost in human rights and human life was simply too great. At the same time, however, the UN Charter's core commitment to national sovereignty seemed an insuperable obstacle to international intervention in conflicts that took place entirely within the boundaries of a State. Non-interference in a nation's domestic affairs remained still the cardinal rule underpinning the global legal order. If, therefore, the call 'never again' were to be made meaningful, new thinking and greater resolve were needed to chart the perilous waters between these apparently irreconcilable legal principles and political commitments.

The dilemma itself was not new. Debates about humanitarian intervention had taken place over centuries (Chesterman, 2001, Ch 1). Nevertheless, the impetus had seemed greater. The scale of recent atrocities, not least in Kigali and Srebrenica, had shocked the world's conscience. And the widespread and rapid acceptance of the understanding that individuals, just as much as States, should be regarded as the subjects of international law and, therefore, that they were deserving of its protection, had elevated human rights concerns to the top table of international political, legal and academic deliberation (Alston and MacDonald, 2008; Fabri, 2008; Peters, 2009).

It was largely by way of cracking that seemingly intractable problem that the idea that nations individually have a responsibility to protect their own citizens and that collectively they may take action to protect those in peril elsewhere has recently been developed and elaborated.[1] As I will argue presently, the 'responsibility to protect' (R2P) has not yet crystallized into a norm of international law. Yet its advance as a widely considered and broadly accepted political doctrine has been remarkably rapid. In the remainder of this chapter I trace this advance and assess the doctrine's contemporary legal and political standing. To do that effectively, however, it may help to contextualize the issue by examining briefly the legal position with respect to its predecessor conception—humanitarian intervention (see Evans, 2006; Janssen, 2008; Evans, 2009).

II. HUMANITARIAN INTERVENTION IN INTERNATIONAL LAW

The *prima facie* position with respect to military interventions undertaken for humanitarian reasons appears to be as follows.[2] Pursuant to Article 2(4) of the United Nations (UN) Charter:

All states shall refrain in their international relations from the threat or use of force against the territorial integrity and political independence of any state, or in any other manner inconsistent with the purpose of the United Nations

This injunction against the use of force is reinforced by the terms of Article 2(7) which declares: 'Nothing in the present Charter shall authorize the UN to intervene in matters which are essentially within the domestic jurisdiction of any state'. The principle of non-intervention, together with that of the sovereign equality of States, is designed to ensure that each State respects the prerogatives and entitlements of every other State.

There are only two exceptions in the Charter to the Article 2(4) prohibition. First, Chapter VII of the Charter empowers the Security Council to authorize the use of force in response to threats and breaches of international peace and security. Pursuant to Article 39, therefore, the Security Council may make recommendations as to what measures, including the use of armed force, should be taken to address an identified threat to

---

[1] See the International Commission on Intervention and State Sovereignty (2001), *The Responsibility to Protect: Report of the International Commission on Intervention and State Sovereignty*, Ottawa: International Development Research Centre.

[2] See generally, Chesterman, 2001, ch 2; Farer, 2003; Franck, 2003; Wheeler, 2004; Welsh, 2004; Triggs, 2006, p 598; Gray, 2008, p 33.

international peace and security or to any act of aggression. Secondly, in accordance with Article 51, member States of the United Nations may take measures, whether individually or collectively, in pursuit of their inherent right to self-defence should they be subject to armed attack. Such action in self-defence may continue until the Security Council itself has instituted whatever further measures are necessary to maintain international peace and security.

When laid down plainly in this way, it is apparent that the express terms of the Charter do not readily embrace either humanitarian intervention or a responsibility to protect. The principle of non-intervention stands steadfastly in their path. The UN Declaration on Friendly Relations of 1970 states the duty in similar and compelling fashion:[3]

No State or group of states has the right to intervene directly, or indirectly, for any reason whatsoever in the international external affairs of any other State. Consequently, armed intervention and all other forms of interference or attempted threats against the personality of the state or against its political, economic and cultural elements are in violation of international law.

Of course, the Charter's provisions are capable of competing interpretations. These can occupy the full spectrum from the literal to the liberal. International lawyers, for example, have argued that, despite what appear to be the plain words of the Charter text, a doctrine of humanitarian intervention may be insinuated into its interstices (Chesterman, 2001, p 47; Farer, 2003; Holzgrefe, 2003, p 53). One argument that has been made is that Article 2(4) prohibits the use of force only against 'the territorial integrity or political independence of a state'. If, therefore, force is used in the pursuit of some other objective, particularly one that is consistent with the objects of the Charter, it may be permissible. A humanitarian intervention, properly conducted, may pose no long-term threat either to the territorial integrity or political autonomy of a State. Its sole purpose may be said to be to prevent the further commission of atrocities pending the restoration of stability.

Such an interpretation faces great difficulty, however, because it creates the prospect of a damaging ambiguity in the Charter's interpretation. Even a brief look at the *travaux preparatoire*, as a means of resolving such an ambiguity, demonstrates clearly that such an adventurous interpretation of the qualification has little if any plausible foundation. Instead, the original aim of the non-intervention principle appears to have been to protect smaller States and the words 'territorial integrity and political independence' were added as supplements to, not as detractions from, the general prohibition on the use of force (Triggs, 2006, p 569).

Next, it may be suggested that the use of force is permitted so long as it is not, in the terms of Article 2(4), 'in any other manner inconsistent with the purposes of the United Nations'. Clearly, if the objective of the intervention is to prevent gross violations of human rights, it could not be said to be anything other than consistent with the Charter's fundamental purposes. The argument runs into immediate problems, however, not the least of which is that even if the disputed intervention is aimed at protecting and preserving the human rights of the afflicted people of a nation, the Charter's express prohibition of infringements

---

[3] Declaration on Principles of International Law Concerning Friendly Relations and Co-operation among States in accordance with the Charter of the United Nations, October 1970, Article 1.

upon the territorial integrity and political independence of a sovereign State still stands. It is unlikely that a vague reference to humanitarian purpose is sufficient to displace it.

Alternatively, a right or obligation of humanitarian intervention may arise in consequence of its progressive acceptance as part of customary international law (Cassese, 1999; Chesterman, 2001, Ch 2; Corten, 2008). There are significant methodological and practical problems, however, that stand in the path of humanitarian intervention's recognition as a customary rule. The International Court of Justice, for example, has had only limited opportunity to develop the rules governing the use of force.[4] In so far is the Court has considered the matter, it has come down steadfastly against any broadly applicable doctrine of permissible intervention. Nations themselves are not often clear or straightforward about their motivations for acting and mix legal justifications with political and security concerns in a way that makes the interpretation of State action an uncertain exercise. The UN's norm-creating bodies, in particular the Security Council and General Assembly, may not always be at one in their judgment of events, raising complex questions about the weight to be given to the opinions of each and the relative merits of both.

Such methodological difficulties have plainly been present in the most recent examples of international military interventions claimed to have had an humanitarian foundation. These are worth examining more closely. Two classes of case may be identified: those where the UN Security Council has sanctioned purported humanitarian interventions and those where it has not.

A. INTERVENTION WITH SECURITY COUNCIL AUTHORIZATION

In the first category are the cases of international intervention in Somalia, Rwanda and Bosnia (Weiss, 2007, p 27; Evans, 2008). The Somali operation was justified principally on the basis that the obstacles being placed in the way of urgently required humanitarian assistance to the country's distressed population were, in the opinion of the Security Council, such as to constitute a threat to international peace and security. The Council, therefore, authorized the international community pursuant to Chapter VII to use all necessary means to establish a secure environment for international relief operations.[5] The UN Secretary-General later expressed his opinion that the Somali operation constituted a new precedent for the Council. It had, for the first time, authorized a military intervention for purely humanitarian purposes.[6]

All too late, the Security Council authorized French military intervention to prevent further mass atrocities in Rwanda. It had previously determined that the Rwandan genocide had constituted a threat to international peace and security and therefore that safe-havens were required for those fleeing the genocide. In its primary resolution the Council also referred specifically to the wider disruption to cross-border security that had been created by the mass internal displacement of Rwandan citizens. Again, the Council authorized all necessary means to achieve the primary humanitarian objective. To that end, it instructed the French interveners to create a safe haven in which those fleeing the wider conflict could

---

[4] See in particular *Military and Paramilitary Activities in and against Nicaragua (Nicaragua v United States of America), Merits, Judgment, ICJ Reports 1986*, p 14; *Legality of Use of Force (Yugoslavia v Belgium), Provisional Measures, Order of 2 June 1999, ICJ Reports 1999*, p 124.

[5] SC Res 794 (3 December 1992).   [6] [1993] *UNYB* 51.

find security.[7] The French were also clear that any intervention on their part had to be founded upon the Security Council's mandate, even if delay were the result.[8]

The Security Council's many resolutions in relation to Bosnia and Herzegovina were directed principally at ending civil conflict consequent upon the dissolution of the former Yugoslavia rather than having a primarily humanitarian objective, although the latter remained significant. Resolution 770 (1992), for example, called upon States to take the measures necessary to facilitate the delivery of humanitarian and assistance to Sarajevo and other parts of the country as needed. It went further to authorize the UN intervention force to act in self-defence where necessary in order to reply to bombardments of established safe havens or to armed incursion into them and to take all necessary measures including the use of air power in and around the internationally protected safe areas to support its protective objective.[9] Again these resolutions proceeded from the Council's earlier determination that the conflict in Bosnia-Herzegovina constituted a threat to international peace and security.

These three cases suggest that since 1990, a highly circumscribed recognition of a right of humanitarian intervention may have been developing gradually within customary international law. The legal preconditions for such a nascent right were first that an existing or potential humanitarian catastrophe must be identified. Secondly, the catastrophe and its wider effects must be such as to constitute, in the opinion of the Security Council, a threat to international peace and security. Thirdly, the Security Council must explicitly authorize any subsequent military intervention. Fourthly, and implicitly, the authorization and conduct of the intervention must be an act of last resort (see Gazzini, 2005, p 174; Corten, 2008, p 106).

B. INTERVENTION WITHOUT SECURITY COUNCIL AUTHORIZATION

Following the defeat of the Iraqi army in Kuwait and its subsequent withdrawal from that country, in 1991 the Kurdish peoples in the north of the country sought to assert their right to political independence. This uprising was met with brute military force by troops loyal to the Hussein regime and, after it was put down, the government embarked upon further, genocidal, repression of the Kurdish population. In response, the Security Council adopted Resolution 688. The resolution condemned the repression of the Iraqi civilian population, demanded that Iraq end this oppression and insisted that Iraq allow international humanitarian organizations immediate access to all those in need of assistance. The Council also appealed to all member States and humanitarian organizations to continue their humanitarian relief efforts. Despite its strong language, however, the resolution did not contain any express authorization for military action pursuant to Chapter VII.[10]

Nevertheless, on the same day, the US administration announced that it would commence dropping food and other forms of material aid over Northern Iraq in partnership

---

[7] SC Res 929 (22 June 1994).

[8] 40 *Annuaire Francais de Droit International Public* (1998) 429–430.

[9] SC Res 770 (13 August 1992) and see further SC Res 814 (26 March 1993); SC Res 816 (31 March 1993); SC Res 844 (19 June 1993); and SC Res 871 (2 October 1993).

[10] SC Res 688 (5 April 1991).

with France and the United Kingdom. Then, 11 days later when it appeared as if the aid effort was being substantially compromised by mountainous and inhospitable terrain into which the aid was being delivered, President Bush announced unilaterally that US troops would enter Northern Iraq in order to establish safe havens for the beleaguered Kurdish population.

When these interventions were challenged by Iraq in the Security Council, the coalition partners contended that their actions were justified on purely humanitarian grounds. They also sought to establish legal legitimacy for their interventions by arguing that Resolution 688 had provided implicit legal authorization for them. The argument that humanitarian intervention might legally be supported by such implicit authorization was difficult to justify. This was because the express terms of the relevant Resolution did not appear to allow for such an expansive interpretation. The Resolution itself was the first of fourteen that had not been adopted under Chapter VII. And in the Council debates that led to its adoption, the prospect of military intervention had never explicitly been contemplated. However strongly founded in humanitarian concern, then, the arguments put in favour of the right of a State or States to engage unilaterally in humanitarian intervention without express Security Council authorization seemed, at least at that stage, to have only the most tenuous foundation.

The question as to the legality of unilateral humanitarian intervention emerged for consideration again in 1999 in relation to the controversial intervention by NATO in defence of the ethnic Albanian people of Kosovo.[11] So as to protect the Kosovar Albanians from violence and ethnic cleansing at the hands of Serbian forces, NATO conducted some thousands of bombing raids on Kosovo and surrounding areas over several months. Prior to this, the Security Council had adopted three resolutions concerning the deteriorating military and humanitarian situation.

Resolution 1160 condemned the use of excessive force by Serbian police, imposed an arms embargo and expressed support for a political solution based on the territorial integrity of the FRY with greater autonomy for the Kosovar Albanians.[12] Resolution 1199 recognized the deteriorating humanitarian situation, one that had already resulted in numerous civilian casualties and the displacement of 230,000 people from their homes. It declared the situation as one constituting a threat to international peace and security and, acting under Chapter VII, demanded a ceasefire and action to improve the humanitarian position.[13] In Resolution 1203, finally, the Council decided that should the concrete measures it had demanded not be taken, and should Serbia not comply with the terms of the agreement reached with NATO and the OSCE to end the hostilities, it would *consider* further action and additional measures to maintain or restore peace and stability in the region.[14] These resolutions fell far short of authorizing any international military intervention to achieve that aim.

Certainly, the Council had determined that the deterioration of the situation in Kosovo threatened regional peace and security. And, in Resolution 1199, the Council had demanded an immediate end to the hostilities and the maintenance of a ceasefire. It had also demanded immediate measures to avert an imminent catastrophe. Not once, however,

---

[11] See Simma, 1999; Kritsiotis, 2000; Chinkin, 2000; Bilder, 2008; Gray, 2008, p 39.
[12] SC Res 1160 (31 March 1998).   [13] SC Res 1199 (23 September 1998).
[14] SC Res 1203 (24 October 1998).

had the Council authorized the use of force by the international community in order to advance these objectives. Instead, in Kosovo, NATO took upon itself the task of pursuing and achieving them without further reference to the Council.

The bones of NATO's legal argument were straightforward. The Security Council had adopted resolutions under Chapter VII that demanded that the Yugoslavian authorities halt their brutal repression of ethnic Albanians. The authorities had refused to comply with these resolutions and the prior, brokered agreements to which they referred. Consequently, NATO member States presumed unilaterally to act in support of those resolutions by intervening to prevent further violations.

However forcefully legal arguments in favour of the NATO action were put, formidable obstacles remained in the path of their acceptance. The argument that NATO's intervention was implicitly justified as a means of enforcing prior Security Council resolutions again was weak. This was because the wording of the resolutions did not at all appear to authorize any subsequent unilateral military action and it left for the Council's further consideration any decision as what additional measures might be necessary to pursue and enforce its demands (Corten, 2008). Quite apart from this, the idea that a State or group of States could or should act unilaterally to enforce Council resolutions without any subsequent Council involvement or authorization could open the door to opportunistic interventions of any and every kind.[15] Finally, even if it had been accepted prior to Kosovo that the protection of non-derogable human rights had achieved the status of *jus cogens* and therefore obliged the UN to protect them, it by no means followed that the unilateral employment of military force, outside the UN, to secure them had also become part of customary international law (Alston and MacDonald, 2008).

Taking all this into consideration the conclusion of the Independent Commission Report on Kosovo (2000) is apt:

Far from opening up a new era of humanitarian intervention the Kosovo experience seems, to this Commission at least, to teach a valuable lesson of skepticism and caution. Sometimes, and Kosovo is such an instance, the use of military force may become necessary to defend human rights. But the grounds for its use in international law urgently need clarification and the tactics and rules of engagement for its use needs to be improved. Finally, the legitimacy of such use of force will always be controversial, and will remain so, as long as we intervene to protect some people's lives but not others.

III. THE BIRTH OF THE 'RESPONSIBILITY TO PROTECT'

In the decade following Kosovo, there have been no significant instances of humanitarian military interventions in which the international community has engaged. State practice, therefore, has provided no further guidance as to the doctrine's further development in international law. At the same time, however, conceptual and political developments have been quick. These political developments have focused not upon humanitarian intervention per se, but rather on a bold endeavour, by those concerned to prevent mass atrocity

---

[15] See to similar effect the statement by the Permanent Representative of India during Security Council debate, SC/1035 (24 March 1999), p 3 at p 10.

crimes, to craft a new, more thoughtful and more measured doctrine to build upon and at the same time differentiate it from its humanitarian predecessor. In just a few years the idea of humanitarian intervention has been displaced by what has come to be known as the 'responsibility to protect'.

Speaking in an address to the UN General Assembly in 1999, the UN Secretary-General challenged member States to resolve what he saw as the conflict between the principle of non-interference with State sovereignty, embodied in Article 2(4) of the Charter, and the responsibility of the international community to respond to massive human rights violations and ethnic cleansing. He posed what he described as a tragic dilemma. Kofi Annan stated the dilemma as follows:

> To those for whom the greatest threat to the future of the international order is the use of force in the absence of a Security Council mandate, one might ask . . . in the context of Rwanda: if in those dark days and hours leading up to the genocide a coalition of states had been prepared to act in defence of the Tutsi population, but did not receive prompt Security Council authorization, should such a coalition have stood aside and allowed the horror to unfold?

> To those for whom the Kosovo action heralded a new era when States and groups of States can take military action outside the established mechanisms for enforcing international law, one might ask: is there not a danger of such interventions undermining the imperfect, yet resilient, security system created after the Second World War, and of setting dangerous precedents for future interventions without a clear criterion to decide who might invoke these precedents, and in what circumstances?[16]

To steer between the Scylla and Charybdis of the problem, Annan argued that the Security Council must be able to agree on effective action to defend fundamental human rights. He proposed that the core challenge to the Council in the twenty-first century was: 'To forge unity behind the principle that massive and systematic violations of human rights— wherever they may take place—should not be allowed to stand.'[17]

The Secretary-General's call to action met with a mixed and in some quarters hostile response in the General Assembly. Nevertheless, it prompted the Canadian Government, in a singular initiative, to form an international panel of experts, the International Commission on Intervention and State Sovereignty (ICISS), to address the problem thus stated. The Commission consulted widely with governments, non-governmental organizations, inter-governmental organizations, universities and think-tanks. On the basis of these extensive consultations, the Commission produced its final report, *The Responsibility to Protect*.[18] The report radically altered the terms of the ensuing political debate. This it did in three inter-related ways.

First, it re-conceptualized forcible international action in defence of peoples at risk of mass atrocity. The international community would no longer engage in 'humanitarian intervention' but would instead exercise a broader 'responsibility to protect' nations at risk of failure and descent into violence. Secondly, the new approach attributed primary

---

[16] Address by Kofi Annan to the 54th Session of the UN General Assembly, 20 September 1999.
[17] Ibid.
[18] International Commission on Intervention and State Sovereignty (2001), *The Responsibility to Protect: Report of the International Commission on Intervention and State Sovereignty*, Ottawa, International Development Research Centre.

responsibility for taking action to prevent humanitarian disaster upon the sovereign government of the nation in which might occur. Only if and when that responsibility had not been exercised would the larger global community's parallel responsibility to intervene in the national and international interest be engaged. Thirdly, new rules of engagement should be developed to ensure that any such intervention would have the maximum possible opportunity for success (see Acharya, 2002; Evans and Sahnoun, 2002; Thakur, 2006; Bellamy, 2008a).

The Commission asserted, more in hope than expectation given its novelty, that the 'responsibility to protect' reflected an emerging norm of international law and behaviour:

Based on our reading of state practice, Security Council precedent, established norms, guiding principles, and evolving customary international law, the Commission believes that the Charter's strong bias against military intervention is not to be regarded as absolute when decisive action is required on human protection grounds.[19]

As to the vexed question of military intervention, ICISS recommended that it should take place pursuant to authorization by the Security Council and only then after the careful consideration of five criteria of legitimacy. These were that:

- The threatened harm must be serious, ie it must involve genocide, war crimes, crimes against humanity, or ethnic cleansing.
- The primary purpose of the intervention must be to halt the threatened humanitarian catastrophe.
- Military intervention must be adopted only as a measure of last resort.
- The proposed military action must be proportionate to the threat.
- The adverse consequences flowing from the military intervention should clearly be less than the consequences of inaction (see Evans 2008, p 139).

Finally, ICISS developed its conceptual framework by proposing that three different forms of responsibility were engaged. The responsibility to protect should best be exercised initially through prevention. This 'responsibility to prevent' spoke to the need to take every reasonable step to ensure that predicted humanitarian catastrophes would not occur. Preventive strategies such as good governance and human rights, together with international aid and development assistance should be the first to be deployed. Next, 'the responsibility to react' emphasized that in the exercise of its preventive role, the international community should always prefer non-forcible measures, such as diplomatic negotiations and economic sanctions, to instigating armed intervention. Once a crisis had been averted, whether militarily or otherwise, a 'responsibility to rebuild' would be assumed. In this, the international community would involve itself in peacekeeping, economic and social reconstruction and other similar developmental initiatives.

The central thrust of the report, then, was upon the prevention of conflict through a range of non-military measures that would likely entail significant transfers of wealth, expertise and opportunity from developed to developing countries. It would involve taking Third World development seriously (see Byers, 2005, p 111). Only once such measures had failed to avert an anticipated humanitarian crisis would more coercive means be considered.

---

[19] Ibid, p 16.

IV. THE 2005 WORLD SUMMIT

A. TOWARDS THE 2005 WORLD SUMMIT

Three years after ICISS had reported, its recommendations received powerful endorsement from the Secretary-General's High-Level Panel on Threats, Challenges and Change (HLP). The Panel adopted the conceptual framework embodied in the idea of the 'responsibility to protect'. It favoured the ICISS's conclusion that any such responsibility should be exercised only with the endorsement of the Security Council. And it incorporated, with some minor alterations, the legitimacy criteria that had been set down in the original report.[20]

Addressing the relevant legal issues, the Panel observed that the Charter reaffirmed a fundamental faith in human rights but did not do much to protect them. Article 2(7) prohibits intervention in matters which are essentially within the jurisdiction of any State. Nevertheless, the Panel asserted that the principle of non-intervention embodied in that Article could not be used to shield nations from the consequences of state-sponsored genocidal acts or other atrocities. These should properly be considered as threats to international peace and security under Article 24 and, as such, might with legal justification provoke a response from the Security Council.

We endorse the emerging norm that there is a collective international responsibility to protect, exercisable by the Security Council, authorizing military intervention as a last resort, in the event of genocide and other large-scale killing, ethnic cleansing or serious violations of international humanitarian law which sovereign governments have proved powerless or unwilling to prevent.[21]

Taking his lead from the Panel, the Secretary-General recommended that the World Leaders' Summit in 2005 adopt the 'responsibility to protect'.[22] Even so, it was unclear whether his recommendation would survive the exhaustive and exhausting negotiations that would occur in six months preceding the Summit. The principal line of objection was clear. Some States would argue strongly in favour of the international community's entitlement to intervene in the face of genocide, crimes against humanity and other mass atrocities committed by a State. Others, however, would maintain that the Security Council was prohibited legally from authorizing coercive action against sovereign nations in relation to any matter that occurred within their borders. As the Permanent Representative of Algeria put the matter in an early discussion on the Secretary-General's report:

...interference can occur with the consent of the State concerned...we do not deny that the United Nations has the right and duty to help suffering humanity. But we remain extremely sensitive to any undermining of our sovereignty, not only because sovereignty is our last

---

[20] *A More Secure World: Our Shared Responsibility*, the Report of the High-Level Panel on Threats, Challenges and Change, UN Document A/59/565, 2004.

[21] Ibid; and for an analysis of the assertion see Corten, 2008, p 127.

[22] *In Larger Freedom: Towards Development, Security and Human Rights for All*, Report of the Secretary-General, UN Document A/59/2005, 2005, p 35.

defence against the rules of an unequal world, but because we are not taking part in the decision making process of the Security Council…[23]

Generally speaking, the Western Europe and Others Group (WEOG) nations supported the inclusion of a resolution in favour of the responsibility to protect in the World Summit outcome document. The United States, however, had significant reservations. A powerful bloc in the Non-Aligned Movement (NAM) either opposed its inclusion or sought significant amendments to the basic principles that had been set down. Several Latin American nations also expressed their disquiet. The most interesting and crucial aspect of these pre-summit discussions was the strong support for the doctrine provided by the nations of Africa. In a sense, this was not surprising. It has been in Africa—perhaps more than in any other region of the world—that mass violations of human rights of the kind sought to be prevented here, have occurred. African nations had first-hand, or near-hand, experience of the atrocities and consequent human suffering with which the doctrine was concerned and an intimate and devastating knowledge of the consequences of both State and international failure.[24] In this context, the Tanzanian President had made the case plainly:

We must now stop misusing the principles of sovereignty and non-interference in the internal affairs of states to mark incidences of poor governance and unacceptable human rights abuses…In the aftermath of the genocide in Rwanda, and in light of the massive influx of refugees in the Great Lakes Region, it is inevitable to conclude that the principle of non-intervention in the internal affairs of a state can no longer find unqualified, absolute legitimacy…Governments must first be held responsible for the life and welfare of their people. But, there must also be common agreed rules and benchmarks that would trigger collective action through our regional organizations and the United Nations against governments that commit unacceptable human rights abuses.[25]

B. THE WORLD SUMMIT RESOLUTION

Under heavy pressure to adopt some form of the 'responsibility to protect' formula, diplomatic representatives in New York haggled into the last week before the Summit to try to find the words that might permit a compromise text to go to the world's leaders for endorsement.[26] After frenzied last minute negotiations, the final text was concluded. It was hedged with qualifications and therefore weaker than that which had been proposed in the ICISS and High-Level Panel reports. Nevertheless, the very fact that the concept and principle had been agreed to at the World Summit represented a substantial success. The concluded wording was as follows:

138. Each individual State has the responsibility to protect its populations from genocide, war crimes, ethnic cleansing and crimes against humanity. This responsibility entails the

[23] Abdallah Baali, Permanent Representative of Algeria, Statement to the Informal Thematic Consultations of the General Assembly to Discuss the Four Clusters Contained in the Secretary-General's Report 'In Larger Freedom', Cluster III: Freedom to Live in Dignity, 19 April 2005.

[24] For that reason the African Union had previously inserted a provision embodying a doctrine resembling the responsibility to protect into its Constitutive Act. See Article 4(h).

[25] President of Tanzania, Benjamin Mkapa, Address to the First Summit of the International Conference of the Great Lakes, Dar-es-Salaam, November 2004.

[26] As to the General Assembly Debate prior to the World Summit see Bellamy, 2008a; Zifcak 2009, Ch 6.

prevention of such crimes, including their incitement, through appropriate and necessary means. We accept that responsibility and will act in accordance with it...

139. The international community, through the United Nations, also has the responsibility to use appropriate diplomatic, humanitarian and other peaceful means, in accordance with Chapters VI and VII of the Charter, to help protect populations from genocide, war crimes, ethnic cleansing and crimes against humanity. In this context, we are prepared to take collective action, in a timely and decisive manner, through the Security Council, in accordance with the Charter, including Chapter VII, on a case-by-case basis and in cooperation with relevant regional organizations as appropriate, should peaceful means be ineffective... We stress the need for the General Assembly to continue considerations of the responsibility to protect populations from genocide, war crimes, ethnic cleansing and crimes against humanity and its implications, bearing in mind the principles of the Charter and international law. We also intend to commit ourselves, as necessary and appropriate, to helping states build capacity to protect their populations from genocide, war crimes, ethnic cleansing and crimes against humanity and to assisting those which are under stress before crises and conflicts break out.[27]

Despite this success, a close look at the Summit resolution makes it plain that several of the doctrine's underlying principles are likely to be qualified heavily in practice. In the process of negotiating the final text, victory went to those favouring the acceptance of the new doctrine. However, those opposing it, whether absolutely or conditionally, managed to extract substantial concessions. A close reading of the text reveals the following qualifications:

- The crimes in relation to which a responsibility to protect may arise are limited to genocide, war crimes, ethnic cleansing and crimes against humanity. A suggestion from the United States that an additional phrase 'or other major atrocities' be added to avoid further definitional argument was not adopted (see Scheffer, 2009).

- The international community is enjoined in the first instance to exercise its responsibility by using all appropriate diplomatic, humanitarian and other peaceful means in accordance with the Charter. Collective action will be triggered only when such peaceful means are considered to have been inadequate.

- The international community, in its Summit embodiment, has indicated that it is 'prepared to take collective action'. Following from an American recommendation, the words 'we recognize our shared responsibility to take collective action' were removed.

- Collective action by the international community must be authorized by the Security Council in accordance with the terms of Chapter VII of the Charter. The idea, referred to briefly by the High-Level Panel, that there may be certain circumstances in which intervention may be countenanced without such authorization did not make its way into the text.

- No criteria of legitimacy are set down. Instead, the international community, through the United Nations, will determine on a 'case-by-case' basis whether collective action to defend populations from criminal activities is required. This was a late insertion, at the behest of the United States and China.

---

[27] 2005 World Summit Outcome, UN Doc. A/60/L.1.

- Collective action under Chapter VII will be considered only where national authorities 'manifestly fail to protect their populations' from the relevant crimes. This is a standard considerably higher than that initially suggested.

- A recommended constraint—that the permanent members of the Security Council should refrain from exercising the veto in cases of genocide, war crimes, ethnic cleansing and crimes against humanity—was rejected.

There is no doubt that the formal recognition of the new doctrine of the responsibility to protect by the world's political leadership stood as one of the principal achievements of the World Summit. And for such a doctrine to achieve consensus agreement within five years of its first formulation is almost unprecedented. However, as is plain from this analysis of the resolution's text, there remains ample room for argument as to its meaning, standing, and exercise (Focarelli, 2008).

V. POST WORLD SUMMIT RECOGNITION OF THE DOCTRINE

Since the World Summit, the most significant development with respect to the responsibility to protect has been its recognition by the Security Council. In the context of a debate upon the protection of civilians in armed conflict, the Security Council approved Resolution 1674 dealing with all aspects of that question, including the promotion of economic growth, poverty eradication, national reconciliation, good governance, democracy, the rule of law and the protection of fundamental human rights.[28] This resolution reaffirmed 'the provisions of paragraphs 138 and 139 of the 2005 World Summit Outcome Document regarding the responsibility to protect populations from genocide, war crimes, ethnic cleansing and crimes against humanity'. Apart from the normative importance of this reaffirmation, the adoption of the resolution marked the first occasion upon which the Security Council acknowledged expressly that its role may extend not just to the prevention of threats to international peace and security but also to the cessation of mass atrocities taking place within State borders.[29]

Soon after, without any further elaboration of the doctrine, the Security Council invoked the new norm for the first time—in relation to the situation in Darfur. In Resolution 1706, the Council resolved, among other things, to deploy a UN peacekeeping force in Darfur and sought the consent of the Sudanese Government to do so.[30] In its preliminaries, the Resolution recalled Resolution 1674 and its endorsement of the terms of the World Summit Outcome in this respect. It reaffirmed the Council's strong commitment to the sovereignty, unity, independence and territorial integrity of Sudan but made clear its view that the nation's sovereignty would not be adversely affected by the transition to a UN force devoted to the cause of peace.

---

[28] SC Res 1674 (28 April 2006).

[29] The Security Council recognized and approved the 'responsibility to protect', again in a more recent resolution with respect to the protection of civilians in armed conflict: see SC Res 1894 (11 November 2009).

[30] SC Res 1704 (25 August 2006).

A. THE SECRETARY-GENERAL'S ELABORATION OF THE RESPONSIBILITY TO PROTECT

The resolutions with respect to the responsibility to protect, although adopted by consensus, were highly general in nature and much work remained to be done to put flesh on their bones. To assist with this task Ban Ki-moon appointed Professor Edward Luck to be his special adviser on the subject and Luck went to work to make the doctrine comprehensible and concrete. The product was the Secretary-General's report to the General Assembly on the implementation of the responsibility to protect which was tabled in January 2009.[31]

The report was a detailed encapsulation and explication of the new doctrine's principal parameters. It drew heavily on the work of ICISS and the High-Level Panel but its cast was much more pragmatic. The report made clear that Kofi Annan's successor was also committed to the doctrine. In elaborating upon it, a three-pillar approach to its implementation was proposed.

In the first, the nation in which a humanitarian catastrophe is in prospect must assume responsibility for taking timely and appropriate preventative measures. These may include intensive diplomatic steps to mediate impending conflict, the adoption of anti-corruption strategies, the early prosecution of those engaging in violent activity, the promotion of human rights and efforts to establish more effective governance.[32] The second pillar involves a calibrated reaction by the international community. Here, concerted and directed assistance in the form of development aid, foreign investment, technical assistance, economic incentives, rapid police responsiveness, and more general capacity building will be crucial. Under the third pillar, these measures may be supplemented initially by 'soft' coercion which may include international fact finding, the deployment of peacekeepers, the imposition of arms embargoes, the application of diplomatic and economic sanctions and the creation of safe-havens and no-fly zones. Then, when all else has failed, the Security Council may authorize military intervention as the measure of last resort.

The Secretary-General sought to clarify certain issues about which there had been considerable confusion or dissension since the World Summit. He made clear that the responsibility to protect applies only in relation cases of genocide, war crimes, crimes against humanity and ethnic cleansing. It does not detract from existing international commitments under international humanitarian law, human rights law or refugee law. Collective action in the use of force must be undertaken with the authority of the Security Council and in accordance with Chapter VII of the Charter. The responsibility to protect provides no support, therefore, for unilateral military interventions. The doctrine is to be distinguished from 'humanitarian intervention'. Humanitarian intervention, the report said, posed a false choice between either standing by in the face of catastrophe or deploying coercive military force to protect populations that were threatened. The responsibility to protect seeks to overcome this binary divide by recasting sovereignty as responsibility and then defining in some detail what the respective duties and obligations of nations and the international community to prevent humanitarian disaster should be.

---

[31] Report of the Secretary-General, *Implementing the Responsibility to Protect*, UN Doc. A/63/677; and see further Luck, 2009.

[32] On prevention, see Bellamy, 2008b.

B. THE GENERAL ASSEMBLY'S 2009 DEBATE

In his report, the Secretary-General had urged the UN General Assembly to consider and endorse his report. This was a course not without risk. In the four years between the World Summit and the report, there had been strongly conflicting opinions expressed by UN member States as to the doctrine's standing, relevance, and acceptability.[33] Among nations that supported it, there had been widespread anxiety that its reintroduction into discussion in the General Assembly might well result in its substantial dilution or even abandonment. After six months of wrangling, however, the President of the General Assembly finally agreed to hold an informal interactive dialogue on the Secretary-General's report in late July 2009.

The proceedings began controversially when the Assembly President distributed a concept note to member States prior to the dialogue outlining his reservations with respect to R2P.[34] In this note, the President argued that it had no binding status in international law, that there had been no genuine agreement as to its terms, and that it was not the absence of such a doctrine that had impeded necessary intervention to prevent humanitarian disaster. Instead it had been the unrepresentative composition of the Security Council, the inappropriate use of the veto and a lack of political will that had impeded action. National sovereignty, he concluded, demanded that no external military intervention into the exclusively domestic affairs of a State should be either contemplated or permitted.

Soon after this faltering start, however, it became apparent that the President's intervention had been neither appreciated nor influential. To the surprise of most observers, member States expressed substantial concordance with the Secretary-General's report. Ninety-four States took part in the dialogue and their views were representative of approximately 180 of the Assembly's 192 members. A very clear majority supported the terms of the World Summit resolutions and backed the Secretary-General's three-pillar approach to their implementation. It was highly significant that many powerful States outside the P-5, which had previously expressed substantial doubt about the merits of the doctrine, now chose to provide cautious support for it. Nations such as Brazil, South Africa, Chile, India, Egypt, and Algeria each moderated their previously skeptical positions.[35] Clear dissentients numbered only four of those nations that took part.[36] The most important matters that emerged from the Assembly's deliberations may be summarized as follows.[37]

1. Matters on which nations agreed

Most member States stated unequivocally that the dialogue should not be devoted to a renegotiation of the World Summit Outcome resolutions. They made plain their intention

---

[33] See for example, in the General Assembly debate on the 'Protection of Civilians in Conflict', S/PV.6066, 14 January 2009.

[34] Office of the President of the General Assembly, *Concept Note on the Responsibility to Protect Populations from Genocide, War Crimes, Crimes against Humanity and Ethnic Cleansing*, 16 July 2009.

[35] See for example, Statement by H.E. Hardeep Singh Puri, Permanent Representative of India to the United Nations at the General Assembly Plenary Meeting on Implementing the Responsibility to Protect, 24 July 2009.

[36] These were Venezuela, Cuba, Sudan, and Nicaragua.

[37] See also The Global Centre for the Responsibility to Protect (2009), *Implementing the Responsibility to Protect: the 2009 General Assembly Debate, an Assessment*, August 2009; The International Coalition for the Responsibility to Protect (2009), *Report on the General Assembly Plenary Debate on the Responsibility to Protect*, September 2009.

to move forward to a practical understanding of the resolutions rather than to re-open the debate on whether or not the responsibility to protect should be recognized or acted upon. The member States' re-affirmation of the resolutions made plain, however, that they regarded them as expressly limited by their terms. All agreed, therefore, that the responsibility to protect would apply only in situations that involved the commission of genocide, war crimes, crimes against humanity, or ethnic cleansing. Any expansion of the doctrine to cover the consequences of climate change, cyclones, counter-terrorism, external aggression, or internal repression was roundly rejected.

Member States almost without exception welcomed the three-pillar conception outlined in the Secretary-General's report. In this respect, there was concordance with the general principle that sovereignty should be defined as responsibility and that the first responsibility of sovereign States should be to protect the rights and interests of their peoples. Pillar 1 encapsulated that understanding. Member States regarded Pillar 2 as the most novel part of the doctrine. The idea that the international community should and would provide early assistance to States at risk of failure was one that was greeted with approval. Unsurprisingly, Pillar 3 was the subject of most contention. Nevertheless, even here there appeared to be agreement that where one of the four defined crimes was either in prospect or in the course of commission, the international community had a responsibility to intervene, but, in the case of military intervention, only if Security Council authorization had been previously been obtained.

A substantial body of member States seemed willing to endorse the idea that the commission of mass atrocities within a single member State may nevertheless, and depending on the specific circumstances, be regarded as constituting a threat to international peace and security.[38] In such a case, the operation of Chapters VI and VII of the UN Charter could be attracted.

2. Matters in relation to which there was continuing concern

The position of State sovereignty in relation to the responsibility to protect was the subject of continuing contention. Several States declared that sovereignty was inviolable and that nothing in the new doctrine should be permitted to undermine that inviolability.[39] Even in relation to the four crimes specified, therefore, they argued that international intervention should be countenanced only if requested by the State concerned. At the other end of the spectrum were member States which strongly supported the doctrine and who, therefore, were willing to countenance some compromise to sovereignty in the interests of avoiding atrocity. None, however, endorsed unilateral intervention and all agreed that military intercession could proceed only if the Security Council authorized it.[40]

Developing nations forcefully expressed their concern that the doctrine may be used selectively and in particular by more powerful States as a means to interfere with the rights and interests of the less powerful. To counter that possibility many developing countries insisted that decisions as to whether a nation had failed in its responsibility to protect its

---

[38] See Statement on behalf of the European Union by H.E. Mr Anders Liden, Permanent Representative of Sweden to the United Nations, at the General Assembly Dialogue on the Responsibility to Protect, 23 July, 2009.

[39] These States included, for example, Cuba, Iran, Sudan, North Korea, Pakistan, and Nicaragua.

[40] These States included the Netherlands, Austria, Australia, New Zealand, Canada, Denmark, and Costa Rica.

own people had to be taken without fear or favour and with the application of identifiable and identical standards.[41] The Security Council's manifest failure to take action with respect to the Israeli invasion of Gaza in January 2009 was commonly cited as an example of the double standards that may and can apply.

Member States put competing views with respect to the Security Council's recommended role as the arbiter of Pillar 3 interventions. There was agreement that the Council should exercise that role but disagreement about the extent to which, if at all, the General Assembly should also play some part. Many nations, including especially those who aspired to permanent membership of the Council, conditioned their support on comprehensive Security Council reform. Still more expressed the view that the P-5 should agree voluntarily to refrain from the use of the veto in situations in which action with respect to genocide, war crimes, crimes against humanity, and ethnic cleansing was the subject of Council consideration. The P-5 made no contribution as to the question.

3. Matters in relation to which further clarification was required

Many States expressed uncertainty as to the circumstances in which international aid, assistance, or intervention should be triggered. The World Summit resolutions stated, for example that the international community was committed to helping States build capacity to protect their populations from the commission of mass atrocities, as necessary and appropriate. At what stage, then, and under what circumstances would the criteria of necessity and appropriateness properly be engaged? Similarly, the international community had stated its preparedness to take collective action through the Security Council should peaceful means be inadequate and national authorities manifestly fail to protect their populations. Member States expressed the view that the phrase 'manifestly fail to protect their populations' was vague and therefore provided very uncertain guidance as to when the Security Council should consider any consequential action.

Several nations observed that the World Summit resolutions referred to mass atrocities consequent upon State failure. Nothing there appeared referable, however, to crises which had been caused by the actions of non-State actors. In what circumstances the international community might intervene to prevent atrocities at the hands of such actors, therefore, was a matter placed on the table for further deliberation.

Finally, member States seemed quite unclear as to the standing of the responsibility to protect in international law. In line with the opinions expressed by the High-Level Panel and the former Secretary-General in his report to the World Summit, some member States were sufficiently confident to declare the doctrine either as a norm of international law or at least as a principle that was near to maturing into such a norm. Others, however, regarded the doctrine not as legal but as political. It represented a political commitment by most nations to take steps to prevent mass atrocities but brought with it no specific legal content or obligation. Still others maintained that the responsibility to protect could more than adequately be contained within and elaborated from the existing law of the United Nations Charter. Those opposed to the advance of the doctrine made clear their view that it had no legal standing whatever. In the final section of this chapter, therefore, I take a closer look at the legal standing of the doctrine by way of further clarification.

---

[41] See for example, the Statement by Vanu Gopala Menon, Permanent Representative of Singapore at the General Assembly Dialogue on the Responsibility to Protect, 24 July 2009.

VI. THE RESPONSIBILITY TO PROTECT AS INTERNATIONAL LAW

Politically speaking, it is fair to say that there has been a progressive convergence of opinion amongst member States of the United Nations that they bear a responsibility individually and collectively to protect their peoples from the commission of mass atrocity crimes. Concentrating in particular on those elements of the doctrine that appear to have achieved the support of most UN member States, its present parameters as elaborated in debate prior to the World Summit and at the 2009 General Assembly Debate may be summarized in the following terms. It appears to be agreed that:

1. The primary responsibility for protecting its peoples from the commission of mass atrocity crimes rests with the sovereign nation within which such crimes are at risk of being committed.

2. The mass atrocity crimes with which the responsibility is concerned are limited to genocide, war crimes, crimes against humanity, and ethnic cleansing.

3. The responsibility of the international community with respect to the prevention of and protection against such crimes is engaged only when it appears that the sovereign nation concerned may be unable to prevent the escalation of civil strife so as to avert the danger of the defined international crimes being committed.

4. In that instance, the international community's primary and preventative responsibility is to provide aid, expertise, resources and other similar forms of assistance so as to build the affected nation's capacity to deal with an impending humanitarian crisis.

5. Where, however, it becomes apparent that a State has manifestly failed to exercise its sovereign obligations, and where the international community's assistance has proven ineffective, the primary responsibility to prevent or protect against the commission of the international crimes shifts from the State to the international community.

6. The international community in exercising this responsibility may, on a case-by-case basis, take coercive measures to achieve the objective of maintaining or restoring peace and security. Such measures may, as a last resort, include internationally mandated military intervention.

7. These coercive measures, however, may be adopted and authorized only by the UN Security Council acting in accordance with its powers under Chapter VI and Chapter VII of the UN Charter. Unilateral humanitarian intervention is impermissible.

8. Where the international community has intervened in the domestic affairs of a nation whether militarily or in some other coercive manner, it assumes a further responsibility upon the restoration of peace and security to facilitate and assist with peacekeeping, peacebuilding, and other forms of national reconstruction.

It should be apparent that these heads of agreement are in the nature of a joint *political* commitment. The question remains, then, as to whether any segment of this common acknowledgment and understanding has become part of or is reflected in international law. With one or two minor caveats, the answer would appear to be no.

The responsibility to protect is not embodied in any treaty.[42] Consequently, the most likely way that it could be considered as a norm of international law would be by way of its acceptance as part of customary international law. A doctrine or principle will form part of customary law if two broad conditions are met. First, it must be a matter of State practice and that practice must be recurrent and widely observed. Secondly, there must be a conviction among nations that the practice is sufficiently consistent and of sufficiently general application as to be regarded as a compulsory rule.[43] In other words, it should come to be understood that the practice is dictated by international law (*opinio juris*).

Applying these conditions to the responsibility to protect it is evident immediately that State practice in conformity with the doctrine is almost non-existent. The doctrine was conceived only in 2002 and no nation or international organization has legitimately claimed to have acted in accordance with its terms since that time.[44] It could be argued that relevant State practice occurred in the context of humanitarian intervention that preceded that concept's recent reconceptualization as the responsibility to protect. Given, however, that the new doctrine's sponsors have been at great pains to distinguish it from humanitarian intervention, and that many in the General Assembly have repudiated the latter, the argument cannot be accorded much weight.[45]

Still, there is one current of thought that suggests that the existence of well-settled State practice may not be absolutely critical in the formation of customary rules. So for example, within the framework of international humanitarian law, an imperative of moral behaviour and the dangers attendant upon its abuse may be such as to make the observance of a particular rule of war absolutely necessary even prior to recurrent State practice having been established. In this case, 'the laws of humanity' and the 'dictates of public conscience' are put on the same footing as State practice in the formation of international law (Cassese, 2005, pp 160–161). In that context it might reasonably be accepted that the principle that States have an individual and collective responsibility to protect their peoples from genocide, war crimes, crimes against humanity and ethnic cleansing is a 'law of humanity' of a similar kind and standing. But that is still far from confirming that every one of the core elements of the doctrine has similar force and effect. Quite apart from anything else, the principle is capable of achievement by very diverse means of which the key components comprising the responsibility to protect are but one.

The second condition to be met is that there should be a mutual conviction among nations that the doctrine or principle in question should have the character of a binding

---

[42] The doctrine, however, is closely related to the objectives and provisions of of existing international treaties including for example, the International Convention on the Prevention and Punishment of the Crime of Genocide (1948), the Geneva Conventions (1949), and the Rome Statute of the International Criminal Court (2002). See further Barbour and Gorlick, 2008.

[43] *North Sea Continental Shelf, Judgment, ICJ Reports 1969*, p 3, para 77.

[44] It has been claimed that Kofi Annan's mediation in the tribal conflict following Kenya's recent election is an example of R2P at work. It seems no different, however, to traditional international mediation of a kind that has been known and exercised many times before.

[45] See Ban Ki-Moon, 'Responsible Sovereignty: International Co-operation for a Changed World', Speech delivered in Berlin, 15 July 2008; Sahnoun, M, 'Africa: Uphold Continent's Contribution to Human Rights', *AllAfrica.com*, 21 July 2009; Evans, G, Statement delivered to the UN General Assembly Interactive Thematic Dialogue on the Responsibility to Protect, 23 July 2009.

rule of law. In the present case, the existence of this 'opinio juris' is difficult to discern or to justify. Certainly, the responsibility to protect has been the subject of consideration, elaboration, and recommendation by international commissions of stature. It has been embodied, though not without considerable prior political division, in the resolutions of the most important Summit of World leaders held in the past decade. It has been referred to and endorsed in general terms in subsequent Security Council resolutions. And at least in relation to its core components, it generated a surprising measure of acceptance at the most recent General Assembly debate.

Yet the idea that it might constitute a legal rule that binds nations to it by common consent is not a position that has yet been reached. This point is illustrated clearly when one considers the content of the recent General Assembly debate. As previously noted member States in the debate had significantly differing views as to the legal standing of the doctrine. Such diverse conceptions do not inspire confidence that a customary rule accepted in common as binding is anywhere near maturity. It is also the case, regrettably, that many nations participating in the debate and addressing international law had but a thin conception of its nature and requirements. Among those that did, the most considered view expressed was that the responsibility to protect was a doctrine primarily of a political rather than legal character. The Brazilian position is illustrative:

In Brazil's view, (the responsibility to protect) is not a principle proper, much less a novel legal prescription. Rather it is a powerful political call for all States to abide by legal obligations already set forth in the Charter, in relevant human rights conventions and international humanitarian law...[46]

It is clear, further, that although the doctrine's core elements as enumerated above are the subject of substantial political agreement, there remain significant areas of concern with respect to its operational scope and important matters as to its meaning and effect that require much further clarification. Until these doubts and concerns have been satisfactorily addressed, it is difficult to contend that in this instance some new, generally accepted legal norm governing the conduct of nations has come to fruition.

Finally, it should be noted that the recent General Assembly deliberation was in the form of an informal interactive dialogue. In other words, it was a session designed to encourage States to express their views with respect to the responsibility to protect without any necessary anticipation that there would be any concrete outcome. As to an outcome, some nations argued that a resolution providing a firm re-endorsement of the doctrine as expressed in the World Summit Outcome document would be appropriate and constructive. Others argued that neither an endorsement nor a resolution should be put. In the end, a weak procedural resolution went forward noting (amended from welcoming) the Secretary-General's report and recommending that the General Assembly continue to consider the matter.[47] Plainly, then, the thought that the interactive dialogue may produce some confirmation of the existence of a new binding rule of international law was far from most delegates' minds.

---

[46] Statement by H.E. Maria Luiza Ribiero Viotti, Permanent Representative of Brazil, at the General Assembly informal dialogue on the Responsibility to Protect, 23 July 2009.
[47] A/Res/63/608.

On this basis the best that can be said is that core of the doctrine previously delineated constitutes but a fledgling rule of international customary law. It has quite some considerable way to go, however, before it can be regarded as having been adopted in practice and obtained the requisite international acceptance to be considered as fully formed.

One final legal matter should be considered. As explained at the commencement of this chapter, the UN Charter's provisions, and in particular the terms of Articles 2(4) and 2(7), have proven exceptionally difficult to reconcile with any doctrine of external intervention in a nation's domestic affairs. Article 2(7) relevantly provides however that this principle of non-interference is not to prejudice the application of enforcement measures under Chapter VII. Chapter VII enforcement measures may be pursued where the Security Council has determined the existence of any threat to the peace, breach of the peace or act of aggression. It has generally been assumed that any such threat must be to international peace and security as Chapter VII measures are authorized in accordance with Articles 41 and 42 only to restore international peace and security.

However, the sole arbiter of whether there exists a threat to international peace and security remains the Security Council itself. And in recent years it has become apparent that the Council is now more willing than it has been previously to determine the existence of such a threat even where conflict or strife is taking place entirely within the boundaries of one State. Generally speaking the Council has made such a determination only where, for example, the 'international dimension' is constituted by some cross-boundary ramification of the primary conflict, such as massive consequential refugee flows. In the past two decades or so, however, it has seemed prepared to go one step further where a humanitarian disaster is in prospect and declare a threat even where cross-boundary consequences have not plainly been in evidence. The Council's resolutions in relation to Somalia, Bosnia-Herzegovina, and Rwanda provide relevant examples.[48] In the absence of a power of judicial review of Security Council decision-making, the Council will continue to have very considerable flexibility when determining whether threats to international peace and security are present. And, further, it does not need to give reasons for its decisions.

The broad exercise of Security Council discretion in humanitarian cases suggests that there may be one further, legally recognized way in which the competing demands of sovereignty and the prevention of atrocity may eventually be capable of reconciliation within the framework of the UN Charter itself. On the basis of the emerging trend, it could over time become standard Security Council practice to interpret the threshold requirement of a threat to peace and security as existent in situations of humanitarian crisis, even where the crisis is contained entirely within a State. Were this practice to become recurrent and internationally recognized as necessary and appropriate, a new customary rule, as embodied in Council practice, may eventually crystallize as part of international law.[49] This rule would allow for an exception to Article 2(4) by sanctioning intervention by the international community to prevent a humanitarian catastrophe occurring entirely within the boundaries of one State pursuant, first, to a preliminary determination by the

---

[48] See SC Res. 794 (3 December 1992: Somalia); SC Res 770 (13 August 1992: Bosnia-Herzegovina); SC Res 929 (22 June 1994: Rwanda). See also Chesterman, 2001, pp 140–151.

[49] In an analogous case, the International Court of Justice determined in an Advisory Opinion that the United Nations had international legal personality partly based on the practice of the United Nations in concluding international conventions. *See Reparation for Injuries Suffered in the Service of the United Nations, Advisory Opinion, ICJ Reports 1949*, p 174.

Security Council under Article 39 of a threat to international peace and security followed, secondly, by authorized international intervention in accordance with Articles 41 and 42.

This is not to suggest that international law has arrived at such a normative recognition yet. Security Council practice in the relevant respect has neither solidified nor attained a requisite measure of consistency (see McClean, 2008). And to achieve recognition as institutional custom, an enormous stretch in the interpretation of the language of the Charter would still be required. It is apparent, however, from the General Assembly dialogue that many more nations than previously have seemed willing to countenance wider Security Council discretion in cases of humanitarian need. And it is not too great a leap to suggest that in an increasingly interconnected and interdependent world, few conflicts or catastrophes remain entirely local in their ramifications.

Consequently, the promise of eventual legal recognition is there and with it the foundation so necessary for accepting the international legitimacy of the responsibility to protect may in time become more firmly established.

REFERENCES

ACHARYA, A (2002), 'Redefining the Dilemmas of Humanitarian Intervention', 56 *Australian Journal of International Affairs* 373.

ALSTON, P and MacDONALD, E (2008), 'Sovereignty, Human Rights, Security: Armed Intervention and the Foundational Problems of International Law' in Alston, P and MacDonald, E (eds), *Human Rights, Intervention, and the Use of Force* (Oxford: Oxford University Press), p 1.

BARBOUR, B and GORLICK, B (2008), 'Embracing the Responsibility to Protect: A Repertoire of Measures including Asylum for Potential Victims, 13 *Journal of Conflict and Security Law* 541.

BELLAMY, A (2008a), *The Responsibility to Protect* (Cambridge: Polity Press).

—— (2008b), 'The Responsibility to Protect and Conflict Prevention', 14 *Global Governance* 135.

BILDER, R (2008), 'The Implications of Kosovo for International Human Rights Law', in Alston, P and MacDonald, E (eds) (2008), *Human Rights, Intervention and the Use of Force* (Oxford: Oxford University Press), p 139.

BYERS, M (2005), *War Law* (London: Atlantic Books).

CASSESE, A (1999), 'Follow Up: Forcible Humanitarian Countermeasures and *opinio necessitas*', 10 *EJIL* 791.

—— (2005), *International Law*, (Oxford, Oxford University Press).

CHESTERMAN, S (2001), *Just War or Just Peace: Humanitarian Intervention and International Law* (Oxford: Oxford University Press).

CHINKIN, C (2000), 'The Legality of NATO Action in the Former Republic of Yugoslavia (FRY) under International Law', 49 *ICLQ* 910.

CORTEN, O (2008), 'Human Rights and Collective Security: Is there an Emerging Right to Humanitarian Intervention?' in Alston, P and MacDonald, E (eds), *Human Rights, Intervention, and the Use of Force* (Oxford: Oxford University Press), p 87.

EVANS, G (2006), 'From Humanitarian Intervention to the Responsibility to Protect', 24 *Wisconsin International Law Journal* 703.

EVANS, G (2008), *The Responsibility to Protect: Ending Mass Atrocity Crimes Once and for All* (Washington: The Brookings Institution Press).

———(2009), 'The Responsibility to Protect: From and Idea to an International Norm', in Cooper, R and Volnov, J, *Responsibility to Protect: Global Compact for the 21st Century* (New York: Palgrave MacMillan), p 15.

——— and SAHNOUN, M (2002), 'The Responsibility to Protect', 81 *Foreign Affairs* 99.

FABRI, H (2008), 'Human Rights and State Sovereignty: Have the Boundaries been Significantly Redrawn?', in Alston, P and MacDonald, E (eds) (2008), *Human Rights, Intervention, and the Use of Force* (Oxford: Oxford University Press), p 33.

FARER, T (2003), 'Humanitarian Intervention Before and After 9/11: Legality and Legitimacy', in Holzgrefe, J and Keohane, R (eds), *Humanitarian Intervention* (Cambridge: Cambridge University Press), p 53.

FOCARELLI, C (2008), 'The Responsibility to Protect and Humanitarian Intervention: Too many Ambiguities for a Working Doctrine', 13 *Journal of Conflict and Security Law* 191.

FRANCK, T (2003), 'Interpretation and Change in the Law of Humanitarian Intervention', in Holzgrefe, J and Keohane, R (eds), *Humanitarian Intervention* (Cambridge: Cambridge University Press), p 204.

GAZZINI, T (2005), *The Changing Rules on the Use of Force in International Law* (Manchester: Manchester University Press).

GRAY, C (2008), *International Law and the Use of Force,* 3rd edn (Oxford: Oxford University Press).

HOLZGREFE, J (2003), 'The Humanitarian Intervention Debate', in Holzgrefe, J and Keohane, R (eds), *Humanitarian Intervention* (Cambridge: Cambridge University Press), p 53.

INDEPENDENT INTERNATIONAL COMMISSION ON KOSOVO (2000), *Kosovo Report, Conflict, International Response, Lessons Learned* (Oxford: Oxford University Press).

JANSSEN, D (2008), 'Humanitarian Intervention and the Prevention of Genocide', 10 *Journal of Genocide Research* 289.

KRITSIOTIS, D (2000), 'The Kosovo Crisis and NATO's Application of Armed Force against the FRY', 49 *ICLQ* 330.

LUCK, E (2009), 'Sovereignty, Choice and the Responsibility to Protect', 1 *Global Responsibility to Protect* 1.

McCLEAN, E (2008), 'The Responsibility to Protect: The Role of International Human Rights Law', 13 *Journal of Conflict and Security Law* 135.

PETERS, A (2009), 'Humanity as the Alpha and Omega of Sovereignty', 20 *EJIL* 513.

SCHEFFER, D (2009), 'Atrocity Crimes Framing the Responsibility to Protect' in Cooper, R and Voiner Kohler, J (eds), *Responsibility to Protect: The Global Moral Compact for the 21st Century* (London: Palgrave Macmillan), p 77.

SIMMA, B (1999), 'NATO, the UN and the Use of Force: Legal Aspects' (1999) 10 *EJIL* 1.

THAKUR, R (2006), *The United Nations, Peace and Security* (Cambridge, Cambridge University Press), p 250.

TRIGGS, G (2006), *International Law: Contemporary Principles and Practices* (Lexis Nexis Butterworths), p 598.

WEISS, T (2007), *Humanitarian Intervention* (Cambridge: Polity Press), p 40.

WELSH, J (2004), 'Conclusion: The Evolution of Humanitarian Intervention in International Society', in Welsh, J (ed) *Humanitarian Intervention and International Relations* (Oxford: Oxford University Press), 176.

WHEELER, N (2004), 'The Humanitarian Responsibilities of Sovereignty: Explaining the Development of a New Norm of Military Intervention for Humanitarian Purposes in International Society', in Welsh, J (ed), *Humanitarian Intervention and International Relations* (Oxford: Oxford University Press), p 32.

ZIFCAK, S (2009), *United Nations Reform: Heading North or South?* (London: Routledge).

FURTHER READING

INTERNATIONAL COMMISSION ON INTERVENTION AND STATE SOVEREIGNTY (2001), *The Responsibility to Protect: Report of the International Commission on Intervention and State Sovereignty*, Ottawa, International Development Research Centre. The Canadian Commission Report in which the Responsibility to Protect was first conceptualized.

REPORT OF THE SECRETARY-GENERAL, *Implementing the Responsibility to Protect*, UN Doc A/63/677 (2009). The UN Secretary-General's most recent elaboration of the core elements of the Responsibility to Protect.

ALSTON, P and MACDONALD, E (2008), (eds), *Human Rights, Intervention, and the Use of Force* (Oxford: Oxford University Press). A fine contemporary overview of the inter-relationship between sovereignty, armed intervention and human rights under international law.

BELLAMY, A (2008), *The Responsibility to Protect* (Cambridge: Polity Press). A clear introduction to the idea and practice of the Responsibility to Protect from a political science perspective.

CHESTERMAN, S (2001), *Just War or Just Peace: Humanitarian Intervention and International Law* (Oxford: Oxford University Press). The most comprehensive overview of the law with respect to humanitarian intervention.

EVANS, G (2008), *The Responsibility to Protect: Ending Mass Atrocity Crimes Once and for All* (Washington: The Brookings Institution Press). The key text in the field written by one of the co-authors of the original Canadian Commission report.

PART VI

RESPONDING TO BREACHES OF INTERNATIONAL OBLIGATIONS

18

COUNTERMEASURES AND SANCTIONS

Nigel White and Ademola Abass

SUMMARY

The issue of enforcement by means of non-forcible measures is one of the least developed areas of international law. Two legal regimes are relatively clear—non-forcible countermeasures taken by States (countermeasures) and non-forcible measures taken by international organizations (sanctions). The manifestation of a restricted doctrine of countermeasures as the modern acceptable form of self-help is considered, along with the partial centralization of coercion in international organizations. The problems within each of these regimes are examined, along with the limitations that have been placed upon their application. The co-existence of countermeasures based on a traditional view of international relations, alongside the post-1945 development of centralized institutional responses, is explored. Moreover, the range of State and institutional practice that seems to lie somewhere between the basic right of a State to take countermeasures to remedy an internationally wrongful act, and the power of international organizations to impose sanctions in certain circumstances, is considered. The legality of the continued use by States of non-forcible reprisals, retorsion, and wider forms of economic coercion is explored, as is the issue of collective countermeasures imposed either multilaterally or institutionally.

I. INTRODUCTION: SELF-HELP IN INTERNATIONAL LAW

Traditionally, States co-exist in a legal system that is essentially consensual. States, no matter their disparities in size or strength, are sovereign and equal. Obligations are accepted by States either in treaty or custom by consent, they are not imposed by any higher authority. In its purest form such a legal condition existed in the eighteenth and nineteenth centuries. This period was one of self-help, in that if a State breached one of its obligations, the victim State(s) of such a breach could take both non-forcible and forcible measures to remedy or to punish that breach. Forcible measures could range from measures short of war, such as armed reprisals,[1] or could take the form of war. War itself could be a relatively minor exchange of fire, even mere confrontation without hostilities, or it could be a full-scale bloody conflict the causes of which could be relatively minor.

Before this period of absolute sovereignty and its accompanying self-help regime of enforcement, theories of natural law argued for a hierarchy of norms within the concept of an international society (Bull, 1992, pp 71–72). Moving forward to the advent of the League of Nations in 1919, created in the aftermath of the manifest failure of the existing system, there emerged structures as well as norms that were again suggestive of a more hierarchical approach. The Covenant of the League of Nations purported to regulate, if not prohibit, war, and the organization it established potentially had weak authority over States. Brierly argued that the League was based on the principles of consensuality and voluntarism (Brierly, 1946, p 92), a view that would suggest that the organization did not upset the pre-existing order. McNair on the other hand thought that the League marked a move away from a system of purely private law between consenting States towards a system of public law (McNair, 1930, p 112) indicating a more vertical system of regulation.

Whatever its nature, the idea of an international organization, with some measure of authority over States, took an even firmer grip on the imagination of States during the Second World War. The United Nations was created in 1945, its Charter containing in Article 2(4) a basic rule prohibiting the threat or use of force in international relations, and creating machinery to promote and restore international peace and security. The prohibition of force, which itself formed a core norm in an emerging corpus of peremptory norms of international law (*jus cogens*) from which States could not derogate, immediately cut back on the type of measures a State could take in response to a breach of international law. Self-help was thus cut down to half its former size by the UN Charter. Though States were still permitted to take forcible action in self-defence in response to an armed attack against them, forcible measures beyond that were prohibited by the new legal regime initiated by the Charter. Though some States and writers have repeatedly tried to resurrect the concept of armed reprisals (Bowett, 1972a) there does not appear to be any general acceptance of an erosion of the statement of law made by member States of the UN in 1970—'States have a duty to refrain from acts of reprisal involving the use of armed force'.[2]

The prohibition in 1945 of forcible measures of self-help left the position of non-forcible measures untouched but at the same time unclear. Clarity was lacking because the doctrines that had emerged over the centuries were inevitably subject to many interpretations. In addition, the UN itself was given significant power to impose on member States obligations to impose non-forcible measures against miscreant member States by virtue of Article 41 of the Charter. The developing Inter-American system of collective security also provided for the application of such measures,[3] a trend that was to be followed by some other regional organizations. A self-help system of non-forcible measures deriving from an earlier period of international relations, had to co-exist with a system of centralized 'sanctions' based on notions of hierarchy and governance. In addition to the uncertainty that existed between the institutional level and the customary level, there was also a lack

---

[1] *Naulilaa* case (1928) 2 *RIAA* 1052.
[2] *Declaration on Principles of International Law concerning Friendly Relations and Co-operation among States in Accordance with the Charter of the United Nations*, UN Res 2625 (XXV) (24 October 1970).
[3] Articles 8, 17, 20 Rio Treaty, 1947, 21 UNTS 77.

of clarity in the relationship between the universal organization (the United Nations) and other organizations. Article 53(1) of the UN Charter seemed to provide that any non-forcible measures taken by regional organizations that amounted to 'enforcement action' would require the authorization of the Security Council.

Certainly the concept of lawful non-forcible measures survived the new world order of the post-1945 period. Article 2(4) of the Charter prohibited the 'threat or use of force', and this was clearly construed as military force (Dinstein, 2005, p 86). State practice in the immediate post-1945 period provided evidence of the continuation of the concept of non-forcible measures. As Elagab states '[r]egardless of whether the conditions of legality had been complied with in each case, the crucial feature was the very fact of such claims being staked at all. This provides a presumption of continuity of counter-measures as a viable mode of redress' (Elagab, 1988, p 38). In the first decade after the UN Charter the US adopted, *inter alia*, measures freezing the assets of China, Bulgaria, Romania, and Hungary. The coinage of the term, countermeasures in the *Air Services Agreement* case of 1978[4] and the codification of countermeasures by the International Law Commission (ILC), culminating in Chapter III of the Articles on State Responsibility of 2001,[5] represent the continuation and development of the concept in international law.

Indeed, despite the proliferation of international institutions since 1945, the ILC was confident in asserting in 2001 that countermeasures are inherent in a decentralized system where 'injured States may seek to vindicate their rights and to restore the legal relationship with the injured State which has been ruptured by' an unlawful act.[6] As noted by Alland—'countermeasures are a mechanism of private justice', the result of which are 'contradictions inherent in a self-assessed (ie, auto-interpreted or auto-appreciated) decentralized policing of an international *ordre public*' (Alland, 2002, p 1223, p 1235). Provost is even more explicit in depicting the weaknesses of such a system when he writes that 'the right of states unilaterally to assess a breach by another state and to validate what would otherwise be an illegal act has the potential of significantly destabilizing international relations' (Provost, 2002, p xv). Nevertheless, as has been stated above, a totally decentralized system no longer exists (but see Zoller, 1984, p xiii). While injured States are entitled to take certain non-forcible actions within a bilateral context against States responsible for a breach of international law, sanctions imposed by the UN and other international organizations create a vertical relationship between the organization and the implementing States (Gowlland-Debbas, 2001, p 2). Essentially the horizontal system of self-help has been supplemented by the creation of organization(s) with the competence to create vertical relationships. After 1945, and arguably in a weaker sense, after 1919 (but see Brierly, 1932, p 68), there no longer exists a pure system of self-help, and this has affected practice as shall be seen. States wanting to take measures against a responsible State may go to international bodies for authority/legitimacy, indeed it could be argued that they ought to do this when they are not the direct victims of the unlawful act.

---

[4] *Air Services Agreement* case (1978), 54 ILR 303.
[5] See Report of the International Law Commission on the work of its 53rd Session, UN Doc A/56/10, adopted 9 August 2001. The Articles and the Commentary are found in Crawford, 2002. The Articles will be referred to as ARSIWA (Articles on Responsibility of States for Internationally Wrongful Acts). The references to the Commentary are to Crawford's text.
[6] Crawford, 2002, p 281.

II. COUNTERMEASURES

A. DEFINITION OF COUNTERMEASURES

It is true to say that since the first use of the term in 1978 by the arbitral tribunal in the *Air Services Agreement* case, international lawyers have used the term countermeasures to indicate non-forcible measures. However, the discussion below will illustrate that this has not necessarily clarified the matter, for the related doctrines of retorsion, reprisals (in a non-forcible sense), economic coercion, and economic sanctions remain. In effect, as will be seen, after the ILC Articles of 2001 the concept of countermeasures is a fairly narrow one at one end of a spectrum of non-forcible measures that may be taken in international relations. At the other end of the spectrum are sanctions undertaken by international organizations. In between there is something of a grey area where regulation is rudimentary, indeed, arguably, non-existent. In this section, the focus will be on countermeasures on the grounds that they have become perhaps the most clearly defined type of non-forcible measures, having been the subject of many years of study by the ILC. The ILC's concept of countermeasures is the one portrayed here, though it must be noted that it may well constitute an example of the ILC progressively developing international law. It should be noted that the ILC's Special Rapporteur on the matter, James Crawford, commented only a few years before the adoption of the Articles that 'at present there are few established legal constraints on non-forcible counter-measures' (Crawford, 1994, p 65). As Bederman suggests 'the central conceptual mission' of the ILC's articles on countermeasures, is 'the search for a polite international society' (Bederman, 2002, p 819). Further he contends that the countermeasures articles represent a 'profound impulse toward social engineering for international relations... imagining a time in international life when unilateral and horizontal means of enforcement through robust self-help will be a thing of the past' (Bederman, 2002, p 831). Nevertheless, while the ILC does purport to define and constrain countermeasures, in so doing it leaves question marks hanging over the legality of a large segment of State practice on wider non-forcible measures.

Countermeasures 'are intrinsically unlawful, but are justified by the alleged failing to which they were a response' (Alland, 2002, p 1221). In its final Articles on State Responsibility of 2001, the ILC defined countermeasures as non-forcible measures taken by an injured State in response to a breach of international law in order to secure the end of the breach and, if necessary, reparation.[7] Non-forcible countermeasures may only be taken in response to an internationally wrongful act, and only against the State responsible for that act.[8] If such measures are taken without fulfilling these conditions, they themselves will constitute an internationally wrongful act, giving rise to State responsibility and possible countermeasures. According to the ILC, countermeasures are limited to the temporary non-performance of one or some of the international obligations of the injured State owed to the responsible State.[9] Cassese's summation is perhaps stronger than that of the ILC, but useful nonetheless. He states that 'in the event of a breach of international

---

[7] Ibid, p 281.
[8] Article 49(1) ARSIWA. See also *Gabčíkovo-Nagymaros Project (Hungary/Slovakia), Judgment, ICJ Reports 1997*, p 7, paras 83–85.
[9] Article 49(2)(3) ARSIWA.

law, the injured State is legally entitled to disregard an international obligation owed to the delinquent State' (Cassese, 2005, p 302). In ILC terms, countermeasures are not intended to be punishment for illegal acts but as 'an instrument for achieving compliance with the obligations of the responsible State' (but see Alland, 2002, pp 1226–1228). Countermeasures are taken 'as a form of inducement, not punishment'. The ILC's definition does not restrict States taking countermeasures to suspension of performance of the same or very similar obligation. Countermeasures though are more likely to accord with the conditions of proportionality and necessity if they are so taken. Such measures which correspond to the obligation breached by the responsible State are sometimes called 'reciprocal countermeasures'.[10]

The suspension or temporary non-performance of a treaty obligation, quite often the suspension of a trade agreement, and the freezing of the assets of a State under international obligations, are primary examples of countermeasures.[11] In ILC terms the paradigmatic case is the *US-French Air Services Arbitration* of 1978. This case concerned the application of the bilateral air services agreement that existed between the two countries. France had objected, as being incompatible with the treaty, to the so-called 'change of gauge' or change of type of aircraft by PanAm on its flight from the US to Paris via London. The French authorities prevented PanAm passengers from disembarking in Paris. By the time of arbitration the US had initiated (but had not implemented) measures which would have prohibited certain French flights to the US. The arbitral tribunal found that the change of gauge by PanAm was permitted under the treaty and that the US retaliatory measures were permissible countermeasures, which were not disproportionate to the violative actions taken by France. The arbitral tribunal stated '[i]f a situation arises, which in one State's view, results in the violation of an international obligation by another State, the first State is entitled, within the limits set by general rules of international law, pertaining to the use of armed force, to affirm its rights through "countermeasures".'[12] Of course, the case reveals the inherent problem with countermeasures, indeed with measures of self-help more generally, in that the crucial element, the determination of the initial wrongful act, is a subjective one. Both France and the US believed that they were acting in accordance with international law—the US in terms of treaty compliance and France in terms of taking countermeasures. It turns out that the US was correct so that the French measures were not lawful but a breach of treaty justifying US countermeasures. While the doctrine of countermeasures looks neat on paper its very messy in practice.

Countermeasures are distinct from suspension or termination of treaty obligations due to material breach within the meaning of Article 60 of the 1969 Vienna Convention on the Law of Treaties (VCLT). Measures taken under Article 60 affect the substantive legal obligations of the State parties while countermeasures are concerned with the responsibility that has arisen as a result of the breach. Their aim is to rectify the legal relationship and their application should always be temporary.[13] Article 60 of the VCLT also deals with 'material breach' of the treaty, countermeasures may be taken in response to any breach, as long as they are proportionate. Article 60 specifies a procedure for suspension or termination of treaty obligations for material breach, which differs from the procedures required to take countermeasures. Action under Article 60 of the VCLT must be confined to the

10 Crawford, 2002, pp 282–286.
11 Ibid, p 286.
12 *Air Services Agreement* case (1978) 54 ILR 303 at p 337.
13 Crawford, 2002, p 282.

treaty being breached, while countermeasures are not so confined (Elagab, 1988, p 164). Article 60 of the VCLT provides for the possibility of termination of the treaty, or obliga-tion, while, in principle, countermeasures are only temporary.

Given the growth of international organizations possessing international legal per-sonality, with rights and duties under international law, there appears no reason why countermeasures cannot be taken by States or other organizations against international organizations that have committed internationally wrongful acts, or by organizations that are the victims of internationally wrongful acts. In principle countermeasures must be available to any entity possessing international legal personality, though in the current state of international legal development such actors are generally confined to States and (most) inter-governmental organizations. The ILC's work on the responsibility of inter-national organizations, started in 2002, made good progress until it came to the issue of countermeasures in its 2008 report.[14] Though certain draft articles on countermeasures are posited in the report,[15] there is clearly some disagreement among the members of the ILC as to the value of including articles on countermeasures by and against international organizations.[16] Most of the suggested draft articles are similar in content to those gov-erning State responsibility, but one of the contentious draft articles states that 'where an international organization is responsible for an internationally wrongful act, an injured member of that organization may take countermeasures against the organization only if it is not inconsistent with the rules of the same organization'.[17] The desire is to pre-vent member States precipitously taking unilateral countermeasures against the organ-ization for perceived internationally wrongful or *ultra vires* acts. Given the problems the UN has been faced with in the past with France and the Soviet Union withholding their peacekeeping contributions on the basis of the alleged *ultra vires* actions of the General Assembly in mandating peacekeeping forces in the Middle East and the Congo (leading to an advisory opinion in 1962), and of the withholding practice of US in the 1980s and 1990s, there is clearly a problem in recognizing that member States can take counter-measures against organizations. Arguably though, member States that believe they are victims of unlawful actions by the organization (for example being subjected to economic sanctions) have very limited options to challenge the legality of such measures (with no access to the International Court for instance). Without giving member States means of holding organizations to account, arguably they should have the right to take counter-measures against the organization (O'Connell, 2008, pp 267, 271). Organizations, on the other hand, normally possess a number of means of controlling their members—expul-sion, suspension, and sometimes other non-forcible measures such as sanctions. The ILC itself was uncertain whether institutional (specifically Security Council) sanctions could be regarded themselves as countermeasures. Some members thought that they were differ-ent since they were coercive and were directed at issues of peace and security, while others thought that in certain instances they could be viewed as countermeasures as they were directed at terminating internationally wrongful acts.[18] Clearly further work and clarifi-cation will be needed to avoid the position where additional uncertainty is introduced into the relationship between an organization and its member States.

---

[14] ILC Report of Sixtieth Session (2008), A/63/10.   [15] Ibid, paras 141–144.
[16] Ibid, paras 148, 163.   [17] Ibid, para 141.
[18] Ibid, para 152.

B. REPRISALS AND RETORSION

The ILC's definition of countermeasures has internal coherency. But its failure to address the related concepts of non-forcible reprisals and retorsion leaves the impression that other types of non-forcible action taken by States (as opposed to institutions) remain unregulated, and therefore arguably permitted.[19] This means that in reality while States can engage in countermeasures that are quite specific, they may also be able to engage in wider non-forcible measures. The aim of these measures may be to punish the responsible State (reprisals) as opposed to inducing it into compliance (countermeasures); or which are not limited to the suspension of international obligations owed to the responsible State (retorsion). On the other hand, it could be argued that this approach, essentially permitting other non-forcible measures to be taken by States makes something of a nonsense of the painstaking process of defining countermeasures. Why spend so many years defining lawful countermeasures, unless it is based on a presumption that wider action by States is unlawful? There has certainly been a move by the ILC in its recent revisions away from conflating countermeasures and reprisals, and countermeasures and sanctions.[20] The separation of these concepts though is not, by itself, concrete evidence that unilateral non-forcible measures, not coming within the ILC's doctrine of countermeasures, are unlawful. This issue will be returned to in particular when looking at the wider concept of economic coercion.

Retorsion is conduct that does not involve the suspension of international obligations owed by the injured State to the responsible State, even though usually taken in response to unlawful acts on the part of the responsible State. 'Acts of retorsion may include the prohibition of or limitations upon normal diplomatic relations or other contacts, embargoes of various kinds or withdrawal of voluntary aid programs'.[21] Countermeasures could take the form of a suspension of a trade agreement; whereas acts of economic retorsion are based on a State's freedom to trade or not to trade (or deal more generally) with other States. 'An act of retorsion is an unfriendly but nevertheless lawful act by the aggrieved party against the wrongdoer. As such retorsion is not circumscribed by the international legal order' (Zoller, 1984, p 5). Some writers, however, see countermeasures as encompassing both non-forcible reprisals and retorsion (Abi-Saab, 2001, p 38, citing Schachter, Virally, and Leban in support). In general Abi-Saab sees them as 'reactions permitted in international law to illegality' (Abi–Saab, 2001, p 37). However, that view was not adopted by the ILC, which, at least in its final Articles, keeps the concepts distinct and only concerns itself with delimiting countermeasures, keeping them apart from retorsion. Furthermore, the ILC, together with the International Court of Justice, distinguish countermeasures from reprisals by saying that countermeasures are instrumental while reprisals are punitive.[22]

Thus measures taken by a State may constitute countermeasures if they arise as a result of the suspension of international obligations owed to the responsible State. If they are not the result of the non-fulfilment of an international obligation owed to the responsible State

---

[19] See 'Lotus', Judgment No 9, 1927, PCIJ, Ser A, No 10 at p 18.

[20] See the writings of earlier ILC Rapporteurs where these terms were used without real distinction; Arangio-Ruiz, 1994, p 21; Ago, 1979, p 47.

[21] Crawford, 2002, p 281.

[22] Gabčíkovo-Nagymaros Project (Hungary/Slovakia), Judgment, ICJ Reports 1997, p 7, paras 83–85.

then they may be acts of retorsion. Whether this means that victim States have freedom to impose sanctions against States that have violated international law will be considered below. At first sight it seems odd that acts of retorsion which could be more damaging than countermeasures may be acceptable but this seems to reflect the under-developed state of international law in this area. It is the case that acts of retorsion, while not governed by a specific bilateral legal relationship between the responsible State and the injured State, are still governed by the limitations of necessity and proportionality, and by general principles of international law, such as those prohibiting intervention or violation of basic human rights norms. Furthermore, if the ILC's doctrine of countermeasures is to make complete sense, retorsion arguably should be viewed as a residual remedy in the case of a State injured by a breach of international law where the injured State does not have any existing specific obligations to the responsible State that it is able to suspend. It may, in these circumstances, take limited proportionate non-forcible measures that are an attempt to remedy that breach.

Cassese defines retorsion as 'any retaliatory act by which a State responds, by an unfriendly act not amounting to a violation of international law, to either (a) a breach of international law or (b) an unfriendly act, by another State'. He gives examples of the breaking off of diplomatic relations, discontinuance or reduction of trade/investment, withholding economic assistance, expulsion of nationals, heavy fiscal duties on goods from the offending State, or strict passport regulations. As can be seen these measures may be much more damaging than the fairly restrictive doctrine of countermeasures. Cassese cites as an example of retorsion the measures adopted since 1989 by the US against Burma for its poor human rights record. The United States suspended Burma's eligibility for trade preferences and export licences for munitions, as well as prohibiting bilateral aid and new investment (Cassese, 2005, p 310). These are not characterized by Cassese as countermeasures for 'aggravated responsibility' (see below), presumably because they were not all in the nature of suspension of obligations owed by the US to Burma, but neither do they really seem to be acts of retorsion as suggested by him. Burma's violations of international law were not directed against the US, nor could they be seen as unfriendly actions towards the US. This example of State practice and its analysis illustrates both doctrinal confusion, as well as the fact that practice does not seem to neatly fit any of the categories mentioned. The US actions against Burma were non-forcible measures (not purely countermeasures as defined by the ILC) taken on behalf of the international community (but not authorized by an international organization) to enforce community norms. The legality of this type of action will be returned to.

C. LIMITATIONS UPON COUNTERMEASURES AND OTHER NON-FORCIBLE MEASURES TAKEN BY STATES

The doctrine of countermeasures as defined by the ILC is specific. First of all the response to an unlawful act can only be the suspension of an international obligation owed to the responsible State. This distinguishes countermeasures from reprisals and retorsion. Further, there are numerous other limitations governing the form and extent of that suspension. Whether some or all of these limitations are also applicable to acts of retorsion and reprisal is unclear though it may be suggested that a number are. These will be mentioned below. Of course this assumes that such actions are by themselves lawful, an issue that will be returned to.

Countermeasures must not be forcible. This clearly applies to other types of non-forcible measures.[23] Furthermore, 'anticipatory non-forcible counter-measures are unlawful; since by definition they precede actual occurrence of breach' (Elagab, 1988, p 63). The same principle must be applicable to all non-forcible measures taken by States, since they are based on the occurrence of unlawful or unfriendly acts. Countermeasures should be directed against the responsible State and not third party States.[24] This too seems applicable to other non-forcible measures.

Countermeasures are temporary and should, whenever possible, be reversible so the future legal relations between victim State and responsible State can be restored.[25] If the measures taken punish the responsible State by inflicting irreparable damage on it, then they are not countermeasures.[26] Such punitive measures would appear to be non-forcible reprisals, the legality of which is not discussed by the ILC, but that body's movement away from the notion of punishment as the rationale for countermeasures, indicates uncertainty about the legality of reprisals. This is supported by the International Court's statement in the *Gabčíkovo* case that the purpose of countermeasures is to 'induce the wrongdoing State to comply with its obligations under international law, and that the measures must therefore be reversible'.[27] It is noticeable that James Crawford, then Rapporteur, stated that the 'international community has moved away from the classical terminology of reprisals and towards the notion of countermeasures as temporary, reversible steps' (Crawford, 2001, p 66). As with many changes in international law it is not possible to draw a clear line between the demise of one concept or principle and the emergence of another; the transition is gradual.

Countermeasures must be proportionate. According to the ILC, they 'must be commensurate with the injury suffered, taking account of the gravity of the internationally wrongful act and the rights in question'.[28] Disproportionate countermeasures give rise to the responsibility of the State taking them.[29] Taking a different approach Franck asserts that the response must be proportionate to the initial unlawful act, equivalent to the biblical eye for an eye, tooth for a tooth approach (Franck, 2008, pp 715, 763). However, there appears to be difficulties in both the approaches of the ILC and Franck. The issue ought not to be one of proportionality to the unlawful act or the injury it causes, because this would suggest that countermeasures are taken to punish the responsible State, thus confusing countermeasures with reprisals. As Cassese states 'in current international law the purpose of countermeasures must be seen . . . in impelling the offender to discontinue its wrongful conduct or to make reparation for it. If this is so, the proportionality must be

---

[23] Article 50(1)(a), ARSIWA; Article 2(4) UN Charter; *Declaration on Principles of International Law Concerning Friendly Relations and Co-operation among States in Accordance with the Charter of the United Nations*, UN Res 2625 (XXV) (24 October 1970).

[24] Article 49(1)(2), ARSIWA.   [25] Articles 49(2)(3), 53, ARSIWA.

[26] Crawford, 2002, p 287.

[27] *Gabčíkovo-Nagymaros Project (Hungary/Slovakia), Judgment, ICJ Reports 1997*, p 7, paras 56–57.

[28] Article 51, ARSIWA.

[29] Crawford, 2002, p 294. See *Naulilaa* case (1928) 2 *RIAA* 1052 (disproportionate); *Gabčíkovo-Nagymaros Project (Hungary/Slovakia), Judgment, ICJ Reports 1997*, p 7, para 87 (disproportionate); *Air Services Agreement* case (1978), 54 ILR 303 (proportionate).

appraised by establishing whether the countermeasure is such as to obtain this purpose'. This should mean that in certain cases a weak State may be subject to countermeasures that are quantitatively less than the injury suffered by a powerful State, if the measures are sufficient to bring an end to the illegal act (Cassese, 2005, p 306). The International Court has found that non-forcible countermeasures were disproportionate in the *Gabčíkovo-Nagymaros* case, though it provided little by way of explanation of why Czechoslovakia's assumption of control of part of the Danube in response to Hungary's violation of a treaty obliging it to undertake construction to aid shipping, energy development and flood control on the section of the Danube shared by both countries, was disproportionate.[30] This adds to the impression of indeterminacy in the principle of proportionality despite its elevation to a general principle of international law (Franck, 2008, p 716).

According to the ILC, countermeasures must not violate basic obligations under international law (namely those prohibiting the threat or use of force, protecting fundamental human rights,[31] concerning obligations of a humanitarian character), and those arising under *jus cogens*. Countermeasures should not affect dispute resolution procedures that are applicable. Countermeasures cannot be taken to impair consular or diplomatic inviolability.[32] Diplomatic law provides its own legal regime for dealing with illicit activities by members of diplomatic or consular missions.[33] 'If diplomatic or consular personnel could be targeted by way of countermeasures, they would in effect constitute resident hostages against perceived wrongs of the sending State, undermining the institution of diplomatic and consular relations'.[34] Countermeasures must follow an unsatisfied demand by the injured State that the responsible State comply with its international obligation(s). The injured State must also notify the responsible State that it intends to take countermeasures and offer to negotiate, except in the case of urgent countermeasures necessary to preserve the injured State's rights (eg, temporary staying orders or the temporary freezing of assets).[35] Further they must be suspended if the wrongful act has ceased and the dispute has been submitted to a tribunal with binding authority.[36]

The above limitations are arguably applicable to other more controversial claims to non-forcible measures, with the exception of the suspension of diplomatic relations that seems to be an accepted act of retorsion in international relations. This seems to contradict the 'resident hostages' argument mentioned above. This is illustrative of the problem in defining countermeasures without addressing the issue of retorsion. In general Elagab states that in the case of a 'self-contained regime' where such a regime 'possesses its own mechanism for redressing the wrongful conduct, countermeasures should not be imposed' (Elagab, 1988, p 218). He refers to diplomatic law, but the same can be said of the WTO's procedures for dispute settlement, followed, if necessary by a form of

---

[30] *Gabčíkovo-Nagymaros Project (Hungary/Slovakia), Judgment, ICJ Reports 1997*, p 7, para 87. See also Scobbie, 2004, p 1129 for discussion as to whether Israel's construction of a security wall is better analysed as a purported non-forcible countermeasure rather than the purported exercise of the right of self-defence, dismissed by the International Court in *Legal Consequences of the Construction of a Wall in the Occupied Palestinian Territory, ICJ Reports 2004*, p 136 at paras 139–140.

[31] Especially the non-derogable rights contained in the International Covenants—Crawford, 2002, p 289. See also CESCR General Comment No 8 (1997), UN Doc E/C.12/1997/8, 5 December 1997, paras 1 and 5.

[32] Article 50(1)(2) ARSIWA.

[33] *United States Diplomatic and Consular Staff in Tehran, Judgment, ICJ Reports 1980*, p 3, paras 84–86.

[34] Crawford, 2002, pp 292–293.   [35] Ibid, p 299.

[36] ARSIWA, Article 52.

institutionalized countermeasures. Although they look like countermeasures, they are not measures imposed by dint of custom but by reason of the GATT treaty regime. They are thus similar in appearance to countermeasures but the source of the rights and duties is the special treaty regime, and the limitations may be different (but see Gazzini, 2006, pp 737–741).

Thus, countermeasures may be excluded by special rules (eg, a treaty which states that its provisions cannot be suspended)[37] or a regime which dictates the way in which measures are taken by victim States (the primary example is the WTO).[38] Countermeasures are thus said to be 'residual' remedies,[39] reflecting the fact States may choose to move away from a decentralized system of self-help by developing treaty regimes with their own processes of enforcement.

D. COUNTERMEASURES AND THIRD STATES

We turn now to the question of whether countermeasures as defined by the ILC can be taken by States other than the State directly injured. The issue of whether third States can also take other forms of non-forcible measures will be returned to in the next section. According to the ILC, countermeasures are normally taken by a State injured by an internationally wrongful act of another State. However, responsibility may be invoked by States other than the injured State acting in the collective interest.[40] Responsibility is not invoked by these third States as a result of injury to themselves but as a result of breach of an obligation to a group of States of which it is a member—obligations *erga omnes partes* (eg, regional environmental or human rights regimes), or to the international community as a whole—obligations *erga omnes* (eg, laws prohibiting genocide, aggression, slavery, racial discrimination, self-determination).[41]

However, the ILC is careful to distinguish third States invoking responsibility from them taking countermeasures. The latter issue is left much more open. Such third States can demand cessation and performance in the interests of the injured States or the beneficiaries of the obligation breached.[42] 'The question is to what extent these States may legitimately assert a right to react against unremedied breaches',[43] *viz* by taking countermeasures against the responsible State. One problem in taking collective countermeasures is that of proportionality, though it is difficult to prove a violation of this principle if the aim is to stop a breach of an obligation owed *erga omnes*. In the absence of institutional sanctions imposed for example by the UN Security Council under Chapter VII of the Charter,[44] the legality of such measures is in doubt, though there seems to be some State and institutional practice to support the proposition that such measures are allowed. However, practice is inconsistent, making the drawing of any conclusions as to *opinio juris* extremely difficult if not impossible.

---

[37] EU treaties provide for their own system of enforcement—Crawford, 2002, p 291.

[38] The WTO system requires authorization from the Dispute Settlement Body before a member can take measures against another—Crawford, 2002, p 291.

[39] Crawford, 2002, p 283.   [40] Ibid, p 276.

[41] Article 48(1) ARSIWA. See *Barcelona Traction, Light and Power Company, Limited, Second Phase, Judgment, ICJ Reports 1970*, p 3, paras 33–34; *East Timor (Portugal v Australia), Judgment, ICJ Reports 1995*, p 90, para 29.

[42] Article 48(2) ARSIWA.   [43] Crawford, 2002, p 302.   [44] Ibid.

Further, it is inaccurate to portray such 'collective' countermeasures as a replacement for centralized collective action through an international organization. The term 'collective countermeasures' 'gives the illusion of concerted action when in reality such collective countermeasures are really individual initiatives—even though there is more than one such initiative at the same time' (Alland, 2002, p 1222). In addition, the subjective assessments of States as to whether to impose such countermeasures undermines the enforcement of these crucial norms (Alland, 2002, p 1237). However, it is true to say that to expect international institutions such as the UN Security Council to replace this subjective assessment with something more objective when considering whether to impose non-forcible measures under Chapter VII of the UN Charter would, in reality, 'be replacing one subjectivity (of states) by another (of the Security Council)' (Klein, 2002, p 1249). It is thus premature to argue that the UN Security Council's sanctioning machinery has, or indeed should, replace a system of collective countermeasures even though that system is very weak. In reality there currently exist two weak systems of non-forcible sanctions, one decentralized and one (partly) centralized, for the enforcement of community norms.

Indeed, the practice coming from the decentralized system mentioned in its commentary by the ILC leads it to conclude that 'the current state of international law on countermeasures taken in the general or collective interest is uncertain. State practice is sparse and involves a limited number of States. At present there appears to be no clearly recognized entitlement of [third] States…to take countermeasures in the collective interest'.[45] Hence Article 54 of the ILC Articles states that a third State's right to take 'lawful' measures is not prejudiced by any of its other provision on countermeasures. What are lawful measures in this context is an issue that is, in effect, left open (Klein, 2002, pp 1253–1255; but see Alland, 2002, p 1233). Bederman's summary of the ILC's position on collective countermeasures characterizes it as the 'only possible political solution' was 'to defer debate to another day and to allow customary international lawmaking processes to elaborate any conditions on the use of collective countermeasures' (Bederman, 2002, p 828).

The ILC[46] mentions the US prohibition in 1978 of export of goods and technology to Uganda and all imports from Uganda in response to alleged genocide by the government of Uganda. This certainly appears to be a response to a breach of an obligation owed *erga omnes*, but it did not only concern the suspension of US treaty obligations, and therefore goes beyond countermeasures as defined by the ILC. Again, as with the case of Burma above, they appear to be unilateral non-forcible measures, in effect sanctions, imposed to enforce community norms. The ILC also refers to measures taken by Western States against Poland and the Soviet Union in 1981 in response to internal repression by the Polish government. Measures included suspension of treaty landing rights for scheduled civilian aircraft. These actions seemed to take the form of countermeasures but were they a response to a breach of an obligation owed *erga omnes*? It is still difficult, though not impossible, to argue for a right to democracy in the twenty-first century, but in 1981 such an argument was mainly a political, not legal, one. The US countermeasures in the form of the suspension of treaty landing rights against South African airlines in 1986 seem to be

---

[45] Ibid, p 305.   [46] Ibid, pp 302–304.

a clearer example given the odium attached to the system of apartheid, and its categorization as a crime against humanity.

The examples cited by the ILC of non-forcible measures imposed by regional organizations, mainly the EC, illustrates the even greater legal confusion when the analysis of such measures is elevated from the purely bilateral. In 1982 the EC, along with Australia, Canada, and New Zealand adopted trade sanctions against Argentina in response to its invasion of the Falklands. Before the GATT, the EC justified these as measures taken by the 'Community and its Member States' on the basis of their 'inherent rights', meaning the right of self-defence (Zoller, 1984, p 105). In 1990 (before the UN Security Council imposed sanctions) the EC and US imposed trade sanctions and froze Iraqi assets in response to Iraq's invasion of Kuwait. In both of these episodes the non-forcible measures were in response to a breach of an obligation owed *erga omnes* (aggression) but they seemed to extend beyond mere countermeasures to take the form of multilateral economic sanctions. In 1998, in response to the crimes against humanity being committed in Kosovo, the EC imposed a flight ban and froze Yugoslav assets in response to the humanitarian crisis in Kosovo. In some countries the flight ban was a product of the suspension of treaty rights. The suspension of treaty rights and the freezing of assets seem to be clear examples of countermeasures undertaken in response to a breach of a fundamental norm. Nevertheless, the EC does not limit itself to clear countermeasures in other instances. In response to violence and human rights violations that marred the run-up to the Presidential elections in Zimbabwe in March 2002, the EU imposed a travel ban, a freeze on financial assets, and an arms embargo. The Commonwealth, on the other hand, simply suspended Zimbabwe from membership, a power that is purely institutional. Both institutional responses do show, however, that there is practice that suggests that denial of democracy could now be seen as a breach of an obligation owed *erga omnes*. It is too early to state that this has crystallized into a rule of customary law given the uncertainty about the legal status of third party countermeasures.

What the above examples show is that State and institutional practice is confused in a number of ways. First the wrongful acts involved are not always clearly breaches of obligations owed *erga omnes*. Secondly, non-forcible measures, especially trade sanctions are not always a product of non-performance of existing obligations. Thirdly, some of the practice is institutional rather than by individual States, though the line between them is not clear. Zoller expresses doubts about the imposition of sanctions by regional organizations, in the sense of whether they are actually deploying sanctions as international legal persons, or whether, in reality 'the organization acts less as an organization than as a collectivity of the members states as a whole. When countermeasures are undertaken under these circumstances, it is legally hazardous to consider that they can genuinely be attributed to the organization as such' (Zoller, 1984, p 104). Zoller views the EC measures taken against Argentina in 1982 following its invasion of the Falklands, and against the Soviet Union in 1981 following the imposition of martial law in Poland, as a product of political cooperation by States, despite the fact that the measures against Argentina were imposed by a regulation adopted under Article 113 of the EEC Treaty (Zoller, 1984, pp 104–105).

Crawford casts further doubts on the role in international law of obligations *erga omnes*. The ICJ inspired the concept in the *Barcelona Traction* case but in a dictum wholly inapplicable to the case. When the Court was faced in the *Second South West Africa*[47] and the *East Timor* cases with concrete arguments based on *erga omnes*, it shied away from the application of the concept (Crawford, 2001, p 64). This may indicate doubts about whether collective measures taken outside the UN, by other organizations or third States, can constitute lawful countermeasures. In reality they are a modern form of non-forcible measure or sanction that are outside the narrowly defined countermeasures regime. They are in essence, in the grey area between the doctrine of countermeasures as defined by the ILC, and the imposition of centralized sanctions.

If an analogy is drawn with the use of force in international relations, there is clear legality at each end of a spectrum, which has the unilateral rights of States to take forceful action in self-defence at one end, and the use of force taken under Security Council authority at the other. In between these two poles we have lack of clarity. For example, actions in collective defence blur into actions taken under UN authority, as in the cases of Korea in 1950 and Kuwait in 1990. Furthermore, action is taken by regional organizations to deal with threats to the peace without any clear UN authority, for example NATO's bombing of the FRY in 1999 and ECOWAS's involvement in Liberia in the early 1990s. Moving to the sphere of non-forcible measures a similar clouded picture emerges. At one end of the spectrum, unilateral countermeasures as defined by the ILC and the *Air Services* arbitration are clearly lawful. At the other end are non-forcible measures or sanctions adopted by the Security Council, clearly lawful under the UN Charter. In between we have the grey area of measures taken by States which are more coercive or punitive than those allowed under countermeasures, measures taken by third States, and measures taken by other organizations without UN authority.

On the issue of measures taken by third States, these can only be taken in response to a breach of an obligation owed *erga omnes* or *erga omnes partes*. Here there is an overlap with the activities of regional and other organizations. The lack of clarity on the legality of individual third States having such rights leads those States (as the practice of the EC above shows) to seek authority and legitimacy from international organizations. The question whether some, or all, intergovernmental organizations can take such measures will be returned to.

Cassese suggests that in the case of countermeasures taken by third States in response to 'aggravated responsibility' (ie, breach of fundamental rules), then a precondition is that they have sought to bring the matter before an international organization. This can be the UN or a regional organization, with a view to settlement or the adoption of sanctions. This precondition is 'dictated by the inherent nature of this class of responsibility. This responsibility arises out of a gross attack on community or "public" values. The response to the wrongdoing must therefore be as much as possible public and collective'. However, 'if those bodies take no action, or their action has not brought about cessation of the wrong or adequate reparation... all States are empowered to take peaceful countermeasures on an individual basis' (Cassese, 2005, p 274). Although this seems to be a useful suggestion, it is more by way of *de lege ferenda*, given that States do not always report to IGOs first. It also shows that Cassese certainly does not think that regional or indeed individual countermeasures are subject to any need for prior UN *authorization*.

---

[47] *South West Africa, Second Phase, Judgment, ICJ Reports 1966*, p 6.

It certainly seems to be the case that regional organizations have in their practice taken non-forcible measures against member and non-member States without seeking authority from the Security Council. Practice by the OAS against Cuba and Venezuela in the early 1960s and against Haiti in the early 1990s, as well as the measures taken by the EC against Yugoslavia in the 1990s, all without UN authority or preceding UN measures, suggest that the requirement in Article 53 of the UN Charter that 'enforcement action' requires the authorization of the Security Council does not cover non-military, as opposed to military, coercive measures. Of course, if the Security Council goes on to take non-forcible measures under Article 41 of the UN Charter after determining that the situation of 'aggravated responsibility' is also a threat to the peace, the Security Council 'takes over, and individual States may only take action to the extent allowed by the UN Charter (individual or collective self-defence), or recommended, authorized, or decided upon' by the Security Council (Cassese, 2005, p 275). This is achieved by dint of Article 25 of the Charter, which makes Security Council decisions binding on members of the UN. Article 103 gives obligations arising out of the UN Charter pre-eminence over obligations arising under any other international treaty, though it is not clear that this affects member States' customary duties.

III. ECONOMIC COERCION

While there does appear to be a general trend towards seeking collective endorsement of non-forcible measures for breach of community norms, this still leaves the issue of measures imposed unilaterally by States beyond those allowed by the doctrine of countermeasures. Cassese allows for this in relation to breach of community norms as long as organizational avenues have been exhausted, but this still leaves open unilateral actions taken in response to ordinary breaches of international law. As suggested above an application of the doctrine of countermeasures to non-forcible reprisals would indicate their illegality, since the concept of lawful countermeasures does not include the element of punishment. It has been suggested that retorsion, on the other hand, remains as a residual remedy when no countermeasures in the strict sense are available to injured States.

However, while the ILC has defined lawful countermeasures with a high degree of abstraction and in quite a narrow way thereby implicitly excluding reprisals, the reality of international relations seems to be very different. Powerful States do not always appear to be constrained by the niceties of the requirements of countermeasures, they do not simply suspend obligations, they do not simply seek to remedy the illegality, what they seek is coercion and punishment by the application of sanctions often of an economic nature, not countermeasures. While preferring a collective umbrella for these actions if possible, the United States, for example, is prepared to go it alone if necessary. Its sanctions regimes against Iran first imposed in 1979 and those against the Soviet Union in 1980 are cases in point. Neither could be authorized by the Security Council, and so the US imposed them unilaterally. This has led one leading US commentator to state that 'the suggestion that economic sanctions are unlawful unless approved by the Security Council (or by a regional organization such as the OAS) is obsolete'. Furthermore, he states that 'sanctions have become sufficiently common—and often better than the alternatives—to have become tolerated (not to say accepted) as a tool of foreign relations' (Lowenfeld, 2001, p 96). Furthermore US practice includes the imposition of extraterritorial sanctions.[48] Even when the Security Council does agree on sanctions, for instance against North Korea for WMD proliferation,[49] the United States' own non-forcible measures, though largely similar, make no reference to them.[50]

This reflects a pre-1945 view of international law. Writing in 1933 Lauterpacht stated that 'in the absence of explicit conventional obligations, particularly those laid down in commercial treaties, a state is entitled to prevent altogether goods from a foreign state from coming into its territory'. The prevention of trade from reaching the responsible State seemed equally permissible in the pre-Charter period. Further, this is justified on the basis that 'in a community from which war in its technical sense has been eliminated and which has not reached the stage of moral perfection, pacific means of pressure are unavoidable. To prohibit them would mean to court the more radical remedy of war' (Lauterpacht, 1933, pp 130, 140). In a modern sense this still appears to be the case, subject to the requirements of the multilateral regime of the WTO. Non-forcible measures, ranging from counter-measures in the ILC sense to punitive economic sanctions, can be justified under the view that 'restrictions upon the independence of States, cannot be presumed',[51] in other words on the basis of a State's freedom to trade. However, this basic tenet of sovereignty has to be balanced against another tenet—that of non-intervention. The sovereign freedom of a State must always be balanced against the infringement of the sovereignty of other States.

What are the limitations upon non-forcible measures that go beyond the doctrine of countermeasures as defined by the ILC and the *Air Services* case? To take two obvious instances—the Arab oil embargo of 1973–74, and the US embargo against Cuba in place since 1960. These were much more coercive, hurtful, and intrusive than the regime of countermeasures suggested by the ILC. Their motivations were political—to support the Palestinians and to undermine a communist regime respectively—they were not simply about the suspension of obligations in response to an illegal act in order to try and remedy that act.

Suggestions that these measures might breach Article 2(4) of the Charter, since force in that provision remains undefined (Paust and Blaustein, 1974, p 417), seem to be stretching the axioms of treaty interpretation to breaking point. However, they do appear to breach the law as stated in several General Assembly resolutions that seem to prohibit coercive economic intervention that is intended to undermine the territorial integrity or political independence (and arguably other sovereign rights) of the target States.[52] It is interesting to note too that the General Assembly has regularly called for the ending of the US economic, commercial, and financial embargo against Cuba and in so doing, it recalls the principle of non-intervention.[53] The problem is that State practice does not appear in conformity with

---

[48] See US Helms-Burton Act 1996 and the D'Amato-Kennedy Act 1996 discussed in Cassese, 2005, p 305.

[49] See, for example, most recently SC Res 1874 (12 June 2009).

[50] Executive Order 13466, promulgated by President Bush on 26 June 2008, renewed by President Obama on 24 June 2009.

[51] 'Lotus', Judgment No 9, 1927, PCIJ, Ser A, No 10 at p 18.

[52] GA Res 2131 (21 December 1965: Non-intervention); GA Res 2625 (24 October 1970: Friendly Relations); GA Res 3171 (17 December 1973: Permanent Sovereignty over Natural Resources); GA Res 3281 (12 December 1974: Charter of Economic Rights and Duties of States).

[53] Starting with GA Res 47/19 (24 November 1992). For latest see GA Res 63/7 (11 December 2008).

this law (Bowett, 1972b, p 4). Lillich outlines a 'general principle that serious and sustained economic coercion should be accepted as a form of permissible self-help only when it is also compatible with the overall interests of the world community, as manifested in the principles of the UN Charter or in decisions taken or documents promulgated thereunder' (Lillich, 1975, p 366). However, this is suggested by way of *de lege ferenda*. Furthermore, the approach advocated by Lillich and Bowett is that non-forcible, principally economic activity and measures must be presumed to be lawful unless there is evidence of intent by the sanctioning State—'measures not illegal *per se* may become illegal only upon proof of an improper motive or purpose' (Bowett, 1972b, pp 3–7). Given the unclear state of international law, that presumption could equally be replaced by the opposite proposition that such measures that interfere with the sovereign rights of another State are unlawful—that is certainly the General Assembly's view.

In considering the state of customary law on the question of economic coercion, it is necessary to recall the International Court's approach that for a rule to be customary 'the corresponding practice [need not] be in absolute rigorous conformity with the rule'. Further, 'the conduct of States should, in general, be consistent with such rules, and that instances of State conduct inconsistent with a given rule should generally be treated as breaches of that rule, not as indications of the recognition of a new rule'.[54] The Assembly's general pronouncements on the illegality of economic coercion and its attitude to the clearest instance of a continuing punitive embargo (against Cuba) together suggest the illegality of such activities.

However, one must not forget that the International Court also stated that a customary rule is reinforced if the State acting against it actually tries, no matter how disingenuously, to fit its conduct into the rule or its exception.[55] There is no indication that the US views its actions against Cuba, for instance, as unlawful. Initially, the Cuban embargo was justified by the US as a response to Cuban support for insurgencies in other States. However, the underlying justification for the continuation and intensification of the non-forcible measures was made clear by the US in 1991, when it stated that 'every government has a right and responsibility to choose the governments with which it wishes to have commercial and political relations'. It stated further that 'bilateral trade is first and foremost a question of national sovereignty. Governments make decisions to initiate trade and to restore trade based on national interest'[56] (Krinsky and Golove, 1993, pp 37, 135, 233). In other words, the US is stating that is has the clear right to take these non-forcible measures. Such measures are normally economic, hence the term economic coercion, and can include trade, financial, commercial, and arms embargoes, but can include non-economic aspects such as political, diplomatic, sporting, cultural, and educational ties.

Elagab considers State practice and Assembly resolutions and concludes rather ambivalently (but perhaps accurately) that 'there are no rules of international law which categorically pronounce either on the prima-facie legality or prima-facie illegality of economic coercion'. However, he is of the opinion that this does not leave economic coercion unregulated by international law, rather that 'individual rules of international law may be applied to determine the legality of economic conduct on a given occasion'. He seems

[54] *Military and Paramilitary Activities in and Against Nicaragua (Nicaragua v United States of America), Merits, Judgment, ICJ Reports 1986*, p 14, para 186.
[55] Ibid.   [56] UN Press Release USUN 90–(91), 13 November 1991.

to suggest that while non-forcible measures may involve some element of coercion, their regulation is subject to a separate legal regime (Elagab, 1988, pp 212–213), though this regime is subject to limitations including principles of international law. Thus the sanctions against Cuba by the US go far beyond countermeasures (and, indeed, reprisals and retorsion); they amount to coercion. This is then subject to applicable rules of international law, such as *jus cogens* and fundamental human rights standards, and, it is argued here, by the principle of non-intervention, which (despite significant erosion over the years) has a core element, prohibiting coercion of political independence.

If a State wishes to overcome the principle of non-intervention then it has to seek authority from an international organization to impose sanctions, even in the case of breaches of obligations owed *erga omnes*, unless the State confines itself to countermeasures. The UN clearly has the competence to override the domestic jurisdiction limitation in Article 2(7) when acting under Chapter VII of the UN Charter. The issue of whether other international organizations have this competence will be turned to. It is worth noting at this point that the Arab oil embargo of 1973–74 was imposed by the Organization of Arab Oil Producing Countries (OAPEC). Does this institutional involvement cure the illegalities with which the action was otherwise tainted?

IV. SANCTIONS

A. DEFINITION OF SANCTIONS

Non-forcible countermeasures, reprisals, and acts of retorsion clearly continue to exist in international relations. Analysis so far has raised a presumption against the legality of non-forcible measures wider than countermeasures as defined by the *Air Services* case, unless they are imposed for breaches of community norms (*erga omnes*), normally through institutional mechanisms. Reprisals are therefore illegal if they are imposed with the purpose of punishment or coercion of the sovereign will of the target State, and by means that are designed to achieve these ends. Punitive measures and deeper coercion than necessary to force the responsible State to stop its illegal act are best seen as sanctions. Of course, in a general sense all measures designed to enforce the law can be seen as sanctions.

There does exist sanction behind the law. Kelsen sees law as essentially a coercive order, an organization of force, a system or norms providing for sanctions (Kelsen, 1945). Brown-John argues that 'in a juristic sense a sanction is a hyphen between prescribed law and law enforcement, although certainly sanctions tend to be more closely related to enforcement than a prescribed law' (Brown-John, 1975, p 2). But despite the fact that sanctions exist under international law, their nature is less precise compared to sanctions under the domestic system, a disparity that has led to controversy about whether sanction exists at all in international law.

According to Brierly the 'real difference...between municipal and international law is not that one is sanctioned and the other is not, but that in the one the sanctions are organized in a systematic procedure and that in the other they are left indeterminate. The true problem for consideration is therefore not whether we should try to create sanctions for international law, but whether we should try to organize them in a system' (Brierly, 1932, p 68). Kunz speaks in the same language when he writes that 'the alleged absence of sanctions has been and is today the principal argument of those who deny that the rules of international law have the character of legal rules. But general international law *has* sanctions…This is not a unique feature of international law, but it is common to all primitive, highly decentralised legal orders, whether municipal or international. Such legal orders have no central organs either for the making or application of legal rule or for the determination of the delict or the execution of sanctions. All these functions must be left to the members of the legal community; in international law, to the sovereign states. There are no collective but only individual sanctions, carried out by way of self-help; there is no monopoly of force at the disposal of a central law-enforcing organ; there is no distinction between criminal and civil sanctions; the sanctions are based on collective, not individual responsibility' (Kunz, 1960, p 324). While Kunz was writing at the height of the Cold War, with no real practice by the UN on sanctions, in the post-Cold War it might be argued that there now exists a central sanctioning organ—the Security Council.

Schachter attributed the decentralized nature of sanctions under international law to a indifferent attitude in the international legal community to enforcement in general rather than to a formal system of structuring between law and politics. As he observes, 'for a long time compliance and enforcement were on the margins of UN concern. Like somewhat backward members of a family, their place was vaguely recognized, but not much was expected from them. The busy world of UN law-making and law applying carried on pretty much without serious consideration of means of ensuring compliance. Some prominent international lawyers dismissively referred to enforcement as a political matter outside the law. Within UN bodies comfort was taken in the pious hope that governments which acknowledged their legal obligations would carry them out, at least most of the time. It was far from evident that they generally did so in some areas, but measures such as compulsory jurisdiction, mandatory fact finding and coercive sanctions were not considered acceptable or feasible' (Schachter, 1994, pp 9–10). Schachter, though, also points to the progress made on enforcement and compliance in the post-Cold War period.

Sanctions are different from countermeasures. Zoller is clear on this when she states that '[a]s opposed to countermeasures, sanctions are very specific measures. A countermeasure is a measure which has temporary effects and a coercive character, while a sanction has final effects and a punitive character. Moreover, sanctions have an exemplary character directed at other countries which countermeasures do not have' (Zoller, 1984, p 106). For instance, the Security Council through Resolution 1343, imposed sanctions on Liberia in 2001 following its determination that its government was supporting the Revolutionary United Front (RUF), in Sierra Leone, in violation of SC Resolution 1132 which had imposed sanctions against the rebel group. This was the first time the Security Council had imposed sanctions against a country because of its refusal to comply with sanctions against another country (Cortright and Lopez, 2002, p 82). Zoller further argues that '…countermeasures should always be temporary measures, they draw a line between the consequences of unlawful conduct in international law; they underline the difference between them and those measures which impose a final harm on the defaulting party and which could properly be designated by the term "sanctions"'. For this reason, '[c]ountermeasures…have to be placed within reparation and outside punishment' (Zoller, 1984, p 75).

The adoption of unilateral sanctions in the sense used by Zoller is unlawful. To be lawful, sanctions have to be pursued by international organizations, representing the 'centralized mechanisms' hinted at by Brierly (Gowlland-Debbas, 2001, p 6). The issue is not simply how many States were involved in the decision to impose sanctions but rather whether the decision was taken by those States acting under the auspices of an organization competent to do so. The British Royal Institute of International Affairs recognized the element of collectivity when in 1938 it defined sanctions as 'action taken by members of the international community against an infringement, actual or threatened, of the law' (Brown-John, 1975, p 5), though it is uncertain whether 'international community', as used in this context, equates to international organizations for the purpose of establishing the legality of sanctions. Abi-Saab defines sanctions as 'coercive measures taken in execution of a decision of a competent social organ ie an organ legally empowered to act in the name of the society or community that is governed by the legal system'. He distinguishes them sharply from 'coercive measures taken individually by States or group of States outside a determination and a decision by a legally competent social organ', including countermeasures. These 'are manifestations of "self-help" or "private justice", and their legality is confined to the very narrow limits within which "remnants" of "self-help" are still admitted in contemporary international law' (Abi-Saab, 2001, p 32).

Cassese notes the trend in the 'international community is for international bodies, and principally international organizations, to react to gross breaches of international law' by means of sanctions (Cassese, 2005, pp 310–311). This practice became more evident after the end of the Cold War. One common trait of this practice is the utilization of sanctions by international organizations to counter unconstitutional removals of governments among their membership. Witness the use of sanctions by the OAS against the military junta in Haiti in 1992 and similar scenarios with regard to ECOWAS in Liberia (1989–1997) and Sierra Leone (1997–2001). This practice has been further entrenched by the use of sanctions by ECOWAS to reverse an unconstitutional governmental take-over in Togo in February 2005.

While countermeasures are taken by individual States, sanctions are imposed within a collective context, normally an international organization. This development corresponds to the growth in recognition of community interests, representing the 'creation of international institutional responses to violations of such core norms' (Gowlland-Debbas, 2001, p 7). However, the distinction between countermeasures and sanctions should not be read as suggesting that countermeasures can only be taken on an individual basis. Certainly, countermeasures, like sanctions, can also be taken collectively. Elagab recognizes this possibility with regard to countermeasures taken by international institutions although he doubted that there is a 'generalized theory of countermeasures taken by international institutions' (Elagab, 1988, p 1).

Sanctions imposed by the Security Council under Article 41 of the Charter can include full or partial trade, financial, commercial, and arms embargoes, and are therefore, generally, of an economic nature. Schachter states that 'sanctions under Article 41 have come to be seen as quintessential type of international enforcement. The language of Article 41 is broad enough to cover any type of punitive action not involving use of armed force'. (Schachter, 1994, p 12). Gowlland-Debbas argues that although Chapter VII measures imposed by the Security Council were not intended to be restricted to cases of non-compliance with international law, the practice of the Council has moved considerably towards dealing with responsibility of States for breaches of international law (Gowlland-Debbas, 2001, p 9; cf Zoller, 1984, pp 106–107). The determination of Iraq's guilt for its invasion of Kuwait, and the requirement for it to pay compensation is a case in point.[57] Before taking action under Chapter VII, the Council is required by Article 39 of the UN Charter to determine the existence of a 'threat to the peace', 'breach of the peace', or 'act of aggression'. The Council can thus deal with threats to or breaches of the peace that do not constitute internationally wrongful conduct. Aggression would appear to be more a determination of breach of international law, although the history of the definition of aggression shows that there is a reluctance to delimit the Security Council's competence in purely legal terms. Thus it is true to say that sanctions imposed by the UN serve much wider purposes than the concept of unilateral, or even collective, countermeasures as defined by the ILC.

It is relevant to ask whether economic measures taken by regional organizations are subject to the legal regime governing sanctions (as with the UN) or the legal regime governing countermeasures. Economic sanctions based on Chapter VII are to be distinguished from economic countermeasures in that, unlike sanctions, the latter are bilateral, imposed in peacetime, and generally considered to be lawful unless prohibited by national law (Kondoch, 2001, p. 269). Countermeasures are not punitive, they are taken to ensure that the responsible State ceases its violation, and, if applicable, provides reparation. They are instrumental—their aim is to achieve a restitution of a legal relationship (Crawford, 2001, p 61). Thus there is clear autonomy for regional organizations to authorize the imposition of countermeasures against a State for breach of either regional or international community norms. Action taken by the regional organization outside its membership must be justified as countermeasures for breach of an international community rule, not merely a regional one.

Given the requirements of Article 53 of the UN Charter, question marks may be raised against action beyond countermeasures, for example measures taken by regional organizations that are designed to be punitive or aimed at achieving a change in regime. Such actions beyond countermeasures are a slippery slope that threatens to blur the distinction between sanctions and countermeasures. The imposition of measures designed to achieve a regime change in another country is an action beyond the doctrine of countermeasures since the original action by the target State may not necessarily constitute a breach of an obligation owed to any of the imposing States. In March 2005, ECOWAS imposed sanctions against Togo in order to reverse the unconstitutional take-over of government in that country. Clearly these were coercive measures designed to achieve regime change, albeit, in response to an earlier unconstitutional regime change in that country. It could be argued, however, that the sanctions imposed by ECOWAS on Togo were not illegal under Article 53 of the Charter since Togo, as an ECOWAS member State, had agreed to an ECOWAS treaty that entitles ECOWAS to take such measures against any member State under specific circumstances (see Abass, 2004, p 163). This is different to a situation where a regional organization imposes sanctions on a non-member State. The imposition of sanctions by the EU on Zimbabwe in 2002 seems to depart from Article 53 given that Zimbabwe is not an EU member State, although there may be arguments of violations of obligations owed *erga omnes*. However, there is institutional practice by the EC and OAS, reviewed above, on which it may be argued that Article 53 does not pose an absolute prohibition on unauthorized regional action of a non-forcible kind, subject to

---

[57] SC Res 687 (3 April 1991).

the caveat that the Security Council still has the power to condemn autonomous regional activity as a breach of the Charter.

B. LIMITATIONS UPON SANCTIONS

One effect of Article 103 of the UN Charter seems to be that mandatory sanctions resolutions adopted by the Security Council under Article 41 of the UN Charter result in obligations for member States that prevail over obligations arising under other international treaties. The Security Council has adopted Article 41 sanctions in a number of instances (eg, Southern Rhodesia, South Africa, Iraq, the Federal Republic of Yugoslavia, Libya, Somalia, Haiti, Sudan, UNITA areas of Angola, Liberia, Sierra Leone, Rwanda, and Afghanistan) (Conforti, 2000, pp 185–194). Sanctions regimes have proliferated since the end of the Cold War, with the comprehensive regime against Rhodesia (1966–79) and the arms embargo against South Africa (1977–94) being the only instances of *mandatory* sanctions imposed by the Security Council during the Cold War. It has also adopted measures directed at stopping assistance to terrorists in the wake of the attacks against the United States on 11 September 2001,[58] and has followed this up with general measures aimed at preventing the spread of weapons of mass destruction, especially to non-State actors.[59] These measures are binding on all States and are directed at *activities* (for example financing terrorists) rather than the past sanctions regimes that were binding on all States but were targeted at *certain States*, including those allegedly supporting terrorism (Libya, Sudan, and Afghanistan). This apparent expansion in the legislative powers of the Security Council has caused considerable discussion (Happold, 2003; Talmon, 2005).

As a consequence of UN sanctions regimes, member States may be required to suspend some of their treaty relations with the target State—eg, trade treaties or civil aviation treaties. Article 103 of the Charter provides a dispensation for implementing States from the performance of these treaty obligations (Gowlland-Debbas, 2001, p 18). The justification for this must be that the UN was established, or has become recognized, as having the competence to uphold and protect community norms, and can therefore direct a collection of States to take measures which would otherwise be unlawful. This partial constitutionalization would also suggest that non-members should also comply with UN directives, certainly to the extent that the Council requires them to take action to combat breaches of fundamental rules. Requiring non-member States to take action beyond that is problematic, although Article 2(6) of the Charter suggests that non-member States should comply if this is deemed necessary to maintain international peace and security. It is questionable whether other organizations have this competence in theory, though they may take collective countermeasures within their region on the basis of regional laws (*erga omnes partes*). In practice, regional organizations have taken wider non-forcible measures or sanctions to enforce obligations owed *erga omnes* as well as *erga omnes partes*, though this practice can be said to have only taken hold because the UN has ultimately not condemned it either specifically or in a general sense.

If the Security Council or the General Assembly only recommend sanctions, it is questionable whether this entitles States (if they choose) to suspend treaty obligations. Since

---

[58] SC Res 1373 (28 September 2001).   [59] SC Res 1540 (28 April 2004).

there are no legal obligations created by a recommendatory resolution (except perhaps a duty to consider), Articles 25 and 103 do not come into play, although some commentators argue that the authority of the UN is sufficient to entitle member States to breach trade agreements (Lowenfield, 2001, p 97). Even mandatory sanctions imposed by the Security Council do not *ensure* that all members comply. The sanctions committees established by the Council to oversee implementation try to ensure this but there has been little attempt to force non-complying States into action.

There is generally no real investigation into the effective execution of sanctions by those States purportedly complying with Council decisions though there are indications that more supervision is occurring. In 2001, Charles Taylor's government in Liberia reported that it was no longer supporting the RUF following SC Resolution 1343 (see above). Liberia's claim was independently confirmed by an ECOWAS delegation which reported that Liberia 'seemed serious in meeting the demands of the Security Council' (Cortright and Lopez, 2002, p 84). Furthermore, with respect to the effect of the sanctions imposed by SC Resolutions 1127 and 1178 on Angola/UNITA, both the mission headed by the Canadian Representative to the UN, Robert Fowler, and the panel of experts, reported the effectiveness of the sanctions against UNITA (Cortright and Lopez, 2002, p 63). Additionally, in relation to the non-forcible measures directed against terrorism after 11 September 2001, the Counter Terrorism Committee established by the Security Council is actively supervising their implementation (Ward, 2003).

It is only with the adoption of comprehensive regimes, especially that imposed against Iraq in the period 1990–2003, that the focus has turned to the limitations upon sanctions in terms of their effects. The Committee on Economic, Social and Cultural Rights produced an opinion in 1997 that stated that sanctions regimes should not violate basic economic, social, and cultural rights, on the basis that unlawfulness of one kind should not be met with unlawfulness of another.[60] In 2000, the Bossuyt Report, which emerged at the behest of Sub Commission on the Promotion and Protection of Human Rights, proposed six tests for evaluating the effectiveness of sanctions.[61] Like a study commissioned by the UN Department of Humanitarian Affairs in 1998,[62] the Bussuyt Report recommended that sanctions be based on a valid reason, specifically target the parties responsible for the threat or breach of peace, exclude the targeting of humanitarian goods, and be imposed for a limited time.

The UN may impose sanctions not on the basis of a breach of international law but with the aim of restoring peace and security. It must be the case that in these situations, *a fortiori*, it must protect the human rights of the target State's population. If the International Court actively reviews a sanctions regime in the future—a possibility raised by the *Lockerbie* cases, 'considerations of proportionality might be examined by the Court'. 'If a particular form of sanctions results in injury to innocent civilians or causes serious harm to the environment and has no discernible impact on the targeted delinquent regime, would it be improper for the Court to say that the measures taken are disproportionate to the goals to be achieved?' (Dugard, 2001, pp 88–89). In reality there are two limitations here, namely

[60] General Comment No 8, UN Doc E/C.12/1997/8, (1998) 5 *IHRR* 302.
[61] The Adverse Consequences of Economic Sanctions on the Enjoyment of Human Rights (The Bossuyt Report), E/CN.4/Sub.2/2000/33, 21 June 2000.
[62] Bruberlin, 1998; cited by Kondoch, 2001 at p 273.

those of human rights norms as well as the general principle of proportionality, although the two are closely related. Sanctions regimes must not cause serious human rights violations, though causation is notoriously difficult to prove in these situations, especially when sanctions regimes always contain an exception for humanitarian supplies. In addition, they must be proportionate to the end being aimed at, either the restoration of peace and security by the withdrawal of an aggressor State,[63] or some specific acts that would lead to the termination of a threat to the peace. For example in the case of Libya, this amounted to the handing over of the two suspects and the renunciation of terrorism by Libya.[64] In the case of Rhodesia, the first attempt by the UN at a comprehensive sanctions regime,[65] the aim was to end white minority rule in that country.

However, to adapt Zoller's words, it is true to say that '[i]n the field of countermeasures and law enforcement, the international legal order has not yet reached a very advanced stage. Most of the time, as the rain in the New Testament, [sanctions] draw no distinction between the just and the unjust; they affect both the state and its citizens, or more precisely the state through its citizens. This situation is a direct result of the primitive doctrine of collective responsibility' (Zoller, 1984, p 101). The Iraqi citizens suffered from the effects of sanctions in the period 1990–2003 because of the guilt of their government. The response has been to modify and target sanctions more accurately on those who are really responsible—the leaders of the regimes, or non-State actors responsible, for example, for acts of terrorism or for supporting terrorism. The irony is that while the Security Council has tempered its general sanctions regimes out of concern for the human rights of the general population, preferring instead targeted or smart sanctions against individuals, those more directed measures can also be seen as falling foul of human rights protections of the targeted individuals. Since 1999, starting with Resolution 1267, the Security Council has in place a scheme of targeted measures, under Chapter VII of the Charter,[66] whereby an individual whose name is placed on the Security Council's list of individual members, or supporters, of the Taliban or Al-Qaeda has his assets and funds frozen by relevant member States, as well as being subject to a travel embargo. Though there is some debate as to whether these sanctions are 'administrative' rather than 'criminal', 'preventive' rather than 'punitive' (Bianchi, 2006, pp 905–907); thereby causing uncertainty as to the human rights of the individuals listed, there seems to be increasing judicial recognition that such measures, without any safeguards, violate the human rights of the individuals concerned (Keller and Fischer, 2009, p 257). In the *Kadi* judgment of 2008 the European Court of Justice found that the EU's incorporation of obligations under SC Resolution 1267 violated European fundamental rights of Mr Kadi who had been listed by the Council's 1267 Committee and therefore had his assets frozen without recourse to a remedy, but the Court gave the European bodies the chance to redraft the regulations in a way that was human-rights compliant.[67] The argument that Article 103 of the Charter means that the obligations

---

[63] SC Res 661 (6 August 1990) (Iraq).   [64] SC Res 748 (31 March 1992).

[65] SC Res 253 (29 May 1968).

[66] SC Res 1267 (15 October 1999, against the Taliban) and SC Res 1333 (19 December 2000, against Al-Qaeda).

[67] See decision of the European Court of Justice in *Kadi and Al Barakaat International Foundation* v *Council*, Joined Cases 402/05 and 415/05, Judgment of 3 September 2008, nyr. See also the decision of the Human Rights Committee in *Sayadi and Vinck* v *Belgium* (2009) 16 IHRR 16.

created by Resolution 1267 prevailed over human rights treaty obligations did not prevail, at least in that case (Cardwell, French, and White, 2009, p 237).

The development of 'smart sanctions' (Cortright and Lopez, 2000, pp 4–5) is a recent one, and the question of whether they will be effective in achieving their aims by targeting the regimes and leaders of States as well as individuals such as terrorist suspects while alleviating the suffering of the civilian population remains to be seen. Indeed, in terms of success, sanctions in their raw form rarely achieve their primary purposes. Sometimes it is the combination of economic and military measures that produces the required change in the targeted State; for example Rhodesia in 1979 (guerrilla campaign); Haiti in 1994 (threat of force by the United States); Serbia in 1995 (use of force by NATO and Muslim/Croat army); and Iraq in 1991 (Coalition action). On other occasions it is the combination of sanctions plus diplomacy, as in the majority of other cases of sanctions mentioned above. Thus it appears that economic sanctions are not by themselves an alternative to military coercion (or indeed diplomacy), but must be used in combination with other foreign policy tools. Normally, they must be used in combination with diplomacy, only exceptionally should they be used in combination with military action when States are acting under the right of self-defence or under the authority of the UN. The UN Secretary-General recognized this when he observed that 'sanctions, as preventive or punitive measures, have the potential to encourage political dialogue, while the application of rigorous economic and political sanctions can diminish the capacity of the protagonists to sustain a prolonged fight' (Cortright and Lopez, 2000, p 2).

V. CONCLUSION

This chapter has demonstrated that there are only two clear issues of law here. These are that countermeasures taken under the doctrine enunciated by the ILC and the *Air Services* case are lawful (subject to limitations concerning, *inter alia*, human rights and proportionality). Non-military sanctions imposed by the UN Security Council under Chapter VII are lawful (subject to the limitations of human rights and proportionality). This would suggest that the topic dealt with under the title of this chapter 'Countermeasures and Sanctions' is straightforward—unfortunately it is not. The clashes between the continuance (at least in the non-forcible realm) of self-help with greater centralization in the post-Charter era, combined with the perennial clash between States' freedom of action and the principle of non-intervention, means that much of the area in the middle between countermeasures and UN sanctions is unclear. However, the above analysis shows that measures in that space are, on balance, illegal, with the probable exceptions of countermeasures imposed by third States for breaches of obligations owed *erga omnes* or *erga omnes partes*, and retorsion in a residual sense. Such measures can be taken through organizations other than the UN as can more punitive or coercive economic sanctions, subject to censure by the Security Council, or arguably, the General Assembly. In convincing the world of the legality and therefore the legitimacy of non-forcible measures, States are best advised to stick to the doctrine of countermeasures. If they want to take deeper, more punitive or coercive measures, they should seek authority of a regional organization, and preferably, though not necessarily, the UN. The requirement of convincing an organization attempts to ensure that such measures are taken for the purpose of protecting a community norm, and are not taken out of pure self-interest. Thus, although there may be remaining doubts about some of the legal conclusions drawn here, there is no doubt that the legitimacy of non-forcible measures in international relations is vastly increased if they are channelled through a competent international organization.

REFERENCES

ABASS, A (2004), *Regional Organisations and the Development of Collective Security. Beyond Chapter VIII of the UN Charter* (Oxford: Hart Publishing).

ABI-SAAB, G (2001), 'The Concept of Sanction in International Law', in Gowlland-Debbas (ed), p 38.

AGO, R (1979), 'Eighth Report', *YBILC*, vol II, part one, 47.

ALLAND, D (2002), 'Countermeasures of General Interest', 13 *EJIL* 1221.

ARANGIO-RUIZ, G (1994), 'Countermeasures and Dispute Settlement: The Current Debate within the ILC', 5 *EJIL* 20.

BEDERMAN, DJ (2002), 'Counterintuiting Countermeasures', 96 *AJIL* 817.

BIANCHI, A (2006), 'Assessing the Effectiveness of the UN Security Council's Anti-terrorism Measures: The Quest for Legitimacy and Cohesion', 17 *EJIL* 881.

BOWETT, DW (1972a), 'Reprisals Involving Recourse to Armed Force', 66 *AJIL* 1.

—— (1972b), 'Economic Coercion and Reprisals by States', 13 *Virginia JIL* 1.

BRIERLY, JL (1932), 'Sanctions', 17 *Transactions of the Grotius Society* 68.

—— (1946), 'The Covenant and the Charter', 23 *BYIL* 83.

BROWN-JOHN, LC (1975), *Multilateral Sanctions in International Law: A Comparative Analysis* (New York: Praeger).

BULL, H (1992), 'The Importance of Grotius in the Study of International Relations', in Bull H, et al (eds), *Hugo Grotius and International Relations* (Oxford: Oxford University Press).

BRUBERLIN, C (1998), 'Coping with the Humanitarian Impact of Sanctions', http://www.reliefweb.int/ocha_ol/pub/sanctions.html

CARDWELL, PJ, FRENCH, D, and WHITE, ND (2009), 'Yassin Abdullah Kadi', 58 *ICLQ* 229.

CASSESE, A (2005), *International Law*, 2nd edn (Oxford: Oxford University Press).

CONFORTI, B (2000), *The Law and Practice of the United Nations*, 2nd edn (The Hague: Kluwer).

CORTRIGHT, D and LOPEZ, GA (2000), *The Sanctions Decade: Assessing UN Strategies in the 1990s* (Boulder, Colo.: Lynne Rienner).

—— (2002), *Sanctions and the Search for Security: Challenges to UN Action* (Boulder, Colo.: Lynne Rienner).

CRAWFORD, J (1994), 'Counter-Measures as Interim Measures', 5 *EJIL* 65.

—— (2001), 'The Relationship between Sanctions and Countermeasures', in Gowlland-Debbas (ed), p 57.

—— (2002), *The International Law Commission's Articles on State Responsibility* (Cambridge: Cambridge University Press).

DINSTEIN, Y (2005), *War, Aggression and Self-Defence*, 4th edn (Cambridge: Cambridge University Press).

DUGARD, J (2001), 'Judicial Review of Sanctions', in Gowlland-Debbas (ed), p 8.

ELAGAB, OY (1988), *The Legality of Non-Forcible Counter-Measures in International Law* (Oxford: Clarendon Press).

FRANCK, TM (2008), 'On Proportionality of Countermeasures in International Law', 102 *AJIL* 715.

GAZZINI, T (2006), 'The Legal Nature of WTO Obligations and the Consequences of their Violation', 17 *EJIL* 723.

GOWLLAND-DEBBAS, V (ed) (2001), *United Nations Sanctions and International Law* (The Hague: Kluwer).

HAPPOLD, M (2003), 'Security Council Resolution 1373 and the Constitution of the United Nations', 16 *Leiden JIL* 593.

KELLER, H and FISCHER, A (2009), 'The UN Anti-terror Sanctions Regime under Pressure', 9 *Human Rights Law Review* 257

KELSEN, H (1945), *General Theory of Law and State* (Cambridge: Harvard University Press).

KLEIN, P (2002), 'Responsibility for Serious Breaches of Obligations Deriving From Peremptory Norms of International Law and United Nations Law', 13 *EJIL* 1241.

KONDOCH, B (2001) 'The Limits of Economic Sanctions under International Law: The Case of Iraq', 7 *International Peacekeeping* 267–294, also available at http://www. casi.org.uk\info\kondoch01.pdf accessed on 20 September 2009.

KRINSKY, M and GOLOVE, CD (eds) (1993), *United States Economic Measures against Cuba* (Northampton, Mass.: Aletheia Press).

KUNZ, LK, (1960) 'Sanctions in International Law' 54(2) *AJIL* 324.

LAUTERPACHT, H (1933), 'Boycott in International Relations', 14 *BYIL* 125.

LILLICH, RB (1975), 'Economic Coercion and the International Legal Order', 51 *International Affairs* 358.

LOWENFELD, AF (2001), 'Unilateral versus Collective Sanctions: An American Perception', in Gowlland-Debbas (ed), p 95.

MCNAIR, AD (1930), 'The Functions and Different Legal Character of Treaties', 11 *BYIL* 100.

O'CONNELL, ME (2008), *The Power and Purpose of International Law* (Oxford: Oxford University Press).

PAUST, J and BLAUSTEIN, AP (1974), 'The Arab Oil Weapon—A Threat to International Peace', 68 *AJIL* 410.

PROVOST, R (2002), *State Responsibility in International Law* (Aldershot: Ashgate).

SCOBBIE, I (2004), 'Smoke, Mirrors and Killer Whales: the International Court's Opinion on the Israeli Barrier Wall', 5 *German Law Journal* 1107.

SCHACHTER, O (1994) 'United Nations Law' 88 *AJIL* 1.

TALMON, S (2005), 'The Security Council as World Legislature', 99 *AJIL* 175.

WARD, CA (2003), 'Building Capacity to Combat International Terrorism: The Role of the United Nations Security Council', 8 *Journal of Conflict and Security Law* 289.

ZOLLER, E (1984), *Peacetime Unilateral Remedies: An Analysis of Countermeasures* (Dobbs Ferry, NY: Transnational).

FURTHER READING

CORTRIGHT, D and LOPEZ, GA (2000), *The Sanctions Decade: Assessing UN Strategies in the 1990s* (Boulder, Colo.: Lynne Rienner). A very good examination of the issues and problems of recent and current UN sanctions regimes.

CRAWFORD, J (2002), *The International Law Commission's Articles on State Responsibility: Introduction, Text and Commentaries* (Cambridge: Cambridge University Press). An essential collection of International Law Commission materials necessary for an understanding of the nature, role, and function of countermeasures.

ELAGAB, OY (1988), *The Legality of Non Forcible Counter-Measures in International Law* (Oxford: Clarendon Press). A very thorough exposition of the history and development of countermeasures.

FARRALL, JM (2007), *United Nations Sanctions and the Rule of Law* (Cambridge: Cambridge University Press). A thorough review of sanctions practice by the Security Council and an evaluation of its legal shortcomings.

GOWLLAND-DEBBAS, V (ed) (2001), *United Nations Sanctions and International Law* (The Hague: Kluwer). An excellent collection of essays, exploring, *inter alia*, the boundaries between countermeasures and sanctions.

O'CONNELL, ME (2008), *The Power and Purpose of International Law* (Oxford: Oxford University Press). A clear reconsideration of the theory and practice of the enforcement of norms of international law, by both forcible and non-forcible means.

SICILIANOS, L-A (1990), *Les Réactions Décentralisées Á L'Illicite: Des Contre-Mesures Á La Légitime Défense* (Paris: Librarie Générale de Droit et de Jurisprudence). Leading non-English text on the subject matter of countermeasures.

ZOLLER, E (1984), *Peacetime Unilateral Remedies: An Analysis of Countermeasures* (Dobbs Ferry, NY: Transnational). A useful conceptual analysis of countermeasures.

19

THE MEANS OF DISPUTE SETTLEMENT

John Merrills

SUMMARY

The peaceful settlement of disputes occupies a central place in international law and international relations. A range of methods of handling international disputes has been developed and this chapter explains what the relevant techniques and institutions are, how they work, and when they are used. Because important distinctions are to be found between the various diplomatic means of settlement (negotiation, mediation, inquiry, and conciliation) and the legal means of arbitration and judicial settlement, the two categories are examined separately. Also considered is the role of the United Nations and regional organizations.

In the light of current international practice two main conclusions emerge: first that enormous progress has been made in refining and developing the means available for dealing with disputes; and secondly that while the various methods have distinctive features which determine how and when they are likely to be used, the key to resolving disputes often lies in their use in combination and interaction.

I. INTRODUCTION

The idea that international disputes should be settled by peaceful means rather than by the use of force has a long history. The attempt to construct institutions and develop techniques with this objective is a more recent phenomenon, however, much of what exists today having been created in the twentieth century and a significant proportion since 1945. This chapter is concerned with the result of that effort in the form of the means currently available for resolving international disputes peacefully. Initially, though, and to put the present arrangements in context, two questions need to be considered: what we mean by an 'international dispute', and what the law has to say about States' obligations.

A 'dispute' is a disagreement about something and an 'international dispute' is a disagreement, typically but not exclusively between States, with consequences on the international plane. However, a dispute is not just any disagreement, but a disagreement about something fairly specific. So the Arab-Israeli problem, for example, is not really a dispute, but because it is so complex is better described as a 'situation'. Of course, 'situations' generally contain specific disputes within them and the international community has to be concerned with both.[1] Nevertheless this chapter is mainly concerned with methods for dealing with disputes, rather than situations, so the distinction is worth bearing in mind.

What sort of specific disagreements qualify as disputes? Or to put the question another way, what is the subject matter of disputes? This is easily answered. International disputes can be about almost anything. A dispute within the European Union, for instance, about the need for closer political integration, would be a dispute about policy. In contrast, most disputes about boundaries or territorial issues involve a disagreement about legal rights. Disputes can also sometimes be about issues of fact. Where was State A's ship when it was intercepted by State B? What was it doing there? Did it have permission? And so on. Clearly these various sources of disagreement (fact, law, and policy) are not mutually exclusive and in many disputes are mixed up together. Separating the different elements, as we shall see, may be a key move in dealing with such disputes effectively.

What, then, are States' legal obligations in this field? A comprehensive statement can be found in an important resolution of the UN General Assembly, the 1982 Manila Declaration on the Peaceful Settlement of International Disputes,[2] which confirms and elaborates the relevant provisions of the United Nations Charter and the General Assembly's earlier Declaration on Principles of International Law concerning Friendly Relations and Co-operation among States of 1970.[3] Thus paragraph 2 of Section I of the Manila Declaration, like Article 2(3) of the Charter, requires every State to 'settle its international disputes exclusively by peaceful means in such a manner that international peace and security and justice, are not endangered'. And paragraph 5, echoing Article 33, lists the means available, calling for States to 'seek in good faith and in a spirit of co-operation an early and equitable settlement of their international disputes by any of the following means: negotiation, inquiry, mediation, conciliation, arbitration, resort to regional arrangements or agencies or other peaceful means of their own choice including good offices'. Acknowledging the range of contingencies, the paragraph then concludes, 'In seeking such a settlement the parties shall agree on such peaceful means as may be appropriate to the circumstances and the nature of their dispute'.

It should also be noted that the Declaration says that in the event of the failure of the parties to reach an early solution 'they shall continue to seek a peaceful solution' and 'consult forthwith on mutually agreed means' (paragraph 7), adding in the next paragraph that the parties to a dispute and other States 'shall refrain from any action whatsoever which may aggravate the situation so as to endanger the maintenance of international peace and security and make more difficult or impede the peaceful settlement of the dispute...' The obligation, then, is not just to give peaceful methods a try, but to persevere for as long as necessary, whilst at the same time avoiding action which could make things worse. In other words, if a dispute cannot be settled, States must at least manage it and keep things under control. What the various methods are and how they are used will therefore now be considered.

---

[1] On the significance of 'situations' with particular reference to the role of the United Nations, see Koufa, 1988.

[2] GA Res 37/10 (1982) 21 ILM 449.

[3] GA Res 2625 (XXV) (1970) 9 ILM 1292. See further Merrills, 1994.

II. DIPLOMATIC METHODS

A. NEGOTIATION

The methods of peaceful settlement listed in the Manila Declaration are not set out in order of priority, but the first mentioned, negotiation, is the most widely used way of dealing with international disputes.[4] In fact, negotiation is used more often in practice than all the other methods put together. Often, indeed, negotiation is the only means employed, not just because it is normally the first to be tried and is often successful, but also because its advantages may appear so great as to rule out other methods, even where the chances of a negotiated settlement are slight. When other methods are chosen, negotiation is not supplanted but used to resolve instrumental issues, the terms of reference for an inquiry commission, for instance, or the arrangements for implementing an arbitral award.

Since negotiation allows the parties to retain control of a dispute without involving third parties, it is not surprising that governments find it so attractive. However, the decision to negotiate can itself be controversial, acknowledging as it does both the other party's standing and the legitimacy of its interests. Consequently, on sensitive subjects such as sovereignty, if it is possible to negotiate at all, it may be necessary to restrict discussions to relatively uncontentious issues at least to start with, leaving the bigger problems until later. In 1973, for example, the United Kingdom succeeded in negotiating an Interim Agreement during its fishing dispute with Iceland[5] and following the Falklands War of 1982 was likewise able through diplomatic contact to establish a *modus vivendi* with Argentina (Evans, 1991; Churchill, 1997). It would therefore be a mistake to see negotiation as concerned only with settling international disputes. Its function in 'managing' disputes, ie, containing them in order to preserve other aspects of the parties' relationship, may be equally significant.

Because negotiation is fundamental it should be thought of not so much as a first stage in the conduct of virtually all disputes, but rather as an option available to the parties at any time, for use either alongside, or as part of, other processes. Thus, as the International Court indicated in the *Aegean Sea Continental Shelf* case, the fact that negotiations are being pursued during litigation is no bar to the exercise of the Court's powers and *vice versa*.[6] As a result, it is not at all uncommon for cases to be resolved by negotiation in the course of litigation, as happened in 1996 in the Iran-United States *Aerial Incident* case.[7] Similarly, a State may decide to take a dispute to a political body like the Security Council or General Assembly but at the same time continue bilateral discussions. Such twin-track approaches, employing both public and private diplomacy, are perfectly permissible and show the adaptability of negotiation.

Important though negotiation is, it cannot guarantee that a dispute will be settled, or even managed, because it is limited in various ways. It may be impossible if the parties

---

[4] For more detailed discussion of negotiation see Merrills, 2005, Ch 1 and Anderson, 1998.

[5] See *Fisheries Jurisdiction (United Kingdom v Iceland), Merits, Judgment, ICJ Reports 1974*, p 3, paras 37–39.

[6] See *Aegean Sea Continental Shelf, Judgment, ICJ Reports 1978*, p 3, para 29.

[7] See *Aerial Incident of 3 July 1988, Order of 22 February 1996, ICJ Reports 1996*, p 9. See also (1996) 90 *AJIL* 278.

refuse to speak to each other and it will be ineffective if their positions are too far apart, although in both situations, as we shall see, mediation or good offices can help. If a procedure for dealing with the dispute, such as arbitration, has already been agreed, one party may see no point in further negotiation, especially if it is confident of its legal position. More generally, the objective of resolving disputes 'equitably' and in accordance with justice, which are what the Manila Declaration prescribes, sits uneasily with the prospect of having to negotiate in a situation of grossly unequal political power. Accordingly, though negotiation is often called for by the strong, the weak may be justified in declining the invitation.

Negotiation, however, is not always a matter of free choice. Quite apart from the force of circumstances which may mean that refusing to negotiate is not an available option, a State may bind itself to negotiate in a treaty, or find that an obligation to negotiate arises under the general law. In the *North Sea Continental Shelf* cases, for instance, the International Court decided that according to customary international law the delimitation of continental shelf boundaries between neighbouring States 'must be effected by agreement in accordance with equitable principles'.[8] Of course, an obligation to negotiate on this or any other subject is not the same as an obligation to agree, nor does it exclude recourse to other procedures. What the Court wished to emphasize here was simply that as each party had rights in the disputed area, the boundaries in question were not subject to unilateral determination, and unless resolved by another procedure, had to be settled by negotiation.

The duty to negotiate sometimes laid down in treaties may be compared with related, but lesser, obligations which are an alternative. The 1994 World Trade Organization (WTO) Agreement requires its parties to 'enter into consultations' over trade issues when requested by another party,[9] which is an obligation to negotiate, whereas the 1982 Law of the Sea Convention calls only for the parties to a dispute to 'proceed expeditiously to an exchange of views' as to the means of settlement to be used.[10] It is, however, worth stressing that just as there is no general duty to consult before taking action which may affect others, so there is no general duty to seek negotiated settlements. The various methods of settlement available in international law are listed as alternatives. Negotiation is simply one possibility and in the absence of a specific duty to negotiate, such as in the WTO Agreement, States can use it or not as they see fit.

Despite this essential qualification, negotiation is an extremely important means of dealing with disputes and international relations would be unimaginably different without it. In almost all cases diplomatic exchanges will have to take place before a disagreement becomes specific enough to be described as a dispute—that is in order for the parties to establish what, if anything, they disagree about. And once it is clear a dispute exists, negotiation will often provide the best prospect of a solution, whether permanent or provisional, and for cases involving major differences as well as routine friction. It is evident, however, that although negotiation must be regarded as basic, it may not be sufficient, without more, either to resolve a dispute, or even supply a *modus vivendi*. The other methods mentioned in the Declaration must therefore now be considered.

[8] *North Sea Continental Shelf, Judgment, ICJ Reports 1969*, p 3, para 85.
[9] WTO Understanding on Rules and Procedures Governing the Settlement of Disputes (1994), Article 4(3). Text in (1994) 33 ILM 1226.
[10] United Nations Convention on the Law of the Sea (1982), Article 283(1). Text in (1982) 21 ILM 1245.

B. MEDIATION

Mediation is essentially an adjunct of negotiation and involves a third party. If the latter does no more than encourage the protagonists to resume negotiations, or simply acts as a channel of communication, the role is described as one of 'good offices'. A mediator, on the other hand, is an active participant, authorized, and indeed expected, to advance fresh ideas and to interpret, as well as to transmit, each party's proposals to the other.[11] Mediation therefore has much in common with conciliation, although a mediator usually makes proposals informally and on the basis of information supplied by the parties, rather than through independent investigations which are a feature of conciliation. In practice, however, these distinctions tend to be blurred. In a given case it may therefore be difficult to draw the line between mediation and conciliation, or to say exactly when good offices ended and mediation began.

Mediation can only take place if the parties to a dispute consent and a mediator willing to act in that capacity is available. The United Nations and several regional organizations are charged with the resolution of disputes as an institutional objective and as a result the Secretary-General and his regional counterparts often find themselves providing good offices and mediation. Non-governmental organizations too, such as the International Committee of the Red Cross, can act as mediators (Forsythe, 1985). Since it offers an opportunity to become involved in a dispute and to influence its outcome, the role of mediator also has attractions for States, or individuals, with the necessary qualifications. Accordingly, it is not unusual for the course of significant international disputes to be punctuated by offers of mediation from one or more outside sources.

Since mediation cannot be forced on the protagonists, unless they take the initiative and invite outside involvement, an unwillingness even to consider this form of assistance may frustrate the efforts of would-be mediators. If a party is unwilling to negotiate, or to contemplate any modification of its position, its acceptance of mediation (which would imply the opposite) is clearly very unlikely. On the other hand, States normally have an interest in resolving their disputes and while the terms of any settlement are plainly important, intransigence may be too expensive politically for a blank refusal of mediation to be feasible. In 1982, for example, Argentina and the United Kingdom were willing to accept good offices from the UN Secretary-General, and then mediation from the United States, because neither government could afford to alienate potential supporters.[12] It was clear at the time that something of a miracle would be needed to avoid further conflict, but for the sake of appearances, if for no other reason, they had to show willing.

Once mediation has been accepted, the task of the mediator is to devise or promote a solution which both sides can accept. Here much can be achieved by simply providing good offices and facilitating communication, especially if the parties are unable to deal with each other directly. This was the situation in both the Falklands crisis and the Diplomatic Hostages dispute of 1980, where Algeria acted as intermediary between Iran and the United States (Sick, 1985; Slim, 1992). As well as acting as a channel for information, a mediator can remind the parties of their real objectives, or encourage rethinking,

---

[11] For more detailed discussion of mediation see Bercovitch and Rubin, 1992; Greenberg, Barton, and McGuiness, 2000; Merrills, 2005, Ch 2.

[12] For an account of these initiatives and the subsequent efforts of the President of Peru, see Freedman and Gamba-Stonehouse, 1990, pp 150–323.

and devise suitable compromises, as the Papal mediator in the Beagle Channel dispute eventually succeeded in doing (Laudy, 2000). A powerful mediator may also be able to influence the parties by exploiting the role, offering inducements to agree in the form of rewards, or indicating that a failure to do so will be costly.

Normally, a mediator's main concern is only to find terms the parties can accept; in some types of mediation, however, any settlement must also meet certain external criteria. Thus according to Article 38 of the European Convention on Human Rights, one of the functions of the European Court of Human Rights is to 'place itself at the disposal of the parties concerned with a view to securing a friendly settlement of the matter *on the basis of respect for human rights*' as defined in the Convention and its Protocols. In this provision, which has its counterpart in other human rights treaties, the Court is, in effect, required to act as mediator, while at the same time respecting the Convention's basic values. A significant number of individual claims have been resolved using the friendly settlement procedure,[13] demonstrating that mediation with a substantive dimension is both workable and appropriate in the human rights field.

As a means of dispute settlement mediation is clearly subject to important limitations. A mediator must be available and the parties must be willing to accept mediation. When mediation has begun the prospects of success rest largely on the parties' readiness to compromise which means that timing is often crucial. In both the Diplomatic Hostages crisis and the Beagle Channel dispute mediation occurred at an opportune moment and a peaceful resolution of the situation was achieved. In the Falklands crisis, on the other hand, the aims of Britain and Argentina were diametrically opposed and as neither was willing to yield on the crucial issue of sovereignty, the matter was eventually resolved by armed conflict.

Mediation, then, is as effective as the disputants allow it to be and their attitudes are likely to be governed by their immediate situation. This restricts the possibilities of mediation, but does not destroy its value. A mediator does more than perfect an inchoate settlement. By facilitating the parties' dialogue, providing them with information and suggestions, identifying and exploring their aims, and canvassing possible solutions, intercession may be vital in moving them towards agreement. Success will often be incomplete and failure sometimes unavoidable. The mediator, however, must spare no effort and trust that the parties reciprocate.

C. INQUIRY

Inquiry in the context of dispute settlement is a term used in two distinct, but related senses. In the broader sense it refers to the process performed whenever a court or other body attempts to resolve a disputed issue of fact. Since most international disputes raise such issues, even if questions of law or policy are also present, it is clear that inquiry in this operational sense must play a large part in arbitration, conciliation, the work of international organizations, and other methods of peaceful settlement. Inquiry can, however, also be used in a narrower sense, not as a process of general relevance and application, but as a specific institutional arrangement which may be selected instead of arbitration or

---

[13] For an account of practice under Article 38 (ex 28) of the European Convention, see Merrills and Robertson, 2001, pp 279–282, 318–319. See also Koopmans, 2008, pp 184–199.

other techniques to establish the facts. In its institutional sense, then, inquiry refers to a particular type of international tribunal, known as the commission of inquiry and introduced by the 1899 Hague Convention.[14]

The delegates to the first Hague Peace Conference were prompted to address the issue of fact-finding by an incident the year before in which the unexplained destruction of the United States battleship *Maine* had precipitated a Spanish-American war. In an effort to minimize such problems in the future the Conference suggested the appointment of international commissions of inquiry for impartial fact-finding and arrangements to this effect were incorporated in the 1899 Hague Convention. Soon afterwards in 1904 they were used for the first time in a curious episode known as the Dogger Bank incident when the Russian fleet, wrongly believing it was under attack, fired on and damaged a number of British trawlers. A commission of inquiry appointed by the two governments established that a mistake had been made and on payment of suitable compensation the incident was declared closed (Bar-Yaacov, 1974, pp 72–81).

The Dogger Bank episode was a striking example of the value of fact-finding in the settlement of international disputes. However, it also revealed certain weaknesses in the provisions of the Hague Convention which were conspicuously lacking in detail. Accordingly, the Hague Convention of 1907 expanded the earlier scheme with a series of Articles devoted to organization and procedure. These arrangements were then used in a group of cases over the next two decades involving incidents at sea, where once again establishing the facts enabled the disputes to be disposed of.[15] This was also the outcome in the *Red Crusader* case[16] in 1962 in which the United Kingdom and Denmark set up an inquiry commission to deal with a dispute arising out of an attempt to arrest a British trawler.

Following the 1907 Hague Convention the United States concluded treaties with France and Great Britain, known as the Taft treaties, providing for commissions of inquiry with expanded powers and a further series, known as the Bryan treaties, featuring further variations. A number of other States concluded agreements along similar lines. All this treaty practice failed to produce a sequence of inquiries like those generated by the Hague Conventions, although in 1992 one of the Bryan treaties was used in the *Letelier and Moffitt* case[17] to resolve a dispute over compensation between the United States and Chile. But if in terms of case law the significance of these bilateral treaties was negligible, they were important more generally because the idea of combining inquiry with the power to make recommendations produced the institutional arrangement known as conciliation described further in the next section.

Inquiry is clearly a very flexible method having been used both for 'pure' fact-finding, as in some of the early cases, and for situations where legal questions were prominent, as in *Letelier and Moffitt*. Why, then, is it so rarely used? One explanation is that today when an inquiry is needed it can sometimes be carried out through an international organization without using the Hague Conventions. The Security Council, for example, sets up

[14] For more detailed discussion of inquiry see Bar-Yaacov, 1974; Merrills, 2005, Ch 3.

[15] For a summary of these cases see Bar-Yaacov, 1974, pp 141–179.

[16] The text of the Commission's Report can be found in 35 ILR 485. For discussion of the case see Bar-Yaacov, 1974, pp 179–196.

[17] *Letelier and Moffitt* case (Chile-United States), 88 ILR 727 and (1992) 31 ILM 1. For comment see Merrills, 2005, Ch 3.

fact-finding commissions from time to time, as do the Specialized Agencies and in 1993 the World Bank introduced a unique Inspection Panel procedure[18] to investigate development projects. These institutional developments account, at least in part, for the relatively small number of cases using the Hague procedure. There is, however, a more fundamental explanation.

All forms of third party settlement have proved less popular than was once anticipated. The root of the problem is that States are often less interested in settling a dispute than in having their own views prevail. It is therefore only when certain special conditions are satisfied that there is usually scope for setting up an inquiry commission. These are that the disputed issue is largely one of fact, that no other procedure is being employed and, most important of all, that the parties are willing to accept that their version of events may be shown to be wrong. Such a combination evidently does not occur very often. When it does, the highly satisfactory outcome of the *Red Crusader* episode shows that the international commission of inquiry can still produce useful results.

D. CONCILIATION

Conciliation has been defined as:

A method for the settlement of international disputes of any nature according to which a Commission set up by the Parties, either on a permanent or an ad hoc basis to deal with a dispute proceeds to the impartial examination of the dispute and attempts to define the terms of a settlement susceptible of being accepted by them, or of affording the Parties with a view to its settlement, such aid as they may have requested.[19]

If mediation is essentially an extension of negotiation, conciliation puts third party intervention on a formal footing and institutionalizes it in a way comparable, but not identical, to inquiry or arbitration. For the fact-finding exercise that is the essence of inquiry may or may not be present in conciliation, while the search for terms 'susceptible of being accepted by the parties' but not binding on them, contrasts sharply with arbitration and forms a link between conciliation and mediation.

Like other institutional methods, conciliation is normally entrusted to commissions containing several members. However, it is also possible to refer a dispute to a single conciliator and this procedure was adopted in 1977 when Kenya, Uganda, and Tanzania asked the experienced Swiss diplomat, Dr Victor Umbricht, to make proposals for distributing the assets of the former East African Community (EAC). As the extent of the assets was unknown, the conciliator had to begin by conducting a wide ranging inquiry, first to identify and then to value the assets, after which he could consider their distribution. Although in the final negotiated settlement the division of assets differed slightly from that proposed by Dr Umbricht, it is clear that his activities, which included mediation as well as conciliation and inquiry, and extended over seven years, made a vital contribution to the eventual settlement (Umbricht, 1984).

[18] See Collier and Lowe, 1999, pp 119–121; Gowlland Gualtieri, 2001; and Koopmans, 2008, pp 212–217. The Inter-American Bank and the Asian Development Bank have established similar panels.

[19] The quotation is from Article 1 of the Regulations on the Procedure of International Conciliation, adopted by the Institute of International Law in 1961. For more detailed discussion of conciliation see Cot, 1972; Bar-Yaacov, 1974, pp 198–248; Merrills, 2005, Ch 4; and Koopmans, 2008.

A more straightforward dispute which was resolved at about the same time involved a commission of the type familiar from previous conciliations. In 1980 Iceland and Norway set up a commission to make recommendations with regard to the dividing line for the area of continental shelf between Iceland and Jan Mayen Island. The Commission was instructed to take into account Iceland's 'strong economic interests' in the sea areas in question, along with various other factors. Following a detailed investigation of geological and other evidence, the Commission proposed both a boundary line and a joint development agreement for the area where oil deposits might exist (Churchill, 1985; Richardson, 1988). This recommendation, typical of the kind of constructive compromise which conciliation can generate, was accepted by the parties and in 1981 was incorporated in a treaty which ended the dispute.

Bilateral agreements providing for the reference of future disputes to conciliation were quite common in the League of Nations era after the First World War, but are now quite rare. When States use conciliation in a bilateral treaty today it is therefore usually in order to deal with a specific dispute, as in the two cases just mentioned. Multilateral treaties, however, show a quite different pattern and in recent practice agreements providing for conciliation, often in conjunction with other procedures, have been concluded on a variety of topics. Among treaties demonstrating the relevance of conciliation to dispute settlement in different fields are the 1969 Vienna Convention on the Law of Treaties, the 1981 Treaty establishing the Organization of Eastern Caribbean States, the 1982 Convention on the Law of the Sea, and the 1992 Convention on Biological Diversity.[20]

The 1987 Montreal Protocol on Substances that Deplete the Ozone Layer is also worth mentioning here as it establishes a novel 'non-compliance procedure', constituting a special kind of conciliation. Under the procedure an Implementation Committee consisting of 10 parties to the Protocol hears submissions relating to a party's non-compliance which may be put forward by the Secretariat or any other party. The Committee may then make recommendations 'with a view to securing an amicable solution of the matter on the basis of respect for the provisions of the Protocol'. Chinkin (1998, p 129) points out that a process such as this, dealing as it does with disputes both 'in-house' and informally, is particularly suitable for an evolving regulatory regime, as it can reflect the expectations and understandings of the parties, but at the same time avoid crystallizing the law in a fast changing area. Following the example of the Montreal Protocol, non-compliance procedures have been included in a number of other environmental treaties, including the 1997 Kyoto Protocol and the 1998 Aarhus Convention.

The Law of the Sea Convention, which includes conciliation as part of elaborate arrangements for the settlement of disputes, lays down the procedure to be followed in setting up commissions, together with details of their organization and jurisdiction.[21] Other multilateral treaties contain similar provisions, though with various differences of detail. For States wishing to establish an ad hoc commission the United Nations General Assembly has produced a set of model rules covering all aspects of conciliation which were approved in 1995. In the following year the Permanent Court of Arbitration produced its own

---

[20] See also the 1997 UN Convention on the Law of the Non-Navigational Uses of International Watercourses, Article 33 of which provides for Commissions charged with inquiry and conciliation.

[21] For analysis of these arrangements and their relation to the Convention's other provisions see Merrills, 2005, Ch 8.

optional rules for States wishing to use the Court and the United Nations Commission on International Trade Law (UNCITRAL) adopted rules in 1980 for conciliation in international commercial disputes.[22]

Although conciliation is now regularly included in provisions on dispute settlement, the number of cases in which it has actually been used remains very small. Moreover, since a commission's proposals are not binding, even when conciliation is attempted, there can be no guarantee it will be successful. Conciliation, nevertheless, has a value. Compulsory procedures of any kind, by their very existence, tend to discourage unreasonable claims, while conciliation in practice has proved particularly useful for disputes like the *Jan Mayen* case where the main issues are legal, but the parties are seeking an equitable compromise. Like inquiry, the process from which it developed, conciliation offers a procedure adaptable to a variety of needs and shows the advantage to be gained from a structured involvement of outsiders in the settlement of international disputes.

III. LEGAL METHODS

A. ARBITRATION

The oldest of the legal methods of dispute settlement is arbitration, the origins of which in current international practice can be traced back to the 1794 Jay Treaty between Great Britain and the United States. A distinctive feature of arbitration is that the parties themselves set up a tribunal to decide a dispute, or a series of disputes, usually on the basis of international law, and agree to treat its decisions as binding. Since form is subordinate to function in international relations, variations on the basic pattern are possible, but the standard form of arbitration is now well-established and regularly used for many kinds of international disputes.[23]

Traditionally, arbitration has been used for disputes in which the issues are legal and the need to remove an obstacle to good relations makes the idea of a binding settlement attractive. Territorial and boundary disputes, for example, often fall into this category. Because the parties define the question to be answered and can specify the basis of the decision, they exercise a degree of control over the process which is a further advantage. Moreover, the parties are entitled to choose the arbitrators. Although this, like other elements of an arbitration, requires agreement and so may cause delay, it means that the dispute will eventually be decided by a tribunal which the parties believe they can trust, a factor of fundamental importance in international litigation. Over the years the reference of disputes to arbitration has generated a significant and influential case law, prominent awards including those in the *Tinoco* case[24] (1923), the *Island of Palmas* case[25] (1928), and the *Trail Smelter* case[26] (1938–41). More recently, the value of arbitration has been further demonstrated in the *Taba* case[27] (1988) between Egypt and Israel, where a land boundary was in issue, the *Guyana/Suriname* case[28] (2007) involving a maritime boundary, and the

---

[22] See the Annex to GA Res 35/52 (4 December 1980) and Collier and Lowe, 1999, p 31.

[23] For useful surveys of the development and current role of arbitration see: Simpson and Fox, 1959; Gray and Kingsbury, 1992; Collier and Lowe, 1999, pp 189–279; Merrills, 2005, Ch 5.

[24] 1 *RIAA* 369.   [25] 2 *RIAA* 829.   [26] 3 *RIAA* 1905.   [27] 80 ILR 224.

[28] (2008) 47 ILM 164.

two-stage *Red Sea Islands* case[29] (1998–99) between Eritrea and Yemen, where territorial sovereignty and maritime delimitation were both in issue. Among notable arbitrations where boundary issues were not involved are the two arbitrations in the *Rainbow Warrior* case[30] (1986 and 1990) between France and New Zealand, the *OSPAR (Article 9)* case[31] (2003) between Ireland and the United Kingdom and the *Iron Rhine Railway* case (2005) between Belgium and the Netherlands.[32]

Arbitration, like conciliation, is a method which can be employed ad hoc when a dispute arises, or provided for in advance by appropriate arrangements in a treaty. It is therefore to be found in the dispute settlement provisions of multilateral and bilateral conventions on a wide variety of subjects, as either an optional or a compulsory procedure, and often in combination with other methods. The 1982 Law of the Sea Convention, for example, gives a very prominent role to arbitration, as do the 1992 Stockholm Convention on Conciliation and Arbitration within the CSCE and a number of recent conventions concerned with the environment.[33] In the WTO's dispute settlement system, similarly, though the general emphasis is on panel proceedings (described below), arbitration is also an option and for certain disputes is even mandatory.

The use of arbitration to decide inter-State disputes must be distinguished from its use in a related context, to deal with disputes between a State on one side and an individual or corporation on the other. In cases of this type, known as mixed arbitrations,[34] the tribunal's jurisdiction may derive from a contract rather than a treaty, but in either event has international implications that are likely to be significant. The Iran-US Claims Tribunal,[35] for example, was set up in 1981 to handle a large number of disputes arising from the Islamic revolution in Iran and has jurisdiction over both inter-State and private claims. Its decisions, which now run to more than 30 volumes, not only show the value of arbitration as a procedure for resolving serious and complex disputes of a commercial character, but because the Tribunal has had to address issues such as expropriation and State responsibility, have also made a significant contribution to international law.

Arbitration, then, is an important means of handling international disputes. It does, however, have significant limitations. As we shall see in the next section, States are reluctant to make general commitments to judicial settlement and for much the same reasons often resist the idea of arbitration. When a specific dispute arises, however, negotiation or another diplomatic method may be preferred on the ground that it keeps the solution firmly in the hands of the parties. Another limitation concerns enforcement. Although arbitration produces a binding decision, it can be difficult to ensure that the losing party carries out the award. This does not mean that arbitral decisions are widely disregarded, but nonetheless is a real weakness. Ways of encouraging compliance are available and can be useful, but the answer really lies with the protagonists. Arbitration, like other means

---

[29] (2001) 40 ILM 900 and 983.   [30] 74 ILR 241 and 82 ILR 499.

[31] (2003) 42 ILM 330.

[32] Available at http://www.pca-cpa.org.

[33] See Merrills, 2005, Chs 5 and 8 and for the use of arbitration in earlier treaties, Sohn, 1982–83.

[34] For a good account of mixed arbitration, including the work of the International Centre for the Settlement of Investment Disputes (ICSID), and the related topic of international commercial arbitration, see Collier and Lowe, 1999, pp 45–84.

[35] For a more detailed account of the Tribunal and its work see Brower, 1998.

of settling disputes in a world of sovereign States, relies for its effectiveness on responsible behaviour from the parties.

B. THE INTERNATIONAL COURT OF JUSTICE

Judicial settlement involves the reference of disputes to permanent tribunals for a legally binding decision. It is listed in the Manila Declaration after arbitration, from which it developed historically, and is currently available through a number of courts with general or specialized jurisdiction. The only court of general jurisdiction is the International Court of Justice (ICJ) at The Hague, details of which will be found in Chapter 20. Courts with specialized jurisdiction include human rights courts and various tribunals considered in the next section and the European Court of Justice (ECJ), a regional organ with extensive powers over the member States of the European Community, Community organs, and natural or legal persons. It is interesting to note that the ECJ and the other specialized courts have all been created since 1945 and reflect the increasing complexity of international relations. Our review must begin, however, with the ICJ.[36]

The Court's authority to decide cases is conferred by its Statute and is based on the principle of consent. It is therefore open to States to agree to take future disputes, or any particular dispute, to the Court by concluding a treaty in appropriate terms, or to make a unilateral acceptance of jurisdiction in the form of a declaration under Article 36(2) of the Statute, known as the Optional Clause.[37] In the event of a disagreement as to whether jurisdiction has been accepted the matter is decided by the Court, whose decision, according to Article 36(6), is final. Only States may be parties in cases before the Court, although under Article 65 it may also give advisory opinions on legal questions for the benefit of international organizations.

The Court is composed of 15 judges who are elected for nine-year terms by the Security Council and General Assembly of the United Nations. The Statute requires the judges to be broadly representative of 'the main forms of civilization and of the principal legal systems of the world', but they sit as independent judges, not as representatives of their national States. However, if a party to a dispute does not currently have a judge of its nationality on the Bench, it is entitled to appoint an ad hoc judge who becomes a member of the Court for that case only. Cases are normally heard by the full Court, but if the parties wish, they can instead refer it to a smaller chamber (normally five judges). The composition of a chamber is in practice determined by the parties, making the process similar in this respect to arbitration.[38]

The Court's function is described in Article 38(1) of the Statute as 'to decide in accordance with international law such disputes as are submitted to it...' and the list of materials which follows, beginning with 'international conventions' and ending with 'judicial decisions' and 'the teachings of... publicists', has come to be seen as the core of modern international law. As well as interpreting and applying the law, the Court must, of course, also

[36] For more detailed treatment of the International Court and its work see Merrills, 2005, Chs 6 and 7; Collier and Lowe, 1999, pp 124–189 and the essays in Muller, Raic, and Thuranszky, 1997.

[37] For discussion of the Optional Clause, with particular reference to recent State practice, see Merrills, 2002 and for an earlier survey, Merrills, 1993.

[38] For discussion of this and other aspects of the chambers procedure see Ostrihansky, 1988; Valencia-Ospina, 1996.

resolve any issues of fact that may be necessary and for this purpose receives and assesses documentary or other evidence brought forward by the parties, the quantity of which may sometimes be extremely large. This may include the evidence of witnesses or experts and the Court itself may decide to visit the scene, as happened in 1997 in the *Gabčíkovo-Nagymaros Project* case.[39]

Under Article 38(2) of the Statute the Court may at the request of the parties give a decision *ex aequo et bono* instead of on the basis of law. However, this provision, which blurs the distinction between adjudication and conciliation, has never been used. A less drastic alternative is to refer a case to the Court for a decision on an agreed basis. Like the chambers procedure, this again brings adjudication close to arbitration, although the Court's powers must always be exercised within the Statute. A further possibility is for the Court to extend its function on its own initiative by utilizing equitable considerations of various kinds. Whilst this is not a licence for freewheeling judicial legislation, it introduces an element of flexibility into the Court's decisions which can sometimes be useful (Weil, 1996).

When the Court decides a case its judgment is binding on the parties and is final and without appeal. Whether it actually resolves the dispute, however, depends partly on whether the parties accept it, that is are prepared to treat it as binding, and partly on the precise question referred. States may, for example, decide to use the Court only to obtain a ruling on applicable rules and principles,[40] or to determine whether a dispute is subject to compulsory arbitration[41] and in cases such as these further steps may be needed to achieve a final settlement. As regards the acceptance of decisions, difficulties can sometimes arise, especially where the unsuccessful party has sought to challenge the Court's jurisdiction. On the other hand, disputes are often taken to the Court and resolved there without acrimony because the States concerned want a settlement. In such cases repudiation of the decision would merely return the dispute to the political arena and therefore be self-defeating.

C. OTHER COURTS AND TRIBUNALS

Among the various courts with specialized jurisdiction the most spectacular developments have unquestionably been those associated with human rights tribunals, notably the European Court of Human Rights at Strasbourg and the Inter-American Court in San José. Before 1970 the former was rarely employed and the American Court was not inaugurated until 1979. Today, however, the European Court, which was reconstructed in 1998, has a flourishing jurisprudence[42] and although the American Court is not as busy, it has made its mark with both contentious cases and advisory opinions (Pasqualucci, 2003). The work of these courts stems mainly from cases brought by individuals, but both courts have jurisdiction over inter-State disputes and deal with such cases from time to time. More importantly, as human rights are now an international issue, procedures for adjudicating

---

[39] *Gabčíkovo-Nagymaros Project (Hungary/Slovakia), Order of 5 February 1997, Judgment, ICJ Reports 1997*, p 7.

[40] As in the *North Sea Continental Shelf, Judgment, ICJ Reports 1969*, p 3.

[41] As in *Ambatielos, Merits, Judgment, ICJ Reports 1953*, p 10.

[42] For an account of the Court and its work, including the changes made in 1998, see Merrills and Robertson, 2001.

claims help to promote friendly relations whether or not they are brought by States. The activities of human rights courts thus certainly fall within the Manila Declaration.

Courts with specialized jurisdiction of a quite different type are to be found in the 1982 Law of the Sea Convention. For among several new institutions created by the Convention is a new court, the International Tribunal for the Law of the Sea (ITLOS), and a separate subsidiary organ, the Sea-Bed Disputes Chamber (SBDC).[43] ITLOS reflects the preference which many States had for a special tribunal to handle disputes arising out of the new law contained in the 1982 Convention, and starting with the *M/V Saiga* case[44] in 1997, the Court has begun to develop its own distinctive jurisprudence. In the same way the SBDC was set up because the complex arrangements in the Convention for exploiting the deep sea-bed were thought unsuitable for adjudication in the main Tribunal. Unlike its parent body, however, the SBDC has no case law, as yet.

The arrangements pertaining to the organization and jurisdiction of ITLOS and the SBDC and the choice of law to be applied are set out in great detail in the 1982 Convention and show the thinking behind their creation. Among points particularly worth noting are that the jurisdiction of ITLOS is based on the principle of free choice of means, since it depends upon States making a declaration nominating the Tribunal as their preferred option. The SBDC, on the other hand, has a jurisdiction which is automatically accepted by all the parties to the Convention. Both tribunals, unlike the International Court, are open not just to States, but also to other entities, including organizations, and each is permitted to split into smaller chambers, in order to provide the parties, if they wish, with some of the advantages of arbitration.

Functioning in a quite different sphere of operation is the dispute settlement system of the World Trade Organization, set up when the Organization was created in 1994. This complex system exists to deal with disputes concerned with trade agreements and utilizes consultations between the parties, mediation, conciliation, and arbitration in elaborate provisions details of which must be sought elsewhere.[45] At the centre of the system is an arrangement for referring disputes to panels made up of independent experts whose role resembles that of arbitrators. Panel reports are then liable to review by the members of an organ called the Appellate Body, which further emphasizes the juridical nature of the process.

A feature of the WTO system is that the principle of free choice of means, normally so important in dispute settlement, is largely absent. Whilst States are encouraged to settle disputes by agreement, if they fail to do so, the complaining party is entitled to request a panel. When the panel has reported, recourse to the Appellate Body is again a matter of right, and when the litigation stage is complete, a political organ, called the Dispute Settlement Body, takes over to ensure implementation. Notice also that by subscribing to the WTO Agreement States not only forgo the remedy of self-help, but also undertake to use its procedures exclusively. So, for example, if a dispute could be dealt with either through the WTO, or through a regional system, the former should be given priority.

---

[43] On the arrangements relating to ITLOS and its place in the dispute settlement arrangements of the Convention, see Klein, 2005; Merrills, 2005, Ch 8; Collier and Lowe, 1999, pp 84–96.

[44] (1998) 37 ILM 360.

[45] There is already a large literature on the WTO system, including Kennedy and Southwick, 2002 and a detailed treatment by Petersmann, 1997. For more concise treatments see Merrills, 2005, Ch 9 and Collier and Lowe, 1999, pp 94–104.

Although the WTO system is relatively new, it is in constant use and regularly proves its worth. Trade disputes are complex, often involve shifts in economic and political forces and are capable of arousing strong passions. If this makes peaceful methods for resolving such disputes essential, it also means that methods which encourage accommodation are no less important than those that seek to enforce rules. That is why the WTO system features diplomatic as well as legal processes. Moreover, in international trade law, as elsewhere, adjudication works best when rules are not just applied impartially, but also command general acceptance. As the fairness of trade rules depends on the policies of the major players in the WTO, their responsibility as legislators underpins its system for dealing with disputes.

D. THE PLACE OF LEGAL METHODS

To understand the significance of arbitration or other legal methods and how they are used in practice it is important to appreciate at the outset that courts and tribunals do not operate in isolation, but regularly interact with political institutions and processes. So, for example, the reference of a dispute to the ICJ may be prompted by the efforts of a regional organization, negotiations may be necessary to establish the question asked, and may well continue on substantive matters once litigation is in progress. At the post-adjudication stage, likewise, technical assistance from the UN, or further negotiations, perhaps assisted by a mediator, may be needed to deal with boundary demarcation, or similar issues concerning implementation.[46]

When considering the role of adjudication it is also as well to recognize that courts and tribunals have no all-embracing ability to solve international problems, but occupy a specialized place among the instruments of dispute settlement. Not only are they limited to deciding disputes and so lack competence to deal with broader 'situations', but as their normal function is to decide cases by applying law, many problems are unsuited to adjudication because they do not raise legal issues. Thus the International Court has indicated that as a general rule it cannot deal with issues requiring, say, a political or economic assessment, rather than a legal decision, and by the same token it will decline to answer questions which are moot or only of historical interest.[47]

What, then, is the value of legal methods? Because the decisions of courts and tribunals are binding, litigation is a good way of disposing of troublesome issues the resolution of which is considered to be more important than the actual result. Conversely, when the result is all-important adjudication is likely to be unattractive because it is simply too risky, a point which is reinforced by the fact that adjudication is not merely dispositive, but tends to produce a winner-takes-all type of solution. This explains why States are notoriously reluctant to make a general commitment to take their disputes to the International Court, but may be willing to do so in individual cases. It also explains the popularity of ITLOS and the WTO panels system, which are designed for a specific purpose, where the

---

[46] For discussion of the issue of compliance and implementation generally see Paulson, 2004 and Schulte, 2004.

[47] See *Haya de Torre, Judgment, ICJ Reports 1951*, p 71; *Northern Cameroons, Preliminary Objections, Judgment, ICJ Reports 1963*, p 15; *Nuclear Tests (Australia v France), Judgment, ICJ Reports 1974*, p 253, and *Nuclear Tests (New Zealand v France), Judgment, ICJ Reports 1974*, p 457.

parties' commitments are defined and the judges have special expertise. It is worth bearing in mind, however, that when arrangements of this kind are set up they are not mutually exclusive. Consequently, an unavoidable effect is to create situations of overlapping competence, where several courts or tribunals may have jurisdiction over the same dispute, or different aspects of it. If, as may happen in such circumstances, the parties elect to refer a dispute to different legal bodies, difficult questions can arise as to which, if either, should have priority (Shany, 2003; Merrills, 2007).

Are international courts capable of deciding disputes with a strong political element? The answer is to be found in a firmly established principle which is really quite basic to international adjudication. It is that courts and tribunals are set up to resolve legal issues and so, provided a case presents a legal issue, they are not prevented from deciding it merely because it also has political elements.[48] It is easy to see that such an attitude is essential if adjudication is to function. All disputes between States have political elements because States are political bodies. Therefore to concede that a case could not be decided if it had political elements would be to enable any case to be blocked. Quite rightly, this absurd conclusion has been rejected.

Since international disputes often have both a legal and a political dimension, it is no surprise to find that on occasion disputes are referred to legal and political institutions simultaneously. The Tehran hostages dispute, for example, between the United States and Iran was considered by both the ICJ and the UN Security Council in 1980 and there have also been cases involving regional organizations. Such cases clearly raise the question of the relation between the legal and the political process, on which the Court's view, as might be expected, is that each has its own sphere and neither is entitled to priority as a matter of principle.[49] This is useful as far as it goes, but leaves open questions such as how far the legality of the Security Council's actions may be challenged before the Court, a problem to which as yet there is no clear answer.[50]

When the parties to a dispute decide to employ adjudication by, for example, concluding an arbitration agreement, or jointly referring a case to the International Court they are, in effect, agreeing that the legal and political aspects of the dispute should be separated. When, on the other hand, a case is referred unilaterally, it may be because the parties view the dispute differently, the applicant seeing the legal aspect as paramount, but the respondent emphasizing its political aspects and so regarding it as unsuitable for adjudication. As already noted, a court can decide such a case, notwithstanding the conflict of characterization, but does so by isolating the legal element, thereby effecting a 'depoliticization' which the parties were unable to achieve consensually.

The point just made is critical because it means that although courts and tribunals are competent to deal with disputes which present legal issues, however complex their political background, the party whose concerns are with the non-legal elements of the dispute may be unwilling to accept the decision. This clearly limits the contribution which adjudication can make to the resolution of international disputes in practice. It is also

[48] For discussion of the cases in which this point has been made, including the *Diplomatic Staff in Tehran* case and the *Nicaragua* case, see Merrills, 2005, Ch 7.

[49] For discussion of the 1993 *Genocide* case and earlier cases in which this point has been made see Merrills, 2005, Ch 10.

[50] For discussion of the *Lockerbie* cases which raised this point see Akande, 1997; White, 2002, pp 119–130; Merrills, 2005, Ch 10.

why appreciating the interaction of legal and political processes is so vital and why, when describing the WTO system, we noticed the role of consultation and the need for trade rules which all States can regard as legitimate. It is not enough to have courts and tribunals capable of handing down legal decisions. Persuading States to use them, and making their decisions effective, are problems grounded in the political context.

IV. INTERNATIONAL ORGANIZATIONS AND DISPUTE SETTLEMENT

A. REGIONAL ORGANIZATIONS

The reference in the Manila Declaration to 'resort to regional agencies or arrangements' relates to bodies such as the Organization of American States (OAS), the African Union (AU), formerly the Organization of African Unity (OAU), NATO, and the EEC, which are recognized in Article 52(2) of the UN Charter as relevant to the settlement of local disputes.[51] There is no reference in the Declaration's list to the UN's own procedures, although these are covered in some detail in later provisions which, as well as mentioning the ICJ, deal also with the Security Council and the General Assembly. Thus the Declaration acknowledges the role of international political organizations in dispute settlement at both the regional and universal levels.

One of the main functions of regional organizations is to provide governments with opportunities for diplomatic contact in a structured setting. Although such contact serves many purposes, it is something which may be particularly useful when there are disputes between member States because it can provide them with an opportunity to discuss their differences when tension may have disrupted normal communication. Such contact, moreover, is by no means restricted to the speech-making and formal proceedings of the organization, but also includes behind the scenes activity where the real work is often done. Indeed, informal contact of this kind may well be more valuable for parties with a dispute since it enables other States to use their influence without having to take a public position.

Negotiations, whether formal or informal, are the basic method of dealing with disputes, but, as noted earlier, may benefit from the presence of an outsider to encourage the dialogue and keep it going, or to make an independent contribution. Regional organizations provide opportunities for both good offices and mediation, as may be seen, for example, in the OAU which frequently provided these services in disputes between African States (Maluwa, 1989) and the European Union which attempted mediation during the break-up of Yugoslavia. Some of these efforts, including the last, were unsuccessful, but then mediation, it will be recalled, is about facilitating negotiations, not imposing solutions.

More formal than mediation are the other diplomatic methods—inquiry and conciliation—and these too can be used by regional organizations. Inquiry, as we have seen, is essentially a fact-finding exercise, whereas conciliation involves presenting the parties with specific recommendations. Both processes need an individual or a commission to

---

[51] On the role of regional organizations in general see Fawcett and Hurrell, 1995 and in relation to disputes specifically Merrills, 2005, Ch 11.

do the necessary fact-finding or conciliation and the two can sometimes be combined. In 1929, for example, the Conference of American States established a body called the Chaco Commission to investigate a dispute between Bolivia and Paraguay and to make proposals for a settlement. This involved both inquiry and conciliation and the Commission produced recommendations which the parties accepted, so demonstrating the value of this type of initiative (Bar-Yaacov, 1974, pp 199–211). So far we have really been considering ways in which disputes can be handled *through* regional organizations, rather than ways in which they can be handled *by* them. Negotiation and the other diplomatic methods are all processes which States can, and often do, employ on their own initiative without involving a regional organization at all. This does not make such organizations irrelevant because they may provide the spur to make things happen. It does, however, prompt the question whether there is action in relation to disputes which only organizations can take. Is there, in other words, a contribution from regional organizations that is uniquely their own?

The answer is yes, as may be seen from the following examples. First, a collective declaration of policy, such as the OAU's 1964 declaration on respecting African boundaries,[52] can both reduce the likelihood of disputes and provide a basis for dealing with them when they arise. Secondly, though the powers of regional organizations are subject to international law and not unlimited, in some circumstances they are entitled to impose sanctions on a recalcitrant member.[53] And thirdly, regional organizations can play a role in international peace-keeping,[54] or in support of action by the Security Council under Chapter VII of the Charter. Such measures show how collective action may be used to pursue goals not open to States acting separately and the variety of ways in which regional organizations may be involved in international dispute settlement.

B. THE UNITED NATIONS

Article 1 of the UN Charter sets out the purposes of the United Nations which are: to maintain international peace and security; to develop friendly relations among nations; to achieve international cooperation in solving problems of an economic, social, cultural, or humanitarian character and in promoting human rights; and to be a centre for harmonizing the actions of States in attaining these ends. These are inter-related purposes, but the maintenance of international peace and security occupies a primary place, the UN having a responsibility to bring about cessation of conflict whenever it occurs and to assist the parties to international disputes to settle their disputes by peaceful means. Clearly, then, dealing with disputes is a central function of the Organization according to the Charter.[55]

---

[52] See on the declaration Zartman, 1991. Another example is the adoption in 1991 of a common policy on recognition towards the States of Eastern Europe by the members of the European Union on which see Warbrick, 1992.

[53] For an example see Macdonald, 1963–64, pp 367–372.

[54] For a general survey see McCoubrey and Morris, 2000. An interesting illustration of such activity is provided by the operations carried out by the Commonwealth of Independent States (CIS) in several parts of the former Soviet Union, which are described by Webber, 1996.

[55] From the vast literature on the United Nations the following relate specifically to the issues discussed in the text: Peck, 1996; White, 1997; Merrills, 2005, Ch 10.

How is this to be done? The Charter assigns a key role to the Security Council and gives it the relevant powers in Chapter VI, which is wholly concerned with the peaceful settlement of disputes. Although the Council may make recommendations with a view to the settlement of any dispute, if all the parties so request, and under Article 34 can investigate any dispute or threatening 'situation', its general competence is limited to disputes 'the continuation of which is likely to endanger the maintenance of international peace and security'. It is therefore clear that although Article 2(3) imposes a quite general obligation on member States to settle disputes by peaceful means, only the more serious disputes, or those which may become serious, are regarded as the Council's concern.

The particular role of the Security Council is further emphasized in Article 33(1) which provides that the parties to a dispute within its remit should 'first of all' seek a solution by negotiation or another peaceful means of their own choice, and Article 52(2), which provides that members of regional arrangements or agencies 'shall make every effort to achieve peaceful settlement of local disputes' through such arrangements or agencies before referring them to the Security Council. However, despite these priorities, the Council has the right under Article 36(1) to recommend appropriate procedures at any time. Moreover, its authority to consider these issues comes from the relevant provisions of the Charter. Thus, unlike a court of arbitration or conciliation commission, the Security Council does not require the consent of the States concerned in order to become involved.

A final point to make about Chapter VI is that the provisions in this part of the Charter, which are all concerned with encouraging States to use peaceful methods of settlement, need to be read alongside those of Chapter VII, which give the Security Council power to impose sanctions. The structure of the Charter can therefore be seen as designed first and foremost to help States with their problems, but in the last resort to back this up with coercive measures in disputes or situations which lead to a 'threat to the peace, breach of the peace or act of aggression'. How well this has worked in practice is another matter, but in theory at least the Charter equips the Security Council with enforcement powers to use when they are needed.

Because the Charter envisages the Security Council playing the main role in UN dispute management, there is nothing as elaborate as Chapter VI or Chapter VII conferring powers on the General Assembly or Secretary-General. However, these organs too are given a role. Thus the General Assembly has broad powers of discussion and recommendation under Articles 10 to 14. These are wide enough to cover, for example, the recommendation of 'measures for the peaceful adjustment of any situation, regardless of origin, which it deems likely to impair the general welfare or friendly relations among nations' (Article 14), although this provision, like others relating to the General Assembly, is subject to Article 12, which preserves the primacy of the Security Council.

The role of the Secretariat is set out in Articles 98 and 99 of the Charter which, though brief, are very important. Article 98 speaks of the Secretary-General performing secretarial (ie, administrative) functions for the General Assembly, the Security Council, and the other principal organs and performing 'such other functions as are entrusted to him by these organs'. Under this provision, then, tasks relating to disputes and other matters may be delegated to the Secretariat. Article 99, on the other hand, refers to the Secretary-General bringing 'to the attention of the Security Council any matter which in his opinion may threaten the maintenance of international peace and security'. Here therefore the

Secretary-General is given a power of initiative which, as will be seen, has proved highly significant.

C. THE CHARTER SYSTEM IN PRACTICE

The United Nations is often criticized for failing to solve the world's problems and the validity of this criticism, at least in relation to disputes, is something we must consider. Before doing so, however, something should be said about what the UN has been able to achieve, beginning with the work of the political organs. As noted above, both the General Assembly and the Security Council are entitled to make recommendations and both organs have used this power extensively, to try to calm disputes, to urge the use of particular methods, or in some cases to recommend specific terms for a settlement. As these are merely recommendations, they can be, and often are, ignored. On the other hand, such UN involvement has the effect of bringing diplomatic pressure to bear and is sometimes helpful in providing States which may be locked on a collision course with a way out of their difficulty.

It was pointed out earlier that the existence of regional organizations stimulates negotiation by bringing States together in a setting where diplomatic contact is easy and can be encouraged by others. The United Nations functions in a similar way with the advantage that at the UN diplomacy is possible not just among States which are neighbours, but on a worldwide scale. Providing a setting for diplomatic contacts is useful in itself, but it is often possible to go further and use the Organization's own machinery to facilitate negotiations. One rather formal method is to appoint a committee of selected member States to assist negotiations, as was done for discussions on Indonesia's independence in 1947. Another is to use individuals as mediators or conciliators, which has been one of the Secretariat's most significant activities.

The contribution which fact-finding can make to the resolution of certain types of disputes has also already been mentioned. This too is a matter on which the UN may be able to help and there are many examples of the Security Council or the General Assembly creating subsidiary organs for this purpose.[56] As we have seen, this is something which the States concerned could do for themselves utilizing the inquiry procedure of the Hague Conventions, but this requires the parties to agree and by the time a dispute reaches the UN it is usually plain they are not going to do so. The Organization's contribution is therefore to fill this gap by promoting the necessary investigation, in an attempt to bring the parties closer together.

If the political organs cannot help directly, or do not wish to do so, they can refer a dispute to another body, a regional organization, for example, or another UN organ. So long as it is not merely a way of evading responsibility (as it can sometimes be), passing a dispute on in this way may be a desirable step. A case in point is legal disputes, which Article 36(3) says should 'as a general rule' be referred to the International Court. The General Assembly and the Security Council may also ask the Court for advisory opinions and this power is potentially very important in disputes like that in the *Western Sahara* case[57]

---

[56] For a review of early UN practice, examining the value and limitations of this form of activity see Plunkett, 1968–69.

[57] *Western Sahara, Advisory Opinion, ICJ Reports 1975*, p 12. See also the *Namibia* case, *Legal Consequences for States of the Continued Presence of South Africa in Namibia (South West Africa) notwithstanding Security Council Resolution 276 (270), Advisory Opinion, ICJ Reports 1971*, p 16.

which involve decolonization or other United Nations policies. Accordingly, the Court responded positively when the General Assembly asked recently for an advisory opinion on the legal consequences of Israel's construction of a security barrier in the occupied Palestinian territory.[58] It cannot be said, however, that the political organs use the Court as often as they might with the result that opportunities to engage it in their work have been somewhat neglected.

The political organs, and the Security Council in particular, though active in the ways described, have frequently been slow to act; however, the same cannot be said for the Secretary-General, whose work under Articles 98 and 99 has often formed the main, or even the only element in a United Nations response (Chesterman, 2007). As regards Article 98, one of the most important contributions has been to provide good offices and mediation when the authorizing organ perceives a need to help the parties with negotiations (Franck and Nolte, 1993; Skjelsbaek and Fermann, 1996). In such cases introduction of the Secretary-General as a neutral third party, supported by the Security Council or the General Assembly can be a constructive move. Among the many examples of such involvement are the Secretary-General Waldheim's creation of a fact-finding and conciliation commission, together with the provision of good offices, in the Diplomatic Hostages crisis of 1979, and the good offices of Secretary-General Boutros-Ghali, following the invasion of Kuwait in 1990.

The powers of initiative possessed by the Secretary-General under Article 99 have been interpreted broadly which has made this provision just as important in practice as Article 98. Consequently, a similar range of activities has been undertaken. It is important to appreciate, however, that even when exercising initiative under Article 99, the Secretary-General has always been careful to coordinate his work with that of the political organs, especially the Security Council (Perez de Cuellar, 1993). This underlines the point that the primary responsibility for making the UN system work lies with the member States. If they fail to play their part it is pointless expecting the Secretary-General to fill the gap and blaming him when things go wrong. The Secretary-General has a key role, but cannot carry the whole burden of dispute management for the United Nations.

D. THE VALUE AND LIMITATIONS OF ORGANIZATIONS

Enough has been said to indicate that political organizations can make a useful contribution to the management and resolution of international disputes. However, various factors which can limit their activity must now be noted. To take regional organizations first, one very obvious limitation is that they are unlikely to be very effective in disputes which cross regional boundaries, ie, in disputes between States from different regions. Another, no less significant, limitation is that regional organizations are often reluctant to become involved in disputes within States, for example, civil wars and other internal conflicts. A further limitation is that most regional organizations lack resources and so may simply be unable to undertake the more expensive kinds of institutional activities such as peace-keeping.

Turning to the United Nations, its involvement in disputes has tended to reflect the extent to which the major States have seen UN action as something which is in their interests. This means that in many disputes there has been little UN involvement, or its contribution

---

[58] *Legal Consequences of the Construction of a Wall in the Occupied Palestinian Territory, Advisory Opinion, ICJ Reports 2004,* p 136.

has been only marginal. Where the UN has been involved, the record underlines the point made at the beginning about the need to manage international disputes when they cannot be settled. Not many disputes have been settled through the UN, compared with the large number which have been managed, in the sense of being dealt with in some way, through the Organization's processes. This is particularly clear in the case of peace-keeping operations, for example, which have almost always been concerned with stabilizing situations, so as to create conditions in which other processes can be used.

To see why all this is so is to begin to understand the nature and limitations of the UN system. The Organization is a reflection of the social and political relations of States. Although constructive steps have sometimes been taken, effective action is usually possible only insofar as States are prepared to relinquish claims to exclusive control and seek assistance. When things become sufficiently serious, a UN presence or other initiative may be acceptable, but unless what is wanted is simply a face-saving arrangement, settling the basic problem is likely to be much more difficult. As a consequence, in very many cases prophylactic measures may be all that is politically possible, yet the fact that a festering dispute remains unresolved will be accounted another failure of the Organization.

In *An Agenda for Peace*,[59] his 1992 report to the Security Council, Secretary-General Boutros-Ghali examined the potential of the United Nations in the fields of preventive diplomacy, peace-keeping, peace-making and post-conflict peace-building. The report described what the Secretary-General saw as the contribution which regional organizations could make to resolving disputes, emphasizing, as might be expected, that they must act in a manner consistent with the Charter and that the Security Council has primary responsibility for maintaining international peace and security. However, provided these constitutional limitations are respected, regional action could lighten the Security Council's burden and 'contribute to a deeper sense of participation, consensus and democratization in international affairs'.[60]

As the Secretary-General indicated, cooperation between regional organizations and the UN is particular useful in situations which call for peace-keeping forces or related action and recent events have demonstrated how institutions can perform complementary functions when the political atmosphere is favourable. In the complex situation in Central America in the 1980s, for example, the main diplomatic work was carried out through the regional Contadora process, but when security arrangements were needed, a UN force (ONUCA) was established by the Security Council (White, 1993, pp 226–227). Similarly, in the Liberian crisis of 1990 peace-keeping forces were supplied by the local sub-regional organization (ECOWAS) and subsequently supported both politically and on the ground by the UN (White, 1996, pp 217–219). It is scarcely necessary to add that cooperation between organizations presents many difficulties and is not a panacea. But if there is still far to go before we can speak of a global-regional peace-making system, what *An Agenda for Peace* calls 'this new era of opportunity',[61] makes it worth working for.

The Charter, as already noted, puts the Security Council at the centre of the collective security system. It was therefore fitting that following the controversial invasion of Iraq in 2003, which lacked explicit authorization from the Council, Secretary-General Kofi

---

[59] SC Doc S/24111, 17 June 1992. Text in (1992) 31 ILM 953.
[60] Ibid, para 64.   [61] Ibid, para 63.

Annan established a High Level Panel to bring forward new ideas on collective security, including a re-evaluation of the role of the principal organs of the UN (Slaughter, 2005). The Panel's report,[62] which appeared in 2004, adopted a radical approach, proposing, among other steps, that the Security Council should employ five criteria to guide its decisions on the use of force. In response, the Secretary-General produced his own report, *In Larger Freedom: Towards Development, Security and Human Rights for All*,[63] in which he largely endorsed the Panel's conclusions. However, the UN World Summit in September 2005 did not support the five criteria, although another of the Panel's proposals, the concept of a 'responsibility to protect' was accepted (Gray, 2007). Collective security is, of course, only one aspect of dispute settlement. Likewise, the prominence of the Security Council in this field should not prevent the potential of other organs from being recognized. The report of the High Level Panel and the response of the Secretary-General are nonetheless important for both their content and as a reminder of how hard it can be to secure political support for institutional changes.

One final point. Institutions exist to help with disputes which States are incapable of dealing with themselves. It follows that these will tend to be the more difficult cases and it should be no surprise if even moderate success is often elusive. However, whether a dispute is referred to an organization or not, the primary responsibility remains with the governments concerned. Organizations are valuable and worth improving, but institution building is no more a substitute for responsible behaviour internationally, than it is in domestic affairs.

V. CONCLUSION

International law requires States to resolve their disputes peacefully and the primary means available for them to do so remains negotiation, sometimes assisted by good offices and mediation from third parties, and including today new forms of diplomacy associated with the ever-expanding role of international organizations. With the introduction of inquiry and conciliation we find third party assistance formalized in processes which provide the benefit of independent findings or recommendations, but with no prior commitment to accept the result. The non-binding character of these methods means they should be thought of more as ways of moving a dispute forward than of settling it, but their value and flexibility may be seen in international practice.

States which are prepared to relinquish control over their disputes can reap the additional advantages of judicial settlement or arbitration. Legal means, including the dispute settlement system of the WTO, and an increasing number of specialized courts, provide a way of obtaining binding decisions for individual cases, or whole classes of disputes. Moreover, access to such procedures need not, as hitherto, be confined to States, but is now sometimes available to international organizations, companies, or individuals. Important as they are, however, courts and tribunals are not suitable for all disputes and even when available, may not always be utilized, or be effective. Thus legal methods must be seen in their political context.

---

[62] *A More Secure World: Our Shared Responsibility*, UN Doc A/59/565.
[63] UN Doc A/59/2005.

Organizations are also important. However, the United Nations is not a world government, but essentially a body through which pressure and influence can be exerted on States when their disputes come before the Organization. Of course, many disputes never reach the UN, while many of those that do remain unsettled. Regional organizations can sometimes help by providing a diplomatic forum, or involving regional neighbours in the capacity of mediators or conciliators. There is also now the possibility of combining regional action with action by the United Nations. In both fora though, institutional action will often be less important in practice than the parties' own initiatives. Organizations, then, bring new possibilities, but for much of the time are no more than a further arena in which the sovereign State can exercise its traditional power to settle, or not to settle, its international disputes.

No student of current affairs needs to be told that dispute settlement is a subject on which the gulf between rhetoric and reality is conspicuously wide. All too often governments express support for general propositions like those to be found in the UN Charter, the Declaration on Friendly Relations, and the Manila Declaration, only to follow quite different precepts in their international behaviour. But realism is not cynicism and any dispassionate observer must recognize that since the landmark 1899 Hague Convention enormous progress has been made in refining the methods available for resolving international disputes and in developing States' obligations. The challenge for the twenty-first century is to see that current arrangements, which unquestionably provide the means for dealing with disputes, continue to be used in international practice.

REFERENCES

AKANDE, D (1997), 'The International Court of Justice and the Security Council: Is there Room for Judicial Control of Decisions of the United Nations?', 46 *ICLQ* 309–344.

ANDERSON, D (1998), 'Negotiation and Dispute Settlement', in Evans (ed), pp 111–121.

ANDO, N, MCWHINNEY, E, and WOLFRUM, R (eds) (2002), *Liber Amicorum Judge Shigeru Oda* (The Hague: Kluwer).

BAR-YAACOV, N (1974), *The Handling of International Disputes by Means of Inquiry* (Oxford: Oxford University Press).

BERCOVITCH, DJ and RUBIN, JZ (eds) (1992), *Mediation in International Relations* (London: St Martin's Press).

BERCOVITCH, J (ed) (1996), *Resolving International Conflicts: The Theory and Practice of Mediation* (London: Lynne Rienner).

BROWER, CN (1998), *The Iran-United States Claims Tribunal* (The Hague: Kluwer).

CHESTERMAN, S (ed) (2007), *Secretary or General? The UN Secretary-General in World Politics* (Cambridge: Cambridge University Press).

CHINKIN, C (1998), 'Alternative Dispute Resolution under International Law', in Evans (ed), pp 123–140.

CHURCHILL, RR (1985), 'Maritime Delimitation in the Jan Mayen Area', 9 *Marine Policy*, 16–38.

—— (1997), 'Falkland Islands: Maritime Jurisdiction and Co-operative Arrangements with Argentina', 46 *ICLQ* 463–478.

COLLIER, J and LOWE, AV (1999), *The Settlement of Disputes in International Law* (Oxford: Oxford University Press).

COT, J-P (1972), *International Conciliation* (London: Europa).

Deng, FM and Zartman, IW (1991), *Conflict Resolution in Africa* (Washington, DC: The Brookings Institute).

Evans, MD (1991), 'The Restoration of Diplomatic Relations between Argentina and the United Kingdom', 40 *ICLQ* 473–482.

——— (ed) (1998), *Remedies in International Law: The Institutional Dilemma* (Oxford: Hart Publishing).

Fawcett, L and Hurrell, A (eds) (1995), *Regionalism in World Politics* (Oxford: Oxford University Press).

Forsythe, DP (1985), 'Humanitarian Mediation by the International Committee of the Red Cross', in Touval and Zartman (eds), pp 233–249.

Franck, TM and Nolte, G (1993), 'The Good Offices Function of the Secretary-General', in Roberts and Kingsbury (eds), pp 143–182.

Freedman, L and Gamba-Stonehouse, V (1990), *Signals of War: The Falklands Conflict of 1982* (London: Faber & Faber).

Gowlland Gualtieri, AN (2001), 'The Environmental Accountability of the World Bank to Non-State Actors: Insights from the Inspection Panel', 72 *BYIL*, 213–255.

Gray, C (2007) 'A Crisis of Legitimacy for the UN Collective Security System?' 56 *ICLQ* 157–171.

———, and Kingsbury, B (1992), 'Developments in Dispute Settlement: Inter-State Arbitration since 1945', 63 *BYIL* 97–135.

Greenberg, MC, Barton, JH, and McGuiness, ME (eds) (2000), *Words over War. Mediation and Arbitration to Prevent Deadly Conflict* (Lanham, Md.: Rowman and Littlefield).

Kennedy, DLM and Southwick, JD (eds) (2002), *The Political Economy of International Trade Law* (Cambridge: Cambridge University Press).

Klein, N (2005), *Dispute Settlement in the UN Convention on the Law of the Sea* (Cambridge: Cambridge University Press).

Koopmans, SMG (2008), *Diplomatic Dispute Settlement* (The Hague: TMC Asser Press).

Koufa, KK (1988), 'International Conflictual Situations and their Peaceful Adjustment', 18 *Thesaurus Acroasium* 7–51.

Laudy, M (2000), 'The Vatican Mediation of the Beagle Channel Dispute', in Greenberg, Barton, and McGuiness (eds), pp 293–321.

Lowe, AV and Warbrick, C (eds) (1994), *The United Nations and the Principles of International Law* (London: Routledge)

——— and Fitzmaurice, M (eds) (1996), *Fifty Years of the International Court of Justice* (Cambridge: Cambridge University Press).

McCoubrey, H and Morris, J (2000), *Regional Peace-keeping in the Post Cold War Era* (The Hague: Kluwer).

Macdonald, RStJ (1963–64), 'The Organisation of American States in Action', 15 *University of Toronto LJ* 359–430.

Maluwa, T (1989), 'The Peaceful Settlement of Disputes among African States, 1963–1983: Some Conceptual Issues and Practical Trends', 38 *ICLQ* 299–321.

Merrills, JG (1993), 'The Optional Clause Revisited', 64 *BYIL* 197–245.

——— (1994), 'The Principle of Peaceful Settlement of Disputes', in Lowe and Warbrick (eds), pp 49–65.

——— (2002), 'The Optional Clause at Eighty', in Ando et al (eds), pp 435–451.

——— (2005), *International Dispute Settlement*, 4th edn (Cambridge: Cambridge University Press).

——— (2007), 'The Mosaic of International Dispute Settlement Procedures: Complementary or Contradictory?' 54 *Netherlands ILR* 361–395.

MERRILLS, JG and ROBERTSON, AH (2001), *Human Rights in Europe*, 4th edn (Manchester: Manchester University Press).

MULLER, AS, RAIC, D, and THURANSZKY, JM (eds) (1997), *The International Court of Justice* (The Hague: Kluwer).

OSTRIHANSKY, R (1988), 'Chambers of the International Court of Justice', 37 *ICLQ* 30–53.

PASQUALUCCI, JM (2003), *The Practice and Procedure of the Inter-American Court of Human Rights,* (Cambridge: Cambridge University Press).

PAULSON, C (2004), 'Compliance with Final Judgments of the International Court of Justice since 1987', 98 *AJIL* 434–462.

PECK, C (1996), *The United Nations as a Dispute Settlement System* (The Hague: Kluwer).

PEREZ DE CUELLAR, J (1993), 'The Role of the UN Secretary-General', in Roberts and Kingsbury (eds), pp 125–142.

PETERSMANN, E-U (1997), *The GATT/WTO Dispute Settlement System* (Dordrecht: Kluwer).

PLUNKETT, EA (1968–69), 'UN Fact-Finding as a Means of Settling International Disputes', 9 *Virginia JIL* 154–184.

RICHARDSON, EL (1988), 'Jan Mayen in Perspective', 82 *AJIL* 443–459.

ROBERTS, A and KINGSBURY, B (eds) (1993), *United Nations, Divided World. The UN's Roles in International Relations*, 2nd edn (Oxford: Clarendon Press).

SCHULTE, C (2004), *Compliance with Decisions of the International Court of Justice* (Oxford: Oxford University Press).

SHANY, Y (2003), *The Competing Jurisdictions of International Courts and Tribunals* (Oxford: Oxford University Press).

SICK, G (1985), 'The Partial Negotiator: Algeria and the US Hostages in Iran', in Touval and Zartman (eds), pp 21–67.

SIMPSON, JL and Fox, H (1959), *International Arbitration: Law and Practice* (London: Stevens).

SKJELSBAEK, K and FERMANN, G (1996), 'The UN Secretary-General and the Mediation of International Disputes', in Bercovitch (ed), pp 75–104.

SLAUGHTER, AM (2005), 'Security, Solidarity and Sovereignty: The Grand Themes of UN Reform', 99 *AJIL* 619–632.

SLIM, RM (1992), 'Small State Mediation in International Relations: The Algerian Mediation in the Hostage Crisis', in Bercovitch and Rubin (eds), pp 206–232.

SOHN, LB (1982–83), 'The Role of Arbitration in Recent Multilateral Treaties', 23 *Virginia JIL* 171–189.

TOUVAL, S and ZARTMAN, IW (eds) (1985), *International Mediation in Theory and in Practice* (Boulder, Colo.: Westview Press).

UMBRICHT, V (1984), 'Principles of International Mediation. The Case of the East African Community', 187 *Hague Recueil des Cours* 307–389.

VALENCIA-OSPINA, E (1996), 'The Use of Chambers of the International Court of Justice', in Lowe and Fitzmaurice (eds), pp 503–527.

WARBRICK, C (1992), 'Recognition of States', 41 *ICLQ* 473–483.

WEBBER, M (1996), 'Coping with Anarchy: Ethnic Conflict and International Organisations in the Former Soviet Union', 13(1) *International Organisation* 1–28.

WEIL, P (1996), 'L'Equité dans la Jurisprudence de la Cour Internationale de Justice', in Lowe and Fitzmaurice (eds), pp 121–144.

WHITE, ND (1993), *Keeping the Peace* (Manchester: Manchester University Press).

—— (1996), *The Law of International Organisations* (Manchester: Manchester University Press).

—— (1997), *Keeping the Peace*, 2nd edn (Manchester: Manchester University Press).

—— (2002), *The United Nations System* (London: Lynne Rienner).

ZARTMAN, IW (1991), 'Conflict Reduction: Prevention, Management and Resolution', in Deng and Zartman (eds), pp 299–320.

FURTHER READING

COLLIER, J and LOWE, AV (1999), *The Settlement of Disputes in International Law* (Oxford: Oxford University Press). A wide-ranging survey with the focus on institutions and procedures for dealing with disputes involving individuals, corporations, and other non-State actors, as well as States.

MERRILLS, JG (2005), *International Dispute Settlement*, 4th edn (Cambridge: Cambridge University Press). A review of dispute settlement in its legal and political context, explaining what techniques and institutions exist for dealing with disputes involving States, how they work and when they are used, and containing many practical examples.

PECK, C (1996), *The United Nations as a Dispute Settlement System* (The Hague: Kluwer). A comprehensive study of the characteristics of the United Nations system from a dispute settlement perspective with some perceptive observations about its potential for further development.

UNITED NATIONS (1992), *Handbook on the Peaceful Settlement of Disputes between States* (New York: United Nations). A succinct account of the means available, covering diplomatic and legal methods, as well as the role of political organizations. Very good at a descriptive level and as a source of reference, though rather short on critical evaluation.

20

THE INTERNATIONAL COURT OF JUSTICE

Hugh Thirlway

SUMMARY

The International Court of Justice, the principal judicial organ of the United Nations, is a standing tribunal to which States may bring their disputes, and which is empowered to give advisory opinions to United Nations organs and specialized agencies. Its jurisdiction derives from the consent of the States parties to the case, which may be given either directly in respect of a specific dispute, or in advance in respect of a defined class or category of disputes; the Statute of the Court also provides for acceptance of a general 'compulsory' jurisdiction by simple declaration, which may however be subject to reservations. Decisions of the Court, given after an extensive written and oral procedure, are binding on the parties in respect of the case, but not otherwise.

I. INTRODUCTION

The International Court of Justice (ICJ) is often referred to in non-technical contexts as the 'World Court', but this is perhaps misleading. Such an appellation may suggest the international equivalent of a national supreme court, a body of worldwide jurisdiction, empowered to pass judgment on the legal rights and duties of all States from a position of superiority and supervision. No such tribunal however exists. The International Court can better be seen as a standing mechanism available for the peaceful settlement of disputes between States, to the extent that they wish to make use of it. No dispute can be the subject of a decision of the Court unless the States parties to it have consented to the Court's jurisdiction over that specific dispute, or over a class of disputes of which that dispute is one. Access to the Court is enjoyed by all members of the United Nations, but its 'compulsory jurisdiction' (also a somewhat misleading term) is accepted by only a fairly small number of States, and for the most part with reservations that limit effective jurisdiction to certain classes of dispute.

The Court is defined in the United Nations Charter (Article 92) as the 'principal judicial organ' of the Organization, but here also the term 'judicial' serves to distinguish the role of the Court from that of the political organs, the General Assembly and Security Council. It does not signify that the Court enjoys, within the Organization, any position resembling that of the supreme court or constitutional court of a State. It has, for example, no overriding power to interpret the Charter, and the question whether it is entitled to examine the legality of a decision adopted by one of the other principal organs is controversial.[1]

Despite these limitations, the Court has, as we shall see, an important role to play in the settlement of disputes, and thus the maintenance of international peace, and in the development of international law. Its function is defined by its Statute (Article 38) as being 'to decide, in accordance with international law, such disputes as are submitted to it'. It is further empowered to give advisory opinions on legal questions at the request of the Security Council or the General Assembly; subject to certain limitations (to be examined below), such opinions may also be requested by other organs and agencies authorized by the General Assembly.

II. HISTORY

The present Court was established by the United Nations Charter, and came into existence with the election of the first members in February 1946. It was however created as the successor to the Permanent Court of International Justice (PCIJ), established pursuant to Article 14 of the Covenant of the League of Nations in 1921, and was modelled closely on that body.

The move towards the creation of a standing international judicial body came as the culmination of the trend, throughout the nineteenth and early twentieth centuries, to make increasing use of arbitration as a means of settling international disputes. (The development of arbitration, its operation, and its advantages and disadvantages, are dealt with in Ch 19 above.) Two practical problems however stood in the way of implementing proposals for the establishment of such a permanent body. When an existing dispute was taken to arbitration, the arbitrators were appointed by the States parties to the dispute (or by a third party nominated by them), and the expenses of the arbitration were borne by the parties. If a standing tribunal were set up to try *future* disputes, how were its judges to be appointed, and how should it be financed? The Permanent Court of Arbitration, created in 1899, had gone some way to meet the difficulty, by establishing a large panel of potential arbitrators from whom States could choose for a particular dispute, and by setting up a small standing secretariat, but this did not amount to a true court. With the creation of the League of Nations, it became possible to set up a system of election of members of the new Court by the League Council and Assembly, and for the expenses of the Court to be met out of the budget of the League.

It was originally hoped that the new Court would have a status approximating to that of a 'World Court' as described above, and in particular that it would have universal compulsory jurisdiction, at least over members of the League. This proved over-optimistic; the new Court's jurisdiction had to be the subject of general acceptance, and it was too much

---

[1] The question has been debated before the Court in the cases of the *Aerial Incident at Lockerbie (Libya* v *United Kingdom, Libya* v *United States)*, but the cases were discontinued by agreement before the Court had ruled on the point.

to expect States to give a new and untried body such a wide mandate. Jurisdiction could be conferred ad hoc by agreement, or accepted by treaty in advance for defined categories of disputes; and the 'optional clause' of Article 36(2) of the PCIJ Statute, whose operation is explained below, went as far as was possible for the time in the direction of compulsory jurisdiction.

The history of the Permanent Court during the inter-war period was generally a satisfactory one; it gave a number of judgments and advisory opinions, some on matters of acute political or legal delicacy, and its operation inspired increasing confidence. The fact of its existence was also a force for peaceful settlement, since the possibility that a dispute might be brought before it, with the attendant publicity, was an inducement to reach a negotiated settlement. However, although not formally an organ of the League, its fortunes were bound up with those of the League; and the paralysis of the League caused by the outbreak of the Second World War had already impeded the Court's work even before the German invasion of the Netherlands, where the Court had its seat, brought it completely to a halt.

The Allies' plans for a new post-war international organization included provision for a judicial body; the possibility of keeping the Permanent Court in being was considered, but it was thought better to let it disappear with the League of Nations, and set up a new Court to continue its work. However, the new International Court of Justice was not only to take over the premises and archives of the pre-war Court, but also, so far as possible, to inherit its jurisdiction. Numerous treaties had been concluded providing for settlement of disputes by the Permanent Court; the Statute of the new Court provided that, as between parties to that Statute, such treaties should be read as referring to the new Court.[2]

III. STRUCTURE AND COMPOSITION

The Court consists of 15 judges, elected by the Security Council and the General Assembly for terms of nine years; the elections are staggered so that five judges complete their terms of office every three years. A judge may be re-elected (and this has frequently occurred), but the system thus ensures that a regular renewal of the bench is possible, while at the same time preserving continuity. Judges are elected as individuals, not as representatives of their countries, and are required to make a solemn declaration in open court of impartiality in the exercise of their functions. They may not engage in any other occupation during their period of office.

No two members of the Court may be of the same nationality.[3] The Statute (Article 9) directs that the election be such as to ensure the representation of 'the main forms of civilization and of the principal legal systems of the world'. There is no official allocation of seats on this (or any other) basis, but it is a long-standing convention that the candidate

---

[2] Similarly, pre-war 'optional clause' jurisdiction was preserved, so far as possible: see n 23 below. These provisions of the Statute did not specifically regulate the position of States parties to the Statute of the Permanent Court who did not become members of the United Nations, and thus parties to the Statute of the new Court, until many years after the Permanent Court had ceased to exist. For the handling of lacunas of this kind, see *Temple of Preah Vihear, Preliminary Objections, ICJ Reports 1961*, p 17; *Barcelona Traction, Light and Power Company, Preliminary Objections, ICJ Reports 1964*, p 6.

[3] But a judge ad hoc (see below) may have the same nationality as an elected member of the Court.

of each of the permanent members of the Security Council will always be elected, and the other seats are unofficially distributed between various regions of the world.

The salaries of the judges, and the other expenses of the Court, are borne by the United Nations, as part of the regular budget. The seat of the Court is at The Hague, in the Peace Palace, where the Court occupies premises under an agreement between the United Nations and the Carnegie Foundation, the owner of the building. The President of the Court (elected triennially by his colleagues) is to 'direct the work and supervise the administration of the Court' (Rules, Article 12). The day-to-day administration of the Court is the responsibility of the Registry, headed by a Registrar, elected by the Court for a seven-year term.

Cases are heard by the full Court unless the parties to a case agree that it shall be heard by a chamber (see below). A judge is not required to withdraw if a case is brought by the State of which he is a national; on the contrary, he is bound to sit in all cases before the full Court, unless there are special reasons, other than the mere fact of nationality, why it would be inappropriate for him to sit. (If however the President of the Court is a national of one of the parties to a case, he does not preside in the case, but hands over the presidency to the Vice-President or senior judge.) The disqualification or withdrawal of a judge from a case is dealt with by Articles 17 and 24 of the Statute: the commonest reason for exclusion is that the judge has, prior to his election, already been involved in the case, for example, as having advised one of the parties.

The possible presence on the bench of a judge of the nationality of one of the parties was seen, when the Statute was drafted, as suggestive of inequality, despite the fact that members of the Court are required to act impartially. This view is defended on the ground that the presence of a 'national judge', even one bound to decide impartially, is still valuable for ensuring justice for the State of which he is a national, since he can ensure that the case presented by his country is fully understood. Rather than requiring withdrawal of the judge in such circumstances, the Statute ensures equality by enabling the other party to a case of this kind to nominate a person to sit as judge solely for that case, with the title of judge ad hoc.[4] The Statute also provides, consistently with the idea of the benefit of a 'national judge', that in a case where neither party has a judge of its nationality on the Bench, and thus there is no inequality between the parties, each party may choose a judge ad hoc. In such cases, the parties however quite often agree that neither of them will exercise their right to a judge ad hoc.

Elected members of the Court not infrequently vote against the State of their nationality, but to date judges ad hoc have nearly always voted in favour of the State that appointed them; and it is perhaps too much to expect that they should do otherwise.

In addition to certain standing chambers (in practice virtually never used),[5] a chamber may be formed by the Court to deal with a specific case, if the parties so request. The

---

[4] There is however no requirement that the judge ad hoc be of the nationality of the party appointing him, and this is frequently not the case. For an analysis of the function of a judge ad hoc, see the dissenting opinion of Judge ad hoc Franck in the case of *Sovereignty over Pulau Ligitan and Pulau Sipadan, ICJ Reports 2002*, p 625, paras 9–12, quoting the Separate Opinion of Judge ad hoc Elihu Lauterpacht in the *Application of the Convention on the Prevention and Punishment of the Crime of Genocide, Provisional Measures, Order of 13 September, ICJ Reports 1993*, p 325, at pp 408–409, paras 4–6.

[5] The experience with special chambers suggests that the reason for the neglect of the standing chambers is probably that their composition is determined in advance by the Court, and the parties have no say in it.

number of judges to constitute such a chamber is determined by the parties, but the individual judges to be members of it are elected by the Court, and the composition of the chamber is thus, theoretically, outside the control of the parties. In practice however it has become accepted that if the parties indicate that certain names would be acceptable, the Court is virtually certain to elect them, if only because the creation of a chamber composed otherwise than as desired by the parties would be likely to result in the case being withdrawn and referred to some other method of settlement.[6]

Reference of a case to a special chamber of the Court, a procedure long neglected, became more popular between 1984 and 2002, but may now be in decline.[7] To some extent the use of chambers makes for greater flexibility and thus tends toward speedier settlement of cases; but simultaneous operation of two chambers is only practicable for this purpose if no member of one chamber is also a member of the other. In tribunals where the chambers are established by the tribunal itself, as sub-units (eg, the International Criminal Tribunal for the Former Yugoslavia and the International Criminal Court), this can be arranged; but where the membership of chambers is in effect left to the parties to determine, experience shows that overlapping membership is frequent. The use of chambers has thus not appreciably accelerated the procedure of the International Court.

IV. PROCEDURE

The procedure before the Court is regulated primarily by its Statute. Under Article 30 of the Statute the Court has power to make rules 'for carrying out its functions', including rules of procedure. The Rules of Court adopted in 1946 were modelled closely on those drawn up by the Permanent Court; they were revised in part in 1972, and more radically in 1978. Further revisions of detail have been effected in more recent years. The Court has recently found it useful to regulate detailed matters of procedure in a more informal way, by issuing 'Practice Directions' interpreting and implementing the Statute and Rules. The hierarchy of norms is of course that Practice Directions cannot be inconsistent with the Rules or the Statute, and the Rules cannot depart from the Statute.[8] Generally, the extent to which the broad lines of the procedure laid down in the Statute of the Permanent Court, and in the Rules adopted by that body, have been maintained, is a tribute to the work of the jurists of the inter-war period. The official languages of the Court are French and English.

---

[6] The first request for a special chamber, by the United States and Canada in the *Gulf of Maine* case, was made pursuant to a treaty which provided explicitly that the case would be transferred to arbitration if the Chamber was not formed as the parties wished. Subsequent approaches to the Court have been more tactful.

[7] The following cases have been decided by chambers: *Gulf of Maine* (1984); *Frontier Dispute (Burkina Faso/Mali)* (1986); *Elettronica Sicula* (1989); *Land, Island and Maritime Frontier Dispute* (1992). Chambers have been established to hear the following further cases: *Application for Revision of the Judgment of 11 September 1992 in the Land, Island and Maritime Frontier Dispute* (2002); *Frontier Dispute (Benin/Niger)* (2002).

[8] For an example of a challenge to a provision in the Rules on the ground that it was inconsistent with the Statute, see the dissenting opinion of Judge Shahabuddeen in the *Land, Island and Maritime Frontier Dispute, (El Salvador/Honduras), Application to Intervene, Order of 28 February 1990, ICJ Reports 1990*, p 3 at pp 18ff.

The proceedings in contentious cases are set in motion in one of two ways. If the parties have concluded an agreement (*compromis* or Special Agreement) to bring the dispute before the Court, the case begins with the notification of this to the Court. If not, one State may file an application instituting proceedings against another State, and the Registrar communicates this to that State. In either event, all other States entitled to appear before the Court are notified of the institution of proceedings. The procedure thereafter represents something of a blend of the continental system of extensive written pleadings, and the Anglo-American common law system in which the hearing, the 'day in court', is the essential element. In a first stage, the parties exchange written pleadings (Memorial by the applicant, Counter-Memorial by the respondent; in some cases followed by a Reply (applicant) and a Rejoinder (respondent), but these additional pleadings are now exceptional). There then follows a hearing, usually taking several days or even weeks, at which the parties address their arguments to the Court in the same order: a presentation by the applicant, followed by a presentation by the respondent, and a much briefer 'second round' devoted to refutation of the opponent's contentions. When the case is brought by special agreement, rather than by a unilateral application filed by one State against another, neither party is, strictly speaking, in the position of applicant or respondent; the order of speaking is determined by the Court, taking into account the views of the parties.[9] The hearing is open to the public; the Court has power to hold a closed hearing (Statute, Article 46), but has done so only on two occasions.[10] The written pleadings are normally made available to the public (in particular, on the Court's website) at the time of the opening of the oral proceedings (Rules, Article 53(2)).

Evidence is normally submitted in the form of documents, though it may of course take other forms (eg, photographs, physical objects); witnesses may give written evidence, or appear at the hearing to give their evidence orally, in which case they may be cross-examined by the other party. The procedure in this respect is modelled broadly on Anglo-American practice. Hearsay evidence does not carry weight;[11] and in the case of *Military and Paramilitary Activities in and against Nicaragua* the Court expressed some reservations as to the value of evidence of government ministers and other representatives of a State, who could be taken to have some personal interest in the success of their government's case.[12]

The burden of proof of fact, in accordance with general procedural principles, rests upon the party alleging the fact. In accordance with the principle *iura novit curia* (the law is known to the Court), the parties are not required to prove the existence of the rules of international law that they invoke; the Court is deemed to know such rules. An exception to this is where a party relies on a customary rule which is not one of general law (local or special custom): in this case, the party must 'prove that this custom is established in such

---

[9] The order of speaking is different in proceedings on preliminary objections or requests for the indication of provisional measures; these proceedings are explained below.

[10] *South West Africa, Pleadings, Oral Arguments, Documents*, Vol VIII, p 4; *Legal Consequences for States of the Continued Presence of South Africa in Namibia (South West Africa) Notwithstanding Security Council Resolution 276 (1970) Pleadings, Oral Arguments, Documents*, Vol II, p 3. In the latter case, the verbatim record of the closed sitting was later made public (ibid).

[11] Cf *Corfu Channel, Merits, Judgment, ICJ Reports 1949*, p 4 at pp 16–17; *Military and Paramilitary Activities in and against Nicaragua (Nicaragua v USA), Merits, Judgment, ICJ Reports 1986*, p 42, para 68.

[12] Ibid, para 70.

a manner that it has been binding on the other Party'.[13] In practice, particularly where the existence of a particular rule of general law is controversial, States will devote much argument to demonstrating that it does, or does not, exist, citing the facts of State practice in support.

The sources of international law to be applied by the Court, enumerated in Article 38 of the Statute, have been discussed in Chapter 4 above: international treaties and conventions; international custom; general principles of law; and the subsidiary sources, ie, decisions of tribunals[14] and opinions of jurists.

The decision of the Court is adopted by majority vote, the President of the Court having a casting vote in the event of a tie. Every judge has the right to append to the decision an individual statement of his views, entitled 'separate opinion' if he agrees with the decision, or 'dissenting opinion' if he does not (the non-statutory term 'declaration' is also used). Until 1978, the way in which a judge had voted would not become public unless he chose to attach such an opinion; but the revised Rules of Court adopted in that year provided that in future the decision would indicate not only the numbers of the votes on each side, but also the names of the judges.

V. THE COURT'S JURISDICTION

Emphasis has already been laid on the fact that the jurisdiction of the Court, like that of any international judicial or arbitral body, is based upon the consent of States. The application of this principle is however complicated as a result of the fact that the Court is a permanent institution.

In the first place, the Court is a treaty-based institution, created and regulated by the United Nations Charter and the Statute of the Court (which is in fact an 'integral part' of the Charter: Article 92); this means that the general scope of its jurisdiction, and the conditions of its exercise, are defined *ne varietur* by those instruments. Jurisdiction in this sense, relating to access to the Court, and to the general nature of the powers it possesses, is thus a function of the will of the body of States parties to the Charter and Statute, not of the will of the specific parties to a given dispute. The consent of the parties to the dispute cannot therefore abrogate or modify statutory provisions of this kind;[15] it is in fact those provisions that determine how, for example, the necessary consent may be given for the creation of jurisdiction in specific cases.

Secondly, the jurisdiction of the Court may be, and frequently is, asserted on the basis of treaty instruments of a general nature conferring future jurisdiction over a range or category of disputes. When the instrument was concluded, no such disputes may yet have been in existence, but the possibility that such may arise will have been foreseen, and consent given in advance to the binding determination of them by the Court. When a dispute

---

[13] *Asylum, Judgment, ICJ Reports 1950*, p 266 at p 276. For the distinction between general and special custom, see above, Ch 4, Section II B.

[14] For the treatment by the Court of its own decisions, see Section VII below.

[15] Discussing Article 35, para 2, of the Statute, the Court has observed that 'it would have been inconsistent with the main thrust of the text to make it possible in the future for States to obtain access to the Court simply by the conclusion between themselves of a special treaty…': *Legality of the Use of Force (Serbia and Montenegro v Belgium), Judgment, ICJ Reports 2004*, p 319, para 102.

is subsequently brought before the Court on the basis of a clause of this kind, that advance consent creative of jurisdiction is still operative (assuming that the treaty has not been denounced), but it may well not be accompanied, at the time that the matter is brought to the Court, by actual contemporary consent or willingness to have that particular dispute settled by decision of the Court. The respondent State may therefore seek to deny that the general consent given in the past applies to the specific dispute, because, for example, it does not really fall within the category of disputes contemplated, or because any conditions attached to it have not been met in the specific case. The Court, in order to be satisfied that consent to its dealing with the dispute has actually been given, will have to analyse, in some-times painstaking detail, the provisions of the relevant instruments in order to trace a link between the consent given, often in wide general terms, by the respondent and the facts of the particular case. The principle remains simple: has the respondent State given consent to jurisdiction? Its application may however involve much subtle and complex argument.

A. JURISDICTION: STRUCTURAL LIMITATIONS

The most basic limitation on the Court's jurisdiction is that provided in Article 38 of the Statute: 'Only States may be parties to cases before the Court'. The reference is of course to sovereign States in the sense of the principal category of subjects of international law, and excludes the component States of federations, for example. A case cannot be brought by or against a non-State entity, such as an individual, a non-governmental organization, or a multinational, even if the other party is a State and consents to the case being brought.[16] Nor can an intergovernmental international organization (not even the United Nations itself) be a party, though the major ones are empowered to ask the Court for advisory opinions.

To be a party to a case, a State must also be one of those to which the Court is 'open', or having 'access' to the Court, under Article 35 of the Statute. The principal category of States with such access is that of parties to the Statute of the Court (Article 35(1)); this category automatically includes the members of the United Nations.[17] It is possible for a State to become a party to the Statute without joining the United Nations; Article 93(2) of the Charter provides that the conditions for this are to be laid down by the General Assembly,

---

[16] The position is apparently different in advisory proceedings, in which there are strictly speaking no 'parties': cf the participation by Palestine in the case concerning *Legal Consequences of the Construction of a Wall in the Occupied Palestinian Territory, ICJ Reports 2004*, p 136, para 4; Order of 17 October 2008 in the case of *Accordance with International Law of the Unilateral Declaration of Independence by the Provisional Institutions of Self-Government of Kosovo*. The Court has also indicated in Practice Direction XII that where an international non-governmental organization submits a statement in advisory proceedings, while 'it is not to be considered part of the case-file', the Court may refer to it as 'a publication readily available', and it may thus be referred to by, and before, the Court.

[17] UN Charter, Art. 93, para 1 Paragraph 2 of Article 35 of the Statute contains an obscure reference to 'the special provisions contained in treaties in force'. At the provisional measures stage of the *Bosnia v Yugoslavia* case, the Court took the view that this might authorize proceedings against a State which was not a party to the Statute and had not complied with the conditions laid down by the Security Council: *Application of the Convention on the Prevention and Punishment of the Crime of Genocide, Provisional Measures, Order of 8 April 1993, ICJ Reports 1993*, p 3, paras 18–19. The Court however took the opposite view in the NATO cases: see for example *Legality of the Use of Force (Serbia and Montenegro v Belgium), Judgment, ICJ Reports 2004*, p 279, paras 113–114.

on the recommendation of the Security Council.[18] Furthermore, under Article 35(2) of the Statute, the Security Council is empowered to lay down the conditions on which other States not parties to the Statute may have access to the Court. Security Council Resolution 9 (1946) implements this provision, and provides for the deposit with the Secretary-General of a declaration accepting the jurisdiction of the Court and undertaking to comply with its decisions.

The application of these provisions is normally simple, inasmuch as it is generally evident at the outset of a case whether the parties are States having access to the Court;[19] and if one of them is not, then the case cannot proceed, even with the consent of the other party. If for example an individual attempts to bring a case before the Court (as frequently happens), the Registrar draws his attention to the provisions of Article 38, and no further action is necessary.

A similar limitation is imposed by the provisions of the Statute concerning the nature of the Court's judgment, which is 'final and without appeal'. The Court cannot, even at the request of the parties, give a provisional or conditional judgment (though it can give a declaratory judgment, confined, for example, to certain aspects of a dispute). For example, parties to a case before the Permanent Court of International Justice requested the Court to give an informal and non-binding indication of how it was minded to decide, so that they could negotiate a settlement on that basis; but the Court declined, on the basis that it had no power to give a ruling of this kind, which would be dependent for its implementation on the wishes of the parties.[20]

B. JURISDICTION IN PARTICULAR CASES

1. Special agreements and compromissory clauses

The simplest means of putting into effect the principle that jurisdiction is conferred on the Court by the consent of the parties is for two States that wish a dispute to be settled by the Court to enter into an agreement to that effect. This is the classic *compromis* or Special Agreement, used for many years prior to the establishment of the Court for the

---

[18] This procedure was followed for Switzerland (1946), Liechtenstein (1949), San Marino (1953), and Nauru (1987).

[19] An exception is the case of the *Application of the Convention on the Prevention and Punishment of the Crime of Genocide.* Following the break-up of the former Socialist Federal Republic of Yugoslavia, for a time the new Republic of Yugoslavia (Serbia and Montenegro) was treated by the United Nations as the successor of the old Yugoslavia, and on that basis it was made respondent to the proceedings before the Court. On 1 November 2002, however, after the Court had indicated certain provisional measures in the case, and had given judgment dismissing certain preliminary objections, the new Yugoslavia was admitted to the United Nations as a new member. Yugoslavia filed an Application for Revision of the Court's judgment on the preliminary objections on the basis that this admission showed that it had not previously been a party to the Statute. The Court however dismissed the Application on the ground that this event was not a 'new fact' within the meaning of Article 61 of the Statute (see Section VI C, below). The question then arose again in the cases brought by Yugoslavia against 10 member States of NATO: at a late stage in the proceedings, Yugoslavia withdrew its claim to have been a party to the Statute (and to the Genocide Convention) and invited the Court 'to decide on its jurisdiction'. The Court ruled that Yugoslavia had not been a member of the United Nations when its Application was filed, and consequently declined jurisdiction: *Legality of the Use of Force,* eight judgments dated 15 December 2004.

[20] *Free Zones of Upper Savoy and the District of Gex, Order of 6 December 1930,* PCIJ, Ser A, No 24, at p 14.

submission of a dispute to arbitration. Such an agreement will define the dispute and record the agreement of the parties to accept the Court's decision on it as binding—this last being theoretically unnecessary in view of the provisions of the Charter and Statute. It may also contain provisions as to the procedure to be followed (number and order of written pleadings, possibly waiver of the right to appoint judges ad hoc, etc). Normally no jurisdictional problems arise in a case brought before the Court by special agreement, since the consent of the parties is real and contemporaneous, rather than given in advance and in general terms.[21] When a special agreement has been concluded, the procedural step by which a case is brought before the Court—in technical language the 'seising' of the Court—is the notification of the agreement to the Court. Whether this is done by one party or by both parties jointly, the essence of a case of this kind is that it is a joint approach to the Court, not an action commenced by one party against the other.

Where jurisdiction is asserted on the basis of some instrument other than a special agreement, the Court is seised unilaterally, by an application, indicating the subject of the dispute and the parties. The applicant State claims that the other party to the dispute has in the past consented to settlement of disputes of a particular category being referred unilaterally to the Court for settlement, and that the current dispute falls into that category. In a case of this kind, the consent creative of jurisdiction will, according to the applicant, have been given in advance. It may take the form of a compromissory clause, that is to say a clause in a treaty providing that all disputes relating to the application or interpretation of the treaty may be brought by one or the other party before the Court by unilateral application. Alternatively, the treaty itself may have been concluded for the purpose of making advance provision for the settlement by the Court of all disputes (or certain categories of disputes) that may subsequently arise between the parties: a treaty of judicial settlement (often combined with a treaty of friendship or commercial relations).

If a case is brought before the Court by unilateral application, there is thus normally a pre-existing title of jurisdiction in the form of a treaty between the parties of this kind, or in the form of acceptances of jurisdiction under the 'optional clause', to be discussed below. This does not mean, however, that an application that fails to specify such a pre-existing title is invalid; the Statute of the Court (Article 40) only requires an application to specify 'the subject of the dispute and the parties', and the Rules of Court (Article 38(2)) only require that it indicate 'as far as possible' the basis of jurisdiction relied on. Consequently, an application may be made which in effect invites the State named as respondent to consent to jurisdiction simply for the purposes of that particular case, a process known as *forum prorogatum*. At one time this possibility was being abused for political ends, applications being made simply for publicity purposes against States whose known attitude to judicial settlement made it certain that no such consent would be forthcoming. As a result, a special provision (Article 38(5)) was included in the Rules of Court in 1978 whereby an application of this kind is treated for procedural purposes as ineffective until the consent of the named respondent is forthcoming—usually it is not, but in the recent case of *Certain Questions of Mutual Assistance in Criminal Matters (Djibouti v France)*, following

---

[21] There may however be limitations on the exercise of jurisdiction: see the *Monetary Gold Removed from Rome in 1943, Judgment, ICJ Reports 1954*, p 19; Section VII below.

an Application by Djibouti instituting proceedings against France, the State named as Respondent gave its consent to ad hoc jurisdiction.[22]

2. The 'optional clause' system

At the time of the drafting of the Statute of the Permanent Court in 1920, it was first envisaged that the new Court would have universal compulsory jurisdiction, in the sense that any State party to the Statute could bring before the Court, by unilateral application, any dispute whatever with another State party to the Statute. The necessary consent conferring jurisdiction would thus be given simply by accession to the Statute. However, as noted above, it was soon realized that the majority of States were not ready for so radical an innovation, and the optional clause system was devised as being the furthest that it was then possible to go in the direction of compulsory jurisdiction. This system was carried over, without change of substance, into the Statute of the post-war Court, and it is in that context that it will be examined here.[23]

Under Article 36(2) of the Statute, a State may deposit with the UN Secretary-General a declaration that it accepts the jurisdiction of the Court for disputes in respect of all or some of a number of matters enumerated in Article 36 (in effect, all international legal disputes), 'in relation to any other State accepting the same obligation'. The intended effect of this was that those States that were ready to accept compulsory jurisdiction could do so among themselves, while other States would have to rely on obtaining the consent ad hoc of any State with which they might have a dispute, if that dispute were to be brought before the Court. There would be two classes of 'clients' of the Court, those within the 'optional clause' system and those outside it. This simple vision became complicated however as a result of the recognition by Article 36 of the possibility of making reservations to an optional clause declaration. Specifically, the reservations foreseen were 'a condition of reciprocity on the part of several or certain States' and acceptance 'for a certain time'. The simplicity of the system was already compromised by this facility; but the question soon arose whether any *other* reservations were effective (eg, the exclusion of disputes of a specified type, or of disputes arising before or after a specified date). No reservation was challenged before the Permanent Court as being unauthorized by the Statute, and the inclusion of reservations became standard State practice. The prevailing view became that, since a State was free to decide to accept or not to accept the optional clause jurisdiction in its entirety, it was also free to accept it subject to whatever reservations it saw fit to make.[24]

Furthermore, Article 36(2) of the Statute employed the term 'reciprocity', and provided for acceptances of jurisdiction 'in relation to any other State accepting *the same obligation*'. If a State which had made a reservation to its acceptance brought proceedings against

---

[22] See *Certain Questions of Mutual Assistance in Criminal Matters (Djibouti v France), Judgment of 4 June 2008*, paras 39–43 and 63–95 for the complications involved in ascertaining the precise extent of such jurisdiction.

[23] Article 36(5) of the Statute of the post-war Court preserves, as between parties to that Statute, any declarations of acceptance of jurisdiction made under the PCIJ Statute: cf *Military and Paramilitary Activities in and against Nicaragua (Nicaragua v USA), Jurisdiction and Admissibility, Judgment, ICJ Reports 1984*, p 392, para 14. (See also n 2 above.)

[24] See the statement in the report of Subcommittee IV/1/D of the San Francisco Conference that drafted the Statute of the post-war Court: UNCIO, vol 13, pp 391, 559. The League Assembly had taken the view as early as 1928 that reservations were not limited to those specifically contemplated in the Statute: see the resolution of the Assembly quoted in *Aerial Incident of 10 August 1999 (Pakistan v India), Jurisdiction, ICJ Reports 2000*, p 12, para 37.

a State which had made none, was the jurisdiction of the Court affected by the reservation? The Permanent Court held that it was; that the respondent State could invoke the applicant State's reservation, or to put it another way, that the Court's jurisdiction was defined by the narrower of the two acceptances.[25] Some of the cases concern reservations that must necessarily operate bilaterally, for example the reservation limiting jurisdiction to disputes arising after a certain date: if a dispute arises after such date for one party to it, then it must equally do so for the other.[26] A more striking example of the application of this principle is afforded by the *Certain Norwegian Loans* case, in which the reservation made by France, the applicant, excluding disputes within the domestic jurisdiction of France could be turned against it by Norway, the respondent, so as to exclude a dispute on the ground that it was within the domestic jurisdiction of Norway.[27]

The consequence was that, instead of the simple system of universal compulsory jurisdiction within a limited group of States, foreseen by the draftsmen of the Statute, the jurisdiction of the Court under Article 36(2) became a complex network of bilateral relationships. The fact that two States have each made a declaration of acceptance no longer signifies that any dispute between them can be brought by either of them unilaterally before the Court, unless both acceptances are entirely without reservations. If that is not so, it is necessary to find the lowest common denominator of the jurisdiction *not* excluded by reservations on each side, and consider whether the particular dispute falls within it.

Another disruptive development, though one that has now more or less passed out of use, was the invention of the 'self-judging' reservation, designed to retain control of the extent of the jurisdictional obligation in the hands of the State making the declaration. In the form pioneered by the United States, and known as the 'Connally reservation', this was a reservation excluding matters within the domestic jurisdiction of the reserving State *as determined by the reserving State*. This reservation apparently enabled the reserving State to declare, even after the Court had been seised of a dispute on the basis of the optional clause declaration, that the dispute was a matter of domestic jurisdiction, and that the Court had therefore no jurisdiction. It was generally felt that a reservation of this kind was objectionable as being incompatible with the system of Article 36, and in particular with the principle of the *compétence de la compétence* stated in Article 36(6) (see below), but the Court nevertheless gave effect to the reservation. It has been convincingly argued that to rule that the reservation was invalid would lead to the consequence that the whole declaration of acceptance was invalid, so that the reserving State would still be able to escape the jurisdiction of the Court.[28]

[25] *Electricity Company of Sofia and Bulgaria, Judgment, 1939, PCIJ, Ser A/B, No 77*, p 64 at p 81; see also *Certain Norwegian Loans, Judgment, ICJ Reports 1957*, p 9 at p 24. For a fuller examination of the problem, see Thirlway, H, 1984.

[26] See, eg, the Orders on provisional measures in the cases concerning the *Legality of Use of Force*, brought by Yugoslavia against the member States of NATO: eg, *Yugoslavia v Belgium, Provisional Measures, Order of 2 June 1999, ICJ Reports 1999*, p 124, paras 22ff.

[27] *Certain Norwegian Loans, Judgment, ICJ Reports 1957*, p 9: the reservation was in fact of the 'Connally' type (see below). Cf also the *Aegean Sea Continental Shelf, Judgment, ICJ Reports 1978*, p 3, where a reservation made by Greece (applicant) excluding matters of the 'territorial integrity' of Greece applied to exclude a matter concerning the territorial integrity of Turkey (respondent), though this case related, not to Article 36(2) of the Statute, but to the 1928 General Act for the Pacific Settlement of International Disputes.

[28] See *Certain Norwegian Loans, Judgment, ICJ Reports 1957*, p 9, Separate Opinion of Judge Lauterpacht, p 34 at pp 56ff. This was on the basis that it would not be proper to 'sever' the reservation from the acceptance, since to do so would be to impose on the State concerned an obligation that it had clearly not consented to

There is however nothing illicit about attaching even extensive reservations to an acceptance of jurisdiction. The Court has had occasion to emphasize the 'fundamental distinction between the acceptance by a State of the Court's jurisdiction and the compatibility of particular acts with international law'.[29] The fact that a reservation to an optional-clause declaration excludes jurisdiction over acts of which the legality may be doubtful does not render the reservation invalid; the reservation may have been made specifically because there is doubt about the matter, and this does not mean that the reserving State is claiming a licence to commit wrongful acts with impunity. This is another application of the principle that, since a State is free not to accept the jurisdiction of the Court at all, it must also be free to decide for itself what limitations it will impose on such acceptance as it does consent to make.

C. JURISDICTION AND ITS EXERCISE

In principle, if the Court finds that it has jurisdiction to entertain a particular case, it is under a duty to exercise that jurisdiction, to the extent that it has been conferred and to the extent of the claims of the parties before it (the rule *ne ultra petita*). In a few cases, the Court has however found that, even before inquiring into the existence of jurisdiction, it sees reasons for not exercising it. One example of a category of cases of this kind is where to decide the case would involve deciding the legal situation of a State not a party to the case (the *Monetary Gold* principle, examined further in Section VII below). Another is where any judgment given would be ineffective, because the legal situation is such that the decision would have no 'forward reach',[30] or because the claims of the applicant have in effect been satisfied, so that the case has become 'without object' or 'moot'.[31] Since a refusal to exercise jurisdiction would normally be a renunciation of the very function of the Court, these cases are however highly exceptional.[32]

D. VERIFICATION OF JURISDICTION AND ADMISSIBILITY: PRELIMINARY OBJECTIONS

A well-established principle of the law relating to international arbitral and judicial proceedings is that a tribunal (arbitral or judicial) has power to decide, with binding effect for the parties, any question as to the existence or scope of its jurisdiction.[33] This

accept. The European Court of Human Rights, on the basis of a virtually identical provision in its constituent instrument, has however taken a different view on this point: see *Belilos* v *Switzerland*, Judgment of 29 April 1988, Ser A, no 132; 10 *EHRR* 418, and *Loizidou* v *Turkey (Preliminary Objections)*, Judgment of 23 March 1995, Ser A, no 310, 20 *EHRR* 99.

[29] *Fisheries Jurisdiction (Spain v Canada), Jurisdiction of the Court, Judgment, ICJ Reports 1998*, p 432, para 55.

[30] *Northern Cameroons, Judgment, ICJ Reports 1963*, p 15 at p 37.

[31] *Nuclear Tests (Australia v France), Judgment, ICJ Reports 1974*, p 253, paras 55ff.

[32] When a point of this kind was raised in the cases concerning the *Aerial Incident at Lockerbie*, the Court declined to deal with it as a preliminary issue (and the cases were subsequently discontinued). See *Questions of Interpretation and Application of the 1971 Montreal Convention arising from the Aerial Incident at Lockerbie (Libyan Arab Jamahiriya v United Kingdom), Preliminary Objections, Judgment, ICJ Reports 1998*, p 9, paras 46–50.

[33] It even extends to ruling on a claim that the tribunal itself has no legal existence: see the decision of the Appeals Chamber of the ICTY in *Prosecutor v Dusko Tadić, Decision on the Defence Motion for Interlocutory Appeal on Jurisdiction (Interlocutory Appeal)*, Case No IT-94-1-AR72 (2 October 1995).

principle is known as that of the *compétence de la compétence*, the jurisdiction to decide jurisdiction. It is in fact inherent in the concept of consensual jurisdiction: if a party, having consented to dispute settlement by a third party, were then to claim the right to determine for itself the extent of the third party's jurisdiction, it would be in effect withdrawing the consent given.

The principle is stated as applicable to the Court by Article 36(6) of the Statute: 'In the event of a dispute as to whether the Court has jurisdiction, the matter shall be settled by the decision of the Court'. The text makes it clear that if the two parties agree on the extent of jurisdiction, the Court can and must accept that agreement (provided the question is one of consensual jurisdiction—see above); and that the decision of the Court on a jurisdictional question is binding on the parties.[34] The matter is however not merely one of application of the Statute: the principle of the *compétence de la compétence* is a general one, which would operate even if Article 36(6) were not included in the Statute.[35]

The Court must exercise this power in any case in which the existence of its jurisdiction is disputed. It is not merely debarred from *deciding* a case in which the parties have not conferred jurisdiction upon it by consent: it may not even entertain it, that is to say begin to receive written or oral argument upon it. The existence of a special agreement will of course guarantee jurisdiction; in the case of an application, the ground of jurisdiction relied on will normally be indicated (and if it is conceded that there is no pre-existing jurisdiction, the case will not proceed, as explained above). Sometimes the attitude of the respondent State in disputing jurisdiction is fully justified: the applicant State may be trying to extend a limited acceptance of jurisdiction by its opponent to cover a dispute of a kind that was never contemplated in the instrument relied on. Sometimes, on the other hand, the respondent is trying to evade its obligation to accept settlement of the dispute by the Court because the ruling, or even any discussion of the matter before the Court, is likely to cause political embarrassment. The Court has also indicated that if the jurisdictional issue is one that cannot be waived by agreement of the parties (tacit or otherwise), then it is 'one which the Court is bound to raise and examine, if necessary, *ex officio*'.[36]

A State named as respondent that considers that the case has been brought without a jurisdictional title will normally raise this at an early stage, and the usual procedure is to file a 'preliminary objection', defined by the Rules of Court as 'Any objection by the respondent to the jurisdiction of the Court or to the admissibility of the application, or other objection the decision upon which is requested before any further proceedings on the merits...' (Article 79(1)).[37] Such an objection is usually presented in response to the Memorial filed by the applicant (though it may be filed earlier). Objections to jurisdiction

---

[34] Note that the matter is 'settled' by a 'decision', and under Article 59 of the Statute the decision has 'binding force' for the parties in respect of that particular case.

[35] Consequently it is equally applicable in advisory proceedings: cf the PCIJ advisory opinion on *Interpretation of the Greco-Turkish Agreement of December 1 1926, PCIJ Ser B, No 16,* p 20.

[36] *Application of the Convention on the Prevention and Punishment of the Crime of Genocide (Bosnia and Herzegovina v Serbia and Montenegro),* Judgment of 26 February 2007, para 122. The Court had however in that case not in fact done so, or at least not explicitly. Cf Article 79, para 8, of the Rules of Court.

[37] It was at one time unclear whether a State that failed to present a timely preliminary objection was to be taken to have renounced the objection; but in the *Avena* case the Court made it clear that 'a party failing to avail itself of the [preliminary objection] procedure may forfeit the right to bring about a suspension of the proceedings on the merits, but can still argue the objection along with the merits' (*Avena and other Mexican Nationals (Mexico v United States of America), ICJ Reports 2004,* p 12, para 24).

are of course denials that the respondent State ever gave its consent to the particular dispute being brought before the Court, or that the particular dispute falls within a category
of disputes for which it did accept jurisdiction. Objections to admissibility are less easy to
define, except negatively, as contentions that are neither matters of jurisdiction, nor questions of the merits. Examples are the contention that the applicant lacks *locus standi* (ie,
has no legally protected interest), that local remedies have not been exhausted; that the
case is, or has become, 'without object' or moot; that the presence as a party of a third State
is essential to the proceedings (see Section VII below), etc.

In accordance with the principle mentioned above, the effect of a preliminary objection
is that the proceedings on the merits of the case (the actual dispute brought before the
Court) are suspended (Rules, Article 79(3)), and will never be resumed if an objection to
jurisdiction is upheld (some objections to admissibility may be 'curable' and make the continuation of the proceedings possible after certain steps have been taken). A separate phase
of the proceedings is opened to deal with the objection: the applicant has the opportunity
of responding in writing to the objection, in a pleading entitled 'Observations', and in the
subsequent oral proceedings the respondent speaks first to present its objection, and the
applicant replies. This is the application of a principle of procedural law, *in excipiendo reus
fit actor* (by submitting an objection the defendant becomes the plaintiff). The Court may
uphold an objection or reject it; but it may also 'declare that the objection does not possess,
in the circumstances of the case, an exclusively preliminary character' (Article 79(7)). This
possibility, introduced in the revision of the Rules of 1978, was at first somewhat obscure,
but it is now clear that its effect is that the objection is not determined at the preliminary
stage, but may be re-presented and re-argued along with the merits.[38]

VI. OTHER INCIDENTAL PROCEEDINGS

A. REQUESTS FOR THE INDICATION OF PROVISIONAL MEASURES

The power of a tribunal to determine its own jurisdiction is one that belongs to all
national judicial bodies, and its attribution to international judicial and arbitral organs
is not in doubt. More controversial is the question whether the power, also enjoyed by
most, if not all, municipal courts, to issue binding interim injunctions, that is to say
directives requiring or prohibiting certain action pending settlement of the case before
the court, is also a necessary and essential part of the armoury of international courts
and of the International Court of Justice in particular. The Statute (Article 41) does
in fact include a power of the Court to 'indicate, if it considers that circumstances so
require, any provisional measures which ought to be taken to preserve the respective
rights of either party'; the debate is therefore in this instance not about the existence of
some power of this kind, but whether the measures so indicated create an obligation to
respect them, binding on the States addressed. The wording of the Statute is, to say the
least, ambiguous, inasmuch as it uses such mild terms as 'indicate' and 'measures which

---

[38] See the Judgments on preliminary objections in the cases concerning *Questions of Interpretation
and Application of the 1971 Montreal Convention arising from the Aerial Incident at Lockerbie (Libyan
Arab Jamahiriya v United Kingdom) (Libyan Arab Jamahiriya v United States of America)*, ICJ Reports
1998, pp 9, 115.

ought to be taken' (rather than 'direct' or 'order', and 'measures which shall be taken'); and the trend of the *travaux préparatoires* of the drafting of the PCIJ Statute is rather such as to suggest that, like universal compulsory jurisdiction, a power of the new Court to indicate binding measures at a preliminary stage may have been regarded as more than States were ready to accept. Some scholars have been ready to appeal to the idea that a power to indicate binding measures is bound up with the power to settle disputes by binding final decisions, and thus belongs in principle to all international judicial bodies; from this they conclude that the power conferred by Article 41 must be interpreted in this sense.

The question long remained unsettled; but in the *LaGrand* case, the Court decided that provisional measures addressed to the United States, which had not been complied with, had created a legal obligation, the breach of which gave rise to a duty of reparation, independently of the rights and duties of the parties in respect of the original dispute.[39] It did not however base this conclusion on any general principle, analogous to that of the *compétence de la compétence*, but on an interpretation of Article 41 as having been intended to achieve that result.[40]

There is no doubt that the Court has incidental jurisdiction under Article 41 to indicate measures; but a question that has given rise to some difficulty is the relationship between this incidental jurisdiction and the jurisdiction of the Court to hear and determine the merits of the case in which measures are requested. The problem only arises at the international level, because of the principle that international jurisdiction rests on consent, and consent has therefore to be proved in each case. If an indication of measures is requested in a case in which the respondent State has already made it clear that it denies the existence of jurisdiction over the merits, what is the relevance of this circumstance to the exercise of the power to indicate measures? At one extreme, it might be argued that if the Court has no jurisdiction to hear the case at all, then it has no power to indicate measures; at the other extreme, it might be said that, since Article 41 confers an independent power (and contains no reference to the question of merits jurisdiction), the Court could indicate measures, if it saw fit, in a case where it was very doubtful whether it had any jurisdiction over the merits, or even where it was almost certain that it had none.

The first view has the obvious defect that it tends to rob the provisional measures procedure of all meaning: if no measures can be indicated until the disputed question of merits jurisdiction has been thrashed out, then the measures cannot serve to meet the urgent needs that they were designed for.[41] The second view may however be seen as a threat to the principle of consensual jurisdiction, or even to the sovereign independence of States, if a State can be subjected to an order indicating measures that it is to comply with, in a case in which it asserts (justifiably, as it later turns out) that it has never consented to the Court having any jurisdiction at all.[42]

---

[39] *LaGrand (Germany v United States of America), Merits, Judgment, ICJ Reports 2001*, p 466, paras 98ff.

[40] In the light of the *travaux préparatoires* and of the general trend of interpretation of the text in practice, this view of Article 41 may be regarded as somewhat revolutionary: see Thirlway, 2001, at pp 114ff.

[41] This view was nevertheless put forward by dissenting judges in the *Nuclear Tests* case in 1974, but has not been heard of since.

[42] The difficulty is exacerbated by the ruling in *LaGrand* that the measures indicated constitute an independent legal obligation, one which exists even in face of a later finding of lack of jurisdiction, at least up to the moment that that finding is made. Provisional measures lapse when judgment on the merits is given, the

A middle solution has therefore become established in the jurisdiction of the Court: the possibility or probability of establishing jurisdiction over the merits is one of the factors to be weighed by the Court when considering whether to indicate measures. A number of different formulae has been employed to express this relationship. It is however clear that, on the one hand, the Court is not debarred from indicating measures by the existence of an objection to jurisdiction, even one which seems *prima facie* likely to be upheld; and on the other, that it is open to the Court to decline to indicate measures because there is a 'manifest lack of jurisdiction', or even a serious doubt as to the existence of merits jurisdiction. In some of the cases brought by Yugoslavia against members of NATO, the Court found, when examining the request for provisional measures, that it 'manifestly lack[ed] jurisdiction' to entertain the application instituting proceedings; it not only rejected the request for measures, but decided to remove the case from the list at that stage.[43] If the Court's eventual finding on jurisdiction contradicts the expectations on which its decision on provisional measures was founded, this will not retrospectively invalidate that decision: thus if it considers it justified to indicate measures on the basis of a likelihood of jurisdiction over the merits, a subsequent finding against jurisdiction will simply cause the measures to lapse, but they will have been valid until then.[44] If the Court refuses measures because of doubts as to jurisdiction, a subsequent finding upholding jurisdiction might justify a renewed request for measures, but the original refusal would not be undermined.

The purpose of the indication of provisional measures is, as stated in Article 41, 'to preserve the respective rights of either party'; and this means the rights that are in issue in the proceedings, and no others. Thus in a case concerning the formal validity of an arbitral award defining a maritime boundary, the Court declined to indicate measures directed to the conduct of the parties in the maritime areas concerned, since the only question before the Court was the validity or otherwise of the award, not the legal correctness of the boundary indicated.[45]

The indication of measures is an interlocutory measure justified by urgency: there must be a threat to the rights of a party that is immediate in the sense that the final decision in the case may come too late to preserve those rights. If therefore it is to be expected that the case will have been decided before irreparable injury is caused, no measures will be indicated. When Finland complained that the construction by Denmark of a bridge over a particular seaway would block the passage of ships and thus prevent Finland from exercising its rights to pass through the seaway, the Court declined to indicate measures because the timetable for the bridge works was such that there would be no interference with passage within the time likely to be required for the Court to decide the case.[46] The Court however

---

obligations of the judgment being substituted for those under the measures. In the *Avena (Interpretation)* case, provisional measures were indicated forbidding the execution of five named individuals, and in its judgment refusing the Request the Court unanimously found that the execution of one of them had been a breach of the obligations of the USA under the provisional measures Order (see Judgment of 19 January 2009, para 61(2)).

[43] See, eg, *Legality of Use of Force (Yugoslavia v United States of America), Provisional Measures, Order of 2 June 1999, ICJ Reports 1999,* p 916, para 29. Removal of a case from the list, without any decision even on jurisdiction, is an exceptional step, only taken in particular circumstances: see, eg, *Legality of the Use of Force (Serbia and Montenegro v Belgium), ICJ Reports 2004,* p 279, para 33.

[44] See the 2009 decision on the Request for Interpretation in the *Avena* case.

[45] *Arbitral Award of 31 July 1989, Provisional Measures, Order of 2 March 1990, ICJ Reports 1990,* p 64.

[46] *Passage through the Great Belt, Provisional Measures, Order of 29 July 1991, ICJ Reports 1991,* p 12.

included in its order a warning to the parties (and to Denmark in particular) that a party may not better its legal position by modifications it has made to the *status quo*, and that consequently the Court might, if it upheld Finland's claim, order Denmark to demolish works already completed that infringed Finland's rights.

B. PARTIES: JOINDER OF CASES; INTERVENTION BY THIRD STATES

Contentious proceedings before the Court are normally brought either by two States jointly (by Special Agreement), or by one State against another (by application); in either case there are only two parties to the proceedings. It is however possible for two or more States to bring proceedings as joint applicants against another State. In practice, it has been more frequent for two States to bring independent proceedings against the same respondent; and the Court then has power, if it sees fit, to 'direct that the proceedings...be joined' (Rules, Article 47). The cases are then heard and determined together, by a single judgment; and the Court may 'direct that the written or oral proceedings...be in common'. A joinder of this kind was ordered in the two *South West Africa* cases (*Liberia* v *South Africa*; *Ethiopia* v *South Africa*), and in the two *North Sea Continental Shelf* cases (brought by two special agreements: *Denmark/Federal Republic of Germany*; *Netherlands/Federal Republic of Germany*). Joinder has however become less common: it was not ordered in the two *Fisheries Jurisdiction* cases (*UK* v *Iceland*; *FRG* v *Iceland*), the two *Nuclear Tests* cases (*Australia* v *France*; *New Zealand* v *France*), or in subsequent 'pairs' of cases.

Similarly, it is possible for a State to bring proceedings against two or more States as joint respondents, though this has never yet occurred. The legal claim of Nauru against Australia in the case of *Certain Phosphate Lands in Nauru* was in fact asserted also against New Zealand and the United Kingdom, who had constituted, jointly with Australia, the administering authority under a UN Trustee Agreement for Nauru; but Nauru did not choose to bring proceedings against all three States, probably because it was uncertain of being able to establish jurisdiction against the other two. The absence of the other two States was in fact raised by Australia as an objection to the admissibility of the claim, but the Court ruled it admissible.[47] In the two cases concerning the *Lockerbie* incident,[48] and the 10 cases brought by Yugoslavia against the NATO States,[49] the contentions against each respondent in each set of cases were virtually identical, but the applicants nevertheless chose to bring parallel cases, and the Court did not see fit to join them.[50]

Where cases are brought in parallel in this way, but no formal joinder is effected, the Court does, for example, hold hearings in quick succession, deliberate on both cases, and

[47] *Certain Phosphate Lands in Nauru (Nauru* v *Australia), Preliminary Objections, Judgment, ICJ Reports 1992*, p 240, para 457.

[48] *Questions of Interpretation and Application of the 1971 Montreal Convention arising from the Aerial Incident at Lockerbie (Libya* v *UK, Libya* v *USA).*

[49] *Legality of Use of Force (Yugoslavia* v *Belgium, Yugoslavia* v *Canada, Yugoslavia* v *France, Yugoslavia* v *Germany, Yugoslavia* v *Italy, Yugoslavia* v *Netherlands, Yugoslavia* v *Portugal, Yugoslavia* v *Spain, Yugoslavia* v *UK, Yugoslavia* v *USA).*

[50] A controversial question is whether the existence of parallel cases which have not been joined affects the right to appoint a judge ad hoc: see the Joint Declaration of Judges Bedjaoui, Guillaume, and Ranjeva in the *Lockerbie* cases, ibid, *ICJ Reports 1998*, pp 32ff.

issue several judgments on the same day; and the judgments are often identical in much of their reasoning and construction.

The choice of States to be parties is normally therefore in the hands of the State or States commencing proceedings; but it may happen that another State wishes to become involved in the case. The Statute provides two possibilities in this respect. Under Article 63, 'Whenever the construction [ie, interpretation] of a convention to which States other than those concerned in the case are parties is in question' in a case, the other parties to the convention have to be notified, and may choose to intervene in the proceedings: however, it is provided that if they do so, the interpretation of the convention given by the Court will be binding upon them. Possibly as a result of this provision, the faculty of intervention under Article 63 has been very little used. In any event, the interpretation by the Court of a multilateral convention will enjoy authority beyond the parties to the case in which it is given.

Under Article 62, a State may request the Court to permit it to intervene in a pending case if it 'consider[s] that it has an interest of a legal nature which may be affected by the decision in the case'. One specific type of dispute has made intervention under this Article particularly attractive to third States. In a number of cases the Court was asked to rule on the delimitation of seabed areas in a dispute between two States, but in a geographical situation in which the possible rights or interests of other States might be infringed in some way—even if in strict law the decision of the Court would be *res inter alios acta* for those States. These cases showed that application of Article 62, which had long remained virtually unused, gives rise to a number of problems. First of all, what sort of interest is contemplated, and how may it be 'affected' by the decision, given that the judgment is only binding on the parties? Secondly, must the original parties agree to the intervention, and if not, does an objection on their part affect the matter? Thirdly, does the State permitted to intervene become a 'party' to the case, and as such bound by the judgment; or if it is not a party, may it still be bound by the decision? The most controversial question has however been that of the 'jurisdictional link'.

The problem was illustrated by the attempted intervention of Fiji in the *Nuclear Tests* cases. Australia and New Zealand had brought proceedings against France asserting the illegality of atmospheric nuclear tests in the Pacific, and had been able to cite as bases of jurisdiction the French acceptance under the 'optional clause', and a 1928 Treaty. Fiji sought to join in the proceedings, in effect as co-plaintiff, but could not point to any jurisdictional title available to it: it was not a party to the 1928 Treaty, and it could not rely on the optional-clause declaration because it had not deposited one of its own. Accordingly, Fiji could not validly have brought a separate case against France; could it therefore be allowed to jump on the bandwagon, as it were, to reach the same result by taking advantage of the fact that Australia and New Zealand had brought proceedings? The cases came to a premature end before the Court was called upon to decide the point, but some of the judges felt strongly enough to indicate their views upon it in separate or dissenting opinions.[51]

After some judicial hesitation, a chamber of the Court ruled, in the case of the *Land, Island and Maritime Boundary Dispute* between El Salvador and Honduras, that no jurisdictional link was required for an intervention which did not confer the status of

---

[51] A further complication was introduced by the introduction into the new Rules of Court, adopted in 1978, of a text which was (apparently deliberately) ambiguous on the issue (Article 81(2)(c)).

party; and that the objection of the original parties was to be taken into account, but was not decisive.[52] These findings were approved by the full Court in the subsequent cases of *Land and Maritime Boundary between Cameroon and Nigeria*[53] and *Sovereignty over Pulau Ligitan and Pulau Sipadan*.[54] It appears that intervention as a party is also possible, either with the consent of the original parties,[55] or if there exists a jurisdictional title such that the intending intervener could have brought independent proceedings against each of them. If however the intervener is not a party, the chamber in the *El Salvador/Honduras* case held that it is not bound by the judgment, but similarly cannot invoke it against the original parties.[56] These decisions have also clarified the significance of the 'legal interest' and how it was to be 'affected'.

C. INTERPRETATION AND REVISION OF JUDGMENTS

Article 60 of the Court's Statute provides that 'The judgment is final and without appeal'. The text however continues: 'In the event of dispute as to the meaning or scope of the judgment, the Court shall construe it upon the request of any party'. Such a request has been filed in only three cases.[57]

Article 61 further qualifies the finality of a judgment, by providing that:

An application for revision of a judgment may be made only when it is based upon the discovery of some fact of such a nature as to be a decisive factor, which fact was, when the judgment was given, unknown to the Court and to the party claiming revision, always provided that such ignorance was not due to negligence.

The fact is then referred to in paragraph 2 as 'the new fact'; this expression has been a source of confusion, as the fact must be an old fact newly discovered. In the case between Bosnia and Yugoslavia, the Court distinguished between a fact of this kind and 'the legal consequences' as to a pre-existing state of affairs drawn from 'facts subsequent to the Judgment';[58] but the distinction is not entirely convincing.

---

[52] *Land, Island and Maritime Frontier Dispute (El Salvador/Honduras), Application to Intervene, Judgment, ICJ Reports 1990*, p 92.

[53] *Land and Maritime Boundary between Cameroon and Nigeria, Application to Intervene, Order of 21 October 1999, ICJ Reports 1999*, p 1029.

[54] *Sovereignty over Palau Ligitan and Pulau Sipidan (Indonesia/Malaysia), Application to Intervene, Judgment of 23 October 2001, ICJ Reports 2001*, p 575, paras 35–36.

[55] In the *Land and Maritime Boundary between Cameroon and Nigeria (Cameroon v Nigeria: Equatorial Guinea Intervening), Judgment, ICJ Reports 2002*, p 303, para 12, the Court took note of the fact that the parties had no objection to the intervention of Equatorial Guinea, but that State was not seeking to intervene as a party.

[56] The intending intervener (Nicaragua) had in fact announced in advance that it would accept the judgment as binding, but the chamber did not find this acceptance legally effective.

[57] *Request for Interpretation of the Judgment of 20 November 1950 in the Asylum case, Judgment, ICJ Reports 1950*, p 395; *Application for Revision and Interpretation of the Judgment of 24 February 1982 in the Case concerning the Continental Shelf (Tunisia/Libyan Arab Jamahiriya) (Tunisia v Libyan Arab Jamahiriya), Judgment, ICJ Reports 1985*, p 192; *Request for Interpretation of the Judgment of 11 June 1998 in the Case concerning the Land and Maritime Boundary between Cameroon and Nigeria (Cameroon v Nigeria), Preliminary Objections (Nigeria v Cameroon), Judgment, ICJ Reports 1999*, p 31.

[58] *Application for Revision of the Judgment of 11 July 1996 in the Case concerning Application of the Genocide Convention (Bosnia and Herzegovina v Yugoslavia), Preliminary Objections (Yugoslavia v Bosnia and Herzegovina), ICJ Reports 2003*, p 7, para 69.

Requests for interpretation or for revision were formerly comparatively rare, but recent years have seen an increase in their frequency.[59]

VII. EFFECT OF THE DECISIONS OF THE COURT

A judgment of the Court is binding upon the parties to the case in which it is given. As noted above, under Article 60 of the Statute, the judgment is 'final and without appeal', and Article 59 provides that 'The decision of the Court has no binding force except between the parties and in respect of that particular case', implying *a contrario* that, between the parties and in respect of the particular case, it is binding. Furthermore, under Article 94(1), of the Charter, 'Each Member of the United Nations undertakes to comply with the decision of the International Court of Justice in any case to which it is a party'.[60] The only provision for what might be termed enforcement of a judgment of the Court is Article 94(2):

If any party to a case fails to perform the obligations on it under a judgment rendered by the Court, the other party may have recourse to the Security Council, which may, if it deems necessary, make recommendations or decide upon measures to be taken to give effect to the judgment.

Very little use has been made of this faculty, which does not confer any additional powers on the Security Council; the political implications of any attempt to enforce a judgment by this means need not be gone into here.

There is a clear obligation of treaty law to treat a judgment of the Court as binding and to comply with it. In legal theory, however, the judgments of the Court are in principle declaratory of the rights and obligations of the parties, not creative of new rights and obligations.[61] If therefore the Court decides, for example, that under a provision in a treaty, the correct interpretation of which is disputed, one of the parties is under a particular obligation, that obligation results from the treaty (as authoritatively interpreted), but is backed by the obligation to comply with the judgment. The only special status that the existence of the judgment confers on the original obligation is confirmation that it exists, in the sense that no alternative interpretation of the treaty provision is legally possible. The fact that the judgment is binding on the parties does not mean that they may not, by agreement between themselves, depart from it—unless of course the obligation found by the Court to

---

[59] *Application for Revision and Interpretation of the Judgment of 24 February 1982 in the Case concerning the Continental Shelf (Tunisia/Libyan Arab Jamahiriya) (Tunisia v Libyan Arab Jamahiriya), Judgment,* ICJ Reports 1985, p 192; *Application for Revision of the Judgment of 11 July 1996 in the Case concerning Application of the Genocide Convention (Bosnia and Herzegovina v Yugoslavia) (Yugoslavia v Bosnia and Herzegovina), Judgment,* ICJ Reports 2003, p 7; *Application for Revision of the Judgment of 11 September 1992 in the Case concerning the Land, Island and Maritime Frontier Dispute (El Salvador v Honduras: Nicaragua Intervening) (Honduras/El Salvador), Judgment,* ICJ Reports 2003, p 392.

[60] This commitment does not, as such, apply to parties to the Statute that are not UN members, or to States admitted to appear without being parties to the Statute. However, when the General Assembly admits a State, under Article 93 of the Charter, to become a party to the Statute, it always attaches as a condition 'Acceptance of all the obligations of a Member of the United Nations under Article 94 of the Charter' (see GA Res 91 (I)), 11 December 1946 (Switzerland); 3 GA Res 63 (IV), 1 December 1949 (Liechtenstein); GA Res 806.

[61] With the possible exception of Orders indicating provisional measures: see Section VI A above.

exist is one of *jus cogens*.[62] All it means is that neither party may unilaterally act as though the legal situation were other than as declared by the Court.

Some of the relevant texts refer to the 'judgment' of the Court (Statute, Article 60; Charter, Article 94(2)) and others to the 'decision' of the Court (Statute, Article 59; Charter, Article 94(1)). The question has therefore sometimes been raised whether an Order of the Court is binding on the parties. Most orders are procedural, and any sanction for compliance is also procedural: if a party fails to file a pleading within the time-limit fixed by an Order, it may lose the right to file that pleading. A special case is however that of provisional measures, which are invariably indicated in the form of an Order. Now that the Court has decided (see Section VI A above) that the measures themselves constitute a legal obligation, the formal question of the effect of the order as a 'decision' has perhaps lost much of its pertinence.

Article 59 thus excludes any formal impact of the judgment on third parties; and on this basis the Court has, for example, been willing to draw a boundary line between two States in an area where a third State might have valid claims, reasoning that the decision of the Court, like a delimitation agreement between the two States before the Court, would be *res inter alios acta* for the third State, and could not therefore prejudice its position.[63] Other cases however have given rise to a distinction: if the Court finds that the rights and obligations of a third State would not merely be affected by the decision, but would form the very subject matter of the decision, the Court takes the view that it should decline to exercise its jurisdiction. The classic case on the point was that of the *Monetary Gold Removed from Rome in 1943*.[64] The parties to the case were Italy as applicant, and the United Kingdom, France, and the United States as respondents. The disputed gold had been removed from Rome by the Germans during the Second World War, but was subsequently found by an arbitrator to have belonged to Albania. Italy and the United Kingdom however each claimed that gold, on the basis of legal claims by those two States against Albania. The Court found that in order to determine the validity of Italy's claim, it would have to 'determine whether Albania has committed any international wrong against Italy', and thus to 'decide a dispute between Italy and Albania'. However, Albania was not before the Court as a party to the proceedings, and had not consented to the dispute being settled by the Court:

To adjudicate upon the international responsibility of Albania without her consent would run counter to a well-established principle of international law embodied in the Court's Statute, namely that the Court can only exercise jurisdiction over a State with its consent.[65]

It was urged that, under Article 59 of the Statute, the decision would not be binding on Albania; but the Court held that where 'the vital issue to be settled concerns the international responsibility of a third State, the Court cannot, without the consent of that

[62] On the concept of *jus cogens*, see Ch 4, Section III B, and Ch 6 passim.

[63] *Frontier Dispute*, ICJ Reports 1986, p 554, paras 46ff. The position is apparently different in the case of maritime delimitations: see, eg, *Land and Maritime Boundary between Cameroon and Nigeria (Cameroon v Nigeria: Equatorial Guinea Intervening)* ICJ Reports 2002, p 424, para 245.

[64] *Monetary Gold Removed from Rome in 1943, Judgment*, ICJ Reports 1954, p 19.

[65] Ibid, p 32.

third State, give a decision on that issue binding upon any State, either the third State, or any of the parties before it'.[66]

The possibility of intervention (see Section VI B above) has been raised in connection with the principle laid down in the *Monetary Gold* line of cases. If a State, not a party to a case, did not wish its rights and duties to be discussed before the Court in its absence, it was open to such a State, it was said, to intervene. The Court however drew a distinction: if the interests of the absent State would merely *be affected* by the decision, then if that State chose not to exercise its right to request intervention, the proceedings could continue to judgment; but if the legal interests of the absent State 'would form the very subject matter of the decision', then the Court could not exercise its jurisdiction in the absence of that State.[67]

VIII. ADVISORY PROCEEDINGS

In addition to its function of settling international disputes in accordance with international law, the Court is empowered by its Statute to give advisory opinions. The provision to that effect included in the Statute of the Permanent Court was something of an innovation: some, but by no means all, national supreme courts possessed a power of this kind; and on the international level, arbitration proceedings, from which the concept of an international tribunal sprang, were essentially means of reaching a binding settlement of a dispute. It was the organs of the League of Nations that were expected to feel a need for such an opinion, and from the beginning it was only such international organs, and not States, that were to be entitled to ask for advice in this form.

The essence of an advisory opinion is that it is advisory, not determinative: it expresses the view of the Court as to the relevant international legal principles and rules, but does not oblige any State, nor even the body that asked for the opinion, to take or refrain from any action. The distinction, clear in theory, is less so in practice: if the Court advises, for example, that a certain obligation exists, the State upon which it is said to rest has not bound itself to accept the Court's finding, but it will be in a weak position if it seeks to argue that the considered opinion of the Court does not represent a correct view of the law.

The essentially non-binding character of an advisory opinion has in the past given rise to some doubts as to the legal effect of a treaty commitment whereby an opinion of the Court is to be accepted, by the parties to the treaty, as binding. One field in which treaty provisions of this kind have proved useful is the relations between international organizations, particularly the United Nations itself, and States. Since an international organization cannot be a party to proceedings before the Court, a dispute between an organization and a State cannot be settled by contentious proceedings. A device that has been used to meet the difficulty is to provide in a convention (for example the 1946 Convention on the Privileges and Immunities of the United Nations) that, in the event of a dispute of this kind, the General Assembly (or other organ concerned) will ask the Court for an advisory opinion on the point at issue, and that it is agreed in advance that the Court's opinion will be accepted as 'decisive' by the State and the organization. It is established that since the

---

[66] Ibid, p 33.   [67] Ibid, p 32.

essentially non-binding character of the opinion itself is not affected, there is no legal obstacle to the conclusion of an agreement of this kind.

Under the Charter, Article 96(1), the General Assembly and the Security Council are entitled to request the Court 'to give an advisory opinion on any legal question'. This is purely a faculty: nowhere in the Charter is there any obligation to seek the advice of the Court, and the Court has no power to offer it unasked. A proposal during the drafting of the Charter to give the Court responsibility for authoritative interpretations of the Charter was not adopted.

Article 96(2) provides that 'Other organs of the United Nations and specialized agencies, which may at any time be so authorized by the General Assembly, may also request advisory opinions of the Court on legal questions arising within the scope of their activities'.[68] Such authorizations have in fact been given to the Economic and Social Council and to practically all the specialized agencies. The restriction as to the type of questions to be put was however held to debar the World Health Organization, which had received a general authorization from the General Assembly to request opinions, from asking for an opinion on the question whether the use of nuclear weapons by a State would be a breach of its obligations under international law 'including the WHO Constitution'. The Court held that under the 'principle of speciality' the WHO could not deal with matters beyond what was authorized by its Constitution; that the question of the legality of nuclear weapons was outside that Constitution; and accordingly the question was not one 'arising within the scope' of the activities of the Organization.[69] In another case, the question was raised whether a subsidiary organ of the General Assembly, whose sole function was in fact to ask for advisory opinions (on the validity of judgments of the United Nations Administrative Tribunal), had any 'activities' of its own for the purposes of this text; the Court ruled in the affirmative.[70]

The provision in the Statute that corresponds to this Charter text is Article 65, which provides that 'The Court may give an advisory opinion on any legal question' at the request of any authorized body. The use of the word 'may' signifies, as the Court has repeatedly emphasized, that the Court is not bound to give an opinion, but may decline to do so if it considers that course appropriate. It has never in fact done so,[71] but has on a number of occasions considered the possibility of refusal. From the resulting jurisprudence it is clear that the reply of the Court, itself an organ of the United Nations, 'represents its participation in the activities of the Organization and, in principle, should not be refused'; and that only compelling reasons would justify a refusal.[72]

---

[68] The wording of paras 1 and 2 of Article 96 suggests that a request from the Security Council or General Assembly can relate to a question not 'within the scope of their activities', but there are dicta of the Court suggesting that this approach may be too wide: see *Legal Consequences of the Construction of a Wall in the Occupied Palestinian Territory, Advisory Opinion, ICJ Reports 2004*, p 136, para 16, and references there cited.

[69] *Legality of the Use by a State of Nuclear Weapons in Armed Conflict, Advisory Opinion, ICJ Reports 1996*, p 66.

[70] *Application for Review of Judgement No 158 of the United Nations Administrative Tribunal, Advisory Opinion, ICJ Reports 1973*, p 166.

[71] The refusal, referred to in the preceding paragraph, of the opinion requested by WHO was not a matter of discretion but a matter of lack of jurisdiction following the lack of competence of WHO to ask for an opinion on the subject.

[72] See, eg, *Western Sahara, Advisory Opinion, ICJ Reports 1975*, p 12, para 23.

A special problem however arises if the question put to the Court is related to an inter-State dispute, and one of the States concerned in that dispute objects to the Court giving the opinion. The consent of the States parties to a dispute is the basis of the Court's jurisdiction in contentious cases; but since the Court's reply to a request for an advisory opinion has no binding force, 'it follows that no State…can prevent the giving of an Advisory Opinion which the United Nations considers to be desirable in order to obtain enlightenment as to the course of action it should undertake'.[73] The consent of any State party to a dispute underlying a request for advisory opinion is thus not necessary for the opinion to be given; but, as the Court declared in a later case, that concerning *Western Sahara*, 'lack of consent might constitute a ground for declining to give the opinion requested', in the exercise of the Court's discretion, 'if, in the circumstances of a given case, considerations of judicial propriety should oblige the Court to refuse an opinion'.[74] The Court offered as an instance of this (and probably the most compelling instance), 'when the circumstances disclose that to give a reply would have the effect of circumventing the principle that a State is not obliged to allow its disputes to be submitted to judicial settlement without its consent'.[75] This might be so if the object of the requesting organ (*in casu* the General Assembly) were 'to bring before the Court, by way of a request for advisory opinion, a dispute or legal controversy, in order that it may later, on the basis of the Court's opinion, exercise its power and functions for the peaceful settlement of that dispute or controversy'.[76] This criterion appears however to have been tacitly abandoned in the *Wall* case.[77] In no case up to the present has the Court declined to give an opinion on this ground, or any other discretionary ground. It did not even refuse in the case of a dispute between the General Assembly and a State, in which the Assembly, unable to obtain a binding advisory opinion under the provisions of the Convention on the Privileges and Immunities of the United Nations, because of a reservation to that Convention made by the State concerned, sought and obtained a non-binding opinion of the Court on the point in dispute.[78]

A further difficulty that has arisen in connection with requests for advisory opinion in cases involving, or related to, existing international disputes is the extent to which a party, or the parties, to such a dispute should be treated as though they were parties to a contentious case, and in particular should be able to appoint a judge ad hoc. Article 68 of the Statute provides that:

In the exercise of its advisory functions the Court shall further be guided by the provisions of the present Statute which apply in contentious cases to the extent to which it recognizes them to be applicable.

---

[73] *Interpretation of Peace Treaties with Bulgaria, Hungary and Romania, First Phase, Advisory Opinion, ICJ Reports 1950*, p 65 at p 71.

[74] *Western Sahara, ICJ Reports 1975*, p 12, para 32.

[75] Ibid, para 33. This passage was later criticized, by Judge Kooijmans in the *Wall* case, as containing 'purely circular reasoning': *Legal Consequences of the Construction of a Wall in the Occupied Palestinian Territory, ICJ Reports 2004*, p 227, para 27.

[76] *Western Sahara, Advisory Opinion, ICJ Reports 1975*, p 12, para 29.

[77] See the Separate Opinion of Judge Higgins, *Legal Consequences of the Construction of a Wall in the Occupied Palestinian Territory, Advisory Opinion, ICJ Reports 2004*, p 136 at p 210, paras 12–13.

[78] *Applicability of Article VI, Section 22, of the Convention on the Privileges and Immunities of the United Nations, Advisory Opinion, ICJ Reports 1989*, p 177, para 38.

The Permanent Court had recognized that in some cases States should be treated as 'parties' to the extent of appointing judges ad hoc. The Rules of Court make no direct provision for this, but Article 102(2) repeats the text of Article 68, and adds: 'For this purpose, it shall above all consider whether the request for the advisory opinion relates to a legal question actually pending between two or more States'.

Practice has shown that the implementation of these texts in specific cases in relation to the appointment of judges ad hoc is not always straightforward. In the *Namibia* case, South Africa, which had a very special interest in the proceedings, and could claim that there was a 'legal question actually pending' between itself and nearly every other State, was not permitted to appoint a judge ad hoc.[79] In the *Western Sahara* case, Morocco and Mauritania each claimed the existence of special legal ties with the territory, and contested the arguments of Spain, the former colonial power: Morocco was permitted to appoint a judge ad hoc, but Mauritania was not.[80] In the *Wall* case one of the parties to the dispute (Palestine) was not a State for the purposes of the Statute.[81]

IX. THE COURT PAST AND PRESENT: AN ASSESSMENT

For the first 20 years of its existence, the International Court of Justice seemed destined to play a part on the international scene similar to that played by its predecessor, the Permanent Court of International Justice. Cases were submitted to it in a small but regular flow, and a series of requests were made by the General Assembly for advisory opinions; the decisions and advisory opinions given were on the whole well received, and the Court's contribution to the development of law, though necessarily marginal, was significant. While the creators of the Permanent Court, and their successors at the San Francisco Conference in 1946, might have hoped for a more spectacular contribution to international dispute settlement, the experiment begun in 1920 could be regarded as successful.

In the 1960s and 1970s, a marked change was observed. For reasons which need not be gone into here, but which must include the Court's 1966 decision in the *South West Africa* case (which had a devastating effect on the Court's reputation with the developing countries), doubts began to be expressed about the future of the Court, as fewer and fewer States seemed inclined to bring their disputes before it. For a brief period, the Court had no cases whatever on its list. Little by little, however, the situation improved, particularly as a result of the increasing need for impartial settlement of seabed delimitation disputes, where the Court had shown the way in the *North Sea Continental Shelf* case (1969). The formation of a special chamber according to the wishes of the parties in the *Gulf of Maine* case (1984) offered an attractive alternative to submission to the full Court, and it was striking that

---

[79] *Legal Consequences for States of the Continued Presence of South Africa in Namibia (South West Africa) notwithstanding Security Council Resolution 276 (1970), Order of 29 January 1971, ICJ Reports 1971*, p 12, and *Advisory Opinion*, ibid, p 16, paras 35ff.

[80] *Western Sahara, Order of 22 May 1975, ICJ Reports 1975*, p 6.

[81] See the Separate Opinion of Judge Owada, *Legal Consequences of the Construction of a Wall in the Occupied Palestinian Territory, Advisory Opinion, ICJ Reports 2004*, p 136 at p 267, para 19. The problem remained hypothetical, as Israel did not claim the right to appoint a judge ad hoc.

the next request for such a chamber came from two developing countries in sub-Saharan Africa (Burkina Faso and Mali in the *Frontier Dispute*, 1986).

Today, the Court is busier than it has ever been before. Disputes have been submitted to it not only by its more established 'clients', but by States of: Latin America;[82] Eastern Europe;[83] Asia;[84] and Africa.[85] On the other hand, the United States now shows distinct coolness toward the Court, marked by the withdrawal of various long-established bases of jurisdiction, avowedly in response to what it regards as unjustifiedly extensive interpretation by the Court of its jurisdiction over the USA.[86] There has however been increasing use of the possibility of requesting an advisory opinion, including the request by both WHO and the General Assembly for an opinion on the legality of nuclear weapons,[87] and by the General Assembly on an aspect of the Israel/Palestine problem.[88]

On the practical level, there are signs that the Court is becoming victim of its own success. The principle that all cases are heard by the full Court unless the parties agree to a chamber means that there is a limit to the number of cases that can be heard and determined each year; and although the Registry has been enlarged and some of the Court's working methods improved, there are signs of an overload. Judicial settlement has never been a speedy means of resolving disputes, but it is to be feared that States considering bringing a case to the Court may be put off by the likely delay before a decision is given, due to the presence of so many other cases in the queue.

A consistently high standard has however been maintained in the quality of the Court's decisions, even though they have, as always, been exposed to healthy criticism. The bringing of more cases has meant more opportunities for contribution to the development of the law; on a number of occasions, for example, the Court has been able to supplement the work of the International Law Commission by settling authoritatively the customary-law status of a rule embodied in a treaty or other text emanating from the ILC.

---

[82] *Military and Paramilitary Activities in and against Nicaragua (Nicaragua v USA), Border and Transborder Armed Actions (Nicaragua v Honduras, Nicaragua v Costa Rica), Land, Island and Maritime Frontier Dispute (Honduras/El Salvador, Nicaragua intervening), Territorial and Maritime Dispute (Nicaragua v Colombia); Maritime Delimitation between Nicaragua and Honduras in the Caribbean Sea; Avena and other Mexican Nationals (Mexico v USA); Territorial and Maritime Dispute (Nicaragua v Colombia).*

[83] *Gabčíkovo-Nagymaros Project (Hungary/Slovakia), Application of the Convention on the Prevention and Punishment of the Crime of Genocide (Bosnia and Herzegovina v Serbia and Montenegro), Legality of Use of Force (Yugoslavia against 10 NATO countries); Application of the Convention on the Prevention and Punishment of the Crime of Genocide (Croatia v Serbia); Maritime Delimitation in the Black Sea (Romania v Ukraine).*

[84] *Aerial Incident of 10 August 1999 (Pakistan v India); Sovereignty over Pulau Ligitan and Pulau Sipadan (Indonesia/Malaysia); Sovereignty over Pedra Blanca/Pulau Batu Pateh, Middle Rocks and South Ledge (Malaysia/Singapore).*

[85] *Frontier Dispute (Benin/Niger); Ahmadou Sadio Diallo (Republic of Guinea v Democratic Republic of the Congo); Armed Activities on the territory of the Congo (Democratic Republic of the Congo v Rwanda); Arrest Warrant of 11 April 2000 (Democratic Republic of the Congo v Belgium); Armed Activities on the Territory of the Congo (Democratic Republic of the Congo v Burundi; v Rwanda; v Uganda); Certain Criminal Proceedings in France (Republic of the Congo v France).*

[86] The cases of *Armed Activities in and against Nicaragua, Oil Platforms*, and *Avena and other Mexican Nationals* may be mentioned.

[87] Opinions differ, however, as to the wisdom of using the advisory opinion procedure in an area of this kind (see, eg, *Legality of the Threat or Use of Nuclear Weapons, Advisory Opinion, ICJ Reports 1996*, p 226, Dissenting Opinion of Judge Oda, p 330).

[88] *Legal Consequences of the Construction of a Wall in the Occupied Palestinian Territories, Advisory Opinion, ICJ Reports 2004*, p 136.

Considerable use has been made of the possibility of requesting the indication of provisional measures, *inter alia* in situations of armed hostilities. It remains to be seen, however, whether the ruling in the *LaGrand* case, that provisional measures give rise to a binding obligation of compliance, may not have a negative influence on advance acceptance of jurisdiction. The provisional measures procedure has always offered a temptation to States to commence proceedings on a shaky jurisdictional foundation in the hope of getting at least the short-term benefit of an order for provisional measures, and this is all the more attractive if the order is immediately binding. The only defence against such tactics is to limit generalized acceptances of jurisdiction that may be misused.

The prospects as regards acceptance of jurisdiction are otherwise mixed: existing treaties for dispute settlement, compromissory clauses, and optional dispute-settlement protocols continue to provide a solid background of jurisdiction, but the modern trend is to include such clauses less frequently in new multilateral treaties. Nor does the optional clause system seem to be thriving. The number of States having filed declarations of acceptance is not increasing, and the declarations that have been filed are much qualified by reservations. Some disquiet has also been caused by what is perceived as a trend whereby the Court, in order to comment on legal questions of substantial current importance, has been over-generous in its interpretation of texts conferring jurisdiction. The decision in the *Oil Platforms* case[89] in particular has been criticized on this ground.[90] The development of a coherent system of intervention has been valuable, since many modern international disputes are plurilateral rather than bilateral. The Court is clearly alive to the need to review its own procedures, as is shown by the recent revision of Articles 79 and 80 of the Rules, and the use of Practice Directions.

All in all, the prospects for the future role of the Court in the settlement of international disputes are encouraging. While it may not be such a World Court as idealists might like to envisage, in its present structure and operation it remains a real force for peaceful settlement of disputes, and the furthest extension of judicial power to the affairs of States that is likely to be acceptable to the members of the present-day international community.

CITATION OF ICJ CASES

Although cases brought before the Court are numbered consecutively on the Court's General List (Rules, Art 26 (1) (*b*)), these numbers are not used for purposes of citation. The official title of each case is determined by the Court at the outset of the proceedings, on the basis of the document instituting proceedings; considerations of avoiding any appearance of pre-judgment lead to such titles often being somewhat unwieldy. The names of the parties are sometimes included in the official title, particularly when the same title is used for more than one case. Abbreviated titles are therefore often used by scholars in books and articles; unfortunately, there is no generally recognized system for these.

---

[89] *Oil Platforms (Islamic Republic of Iran v United States of America), Judgment, ICJ Reports, 2003*, p 161.
[90] Cf the opinion of Judge Kooijmans in that case, ibid, p 257, para 35, and Small, 2004.

REFERENCES

THIRLWAY, H (1984), 'Reciprocity in the Jurisdiction of the International Court' (1984) 15 *NYBIL* 97.

—— (2001), 'The Law and procedure of the International Court of Justice 1960–1989, Part Twelve', 72 *BYIL* 37.

SMALL, D (2004), 'The Oil Platforms case; Jurisdiction through the Closed Eye of the Needle' (2004) 3 *Law and Practice of International Courts and Tribunals* 113

FURTHER READING

AMR, MSM (2003), *The Role of the International Court of Justice as the Principal Judicial Organ of the United Nations* (The Hague: Kluwer Law International).

BOWETT, D et al (1997), *The International Court of Justice: Process, Practice and Procedure* (London: BIICL (British Institute of International and Comparative Law)). Based on the work of a Study Group set up by the British Institute of International and Comparative Law, this study focuses on the practical aspects of the Court's work and procedures.

ROSENNE, S (1997), *The Law and Practice of the International Court, 1920–1996* (The Hague: Martinus Nijhoff). This is the most complete and authoritative survey of the Court.

A Commentary on the Statute of the International Court of Justice (April 2006), a joint publication of the Max-Planck-Institut, Heidelberg, the Institut für Völker- und Europarecht, Humboldt University, Berlin, and the Walter-Schücking-Institut, University of Kiel.

International Court of Justice: Yearbook. This annual publication contains a wealth of information on current cases and on points of practice and procedure.

The International Court of Justice (1996), 4th edn. This useful handbook is published by the Court and distributed jointly by the Court and the United Nations Department of Public Information.

The International Court of Justice: Questions and Answers about the principal judicial organ of the United Nations (2000), UN Sales No E.99.I.25. This sets out basic facts concerning the Court.

British Year Book of International Law. The jurisprudence of the Court since 1960 has been the subject of detailed comment in a series of articles in vol 60 (1989) onwards.

WEBSITES

http://www.icj-cij.org: the Court's website contains the text in the two official languages (English and French) of the Statute, Rules of Court and Practice Directions, the other texts governing jurisdiction, and full texts of all recent decisions, press releases, and other materials. Once the Court has decided that the pleadings in a case are to be made public, these and the oral arguments will also be on the website, but only in the language in which they were presented. The translations of judges' separate and dissenting opinions may also not be available until some time after the decision itself is given.

21

THE USE OF FORCE AND THE INTERNATIONAL LEGAL ORDER

Christine Gray

SUMMARY

This is one of the most controversial areas of international law. States are divided as to the interpretation of the fundamental rules on the use of force in the UN Charter. The prohibition of the use of force in Article 2(4) is directed at inter-State conflicts; there is disagreement as to whether this allows the use of force for humanitarian intervention. The application of Article 2(4) to civil wars is also problematic. The main exception to the prohibition on the use of force is the right to self-defence under Article 51. It is controversial whether this is a narrow right, available only in response to an armed attack, or whether it allows force in protection of nationals abroad or in response to terrorist attacks. The UN Charter also establishes a collective security system whereby the Security Council may respond to threats to the peace and acts of aggression. This chapter examines the use of enforcement action and the institution of UN peacekeeping as well as the power of regional organizations to assist in peacekeeping and enforcement action.

I. INTRODUCTION

The law on the use of force is one of the most controversial areas of international law and one where the law may seem ineffective. The UN Charter prohibits the use of force by States in Article 2(4), but this has not prevented the occurrence of over 100 major conflicts since 1945 and the deaths of over twenty million people. Difficult questions arise as to how far international law in fact influences State behaviour. In practice States are clearly anxious to avoid condemnation for their use of force and they generally use the language of international law to explain and justify their behaviour—not as the sole justification but as one of a variety of arguments. Thus NATO based its use of force in 'humanitarian intervention' over Kosovo on a mixture of political, moral, and legal arguments. It is tempting to dismiss legal arguments in justification of the use of force by States, especially powerful States, as merely self-interested manipulation of the rules, but in the absence of clear empirical evidence about the nature of decision-making within States this remains an assumption. It may underestimate the genuine differences of viewpoint between opposing States and the commitment of the vast majority of States, especially small, weak States, to the prohibition on the use of force.

A. THE UN CHARTER SCHEME

The UN Charter is the starting point for any discussion of international law on the use of force (Simma, 2002). It was concluded after, and in response to, the experiences of the Second World War, in the same way as the League of Nations Covenant was a response to the First World War. There is disagreement as to whether the prohibition of the use of force in the UN Charter was a revolutionary new provision or whether customary law had already developed along the lines of Article 2(4) by the time of the creation of the United Nations (Brownlie, 1963, p 66). The Charter aims not only to prohibit the unilateral use of force by States by Article 2(4), but also to centralize control over the use of force in the Security Council, acting under Chapter VII.

The Preamble of the Charter begins 'We the peoples of the United Nations determined to save succeeding generations from the scourge of war', and the first purpose of the UN set out in Article 1 is 'To maintain international peace and security, and to that end: to take effective collective measures for the prevention and removal of threats to the peace and for the suppression of acts of aggression or other breaches of the peace'. The original scheme was that the Security Council should respond to threats to the peace, breach of the peace, and acts of aggression, if necessary through its own standing UN army. However, this plan foundered during the Cold War because the veto possessed by the five permanent members of the Security Council—the USA, the USSR (now succeeded by Russia), China, France, and the UK—obstructed effective decision-making by the Security Council (Patil, 1992).

The original Charter scheme has not been implemented; the action taken by the Security Council under Chapter VII has been different from that originally planned. 'Coalitions of the willing' have replaced the plan for a standing UN army: member States have been authorized to use force in major enforcement operations which are perceived to be beyond the resources of the UN. Also the institution of peacekeeping which grew up as a partial substitute for Security Council enforcement action during the Cold War did so without express provision in the Charter.

There is broad agreement between States on the core of the law on the use of force, as set out in the UN Charter and also in regional and collective self-defence treaties. However, early divisions between developed and developing States emerged on the interpretation of the brief provisions of the Charter. The UN General Assembly adopted resolutions on the use of force to elaborate on the Charter, and where these were adopted by consensus they are generally regarded as statements of customary international law or as authoritative interpretations of the UN Charter. But often these resolutions were deliberately ambiguous. The consensus in favour of the *Definition of Aggression*,[1] the *Declaration on*

---

[1] *Definition of Aggression*, GA Res 3314 (XXIX) (14 December 1974).

Friendly Relations,[2] and the *Declaration on the Non-Use of Force*[3] masked the divisions between States on questions such as the scope of the right of self-defence. These divisions were apparent in the debates leading up to the resolutions. The central concerns of developing States have been with disarmament, nuclear weapons, and economic coercion; in general they have favoured a stricter interpretation of the prohibition of the use of force than developed States.

Also important in the interpretation and application of the UN Charter rules on the use of force are the resolutions of the General Assembly and of the Security Council passed in reaction to specific instances of the use of force by States. Of course these are political bodies, but it is generally accepted that a condemnation of a use of force is strong evidence of its illegality. In contrast, a failure to condemn may not be conclusive evidence that the action in question was lawful, given the variety of motives influencing States. The International Court of Justice (ICJ) has also played a significant part in the identification and development of the rules on the use of force in the *Nicaragua* case,[4] the *Legality of the Threat or Use of Nuclear Weapons* Advisory Opinion,[5] the *Oil Platforms* case,[6] and the *Case Concerning Armed Activities on the Territory of the Congo* (DRC v Uganda).[7]

II. THE PROHIBITION OF THE USE OF FORCE IN ARTICLE 2(4) UN CHARTER

Article 2(4) is the basic prohibition on the use of force by States. It provides that 'All Members shall refrain in their international relations from the threat or use of force against the territorial integrity or political independence of any State, or in any other manner inconsistent with the Purposes of the United Nations'. Clearly this is directed at the inter-State use of force, although as it has turned out civil conflicts have been more common than traditional inter-State conflicts since the Second World War. Under Article 2(6) there is a duty on the UN to ensure that even States which are not UN members act in accordance with these principles so far as may be necessary for the maintenance of international peace and security. This brief prohibition of the use of force in Article 2(4) is accepted as representing customary international law and even as *jus cogens*, as was acknowledged by the ICJ in the *Nicaragua* case.[8] But its interpretation has given rise to much debate. General Assembly resolutions give some limited guidance, but gloss over the more fundamental disagreements.

---

2 *Declaration on Principles of International Law concerning Friendly Relations and Co-operation among States in Accordance with the Charter of the United Nations*, GA Res 2625 (XXV) (24 October 1970).

3 *Declaration on the Enhancement of the Effectiveness of the Principle of Refraining from the Threat or Use of Force in International Relations*, GA Res 44/22 (18 November 1987).

4 *Military and Paramilitary Activities in and against Nicaragua (Nicaragua v United States of America)*, Merits, Judgment, *ICJ Reports 1986*, p 14.

5 *Legality of the Threat or Use of Nuclear Weapons, Advisory Opinion*, ICJ Reports 1996, p 226.

6 *Oil Platforms (Islamic Republic of Iran v United States of America)*, ICJ Reports 2003, p 161.

7 *Armed Activities on the Territory of the Congo (Democratic Republic of the Congo v Uganda)*, Judgment, *ICJ Reports 2005*, p 168.

8 *Military and Paramilitary Activities in and against Nicaragua (Nicaragua v United States of America)*, Merits, Judgment, *ICJ Reports 1986*, p 14, para 190.

A. THE USE OF FORCE IN 'INTERNATIONAL RELATIONS'

Article 2(4) prohibits the use of force in 'international relations'; certain States have therefore tried to argue that they were justified in the use of force to recover what they claimed
to be their own territory. Thus, Argentina invaded the Falkland Islands in 1982 in order to
seize them back from the UK whose title to the territory it rejected.[9] Iraq invaded Kuwait
in 1990 on the basis that it had pre-colonial title and therefore was not violating Article
2(4) because the territory belonged to it.[10] These invasions were strongly condemned by the
international community; the actions of Argentina and Iraq were inconsistent with the duty
under Article 2(3) of the UN Charter to settle disputes, including territorial and boundary
disputes, peacefully. This duty was further elaborated in the *Definition of Aggression* and
the *Declaration on Friendly Relations*. Nevertheless, China does not exclude the right to
use force to recover the island of Taiwan on the basis that this is part of China, while other
States have called for a peaceful settlement of the controversy.

Another problem with the interpretation of 'international relations' has arisen over
the categorization of conflicts: is the situation an inter-State conflict to which Article 2(4)
applies or is it an internal conflict governed by different rules? This issue of categorization
was crucial in the Vietnam and Korean Wars during the Cold War; Western States argued
that these were inter-State wars initiated when an aggressor Communist State invaded its
neighbour and that the international community was able to respond in collective self-
defence or collective action under Chapter VII of the UN Charter. The socialist bloc position was that Vietnam and Korea were both unitary States engaged in struggles against
colonial intervention. Disagreements as to whether the conflict was a civil war or an inter-
State conflict also arose with regard to the break-up of the former Yugoslavia.[11]

B. THE MEANING OF 'THREAT OR USE OF FORCE'

Developed and developing States are divided on the meaning of 'force'; the former maintain that this means only armed force, whereas developing States claim that it covers also
economic coercion. However, this division is perhaps more of symbolic than of practical
importance; economic coercion is now expressly prohibited in General Assembly resolutions, such as the *Declaration on Friendly Relations*.

Of greater practical importance with regard to the interpretation of 'force', the ICJ in
the *Nicaragua* case was called on to categorize the various actions of the USA aimed at
the overthrow of the government of Nicaragua. It held that not only the laying of mines
in Nicaraguan waters and attacks on Nicaraguan ports and oil installations by US forces
but also support for *contras* engaged in forcible struggle against the government could
constitute the 'use of force'. The arming and training of the *contras* involved the use of
force against Nicaragua, but the mere supply of funds did not in itself amount to a use
of force.[12]

---

[9] 1982 *UNYB* 1320.   [10] 1991 *UNYB* 189.

[11] See Gray, 1996. See also ICTY, Appeals Chamber, *Prosecutor v Dusko Tadić, Decision on the Defence
Motion for Interlocutory Appeal on Jurisdiction (Interlocutory Appeal)*, Case No IT-94-1-AR72 (2 October
1995).

[12] *Military and Paramilitary Activities in and against Nicaragua (Nicaragua v United States of America)*,
Merits, Judgment, ICJ Reports 1986, p 14, para 228.

The prohibition of the 'threat of force' has attracted less discussion than the actual 'use of force'. The ICJ in the *Nicaragua* case and in the Advisory Opinion on the *Legality of Nuclear Weapons* was faced with questions as to the meaning of 'threat of force' but offered little by way of guidance, limiting itself to the not very surprising conclusion that a threat of force is unlawful where the actual use of the force threatened would itself be unlawful; the Court refused to find that the mere possession of nuclear weapons was an unlawful threat of force.

C. THE USE OF FORCE 'AGAINST THE TERRITORIAL INTEGRITY AND POLITICAL INDEPENDENCE OF ANY STATE, OR IN ANY OTHER MANNER INCONSISTENT WITH THE PURPOSES OF THE UNITED NATIONS'

The most fundamental debate on the interpretation of Article 2(4) is whether it is an absolute prohibition on the use of force or whether it should be interpreted to allow the use of force for aims which are consistent with the purposes of the UN. Can there be a use of force which does not harm the territorial integrity or political independence of a State? There have been debates as to whether the use of force to rescue nationals, to promote democracy, and to further self-determination could be compatible with Article 2(4). States were divided as to whether NATO's forcible humanitarian intervention in Kosovo in 1999 was prohibited by Article 2(4).

During the Cold War some, mostly US, writers argued that Article 2(4) represents only a limited prohibition; they maintained that it should be interpreted in the context of the whole Charter and thus that the prohibition of force depends on the functioning of the Charter scheme for collective security under Chapter VII. In the Cold War the Security Council could not use its powers effectively and therefore Article 2(4) should be interpreted to allow the use of force to further the principles and purposes of the UN. Others rejected this approach, arguing that Article 2(4) should be strictly construed; the non-functioning of the UN system made it all the more important that States should not use force except in self-defence. The debate as to whether Article 2(4) is a wide or a narrow prohibition on the use of force has outlasted the Cold War.

In practice few States openly relied on a narrow interpretation of Article 2(4) to justify their use of force during the Cold War. The apparent adoption of the restrictive argument on Article 2(4) by the UK in the *Corfu Channel* case was exceptional; the UK argued that its forcible intervention in Albanian territorial waters to recover evidence (as to which State was responsible for laying naval mines that had led to the destruction of two British warships) did not violate Article 2(4) because its action did not threaten the territorial integrity or political independence of Albania.[13] The Court rejected this claim, but there was some debate as to whether this was merely a limited rejection of the UK claim on the particular facts or a total rejection of the narrow interpretation of Article 2(4). The ICJ in the *Nicaragua* case seems to have taken the latter view of the ruling.[14] In later incidents the USA and Israel also expressly took a narrow view of Article 2(4) as not prohibiting the

---

[13] *Corfu Channel, Merits, Judgment, ICJ Reports 1949*, p 4 at p 34.

[14] *Military and Paramilitary Activities in and against Nicaragua (Nicaragua v United States of America), Merits, Judgment, ICJ Reports 1986*, p 14, para 202.

rescue of nationals. This was argued by Israel to justify its rescue of nationals on a hijacked plane from Entebbe in Uganda (1976) and by the USA in its more extensive operation in Grenada (1983), but this was not the sole justification for the use of force and was not taken up by other States. In these cases other justifications were also offered by the USA and Israel for their use of force; they did not rely solely on the controversial narrow interpretation of Article 2(4). So express reliance on the argument that Article 2(4) should be interpreted to allow the use of force if this was consistent with the aims of the UN remained exceptional.

1. Force in pursuit of self-determination

During the era of decolonization States were divided as to whether force could be used by colonial peoples in pursuit of the right of self-determination (Wilson, 1988). Former colonies and developing States maintained that Article 2(4) did not prohibit such use of force; Western and former colonial powers did not accept this and voted against the General Assembly resolutions which expressly affirmed a right to use force. Those resolutions which were adopted by consensus, such as the *Definition of Aggression* and the *Friendly Relations Resolution*, were deliberately ambiguous. They spoke of the right of peoples with the right to self-determination to 'struggle' for that end; by this developing States understood armed struggle and the developed States peaceful struggle. There was agreement, however, that force should not be used against a people with the right of self-determination. Even though many groups continue to invoke self-determination and to turn to armed force in pursuit of independence, there is no support by developing States for any legal right to use force other than in pursuit of decolonization. The virtual end of decolonization therefore means that the legal debate does not have great practical significance today, except in the context of the struggle of the Palestinians for self-determination to end the illegal occupation by Israel of the West Bank and Gaza Strip. Even in this context there was little public debate of this legal issue with regard to the Gaza conflict in 2008–09.

2. Force in pursuit of democracy

The claim that pro-democratic force—the use of force to restore a democratic government—is not prohibited by Article 2(4) has been put forward by writers such as D'Amato (1990), but not by States. It is notable that when the USA invaded Panama in 1989 it specifically disavowed any legal doctrine of pro-democratic invasion, preferring to rely instead on self-defence. When the former President Noriega refused to stand down after defeat in the election the USA intervened, claiming that it was acting in self-defence of its nationals in Panama. It distinguished between its political interest in the protection of democracy and its legal justification for intervention.[15] Although the UN may have a power to authorize force to restore democratic government in exceptional cases, such as that of Haiti after its first democratically elected government was overthrown in a coup in 1991, it is not possible to extrapolate from this a right of unilateral intervention by States. It is significant that even though the 2006 *US National Security Strategy* produced during the presidency of George W Bush devoted considerable attention to the promotion of democracy, it did not support the use of force for this end.

---

[15] 1989 *UNYB* 172.

D. HUMANITARIAN INTERVENTION

The NATO action over Kosovo in 1999 led to prolonged debate as to whether Article 2(4) allowed the use of force for humanitarian intervention, and produced a fundamental split between NATO States on the one hand and China, Russia, and the Non-Aligned Movement on the other.[16] Acting in response to Yugoslavia's repression and displacement of ethnic Albanians in Kosovo, NATO conducted a 78-day air campaign starting in March 1999. Although NATO did not offer a fully elaborated legal argument for its air campaign, it seemed to put forward in justification a mixture of implied authorization by the Security Council and humanitarian arguments. Member States set out their legal arguments in the Security Council debates and in their pleadings in the *Legality of Use of Force* case brought by Yugoslavia before the International Court of Justice against NATO States.[17]

The UK more than any other State has developed a doctrine of humanitarian intervention as an autonomous institution. It has argued that the interpretation of Article 2(4) has changed over time; that international law in this field has developed to meet new situations. This apparently new doctrine was first put forward with regard to US and UK action over Iraq. After Iraq invaded Kuwait in 1990 and was driven out by coalition forces in *Operation Desert Storm*, the UN Security Council established a binding cease-fire which was accepted by Iraq. However, the cease-fire regime in Resolution 687 failed to make provision for the protection of human rights in Iraq; Iraq turned on the Kurds of the north and the Shiites and Marsh Arabs of the south. In response the Security Council passed Resolution 688[18] asking Iraq to end its repression and to allow access to humanitarian agencies. This resolution was not a binding resolution passed under Chapter VII; it expressly refers to Article 2(7) UN Charter which provides that nothing in the Charter authorizes UN organs to intervene in matters which are essentially within the domestic jurisdiction of States; it did not authorize force. The USA, the UK, and, to a lesser extent, France nevertheless intervened in Iraq to protect the endangered civilians and subsequently proclaimed no-fly zones over north and south Iraq. The legal basis for this was not made clear at first, but the UK subsequently developed the doctrine of humanitarian intervention. To justify the use of force to protect the no-fly zones over north and south Iraq, the UK said that 'We believe that humanitarian intervention without the invitation of the country concerned can be justified in cases of extreme humanitarian need'. In contrast, the USA and France did not offer humanitarian intervention as the justification for their use of force in Iraq. States became polarized over the legality of the operations in the no-fly zones which continued for over ten years until *Operation Iraqi Freedom*. France withdrew its initial support; China and Russia did not accept the legality of the no-fly zones (Gray, 2002).

Those who support a doctrine of humanitarian intervention often rely on earlier, pre-Iraq, practice; they invoke as precedents India's intervention to end repression and support self-determination in Bangladesh (1971), Tanzania's intervention which overthrew the regime of Idi Amin in Uganda (1979), and Vietnam's use of force which ended the murderous rule of Pol Pot in Cambodia (1978). But in these episodes the States using force did

---

[16] 1999 *UNYB* 332.

[17] *Legality of Use of Force (Yugoslavia v Belgium), Provisional Measures, Order of 2 June 1999, ICJ Reports 1999*, p 124.

[18] SC Res 688 (5 April 1991). This was adopted with ten votes in favour, three against, and with two abstentions.

not actually invoke a doctrine of humanitarian intervention; they preferred to rely on the better established right to self-defence. Several States said that violations of human rights could not justify the use of force. Some commentators attempt to re-write history in order to try to justify the action in Kosovo. This requires that we ignore what the States in question actually said, and therefore seems inconsistent with the approach of the ICJ in the *Nicaragua* case. The Court in considering whether a new doctrine of forcible intervention to help opposition forces to overthrow the government had emerged through State practice put great stress on the fact that neither the USA itself, nor other States, had claimed such a right.[19]

As regards Kosovo there was little express support from States for an autonomous doctrine of humanitarian intervention, other than from the UK. However, Belgium in its arguments to the ICJ did resort to this doctrine on the interpretation of Article 2(4). It said that the NATO campaign was an action to rescue a population in danger and was not directed against the territorial integrity or political independence of Yugoslavia. Other States such as Germany and France stressed the unique nature of the NATO operation and made clear that they did not regard it as a precedent for future humanitarian intervention. Most States arguing in the Security Council and in the ICJ did not rely on humanitarian intervention alone as an autonomous justification for the use of force; they seemed to rely on a combination of humanitarian intervention and implied authorization by the Security Council.

Those against the NATO bombing argued that Article 2(4) should be construed strictly. It was an absolute prohibition of the use of force and it was for the Security Council under Chapter VII to authorize the use of force; unilateral action by NATO was illegal. Yugoslavia's pleadings argue that there is no right of humanitarian intervention in international law. The practice of States after the creation of the UN did not justify any argument that there had been a change in the meaning of Article 2(4). General Assembly resolutions such as the *Definition of Aggression* and the *Declaration on Friendly Relations* excluded intervention in absolute terms. However, the attempt to secure a Security Council resolution condemning the NATO action was rejected, an indication of considerable political sympathy for NATO, if not conclusive as to the legality of its action.

Therefore, even if a legal doctrine of humanitarian intervention could be said to have emerged from the NATO action in Kosovo, its scope is far from clear (Chesterman, 2001). Is humanitarian intervention an autonomous right or does it depend on a prior determination by the Security Council under Chapter VII? Must it always be collective action and if so how many States should be involved? Can a bombing campaign amount to humanitarian action? Yugoslavia argued that even if there is a right of humanitarian intervention the modalities chosen were inconsistent with humanitarian aims: a high-level bombing campaign and the wide range of targets chosen put the population of the whole of Yugoslavia at risk.

There have been attempts by the UK and by scholars to develop a detailed framework for humanitarian intervention.[20] Moreover, Article 4(h) of the African Union Constitutive

---

[19] *Military and Paramilitary Activities in and against Nicaragua (Nicaragua v United States of America)*, Merits, Judgment, *ICJ Reports 1986*, p 14, paras 206–209.

[20] See, for example, (2000) 71 *BYIL* 644, and the *Report of the International Commission on Intervention and State Sovereignty, The Responsibility to Protect* (2001).

Act (2000) includes provision for humanitarian intervention pursuant to a decision of the AU Assembly. But there is still no general agreement on a right of unilateral intervention. Many States in many different fora within and outside the UN after the NATO campaign made a point of condemning the NATO action in Kosovo as illegal. The Non-Aligned Movement rejects humanitarian intervention as having no legal basis in the Charter. The doctrine therefore remains controversial. It is noteworthy that it was not used to justify the use of force against Afghanistan in *Operation Enduring Freedom* or against Iraq in *Operation Iraqi Freedom*, despite the choice of names for these operations.

In recent years attention has shifted away from humanitarian intervention to the concept of the 'Responsibility to Protect' (Stahn, 2007 and see Ch 17, above). Provision for this was included in the 2005 UN World Summit Outcome Document which was adopted unanimously by States. This responsibility arises in cases of genocide, ethnic cleansing or other serious violations of international humanitarian law. When a State fails to act to protect its own citizens, the international community has a responsibility to act, by force if necessary. But the action should be taken through the UN Security Council. There was no agreement on a right of unilateral intervention. The 'Responsibility to Protect' has been invoked by the UN Security Council with regard to the humanitarian catastrophe in Darfur (Sudan) which arose out of the 2003 civil conflict, but the Security Council was slow to react and unwilling to intervene without the consent of the government of Sudan.

III. INTERVENTION, CIVIL WARS, AND INVITATION

The prohibition of the use of force in the UN Charter is directed at inter-State conflict, but apart from the many minor border incidents since the Second World War the most common use of force has been civil war, sometimes purely internal and sometimes fuelled by outside involvement. The rules against forcible intervention in civil conflict have been developed by General Assembly resolutions which elaborate on the Charter provisions on the use of force and complement the prohibitions of intervention in the constitutions of regional organizations. Thus the *Friendly Relations Declaration* (1970) makes clear that every State has the duty to refrain from organizing, instigating, assisting, or participating in acts of civil strife in another State and the duty not to foment incite, or tolerate subversive, terrorist, or armed activities directed towards the violent overthrow of the regime of another State. There is a general consensus between States as to the principles to be applied to forcible intervention in civil conflicts, but their application in particular conflicts has caused fundamental disagreement (Roth, 1999).

The *Nicaragua* case set out the general doctrine in this area.[21] Nicaragua brought this case against the USA not only for unlawful use of force but also for unlawful intervention against the government through its support for the military and paramilitary operations of the *contra* forces. The ICJ affirmed that the principle of non-intervention involves the right of every State to conduct its affairs and to choose its own form of government without outside interference; it acknowledged that breaches of this principle were common but

---

[21] *Military and Paramilitary Activities in and against Nicaragua (Nicaragua v United States of America), Merits, Judgment, ICJ Reports 1986*, p 14, paras 202–209.

nevertheless found that the principle was customary international law. It held that the USA through 'recruiting, training, arming, equipping, financing, supplying and otherwise encouraging, supporting, aiding and directing military and paramilitary actions in and against Nicaragua' had violated international law.

In this case the Court distinguished between assistance to the government of a State and assistance to an opposition forcibly to overthrow the government. The former is allowed, the latter is forbidden. If forcible assistance to the opposition were allowed nothing would remain of the principle of non-intervention. The Court stressed that States in practice had not claimed such a right to help opposition forces against the government outside the context of national liberation movements seeking the right of self-determination and that in the *Nicaragua* case the USA itself had not invoked a right to intervene but had relied on collective self-defence to justify its use of force against Nicaragua. The ICJ reaffirmed this approach in 2005 in *Armed Activities in the Territory of the Congo.*[22]

During the Cold War States which assisted opposition forces generally did so covertly; they also tended to challenge the legitimacy of the governments they were trying to overthrow. Thus when the USA assisted the opposition forces in Angola, Cambodia, and Afghanistan its use of force was covert and it challenged the legitimacy of the government in all these cases. No objective determination of the legitimacy of governments by the Security Council was possible in the Cold War. Since the end of the Cold War it is now possible for the Security Council to determine who is the legitimate government and to distinguish between it and the opposition, for example in the context of arms embargoes. In the case of the complex conflict in the Democratic Republic of Congo (DRC) the Security Council distinguished between those States lawfully in the DRC at the invitation of the government and those unlawfully assisting opposition forces.

As for assistance to the government, the law in this area is complex (Doswald Beck, 1985; Roth, 1999). During the Cold War there was agreement on the principle that during a civil war any form of outside interference was unlawful, but it is clear that States manipulated the rules in pursuit of their own interests. Many States claimed that they were invited by a government; the right to use force to keep a government in power or to maintain domestic order has been taken for granted if the level of unrest falls below the threshold of civil war. The *Definition of Aggression* acknowledges that a State may invite a foreign army into its territory. Thus France repeatedly intervened in its former colonies in Africa, ostensibly to maintain order. Similarly the USA currently denies intervention in a civil war in Colombia, but maintains that it is merely providing assistance to the government to fight the drugs trade and terrorism.

If the conflict amounts to a civil war rather than mere internal unrest it is accepted that there is a duty not to intervene in the absence of UN or regional authorization. States in this situation have often attempted to justify their intervention by claiming that it was in response to a prior foreign intervention against the government. The USSR interventions in Czechoslovakia in 1968 and in Afghanistan in 1979 are examples of such claims. In both cases the claim that there had been an invitation was a fiction as the USSR had itself

---

[22] *Armed Activities on the Territory of the Congo (Democratic Republic of the Congo v Uganda), Judgment,* ICJ Reports 2005, p 168.

installed the government whose invitation it claimed to rely on, and in both the intervention was condemned by the General Assembly.

IV. SELF-DEFENCE

The main exception to the prohibition on the use of force in Article 2(4) is the right of self-defence. There are deep divisions between States and between writers as to whether this right of self-defence is a wide or a narrow right (Alexandrov, 1996). The controversy as to the scope of the right has intensified following the terrorist attacks of 9/11. The basic United Nations Charter provision on self-defence is Article 51, which provides:

Nothing in the present Charter shall impair the inherent right of individual or collective self-defence if an armed attack occurs against a Member of the United Nations, until the Security Council has taken measures necessary to maintain international peace and security. Measures taken by Members in the exercise of this right of self-defence shall be immediately reported to the Security Council and shall not in any way affect the authority and responsibility of the Security Council under the present Charter to take at any time such action as it deems necessary in order to maintain or restore international peace and security.

As a matter of treaty interpretation, the debate centres on whether Article 51 is an exhaustive statement of the right to self-defence or whether there is a wider customary law right of self-defence going beyond the right to respond to an armed attack. Those supporting a wide right of self-defence argue, first, that the reference to 'inherent right' in Article 51 preserves a customary law right of self-defence and, second, that such a customary law right is wider than Article 51 and allows self-defence other than against an armed attack (Bowett, 1958; Arend and Beck, 1993). They argue for a right of anticipatory self-defence and of protection of nationals abroad. Those against a wide view of self-defence argue that this interpretation deprives Article 51 of any purpose; Article 51 imposes restrictions on the right of self-defence in response to armed attack and so it would be strange at the same time to preserve a wider right of self-defence unlimited by these restrictions. Also, as the right of self-defence is an exception to the prohibition on the use of force, it should be narrowly construed (Brownlie, 1963, p 251). Those arguing for a narrow right of self-defence also deny that customary law in 1945 included a wide right of self-defence which was preserved by Article 51. Given this fundamental disagreement on the proper interpretation of the UN Charter, State practice since 1945 is crucial for an understanding of the scope of the right of self-defence.

A. THE SCOPE OF SELF-DEFENCE: NECESSITY
AND PROPORTIONALITY

Despite the fundamental disagreement on the scope of the right of self-defence, all are agreed that self-defence must be necessary and proportionate. This requirement of necessity and proportionality is not explicit in the UN Charter but is part of customary international law. It is generally taken as limiting self-defence to action which is necessary to recover territory or repel an attack on a State's forces and which is proportionate to this end. These customary law requirements of necessity and proportionality have been reaffirmed in the *Nicaragua* case,[23] the *Nuclear Weapons* Advisory Opinion,[24] the *Oil Platforms* case,[25] and *Armed Activities on the Territory of the Congo*.[26] The agreement between States that all self-defence should be necessary and proportionate makes it possible for them to reject many claims to self-defence on this simple basis without going into the more controversial doctrinal debates such as the existence of a right to anticipatory self-defence or the right to protect nationals or self-defence against terrorism.

B. THE MEANING OF 'ARMED ATTACK'

Article 51 specifies that self-defence is permissible in response to an armed attack. The definition of armed attack is left to customary international law. The most straightforward type of armed attack is that by a regular army of one State against the territory or against the land, sea, or air forces of another. The meaning of armed attack at sea was considered in some detail in the recent *Oil Platforms* case; mine and missile attacks aimed at US-flagged military ships could constitute 'armed attacks', but attacks on US-owned ships did not amount to attacks on the State.

'Armed attack' extends beyond attacks by regular forces; it can also cover attacks by armed bands, irregulars, and mercenaries. In the *Nicaragua* case the ICJ used the *Definition of Aggression* paragraph 3(g) to help interpret the meaning of armed attack in customary international law. It held that an armed attack must be understood as including 'the sending by or on behalf of a State of armed bands, groups, irregulars or mercenaries, which carry out acts of armed force against another State of such gravity as to amount to an actual armed attack, or its substantial involvement therein.' But the Court did not consider that the concept of armed attack stretched as far as assistance to rebels in the form of the provision of weapons or logistical or other support.[27] This conception of armed attack as covering the acts of armed bands clearly requires a significant degree of government involvement. But it has been argued that the 11 September 2001 terrorist attacks on the World Trade Center and Pentagon have further expanded the notion of armed attack to cover force by terrorist organizations, even in the absence of State involvement in the attack. The Security Council stopped short of an express pronouncement that the terrorist attack amounted to an 'armed attack', preferring to characterize it as a 'threat to the peace', but it did affirm the right of self-defence in the preambles to Resolutions 1368 and 1373 condemning the attack;[28] this amounts to an implicit acceptance that the terrorist attacks on the USA were armed attacks, but leaves unclear the exact nature of Afghanistan's involvement in the actions of Al Qaida terrorists. Similar questions arose about Hezbollah's attacks on Israel from Lebanon, Hamas' rocket attacks on Israel from

---

[23] *Military and Paramilitary Activities in and against Nicaragua (Nicaragua v United States of America)*, Merits, Judgment, ICJ Reports 1986, p 14, para 194.

[24] *Legality of the Threat or Use of Nuclear Weapons, Advisory Opinion, ICJ Reports 1996*, p 266, para 141.

[25] *Oil Platforms (Islamic Republic of Iran v United States of America), ICJ Reports 2003*, p 161.

[26] *Armed Activities on the Territory of the Congo (Democratic Republic of the Congo v Uganda), Judgment*, ICJ Reports 2005, p 168.

[27] *Military and Paramilitary Activities in and against Nicaragua (Nicaragua v United States of America)*, Merits, Judgment, ICJ Reports 1986, p 14, para 195.

[28] SC Res 1368 (12 September 2001); SC Res 1373 (28 September 2001).

Gaza and attacks by the PKK (Kurdish terrorists) on Turkey from Iraq: could these be classified as armed attacks giving a right to use force in response? What degree of State involvement is necessary to allow self-defence against Lebanon and Iraq? The law on this question remains uncertain, and the ICJ has deliberately avoided pronouncing on it in *Armed Activities on the Territory of the Congo*.[29]

C. THE USE OF FORCE IN PROTECTION OF NATIONALS

One controversy as to the scope of self-defence concerns the right of States to use force to protect their nationals abroad (Ronzitti, 1985). This right has been asserted by developed States such as the USA, UK, and Israel under Article 51; it has been exercised in practice by the USA in the Dominican Republic (1965), Grenada (1983), and Panama (1989), by the UK in Suez (1956) and by Israel in Entebbe (1976). Most recently it has been invoked by Russia to justify its use of force against Georgia (2008). Developing States are more doubtful about the existence of this right. Where the host State consents or acquiesces or where there is no effective government, there is not usually a hostile response by other States if the forcible action is limited to the evacuation of nationals and not a pretext for more far-reaching intervention.

One of the most discussed and most controversial examples of the use of force to protect nationals abroad was by the USA in the small Caribbean island of Grenada.[30] The USA relied on a series of justifications for sending forces into Grenada in response to a coup which brought a socialist government to power. One of its arguments was that US nationals were under threat and that the operation was designed to rescue them. But there was considerable doubt as to the existence of the danger, and the use of force was condemned by the UN General Assembly. In the Security Council the USA vetoed the resolution condemning its intervention. One of the grounds for doubt about the legality of the US operation, insofar as it was based on protection of nationals, was that the use of force went beyond what was necessary and proportionate. All too often the protection of nationals is a mere pretext to mask the real intent of overthrowing the government; this was the case in all the episodes listed above, with the exception of the Entebbe intervention. Even here a majority of States did not accept the legality of the intervention, though there was sympathy for Israel's position.[31]

When Russia invoked the protection of nationals to justify its use of force against Georgia, western States did not oppose this doctrine as a matter of principle. Instead they challenged Russia's motives and the proportionality of its action. In August 2008 Georgia mounted a military action to assert control over separatists in the region of South Ossetia.[32] Russia's response was to send troops into South Ossetia to protect its nationals; many ethnic Ossetians held Russian passports. The conflict spread to Abkhazia, another area of separatist conflict, and Russia went on to attack military bases and transport links throughout Georgia. Georgia was forced to withdraw its forces from South Ossetia and

---

[29] *Armed Activities on the Territory of the Congo (Democratic Republic of the Congo v Uganda), Judgment, ICJ Reports 2005*, p 168, para 147.

[30] 1983 *UNYB* 211.   [31] 1976 *UNYB* 315.

[32] *Keesing's Record of World Events 2008*, p 48740.

Abkhazia which subsequently proclaimed their independence. Western States asserted that Russia's intervention was unlawful because it was not limited to the protection of its nationals, but was really designed to lead to the dismemberment of Georgia and the independence of South Ossetia and Abkhazia.

D. ANTICIPATORY OR PRE-EMPTIVE SELF-DEFENCE

Another major controversy over the scope of self-defence concerns the right of 'anticipatory' self-defence; that is, does the right of a State to self-defence arise only after an armed attack has started under Article 51 or is there a wider right to anticipate an *imminent* attack? The controversy over the legality of anticipatory self-defence was so strong that no provision on self-defence could be included in the UN General Assembly resolutions such as the *Definition of Aggression* and the *Declaration on Friendly Relations*. States such as the USA, the UK, and Israel have claimed a wider right, but the doctrine is so controversial that such claims have been rare in practice. Although the USA has sometimes adopted wide Rules of Engagement which allow its own forces to use force in response to demonstrations of 'hostile intent' by opposing forces rather than requiring them to wait for an actual armed attack, it has tended to play down any anticipatory element in operations such as those by its naval convoys in the Gulf during the 1980–88 Iran/Iraq War, and those by its aircraft over the no-fly zones proclaimed in Iraq to protect the civilian population after Iraq invaded Kuwait in 1990. Thus, in the case of the shooting down of the civilian Iran Airbus by the *USS Vincennes* in 1988, an incident which may be taken to show the hazards of anticipatory self-defence, the USA argued that it had acted in the context of an ongoing armed attack on its naval convoy in the Gulf to respond to what it (mistakenly) believed to be imminent attack by a hostile Iranian military aircraft. Iran took the case to the ICJ, but it was settled without the need for the Court to make any authoritative pronouncement on anticipatory self-defence. Similarly in the *Oil Platforms* case the USA preferred to rely on an extensive notion of armed attack rather than claim any right of anticipatory self-defence.

The express invocation of anticipatory armed attack by Israel to justify its attack on an Iraqi nuclear reactor in 1981 is therefore unusual. Israel argued that the Iraqi reactor under construction was designed to produce nuclear weapons for use against Israel and therefore that it was entitled to take pre-emptive action. This attack was condemned by both the Security Council and by the General Assembly, but the resolutions do not directly address the fundamental doctrinal issue; it is left open to question whether the condemnation should be taken as a total rejection of anticipatory self-defence or just a rejection on the particular facts.[33]

Those in favour of a right to anticipatory self-defence argue that it is not realistic to expect States to wait for an attack before responding; those against argue that anticipatory self-defence involves a risk of escalation in that the State may mistake the intentions of the other or react disproportionately. Insofar as a wide conception of armed attack based on the capabilities of modern weapons is adopted, the gap between the two positions may shrink.

---

[33] 1981 *UNYB* 275.

The ICJ in the *Nicaragua* case deliberately left the matter unresolved.[34] It did so again in *Armed Activities on the Territory of the Congo* (2005), a clear indication of the controversial nature of the doctrine.[35]

E. THE IMPACT OF THE TERRORIST ATTACKS OF 9/11 ON THE LAW OF SELF-DEFENCE

The attacks by Al Qaida on the World Trade Center and the Pentagon on 11 September 2001 brought a revolutionary challenge to the doctrine of self-defence.[36] Before 9/11 the use of force in response to terrorist attacks had been controversial; only Israel and the USA had expressly claimed such a right, and this was generally exercised in response to attacks on nationals abroad. There was no general support for such a right. In response to the 9/11 attacks on US territory, the USA began *Operation Enduring Freedom* with the aim of disrupting the use of Afghanistan as a terrorist base. It relied on self-defence as the basis for its use of force against Afghanistan; in its report to the Security Council under Article 51 the USA claimed to be acting in self-defence. This claim may seem controversial in the light of the previous doubts as to whether the right to self-defence could extend to action against past terrorist attacks, but *Operation Enduring Freedom* received massive support and the action was almost universally accepted as self-defence. NATO invoked Article 5 of the NATO Treaty for the first time; this provides that an attack on one member State is an attack on all. Other collective self-defence organizations, including the Organization of American States (OAS), also took the view that the attack was an armed attack for the purposes of collective self-defence. The EU, China, Russia, Japan, and Pakistan supported this view. Many States have played a role in the military campaign. Only Iran and Iraq expressly challenged the legality of the operation. In Resolution 1368 condemning the attacks the Security Council had expressly recognized the right of self-defence. Subsequently Resolution 1373 on measures against international terrorism also included express reference to individual and collective self-defence. This was the first time that the Security Council had implicitly recognized the right to use force in self-defence against terrorist action.

This use of force against Afghanistan raises many questions about the traditional model of self-defence. It seems that the massive State support for the legality of the US claim to self-defence could constitute instant customary international law and an authoritative re-interpretation of the UN Charter, however radical the alteration from many States' prior conception of the right to self-defence. First, the question arises whether the response to 9/11 widens the concept of armed attack. Article 51 originally envisaged self-defence against an attack by a State and those invoking the right generally took care to attribute responsibility to a State. Now some States argue that a terrorist attack on a State's territory by a non-State actor may be an armed attack which justifies a response against the State which harboured those responsible. However, considerable uncertainty remains

---

[34] *Military and Paramilitary Activities in and against Nicaragua (Nicaragua v United States of America), Merits, Judgment, ICJ Reports 1986*, p 14, para 194.

[35] *Armed Activities on the Territory of the Congo (Democratic Republic of the Congo v Uganda), Judgment, ICJ Reports 2005*, p 168, para 143.

[36] See account of the facts in (2002) 96 *AJIL* 237, and editorial comments in (2001) 95 *AJIL* 833.

as to the degree of State involvement required, and as to whether force could be used in self-defence against terrorists in a State which was not complicit in the terrorist attack (Becker, 2006) The ICJ did not elaborate on the law in this controversial area in *Armed Activities on the Territory of the Congo* and the *Wall* Advisory Opinion. There are few express claims in State practice since 9/11 to support such a wide right of self-defence, but some commentators have taken an extensive view of the legal significance of 9/11 and its aftermath (Tams, 2009).

The right to self-defence claimed by the USA and the UK in response to the 9/11 terrorist attacks was also pre-emptive. Both the USA and the UK in their letters to the Security Council said that their action was in response to the attack on the World Trade Center; for the USA the aim is to deter further attacks on the United States, for the UK 'to avert the continuing threat of attacks from the same source'. That is, although the initial attack had ended and thus it would be difficult to invoke self-defence against that attack, the USA and the UK clearly felt the need to avoid the appearance of punitive (and unlawful) reprisals. Many States in the past have rejected the legality of pre-emptive self-defence, but they accepted a wide right to self-defence by the USA, at least in regard to *Operation Enduring Freedom*. However, there is still controversy as to the scope of this right; it is not clear how far the international response should be construed as a general acceptance of anticipatory or pre-emptive use of force outside the context of terrorism or of *Operation Enduring Freedom*. Another possible restriction on this apparently very wide and, for many States, new doctrine of self-defence is that the right of self-defence against terrorism may exist only in cases where the right has been asserted by the Security Council, as here in Resolutions 1368 and 1373. Several States regarded this Security Council backing as crucial to the US claim to self-defence.

Also questions arise as to necessity and proportionality. The USA at the start of *Operation Enduring Freedom* warned that the 'Global War on Terror' could take many years. In a campaign to prevent future terrorist attacks it is difficult to identify an appropriate end to the action, but the longer it continues and the more destruction it involves the more difficult it is to argue that it is proportionate. If the use of force proves ineffective in deterring terrorist attacks it is also difficult to argue that it is necessary. *Operation Enduring Freedom* in Afghanistan is now in its ninth year. The UN Security Council apparently accepts its legality, but it is not entirely clear whether its legal basis is now the consent of the government of Afghanistan or an independent—and long-lasting—right of self-defence.

1. Lebanon (2006)

Questions concerning the scope of self-defence after 9/11 arose with regard to the 2006 conflict in Lebanon. The conflict began when Hezbollah launched a minor cross-border attack on Israeli forces in northern Israel from Lebanon, killing eight Israeli soldiers and abducting two.[37] In response Israel mounted a month-long land, sea, and air attack on Lebanon causing serious destruction to its infrastructure and massive displacement of its people. In the Security Council States avoided discussion of the fundamental questions whether there could be an 'armed attack' by non-State actors in the absence of Lebanon's involvement, and whether Israel had the right of self-defence against Lebanon under the

[37] Gray, 2008, p 237.

UN Charter, preferring to focus on the issue of proportionality. Most States eventually condemned Israel's use of force as disproportionate. If seen as a response to the minor action by Hezbollah, Israel's action was clearly not proportionate. But Israel, the USA, and the UK took a different approach to proportionality: they argued that terrorist attacks by Hezbollah posed an existential threat to Israel and that massive forcible action to stop future attacks was proportionate to the threat posed.

Similar questions about the scope of self-defence in response to terrorist acts arose with regard to the 2008–09 Gaza conflict and Ethiopia's intervention in Somalia (2006–08). The Gaza conflict was precipitated by Hamas rocket attacks on Israel; Israel responded by three weeks of intense land, sea, and air military action, leading to 1,300 Palestinian deaths and 130 Israeli deaths, and massive destruction of property within Gaza. Was this action justified as self-defence? The fundamental issue was the status of Gaza: it had been taken by force from Egypt in 1967 and remained as occupied territory until 2005. In 2005 Israel withdrew its troops, but maintained control over movement in and out of the territory. If Gaza remained occupied territory under international law in 2008, then the relevant law would be that governing occupation rather than any right of self-defence under Article 51. This is the ICJ view, as expressed in a rather obscure paragraph on self-defence in the *Wall* Advisory Opinion with regard to the occupied West Bank: Security Council Resolutions 1368 and 1373 could not apply to allow self-defence in response to terrorist attacks from occupied territory.[38] In the Security Council debates States were initially broadly sympathetic to Israel, but they preferred to avoid express discussion of the issue whether Israel had a right of self-defence under Article 51, and the related question of the classification of the conflict, instead focusing on the international humanitarian law applicable during armed conflict.

F. A 'BUSH DOCTRINE' OF PRE-EMPTIVE SELF-DEFENCE?

After it had undertaken *Operation Enduring Freedom* in Afghanistan the USA shifted its focus in the 'global war on terror' to the threat posed by the 'Axis of Evil': Iran, Iraq, and North Korea. In the light of the new dangers facing it after 9/11, the USA developed a new *National Security Strategy* (2002): the USA must be prepared to stop rogue States and global terrorists from threatening to use weapons of mass destruction against it.[39] Accordingly there was a need to re-examine the law of self-defence. The USA had always taken the wide view that anticipatory self-defence was lawful in the case of an imminent armed attack, but now it argued that the requirement of imminence should be reconsidered. However, it did not make clear what would trigger such pre-emptive (or preventive) action. The 2006 US *National Security Strategy* repeated the commitment to pre-emptive self-defence, but did not elaborate further.

There is little sign of support for a fundamental transformation of self-defence along the lines suggested in the US *National Security Strategy*. A UN High-level Panel of Experts was set up to respond to the new challenges to the collective security system after 9/11; in its Report of December 2004 it accepted the controversial right of anticipatory self-defence,

---

[38] *Legal Consequences of the Construction of a Wall in the Palestinian Occupied Territories, Advisory Opinion, ICJ Reports 2004*, p 136, para 139.
[39] (2002) 41 ILM 1478.

but firmly rejected the doctrine of pre-emptive self-defence.[40] It said that there is no right to self-defence if the threat of armed attack is not imminent. If there are good arguments for preventive military action, with good evidence to support them, they should be put to the Security Council which can authorize action if it chooses to. A unilateral right of pre-emptive self-defence would be dangerously destabilizing. Thus, the UK supports anticipatory self-defence but rejects a wider doctrine of pre-emptive self-defence. The position of President Obama on this issue is not yet clear.

G. COLLECTIVE SELF-DEFENCE

The express provision for collective self-defence in Article 51 of the UN Charter is generally seen as an innovation, included in response to the desire of Latin American States to retain regional autonomy. The right of collective self-defence formed the basis for the NATO Treaty and the Warsaw Pact and for many regional treaties after the Second World War; these treaties provided that an attack on one was an attack on all and provided for a collective response. As mentioned above, NATO invoked Article 5 for the first time with regard to the attack on the World Trade Center. The USA conducted the major role in *Operation Enduring Freedom* against Afghanistan, but it received some assistance from other States acting in collective self-defence. Opinion is divided as to whether collective self-defence is a valuable safeguard for small States or a dangerous doctrine justifying intervention by distant and powerful States in remote conflicts. It was not often invoked during the Cold War and the few instances where it was invoked—such as the USA in the Vietnam War (1961–75) and in Nicaragua, and the USSR interventions in Hungary (1956), Czechoslovakia (1968), and Afghanistan (1979)—were controversial. In all these cases there was dispute as to whether there had been an armed attack or a genuine request for help from the victim State.

The *Nicaragua* case played a crucial role in establishing the scope of the right of collective self-defence. The USA had attempted to justify its use of force against Nicaragua by relying on collective self-defence, but the ICJ held that the use of force by the USA did not satisfy any of the criteria for legitimate collective self-defence. There had been no armed attack by Nicaragua on Costa Rica, El Salvador, or Honduras, no declaration by any of these States that it was the victim of an armed attack, and no invitation by them to the USA to come to their aid. Finally, the mining of harbours and bombing of ports by the USA was not necessary to repel alleged attacks by Nicaragua on El Salvador, and was not proportionate. The USA had not reported its actions to the Security Council under Article 51. This decision was controversial at the time, but accurately reflects State practice on collective self-defence.

H. THE ROLE OF THE SECURITY COUNCIL

In theory the Security Council has a central role with regard to individual and collective self-defence: States must report their use of force in self-defence to the Security Council

---

[40] Report of the Secretary-General's High-level Panel on Threats, Challenges and Change, UN Document A/59/565. The UN Secretary-General in his response to the High-level Panel, 'In Larger Freedom' (March 2005), also accepted this previously controversial doctrine, although in more cautious terms, saying that 'imminent threats are fully covered by Article 51' (UN Document A/59/2005). The Non-Aligned Movement reaffirmed its rejection of a wide doctrine of self-defence.

immediately and the right of the State to self-defence is temporary until the Security Council takes the measures necessary to maintain international peace and security. In practice the Security Council does not generally make pronouncements on the legality of claims to self-defence. Thus in the case of inter-State conflict between Iran and Iraq (1980–88) and Ethiopia and Eritrea (1998–2000) the Security Council did not initially attribute responsibility for the start of the conflict, and thus did not decide who had the right of self-defence. In contrast when Iraq invaded Kuwait in 1990 the Security Council did expressly uphold the right of Kuwait to self-defence.

States have taken care to report their self-defence to the Security Council, especially since the *Nicaragua* case where the Court held that the failure by the USA to report its use of force to the Security Council was an indication that the USA was not itself convinced that it was acting in self-defence. This approach was followed in *Armed Activities on the Territory of the Congo*[41] and by the Eritrea/Ethiopia Claims Commission.[42] There has in the past been some controversy as to whether the right to self-defence has been terminated because the Security Council has taken action and thus has taken 'measures necessary to maintain international peace and security'. It seems to be generally accepted that it is not enough for the Security Council simply to pass a resolution or even to impose economic measures if the aggressor is left in occupation of territory it has seized illegally. This was the argument of the United Kingdom with regard to the Falkland Islands (Islas Malvinas); it claimed the right to use force in self-defence when Argentina seized the Falklands despite the Security Council resolutions calling for a peaceful resolution. The UK argued that it retained its right to self-defence until Argentina was driven out.[43] Unless the Security Council has expressly passed a binding resolution declaring the right to be terminated, there will be room for doubt on this issue. If a State wishes to make the position clear it should try to secure an express recognition of its right by the Security Council. Thus in the Iraq/Kuwait conflict, even when economic measures were taken by the Security Council, in the same resolution it affirmed the right of self-defence;[44] and in regard to the attack on the World Trade Center the Security Council expressly referred to the continuing right to self-defence.[45]

V. THE USE OF FORCE UNDER CHAPTER VII OF THE UN CHARTER

The original intent behind the UN Charter was that control over the use of force would lie with the Security Council which would have a standing army at its disposal to enable it to take enforcement action against aggression in order to restore international peace and security. This ambitious plan has not been realized and the original Charter scheme has been modified through practice. Under Article 24 of the UN Charter the Security Council has the primary responsibility for the maintenance of international peace and

---

[41] *Armed Activities on the Territory of the Congo (Democratic Republic of the Congo v Uganda), Judgment, ICJ Reports 2005*, p 168, para 145.

[42] See Ethiopia's Ius ad Bellum claims 1–8, (2006) 45 ILM 430.

[43] 1982 *UNYB* 1320.   [44] SC Res 661 (16 August 1990).

[45] SC Res 1368 (12 September 2001), 1373 (14 November 2001).

security, but during the Cold War the veto possessed by the five permanent members of the Security Council under Article 27 generally blocked effective action by the Security Council. Chapter VII sets out the framework for its enforcement powers; under Article 2(7) these powers are not limited by the normal duty on the UN not to intervene in matters essentially within the domestic jurisdiction of States. Thus Chapter VII gives very wide powers to the Security Council. The Council in practice does not generally make express reference to specific Articles within Chapter VII; it more commonly makes a reference to Chapter VII in general terms (Sarooshi, 1999). However, since the use of force against Iraq in 2003, certain members of the Security Council have ensured that its resolutions on Iran and North Korea refer expressly to specific Charter Articles, in order to prevent any invocation of those resolutions to justify the use of force.

Under Article 39 the Security Council is 'to determine the existence of any threat to the peace, breach of the peace or act of aggression' and then to make recommendations or decide measures under Articles 41 and 42. The Council has been reluctant to find an act of aggression under Article 39; rare examples are resolutions condemning South Africa (under the apartheid regime) and Israel for attacks on neighbouring States. In response to inter-State conflicts it has preferred merely to find a breach of the peace, as in the 1980–88 Iran/Iraq conflict and in response to the 1990 Iraqi invasion of Kuwait, or a threat to the peace.

It has consistently taken a wide view of 'threat to the peace' and has been prepared to identify such a threat as arising out of internal conflicts such as those in the DRC and Somalia, overthrow of democratic government as in Haiti, and refusal to act against terrorism in the cases of Libya, Sudan, and the Taliban regime in Afghanistan. It is not clear whether any other body such as the ICJ would have the power to challenge a finding under Article 39 by the Security Council. The Court has never made an authoritative ruling on the matter; it avoided the issue in the *Lockerbie*[46] and *Bosnia-Herzegovina Genocide* cases.[47]

Article 40 provides for provisional measures and the Security Council has invoked this as the basis for its call for cease-fires as, for example, in Resolution 598 (20 July 1987) with regard to the 1980–88 Iran/Iraq conflict. This resolution was unusual in that it made express reference to Articles 39 and 40.

A. MEASURES UNDER ARTICLE 41

Article 41 allows the Security Council to decide on measures not involving the use of armed force to give effect to its decisions; these include 'complete or partial interruption of economic relations and of rail, sea, air, postal, telegraphic, radio, and other means of communication, and the severance of diplomatic relations'. Article 41 was little used in the Cold War: only in the comprehensive trade embargo on the illegal white minority government in Rhodesia (now Zimbabwe) in a series of resolutions from 1965 and in

---

[46] *Questions of Interpretation and Application of the 1971 Montreal Convention arising from the Aerial Incident at Lockerbie (Libyan Arab Jamahirya v United States of America), Preliminary Objections, Judgment,* ICJ Reports 1998, p 115.

[47] *Application of the Convention on the Prevention and Punishment of the Crime of Genocide, Provisional Measures, Order of 8 April 1993, ICJ Reports 1993, p 3, Order of 13 September, ICJ Reports 1993, p 325.*

the arms embargo on South Africa in 1977. But there has been a massive increase in the use of Article 41 since then (Gray, 2008, p 266). Indeed there is now increasing concern about the effects of trade embargoes on 'innocent' populations and the Security Council has attempted to develop 'smart' sanctions, targeted on those responsible for any non-compliance with its decisions. The official position is that Article 41 measures are not punishment but should be designed to secure compliance with decisions of the Security Council. They have been imposed on States and also on non-State actors, such as the Bosnian Serbs and UNITA in Angola. Recently they have been imposed on Iran and North Korea in an attempt to halt their development of nuclear weapons; these resolutions refer expressly to Article 41 in order to prevent any argument that they could be invoked to justify the use of force.

In many civil wars the imposition of an arms embargo is the immediate response of the Security Council to calls for it to act; thus arms embargoes were imposed in response to civil war in Yugoslavia, Somalia and Rwanda, and Liberia. Also, for the first time an arms embargo was imposed on both sides in the inter-State conflict between Ethiopia and Eritrea.

B. THE USE OF FORCE UNDER CHAPTER VII OF THE UN CHARTER

In cases where Article 41 measures would not be sufficient or had proved insufficient to maintain or restore international peace and security the original Charter scheme under Articles 42–49 was that the UN would have its own standing army able to take measures involving armed force. Member States were to make agreements to put troops at the disposal of the Security Council which would 'take such action by air, sea or land forces as may be necessary to maintain or restore international peace and security' under Article 42. But in practice member States did not conclude agreements to put troops at the disposal of the UN under Article 43 and no standing army was created. Cold War divisions help to explain this failure to implement the Charter scheme, but even today States remain unwilling to hand over control of troops for enforcement action. Because of the failure of States to conclude agreements under Article 43 there was a doctrinal debate as to whether the whole Charter scheme was therefore frustrated and Article 42 was inoperative (Simma, 2002, p 628).

However, the Security Council interpreted Chapter VII flexibly to authorize the establishment of a UN force in Korea in 1950. Although it did not make clear the exact constitutional basis for its actions, it referred to Chapter VII in general terms. When North Korea invaded South Korea in 1950 the Security Council intervened, although neither was a member State; it recommended member States to 'furnish such assistance to South Korea as may be necessary to repel the armed attack and to restore international peace and security in the area'. There was heated debate at the time as to the legal basis for this action, especially as the Security Council was able to act only because the USSR had stayed away from the relevant meeting in protest at the representation of China by the Taiwan government rather than the effective Communist government. Commentators disagreed as to whether this was collective security under Article 39, 42, or Chapter VII generally or whether it was only an authorization of collective self-defence. The debate leading to the Security Council decision sheds no light on this dilemma and it appears to have little practical significance.

No further forcible action was authorized under Chapter VII until the end of the Cold War. When Iraq invaded Kuwait in 1990 the Security Council passed Resolution 678 (1990) authorizing member States to use 'all necessary means to secure the withdrawal of Iraqi troops and to restore international peace and security in the area'.[48] It is clear from the Security Council debates that this phrase 'all necessary means' was intended to cover the use of force. The action against Iraq in *Operation Desert Storm* was seen at the time as the beginning of a new era for the Security Council, the start of a New World Order. In contrast with Korea the force did not operate under the UN flag, but it did act under the authorization of the Security Council, even if the precise constitutional basis was again unclear.

This use of Chapter VII to authorize member States to use force has been repeated many times in many different situations. It has certainly become clear that Chapter VII action is not limited to collective self-defence. The Security Council has not again authorized force against an aggressor State, but it has authorized force in internal conflicts, for example in response to non-cooperation with UN-brokered cease-fires; to secure the delivery of humanitarian aid as in Somalia and in Yugoslavia; to protect safe havens and enforce no-fly zones in Bosnia-Herzegovina; to restore democracy in Haiti; to protect a refugee camp in Rwanda; as well as to secure the implementation of economic measures under Article 41. The Security Council has also authorized massive member State forces to maintain order and engage in peace-building after the end of conflicts in East Timor, Kosovo, Afghanistan, and Iraq.

The UN Secretary-General recognizes that the UN does not itself have the resources for enforcement action, and that it will have to continue to turn to 'coalitions of the willing' or to regional organizations, but he acknowledges that there is a danger that the UN may be sidelined. The Security Council has made greater attempts to keep some control of the member State forces since *Operation Desert Storm* when it set no time limit for the operation against Iraq. The mandates authorizing member States to use force are now for a fixed period and stress the need for impartiality; States are required to report regularly to the Security Council.

C. IMPLIED OR REVIVED AUTHORIZATION OF FORCE?

More controversial than the express authorization of member States to use force under Chapter VII has been the issue of implied or revived authorization (Lobel and Ratner, 1999). States seeking legitimacy for their use of force but unable or unwilling to obtain a Chapter VII resolution have sought to rely on implied or revived authorization. Thus, the USA and UK in using force against Iraq in the decade after the cease-fire of Security Council Resolution 687 claimed that Iraq's violations of the cease-fire regime justified them in using force under Chapter VII in 1993 and 1998. The same argument was put forward by several States with regard to Kosovo. NATO's legal justification for its air campaign against the government of Yugoslavia was brief, but there were indications that it claimed implied authorization under Security Council Resolutions 1160 (1998), 1199 (1998), and 1203 (1998). Those impatient with the difficulty of securing agreement from China and Russia to the use of force even after the end of the Cold War argued that there

---

[48] SC Res 678 (29 April 1990).

was no need for express authorization of the use of force. It was enough that the resolutions identified a threat to international peace and security under Chapter VII, made certain demands on Yugoslavia, and determined that it had violated international agreements. This interpretation of the relevant Security Council resolutions was strongly resisted by Russia and China as a distortion of the words of the resolutions, not justified in the light of the Security Council debates, and a dangerous threat to the authority of the Security Council.

1. Operation Iraqi Freedom (2003)

These arguments arose again over *Operation Iraqi Freedom* in March 2003. Deep divisions as to the legality of the use of force against Iraq existed not only between the USA and China and Russia, but also within NATO and Europe. The USA, the UK and Australia (with the support of a 'coalition' of about forty-five other States including Spain, Poland, and others from eastern Europe) undertook *Operation Iraqi Freedom* to secure the disarmament of Iraq of weapons of mass destruction. The legal justification they offered was that they were acting on the basis of Security Council authority under a combination of three resolutions (678, 687, and 1444) adopted under Chapter VII of the Charter.[49] They claimed that military operations were necessary because of the threat posed by Iraq's alleged development of weapons of mass destruction in violation of its disarmament obligations. Other States such as Russia, China, France, and Germany argued for the continuation of UN weapons inspections; military action was not necessary.

Only the USA invoked (pre-emptive) self-defence as a possible basis for *Operation Iraqi Freedom* and it did not provide any detailed justification of this position; the UK and Australia did not rely on this doctrine. After *Operation Iraqi Freedom* drove Saddam Hussein from power in April 2003 it became apparent that Iraq did not possess weapons of mass destruction or the immediate capacity to produce them. Serious doubts emerged about the intelligence on the basis of which the use of force had been justified, and for many this provided a dramatic illustration of the dangers of pre-emptive action.

The argument as to the legality of *Operation Iraqi Freedom* turned on the interpretation of the three Security Council resolutions. Resolution 1441 was passed unanimously in November 2002 to give Iraq a 'final opportunity' to comply with its disarmament obligations imposed under the cease-fire regime.[50] The Security Council recalled its earlier resolutions and, acting under Chapter VII, decided that Iraq had been and remained in material breach of its obligations under Resolution 687 (1991), the cease-fire regime imposed by the Security Council requiring Iraq to disarm its weapons of mass destruction and to cooperate with UN weapons inspectors.[51] The UN weapons inspectors were to return to Iraq under an enhanced system of weapons inspection and Iraq was to provide a complete declaration of all aspects of its weapons programme; any omissions would constitute a further material breach by Iraq. In the event of reports of non-compliance the Security Council would reconvene to consider the situation. Resolution 1441 clearly did not expressly authorize force against Iraq; several permanent members of the Security Council were not willing to agree to such authorization.

---

[49] For the UK case, see 52 *ICLQ* (2003) 811. The US position has been set out in Taft and Buchwald, 2003, p 553. For a description of the sequence of events, see Murphy, 2003, p 419.

[50] SC Res 1441 (8 November 2002).   [51] SC Res 687 (3 April 1991).

Following this resolution Iraq produced a lengthy declaration on the state of its weapons programme and UN weapons inspectors returned to Iraq. Iraq was at first slow to cooperate with the inspectors, but from February 2003 this improved. The USA and the UK argued that Iraq was in material breach of its obligations, but there was no such formal determination by the Security Council itself. The USA and the UK tried to secure a second resolution expressly authorizing force against Iraq but failed to convince other member States that military action was justified. They then proceeded to argue that no second resolution was necessary: Resolution 1441 had not expressly required a second resolution; its effect was to revive the authority to use force given in Resolution 678 (1991) in the event of material breach by Iraq of disarmament requirements under the cease-fire regime established by Resolution 687.

The main problems with this line of argument are, first, that it relies on the revival of Resolution 678, passed ten years earlier in response to Iraq's invasion of Kuwait. Those supporting *Operation Iraqi Freedom* argued that the authorization to use force in Resolution 678 could be revived as it had been suspended but not terminated by the cease-fire in Resolution 687. Resolution 678 did not contain any time limit and Iraq continued to pose a threat to international peace and security. Second, the 'coalition' case assumed that it was possible for them unilaterally to determine that there had been a material breach by Iraq and that the use of force was justified. States opposed to the use of force, such as Russia, China, France, and Germany, argued that such decisions were exclusively for the Security Council; this was also the view of the UN Secretary-General.

VI. UN PEACEKEEPING

A. THE INCEPTION OF PEACEKEEPING

UN peacekeeping is not expressly provided for in the UN Charter; it developed through practice during the Cold War (Higgins, 1969–81). When the UN Security Council proved unable to take action in response to breaches of the peace, threats to the peace, and acts of aggression, because its decision-making was obstructed by the divisions between the Western and Eastern blocs, peacekeeping was developed as a partial substitute. The General Assembly initially took on a (controversial) role in this area under the *Uniting for Peace Resolution* (1950)[52] which allowed it to call emergency meetings and make recommendations to States on the use of force when the Security Council was prevented from acting by the lack of unanimity of the permanent members. The *Certain Expenses* Advisory Opinion[53] considered the constitutionality of a force set up by the General Assembly: could member States be required to pay the expenses of such operations? The ICJ held that, although the Security Council had primary responsibility for the maintenance of international peace and security under Article 24, this was primary and not exclusive; it was open to the General Assembly to recommend peacekeeping but not to decide on enforcement action which was the exclusive province of the Security Council.

---

[52] GA Res 377 (V), (3 November 1950).
[53] *Certain Expenses of the United Nations, Advisory Opinion, ICJ Reports 1962*, p 151.

In practice it has been the Security Council which has subsequently exercised the main responsibility for peacekeeping. The UN Charter does not make any express provision for peacekeeping and its precise constitutional basis remains unclear, but discussion now centres on the nature rather than on the legality of the institution. There was initially a clear distinction between peacekeeping and Chapter VII enforcement action, but the peacekeeping label has come to cover a wide range of operations and the distinctions between peacekeeping and enforcement action have blurred. From 1948–88 15 peacekeeping forces were created (United Nations, 1996). The first major force was UNEF, established by the General Assembly in the Middle East from 1956–67; the principles on which this operation was based provided guidelines for future operations. UNEF was established with the consent of the host State and was terminated when Egypt withdrew its consent; it was an impartial and neutral force and used force only in self-defence. Like UNEF, most Cold War peacekeeping operations functioned between States, and most were limited operations mandated only to monitor cease-fires or borders. The five permanent members of the Security Council generally did not take part in peacekeeping forces in order to insulate peacekeeping from Cold War divisions and States with historic or geographical interests in the conflict were also excluded.

ONUC was the second major peacekeeping operation and it departed to some extent from the above guidelines. It operated within the Congo which had descended into chaos on the withdrawal of the colonial power in 1960. The original mandate of ONUC was expanded to allow the use of force beyond self-defence; the Security Council used the language of Chapter VII in authorizing force to prevent the occurrence of civil war and the secession of the province of Katanga, but made no express reference to it.

Five of the original peacekeeping forces are still in existence: three in the Middle East, one in Kashmir, and one in Cyprus; this reflects the danger that a peacekeeping force may simply freeze a situation.

B. PEACEKEEPING AFTER THE END OF THE COLD WAR

After the end of the Cold War the Security Council expanded its peacekeeping functions and there is now a continuing debate about the nature of peacekeeping. Over forty new forces have been created, most within States. In his 1992 *Agenda for Peace* the UN Secretary-General showed an optimistic and expansionist approach.[54] UN peacekeeping forces played a role in the settlement of Cold War conflicts in Namibia, Angola and Mozambique, Afghanistan, Cambodia, and Central America. These forces are sometimes called the second generation of peacekeeping; they were generally ambitious operations going beyond military and humanitarian operations to bringing about national reconciliation and re-establishing effective government. They met with mixed success and faced serious problems of non-cooperation in Angola and Cambodia.

New conflicts broke out after the Cold War in the Former Yugoslavia, the former USSR, and in Africa and more peacekeeping forces were created. The Security Council took an innovative approach in many ways. The distinction between peacekeeping and enforcement action was blurred; peacekeeping forces were expected to carry out their functions as the same time as member State enforcement forces; UN peacekeeping was combined with

---

[54] (1992) 31 ILM 953.

regional peacekeeping for the first time in the former USSR and in Africa; the first preventive force was created in Macedonia to prevent the spread of the conflict in Yugoslavia (it was withdrawn when China vetoed its renewal in 1997). A third generation of peacekeeping was conceived in 1999 when UNMIK was established in Kosovo and UNTAET in East Timor. The UN Secretary-General said that these were qualitatively different from almost any other the UN had ever undertaken; in each place the UN formed the administration responsible for fulfilling all the functions of a State (Wilde, 2008).

C. THE TRANSFORMATION OF PEACEKEEPING: YUGOSLAVIA AND SOMALIA 1991–95

The peacekeeping operations in Yugoslavia and Somalia will be considered in some detail because they constituted a major challenge to the traditional rules governing peacekeeping. This experiment proved largely unsuccessful and was abandoned in favour of a retreat to the traditional model, but there have recently been new attempts to create a workable model for robust peacekeeping.

The traditional principles of peacekeeping were that it is distinct from enforcement action under Chapter VII of the Charter, and that a peacekeeping force should be impartial, lightly armed, not use force except in self-defence, and operate with the consent of the host State. In Yugoslavia this traditional model was modified with negative results. UNPROFOR was created as a peacekeeping force, first in Croatia and then in Bosnia-Herzegovina, initially without reference to Chapter VII. But there was no effective cease-fire and no proper cooperation from the parties and UNPROFOR was given an ambitious and unrealistic mandate 'to create the conditions of peace and security required for the negotiation of a settlement'. This mandate was incrementally expanded in a long series of resolutions; the first controversial increase was to give UNPROFOR the power to use force to secure the delivery of humanitarian aid. When UNPROFOR met non-cooperation subsequent resolutions were passed under Chapter VII authorizing UNPROFOR to enforce no-fly zones and to protect safe havens declared to protect Bosnian Muslims in Bosnia-Herzegovina. This authority to use force went beyond self-defence and brought UNPROFOR into conflict with the Bosnian Serbs. But member States were not willing to provide enough troops to enable UNPROFOR to carry out its wide mandate. Instead the UN turned to NATO air forces to take enforcement action under Chapter VII.

The UN had a similar experience in Somalia. The Security Council was slow to get involved in the civil war which broke out in 1991. It established a peacekeeping force, UNOSOM, to provide security for those delivering humanitarian aid. When this met non-cooperation on the ground it was supplemented by a US-led member State force. Both were replaced by UNOSOM II, the first UN peacekeeping operation which was actually created under Chapter VII. But UNOSOM II was drawn into the conflict and proved unable to carry out its mandate. In both Yugoslavia and Somalia UN peacekeeping forces on the ground had to try to operate at the same time as member State forces authorized to use force under Chapter VII. Such a combination proved unworkable during ongoing conflict.

The peacekeeping forces subsequently created in Georgia, Liberia, and Tajikistan were not established under Chapter VII, and were not given powers under Chapter VII.

This looked like a return to traditional peacekeeping in response to the experience of Yugoslavia and Somalia. However, the experience in Rwanda brought further reappraisal of peacekeeping.

D. PEACEKEEPING IN AFRICA

The demands of the major operations in Yugoslavia and Somalia made developed States reluctant to intervene in Rwanda in 1994 when the Hutu government turned on the Tutsis and massacred over 500,000 people in three months. A UN force, UNAMIR, had been established to implement a peace agreement, but this mandate was overtaken by events and the relatively small number of UN peacekeeping forces were not authorized or able to prevent the genocide. The Security Council has repeatedly been accused of double stand-ards with regard to its treatment of Africa. However, seven of the 15 current peacekeeping operations are in Africa; these involve two-thirds of all UN peacekeeping personnel. But the UN still encounters difficultie: in securing adequate resources for these operations. There is concern about the unwill ngness of developed States to provide peacekeeping troops in difficult situations, especially in Africa (Berman and Sams, 2000). The call for 'robust peacekeeping' to prevent a recurrence of the failure to prevent the genocide in Rwanda meets the reluctance of developed States to contribute troops in situations where there is no peace to keep and no cooperation on the ground, in the light of their experience in Yugoslavia and Somalia.

E. PEACEKEEPING AFTER THE *BRAHIMI REPORT*

The *Brahimi Report* on peacekeeping was presented at the Millennium Summit of the UN and made proposals for major reform.[55] The most important called for an increase in resources for the UN Department of Peacekeeping to enable it properly to manage com-plex and demanding peacekeeping operations. The report also stressed the need for the Security Council to provide a clear and realistic mandate for peacekeeping forces, and suggested that no resolution creating a peacekeeping force be passed until the Security Council has commitments from member States for troops. The Report also called for better cooperation between the Security Council and troop-contributing countries; this raises issues about control of the force and the balance of power between the Security Council with its primary responsibility for the maintenance of international peace and security and those States contributing troops.

But the most serious problem facing UN peacekeeping remains one of resources; if developed States are unwilling to provide troops and to allow their forces to be placed under UN command in the more complex operations which need better trained and equipped forces, the UN will be unable to take effective action. There has been a major surge in peacekeeping since 2003. This reflects the success of peacekeeping as the 'flagship of the UN', but the increased demand has placed an enormous strain on UN resources and on the ability of member States to provide funds, troops, and equipment. Seven major new operations have been deployed since September 2003. Some of these are complex missions established under Chapter VII. The reforms which followed the *Brahimi Report*

---

[55] (2000) 39 ILM 1432.

have proved insufficient to cope with these increased demands, and a further reform programme is underway. In order to cope with the increasing demands the UN is turning
increasingly to regional organizations.

VII. REGIONAL ACTION UNDER
CHAPTER VIII OF THE UN CHARTER

The Charter provides for UN action to be supplemented by regional action under Chapter
VIII: 'regional arrangements or agencies' are to deal with such matters relating to the
maintenance of international peace and security as are appropriate for regional action,
provided that their actions are consistent with the purposes and principles of the UN
(Article 52). Any enforcement action should be authorized by the Security Council; the
Security Council may choose to utilize regional arrangements for enforcement action
(Article 53). The Charter does not define 'regional arrangements or agencies' but the UN
has accepted that the main regional organizations, the Organization of American States
(OAS), the Organization of African Unity (OAU) (now the African Union (AU)), and the
Arab League come within this heading. Other sub-regional organizations not originally
set up under Chapter VIII have taken on peacekeeping powers and have drawn up new
constitutional instruments to regulate this. These include the Economic Community of
West African States (ECOWAS), the Commission on Security and Cooperation in Europe
(CSCE) (now Organization for Security and Co-operation in Europe (OSCE)), the Southern
African Development Community (SADC), and the Intergovernmental Authority on
Development (IGAD). In its resolutions the Security Council has taken a flexible, non-
formalistic approach to the issue of which organizations come within Chapter VIII.

A. A GREATER ROLE FOR REGIONAL ORGANIZATIONS

Since the end of the Cold War regional organizations have become much more active.
The UN Secretary-General expressed the hope in his *Agenda for Peace* that they could be
used to compensate for the resource problems facing the UN; they should play a greater
role through increased consultation, joint operations, and regional enforcement action
authorized under Chapter VII. There has indeed been a significant increase in cooperation between regional organizations and the UN. UN and regional forces have combined
in Georgia, Tajikistan, Liberia, Sierra Leone, Côte d'Ivoire, the DRC, and Chad/Central
African Republic and have undertaken complementary roles. Developed States have given
significant financial assistance, logistical support and military training to regional and
sub-regional organizations in Africa. They have encouraged the AU to take an increasing
role in peacekeeping; it has deployed peacekeeping forces in Burundi, Darfur (Sudan),
and Somalia. The first hybrid AU-UN operation was established in Sudan in December
2007. But the AU faces serious resource problems and depends on outside support for its
peacekeeping operations. Its forces have struggled to cope with the extremely challenging
conditions in Darfur and Somalia.

    Also, since the end of the Cold War regional organizations have been authorized to use
enforcement action under Chapter VII; in Yugoslavia the Security Council authorized

'member States acting nationally or through regional agencies or arrangements' to use force to implement economic embargoes imposed under Article 41. A similar resolution was passed with regard to the enforcement of economic measures against Haiti after the anti-democratic coup. Although the Security Council did not expressly refer to Article 53, or specify exactly which regional organization was envisaged, it seems that these are the first instances of resort to Article 53. The Security Council has since gone further: acting under Chapter VII it has authorized States acting through regional arrangements or agencies to use force to facilitate the delivery of humanitarian aid in Yugoslavia, to ensure compliance with the ban on flights over Bosnia-Herzegovina, and to protect the safe havens; it has also authorized the member States of ECOWAS to use force in Côte d'Ivoire and Liberia, the EU to conduct operations in the DRC, and the AU to establish a Chapter VII force in Somalia.

B. CONTROVERSY AS TO THE INTERPRETATION OF CHAPTER VIII

During the Cold War and subsequently, the distinction between regional peacekeeping action for which no Security Council authorization was necessary and regional enforcement action which required such authorization has been problematic. When the OAS intervened against Cuba (1962) and the Dominican Republic (1965) there was controversy as to whether this was legal under the UN Charter (Akehurst, 1967). The Eastern and Western blocs were divided as to whether economic measures constituted enforcement action requiring authorization; more recently it seems to have been implicitly accepted with regard to regional sanctions that Security Council authorization is not needed for economic measures. The other main question which arose as to the legality of the OAS actions with regard to Cuba and to the Dominican Republic was whether acquiescence or failure to condemn by the Security Council amounted to authorization of enforcement action under Article 53. Such claims seem far-fetched where it is the veto or the threat of a veto by a permanent member which has led to the failure to condemn.

So long as the use of force by these regional and sub-regional organizations is limited to peacekeeping with the consent of the host State there is no controversy over the question of whether or not the operations are consistent with the constituent treaty of the relevant organization. The crucial question is the compatibility of their actions with the UN Charter. It is when regional organizations go beyond peacekeeping and seem to engage in intervention without Security Council authorization that there is difficulty. During the Cold War there was sometimes suspicion that major powers were manipulating regional organizations to further their own ends. Thus, as well as the concerns about the relation between the USA and the OAS, there was doubt as to whether the Syrian-dominated Arab League intervention in Lebanon (1976–83) was truly impartial peacekeeping in accordance with the purposes and principles of the UN.

C. THE OECS INTERVENTION IN GRENADA (1983)

The Organization of East Caribbean States (OECS) intervention in Grenada provoked lengthy discussion in the Security Council as to whether the action was legitimate peacekeeping or whether it amounted to unlawful interference in the domestic affairs of a State in order to overthrow an unsympathetic government.[56] There was a coup in 1983 and a pro-Cuban government seized power. The USA which was not itself a member of the OECS, led an OECS intervention and oversaw the installation of a new government. It offered a variety of legal justifications for its use of force, including an argument that the intervention was regional action under Chapter VIII at the request of the Governor-General of Grenada. Many States did not accept that the Governor-General had such power to represent the State of Grenada, but the main reason for their criticism of the invasion was that the action went beyond peacekeeping and constituted unlawful intervention. The UN General Assembly and the OAS condemned the intervention; in the Security Council the USA vetoed a resolution calling for the withdrawal of foreign troops from Grenada (Gilmore, 1984).

D. REGIONAL PEACEKEEPING AFTER THE COLD WAR

Questions about the distinction between peacekeeping and enforcement action and concerns about the impartiality of regional action continue to arise after the Cold War, in particular with regard to the CIS operations in Georgia and Tajikistan in the former USSR and also with regard to ECOWAS operations in Liberia (1990–97) and Sierra Leone (1997–2000). ECOWAS, a sub-regional organization of 15 member States, established in 1975 and originally concerned with economic matters, took a major role in attempting to end civil wars in Sierra Leone and Liberia through its Economic Community of West African States Monitoring Group (ECOMOG) force. Commentators expressed doubts as to whether there were genuinely impartial peacekeeping forces or whether the major regional power, Nigeria, was pursuing its own agenda through ECOWAS. In both conflicts ECOMOG seemed to go beyond limited peacekeeping action, but ECOWAS did not openly claim wide powers or seek authorization under Article 53 by the Security Council. Its official position was that ECOMOG used force only in self-defence or, in the case of Sierra Leone, to secure implementation of a UN economic embargo. The Security Council acquiesced in the ECOMOG action; it avoided discussion of constitutionality under the ECOWAS constituent instruments or of legality under the UN Charter, leading some commentators to argue that these operations marked the inception of a new wide right of regional action to restore democracy or to undertake humanitarian intervention. However, the Security Council itself was cautious and did not expressly approve any use of force going beyond self-defence or in performance of the provisions of peace agreements. It is difficult to read approval for any radical change in the doctrine of regional peacekeeping into its resolutions. But some commentators have argued for a reinterpretation of the UN Charter in the light of these developments (Franck 2002, 162). Subsequent regional operations do not support such claims: enforcement action has been expressly authorized by the Security Council. States including China and Russia stress the need for regional action to be conducted strictly in accordance with the Charter framework.

VIII. CONCLUSION

The UN Charter provisions on the use of force by States, Article 2(4) on the prohibition of force and Article 51 on self-defence, have produced fundamental divisions between States. There is disagreement as to whether the prohibition on force should be interpreted strictly

---

[56] 1983 *UNYB* 211.

or whether it allows humanitarian intervention, as in Kosovo. There is also disagreement as to whether the right of self-defence is wide or narrow. The response to the 9/11 terrorist attacks has led to a fundamental reappraisal of the law in this area. As regards collective security, the original scheme of the UN Charter for the Security Council to play a primary role in the maintenance of international peace and security through its own standing army has not been fully implemented. Instead the UN has turned to member States to use force under Security Council authority in 'coalitions of the willing'. It is extremely controversial in the light of *Operation Iraqi Freedom* whether member States may ever use force without express authority. Also, UN peacekeeping has developed through practice. UN peacekeeping forces deployed in ongoing conflicts face a tension between impartiality and effectiveness. The relationship between peacekeeping operations and Chapter VII has yet to be satisfactorily resolved.

REFERENCES

AKEHURST, M (1967), 'Enforcement Action by Regional Agencies, with Special Reference to the OAS', 41 *BYIL* 175.

ALEXANDROV, S (1996), *Self-Defense Against the Use of Force in International Law* (The Hague: Kluwer).

AREND, A and BECK, R (1993), *International Law and the Use of Force* (London & New York: Routledge).

BECKER, T (2006), *Terrorism and the State* (Oxford: Hart Publishing).

BERMAN, E and SAMS, K (2000), *Peacekeeping in Africa: Capabilities and Culpabilities* (Geneva: United Nations Institute for Disarmament Research).

BOWETT, D (1958), *Self-Defence in International Law* (Manchester: Manchester University Press).

BROWNLIE, I (1963), *International Law and the Use of Force by States* (Oxford: Oxford University Press).

CHESTERMAN, S (2001), *Just War or Just Peace? Humanitarian Intervention and International Law* (Oxford: Oxford University Press).

D'AMATO, A (1990), 'The Invasion of Panama was a Lawful Response to Tyranny', 84 *AJIL* 516.

DOSWALD BECK, L (1985), 'The Legal Validity of Military Intervention by Invitation of the Government', 56 *BYIL* 189.

FRANCK, T (2002), *Recourse to Force* (Cambridge: Cambridge University Press).

GILMORE, W (1984), *The Grenada Intervention* (London: Mansell).

GRAY, C (1996), 'Bosnia and Herzegovina: Civil War or Inter-State Conflict?', 67 *BYIL* 155.

——— (2002), 'From Unity to Polarisation: International Law and the Use of Force Against Iraq', 13 *EJIL* 1.

——— (2008), *International Law and the Use of Force*, 3rd edn (Oxford: Oxford University Press).

HIGGINS, R (1969–81), *United Nations Peacekeeping*, vols I–IV (Oxford: Oxford University Press).

LOBEL, J and RATNER, M (1999), 'Bypassing the Security Council: Ambiguous Authorizations to Use Force, Cease-fires and the Iraqi Inspection Regime', 93 *AJIL* 124.

MURPHY, SD (ed) (2003), 'Contemporary Practice of the United States relating to International Law', 97 *AJIL* 419.

PATIL, A (1992), *The UN Veto in World Affairs 1946–1992* (London: Mansell).

RONZITTI, N (1985), *Rescuing Nationals Abroad* (Dordrecht: Martinus Nijhoff).

ROTH, B (1999), *Governmental Illegitimacy in International Law* (Oxford: Oxford University Press).

SAROOSHI, D (1999), *The United Nations and the Development of Collective Security* (Oxford: Clarendon Press).

SIMMA, B (ed), (2002), *The Charter of the United Nations: A Commentary*, 2nd edn (Oxford: Oxford University Press).

STAHN, C (2007), 'Responsibility to Protect', 101 *AJIL* 99.

TAFT, WH and BUCHWALD, TF (2003), 'Pre-emption, Iraq and International Law', 97 *AJIL* 553.

TAMS, C (2009), 'The use of force against terrorists', 20 *EJIL* 359.

UNITED NATIONS (1996), *The Blue Helmets*, 3rd edn (New York, NY: United Nations Dept. of Public Information).

WILDE, R (2008), *International Territorial Administration* (Oxford: Oxford University Press).

WILSON, H (1988), *International Law and the Use of Force by National Liberation Movements* (Oxford: Oxford University Press).

FURTHER READING

GENERAL TEXTBOOKS

BROWNLIE, I (1963), *International Law and the Use of Force by States* (Oxford: Oxford University Press) is still valuable for an historical account of the development of the law and of doctrinal divisions.

FRANCK, T (2002), *Recourse to Force* (Cambridge, Cambridge University Press).

GRAY, C (2008) *International Law and the Use of Force*, 3rd edn (Oxford: Oxford University Press). This is a general book covering the whole of the use of force, both the unilateral use of force by States and the role of the UN and regional bodies.

THE INTERPRETATION OF ARTICLE 2(4)

CHESTERMAN, S (2000), *Just War or Just Peace? Humanitarian Intervention and International Law* (Oxford: Oxford University Press) is a thorough and measured account of this emotive subject.

REISMAN, M (1984), 'Coercion and Self-determination: Construing Charter Article 2(4)' and the reply by SCHACTER, O (1984), 'The Legality of Pro-democratic Invasion', 78 *AJIL* 642, 646, provide a valuable summary of the opposing positions.

STÜRCHLER, N (2007), *The Threat of Force in International Law* (Cambridge: Cambridge University Press).

SELF DEFENCE

BECKER, T (2006), *Terrorism and the State* (Oxford: Hart Publishing).

GREIG, D (1991), 'Self-defence and the Security Council: What Does Article 51 Require?', 40 *ICLQ* 366.

RONZITTI, N (1985), *Rescuing Nationals Abroad* (Dordrecht: Martinus Nijhoff) remains the best work on the protection of nationals.

RUYS, T and VERHOEVEN, S (2005), 'Attacks by Private Actors', 10 *Journal of Conflict and Security Law* 289.

SCHACTER, O (1989), 'Self-defence and the Rule of Law', 83 *AJIL* 259.

UN ENFORCEMENT AND PEACEKEEPING

UN Blue Books series. These provide detailed accounts of UN peacekeeping operations in particular conflicts.

GREENWOOD, C (1992), 'New World Order or Old? The Invasion of Kuwait and the Rule of Law', 55 *MLR* 153 examines the debate about Security Council powers under Chapter VII with regard to the UN authorized action against Iraq.

KONDOCH, B (ed) (2007), *International Peacekeeping* (Aldershot: Ashgate Publishing).

LOWE, AV, ROBERTS, A, WELSH, J, and ZAUM, D (eds) (2008), *The UN Security Council and War* (Oxford: Oxford University Press).

MATHESON, M (2006), *The Council Unbound* (Washington DC: US Institute of Peace Press).

SAROOSHI, D (1999), *The United Nations and the Development of Collective Security* (Oxford: Clarendon Press) examines the Charter framework for the use of force.

WEBSITES

United Nations: **http://www.un.org**

The African Union: **http://www.africa-union.org**

ECOWAS: **http://www.ecowas.int**

NATO: **http://www.nato.int**

PART VII

THE APPLICATION OF INTERNATIONAL LAW

22

THE LAW OF THE SEA

Malcolm D Evans

SUMMARY

Historically, the principal division in the law of the sea was between the territorial seas, which formed a part of the territory of the State but within which other States enjoyed a number of restricted rights, and the high seas which were open to use by all. This has now changed, with the recognition and development of new zones of functional and resource-oriented jurisdiction, accompanied by complex realignments of jurisdictional competences which cut across—and, in the eyes of some, threaten to undermine—the traditional principles of governance at sea. This chapter traces these developments. It also provides an introduction to the basic rules concerning the principle zones of maritime jurisdiction, as well as looking at the rules concerning the construction of baselines—which is foundational to the entire subject—and to the problem of determining boundaries where claims to zones overlap.

I. INTRODUCTION

The law of the sea is regulated in a complex yet subtle manner and provides an interesting contrast to the rather absolutist approach to questions concerning sovereignty and jurisdiction which are still encountered in other areas of international law. Sovereignty and jurisdiction are, of course, of vital importance to the law of the sea: indeed, they provide the basis upon which all else is founded. Over time, they have, however, been moulded and melded in an extremely sophisticated manner in order to better to reflect the changing nature of the competing interests in the utilization of the seas.

For example, some of the earliest doctrinal debates concerning the law of the sea focused on whether the seas could be made subject to the exclusive sovereignty of a State. In the middle ages, before State-sponsored exploration of the oceans and the intensification of international trade by sea, this was hardly a question at all. When the question did emerge in the fifteenth and sixteenth centuries, writers who argued that seas should be 'closed' and subject to the jurisdiction of coastal States did so either for reasons of security (to keep threatening forces at a distance) or for reasons of trade (to operate profitable customs regimes and control navigation). The balance that finally emerged reflected both concerns: whereas States were to enjoy full sovereignty over those waters proximate to their coasts, reflecting their interests in security and control, in the waters beyond, where trade and navigation issues assumed a greater significance, the principle of the freedom of the seas—famously argued for by Grotius in his work *Marem Liberum*—prevailed (Anand, 1993; O'Connell, 1982, pp 18–30).

This, then, established the basic division that dominated the law of the sea for some 350 years; between the territorial sea which was subject to the jurisdiction of the coastal State, and the high seas beyond which were open to all. However, new issues emerged over time as economic and technological developments resulted in changed strategic interests and an increased demand for, and capacity to access and harvest, the resources of the sea. The challenges presented by these changes have been made more complex still by the rapid expansion of the international community, shifts in the political balance of power and the increasing awareness of the need not only to access and exploit the resources of the seas and the marine environment but also to conserve and protect them.

In the early years of the twentieth century ambitious plans were made to 'codify' much of international law in written form, including the law of the sea. Although the overall project made little headway one positive outcome was the 'Hague Codification Conference' held in 1930. This did not produce any finished text but it did provide useful experience which was extensively drawn on when, after the Second World War, the International Law Commission (ILC) decided to examine the subject. In 1956 the ILC produced a set of draft Articles which were considered at the First United Nations Conference on the Law of the Sea (UNCLOS I) held in Geneva in 1958. This conference produced four 'Geneva Conventions' on the Law of the Sea[1] which in part reflected customary international law but also contained much that was 'progressive development'.

Although impressive in their scope, the Geneva Conventions left some key issues open. The most significant of these concerned the vexed question of the breadth of the territorial sea and in 1960 a second UN Conference was convened in Geneva (UNCLOS II) to address this and other related questions but it ended without agreement. One reason for this failure was the mounting pressure for a more fundamental review of the law of the sea which would take account of the growing demands for access to resources and, in the process, erode the rigidity of the territorial sea/high seas dichotomy. Admittedly, the four 1958 Conventions themselves represented a limited break with this approach. Two of those Conventions reflected the traditional divisions, one dealing with the territorial sea (and contiguous zone) and another with the high seas. The other two 1958 Conventions reflected new concerns, these being the continental shelf and fisheries conservation and management. Although the fisheries convention did not gain much international support, and elements of the continental shelf convention have since been jettisoned, adopting 'general' conventions on these 'functional' issues indicated that the way forward did not lie in changing the limits and further refining the concepts of the territorial sea and high seas, but would involve creating new zones and forms of jurisdictional competence that would co-exist alongside them. UNCLOS II had attempted to go down this path by suggesting that States be permitted to exercise exclusive jurisdiction over fishing in a belt outside of

---

[1] These being the Convention on the Territorial Sea and Contiguous Zone (TSC); Convention on the High Seas (HSC); Convention on the Continental Shelf (CSC); and the Convention on Fisheries and Conservation of the Living Resources of the High Seas (CFC).

their territorial sea rather than extend the territorial sea as far seawards as some would have liked. Moreover, this general approach found endorsement in the *North Sea*[2] and *Fisheries Jurisdiction*[3] cases, where the emergence of other forms of jurisdictional zones and competences was acknowledged and accepted by the ICJ.

However, an even more fundamental challenge was also being made to the ordering of the oceans. The basic idea underlying the distinction between the territorial seas and high seas was that it separated out those areas of maritime space over which jurisdiction and control was exercised by a single State from those over which no single State exercised jurisdiction or control and in which activities were 'free' from any form of control (other than that of the State whose nationality a person or vessel on the high seas carried and which it exercised in accordance with international law). In practice, therefore, the resources of the high seas were available for unilateral exploitation by anyone and everyone. As will be seen below, the extension of coastal State jurisdiction over resources located beyond the territorial sea was already having the effect of breaking down this clear distinction but the essence of the underlying approach remained intact. In 1967, however, a more fundamental challenge was made to this traditional approach when the Maltese ambassador to the UN, Arvid Pardo, claimed that the resources of the seabed beyond national jurisdiction should be considered to be the 'Common Heritage of Mankind' and be exploited for the benefit of the international community as a whole (Schmidt, 1989, pp 18–30).

There was, then, a complex matrix of unresolved issues and emerging agendas, and these were considered at the third UN Conference on the Law of the Sea (UNCLOS III) which met from 1974–82 and culminated in the adoption of the 1982 Convention on the Law of the Sea (LOSC). Negotiations at UNCLOS III were tortuous and the convention attempted to balance a myriad of competing interests in a 'package deal' that ultimately satisfied few. Although by the early 1990s the number of ratifications approached the 60 required by LOSC Article 308 for the convention to enter into force there was relatively little support from group of developed States, whose acceptance was critical to the success of the convention. This focused the minds of all concerned and, assisted by changes in the world political order at that time, a rather euphemistically entitled 'Implementation Agreement' was agreed in July 1994 which, in fact if not in name, amended Part XI of the convention (the provisions concerning the 'Common Heritage' and seabed mining in the area beyond national jurisdiction) in order to make it acceptable to a broader range of States (Anderson, 1993; 1995). The LOSC entered into force on 16 November 1994 and at the time of writing there are 160 States parties (including the European Union). The Implementation Agreement entered into force in July 1996 and currently has 138 States parties. However, Article 7 of the 1994 Agreement allowed for its provisional application pending its entry into force and so for those States party to both the 1982 Convention and the 1994 Agreement, the 'original' version of Part XI as set out in the 1982 Convention never became binding on them at all. Much of the 1982 Convention now reflects customary law and so is relevant to the increasingly small number of States which are not bound by it as a matter of treaty law. As a result, it provides the starting point for any presentation of the contemporary law of the sea. However, parts of the convention are of a 'framework' nature and it has been supplemented by a number of other major conventions addressing

---

[2] *North Sea Continental Shelf, Judgment, ICJ Reports 1969*, p 3.
[3] *Fisheries Jurisdiction (United Kingdom v Iceland), Merits, Judgment, ICJ Reports 1974*, p 3.

certain issues in greater detail. Developments in other areas of international law have also had an impact on the Convention framework and customary law continues to play an important role by further supplementing and amplifying its provisions (Boyle, 2005).

Since a chapter of this length cannot be comprehensive, it aims to give a flavour of the convention's approach and illustrate the manner in which competing interests are accommodated in some key areas.

II. CONSTRUCTING BASELINES

A. INTRODUCTION: THE NORMAL RULE

International law parcels the sea into various zones in which States enjoy a variety of jurisdictional competences. The general rule is that coastal States exercise the greatest degree of jurisdictional competence over those zones that lie closest to them. Logically enough, a State exercises full powers of territorial sovereignty within areas of water which are 'internal'. This obviously includes lakes and rivers but also includes harbours and other areas of water which are landward of 'baselines' from which the various zones of seawards jurisdiction are generally[4] measured. Determining baselines is, then, very important and a number of detailed rules were set out in the 1958 TSC and largely repeated in the 1982 LOSC. Most of these rules reflect customary law. Since the further seawards a coastal State is able to 'push' its baselines the further seawards its jurisdiction will extend, the practical application of these rules often gives rise to controversy. It should also be borne in mind that islands of all sizes also have baselines and generate maritime zones, although under LOSC Article 121(3) there is the important exception that 'Rocks which cannot sustain human habitation or economic life of their own shall have no exclusive economic zone or continental shelf'. The scope of this provision is uncertain, with neither the terms 'rock' nor 'economic life' expressly defined (Charney, 2000; Lavalle, 2004; Prescott and Schofield, 2005, pp 61–89). The ICJ has tended to avoid having to address the question when an opportunity to do so has presented itself[5] and it remains doubtful whether this provision reflects customary international law,[6] though obviously it is binding on States party to the convention.

Whether island or mainland territory, '...the normal baseline for measuring the breadth of the territorial sea is the low-water line along the coast as shown by the appropriate symbols on charts officially recognized by the coastal state' (LOSC Article 5). Although relatively easy to apply, this method can produce unwieldy results when a coastline is not comparatively straight and/or there are a considerable number of islands in the vicinity of a mainland coast. Therefore, a number of rules have been devised which address some exceptional situations. States do not have to adopt one method of drawing baselines but may use those methods most appropriate for each portion of their coast (LOSC Article 14).

---

[4] The continental shelf is, in part, an exception to this. See below.

[5] See, for example, *Maritime Delimitation in the Black Sea (Romania v Ukraine), Judgment of 3 February 2009*, nyr, at para 187, concerning Serpents' Island, a 'natural feature' above water at high tide (and thus an island) with an area of 0.17 sq km and a circumference of some 2000m.

[6] Cf Brownlie, 2008, p 183 who is clear that Article 121(3) does not reflect customary law.

B. STRAIGHT BASELINES

In the *Anglo-Norwegian Fisheries* case[7] the UK challenged the right of Norway to claim a territorial sea drawn not from the low water line but from a series of artificial lines linking the outermost points of the 'skaergaard' (a fringe of rocks and islands) that lay off the Norwegian coast. The Court noted that it might be inconvenient to use the low water mark as the baseline in such geographically complicated circumstances and accepted the legitimacy of drawing 'straight baselines' under certain circumstances. The judgment was reflected in TSC Article 4, the essence of which was repeated in LOSC Article 7 (Reisman and Westerman, 1992).

Straight baselines may only be drawn if a coastline is 'deeply indented and cut into' or 'if there is a fringe of islands along the coast in its immediate vicinity' (LOSC Article 7(1)). If these criteria are not met the normal rule applies. Even if straight baselines *may* be drawn, there are limitations upon *how* they are to be drawn. These include restrictions on the use of Low Tide Elevations, that straight baselines 'must not depart to any appreciable extent from the general direction of the coast' and that 'the sea areas lying within the lines must be sufficiently closely linked to the land domain to be subject to the regime of internal waters' (LOSC Article 7(4)). This latter, rather impressionistic, requirement is particularly important. Waters on the landward side of a straight baseline are by definition internal waters over which the coastal State enjoys full territorial jurisdiction and control (subject to an exception to be considered below) and straight baselines must not be used to bring into the territorial domain waters which lack an intrinsic nexus with the coast. That nexus might be established by non-geographic criteria: in keeping with the *Anglo-Norwegian Fisheries* case, LOSC Article 7(5) permits local and well-established economic interests to be taken into account when establishing particular baselines, but only in those situations where the geographical threshold criteria set out in Article 7(1) are met.

C. BAYS

A further exception to the 'normal' rule concerns bays and is addressed by LOSC Article 10, which is generally considered to reflect customary law (Westerman, 1987). The motivation for departing from the normal rule here is not so much based on convenience but to avoid situations in which the territorial sea—or even fingers of high seas—penetrate the mouths of bays and intrude into areas intrinsically connected with the land domain. The problem is greatest where entrances to bays are relatively narrow but open out into broader expanses of water. The aim is to differentiate areas of water which are essentially of an 'internal' nature from those which are not and this is achieved by drawing 'closing lines' across the mouth of bays and using that 'closing line' as the baseline from which the territorial sea and other zones of jurisdiction are measured.[8]

Once again, there are two stages to this process. First, the distance between the 'natural entrance points' of a bay is measured and a semi-circle is drawn along a line of that length. The area of this semi-circle is then compared to the area of water on the landward

---

[7] *Fisheries, Judgment, ICJ Reports 1951*, p 116.

[8] It is important to remember that a bay closing line and a straight baseline are legally speaking two very different types of line, though both have the same general function.

side of the closing line. If the area of the semi-circle is less than that of the area of water, the indentation is, for the purposes of baseline construction, a bay; if the area of the semi-circle is greater than the area of the water on the landward side of the closing line, the indentation is not—for legal purposes—a bay. The second stage is to draw a closing line. If the distance between the natural entrance points used for the previous calculation is less than 24 nautical miles (n. miles), the closing line may be drawn between them. If that distance exceeds 24 n. miles, then a closing line of up to that length can be drawn 'within the bay in such a manner as to enclose the maximum area of water that is possible with a line of that length' (LOSC Article 10(6)). This seemingly simple provision is very complex to apply in practice, with the identification of the natural entry points being a particular problem,[9] and the bay being a 'well marked indentation' another.[10]

It may be the case that the coastline of a bay belongs to more than one State. This poses an additional difficulty since the exceptional rule in LOSC Article 10 only applies to those bays whose coasts belong to a single State. However, in the *Land, Island and Maritime Frontier Dispute* the ICJ sought to identify a concept of a 'pluri-State' bay, where the coasts belong to a number of States yet a closing line might still be drawn.[11] Whilst such an approach might be appropriate if, as in that case, there is a particular historical justification, it is difficult to see how it could be used more generally, if only because the waters behind the closing line would be 'internal' to all of the States concerned and this would simply generate a further need to differentiate between them. It seems to create more problems than it solves and is not found in State practice. In any case, LOSC Article 10(6) expressly renders the convention regime inapplicable to 'historic bays', these being indentations claimed by the coastal State as a part of its internal waters on the basis of a long-standing claim, assertion of jurisdiction, and acquiescence by others' (O'Connell, 1982, Ch 11). This offers an alternative route for States wishing to make claims in respect of indentations which cannot fulfil the criteria set out in the convention. However, such claims are difficult to substantiate and will often meet with considerable protest, as is the case with the Libyan claim to the Gulf of Sirte, a 'bay' nearly 300 n. miles in extent (Ahnish, 1993, Ch 7).

D. ARCHIPELAGOES

The 1951 *Anglo-Norwegian Fisheries* case also addresses what might be called 'coastal archipelagoes'. But what of States comprised wholly or partly of groups of islands? Should the waters be enclosed and treated as internal? What of the navigational rights of third States? At UNCLOS III the interests of archipelagic States, such as Indonesia and the Philippines, and the concerns of adjacent maritime neighbours, such as Australia, combined to produce a particular regime, set out in Part IV of the convention, applicable to 'archipelagic states'. Rather self-referentially, LOSC Article 46 defines an archipelagic State as a State 'constituted wholly by one or more archipelagoes' and other islands, where an 'archipelago' is itself further defined as a group of islands, or parts of islands, and their

---

[9] See, eg, *Post Office* v *Estuary Radio* [1968] 2 QB 740. See also Marston, 2002.

[10] See, eg, the US Supreme Court judgment in *United States* v *Alaska* 545 US 17 (2005), pp 17–20.

[11] *Land, Island and Maritime Frontier Dispute (El Salvador/Honduras: Nicaragua) Judgment of 11 September 1992, ICJ Reports 1992*, p 351, para 395. The entire concept was roundly criticized by Judge Oda in his Dissenting Opinion, ibid, p 732, paras 1–26.

interconnecting waters which are so closely interconnected as to form, or be regarded as forming, an intrinsic entity, or which have been historically regarded as such. Therefore Indonesia, the Philippines, Fiji, Japan, and the UK are archipelagic States for convention purposes and so are entitled to draw archipelagic baselines, whereas island groups such as the Azores (belonging to Spain) and the Galapagos (belonging to Ecuador) are not.

However, not all archipelagic States are able to construct archipelagic baselines since such baselines must conform to strict criteria, the principal elements of which are that they must link the main islands of the group; no baseline may be more than 100 n. miles long, except that 3% of the total may be up to 125 n. miles in length; they must follow the general configuration of the island grouping; and, most importantly, fulfil the requirement that the ratio of water to land within the baselines must be not less than 1:1 and not more than 9:1 (LOSC Article 47). The result is both that those archipelagic States which primarily consist of a few large islands (such as Japan and the UK) and those which are composed of very small and widely spaced islands (such as Kiribati) are unable to draw archipelagic baselines even though they fall within the definition of an archipelagic State. It is the latter category of small and scattered island States which stood to gain most from the concept but they were unable to influence the negotiations in their favour and the details of the regime found in the convention favour the interests of the larger archipelagic States. It may be that, in time, State practice and customary law might develop in a fashion which is somewhat less rigid than the convention regime.

The waters within archipelagic baselines are 'archipelagic waters' rather than internal waters and are subject to special rules concerning, *inter alia*, fishing and navigation which will be considered later (LOSC Articles 49–53). Once again, and whatever its shortcomings, the Archipelagic regime offers another example of the manner in which the convention sought to forge a new approach to the division of jurisdictional competences, and moved away from a strict approach based on the distinction between the territorial and high seas.

III. THE INTERNAL WATERS, TERRITORIAL SEA, AND CONTIGUOUS ZONE

A. INTRODUCTION

The idea that States are entitled to exercise authority over the waters beyond their land territory (and internal and archipelagic waters) is deeply entrenched in international legal thinking. Although it was once argued that the competences States enjoyed within waters off their coasts fell short of territorial sovereignty and had to be positively asserted,[12] it is now clear that this authority flows automatically from the sovereignty exercised over land territory and so all coastal States do in fact have a territorial sea.[13] Practically speaking, however, States need to make some form of pronouncement, if only to determine the extent of their jurisdiction.

---

[12] This view found reflection—somewhat unexpectedly—in *R v Keyn* (1876) 2 Ex D 63, the substance of which was subsequently reversed by the 1878 Territorial Waters Jurisdiction Act.

[13] A view expressed by Judge McNair in his Dissenting Opinion in *Fisheries, Judgment, ICJ Reports 1951*, p 116 at p 160.

The breadth of water over which a State might legitimately exercise sovereign jurisdiction has been the subject of lengthy debate down the ages, but at the dawn of the twentieth century the preponderance of known practice fixed that distance at 3 n. miles. The conflict between those who favoured broadening this zone, in order to enhance coastal State security or to increase access and control over resources, and those who opposed this in the name of the freedom of navigation (and of fishing on the high seas) not only underpinned the development of the various functional maritime zones which will be considered shortly but was also responsible for the failure of UNCLOS I and II to determine the issue. By the time of UNCLOS III, however, it seemed clear that an expansion of territorial seas to 12 n. miles was inevitable and the only question was the price that its opponents could extract from its proponents. LOSC Article 3 now recognizes the right to establish a territorial sea of up to 12 n. miles, the overwhelming majority of States—nearly 140—have done so and this is now the position under customary international law. Although described as the territorial sea, the sovereignty of the State extends to the airspace above and the seabed and subsoil beneath (LOSC Article 2(2)).

It is important that States make their position clear since possession of a territorial sea not only entails rights but also duties: in his Separate Opinion in the *Fisheries Jurisdiction* case Judge Fitzmaurice pointed out that coastal States were obliged to maintain navigational aids within their territorial sea[14] and could be held responsible for damage flowing from the failure to do so. Clearly, the scope of this obligation depends on the extent of the territorial sea.

B. JURISDICTION OF THE COASTAL STATE

Although the coastal State exercises 'sovereignty' within its territorial sea, this sovereignty is circumscribed in a number of ways which will be considered in this section. It is also helpful to consider the jurisdiction enjoyed by a State within its territorial sea alongside that which it may exercise within its internal waters and in the contiguous zone that lies beyond, since these together represent a progression from the strongest to the weakest form of jurisdictional competences over maritime spaces which are grounded upon territorial sovereignty.

1. Internal waters

Predictably, a coastal State exercises sovereignty to its fullest extent within its internal waters. No State is obliged to allow foreign vessels into its internal waters, except in cases of distress and, exceptionally, where drawing straight baselines encloses waters which were not previously regarded as such, the right of innocent passage (described below) applies within internal waters (LOSC Article 8(2)). Otherwise, coastal States are free to restrict or impose whatever conditions they wish upon entry into internal waters, and it should be stressed that this includes entry into its ports, the waters of which form part of its 'internal waters'. Indeed, many international conventions are drawn up which *require* States to prevent unseaworthy vessels from entering ports as a matter of international law.

---

[14] *Fisheries Jurisdiction (United Kingdom v Iceland), Jurisdiction of the Court, Judgment, ICJ Reports 1973,* p 3 at p 27.

Once a foreign vessel has entered internal waters it is subject to the domestic legislation of that State which can, in principle, be enforced against it. On entering a port, the port State (as the coastal State then becomes known) is particularly well-placed to take enforcement action against vessels, if only because it can prevent them from leaving. The expansion of 'port State jurisdiction' over vessels is a feature of contemporary law, particularly as regards vessels which have breached health and safety regulations or have been causing pollution outside of the territorial sea of the State concerned (Özçayir, 2001). Indeed, there is an increasing trend to encourage the use of port State jurisdiction as a means of addressing the failures of flag States to exercise jurisdiction over vessels acting in breach of international standards (see Molenaar, 2006). However, States generally exercise restraint in enforcing local law over incidents taking place on board foreign vessels in their ports, limiting this to matters such as the infringement of customs laws, or activities which threaten to disrupt the peace of the port. This may include offences such as murder,[15] which have an intrinsic gravity that on-board scuffles between crew members lack. States will, however, generally exercise jurisdiction over incidents which involve non-crew members, as these concern more than the 'internal economy' of the vessel, and also take action in situations where the captain requests intervention. Such restraint reflects the temporary nature of the vessel's presence in a port and the fact that the flag State of the vessel itself has the right to exercise jurisdiction and that it is often more appropriate for it do so.

2. Territorial sea

The dominant view is that coastal State jurisdiction automatically extends to the territorial sea, with the logical corollary that the entire body of State law applies there. However, this does not mean that the coastal State has an unfettered discretion regarding the content of that legislation since international law places imposes a number of important restrictions upon what the coastal State might render unlawful activity within the territorial sea, the most important of which concerns vessels exercising the right of innocent passage, considered below. Moreover, logic does not necessarily make for practicality and the full rigours of this approach (assuming it to be doctrinally correct) are mitigated by a more restrictive approach to the enforcement of domestic law within the territorial sea, irrespective of whether a vessel is engaged in innocent passage or not.

It would be odd if States were to enforce their criminal law over vessels merely passing through their territorial seas in circumstances which would not have triggered enforcement within internal waters. Therefore, LOSC Article 27(1) exhorts States to refrain from investigating or arresting those suspected of offences committed on board a vessel unless: the consequences extended to the coastal State; it was of a kind to disturb the peace of the country or the good order of the territorial sea; assistance was requested; or it was necessary for the suppression of illicit traffic in drugs (LOSC Article 27(1)(a)–(d)). If the vessel has just left the State's internal waters it need show no such restraint (LOSC Article 27(2)), but in all cases the coastal State is to have 'due regard to the interests of navigation' when deciding whether, or how, to carry out an arrest within the territorial sea. These provisions apply to the criminal jurisdiction of the State. There are further exhortations against the exercise of jurisdiction over vessels in respect of civil matters, the chief of which is that

[15] Eg *United States* v *Wildenhaus*, 120 US 1 (1887), concerning the assertion of jurisdiction by the local courts over a murder on board a Belgian vessel in New York harbour.

vessels should not be stopped in order to exercise civil jurisdiction over an individual or with regard to actions *in rem*, rather than in respect of the activities of the vessel itself (LOSC Article 28). Finally, and unsurprisingly, coastal States are not permitted to arrest a warship or other vessels being used for governmental purposes which belong to another State. Rather, such vessels may be 'required' to leave the territorial sea immediately (LOSC Article 30) and it is implicit in this that the requisite degree of force necessary to ensure compliance with such a request might be used.

3. Contiguous zone

Traditionally, where the territorial sea ended, the high seas began and the laws of the coastal State no longer applied. However, policing maritime zones is no easy matter and, unlike land boundaries, they are simple to cross and it is therefore easy for vessels to commit offences within the territorial sea but to evade arrest by moving just a little further seawards. The answer was to permit coastal States to arrest vessels outside their territorial seas in connection with offences that either had been committed or which it was suspected were going to be committed within their territorial sea. Under LOSC Article 33 (and following a compromise first agreed upon in the 1958 TSC Article 24), the coastal State is permitted to 'prevent' and 'punish' infringements of some, but not all, of its laws (those concerned being 'customs, fiscal, immigration or sanitary laws and regulations') in a zone which might be up to 24 n. miles from the baselines (thus permitting a State with a three mile territorial sea to have a contiguous zone of up to 21 n. miles). Not all States have declared a contiguous zone, but their usefulness is such that an increasing number do so.[16]

The ability to 'punish' means that vessels that have committed such offences within the territory of the State may be arrested even though they have left the territorial seas. The ability to 'prevent' suggests that a State might stop a vessel from entering its waters when it has reason to believe that such an offence would be committed should that vessel enter. This is clearly open to abuse. Indeed, the entire concept represents a not insignificant extension of coastal State authority and there is a tendency for States to assert jurisdiction for a more ambitious range of matters than those mentioned in the convention text.

C. NAVIGATION IN THE TERRITORIAL SEA

The desire of coastal States to assert their jurisdiction in the waters off their coasts is matched by the needs of the international community to ensure that the seas remain open to navigation. Once again, there has been progressive development in both the range and the content of regimes applicable to navigation within waters over which coastal States exercise sovereignty. The principal regime concerns innocent passage through the territorial sea and the manner in which that regime has sought to the balance the relevant competing interests has shifted over time. In addition, some entirely new regimes of passage have been developed that reflect other developments.

---

[16] Some 84 States currently claim contiguous zones for a variety of purposes (not all in compliance with the LOSC) and the overwhelming majority are of 24 n. miles.

1. Innocent passage

Ships of all States enjoy a right of 'innocent passage' through the territorial seas of coastal States. For these purposes, 'passage' means that the vessel is in the process of travelling through the territorial sea and is doing so in a 'continuous and expeditious' fashion, though there are exceptions for stops which are 'incidental to ordinary navigation' or as a result of *force majeure* (LOSC Article 18). Thus a ship loitering within the territorial sea or traversing in a circuitous manner would not be engaged in 'passage' at all.

Not all passage is 'innocent'. According to the 1958 TSC Article 14(4), 'Passage is innocent so long as it is not prejudicial to the peace, good order or security of the coastal state'. It is, however, unclear who is to make that determination. In the *Corfu Channel* case[17] the ICJ adopted a fairly objective approach, suggesting that the innocent nature of passage was capable of objective assessment, that the opinion of the coastal State was not decisive and the mere fact that a violation of local law had occurred was not in itself sufficient to demonstrate prejudice to the interests of the coastal State. The difficulty that faced the Court was that it needed to allow coastal States sufficient scope to decide whether to take measures against vessels exercising the right of innocent passage but also needed to guard against their acting in an arbitrary and capricious fashion. The approach adopted in the *Corfu Channel* case seemed to favour the interests of ships in passage over that of the coastal State. The balance struck by the 1958 TSC seemed to adopt a rather more subjective and coastal-State oriented approach. It also provided for two special cases in which the very manner of passage would be enough to result in the loss of innocence, irrespective of whether there was in fact any prejudice to the coastal State or not: these concerned infringements by foreign fishing vessels of local legislation concerning fishing in the territorial sea (TSC Article 14(5)) and the requirement that submarines were to 'navigate on the surface and show their flag' (TSC Article 14(6)). Such activities were deemed to be incompatible with 'innocent passage' altogether.

These provisions in the 1958 TSC were widely regarded as unsatisfactory, particularly given the trend towards establishing increasingly broad belts of territorial seas and they were revisited at UNCLOS III. Although LOSC Article 19(1) endorses the general principle established in TSC Article 14(1), it takes a more objective approach to the determination of innocence by setting out in Article 19(2) a considerably longer list of activities and circumstances in which innocence is deemed to be lost, irrespective of whether there is any actual prejudice or infringement of local law. Moreover, these heads are themselves rather open textured, particularly the final catch-all provision of 'any other activity not having a direct bearing on passage' (LOSC Article 19(2)(j). At first sight this might suggest that the right of innocent passage has been limited even further by the LOSC. This has to be balanced against the argument that the list of exceptions is now exhaustive and closed, an argument forcefully put by the USA and former USSR in a joint statement in 1989. However, the wording of the convention is ambiguous on this matter, to say the least. Churchill and Lowe also point out that Article 19(2) refers to 'activities' and so the mere 'presence' of a vessel may no longer be sufficient to deprive it of innocence (Churchill and Lowe, 1999, p 85). It is clear that there is still considerable controversy surrounding this Article, but it would be consonant with the general thrust

---

[17] *Corfu Channel, Merits, Judgment, ICJ Reports 1949*, p 4 at pp 30–31.

of the convention if it were to be understood as representing a modest move towards enhanced, but objectively verifiable, coastal State control over passage through the territorial sea.

Even this assessment must be balanced against developments concerning the other plank of the innocent passage regime. Being engaged in innocent passage does not exempt a vessel from the need to comply with coastal State legislation, but the coastal State may only legislate for the range of issues that are set out in LOSC Article 21. These concern the safety of navigation, cables and pipelines; the conservation of living resources and prevention of infringements of fisheries laws; matters concerning the preservation of the environment and marine pollution, marine scientific research, and prevention of infringements of customs, fiscal, immigration, and sanitary laws. By way of checks and balance, however, the coastal State may not use these legislative competences in ways which hamper innocent passage by, for example, imposing onerous or discriminatory requirements (LOSC Article 24(1)). Moreover, such laws 'shall not apply to the design, construction, manning or equipment of foreign ships unless they are giving effect to generally accepted international rules or standards' (LOSC Article 21(2)), these being those agreed under the auspices of the International Maritime Organization (IMO). The coastal State does have the power to 'suspend temporarily' innocent passage in specified areas, but only if this is non discriminatory, is 'essential for the protection of its security', and is duly publicized (LOSC Article 25(3)).[18]

Vessels violating such laws are liable to arrest in accordance with LOSC Article 27 even though they may be exercising the right of innocent passage through the territorial sea. It would, of course, be in breach of international law for a coastal State to enforce laws on matters other than these upon a vessel simply because it ceased to be engaged in innocent passage by reason of entering internal waters. The more exacting standards that can be applied to ships not engaged in innocent passage can only be enforced against those whose passage ceased to be innocent *whilst in the territorial sea* and in accordance with Article 27.

A final question concerns the range of vessels which are entitled to exercise innocent passage. The convention texts refer to 'ships' and in the *Passage through the Great Belt* case[19] Denmark questioned whether the regime was applicable to structures such as oil rigs. The better view is that a broad, purposive approach should be taken in unusual cases such as this, but the most controversial issue is whether warships can exercise a right of innocent passage. No agreement could be reached on this issue at UNCLOS I or III, and the matter is not dealt with directly by the TSC or the LOSC. The major maritime powers favour warships enjoying the right of innocent passage, but this is opposed by many smaller States or those in strategically sensitive locations.

There are three schools of thought: that the passage of warships requires the prior authorization of the coastal State; that such passage must be notified to the coastal State, though no express authorization need be requested or given; or that such passage is possible provided that it conforms to the general rules on innocent passage as set out in the

---

[18] Notifications made to the UN Secretary-General are publicized on the UN website at http://www.un.org/depts/los.

[19] *Passage Through the Great Belt (Finland v Denmark), Provisional Measures, Order of 29 July 1991, ICJ Reports 1991*, p 12.

convention. For some, this last approach is implausible since the mere presence of a foreign warship within a territorial sea is prejudicial to the coastal State's interests. However, the move towards focusing upon 'activities' rather than the presence of ships within the territorial sea in the LOSC makes this argument less persuasive. Moreover, the convention texts provide some support for warships enjoying innocent passage: the general rules are set out in a section headed 'Rules Applicable to all Ships'; some of the activities listed in Article 19(2) as leading to the loss of innocence can only (or largely) be undertaken by warships; and submarines, most (but not all) of which are warships, can exercise that right if surfaced and showing their flag (Churchill and Lowe, 1999, p 89). None of these arguments is wholly convincing and State practice is as diverse as it is predictable, with major maritime powers such as the UK and the USA (joined by the USSR in their 1989 Joint Statement)[20] arguing in favour of warships enjoying the right of innocent passage and less powerful coastal States enacting legislating requiring authorization or notification. Despite the growing trend towards increased coastal State dominance of offshore areas, the imperatives of essential military interests would suggest that this is likely to remain a matter of controversy for some time to come, though on a day-to-day basis pragmatic approaches are usually found which respect the positions of all concerned.

2. Straits

The regime of innocent passage is a concession by coastal States to accommodate the interests of navigation but, as has been seen, the coastal State still enjoys a formidable array of jurisdictional competences. Whilst this might be acceptable where there is no real need, other than convenience or desire, to enter the territorial seas, different considerations apply to narrow straits wholly comprised of territorial seas but which are also used for international navigation, such as the straits of Dover, Gibraltar, and Hormuz. In such cases, international law shifts the balance somewhat in favour of the freedom of navigation (see generally Nandan and Anderson, 1989; Jia, 1998).

In the *Corfu Channel* case the ICJ concluded that, irrespective of the position more generally, warships were entitled to exercise a right of innocent passage through straits used for international navigation and that coastal States were not entitled to 'suspend' innocent passage within such straits for any form of ship.[21] This variant on innocent passage only applied in straits which linked one part of the high seas with another and which were actually used as a route of international navigation. Importantly, the existence of a relatively convenient alternative (in this case, around the western side of the Island of Corfu) did not deprive it of this status. Arguably, this was an overly generous approach to the interests of the international community at the expense of the coastal State but it was nevertheless reflected in 1958 TSC Article 16(4), which further expanded the regime by applying it to straits linking the high seas with the territorial sea of a third State at the head of a Gulf (this being intended to facilitate access to the Israeli port of Eilat at the head of the Gulf of Aqaba). This latter gloss did not reflect customary law, and was rejected by Arab States, but it was retained in Article 45 of the LOSC which reflects the TSC approach, though now expanded to take account of the Exclusive Economic Zone (EEZ).

---

[20] USA-USSR Uniform Interpretation of Norms of International Law Government Innocent Passage (1989), 14 *Law of the Sea Bulletin* 12. See Schachte, 1993, pp 182–183.
[21] *Corfu Channel, Merits, Judgment, ICJ Reports 1949*, p 4 at p 28.

Under the LOSC, the *Corfu Channel* regime of 'non-suspendable innocent passage' has something of a residual flavour, now applying only to straits not covered by the new regime of transit passage, considered below. However, there is no doubting the customary law status of the *Corfu Channel* regime which provides an assured minimum guarantee of passage though international straits for all vessels, including warships.

3. Transit passage

A major problem facing UNCLOS III concerned the consequences of the breadth of the territorial sea increasing from 3 to 12 n. miles. This meant that many major strategic waterways which had previously been high seas, such as the Straits of Dover, could become entirely territorial seas and at best be subject to the regime of non-suspendable innocent passage. During the Cold War, when super-power security was thought to depend in part on relatively undetectable submarine-based nuclear missiles, the idea that submarines should surface and show their flags when prowling the oceans was an additional concern. The result was a comprise that sought to further reduce the ability of coastal States to restrict passage within their territorial seas.

The LOSC regime of transit passage applies to all straits connecting high seas or EEZs with other areas of high seas or EEZs and which are used for international navigation unless there is a corridor of high seas or EEZ running through it (LOSC Article (36)) or the strait is formed by an island which belongs to the coastal State and seawards of which there is an alternative route (LOSC Article 38(1)). In cases covered by this latter rule, known as the 'Messina Strait' exception (after the Straits between Italy and Sicily), the *Corfu Channel* regime of non-suspendable innocent passage continues to apply. Straits covered by particular treaty regimes, such as the Turkish Straits (the Dardanelles and the Bosphorus), are also expressly excluded from the scope of the provisions concerning transit passage (LOSC Article 35(c)).

Whereas innocent passage only applies to ships and submarines, transit passage also applies to aircraft which are accorded the right of overflight. Although not expressly stated, the regime applies to military ships and aircraft, and submarines may proceed submerged. Ships or aircraft must 'proceed without delay' and 'refrain from any threat or use of force' against the States bordering the strait (thus, for example, hurrying through the Straits of Gibraltar to conduct military activities in the eastern Mediterranean would be permissible). Although ships and aircraft must comply with generally accepted international regulations regarding safety matters (LOSC Article 39), coastal States may themselves only regulate a very circumscribed list of activities: maritime safety (including traffic separate schemes); internationally approved regulations concerning discharges of oil, oily waste, and noxious substances in the strait; with respect to fishing vessels, prevention of fishing and the stowage of fishing gear; and loading and unloading in connection with customs, fiscal, immigration, or sanitary laws (LOSC Article 42(1)). The balance struck clearly favours the freedom of navigation. The customary law status of transit passage has been challenged (de Yturriaga, 1991) and remains unclear, although State practice outside the convention framework increasingly reflects these provisions. Whilst the increasing numbers of States party to the LOSC has taken some of the heat out of this debate, it remains the case that maritime powers which are not party to the Convention may need to rely on the customary status of transit passage in order to be assured of passage for warships and overflight of aircraft through or over straits of key strategic significance.

4. Archipelagic sea lane passage

Drawing archipelagic baselines converts vast tracts of waters which were previously either high seas or territorial seas into 'archipelagic waters'. LOSC Article 52 provides that the right of innocent passage applies throughout such waters and, moreover, Article 53 provides for a right of 'archipelagic sea lane passage' in 'corridors' to be designated by the archipelagic State. Archipelagic sea lane passage is substantially similar to transit passage, meaning that the jurisdiction of archipelagic States over a wide range of matters in waters within their baselines is substantially reduced. As a result, the demands of international navigation have been given precedence over local control.[22]

IV. THE HIGH SEAS

A. THE FREEDOMS OF THE SEAS

The idea that beyond the territorial seas lie the high seas which are free for use by all lies at the heart of the law of the sea. Both the 1958 HSC and the LOSC proclaim the high seas to be free and open to vessels of all States and give non-exhaustive lists of freedoms. The HSC mentions navigation, fishing, overflight, and cable laying (HSC Article 2), and the LOSC adds the construction of artificial islands and marine scientific research. All are to be enjoyed with 'due regard' (in the HSC, 'reasonable regard') to the interests of others (LOSC Article 87).

It has already been seen how that space has been eroded by the expansion of the territorial seas, and some of the balances that have been struck as a consequence. Later sections will look at how the high seas have been further eroded by the creation of zones of functional jurisdiction. This section considers how freedom of navigation on the high seas has fared.

The key to regulating activities within the high seas is the concept of flag State jurisdiction. All vessels must be registered according to the laws of a State and, in consequence, are subject to its legislative jurisdiction and, whilst on the high seas or within its own territorial sea or EEZ, to its enforcement jurisdiction. In principle, a flag State enjoys exclusive jurisdiction over its vessels, although there are exceptions. However, if a ship is stateless, or flies more that one flag so that its true State of registry is not clear, then any State can exercise jurisdiction over it.[23]

Although the content of domestic laws applicable to vessels will vary considerably, there are an increasingly large number of international conventions relating to matters such as pollution control, resource management, and health and safety at sea which seek to ensure as common an approach as possible. Beyond this lies the problem of enforcement. A State is obliged to 'effectively exercise its jurisdiction and control' over ships operating under its flag (LOSC Article 94(1)) but this is often easier said than done. Many States simply do not have the capacity to enforce their laws over vessels flying their flag, (many of which may only rarely, if ever, put into port in their State of registry), whilst others simply lack

---

[22] The first example of a designation was that of Indonesia. See Indonesian Government Reg No 37 on the Rights and Obligations of Foreign Ships and Aircraft Exercising the Right of Archipelagic Sea Lane Passage through Designated Archipelagic Sea Lanes, 28 June 2002 (2003) 52 *Law of the Sea Bulletin* 20.

[23] See, eg, *Molvan v Attorney General for Palestine* [1948] AC 351.

the will to do so. Moreover, States are entitled to set their own conditions for registering ships, and although a 'genuine link' must exist between the vessel and State, attempts to lend greater precision to this requirement have not been successful and the problem of vessels being registered under 'flags of convenience', which exercise little effective control over their activities, remains. It is against this background that the subtle but steady erosion of the exclusive jurisdictional competence of the flag State over its registered vessels must be assessed.

B. THE EXCEPTIONS TO FLAG STATE JURISDICTION

1. Visit

It is axiomatic that the authorities of one State may not board a vessel flying the flag of another without the consent of the flag State. There is, however, an increasingly long and increasingly detailed list of exceptions to this general principle. These exceptions will be outlined below, but since it will not always be immediately apparent whether such action is permissible, international law recognizes an intermediary position in which the authorities of a non-flag State are entitled to board a vessel on the high seas in order to verify whether their suspicions are justified. These instances arise where there are reasonable grounds for suspecting that a ship is engaged in piracy, the slave trade, or unauthorized radio broadcasting (LOSC Article 110(1)(a)–(c)), the consequences of which are considered below. In addition, a ship might be visited to confirm that it is either stateless or, in cases of doubt, that it is in fact of the nationality of the visiting authorities, meaning that the visiting authority can assert its jurisdiction on the basis of the principles outlined in the previous section. In all of these cases a visit and any subsequent action may only be undertaken by a warship or other vessel or aircraft duly authorized and clearly marked (LOSC Articles 110(5) and 107), but the right of visit cannot be exercised in respect of a warship of another State or any other non-flag State vessel entitled to immunity.

2. Piracy

Under both customary international law and the conventions all States may take action on the high seas, or in any other place beyond the national jurisdiction of a State, against individuals or vessels involved in acts of piracy. Those committing acts of piracy are often said to have rendered themselves 'enemies of all mankind' and piracy is the oldest and most well-attested example of an act which attracts universal jurisdiction.[24] However, the LOSC definition of piracy is comparatively narrow, covering only 'illegal acts of violence or detention, or any act of depredation, committed for private ends by the crew or passengers of a private ship or private aircraft and directed (i) on the high seas, against another ship or aircraft, or against persons or property on board such a ship or aircraft; (ii) against a ship, aircraft, persons or property in a place outside the jurisdiction of any State' (LOSC Article 101(a)).

This definition conjures up a vision of pirates roaming the seas in their own private and unregistered vessels, beyond the reach of any flag State, and preying on other vessels whose

---

[24] See, eg, *Arrest Warrant of 11 April 2000 (Democratic Republic of Congo v Belgium), Preliminary Objections and Merits, Judgment, ICJ Reports 2002*, p 3. Separate Opinion of Judges Higgins, Kooijmans, and Buergenthal, para 61; Separate Opinion of President Guillaume, para 5.

own flag State may not be in a position to react or respond. This model reflects historical experience (and Hollywood stereotypes) but it also resonates with the current reality in a number of regions and, in particular where weak or failing States have produced the forms of legal vacuum in which piracy flourishes. The situation off the coast of Somalia has given rise to particular concern in recent times and a number of powers have stationed military vessels in the vicinity in order to deter and offer protection. In June 2008 the UN Security Council, with Somalia's consent and acting under Chapter VII of the UN Charter, adopted Resolution 1816 which called on States to co-operate in tackling piracy off the coast of Somalia and authorized them to enter Somalia's territorial seas in order to exercise enforcement jurisdiction over acts of piracy or armed robbery which had occurred either in international waters or in the territorial sea itself[25] (Guilfoyle, 2008). Later that year, in Resolution 1846, the Security Council went further and authorized States to take action against vessels reasonably suspected of involvement in piracy.[26] Shortly afterwards the Council went further again, calling on States to take all necessary measures within the territory of Somalia itself to suppress piracy and armed robbery at sea[27] (Guilfoyle, 2009, pp 61–78). It remains to be seen whether this innovative and expansive response to piracy off Somalia offers a model which might be employed more generally or whether its relevance is limited by the very particular situation within that country.

Previous responses to the shortcomings of the definition of piracy in LOSC 110 have been enduring in their impact. The *Achille Lauro* incident in the mid-1980s concerned a situation in which a group of passengers turned hijacker and seized control of an Italian cruise liner, and subsequently killed one of the other passengers. Although those responsible were clearly susceptible to, *inter alia*, Italian jurisdiction, this incident prompted the adoption of the 1988 Rome Convention on the Suppression of Unlawful Acts Against the Safety of Maritime Navigation (known as the 1988 SUA Convention). Following the pattern of numerous other international conventions, it sets out an extensive range of offences which States parties must make criminal under their domestic law and obliges them either to extradite or to submit the cases of those suspected of committing such acts to their prosecuting authorities. Although the SUA Convention does not grant States parties further jurisdictional competencies at sea, it does oblige them to extend and use their domestic law against those who imperil the freedom of navigation. Moreover, Article 17 of the SUA Convention sets out a highly developed framework for facilitating cooperation between contracting States, including procedures for flag States to authorize the boarding and searching of vessels suspected of prohibited activities by those requesting to do so. These provisions have been built upon in other contexts, as will be described below.

3. Hot pursuit

The problem of how to deal with vessels which commit offences within internal waters or the territorial sea but evade arrest by moving outside the zones of coastal State jurisdiction has already been mentioned and one response—that of the contiguous zone—has already

---

[25] SC Res 1816 (2 June 2008). This authorization was for a period of six months from the date of the resolution.

[26] SC Res 1846 (2 Dec 2008), extending the authorizations given in SC Res 1816 for a further 12 months. This has recently been extended for a further 12 months by SC Res 1897 (30 November 2009).

[27] See SC Res 1851 (8 December 2008).

been noted. The doctrine of 'hot pursuit' provides another means of addressing the same problem and forms another exception to the principle of exclusive flag State jurisdiction. According to this doctrine, the rather complex details of which are set out at length in LOSC Article 111, warships or military aircraft of a coastal State which have commenced the pursuit of a vessel within their territorial sea (or within their the contiguous zone or EEZ, if the offence in question is one for which an arrest might have been made there) may continue that pursuit outside of it provided that the pursuit is continuous, although the actual ship or aircraft involved in the pursuit might change: indeed, practice suggests that ships or aircraft of several nationalities may cooperate in arresting a vessel in the exercise of a right of hot pursuit.[28]

A further variant on this is 'constructive presence'. Rather than commit an offence within the territorial sea, some vessels choose to remain just outside and dispatch smaller boats, for example, to take illegal goods ashore. Under such circumstances, the 'mother' vessel might be chased and arrested even though it has never entered the territorial sea and the pursuit begins outside of it. The same is true should boats be sent out from the coastal State to meet the 'mother' vessel: in both cases there has been teamwork that implicates the vessel operating outside of the territorial seas with those committing offences within it.

How far can this approach be taken? In *R* v *Mills*, the *Poseidon*, a vessel registered in St Vincent, transferred a consignment of drugs on the high seas to a trawler sailing from Ireland to the UK. Following the arrest of the trawler in the UK, the *Poseidon* was also arrested, this being justified on the basis of 'constructive presence' (Gilmore, 1995). Taken to extremes, this suggests that any vessel which whilst at sea colludes with another vessel in the commission of an illegal act within the jurisdiction of a State is liable to arrest by that State anywhere on the high seas. Though not irreconcilable, this expansive approach sits rather uneasily with the caution expressed by the International Tribunal on the Law of the Sea (ITLOS) in *M/V Saiga (No 2)* in which stressed the need for a strict approach to be taken to the application of LOSC Article 111.[29]

4. Broadcasting

In the 1960s elements of the international community became agitated about the rise of commercial broadcasting into a country from foreign registered vessels on the high seas and over which they could not exercise any control (or extract revenues).[30] Regional State practice to address this problem in the North Sea through co-operative measures was subsequently built on, with the result that LOSC Article 109 permits the arrest and prosecution of any person engaged in 'unauthorized radio broadcasting' from ships or installations on the high seas by a range of States, including the State where the transmissions are received (Anderson, 2006, pp 340–341). A perhaps unexpected consequence of this arose in the early 1990s when a vessel called the *Goddess of Democracy* planned to broadcast messages of solidarity and support for those arrested in the pro-democracy demonstrations in

---

[28] In 2003 the *Viarsa 1* was arrested following a pursuit lasting some 21 days and extending over some 3,900 km and which involved vessels from Australia, South Africa, and the United Kingdom. See Molenaar, 2004.

[29] *M/V Saiga No 2 (St Vincent and the Grenadines* v *Guinea)*, Case No 2, Judgment of 1 July 1999, paras 146–152.

[30] See generally Guilfoyle, 2009, ch 7. A recent film *The Ship that Rocked* (2008) provides an entertaining account of the issues as seen at the time.

Bejing. The Chinese authorities made it clear they would arrest the vessel if it did so, and the mission was aborted.

5. Slavery

The rather heavy-handed approach taken in respect of unauthorized broadcasting contrasts with the comparatively feeble manner in which other, more pressing, issues were tackled. The international prohibition of slavery is well-established in international law yet the 1982 convention does not permit the arrest of vessels engaged in slave trading by non-flag States; it merely provides that a State 'shall take effective measures to prevent and punish the transport of slaves in ships authorized to fly its flag' (LOSC Article 99). Admittedly, that Article also provides that any slave fortunate enough to escape and take refuge on a non-flag State vessel 'shall *ipso facto* be free' and since there is a right to visit vessels suspected of being involved in slave trading (LOSC Article 110(1)(b)) this should not be difficult to manufacture. Nevertheless, it remains difficult to see why those involved in the slave trade, and their vessels, should not be susceptable to arrest under such circumstances without the express authorization of the flag State. More attention has been paid to the related practice of smuggling migrants across boarders and the 'Migrant Smuggling Protocol' to the UN Convention against Transnational Organized Crime adopted in 2000 follows the model of the 1988 Vienna Convention against Illicit Traffic in Narcotics (considered below) in constructing a regime to encourage and facilitate the acquisition of flag-State consent to board and undertake other 'appropriate measures' to 'prevent and suppress' migrant smuggling.[31]

6. Drugs trafficking

As with slavery, the LOSC provisions concerning drugs trafficking have also been found wanting. Article 108 is an anodyne provision which merely provides that States 'shall co-operate' in the suppression of the drugs trade by vessels on the high seas and that a State which suspects a vessel flying its flag is involved in trafficking 'may request the co-operation of other states to suppress such traffic'. This states the obvious. The 1988 Vienna Convention Against Illicit Traffic in Narcotic Drugs and Psychotropic Substances takes the matter further, developing and institutionalizing a more detailed framework for cooperation, but boarding a vessel still requires flag State authorization and there is no right of visit under LOSC Article 110. This was vividly illustrated in *R* v *Charrington* where irregularities in the manner in which the UK Customs and Excise obtained the consent of the Maltese authorities to board a vessel carrying £15m of cannabis resulted in the collapse of the domestic prosecution (Gilmore, 2000). State practice has gone further and, building on the model provided by the 1988 Convention, arrangements for mutual enforcement and assistance have been concluded in a number of spheres, particularly fishing. In addition, the UK has concluded bilateral arrangements permitting US authorities to board British vessels suspected of drugs offences on the high seas within the Caribbean region and has recently concluded a regional treaty to facilitate more widespread cooperation.[32]

---

[31] The Protocol entered into force in 2004 and currently has 123 States parties. See generally Guilfoyle, 2009, pp 184–226 for this and a consideration of related State practice.

[32] Agreement Concerning Co-operation in Suppressing Illicit Maritime and Air Trafficking in Narcotic Drugs and Psychotropic Substances in the Caribbean Area, 10 April 2003. See Gilmore, 2005. For a more general review of the topic see Guilfoyle, 2009, ch 5.

Once again, it may be that long-standing dogmas have stood in the way of devising rather more effective means of tackling a matter of major international concern.

7. Terrorism and weapons of mass destruction

The 1988 SUA Convention was drafted in the wake of a terrorist outrage akin to piracy and so it was not surprising that the response was tailored to that form. As new concerns have emerged they too have been addressed within the model that the SUA provides; that is, through the identification and definition of additional forms of unlawful conduct and the utilization of cooperative arrangements to enable flag State consent to be more readily obtained for boarding, search and, if necessary, arrest of vessels by non-flag States. In October 2005 the International Maritime Organization adopted a Protocol to the SUA which would make it an offence under the convention to engage in an extremely broad range of activities at sea when the purpose of the activity, given its nature and context, is intended to 'intimidate a population, or to compel a Government or an international organization to do or to abstain from any act', or to knowingly transport persons who have committed such unlawful acts.[33] Moreover, the Protocol would permit participating States to notify the IMO Secretary General in advance that permission for boarding and searching is to be presumed if no reply is given to a requesting State within four hours of a request being made. This goes a long way to creating a presumption in favour of boarding by those States with reasonable grounds for suspicion and a heavy onus on those flag States that might seek to deny such a request. At the time of writing, however, the 2005 Protocol has not yet entered into force.[34]

The 2005 Protocol had already been prefigured by the 'Proliferation Security Initiative' (PSI), instigated by the USA in 2003 and which provides an enhanced framework for cooperation between participating States (see Byers, 2004; Guilfoyle, 2009, ch 9). The USA has also entered into reciprocal bilateral treaties with a number of States which, like the 2005 Protocol, provide for a presumption that a request for boarding has been granted if no response if given within a limited period of time.[35] Once again, these developments are consonant with the traditional principles of high seas and flag State jurisdiction, but point to a reality very different from that which those principles suggest for those willing to accept them through participating in the SUA Protocol, PSI or other bilateral arrangements. However, there is as yet no evidence to suggest that such broad-ranging rights and facilitative arrangements for boarding and search—even in this context—are reflective of customary international law.

[33] These acts not only embrace the use or discharge of any explosive, radioactive material or BCN (biological, chemical, nuclear) weapon in a manner that causes or is likely to cause death or serious injury or damage but also include the transportation of explosive or radioactive materials in the knowledge that they are intended to be so used, knowingly transporting a BCN weapon and a further range of related activities including the transportation of any equipment, materials or software or related technology that significantly contributes to the design, manufacture or delivery of a BCN weapon with the intention that they will be used for such purposes. See 2005 Protocol, adding Article 3 *bis* to the SUA.

[34] The Protocol had only attracted ten of the 12 ratifications needed to enter into force.

[35] The USA has so far concluded nine such bilateral agreements, with the Bahamas (2008), Belize (2005), Croatia (2005), Cyprus (2005), Liberia (2004), Malta (2007), Marshall Islands (August 2004), Mongolia (2007), and Panama (May 2004). These States account for much of the registered shipping in the world. The time period for notification before the presumption in its favour takes effect in these agreements is the even shorter period of two hours.

C. CONCLUSION

The freedom of navigation has, then, been the subject of some whittling away, both by reason of the increasing breadth of the territorial sea, outlined in Section III, and by the erosion of exclusive flag-State jurisdiction outlined above. However, the modifications to the regime of innocent passage and the new regime of transit passage, as well as the limited and piecemeal nature of the increased jurisdictional competence over non-flag State vessels, all point in the direction of the continuing significance of the freedom of navigation, albeit that this is 'freedom under the law' (Anderson, 2006, at p. 345). This is further underscored by the remaining sections of this chapter which chart the rise of functional zones of jurisdiction and which, although representing a marked diminution in other freedoms of the high seas, left navigation relatively untouched and also ensured that the increase in the breadth of the territorial sea was kept within modest bands.

V. RESOURCE JURISDICTION

A. THE CONTINENTAL SHELF

During the opening decades of the twentieth century improvements in technology made the exploration and exploitation of seabed and subsoil resources beyond the territorial sea—particularly oil and then natural gas—both increasingly possible and economically viable. In theory, these deposits were available to all since legally speaking they were high seas resources. However, orderly and effective development required some degree of involvement by a proximate coastal State and in the Truman Proclamation (1945), the US President declared 'the natural resources of the subsoil and seabed of the continental shelf beneath the high seas but contiguous to the coasts of the US as appertaining to the US, subject to its jurisdiction and control'.[36] Following consideration by the ILC, the 1958 CSC provided that 'The coastal state exercises over the continental shelf sovereign rights for the purpose of exploring it and exploiting its natural resources' and did so independently of express acts or declarations (Articles 2(1) and 2(3)). In the *North Sea* cases the ICJ recognized this as a statement of customary law, stressing that these rights existed '*ipso facto and ab initio*'.[37] LOSC Article 77 reiterates this approach.

Natural resources include both mineral and other non-living resources of the seabed and subsoil and well as 'sedentary species' (CSC Article 2(4); LOSC Article 77(4)). Thus pearling is clearly covered by this definition, whereas jurisdiction over wrecks is not. Whether crabs and lobsters are continental shelf resources is more controversial, although the EEZ now provides an alternative means of securing coastal State jurisdiction over such resources.

The most vexed question concerns the outer limit of continental shelf jurisdiction. The seabed off a coast may not be a 'continental shelf' in a geophysical sense at all: the coast may swiftly plunge to great depths, as it does off the western coasts of much of South America, or merely be shallow indentations into which water has flooded, as in the Gulf region of the Middle East. The continental shelf proper is merely a component of the 'continental

---

[36] 1 *New Directions in the Law of the Sea* 106.
[37] *North Sea Continental Shelf, Judgment, ICJ Reports 1969*, p 3, paras 19, 39, and 43.

margin' which comprises the gently sloping shelf, which gives way to a steep slope which then levels off into the continental rise that emerges from the ocean floor (sometimes rather prosaically described as the 'Abyssal Plain'). The 1958 CSC did not draw directly on any of these concepts and defined the continental shelf, for legal purposes, as comprising the seabed and subsoil adjacent to the coast but outside the territorial sea, extending to the point where the waters above were 200 metres deep, or as far seawards as it was possible to exploit (CSC Article 1). This was most unsatisfactory since it permitted States to claim ever more distant areas as technology rapidly developed. Moreover it ran into the claim advanced in the late 1960s that the deep seabed was the 'common heritage' of all mankind and not subject to single State jurisdiction. It was, then, necessary to place some limit on the seawards expansion of continental shelf jurisdiction.

In the *North Sea* cases the ICJ argued that the continental shelf represented the 'natural prolongation' of the landmass into and under the sea,[38] implying some limit to its seawards expansion. However, this still did not address the claims of States which had no 'natural prolongation' as such, but who nevertheless sought jurisdiction over offshore seabed and subsoil resources and who therefore argued that the continental shelf should be a fixed distance, measured from the baselines, irrespective of the nature of the seabed. This approach was opposed by some of the so-called 'broad shelf' States which already exercised jurisdiction on the basis of 'natural prolongation' beyond the most likely fixed limit of 200 n. miles.

This conundrum was resolved by the complex compromise found in LOSC Article 76, according to which the continental shelf extends to (a) 200 n. miles from the baselines or (b) to the outer edge of continental margin (this being seen as the natural prolongation), whichever is the further. The outer edge of the margin is calculated with reference to the 'foot' of the continental slope, this being the point where the continental slope gives way to the continental rise. From this point, a State might either exercise jurisdiction for a further 60 n. miles seawards, or as far as a point where the depth of the 'sedimentary rock' (loose, rather than bedrock) overlying the continental rise is more than 1% of the distance of that point from the foot of the slope. These outer lines are then subject to one of two alternative limitations: they cannot be drawn more than 350 miles from the baselines of a State, or more than 100 miles from a point at which the depth of the water is 2,500 metres. Finally, exploitation beyond the fixed 200 n. miles distance is subject to the State making 'payments or contributions in kind' through the International Seabed Authority (LOSC Article 82).

This complicated formula is difficult to apply and its customary law status unclear. It is particularly difficult to see how Article 82 could have a life outside the convention framework. Nevertheless, it is vital to determine the outer limit of each State's continental shelf since the seabed beyond forms part of the 'Area', governed by its own legal regime (considered in subsection D, below). LOSC Article 76(8) therefore establishes the Commission on the Limits of the Continental Shelf, to which States must submit details of their outer limits should they lie beyond 200 n. miles from the baseline. Under the terms of the Convention, States were to submit details of any such claims within 10 years of its entry into force for them, but it was subsequently agreed by the States parties to substitute the fixed date of 13 May 2009 for all States for whom the ten years would previously have expired. Fifty-one

---

[38] Ibid, para 18. For an extended discussion see Hutchinson, 1985.

claims have now been submitted, 16 before the end of 2008 and 36 in the weeks before the deadline elapsed.

The role of the Commission is to examine these submissions and to make recommendations to States 'on the basis of which' the State establishes its final boundary (see generally Cook and Carlton, 2000). This is clearly opaque and since the Commission has so far issued relatively few recommendations (the content of which it does not make public), practice is scant.[39] What is clear is that the entire regime reflects a careful balancing act between the interests of coastal States with varied geo-physical relationships to the sea; to the economic interests of the international community as a whole and to the interests of the freedom of navigation and of the high seas, which it leaves substantially untouched.

B. THE EXCLUSIVE FISHING ZONE

As States watched the international community recognize and legitimate coastal State jurisdiction over the resources of the seabed and subsoil, it was inevitable that the argument would be made that resources of the water column be treated likewise. This was always going to be controversial since the seabed was, by and large, chiefly of potential economic importance, whereas high seas fishing was already of very real economic importance and excluding foreign-flagged fishing vessels from waters beyond narrow belts of territorial seas would have serious consequences for many communities and economies. However, the increased capacity of vessels to harvest fish was putting stocks at risk and so there was a tension between maximizing access to resources and promoting effective conservation. Viewed in this light, increased coastal State control appeared more beneficial than high seas freedoms and this was reflected in the developing law of fisheries. This will be considered further in Section VII but it is important to note here the emergence of the Exclusive Fishing Zone (EFZ) as an autonomous zone of resource jurisdiction.

Neither UNCLOS I nor II could agree upon the establishment of an EFZ but State practice moved steadily in the direction of recognizing the right of a coastal State to assert jurisdiction over fisheries within 12 n. miles of its baselines and in the 1974 *Fisheries Jurisdiction* case the ICJ recognized this as reflecting customary law.[40] By this time claims for zones of up to 200 n. miles were being advanced yet the Court was unwilling to go further and endorse Iceland's claim for an EFZ of up to 50 n. miles. It did, however, suggest that a State might exceptionally be entitled to preferential access to the high seas resources within such a distance under certain circumstances.[41] Such hesitations were subsequently swept away by the development of the EEZ and, although there is no mention of the EFZ as an autonomous regime within the LOSC, it is clear that customary law now recognizes EFZ claims of up to 200 n. miles.[42]

---

[39] Four of the nine recommendations so far communicated to States were adopted in 2009, two in 2008 and two in 2007. For an overview of the practice of the Commission, given against to background of the joint submission made by France, Ireland, Spain, and the UK in 2007 see Llewellyn, 2007. The CLCS issued its recommendations in the light of this submission in March 2009.

[40] *Fisheries Jurisdiction (United Kingdom v Iceland), Merits, Judgment, ICJ Reports 1974*, p 3, para 53.

[41] Ibid, paras 55–60.

[42] See *Maritime Delimitation in the Area between Greenland and Jan Mayen, Judgment, ICJ Reports 1993*, p 316, accepting uncritically the Norwegian claim to an EFZ of this distance.

C. THE EXCLUSIVE ECONOMIC ZONE

The previous sections have already identified the reasons why during the 1960s and 1970s many coastal States wanted to have exclusive access to the resources of the seabed and the water column but were reluctant to extend the breadth of their territorial seas. In order to balance the competing interests, Latin and South American States advanced the claim that there should be a single zone of up to 200 n. miles in which the coastal State enjoyed sovereign rights over all natural living and non-living resources but within which the other freedoms of the seas, and in particular navigation, would be unaffected. Over time, this claim became refined into what is now known as the Exclusive Economic Zone, which became recognized as reflecting customary international law during the UNCLOS III process[43] and, of course, is established as a matter of treaty law by the LOSC itself.[44]

Under the regime established by the Convention, States may claim an EEZ of up to 200 n. miles (LOSC Article 57) within which the range of matters reserved for the coastal State are so extensive that the Zone is comprised of neither territorial seas nor high seas but is considered to be 'sui generis' and subject to a distinct jurisdictional framework (LOSC Article 55). First and foremost, coastal States exercise sovereign rights within the EEZ for the purposes of 'exploring and exploiting, conserving and managing' both its living and non-living natural resources (LOSC Article 56(1)(a)). Although this may seem to be an amalgamation of the jurisdictional capacities which States already were able to enjoy on the basis of the continental shelf and the EFZ regimes, the EEZ does in fact embrace additional elements, including the harnessing of wind and wave power. The coastal State also has jurisdiction, subject to the other provisions of the convention, over the establishment and use of artificial islands and installations, marine scientific research, and the preservation of the marine environment, as well as a range of other matters (LOSC Article 56(b) and (c)).

Despite its 'sui generis' nature, the EEZ is pulled in a number of different directions. As regards jurisdiction over the resources of the seabed and subsoil, it is closely aligned with the continental shelf (LOSC Article 56(3)). Article 58 provides that three of the freedoms of the seas expressly mentioned in the convention—navigation, overflight, and laying cables and pipelines, and related activities—are to be exercised by all States within an EEZ in accordance with the general framework for the high seas, as provided for in Articles 87–116. Thus of the six high seas freedoms identified in the convention, three pass to the predominant control of the coastal State within its EEZ whilst three remain open to the international community at large. This list of freedoms is not exhaustive and in situations not specifically provided for the question of whether a matter falls within the jurisdiction of the coastal State 'should be resolved on the basis of equity and in the light of all the relevant circumstances, taking into account the respective importance of the interests involved to the parties as well as to the international community as a whole' (LOSC Article 59). The *M/V Saiga (No 2)* illustrates the type of problem that might arise. Guinea arrested a vessel in its EEZ and argued, *inter alia*, that it was entitled to do so because the vessel had been 'bunkering' (transferring oil to) a fishing vessel and thereby avoiding customs duties.

---

[43] See *Continental Shelf (Libyan Arab Jamahiriya/Malta), Judgment, ICJ Reports 1985*, p 13.

[44] For general studies of the origins and background of the EEZ see Attard, 1986; Orrego-Vicuna, 1989.

The ITLOS found it unnecessary to decide this point,[45] but it is clear that had bunkering occurred within the territorial sea, and the arrest taken place within internal waters, the territorial sea, or a contiguous zone, the legitimacy of the arrest would not have been an issue at all.

The heart of the EEZ concerns jurisdiction over fisheries and this is considered in Section VII below. However, it should be noted here that coastal States enjoy broad-ranging legislative jurisdiction (LOSC Article 63(4)) and may take measures including 'boarding, inspection, arrest and judicial proceedings' which are necessary to enforce laws and regulations concerning its sovereign right to 'explore, exploit, conserve and manage' living resources of the EEZ (LOSC Article 73). This is not without difficulties. For example, the 1986 *Franco-Canadian Fisheries Arbitration*[46] took the view that a vessel engaged in processing fish at sea fell outside the range of activities over which the coastal State was entitled to exercise and enforce jurisdiction (for criticism see Churchill and Lowe, 1999, p 291). The convention also balances the potentially intrusive power of the coastal State over vessels within its EEZ against the risk of abuse by requiring that vessels or crew arrested 'shall be promptly released upon the posting of reasonable bond or other securities' and by restricting the nature of the penalties to which they might be subject (LOSC Article 73). Moreover, the International Tribunal on the Law of the Sea enjoys an automatic jurisdiction over claims concerning the prompt release of vessels (LOSC Article 292) and this has so far generated the majority of the admittedly modest number of cases that it has considered.[47]

D. THE DEEP SEABED

The final zone of resource jurisdiction which has been carved out of the high seas is the most dramatic in both kind and extent. The claim that the seabed beyond the limits of national jurisdiction form the 'common heritage of mankind', fuelled initially by some near fantastical estimates of the potential mineral wealth at stake, has already been noted. The difficulty lay in translating that idea into a workable regime: the developed world favoured a loosely structured international agency to oversee and regulate activities of those wishing to conduct mining whereas the developing world generally favoured creating a strong international mechanism that would itself undertake mining activity and distribute the proceeds as appropriate, taking account of the needs of developing countries and developing land-based producers. Negotiations at UNCLOS III were tortuous and produced an outcome—Part XI of the LOSC—which satisfied few and was

---

[45] *M/V Saiga No 2* (*St Vincent and the Grenadines* v *Guinea*), Case No 2, Judgment of 1 July 1999, paras 56–59.

[46] *Franco-Canadian Fisheries Arbitration* (1986) 90 *RGDIP* 713.

[47] A total of 16 cases have been submitted to the ITLOS since its inception, nine of which have concerned applications for prompt release. See *M/V Saiga* (*St Vincent and the Grenadines* v *Guinea*), Case No 1, Judgment of 4 December 1997; *Camouco* (*Panama* v *France*), Case No 3, Judgment of 7 February 2000; *Monte Confurco* (*Seychelles* v *France*), Case No 6, Judgment of 19 December 2000; *Grand Prince* (*Belize* v *France*), Case No 8, Judgment of 20 April 2001; *Chaisiri Reefer 2* (*Panama* v *Yemen*), Case No 9, Order of 13 July 2001; *Volga* (*Russian Federation* v *Australia*), Case No 11, Judgment of 23 December 2003; *Juno Trader* (*St Vincent and the Grenadines* v *Guinea-Bissau*), Case No 13, Judgment of 18 December 2004; *Hoshinmaru* (*Japan* v *Russian Federation*), Case No 14, Judgment of 6 August 2007; *Tomimaru* (*Japan* v *Russian Federation*), Case No 15, Judgment of 6 August 2007.

considered completely unacceptable by the developed world in general and the USA in particular (Schmidt, 1989).

Even at the time of its adoption, it was clear that the convention text would need to be modified in some way in order to accommodate the interests of the major industrialized powers whose support would be necessary for the regime to become a practical reality. Some concessions were made in Resolutions I and II which were appended to the Final Act of the Conference. These granted certain privileges to 'pioneer investors', States and companies registered in States which had already made a significant investment in seabed mining. This, however, proved to be too little too late. The breakthrough came in the early 1990s when the likelihood of the convention's entry into force, coupled with the demise of communism and changing economic and geo-political factors, produced a climate in which it was possible to revisit the convention text, sweep away some of the more bureaucratic and arcane layers of regulation and strike a new balance between the interests of those States and those companies which were already practically engaged in activities relating to mining the deep seabed and the more general interests of the international community as a whole. Far reaching changes were made in the 1994 Implementation Agreement which paved the way for widespread ratification of the convention and which has been considered in Section I, above. Underlying this change of approach was the realization that the financial rewards were likely to be considerably less than originally thought—if, indeed, there were likely to be any at all.[48]

Under the current arrangements, resource exploration and exploitation of the seabed and subsoil beyond the limits of national jurisdiction, known as the 'Area', is administered by the International Seabed Authority (ISA) to which applicants must submit 'plans of work'. These must identify two areas of roughly equal mining potential, one of which is to be mined by the applicant whilst the other will be 'reserved' for exploitation by the international community. In the original convention scheme, exploitation of the 'reserved' site would be undertaken by the 'Enterprise', an independent commercial mining arm of the ISA but under the 1994 Agreement the 'Enterprise' was given a considerably reduced role and, at least initially, might only engage in joint ventures. If the Enterprise does not undertake the mining of a reserved site within 15 years, the original applicant may do so. Moreover, if it does seek to mine the site, the original applicant is to be offered the chance to participate in the joint venture. The reality of the situation is that the Enterprise does not yet exist as an entity, and the ISA is currently fulfilling its functions. It will only be established should seabed mining becomes commercially feasible, and it may be that it never will. In the meanwhile, the Authority has since 2001 entered into a number of 15-year contracts with a range of governments, government entities and commercial consortia, whose activities are largely focused on exploration and research at present, in the Clarion-Clipperton Zone in the Pacific Ocean and the Central Indian Ocean Basin.

The details of the regime, and the manner in which it balances the interests of various interest groups—including consumer States, investing States, producing States, developing States, landlocked States, and others—is such as to defy easy and succinct description

---

[48] Indeed, commercial interest was already switching away from polymetallic nodules, primarily located beyond national jurisdiction in the Area, and becoming more focused on polymetallic sulphides which are more usually found within areas of national jurisdiction within the continental shelf and EEZ, further lessening the significance of the Deep Seabed regime.

and may be pursued elsewhere.[49] For current purposes what is significant is the manner in which the international community—after a number of false starts—was able to agree to extract the resource potential of the seabed and subsoil from of the high seas regime and create a further regime of resource jurisdiction whilst preserving the integrity of the general jurisdictional framework applicable to the law of the sea.

VI. DELIMITATION OF MARITIME ZONES BETWEEN OPPOSITE OR ADJACENT STATES

It will often be impossible for States to extend their jurisdiction as far seawards as international law permits because of the claims of other States. The resulting problem of delimiting maritime zones between opposite or adjacent coastal States whose claims overlap is extremely difficult and has given rise to more cases before the ICJ than any other single subject, as well as having generated a considerable number of ad hoc arbitrations.

A. EQUIDISTANCE OR EQUITABLE PRINCIPLES?

LOSC Article 15 provides that, in the absence of agreement to the contrary, States may not extend their territorial seas beyond the median, or equidistance line, unless there are historic or other 'special' circumstances that dictate otherwise. This 'equidistance/special circumstances' rule has been accepted by the ICJ as customary international law[50] and it is clear that only in exceptional cases will the equidistance line not form the basis of the boundary between overlapping territorial seas, although recent practice has in fact produced rather more exceptions than might have been thought probable.[51]

Article 6 of the 1958 CSC adopted the same approach to the delimitation of overlapping continental shelves but its application in this context has had a more chequered history (see generally Evans, 1989; Weil, 1989; Antunes, 2003; Tanaka, 2006). In the *North Sea* cases Denmark and the Netherlands argued that Article 6 represented customary law and so bound Germany, a non-State party. Applying this rule mechanically to the concave Germany coastline sandwiched between Denmark and Norway restricted Germany

---

[49] For details see the information available on the International Sea Bed Authority website: **http://www.isa.org.jm**. For a helpful overview of its work see Nandan, 2006.

[50] *Maritime Delimitation and Territorial Questions Between Qatar and Bahrain (Qatar v Bahrain), Merits, Judgment, ICJ Reports 2001*, p 40, paras 175–176. Cf Separate Opinion of Judge Oda, paras 13–21, who challenged the Court's views of customary law. The Court reaffirmed its view in *Territorial and Maritime Dispute between Nicaragua and Honduras in the Caribbean Sea (Nicaragua v Honduras)*, Judgment of 8 October 2007, nyr, paras 268 and 281.

[51] In the *Territorial and Maritime Boundary Dispute between Nicaragua and Honduras in the Caribbean* the ICJ, whilst emphasizing that equidistance remained the general rule, took the view that both the configuration and unstable nature of the relevant coastal area made it impossible to identify basepoints and construct a provisional equidistance line at all. This amounted to a 'special circumstance' justifying the use of an alternative method, the use of a line which bisected two lines drawn along the coastal fronts of the two States. See *Territorial and Maritime Dispute between Nicaragua and Honduras in the Caribbean Sea (Nicaragua v Honduras)*, Judgment of 8 October 2007, nyr, paras 268–281. Also in that year the Annex VII Arbitration Award in the case concerning *Guyana/Suriname*, 17 September 2007, paras 323–325 concluded that historical and navigational issues were considered to amount to special circumstances justifying a departure from the use of the equidistance line for the territorial sea.

to a modest triangle of continental shelf, to the substantial benefit of its neighbours. Rather than ameliorate this outcome by arguing that the concave nature of the coast was a 'special circumstance' justifying another line, the ICJ decided that Article 6 did not reflect customary law, and that customary law required continental shelf delimitation to be conducted on the basis of equitable principles and taking account of relevant circumstances.[52]

This ushered in a period in which supporters of the more formulaic 'equidistance/ special circumstances' approach vied with supporters of the relatively more flexible 'equitable principles/relevant circumstances' approach—though it is doubtful whether there was ever much to choose between them.[53] At UNCLOS III groups of States championed the approach they considered best suited their interests and, as no consensus could be found, an anodyne formula, applicable to both continental shelf and EEZ delimitation, was adopted in the dying days of the conference. This provides that such delimitations are to be 'effected by agreement on the basis of international law, as referred to in Article 38 of the Statute of the International Court of Justice, in order to achieve an equitable solution'. This avoids mentioning equidistance, equitable principles, special or relevant circumstances—and is virtually devoid of substantive content.

Around this time the ICJ delivered a trilogy of judgments, all of which emphasized the role of equity at the expense of equidistance, though in varying degrees.[54] Perhaps these cases were too close in time to UNCLOS III to shake off the ideological hostility to equidistance. By 1993, however, the Court was prepared to declare in the *Jan Mayen* case that, 'Prima facie, a median line delimitation between opposite coasts results in general in an equitable solution'[55] (Evans, 1999). Although the position regarding the use of equidistance as the starting point for delimitation between adjacent coasts remained less certain, the judgment of the ICJ in the *Qatar v Bahrain* case[56] strongly suggested that equidistance would provide the starting point and this was confirmed in the *Cameroon v Nigeria* case[57] where it said that:

The Court has on various occasions made it clear what the applicable criteria, principles and rules of delimitation are when a line covering several zones of coincident jurisdiction is to be determined. They are expressed in the so-called equitable principles/relevant circumstances method. This method, which is very similar to the equidistance/special circumstances method applicable in delimitation of the territorial sea, involves first drawing an

---

[52] *North Sea Continental Shelf, Judgment, ICJ Reports 1969*, p 3, para 101(c)(1).

[53] Thus the 1977 *Anglo-French Arbitration*, Cmnd 7438, 18 ILM 397, generally considered to lean towards the equitable principles school of thought, proceeded on the basis that although CSC Article 6 and custom were different the practical result of their application would be the same.

[54] *Continental Shelf (Tunisia/Libyan Arab Jamahiriya), Judgment, ICJ Reports 1982*, p 18; *Delimitation of the Maritime Boundary in the Gulf of Maine Area, Judgment, ICJ Reports 1984*, p 246; *Continental Shelf (Libyan Arab Jamahiriya/Malta), Judgment, ICJ Reports 1985*, p 13.

[55] *Maritime Delimitation in the Area between Greenland and Jan Mayen, Judgment, ICJ Reports 1993*, p 316, para 64, a position affirmed in the *Eritrea-Yemen Arbitration, Second Phase, Award of 17 December 1999*, para 131.

[56] *Maritime Delimitation and Territorial Questions between Qatar and Bahrain (Qatar v Bahrain), Merits, Judgment, ICJ Reports 2001*, p 40, para 230.

[57] *Land and Maritime Boundary between Cameroon and Nigeria (Cameroon v Nigeria: Equatorial Guinea Intervening), Merits, Judgment, ICJ Reports 2002*, p 303, para 288. See also *Barbados/Trinidad and Tobago, Award of 11 April 2006*, paras 242–244 and 306.

equidistance line, then considering whether there are factors calling for the adjustment or shifting of that line in order to achieve an 'equitable result'.

After 35 years of hesitation, the ICJ finally accepted what it had rejected in the *North Sea* cases, that the equidistance/special circumstances approach reflects customary international law (Evans, 2006). It has subsequently confirmed that this is the case both for the delimitation of the territorial sea[58] and for the delimitation of the continental shelf, EEZ, or when drawing a single delimitation line.[59]

B. FACTORS AFFECTING DELIMITATION

Even if equidistance provides the starting point, this does not mean it will be the finishing line. All formulations of the rule accept that it can be modified to take account of other factors. Although the categories of potentially relevant factors are never closed, the potential relevance—and irrelevance—of some factors is well established (Brownlie, 2008, pp 217–218). Close attention is usually paid to ensuring that areas appertaining to each State are not disproportionate to the ratio between the lengths of their 'relevant coasts' adjoining the area (though this is clearly open to gerrymandering). Likewise, the presence of islands capable of generating claims to a continental shelf or EEZ is a complicating factor and their impact upon an equidistance line can be reduced or discounted in numerous ways (Jayawardene, 1990). On the other hand, geological factors are not considered relevant where the distance between the coasts is less than 400 n. miles[60] and economic factors are generally considered irrelevant by courts and tribunals, although they probably play a significant role in negotiated boundary agreements.

It is difficult to go beyond this with certainty, and it is certainly not possible to predict how the various factors will be taken into account. Courts and tribunals increasingly refrain from indicating how—or why—the factors considered relevant combine with the chosen methodology to produce the final line. This had led some to observe that some judgments do little more than 'split the difference' between competing claims (Churchill and Lowe, 1999, p 191). However, in the *Cameroon v Nigeria* case the ICJ dismissed the relevance of all the various factors put forward by the parties and used an equidistance line in an unmodified fashion, despite the presence of a number of factors that might have been thought to have some claim to consideration.[61] The subsequent Arbitral Award in the *Guyana/Suriname* case and the judgment of the ICJ in the *Romania v Ukraine* case also dismissed the relevance of all factors put forward by the parties.[62] Whilst it would be a mistake to conclude from this that using an equidistance line alone might itself become seen an producing an equitable outcome, there appears to be an increasing need for caution and clear reasoning when presenting claims which call for a departure from the equidistance

---

[58] *Territorial and Maritime Dispute between Nicaragua and Honduras in the Caribbean Sea (Nicaragua v Honduras)*, Judgment of 8 October 2007, nyr, paras 262–298.

[59] *Guyana/Suriname*, Award of 17 September 2007, paras 376–392; *Maritime Delimitation in the Black Sea (Romania v Ukraine)*, Judgment of 2 February 2009, para 116.

[60] *Continental Shelf (Libyan Arab Jamahiriya/Malta), Judgment, ICJ Reports 1985*, p 13, para 39.

[61] *Land and Maritime Boundary between Cameroon and Nigeria (Cameroon v Nigeria: Equatorial Guinea Intervening), Merits, Judgment, ICJ Reports 2002*, p 303, paras 293–306.

[62] *Maritime Delimitation in the Black Sea (Romania v Ukraine)*, Judgment of 2 February 2009, paras 185–218.

line, and such departures normally should be firmly grounded in factors flowing from coastal geography (see Tanaka, 2004; Evans, 2006).[63] Overall, one must still conclude that, despite the greater certainly concerning the law to be applied, the application of the law pertaining to maritime delimitation remains as unpredictable and as mysterious as ever.

VII. FISHERIES

A. THE BASIC SCHEME OF REGULATION

Given its significance, it is perhaps surprising that the LOSC does not address fisheries as a discrete topic. However, the manner in which the seas are divided for jurisdictional purposes means that one has to look at how fisheries are regulated in each particular maritime zone. The basic scheme seems simple enough; the coastal State exercises sovereignty over the territorial seas and sovereign right to explore, exploit, conserve, and manage fishing in any EEZ or EFZ that it might claim. In the high seas the freedom of fishing remains and fish stocks are open to all, but the activities of fishing vessels are subject to the jurisdiction and control of their flag State. The problems are, however, enormous. Overfishing has endangered many fish stocks and there is a pressing need to agree upon and implement effective strategies for conservation and management in the increased threat from 'Illegal, Unreported and Unregulated' (IUU) fishing. At the same time, the economic and nutritional needs of communities must be borne in mind. The result is that the piecemeal approach to regulation is under increasing pressure and a more holistic approach, built around the idea of sustainable development may be in the process of emerging (see Edeson, 1999; Orrego-Vicuna, 1999). However, any system that is ultimately dependent upon flag State enforcement will be vulnerable to abuse.

One particularly noteworthy trend is the establishment of Regional Fisheries Bodies (RFBs) and Regional Fisheries Management Organisations (RFMOs) which provide means through which States may work together in the conservation, management and development of fishing in particular areas or of particular stocks. Multilateral treaty practice is moving beyond merely encouraging States to participate in such regimes and is increasingly requiring them to do so in order to have access to them. However, such obligations only bind States which become a party to such agreements and many major fishing States simply choose not to do so and continue to claim the right to fish these stocks as an aspect of the freedom of the high seas. An alternative response is to extend coastal State jurisdiction still further seawards but this also runs into fierce opposition. Some years ago Canada adopted a slightly different approach, by asserting its right to enforce conservation and management measures adopted by the relevant regional body (NAFO) over non-flag State vessels fishing beyond its 200 n. mile EEZ. The subsequent arrest in 1995 of the Spanish registered *Estai* on the high seas prompted a serious incident between the EC and Canada[64] and illustrated the difficulty of pursuing the unilateral route. For the moment,

---

[63] See also *Barbados/Trinidad and Tobago*, Award of 11 April 2006, paras 233–240. But cf n 51 above.

[64] See Davies, 1995. Spain subsequently brought a case against Canada before the ICJ which the Court was unable to consider because Canada had previously removed such disputes from the scope of its consent to the Court's jurisdiction. (See de LaFayette, 1999.)

then, we can merely chart the trends in this direction whilst outlining the major elements of the regimes applicable beyond the limits of the territorial seas.

B. MANAGING FISHERIES

1. EEZ

Some 80–90% of all fishing takes place within EEZs. The coastal State does not enjoy a completely unfettered right to exploit the fisheries resources of the EEZ under the LOSC (though this may not be the position in customary law). LOSC Article 61(1) requires the coastal State to 'determine the allowable catch' (known as the TAC) of living resources. A number of factors feed into this determination, including the need to 'ensure through proper conservation and management measures that the maintenance of the living resources . . . is not endangered by over-exploitation' (Article 61(2)). At the same time, these measures must themselves be designed 'to maintain or restore populations of harvested species at levels which can produce the maximum sustainable yield' (Article 61(3)). This, then, looks to conserving stocks, but Article 62(1) switches to the obligation to 'promote the objective of optimum utilization of the living resources of the EEZ' by requiring the coastal State 'to determine its capacity to harvest' them. Where the harvestable capacity falls short of the TAC, the coastal State is to give other States access to that surplus (Article 62(2)), with particular regard being given to the requirements of developing States in the area (Article 62(3)), as well as the interests of landlocked and geographically disadvantaged States (Articles 69 and 70; Vasciannie, 1990) in determining to whom access will be offered.[65] Despite these provisions, since coastal States have their hands on both levers—determining both the TAC and the harvestable capacity—their control over EEZ fisheries is hardly troubled by these provisions which have more symbolic than substantial significance. If it were otherwise, the attraction of declaring an EEZ rather than an EFZ (in which these provisions would not apply) would be significantly diminished.

The convention also provides special rules for particular categories of species, including anadromous stocks, such as salmon, which spend most of their time at sea but spawn in freshwater rivers (LOSC Article 66), catadromous stocks, such as eels, which spawn at sea but spend most of their lives in fresh water (LOSC Article 67) which again reflect the theme of reconciling the interests of the State of origin with the established interests of others, and for marine mammals (LOSC Article 65). The situation regarding 'straddling stocks' and 'highly migratory species' (LOSC Articles 63 and 64) will be considered below.

Although the coastal State in principle enjoys complete control over fishing within the EEZ, this has not prevented overfishing. Some States refuse to accept the need for conservation of fish stocks in the face of more pressing and immediate economic or political interests, whilst others are simply unable to control the fishing activities of foreign-flagged vessels within their EEZ, both licensed and illegal.

2. High seas

It is often forgotten that the freedom of fishing upon the high seas is not unfettered. The 1958 Convention on Fishing and Conservation of the Living Resources of the High Seas

---

[65] Such access can, of course, be subject to licensing and fees and is more generally regulated by LOSC Article 64.

(CFC) had recognized the 'special interest' of the coastal State in fishing activities in areas adjacent to its territorial waters and sought to reflect that through cooperative arrangements with States engaged in high seas fishing in the interests of conservation and management (CFC Article 6). LOSC Article 116(b) now expressly subjects that freedom to the interests that coastal States have in the particular classes of species identified in LOSC Articles 63–67 as well as the more general obligation to conserve the living resources of the high seas by setting total allowable catches, based on the maximum sustainable yield (LOSC Article 119). It has to be said that, to the extent that this implies unilateral determinations and self-imposed restrictions, this is little short of wishful thinking. How can the practice of a single State significantly affect the overall pattern when its self-restraint may simply make more space for others to over-exploit?

The key lies in coordinated and cooperative activities by all involved in fishing a given stock or region and LOSC Article 118 recognizes this by requiring that States 'whose nationals exploit identical living resources, or different living resources in the same area, shall enter into negotiations with a view to taking the measures necessary for the conservation of the living resources concerned. They shall, as appropriate, co-operate to establish sub-regional or regional fisheries organizations to this end'. This approach is not new, having echoes in the 1958 CFC, and, as mentioned above, a considerable number of RFBs and RFMOs have been established.[66] Some have been relatively successful, notably the Northwest Atlantic Fisheries Organization (NAFO) and the Commission for the Conservation of Antarctic Marine Resources (CCAMLR), though even these have suffered from poor records of enforcement at times. Others have been less successful, such as the 1993 Commission for the Conservation of Southern Bluefin Tuna (CCSBT), where some years ago the failure of the three States parties (Japan, Australia, and New Zealand) to agree a TAC and the introduction of an 'experimental fishing programme' by Japan prompted a case under the LOSC dispute settlement provisions (Churchill, 2000; Boyle, 2001). This gives a flavour of the difficulties which need to be overcome.

It is difficult to resist the conclusion that the problems of over-utilization of the living resources of the high seas will remain until the right to exploit them is made conditional upon participation in a unified international regulatory framework. However, the experience of creating the International Seabed Authority suggests this might also be a route to paralysis and is bound to be fraught with difficulties. Unless there is a further expansion of coastal State jurisdiction—itself no panacea since some coastal States have themselves fished their own resources to near extinction—it is difficult to see what the international community can do except continue to press the case for cooperation and coordination. This it continues to do, as illustrated by the most recent addition to the family of regulatory instruments: in November 2009 the FAO built on the trend of utilizing port State jurisdiction by adopting the Agreement on Port State Measures to Prevent, Deter and Eliminate Illegal, Unreported and Unregulated Fishing. It remains to be seen whether moving towards a more enforcement oriented approach is more successful than reliance on restraint, co-operation and self regulation.

---

[66] There are currently 44 Regional Fisheries Bodies, 20 of which are RFMOs. The distinguishing feature of an RFMO is that, unlike a RFB, it is able to adopt measures which are binding on its members. For a full list of regional fishing bodies, and links to their websites, see http://www.fao.org.

3. Straddling stocks and highly migratory species

Fish do not respect man-made boundaries and many stocks 'straddle' the limits of maritime zones. Where stocks straddle boundaries the LOSC provides that those States concerned in the fisheries should, either directly or through appropriate organizations should they exist, agree upon appropriate measures of conservation and development (LOSC Article 63). Other stocks, such as tuna, are highly mobile and travel great distances in the course of their regular life cycle, migrating through both EEZs and high seas making them particularly vulnerable to predatory exploitation as they pass. Once again, the convention's response is to call for cooperation with respect to a list of species contained in Annex I to the convention, with the objective of optimum utilization, and also calls for the establishment of appropriate regional organizations where none exist (LOSC Article 64).

These rather open-textured provisions have since been built upon by the 1995 UN Agreement on Straddling Stocks and Highly Migratory Species (SSC).[67] This, *inter alia*, obliges States parties fishing for such stocks either to become members of those fisheries management organizations that exist for the relevant region or stock, or to agree to apply the measures which such an organization establishes, and States parties to the Agreement which do not do so are debarred from having access to the stock (SSC Articles 8(3) and (4)). In other words, States parties to the Agreement may not fish for such stocks outside of the framework established by any such organization (SSC Article 17). Since most fishing undertaken on the high seas involves either straddling stocks or highly migratory species, this is an extremely significant self-denying ordinance. Moreover, where RFMOs exist, SSC Article 21 permits the authorized inspectors of any State party to board and inspect fishing vessels flying the flag of other State parties in order to ensure compliance with the conservation and management measure that the organization has established and, in cases where there are 'clear grounds' for suspecting that 'serious violations' have occurred, the vessel might be taken to the nearest appropriate port—though it should be noted that in both cases enforcement action against the vessel can only be taken by the flag State or with the flag State's consent.

Once again, it is possible to see in this how the international community is striving to address a complex problem by incremental diminutions in the freedom of the high seas in favour of communal responses, backed by equally incremental incursions into the principle of flag State jurisdiction. However, this is entirely dependent upon States choosing to fetter themselves in this way and many remain reluctant to do so whilst others remain free to take advantage of their self-restraint.[68]

VIII. CONCLUSION

There are a great many important topics that have not been touched upon in this chapter, including, *inter alia*, marine scientific research, pollution and the marine environment, military uses of the seas, and the dispute settlement provisions of the LOSC. Although a

---

[67] See Davies and Redgwell, 1996; Orrego-Vicuna, 1999, Chs 5–9; and the illuminating collection of essays in Stokke, 2001.

[68] The SSC entered into force in December 2001, having secured 30 ratifications. At the time of writing 77 States and other entities (including the European Community) have become a party to it.

number of these topics are touched on elsewhere in this volume, these omissions remain regrettable. However, by focusing in some detail on some foundational aspects of the division of ocean space and its principles of governance, this chapter introduces the complexities that must be grappled with and the manner in which this has been attempted. The underlying tension remains the same as ever: balancing the competing demands of access to ocean space whilst recognizing the need to preserve order and good governance. The law of the sea has undergone a remarkable transformation in the last 50 years yet more still needs to be done if that balance is to be achieved. Perhaps at the end of the day the problem is the perception, uttered by the ICJ in the *North Sea* cases in the context of the delimitation of maritime boundaries, that 'the land dominates the sea'.[69] We are coming to realize that, in many ways, it is the sea that dominates the land and, as they are projected seawards, our concepts of sovereignty, rights, and jurisdiction, no matter how subtle or sophisticated their application, seem increasingly cumbersome instruments for addressing the resulting issues. But for the moment, they remain the best we have.

REFERENCES

AHNISH, FA (1993), *The International Law of Maritime Boundaries and the Practice of States in the Mediterranean Sea* (Oxford: Clarendon Press).

ANAND, RM (1983), *Origin and Development of the Law of the Sea* (The Hague: Martinus Nijhoff).

ANDERSON, DH (1993), 'Efforts to Ensure Universal Participation in the UN Convention on the Law of the Sea', 42 *ICLQ* 654.

—— (1995), 'Legal Implication of the Entry into Force of the UN Convention on the Law of the Sea', 44 *ICLQ* 313.

—— (2006), 'Freedoms of the High Seas in the Modern Law of the Sea' in Freestone, D, Barnes, R, and Ong, D (eds), *The Law of the Sea: Progress and Prospects* (Oxford: Oxford University Press), p 327.

ANTUNES, NM (2003), *Towards the Conceptualisation of Maritime Delimitation* (The Hague: Martinus Nijhoff).

ATTARD, D (1986), *The Exclusive Economic Zone* (Oxford: Clarendon Press).

BOYLE, A (2001), 'The Southern Bluefin Tuna Arbitration', 50 *ICLQ* 447.

—— (2005), 'Further Development of the Law of the Sea Convention: Mechanisms for Change', 54 *ICLQ* 563.

BROWNLIE, I (2008), *Principles of Public International Law*, 7th edn (Oxford: Oxford University Press).

BYERS, M (2004) 'Policing the High Seas: the Proliferation Security Initiative', 98 *AJIL* 526.

CHARNEY, J (2000), 'Rocks that cannot sustain Human Habitation', 96 *AJIL* 863.

CHURCHILL, RR (2000), 'The Southern Bluefin Tuna Cases', 49 *ICLQ* 979.

—— and LOWE, AV (1999), *The Law of the Sea*, 3rd edn (Manchester: Manchester University Press).

COOK, PJ and CARLTON, C (2000), *Continental Shelf Limits* (Oxford: Oxford University Press).

DAVIES, PGG (1995), 'The EC/Canadian Fisheries Dispute in the Northwest Atlantic', 44 *ICLQ* 933.

---

[69] *North Sea Continental Shelf, Judgment, ICJ Reports 1969, p 3*, para 96.

—— and REDGWELL, C (1996), 'The International Legal Regulation of Straddling Fish Stocks', 67 *BYIL* 199.

DE LAFAYETTE, L (1999), 'The Fisheries Jurisdiction Case (*Spain v Canada*)', 48 *ICLQ* 664.

DE YTURRIAGA, JA (1991), *Straights Used for International Navigation* (Dordrecht: Martinus Nijhoff).

EDESON, W (1999), 'Towards Long-term Sustainable Use: Some Recent Developments in the Legal Regime of Fisheries', in Boyle, A and Freestone, D (eds), *International Law and Sustainable Development* (Oxford: Oxford University Press), p 165.

EVANS, MD (1989), *Relevant Circumstances and Maritime Delimitation* (Oxford: Clarendon Press).

—— (1999), 'Maritime Delimitation after *Denmark v Norway*. Back to the Future?', in Goodwin-Gill, GS and Talmon, S (eds), *The Reality of International Law* (Oxford: Clarendon Press), p 153.

—— (2006), 'Maritime Boundary Delimitation: Where Do We Go From Here?', in Freestone, D, Barnes, R, and Ong, D (eds), *The Law of the Sea: Progress and Prospects* (Oxford: Oxford University Press), p 137.

GUILFOYLE, D (2008), 'Piracy off Somalia: UN Security Council Resolution 1816 and IMO Regional Counter-Piracy Efforts', 57 *ICLQ* 690.

—— (2009), *Shipping Interdiction and the Law of the Sea* (Cambridge: Cambridge University Press).

GILMORE, W (1995), 'Hot Pursuit: The Case of *R v Mills* and Others', 44 *ICLQ* 949.

—— (2000), 'Drugs Trafficking at Sea: The Case of *R v Charrington* and Others', 49 *ICLQ* 477.

—— (2005), *Agreement Concerning Co-Operation in Suppressing Illicit Maritime and Air Trafficking in Narcotic Drugs and Psychotropic Substances in the Caribbean Area, 2003* (London: TSO).

HUTCHINSON, D (1985), 'The Seawards Limit to Continental Shelf Jurisdiction in Customary International Law', 56 *BYIL* 133.

JAYAWARDENE, H (1990), *The Regime of Islands in International Law* (Dordrecht: Martinus Nijhoff).

JIA, BB (1998), *The Regime of Straits in International Law* (Oxford: Clarendon Press).

LAVALLLE, R (2004), 'Not Quite a Sure Thing: The Maritime Areas of Rocks and Low Tide Elevations under the UN Convention on the Law of the Sea' 19 *IJMCL* 43.

LLEWELLYN, H (2007), 'The Commission on the Limits of the Continental Shelf: Joint Submission by France, Ireland, Spain and the United Kingdom', 56 *ICLQ* 677

MARSTON, G (2002), 'Redrawing the Territorial Sea Boundary in the Firth of Clyde', 51 *ICLQ* 279.

MOLENAAR, EJ (2004), 'Multilateral Hot Pursuit and Illegal Fishing in the Southern Ocean: The Pursuits of the *Viarsa 1* and *South Tomi*', 19 *IJMCL* 19.

—— (2006), 'Port State Jurisdiction: towards Mondatory and Comprehensive Use', in Freestone, D, Barnes, R, and Ong, D (eds), *The Law of the Sea: Progress and Prospects* (Oxford: Oxford University Press), p 137.

NANDAN, SM (2006), 'Administrating the Mineral Resources of the Deep Sea Bed', in Freestone, D, Barnes, R, and Ong, D (eds), *The Law of the Sea: Progress and Prospects* (Oxford: Oxford University Press), p 75.

—— and ANDERSON, DH (1989), 'Straits Used for International Navigation', 90 *BYIL* 159.

O'CONNELL, DP (1982), *The International Law of the Sea*, vol I (Oxford: Clarendon Press).

ORREGO-VICUNA, F (1989), *The Exclusive Economic Zone* (Cambridge: Cambridge University Press).

—— (1999), *The Changing Law of High Seas Fisheries* (Cambridge: Cambridge University Press).

ÖZÇAYIR, ZO (2001), *Port State Control* (London: LLP Professional Publishing).

PRESCOTT, V and SCHOFIELD, C (2005), *The Maritime Political Boundaries of the World*, 2nd edn, (Leiden: Martinus Nijhoff).

REISMAN, WM and WESTERMAN, GS (1992), *Straight Baselines in International Maritime Boundary Delimitation* (London: Macmillan).

SCHACHTE, WL (1993), 'International Straits and Navigational Freedoms', 24 *ODIL* 179.

SCHMIDT, M (1989), *Common Heritage or Common Burden?* (Oxford: Clarendon Press).

STOKKE, OV (ed) (2001), *Governing High Seas Fisheries* (Oxford: Oxford University Press).

TANAKA, Y (2004), 'Reflections on the Maritime Delimitation in the Cameroon/Nigeria Case', 53 *ICLQ* 369.

—— (2006), *Predictability and Flexibility in the Law of Maritime Delimitation* (Oxford: Hart Publishing).

VASCIANNIE, SC (1990), *Land-Locked and Geographically Disadvantaged States in the Law of the Sea* (Oxford: Clarendon Press).

WEIL, P (1989), *The Law of Maritime Delimitation—Reflections* (Cambridge: Grotius).

WESTERMAN, G (1987), *The Juridical Bay* (Oxford: Clarendon Press).

FURTHER READING

CHARNEY, JI and ALEXANDER, LM (eds), *Maritime Boundary Agreements*, vol I (1993), vol II (1993), vol III (1998), vol IV (2002), vol V (2005) (The Hague: Martinus Nijhoff). A compendium of State practice, with commentaries and an excellent series of essays relating to boundary delimitation.

CHURCHILL, RR and LOWE, AV (1999), *The Law of the Sea*, 3rd edn (Manchester: Manchester University Press). This is the essential *vade mecum* to the subject.

FREESTONE, D, BARNES, R, and ONG, D (2006), *The Law of the Sea: Progress and Prospects* (Oxford: Oxford University Press). An important collection of essays exploring practical and conceptual issues in considerable detail.

NORDQUIST, MN et al, *United Nations Convention on the Law of the Sea 1982: A Commentary*, vol I (1985), vol II (1993), vol III (1995), vol IV (1990), vol V (1989), vol VI (2002) (The Hague: Martinus Nijhoff). This is an excellent source of reference, tracing and commenting upon the evolution of each Article of 1982 Law of the Sea Convention.

O'CONNELL, DP, *The International Law of the Sea*, vol I (1982), vol II (1984) (Oxford: Clarendon Press). Although now considerably out of date, this remains a classic and magisterial point of reference.

PRESCOTT, V and SCHOFIELD, C (2005), *The Maritime Political Boundaries of the World*, 2nd edn (Leiden: Martinus Nijhoff), An excellent overview of the construction of maritime boundaries.

STOKKE, OV (ed) (2001), *Governing High Seas Fisheries* (Oxford: Oxford University Press). This is an excellent collection of essays probing aspects of high seas fishing in depth.

23

INTERNATIONAL ENVIRONMENTAL LAW

Catherine Redgwell

SUMMARY

The development of international environmental law is typically divided into three periods. The first demonstrates little genuine environmental awareness but rather views environmental benefits as incidental to largely economic concerns such as the exploitation of living natural resources. The second phase demonstrates a significant rise in the number of treaties directed to pollution abatement and to species and habitat conservation. Here an overt environmental focus is evident, yet the approach is still largely reactive and piecemeal. The final phase, which characterizes current international environmental law, demonstrates a precautionary approach to environmental problems of global magnitude such as biodiversity conservation and climate change. Concern transcends individual States, with certain global problems now considered the common concern of humankind. This chapter first defines international environmental law, its key sources and actors, and the difficulties of enforcement, before embarking on a sectoral examination of the extensive treaty law applicable in this field.

I. INTRODUCTION: WHAT IS INTERNATIONAL ENVIRONMENTAL LAW?[1]

This chapter addresses one of the more recent areas of development in international law, international environmental law. It is an area of public international law marked by the application of principles which have evolved in the environmental context, such as the precautionary and no harm principles, yet also forms part of, and draws from, the general corpus of public international law elaborated elsewhere in this text such as the sources of public international law principles of the exercise of State jurisdiction, and State responsibility. It is thus part and parcel of general public international law and not an entirely

---

[1] For discussion of *why* the environment is protected, see Gillespie, 1997.

separate, self-contained discipline (Birnie, Boyle, and Redgwell, 2009). In this sense it is analogous to, say, international human rights law, the law of the sea, or international economic law, all applications of international law addressed in this volume. Institutionally it is less well-developed than these fields: there is no 'global environmental organization' with competence over environmental matter analogous to, say, the World Trade Organization (WTO), nor a dispute settlement body analogous to the WTO's Dispute Settlement Body or the Law of the Sea Convention's International Tribunal for the Law of the Sea.

Moreover, notwithstanding significant growth in the body of general and particularized rules governing State conduct in respect of the environment, it remains the case that there is not yet any general customary or treaty law obligation on States to protect and preserve the environment *per se*. To be sure there is a relevant negative obligation found in customary international law—the no harm principle, or the obligation imposed on States not to allow their territory to be used in a such a manner so as to cause harm to the territory of other States, or to the global commons, which may be traced back to the seminal *Trail Smelter Arbitration*.[2] Positive obligations, however, remain largely sectoral in focus, the most outstanding examples being the obligation in Article 192 of the 1982 Law of the Sea Convention to protect and preserve the marine environment and the obligation in Article 2 of the 1991 Protocol on Environmental Protection to the 1959 Antarctic Treaty comprehensively to protect the Antarctic environment and dependent and related ecosystems. But as for a general obligation to protect and preserve the environment wherever situated, one looks in vain. This is partly explained by the piecemeal development of the subject, elaborated in the next section. Early international regulation of environmental activities dealt with conservation of common property resources subject to over-exploitation and customary international law first developed to restrain State actions causing transboundary harm—primarily economic harm—in the territory of another State. International environmental regulation of State behaviour penetrating *within* the State has been less rapid to develop, particularly since it encounters the twin yet related obstacles of State sovereignty and permanent sovereignty over natural resources. Nonetheless it is possible to detect the impact of international environmental law on the evolution of the principle of permanent sovereignty over natural resources, most notably in the concept of sustainable development, importing duties as well as rights in respect of natural resource management (Schrijver, 1997). Undoubtedly one of the challenges facing international environmental law in the twenty-first century is achieving a holistic and integrated approach to environmental regulation which applies within as well as between and beyond States. The 1992 Convention on Biological Diversity is one example of a treaty instrument moving in this direction.

II. DEFINING 'THE ENVIRONMENT'

'The environment' is an amorphous term that has thus far proved incapable of precise legal definition save in particular contexts. Even the Law of the Sea Convention, which comprehensively defines pollution of the marine environment, does not define the marine

---

[2] (1939) 33 *AJIL* 182 and (1941) 35 *AJIL* 684; see also Principle 21 of the 1972 Declaration of the United Nations Conference on the Human Environment (Stockholm) and Principle 2 of the 1992 Declaration of the UN Conference on Environment and Development (Rio) reproduced in Birnie and Boyle, 1995, at pp 1 and 9 respectively.

environment as such. A rare exception is Article 2(10) of the 1993 Council of Europe Convention on Civil Liability for Damage Resulting from Activities Dangerous for the Environment. It defines the environment to include 'natural resources both abiotic and biotic, such as the air, water, soil, fauna and flora and the interaction between the same factors; property which forms part of the cultural heritage; and the characteristic aspects of the landscape'. This broad definition encompasses natural and cultural heritage protection (regulated by the 1972 UNESCO Convention for the Protection of the World Cultural and Natural Heritage for example); species and habitat protection (see, for example, the 1992 United Nations Convention on Biological Diversity); and pollution prevention (regulated, *inter alia*, by the 1972 London (Dumping) Convention and the 1979 UN ECE Convention on Long-Range Transboundary Air Pollution (LRTAP)). As will be seen shortly, this in fact encapsulates the development of international law, especially treaty law, in the field of the environment: from sectoral pollution and conservation treaties to ecosystem and holistic environmental protection, with increasing attention to issues of liability, compensation, and compliance. It demonstrates 'the broad range of issues now addressed by international environmental law, including conservation and sustainable use of natural resources and biodiversity; conservation of endangered and migratory species; prevention of deforestation and desertification; preservation of Antarctica and areas of outstanding natural heritage; protection of oceans, international watercourses, the atmosphere, climate and ozone layer from the effects of pollution; safeguarding human health and the quality of life' (Birnie, Boyle, and Redgwell, 2009).

III. THE DEVELOPMENT OF INTERNATIONAL ENVIRONMENTAL LAW

Although the origins of international environmental regulation may be traced to the nineteenth century, the modern development of the subject dates from the post-Second World War era. Indeed, the development of international environmental law shares much in common with the development of domestic environmental law which arose concomitantly with concerns about environmental degradation highlighted especially in the 1960s. A turning point was undoubtedly the United Nations-sponsored 1972 Stockholm Conference on the Human Environment which produced a non-binding Declaration of Principles and a Programme for Action. Subsequently not only did national departments of environmental protection proliferate, but the United Nations established a specialized subsidiary body of the UN General Assembly—the United Nations Environment Programme (UNEP), headquartered in Nairobi. Today UNEP remains the only international body exclusively concerned with environmental matters, although many other specialized bodies within the United Nations family concern themselves with environmental matters as part of their broader remit, such as the fisheries conservation efforts of the Food and Agriculture Organization (FAO) in Rome and the marine environmental protection activities of the International Maritime Organization (IMO) in London.

The United Nations General Assembly has also played a significant role in shaping international environmental law and policy notwithstanding the absence of any mention of the environment in the UN Charter. Undoubtedly dynamic interpretation of the

Charter—especially of Articles 1 and 55—and the implied powers approach adopted by the ICJ in the *Reparations* case[3] would support reading environmental matters into the competence of the UN. The establishment of UNEP following the Stockholm Conference in 1972, and of the UN Commission on Sustainable Development[4] following the 1992 Rio Conference on Environment and Development, is ample testament to the suppleness of the Charter treaty text. Today a number of significant global treaties has resulted from UN auspices, including the 1992 Conventions on Climate Change and Biological Diversity. The UN has also played a significant role in regional developments through, for example, the regional seas programme of UNEP and the UN's economic commissions. The UN Economic Commission for Europe (ECE) has been particularly active in the environmental field and is responsible for two significant procedural treaties addressing environmental impact assessment (the 1991 Espoo Convention on Environmental Assessment in a Transboundary Context) and access to environmental information, public participation, and access to justice (the 1998 Aarhus Convention on Access to Information, Public Participation in Environmental Decision-Making, and Access to Justice in Environmental Matters) as well as for sectoral pollution regulation (the 1979 Convention on Long-Range Transboundary Air Pollution and the 1992 Conventions on the Transboundary Effects of Industrial Accidents, and on the Protection and Use of Transboundary Watercourses and International Lakes).

It is common to divide the development of international environmental law into three (Francioni, 1994) or four (Sands, 2003; Fitzmaurice, 2001) stages. The first pre-dates the 1972 Stockholm Conference and is characterized by piecemeal and reactive responses to particular problems of resource use and exploitation (eg, the 1946 International Convention for the Regulation of Whaling), including shared resources (eg, the 1909 Treaty Between the United States and Great Britain Respecting Boundary Waters Between the United States and Canada), and pollution (eg, the 1954 International Convention for the Prevention of Pollution of the Sea by Oil). Some writers sub-divide this first stage into two, commencing the second stage with the creation of international institutions from 1945 and seeing its culmination in the 1972 Stockholm Conference on the Human Environment inaugurating on this analysis the third phase of development. It produced a Declaration[5] and an Action Programme, a template followed by the 1992 Rio Conference on Environment and Development 20 years later. In addition, the run-up to and conclusion of the Stockholm Conference stimulated a great deal of regional and global treaty-making activity, much of it directed towards protection of the marine environment. The 1972 London (Dumping) Convention dates from this period, as does the regional seas programme of UNEP which from 1976 onwards has led to the conclusion of a number of regional seas agreements including environmental protection provisions. The terrestrial environment was also the focus of attention, with the conclusion of major treaties regarding the natural and cultural heritage (the 1972 UNESCO Convention Concerning the Protection of the World Cultural and Natural Heritage), species and habitat protection

---

[3] *Reparations for Injuries Suffered in the Service of the United Nations, Advisory Opinion, ICJ Reports 1949*, p 174.

[4] See UN GA Res 47/191 (1992) in Birnie and Boyle, 1995, p 658. See further **http://www.un.org/esa/dsd/csd/csd_aboucsd.shtml**.

[5] For seminal analysis of the Stockholm Declaration on the Human Environment, see Sohn, 1973.

(eg, the 1971 Ramsar Convention on Wetlands of International Importance Especially as Waterfowl Habitat, the 1973 Convention on International Trade in Endangered Species and, in direct response to a recommendation at Stockholm, the 1979 Bonn Convention on the Conservation of Migratory Species of Wild Animals). With one or two exceptions such as the 1980 Convention on the Conservation of Antarctic Marine Living Resources with its novel ecosystem approach, this period of international legislative activity is characterized by a sectoral and fragmented approach to achieving environmental protection.

The third (or fourth) period witnesses instruments adopting a holistic approach to environmental protection and seeks to marry such protection with economic development, embraced in the concept of sustainable development. This was the theme of the 1992 Rio Conference on Environment and Development which, in addition to producing a Declaration of Principles and a programme of action for the twenty-first century (Agenda 21) saw the conclusion of two major treaties under UN auspices—the 1992 Framework Convention on Climate Change and the 1992 Convention on the Conservation of Biological Diversity. It was hoped also to adopt binding texts relating to forests and to deserts, but in the event only a soft law text on forests was also adopted (the 'Non-Binding Authoritative Statement of Principles for a Global Consensus on the Management, Conservation and Sustainable Development of all Types of Forest'). In 1994 the Convention to Combat Desertification was adopted, as was the International Tropical Timber Agreement (ITTA), (replacing a 1983 agreement and itself superceded by a new agreement in 2006). While paying greater attention to sustainable development than its predecessors, the 2006 ITTA is largely concerned with facilitating sustainable timber trade and not with forest biodiversity *per se*, which thus falls under the remit of the Biodiversity Convention. Both forests and deserts have proved resistant to international regulation largely owing to concerns about the infringement of State sovereignty. Nonetheless the general outcome of the Rio Conference, and the conclusion of the Biodiversity and Climate Change Conventions in particular, marked a new phase in international environmental regulation with the acknowledgement in each that the conservation of biological diversity or preventing further adverse changes in the earth's climate are the common concern of humankind. Proposals further to develop the institutional framework of international environmental law to reflect these common and intergenerational concerns have not yet made any significant headway. Suggestions for revamping the UN Trusteeship Council to address matters to do with the global commons have become linked with broader and more vexed questions of UN institutional reform. The 10-year follow-up to the Rio Conference, the 2002 Johannesburg World Summit on Sustainable Development, achieved neither environmental institutional reform nor resulted in significant multilateral law-making, though making a significant contribution, *inter alia*, to developments within the Southern African region.[6]

Thus the past decades have witnessed an evolution in law-making focus from environmental regulation incidental to the primary focus, such as economic regulation of a resource, to an holistic approach to environmental protection within and beyond State borders. These stages are not necessarily sequential, however, with evidence in the present of international rules reflecting each of these stages of evolution. This is particularly evident

---

[6] See the Johannesburg Declaration on Sustainable Development and Plan of Implementation, http://www.johannesburgsummit.org.

in the tension between permanent sovereignty over natural resources and the common concern of humankind contained in the Biodiversity Convention, and in the resistance to international regulation of forest and desertification issues because of the perceived threat to State sovereignty. Moreover what is absent from the corpus of international rules thus developed is a comprehensive codification of the basic rules and principles applicable to international regulation of the environment analogous to the 1948 Universal Declaration of Human Rights or the 1982 Law of the Sea Convention.[7]

IV. KEY ENVIRONMENTAL ACTORS

While States remain the central actors in environmental law-making and enforcement activities, they are not the exclusive actors. The 1992 Rio and 2002 Johannesburg summits evidence a further feature of international environmental law, which is the increased participation of non-State actors, in particular non-governmental organizations (NGOs). Witness the range of actors identified in Section 3 of the Earth's Action Plan agreed at Rio (Agenda 21): women, youth, indigenous peoples, NGOs, local authorities, workers and trade unions, business and industry, the scientific and technological community, and farmers. Of course this is not a unique feature of the environmental field, though particularly marked within it (and in the human rights area, as Ch 26 below attests). The role of NGOs in particular has been significant both in shaping the treaty-negotiating process and also in stimulating subsequent developments within treaty regimes.[8] Perhaps the outstanding example is the influence of the International Council for Bird Preservation (ICBP) and the International Waterfowl and Wetlands Research Bureau (IWRB) in the conclusion and implementation of the 1971 Ramsar Convention, for which the International Union for the Conservation of Nature (IUCN), a unique union of governmental and non-governmental actors, acts as the secretariat.

NGO influence is achieved primarily through the mechanism of participation, viz as observers in international organizations, at treaty negotiations, and within treaty institutions. For example, the meetings of the conference of the parties to the 1992 Climate Change Convention and its subsidiary bodies provide for the participation of NGO representatives to observe with limited scope for active participation. These reflect the diverse constituencies of the convention including business and industry NGOs (principally the major natural resource companies), environmental and local government NGOs. These developments may be viewed as a wider trend towards viewing international society in terms broader than a community of States alone.[9] This is recognized in recent environmental treaties such as the Climate Change and Biodiversity Conventions, where we have seen that the global climate and biological diversity respectively are expressly recognized as the common concern of humankind. However, as yet there is limited participation of non-State actors as treaty parties. A notable exception is the European Community[10]

---

[7] One such attempt is the *International Union for the Conservation of Nature's Draft International Covenant on Environment and Development*, 2nd edn (IUCN, 2000).

[8] See further Chinkin and Boyle, 2007.

[9] See, eg, the Commission on Global Governance, 1995.

[10] The Treaty of Lisbon, recently in force, provides for the legal personality of the European Union.

which possesses international legal personality coupled with the requisite internal constitutional competence to participate in international treaties alongside the member States. Thus, for example, the EC is a party to the 1992 Climate Change Convention and the 1997 Kyoto Protocol which expressly provide for the participation of regional economic integration organizations.[11] Yet it is not a party to 1973 Convention on International Trade in Endangered Species, because there the treaty text does not presently make provision for non-State participation. Thus only the member States may become parties in their individual capacities. This has not prevented the EC from regulating trade in endangered species within the European area, but it does so in the exercise of internal legal competence over the matter and not in furtherance of an expressly undertaken international obligation.

In addition to participation in international environmental law-making, non-State actors may play a significant role in enforcement, whether through transnational litigation before national courts, in treaty compliance procedures (where permitted, as under the Aarhus Convention procedure) or in the indirect enforcement of environmental norms through human rights litigation. Civil liability regimes are concerned with the liability of non-State actors—shipowners under oil pollution liability; nuclear operators under the nuclear liability regimes, for example. Increasing attention is also being paid to corporate environmental accountability; however, corporations are not directly bound by environmental treaties or customary international law, and national courts have not been highly receptive to international environmental law arguments, especially in horizontal litigation.[12] Corporations may nonetheless volunarily adhere to environmental standards (eg ISO 14000 series environmental standards) as a form of corporate self-regulation;[13] corporate social responsibility discussions also evidence an environmental dimension, illustrated by three of the ten principles of the non-binding UN Global Compact.[14]

V. SOURCES OF INTERNATIONAL ENVIRONMENTAL LAW

Since international environmental law is concerned with the application of general international law to environmental problems, it is not surprising that its sources include the traditional ones enumerated in Article 38 of the Statute of the International Court of Justice. However, two points should be highlighted in this context. The first is that treaties are by far and away the most significant source of binding rules of international environmental law. The adoption of consensus and 'package-deal' approaches to treaty negotiation have been particularly beneficial in the environmental context, permitting States to

---

[11] The European Court of Justice has held an environmental treaty to which the EC is a party to be directly effective in the member States 'so that any interested party is entitled to rely on those provisions before national courts': see *Syndicat professionnel coordination des pêcheurs de l'Etang de Berre et de la region* v *Electricité de France*, Case C-213/03, [2004] ECR I-7357, para 47. The provision in question was Article 6(3) of the 1980 Athens Protocol for the Protection of the Mediterranean Sea against Pollution from Land-Based Sources (now Article 6(1) of the amended Protocol, 1996).

[12] See Anderson and Galizzi, 2002.   [13] See Muchlinski, 2007.

[14] Principles 7 (precautionary principle); 8 (environmental responsibility) and 9 (environmentally friendly technologies): see http://www.unglobalcompact.org.

reach agreement on issues such as transboundary air pollution, climate change, and the conservation of biological diversity, even in the face of sharp differences of view about the very existence of the problems and about their solution. Sometimes environmental treaties are preceded by a non-binding instrument—for example, the UNEP Guidelines which preceded the 1989 Basel Convention and the UNEP and FAO Guidelines and Code which preceded the 1998 Rotterdam Convention on the Prior Informed Consent Procedure for Certain Hazardous Chemicals and Pesticides in International Trade. Indeed, the prevalence and importance of such 'soft law' is the other feature of international environmental law meriting closer attention below.[15]

A. TRADITIONAL SOURCES OF INTERNATIONAL ENVIRONMENTAL LAW

The vast bulk of environmental law is contained in treaty texts which are given dynamic force in part because they usually provide an institutional mechanism for their implementation (Churchill and Ulfstein, 2000). A common format is to provide for regular meetings of the Conference of the Parties (COP),[16] a number of subsidiary Committees reporting to the COP, most commonly comprising at least a Committee for Scientific and Technical Advice, and a Secretariat to provide support at and between meetings of these bodies. The dynamic force of many environmental treaties derives from the need to respond to changes in the physical environment regulated thereby and is most generally effected through the COP via a subsidiary scientific body. A significant number of environmental treaties adopt a framework approach to facilitate more rapid change than is generally the case through the normal (and time-consuming) process of treaty amendment. This approach enables the treaty to contain general principles and set forth the organizational structure of the treaty bodies (the framework), whilst further protocols and/or annexes embody specific standards and are generally subject to a more flexible amendment process.

An excellent example of a framework treaty is the regional 1979 ECE Convention on Long-Range Transboundary Air Pollution, now accompanied by eight protocols; the 1992 United Nations Framework Convention on Climate Change and the 1997 Kyoto Protocol is another good example at the global level. More flexible amendment procedures were pioneered by the International Maritime Organization with the use of the 'tacit amendment procedure' with its 1973/78 Convention for the Prevention of Pollution from Ships (MARPOL), to which there are now six annexes. Changes to the annexes come into force for *all* contracting parties within a minimum of 16 months of adoption of the change unless objection is lodged within a certain time period (10 months) by one-third of the contracting parties or by the number of contracting parties whose combined merchant shipping fleets represent at least 50% of world gross tonnage. A more recent and further example of this framework approach is the 1992 Convention for the Protection of the Environment of the North-East Atlantic (OSPAR), where the Convention is accompanied by five annexes and three appendices, with the latter embodying matters exclusively of a technical, scientific, or administrative nature. Both appendices and annexes are more readily amended

---

[15] On environmental treaty-making, see Redgwell, 2000; on the interaction of treaty and soft law, see Boyle, 1999; and on compliance with non-binding norms in the environment and natural resources field, see the case studies in the edited volume by Shelton, 2000.

[16] For recent analysis of the role of the COP, including in compliance procedures, see Brunee, 2002.

and modified than the convention text itself, thus permitting the convention more readily to grow and adapt to changing scientific and other data.[17]

Further flexibility is found in recent treaty texts that allow for differentiation in the implementation obligations for States taking on treaty commitments (French, 2000; Cullet, 2003). For example, Article 3(1) of the Climate Change Convention recognizes the common but differentiated responsibilities and respective capabilities of States in implementing the obligation to protect and preserve the climate system for the benefit of present and future generations (Rajamani, 2000). Developed country parties 'should take the lead in combating climate change and the adverse effects thereof'; indeed, under the Kyoto Protocol it is only Annex I parties (developed country parties) which are subject to specific targets and timetables for greenhouse gas emission reductions. In similar vein a number of the substantive treaty obligations of States party to the 1992 United Nations Convention on Biological Diversity are qualified by the words 'in accordance with [each contracting party's] particular conditions and capabilities'.

While the vast majority of the rights and obligations of States with respect to the environment derive from voluntarily assumed treaty obligations, it would be misleading to suggest that no customary international law norms govern State conduct. State practice has given rise to a number of customary law principles, buttressed by the process of treaty and customary law interaction noted in Chapter 4 above. Of these the most significant is the 'good neighbour' or 'no harm' principle, pursuant to which States have a duty to prevent, reduce, and control pollution and transboundary environmental harm. It has been enunciated in judicial decisions as well as soft law declarations. State practice further supports the customary law obligation to consult and to notify of potential transboundary harm. Other relevant principles of customary international law include the polluter pays principle, the principle of preventive action, and equitable utilization of shared resources. More controversial is the customary law status of the precautionary principle or approach (Birnie, Boyle, and Redgwell, 2009) and the principle of sustainable development *per se* (Lowe, 1999) and of its buttressing principles (eg, sustainable use; intergenerational equity; integration of the environment into economic and development projects; and common but differentiated responsibilities) (Paradell-Trius, 2000; French, 2005).

General principles of law are also of significance in the environmental context, though a distinction needs to be made between the general principles of law referred to in Article 38(1)(c) of the ICJ Statute, and general principles such as those found in the Stockholm and Rio Declarations in international environmental law. To the extent that the former embraces general principles found in national law, these are of limited utility in the international environmental context (though relied on in the seminal *Trail Smelter Arbitration*[18]). If Article 38(1)(c) includes general principles recognized at international law, then the scope is potentially significant, including the polluter pays principle, the precautionary prinicple and the principle of common but differentiated responsibilities. These operate to influence the interpretation of (but not override) treaty provisions, the application of custom, and influence judicial decisions. The reference to 'the concept of sustainable development' by the ICJ in the *Gabcikovo-Nagymaros* case[19] remains the best

[17] For further discussion of the legal implications of such flexible amendment procedures under OSPAR, see de la Fayette, 1999.

[18] See n 2 above.

[19] *Gabčíkovo-Nagymaros project (Hungary/Slovakia), Judgment, ICJ Reports 1997*, p 7.

known example of the influence an internationally recognized principle of international environmental law may wield.

Indeed, as this last example illustrates, although not a formal source of international law as such, judicial decisions provide important authoritative evidence of what the law is, with a growing number of judicial and arbitral awards of importance in the environmental field. These include judgments of the ICJ (eg *Gabcikovo-Nagymaros;*[20] the forthcoming *Pulp Mills*[21]); the PCA (eg *MOX;*[22] *Iron Rhine*[23]); ITLOS (eg *MOX*[24]); arbitral awards (eg *Trail Smelter;*[25] *Metalclad*[26]); and the decisions of human rights courts (eg *Fadeyeva*[27]).

B. SOFT LAW

In addition to the traditional sources of international law identified above, a variety of non-binding instruments such as codes of conduct, guidelines, resolutions, and declarations of principles, may be resorted to by States and non-State actors alike.[28] As discussed in Chapter 5 above, these are non-binding instruments non-compliance with which does not entail international responsibility. Soft law may be employed because its origins are not law-creating either because the body promulgating the 'law' does not have law-making authority (eg, an autonomous treaty supervisory body or an NGO) or because a law-making body chooses a non-binding instrument with which to embody a statement of particular principles (eg, States at the 1992 Rio Conference on Environment and Development adopting the binding 1992 Climate Change Convention and the non-binding 1992 Rio Declaration of Principles on Environment and Sustainable Development). International environmental law is a particularly fertile area for soft law norms, since it allows agreement on collective but non-binding action where, for example, the scientific evidence is inconclusive or the economic costs uncertain. It may, and not infrequently does, lead to 'hard' law, such as the UNEP Guidelines mentioned above.

VI. ENFORCEMENT OF INTERNATIONAL ENVIRONMENTAL LAW

A question of over-arching importance is what happens in the event of the breach of an environmental obligation?[29] Here the traditional rules regarding State responsibility, explored in more depth in Chapter 15, would apply. Yet these rules are of only

---

[20] Ibid.

[21] *Pulp Mills on the River Uruguay (Argentina v Uruguay)*, judgment of 20 April 2010, available at www. icj-cji.org.

[22] *MOX Plant Arbitration (Ireland v United Kingdom), Jurisdiction and Provisional Measures*, PCA, 16 June 2003.

[23] *Iron Rhine Arbitration (Belgium/Netherlands), PCA Award of 24 May 2005*, para 58.

[24] *MOX Plant Case (Ireland v United Kingdom)*, Case No 10, Provisional Measures, Order of 3 December 2001.

[25] See n 2 above.

[26] *Metalclad Corporation v United Mexican States* (ICSID Case No ARB(AF)/97/1), Award of 30 August 2000.

[27] *Fadeyeva v Russia*, no 55723/00, ECHR 2005-IV.

[28] See Chinkin and Boyle, 2007, and Shelton, 2000; on the interaction of treaty and soft law, see Boyle, 1999.

[29] See the contributions to the edited volume by Francioni and Scovazzi, 1991; Wetterstein, 1997; and Wolfrum, 1999.

limited assistance in the environmental field for two reasons. The first is the generally non-reciprocal character of international environmental obligations which render it difficult to meet the requirement of breach of an obligation owed to another State. Both the *Trail Smelter* Arbitration between the United States and Canada[30] and the *Gabčíkovo-Nagymaros Dam* dispute between Hungary and Slovakia[31] saw the application of traditional rules on State responsibility because of the bilateral character of the dispute and of the obligations thereunder. Had it proceeded to the merits, the ICJ case brought in 1974 against France by Australia and New Zealand regarding French atmospheric nuclear testing in the South Pacific would have likewise largely fit within this bilateral model.[32] But what of the example of a breach by a State of its obligation to conserve biological diversity, expressly acknowledged as 'the common concern of humankind'? A complainant State is required to show that the obligation is owed to it and (usually) that injury has resulted to it in order for standing requirements to be satisfied; there is no such thing (yet) under international law as an *actio popularis* whereby a State may bring an action on behalf of the international community.[33] There are glimmerings of such an approach in Articles 42 and 48 of the 2001 Articles on State Responsibility drafted by the International Law Commission, wherein the possibility exists for a State party to a multilateral treaty to complain of breach of a multilateral obligation by another State party[34] but the status of these provisions remains *de lege ferenda*.

There are several consequences of the inadequacies of traditional rules of State responsibility for the development of international environmental law. The first is a relative paucity of cases at the international level in which environmental matters have figured largely. Recourse to the dispute settlement under international environmental treaties is rare, a recent example being the recent invocation of the dispute settlement procedures of the 1982 LOSC and 1992 OSPAR Convention by Ireland against the United Kingdom in connection with radiological pollution from the MOX plant.[35] Moreover, few dispute settlement clauses in international environmental treaties provide for compulsory third-party settlement of inter-State claims (Brus, 1995). Sparse examples include the Ozone Layer Convention and the Montreal Protocol, and the Framework Convention on Climate Change (FCCC) and the Kyoto Protocol. A second consequence has been pressure further to develop the rules of State responsibility, including standing. Few environmental treaties address standing; rarer still is to provide for reciprocal standing for non-State actors. An oft-cited example is the 1974 Nordic Environmental Protection Convention, Article 3 of which addresses access to justice for non-State actors; the 1998 Aarhus Convention may well stimulate further developments in this area.[36]

---

[30] (1939) 33 *AJIL* 182 and (1941) 35 *AJIL* 684.

[31] See n 19 above.

[32] *Nuclear Tests (Australia v France), Interim Protection, Order of 22 June 1973, ICJ Reports 1973*, p 99; *Judgment, ICJ Report 1994*, p 253; *Nuclear Tests (New Zealand v France), Interim Protection, Order of 22 June 1973, ICJ Reports 1973*, p 135; *Judgment, ICJ Report 1994*, p 457.

[33] *South West Africa, Second Phase, Judgment, ICJ Reports 1966*, p 6.

[34] 2001 Articles on State Responsibility, Article 48; for analysis see Peel, 2001.

[35] For discussion of the international and EU law aspects of the proceedings, see Churchill and Scott, 2004.

[36] For analysis of the convention see Davies, 2002; on public participation see generally Ebbesson, 1997.

A third consequence is the development of alternatives to traditional dispute settlement techniques under specific treaty instruments directly to address the issue of non-
compliance with treaty obligations from both a facilitative and a coercive point of view. The
1987 Montreal Protocol is pioneering in this regard, establishing the first non-compliance
procedure in an environmental agreement. A handful of other treaty instruments have
established implementation and compliance procedures, including the 1997 Kyoto Protocol
to the 1992 Framework Convention on Climate Change, the 1989 Basel Convention on the
Transboundary Movement of Hazardous Wastes and their Disposal, the 2000 Cartagena
Protocol to the 1992 Convention on the Conservation of Biological Diversity, and the 1998
Aarhus Convention on Access to Information, Public Participation in Decision-Making,
and Access to Justice in Environmental Matters. These generally exist alongside traditional
dispute settlement clauses and are suspended in the event of the invocation of traditional
dispute settlement procedures (Fitzmaurice and Redgwell, 2000). Finally, a further consequence of the inadequacies of State responsibility in the environmental field is the development of liability regimes which side-step the necessity to rely on the route of inter-State
claims. As we will see, the development of specific liability instruments has been particularly marked in the field of activities with transboundary consequences (eg, nuclear activities, vessel source oil pollution, and hazardous waste movements) and in the protection of
common spaces (eg, liability arising from environmental emergencies in Antarctica under
the 2005 annex to the 1991 Environmental Protocol to the 1959 Antarctic Treaty, and the
responsibility and liability of seabed contractors for environmental damage in the 2000
regulations on prospecting and exploring for polymetallic modules promulgated by the
International Seabed Authority under the 1982 LOSC).

VII. SUBSTANTIVE INTERNATIONAL
ENVIRONMENTAL LAW

From the foregoing it will already be apparent that there exists a considerable body of international rules applicable to environmental protection. The breadth of regulatory activity is
enormous, ranging from liability and compensation for oil pollution damage through to
licensing regimes for the transboundary movement of hazardous waste and the listing of
sites important for wild birds or for the natural and cultural heritage. The purpose of this
section is to provide a flavour of the breadth and depth of international law pertaining to
the environment.

A. PROTECTION OF THE MARINE ENVIRONMENT[37]

The protection of the marine environment was one of the key issues at the 1972 Stockholm
Conference, and is clearly reflected in the flurry of law-making in this area which occurred
in the early 1970s in particular. The negotiation of the 1982 LOSC, which commenced in
1973, likewise had an influence upon (and was influenced by) these developments. Thus
Part XII of the resulting 1982 Convention—with its 46 Articles devoted to the marine

---

[37] For succinct treatment of the extensive law in this area, see Churchill and Lowe, 1999, Ch 15 and Birnie,
Boyle and Redgwell, 2009, Ch 7.

environment—implicitly acknowledges existing marine environment treaties in the areas of dumping at sea[38] and vessel source pollution in particular. Pollution of the oceans, and concerns about their limited absorption capacity, formed a key thrust of these 1970s lawmaking activities: both the global 1972 London (Dumping) Convention and the regional 1972 Oslo Dumping Convention date from this period, as does the 1973 Convention on the Prevention of Pollution from Ships (MARPOL 73/78). UNEP, established it will be recalled after the Stockholm Conference, undertook the establishment of regional seas programmes for which the 1976 Barcelona Convention for the Protection of the Mediterranean Sea Against Pollution, and subsequent protocols, formed the prototype for many other regional seas areas (only the Baltic, the North-east Atlantic/North Sea, Antarctic, and Arctic oceans, are regulated by regional instruments outside UNEP's programme). The Protocols to the Barcelona Convention range in subject matter from pollution caused by dumping, land-based sources, and seabed activities, to cooperation in emergencies, specially protected areas, and transboundary movement of hazardous waste. The convention was substantially revised in 1995 following the Rio Conference, the impact of which is observable in many other areas of regulatory activity where such 'second generation agreements' have been adopted.

Dumping is one area of regulatory activity where this progression is particularly marked. Initially, regional and global dumping conventions adopted the regulatory approach of listing prohibited, dangerous, and other substances, relying on nationally-implemented licensing schemes for their effectiveness. Coastal States exercised the jurisdiction afforded them under international law to do so: territoriality and nationality (of the vessel). There was no presumptive ban operating in respect of dumping at sea, with the regulatory approach essentially one of 'permitted unless prohibited'. Wastes were divided into three categories: Annex I, the 'black list', contained a list of substances prohibited from dumping; Annex II, the 'grey list', those substances the dumping of which required a prior special permit; for all other substances, Annex III (the 'white list') required a prior general permit. However, with the replacement of the 1972 Oslo Convention (and 1974 Paris Convention for the Prevention of Marine Pollution from Land-Based Sources) by the 1992 Convention on the Protection of the Marine Environment of the North-east Atlantic (OSPAR) and the negotiation of the 1996 Protocol to the 1972 London Convention, this philosophy has been replaced by a 'prohibited unless permitted' approach. Dumping is not permitted unless it falls within one of the permitted exceptions to a general ban on dumping. The list is quite restrictive, including bulky matter such a dredged material and sewage sludge and (at least for the moment) offshore installations. The precautionary approach is very much in evidence here, with a significant shift in the burden of proof to the polluter to demonstrate that dumping at sea will not have significant harmful consequences for the marine environment.

Vessel source pollution, though a relatively minor contributor to marine pollution, has nonetheless been subject to extensive international regulation following highly publicized oil spills such as the *Torrey Canyon* in 1967. MARPOL 73/78 adopts a framework approach in that six accompanying annexes embody the technical details of regulating oil discharges (Annex I), noxious liquids in bulk (Annex II), harmful packaged substances

---

[38] For analysis of the relationship between the 1982 LOSC and both prior and subsequent treaties regulating ocean dumping, see Redgwell, 2006a.

(Annex III), sewage (Annex IV), garbage (Annex V), and air pollution (Annex VI). Any State wishing to become a party to MARPOL 73/78 must also adopt Annexes I and II as a minimum. Annex I reflects a particular preoccupation with vessel-source oil pollution, focusing on limiting discharges of oil as part of routine tanker operations. It sets forth oil discharge and tanker design criteria[39] and requires coastal States to provide adequate reception facilities for oily residues. Some maritime areas have been designated as 'special areas' under MARPOL in which no discharge is permitted, including areas such as the North-west Atlantic Ocean and Mediterranean Sea areas, and the Antarctic Southern Ocean.

A key regulatory device under MARPOL is the use of standardized International Oil Pollution Prevention Certificates, the issuance of which is linked to regular surveying and inspection of vessels. This is supplemented by a requirement for tankers and other ships to carry an Oil Record Book itemizing all operations involving oil. In addition to the requirement that this record may be inspected by any other party to MARPOL, it is these documents which in certain circumstances coastal and port States are entitled to inspect under the 1982 LOSC, whether or not a party to MARPOL.[40] Coastal States' enforcement powers are also enhanced under the 1982 LOSC, including the power to investigate, inspect, and, in limited circumstances, to arrest vessels navigating in the Exclusive Economic Zone (EEZ) when a violation of applicable international rules and standards for the prevention, reduction, and control of pollution from vessels, eg, MARPOL 73/78, has occurred which threatens or causes environmental damage.[41] Thus MARPOL 73/78, like the other marine pollution conventions, relies on general public international law and the Law of the Sea Convention in particular for the exercise of legislative and enforcement jurisdiction. As Chapter 22 makes clear, the LOSC constitutes a significant innovation in the development of port State enforcement jurisdiction upon which the success of MARPOL 73/78 has largely rested. Improved exercise of flag State jurisdiction has likewise had beneficial impact on the number of pollution incidents at sea.

Apart from prompting the regulation of marine pollution through routine operational discharges at sea, the oil tanker catastrophes of the 1960s and 1970s in particular led to the development of separate liability conventions, the 1969 Convention on Civil Liability for Oil Pollution Damage (CLC) and the 1971 Convention on the Establishment of an International Fund for Compensation for Oil Pollution Damage (Fund Convention). These follow a pattern found in the nuclear civil liability conventions, which is to limit and channel liability. Risk is assumed by, and liability is channelled through, the shipowner, which is strictly liable for oil pollution damage as defined under the conventions. A monetary ceiling on liability is fixed, enabling the shipowner to obtain insurance cover in the market through P & I Clubs. If this ceiling is exceeded under the CLC, then the Fund Convention may provide a further source of compensation funds for claimants. The Fund is based on levies from oil-importing countries, thus spreading the risk between the shipowner and the risk-creating States. The advantage for claimants in States party to the CLC/Fund regime is the ability to obtain compensation swiftly without recourse to the courts in their own or another State. Both conventions were updated by Protocols in 1992 with an increase in

---

[39] Thus constituting the 'generally accepted international rules or standards' which coastal States may apply to third party shipping traversing the territorial sea fully in accordance with LOSC Article 21(2).
[40] Article 218 LOSC.   [41] Article 220, especially paras (3), (5), and (6).

the compensation limits (further increased in 2000 and 2003), an extension of geographic coverage (to incidents in the EEZ) and the inclusion of pollution prevention costs in the recoverable heads of damage. In 2001, a further convention was concluded on pollution damage from bunker fuel from ships, the International Convention on Civil Liability for Bunker Oil Pollution Damage. Modelled on the CLC, it entered into force in 2008.

Further responses to catastrophic oil spills are reflected in the 1969 Convention Relating to Intervention on the High Seas in Cases of Oil Pollution Casualties—which permits the coastal State to intervene beyond its territorial sea—and the 1990 Oil Pollution Preparedness and Response Convention which requires, *inter alia*, the preparation of emergency response plans for oil spill incidents. These were international legislative responses to the 1967 *Torrey Canyon* and 1989 *Exxon Valdez* oil spill emergencies respectively. In recognition of the fact that the threat to the marine environment from vessel-source pollution extends beyond petroleum, in 1973 the Intervention Convention was extended to apply to hazardous substances other than oil and, in 2000, the OPRC was extended by Protocol to cover hazardous and noxious substances.[42]

B. PROTECTION OF THE ATMOSPHERE

There are three principal areas of international regulatory activity in respect of protection of the atmosphere—transboundary air pollution, ozone depletion, and global warming. All share a transboundary or global dimension and in no case are the existing rules of customary law, including those on State responsibility, adequate to address the problem. In particular the persistence, scope, and intertemporal nature of environmental problems such as global warming necessitates global (preventative) action. A classic case for international regulation, it would seem. Yet in the case particularly of transboundary air pollution and of global warming, there was (and in the case of the latter, still is) scepticism regarding the existence and scope of the problem.

1. Transboundary air pollution[43]

The *Trail Smelter* arbitration referred to above was an early instance of an inter-State claim arising in respect of the harmful transboundary effects of air borne pollutants. Yet this case involved a single detectable source of air pollution (sulphur dioxide emissions from the smelter) causing quantified harm to health and property; today it would most likely be resolved through transnational litigation by access to municipal courts. What if the sources of air pollution are far more diffuse and its harmful effects upon the environment are widespread? These were the difficulties confronting States in negotiating the 1979 LRTAP Convention, added to which was the initial scepticism of some parties as to the very existence and nature of the problem. In fact it remains the only major regional agreement addressed to air pollution, a reflection both of the severity of the problem in Europe (Canada and the US are also parties) and the difficulty in achieving international regulation of an activity impacting on sovereign energy and other choices.

---

[42] The 1996 International Convention on Liability and Compensation for Damage in Connection with Carriage of Hazardous and Noxious Substances by Sea (HNS), also modelled on the CLC, has not yet entered into force.

[43] See generally Okowa, 2000.

The purpose of LRTAP is to prevent, reduce, and control transboundary air pollution from both new and existing sources. 'Air pollution' is defined in terms reminiscent of the marine pollution definition of the 1982 LOSC, and includes harm to living resources, ecosystems, and interference with amenities and legitimate uses of the environment. 'Long-range transboundary air pollution' is defined as adverse effects in the jurisdiction of one State resulting from emissions originating in the jurisdiction of another State yet the individual source of which cannot necessarily be distinguished. The framework character of LRTAP resulted in the absence of specific reduction targets in the treaty itself; rather, an environmental monitoring programme was first put in place to gather data to assess the extent of the problem, followed by the negotiation of specific protocols to reduce emissions of specific air pollutants. In this respect the LRTAP Convention is a good example of the interaction of monitoring and reporting obligations on the one hand and flexible treaty structures, easily adapted to changes in scientific knowledge, on the other. The framework approach of the convention has allowed a step-by-step approach by States allowing 'agreement' at the outset even where there is no consensus regarding the concrete steps to be taken to address a particular environmental problem. To date eight protocols on monitoring and on specific air pollutants with specific reduction targets and timetables[44] have been added to the initial framework convention, significantly expanding the scope of the parties' commitments. Although there are provisions on notification and consultation in cases of significant risk of transboundary pollution, LRTAP does not itself contain provisions on liability nor on compliance. But in 1994 a second sulphur protocol was adopted with a non-compliance procedure based on the experience of the 1987 Montreal Protocol to the Ozone Convention. In 1997 this procedure was subsumed within a broader Implementation Committee established, inter alia, to review compliance by Parties with the reporting obligations of the convention and any non-compliance with the protocols.[45]

2. Ozone depletion[46]

It was UNEP which in 1981 launched negotiations for the conclusion of a treaty to protect the ozone layer, culminating in the adoption of the 1985 Vienna Convention for the Protection of the Ozone Layer (Yoshida, 2001). Like LRTAP, the initial treaty contained little by way of substantive obligations, focusing rather on the need to assess the causes and effects of ozone depletion and cooperation in the exchange of relevant information and technology. This 'largely empty framework' treaty was a result of the divergent interests of States: the US, having taken steps for domestic reduction, was concerned to ensure a level playing field in respect of ozone-depleting substances regulation; developing States were concerned to ensure that any restraints on the use of such substances did not adversely affect industrial development and that if imposed, appropriate access to alternative technology would be assured; while the EC, where many producers were located, was concerned regarding the potential cost of steps to be taken and unconvinced of the scientific case for the harmful effects of the substances (Birnie, Boyle, and Redgwell, 2009).

---

[44] For texts see http://www.unece.org/env/lrtap.

[45] Decision 1997/2. Over a dozen States have been considered by the Implementation Committee for possible non-compliance. For the most recent available report see ECE/EB.AIR/2008/3, 21 December 2008.

[46] See, generally, Benedick, 1998; Yoshida, 2001; Anderson and Sarma, 2002 and http://www.ozone .unep.org.

The 1987 Montreal Protocol—like the 1997 Kyoto Protocol to the Climate Change Convention—radically altered this picture in several respects. In addition to introducing specific targets for the reduction and eventual elimination of ozone-depleting substances, subsequent adjustments or amendments of the Protocol have introduced financial (the Multilateral Fund) and technical incentives to encourage developing country adherence to the Protocol. Implementation and compliance is further secured through the establishment of a non-compliance procedure, the first mechanism of its kind but which is now found in a number of other agreements (see Part VI above). This is a form of 'soft enforcement' designed to address non-compliance by essentially self-implicating States through both facilitation (access to the Multilateral Fund, provision of technical assistance) and/or sanction (issuing of cautions and/or suspension of the Article 5 privilege of delay in implementation for which some 147 developing States are currently eligible). In fact compliance by developed States has been high, and it has been largely former Soviet and East European States which have experienced difficulties with full compliance largely owing to financial and technical constraints. Successive amendments to the Protocol have also set more stringent targets and timetables and added to the list of ozone-depleting substances such that recovery of the ozone layer, including the hole above Antarctica, is hoped for by the mid-twenty-first century.

3. Climate change[47]

It will be recalled that the 1992 UN Framework Convention on Climate Change was one of two treaties adopted at the Rio Conference. Negotiations followed upon recognition by the General Assembly that the atmosphere is 'the common concern of mankind' and the work of the Intergovernmental Panel on Climate Change (IPCC) in providing the scientific guidance necessary to regulate the emission of greenhouse gases on the international level.[48] The principal objective of the Convention is 'stabilization of greenhouse gas concentrations in the atmosphere at a level that would prevent dangerous anthropogenic interference with the climate system'. Although framework in character, the Convention contains specific commitments in Article 4 addressed to all parties and, additionally, specifically to developed country parties. All 194 parties have the obligation to produce inventories of greenhouse gas sources and sinks, to formulate national and, where appropriate, regional programmes to reduce global warming, to cooperate in preparing for adaptation to the impacts of climate change, and to promote scientific research. Since these obligations are addressed to developing as well as developed country parties, the convention qualifies these obligations by permitting parties to 'tak[e] into account their common but differentiated responsibilities and their specific national and regional development priorities'. No such qualification is made of the obligations for developed country parties and other parties (countries with economies in transition)—the 'Annex I' parties to the convention. For these States, Article 4 sets forth the obligation to develop national policies and measures to mitigate the adverse effects of climate change indicating that developed country parties

---

[47] On the negotiation of the convention see Bodansky, 1993; on the protocol see Freestone and Streck, 2005, and on the climate regime see Depledge and Yamin, 2004. For current status and text see http://www.unfccc.int.

[48] The Fourth Assessment Report (AR4) was released in 2007, comprising four volumes (reports of the three working groups and a synthesis report) available at http://www.ipcc.ch. AR5 is scheduled for 2014.

are to take the lead in modifying longer-term trends in anthropogenic emissions. Detailed reports on such policies are to be provided 'with the aim of returning individually or jointly to their 1990 levels...of carbon dioxide and other greenhouse gases not controlled by the Montreal Protocol'. It is also the responsibility of developed country parties to provide new and additional financial resources to meet the agreed full costs incurred by developing country parties in complying with their convention obligations. The financial mechanism under the convention is the Global Environmental Facility (GEF), administered jointly by the World Bank (as trustee), UNEP, and the UN Development Programme. The GEF is also the financial mechanism under the Biodiversity Convention.

Notwithstanding the obligations contained in Article 4, it was not until the negotiation of the 1997 Kyoto Protocol that developed country parties committed themselves to explicit, unambiguous targets and timetables for the reduction of the chief greenhouse gases and to the development of international mechanisms for ensuring the fulfilment of these commitments. The core obligation of the Protocol is contained in Article 3(1) which states that Annex I parties 'shall, individually or jointly, ensure that their aggregate anthropocentric carbon dioxide equivalent emissions' of specific greenhouse gases 'do not exceed their assigned amounts' and that overall emissions of such parties are reduced 'by at least 5 per cent below 1990 levels in the commitment period 2008–2012'. To ensure its effectiveness the Protocol could only enter into force when adhered to by 55 States including Annex I parties representing 55% of that group's 1990 carbon dioxide emissions. Annex I party participation was contingent on satisfactory elaboration of the three 'flexibility mechanisms' in the Protocol for achieving these targets and timetables, namely, joint implementation (projects between Annex I parties), the clean development mechanism (between Annex I and non-Annex I parties), and emissions trading. At COP 7 (2001) significant breakthrough had been achieved in realizing the details of implementation such that both Canada and Russia announced at the Johannesburg summit in 2002 that they would ratify the Protocol. The participation of both States was essential for the attainment of the entry into force threshold of the Protocol given the United States' stated determination to remain outside the Protocol. The Protocol duly entered into force on 16 February 2005,[49] leaving less than eight years remaining for Annex I parties to achieve the reductions mandated for the first commitment period (2008–12). The Protocol has a Compliance Committee, with both a facilitative branch and an enforcement branch, to facilitate, promote, and enforce compliance with the Protocol.[50]

At COP 13 in 2007 the Parties agreed the 'Bali Roadmap' with the aim of reaching agreement on a post-2012 governance framework by COP15/MOP5 to be held in Copenhagen at the end of 2009.[51] Two ad hoc working groups—on long-term cooperation action under the convention, and on further commitments of the Annex I parties to the protocol—prepared draft texts for consideration at Copenhagen. In the event a controverial non-binding 'Copenhagen Accord' was concluded by representatives of major economics and regions, which is not based on the working group drafts, and of which the

---

[49] It presently has 190 parties including the EC (but not the US).

[50] For discussion of the evolution of the mechanism and comparison with the Montreal Protocol non-compliance procedure, see Werksman, 1998; see also Fitzmaurice and Redgwell, 2001.

[51] On the legal implications of the possible outcomes, see Rajamani, 2009.

COP decision to which it is attached as an unofficial document 'took note'.[52] Mechanisms are to be developed to allow for other States to accede to the Accord and to submit their targets for mitigation by 31 January 2010, but this is purely for information; unlike the Kyoto Protocol, the Accord does not contain binding targets for emissions reduction but rather relies on this 'bottom up' approach of pledged reductions. The main achievement of the conference was political agreement on a 2 degree C target, on mitigation actions by both developed and major developing countries, and the pledge of significant finance for developing countries' adaptation and mitigation. The mandate of the two ad hoc working groups was also extended for a further year. Much remains to be fleshed out, including the establishment of the four bodies created in the Accord.[53]

C. NUCLEAR RISKS

The nuclear sector has been the subject of considerable regulatory activity at the international level.[54] Given that nuclear energy activities are ultrahazardous in character with potentially devastating transboundary implications, this degree of international regulatory activity is unsurprising. The first international agreements, at both global and regional level, were concerned with regulating liability and compensation for nuclear damage largely with a view to rendering a fledgling energy industry commercially viable. They also reflected the generally unsatisfactory nature of the general customary international law principles in respect of State responsibility discussed above, as well as the magnitude of the potential harm to humans and the environment.

At the regional level, the 1960 Paris Convention on Third Party Liability in the Field of Nuclear Energy and the 1963 Brussels Supplementary Convention, were adopted under the auspices of the Nuclear Energy Agency of the Organization for Economic Cooperation and Development (OECD). These are designed to elaborate and harmonize legislation relating to third party liability to ensure that compensation is paid for persons suffering nuclear damage, whilst at the same time ensuring that the development and use of nuclear energy remains commercially feasible. Channelling and limiting liability achieves both of these aims, with the nuclear operator initially liable, then the State of operation and, finally, all contracting parties. Financial limits for liability, which is strict, are set for each level. In 2004 amendments to the Paris/Brussels regime (not yet in force) were made which increase compensation levels, enhance operator liability, and enlarge their geographic scope. The definition of nuclear damage thereunder includes not only personal injury and damage to property, but also economic losses such as the cost of preventive measures and of measures to reinstate an impaired environment, which may constitute the major portion of the damage caused by a nuclear incident. However, there has not yet been a serious test of these provisions within Europe. The Chernobyl incident in 1986 did not fall under the Paris/Brussels regime since, as a non-OECD member, the Soviet Union was not a party to the convention (nor is the Russian Federation now) and the convention does not

[52] See Decision 2/CP.15.

[53] A 'REDD-plus' mechanism; a High-Level Panel under the COP to study the implementation of financing provisions; a Copenhagen Green Climate Fund; and a technology mechanism.

[54] For succinct overview, see Ghaleigh in Birnie, Boyle, and Redgwell, 2009, Ch 6. There have been three compliance cases to date, all under the enforcement branch, with respect to implementation of the protocol (Greece, Croatia, and Canada).

apply to incidents outside convention States. In 1988 a Joint Protocol was concluded which links this regional system with the similar global regime, the 1963 Vienna Convention on Civil Liability for Nuclear Damage, with a further 1997 Supplemental Convention (in force 2003) increasing the amount of compensation available for nuclear damage.

These global instruments have been concluded under the auspices of the International Atomic Energy Agency (IAEA), a UN body which was established in 1957 to facilitate the peaceful development of nuclear energy and adherence to non-proliferation safe-guards. Following the Chernobyl accident in 1986, the IAEA concluded two further inter-national treaties addressed to early notification (1986 Convention on Early Notification of a Nuclear Accident or Radiological Emergency) and to assistance in the event of an international nuclear incident (1986 Convention on Assistance in the Case of a Nuclear Accident or Radiological Emergency). The former embraces in treaty form the customary law obligation to notify in the event of serious transboundary harm. In more preventive vein, a further IAEA convention, the 1994 Convention on Nuclear Safety, is designed to ensure the safe operation of land-based nuclear power plants. Safety and security issues form an increasingly important area of the IAEA's activities with the object, *inter alia*, of protecting humans and the environment from harmful radiation exposure. In 1997 a further Joint Convention on the Safety of Spent Fuel and Radioactive Waste Management was concluded, modelled on the 1994 Convention, to ensure high safety standards and the prevention of accidents in the disposal of nuclear waste. In many respects these recent developments of both the OECD and IAEA regimes demonstrate parallels with the regula-tion of oil pollution liability: preventive concern to ensure that the activity is carried out to minimize or avert pollution consequences; emergency response and notification systems; and a liability regime which increasingly acknowledges the environmental costs of pre-vention and of reinstatement.

D. OTHER HAZARDOUS SUBSTANCES AND ACTIVITIES[55]

Apart from the nuclear sector there has also been considerable regulation of other haz-ardous activities and substances, focusing on environmentally sound management and regulation of the transboundary movement of such substances. Four instruments are of particular importance in this area, three of which are of relatively recent origin. The 1989 Basel Convention on the Transboundary Movement of Hazardous Wastes and their Disposal[56] was the first to occupy the field, and was the international response to 'toxic traders' seeking to avoid the increasingly higher costs of hazardous waste disposal in devel-oped countries through cheaper disposal in developing and East European countries. It has had an influence on the scope and application of two other instruments with which it is closely linked, namely, the 1998 Rotterdam Convention on Prior Informed Consent Procedure for Certain Hazardous Chemicals and Pesticides in International Trade and the 2001 Stockholm Convention on Persistent Organic Pollutants. Together these three instruments are intended to provide for the environmentally sound management of

[55] See, generally, Pallemaerts, 2003; Wirth, 2007.

[56] Regional regulation is found in the 1991 Bamako Convention on the Import into Africa and the Control of Transboundary Movement and Management of Hazardous Wastes within Africa and in Protocols to the Regional Seas Agreements discussed in Section VII A above.

hazardous chemicals throughout their life-cycle. Indeed, pursuant to synchronized synergies decisions by each treaty body, cooperation has been enhanced through a UNEP-facilitated synergies oversight team (SOT) mandated, inter alia, with preparing the first trilateral extraordinary meeting of the parties to the three conventions to be held in 2010. The fourth instrument, the 2000 Cartagena Protocol to the 1992 Biodiversity Convention, is addressed to the transboundary movement of living modified organisms, on the hazardous character of which there is as yet no international consensus. Further linkages between these instruments is provided by UNEP, as indicated, which functions as the secretariat for each of the four instruments (jointly with the Food and Agriculture Organization (FAO) in the case of the Rotterdam Convention).

1. 1989 Basel Convention on the Transboundary Movement of Hazardous Wastes and their Disposal[57]

The Basel Convention has achieved widespread adherence with 172 parties at present, including significant developing country participation which was facilitated by the early establishment of a Trust Fund and a Technical Cooperation Fund. It is concerned both with regulating the transboundary movement of hazardous waste and ensuring sound environmental management in respect of its disposal. This is reflected in the annexes to the convention which address not only the categories of waste controlled (Annex I) or requiring special consideration (Annex II) but seeks to standardize the definition of hazardous characteristics (Annex III), regulate disposal operations (Annex IV), and ensure adequate information is provided about hazardous characteristics, etc (Annex V). There is also provision for arbitration (Annex VI) and, concluded in 1999 but not yet in force, a Protocol on Liability and Compensation for Damage (including environmental damage). The convention affirms the sovereign right of States to prohibit imports of hazardous waste and ensures the corresponding export prohibition will be respected by other States parties. Where transboundary movement does take place it must be grounded in the prior consent of the importing State (and any transit States), with both importing and exporting States obliged to ensure that waste is managed in an environmentally sound manner. Trade with non-parties is prohibited; moreover hazardous waste disposal from OECD to non-OECD countries is also now prohibited under the convention. This move to prohibition is characteristic of other pollution treaties, most notably in the case of dumping at sea under both the global 1996 London Protocol and under the regional 1992 Convention for the Protection of the Marine Environment of the Northeast Atlantic. These treaties also share with the Basel Convention (and with the Stockholm Convention) an increasing focus on sound environmental management seeking to eliminate waste generation at source through best environmental practices and available techniques, signalling a shift in emphasis from remediation to prevention. The Basel Convention parties are also increasingly focused on the effective implementation and enforcement of the regulatory framework established over the decade of the 1990s. The convention joins an increasing number of environmental treaties to address not only the liability of non-State actors and compensation for, inter alia, environmental damage (the 1999 Protocol), but also compliance by States with their convention obligations. In 2002 the Basel Convention established a compliance mechanism to facilitate early detection of implementation and compliance

---

[57] For a thorough analysis see Kummer, 2000.

problems such as illegal trafficking or meeting reporting obligations, a move possible only through the establishment of concrete norms and standards against which to benchmark State compliance and the political will of the parties to achieve more effective implementation of its provisions.[58]

2. 1998 Rotterdam Convention on Prior Informed Consent and the 2001 Stockholm Convention on Persistent Organic Pollutants[59]

The Rotterdam and Stockholm Conventions arose from Chapter 19 of Agenda 21 which highlighted the regulatory gap in respect of substances that are 'toxic, persistent and bio-accumulative and whose use cannot be controlled'. Like the Basel Convention, soft law guidance in the form of UNEP/FAO Guidelines preceded their negotiation, with both instruments fairly rapidly entering into force with relatively widespread adherence by States. The Rotterdam Convention was applied provisionally from its conclusion in 1998 until its entry into force on 24 February 2004, and currently has 131 parties. It establishes a prior informed consent regime in respect of the importation of toxic substances, many of which are also subject to the Stockholm Convention. It does not ban outright the import/export of hazardous chemicals and pesticides but rather subjects them to a regime of the prior informed consent of the importing party before export of a banned or severely restricted chemical or severely hazardous pesticide to which the convention applies may take place between parties. These are listed in Annex III of the convention, which provides a mechanism for amending the list of substances through the Conference of the Parties. Ultimately of course the convention relies on exchange of information among parties about potentially hazardous chemicals that may be exported and imported and requires national decision-making processes to be established regarding import and compliance by exporters with these decisions. The 2001 Stockholm Convention entered into force on 17 May 2004 and presently has 168 parties. It initially addressed environmentally sound management of a so-called 'dirty dozen' of toxic substances, to which a further nine chemicals were added at COP4 in 2009. The fundamental objective is to protect human health and the environment from persistent organic pollutants (POPs), which remain intact in the environment for long periods, becoming widely distributed geographically, and accumulate in the fatty tissues of living organisms thus posing a toxic threat both to humans and to wildlife. The Stockholm Convention seeks to eliminate or reduce the release of POPs into the environment through controls over the production or use of intentionally produced POPs (ie, industrial chemicals and pesticides), management and reduction of stockpiles, and minimization and elimination of unintentionally produced POPs (eg, industrial by-products such as dioxins and furans). Unlike the PIC Convention, POPs explicitly relies on a precautionary approach (Article 1).

3. 2000 Cartagena Protocol on Living Modified Organisms[60]

The Cartagena Protocol on Living Modified Organisms (LMOs) to the 1992 Convention on Biological Diversity was concluded in 2000 and entered into force on 11 September 2003. It presently has 157 parties. The focus of the Protocol is upon the transboundary

---

[58] For reports of the seven sessions of the Compliance Committee to date, see http://www.basel.int/legalmatters/compcommitee.
[59] See further http://www.pic.int and http://chm.pops.int, respectively.
[60] See further Redgwell, 2006b; McKenzie et al, 2003; and http://www.cbd.int/biosafety.

movement of LMOs which may have adverse effects on biological diversity and human health. 'LMO' is defined as 'any living organism that possesses a novel combination of genetic material obtained through the use of modern biotechnology'. In fact the Protocol addresses two general categories of LMO: (i) those intended for release into the environment (eg, seeds for cultivation or animal breeding stock); and (ii) those intended for use in food or feed, or for processing (eg, corn, cotton, and soy). The latter was of particular concern to exporters of genetically modified crops (including the United States, though not yet a party to the Protocol), and are subject to a less onerous regime (Article 11) than that applicable to LMOs intended for direct release into the environment (Articles 7–10). The chief regulatory technique employed under the Protocol is the 'advanced informed agreement' (AIA) procedure, which is designed to ensure that contracting parties are provided with the information necessary to make informed decisions before agreeing to the import of LMOs into their territory. AIA marks the Protocol out from the 'prior informed consent' procedures of the 1989 Basel and 1998 Rotterdam Conventions, which are based on prior multilateral agreement on the hazardous substances to be regulated and which are set out in annexes. No such agreement exists regarding LMOs; in consequence, a marked feature of the Protocol is its overtly precautionary approach, with Article 1 making express reference to the precautionary approach contained in Principle 15 of the 1992 Rio Declaration. To facilitate information exchange and to assist with national implementation, a Biosafety Clearing-House has been established. Facilitative financing is also available through the Global Environmental Facility (the financial mechanism for the parent CBD as well). A Compliance Committee, expressly contemplated under the Protocol to address problems of implementation and non-compliance, was established at the first meeting of the parties, and is still at the stage of refining its rules of procedure. It has not yet considered specific instances of non-compliance (a 2009 submission by an NGO regarding a party was held inadmissible) although it has reviewed compliance in general terms based on national reports submitted by the parties after four years' operation of the Protocol. In common with similar mechanisms in other environmental treaties, it is intended to be principally facilitative and non-adversarial in function, with more coercive measures (eg, the issuing of cautions and the publication of non-compliance details in the Biosafety Clearing-House) left to the decision of the Meeting of the Parties under the Protocol.

E. CONSERVATION OF NATURE

The evolution of treaties for the protection of species and habitat reflects in many respects the evolution of international environmental law itself. Some of the earliest treaties in the environmental field were concerned with the incidental regulation of wildlife, though their primary purpose was economic, eg, the 1902 Paris Convention on the Protection of Birds Useful to Agriculture and the 1911 Treaty of Washington on the Protection of Fur Seals. One of the first cases to consider (and reject) the concept of coastal State stewardship over common property resources on the adjacent high seas likewise concerned fur seals, the 1898 *Bering Fur Seals Fisheries Arbitration*.[61] There are now dozens of bilateral, regional,[62]

---

[61] (1893) *Moore's International Arbitrations* 755 (*Great Britain* v *US*).
[62] In particular the 1968 African Convention on the Conservation of Nature and Natural Resources (revised 2003, not yet in force), the 1979 Council of Europe Convention on the Conservation of European Wildlife and Natural Habitats (Berne Convention).

and multilateral treaties concerned with species and habitat protection, ranging from the protection of seals, bears, whales, and turtles, to holistic environmental regulation of the Antarctic environment.[63] For present purposes it is not intended exhaustively to scrutinize the detailed legal mosaic of species and habitat regulation at the bilateral and regional levels, but rather to focus upon the 'big five' of multilateral species and habitat treaties, namely, the 1971 Ramsar Convention on Wetlands of International Importance Especially As Waterfowl Habitat (Ramsar Convention); the 1972 UNESCO Convention Concerning the Protection of the World Cultural and Natural Heritage (WHC); the 1973 Convention on International Trade in Endangered Species of Wild Fauna and Flora (CITES); the 1979 Bonn Convention on the Conservation of Migratory Species of Wild Animals (Bonn Convention); and the 1992 Convention on the Conservation of Biological Diversity (CBD) (see Bowman, Davies, and Redgwell, 2010).

1. 1971 Convention on Wetlands of International Importance (Ramsar Convention)[64]

The Ramsar Convention is the only global environmental treaty addressed to a particular ecosystem, the conservation and wise use of wetlands primarily as habitat for wildbirds. The mission of the convention has broadened over time, so that today 'wise use' is interpreted to mean 'sustainable use' and the concept of wetlands now embraces fish as well as bird species and habitat. Integration of the conservation of wetland biodiversity with sustainable development, considered as synonymous with the convention's concept of 'wise use', is at the heart of the current strategic plan for the convention. There are currently 159 contracting parties to the Ramsar Convention, with 1,880 sites designated for the List of Wetlands of International Importance covering a total surface area of nearly 185 million hectares (larger than the combined surface area of France, Germany, and Switzerland).

Much has been accomplished under a convention of initially rather unpromising beginnings. It is still an extraordinarily brief instrument of only 13 articles, but these have been subject to extensive elaboration through the Guidelines issued by the Regular Meetings of the COP. The chief regulatory device of the convention is the listing of sites for protection that is then afforded such sites under national laws. Each contracting party is required to designate 'suitable wetlands' within its territory for inclusion on the List of Wetlands of International Importance, the 'flagship' of the convention. Indeed, a State is not considered a full party to the convention unless and until a site has been designated (in contrast with the World Heritage Convention, for example). So long as the proposed site fulfils one of the Criteria for Identifying Wetlands of International Importance and has been designated by the appropriate national authority it will be added to the list. Contracting parties are required to submit triennial reports on the implementation of the treaty to the contracting parties, thus providing an opportunity for review of national implementation measures.

Once designated, Ramsar sites are to be protected under national law but also acquire recognition under international law as being significant for the international community as a whole. Failure to promote the conservation of wetlands on the list and their wise use

---

[63] On which see Rothwell, 1996, Ch 9; and Redgwell, 1994.
[64] See http://www.ramsar.org; Ramsar Convention Secretariat, 2007. *Ramsar handbooks for the wise use of wetlands*, 3rd edn; and Ch 13 in Bowman, Davies, and Redgwell, 2010.

may lead to listing on the 'Montreux Record of Ramsar sites requiring priority attention', established in 1990, and which highlights threats to designated sites. The ultimate sanction is de-listing because of the irremediable loss of the values which led to Ramsar listing in the first instance. This has never occurred; nor have any sites been deleted owing to 'urgent national interests' as provided for in the convention.[65] The only instance of removal was of three sites designated before the development of the Criteria which they then failed to meet, and were replaced with other designations.

Sites requiring priority attention may not formally be added to the Record without the consent of the State concerned. There are currently 50 sites which have been added to the Montreux Record with the consent of the States concerned.[66] An additional and facilitative feature of the Ramsar Convention is the awareness that failure to conserve wetlands may result from lack of capacity. Thus, a Small Grants Fund for Wetland Conservation and Wise Use was also established in 1990 with the express purpose of facilitating compliance, along with other forms of technical assistance, and the Ramsar Advisory Mission was established as a technical assistance mechanism to provide further advice regarding the problems or threats which have caused Montreux listing to be contemplated. Site visits are an integral part of this mechanism and, as with the Montreux listing procedure itself, are conditional upon the agreement of the contracting party concerned. For sites covered by both Ramsar and the World Heritage Convention, such visits may be requested and carried out jointly. For example, Ichkeul National Park in Tunisia is on both the Ramsar Montreux Record and the WHC Heritage in Danger List owing to the impact of dam projects on the river flowing into Ichkeul.[67] Conservation efforts may be assisted by listing on the Montreux Record with consequent access to technical assistance and facilitative financing under the Convention and elsewhere: the listing of the Azraq Oasis in Jordan assisted in obtaining funding from the Global Environmental Facility and of the Austrian Donau-March-Auen in obtaining European Commission funding.

2. The World Heritage Convention[68]

The World Heritage Convention (WHC) was adopted on 16 November 1972 under UNESCO auspices, mere months after the 1972 Stockholm Conference. There are presently 186 States party to the convention. Participation by developing States in particular is enhanced through the World Heritage Fund, a trust fund constituted by compulsory and voluntary contributions made by States parties to the convention. The purpose of the WHC is the identification, protection, conservation, presentation, and transmission to future generations of the cultural and natural heritage. The WHC is thus unusual in its express linkage of nature conservation and preservation of cultural properties, seeking

---

[65] Article 2.5 provides that in the urgent national interest the boundaries of a site may be deleted or restricted. Parties have invoked the 'urgent national interest' clause to *restrict* the boundaries of a Ramsar site on three occasions only: Belgium in the 1980s, Australia in 1997 (though not ultimately implemented) and Germany in 2000. Further guidance on implementation of Article 2.5 is found in Resolution VIII.20 (2002).

[66] See http://www.ramsar.org; and Ch 13 in Bowman, Davies and Redgwell, 2010.

[67] In fact, the Park is one of a few sites which are protected by listing under three agreements: Ramsar (1980), WHC (1979), and Biosphere Reserve (1977). Details of listings can be found on the Ramsar website: http://www.ramsar.org.

[68] For commentary on the Convention, see Francioni with Lenzerini, 2008.

to achieve a balance between the two. Protection of designated natural and cultural heritage is conferred by inscription on the World Heritage List of natural and cultural sites satisfying the inscription criteria under the convention. At present there are 890 properties on the list, 689 cultural, 176 natural, and 25 mixed properties in 148 States parties. However, unlike under the Ramsar Convention, it is not necessary to have a site listed to become a full participating party to the WHC.[69] The effectiveness of the convention is thus dependent upon States parties offering up sites for designation since UNESCO has no independent listing power. Independent evaluation of proposed sites is carried out by two advisory bodies, the International Council on Monuments and Sites (ICOMOS) in respect of cultural properties and the World Conservation Union (IUCN) in respect of natural properties. The criteria for inscription on the World Heritage List are set forth in *Operational Guidelines* which are revised regularly by one of the convention bodies, the World Heritage Committee, in order to reflect changes in the concept of world heritage.

Listing applications must include details of how the site is managed and protected under national legislation. Subsequent protection is thus a task for national law, subject to the general treaty obligation already indicated to protect and preserve such heritage. The convention makes clear that *international* protection of the world cultural and natural heritage is limited to 'the establishment of a system of international cooperation and assistance designed to support States parties to the convention in their efforts to conserve and identify that heritage'. The chief regulatory tools at the disposal of the convention organs for the achievement of such international protection are monitoring entry to and departure from listed status of sites of world natural and/or cultural heritage based on the data supplied by States parties in their national inventory and implementation reports and providing international assistance, including access to the resources of the World Heritage Fund.

In addition to stipulating the criteria for listing, published in the *Operational Guidelines*, the World Heritage Committee is also responsible for establishing the 'List of World Heritage in Danger', the latter designation signalling that major operations are necessary to conserve the site and for which assistance has been requested under the convention. The ultimate consequence of a State's failure to fulfil its obligations under the convention is deletion from the World Heritage List. Unlike Ramsar, there have been two deletions from the World Heritage List: the Arabian Oryx Sanctuary in Oman (2007) and the Dresden Elbe Valley in Germany (2009). Danger listing may be perceived either as a form of 'name and shame' or 'dishonour', or as a means of highlighting for the international community difficulties in conserving heritage values and seeking assistance in addressing them. Whatever the perception, the clear expectation upon danger listing is that steps will be taken by the State party concerned to reduce and/or eliminate the danger posed to the world cultural and natural heritage, often in consultation with the key stakeholders in the site and activities related thereto. At present there are thirty-one properties on the danger list.

3. 1973 Convention on International Trade in Endangered Species[70]

Unlike the other treaties considered here, the direct purpose of the 1973 Convention on International Trade in Endangered Species (CITES) is not the protection of animal and

---

[69] For a full list by country and property, see http://whc.unesco.org.
[70] See http://www.cites.org; and Ch 15 in Bowman, Davies, and Redgwell, 2010.

plant species or habitat *per se*. Rather, its objective is to control or prohibit trade in species or their products where those species are in danger of extinction. It addresses one of the reasons for species decline apart from loss of habitat, which is increased exploitation to which commercial trade is a contributory factor. Over 5,000 animal species 'from leeches to lions' and 25,000 plant species 'from pine trees to pitcher plants' are now covered in the 175 States presently parties to CITES.

The convention controls the import and export of endangered species and products on a global scale through a permitting system operated by designated national authorities, a procedure familiar from the discussion of the dumping conventions above. Three appendices are used. Appendix I forbids trade in the listed species which are in danger of extinction, subject to some exceptions which are controlled by export, re-export, and import permits as required. Appendix II permits trade subject to certain restrictions in the species listed therein which are not threatened with extinction but may become so if trade is not controlled and monitored. Here only export (or re-export) permits apply. Appendix III encompasses species covered by national regulation where a State seeks international cooperation in controlling (external) trade, in which case an export permit is required. As may be expected, much of the controversy surrounding CITES has focused on listing (and de-listing) in the Appendices, with the listing of the African elephant particularly contentious. For a short time the African elephant was on Appendix I, but the adverse socio-economic consequences for Range States led to a partial relaxation in the ban in an attempt to seek a compromise between wildlife protection and human development. Populations in Botswana, Namibia, South Africa and Zimbabwe are presently on Appendix II, with one-off sales of existing ivory stocks permitted in 1997 and 2007 (following the establishment of baseline data on poaching and wild populations).

In common with the other treaties examined here, the effectiveness of CITES is dependent on national implementation. Each party is required to establish at least one Management Authority and Scientific Authority to implement the permitting scheme, while the CITES Secretariat is responsible for monitoring the overall operation of the Treaty and facilitating exchange of information obtained through performance of States' monitoring and (annual) reporting obligations. NGOs also play a significant role under CITES in monitoring trade, such as the Wildlife Trade Monitoring Unit and IUCN/WWF's TRAFFIC (Trade Records Analysis of Flora and Fauna in Commerce). CITES' compliance review process is based on infractions reports by the Secretariat to the COP with the effective sanction for non-compliance being suspension of trade in specimens of CITES-listed species with the non-complying party. Presently there are 24 States subject to a recommendation to suspend trade in certain species, including four non-Parties (Bahrain, Haiti, Iraq, and Tajikistan). In practice this has served as a potent tool for ensuring proper national implementation of CITES' obligations to enact legislation, develop work plans, control legal/illegal trade, and/or improve the basis for government decision-making (Yeater and Vasquez, 2001).

4. 1979 Convention on the Conservation of Migratory Species[71]

The Convention on the Conservation of Migratory Species (Bonn Convention) is not quite a pygmy amongst the giants of the other 'big five' species and habitat treaties, but it

---

[71] See, generally, http://www.cms.int and Ch 16 in Bowman, Davies, and Redgwell, 2010.

certainly has the lowest profile. This is in part due to its relatively slow start; however, today there are 112 parties, of whom about half are developing countries. Activity under the convention was also hampered by the failure of many States parties to pay their contributions and expenses, which led to the Bonn Secretariat being chronically short-staffed and underfunded. Nonetheless the Bonn Convention has achieved some modest success in its primary objective, which is to conserve habitat and protect migratory species threatened with extinction. The need for such regulatory action was highlighted in the Stockholm Action Plan in 1972, offering an holistic approach to protection of both land-based and marine migratory species not readily afforded by other international instruments. The two techniques employed under the convention are first to impose obligations on Range States to protect migratory species through restoration of habitat and removing obstacles to migration of species listed in Appendix I as endangered throughout all or a significant portion of their range. Taking of such species must be prohibited under domestic law. Secondly, the convention provides for the conclusion of conservation 'AGREEMENTS' (including Memoranda of Understanding) between Range States for the conservation and management of migratory species listed in Appendix II as having 'unfavourable conservation status' requiring international agreement,[72] or at least which would benefit significantly from international cooperation. The Bonn Convention thus has a framework character, encouraging Range States to conclude regional or global AGREEMENTS in respect of Appendix II species. In practice it is possible for dual-listing of species under the Bonn Convention and for species also to be subject to protection under other existing international agreements (marine mammals in particular fall into this category). Thus in concluding AGREEMENTS parties to the Bonn Convention are to ensure that rights and obligations under other treaties are not affected.

5. 1992 United Nations Convention on Biological Diversity[73]

Notwithstanding the extent of international environmental regulation of species and habitat protection outlined above, a gap persisted: no global instrument regulated the interaction of species and habitat, and of ecosystems, in a holistic rather than a piecemeal manner.[74] The closest perhaps is the regional Convention on the Regulation of Antarctic Marine Living Resources which expressly adopts an ecosystem approach but this applies only to the southern ocean and, at the time of the adoption of the CBD in 1992, had yet successfully to operationalize its novel ecosystem approach. UNEP perceived this 'biodiversity gap' and initiated negotiations to conclude a Convention on Biological Diversity (CBD) in time for signature at Rio. This was duly accomplished, and the convention entered swiftly into force a mere 18 months later.[75] Today it has virtually universal support with 193 States parties (including the EC and all of its member States). This includes significant developing country participation, crucial to the effectiveness of the convention given that the most biologically rich parts of the planet are located within developing equatorial

---

[72] For an example of such international cooperation see the 1991 Agreement on the Conservation of Small Cetaceans of the Baltic and North Seas (ASCOBANS). For a full list of the Agreements and Memoranda of Understanding concluded within the framework of the Bonn Agreement see http://www.cms.int.

[73] See, generally, http://www.cbd.int; Ch 17 in Bowman, Davies, and Redgwell, 2010; and the CBD Handbook, 3rd edn, available at http://www.cbd.int/handbook.

[74] For contributions placing the CBD in its broader context, see Bowman and Redgwell, 1996.

[75] For discussion of the 2000 Cartagena Protocol to the CBD, see Section VII D.3 above.

States. Participation is facilitated through funding (the GEF is the funding mechanism for the CBD) and differentiation of implementation obligations through 'according to respective capabilities' language. The convention also provides a framework for national regulation of access to biological resources ('bioprospecting') on mutually agreed terms and benefit-sharing where such resources are exploited for commercial benefit. The role of indigenous peoples' knowledge and the application of traditional intellectual property rights principles remain areas of acute controversy under the convention though without impairing developing country participation. Here it is developed States, in particular the United States, which expressed concerns regarding the intellectual property and technology transfer provisions of the convention (Articles 15 and 16) and has remained outside the convention regime.

In its role as 'biodiversity gap-filler' the CBD defines biodiversity broadly to encompass the variability among living organisms from all sources, including, *inter alia*, terrestrial, marine, and other aquatic ecosystems and the ecological complexes of which they are part. The CBD's objectives are: the conservation of biological diversity; sustainable use of its components; and fair and equitable sharing of the benefits arising out of the utilization of genetic resources, including by appropriate access to genetic resources; transfer of relevant technologies, taking into account all rights over those resources; and funding. Each is addressed in further detail in the body of the CBD. Significant reliance is placed upon national measures for implementation, in accordance with each State's particular conditions and capabilities. It is thus up to individual contracting parties to determine the manner of implementation of their obligations, subject of course to scrutiny of national implementation by the COP through the reporting requirements of the convention. Concrete obligations are few and far between in the convention, a reflection both of the resistance to targets, lists, and the identification of species and sites for protection (though some States such as France preferred to adopt the listing model of the WHC for the CBD) and of the realization that there already exist a number of conventions with concrete obligations in respect of species and habitat such as Ramsar and the WHC. Indeed, cooperation with other closely linked treaties regimes has been facilitated by the conclusion of memoranda of understanding between secretariats. In addition, the CBD COP and its subsidiary organs have continued to supplement the treaty text principally through seven thematic work programmes comprising: marine and coastal biodiversity; mountain biodiversity; agricultural biodiversity; forest biodiversity; inland waters biodiversity; dry and sub-humid lands biodiversity; and island biodiversity. These are buttressed by a number of cross-cutting issues such as access to genetic resources and benefit sharing, alien species, biodiversity and tourism, and sustainable use of biodiversity. As discussed above, the 2000 Cartegena Protocol addresses one of the issues outstanding from Rio, namely, the impact upon biological diversity of the transboundary movement of living modified organisms.

The CBD constitutes an important milestone in its preambular recognition of the intrinsic value of biodiversity and of the conservation of biodiversity as a 'common concern of humankind'. However, it should be observed that this falls far short of any internationalization of biological resources either in their ownership or in their control—common concern is thus not akin to the 'common heritage of mankind' concept applicable to the resources of the deep seabed. Indeed, there is an inherent tension in the CBD in that the preamble also reaffirms States' permanent sovereignty over their natural resources. Linkage between these concepts is found in the responsibility of States for conserving their biological diversity and for using their biological resources in a sustainable manner (Glowka, 1994). Permanent sovereignty is thus responsible sovereignty under the CBD, a theme which pervades many of the instruments discussed above.

F. CONSERVATION OF MARINE LIVING RESOURCES

Regulation of marine living resources was one of the first areas of international environmental regulatory activity, stimulated by the need to regulate common property resources of significant economic value such as seals, whales, and fish stocks. Of course in the nineteenth and early twentieth centuries, most coastal States claimed only a 3 mile territorial sea with the seas beyond regarded as high seas open to exploitation of the resources therein. The Bering Fur Sea Arbitration established that adjacent coastal States had no legal interest in the protection of living resources beyond their initial belt of territorial sea. Today of course the picture is rather different, particularly with the development of the 200 mile Exclusive Economic Zone which accords coastal States exclusive rights over the living resources of this zone (see Ch 22, Sections V C; VII B.1). International regulation of marine living resources tends to focus on areas beyond national jurisdiction—high seas fisheries for example—and/or fish stocks which are straddling or highly migratory, spending at least part of their life-cycle beyond coastal State zones. In 1995 the Straddling Stocks Agreement was concluded to address this problem, supplementing not only the 1982 LOSC but also the myriad regional fisheries organizations (RFOs) regulating such stocks (see Ch 22, Section VII B.2–3). Of particular note in the latter context is the North Atlantic Fisheries Convention and the 1980 Convention on the Regulation of Antarctic Marine Living Resources (CCAMLR) with its ecosystem approach.

The approach of most fisheries treaties is to establish a fixed quota (a total allowable catch) for particular stocks, regulate fishing methods (eg, stipulated mesh size, open and close fishing seasons, and/or a prohibition of certain methods such as drift or purse seine nets) and to require monitoring and reporting obligations to be observed. Some form of inspection system is also common, as is the establishment of a scientific body to assess catch data and generally to advise on sustainable levels of fishing activity. In the Antarctic context the determination of permissible fishing effort is related not only to an analysis of the individual stocks but also of the interaction between predator and prey, in order to set a level of catch consistent with maintenance of the marine ecosystem as a whole. Common to all these instruments, however, is the persistent problem of illegal fishing, usually by 'free riders' outside the relevant treaty and thus exercising the high seas freedom to fish. The 1995 SSA seeks to encourage participation in RFOs where established for the areas in question, though here again such provision depends on the free rider States being party to the SSA. There have also been unilateral attempts to address illegal fishing, whether by States party to an RFO (eg, Canada's arrest of the Spanish trawler the *Estai* outside its 200-mile EEZ for violation of NAFO measures)[76] or

---

[76] For analysis see Davies, 1995; more generally on straddling stocks, Davies and Redgwell, 1996.

by coastal States exercising control over landing rights the exercise of which are crucial in ensuring transit of fresh fish to lucrative European and other markets.[77] Particular fish stocks, such as highly migratory tuna stocks,[78] are the subject of species specific regulation as are a wide range of marine mammals such as dolphins,[79] seals,[80] and whales (which are also protected under CITES). Here we see a shift in regulatory focus, for whilst fisheries regulation continues to be primarily concerned with conserving the economic value of the resource through good fisheries management practices, there is no doubt the 1946 International Convention for the Regulation of Whaling has seen a shift in approach from regulation of the (over) exploitation of an economic resource to a moratorium on whaling based at least in part on the more diffuse anthropocentric concern to protect the species.[81]

VIII. CONCLUSION

The breadth and scope of international environmental law is of course much greater than that briefly introduced in this chapter. Regional regulation of the Antarctic has contributed much to international environmental protection of both marine living resources and the terrestrial Antarctic environment; the regulation of the non-navigable uses of international watercourses has recently been codified and rests alongside extensive regional and bilateral regulation of riparian uses, including those which may have significant environmental impact; and marine living resources, from fish to mammals, have been subject to a myriad of global, regional, and bilateral arrangements only touched on here. Fertile areas for further exploration are the intersection of international environmental law with other areas addressed in this volume, most notably human rights (including access to environmental justice and public participation in environmental decision-making) and trade, as well as the effect of armed conflict on the environment.

With its development over the last several decades, international environmental law has been transformed from mere incidental regulation of the environmental effects of human activities, to holistic regulation of global issues of common and intertemporal concern reaching both within and beyond the State. Its maturation is reflected in present concerns regarding State compliance with international obligations, reflected in the growing number of treaty-based compliance mechanisms, and in the crucial importance of effective domestic implementation and enforcement. Future developments will therefore see significant emphasis upon the effective enforcement of international environmental law at the global, regional, national, and local levels, with less emphasis on the generation of new rules.

[77] See the Special Chamber of the ITLOS established on 20 December 2000 in the *Case Concerning the Conservation and Sustainable Exploitation of Swordfish Stocks in the South-Eastern Pacific Ocean (Chile/European Community)* (proceedings suspended by agreement).

[78] See the 1949 Convention for the Establishment of an Inter-American Tropical Tuna Commission.

[79] See, eg, the 1991 ASCOBANS, n 72 above.

[80] Such as the 1972 Convention on the Conservation of Antarctic Seals.

[81] See Birnie, 1997, and Ch 6 in Bowman, Davies, and Redgwell, 2010.

REFERENCES

ANDERSON, M and GALIZZI, P (eds) (2002), *International Environmental Law in National Courts* (London: British Institute of International and Comparative Law), ch 1.

ANDERSON, S and SARMA, K (eds) (2002), *Protecting the Ozone Layer; The United Nations History* (London: Earthscan Publications Limited).

BENEDICK, R (1998) *Ozone Diplomacy: New Directions in Safeguarding the Planet*, enlarged edn (Cambridge, Mass.: Harvard University Press).

BIRNIE, P (1997), 'Are Twentieth Century Marine Conservation Conventions Adaptable to Twenty-First Century Goals and Principles?', 12 *IJMCL* 307 and 488.

—— and BOYLE, A (1995), *Basic Documents on International Law* (Oxford: Oxford University Press).

——, ——, and REDGWELL, C (2009), *International Law and the Environment*, 3rd edn (Oxford: Oxford University Press).

BODANSKY, D (1993), 'UN Convention on Climate Change', 18 *Yale ILJ* 451.

BOWMAN, M and REDGWELL, C (eds) (1996), *International Law and the Conservation of Biological Diversity* (The Hague: Kluwer).

——, DAVIES, P, and REDGWELL, C (2010), *Lyster's International Wildlife Law*, 2nd edn (Cambridge: Cambridge University Press).

BOYLE, A (1999), 'Some Reflections on the Relationship of Treaties and Soft Law', 48 *ICLQ* 901.

BRUNNEE, J (2002), 'Coping with Consent: Law-Making under Multilateral Environmental Agreements', 15 *Leiden JIL*, pp 26–29.

BRUS, M (1995), *Third Party Dispute Settlement in an Interdependent World* (The Hague: Martinus Nijhoff).

CHINKIN, C and BOYLE, A (2007), *The Making of International Law* (Oxford: Oxford University Press), ch 2.

CHURCHILL, RR and LOWE, AV (1999), *The Law of the Sea*, 3rd edn (Manchester: Manchester University Press).

—— and SCOTT, J (2004), 'The MOX Plant Litigation: The First Half-Life', 53 *ICLQ* 643.

—— and ULFSTEIN, G (2000), 'Automomous Institutional Arrangements in Multilateral Environmental Agreements: A Little-Noticed Phenomenon in International Law', 94 *AJIL* 623.

COMMISSION ON GLOBAL GOVERNANCE (1995), *Our Global Neighbourhood* (Oxford: Oxford University Press).

CULLET, P (2003), *Differential Treatment in International Environmental Law* (Aldershot: Ashgate).

DAVIES, PGG (1995), 'The EC/Canadian Fisheries Dispute in the Northwest Atlantic', 44 *ICLQ* 933.

—— (2002), 'Public Participation, the Aarhus Convention, and the European Community', in Zillman, D, Lucas, A, and Pring, G (eds), *Human Rights in Natural Resource Development: Public Participation in the Sustainable Development of Mining and Energy Resources* (Oxford: Oxford University Press), p 155.

—— and REDGWELL, C (1996), 'The International Legal Regulation of Straddling Fish Stocks', LXVII *BYIL* 199.

DE LA FAYETTE, L (1999), 'The OSPAR Convention Comes into Force: Continuity and Progress', 14 *IJMCL* 247.

DEPLEDGE, J and YAMIN, F (2004), *The International Climate Change Regime: A Guide to Rules, Institutions and Procedures* (Cambridge: Cambridge University Press).

EBBESSON, J (1997), 'The Notion of Public Participation in International Environmental Law', 8 *YBIEL* 51.

FITZMAURICE, M (2001), 'International Environmental Protection of the Environment', 293 *Recueil des Cours* 13.

—— and REDGWELL, C (2000), 'Environmental Non-Compliance Procedures and International Law', XXXI *NYIL* 35.

FRANCIONI, F (1994), 'Developments in Environmental Law from Sovereignty to Governance: The EC Environmental Policy', in Markesinis, B (ed), *The Gradual Convergence: Foreign Ideas, Foreign Influences, and English Law on the Eve of the 21st Century* (Oxford: Clarendon Press), p 205.

—— and SCOVAZZI, T (eds) (1991), *International Responsibility for Environmental Harm* (Dordrecht: Kluwer).

—— with LENZERINI, F (eds) (2008), *The 1972 World Heritage Convention A Commentary* (Oxford: Oxford University Press).

FREESTONE, D and STRECK, C (eds) (2005), *Legal Aspects of Implementing the Kyoto Protocol* (Oxford: Oxford University Press).

FRENCH, D (2000), 'Developing States and International Environmental Law: The Importance of Differentiated Responsibilities', 49 *ICLQ* 38.

—— (2005), *International Law and Policy of Sustainable Development* (Manchester: Juris Publishing/Manchester University Press).

GILLESPIE, A (1997), *International Environmental Law, Policy and Ethics* (Oxford: Oxford University Press).

GLOWKA, L, et al (1994), *A Guide to the Convention on Biological Diversity*, IUCN Environmental Policy and Law Paper No 30.

IUCN (2000), *Draft International Covenant on Environment and Development*, 2nd edn (IUCN).

KUMMER, K (2000), *International Management of Hazardous Wastes* (Oxford: Clarendon Press).

LOWE, AV (1999), 'Sustainable Development and Unsustainable Arguments', in Boyle, AE and Freestone, D (eds), *International Law and Sustainable Development: Past Achievements and Future Challenges* (Oxford: Oxford University Press).

MCKENZIE, R et al (2003), *An Explanatory Guide to the Cartagena Protocol on Biosafety* (Gland: IUCN Environmental Policy and Law Paper No. 46).

MUCHLINSKI, P (2007), *Multinational Enterprises and the Law* (Oxford: Oxford Univerisity Press), ch 14.

OKOWA, P (2000), *State Responsibility for Transboundary Air Pollution in International Law* (Oxford: Oxford University Press).

PALLEMAERTS, M (2003), *Toxics and Transnational Law* (Oxford: Hart Publishing).

PARADELL-TRIUS, L (2000), 'Principles of International Environmental Law: an Overview', 9:2 *RECIEL* 93.

PEEL, J (2001), 'New State Responsibility Rules and Compliance with Multilateral Environmental Obligations—Some case studies of how the new rules might apply in the international environmental context', 10:1 *RECIEL* 82.

RAJAMANI, L (2000), 'The Principle of Common but Differentiated Responsibility and the Balance of Commitments under the Climate Regime', 9 *RECIEL* 120.

—— (2009), 'Addressing the "Post-Kyoto" Stress Disorder; Reflections on the Emering Legal Architecture of the Climate Regime' 58 *ICLQ* 803.

REDGWELL, C (1994), 'Environmental Protection in Antarctica: the 1991 Protocol', 43 *ICLQ* 599.

—— (2000), 'Multilateral Environmental Treaty-Making', in Gowlland-Debbas, V (ed), *Multilateral Treaty-Making: The*

Current Status of Challenges to and Reforms Needed in the International Legislative Process (The Hague: Martinus Nijhoff), p 89.

—— (2006a), 'From Permission to Prohibition: the 1982 LOSC and Protection of the Marine Environment', in Freestone, D, Barnes, R, and Ong, D (eds), *The Law of the Sea: Progress and Prospects* (Oxford: Oxford University Press), p 180.

—— (2006b), 'Biotechnology, Biodiversity and International Law', in Holder, J (ed), *Current Legal Problems* (Oxford: Oxford University Press), p 543.

ROTHWELL, D (1996), *The Polar Regions and the Development of International Law* (Cambridge: Cambridge University Press).

SANDS, P (2003), *Principles of International Environmental Law,* 3rd edn (Cambridge: Cambridge University Press).

SCHRIJVER, N (1997), *Sovereignty Over Natural Resources: Balancing Rights and Duties* (Cambridge: Cambridge University Press).

SHELTON, D (ed) (2000), *Commitment and Compliance: The Role of Non-Binding Norms in the International Legal System* (Oxford: Oxford University Press).

SOHN, L (1973) 'The Stockholm Declaration on the Human Environment', 14 *Harv ILJ* 423.

WERKSMAN, J (1998), 'Compliance and the Kyoto Protocol: Building a Backbone into a "Flexible" Regime', 9 *YBIEL* 48.

WETTERSTEIN, P (ed) (1997), *Harm to the Environment: The Right to Compensation and the Assessment of Damages* (Oxford: Clarendon Press).

WIRTH, D (2007), 'Hazardous Substances and Activities', in Bodansky, D, Brunnee, J, and Hey, E (eds) (2007), *The Oxford Handbook of International Environmental Law* (Oxford: Oxford University Press).

WOLFRUM, R (1999), 'Means of Ensuring Compliance with and Enforcement of International Environmental Law', 272 *Recueil des Cours* 9.

YEATER, M and VASQUEZ, J (2001), 'Demystifying the Relationship between CITES and the WTO', 10:3 *RECIEL* 271.

YOSHIDA, O (2001), *The International Legal Regime for the Protection of the Stratospheric Ozone Layer* (The Hague: Kluwer).

FURTHER READING

BIRNIE, P, BOYLE, A, and REDGWELL, C (2009), *International Law and The Environment,* 3rd edn (Oxford: Oxford University Press). Of the general textbooks on international environmental law, this is the best and one of the most recent.

BODANSKY, D, BRUNNEE, J, and HEY, E (eds) (2007), *The Oxford Handbook of International Environmental Law* (Oxford: Oxford University Press). This edited volume follows the pattern of this work, with chapters submitted by the leading authorities in the international environmental field. An invaluable source to supplement the standard texts and specialized edited collections.

BOWMAN, M, DAVIES P, and REDGWELL, C (2010), *Lyster's International Wildlife Law,* 2nd edn (Cambridge: Cambridge University Press). This is the much anticipated second edition of a highly readable account of the principal treaties concerned with wildlife protection.

BOYLE, A and ANDERSON, M (eds) (1996), *Human Rights Approaches to Environmental Protection* (Oxford: Clarendon Press). A splendid overview of the intersection of human rights and the environment.

—— and FREESTONE, D (eds) (1999), *International Law and Sustainable Development: Past Achievements and Future Challenges* (Oxford: Oxford University Press). A valuable resource not only for discussion of sustainable development but for contextual analysis drawing on many topical international environmental issues.

FITZMAURICE, M (2001), 'International Protection of the Environment', 293 *Recueil des Cours* 13. These Hague Academy lectures on international environmental law provide a helpful overview of the subject with case studies of the ozone layer protection and international watercourses.

FRANCIONI, F (ed) (2001), *Environment, Human Rights and International Trade* (Oxford: Hart Publishing). This contains a number of stimulating contributions not only on the general issue but also examining the compatibility of specific environmental treaties, in particular the Cartagena Protocol, with the WTO agreements.

HURRELL, A and KINGSBURY, B (eds) (1992), *International Politics of the Environment* (Oxford: Clarendon Press). This places environmental issues in their international relations context.

MORRISON, FL and WOLFRUM, R (eds) (2000), *International, Regional and National Environmental Law* (The Hague: Kluwer). This edited volume includes chapters on the EC and North American cooperation, and in-depth analysis of German and US law.

SANDS, P (2003), *Principles of International Environmental Law*, 2nd edn (Cambridge: Cambridge University Press). Another very useful textbook with detailed treatment of principles and of specific treaty regimes.

The principal treaty texts are compiled with useful commentary and guidance for further reading in Birnie, P and Boyle, A (1995), *Basic Documents on International Law and the Environment* (Oxford: Oxford University Press) and in Galizzi, P, and Sands, P (2004), *Documents in International Environmental Law* (Cambridge: Cambridge University Press).

Finally, the major cases on international environmental law may be found in Robb, C (ed), *International Environmental Law Reports* (Cambridge: Cambridge University Press), four volumes to date addressed to early decisions, trade and environment, human rights and environment, and international environmental law in national courts.

WEBSITES

Those searching for access to the web pages of the key environmental treaties will find the UNEP (http://www.unep.org) and

IMO (http://www.imo.org) sites useful gateways.

24

INTERNATIONAL
ECONOMIC LAW

Gerhard Loibl

SUMMARY

International economic law covers a very broad range of topics as it deals with all economic aspects of relations between States. Thus, international trade law, international fiscal law, and investment law fall within the scope of international economic law. Customary international law has only developed very general rules in the area of international economic law. Thus, international economic relations between States are mainly based on treaties. The current international economic system has been elaborated in the aftermath of the Bretton Woods conference. In the last decades this system has been adapted to deal with new challenges.

I. INTRODUCTION

International economic law may be described in various ways. No clear definition has developed in practice or in theory. Both broad and more restricted descriptions have been put forward. In the broadest sense, international economic law could be defined as including all legal subjects which have both an international and an economic component.

The Third Restatement (American Law Institute, 1987, vol 2, p 261) has described international economic law very comprehensively:

The law of international economic relations in its broadest sense includes all the international law and international agreements governing economic transactions that cross state boundaries or that otherwise have implications for more than one state, such as those involving the movement of goods, funds, persons, intangibles, technology, vessels or aircraft.

It has been suggested that international economic law embraces the following areas: the law of establishment, the law of investment, the law of economic relations, the law of economic institutions, and the law of regional economic integration (cf Carreau and Julliard, 1998, p 6). But of course there are other areas which could be seen as part of international economic law, such as the question of economic development or the relationship between economic issues and environmental protection or human rights. This chapter will concentrate on those areas of international economic law which govern the relations between subjects of international law and thus will include international financial issues, international trade, and issues concerning foreign investment. Furthermore, organizational matters of the organizations dealing with international economic issues will be taken into account.

International economic law has developed rapidly since the end of the Second World War. The current international economic system is based on the international regulations established by the Bretton Woods Conference in 1944 (Coing, 1992, pp 494–495). The main objective of the Conference was to avoid the monetary disorders of earlier decades in the future and to ensure international trade discipline. Central to this system are the economic theories of comparative advantage and economies of scale.[1] The main influences were the proposals of John Maynard Keynes (United Kingdom) and Harry Dextor White (USA).

As a result of the Bretton Woods Conference three main international institutions were established which form the backbone of the current international economic legal system: the International Monetary Fund (IMF), the International Bank for Reconstruction and Development (IBRD, better known under the name 'World Bank'), and the General Agreement on Tariffs and Trade (GATT), which was replaced by the World Trade Organization (WTO) in 1995. The evolution of these institutions is described later in this chapter.

In addition, a number of other international organizations and institutions have been set up which are important for the further development of international economic law. The Organization for Economic Cooperation and Development (OECD),[2] established in 1960 as the successor to the Organization for European Economic Cooperation (OEEC) which was set up to administer the Marshall Plan aid provided by the United States to Europe after the end of the Second World War, plays an important role in the elaboration of principles for international economic transactions, such as capital movements and investments.[3] Moreover, specialized agencies of the United Nations have been set up or have continued to operate, such as the Food and Agriculture Organization (FAO), the World Intellectual Property Organization (WIPO), and the International Labour Organization (ILO). The United Nations Conference on Trade and Development (UNCTAD) was established in 1965 by the UN General Assembly to give more weight to the interests of developing countries.

On the regional level a number of international organizations or institutions have been set up to ensure closer economic cooperation between States, such as the European

---

[1] The theory of economies of scale is built on the idea that specialization in the production of goods and services leads to lower (average) production costs. The economic theory of comparative advantage states that countries will produce goods where they have a comparative advantage.

[2] Currently the OECD has 30 member countries. They compromise the 15 'old' member States of the European Union, as well as the Czech Republic, Hungary, Poland, and the Slovak Republic. Thus, not all of the 27 members of the European Union have yet become members of OECD. The other members of OECD are Australia, Canada, Iceland, Japan, Korea, Liechtenstein, Mexico, New Zealand, Norway, Switzerland, Turkey, and the United States of America. The Commission of the European Union takes part in the work of the OECD (based on Supplementary Protocol No 1 to the Convention on the OECD from 1960).

[3] Cf the OECD Code of Liberalization of Current Invisible Transactions and the OECD Code of Liberalization of Capital Movements.

Community (EC), the North American Free Trade Agreement (NAFTA), the Southern African Development Community (SADC), the West African Economic and Monetary Union (Union Economique et Monétaire Ouest-Africaine) (UEMO), the Association of Southeast Asian Nations (ASEAN), MERCOSUR (Mercado Común del Sur or Mercado Común del Cono Sur), and the Central American Free Trade Agreement (CAFTA). Moreover, numerous bilateral freetrade agreements have been concluded in the last few years. The degree of organizational integration achieved by these agreements as well as the economic topics covered by them varies.

II. INTERNATIONAL FINANCE LAW

The Bretton Woods institutions are the backbone of today's international finance system. It has adapted to new challenges and issues which have come up in the last decades. Over the years it has been able to provide the stability and flexibility necessary to ensure a stable environment for the world economy as well as to provide financial resources for development.

A. THE INTERNATIONAL MONETARY FUND (IMF)

1. Purposes and activities of the IMF

The IMF was established to promote international monetary cooperation and exchange rate stability, to assist in the establishment of a multilateral system of payments for current transactions between members, and to assist in the elimination of foreign exchange restrictions that hamper the growth of world trade and to provide temporary, ie, short term, assistance to correct balance of payments imbalances (Shihata, 2001, p 111). Article I of the Articles of Agreement which established the IMF states the following purposes:

 (i) To promote international monetary cooperation through a permanent institution which provides the machinery for consultation and collaboration on international monetary problems.

 (ii) To facilitate the expansion and balanced growth of international trade, and to contribute thereby to the promotion and maintenance of high levels of employment and real income and to the development of the productive resources of all members as primary objectives of economic policy.

 (iii) To promote exchange stability, to maintain orderly exchange arrangements among members, and to avoid competitive exchange depreciation.

 (iv) To assist in the establishment of a multilateral system of payments in respect of current transactions between members and in the elimination of foreign exchange restrictions which hamper the growth of world trade.

 (v) To give confidence to members by making the general resources of the Fund temporarily available to them under adequate safeguards, thus providing them with the opportunity to correct maladjustments in their balance of payments without resorting to measures destructive of national or international prosperity.

 (vi) In accordance with the above, to shorten the duration and lessen the degree of disequilibrium in the international balances of payments of members.

The Agreement establishing the IMF provided for a fixed parity between all currencies and gold. This was based on the agreement of the USA to fix the convertibility of the US dollar into gold at the rate of 35 US dollar per ounce (gold exchange standard). All other currencies had a fixed exchange rate to the US dollar. However, the system based on the gold standard was terminated in 1971 when the USA suspended its obligation unilaterally. In 1978 an amendment to the Articles of Agreement entered into force, allowing member States to choose their exchange rate system freely with the aim to assure orderly exchange arrangements and to promote a stable system of exchange rates (Article IV).[4]

Furthermore, according to the Articles of Agreement a multilateral system of payments and transfers for current international transactions to facilitate the growth of international trade and services was established (Article VIII). It ensures that governments do not prohibit, delay, or otherwise hinder the availability or use of their own or another member's currency for making current international transactions. However, as not all members are able to implement the obligations under Article VIII, Article XIV provides for transitional arrangements which allow members to maintain restrictions on current international transactions. In addition, exceptions may be granted by the IMF if they are deemed temporarily necessary (Qureshi, 1999, pp 138–158). Capital transfers may be regulated by members in a manner not to impede the multilateral system (Article VI). A major activity of the IMF, considered in more detail later, is to provide loans to member countries. In order to ensure that member States meet their obligations a process of reporting, monitoring, and consultations (surveillance) has been established.

2. Organizational structure of the IMF

The main organs of the IMF are: the Board of Governors, the International Monetary and Financial Committee, the Executive Board, and the Managing Director. All member States (in 2009, 186 in number) are represented in the Board of Governors, while the Executive Board conducts the day-to-day business of the IMF. It consists of a limited number of Executive Directors (currently 24 members). Eight Executive Directors representing individual countries (five appointed by France, Germany, Japan, the United Kingdom, and the United States; three elected by the votes of China, Russia, and Saudi Arabia); the other 16 members represent groupings of countries, so-called constituencies. The Executive Board is responsible for conducting the business of the Fund, and the Managing Director, who is selected by the Executive Board, conducts ordinary business under the direction of the Executive Board. The decision-making process in the IMF is based on weighted voting, ie, each member's voting power is based on its quota. But the general practice of the IMF is to avoid voting and to take decisions by consensus.

The quota of each member is determined in general by its economic position relative to other members. A number of economic factors are considered in determining quotas, including GDP, current account transactions, and official reserves. The largest quota is currently held by the United States (17.09%), the smallest by Palau (0.001%). The quota determines various aspects of a member's relations with the IMF, including its subscription, voting power, access to financing, and its SDR allocation (see below).

[4] For the economic background on the evolution of the IMF see Krugman and Obstfeld, 2000, p 546.

3. Loans facilities

One of the main functions of the IMF is to provide loans to member countries which experience balance-of-payments problems. Since its creation, the IMF has developed a number of different loan facilities, including non-concessional and concessional lending. Whereas in the first case the interest rate is market based and a surcharge is paid, the interest rate in the latter case is only 0.5% and the repayment period is longer.[5]

The non-concessional lending include, *inter alia*, Stand-By Arrangements to address short-term balance-of-payments problems, the Extended Fund Facility to meet balance-of-payments problems caused by structural problems of the economy, and the Supplemental Reserve Facility to meet needs for very short-term financing on a large scale caused by sudden loss of market confidence. The Poverty Reduction and Growth Facility provides concessional loans to low income countries. The amount of borrowing from the IMF for a member State is limited in general to 100% of its quota annually and 300% cumulatively.

The Fund makes its resources available to a member subject to certain conditions (IMF Conditionality), ie, financial conditionality (eg, repurchase obligations or charges) and economic conditionality (eg, reduction of food subsidies or devaluation).[6] This practice has given rise to wide criticism as such measures have not always been successful in economic terms and have sometimes led to negative social developments.

4. Financial resources of the IMF

The financial resources of the IMF are provided by the members based on their quotas. Of these quotas, 25% (so-called subscriptions) have to be paid in Special Drawing Rights or other reserve currencies determined by the IMF. The remaining 75% may be paid in the State's national currencies. The financial resources have been increased several times. An increase of subscriptions was agreed by the Board of Governors in 1998 and also led to a change in quotas. A further change was agreed at the G-20 meeting at Pittsburgh in 2009 when it was decided that the 'voting power of emerging market and developing countries' was to be increased by at least 3%.

The quotas of the members are the principal source of financing for the IMF. In addition, a number of members are ready to lend supplementary funds to the IMF if these were needed in order to forestall or cope with an impairment of the international monetary system, or to deal with an exceptional situation that threatens the international monetary system. For this purpose, as supplementary sources of financing, the General Arrangements to Borrow (GAB) was established in 1962 and the New Arrangements to Borrow (NAB) was introduced in 1998. GAB enables the IMF to borrow specified amounts of currencies from eleven industrial countries (or their central banks) under certain circumstances and at market-related rates of interest. NAB provides supplementary resources to the IMF from 25 countries (including countries such as Malaysia, Saudi Arabia, Singapore, and Thailand).

5. Special Drawing Rights

In 1969, the Articles of the IMF were amended to create Special Drawing Rights (SDR) as an international reserve asset to supplement members' existing reserve assets (Article

---

[5] The IMF website has further details: **http://www.imf.org**.
[6] See Quereshi, 1999, p 176; Denters, 1996.

XVIII section 2(a)). This was necessary because of the pressure which the IMF fixed exchange rate system came under in the 1960s, lacking as it did a mechanism for regulating reserve growth to finance the expansion of world trade and financial development. At that time, gold and the US dollar were the two main reserve assets but gold production had become an inadequate and unreliable source of reserve supply and the continuing growth of international payments posed a threat to the value of the US dollar. SDRs were created to address this inadequacy of international liquidity. Physically, SDRs are simply book-keeping entries at the IMF in accounts for member countries and the Fund itself, proportionate to their quotas in the Fund (Ethier, 1988, p 455).

SDRs were allocated in the 1970s, the 1980s and in 2009 according to the quotas of the then member States. A special one-time allocation of SDRs which was made in 1997 only met with the approval of the necessary 85% majority in 2009. The value of the SDR is determined by a basket of currencies that currently consists of the euro, Japanese yen, pound sterling, and US dollar. The role of the SDRs as a reserve asset is limited. By the end of the year 2001 SDRs accounted for less than 1.17% of IMF members' non-gold reserves. But SDRs have been accepted as a currency of accounting not only within the IMF but also in other areas of international economic law, eg, in international commodity agreements.

B. THE WORLD BANK GROUP

The International Bank on Reconstruction and Development (IBRD), also known as the World Bank, was established in 1944. Since then a number of new institutions have been established under the auspices of the IBRD in order to deal with new challenges. Thus, the International Finance Cooperation (IFC), the International Development Association (IDA), the International Centre for the Settlement of Investment Disputes (ICSID), and the Multilateral Investment Guarantee Agency (MIGA) were established to supplement the activities of the IBRD. Although each of these institutions is a separate legal entity, they collaborate closely towards a common objective: the transfer of resources and the promotion of investment for developing countries. Together they form the World Bank Group. Furthermore, the Global Environmental Facility (GEF) was created by the IBRD together with the United Nations Environment Programme (UNEP) and the United Nations Development Programme (UNDP). The institutions of the World Bank Group share similar organizational structures and decision-making processes. Furthermore, there are overlaps in personnel, this sometimes being expressly required by the relevant treaties whilst in other instances it is a product of practice. This ensured a consistent policy across the World Bank Group.

1. International Bank of Reconstruction and Development (IBRD)

Membership of the IBRD requires membership of the IMF. Therefore, both organizations have the same circle of member States. The World Bank was created to mobilize financial resources with a view of lending to those States in need of foreign investment. According to Article I of the Articles of Agreement the purposes of the World Bank are to assist in the reconstruction and development of territories of members by facilitating the investment of capital for productive purposes; to promote private foreign investments by means of guarantees or participation in loans and other investments made by private investors;

to supplement private investment by providing, on suitable conditions, finance for productive purposes; to promote the long-range balanced growth of international trade and the maintenance of equilibrium in balances of payments by encouraging international investment for the development of the productive resources; to arrange the loans made or guaranteed by it in relation to international loans through other channels so that the more useful and urgent projects, large and small alike, will be dealt with first; and to conduct its operation with due regard to the effect of international investment on business conditions in the territories of members.

After the Second World War the World Bank concentrated its activities on reconstruction. Today, the World Bank concentrates primarily on the financing of projects in developing countries. According to a narrow interpretation of the purposes of the World Bank, its role may be restricted to financing or facilitating investments for productive purposes. Moreover, Article III, section 4(iii) provides that its loans and guarantees shall, except in special circumstances, be for the purpose of specific projects of reconstruction or development. Thus, the World Bank in its early years financed construction programmes in Europe and economic development projects in developing countries. It only started slowly to finance social projects.

Based on the special circumstances exception, in 1980 the IBRD started to provide structural adjustment loans and in 1984 sectorial adjustment loans. These provide cash to support structural (policy and institutional) reforms in the economy as a whole or in a specific sector (Shihata, 2001, p 121), including in particular support for legal, regulatory, judicial, and civil service reforms as well as loans for the privatization of public enterprises. These activities are considered to fall within the scope of Article I as they further the Bank's objective of facilitating investment for productive purposes. According to Article III section 4(i) of the Articles of Agreement any loan (or guarantee of loan) made by the Bank needs sovereign involvement, ie, it has to be guaranteed by the member (or its central bank or some comparable agency of the member) in whose territory the project is located. The IBRD provided its first guarantee for a private investment loan as set out in Article III in 1984.

Furthermore, according to Article III section 4(v) the IBRD shall pay due regard to the prospects that the borrower, and, if the borrower is not a member, that the guarantor, will be in a position to meet its obligations under the loan. Thus, the World Bank may not provide loans or guarantees on a concessional basis. It charges interests which reflect its costs. Loans must be repaid in 15 to 20 years and there is a grace period of three to five years before repayments of the principal begin.

The capital of the World Bank is provided by its member States. These shares differ in accordance with their quota which is based on their relative economic strength (the United States is the biggest shareholder). The members pay only a small portion of the value of their shares (5%). The unpaid balance is due if the IBRD is unable to pay its creditors (which has not happened so far). IBRD rules require that loans outstanding and disbursed do not exceed the combined total of capital and reserves. The IBRD raises the money for its activities in financial markets (eg, by selling debt securities to pension funds, insurance companies, corporations, and other banks). Furthermore, the Bank earns interest on its lending, the commissions and charges arising from the granting of loans.

The organizational structure of the IBRD is similar to the IMF. The central organ is the Board of Governors, consisting of a Governor and an alternate appointed by each member

State. Decisions are taken by weighted voting: each member has the same basis number of votes (250), plus votes allocated on the basis of its quota. The daily business is conducted by the Executive Board, currently consisting of 24 Directors: five of the Directors are appointed by the members having the highest quotas, the rest elected by constituencies (as in the IMF). The President is elected by the Executive Board.

In response to criticisms by the public (and in particular the NGO community) the World Bank has elaborated a set of operational policies and procedures addressing social and environmental concerns that could result from projects financed by the World Bank. Each project is screened according to these policies and procedures (eg, operational policies and procedures have been established for environmental impact assessment, forestry, involuntary resettlement, indigenous people, and natural habitat).[7]

Furthermore, the World Bank Inspection Panel was established in 1993 (the resolutions establishing the Panel have been amended since then) to deal with complaints from 'affected persons', ie, two or more persons, who allege that their rights or interests have been, or could be, negatively affected by a project financed by the Bank (or IDA). The Panel, consisting of three individuals, makes recommendations to the Bank's management which makes recommendations to the Board of Directors. The Board of Directors decides finally on necessary action to be taken in order to be in compliance with the Bank's policies and procedures.[8]

2. International Finance Cooperation (IFC)

The IFC was established in 1956 to provide financial resources without any government guarantees to private enterprises in developing countries.[9] Article I of the Articles of Agreement states that the purpose of the IFC is to further economic development by encouraging the growth of productive private enterprise in member countries, particularly in less developed areas, thus supplementing the activities of the IBRD. In carrying out this purpose, the IFC shall:

(i) in association with private investors, assist in financing the establishment, improvement and expansion of productive private enterprises which would contribute to the development of its member countries by making investments, without guarantee of repayment by the member government concerned, in cases where sufficient private capital is not available on reasonable terms;

(ii) seek to bring together investment opportunities, domestic and foreign private capital, and experienced management; and

(iii) seek to stimulate, and to help create conditions conducive to, the flow of private capital, domestic and foreign, into productive investment in member countries.

Financing by the IFC may take the form of loans, guarantees, or even equity participation (Article III section 2). As the IFC is to invest in private enterprises, its investment activities are heavily dependent on the decisions of private investors, who in turn are influenced by their perceptions of the business climate and opportunities. Therefore, one of the IFC's

---

[7] Cf Shihata, 1998; Loibl, 1998. On the policies of the World Bank Group see *Pollution Prevention and Abatement Handbook*, effective July 1998 (**http://www.ibrd.org**).

[8] For a detailed description on the structure and operation of the Inspection Panel see Shihata, 2000. The reports of the Panel can be found on the website of the World Bank Inspection Panel.

[9] See above the requirements set by the Articles of Agreement of the World Bank (Article III para 4(i)).

main activities is also to develop investment opportunities through its promotional work and to help raise the level of investor confidence in selected projects by working with local investors, foreign partners, other financial institutions, and host governments.[10]

Investment decisions by the IFC are based on there being an adequate financial return to the IFC and an adequate economic return in the country in which the investment is made. Moreover, the IFC will only provide financial resources for projects which it considers would not otherwise be capable of attracting private resources on reasonable terms (Golsong, 1992). Furthermore, the IFC shall not assume responsibility for managing any enterprise in which it has invested and shall not exercise voting rights for such purpose or any other purpose which, in its opinion, is properly within the scope of managerial control (Article III section 3(iv)). As with the World Bank, each project is screened for its social and environmental impacts. The organizational structure of the IFC follows the pattern of the IBRD. Its share capital, which is paid by member countries (in 2009, 182 in number), is similar to the IBRD. Voting rights are proportionate to the number of shares held.

In 1999 a Compliance Advisor/Ombudsman was established by the IFC (and MIGA) which has a function similar to that of the World Bank's Inspection Panel for the IBRD and IDA. Its mandate is to assist the IFC and MIGA to address complaints of people affected by projects in a fair, objective, and constructive manner and to enhance the social and environmental outcomes of projects in which these institutions play a role.[11]

3. International Development Association (IDA)

The International Development Association was established in 1960 to provide concessional financing to developing countries. Many developing countries that became members of the IBRD did not meet the condition of creditworthiness set by the IBRD' s Articles of Agreement,[12] so a new mechanism had to be created to provide them with loans and guarantees.

Article I of the Articles of Agreement states that the purposes of IDA are:

to promote economic development, increase productivity and thus raise standards of living in the less-developed areas of the world included within the Association's membership, in particular by providing finance to meet their important developmental requirements on terms which are more flexible and bear less heavily on the balance of payments than those of conventional loans, thereby furthering the developmental objectives of the IBRD and supplementing its activities.

Out of the 163 members, 79 countries are currently eligible to borrow from IDA.[13] Some countries that have borrowed from IDA in the past are now too prosperous to do so, including China, Costa Rica, Chile, Egypt, Morocco, Thailand, and Turkey.

Loans by IDA are made on concessional terms: no interest charge, a service charge of three-quarters of 1% per annum, a long repayment period (35 to 45 years) and a

---

[10] See http://www.ifc.org.

[11] See Operation Guidelines for the Office of the IFC/MIGA Compliance Advisor/Ombudsman (www .cao-ombudsman.org).

[12] Ibid, Article III section 4(v).

[13] In the year 2000, for example, IDA lent to countries that had a per capita income of less than US$885 and lacked the financial ability to borrow from the IBRD.

10-year grace period. The financial resources of IDA are provided through subscriptions and contributions by the richer members. They are replenished from time to time (13 replenishments have taken place so far). Furthermore, IBRD has also granted loans to IDA. Additional funds come from repayments of previous IDA credits. The organizational structure and the decision-making process follow those of the World Bank (and IFC).

4. Global Environmental Facility (GEF) and other trust funds

To further the World Bank's purposes a number of trust funds have been set up to finance specific activities. They are funded by donors and are administered by the Bank, examples being the Brazilian Rainforest Trust Fund and the HIPC (Heavily Indebted Poor Countries) Trust Fund to support the HIPC initiative to reduce the debt burden. In 1994 the Global Environmental Facility (GEF)[14] was set up jointly by IBRD, UNEP, and UNDP, in order to meet incremental costs of projects and programmes aiming to achieve global environmental benefits in the four focal areas—climate change, biological diversity, international waters, and ozone layer depletion—and activities concerning land degradation relating to those four areas. In 2002 two more focal areas were added (desertification and persistent organic pollutants). The GEF also operates as the financial mechanism for a number of conventions (eg, United Nations Framework Convention on Climate Change, Convention on Biodiversity).

C. REGIONAL DEVELOPMENT BANKS

Regional development banks have been founded to supplement the activities of the IBRD, IDA, and IFC as well as bilateral development cooperation. Their task is to give closer attention to specific regional needs and priorities. In general, their membership comprises both countries of the region in question and countries from Europe and North America. Examples of such regional banks are the Inter-American Development Bank, the African Development Bank, the Asian Development Bank, and the European Bank for Reconstruction and Development.

D. CONCLUDING REMARKS

The international financial system has been criticized in the last few years for not being able to address the new challenges which have arisen. However, as its evolution shows, the international financial system has in the past been adapted to deal with new issues and it is to be hoped that legal norms and institutional structures will be further adjusted to meet future challenges. Although it seemed clear when they were established that the IMF and World Bank would serve different purposes, practice over the years has demonstrated that their activities overlap to a certain extent and one future task is to draw a clear distinction between them. Furthermore, the finance institutions have elaborated new mechanisms to take into account the concerns of civil society. The World Bank's Inspection Panel and similar institutions of other finance institutions are examples for their changed attitude towards social and environmental concerns.

---

[14] The Global Environmental Facility had been operating since 1991 on an interim basis.

III. INTERNATIONAL TRADE LAW

A. THE GENERAL AGREEMENT ON TARIFFS AND TRADE (GATT) AND THE WORLD TRADE ORGANIZATION (WTO)

In addition to creating financial institutions, there was also need to establish an international system to abolish trade barriers. Following the Second World War, a charter for an International Trade Organization (ITO) was drafted to deal with trade in goods. This was adopted in Havana in 1948, but it failed to enter into force since the United States Congress did not approve it and other States did not want to establish a global trading system without the largest economy in the world. Instead, international trade after the Second World War was based on the General Agreement on Tariffs and Trade (GATT), a multilateral treaty that was designed to operate under the umbrella of the ITO. It entered into force on a provisional basis in 1948 and stayed in force until 1995 and was known as GATT 1947.

Since then six general tariff negotiations rounds (multilateral negotiations rounds) have taken place: Annecy (1949), Torquay (1951), Geneva (1956), the Dillon Round (1960–62), the Kennedy Round (1964–67), and the Tokyo Round (1973–79). Whereas the earlier rounds centred on tariff reductions, the later rounds resulted in the conclusion of new multilateral agreements. The Uruguay Round (1986–94) led to the establishment of the World Trade Organization (WTO). The WTO entered into force on 1 January 1995 and established a comprehensive single international trade organization (incorporating the multilateral trade agreements which had been the result of the multilateral negotiation rounds and whose membership differed for each of these agreements) as had been envisaged by the ITO. GATT 1947 was terminated by a decision of the GATT contracting parties.

B. THE WORLD TRADE ORGANIZATION

1. Introduction

The WTO was established by the Marrakesh Agreement 1994. States and separate customs territories (eg, the European Community, Hong Kong, Macao) may become members of the WTO, which currently number 148. It is built on four main pillars: GATT 1994 (GATT 1947 supplemented by a number of understandings of interpretation and decisions), the General Agreement on Trade in Services (GATS), the Agreement on Trade-Related Aspects of Intellectual Property Rights (TRIPS), and the Dispute Settlement Understanding. The following sections describe each of these pillars. GATT 1994 has itself been supplemented by 12 international agreements dealing with trade in goods. Moreover, four Plurilateral Trade Agreements (eg, the Agreement on Trade in Civil Aircraft or the Agreement on Government Procurement) are administered by the WTO Secretariat, but do not form part of the WTO as such.

A State or separate customs territory which wants to become a member of WTO has to accept all agreements and understandings that form the WTO.[15] The terms of accession

---

[15] Under GATT 1947 and the multilateral trade agreements, each State or separate customs territory could choose which agreements they wished to be a party to.

must be agreed between the applicant and WTO members and this can be a lengthy process.[16]

The WTO has three main organs: the Ministerial Conference which meets at least once every two years, the General Council which is composed of representatives of all members, and the Secretariat, headed by the Director-General (Article IV of the Marrakesh Agreement). The General Council also operates as the Dispute Settlement Body and the Trade Policy Review Body. Three councils operate under the general guidance of the General Council: a Council for Trade in Goods, a Council for Trade in Services, and a Council for Trade-Related Aspects of Intellectual Property Rights. Other committees have been established by the Ministerial Conference such as the Committee on Trade and Development or the Committee on Trade and Environment.

As was the case with GATT 1947, decision-making is based as far as possible on consensus. Only if there is no consensus is the matter decided by majority vote (Article IX para 1 Marrakesh Agreement), although a three-quarters majority is needed in some cases, such as decisions relating to the interpretation of the WTO Agreement and multilateral trade agreements (Article IX para 2 Marrakesh Agreement). Each member has one vote, although the European Community is covered by special provisions.[17]

2. Multilateral agreements on trade in goods

The multilateral agreements on trade in goods comprise the GATT 1994 and other multilateral agreements. As stated above GATT 1994 basically maintained GATT 1947 supplemented by a number of understandings on interpretation and decisions, such as the Understanding on the Balance-of-Payments Provisions of the General Agreement on Tariffs and Trade 1994 or the Understanding in Respect of Waivers of Obligations under the General Agreement on Tariffs and Trade 1994.

The other 12 multilateral agreements deal with the following matters: agriculture, sanitary and phytosanitary standards, textiles and clothing, technical barriers to trade, trade-related investment measures (TRIMs), customs valuation, anti-dumping measures, pre-shipment inspection, rules of origin, import licensing procedures, subsidies and countervailing measures, and safeguards. These agreements provide detailed provisions which limit members' discretion in implementing GATT in these areas. Although the WTO allows waivers (ie exceptions to certain obligations) to be granted to members by the Ministerial Conference under exceptional circumstances for a limited period of time and under specific terms and conditions, their use has been limited compared to GATT 1947. Moreover, waivers are reviewed on a regular basis.[18]

GATT is based on the following main principles:

(i) Most-Favoured-Nation Treatment (Article I): this obliges members to grant each other unconditional most-favoured nation treatment in their mutual trade relations, ie, any tariff or other concession given by a GATT/WTO member to

---

[16] For example, the terms of accession for China and the Separate Customs Territory of Tawain, Penghu, Kinmen, and Matsu were negotiated over a number of years and they only became WTO members in 2001 and 2002 respectively.

[17] When it exercises its right to vote, the EC has a number of votes equal to the number of EC member States which are WTO members (Article IX para 1 Marrakesh Agreement).

[18] Article IX paras 3 and 4 Marrakesh Agreement. See Jackson, 1997, p 55.

a product originating from or destined for any other country must be given immediately and unconditionally to like products originating from or destined for all other members (Janeke, 1995, pp 502, 504; Jackson, 1997, p 157). However, although WTO members may not discriminate between like products, this does not mean that products must be treated alike. This depends on the treatment established by a member for specific products. The meaning of the term 'like product' has, in general, to be determined on a case-to-case basis and it has been at the centre of a number of disputes. Factors that have to be taken into account include the product's end use in a given market, consumer tastes and habits, or the properties of the product.[19]

(ii) National treatment (Article III): WTO members are obliged to treat products imported from other members on the basis of complete equality with like products of domestic origin. This should ensure that internal taxes, regulations, and requirements are not used to discriminate against foreign products and thus to protect domestic products.

(iii) Schedule of Concessions (Article II): although GATT does not prohibit tariffs, the successive rounds of multilateral trade negotiations have led to a reduction of tariffs (eg, the Uruguay Round led to a 40% reduction of tariffs). These tariff concessions (the so-called bound rate) are contained in the schedule of concessions for each member which is annexed to GATT. Members are obliged to treat other members' products no less favourably than is stated in the respective schedule.

(iv) Quantitative Restrictions (Article IX): quantitative import or export restrictions of any kind (eg, import or export quotas, restrictive use of import or export licences, controls of international payments for imported or exported products) are generally prohibited because of their possible distorting effect on the normal flow of trade. Restrictions may be imposed only in accordance with the conditions set out by GATT.

(v) Transparency (Article X): members are obliged to publish all trade and trade-related measures to ensure certainty, predictability, and accountability of governmental measures.

(vi) Exceptions: GATT provides a number of exceptions to the general rule of liberalization. Article XIX allows emergency action regarding the import of particular products. Moreover, members may impose restrictions to safeguard their balance of payments (Article XII). Article XX allows restrictions for particular purposes, such as the protection of public morals or the protection of human, animal, or plant life or health.[20] Furthermore, Article XXI permits restrictions

---

[19] See *United States—Standards for Reformulated and Conventional Gasoline*, Appellate Body Report, WT/DS2/AB/R (29 April 1996); *EC Measures affecting Asbestos and Asbestos-Containing Products*, Panel Report, WT/DS135/R (18 September 2000); Appellate Body Report, WT/DS135/AB/R (12 March 2001).

[20] See, eg, *United States—Restriction on the Imports of Tuna*, GATT Panel Report, (1991) 30 ILM 1594; *United States—Import Prohibition of Certain Shrimp and Shrimp Products*, Appellate Body Report, WT/DS58/AB/R (12 October 1998). The relationship between trade and environment has been discussed intensively in the last decades both in practice and academic writings. See Schoenbaum, 1997; Brown-Weiss, Jackson, and Bernasconi-Osterwalder, 2008; McRae, 1996 at p 194.

pertaining to national security.[21] Under Article XXV para 5, members may vote to waive certain obligations of a member.[22] Article XXIV provides exceptions for free-trade areas and customs unions, thus allowing preferential treatment between members of such special agreements (eg, European Community, Mercosur, or NAFTA).

(vii) Specific provisions on developing countries: already in the 1950s changes beneficial to developing countries were introduced to GATT 1947 and in 1965 Part IV on Trade and Development was added to the Agreement. The concepts of differentiated and more favourable treatment for developing countries and the principle of non-reciprocity in trade negotiations were further elaborated in 1979 by the so-called 'enabling clause'. This provides the legal basis for the Generalised System of Preferences (ie, that developed countries give developing countries non-reciprocal preferential treatment for products originating from them) and the Global System of Trade Preferences (ie, that developing countries exchange trade concessions among themselves).[23]

3. General Agreement on Trade in Services (GATS)

The growing importance of services for the world economy led to the conclusion of GATS, which provides for a liberalization of trade in services. Its structure is similar to GATT. GATS consists of a framework agreement and annexes, schedules of specific commitments, and the list of exemptions submitted by member countries.

According to GATS Article I para 2:

trade in services is defined as the supply of services:

(a) from the territory of one Member into the territory of any other Member;

(b) in the territory of one Member to the service consumer of any other Member;

(c) by a service supplier of one Member, through commercial presence in the territory of any other Member;

(d) by a service supplier of one Member, through presence of natural persons of a Member in the territory of any other Member.

The general obligations of GATS, such as the most-favoured-nation treatment (Article II) and transparency on measures taken by a country that could affect trade in services (Article III), apply to all services. Exemptions are only possible if requested before GATS entered into force. New exemptions are only granted to new members at the time of their

---

[21] Although Article XXI (National security) has been invoked by members it has never been scrutinized in dispute settlement proceedings. For example, the USA invoked Article XXI as a justification for the Helms-Burton Act, which enables claimants to sue before US courts third-country nationals 'trafficking' in Cuban property formerly owned by US nationals. A solution was found between the European Community and the USA without having resort to the WTO dispute settlement procedures ((1997) 36 ILM 529ff). Cf Reiterer, 1997.

[22] Cf also Article IX paras 3 and 4 Marrakesh Agreement and the 1994 Understanding in Respect of Obligations under the General Agreement of Tariffs and Trade. Such waivers were granted to the European Community regarding the transitional regime for the EC autonomous tariff rate quotas on the import of bananas ((2002) 41 ILM 770ff) and regarding the ACP–EC partnership agreement ((2002) 41 ILM 767ff) by the Doha Ministerial Conference 2001.

[23] Cf Hudec, 1987; Cassese, 2005, p 517.

accession, and to existing members by waiver under the WTO Agreement. All exemptions are subject to review and should, in principle, last no longer than 10 years. Restrictions to safeguard the balance of payments may be taken if there are—or if there is a threat of—serious balance-of-payments and external financial difficulties. GATS also provides general and security exemptions similar to GATT Articles XIX and XX (the protection of public morals or for the protection of human, animal, or plant life and health). Finally, GATS allows members to enter into economic integration agreements or to mutually recognize regulatory standards in accordance with certain conditions.

Specific obligations for liberalizing trade in services are contained in country-specific schedules. These list services for which market access and national treatment are guaranteed and limitations which may be attached, concerning, for example, the number of service operations or employees in a sector, the value of transactions, or the legal form of the service supplier. The scope of these individual country schedules may vary widely between members. Some may contain only few services, others concern over 120 types of services. Additional sector-specific commitments can be the subject of protocols negotiated between WTO members and such protocols have been concluded on financial services (1995 and 1997), basic telecommunications (1997), and the movement of natural persons (1995).

4. Agreement on Trade Related Intellectual Property Rights (TRIPS)

The TRIPS Agreement links the international trading system to the legal provisions laid down by international agreements on intellectual property rights, such as the Paris and Berne Conventions administered by the World Intellectual Property Rights Organization (WIPO). The TRIPS Agreement provides for the application of the principle of national treatment and the most-favoured-nation treatment and sets standards concerning the availability, scope, and use of intellectual property rights. The categories of intellectual property rights covered by the TRIPS Agreement are: copyright and related rights, trademarks, geographical indications, industrial designs, patents, and the protection of undisclosed information. Furthermore, the TRIPS Agreement provides standards for the enforcement of intellectual property rights by means of civil and administrative procedures and remedies as well as criminal procedures.

5. Trade Policy Review Mechanism (TPRM)

The purpose of the TPRM is to improve adherence by all members to rules, disciplines, and commitments made under the Multilateral Trade Agreements and, where appropriate, the Plurilateral Agreements by achieving greater transparency in, and understanding of, the trade policies and practices of WTO members. Reviews take place at regular intervals based on the reports of WTO members (every two years for the USA, the EC, Japan, and Canada; every four years for other industrialized countries; and every six years for all other members).

6. Dispute Settlement Understanding (DSU)

The DSU builds on the experience of GATT 1947. Dispute settlement under GATT 1947 was centred on the use of ad hoc panels consisting of three or five individuals. Although quite successful, decisions had to be taken by consensus by all GATT contracting parties, including the parties to the dispute who could therefore delay or even block the decision-making process. This led some parties to take unilateral measures. Furthermore, there was no time frame for the decision-making process. The DSU strengthened the rule of law in the world trading system by setting strict time limits for the different stages of the dispute settlement process, by providing for a negative consensus and by obliging parties to refrain from taking unilateral measures (see Petersmann, 1997; Merrills, 2005, pp 235–236).

If a dispute arises between WTO members, obligatory consultations must take place. If no solution is achieved within 60 days, any party to the dispute may request the establishment of a panel. The Dispute Settlement Body (DSB, consisting of representatives of all WTO members) must then establish a panel unless it decides otherwise by consensus. A panel consists of three individuals agreed upon by the parties concerned. If the parties cannot agree on the composition of the panel within 20 days, the Director-General appoints the panel members after consultations. The panel makes an objective assessment of the matter, based on the submissions of the parties to the dispute and of other members having a substantial interest in the matter before the panel as well as upon information and technical advice sought by the panel itself (DSU Article 13). The panel produces a report containing its findings and recommendations to the DSB within six months.[24] The report is adopted by the DSB unless it decides not to do so by consensus (negative consensus) or unless a party to the dispute appeals to the Standing Appellate Body. The latter shall deliver its report on legal issues arising from the panel report within 90 days. The Appellate Body's report is itself to be adopted by the DSB unless it decides otherwise by consensus.

The reports have to be implemented by the parties, normally within 15 months, under the surveillance of the DSB. If there are disagreements on the measures taken in implementing the panel report, these are themselves to be decided through the dispute settlement procedures, including resort to the original panel. The DSB may authorize countermeasures (by the affected party), including compensation or the suspension of concessions or other obligations, if the report is not implemented. Disputes concerning the scope of countermeasures are to be referred to arbitration, conducted either by the original panel or by an arbitrator appointed by the Director-General, within 60 days. All these dispute settlement procedures were used in the *Bananas*[25] and *Beef Hormones* cases,[26] which also showed the shortcomings of the DSU system, including, for example, a lack of clarity concerning the exact point at which countermeasures might be authorized.

Under the DSU, any WTO member may intervene in proceedings if its interests are affected. In recent years the question has been debated if other entities, such as non-governmental organizations, may make submissions. The DSU does not address this and although the Appellate Body allowed this in the *Shrimp-Turtle* case, the DSB has requested caution in this regard (Wirth, 2002, pp 437–439).

The *Beef Hormones* cases brought by the USA, and subsequently Canada, against the European Community illustrate both the operation of the WTO dispute settlement system, its effectiveness, and its shortcomings. In accordance with DSU Article 4 and

---

[24] The panel may inform the DSB in writing that it needs more time but the maximum period from the establishment of the panel to the circulation of its report is nine months (DSU Article 12(9)).

[25] Case concerning *European Communities—Regime for the Importation, Sale and Distribution of Bananas*.

[26] Case concerning *European Communities—Measures Concerning Meat and Meat Products (Hormones)*.

relevant provisions of other WTO Agreements, the USA requested consultations with the EC in January 1996 (Canada in June 1996) concerning an EC import ban on meat and meat products from cattle to which either natural or synthetic hormones had been admin- istrated for growth purposes. Australia, New Zealand, and Canada requested to join these consultations. Joint consultations were held in March 1996 (Canada in September 1996) but reached no result. In April 1996 the United States requested that a panel be established with standard terms of reference pursuant to DSU Article 6 and in May 1996 (Canada in October 1996) a panel was established and its composition agreed upon in early July 1996 (Canada and the EC subsequently agreed to its panel having the same composition as that set up with the USA). The panel met several times with the parties to the dispute and consulted scientific and technical experts. Final reports were provided to the parties on 30 June 1997 and to the WTO members on 18 August 1997.[27] In accordance with DSU Article 12(9) the DSU had previously informed the DSB that the report would take more than six months to produce.

Both the EC and the USA and Canada notified the DSB that, pursuant to DSU Article 16.4, they would appeal certain issues of law addressed in the panel reports (24 September 1997 and 9 October 1997, respectively) and Australia, New Zealand, and Norway filed sep- arate third participants' submissions. All submissions were heard by the Appellate Body on 4 and 5 November 1997 and its report[28] (along with the panel reports, as modified by the Appellate Body report) were adopted by the DSB on 13 February 1998. One month later, on 13 March 1998 the EC informed the DSB, pursuant to DSU Article 21.3, that it intended to fulfil its obligations, that it had initiated the process to examine the options for compliance with a view to implementation in as short a period of time as possible, and that it would require a 'reasonable period of time' for this process. Consultations were held between the EC, the USA, and Canada on 26 March 1998 and further writ- ten communications between the parties failed to resolve the issue of what constituted a 'reasonable period of time' and so on 8 April 1998 the EC requested that the 'reasonable period of time' be determined by binding arbitration in accordance with DSU Article 21.3(c). As no agreement on the appointment of an arbitrator was reached within 10 days, an arbitrator was appointed by the Director-General who then determined that the 'rea- sonable period of time' would expire on 13 May 1999 (15 months after the adoption of the reports by the DSU).[29]

The USA informed the DSB on 17 May 1999 that the EC had failed to implement the recommendations and rulings of the DSB with respect to its hormones measures by 13 May 1999 and requested authorization to suspend the application of tariff concessions and related obligations under the GATT 1994 towards the EC and its member States, covering US$202 million worth of trade, a sum equal to the loss in US exports consequent upon the ban. The EC objected to the magnitude of the proposed suspensions and requested that the matter be referred to arbitration pursuant to DSU Article 22.6. The arbitration was carried out by the original panel, which determined the level of nullification or impairment suf- fered by the USA to be US$116.8 million per year and that the USA could take suspensive

[27] *EC Measures Concerning Meat and Meat Products (Hormones)*, Panel Report, WT/DS26/R/USA, WT/ DS48/R/CAN (18 August 1997).

[28] *Beef Hormone Case*, Appellate Body Report, WT/DS26/AB/R, WT/DS48/AB/R (16 January 1998).

[29] Arbitration under Article 21.3(c) DSU (WT/DS26/15 and WT/DS48/13 dated 29 May 1998).

measures to that amount,[30] this being subsequently authorized by the DSB in accordance with DSU Article 22.7. Thus although the dispute settlement proceedings did not lead to a settlement as such within the time period set by the DSU, a solution was found that avoided a 'trade war' between disputants.

The EC demanded the lifting of the sanctions imposed by the USA and Canada in 2003 after a new directive entered into force concerning the prohibition on the use in stockfarming of certain substances having a hormonal or thyrostatic action and of beta-agonists. The EC argued that it was based on a comprehensive risk assessment, which had indicated that the hormones in question in the dispute were a risk to human health. Thus, the EC legislation was in conformity with WTO law. The USA and Canada considered the new Directive to be inconsistent with the EC's obligations under WTO law, but refused to initiate dispute settlement procedures under Article 21.5 of the DSU in order to obtain a review the consistency of the new Directive with the recommendations and the rulings of the DSB. Thus the EC requested consultations with the USA and Canada which failed to resolve the dispute. At the request of the EC a panel was established on 17 February 2005 to address, *inter alia*, the question whether the USA and Canada violated WTO law by not removing the retaliatory measures. The DSB adopted the Appelate Body report and the Panel report on 14 November 2008.[31] It held that it had been unable to establish whether the directive had brought the EC into substantive compliance within the meaning of DSU Article 22.8. The DSB requested the US, Canada and the EC to initiate proceedings under DSU Article 21.5 in order to settle the dispute on whether the EC has removed the measures which had been found inconsistent with the WTO law in the *Beef Hormones* cases.

7. Concluding remarks

Although the WTO established a comprehensive international legal and institutional framework for international trade, a number of issues remain to be addressed. Some further areas might become subject to new agreements, such as foreign investment and international competition rules. Furthermore, human rights, social, health, and environmental standards will become central issues in negotiations for further development of the international trade system.[32] Thus, the WTO needs to cooperate closely with other international organizations and institutions (such as the International Labour Organization) dealing with these matters. The Ministerial Conference, held in Doha, Qatar in 2001, has made development issues a central topic for the further development of WTO law.[33] The new round of negotiations ('Doha Round'), which was started by the Doha Ministerial Conference, deals with a range of subjects, such as agriculture and non-agricultural market access, services, environment and investment, technical cooperation and capacity-building as well as issues related to the implementation of agreements which have been the result of the Uruguay Round. Although the GATT/WTO legal system has been altered

[30] Decision by the Arbitrators under DSU Article 22.6 (WT/DS26/ARB dated 12 July 1999).

[31] *US-Continued Suspension of Obligations in the EC-Hormones Dispute*, Panel Report, WT/DS320/R (31 March 2008); Appellate Body Report, WT/DS320/AB/R (16 October 2008).

[32] For example the implications of the principle of precautionary approach as stated in the 1992 Rio Declaration on Environment and Development already gave rise to a number of controversies between WTO members.

[33] See in particular paras 38–44 of the Work Programme adopted by the Fourth WTO Ministerial Conference in Doha, Qatar, 2001 (2002) 41 ILM 746.

to take account of the concerns of developing countries, further changes are necessary to address their specific needs. The WTO will need to succeed in its efforts to include these new issues within its legal framework if it is to establish a stable and predictable system for international trade relations in the future. A successful outcome of the Doha Round is therefore essential as the new 'economic realities' have to be taken into account.

C. INTERNATIONAL COMMODITY AGREEMENTS

Specific rules have been established regarding the production of and international trade in commodities, that is, primary commodities or raw materials (GATT Article XX(h)). These products provide an important source of export earnings for the great majority of developing countries but price fluctuations hamper their long-term economic planning activities. Therefore, international agreements have been set up which aim to secure stable prices and demand, assist in establishing predictable incomes for developing countries, and secure supplies for the consumer countries. Such arrangements have been concluded for a number of commodities, including wheat, coffee, cocoa, olive oil, and tin. These agreements last for specific time periods—the International Coffee Agreement 2001, for example, has a duration of six years—so they can be modified periodically to reflect changing economic conditions. International commodity agreements should not be seen as instruments to bolster prices, but rather as mechanisms designed to stabilize prices without distorting long-term market trends.

A number of market regulation mechanisms have been developed, the most prominent being buffer stocks and export quotas. Buffer stocks aim at ensuring that the price remains within a given price range by selling when the market price exceeds the maximum intervention price and by buying when the price falls below the minimum price. A system of export quotas for producers might be combined with a buffer stock. Such mechanisms were used in a number of commodity agreements in the 1960s and 1970s (eg tin, sugar, and coffee). At first, buffer stocks were financed by the producers but in the 1970s consumer countries agreed to contribute, because they benefited from the buffer stocks as well. However, the failure of the sixth International Tin Agreement in 1985 due to insolvency[34] led to a change of the structure of international commodity agreements.

Today's agreements do not contain market intervention mechanisms but have set new objectives. The 2001 International Coffee Agreement has the following aims: to encourage members to develop a sustainable coffee economy, promote coffee consumption, promote quality, provide a forum for the private sector, promote trading and information programmes designed to assist the transfer of technology relevant to member countries, and analyse and advise on the preparation of projects to the benefit of the world coffee economy. Similar objectives are set out in the 2001 Sixth International Cocoa Agreement and the 1994 International Tropical Timber Agreement.

---

[34] The International Tin Council was set up as an agreement between producer and consumer States and had a buffer stock of 50,000 tons and operated a system of export controls. It failed because major producer and consumer States did not become parties to the agreement and because the Tin Council had to buy large quantities of tin on the international market in order to ensure a stable market price. In 1985 its financial resources were exhausted and it had borrowed £900 million from banks and brokers. For further details on the collapse of the ITC, see McFadden, 1986.

All international commodity agreements set up at least one organ: a council comprising representatives of all member countries. Voting under international commodity agreements is based on weighted votes. Both producer and consumer countries are given an equal number of total votes, normally 1,000 votes. Each member is given a basic number of votes and the remaining votes are distributed according to the percentage of imports or exports during a reference period. Decisions and recommendations are adopted by a distributed simple majority, ie, a simple majority of both producer and consumer countries, although some decisions might require a two-thirds majority of both producer and consumer countries. To be effective, such agreements need a minimum membership which represents a considerable percentage of both producers and consumers. For example, Article 45 of the 2001 International Coffee Agreement provides that the agreement only enters into force when at least 15 exporting members holding at least 70% of the votes of the exporting members and at least 10 importing members holding at least 70% of the votes of the importing members have deposited instruments of ratification, acceptance, or approval.

The practical impact of international commodity agreements has decreased in recent years. This is evident not only from the decline in market regulation mechanisms used in such agreements but also from the decreasing number of such agreements. For example the International Rubber Agreement was suspended in 1999 by the International Rubber Council after a number of the main producing countries withdrew from the Agreement. Thus, as the example of the 2001 Cocoa and Coffee Agreements shows, the direct influence of such agreements on the market will be comparatively limited in future. Their main aim is to encourage cooperation not only between governments, but also to include the private sector in their efforts to promote the commodity in question. Furthermore, projects to improve the quality of the commodity, to combat diseases, and to diversify products aim at assisting developing countries in their efforts to achieve sustainable development. The 2007 Coffee Agreement, which is expected to replace the 2001 Coffee Agreement, includes provisions on development and funding of coffee development projects and the establishment of a consultative forum on coffee sector finance in order to take into account in particular the needs of small- and medium-scale prducers and local communities in coffee producing areas.

In 1989 the Agreement Establishing the Common Fund for Commodities entered into force. The Agreement was negotiated in the United Nations Conference on Trade and Development (UNCTAD). The Fund, in line with its market-oriented approach, concentrates on commodity projects financed from its resources. These projects aim at improving the structural conditions in markets and at enhancing the long-term competitiveness and prospects of particular commodities. Commodity producers in developing countries and countries in transition are assisted in transforming regulated into liberalized market systems. The Fund currently concentrates on commodities which are of interest to Least Developed Countries. It also closely cooperates with the institutions established by the international commodity agreements.

In addition to international commodity agreements, international commodity cartels have also been established. Their membership comprises countries producing a given commodity. The most well-known example is the Organization of Petroleum Exporting Countries (OPEC), which was set up in 1960 and which plays an important role in determining global oil supply and prices. The effectiveness of such organizations largely depends on the percentage of market supply controlled by members and the degree of cooperation achieved between them.

IV. INTERNATIONAL INVESTMENT LAW

A. INTRODUCTION

The expansion of Western economies since the nineteenth century has resulted in considerable levels of investments in other States, both developed and developing. But the degree of control over local economies that follows from this has given rise to conflicts between capital exporting and capital importing countries. On the one hand, capital exporting countries require protection and security for the investments made by their nationals, whilst, on the other hand, the capital importing countries demand the ability to regain or retain control over certain (key) parts of their economies and numerous countries, both developing and developed, have expropriated foreign property to achieve this (Shaw, 2008, p 828).

Under customary international law, expropriation of foreign property is legitimate if it takes place under certain conditions: the expropriation must be in the public interest, without discrimination on the basis of nationality and be accompanied by the payment of appropriate compensation. In the last decades the amount of compensation to be paid by the expropriating State has been a source of controversy[35] between developed and developing countries. UNGA Resolution 1803 (XVII) 1962 on permanent sovereignty over natural resources states that appropriate compensation has to be paid, whereas UNGA Resolution 3281 (XXIX) 1974, the Charter of Economic Rights and Duties of States, adopted in the General Assembly against the votes of the OECD member countries, provides that appropriate compensation should be paid and that disputes are to be settled by the tribunals of the nationalizing State applying its domestic law, unless it is freely and mutually agreed otherwise by all States concerned. Against this, a number of capital exporting countries have argued that compensation should be prompt, adequate, and effective—the so-called Hull Formula.[36]

In recent years, issues concerning establishment in a host country have also become a focal point in efforts to promote foreign direct investment. Under customary international law the host country determines the conditions of establishment of foreigners within its territory. The resulting legal uncertainties led to calls for new legal instruments to encourage investment flows between countries and a number of instruments have been developed to create a favourable investment climate under public international law: bilateral investment treaties (BITs), investment insurance schemes, and investment dispute settlement mechanisms. Moreover, multilateral instruments such as GATS, TRIMS, and TRIPS also address investment issues.

B. DEFINITION OF INVESTMENT

The term investment in international law should be understood in a very broad way as it comprises all kinds of assets, including all categories of rights and interests. Most BITs

---

[35] Eg, *Texaco Overseas Petroleum Co* v *Libyan Arab Republic*, Arbitral Award (1977), 53 ILR 389.

[36] On the issue of expropriation of foreign property and case law see Brownlie, 2008, p 531; Shaw, 2008, p 827.

include elaborate descriptions of investments, although such descriptions are themselves non-exhaustive. An example of a definition of investment may be found in Article 1(a) of the 1989 Agreement between the Russian Federation and the UK:[37]

the term investment means every kind of asset and in particular, though not exclusively, includes:

(i) movable and immovable property and any other related property rights such as mortgages;

(ii) shares in, and stocks, bonds and debentures of, and any other form of participation in, a company or business enterprise;

(iii) claims to money, and claims to performance under contract having a financial value;

(iv) intellectual property rights, technical processes, know-how and any other benefit or advantage attached to a business;

(v) rights conferred by law or under contract to undertake any commercial activity, including search for, or the cultivation, extraction or exploitation of natural resources.

C. BILATERAL INVESTMENT TREATIES

Bilateral investment treaties aim to encourage and protect investments in the territories of the contracting States. The first bilateral investment agreement was concluded between Germany and Pakistan in 1959 since which time their number has increased enormously: Germany has concluded more than 110 BITs, the UK over 80, France more than 60, and the USA around 40. BITs have been concluded between developed and developing countries, but in recent years also between developing countries.[38] In general, BITs provide that nationals and companies of the State parties should enjoy non-discriminatory treatment, protection, and security, prompt, adequate, and effective compensation in the event of expropriation, and freedom from currency transfer restrictions.

The USA started to conclude BITs in the early 1980s. However, it had already begun to enter into Friendship, Commerce and Navigation (FCN) Treaties in the 1920s and concluded such treaties with most developed countries. But developing countries were reluctant to accept such a comprehensive liberalization of economic relations. Therefore the USA followed the example of the European countries by concluding BITs that are limited to the promotion and protection of investments.

Most BITs are based on a OECD model agreement developed in the 1960s and further elaborated since. Their importance is underlined by the fact that the African Asian Legal Consultative Committee (AALCC) has also elaborated several models for BITs which follow a similar pattern to the OECD model, although the AALCC models put more emphasis on the promotion of investments (Dolzer and Stevens, 1995, p 5).

Efforts to ensure stable conditions for foreign investments in the energy sector within the territory of the former Soviet Union led to the conclusion of the 1994 Energy Charter

---

[37] (1990) 29 ILM 366. [38] Eg, China has concluded BITs with the central Asian republics.

Treaty.[39] This comprehensive multilateral agreement establishes a non-discriminatory investment, trade, and transit regime for the energy sector (Walde, 1996, p xx). Similar provisions to those contained in BITs are also found in Chapter XI of the North American Free Trade Agreement (NAFTA) between Canada, Mexico, and the USA (Sacerdoti, 1997, p 333).

Although BITs do not conform to a common standard, they do have a number of common features and tend to address the following issues (Sacerdoti, 1997, p 298; Sornarajah, 1994, p 277):

- *The definition of the investor*: the main question here concerns whether the treaty protects companies that have been established under the law of the host State but which are owned by nationals of the other party.

- *Conditions for admission of investments*: although BITs do not establish a right to invest in the territory of a State, a number of BITs provide that investments should be admitted in accordance with the State's legislation and that favourable conditions for investments should be created. Earlier BITs required foreign investments to fit into national development plans and underlined the need for specific approval by the host State authorities (Sacerdoti, 1997, pp 328–329).

- *Treatment of investments*: BITs provide standards regarding the treatment of foreign investments reflecting the following principles:
  - fair and equitable treatment
  - full protection and security
  - non-discrimination
  - national treatment
  - most-favoured nation treatment.

In general, BITs provide for a combination of these standards, eg, the obligation to provide fair and equitable treatment is combined with the principle of non-discrimination, and national treatment is combined with most-favoured-nation treatment. Recent agreements have extended these treatment standards also to the pre- and post-establishment phases.[40]

- *Protection against political risks*: explicit provisions provide that if expropriation occurs, compensation shall be paid according to the Hull Formula. Furthermore, transfer restrictions are only permitted in cases of emergency.

- *Dispute settlement provisions*: BITs provide for dispute settlement mechanisms both between the States party to the BIT and between the host State and the foreign investor. As regards dispute settlement between the States, traditional patterns of dispute settlement are envisaged.[41] For dispute settlement between the host State and the foreign investor, most BITs provide that the foreign investor may choose from the following possibilities:
  - settlement before a court of the host State;

---

[39] (1995) 34 ILM 360.
[40] See Salacuse, 1996, p 335. Cf UNCTAD Series on issues in international investment agreements.
[41] Cf Article 33 of the UN Charter.

- arbitration through ICSID; and

- arbitration using the UNCITRAL rules of arbitration.

D. IS THERE A NEED FOR A MULTILATERAL INVESTMENT AGREEMENT?

So far efforts to create a multilateral agreement on the promotion and protection of foreign investments on a global level have failed. The most recent effort was undertaken within OECD. The negotiations on a Multilateral Agreement on Investment (MAI) aimed to provide high standards for the liberalization of investment regimes and investment protection between the OECD member countries and, eventually, other interested non-OECD member States. But the negotiations on the MAI were suspended and finally discontinued as a number of key issues could not be solved during the negotiations, chiefly concerning the definition of investment, exceptions to national and most-favoured-nation treatment, intellectual property rights, the cultural exception clause, labour and environmental issues, regulatory takings, and the settlement of disputes. This was partly due to the opposition of NGOs (trade unions, environmental groups, and human rights groups) and partly due to the lack of support by the business community since the MAI failed to offer any significant shift towards liberalization. Proposals have recently been put forward to establish a multilateral framework for foreign investments within the WTO, but no consensus has been reached on this issue (Sacerdoti, 1997, p 297).

E. INVESTMENT INSURANCE SCHEMES AT THE NATIONAL LEVEL

In order to provide security for investors against the political risks involved in investing in other countries, a number of capital exporting countries have established national investment insurance schemes. The risks covered are: expropriation, transfer restrictions, and war or civil unrest. Most industrialized countries—and some newly industrialized countries, such as Malaysia—provide insurance schemes against political risks (Loibl, 1987, pp 102–115). In the United Kingdom the Export Credits Guarantee Department (a separate Department of the British Government) provides political risk insurance for UK investors. In the United States the Overseas Private Investment Cooperation (a US government agency) assists US private investors overseas. Political risk insurance coverage is also offered by a number of insurance companies. Various efforts have been undertaken at the regional and international level to establish such investment insurance schemes, eg by OECD and the European Community, but these were unsuccessful. The only regional investment insurance scheme currently in existence is the Inter-Arab Investment Guarantee Corporation.

F. THE MULTILATERAL INVESTMENT GUARANTEE AGENCY (MIGA)

The idea of establishing a multilateral investment insurance agency dates back to the 1950s. In 1985 international efforts resulted in the adoption of an agreement on the establishment of the Multilateral Investment Guarantee Agency (MIGA) under the auspices of the World Bank which entered into force in 1988 and currently has 164 parties. Article 2 provides that MIGA's objective is to encourage the flow of investments for productive purposes among member countries, and in particular to developing member countries, thus supplementing the activities of the IBRD, the IFC, and other international development finance institutions. The organizational structure of MIGA follows that of the other World Bank institutions. Although MIGA could have its own President and Board of Directors, these roles have, so far, been undertaken always by the President and Directors of the World Bank.

MIGA issues guarantees, including co-insurance and reinsurance, against non-commercial risks concerning investments in a developing member country that flow from other member countries and promote investments. According to MIGA Article 11(a) the following political risks may be covered:

- *Currency transfer*: any introduction attributable to the host government of restrictions on the transfer outside the host country of its currency into a freely usable currency or another currency acceptable to the holder of the guarantee, including failure of the host government to act within a reasonable period of time on an application by such holder for such transfer;

- *Expropriation and similar measures*: any legislative action or administrative action or omission attributable to the host government which has the effect of depriving the holder of a guarantee of his ownership or control of, or a substantial benefit from his investment, with the exception of non-discriminatory measures of general application which governments normally take for the purpose of regulating economic activity in their territories;

- Breach of contract: any repudiation or breach by the host government of a contract with the holder of a guarantee, when (a) a holder of a guarantee does not have recourse to a judicial or arbitral forum to determine the claim of repudiation or breach, or (b) a decision by such forum is not rendered within a reasonable period of time as shall be prescribed in the contracts of guarantee pursuant to the Agency's regulations, or (c) such a decision cannot be enforced; and

- War and civil disturbance: any military action or civil disturbance in any territory of the host country to which the convention applies.

MIGA only guarantees investments in developing countries and certain transition countries (Article 14) and the host government must approve the issuance of the guarantee by the Agency against the risks to be covered (Article 15). If compensation is paid by MIGA to a holder of a guarantee, any rights that that holder may have against the host country or others pass to the Agency (Article 18). Furthermore, Article 23 determines that MIGA is to carry out research, undertake activities to promote investment flows, and disseminate information on investment opportunities in developing countries, with a view to improving the environment for foreign investment flows to such countries.

Contrary to initial speculation, there has been a high demand for MIGA's services and this continues to rise with the growth of foreign direct investment to developing countries and to countries in transition.

G. INVESTMENT DISPUTE SETTLEMENT MECHANISMS

There is a long history of settling disputes between foreign investors and host countries by mixed arbitration, ie arbitration between a State and a non-State entity. The most well-known mixed arbitration mechanism established, on a permanent basis, to deal with investment disputes is the International Centre for the Settlement of Investment Disputes (ICSID). The convention creating ICSID was elaborated under the auspices of the World Bank, was opened for signature in 1965, entered into force in 1966, and currently has 144 States parties.

ICSID is not a tribunal itself, but rather a framework within which arbitration and conciliation can occur (Collier and Lowe, 1999, p 60). Each member State has one vote in the Administrative Council which is chaired by the President of the World Bank. The Administrative Council supervises the operation of ICSID and adopts rules of procedure for conciliation and arbitration. The ICSID secretariat screens requests for arbitration in order to ensure that they are not manifestly outside the jurisdiction of ICSID and it also provides institutional support.

ICSID Article 25 (1) provides that:

The jurisdiction of the Centre shall extend to any legal dispute arising out of an investment, between a Contracting State (or any constituent subdivision or agency of a Contracting State designated to the Centre by that State) and a national of another Contracting State, which the parties to the dispute consent in writing to submit to the Centre. When the parties have given their consent, no party may withdraw its consent unilaterally.

Thus ICSID jurisdiction is limited to legal disputes arising out of an investment dispute. Moreover, both the home State of the foreign investor and the host State must be parties to the Convention, and the parties to the dispute must have given explicit agreement to ICSID arbitration. The latter consent may be given in various forms, eg, in a concession agreement between the host State and the foreign investor, in a bilateral investment agreement[42] or in the investment laws of the host State. However, an Additional Facility has extended the jurisdiction of ICSID to non-investment disputes and to disputes in which only the host State or the State whose national is the other party to the dispute is a party to the ICSID Convention. Moreover, a fact-finding procedure has been established.

ICSID maintains lists of persons who may serve as conciliators or arbitrators. If a request for arbitration is made, the parties to the dispute choose an uneven number of arbitrators and the persons to act as arbitrators. If the parties do not appoint the arbitrators within the set time, they are appointed by the ICSID Chairman.[43]

Arbitration awards are not subject to judicial review by national courts (Article 53) although they could be subject to an internal annulment procedure through an ad hoc ICSID Committee (Article 52).[44] Each contracting party is obliged to recognize awards as

---

[42] Eg, Article 8 of the Argentine-French BIT and *Compania de Aguas del Aconquija, SA & Compagnie Générale des Eaux* v *Argentine Republic*, Case No ARB/97/3.

[43] According to Article 5 the President of the World Bank is ex officio ICSID Chairman.

[44] Such annulment procedures have been relatively rare in practice. Examples include *Amco Asia Corp* v *Republic of Indonesia*, (Case No ARB/81/1); *Compania de Aguas del Aconquija, SA & Compagnie Générale des Eaux* v *Argentine Republic* (Case No ARB/97/3) and *CMS Gas Transmission Company* v *Argentine Republic* (Case No ARB/01/8).

binding and to enforce pecuniary obligations imposed by awards within its territories as if it were a final judgment from a court in that State (Article 54).

ICSID has been used to solve a growing number of investment disputes. Its success is closely linked to the growth of BITs, since most of these treaties specify ICSID as an alternative for the settlement of investment disputes. Thus an effective mechanism has been established to settle disputes between foreign companies and host States.[45] This has helped to depoliticize conflicts between capital exporting and capital importing countries since the home State of the foreign investor is no longer drawn directly into the dispute, and it is left to the investor and the host country to settle their differences by judicial means.

V. REGIONAL ECONOMIC INTEGRATION ARRANGEMENTS

Since the end of the Second World War the number of regional economic arrangements has grown steadily in all parts of the world. Although they differ greatly in their institutional structure and in the range of economic activities covered, most have followed the example of European regional cooperation and integration by first concentrating on establishing free trade areas or customs unions for trade in goods. Only at a later stage in their evolution are other areas of economic activity, such as trade in services and investment issues, subjected to regulation at the regional level. The success of these organizations in ensuring closer economic cooperation and integration differs. Some, such as the European Community or the North American Free Trade Area, have reached a high degree of integration of their member States' economies, whereas others have not yet achieved this.

VI. CONCLUDING REMARKS

As international economic relations have expanded in the last decades other areas of international relations have become increasingly important. Discussions concerning the inter-relationship between international economic law and human rights as well as international environmental law have made it clear that these areas can no longer be separated. Recent developments in the area of international financial law, international trade law, and investment law demonstrate that other areas of international regulation have a decisive influence on international economic law. Moreover, international economic law is more and more addressing development concerns. In some areas specific rules have been elaborated to deal with the needs of the developing countries whilst the World Summit for Sustainable Development in Johannesburg in 2002 has underlined the need to address international economic issues in a broader context in order to achieve sustainable development. International economic law can no longer be seen in isolation from other areas of international law.

---

[45] For ICSID cases see the website of ICSID (**http://icsid.worldbank.org/ICSID/Index.jsp**), the ICSID Review, and the Foreign Investment Law Journal. Most cases are made public.

REFERENCES

AMERICAN LAW INSTITUTE (1987), *Restatement of the Law of the Foreign Relations Law of the United States* (St Paul, Minn.: American Law Institute Publishers).

BLOKKER, NM and SCHERMERS, HG (eds) (2001), *Proliferation of International Organizations* (The Hague: Kluwer Law International).

BROWN-WEISS, E, JACKSON, JH, and BERNASCONI-OSTERWALDER, N (eds) (2008), *Reconciling Environment and Trade* (New York: Transnational Publishers).

BROWNLIE, I (2008), *Principles of Public International Law*, 7th edn (Oxford: Oxford University Press).

CARREAU, D and JULLIARD, P (1998), *Droit International Économique*, 4th edn (Paris: Librairie générale de droit et de jurisprudence).

CASSESE, A (2005), *International Law*, 2nd edn (Oxford: Oxford University Press).

COING, H (1992), 'Bretton Woods Conference 1944', in Bernhardt, R (ed) *Encyclopaedia of Public International Law*, vol I (Amsterdam: North-Holland), pp 494–495.

COLLIER, J and LOWE, AV (1999), *The Settlement of Disputes in International Law Institutions and Procedures* (Oxford: Oxford University Press).

DENTERS, E (1996), *Law and Policy of IMF Conditionality* (The Hague: Kluwer Law International).

DICKE, DC (ed) (1987), *Foreign Investment in the Present and a New International Economic Order* (Fribourg: University Press).

DOLZER, R and STEVENS, M (1995), *Bilateral Investment Treaties* (The Hague: Kluwer Law International).

GOLSONG, H (1995), 'International Finance Corporation', in Bernhardt, R (ed), *Encyclopaedia of Public International Law*, vol II (Amsterdam: North-Holland), pp 1142–1143.

HUDEC, RE (1987), *Developing Countries in the GATT Legal System* (London: Trade Policy Research Centre).

JACKSON, JH (1997), *The World Trading System Law and Policy of International Economic Relations*, 2nd edn (Cambridge, Mass.: MIT Press).

JANEKE, G (1995), 'General Agreement on Tariffs and Trade (1947)', II *EPIL* 502–510.

KRUGMAN, R and OBSTFELD, M (2000), *International Economics—Theory and Politics*, 5th edn (Reading, Mass.: Addison-Wesley Publishing).

LOIBL, G (1987), 'Foreign Investment Insurance Systems', in Dicke, DC (ed), *Foreign Investment in the Present and a New International Economic Order* (Fribourg: University Press), pp 102, 115.

—— (1998), 'The World Bank Group and sustainable development', in Weiss, F, Denters, E, and De Waart, P (eds) *International Economic Law with a Human Face* (The Hague: Kluwer Law International), pp 513–532.

McFADDEN, JM (1986), 'The Collapse of the Tin: Restructuring a Failed Commodity Agreement', 80 *AJIL* 811–830.

McRAE, DM (1996), 'The Contribution of International Trade Law to the Development of International Law', 260 *Recueil des Cours* 99.

MERRILLS, JG (2005), *International Dispute Settlement*, 4th edn (Cambridge: Cambridge University Press).

PETERSMANN, E (1997), *The GATT/WTO Dispute Settlement System* (The Hague: Kluwer Law International).

QURESHI, AH (1999), *International Economic Law* (London: Sweet & Maxwell).

REITERER, MA (1997), 'Article XXI GATT—Does the National Security Exception Permit "Anything Under the Sun"?', 2 *Austrian Rev of Int'l and European L* 191–212.

SACERDOTI, G (1997), 'Bilateral Treaties and Multilateral Instruments on Investment Protection', 269 *Recueil des Cours* 251.

SALACUSE, JW (1996), 'The Energy Charter Treaty and Bilateral Investment Treaty Regimes', in Wälde (ed), p 321.

SCHOENBAUM, T (1997), 'International Trade and the Protection of the Environment. The Continuing Search for Reconciliation', 91 *AJIL* 268–313.

SHAW, MN (2008), *International Law*, 6th edn (Cambridge: Cambridge University Press).

SHIHATA, I (1998), 'The World Bank's Contribution to the Development of International Environmental Law', in Hafner, G et al (eds), *Liber Amicorum for Professor Ignaz Seidl-Hohenveldern* (The Hague: Kluwer), pp 631–657.

—— (2000), *World Bank Inspection Panel*, 2nd edn (Oxford: Oxford University Press).

—— (2001), 'Techniques to Avoid Proliferation of International Organisations—The Experience of the World Bank', in Blokker, NM and Schermers, HG (eds) *Proliferation of International Organizations* (The Hague: Kluwer Law International), pp 111–134.

SORNARAJAH, M (1994), *The International Law on Foreign Investment* (Cambridge: Cambridge University Press).

WÄLDE, T (ed) (1996), *The Energy Charter Treaty, An East-West Gateway for Investment and Trade* (The Hague: Kluwer Law International).

WEISS, F, DENTERS, E, and DE WAART, P (eds) (1998), *International Economic Law with a Human Face* (The Hague: Kluwer Law International).

WIRTH, D (2002), 'Case Report. European Communities—Measures Affecting Asbestos and Asbestos-Containing Products', 96 *AJIL* 435.

FURTHER READING

CARREAU, D and JUILLARD, P (1998), *Droit International Économique*, 4th edn (Paris: Librairie générale de droit et de jurisprudence): a most comprehensive treatise on international economic law, in particular dealing with the transnational monetary and financial system.

GOLD, J (1996), *Interpretation: The IMF and International Law* (The Hague: Kluwer Law International): the most comprehensive work on the operation of the IMF and the legal issues arising within the IMF.

JACKSON, JH (1997), *The World Trading System Law and Policy of International Economic Relations*, 2nd edn (Cambridge, Mass.: MIT Press): a thorough work on the functioning of the World Trading System.

LOWENFELD, AF (2002), *International Economic Law* (Oxford: Oxford Unversity Press): an outstanding treatise on international economic law.

MATSUSHITA, M, SCHOENBAUM, TJ, and MAVROIDIS, PC (2006), *The World Trade Organisation—Law, Practice and Policy*, 2nd edn (Oxford: Oxford University Press): an excellent and detailed analysis of the current status of the World Trade Organization.

SACERDOTI, G (1997), 'Bilateral Treaties and Multilateral Instruments on Investment Protection', 269 *Recueil des Cours* 251–460: an analysis of the current status of investment protection under international law.

SCHREUER, C (2001), *The ICSID Convention: A Commentary* (Cambridge: Cambridge University Press): the leading work on the practice of ICSID.

SEIDL-HOHENVELDERN, I (1999), *International Economic Law* (The Hague: Kluwer Law International): the most comprehensive work on rules of public international law directly concerned with economic exchanges.

SHIHATA, I (1998), *World Bank Inspection Panel*, 2nd edn (Oxford: Oxford University Press): this work gives an insight into the operation of the World Bank Group.

VAN DEN BOSSCHE, P (2008), *The Law and Policy of the World Trade Organization*, 2nd edn (Cambridge University Press): a comprehensive book on the functioning and operation of the WTO.

WEBSITES

http://www.imf.org

http://www.worldbank.org

http://icsid.worldbank.org/ICSID/ Index.jsp

http://www.ifa.org

http://www.itto.int

http://www.miga.org

http://www.wto.org

http://www.un.org

http://www.unctad.org

25

INTERNATIONAL CRIMINAL LAW

Robert Cryer

SUMMARY

This chapter deals with international crimes in the narrow sense. These are those crimes which are directly criminalized by international law. It therefore discusses the material and mental aspects of the four crimes that quality as such crimes: genocide, crimes against humanity, war crimes, and aggression. As international criminal law directly criminalizes those offences, this chapter also covers some of the general principles of liability and defences that are of particular relevance to international crimes. Therefore it explains and critiques joint criminal enterprise, co-perpetration, command responsibility, and the defence of obedience to superior orders. The chapter then looks at the international and, briefly, the national prosecution of international crimes. It covers, in particular, the Nuremberg and Tokyo Trials, the International Criminal Tribunals for former Yugoslavia and Rwanda, and the International Criminal Court. Reference is also made, *inter alia*, to the Special Court for Sierra Leone, the Special Tribunal for Lebanon, the Iraqi High Tribunal, and purely national prosecutions such as *Eichmann*. As prosecution is not the only, or predominant, response to international crimes, the chapter concludes with a discussion, and evaluation, of alternatives and complements to prosecution, such as amnesties, and truth and reconciliation commissions.

I. INTRODUCTION

There are various different ways of defining international criminal law. These include those aspects of international law involving allocation of jurisdiction, or international cooperation in criminal matters (Schwarzenberger, 1950). However international criminal law, for the purposes of this chapter, is the branch of public international law that deals with the direct criminal responsibility of individuals under that law. It can be summed up in the famous statement of the Nuremberg International Military Tribunal (IMT) that 'Individuals have international duties which transcend the national obligations of obedience imposed by the individual State ... crimes against international law are committed by men, not by abstract entities, and only by punishing individuals who commit such crimes can the provisions of international law be enforced.'[1] For international crimes, the locus of the criminal prohibition is the international legal order (although it may also be the case that such crimes are also criminalized in domestic legal orders). There are only four clear examples of international crimes in this sense: genocide, crimes against humanity, war crimes, and aggression.

There have been some suggestions that there are other international crimes, most notably terrorism and individual acts of torture (Cassese, 2008, Chs 7–8). Terrorism or torture may fall under the definitions of other international crimes (in particular crimes against humanity or war crimes), and when they do so they may be prosecuted as such. However, as it stands, there is insufficient practice indicating acceptance of the idea that they exist as separate categories of international crimes (Simma and Paulus, 1999, p 313, Saul, 2006, Ch 4).

This is not to say that acts of terrorism and torture not amounting to genocide, war crimes, or crimes against humanity are entirely unregulated by international law. There are numerous treaties dealing with aspects of terrorism,[2] and individual acts of torture are dealt with by the 1984 UN Convention Against Torture.[3] However, these are examples of what are known as 'transnational crime' conventions (Boister, 2003). These do not, in themselves create direct liability international crimes: As much can be seen from a comparison of the Torture Convention and the Genocide Convention. Article 4(1) of the Torture Convention provides that 'Each State Party shall ensure that all acts of torture are offences under its criminal law. The same shall apply to an attempt to commit torture and to an act by any person which constitutes complicity or participation in torture'. Article 1 of the Genocide Convention[4] provides that 'The Contracting Parties confirm that genocide, whether committed in time of peace or in time of war, is a crime under international law which they undertake to prevent and to punish.' There was a proposal by the International Association of Penal Law draft of the Torture convention to provide that 'Torture is a crime under international law', however, this did not make it into the first draft of the convention written by a State (Sweden).[5] Therefore, what the Torture Convention does is not create a crime itself, but oblige States to domestically criminalize Torture. The *locus* of the criminal prohibition is thus the domestic, not the international, legal order.

It is sometimes thought that the question of whether torture is an international crime turns, at least in part, on whether the Torture Convention has achieved customary status (Cassese, 2008, p 151). However, since the Convention itself does not create a direct criminal prohibition, it cannot form the basis of a customary prohibition of this type. If the Torture Convention is customary, then all States are obliged to prohibit torture domestically, not accept the existence of a direct criminal prohibition on torture in customary international law.

---

[1] Nuremberg IMT, 'Judgment and Sentence' (1947) 41 *AJIL* 172, 221, 223.

[2] For example, Convention for the Suppression of Unlawful Seizure of Aircraft 860 UNTS 105, International Convention for the Suppression of the Financing of Terrorism GA Res 54/109.

[3] 1465 UNTS 85.

[4] Convention on the Prevention and Punishment of the Crime of Genocide 78 UNTS 277.

[5] Draft Convention for the Prevention and Suppression of Torture, Submitted by the International Association of Penal Law, UN Doc E/CN.4/NGO/213, Article 1, Draft Convention Against Torture and Other Cruel, Inhuman and Degrading Treatment or Punishment (Sweden), UN Doc E/CN/4/1285.

As a final introductory point, sometimes international crimes are referred to as '*jus cogens* crimes' (eg Sadat, 2007, p 231). Although there is considerable overlap between *jus cogens* norms and international crimes (genocide, for example was considered by the ICJ to be 'assuredly' a *jus cogens* prohibition[6]), the term '*jus cogens* crime' can be apt to mislead. An international crime is created when international law directly criminalizes something. It is not required that the rule doing so has *jus cogens* status. Indeed, international crimes arose at the very latest in the Nuremburg and Tokyo IMTs, nearly 25 years before the concept of *jus cogens* was accepted in the Vienna Convention on the Law of Treaties.[7] Similarly, that a prohibition has reached the status of *jus cogens* does not mean that it is automatically an international crime. The prohibition of torture is a *jus cogens* norm,[8] however, that has not been considered, in and of itself to make the case that torture is an international crime, even amongst those that consider it to be such a crime (Cassese, 2008, p 151). In spite of this, the vast majority of international criminal law finds its basis in customary international law, and thus is applicable throughout the world. There are those that question the cultural sensitivity of this (Clarke, 2009). However, there is very considerable agreement about the relevant norms,[9] even if the way in which they are implemented and enforced is sometimes the matter of more debate.

A. INTERNATIONAL AND CRIMINAL LAW

International criminal law is an amalgam of international and criminal law. As such its sources are those of international law, which has its own methods and mentality, and criminal law, which has its own, often different, approach to critique. An understanding of both is necessary for a full understanding of international criminal law. Sometimes, the dual nature of international criminal law has led to critique, particularly from those in civilian systems where the principle of non-retroactivity of criminal prohibitions prohibits the reliance on non-written law (*nullum crimen sine lege scripta*: no crime without written law). The international legal system's acceptance of customary law is a problem for such scholars (eg Djuro-Degan, 2005, p 67). However, the *nullum crimen sine lege* principle, as it is protected at the international level does not prohibit the use of custom (Gallant, 2008, p 354), and the International Criminal Tribunal for the former Yugoslavia (ICTY), in particular, has made considerable use of customary law.[10]

II. THE CRIMES

As mentioned above, there are four international crimes, these are genocide, crimes against humanity, war crimes and aggression.

---

[6] *Armed Activities on the Territory of the Congo (New Application: 2002) (Democratic Republic of the Congo* v *Rwanda), Jurisdiction and Admissibility, Judgment, ICJ Reports 2006*, p 6, para 64. This case was also the first time the ICJ had used the term *jus cogens*.

[7] 1155 UNTS 331, Article 53. See Ch 6 above.

[8] ICTY Trial Chamber II, *Prosecutor* v *Furundžija, Judgment*, Case No IT-95-17/1-T, 10 December 1998, para 153.

[9] Although see Kelsall, 2009, Chs 3–5.

[10] See, in particular, ICTY Appeals Chamber, *Prosecutor* v *Tadić, Decision on the Defence Interlocutory Appeal on Jurisdiction*, Case No IT-94-1-AR72, 2 October 1995 (hereafter, cited as '*Tadić* Appeal').

A. GENOCIDE

Genocide, considered by some to be the 'crime of crimes' (Schabas, 2008a), is also arguably the youngest international crime. The term itself was invented by Raphael Lemkin in 1944 to describe the Holocaust (Lemkin, 1944). The tem was created by combining the Greek *'genos'* (people, or race) and the Latin *'cide'* (to kill), and this provides an insight into the underlying focus of the crime. The crime focuses on crimes that relate to threats to the existence of groups. Although the term was referred to in the Nuremberg IMT indictment, genocide was not prosecuted separately there. The first time the term genocide was used internationally in an official context was in General Assembly Resolution 96(I) (1946).

The first express definition of genocide as an international crime was in the Genocide Convention in 1948. The Convention came into force in 1951. In the same year the ICJ, in the *Reservations to the Genocide Convention* Case, determined that 'the principles underlying the Convention are principles which are recognized by civilized nations as binding on States, even without any conventional obligation.'[11] It has also been determined that the prohibition has achieved *jus cogens* status.[12]

Genocide is defined in Article II of the Genocide Convention (which is repeated practically verbatim in the ICTY, International Criminal Tribunal for Rwanda (ICTR) and International Criminal Court (ICC) Statutes). Article II reads that genocide is:

any of the following acts committed with intent to destroy, in whole or in part, a national, ethnical, racial or religious group, as such:

  (a) Killing members of the group;

  (b) Causing serious bodily or mental harm to members of the group;

  (c) Deliberately inflicting on the group conditions of life calculated to bring about its physical destruction in whole or in part;

  (d) Imposing measures intended to prevent births within the group;

  (e) Forcibly transferring children of the group to another group.

Genocide is characterized in particular by its mental element, but before moving on to discussion of that, it is worth looking at the controversies that have surrounded the conduct element.

1. Conduct element

Perhaps the classic example of the conduct element of genocide is killing. This has not caused too many difficulties in practice, although 'killing' does not define the mental element that accompanies that conduct. It is generally accepted, however, that the killing has to be intentional.

Genocide may also be committed in the other manners provided for by Article II. The second means of committing genocide is causing serious bodily or mental harm. The former was given a progressive (but entirely defensible) interpretation by the ICTR in the *Akayesu* case.[13] In this case the ICTR accepted that rape and other forms of sexual

---

[11] Reservations to the Convention on the Prevention and Punishment of the Crime of Genocide, Advisory Opinion, ICJ Reports 1951, p 15 at p 23.

[12] See above, n 6.

[13] ICTR Trial Chamber I, *Prosecutor* v *Akayesu*, Judgment, Case No ICTR-95-4-T, 2 September 1998, para 731 (hereafter, cited as '*Akayesu*').

violence are covered by this provision. The Elements of Crimes for the ICC confirm this.[14] The third means, deliberately inflicting conditions of life designed to destroy a group, like most of the acts of genocide, track Nazi policies. The Elements of Crimes for the ICC provide that 'The term "conditions of life" may include, but is not necessarily restricted to, deliberate deprivation of resources indispensable for survival, such as food or medical services, or systematic expulsion from homes.'[15] It is not enough that these conditions are imposed, they must also be calculated to destroy the group, which is a *mens rea* issue. Imposing measures intended to prevent births within the group is the fourth means of committing genocide, and this is a response to Nazi forced sterilization policies. The Elements of Crimes do not contain much elaboration of the crime; however, the ICTR has made clear that the measures may be physical or mental.[16] Finally, the fifth means of committing genocide is transferring children of a group to another group. For this purpose, children are those under 18 years old, and forcible does not only include physical force, but also mental coercion, 'such as that caused by fear of violence, duress, detention, psychological oppression or abuse of power, against such person or persons or another person, or by taking advantage of a coercive environment.'[17] This last phrase is rather vague, and will need judicial interpretation, although to date, there have been no authoritative rulings on this means of committing genocide.

The final part of the physical form of genocide is a matter of some controversy. The Elements of Crimes require that for all forms of genocide 'The conduct took place in the context of a manifest pattern of similar conduct directed against that group or was conduct that could itself effect such destruction.'[18] It is controversial whether this is something inherent in the concept of genocide, or a non-customary addition to the crime solely for the purposes of the ICC. The ICTY in the *Krstić* case took the view that the element was not present in customary law.[19] However, a Pre-Trial Chamber in the ICC, whilst not taking a stand on the customary status of the element, applied it in the *al-Bashir* arrest warrant decision, on the basis of its determination that the element was not in 'irreconcilable contradiction' with the ICC Statute.[20]

2. Mental element

The factor that distinguishes genocide from 'mere' mass killing is the requirement that the conduct is undertaken with the 'intent to destroy, in whole or in part, a national, ethnical, racial or religious group, as such.' This is the controversial. Some would interpret the mental element broadly, to catch more killings and the like with the term 'genocide' to track more closely its popular conception. Against this are restrictionist scholars, such as William Schabas, who take the view that the mental element must be kept narrow, for fear of diluting the opprobrium that attaches to conduct legally defined as genocide (Schabas, 2008a, pp 10–11).

---

[14] Elements of Crimes for Article 6(b) footnote 3.
[15] Elements of Crimes for Article 6(c), footnote 4.
[16] *Akayesu* paras 507–508.   [17] Elements of Crimes for Article 6(e) element 5 and footnote 5.
[18] Eg Elements of Crimes for Article 6(a) element 4.
[19] ICTY Appeals Chamber, *Prosecutor* v *Krstić, Judgment*, Case No IT-98-33-A, 19 April 2004, para 224 (hereafter, cited as '*Krstić* Appeal').
[20] ICC Pre Trial Chamber 1, *Prosecutor* v *al-Bashir*, Case No 02/05-01/09 4 March 2009, para 132 (hereafter, cited as '*al-Bashir*').

On a more doctrinal level, there are also major controversies that surround the interpretation of the mental element of genocide. The first is whether intent means motive, direct, or indirect intention.[21] It is now clear that intention here does not mean motive.[22] The ICJ, ICC, as well as the ICTY have taken the view that direct intention is necessary for genocide; indirect intent will not suffice.[23] There are those that criticize this (Greenawalt, 1999). In part as a result of the Tribunals' approach, proving genocidal intent is difficult, and the ICJ could only find genocidal intent in former Yugoslavia in Srebreniča.[24] In the absence of a confession, proof of intent often depends on various circumstantial factors. The ICTR has identified, *inter alia*, the following as probative:

The overall context in which the crime occurred, the systematic targeting of the victims on account of their membership in a protected group, the fact that the perpetrator may have targeted the same group during the commission of other criminal acts, the scale and scope of the atrocities committed, the frequency of destructive and discriminatory acts, whether the perpetrator acted on the basis of the victim's membership in a protected group and the perpetration of acts which violate the very foundation of the group or considered as such by their perpetrators.[25]

The second controversy is whether the intention to destroy refers to physical or cultural destruction. Some support the idea of 'cultural genocide',[26] however, this has been rejected as a matter of law by various courts, probably most authoritatively by the ICJ in the *Bosnian Genocide* case.[27] As the ICJ said in that case though, 'where there is physical or biological destruction there are often simultaneous attacks on the cultural and religious property and symbols of the targeted group as well, attacks which may legitimately be considered as evidence of an intent to physically destroy the group'.[28]

Some of the thorniest issues relate to the question of defining the protected groups. Although one Trial Chamber in the ICTR argued that the convention protects all stable and permanent groups,[29] this is not the generally accepted position in law, as the ICJ has said: 'the essence of the intent is to destroy the protected group, in whole or in part, as such. It is a group which must have particular positive characteristics-national, ethnical, racial or religious...'[30] In this case the ICJ also rejected the idea that a group could be defined negatively, eg as all 'non-Serbs'.[31]

---

[21] The direct intention being wanting something to occur, indirect intention is present when a person, whilst not wanting something to occur, accepts it as a virtually certain consequence of conduct, and undertakes that conduct anyway.

[22] *Application of the Convention on the Prevention and Punishment of the Crime of Genocide (Bosnia and Herzegovina v Serbia and Montenegro), Merits, Judgment*, 26 February 2007, para 189 (hereafter, cited as 'Bosnian Genocide'); *ICTY Appeals Chamber Prosecutor v Jelesić, Judgment*, Case No IT-95-10-A, 5 July 2001, para 49.

[23] *Bosnian Genocide*, para 188; *al Bashir*, para 114; ICTY Trial Chamber II, *Prosecutor v Kupreškić et al, Judgment*, Case No IT-95-16-T, 14 January 2000, para 636 (hereafter, cited as 'Kupreškić').

[24] *Bosnian Genocide*, paras 278–297.

[25] ICTR Trial Chamber III, *Prosecutor v Ncamihigo, Judgment*, Case No. ICTR-01-63-T, 12 November 2008, para 331.

[26] See the discussion in Schabas, 2008a, pp 207–221.

[27] *Bosnian Genocide*, para 344.   [28] Ibid. This picked up on the ICTY's approach.

[29] *Akayesu*, para 516.   [30] *Bosnian Genocide*, para 193.

[31] Ibid.

Equally, the question of group existence and membership is not simple. In the *Akayesu* case the ICTR tried to define each of the terms and take them separately. This proved to be problematic, not least as on the definitions of the terms that the Trial Chamber gave, there was no relevant distinction between the Hutus and the Tutsis. A more satisfactory approach was taken by the ICTY in the *Krstić* case, in which the Trial Chamber explained:

The preparatory work of the convention shows that setting out such a list was designed more to describe a single phenomenon, roughly corresponding to what was recognized, before the second world war, as 'national minorities', rather than to refer to several distinct prototypes of human groups. To attempt to differentiate each of the named groups on the basis of scientifically objective criteria would thus be inconsistent with the object and purpose of the Convention.[32]

Part of the difficulty is that groups exist, at least in part, in perceptions, and differences are perceived (Cryer, Friman, Robinson, and Wilmshurst, 2010, pp 211–213). For example in Darfur, the 'Arab/African' distinction is modern, and has been consciously fostered by some. In addition, group membership is not simple, as some people may not consider themselves a member of a group, but others may do so, and *vice versa* (Schabas, 2008a, pp 124–129). As a result of these issues, the ICTR has adopted that if such a group is considered to exist in the relevant cultural context, then the perception of the perpetrator that the victim is a member of that group suffices for that person to be considered a member for the purposes of genocide.[33] The ICJ has noted this approach, but has not expressly endorsed it, on the basis that the parties were agreed on that approach and that the issue did not arise in the case.[34]

Finally, as can be seen from the language of the Genocide Convention, it suffices if the perpetrator intended to destroy a part of the group. It therefore becomes very important to define what the group is (for example, is it all Christians, all Christians in the UK, or all members of a particular church?) and what size a part of the group has to be. The ICTY has tended to take the view that it is all of the group in the country. So, for example, in the *Krstić* case, the Prosecution argued that the relevant group was the Bosnian Muslims of the Srebreniča area. The ICTY disagreed, saying that the relevant group was the Bosnian Muslims, and the Bosnian Muslims of the Srebreniča area were a part of the group.[35] They also determined that the part of the group must be 'substantial',[36] something the ICJ has expressly accepted:

the intent must be to destroy at least a substantial part of the particular group. That is demanded by the very nature of the crime of genocide: since the object and purpose of the Convention as a whole is to prevent the intentional destruction of groups, the part targeted must be significant enough to have an impact on the group as a whole.[37]

B. CRIMES AGAINST HUMANITY

Crimes against humanity were first defined in Article 6(c) of the Nuremberg IMT Statute, as 'murder, extermination, enslavement, deportation, and other inhumane acts committed

---

[32] ICTY Trial Chamber I, *Prosecutor v Krstić, Judgment*, Case No. IT-98-33-T, 2 August 2001, para 556.

[33] See eg ICTR Trial Chamber I, *Prosecutor v Semanza, Judgment*, Case No ICTR-97-20-T, 15 May 2003, para 317.

[34] *Bosnian Genocide*, para 191.   [35] *Krstić* Appeal, para 12.

[36] Ibid.   [37] *Bosnian Genocide*, para 198.

against any civilian population, before or during the war; or persecutions on political, racial or religious grounds in execution of or in connection with any crime within the jurisdiction of the Tribunal, whether or not in violation of the domestic law of the country where perpetrated.' Since then there have also been definitions in, *inter alia*, the Tokyo IMT Statute (Article 5(c)), the ICTY (Statute, Article 5), ICTR (Statute, Article 3), and SCSL (Statute, Article 2). Unfortunately none of these definitions are the same, and this has led to calls for a comprehensive convention on crimes against humanity (Bassiouni, 1994).

The most widely ratified definition of crimes against humanity is now that in Article 7 of the Rome Statute of the International Criminal Court. This reads:

1. For the purpose of this Statute, 'crime against humanity' means any of the following acts when committed as part of a widespread or systematic attack directed against any civilian population, with knowledge of the attack:

    (a) Murder;

    (b) Extermination;

    (c) Enslavement;

    (d) Deportation or forcible transfer of population;

    (e) Imprisonment or other severe deprivation of physical liberty in violation of fundamental rules of international law;

    (f) Torture;

    (g) Rape, sexual slavery, enforced prostitution, forced pregnancy, enforced sterilization, or any other form of sexual violence of comparable gravity;

    (h) Persecution against any identifiable group or collectivity on political, racial, national, ethnic, cultural, religious, gender as defined in paragraph 3, or other grounds that are universally recognized as impermissible under international law, in connection with any act referred to in this paragraph or any crime within the jurisdiction of the Court;

    (i) Enforced disappearance of persons;

    (j) The crime of apartheid;

    (k) Other inhumane acts of a similar character intentionally causing great suffering, or serious injury to body or to mental or physical health.[38]

Crimes against humanity are a complex crime, and there are many definitional controversies, not all of which are easily resolved. The crime, like many international crimes has a conduct element, a contextual element, and a mental element.[39] They will be dealt with in turn.

1. Conduct element

For reasons of space, it is not possible to deal with all of the conduct elements in great detail. However, Article 7(2) and the Elements of crimes provide further elaboration of the various conduct criminalized under this head. For example, Article 7(2)(c) defines

---

[38] Although it must be noted that this definition is not necessarily entirely reflective of customary international law on point: Cassese, 2008, pp 123–126.

[39] The question of whether or not genocide has a contextual element is controversial, see above.

enslavement as 'the exercise of any or all of the powers attaching to the right of owner-ship over a person and includes the exercise of such power in the course of trafficking in persons, in particular women and children.' One of the more controversial defini-tions was that of enforced pregnancy. Article 7(2)(f) defines that crime as 'the unlawful confinement of a woman forcibly made pregnant, with the intent of affecting the ethnic composition of any population or carrying out other grave violations of international law. This definition shall not in any way be interpreted as affecting national laws relating to pregnancy'. The additional intent requirement was included, as well as the last sentence, were added at the insistence of some States, who thought that this crime could poten-tially be used to condemn domestic laws limiting or prohibiting abortion (von Hebel and Robinson, 1999, p 100). The additions render the crime narrower than customary law requires (Cryer, 2005, p 258).

Another controversial addition to the requirements set by customary law is the con-dition in Article 7(1)(h) that persecutions can only be prosecuted before the ICC if they occur 'in connection with any act referred to in this paragraph or any crime within the jurisdiction of the Court'.[40] This was included on the basis that some States felt that some of their family laws could be interpreted as contrary to the prohibition of gender-based persecutions.[41]

2. Contextual element

The core of crimes against humanity, the thing that renders what are generally domestic crimes (such as rape and murder) into international crimes is the contextual element. The context for crimes against humanity though is controversial, and there have been various conflicting definitions. For example, in the Nuremberg and Tokyo IMTs' definitions there was a requirement of the existence of an armed conflict.[42] This is no longer the case in cus-tomary law,[43] and it does not appear in any later definitions.

The core of the contextual element, in customary law is that the conduct occurs in the context of a widespread or systematic attack on the civilian population. As the ICTY has said ' "Widespread" refers to the large-scale nature of the attack and the number of victims, while the phrase "systematic" refers to the organized nature of the acts of violence and the improbability of their random occurrence.'[44] In Rome the question of whether widespread and systematic ought to be included as alternatives, or cumulatively (ie whether it was widespread and systematic or widespread or systematic). The latter was chosen, however, as part of the compromise, Article 7(2) defines an attack on the civilian population as being 'a course of conduct involving the multiple commission of acts referred to in para-graph 1 against any civilian population, pursuant to or in furtherance of a State or organ-izational policy to commit such attack'. This definition means that if the Prosecution seeks to prove a crime against humanity on the basis that it was widespread they will also have to prove a more limited form of the systematic element (a 'policy') whilst if they seek to prove

---

[40] The ICTY has unequivocally rejected this as the customary standard: *Kupreškić*, para 580.
[41] The definition of gender was similarly controversial (von Hebel and Robinson, 1999, p 101).
[42] London Charter, Article 6(c), Tokyo IMT Charter, Article 5(c).
[43] *Tadić* Appeal, para 141.
[44] ICTY Appeals Chamber, *Prosecutor v Kunarac, Kovać and Vuković*, Judgment, Case No IT-96-23/1-A, 12 June 2002, para 94 (hereafter, cited as '*Kunarac* Appeal'). The ICC has, so far, agreed, *al-Bashir*, para 81.

the crime against humanity no the basis that the attack was systematic, they will have to prove a more limited version of the widespread requirement (Robinson, 1999, pp 459–451). The ICTY expressly rejected the customary basis of requiring the proof of a policy in the *Kunarac* case,[45] although the rather conclusionary nature of the discussion in that case has been criticized (Schabas, 2008b, pp 958–969).

The question of what amounts to a civilian population, and who can be a victim of a crime against humanity have also been controversial. On the former point, the ICTY has adopted the view that:

the use of the word population does not mean that the entire population of the geographical entity in which the attack is taking place must have been subjected to that attack. It is sufficient to show that enough individuals were targeted in the course of the attack, or that they were targeted in such a way to satisfy the Chamber that the attack was in fact directed against a civilian population, rather than against a limited and randomly selected number of individuals.[46]

Furthermore, the presence of some non-civilians in a population does not render that population non-civilian so long as it is 'predominantly' so.[47] In wartime situations, who is a civilian is to be interpreted in accordance with the relevant applicable humanitarian law.[48] It was often thought that only civilians can be the victims of crimes against humanity. However, what is required is that the attack is against the civilian population. As a result, the ICTY has held that those non-civilians who are *hors de combat* (such as PoWs) may also be the victims of crimes against humanity so long as the overarching attack is directed at the civilian population.[49]

3. Mental element

The mental element applicable to crimes against humanity is, firstly, that the person had the mental element required for the underlying crime (murder etc). In addition, however, they have to have knowledge of the broader context in which their crimes are committed, in other words, that they took place in the context of a widespread or systematic attack on the civilian population, or intended it to be. There is nothing which excludes a personal motive from co-existing with this knowledge though.[50] For persecutive crimes against humanity there is an additional mental element that the perpetrator has to intend to discriminate against those persecuted.[51] The Elements of Crimes require that the perpetrator 'targeted' the members of the relevant group, which probably implies the same mental element.

---

[45] Ibid, para 98.

[46] *Kunarac* Appeal, para 90.

[47] ICTY Trial Chamber II, *Prosecutor v Tadić*, Opinion and Judgment, Case No IT-94-1-T, 7 May 1997, para 638.

[48] ICTY Appeals Chamber, *Prosecutor v Blaškić*, Judgment, Case No IT-95-14-A, 29 July 2004, para 113–115.

[49] ICTY Appeals Chamber, *Prosecutor v Martić* Judgment, Case No IT-95-11-A, 8 October 2008, para 313.

[50] ICTY Appeals Chamber, *Prosecutor v Tadić*, Judgment, Case No IT-94-1-A, 15 July 1999, para 248 (hereafter cited as '*Tadić* Appeal 1999').

[51] ICTY Trial Chamber II, *Prosecutor v Krnojelac*, Judgment, Case No IT-97-25-T, 13 March 2002, para 435.

C. WAR CRIMES

The law of war crimes is probably the oldest part of international criminal law. It is, in essence, the criminal phase of humanitarian law. As such most of the conduct criminalized by the law of war crimes (and some of the mental elements) is prohibited by that law, which is discussed in Chapter 27. There are three main views on the relationship between humanitarian law and the law of war crimes. The first is that all violations of humanitarian law are war crimes (Nuremberg IMT Statute, Article 6(b)). This would almost fuse the substantive norms of humanitarian law and the law of war crimes. There are those that have argued that since some norms of humanitarian law (particularly some of the highly detailed technical rules governing PoWs) are not well suited to criminal enforcement, the most appropriate position is that all serious violations of humanitarian law amount to war crimes (Greenwood, 1996, pp 279–280). This is the view with the most support in practice, but some go further, arguing that there has to be a separate rule criminalizing each rule of humanitarian law (Abi-Saab, 2001, p 112). This has been the position adopted by the ICTY,[52] although the reasoning adopted to support it is rather strained, and the search for such rules has not been the most convincing part of the proof of custom that the ICTY has engaged in.

As with humanitarian law more generally, the law of war crimes differs depending on whether the armed conflict is international or non-international. In international armed conflicts, there are treaty-based and customary norms that are relevant. Of the treaty-based norms, possibly the most important are grave breaches of the Geneva Conventions, these are explained in Article 8(2)(a) of the ICC Statute as being:

any of the following acts against persons or property protected under the provisions of the relevant Geneva Convention [essentially the wounded, sick, shipwrecked, PoWs and interned civilians and civilians in occupied territory] ... :

  (i) Wilful killing;

  (ii) Torture or inhuman treatment, including biological experiments;

  (iii) Wilfully causing great suffering, or serious injury to body or health;

  (iv) Extensive destruction and appropriation of property, not justified by military necessity and carried out unlawfully and wantonly;

  (v) Compelling a prisoner of war or other protected person to serve in the forces of a hostile Power;

  (vi) Wilfully depriving a prisoner of war or other protected person of the rights of fair and regular trial;

  (vii) Unlawful deportation or transfer or unlawful confinement;

  (viii) Taking of hostages.

Outside the ICC, such acts are also subject to mandatory prosecution on the basis of universal jurisdiction (eg Geneva Convention I, Article 49). There are also grave breaches provisions in Additional Protocol I.

Although the Nuremberg (Statute, Article 6(b)) and Tokyo (Statute, Article 5(b)) IMTs, as well as the ICTY (Statute, Article 3) all were granted jurisdiction granted over an

---

[52] *Tadić* Appeal, para 94.

open-ended list of war crimes, and were thus able to prosecute any customary war crime applicable in international armed conflict. The ICC, on the other hand, has been granted jurisdiction over (in addition to grave breaches of the Geneva Conventions (ICC Statute, Article 8(2)(a)) a closed list of twenty-six customary crimes, which include those relating to a limited number of weapons offences (eg Article 8(2)(b)(xviii) (employing chemical weapons contrary to the 1925 Geneva Gas Protocol)); declaring no quarter (Article 8(2)(b) (xii)); sexual offences (Article 8(2)(b)(xxii)); attacking civilians (Article 8(2)(b)(i)); using human shields (Article 8(2)(b)(xxiii)); and launching an attach which will cause disproportionate collateral damage (Article 8(2)(b)(iv)). The definitions in, and the inclusions and exclusions from, the list were extremely controversial.

Turning to non-international armed conflict, the ICTR (Statute, Article 4), Special Court for Sierra Leone (Statute, Article 3) and the ICC (Statute, Article 8(2)(c)) all have jurisdiction to prosecute violations of common Article 3 to the Geneva Conventions,[53] which reads (in relevant part):

Persons taking no active part in the hostilities, including members of armed forces who have laid down their arms and those placed hors de combat by sickness, wounds, detention, or any other cause, shall in all circumstances be treated humanely, without any adverse distinction founded on race, colour, religion or faith, sex, birth or wealth, or any other similar criteria. To this end, the following acts are and shall remain prohibited at any time and in any place whatsoever with respect to the above-mentioned persons:

(a) violence to life and person, in particular murder of all kinds, mutilation, cruel treatment and torture;

(b) taking of hostages;

(c) outrages upon personal dignity, in particular humiliating and degrading treatment;

(d) the passing of sentences and the carrying out of executions without previous judgment pronounced by a regularly constituted court, affording all the judicial guarantees which are recognized as indispensable by civilized peoples.

The ICTR (Statute, Article 5) and SCSL (Statute, Article 3) also have jurisdiction over violations of Additional Protocol II, as those States were parties to that treaty before the beginning of the respective Court's jurisdictions. The SCSL has jurisdiction over three named offences comissable in non-international armed conflict (Statute, Article 4—attacking civilians, attacking peacekeepers entitled to protection as civilians, and 'Conscripting or enlisting children under the age of 15 years into armed forces or groups or using them to participate actively in hostilities'). The ICC has a closed list of 12 customary war crimes for non-international armed conflicts (Statute, Article 8(2)(e)). In addition to those included in the SCSL Statute, these include prohibitions on pillage (Article 8(2)(e)(v)), perfidy (Article 8(2)(e)(ix)) and sexual offences (Article 8(2)(e)(vi)). As identified in the *Tadić* decision, there is a body of customary war crimes law, applicable to both international and non-international conflicts not limited to these offences.

As with much of the conduct that amounts to a crime against humanity, many war crimes would also normally be domestic crimes, and domestic crimes do also occur in times of armed conflict and occupation. As a result, for conduct to amount to a war crime,

---

[53] The ICTY also has jurisdiction over this, as it interpreted Article 3 of its Statute to cover all applicable humanitarian law in force during the Yugoslav wars of dissolution, *Tadić* Appeal, paras 86–93.

there has to be a 'nexus' between that conduct and the armed conflict. The ICTY has explained the position as follows: 'what distinguishes a war crime from a purely domestic offence is that a war crime is shaped by and dependent upon the environment—the armed conflict—in which it was committed'.[54] This means that:

The armed conflict need not have been causal to the commission of the crime, but the existence of an armed conflict must, at a minimum, have played a substantial part in the perpetrator's ability to commit it, his decision to commit it, the manner in which it was committed or the purpose for which it was committed...In determining whether or not the act in question is sufficiently related to the armed conflict, the Trial Chamber may take into account, *inter alia*, the following factors: the fact that the perpetrator is a combatant; the fact that the victim is a non-combatant; the fact that the victim is a member of the opposing party; the fact that the act may be said to serve the ultimate goal of a military campaign; and the fact that the crime is committed as part of or in the context of the per-petrator's official duties.[55]

There is no current reason to believe that the ICC's views on this will be significantly different.

D. AGGRESSION

Aggression remains a controversial crime in international criminal law. It was first pros-ecuted (as 'Crimes Against Peace') before the Nuremberg IMT. The prosecution proceeded on the basis of Article 6(a) of the Nuremberg IMT Statute, which criminalized 'planning, preparation, initiating or waging of a war of aggression, or a war in violation of inter-national treaties, agreements or assurances, or participation in a common plan or conspir-acy for any of the foregoing'. The article (to which Article 5(a) of the Tokyo IMT's Statute is in essence the same) does not provide a definition of the crime. It is also highly doubtful that aggression was criminal prior to the war; although the Kellog-Briand pact rendered recourse to non-defensive force unlawful, it did not contain any hint of criminal responsi-bility for its breach (Schwarzenberger, 1947, pp 346–348).

Unfortunately neither the Nuremberg or Tokyo IMTs (nor the later Control Council Law 10 trials) provided a direct definition of aggression, although all made determin-ations of whether or not particular conflicts were aggressive or not, thus giving sufficient practice to induct, if needs (or wants) be, a definition.[56] However, it was on the question of aggression that the project for a permanent international criminal court stalled in the 1950s, and even after the General Assembly created a definition of the concept (not neces-sarily the crime) of aggression in 1974 in Resolution 3314, this did not bring matters to fruition. None of the ICTY, ICTR, or Special Court for Sierra Leone (SCSL) have jurisdic-tion over aggression. The matter was deeply controversial in the negotiations that led up to the Rome Statute. As a result, aggression is said to be in the jurisdiction of the court by Article 5(1). But what Article 5(1) gives, Article 5(2), essentially, takes away by declaring that the ICC may not exercise its jurisdiction over aggression unless and until a definition is included in the Statute by the (difficult) amendment process. A review conference in

---

[54] *Kunarac* Appeal, para 58.
[55] Ibid, paras 58–59.   [56] *R v Jones et al* [2006] UKHL 16, para 19.

Kampala, Uganda is due to consider the matter in 2010, and current proposals are for the elements of the crime to be are as follows:

1. The perpetrator planned, prepared, initiated or executed an act of aggression.

2. The perpetrator was a person in a position effectively to exercise control over or to direct the political or military action of the State which committed the act of aggression.

3. The act of aggression—the use of armed force by a State against the sovereignty, territorial integrity or political independence of another State, or in any other manner inconsistent with the Charter of the United Nations—was committed.

4. The perpetrator was aware of the factual circumstances establishing the inconsistency of the use of armed force by the State with the Charter of the United Nations.

5. The act of aggression, by its character, gravity and scale, constituted a manifest violation of the Charter of the United Nations.

6. The perpetrator was aware of the factual circumstances establishing such a manifest violation of the Charter of the United Nations.

Some of the aspects of this definition, such that the perpetrator must be in a high leadership position, are relatively uncontroversial. However, others, such as what amounts to a 'manifest' violation of the UN Charter, are the subject of deep division. In addition, the 'preconditions to the exercise of jurisdiction' (a euphemism for whether the Security Council, General Assembly or the ICJ should have role in determining an act of aggression prior to the ICC prosecuting anyone) remain highly contentious, and agreement is unlikely to be easily found.

III. PRINCIPLES OF LIABILITY AND DEFENCES

International law also provides for principles of liability and defences. Many of them, such as aiding, abetting, duress, and self-defence will be familiar to those who have a grounding in domestic criminal law (although the precise details of the principles may differ).[57] However, international law does have a number of specialized forms of liability and defences that are worthy of note. On the liability side, these are joint criminal enterprise, co-perpetration and command responsibility. For defences, the defence of superior orders is highly relevant, but controversial.

A. JOINT CRIMINAL ENTERPRISE

It is a characteristic of many (although not all) international crimes that they tend to be committed by groups of people, some of whom are remote from the actual scene of the commission of the actual crime. As a result, the ICTY has adopted a theory of liability claimed to exist in customary law, of joint criminal enterprise. The objective element of this form of liability is tripartite; set out authoritatively in the *Tadić* case as being:

    i. A plurality of persons.

[57] See ICC Statute, Article 25 and 31.

ii. The existence of a common plan, design or purpose which amounts to or involves the commission of a crime provided for in the Statute.

iii. Participation of the accused in the common design involving the perpetration of one of the crimes provided for in the Statute.[58]

The mental element is an intention that the group commit the crime or, more controversially:

the *intention* to participate in and further the criminal activity or the criminal purpose of a group and to contribute to the joint criminal enterprise or in any event to the commission of a crime by the group. In addition, responsibility for a crime other than the one agreed upon in the common plan arises only if, under the circumstances of the case, (i) it was *foreseeable* that such a crime might be perpetrated by one or other members of the group and (ii) the accused *willingly took that risk*.[59]

The last part, often known as 'type three' joint criminal enterprise expands liability a long way. This, alongside the fact that the direct perpetrators of the offences do not have to be a part of the joint criminal enterprise ensures that the doctrine provides for liability of policy-makers, but also renders the doctrine, for some, to be excessively broad and vague.[60]

B. CO-PERPETRATION

It is notable that the ICC has not adopted joint criminal enterprise in this form. They have, instead, relied on 'co-perpetration', including 'co-perpetration by means' (where the perpetration is done through other people, whether or not they are innocent agents). This form of liability has its basis in Article 25(3)(a) rather, probably, than customary law.[61] This manner of 'committing' international crimes has two objective aspects, and three subjective ones.

The objective aspects are the existence of an explicit or implicit agreement or common plan between the co-perpetrators and a coordinated essential contribution by the suspect which was essential for the commission of the objective elements of the crime.[62] This contribution can be made through control of an hierarchically structured organization in which interchangeable subordinates can be relied upon to carry out orders.[63]

In relation to the subjective elements, it is necessary that the defendant has the mental element required for the relevant offence, the co-perpetrators realize that the common plan will result in that crime,[64] and that the defendant is aware of the circumstances that allow them to jointly control the crime.[65] This is similar to, but narrower than, joint

---

[58] *Tadić* 1999 Appeal, para 227.   [59] Ibid, para 228.

[60] See eg Ohlin, 2007, Danner and Martinez, 2005, although for a contrary view see Cassese, 2007.

[61] ICTY Appeals Chamber, *Prosecutor v Stakić*, Judgment, Case No IT-97-24-A, 22 March 2006, para 62.

[62] ICC Pre-Trial Chamber I, *Prosecutor v Lubanga, Decision on the Confirmation of Charges*, Case No ICC-01/04-01/06, 29 January 2007, paras 343–348 (hereafter, cited as '*Lubanga*').

[63] ICC Pre-Trial Chamber *Prosecutor v Katanga and Ngudjolo, Decision on the Confirmation of Charges*, Case No ICC-01/04-01/07, 30 September 2008, paras 500–510.

[64] ICC Pre-Trial Chamber II *Prosecutor v Bemba Gombo, Decision on the Confirmation of Charges*, Case No ICC-01/05-01/08, 15 June 2009 paras 352–369 (hereafter, cited as '*Bemba Gombo*').

[65] *Lubanga*, paras 349–367.

criminal enterprise. Some of the critiques that have been brought to bear on that principle of liability, thus, are not applicable to co-perpetration to the same extent.

C. COMMAND RESPONSIBILITY

Command responsibility is the responsibility of those who have effective control over subordinates for offences committed by them, where they failed to prevent them. In spite of a lengthy pre-history, it received its first modern judicial confirmation in the controversial *Yamashita* case in 1945.[66] The most recent treaty-based statement of this principle of liability comes in Article 28 of the Rome Statute, which does not necessarily, though, entirely reflect custom. Article 28 reads:

In addition to other grounds of criminal responsibility under this Statute for crimes within the jurisdiction of the Court:

(a) A military commander or person effectively acting as a military commander shall be criminally responsible for crimes within the jurisdiction of the Court committed by forces under his or her effective command and control, or effective authority and control as the case may be, as a result of his or her failure to exercise control properly over such forces, where:

   (i) That military commander or person either knew or, owing to the circumstances at the time, should have known that the forces were committing or about to commit such crimes; and

  (ii) That military commander or person failed to take all necessary and reasonable measures within his or her power to prevent or repress their commission or to submit the matter to the competent authorities for investigation and prosecution.

(b) With respect to superior and subordinate relationships not described in paragraph (a), a superior shall be criminally responsible for crimes within the jurisdiction of the Court committed by subordinates under his or her effective authority and control, as a result of his or her failure to exercise control properly over such subordinates, where:

   (i) The superior either knew, or consciously disregarded information which clearly indicated, that the subordinates were committing or about to commit such crimes;

  (ii) The crimes concerned activities that were within the effective responsibility and control of the superior; and

 (iii) The superior failed to take all necessary and reasonable measures within his or her power to prevent or repress their commission or to submit the matter to the competent authorities for investigation and prosecution.

The ICTY, in the in *Čelebići* case agreed with the International Committee of the Red Cross's commentary on Article 86 of Additional Protocol I, and sought to elaborate the elements of command responsibility under customary law. These are (i) a superior/subordinate relationship; (ii) the 'mental element' and (iii) a failure to take reasonable

---

[66] *Application of Yamashita* (1946) 327 US 1.

measures to prevent or punish international crimes.[67] The ICC Statute also requires that a failure of the defendant's command had a causal relationship to the commission of the crimes.

The superior/subordinate relationship is framed, for both military and civilian superiors, as requiring 'effective control', although it is accepted that the manner in which such control is exercised may differ between those superiors. Effective control means 'a material ability to prevent or punish criminal conduct', alongside a formal, or informal hierarchy.[68] A legal position of superiority is not necessary, but such a position may be useful, albeit not conclusive, evidence of effective control.[69]

The mental element of command responsibility is not simple, or agreed upon. Early cases, such as *Yamashita*, took the view that the *mens rea* was that the defendant 'knew, or should have known'; of the offences. The ICTY, however, interpreting the standard in its Statute (Article 7(3)) that the defendant 'knew, or had reason to know', of possible, or committed offences by subordinates, opined that

[A superior]...may possess the *mens rea* for command responsibility where: (1) he had actual knowledge, established through direct or circumstantial evidence, that his subordinates were committing or about to commit crimes...or (2) where he had in his possession information of a nature, which at the least, would put him on notice of the risk of such offences by indicating the need for additional investigation in order to ascertain whether such crimes were committed or were about to be committed by his subordinates.[70]

This standard is the one accepted by later cases both in the ICTY and ICTR;[71] it is somewhat narrower than the 'should have known' standard, and, in the view of many, customary law (Dinstein, 2004, p 24; Kolb, 2000, p 301). The ICC, with respect to military superiors has, in its only decision on point so far, taken the view that the 'should have known' standard in Article 28 of the Rome Statute is a little broader, and includes a negligent failures to obtain information, something not covered by the ICTY's formulation of the mental element.[72] It is notable, on the other hand, that the Rome Statute, for the first time, distinguishes military and civilian superiors, and the mental element applicable to civilian superiors, that they 'knew, or consciously disregarded information that clearly indicated' that international crimes had occurred, or were going to, is a novelty in international law, and not necessarily a welcome one (Vetter, 2000).

What the precise measures that the superior has to take in relation to subordinates has been said by the ICTY to be those which

can be taken within the competence of a commander as evidenced by the degree of effective control he wielded over his subordinates...What constitutes such measures is not a matter of substantive law but of evidence.[73]

---

[67] ICTY Trial Chamber II, *Prosecutor v Delalić, Mučić, Delić and Landžo*, Judgment, Case No IT-96-21-T, 16 November 1998, para 344.

[68] ICTY Appeals Chamber, *Prosecutor v Delalić, Mučić, Delić and Landžo* Judgment, Case No IT-96-23-A, 20 February 2001, para 256. See generally Mettraux, 2009.

[69] *Čelelbići* Appeal, para 197.   [70] Ibid, paras 223 and 241.

[71] *Blaškić* Appeal, paras 58–64.

[72] *Bemba Gombo*, para 432–434.

[73] *Blaškić* Appeal, para 72.

Relevant evidence according to the ICC, which has largely accepted the ICTY's jurisprudence here, includes, *inter alia*, activities:

(i) to ensure that superior's forces are adequately trained in international humanitarian law;

(ii) to secure reports that military actions were carried out in accordance with international law;

(iii) to issue orders aiming at bringing the relevant practices into accord with the rules of war;

(iv) to take disciplinary measures to prevent the commission of atrocities by the troops under the superior's command.[74]

When it comes to punishment, it is perfectly possible that the superior will not be able to punish the person personally, where this is the case it can be sufficient that the superior 'submit the matter to the competent authorities for investigation and prosecution.'[75]

As mentioned above, the ICC Statute adds a requirement that the international crimes occur as a result of the superior's failure to exercise control over their subordinates. This creates a difficult issue relating to causation. This ICTY has consistently rejected such a requirement.[76] Probably against this background, the ICC, has done its best to minimize this requirement, by saying that

There is no direct causal link that needs to be established between the superior's omission and the crime committed by his subordinates. Therefore, the Chamber considers that it is only necessary to prove that the commander's omission increased the risk of the commission of the crimes charged in order to hold him criminally responsible under article 28(a) of the Statute.[77]

This requirement, in some respects, raises the question of the nature of command responsibility, which is not entirely agreed upon. Early case law considered it a form of liability for the underlying crimes (Meloni, 2007, pp 621–623). However, amongst the judges in the ICTY, there is an increasing view that command responsibility is a *sui generis* form of liability, and that 'Command responsibility imposes responsibility on a commander for failure to take corrective action in respect of a crime committed by another; it does not make the commander party to the crime committed by that other.'[78] This view, which is highly controversial (Meloni, 2007), nonetheless, has implications for the ambit of command responsibility, as the ICTY accepted, in particular in relation to the question of whether a commander could be responsible for offences that occurred prior to him or her taking up that post. The ICC Statute makes it clear that for the ICC command responsibility is a form of liability for the underlying offences, which might be related to the causation requirement it contains, as well as the fact that the nature of command responsibility (as a form of liability for the underlying offences) was not really a matter of controversy between States in 1998.

---

[74] *Bemba Gombo*, para 438.

[75] Rome Statute, Articles 28(a)(ii) and 28(b)(iii).

[76] ICTY Appeals Chamber, *Prosecutor v Hadžihasanović* Judgment, Case No IT-01-47-A, 22 April 2008, para 39 (hereafter, cited as '*Hadžihasanović* Appeal').

[77] *Bemba Gombo*, paras 424–425.

[78] *Hadžihasanović* Appeal, Judge Shahabuddeen, para 33.

D. DEFENCES

Defences are often a taboo amongst international criminal lawyers (Eser, 1996, p 251). However, the defences that are applicable to international crimes, such as self-defence, duress, necessity, insanity, and intoxication[79] are similar to those in most domestic systems.[80] The defence that has caused most comment in international criminal law is obedience to superior orders.[81] It is also frequently raised. The first major international document dealing with superior orders was the Nuremberg IMT Statute, Article 8 of which excluded reliance on the defence, a position that was probably not in accordance with custom at the time. However, the defence was also excluded in the Tokyo IMT (Statute, Article 7) the ICTY (Statute, Article 7(4)), ICTR (Statute, Article 6(4)) and SCSL (Statute, Article 6(4)). The ICC Statute, on the other hand, permits the defence in narrow circumstances for war crimes (Statute, Article 33). That provision reads:

1. The fact that a crime within the jurisdiction of the Court has been committed by a person pursuant to an order of a Government or of a superior, whether military or civilian, shall not relieve that person of criminal responsibility unless:

    (a) The person was under a legal obligation to obey orders of the Government or the superior in question;

    (b) The person did not know that the order was unlawful; and

    (c) The order was not manifestly unlawful.

2. For the purposes of this article, orders to commit genocide or crimes against humanity are manifestly unlawful.

The provision is quite tightly drafted, and all three conditions (that the person was under a duty to obey orders, that they did not know the order was unlawful, and that it was not manifestly unlawful) must be fulfilled before the defence may be relied on. Not all issues are entirely clear; for example like earlier formulations, this provision does not clarify to whom the illegality must be manifest. In addition, the customary status of Article 33 is controversial (Gaeta, 1999; Garraway, 1999).

IV. PROSECUTION OF INTERNATIONAL CRIMES

A. THE NUREMBERG AND TOKYO IMTS[82]

Prosecutorial responses to international crimes have occurred at both the national and international levels, with varying degrees of success. The first international tribunal was the Nuremberg IMT, which sat between 1945 and 1946 to prosecute high-ranking Nazis. It was set up by France, the UK, the US and the USSR, all of whom appointed a lead and an alternate judge to the panel. Pursuant to Article 6 of its Charter, the Tribunal had jurisdiction over crimes against peace (aggression), crimes against humanity, and war crimes.

---

[79] See ICC Statute, Article 31.

[80] One difference to UK law though is that duress is not *a priori* excluded for intentional killings (Article 31(d)), although the ICTY has, by a bare majority, taken a different view ICTY Appeals Chamber, *Prosecutor v Erdemović*, Judgment, Case No IT-96-22-A, 7 October 1997.

[81] See, eg Dinstein, 1965.   [82] See, eg Taylor, 1992, Boister and Cryer, 2008.

Pursuant to Articles 9 and 10 of its Statute, it was also permitted to make declarations of criminality against organizations, to pave the way for domestic prosecutions of their members for that membership. Six such organizations were prosecuted: the SS, SD, SA, High Command, Leadership Corps of the Nazi party and the Gestapo, alongside 24 individuals. They were chosen for their representative nature of the Nazi party, the Army, Navy, and civilian supporters of the regime. The most famous of the defendants was Hermann Göring. Three of the indicted organizations were acquitted (the SA, High Command, and Leadership Corps). Three of the defendants (Schacht, Fritzsche, and von Papen) were also acquitted. All the other defendants were convicted, although not of all charges laid against them. The judgment is a seminal document in international criminal law, albeit not persuasive on all the legal points it sought to prove. The trial, in spite of its flaws, was basically fair, certainly by the standards of the time. There were critiques of the Nuremberg Trial, many of which focus on the crimes against peace charge, which was novel in 1945 (Schwarzenberger, 1947, pp 346–348), and the fact that allegations of war crimes by Allied forces were not heard. This latter claim has some validity, but this is not generally thought to entirely undermine the legitimacy of the Nuremberg trial.

There was lesser-known counterpart to Nuremberg in Tokyo, designed to prosecute the leaders of martial Japan. It was set up by Australia, Canada, China, India, France, the Netherlands, New Zealand, the Philippines, the UK, the US, and the USSR, all of whom appointed one judge. Article 5 of the Tokyo IMT Statute gave that Tribunal jurisdiction over crimes against peace, crimes against humanity and war crimes. The indictment charged 28 military and civilian Japanese leaders, with crimes against peace, war crimes, and murder. These last charges were based on the Prosecution's theory that killings in aggressive wars were not covered by belligerent privilege, and were therefore, simply, murder. The Tribunal considered these charges as overlapping with the crimes against peace charges, so did not pronounce on their validity.[83]

The judgment, delivered in 1948, largely followed the Nuremberg judgment on issues of law such as the criminality of crimes against peace,[84] but, unlike Nuremberg also dealt with command responsibility, including of civilian superiors.[85] The judgment was a majority one, and the bench was by no means unanimous in its reasoning or result. One of the judges, Judge Bernard thought that the proceedings were so flawed that he could not determine the charges against the defendants.[86] Judge Jaranilla, on the other hand, was of the view that the tribunal had been too lenient, both in terms of the charges that were not pronounced upon and the sentences imposed.[87] Judge Webb, who presided over the trial, used his Opinion to criticize the absence of the Emperor of Japan from the dock.[88] Judge Röling doubted the existence of a crime against peace in international law at the time, but argued that those responsible for such offences could lawfully be interned in the interests of international security.[89] He also raised factual doubts about some of the convictions.[90] The largest, and most famous, dissent was that of the Indian justice, Judge Pal.

---

[83] Tokyo IMT Judgment, pp 48, 449.   [84] Ibid, pp 48,437–448, 439.
[85] Ibid, pp 48,443–448, 447.
[86] Dissenting Opinion of the Member from France, pp 18–23.
[87] Concurring Opinion of the Member from the Philippines, pp 7–10, 32–35.
[88] Separate Opinion of the President, pp 18–20.
[89] Opinion of the Member for the Netherlands, pp 10–53.
[90] Ibid, pp 178–249.

Pal denied the existence of crimes against peace,[91] thought that the defendants could not be found guilty of such crimes anyway,[92] and believed that none of the war crimes found were attributable to the defendants.[93] He would have acquitted them all and gave a scathing critique of the Western powers, arguing that their record of colonialism and use of the atomic bomb in Hiroshima and Nagasaki rendered their condemnation of Japan hypocritical.[94] The general critiques of the Tokyo IMT (ie those on the *nullum crimen* bases, and the refusal to hear allegations about possible Allied war crimes) are similar to those of the Nuremberg IMT, although there has, in addition, also been significant, and not wholly unjustifiable, criticism of the running of the trial.[95]

B. THE ICTY AND ICTR[96]

There were no international proceedings after the Nuremberg and Tokyo IMTs until after the end of the Cold War. Then in 1993 the Security Council, responding to atrocities in the former Yugoslavia, created the ICTY under its powers under Chapter VII of the UN Charter, in Resolution 827 (25 May 2003).[97] The Tribunal has jurisdiction over grave breaches of the Geneva Conventions (Statute, Article 2), other war crimes (Article 3), crimes against humanity (Article 4), and genocide (Article 5) committed in former Yugoslavia since 1 January 1991 to date. The ICTY has primacy over national courts.[98] This means that the Tribunal may require States to defer any proceedings they were contemplating or undertaking to it.[99] The Tribunal may also order any State to co-operate with the Tribunal.[100]

The early practice of the ICTY was hampered by the refusal of a number of the former Yugoslav States to co-operate: only the central government in Bosnia was supportive. Many of those thought responsible for crimes were still in high-ranking positions in Serbia, Croatia, or *Republika Srpska*. As a result of those entities' refusal to hand over suspects, early cases at the Tribunal tended to be of low-ranking soldiers, which caused criticism (Verrijn Stuart and Simons, 2009, p 53). These early cases did, however, allow the ICTY to considerably develop their processes and also international law, in particular in the *Tadić* case.[101] By 1996 the end of the war and some political developments caused co-operation to improve in the area, other than by Serbia. Serbia only began to co-operate with the Tribunal in any meaningful way in 2001, when, encouraged by pressure from Western powers, ex-president Milošević was surrendered to the Tribunal.

A year before that, in 2000, the judges realized that their work could take more than another 15 years. As a result they asked the Security Council to take measures to ensure

---

[91] Dissenting Opinion of the Member for India, Parts 1 and 2.
[92] Ibid, part 4.   [93] Ibid, part 6.   [94] Ibid, Recommendation.
[95] On such critiques, see Boister and Cryer, 2008, Ch 4.
[96] See generally Schabas, 2006.
[97] The legality of this was doubted by some (Rubin, 1994) but confirmed by the ICTY in the *Tadić* Appeal.
[98] ICTY Statute, Article 9(1).
[99] Eg *In the Matter of a Proposal for a Formal Request for Deferral to the Competence of the Tribunal Addressed to the Republic of Bosnia and Herzegovina in Respect of Radovan Karadzic, Ratko Mladic and Mico Stanisic*, IT-95-5-D, T.Ch. 16.5.1995.
[100] ICTY Statute, Article 28.   [101] *Tadić* Appeal.

a 'completion strategy'. The Security Council responded in Resolution 1329 (5 December 2000), which allowed for the appointment of additional judges. On its side, in 2002, the ICTY adopted Rule of Procedure and Evidence 11*bis*, which allowed it to refer cases back to national courts, effectively outsourcing its work. The completion strategy was further developed in 2003 by Resolution 1503 (28 August 2003) and in 2004 by Resolution 1534 (26 March 2004), which, between them, directed the Prosecutor to focus on those bearing the greatest responsibility for crimes, the judges to confirm that this was the case when reviewing indictments, and gave a timetable for the completion of investigations, trials and appeals. The timeframe for completion of the latter two aspects has had to slide. As of November 2009, the Tribunal had, of the 161 people charged, 36 in custody, 2 on provisional release, and had completed proceedings against 121 accused with 61 convictions and 11 acquittals. It is continuing proceedings against 40 accused (others have had their indictments withdrawn or have died).[102] There are only two people currently indicted who have not appeared before the court, one Bosnian Serb, Ratko Mladić, and one Croat, Göran Hadžić.

The ICTY itself has set out a number of its achievements.[103] These are, *inter alia*, that it has promoted accountability rather than impunity, including of leaders, established the facts of the crimes in former Yugoslavia, brought justice to victims and given them a voice, developed international law and strengthened the rule of law. The Tribunal has, to some extent, fulfilled these goals, although critiques of the Tribunals that they are expensive and slow are not entirely untrue (Zacklin, 2004, pp 543–544).

Shortly after the creation of the ICTY, the Security Council built upon that precedent to create the ICTR, to prosecute international crimes committed in Rwanda in 1994. Notably, Rwanda was, at the time a non-permanent member of the Security Council. Although it was initially supportive of the creation of the ICTR, owing to the refusal of other members to include the death penalty in the sentencing regime of the court, it voted against the Resolution that established the Court (Resolution 955 (8 November 1994)). The ICTR has jurisdiction over genocide (Statute, Article 2), crimes against humanity (Article 3) and some war crimes-violations of common Article 3 and Additional Protocol II (Article 4). It has the same powers in relation to primacy and cooperation as the ICTY. They also have a joint appeals chamber, to ensure consistency of their jurisprudence.[104]

Some African States were quick to co-operate with the ICTR, although Rwanda was not always amongst them. This was a problem, as most of the evidence and witnesses, and many of the suspects, were in Rwanda. The ICTR was initially slow to move, and there were staffing problems. A report on the management and administration of the ICTR in 1997 was both careful and damning of all aspects of the Tribunal other than the judges. Measures were taken to resolve all of the outstanding difficulties.[105]

Things appeared to be improving in 1998, when the ex-Prime minister of Rwanda, Jean Kambanda, pled guilty to genocide, admitting that this crime had occurred in Rwanda. The first trial, of Jean-Paul Akayesu, proceeded to judgment in September 1998. 1999 proved more difficult. In protest at a decision of the Appeals Chamber in the *Barayagwiza* case to release a defendant whose human rights had been violated in pre-trial detention in

---

[102] http://www.icty.org/sections/TheCases/KeyFigures.
[103] http://www.icty.org/sid/324.   [104] ICTR Statute, Article 12(2).
[105] *Report of the Secretary-General on the Activities of the Office of Internal Oversight Services*, A/51/789.

Cameroon,[106] Rwanda refused to co-operate with the ICTR at all. This caused trials practically to stop. The Appeals Chamber revisited its decision in early 2000, and determined
that Barayagwiza should remain in detention and be sent for trial.[107] Rwanda resumed
co-operation as a result. Some have suggested that this showed the extent that Rwanda was
able to guide the practice of the Court (Schabas, 2000, p 565).

In 2003 the ICTR also was given a very similar completion strategy to that of the ICTY
by the Security Council in the same Resolutions. As a result, the ICTR has also begun to
transfer cases back to national jurisdictions pursuant to its own Rule of Procedure 11*bis*.
As of May 2009, the Tribunal had tried 44 people, 35 of whom were convicted, and was in
the process of trying, or was about to, try 32 more.[108] Although it has not obtained all of
the ringleaders of the genocide, it has many of them (van den Herik, 2005, p 263). There
has been criticism of the ICTR for failing to prosecute possible offences committed by the
Rwandan Patriotic Front (RPF) in the aftermath of the genocide. It has been suggested that
this is because the RPF, having defeated the *génocidaires* in 1994, took over Rwanda, and
control co-operation with the ICTR. The ICTR prosecutor has argued, on the other hand,
that the allegations are less serious than those against Hutu defendants and, because of the
completion strategy, there is no time to engage in prosecution of allegations against the
RPF (Peskin, 2008, Ch 8; Thalman, 2008, pp 1001–1002).

C. THE INTERNATIONAL CRIMINAL COURT (ICC)

Probably the most important development in international criminal law, at least since
Nuremberg, is the creation of the ICC.[109] The ICC Statute was finalized in 1998 after difficult negotiations in Rome. The ICC, as an international organization, actually came into
being in 2002, when the required 60 ratifications of the ICC Statute were obtained. There
are currently 111 States parties to the Statute. A number of major powers, such as the US,
China, India, and Russia, are still non–parties, and the question of if they will become so
in the foreseeable future remains open.

As mentioned above, the Court currently may exercise jurisdiction over genocide,
crimes against humanity, and a closed list of war crimes (ICC Statute, Articles 5–8).[110]
Again, as alluded to above, the ICC also has a dormant jurisdiction over the crime of
aggression, but it is not permitted to exercise that jurisdiction unless and until a definition
of aggression is included by an amendment to the Statute (Article 5(2)).

The jurisdiction of the Court is over crimes committed by nationals of States parties or
on their territories (Article 12), or over any situation referred to it by the Security Council
(Article 13(b)). The jurisdiction of the ICC is prospective; it began, for its original State parties, at that date in 2002 when the court came into being (Article 11(1)). For States that were
not party at that date, unless they make a specific declaration that it may, the ICC can only

---

[106] ICTR Appeals Chamber, *Prosecutor* v *Barayagwiza*, Decision, ICTR-97-19-AR72, 19 November
1999.
    [107] ICTR Appeals Chamber, *Prosecutor* v *Barayagwiza*, Decision (Prosecutor's Request for Review or
Reconsideration) ICTR-97-19-AR72, 31 March 2000.
    [108] Report of 14 May, annex 1.   [109] See generally, Triffterer, 2008.
    [110] Owing to concerns about the possible limiting effect the Statute's definitions on customary law, Article
10 provides that 'Nothing in this Part shall be interpreted as limiting or prejudicing in any way existing or
developing rules of international law for purposes other than this statute.'

exercise its jurisdiction in relation to the relevant offences committed after the entry into force of the Statute for Article 11(2)).

There are three ways in which the Prosecutor may initiate an investigation. The first is after a referral of a situation by a State party to the Rome Statute (Article 12(a)). Contrary to expectations, this provision has led to the practice of 'Self Referrals' where States refer the situations in their own territories to the ICC (Arsanjani and Reisman, 2005). This has happened three times, with references by Uganda, the DRC, and the Central African Republic. There is nothing in the Statute to prevent this, but there have been suggestions that accepting such referrals has led the ICC being too close to governments who wish it to prosecute offences by rebels rather than their own infractions. The next way the ICC may begin an investigation is that the Prosecutor may, with the consent of a Pre-Trial Chamber, initiate an investigation on his own motion (Article 15). This was controversial at Rome, but has recently been invoked by the Prosecutor in relation to post-election violence in Kenya,[111] albeit in a situation where there has been some support for the move from many parties in Kenya.

The Security Council also has the power to refer a situation anywhere in the world to the ICC (Article 13(b)). The Security Council has done this once, referring the situation in Darfur, Sudan, to the ICC in 2005 in Resolution 1594 (Cryer, 2006). Conversely, the Security Council has, controversially, the power under Article 16 of the ICC Statute to require the Prosecutor to defer an investigation or prosecution for a one-year period that can be renewed indefinitely. Its practice under this Article, in Resolutions 1422 and 1487 has proved divisive, and the Council has not respected the limits that Article 16 sets, in particular that an existing specific investigation or prosecution be identified (Jain, 2005). As such it is very doubtful that those Resolutions which have now lapsed, bound the ICC, as opposed to States which are UN Members.

In contrast to the ICTY and ICTR, which enjoy primacy over national courts, the ICC's jurisdiction is said to be 'complementary' to domestic jurisdictions (Article 1).[112] This means that the ICC can only exercise jurisdiction where it determines that a competent national court is 'unwilling or unable genuinely' to prosecute a case itself (Article 17). The concept of unwillingness is elaborated upon by Article 17(3) which explains that such genuine unwillingness is absent if:

(a) the proceedings were or are being undertaken or the national decision was made for the purpose of shielding the person concerned from criminal responsibility for crimes within the jurisdiction of the court referred to in Article 5;

(b) there has been an unjustified delay in the proceedings which in the circumstances is inconsistent with an intent to bring the person concerned to justice;

(c) the proceedings were not or are not being conducted independently or impartially, and they were or are being conducted in a manner which, in the circumstances, is inconsistent with an intent to bring the person concerned to justice.

Inability is the subject of Article 17(3), which reads '[i]n order to determine inability in a particular case, the Court shall consider whether, due to a total or substantial collapse or unavailability of its national judicial system, the State is unable to obtain the accused or the necessary evidence and testimony or otherwise unable to carry out its proceedings.'

---

[111] Request for Authorisation of an Investigation Pursuant to Article 15, ICC-01/09, 26 November 2009.
[112] See generally Kleffner, 2008.

The precise interpretation of these terms will be an important task for the Court. This is a process which is currently embryonic, although the ICC's Appeals Chamber has made clear that where there is inactivity by the relevant State, the case is admissible without it being necessary to determine unwillingness or inability.[113]

The definition of a 'case' in the complementarity context has proved difficult. The early practice of the Court has said that a 'case' encompasses both a personal and a conduct-based element. In other words, the person must be being investigated and/or prosecuted for the conduct that forms the basis of the proposed arrest warrant before a case can be declared inadmissible on the basis of Article 17.[114] This is a surprisingly stringent requirement for inadmissibility, and has been criticized as one which may cause concern to many States (Schabas, 2008c, p 184).

There are both legal and political critiques of the ICC. It is sometimes the case that the former reflect the latter. The main legal challenge, which was first raised by the US government, is the allegation that as the ICC can exercise its jurisdiction over nationals of non-State parties (where they commit international crimes on the territory of States parties) this violates international law (Scheffer, 1999, p 71). The most sophisticated version of this critique does not deny that States can exercise their own territorial jurisdiction over non-nationals, but that they cannot delegate that power to an international organization (Morris, 2001, pp 26–52). However, there is no existing prohibition of this in international law (Akande, 2003, pp 625–634).

Some of the early practice of the ICC, in particular that all the Prosecutor's investigations relate to situations in Africa, has led to accusations from some quarters that the Prosecutor is acting selectively, concentrating on less powerful States. The ICC's Office of the Prosecutor has responded strongly, arguing that it only applies the law, and that the situations that are currently subject to investigation are the most serious events over which the Prosecutor has jurisdiction, and in addition, that the critique ignores the African victims.[115] It might also be noted that three of the situations in Africa were referred by those States themselves. Still, the indictment of President al-Bashir of Sudan has caused some to question whether the possibility of peace is being sacrificed on the altar of justice.[116] Such claims are perhaps best addressed to the UN Security Council, which has the power under Article 16 to defer investigations before the ICC in the interests of peace, rather than criticizing the ICC for doing what it was designed to do: investigate and prosecute international crimes.

D. 'INTERNATIONALIZED' AND NATIONAL COURTS

There are also a diverse group of courts which come under the heading of 'internationalized'.[117] Some, such as the SCSL, and the Special Tribunal for Lebanon

---

[113] *ICC Appeals Chamber, Prosecutor v Katanga and Chui, Judgment on the Appeal of Mr Germain Katanga against the Oral Decision of Trial Chamber II of 12 June 2009 on the Admissibility of the Case*, ICC-01/04-01/07, 25 September 2009, paras 1–2.

[114] *Prosecutor v Lubanga, Decision on the Prosecutor's Application for a Warrant of Arrest, Article 58*, ICC-01-04-01/06, Pre-Trial Chamber I, 10 February 2006, paras 37–39.

[115] Deputy Prosecutor's Remarks, 'Introduction to the Rome Statute Establishing the ICC and Africa's Involvement with the ICC', 14 April 2009.

[116] See the Decision of the African Union Assembly/AU/Dec.245 (XIII) 3 July 2009.

[117] See generally, Cryer, Friman, Robinson, and Wilmshurst, 2010, Ch 9.

(STL) are more or less akin to international courts than domestic courts, as their founding documents are treaties or Security Council Resolutions rather than domestic legislation. Others, such as the Iraqi High Tribunal and the Extraordinary Chambers in the Courts of Cambodia are far closer to ordinary domestic courts, as their jurisdiction is founded on domestic law—they simply have some form of international support, usually in the form of international staff. Each such court is rather different, both in the level of internationalization and jurisdiction. The SCSL, for example, was described by the Secretary-General as 'a treaty-based *sui generis* court of mixed jurisdiction and composition'.[118] It has jurisdiction over international crimes, such as crimes against humanity and some war crimes (Statute Articles 2–4) and domestic offences, such as arson (Article 5). The Special Tribunal for Lebanon, on the other hand has jurisdiction over Lebanese domestic crimes only, although it uses international law principles of liability (Statute, Articles 2–3). The Iraqi High Tribunal and Extraordinary Chambers prosecute purely domestic crimes, but which are based on implementations of international criminal law. As such, generalizations about these courts and their powers are often unhelpful.

The bulk of prosecutions of international crimes are intended to be in domestic courts. States are entitled to assert universal jurisdiction over genocide, crimes against humanity and war crimes.[119] However, in spite of a number of well-known trials, such as the *Eichmann* trial,[120] for the most part domestic courts have been slow to react to international crimes. Often political difficulties in territorial or national jurisdictions impede prosecutions, and other States are unwilling to become involved. There are some signs that there is an increased willingness of domestic courts to prosecute international crimes. Part of the reason for this is a positive side-effect of the complementarity provisions of the ICC Statute, which create an incentive for domestic courts to prosecute international crimes rather than see them prosecuted internationally. This (welcome) development is nonetheless a matter of controversy at the political level. The law is tolerably clear, however, that universal jurisdiction exists over such crimes (O'Keefe, 2004).

V. NON-PROSECUTORIAL RESPONSES TO INTERNATIONAL CRIMES

Although there is an historic and increasing swing towards prosecution of international crimes, there are other methods of dealing with international crimes. The lawfulness of some of these methods is increasingly being contested. Whatever the merits of non-prosecutorial options, at least some of them can be seen as complementary to prosecution, although others (such as amnesties) have to be seen as alternatives. The law, practicality, and morality of this area of international criminal law, and their interrelationship, is the subject of considerable disagreement.

---

[118] Report by the Secretary-General on the Establishment of a Special Court for Sierra Leone, UN Doc S/2000/915 of 4.10.2000 para 9.

[119] See Ch 11 above.

[120] *Attorney-General of the Government of Israel* v *Eichmann* (1961), 36 ILR 5.

A. AMNESTIES

Amnesties are conferred under a law that blocks criminal action against people in the State in which it is passed. At the end of a conflict, the practice was, until recently, frequently to offer an amnesty to all of those who committed crimes as a gesture intended to allow people to move on. They were very controversial in the 1980s when various military regimes granted themselves amnesties, or required them as a condition for handing over power. The most well-known amnesty offered in the recent past was that in South Africa, following the transfer of power from the *apartheid* regime to the democratically-elected African National Congress.

There are various types of amnesties,[121] which run from those granted by regimes to themselves to those which are voted upon by the population. Although the latter are usually thought more legitimate than the former, it must also be said that the often there is little practical choice for the electorate.[122] A further distinction must be made between 'blanket' amnesties, which prevent legal proceedings against all persons without distinction, and those, such as the South African amnesty legislation, which required certain conduct (often full confession of crimes) and/or certain motivations for the crimes (usually political ones) before an amnesty was granted. The latter seem to obtain a greater level of support.

The legality of amnesties is hotly contested. There are those who argue that amnesties are inevitably unlawful (Orentlicher, 1991). These arguments tend to rely on either human rights concerns, or the assertion that there is an all-encompassing duty to prosecute international crimes. It is true that there are certain treaties which impose a duty to prosecute certain international crimes, such as the Geneva Conventions grave breaches regime (eg Geneva Convention 1 Article 49), the Genocide Convention (Articles IV, VI), and the Torture Convention (Article 5). However, these do not cover, for example, crimes against humanity or war crimes other than grave breaches. Therefore, authors supporting the existence of this duty are required to revert to customary law. However, there is not sufficient State practice yet to assert that customary law imposes a duty to prosecute all international crimes, and certainly not on the basis of universal jurisdiction.[123]

Looking to the human rights arguments, the Inter-American Court of Human Rights and Commission have been the most strident in declaring amnesties unlawful:

This Court considers that all amnesty provisions, provisions on prescription and the establishment of measures designed to eliminate responsibility are inadmissible, because they are intended to prevent the investigation and punishment of those responsible for serious human rights violations such as torture, extrajudicial, summary or arbitrary execution and forced disappearance, all of them prohibited because they violate non-derogable rights recognized by international human rights law.[124]

However, it is by no means clear that this is reflective of a more general principle of human rights law, and probably has much to do with the particular context of Latin America

---

[121] For a detailed survey see Mallinder, 2008.   [122] Osiel, 1997, 138.

[123] SCSL Appeals Chamber, *Prosecutor v Kallon and Kamara*, Decision on Challenge to Jurisdiction: Lomé Amnesty Accord, SCSL-2004-15-AR72(E) and SCSL-2004-16-AR72(E), 13 March 2004, para 82.

[124] *Chumbipuma Aguirre et al v Peru (Barrios Altos Case)*, Judgment of 14 March 2001 Ser C, no 75; [2001] IACHR 5, para 41.

and the fact that the Peruvian amnesty under discussion was granted by a regime to itself in a developed State.[125] The other regional human rights courts, and the Human Rights Committee, have not gone so far as the Inter-American Court, and so despite the fact that the scope for lawful amnesties appears to be narrowing, it has not been completely removed.[126]

B. TRUTH AND RECONCILIATION COMMISSIONS

A response to international crimes that has often been employed is a truth and reconciliation commission (TRC). These have been defined as bodies that '(1) investigate the past (2)…investigate a pattern of abuses over a period of time, rather than a specific event, (3)…[are] temporary…completing…[their]…work with the submission of a report and (4)…are officially sanctioned, authorized or empowered by the State'.[127] One of the most famous of these was the South African TRC. However, there have also been TRCs in, for example, Guatemala, Liberia, and Sierra Leone. In the latter case, difficulties were encountered, as there were also proceedings ongoing before the SCSL and the TRC wanted to testimony from some of this indicted before the Tribunal. This led to tensions as the Special Court was unwilling to allow this on the terms the Commission wanted.[128]

The success or otherwise of TRCs depends on various factors, including the terms of reference that they have and the personal qualities of the commissioners. A great deal also depends on the quality of the information that they can obtain. This can be difficult, as perpetrators are unlikely to be willing to fully confess their activities without some promise of amnesty or immunity, and victims may be unwilling to talk about sensitive matters. Although sometimes the hearings can be cathartic affairs, this is not always the case, and some victims are not satisfied with truth without more. It has also been questioned if truth-telling does lead to reconciliation (Hayner, 2001, pp 155–161). Similarly, it has been doubted if truth and reconciliation are congruent goals. However, most take the view that there is a relationship (ibid).

C. OTHER RESPONSES

One way in which some countries have dealt with large scale criminality is by lustration, which is the compulsory removal of people from their jobs.[129] This is usually done on a mass, rather than individual, basis and as such has fallen from favour, as the innocent are punished alongside the guilty. There were elements of lustration involved in the de-Baathification of Iraq, which was, in itself, controversial.

In some countries civil claims are permitted. Whether these are sufficient is sometimes the subject of doubt, but in the absence of prosecutions such proceedings can find the facts and provide some measure of justice for victims, even if where they occur outside

---

[125] Siebert-Fohr, 2009, p 109.

[126] SCSL Appeals Chamber, *Prosecutor v Kondewa, Decision on Lack of Jurisdiction/Abuse of Process: Amnesty provided by the Lome Accord*, SCSL-2004-14-AR72(E) 25 May 2004, para 48, although see Bell, 2008, pp 240–241.

[127] Hayner, 2001, p 14.

[128] *Report of the Truth and Reconciliation Commission for Sierra Leone*, vol 3b, ch 6.

[129] See generally Teitel, 2002, Ch 5.

the *locus delicti*, enforcing such awards can be very difficult. Immunities can also be a problem in third States where government behaviour is at issue. In many societies where there have been international crimes, there simply are insufficient resources to satisfy claims.

In some societies, it is suggested that rather than prosecution, people ought to undergo culturally appropriate traditional justice mechanisms aimed at reconciliation rather than prosecution. Local justice mechanisms are supported by many, on the basis that they 'may have greater legitimacy and capacity than devastated formal systems, and they promise local ownership, access and efficiency.' (Waldorf, 2006, p 4). However, critics have said that they can also be exclusionary, in fact government, not people-led, anachronistic, not designed to deal with international crimes, and dubious on human rights grounds. (Drumbl, 2005, p 549). As is very often the case, a great deal depends on the particular process and its context, making sweeping acceptances or rejections ill-advised.

REFERENCES

ABI-SAAB, G (2001), 'The Concept of War Crimes', in Sienho Yee and Wang Tieya, *International Law and the Post-Cold World: Essays in Honour of Li Haopei*, (London: Routledge), p 99.

AKANDE, D (2003), 'The Jurisdiction of the International Criminal Court Over Nationals of Non-Parties: Legal Basis and Limits', 1 *JICJ* 618.

ARSANJANI, M and REISMAN, R (2005), 'The Law-in-action of the International Criminal Court', 99 *AJIL* 385.

BASSIOUNI, M C (1994), 'Crimes Against Humanity: The Need for a Specialized Convention', 31 *Columbia Journal of Transnational Law* 457.

BELL, C (2008), *On the Law of Peace: Peace Agreements and the Lex Pacificatoria* (Oxford: Oxford University Press).

BOISTER, N (2003), 'Transnational Criminal Law?', 14 *EJIL* 953.

—— and CRYER, R (2008), *The Tokyo International Military Tribunal: A Reappraisal* (Oxford: Oxford University Press).

CASSESE, A (2007), 'The Proper Limits of Criminal Liability Under the Doctrine of Joint Criminal Enterprise', 5 *Journal of International Criminal Justice* 109.

—— (2008), *International Criminal Law*, 2nd edn (Oxford: Oxford University Press).

CLARKE, KM (2009), *Fictions of Justice: The International Criminal Court and the Challenge of Legal Pluralism in Sub-Saharan Africa* (Cambridge: Cambridge University Press).

CRYER, R (2005), *Prosecuting International Crimes: Selectivity and the International Criminal Law Regime* (Cambridge: Cambridge University Press).

—— (2006), 'Sudan Resolution 1654 and International Criminal Justice', *Leiden Journal of International Law* 195.

——, FRIMAN, H, ROBINSON, D, and WILMSHURST, E (2010), *An Introduction to International Criminal Law and Procedure*, 2nd edn (Cambridge: Cambridge University Press).

DANNER, AM and MARTINEZ, JS (2005), 'Guilty Associations: Joint Criminal Enterprise, Command Responsibility and the Development of International Criminal Law', 93 *California Law Review* 75.

DINSTEIN, Y (1965) *The Defence of 'Obedience to Superior Orders' in International Criminal Law* (Leyden: A W Stijhoff).

—— (2004), *The Conduct of Hostilities Under the Law of International Armed Conflict* (Cambridge: Cambridge University Press).

DJURO-DEGAN, V (2005), 'On the Sources of International Criminal Law', 4 *Chinese Journal of International Law* 45.

DRUMBL, M (2005), 'Collective Violence and Individual Punishment: The Criminality of Mass Atrocity', 99 *Northwestern University Law Review* 539.

ESER, A (1996), 'Defences in War Crimes Trials', in Dinstein, Y and Tabory, M (eds), *War Crimes in International Law* (Dordrecht: Martinus Nijhoff), p 251.

GAETA, P (1999), 'The Defence of Superior Orders: The Statute of the International Criminal Court Versus Customary International Law', 10 *EJIL* 172.

GALLANT, K (2008), *The Principle of Legality in International and Comparative Law* (Cambridge: Cambridge University Press).

GARRAWAY, C (1999), 'Superior Orders and the International Criminal Court: Justice Delivered or Justice Denied?', 836 *International Review of the Red Cross* 785.

GREENAWALT, AKA (1999), 'Rethinking Genocidal Intent: The Case for a Knowledge-Based Interpretation', 99 *Columbia Law Review* 2265.

GREENWOOD, C (1996), 'International Humanitarian Law and the Tadić Case' (1996) 7 *EJIL* 265.

HAYNER, P (2001), *Unspeakable Truths: Confronting State Terror and Atrocity* (London: Routledge).

JAIN, N (2005), 'A Separate Law for Peacekeepers; the Clash between the Security Council and the International Criminal Court', 16 *EJIL* 239.

KELSALL, T (2009), *Culture Under Cross-Examination: International Justice and the Special Court for Sierra Leone* (Cambridge: Cambridge University Press).

KLEFFNER, J (2008), *Complementarity in the Rome Statute and National Criminal Jurisdictions* (Oxford: Oxford University Press).

KOLB, R (2000), 'The Jurisprudence of the Yugoslav and Rwandan Criminal Tribunals on Their Jurisdiction and on International Crimes', 69 *BYIL* 259.

LEMKIN, R (1944), *Axis Rule in Occupied Europe* (New York; Carnegie Endowment for International Peace).

MALLINDER, L (2008), *Amnesty, Human Rights and Political Transitions: Bridging the Gap in International Law* (Oxford: Hart).

MELONI, C (2007), 'Command Responsibility: Mode of Liability for Subordinates or Separate Offence of the Superior?', 5 *JICJ* 619.

METTRAUX, G (2009), *The Law of Command Responsibility* (Oxford: Oxford University Press).

MORRIS, M (2001), 'High Crimes and Misconceptions: The ICC and Non Party States', 64 *Law and Contemporary Problems* 131.

OHLIN, J (2007), 'Three Conceptual Problems with the Doctrine of Joint Criminal Enterprise', 5 *Journal of International Criminal Justice* 69.

ORENTLICHER, D (1991), 'Settling Accounts: The Duty to Prosecute Violations of a Prior Regime', 100 *Yale Law Journal* 2537.

OSIEL, M (1997), *Mass Atrocity, Collective Memory and the Law* (New Brunswick: Transaction).

PESKIN, V (2008), *International Justice in Rwanda and the Balkans: Virtual Trials and the Struggle for State Cooperation*

(Cambridge: Cambridge University Press).

O'KEEFE, R (2004), 'Universal Jurisdiction: Clarifying the Basic Concept' 2 *Journal of International Criminal Justice* 735.

RUBIN, A (1994), 'An International Criminal Tribunal for Former Yugoslavia', 6 *Pace International Law Review* 7.

SADAT, L (2007), 'The Effect of Amnesties Before Domestic and International Tribunals, Law, Morality, Politics' in Hughes, E, Schabas, W and Thakur, R (eds), *Atrocities and International Accountability: Beyond Transitional Justice* (Tokyo: UN University Press).

SAUL, B (2006), *Defining Terrorism in International Law* (Oxford: Oxford University Press).

SCHABAS, W (2000), 'Prosecutor v. Barayagwiza', (2000) 94 *AJIL* 563.

—— (2006), The UN International Criminal Tribunals: Yugoslavia, Rwanda, Sierra Leone (Cambridge: Cambridge University Press).

—— (2008a), *Genocide In International Law: The Crime of Crimes*, 2nd edn (Cambridge: Cambridge University Press).

—— (2008b), 'The State Policy as an Element of International Crimes', 98 *Journal of Criminal Law and Criminology* 953.

—— (2008c), *An Introduction to the International Criminal Court*, 3rd edn (Cambridge: Cambridge University Press).

SCHEFFER, D (1999), 'The International Criminal Court: The Challenge of Jurisdiction', 63 *ASIL Proceedings* 68.

SCHWARZENBERGER, G (1947), 'The Judgment of Nuremberg', 21 *Tulane Law Review* 329.

—— (1950), 'The Problem of an International Criminal Law', 3 *Current Legal Problems* 263.

SIEBERT-FOHR, A (2009), *Prosecuting Serious Human Rights Violations* (Oxford: Oxford University Press).

SIMMA, B and PAULUS, A (1999) 'The Responsibility of Individuals for Human Rights Violations in Internal Conflicts: A Positivist View', 93 *AJIL* 302.

TAYLOR, T (1992) *The Anatomy of the Nuremberg Trial* (London: Bloomsbury).

TEITEL, R (2002), *Transitional Justice* (New York: Oxford University Press).

VAN DEN HERIK, L (2005), The Contribution of the Rwanda Tribunal to the Development of International Law (The Hague: Brill).

THALMAN, V (2008), 'French Justice's Endeavours to Substitute for the ICTR', 6 *JICJ* 995.

TRIFFTERER, O (2008), Commentary on the Rome Statute of the International Criminal Court (Oxford: Hart).

VERRIJN STUART, H and SIMONS, M (2009), (eds) *The Prosecutor and the Judge: Benjamin Ferencz and Antonio Cassese: Interviews and Writings* (Amsterdam: Amsterdam University Press).

VETTER, G (2000), 'Command Responsibility of Non-Military Superiors in the International Criminal Court (ICC)' 25 *Yale Journal of International Law* 89.

VON HEBEL, H and ROBINSON, D (1999), 'Crimes Within the Jurisdiction of the Court', in Lee, R (ed), *The International Criminal Court* (The Hague: Martinus Nijhoff).

WALDORF, L (2006), 'Mass Justice for Mass Atrocity: Rethinking Local Justice as Transitional Justice', 79 *Temple Law Review* 1.

ZACKLIN, R (2004), 'The Failings of ad hoc International Tribunals', 2 *JICJ* 541.

FURTHER READING

ALVAREZ, J (1999), 'Crimes of Hate/Crimes of State, Lessons from Rwanda', 24 *Yale Journal of International Law* 365.

BASSIOUNI, MC (ed), (2008), *International Criminal Law*, 3rd edn (The Hague: Martinus Nijhoff).

CASSESE, A, GAETA, P, and JONES, J (eds) (2002), *The Rome Statute: A Commentary* (Oxford: Oxford University Press).

CASSESE, A et al (eds) (2008), *The Oxford Companion to International Criminal Justice* (Oxford: Oxford University Press).

MCGOLDRICK, D, ROWE, P, and DONNELLY, E (eds) (2004), *The International Criminal Court: Legal and Policy Issues* (Oxford, Hart).

MINOW, M (1998), *Between Vengeance and Forgiveness* (Boston: Beacon Press).

RATNER, S, ABRAMS, J, and BISCHOFF, J (2009), *Accountability for Human Rights Atrocities in International Law: Beyond the Nuremberg Legacy*, 3rd edn (Oxford: Oxford University Press).

SADAT, L (2002), *The International Criminal Court and the Transformation of International Law: Justice for a New Millennium* (Ardsley: Transnational Publishers).

WERLE, G (2009), *Principles of International Criminal Law*, 2nd edn (Cambridge: Cambridge University Press).

ZAPPALÀ, S (2003), *Human Rights in International Criminal Proceedings* (Oxford: Oxford University Press).

26

INTERNATIONAL PROTECTION
OF HUMAN RIGHTS

Henry J Steiner

SUMMARY

The international protection of human rights cannot be described without consideration of the State systems that offer the first line of defence and that are so complexly intertwined with international organizations and processes. The very notion of protection must be reconsidered in the context of human rights, so that it reaches beyond conventional understandings of judicial or other enforcement of the law and the related provision of civil remedies. The need for reconsideration stems from several characteristics of the human rights movement that distinguish it from most fields of international law. Those characteristics emphasize how deeply human rights and their violations implicate a State's political and social structures and culture. In many authoritarian States and conflict-riven States of the developing world, it is more productive to understand protection as extending to ways of changing the political and cultural understandings and assumptions that may underlie violations. Without such changes, violations may be temporarily arrested but the risk of their recurrence remains high. In light of these observations, many civil and political rights will be capable of only progressive realization, particularly outside the world of liberal democracies where such kinds of rights are familiar and entrenched and where ongoing elaboration of and innovations in such rights are more readily absorbed. Assessment of the effectiveness of human rights treaties in expanding protection of human rights cannot then stop with inquiry into current compliance but must take account of longer-run possibilities stemming from political and cultural transformation. Different views of these matters and a different rhetoric about immediate or progressive realization may naturally prevail within the distinct but related worlds of victims of violations, human rights advocates, and academic and other critical observers of the human rights movement.

I. INTRODUCTION

The request to write a chapter for this volume on the 'international protection of human rights' evoked at the start a fairly clear image of the task. The topic had a deceptive simplicity. It appeared to *restrict* inquiry to the international norms, organizations, and processes that contributed to protection of human rights, rather than include the variety of States' legal and political institutions that could offer the first line of defence against violations. What came to mind regarding international protection was the range of pressures applied by international bodies or by States themselves against delinquent States—critical diplomatic notes, investigative reports and recommendatory resolutions; judgments by courts or other dispute-resolution bodies; threats to withhold trade or aid; boycotts and embargoes; exclusion from the global financial system; military interventions—in the effort to arrest violations and increase the likelihood of compliance.

These images soon gave way to a more problematic view of the topic. What comprised an *international* system of protection? In the world of human rights that so pervasively affects the internal life of States, can we mark a clear boundary between national and international institutions and processes, at least those international institutions in which States themselves (rather than independent experts elected by States) are the active, voting participants? Should a State's internalization and *application* of an international norm be understood purely as a matter of domestic law? Or are international and national legal and political systems so pervasively and intricately intertwined in the field of human rights that analysis of international protection cannot be an isolated inquiry into either system alone but must embrace the many inter-relationships and complementary roles?

So the term *international* required a broadening and re-imagination. It was not alone. The problematic aspect of the notion of *protection* concerned how far that notion reached and what strategies and methods it employed. Can we grasp the distinctive needs and challenges of the human rights movement if we reduce the international protection of rights to the popular meaning of protection: maintaining compliance with the law through its enforcement, subject (within liberal States) to the constraints of the rule of law? Should the idea of human rights protection include, for example, inquiry into the background conditions and traditional attitudes that may foster violations, followed by efforts to change those conditions and attitudes in such a way as to bring about greater acceptance of human rights norms?

Such questions about the international dimension of human rights and the notion of protection give this chapter its structure. We start with the more formal and positive dimension of our inquiry. Section II describes the formal structure, powers, and functions of some leading international organizations and organs concerned with human rights, to indicate their links to States and to underscore the widely varying kinds of *protection* that they may offer. Section III analyses five characteristics of the human rights movement that distinguish it from many other bodies of international law and that present some puzzling questions about the kinds of international protection that are desirable and workable. Some of the characteristics portrayed—the relationships between human rights violations and deep political and cultural features of the State, the progressive achievement of civil and political rights—appear to be at odds with much of the prevailing discourse about the nature of those rights and the means for their protection. Section IV suggests why victims of violations, human rights activists, and academic and other critical observers who are committed to human rights ideals may naturally speak with different voices and use different language to describe the reality and promise of international protection.

The chapter concentrates on the universal human rights system—universal in membership and in asserted reach—that is so closely linked to the United Nations. That system presents far greater variety among its global participants in ideological, cultural, political, and socio-economic terms than do any of the three regional human rights regimes in Africa, the Americas, and Europe. Such diversity puts the questions here examined under the harshest light, and greatest strain.

The discussion refers almost exclusively to civil and political rights. Given their intrinsic importance and status of equality within the human rights corpus, economic and social rights merit equal attention here. They raise, however, too many distinctive issues to be examined within the available space. The same reason for omission applies to a field of ever closer interaction with human rights, the humanitarian laws of war.

II. THE KINDS OF PROTECTION PROVIDED BY INTERNATIONAL ORGANIZATIONS

A. WHY CREATE INTERNATIONAL ORGANIZATIONS?

Is it necessary or even useful to create intergovernmental human rights organizations (IGOs) to debate, interpret, develop and apply customary and treaty law? Are not matters like implementation and protection better left in the hands of governments and civil society in the different States, particularly since human rights issues are imbedded in national (and sub-national, local) governments, traditions, and cultures? In such respects, the field of human rights differs from situations presented by, for example, international trade or environmental law, where a State's violation of a treaty adversely affects other treaty parties' interests as or (usually) more severely than it does its own population. In such treaty regimes based on reciprocity, the relevant issues about trade or environment may be very significant for a State but are not rooted in its political structures, traditional practices, and cultural underpinnings. Unlike many human rights issues, they only rarely implicate constitutional principles and text. Hence enforcement of treaty commitments and dispute settlement may more readily be entrusted to IGOs.

These doubts become the more plausible when we take into account that even in the absence of substantial enforcement powers in IGOs, standard-setting by itself—the declarations and treaties that dominated the early decades of the human rights movement, and the related spread to interest groups, media and the general population of this new discourse of international human rights—will advance the cause of human rights. The internalization and constitutionalization of treaty norms by many States has made those norms a key ingredient of the domestic legal system. They become institutionalized, and infiltrate political and popular debate. In the longer run, they will influence how some or many people think about issues.

As a consequence, human rights advocates and politically mobilized groups may come to base their demands for political and social change primarily on their State's international commitment and its related internal law that was enacted because required by the terms of that (treaty) commitment. Disaffected citizens can invoke the State's own words against it rather than invoke only 'foreign' or 'international' texts or the more amorphous customary international law, all of which the State may have ignored or explicitly rejected. The gap between the treaty commitment and government policy, between assurance of human rights norms and peoples' precarious lives, becomes strikingly and publicly apparent. The resulting cognitive dissonance as official State norms clash with State conduct may itself generate unrest and demands for change. In such ways, the treaty text itself can serve to empower a population, spur demands for reform, and heighten the pressure on a State. That text can itself serve as the first line of protection of the rights it assures. Its effects may well grow with time.

One can question the need for IGOs from another perspective. We can imagine a world where all States are committed in good faith to observe human rights, and hence where international organizations would be redundant. But even in this ideal world, disputes will inevitably arise over questions of interpretation stemming from conflicts between rights, diverse political and cultural understandings about the meaning of a term in the treaties, and the effect of such changed global circumstances as the end of the Cold War on the human rights corpus. IGOs appear at least useful, perhaps essential, to contribute to resolving such disputes. The possibilities range from merely a forum for States to explore such disputes, to an international court whose opinions could have an advisory character or stand as judgments binding on respondent States.

More to the point, the assumption of a good-faith commitment of all States to a human rights regime defies our knowledge of the world and of the human rights movement's history. Massive violations of basic physical security norms including genocide have captured the world's attention. Cambodia and Rwanda offer extreme examples. As most of these episodes demonstrate, we have no basis for relying on other States to apply economic or military force against such systemic violations, whether unilaterally or through coordinated action—let alone against delinquent States committing less dramatic violations of rights, perhaps related to a free press or imprisonment of dissenters.

If then the human rights treaties were left free floating rather than anchored in intergovernmental organizations endowed with some powers to monitor, report and protect, the movement would have achieved some but a very modest advance. Nonetheless, the conclusion that IGOs are indispensable for an effective movement raises a host of questions: How should membership in such organizations be organized, what relationships should they bear to national systems, what powers and functions should they exercise vis-à-vis States? Moreover, what duties should States bear toward IGOs or their decisions?

Such issues were never systematically examined for IGOs as a group during the evolution of the universal human rights system. The UN Charter and UN organs created or authorized the creation of the major bodies and official posts that are now concerned with human rights issues: the Security Council and General Assembly; the UN Commission on Human Rights, replaced in 2006 by a newly created Human Rights Council, related working groups and rapporteurs; and the Office of the High Commissioner of Human Rights. In addition, each of eight human rights treaties is serviced by its own committee, the so-called treaty bodies or organs. These committees bear a close family resemblance, and as a whole differ markedly from the former UN Commission and new Human Rights Council.

This range of universal organizations and organs was created at different times and in different contexts over a half century; indeed, many of them have played significant roles only over the last quarter century. Moreover, each of them has experienced independent and ongoing internal development with respect to its powers and functions, such that the original understandings about such matters now appear more modest. In the last decade, institutions and centres like the World Bank and the UN Development Programme, as well as the International Criminal Tribunals and the new International Criminal Court, have become important actors in the field of human rights, further expanding the types of pressure against and forms of dialogue with delinquent States.

Starting in the 1970s, non-governmental human rights organizations (NGOs) steadily gained power and influence. In addition to their independent activities of monitoring, reporting, and lobbying in national and international institutions, they have interacted closely with and left a strong imprint on the broad network of IGOs. Today a far greater number of NGOs constitute an indispensable element of the broader human rights movement, including its capacity for protection of human rights.

Substantive provisions of the human rights treaties—so-called standard setting—drew on several centuries of an evolving tradition of rights. But neither the architecture nor powers and functions of most of the intergovernmental institutions seemed obvious at the time of the drafting of their constitutive instruments. We can contrast a State in a period of transition from a repressive authoritarian regime to political democracy. Planners of the structure of its new governmental regime might well adopt broadly understood principles for democratic government like equal protection and the rule of law with its related imperative of separation of powers. But no common stock of principles was available to suggest the design of IGOs intended to protect human rights. In the universal system, close analogies to national legal-political institutions such as a world court of human rights lay beyond political possibility or even imagination.

The inevitably novel architecture and powers of these new institutions raised deep concerns among their planners—and potential members. After all, the IGO under negotiation might have power to implement a treaty through authoritative interpretation or even to apply telling pressure against a member State. Such powers would pose a far greater threat to a State's sovereign control over its own territory and population than would its bare agreement to observe treaty norms. Indeed, many States viewed even that bare agreement as a significant qualification of their exclusive sovereign control over their own citizens (with respect to internal conduct) that was thought to inhere in statehood. If IGOs gained in stature and increased their armoury of pressures against violator States, they could cut to the very bone of sovereignty. They could effectively narrow the boundaries of domestic jurisdiction.

Negotiations during the drafting of the treaties over powers and functions of IGOs were notoriously contentious. The inevitable compromises sometimes led to terse and vague provisions that left much for future decision. Neither basic principles nor a master plan explain our present institutional arrangements. Rather, we must be attentive to contingent compromises over time responsive to the positions of the great powers and of regional or ideological blocs of countries, all as supplemented by a gradual increase in powers of international organizations through their internal development. However qualified and inadequate those arrangements now appear, we should keep in mind how radical and politically implausible they would have seemed when the human rights movement was born.

B. IGOS AND NGOS

This brief look at the structure, powers, and functions of several IGOs concerned in significant ways with human rights[1] includes the UN Security Council, the UN Human

---

[1] I am indebted to Philip Alston, Professor at the New York University School of Law, for his assistance in updating the information in this section about IGOs for the years since this chapter was published in the second edition (2006) of this book.

Rights Council as successor to the UN Commission on Human Rights, the Human Rights Committee, the Office of the High Commissioner for Human Rights, and international tribunals with jurisdiction to try individuals for certain international crimes. The formal descriptions, which illustrate the range of powers and functions of universal intergovernmental human rights organizations as a whole, provide essential information for the discussion in Section III of the distinctive character of the human rights movement.[2] This section also sketches recurrent interactions between IGOs and NGOs.

The evident inadequacies and gross failures of these institutions in curbing human rights violations may well be better known than their success in implanting a new discourse of human rights throughout the world, persuading numbers of States to greater compliance, and developing the human rights movement as a whole in both normative and institutional ways. Some causes of the failures have long been apparent, such as the limited powers granted to these institutions, and the many ways in which the play of national interests of their members, as well as of global politics and related bloc voting, betrayed States' and IGOs' original commitments to advance the protection of human rights. Other less tangible and more complex explanations stem from the characteristics of the human rights movement that Section III will examine.

1. UN Security Council

The Security Council[3] is a 'principal organ' of the UN and consists of 15 State members, five of which are permanent (China, France, Russia, the United Kingdom, and the United States) and possess a veto power with respect to all Council decisions on non-procedural matters. Member States of the UN confer on the Council 'primary responsibility' to maintain international peace and security, and agree to 'accept and carry out' the Council's decisions in accordance with the Charter.

The Council can act under Chapter VI of the Charter (Articles 33–38) to achieve the pacific settlement of 'any dispute, the continuance of which is likely to endanger the maintenance of international peace and security'. It is empowered to investigate such disputes and recommend 'appropriate procedures or methods of adjustment'. The greater power lies in Chapter VII (Articles 39–51), which goes beyond recommendation. If the Council determines 'the existence of any threat to the peace, breach of the peace, or act of aggression', it can call on member States to apply sanctions of various kinds, including boycotts and embargoes (Article 41), or to take such military action 'as may be necessary to restore international peace and security' (Article 42). The powers conferred by Articles 39–42 well illustrate the initial conception of the Council as a body not to be occupied with the conventional tasks of monitoring or criticism of States—more the province in human rights of the UN Human Rights Council (and later of the treaty bodies described below)—but rather to respond to emergency situations threatening international peace and security. The agreement among UN members that Article 43 contemplates, incorporating a commitment by member States to make available to the Security Council armed forces to maintain international peace and security, remains a dead letter.

These provisions do not confer on the Security Council any powers or functions specifically related to human rights. In effect, human rights constitute for the Council a

---

[2] For illustrations of these institutions in action, see Steiner, Alston, and Goodman, 2008, chs 9–11.
[3] See UN Charter, Articles 23–29.

second-order consideration that becomes relevant to its resolutions and exercise of powers under Articles 41 and 42 only insofar as actual or threatened violations of rights bear on the Council's responsibility for international peace and security. When acting under Chapter VII in ways that address human rights issues, the Council has described violations of rights as constituting a threat to international peace and security, and has characterized the action stemming from its decision as contributing to the maintenance or restoration of the peace. The circumstances in a delinquent State leading to such characterization and action have naturally been extreme, involving systemic repression like apartheid, brutality, and often massive loss or threatened loss of life.

The causal links implicit in these decisions are not difficult to see. Severe human rights violations in one State may prompt flows of refugees to other States, enrage populations in other States who are ethnically or religiously related to the oppressed minority in the delinquent State, or threaten to destabilize an entire region. From its early significant involvement in the effort to end South African apartheid, the Council has played an important role in this field, often through its resolutions that address human rights issues in particular national contexts or international conflicts.

Since the end of the Cold War, the Council has given more attention in its decisions under Chapter VII to human rights issues, often in the form of resolutions addressing a particular conflict or country. These decisions have generally responded to serious situations involving physical harm, rather than other kinds of systemic violations like severe gender discrimination or repression of speech and association. The Council has here shown greater awareness of the relevance of human rights concerns to the resolution of conflicts, as well as the relevance of punishment as a response to major human rights abuses in the context of civil war or ethnic conflict.

The great powers that the Council may exercise under Chapter VII have reinforced its political character, manifested from the outset by the permanent members' veto power. Extensive negotiations among the Council's member States take place before critical votes, such as those preceding the first Gulf War as well as those surrounding the arms inspection regime in Iraq prior to the second Gulf War. Major States supporting or opposing a given course of action intensively lobby other Council members for their vote, using when necessary carrots and sticks like increasing or decreasing trade or aid.

Members of the Council and the Council itself form a complex amalgam. The members may argue and vote as independent States advancing their distinctive interests in the debates leading to a particular institutional decision. At such times, the Council appears less as a distinct actor than as a debating forum for its members. Nonetheless, what is ultimately voted under Chapter VI or VII—recommendation, resolution, decision—constitutes an act of the Council as a body separate from its members exercising certain powers that only it possesses.

It can cause no surprise that an organ as politically constituted as the Council and empowered to authorize the use of economic and military force has acted inconsistently in deciding whether and how to react to gross human rights crises in a timely effort to forestall or arrest violence. Intense political pressures exerted by its permanent members and other powerful states or coalitions can decide the outcome. At times the use or threat of use of the veto power has blocked the Council from action. Kosovo and Rwanda offer two major illustrations of the Council's failure to act under Chapter VII, although in the first case a NATO-led coalition of States forcefully intervened despite the absence of authorization by the Council. The invasion of Iraq in 2003 by the United States and several allied States and the resulting war were also launched without the Council's authorization.

Proposals for reform of the Council have received serious attention in political and academic circles for a number of years. The UN Secretary-General and numbers of States advocated that the Council become more broadly representative of the international community as a whole, as well as of current geopolitical realities.

2. The Human Rights Council

The Human Rights Council was established in 2006 as a subsidiary organ of the General Assembly.[4] It is the successor to the Commission on Human Rights whose creation was mandated by Charter Article 68. The Commission was established in 1946 and consisted of 53 member States elected for three-year terms. Like the Security Council, both the Commission and the Council are made up of States rather than independent experts.

The Council was created after sharp criticism of the Commission and its work, spurred not only by the extreme politicization of its proceedings but also by the controversy generated by the important roles played in it by members like Cuba, Libya, and Sudan that stood broadly accused of severe human rights violations. The new Council was designed to respond in several respects to criticism of the Commission's membership and politics. Its 47 members (spread among regional groups to achieve equitable geographical distribution) are elected for three-year terms by secret ballot by an absolute majority (now 96 members) of the GA. By a two-thirds majority of those present and voting, the GA can suspend membership rights of a Council member 'that commits gross and systematic violations of human rights.' Members are not eligible for re-election after two consecutive terms.

The most important procedural innovation introduced by the Council is a system of 'universal periodic review' under which the human rights record of each State is examined by the Council every four years.[5] Whereas the Commission met for a single session annually, the Council must meet at least three times in the course of the year. Special sessions, called to examine an urgent issue, have been far more frequent under the Council than was the case under the Commission. In most other respects, the Council retains the powers and operational functions of the Commission and, in recognition of this formal as well as actual continuity, the following description addresses both the Commission and the Council.

The Commission and the Council have played important roles in standard-setting, both through the drafting of treaties subsequently approved by the General Assembly and submitted to States for ratification, and the adoption of non-binding but often very influential standards. But the biggest challenge has been that of responding to claims of substantial violations of rights by States. The Commission developed many of its procedures in the context of the worldwide campaign to end South African apartheid, but it soon came to apply its powers of discussion, debate and passage of critical resolutions to a growing number of States.

The politics of the Cold War frequently set the tone for argument and the voting within the Commission. Certain States were favoured targets, whereas others, particularly those in the Communist bloc, were effectively immune from inquiry. Since the collapse of the

---

[4] GA Res 60/251 (15 March 2006).   [5] Steiner, Alston, and Goodman, 2008, pp 806–810.

Soviet Union, the political factors influencing debate and decisions of the Commission were perhaps less notorious, but nonetheless decisive with respect to proposed action against a number of States. Dramatic illustrations include the efforts of the United States to have human rights problems in China and Cuba brought into the Commission's procedure for country-specific debates and resolutions. As with proposals for resolutions before the Security Council, negotiations and lobbying among States with a full armoury of carrots and sticks characterized the most intense of these debates.

The Commission's investigative and monitoring functions, as well as its resolutions responding to violations, fell within three broad categories: (1) public debate about a country's problems under what was known as the 1235 procedure—that is, authorized by ECOSOC Resolution 1235 (XLII) of 1967; (2) confidential (within limits) consideration of a given country's human rights problems under the 1503 procedure, authorized in ECOSOC Resolution 1503 (XLVIII) of 1970 (as amended by ECOSOC Resolution 2000/3); and (3) creation by the Commission of 'special procedures' in the form of thematic rapporteurs or working groups charged with investigating and reporting not on States as such but on types of violations such as violence against women.

The 1503 procedure has been retained by the Council in the name of a 'complaint procedure' pursuant to Council resolution 5/1 of 18 June 2007. But while the political symbolism of 1503 was important, its results appear to have been meagre, and there is no reason to expect that its successor will pack any more punch. The 1235 procedure, like the 1503 procedure, addressed situations revealing a 'consistent pattern' of substantial violations of human rights. It involved a 'thorough study' and debate of a situation, sometimes followed by the adoption of 'recommendations thereon', frequently expressed in resolutions voted by its members. However strongly phrased and however successful in applying pressure to the addressee State, these recommendations lacked the obligatory character of Security Council decisions under Chapter VII.

At its annual session, the Commission held a public debate focusing on gross violations in a number of States. Governments, and those NGOs which had entered into consultative relations with the UN, had the opportunity at such debates to identify States that, in their view, should be subject to the Commission's public scrutiny. The number of States singled out for action of some sort varied considerably from session to session. The debate might have varied consequences, such as formulation of a resolution ranging from the gentle and diplomatic to the harsh that would then be put to the vote. Depending on the State, the nature and evidence of the violations, and the contextual politics of the time, the proposed resolution would succeed or fail, and if the former, by votes ranging from bare and contested majorities to near unanimity. In 2005, when the Commission was wound up, there were 12 mandates growing out of this process for special scrutiny, each focused on a specific country.

The Council has continued the same practice, although the Asian and African States have generally sought to eliminate most such country mandates. In 2009 the number was reduced to eight mandates. The process involves the appointment of a special rapporteur, a representative, or a working group to investigate a given country and submit a report on it. Most such independent experts are appointed for a year at a time, and renewed regularly. The approach adopted follows no particular pattern. An on-site visit may or may not be permitted by the target country. Where it is not, the appointed expert seeks information from outside the country from victims of violations, refugees, and other sources. Where a visit is permitted, the fact-finding may last for a week or two and involve extensive travel within the country. The resulting reports generally contain extensive information and recommendations. The tone varies from the conciliatory and complimentary (when a State acts to end violations) to the harshly condemnatory. In principle, the decision to renew the mandate or not is strongly influenced by the nature of the report.

Thematic mandates involve the appointment of issue-specific rather than country-specific rapporteurs. They have increased substantially since the first such mechanism, the Working Group on Disappearances, was established in 1980. By 2009, there were 30 mechanisms focused on themes including torture, independence of judges, religious intolerance, children in armed conflict, violence against women, foreign debt, structural adjustment policies, and the rights to education, food, health and water. There are four working groups (focused on disappearances, arbitrary detention, mercenaries, and people of African descent) and the rest of the mandates involve individual experts. The appointment of thematic rapporteurs has been seen by governments to be much more palatable than country-specific rapporteurs. No government likes to be singled out for public scrutiny about abuse of its citizens; no government likes to be shamed by a critical discussion and resolution.

In its early years, the politicization of the Commission's decision-making process stemmed primarily from the divisions of the Cold War. Thereafter politicization of decision-making came to reflect the different interests and rhetoric of the post-colonial States, or particular groupings or blocs within that broad category such as Arab or sub-Saharan States, or the developed States of the capitalist world. These blocs are not monolithic but can reveal serious internal divisions, as they do in other fora such as the General Assembly.

The intense but only occasionally successful campaigns directed at China during the 1990s provoked strong efforts by that government to avoid public discussion by the Commission of its human rights problems. These efforts illustrate the anxiety of a State—in this case, a State seeking a leadership role in global politics—facing the threat of a strong, adverse resolution. The struggles to pass or block a condemnatory resolution, or even to block any substantive discussion of the resolution, involve the typical inducements or threats of the protagonists directed to other States whose votes may determine the outcome—trade agreements, aid, investment permissions, special contracts, support of such States if they themselves are threatened with public debate. All too frequently, bloc voting of a regional or ideological character exercises a telling influence on the outcome. Since the establishment of the Council, the African and Asian groups, often in conjunction with members of the Organization of the Islamic Conference, have exercised a dominant influence in relation to many of the country-specific and thematic debates.

What effect critical resolutions alone may have on the behaviour of the State under discussion depends greatly on context. The State may lose prestige and influence. A condemnatory resolution may spur political debate within a democratic regime, and give courage to and animate dissenters within a repressive State. It may mobilize the support of other States for applying pressure against the violator. But even strong resolutions voted by large majorities may have a negligible effect on the State involved, or on other States with little inclination to invest their energy or political capital in responding to the violations.

The emphasis in this description on politicization of the work of both the Commission and the Council simply corresponds to their composition and power in the context of human rights. The member States have varying power, interests, ideology, and influence, and they develop and apply foreign policies involving many factors that include the human rights practices of other States. Their particular forms of government, as well as locations in and perspectives on regional or global politics, shape such policies to one or another degree. At international organs like the Security Council and Human Rights Council, their representatives (usually with the rank of ambassadors) are instruments for carrying out those policies through the debates and votes about what action the organ should take. The contrast could not be more striking between such 'political' organizations charged to implement the goals stated in the Charter and human rights instruments, and the quintessential 'legal' organizations that play a more limited a role in the universal human rights movement—above all courts, but also the quasi-judicial jurisdiction of several treaty bodies. The preceding observations and structural similarities between the Commission and the Council suggest in good part why initial hopes that the Council would improve on the human rights record of the Commission have not been realized.

3. Treaty bodies

This chapter discusses three of the eight human rights treaties that are implemented by a separate treaty body confined in its work to matters arising under that treaty: the International Covenant on Civil and Political Rights (ICCPR),[6] the International Covenant on Economic, Social and Cultural Rights (ICESCR),[7] and the Convention on the Elimination of All Forms of Discrimination against Women (CEDAW).[8] The other five treaties concern torture, racial discrimination, children's rights, migrant workers, and persons with disabilities.[9]

The Human Rights Committee (referred to below as the Committee) created under Article 28 of the ICCPR remains the most significant of the treaty organs. It consists of 18 independent experts who are to perform their work 'impartially'. These Committee members are instructed to serve 'in their personal capacity' rather than as representatives of their States of nationality. Hence they are not (in theory) subject to instructions from governments of their country of citizenship about what positions to assert in argument and how to vote. The Committee performs three functions that generally characterize the treaty bodies as a group:

(i)   ICCPR Article 40 requires treaty parties to 'submit reports on the measures they have adopted which give effect to the rights recognized herein and on the progress made in the enjoyment of those rights'. The reports are to 'indicate the factors and difficulties, if any, affecting the implementation' of the Covenant. The Committee has stressed that it intends the reports to offer a realistic description of a State's application of human rights norms and of a State's relevant conduct, rather than to

---

[6] Adopted 1966, entered into force 1976.   [7] Adopted 1966, entered into force 1976.
[8] Adopted 1979, entered into force 1981.
[9] Convention against Torture and Other Cruel, Inhuman or Degrading Treatment or Punishment, adopted 1984, entered into force 1987; International Convention on the Elimination of All Forms of Racial Discrimination (CERD), adopted 1965, entered into force 1969; Convention on the Rights of the Child, adopted 1989, entered into force 1990; International Convention on the Protection of the Rights of all Migrant Workers and Members of their Families, adopted 1990, entered into force 2003; and Convention on the Rights of Persons with Disabilities, adopted 2006, entered into force 2008.

assume a formal and abstract character by emphasizing laws on the books without regard to their enforcement and effects.

The reports are discussed in public proceedings in which a representative of the State participates. These dialogues between the State and the Committee can become occasions for serious probing of States' human rights problems. At the other extreme, they may amount to a formal presentation by the State that conceals more than it reveals, followed by an exchange of views without consequence. The Committee presents its reactions to the report in a single document arrived at by consensus and termed 'concluding observations'. Although politely phrased, the observations may sharply criticize the State and recommend substantial changes in policy and conduct. Those observations may be reported by media or NGOs; they can lead to public debate in the home State; they may go unnoticed.

Over recent decades, a practice has developed of informal involvement by NGOs in the discussion of State reports. At the start of a three-week session of the Committee (held three times annually), an NGO or a group of NGOs knowledgeable about the human rights problems in the State under discussion will invite Committee members to a meeting to discuss the State's report. NGOs often may prepare and present 'alternative reports', giving a different picture to that of the State.

(ii) The Committee also issues General Comments that generally consist of substantive interpretations of treaty provisions on a large range of topics like privacy, torture, non-discrimination, the right to life, and states of emergencies. In earlier years, the Committee drafted and approved General Comments in a closed process that excluded any possibility of participation. Now they are generally discussed in public meetings, and comments of other treaty bodies and interested parties like States are solicited.

(iii) An Optional Protocol to the ICCPR creates a complaints procedure against a State party to that Protocol that can be invoked by citizens of that State.[10] A number of conditions must be satisfied, including the familiar requirement of exhaustion of local remedies. Of the States parties to the ICCPR, 112 are also parties to the Protocol. The complaint, termed a 'communication', must allege a violation of the ICCPR itself. The Committee examines communications in closed meetings, and all proceedings are written. It decides whether a violation has occurred, and is instructed by the treaty to 'forward its views' to the State and the individual complainant. No text defines the form or status of these 'views'—hortatory, recommendatory, or binding—or refers to remedies. The Committee has long asserted that the views are morally binding on States, and in recent years has taken the bolder position that its views are binding.

Given the Committee's other demanding tasks and the one-month duration of each of its three annual sessions (including one week for working group), knowledgeable observers have estimated that it is capable of adopting only about 80 decisions (views and

---

[10] Optional Protocol to the International Covenant on Civil and Political Rights, adopted 1966, entered into force 1976.

decisions on admissibility) annually. The number of views, the most significant output of the Committee under the Optional Protocol, would be considerably less. But well over a billion people inhabit the States that are parties to the Protocol, including many States with poor human rights protection and judiciaries that are likely to produce greater resort to the Committee. Although the Committee has produced a large and important body of views over the years that develop the Covenant's provisions, it seems evident that the complaints procedure cannot serve as an effective 'review' of human rights violations that would assure individual justice and the rule of law within the States parties to the Protocol. Moreover, the record of compliance by a number of States with views of the Committee providing for damages or release of a prisoner is spotty.

Like the UN Commission and the Human Rights Council, the Human Rights Committee and the other treaty bodies have evolved in significant ways through internal decisions. This evolution has expanded the committees' power—for example, by providing a follow-up procedure to ascertain how States have responded to concluding observations. Several treaties have been amended to increase powers. Treaty provisions differ to some degree for the eight committees. For example, some treaty organs are empowered to conduct on-site visits under certain conditions, and to refer especially problematic cases to the General Assembly.

4. The Office of the High Commissioner of Human Rights

The mandate of the High Commissioner of Human Rights (HCHR) was originally spelled out in GA Resolution 48/141 of 1993. Except for the Secretary-General, the HCHR is the UN official with principal responsibility for human rights. The tasks of the High Commissioner include promotion and protection of the effective enjoyment of rights, provision of technical assistance to States in the field of human rights, engagement of governments in dialogue to secure respect for human rights, and enhancement of international cooperation. The Office of the High Commissioner for Human Rights has paid growing attention to creating and strengthening national human rights institutions.

The present High Commissioner, who took office in September 2008, has emphasized the importance of the principles of impartiality, integrity, and independence in guiding the work of her Office. She has also called upon the Human Rights Council to improve its ability to deal with urgent human rights issues, to hold special briefings on matters of concern, to reach out creatively to the outside world, to make more effective use of the special procedures as well as the treaty bodies, and to involve civil society more thoroughly in its deliberations.

5. The International Criminal Tribunals and International Criminal Court

Over the past 15 years, several international tribunals have enriched the array of international institutions designed to protect international human rights. The International Criminal Tribunals for the Former Yugoslavia and for Rwanda cover regional conflicts but have exerted a considerable influence on the human rights movement as a whole. The International Criminal Court, the first of its kind in its permanent character and universal reach, has started to hear its first cases. 'Hybrid' tribunals, whose structure is part international and part national, have also been established in Sierra Leone, East Timor, Kosovo, Cambodia and Lebanon (Steiner, Alston, and Goodman, 2008, pp 1244–1318).

These tribunals apply the international-law norms set forth in their governing statutes—crimes against humanity, genocide, and war crimes—to impose a criminal liability on individual violators. The conduct covered by those norms involves both international humanitarian law and international human rights; the once-clear boundaries between the two have faded over the decades.

Complementing State courts (where criminal trials may be conducted under jurisdictional principles including universal jurisdiction), international criminal tribunals may represent for most observers the closest approximation among international institutions of State institutions charged with the protection of rights, particularly within liberal democracies where the imagination of law, the rule of law, and related notions of protection are strikingly court-centric. Such goals of criminal punishment as retribution and deterrence might first appear to be similar for ordinary crimes within States and for massive crimes tried by the international tribunals. But the situations leading to international criminal prosecutions are often strikingly different from ordinary crimes. For example, the ordinary criminal stands in the eyes of most people as an 'outlaw', a person acting outside the law and drawing broad public censure. But the wrongdoers committing war crimes or crimes against humanity may be responding to 'official orders' and be among a multitude of wrongdoers following the 'law' in effect and viewed by many fellow citizens as doing their duty. That is, peer pressure may encourage and support their conduct. For this and similar reasons, the creation of a criminal court, however promising, holds a more qualified promise for serving a goal like deterrence. Experience with the tribunals has been too short to permit informed answers to such questions.

One central concern informs the question of prosecutions. The task after violence has ended may be primarily to rebuild, to lay the foundations for a society more respectful of basic human rights values that extend from control of violence to institutionalization of political participation, and to achieve some degree of reconciliation that will permit the society to move forward. In such circumstances, prosecutions may hold risks as well as promise, and may be seen as one among several plausible responses to mass and brutal violations. The choices include truth commissions, lustration, and selective or general amnesties that may rest on a popular vote and may involve some quid pro quo on the part of those gaining amnesty, or some combination thereof.

The different constraining conditions facing reform governments of States experiencing deep political change like Chile or South Africa highlight the difficulty of deciding how to deal with violations committed during a recent period of violence and repression. They suggest how contextual these decisions must be, for they have consequences affecting a long-run process of change.

C. INTERACTION AMONG INSTITUTIONS AND SYSTEMS IN EXERTING PRESSURE ON DELINQUENT STATES

The universal system of protection has been no more static than the content of human rights norms. Each has experienced dynamic change over this half century, whether through additional treaties and institutions or through internal expansion of an institution's powers and functions by its organs' interpretation and elaboration of governing texts. That change has made additional routes available for putting pressure on delinquent States. One way of illustrating today's possibilities for exerting pressure (excluding

the earlier-discussed powers of the Security Council under Chapter VII to authorize boycotts, embargoes, and military action) is to sketch the complex interactive network of
IGOs and NGOs.

(i)   Suppose that State X, a party to the basic treaties, severely represses an ethnic
      minority or political opposition. If independent NGOs can function within the
      political environment of X, they and other groups of X's civil society may well
      form the first line of organized protest by lobbying, monitoring and issuing reports
      about the internal situation. International NGOs (INGOs), generally based in the
      liberal democratic States, may direct their attention to X, independently or in
      cooperation with the local NGOs. The reports by NGOs following investigative
      missions will reach the media, governments of other States, and universal as well
      as regional IGOs. They may be accompanied by the lobbying by INGOs or local
      NGOs of executive officials or legislatures in other States with influence over X's
      policies through their financial, trade, and political relationships. NGOs may seek
      to persuade other States to initiate political processes against X in any IGO in
      which they participate, such as the UN Human Rights Council or international
      financial institutions involved in X's economy.

(ii) At the same time, INGOs or local NGOs themselves could attempt to involve
      IGOs. For example, they may have gained the right of access to the Human Rights
      Council to participate in a complaints procedure. If State X was about to submit a
      periodic State report to the Human Rights Committee, NGOs could prepare an
      alternative report presenting relevant facts and circumstances from their own
      critical perspectives. If X were a party to the Optional Protocol, any of its aggrieved
      citizens could file a communication to initiate a proceeding against it.

(iii) State members of the Council could attempt to initiate a course of action against
      X under or independently of a complaints procedure, most likely seeking a
      condemnatory resolution, and possibly the appointment as well of a country-
      specific rapporteur. They could request involvement of the Office of the Secretary-
      General or of the High Commissioner of Human Rights.

(iv) Rapporteurs, special representatives, and working groups appointed by the
      Council or office of the Secretary-General may give heightened attention to the
      situation in X by making investigative trips and issuing reports that would be
      given wide distribution.

(v)   The scheme is hardly complete. Other institutions such as the World Bank or
      International Monetary Fund may become involved in putting pressure on X
      because of their own interests related to their financial involvement in X.

This schematic presentation tells us nothing about the effectiveness of pursuing such strategies, measured in terms of X's moves toward greater compliance. At a minimum, the universal system will generate much knowledge about what is happening in X. But efforts to
organize substantial international pressure might fail for any of the previously indicated
reasons.

The three regional systems play an important role in exerting pressure for compliance
on States. The regional and universal systems are involved in each other's activities and
linked in many ways. In the schematic description above, individuals might well have

invoked the processes of regional human rights institutions if X were located in Africa, the Americas, or Europe. Arrangements become necessary to work out questions of priority among systems, as well as the effect of a decision made by an IGO in one system upon an advocate's efforts to invoke another.

Indeed, the more cohesive and authoritative European Convention on Human Rights[11] may effectively displace the universal system for many disputes generated within its member States. Most of those States will also be parties to the ICCPR and other universal human rights treaties, and often parties to the ICCPR Optional Protocol as well. Nonetheless, individuals challenging their States' conduct often prefer to bring disputes (after exhausting national remedies) over the interpretation or application of rights declared in the Convention before the European Court of Human Rights created by the European Convention, through an application to the Court against their State. That Convention is apt to be better known. Its processes for relief for an aggrieved individual are more effective than those available in the universal system, for its States parties commit themselves to comply with its Court's decisions. In the large majority of cases, compliance with the Court's adverse judgments—damages, release of a prisoner, repeal or revision of a law or policy found by the Court to violate the Convention—has been reasonably prompt. These observations, to be sure, apply to a regional system where the original States parties were long familiar with conceptions of right, and hence could more readily absorb elaborations of and innovations in the rights declared in the Convention as expounded in the European Court's decisions.

Through its investigative missions to the member States and related reports, the Inter-American Commission on Human Rights brings publicity to violations and exerts pressure on the violator. Its complaints procedure for individuals challenging their own State's conduct may lead to recommendations adverse to the State, though the record of compliance is not impressive. The Inter-American Court of Human Rights slowly builds its case law, enjoys a growing sense of its legitimacy among member States, and becomes a more familiar resource throughout the region for victims of violations (Harris, 1998). The younger African system gradually expands its reach and influence (Evans and Murray, 2008).

III. CHARACTERISTICS OF INTERNATIONAL HUMAN RIGHTS RELEVANT TO THE NATURE OF PROTECTION

We have seen that the human rights movement has generated a diverse armoury of pressures against delinquent States that other States, IGOs, and NGOs can apply—only in rare circumstances extending to internationally organized trade and investment restrictions or the use of force. This section develops five inter-related and distinctive characteristics of international human rights. Together they suggest why international protection is weak in comparison with the ordinary sanctions of national legal-political systems or with some different types of international regulatory regimes, and frequently has so hortatory, dialogic, and recommendatory a nature.

---

[11] Adopted 1950, entered into force 1953.

These characteristics demonstrate the need for a different and expanded conception of what the protection of human rights amounts to through the universal human rights system. Such a conception would emphasize pressures against a State to arrest violations, but at the same time, would urge assistance to that State to find plausible paths toward reform and compliance. It would look beyond current violations to ways of forestalling their recurrence in later years, most importantly by fostering change in the background circumstances and culturally rooted understandings that often underlie violations. The task of protection would incorporate strategies traditionally associated with fostering processes of social and cultural transformation. It could not be analogized to conventional modes of protection in developed countries like arrest and criminal trial or tort remedies. It requires a grasp of context, persistence, and time.

The following analysis of these characteristics is not meant to express pessimism or scepticism about the movement's ideals or possibilities. It simply attempts to describe the human rights movement as it is, no matter what the correspondence between that description and assumptions in the authoritative texts or frequently expressed views by many advocates of human rights. Far from defeatist, a realistic portrayal of the complexity and duration of the task should point towards the more fruitful paths for international protection to follow in order to achieve greater realization of human rights ideals.

A. HUMAN RIGHTS VIOLATIONS GENERALLY OCCUR WITHIN AND AFFECT ONLY PEOPLE WITHIN A SINGLE STATE

Conduct amounting to a violation of international law frequently takes place outside the territory of the delinquent State. But the operative events may also occur entirely within that territory: arrest of an ambassador, abusive treatment of an alien, or the refusal to honour a treaty commitment permitting an alien to do business. Nonetheless each illustration implicates other States and international order: the ambassador was entitled to an immunity from arrest, the maltreatment of the alien violated the law of State responsibility, or a treaty with the alien's State of nationality was broken. Each is as 'international' in its effects as the familiar violations of international law through extraterritorial conduct.

Human rights law differs. In the treaty and customary law of the last half century, no trace of a foreign element is essential to the conclusion that a State has violated its international obligations regarding individual rights. In all but a few respects, treaties and customary law abolish the citizen-alien distinction that long decided whether State abuse amounted to an international wrong. Citizens have rights under international law against their own State with respect to its violations that have only internal effects.

For many kinds of violations—police brutality, press censorship, bribed or coerced judges—only the population of the delinquent State is likely to feel the effects. Other States are unlikely to protest, let alone take weightier measures to end the violations, even though the violator may have broken its obligations *erga omnes*, vis-à-vis all other States or at least those within a given treaty regime.[12] These other States lack any narrowly conceived interest to act—that is, material interest related characteristically to power or resources. The general populace or significant interest groups are not likely to put serious pressure on the

---

[12] *Barcelona Traction, Light and Power Company, Limited, Second Phase, Judgment, ICJ Reports 1970,* p 3, paras 33–34.

government to impose significant sanctions against the delinquent State—selective trade barriers, general embargoes or boycotts including financial transactions like bank loans. Reducing or cancelling military support or financial aid has occurred somewhat more frequently. The potential costs to an enforcing State and its citizens, in funds and in lives, escalate when military intervention (with or without Security Council authorization) may be the only way to arrest massive killings, at the extreme a genocide as in Rwanda. Internally, a government may be more likely to suffer rather than gain politically in such a venture, particularly as costs mount and 'exit' always seems to be tomorrow's possibility.

At the same time, the classical self-help remedies or countermeasures allowed by treaty or customary law for injuries to a State caused by the delinquent State's breach of a reciprocal obligation—for example, suspending obligations to the delinquent State that are proportionate to the broken promises made by that State in a tax or trade treaty—lose meaning. A State hardly responds to State X's maltreatment of citizens of X by in turn maltreating its own.

This observation about differences between human rights and many other fields of international law has its exceptions, some of growing currency. Human rights treaties are multilateral; many create treaty organs. The treaties may empower other State parties to bring actions against State X for violations of treaty norms that affect only its own citizens. At the extreme, as with respect to genocide, States come under certain limited obligations to act. Within the European human rights system, States have several times brought actions before the European Court to protest another member State's internal conduct, such as Greece's repression of political life during the reign of its colonels. Moreover, as previously noted, other States may be adversely affected by a delinquent State's internal repression or brutality because of consequences like refugee flows or political support of the oppressed group in X by groups of the same ethnicity or religion who are citizens of and live in other States.

The reluctance of other States to become directly involved in responding to violations elsewhere as serious as gender discrimination, press censorship, or corrupt political trials underscores the need for a system of international organizations. Else victims would be close to where they were when the human rights movement began, with little choice other than continuing an internal struggle for change without benefit of meaningful international support.

B. HUMAN RIGHTS VIOLATIONS OFTEN HAVE A SYSTEMIC CHARACTER AND REFLECT DEEP ASPECTS OF A STATE'S POLITICAL STRUCTURE

Although human rights treaties do not require that State action have a systemic character before it can constitute a violation, in practice other States and international organs are likely to take notice only when such is the case. The conditions for invoking the 1235 and 1503 procedures of the UN Commission and the complaints procedures of the Human Rights Council, mentioned above, so suggest. Actions brought against a State before an international body like the Human Rights Committee or the European Court of Human Rights will in fact allege an individual injury. But the violation and injury are rarely idiosyncratic, disconnected from a larger political system or prevailing cultural practices. They tend to fall within a practice or pattern—perhaps widespread torture or abuse of prisoners, electoral fraud, repression of religious worship, gender discrimination, or disappearance of political dissenters.

Human rights norms may then threaten a State's political structure and ideology, for often government practices and policies that amount to systemic violations of human rights will appear essential to maintaining authoritarian rule. To the extent successful, pressure by other States or international organs to terminate the violations may therefore have deep and widespread structural effects within the delinquent State, far more so than would international responses to a State's violation of trade, commercial, or environmental treaties, or rules of the law of the sea.

South Africa provides a powerful illustration. The enfranchisement of the non-white population within the principle of equal protection brought about a landmark shift in political power, and hence the promise or potential of redistribution of economic and other forms of power. Commonplace illustrations of systemic violations whose termination would shake the viability of authoritarian regimes and increase the chances for fundamental change include denial of the right to associate and suppression of an independent press. Unlike violations of treaties regulating, say, economic intercourse, such violations often pose issues of constitutional breadth and significance. Acute conflict may result between the State's 'supreme law' and international norms, between a traditional conception of State sovereignty and international human rights.

Within the liberal democracies, violations are less likely to reach to the foundations of a social, economic, or political system. The cases brought before the European Court of Human Rights that involve individual complaints against one of the many stable democracies in this region address issues of undeniable legal and moral significance that may deeply engage the population and have important statewide effects—aspects of religious freedom or free speech, criminal procedure, or discrimination on grounds of gender or sexual orientation. Nonetheless, these are violations that, once resolved, are not likely to transform the basic character of the country. Political, social, and cultural life may experience a lengthy period of adjustment, and many lives will be profoundly changed. But basic structures of government and power will adapt rather than collapse or be displaced. Even within the European regime, however, recent entrants like Turkey or some East European States become parties to disputes that may affect the core of the political system—for example, the banning in Turkey of a number of political parties.[13]

It follows that a decision by an IGO to react to serious and systemic violations by an authoritarian State may raise complex questions of strategy and of the relevant time frame. The task is to solve the problem not only for today but for later days as well. Perhaps there must be an uprooting, a reinterpretation or transformation or abolition of the social and political structures underlying the violations. Such a notion of the involvement of human rights institutions in ongoing reform-oriented change within a State amounts to an enlarged conception of protection of human rights. Surely it puts extra burdens on any international mechanism. It also suggests that carving the paths toward effective long-run change requires a sophisticated understanding of many aspects of the State involved. Contrast a once-and-forever order by an international organ settling a dispute over a trade, tax, or environmental treaty.

---

[13] See, eg, the decision of the European Court of Human Rights in *United Communist Party of Turkey* v *Turkey*, 30 January 1998, *RJD* 1998-I; 26 *EHRR* 121.

C. THE EXPANSIVE REACH OF HUMAN RIGHTS DUTIES
TO NON-STATE (PRIVATE) ACTORS

International law, classically defined as the law among States, breaks dramatically with this tradition in its human rights instruments. The regulated relationships are principally between the duty-bearing State and rights-bearing non-State actors—that is, individual or institutional actors that are neither part of government, nor so closely associated with the State as to have their actions attributed to it. With few exceptions, States alone are charged with the duties imposed by international law, principally the duty to respect the declared rights. Failure to fulfil these duties constitutes a violation of international law.

Like many liberal constitutions, the treaties rest on the assumption that the State constitutes the primary threat to individual rights (as well indeed as the prime agency for their protection). Hence they stress the duty to respect individual rights by not interfering or acting inconsistently with them. But of course non-State actors (sometimes referred to as 'private' actors, as distinct from the 'public' realm of government) themselves fail to respect others' rights. The rapist or the abusing spouse violates the right to physical security; the discriminatory employer violates equal protection norms; partisans of the dominant political party curb the right to political participation by threatening harm to those supporting the opposition. A few rights such as guarantees of a fair judicial process, however, are by definition open to violation only by the State.

To say solely as a matter of description that non-State actors violate rights is not necessarily to say that these actors, like States, are subjects of international law that imposes duties directly on them. (Of course, such conduct may lead to tort or criminal liability of such actors under State law.) It is true that international law does directly subject non-State as well as State-related violators to criminal liability—with respect, for example, to war crimes, crimes against humanity, and genocide, as well as to distinct categories of crimes like airplane hijacking. But the number of such international crimes is limited, and the human rights treaties do not often make non-State violators subjects of international law and potentially liable under that law.

Nonetheless, the conduct of non-State actors is frequently *indirectly* regulated by international human rights law. States' obligations under most treaties reach beyond the duty to refrain from interfering with (that is, the duty to respect) the declared rights. They also include duties of 'protecting' or 'ensuring' rights-holders from interference by non-State actors, fulfilled in most instances by regulating those actors' conduct.[14] Much of the significance of the State/non-State (public-private) distinction with respect to the reach of international law in general thereby collapses with respect to human rights. The State is obligated to afford reasonable protection to rights-bearing individuals, and thus to act diligently to prevent violations by non-State actors like the rapist, discriminatory employer, or political partisan. It is the State that will be charged with a violation of its treaty obligations if it fails to take reasonable and appropriate measures to protect— through police, due investigation, prosecutions, punishment, civil remedies, regulatory legislation, and so on.[15]

[14] See, eg, Article 2 of the ICCPR, Article 2 of CEDAW, and Article 1 of the American Convention on Human Rights, entered into force 1978, OASTS 36.
[15] See the reasoning of the Inter-American Court of Human Rights in *Velásquez-Rodríguez v Honduras*, Merits, Judgment of 29 July 1988, Ser C, no 4.

Some treaties make this duty specific. Article 11 of CEDAW, for example, requires a State to assure gender equality in the field of employment. Articles 2(e), 2(f), and 11 obligate the State to take 'appropriate measures' to eliminate discrimination against women by 'any person, organization or enterprise', and to modify or abolish laws, customs, or practices constituting such discrimination.

In order to fulfil this duty, the State must develop a complex web of government policy and legislation, including proactive measures, that will be extremely context-sensitive. Considerable discretion must be allowed the State in deciding on strategies and working out the 'appropriate measures'. Consider, for example, the requirement in CEDAW that parties eliminate discrimination in employment. Should the State criminalize discrimination by corporate officials in hiring or advancement? Would it be preferable to provide only for civil suits for injunctions and damages? Or mandate a policy of affirmative action? Or appoint members of the discriminated-against group to high public office to set an example? Or establish a supervisory agency to which corporations submit periodic reports and enter into public discussion about their employment practices? Or provide funds for discussion groups between employers and the relevant group of employees?

Such discretion of State officials to determine which measures are 'appropriate' is perhaps most suited to overcoming entrenched forms of resistance and transforming certain cultural assumptions and older practices. It demands a fine sense of context, of understanding the local. Surely one useful function of IGOs and NGOs would be to engage in discussion with the State about those measures and to apply appropriate pressures to assure that reasonable steps are being taken toward the goal of non-discriminatory hiring and promotion. Ongoing dialogue with the delinquent State naturally forms an integral part of this enlarged process of protection.

D. THE PROGRESSIVE REALIZATION OF CIVIL AND POLITICAL RIGHTS

Most treaties express at their creation a convergence of interests of States parties, or a compromise of divergent interests shaped by the distribution of power and influence among the parties. The rules stated in a multilateral treaty are not exactly those that any one party would have initially proposed. The treaty regimes intend those rules to regulate State behaviour from the moment of ratification—diplomatic immunities, treaties on intellectual property, commercial or environmental treaties, the law of the sea. If there are to be transitional periods in which a party's duty is met through progressive steps to achieve compliance, the treaty will explicitly provide for them.

Human rights treaties differ. Far from representing compromises of points of view between, say, liberal democratic and authoritarian polities, far from accepting the interests or practices of most or all major States as decisive, these treaties declare ideals of State conduct that no State can fully achieve, and that tower above many States' conduct. In the light of their mandatory character as solemn commitments of their parties, the treaties represent at their core, in the words of the Universal Declaration, a 'common standard of achievement' toward which the treaty parties are obligated to move. The descriptions in this section about four other related characteristics of the human rights movement underscore this idea of progressive realization.

The size of the gap between treaty norms stating civil and political rights and State behaviour varies dramatically among States. It is at its narrowest for the liberal democracies of the developed world whose rights tradition so influenced the international norms. It is at its broadest in many authoritarian States (military rule, 'strong man' charismatic leadership, a governing élite, theocracy, communist or nationalist ruling parties, monarchic rule) without earlier traditions of right, as well as in developing countries where socio-economic conditions, political structures, and cultural and religious foundations differ most sharply from those democracies. In such circumstances, there can be little hope in many States that norms like freedom of association or an independent judiciary will be immediately realized, rather than long remain goals toward which good-faith governments will work. But even the established, stable democracies must confront violations so deeply rooted that their immediate termination by the State and non-State actors sets an impossible goal—in the United States, for example, overcoming racial segregation, or achieving adequate protection against domestic violence against women.

In many instances the common expectation must be that a State joining a human rights treaty will be in violation of some of its major obligations from the outset. If China were to ratify the ICCPR tomorrow without reservations, a long internal struggle would doubtless precede implementation of rights to speech and association, not to mention the right to vote at periodic and genuine elections 'guaranteeing the free expression of the will of the electors'. Nonetheless other States, IGOs, and NGOs would not protest and condemn China for entering a treaty that it would surely continue to violate in serious and systemic ways. Rather the human rights community would applaud the move as a vital first step that might over time lead to China's deeper sensitivity to and engagement with the *human rights* movement and heightened degree of compliance.

Consider the famous provision in Article 2 of the ICESCR requiring States to take steps 'with a view to achieving progressively the full realization' of the rights stated in that Covenant.[16] As the Committee on Economic, Social and Cultural Rights has made clear, that notion of progressive realization or achievement in no sense invalidates or compromises the idea of State obligation. The obligation is to take steps—one could say as large and frequent steps as are plausible in context—toward the goal. The Committee has stated that the steps forming part of progressive achievement 'must be taken within a reasonably short time' after ratification. They must be 'deliberate, concrete and targeted' toward meeting the State's obligations.[17]

These observations refer to the reality of progressive achievement and the strategic necessity to think in such terms with respect to many fundamental rights. In no sense, however, do they qualify the necessity of action as prompt and effective as possible to arrest immediately, not progressively, systematic violations of the right to life like massacres or genocidal attacks, or abusive discrimination. The urgent first step must be to stop the killing, as the Security Council has apparently concluded in some of

---

[16] There are indications in a few human rights treaties of longer-run achievement of goals, such as ICCPR Article 2(3)(b) that requires States to 'develop the possibilities of judicial remedy'. CEDAW represents the most important exception to this characteristic of civil-political rights treaties, for States 'agree to pursue by all appropriate means and without delay, a policy of eliminating discrimination...' Other provisions of CEDAW like Article 5 refer to aspects of cultural change over time.

[17] Committee on Economic, Social and Cultural Rights, General Comment No 3 (1990), UN Doc E/1991/23, Annex III, para 2.

its decisions under Chapter VII. The second and ongoing steps aim at preventing its recurrence.

It is however the fact that most of the civil-political rights treaties make no allowance on their face for gradual implementation over a period of time. The command is unambiguous: comply now with your duty to respect, and to protect or ensure. The ICCPR, for example, does not provide that States incapable of rapid compliance are permitted to work for a decade toward the goal of an independent judiciary, perhaps through such diverse strategies as reform of legal education and training for judges, or that racial segregation is to be undone with, say, 'all deliberate speed'.

But common sense as well as the practice of IGOs and NGOs suggest the inevitability of that kind of process for many basic rights. The direction in which State X is moving noticeably influences IGOs and NGOs in the tone and content of their reports and resolutions on X. If the State extends the suffrage to women and provides for its first popularly elected government body, reaction will be favourable and encouraging, and criticism will be relatively muted, despite continuing discrimination in other sectors and the long path that X must travel before complying with requirements about elections. Evaluation and criticism will depend greatly on the pace and significance of the steps that X must continue to take. (South Africa did manage to make this transition all at once, by extending an existing limited participatory regime to its entire population as part of a process of fundamental transformation.)

Awareness of these considerations informs the ICCPR's requirement in Article 40(1) that a State's periodic reports to the Human Rights Committee about its protection of rights include information about 'the progress made in enjoyment of those rights'. Many comments of the Committee that are set forth in its concluding observations expressly compliment States for progress thus far made (even though the goal may be far from reached) and recommend feasible further steps. Within such a framework, criticism should intensify when progress slackens or stops, and become most insistent on signs of backsliding.

E. THE STATE'S DUTY TO PROMOTE AND TRANSFORM: CULTURAL OBSTACLES

As human rights treaties were negotiated at different times over several decades, they changed in both substance and strategy. To some extent, those changes were related to the ever-greater specificity of the subject matter—from a broad initial declaration covering much of the field, to the two covenants giving far more detail, and ultimately to the proliferation of treaties and declarations on topics like race, gender, children, torture, religion, and disabilities. But they likely stem as well from a deeper awareness of the obstacles to realization of the human rights norms.

The overtly political obstacles to change were evident enough from the start. Authoritarian regimes could accept norms like free speech, free association, or physical security of the person only at great risk to their survival. The new movement confronted political ideologies hostile to its threshold notion of rights against government.

What may have been less evident at the time of the human rights movement's birth were cultural obstacles of a deeper, more diffuse and tenacious character—those aspects of culture that draw on religious belief, political ideology, cosmology, traditional practice and ritual, myth, and symbolic representation. Consider, for example, the structure of the ICCPR, drafted in the first decades of the human rights movement and innocent of any explicit notion of or response to obstacles to change. Article 2 sets forth the obligations of States to 'respect and ensure' to all individuals within their territory the recognized rights, and to take 'necessary steps' to adopt legislative or other measures to give effect to those rights. States also undertake to 'ensure...an effective remedy' to persons whose rights are violated that will allow those rights to be determined 'by competent judicial, administrative or legislative authorities...and to develop the possibilities of judicial remedy'. Finally, States promise to ensure that any granted remedies are enforced.

The image is one of the rule of law within a liberal democracy; the assumption is that legal processes and institutions are in place or will become available to vindicate claims of right. The Covenant has nothing to say about how to get 'from here to there', how to achieve in government and civil society the observance of deep human rights norms that stand in sharp contradiction to existing practices. Surely there is no recognition in the treaty of cultural relativism or diversity. The individual endowed with rights is indeed universal, shorn of all attributes that speak to a particular identity, tradition or culture, abstracted from all context.

Some later conventions evidence a heightened awareness of the need to transform certain assumptions and practices. Within this evolving framework of thought about human rights, police and courts and other familiar State institutions within a conventional understanding of the rule of law can best be understood as essential but insufficient instruments for achieving compliance with the treaties.

CEDAW is most striking. States undertake to ensure the 'full development and advancement of women' (Article 3), and must take 'appropriate measures' to modify 'social and cultural patterns of conduct' to achieve elimination of prejudices and of practices based on the idea of the inferiority of either sex or on stereotyped roles of either sex (Article 5(a)). To achieve such goals, States must encourage appropriate education, revise textbooks and school programmes, and introduce new teaching methods (Article 10(c)). Article 7 of CERD has a similar agenda; States must adopt 'immediate and effective measures, particularly in the fields of teaching, education, culture and information', to combat prejudice and promote understanding and tolerance. The Children's Convention suggests the need for similar strategies of re-education to introduce new cultural understandings, as in the requirement of Article 12(1) that States 'assure to the child who is capable of forming his or her own views, the right to express those views freely in all matters affecting the child, the views of the child being given due weight in accordance with the age and maturity of the child'.

These and similar provisions in other human rights instruments have created what may now be described as a necessary function, if not quite a general duty, of States. That function is to *promote* new understandings with respect to both State-citizen relationships and to interactions among non-State actors in contexts ranging from the family or market to institutions of civil society.[18] These understandings may reach into the most significant and intimate aspects of public action and personal lives. Now that promotion has come to include, as it must, efforts to change aspects of a culture that embraces the rulers and the

---

[18] Compare Article 7(2) of the South African Constitution (1996): 'The state must respect, protect, promote and fulfil the rights in the Bill of Rights'.

ruled, the human rights movement has further eroded the traditional distinction between State and non-State actors. If the State's duty to respect rights were at the forefront in the early years of the movement, the related tasks of protection and promotion have become ever more prominent, both tasks pointing toward the necessity of a proactive State attentive to cultural obstacles.

This attention to the imprint of history—rooted practices, traditional understandings, theological premises, broadly speaking 'culture'—suggests both the movement's greater realism in seeking change and its continuing optimism. However high the barriers, change is possible, if not at the pace and with the single-stroke solutions suggested by the earlier texts. What is rooted may be uprooted or transformed. Culture is plastic, made and remade through the course of history, not unshakable and essentialist in character but in many respects contingent, open to evolution and to more radical change through purposeful human agency informed by human rights ideals.

This instrumental perspective on culture—that it must sometimes be developed or transformed in one or another respect to advance human rights, that States and civil society must devise appropriate strategies for this task—should be understood as distinct from a different perspective on culture that has long inhabited human rights scholarship and discourse. The universal aspirations of human rights have from the start stood in tension with the claims of cultural relativism. Broadly speaking, the term 'universal' has been applied to the norms set forth in the basic treaties and generally understood within the liberal democracies as having universal validity and reach, without consideration of the history or culture of a given State. Claims of cultural relativism insisting that asserted universal norms cannot displace the basic, sometimes different and even contradictory norms of a particular culture issue from a good number of developing States. Within this debate, the 'universal' can be associated with the 'general' or 'essential' in the understanding of human rights norms, while the 'culturally relativist' position can be associated with the 'particular' and the 'contingent'.

The principal fields in which the battles have been waged address the related issues of family, personal law, gender, sexuality, and children, all as informed by religious belief or traditional practice. But the debate has extended to other fields, such as aspects of the criminal law and punishment. It ultimately raises deep issues about the assumptions and explicit premises underlying human rights norms—for example, the competing claims of individualism or community as a foundational characteristic of social organization, or the use of the language of rights as opposed to that of duties as the appropriate moral and conceptual structure for determining relationships within a State or culture.

This chapter has not explored such issues. Rather, it has assumed that the human rights norms here used as illustrations of arguments have a strong foundation as universal rights, or at least command growing support throughout the world as the human rights movement has developed. The claims of cultural relativism are then bypassed, rather than debated and agreed with or dismissed.

Let us turn to two illustrations of the kind of instrumental approach to culture stressed in this chapter:

Gender issues have figured importantly in the human rights movement over the last two decades. They range from straight-out matters of discrimination in employment or qualifications for political office to problems stemming from customary-law distinctions between men and women with respect to inheritance or the issue of female genital mutilation/circumcision (fgm). It is possible for a State to employ the criminal or civil law to end employment discrimination, or to invalidate all customary norms that discriminate with respect to gender. But as CEDAW makes clear, the more effective and pervasive challenge to gender discrimination is likely to stem less from one or another form of State coercion to end a given practice (as important as that might be) than from a transformation in popular attitudes about gender-related distinctions.

Surely education will play a role, as stereotypical gender roles are challenged through textbooks and academic instruction, and through different patterns of participation in the classroom. Government can influence prevailing views by, for example, appointing women to high political or other office, or instituting programmes such as childcare that enable women to work in the public sector. Institutions of civil society can provide their own examples of absorbing women into all levels of their activities. Women's groups may urge and contribute to all such steps. The routes are many, and the task is best spread among many groups to achieve both top-down and bottom-up pressures and ideas for change. Indeed, the dialogue between grassroots (bottom-up) and élite (top-down) movements will often enjoy a particular potency.

With respect to customary practices such as fgm, internal dialogue within the community between proponents and opponents of the practice may open a path to change more likely to succeed than a State's effort to prosecute those authorizing or performing the ritual surgery. Other strategies could include educating women about the adverse health consequences of the practice and related pain, substituting other rituals to symbolize the entrance into adulthood, or postponing the practice until an age where free consent can plausibly be given. Intelligent choices among these and other strategies require a sensitivity to the cultural environment, and the strong engagement in these processes of change of the women most affected by the practice.

The second illustration concerns political participation. The Universal Declaration tells us that 'the will of the people shall be the basis of the authority of government' while the ICCPR proclaims the right of all citizens to vote 'at genuine periodic elections which shall be by universal and equal suffrage and shall be held by secret ballot, guaranteeing the free expression of the will of the electors'. These rare statements in human rights treaties of a theory of political legitimacy fall clearly within the liberal tradition. How then should the human rights movement react to the fact that equal political participation is alien to authoritarian societies, and that authoritarian governments will inevitably see in the free vote their own destruction?

The question of how to introduce the idea of a right to political participation and to institute democratic government has become of increasing salience in a world caught up in the rhetoric of democratization. The current debates over and planning for nation-building in light of the West's experiences in such states as Afghanistan and Iraq give a central place to the difficulties and duration of these culture-influenced processes of political transformation.

Inevitably the process will be gradual, even if a vote is instituted at the first moment of transition. Complementary institutions and processes must ultimately be put in place, and for the while, a healthy experimentalism including grassroots innovations may heighten chances for success far more than would an imposed blueprint from a stable democracy. A reformed education system will play a role both in explaining and justifying the human rights norms within the framework of the relevant culture. New methods and processes of the classroom could stress basic notions of students' participation, voice, and inquiry that would challenge a culture of authoritarianism.

But the goal may not take decades to reach. The outside observer can readily overstate the uniformity and tenacity of popular attitudes and cultural beliefs, whereas the relevant culture may have long experienced a process of erosion and reconstruction. That process publicly calls into question the asserted stability and depth of the culture, which may in fact be far more fragmented, fragile, and fluid than imagined. These days it may be sharply influenced by globalization, by the transnational flow of information and images, and by urbanization and large migrations. The criticisms and proposals stemming from the human rights movement may then enjoy a more hospitable reception among the population than imagined.

Pressure to take steps toward longer-run change, and assistance in taking them, must come from the IGOs and NGOs. But other political, professional, and academic groups will participate with a broader public, as the issue becomes domesticated in the target State and the political battles for change are fought internally at both grassroots and élite levels.

One upshot of this discussion of the characteristics of human rights bearing on protection concerns the question of how to assess States' observance of these mandatory norms. Consider the apparently simple notion of compliance: does or does not a State party comply with certain treaty norms? Does it continue to repress association, systematically torture, censor political news, control decisions of its courts? Do observers' answers about these issues of State protection change, and for the better, after a State's ratification of the relevant treaty? Or do many States parties, particularly authoritarian regimes and States of radically different traditions in the developing world, continue to violate one or several of the treaty's provisions, perhaps leading observers to conclude that the treaty is without effect, a hollow gesture that may serve some State interest such as appearing to join the community of the righteous.

These are vital questions from the perspectives of many kinds of observers, ranging from current or prospective victims of violations to other States, IGOs, and NGOs. But do the answers hold the same salience as if they addressed tax, trade, commercial, or transportation treaties? In those circumstances, treaty parties appropriately expect immediate and ongoing compliance; a party injured by an alleged breach will take such measures as are available to restore compliance, receive compensation, or deny the treaty breaker equivalent treaty benefits. As this chapter has argued, a longer-run perspective and time frame often become essential for human rights.

To return to an earlier example, the vital questions if China were to ratify the ICCPR would address the process of change and commitment to it—continuity, depth, apparent strength, the alignment of internal forces, speed of reforms in relation to observers' assessments of what was realistically possible. Answers to those questions would appear to be more relevant than the fact of continuing violations—in China's case, for example, denial of genuine elections contested by independent political parties—to the decisions of IGOs, other States, and NGOs about strategies and pressures for encouraging change. Such assessment of progress—in a sense, of 'compliance'—would lack the certainty and finality of measurement that a simpler 'yes, no' approach might yield with respect to current practice. It will complicate the question of what external pressures are appropriate. Despite such drawbacks, a longer time frame will permit the key questions to be examined. The findings about current violations become the start rather than end of inquiry into treaties' effectiveness.

IV. CONCLUSION: PERSPECTIVES AND VOICES

The claim that civil and political rights are often progressively realized, indeed often expected to be progressively realized, rests on the several related observations of Section III. Perhaps it is inaccurate to describe this claim as contradicting the broadly accepted understandings about the need everywhere for immediate realization of civil and political rights. Perhaps different notions about the time frame for the realization of rights are all intelligible, indeed potentially complementary and helpful. Perhaps it is a matter of voice. Description and evaluation may depend on who is speaking, out of what role or from what perspective.

Consider the victims who demand full and immediate protection against their victimizers. Assume that the violations are widespread, perhaps imbedded in understandings of religious texts or traditional practices, perhaps a consequence of a long-reigning culture of political authoritarianism. The claims of victims are not apt to be qualified by their attention to the difficulties of achieving change. They are not likely to invoke the notion of progressive realization of rights, and insist only that the State now take the first of many steps over many years.

Few victims of torture, even recognizing that the road toward termination of the practice may involve time-consuming re-education of police or training of lawyers and judges, will limit their demands. To the contrary, victims inevitably insist that the offensive practice stop now, once and for all. Gay people will seek immediate protection of privacy and equal-protection rights without reference to the cultural obstacles and the ongoing 'culture war'. The voice of the victim will be urgent, insistent on release from oppression and humiliation—and so it should be. Such expressions of moral and political outrage and of pain not only speak to dire circumstances and inner feelings, but also put maximum pressure on those who can initiate the process of achieving compliance. The demands' very urgency arouses public attention.

IGOs and NGOs may speak in a different voice. They occupy a more ambivalent position, distanced from the brutal experiences and personal losses of the victims, yet charged with their protection. Frequently, though not invariably, IGOs' and NGOs' criticism of States, recommendations through resolutions and reports, and public pronouncements may use the rhetoric of immediacy, even while their officials are well aware of obstacles. That rhetoric may frequently be accompanied by more nuanced discussions or negotiations with delinquent States that lead to more measured assessments of what can immediately be achieved and of what are the next steps to be taken. But if the proposals for change sound too muted and cautious, allowing a substantial period for the government to reform itself and curb violations by non-State actors, these human rights organizations may lose influence, credibility, and effectiveness. The battle cry for prompt and dramatic change may well achieve more than a meticulous cost-benefit statement about the hows and whens of progress.

Nonetheless, in practice the idea of progressive realization comes into play. Advances by a delinquent State in the protection of rights are strongly praised, even though much *may* remain to be done. The dialogue between the Human Rights Committee and States that have filed reports under ICCPR Article 40 often lead to the Committee's recommendations of steps to be taken, of ways to approach the goal of, say, religious freedom or a judicial system responsive to the rule of law. Moreover, IGOs and NGOs and offices such as the High Commissioner for Human Rights may assist States in planning strategies of change that inherently rest on the premise of progressive realization. Their tasks are various: sources of pressure; providers of assistance; partners in planning change.

Finally, we can talk of the observers, analysts, and planners in academic life, think tanks, State governments, or IGOs—people who are working to realize human rights goals. Events on the ground can well appear more remote, for such people are neither victims nor engaged in active advocacy. Their intention may be to assess what has been achieved and what has failed in the human rights movement, to assess that movement critically, to probe basic assumptions, and to explore the obstacles to the kinds of cultural change that alone may succeed in curbing violations over the long run. To achieve such purposes, these actors must strive to see the range of choices that exist among practical strategies toward change.

All these voices—those in pain who cry out for immediate relief and change, the advocates applying what pressures are available against the delinquent State, the observer and analyst engaging in realistic description and prescription—may work at cross-purposes. This cacophony within the movement may limit its effectiveness; the diverse descriptions and proposals may blunt its message. More likely, this pluralism of voices committed to human rights ideals will strengthen the movement, by providing diverse insights, internal debate and criticism, and better-considered strategies for change. From this perspective the different voices can be understood as complementary, in the sense that they serve distinct but inter-related purposes in giving hope to victims, animating people to resist oppression, placing all possible pressure on violators, and working toward effective social and cultural change.

REFERENCES

EVANS, M and MURRAY, R (eds) (2008), *The African Charter on Human and Peoples' Rights: The System in Practice, 1986–2006*, 2nd edn (Cambridge: Cambridge University Press).

HARRIS, D (1998), 'Regional Protection of Human Rights: The Inter-American Achievement', in Harris and Livingstone (eds), *The Inter-American System of Human Rights* (Oxford: Clarendon Press), p 1.

STEINER, H, ALSTON, P, and GOODMAN, R (2008), *International Human Rights in Context: Law, Politics, Morals*, 3rd edn (Oxford: Oxford University Press).

FURTHER READING

The following readings offer diverse perspectives on human rights and international law that are germane to this chapter:

ALVAREZ, J (2005), *International Organizations as Law Makers* (Oxford: Oxford University Press). A comprehensive, richly descriptive and analytic work on the character, role and development of international institutions.

HENKIN, L (1995), *International Law: Policies and Values* (The Hague: Kluwer Academic Publishers). A lucid account incorporating human rights into a larger framework of international law.

ISHAY, M (ed) (1997), *The Human Rights Reader* (New York: Routledge). A rich collection of excerpts from ancient times to the present of religious, political and moral writings bearing on human rights.

KOSKENNIEMI, M (1989), *From Apology to Utopia: The Structure of International Legal Argument*, 2005 reissue (Cambridge: Cambridge University Press). A challenging analysis of legal argument that opens useful ways of thinking of international human rights.

LAUTERPACHT, H (1950), *International Law and Human Rights* (New York: FA Praeger). The views of a leading jurist about human rights at the time of birth of the human rights movement.

MUTUA, M (2002), *Human Rights: A Political and Cultural Critique* (Philadelphia, Pa.: University of Pennsylvania Press). A critique of human rights from the perspective of the third world and cultural relativism.

27

THE LAW OF ARMED
CONFLICT (INTERNATIONAL
HUMANITARIAN LAW)

*David Turns**

SUMMARY

The international law of armed conflict (also known as international humanitarian law, also known as the law of war) regulates the conduct of hostilities—including the use of weaponry—and the protection of victims in situations of both international and non-international armed conflict. Rooted in customary law, often of very great antiquity, since the late nineteenth century it has become one of the most intensively codified areas of international law. The 1949 Geneva Conventions, which form the cornerstone of contemporary humanitarian law, have been ratified by every single State on the face of the planet; yet implementation and enforcement are, if anything, even more problematic in this than in other areas of public international law, which has led to a symbiotic link between international humanitarian and international criminal law. Indeed, it was the creation of international criminal tribunals to deal with the aftermath of appalling atrocities in the former Yugoslavia and Rwanda, in the early 1990s, which sparked a renewal of interest in substantive humanitarian law, leading to its reaffirmation and development. This chapter outlines the scope of application of the law, issues of personal status (combatants and civilians), the conduct of hostilities (methods and means of warfare, including choice of weapons and targeting operations), the protection of victims (sick, wounded, shipwrecked, prisoners of war, and civilians), and various ways of securing the law's implementation and enforcement.

I. INTRODUCTION

It is a fact of life that armed conflict—the resort to organized force between States or within States—is, and always has been, an integral part of the human condition. Disregarding such

* The views expressed here are purely personal and do not necessarily represent any position of the British Government or the Ministry of Defence.

indicia as the duration or intensity of the fighting, the number of casualties incurred or whether hostilities are active or 'frozen', there are currently some 41 situations in the world where there is either an actual armed conflict or a degree of tension so heightened that there is a real risk of resort to force. Given this state of affairs, coupled with the increase in humanitarian activism, the so-called 'CNN effect' of constant televised reporting from conflict zones, and enhanced mechanisms for securing the international legal liability of both governments (under the doctrine of State responsibility) and individuals (under the doctrine of individual criminal responsibility), it is unsurprising that international humanitarian law (IHL) has re-emerged from the shadows of public international law during the last two decades. The well-known aphorism, 'If international law is in some ways at the vanishing point of law, the law of war is, perhaps even more conspicuously, at the vanishing point of international law' (Lauterpacht, 1952, p 382), may have been accurate enough half a century ago, but it is certainly no longer so today. Although the First Gulf War (1991) was the first modern armed conflict of which it could be said that, '[d]ecisions were impacted by legal considerations at every level, [the law] proved invaluable in the decision-making process',[1] the law of war—now more commonly referred to as IHL or, alternatively, the law of armed conflict (LOAC)[2]—is of very much greater antiquity (Green, 2008, pp 26–45).

For much of its existence, the primary purpose of the law of war was to regulate in a technical sense the conduct of hostilities between belligerents. In the golden age of chivalry, during the Middle Ages in Europe, war was regarded as a kind of game played by princes, nobles, and knights on horseback; like any game, it had to have a set of rules. The Second Lateran Council's ban on the crossbow in 1139, for instance, was apparently formulated not by reason of the pain and suffering which the weapon might cause to anyone unfortunate enough to be struck by one of its bolts, but because, by enabling a man to strike from a distance without himself being struck, it was considered a disgraceful and ignoble weapon which violated the concept of chivalry (Draper, 1965, pp 18–19).

The 'rules of the game' that constituted the laws of war at this time, however, were of little relevance to the feudal peasants who constituted the foot soldiery of European armies, nor were they believed to be of any application to wars against 'uncivilized enemies'—infidels and 'primitive peoples'. By the time of the Peace of Westphalia (1648), war had become a more public activity, in which uniformed regular armies fought on behalf of their countries, rather than as a feudal obligation to their overlords. This contributed during the eighteenth century to the growth of the concept of reciprocity: captured enemy soldiers, for example, needed to be well treated because there was a vested interest in having the adverse party accord the same treatment to one's own soldiers who were captured on the battlefield.

The law at this time was almost exclusively customary in nature, encompassing a wide variety of rules and practices that had been mutually observed by warring forces for many centuries. By the mid-nineteenth century and such conflicts as the Crimean (1853–1855) and Franco-Austrian (1859) Wars, the exponential growth in human suffering, caused by a combination of developing military technology and inadequate provision for military medical facilities, together with increased reporting of the battlefield (the latter developed

---

[1] General Colin Powell, Chairman of the United States Joint Chiefs of Staff, cited in US Department of Defense, *Final Report to Congress on the Conduct of the Persian Gulf War, Appendix O* (1992) 31 ILM 615.

[2] The terms 'IHL' and 'LOAC' are synonymous and are used interchangeably throughout this chapter. The term 'law of war', while still appropriate in an historical context, has been generally abandoned in the contemporary legal discourse.

further by the advent of war photography in the American Civil War, 1861–1865), led to the rise of humanitarianism as a major concern in the regulation of conflicts. This desire to provide for the protection of 'victims' of hostilities in turn encouraged the increasing use of multilateral treaties to codify the existing rules—and develop new ones.

Today IHL is very largely codified in a series of some 57 multilateral treaties. However, the customary laws of war continue to retain considerable significance, in part because of the recognition (as long ago as 1899)[3] that treaties could not cover every eventuality that might arise in an armed conflict; the International Committee of the Red Cross (ICRC) has reinforced this with the publication of a major piece of research identifying 161 'rules' of customary international humanitarian law and collating the evidence (examples of State practice and *opinio juris sive necessitatis*) on which they are based (Henckaerts and Doswald-Beck, 2005). Furthermore, the 1949 Geneva Conventions are now so widely accepted—they attained their 194th ratification (by Montenegro) in 2006—that they are considered to have passed in their entirety into customary international law. This enabled them to be applied in arbitration proceedings between Ethiopia and Eritrea relating to their 1998–2000 conflict: Eritrea, having attained independence only five years before the commencement of hostilities, had not at the time become a party to the Geneva Conventions. Nevertheless, it accepted their application *ex post facto* on the basis of their universal acceptance as customary law.[4]

For all their etymological similarity to each other, and notwithstanding the fact that the language of many provisions of humanitarian law relating especially to non-international armed conflicts is clearly influenced by the language of human rights,[5] it is important to emphasize that international humanitarian law and international human rights law are not the same thing at all. If humanitarian law has been characterized by the International Court of Justice (ICJ) as the *lex specialis* applicable in situations of armed conflict and mostly concerned with how belligerent States treat nationals of the adverse and neutral parties, human rights law is better viewed as a *lex generalis* broadly applicable in all situations—both peace and war—and mostly concerned with how States treat their own nationals. In relation to situations of armed conflict, humanitarian law is almost invariably more detailed and comprehensive, and of greater usefulness to all concerned, than the law of human rights.[6] That said, the boundary between these two bodies of law has become increasingly blurred in recent years, largely in consequence of a complaint brought to the European Court of Human Rights (ECtHR) by Serbs in relation to the bombing of the Federal Republic of Yugoslavia (FRY) by air forces of the North Atlantic Treaty Organisation (NATO) in 1999.

The applicants in that case sought to argue that the NATO States had violated the right to life of Serbs in the FRY by the conduct of their bombing campaign, specifically in relation to the destruction of the Serbian Radio and Television studios in Belgrade. In dismissing the application, the ECtHR found that FRY nationals were not 'within the

---

[3] In the 'Martens Clause', Preamble to The Hague Convention II with Respect to the Laws and Customs of War on Land (1899).

[4] Ethiopia-Eritrea Claims Commission, *Partial Awards on the Claims Relating to Prisoners of War* (2003) 42 ILM 1056 and 1083.

[5] This is especially the case in respect of Additional Protocol (AP) II (1977).

[6] *Legality of the Threat or Use of Nuclear Weapons, Advisory Opinion*, ICJ Reports 1996, p 226, paras 24–25.

jurisdiction' of the NATO States in the terms of Article 1 of the European Convention of Human Rights (ECHR) because, *inter alia*, bombing an area from 30,000 feet did not amount to having 'effective control' of that area for the purposes of applying human rights obligations.[7] An aerial bombing campaign, however, is distinguished for the purposes of ECHR application from a military occupation: thus, Turkey has been held responsible for the application of the ECHR in the 'Turkish Republic of Northern Cyprus' because it has 'effective control' over that territory.[8] A series of recent decided cases in the United Kingdom has indicated that, as a matter of domestic legal obligation, human rights law is applicable in respect of certain situations that may arise during military operations overseas, most notably where British forces are in occupation of territory and have physical custody of individuals (which the House of Lords in *Al-Skeini* likened to having extraterritorial 'effective control' of a prison).[9] All this is not to say, however, that human rights law regulates *prima facie* the conduct of soldiers during active hostilities on the battlefield; indeed, it would be entirely counterintuitive to reach that conclusion. One of the most basic human rights is the right to life; yet it is precisely that right that may, with certain limitations, be lawfully and violently taken away in armed conflicts. Humanitarian law has evolved highly detailed and technical provisions to govern soldiers' and civilians' conduct in such situations, and it will continue to be the primary body of law applicable in all situations of armed conflict.

II. SCOPE OF APPLICATION OF HUMANITARIAN LAW

The international law of armed conflict applies in all armed conflicts, however they are characterized, and applies to all parties in a conflict, irrespective of the legality of the resort to force. There is no direct relationship at all between *jus ad bellum* and *jus in bello*: the application of the latter has no legal implications for the former, and the legality of a conflict as such has no bearing whatsoever on the use of IHL. It would thus be quite incorrect to suggest that, for instance, every battlefield action of an agressor State is *ipso facto* a violation of IHL, or conversely that the victim of an act of aggression has the right to attack the civilian population of the aggressor.[10] The question, however, of when and how humanitarian law applies ('scope of application') is not quite as straightforward as it might initially seem. This is partly because of some uncertainties surrounding the

---

[7] *Banković et al* v *Belgium et al* (Dec) [GC], no 52207/99, paras 67–81, ECHR 2001-XII; 123 ILR 94. For detailed discussion of this and other cases concerning extraterritorial jurisdiction under the ECHR, see Byron, 2007, pp 869–878.

[8] *Loizidou* v *Turkey (Preliminary Objections)*, Judgment of 23 March 1995, Ser A, no 310, 20 *EHRR* 99, paras 56–64. On the applicability of human rights law in territory under belligerent occupation, see *Legal Consequences of the Construction of a Wall in the Occupied Palestinian Territory, Advisory Opinion*, ICJ *Reports 2004*, p 136, paras 105–113.

[9] *R (Al-Skeini and others)* v *Secretary of State for Defence* [2007] UKHL 26; [2008] 1 AC 153; *R (Al-Jedda)* v *Secretary of State for Defence* [2008] 1 AC 332; *R (Al-Saadoon and Mufdhi)* v *Secretary of State for Defence* [2009] EWCA Civ 7; see also *Secretary of State for Defence* v *R (Smith)* [2009] EWCA Civ 441.

[10] Some advocates of the Palestinian cause aver that, because Israel is illegally occupying Palestinian land, it is legitimate to target Israeli civilians: see, eg, *The New York Times*, 5 May 2009.

definition of armed conflict itself, and partly because of the different types of armed conflicts that are recognized in the contemporary law.

Traditionally, application of the law of war was triggered by a declaration of war, which
had the legal effect of suspending most peacetime legal relations between belligerent States.
Although a declaration of war did not invariably precede the actual start of hostilities,[11] it
usually followed in due course once hostilities were under way; conversely, although there
did not need to be active hostilities in progress at all times after a declaration of war had
been issued, the existence of such a declaration was conclusive evidence as to the existence
of a formal state of war. The state of war would normally be terminated only by a peace
treaty, at which point the international law of peacetime relations would resume and the
law of war would no longer be operative.[12] However, as has been conservatively suggested
in recent years:

Developments in international law since 1945, notably the United Nations (UN) Charter,
including its prohibition on the threat or use of force in international relations, may well
have made the declaration of war redundant as a formal international legal instrument.[13]

In point of fact, there have been no formal declarations of war since the Soviet declaration
of war on Japan in August 1945; the association of such declarations with the appearance
of aggression has led to the procedure becoming obsolete. The kind of confusion implicit in
British Prime Minister Anthony Eden's statement in 1956, that the UK was not at war with
Egypt during the Suez Crisis but merely in a state of armed conflict with that country,[14] is
now a thing of the past in international law: the term 'armed conflict' is preferred to the
term 'war',[15] as the former is a purely factual description of a situation, without connota-
tions of right and wrong as regards the *jus ad bellum*. It is additionally often perceived to
be in a State's interest to refrain from such an unequivocal declaration of hostile intent,
as the *status mixtus*—simultaneously observing the law of war for some purposes and
the law of peace for others—affords more room to manoeuvre, both diplomatically and
politically. This may be the case especially in a 'low-intensity conflict', wherein neither
side provokes the other into escalation, resulting in a conflict that is relatively limited and
easily contained, from which belligerents may back away without necessarily appearing
to have been defeated in a military sense (Green, 2008, pp 91–93). During Indonesia's policy of *Konfrontasi* ('Confrontation') with Malaysia from 1962 to 1966, British troops were
actively engaged in armed hostilities against Indonesian forces in North Borneo, but diplomatic and commercial relations between the UK and Indonesia continued throughout
the four years over which the Confrontation persisted.[16]

---

[11] Eg the Japanese surprise attacks on the Imperial Russian Far East Squadron in Port Arthur (1904) and
the United States Pacific Fleet in Pearl Harbor (1941).

[12] The lack of peace treaties between Israel and its Arab neighbours (with the exception of Egypt and
Jordan) could be said to imply that those countries remain in a state of war with each other, as the Armistice
Agreements of 1949 did not terminate hostilities, but merely suspended them: Maoz, 2005, pp 36–44.

[13] House of Lords Select Committee on the Constitution, 15th Report of Session 2005–06, *Waging war:
Parliament's role and responsibility, Volume I: Report* (HL Paper 236-I, 27 July 2006), para 10.

[14] See *Hansard, HC Debs*, 1 November 1956, vol 558, cols 1639–1643. Regarding legal characterization of
the Korean War, see Jessup, 1954.

[15] On the official characterization of hostilities between the UK and Iraq in 2003 as 'armed conflict' but
not 'war', see *Amin v Brown* [2005] EWHC 1670 (Ch).

[16] See *Hansard, HL Debs*, 14 November 1963, vol 253, cols 153–155.

In any event the application of humanitarian law in no way affects the legal status of parties to a given conflict; it depends on neither the legality of the initial resort to force, nor the formal recognition of a state of war or armed conflict by the belligerents. The Geneva Conventions, for example, are expressly stated to apply to 'declared war or any other armed conflict'.[17] In 1982 during the Falklands War, the UK publicly denied that it was at war with Argentina, yet it applied the law of armed conflict in all its military operations.[18]

The difficulty lies in the fact that the law of armed conflict nowhere defines precisely what an 'armed conflict' is for the purposes of application of the law, despite the use of the phrase in the Geneva Conventions and other treaties that constitute this body of law. The ICRC indicates that, 'any difference arising between States and leading to the intervention of members of the armed forces is an armed conflict' (Pictet, 1952, vol I, p 32), but this is problematic because, in its reference to States alone, it takes no account of non-international armed conflicts; it also implies that even a very limited military operation of only a few hours' duration and not followed by any other hostilities would have to be considered an armed conflict, a position which is not supported by State practice. Although there are court decisions on point from various national jurisdictions (including the UK),[19] these invariably have been concerned with defining 'war' in municipal law for such purposes as interpreting liability exclusion clauses in insurance contracts, rather than having anything to do with IHL. In 1995 the International Criminal Tribunal for the Former Yugoslavia (ICTY) held that:

an armed conflict exists whenever there is a resort to armed force between States or protracted armed violence between governmental authorities and organized armed groups or between such groups within a State. International humanitarian law applies from the initiation of such armed conflicts and extends beyond the cessation of hostilities until a general conclusion of peace is reached; or, in the case of internal conflicts, a peaceful settlement is achieved. Until that moment, international humanitarian law continues to apply in the whole territory of the warring States or, in the case of internal conflicts, the whole territory under the control of a party, whether or not actual combat takes place there.[20]

The statement in *Tadić* has since come to be widely accepted as a useful formulation of the concept of an armed conflict in general international law. At least implicit in the formulation is the requirement that hostilities be 'substantial', 'protracted' and 'large-scale'.[21] Thus, it is possible for a very brief or limited military operation to be taking place, yet for there to be no armed conflict between the States involved, as in the Entebbe Raid (1976), when Israel mounted a military operation to rescue the hostages being detained by hijackers on

---

[17] Geneva Conventions (GC), Common Article 2 (1949).

[18] See, eg, *Hansard, HC Debs*, 26 April 1982, vol 22, col 616 (on the treatment of Argentine prisoners of war—the Prime Minister's statement that they were not prisoners of war because the UK was 'not at war' with Argentina was subsequently retracted, and all captured Argentine soldiers were treated in accordance with GCIII); ibid, 11 June 1982, vol 25, col 170W (on the repatriation of Lieutenant-Commander Alfredo Astiz of the Argentine Navy); ibid, 14 June 1982, col 611 (on the establishment by the ICRC of a neutralized zone in Port Stanley, in accordance with GCIV Article 15).

[19] Eg *Kawasaki Kisen Kabushiki Kaisha of Kobe v Bantham Steamship Co* [1939] KB 544.

[20] *Prosecutor v Dusko Tadić*, Decision on the Defence Motion for Interlocutory Appeal on Jurisdiction (Interlocutory Appeal), Case No IT-94-1-AR72 (2 October 1995) 35 ILM 35, para 70.

[21] Ibid.

Ugandan territory. Although Ugandan soldiers did resist the Israelis and there were some exchanges of fire between them, resulting in casualties on both sides and the destruction of several Ugandan Air Force fighters, it was never suggested that there was an armed conflict between Israel and Uganda.

Notwithstanding the possibility that military forces might be deployed on active operations absent a state of armed conflict, the military doctrine of many major military powers today requires that their armed forces comply with the spirit and principles of LOAC in all their operations, irrespective of whether they are formally considered to be in a state of armed conflict.[22] It is not necessary for there to be actual fighting at all times in an armed conflict for the law to be applicable. Some of the treaties that constitute LOAC also apply in situations where actual fighting may no longer be taking place: eg prisoners of war continue to benefit from protection under the law until their final release and repatriation,[23] while the law relevant to military occupation and protection of the civilian population continues to apply as long as an occupation subsists, even if other substantive military operations ceased at an earlier date.[24]

Until the mid-twentieth century, international law only recognized armed conflicts between States as being subject to its legal regulation. This was partly because of the dominant concept of State sovereignty over internal affairs and partly because of the then-prevalent view that international law was concerned only with the regulation of international relations between States. Possibilities for extending the reach of international law to such conflicts were traditionally limited although some did exist, even before 1949 (Moir, 2002, pp 4–18). In that year, Common Article 3 of the Geneva Conventions extended certain basic humanitarian rules of protection to 'armed conflicts not of an international character'; these were supplemented in 1977 by Additional Protocol II. A recent trend has also emerged whereby certain rules are extended to all types of armed conflict, irrespective of their classification (Henckaerts and Doswald-Beck, 2005).[25] This trend is particularly apparent in, though not limited to, the treaties regulating weaponry (Turns, 2006).[26] While fulfilment of the trend would have the virtue of simplifying greatly the legal standards and their consistent application in all armed conflicts, however, the distinction between international and non-international conflicts retains its traditional importance in respect of several key legal provisions. 'Grave breaches' of the Geneva Conventions, for example, exist and may be punished exclusively in the context of international armed conflicts;[27] the distinction between combatants and civilians, so crucial to targeting operations, does not exist in non-international armed conflicts.

Armed conflicts today, therefore, are normally classified into one of two types: international or non-international (internal). In addition, a non-international armed conflict may become 'internationalized' in certain circumstances by the participation of forces from another State (Byron, 2001). The *lex lata* essentially restricts the internationalizing effect of such interventions to cases where the foreign State is intervening on the side of

---

[22] Eg US Department of Defense, Directive 2311.01E, 9 May 2006, *DoD Law of War Program*, para 4.1.
[23] GCIII Article 5.   [24] GCIV Article 6.
[25] *Prosecutor* v *Dusko Tadić*, Decision on the Defence Motion for Interlocutory Appeal on Jurisdiction (Interlocutory Appeal), Case No IT-94-1-AR72 (2 October 1995), paras 97–127.
[26] Eg UN Convention on Conventional Weapons (1981), Amended Article 1 (2001).
[27] *Prosecutor* v *Dusko Tadić*, Decision on the Defence Motion for Interlocutory Appeal on Jurisdiction (Interlocutory Appeal), Case No IT-94-1-AR72 (2 October 1995), paras 79–84; cf ibid, Separate Opinion of Judge Abi-Saab..

insurgents in an internal conflict, because then the requirement of an international armed conflict, for two or more *States* to be in conflict with each other, is met. On the other hand, situations where a State intervenes in an internal conflict by providing assistance to *government* forces fighting against insurgents are said to remain non-international in nature, because the intervening State is not fighting against the host State. Thus, the UK technically considers itself to be engaged in a non-international armed conflict in Afghanistan since the Taliban were displaced as the *de facto* government of that country in December 2001.[28] The international law basis for this somewhat counterintuitive position derives exclusively from the practice of the Coalition States presently operating in Afghanistan and admittedly is supported by a strict interpretation of the wording of Common Article 2 of the Geneva Conventions, but otherwise lacks any doctrinal support in decided case law and is not unproblematic, in that the 'inviting' government may actually lack the legitimacy genuinely to invite foreign forces onto the State's territory. It also takes no account of the UN Security Council's role in 'internationalizing' a previously internal situation. Nevertheless, it does seem to represent the current received opinion.

Under the Geneva Conventions an international armed conflict is defined as 'all cases of declared war or of any other armed conflict which may arise between two or more of the High Contracting Parties',[29] while an armed conflict 'not of an international character' simply has to occur 'in the territory of one of the High Contracting Parties'.[30] The rather formalistic requirement that the conflict be between two or more 'High Contracting Parties' was a direct descendant of the stipulation, in the 1899 and 1907 Hague Conventions, that their provisions applied only 'between contracting Powers, and then only if all the belligerents are parties to the Convention'.[31] These 'all-participation clauses' had to some extent already been discredited by notable abuse by Germany and Japan during World War II, when the Germans refused to apply the 1929 Geneva Convention on the Treatment of Prisoners of War *vis-à-vis* the Soviet Union, ostensibly on the grounds that the latter was not a party to that instrument.[32] Japan, also not a party to the Geneva Convention, punctiliously sent diplomatic notifications to the governments responsible for Allied forces in the Far East, stating that it would nevertheless apply the terms of that Convention, *mutatis mutandis*—and then went on to treat captured Allied nationals with systematically casual cruelty.[33] With both the Geneva Conventions and The Hague Regulations considered as customary international law, however, the 'all-participation clauses' are considered redundant today: IHL is truly universal in its application once there is a factual situation of armed conflict.

The scope of application provisions of the two 1977 Additional Protocols, which added to the definitions of armed conflicts, have been a major reason for some States' unwillingness to apply certain aspects of the Protocols in practice. Article 1(4) of Protocol I extends the Protocol's scope of application to include:

armed conflicts in which peoples are fighting against colonial domination and alien occupation and against racist regimes in the exercise of their right to self-determination, as enshrined in the Charter of the United Nations and the Declaration on Principles of

---

[28] *GS v Secretary of State for the Home Department* [2009] UKAIT 00010.

[29] Common Article 2.   [30] Common Article 3.

[31] The Hague Convention (HC) IV, Article 2 (1907).

[32] *The Trial of German Major War Criminals*, 1946, Judgment, pp 46–48. A 1941 Soviet offer to apply the Geneva Convention *mutatis mutandis* was left unanswered by Germany.

[33] *International Military Tribunal for the Far East*, 1948, Judgment, pp 1096–1106.

International Law concerning Friendly Relations and Co-operation among States in accordance with the Charter of the United Nations.

Article 96(3) of the Protocol further provides that an 'authority' representing a people engaged in such an armed conflict may unilaterally undertake to apply the Geneva Conventions and the Protocol by means of a declaration to that effect.

With the stroke of a pen, the Protocol thus made armed struggles that had traditionally always been seen as internal to individual States, matters for international regulation. After 1977, acts of violence committed by non-State actors could be viewed as legitimate acts of war if the persons committing them claimed to be acting in the name of national liberation or self-determination. Naturally enough, those States that are engaged in armed struggles against such groups have opposed the imposition of international regulation for their conflicts against what they often style mere 'criminals' or 'terrorists'. In many cases this has resulted in important military powers either not becoming parties to the Protocol at all,[34] or becoming parties, but with substantial reservations that have the specific effect of negating the expanded scope of application. The Irish Republican Army (IRA), in its long armed struggle against the UK security forces in Northern Ireland during 'the Troubles', sought to claim that it was acting on behalf of the Irish people in pursuit of their self-determination, to 'liberate' Northern Ireland from 'illegal British occupation', and was thus engaged in an international armed conflict against the UK. This led the IRA to demand prisoner of war (POW) status for its captured operatives. The UK, for its part, consistently denied that there was an armed conflict of any kind in Northern Ireland[35]—and specifically denied the entitlement of captured IRA members to any special status akin to that of a POW, preferring to regulate their activity under national law and regarding them as nothing more than common criminals (Walker, 1984). Concern about attempts to apply the Protocol to Northern Ireland contributed to the UK's decision to delay ratification of the Protocol: although it signed the instrument in 1977, the UK did not ratify it until 1998. Moreover, upon ratification, the UK was careful to enter the following 'statement of understanding' in respect of Articles 1(4) and 96(3):

It is the understanding of the UK that the term 'armed conflict' of itself and in its context denotes a situation of a kind which is not constituted by the commission of ordinary crimes including acts of terrorism whether concerted or in isolation.

The UK will not, in relation to any situation in which it is itself involved, consider itself bound in consequence of any declaration purporting to be made under [Article 96(3)] unless the UK shall have expressly recognized that it has been made by a body which is genuinely an authority representing a people engaged in an armed conflict of the type to which [Article 1(4)] applies.[36]

There has to date been no successful attempt to invoke Article 1(4) as the basis for applying the law of international armed conflict to any situation, although in 1989 the Palestine Liberation Organisation (PLO) notified the Swiss Government (as the depositary of the

---

[34] Eg the USA, Turkey, Israel, India, Pakistan, and Indonesia. On the official US attitude to the Protocol, see President Ronald Reagan, *Message to the Senate Transmitting a Protocol to the 1949 Geneva Conventions* (1987) 26 ILM 561.

[35] See, eg, *Hansard, HC Debs*, 14 December 1977, vol 941, col 237W.

[36] Roberts & Guelff, 2000, p 510.

Geneva Conventions and the Additional Protocols) of its decision to adhere to those instruments as an international legal aid in its violent struggle against Israel. The Swiss Government declined to confirm that the PLO's decision was a valid accession to the instruments, '[d]ue to the uncertainty within the international community as to the existence or the non-existence of a State of Palestine'.[37]

If the expanded definition of international armed conflicts has proved controversial, that of non-international conflicts has been all but unworkable. Article 1 of Protocol II defines non-international armed conflicts to which it applies as:

all armed conflicts which are not covered by Article 1 of Protocol I and which take place in the territory of a High Contracting Party between its armed forces and dissident armed forces or other organised armed groups which, under responsible command, exercise such control over a part of [the State's] territory as to enable them to carry out sustained and concerted military operations and to implement this Protocol.

This Protocol shall not apply to situations of internal disturbances and tensions, such as riots, isolated and sporadic acts of violence and other acts of a similar nature, as not being armed conflicts.

Quite apart from the fact that States with internal conflicts on their territories have been unsurprisingly reluctant to submit to international legal regulation of their violent struggles against 'bandits' or 'terrorists', the main problem with the definition of non-international conflicts, which has largely sabotaged attempts to apply the Protocol in practice, is the requirement for the dissident party to be in control of territory. Illogically enough, this requirement is placed at a higher threshold than is required for national liberation movements in Additional Protocol I, which do not have to control any territory in order to have their struggle legally classified as an *international* armed conflict. The requirement that dissident movements be able to carry out 'sustained and concerted military operations' and to implement the Protocol has been a gift to States seeking to deny the Protocol's applicability to their own internal conflicts, as rebel movements are rarely in such a strong position and rarely have any incentive to apply international humanitarian law in their operations.[38] In effect, the definition of a non-international armed conflict under Protocol II has a threshold so high as to preclude the vast majority of armed rebellions from being subject to its regulation. To date fewer than half a dozen States, and even fewer insurgent movements, have indicated any willingness to be bound by the Protocol in the conduct of their respective internal conflicts (Moir, 2002, pp 119–32). During the Sri Lankan Civil War (1983–2009), the Liberation Tigers of Tamil Eelam (LTTE) undeniably controlled substantial parts of the north-east of the country and mounted 'sustained and concerted' military operations against government forces; yet Sri Lanka is not a party to Protocol II and neither the government nor the LTTE showed any effective application of IHL.

The technicalities of the definitions of international and non-international armed conflicts make it difficult for military personnel to know when to treat irregular opponents as legitimate combatants, civilians directly participating in hostilities, 'dissident armed forces' under Protocol II, a national liberation movement under Protocol I, or common criminals engaged in violence and entitled to no specific protections under IHL. This has led to an increase in the importance of governmental determinations as to the

---

[37] Ibid, p 362.   [38] Cf Sivakumaran, 2006.

classification of armed conflicts in which regular forces are engaged and as to the relevant scope of application of IHL. Unfortunately, as the official US reaction to the events of 11 September 2001 in terms of the treatment of detainees captured in the course of the new 'Global War on Terror' showed, such determinations may do more harm than good. The US Administration of George W Bush persisted in viewing the 'War on Terror' as an international armed conflict within the LOAC paradigm, albeit one in which captured enemy combatants could be detained until the end of 'active hostilities'[39] but were not entitled to be treated as POWs under Geneva Convention III.[40] The US Supreme Court, however, took a radically different view in one of their more celebrated decisions regarding the status and treatment of detainees captured by US forces and held in Guantánamo Bay, Cuba. The plurality of the court held, *obiter*, that because the conflict between the USA and Al-Qaeda terrorists was not against a High Contracting Party to the Geneva Conventions it was by default an 'armed conflict not of an international character' in the terms of Common Article 3.[41]

It is worth noting that virtually no other State agreed with the US legal approach to this situation and, indeed, the Administration of Barack Obama has abandoned such contortions of logic since its first days in office in January 2009. In Israel it has been suggested that such conflicts are better viewed as being in the nature of international armed conflicts, to which the fullest possible extent of IHL should be applied, by reason of the transnational nature of such conflicts—ie the fact that they cross international borders—and the military capabilities of modern terrorist organizations.[42] In the UK, determinations about the existence and characterization of an armed conflict are made as a matter of policy, depending on the facts on the ground and the status of the parties to the conflict.[43] It follows that the UK does not accept that there is a single armed conflict between itself and Al-Qaeda; rather, there are discrete conflicts in theatres such as Iraq (until the withdrawal of British forces in 2009) and Afghanistan. IHL is applied by British forces in all such military operations.

The spectrum of conflict is well illustrated by the case of Iraq since 2003: after an initial phase of full-scale international armed conflict (March–April 2003) to which the fullest extent of LOAC applied, there followed a period of belligerent occupation (April 2003–June 2004) during which certain parts of IHL (notably Geneva Convention IV) continued to be applicable. After the formal end of occupation, however, the legal position became substantially less clear in that Coalition forces were operating extraterritorially against non-State actors; this resulted in the haphazard application of an ad hoc hodgepodge of rules cobbled together from the laws relating to both international and non-international armed conflicts, supplemented by a dose of human rights law

---

[39] GCIII Article 118.

[40] GCIII Article 5 requires that if there is any doubt as to a detainee's status under LOAC, s/he shall be treated as a POW until his/her status is determined by a competent tribunal. Cf President Bush, *Military Order: Detention, Treatment and Trial of Certain Non-Citizens in the War Against Terrorism* (2001) 41 ILM 252; Attorney-General Alberto Gonzales, *Memorandum to the President re Application of the Geneva Convention on Prisoners of War to the Conflict with Al Qaeda and the Taliban* (2002) (reproduced in Greenberg and Datrel, 2005, p 118).

[41] *Hamdan* v *Rumsfeld* (2006) 548 US 557.

[42] *Public Committee against Torture in Israel* v *Government of Israel (targeted killings)* HCJ 769/02; (2006) 46 ILM 375.

[43] UK Ministry of Defence, 2004, paras 3.1–3.13.

and overshadowed by the significance of UN Security Council resolutions regarding the rights of foreign forces in Iraq.

III. THE ACTORS IN HUMANITARIAN LAW

Once the scope of application of IHL has been determined, the crucial feature of the modern law in international armed conflicts is the distinction between combatants and civilians. The former may legitimately be targeted in military operations, while the latter—subject to certain exceptions[44]—may not. Conversely, and as a direct consequence of their status, the former are entitled to certain rights and privileges upon capture, while the latter— again, subject to certain exceptions—are not. Therefore, in the planning and execution of military operations, a distinction must always be made between combatants on the one hand, and civilians on the other. This was an easy enough task when battles were fought by organized armies on discrete (mostly rural) battlefields largely denuded of their civilian inhabitants; however, the proliferation of irregular forces in modern warfare, which also is frequently conducted in an urban environment where the civilian population remains present, has made distinction exceedingly difficult in practice.

Historically, the laws of war did not provide a definition of the concept of a 'combatant'. Warfare was carried on by soldiers, who generally were easily distinguishable from the civilian population. This was so even before the issue of standardized uniforms to European armies began to become common practice in the late seventeenth century. Although a concept of lawful combatancy was present in the literature by the late eighteenth century (Green, 2008, pp 125–128), there was little controversy in practice before the Franco-Prussian War (1870–1871). In that conflict, the swift advance of Prussian forces into French territory led to the definition of two new categories of persons whose proper combatant status was initially a matter of some legal uncertainty: *francs-tireurs* and the *levée en masse*. The latter category ('mass levy') had been recognized since its use by the French Republic in 1793[45] and referred to the spontaneous requisitioning of the civilian population of an invaded—but unoccupied—territory, without time for military organization; its members are regarded as combatants, provided they 'carry arms openly and . . . respect the laws and customs of war'.[46] They are entitled to POW status upon capture.[47]

The former category ('free-shooters'), on the other hand, referred to civilians who— whether in occupied territory or not—take up arms on their own initiative to fight, independently of any governmental or military control, against an invading army. In 1870, members of rifle clubs or unofficial paramilitary shooting societies in eastern France formed irregular bands that carried out ambushes and attacks on Prussian lines of communication, isolated military posts and reconnaissance patrols; nominally under the control of the French Ministry of War, they were in fact entirely outside any military discipline, wearing no uniforms and electing their own officers. Prussian practice was to treat captured *francs-tireurs* as non-combatants found illegally participating in hostilities, and

---

[44] Principally, if civilians directly participate in hostilities, they lose their protected status and may legitimately be targeted 'for such time' as they do so: see ICRC, *Interpretive Guidance on the Notion of Direct Participation in Hostilities under International Humanitarian Law* (2008) 90 IRRC 991.

[45] French National Convention, Decree of 23 August 1793.

[46] The Hague Regulations (HR), Article 2 (1907).   [47] GCIII Article 4(A)(6).

to execute them as such. Their activities also often led to reprisal actions being conducted against nearby French villages. This pattern of conduct occasioned some legal controversy when it was repeated in World War II, with the Germans treating members of the French Resistance as *francs-tireurs* not entitled to any protection under the laws of war, while the Allies insisted that their degree of organization and allegiance to the French Government-in-Exile entitled them to POW status upon capture. Although one prominent subsequent war crimes trial of German generals found that captured partisans in the Balkans had been correctly subjected to the death penalty as *francs-tireurs*,[48] treaty law since has endorsed the contrary position.

As it was generally understood at the turn of the twentieth century that members of regular armies were combatants who were subject to the rights and duties of the laws of war, the main legal issue became how to define *others* who might be so entitled. Article 1 of the 1907 Hague Regulations accordingly provides that:

The laws, rights, and duties of war apply not only to armies, but also to militia and volunteer corps fulfilling the following conditions:

1. To be commanded by a person responsible for his subordinates;

2. To have a fixed distinctive emblem recognizable at a distance;

3. To carry arms openly; and

4. To conduct their operations in accordance with the laws and customs of war.

Apart from designating those persons who can lawfully be attacked in wartime, the other principal significance of the concept of lawful combatancy is that it entitles a person, on capture, to the benefit of treatment as a POW. In 1949, Article 4 of Geneva Convention III expanded entitlement to POW status to the following principal groups:

1. members of the regular armed forces,[49] and of militias or volunteer corps forming part of the armed forces, of a party to the conflict;[50]

2. members of *other* militias or volunteer corps of a party to the conflict, including organised resistance movements, provided that they satisfy the requirements for lawful combatancy listed in Article 1 of The Hague Regulations;

3. authorised persons who accompany the armed forces without actually being members thereof, e.g. war correspondents,[51] supply contractors, members of military labour units etc.; and

4. participants in a *levée en masse*.

Military medical and religious personnel, on the other hand, are non-combatant members of the armed forces. They may if captured be retained by the Detaining Power in order

---

[48] *The Hostages Trial (United States of America v Wilhelm List and Others)* [1949] VIII Law Reports of Trials of War Criminals 38.

[49] Including paratroopers, marine commandos or other special forces, as long as they fight in their correct uniform and with the appropriate unit badges: see Parks, 2003.

[50] The criterion of belonging to a State has been used to deny POW status to captured guerrillas: *Prosecutor v Kassem* (1969), 42 ILR 470.

[51] Journalists not formally accredited as war correspondents are treated as civilians: API, Article 79 (1977).

to assist POWs, and benefit from the protections of the Geneva Convention, but are not formally considered as POWs.[52]

This comparatively simple regime was supplemented in 1977 by the controversial provisions of Additional Protocol I, which set up a new regime with regard to lawful combatant and POW status; this inevitably is distinctly favourable to the national liberation movements whose conflicts were recognized by the Protocol as being international in nature. Article 43 of the Protocol defines the armed forces, and accordingly lawful combatants, as, 'all organized armed forces, groups and units which are under a command responsible to [a Party to the conflict] for the conduct of its subordinates, even if that Party is represented by a government or an authority not recognized by an adverse Party'. This means that, rather than the recognition of there being a state of war or not being irrelevant to the applicability of the Convention's provisions, as stipulated in Common Article 2 of the 1949 Conventions, it becomes the question of whether a party to the conflict is recognized or not which is rendered irrelevant: a change very much to the benefit of non-State actors, who are seldom if ever legally recognized by the States against which they are fighting. It is not hard to see why certain States continue to object to this formulation.

Lawful combatants, as defined in Article 43, are entitled on capture to POW status,[53] subject to the following:

In order to promote the protection of the civilian population from the effects of hostilities, combatants are obliged to distinguish themselves from the civilian population while they are engaged in an attack or in a military operation preparatory to an attack. Recognizing, however, that there are situations in armed conflicts where, owing to the nature of the hostilities an armed combatant cannot so distinguish himself, he shall retain his status as a combatant, provided that, in such situations, he carries his arms openly:

    (a) during each military engagement; and

    (b) during such time as he is visible to the adversary while he is engaged in a military deployment preceding the launching of an attack in which he is to participate.[54]

The first sentence relaxes the pre-existing standard in that it does not specify the way in which combatants must distinguish themselves from civilians (as opposed to The Hague Regulations' requirement of a 'fixed, distinctive sign'); it also requires such distinction to have effect only during 'an attack or…a military operation preparatory to an attack' (whereas The Hague Regulations contain no temporal element as regards lawful combatancy). The second sentence, however, goes even further towards accommodating guerrillas, and remains deeply controversial for several States. Its assumption that there are situations in which a combatant *cannot* distinguish himself is limited—the UK considers that these can only arise in occupied territory or in respect of national liberation movements (NLMs)[55]—and the interpretation favoured by some NLMs, to the effect that arms need only be carried openly immediately before opening fire (as opposed to continually while visible to the enemy and moving into an attack position), have received little support in the literature or State practice.[56] States not party to the Protocol continue to be bound only by the stricter standards from The Hague Regulations and Geneva Convention III.

---

[52] GCIII Article 33.   [53] API Article 44(1).   [54] Ibid, Article 44(3).
[55] Roberts & Guelff, 2000, p 510.   [56] For the UK position on this point, see ibid.

Thus, there are effectively two different legal standards for the determination of lawful combatancy; the undesirability of this situation has been plainly demonstrated by the conflict in Afghanistan since 2001. US President Bush's determination that Al-Qaeda and Taliban fighters captured by US forces were 'unlawful combatants' who were not entitled to POW status, could be detained indefinitely without charge and (eventually) prosecuted for war crimes generated enormous controversy in theory and proved unworkable in practice.[57] On his second day in office, President Obama announced the intended closure of the detention facility at Guantánamo Bay, Cuba;[58] the eventual fate of the detainees still in custody has yet to be determined.

Any 'person who takes part in hostilities' without being a combatant under the terms of the Protocol shall upon capture be presumed to be a POW and therefore entitled to protection under IHL, unless and until a competent tribunal decides otherwise.[59] This provision is in essence the same as that in Article 5 of Geneva Convention III, but its ambit is more controversial. It applies a *presumption of actual POW status* (as opposed to Article 5's assertion that a captive of doubtful legal status will be *treated as if he were a POW* until a competent tribunal determines his actual status) to all persons participating in hostilities in armed conflicts covered by the Protocol. The overall effect of Articles 43–45 is to shift the balance of presumptions and entitlements very much in favour of a captive who, prior to the Protocol, would not have had such benefits under traditional LOAC but would have been automatically subject to trial merely for illegally participating in hostilities. Now the Protocol necessitates charges of specific criminal conduct, as opposed to mere participation in hostilities, if any trial is to take place.

Although in mediaeval Europe and until the advent of mass-recruited citizen armies in the late seventeenth century the use of mercenaries was lawful and indeed widespread,[60] the post-1945 decolonization period saw large numbers of demobilized professional soldiers from Western nations enrolling for financial gain in the armies of colonial powers in Africa who were fighting against NLMs claiming self-determination (or, as in the Congo and Nigeria, for secessionist rebellions). Condemnation of mercenarism consequently became widespread and it is not surprising that special provision for it was eventually made in Additional Protocol I, Article 47 of which removes any possibility of mercenaries being regarded as lawful combatants entitled to POW status if captured. The salient features of the definition of a mercenary are that his motivation is the desire for private gain, and that he is neither a national nor a resident of a party to an armed conflict, nor a member of the armed forces thereof. This was subsequently added to by the UN General Assembly's International Convention against the Recruitment, Use, Financing

---

[57] *Military Order*. In *Rasul* v *Bush* (2004) 542 US 466 the US Supreme Court held that detainees were entitled to challenge in the US courts the legality of their detention by US forces. In *Hamdan* v *Rumsfeld* (2006) 548 US 557 the Court held that the Military Commissions established by the Bush Administration for the trial of 'unlawful combatants' did not meet the requirements of the Geneva Conventions. On 4 June 2007 the original charges in the first two substantive cases to be tried by Military Commissions, *United States* v *Hamdan* and *United States* v *Khadr*, were both dismissed for lack of jurisdiction on the grounds that the defendants' status under LOAC had not been properly determined: 1 MC 6 & 152.

[58] Executive Order 13,493 (22 January 2009), 74 Fed Reg 4901.

[59] API Article 45(1).

[60] Mercenaries are not to be confused with the foreign professional soldiers used in certain armies, eg the British Army's Brigade of Gurkhas and the French Foreign Legion. These units are regularly constituted and subject to the discipline of the armies in which they serve, and are lawful combatants.

and Training of Mercenaries, which extended the Protocol's definition of a mercenary to include the purpose of 'participating in a concerted act of violence aimed at overthrowing a government or otherwise undermining the constitutional order...or...the territorial integrity of a State'.[61] The Convention offence is committed even if a person recruited as a mercenary does not actually take part in a conflict—a departure from Article 47's requirement that he take a direct part in hostilities.

These provisions have not managed to prevent or deter the repeated use of mercenaries since the early 1990s in conflicts such as those in the former Yugoslavia and Sierra Leone.[62] The issue continues to be pertinent in light of the 'privatization of war' in the first decade of the twenty-first century: since the occupation of Iraq in 2003–2004, several States have increasingly outsourced many military services and types of expertise to a growing array of private contractors or 'private military security companies' (PMSCs). These are generally composed of former military personnel who undertake a range of duties from serving as bodyguards for political leaders and diplomats, through the provision of training and advice in the reorganization of State military capabilities in countries such as Nigeria and Bulgaria, to actual military missions in countries such as Colombia (where they have piloted aircraft and helicopter gunships engaged in the destruction of coca crops). Their tendency, exhibited in Iraq, to be somewhat 'trigger-happy' has attracted considerable notoriety.[63] US and British PMSCs operate under national regulation[64] but their legal position under LOAC is uncertain. The UN General Assembly has condemned them as one of 'the new modalities of mercenarism',[65] but they could also arguably be assimilated in certain circumstances to 'supply contractors' who benefit from POW status,[66] and their right to use force in self-defence is lawfully mandated under their contracts of employment. Ultimately, their status under LOAC is most likely to be that of civilians, since they are not part of the armed forces and cannot be regarded as militia; the legal issue is then whether or not their precise function in a given situation involves direct participation in hostilities.

It is a tragic reality of modern warfare, particularly in certain parts of Africa, that child soldiers form a significant part of the combatant forces. This has been notably evident in such cases as the Lord's Resistance Army in Uganda and the Revolutionary United Front in Sierra Leone; in the latter country especially, many of the worst atrocities in the conflict were committed by children (Happold, 2005).[67] Article 77 of Protocol I requires States to 'take all feasible measures in order that children who have not attained the age of fifteen years do not take a direct part in hostilities and, in particular, [to] refrain from recruiting them...'. Measures for the protection of children in armed conflicts are

---

[61] GA Res 44/34 (1989), Article 1(2)(a).

[62] The UN Convention on Mercenaries entered into force in 2001 but still has only 32 States parties.

[63] In *United States* v *Slough et al*, five employees of the PMSC Blackwater Worldwide were charged with manslaughter in connection with the killing of 17 unarmed Iraqi civilians in Baghdad: *The New York Times*, 8 December 2008.

[64] In the USA, PMSCs are now subject to the Uniform Code of Military Justice: HR 5122, John Warner National Defense Authorization Act for Fiscal Year 2007, Section 552. In the UK, Section 370 of, and Schedule 15 to, the Armed Forces Act 2006 make civilians accompanying the armed forces in certain circumstances subject to military law.

[65] GA Res 62/145 (4 March 2008).   [66] GCIII Article 4(A)(4).

[67] *Prosecutor* v *Sesay, Kallon & Gbao*, Trial Chamber Special Court for Sierra Leone, Judgement of 25 February 2009, pp 482–519.

repeatedly called for by the UN Security Council[68] and provided for in legal terms also by the 1989 UN Convention on the Rights of the Child and its 2000 Optional Protocol on the Involvement of Children in Armed Conflict, although these instruments use a higher cut-off age of 18 years.

IV. CONDUCT OF HOSTILITIES

The 1907 Hague Regulations, together with certain provisions of 1977 Additional Protocol I, are the modern sources of the law on the conduct of hostilities—a topic often referred to as 'methods and means of warfare'—but their much older genesis lies in the interaction of the customary principles of humanity, chivalry and military necessity. Nowhere is this truer than in the context of the law of targeting, which is dominated by what the ICJ has termed the two 'cardinal' principles of IHL: the rule of distinction, and the prohibition of the use of weapons causing unnecessary suffering or superfluous injury.[69] The law on the conduct of hostilities also determines the difference between battlefield practices that are forbidden, and those that are permitted, although it should be noted that even if a given practice is allowed under international LOAC, it may well be prohibited under the national law of the belligerents. Thus, while The Hague Regulations do not forbid such classic wartime activities as espionage or sabotage, a spy or saboteur who is captured out of uniform will be tried as such and, under the national laws of many States, may be sentenced to death.[70] Other practices, such as perfidy—'[a]cts inviting the confidence of an adversary to lead him to believe that he is entitled to, or is obliged to accord, protection under the rules of [LOAC], with intent to betray that confidence'[71]—and denial of quarter, are clearly forbidden under LOAC.

A. DISTINCTION AND PROPORTIONALITY

Given the importance which attaches to personal status in international armed conflicts, it is logical that the principle of distinction should lie at the heart of modern LOAC, notably in relation to targeting operations; as such it forms part of customary international law, although it is codified in Article 48 of Additional Protocol I. It requires belligerents at all times to distinguish between combatants and military objectives on the one hand, and civilians and civilian objects on the other, and to attack the former only (subject to certain exceptions which will be detailed below). Basically, anyone who is not a combatant is a civilian, but because in contemporary warfare the two types of person are not always clearly distinguishable from each other, the principle of distinction is moderated by a proportionality test. The law recognizes the permissibility of civilian casualties or damage to civilian objects, during an otherwise lawful attack on a military target, by the grim but functional doctrine of 'collateral damage': such casualties or damage will be proportionate

---

[68] Eg SC Res 1882 (4 August 2009).
[69] *Legality of the Threat or Use of Nuclear Weapons, Advisory Opinion, ICJ Reports 1996*, p 226, para 78.
[70] Eg *Ali* v *Public Prosecutor* [1969] 1 AC 430.
[71] API Article 37(1). Examples of perfidious conduct include feigning any of the following: intent to surrender, incapacitation by wounds or sickness, or non-combatant status.

if it is not excessive in relation to the concrete and direct military advantage anticipated from the attack.[72] In effect, the law accepts that at least *some* civilian casualties or *some* damage to civilian objects will be inevitable in *most* military operations, however carefully conducted. In both World Wars it was considered acceptable to attack the enemy civilian population's morale as such, but such practices would be clearly illegal today: Article 51(2) of Protocol I prohibits attacks designed to spread terror among the civilian population. The key question, then, is: what constitutes a military target?

Article 52(2) of the Protocol defines military objectives as, 'those objects which by their nature, location, purpose or use make an effective contribution to military action and whose total or partial destruction, capture or neutralization, in the circumstances ruling at the time, offers a definite military advantage'. Thus, while certain objects—such as an airforce base—are intrinsically military in nature, others—an apartment block, for example—may be located, or used by the enemy, in such a way that it makes an effective contribution to military action. On the other hand, blanket determinations of military significance for objects which are not intrinsically military but clearly have military uses in wartime, such as roads, railways, or bridges, are not allowed.[73] The Protocol requires a presumption, in case of doubt as to whether a civilian object is actually being used to make an effective contribution to military action, that it is not in fact being so used; it also requires the commander to take all feasible precautions in planning and launching an attack, to warn the civilian population of an impending attack and to cancel or suspend an attack if it becomes apparent that the object is not a military objective or that the attack cannot be executed without disproportionate collateral damage.[74] A particularly important aspect of these provisions is the heavy burden they place on the attacking commander: the law effectively expects him to place the safety of the civilian population ahead of that of his own troops or his legitimate military objectives. Despite widespread condemnation of Israeli operations in the Gaza Strip since 2000, on a number of occasions Israeli military commanders have cancelled planned airstrikes that would have eliminated senior Palestinian militant leaders when it became apparent that Palestinian civilians were flocking to the area in question in an attempt to shield the target.[75]

With so-called 'dual-use objects', a case-by-case determination must be made as to whether a definite military advantage would be obtained by attacking that object, not tomorrow or the day after, but today. It would also be reasonable, however, to take into account longer-term military advantages and effects on the civilian population, such as the eventual strategic consequences of an attack, or impairment of the civilian population's means of survival.[76] The Protocol unhelpfully does not mention dual-use objects as such, but the principles for determining the legality of an attack on such targets are the same as those of general application. The critical issue will generally be whether the anticipated collateral damage (if any) would be proportionate to the military advantage expected. In 1999 NATO treated the Serbian Radio and Television building in Belgrade as a military target, because in addition to its normal function of providing entertainment

---

[72] API, Article 57(2).

[73] Certain objects may never be attacked (unless they are being abused by the enemy): eg medical facilities, personnel and transport, and cultural property.

[74] API, Article 57.   [75] *The Jerusalem Post*, 19 November 2006.

[76] API Article 56 prohibits attacks on dams, dykes, and nuclear electrical generating stations if such attack is likely to release dangerous forces which would cause severe losses to the civilian population.

and information to the civilian population, it also in wartime served as a back-up communications network for the Serbian armed forces. As it was located in the middle of Belgrade, the required assessment of collateral damage had to estimate how many civilians were likely to become casualties in the attack, and whether such casualties would be proportionate to the military advantage which would be gained by knocking out a back-up military communications network. In the event, NATO proceeded with the attack in the middle of the night, when the smallest possible number of civilian employees was likely to be present in the building: in the event, 16 civilians died and broadcasting resumed from a back-up transmitter in a secret location within 24 hours. Although it was unfortunate that 16 civilians died, NATO took the required precautions in attack and made a proper assessment of likely collateral damage and proportionality. The circumstances disclosed no *prima facie* violation of LOAC on NATO's part.[77]

It is important to emphasize that there is no mathematical formula for deciding what would, or would not, be a proportionate level of collateral damage in any given case. Everything depends on the circumstances ruling at the time and the operational context; the decision whether or not to attack a given target is that of the commander, who must base his assessment on the intelligence that is reasonably available to him, in the light of recommendations by his military legal adviser. It is wrong, therefore, to assume that any case of civilians being killed in a military operation *ipso facto* constitutes a war crime: as long as the target was a military objective or a dual-use object and the attacking force undertook the required precautions in attack to the best of their ability in the circumstances ruling at the time, the relevant rules of IHL have been complied with. Civilian deaths or damage to civilian objects in these circumstances is a tragedy, to be sure; but it is one that the law factors into its strictures.

B. WEAPONS

Article 22 of The Hague Regulations lays down a general principle that, 'The right of belligerents to adopt means of injuring the enemy is not unlimited.' From this, and from the principle of distinction, flow two specific customary rules affecting the choice of weaponry in armed conflicts:

1. it is forbidden to employ methods or means of warfare that may be expected to cause superfluous injury or unnecessary suffering;[78] and

2. it is forbidden to employ methods or means of warfare that are indiscriminate, i.e. cannot be directed against a specific military objective.[79]

In addition, there are specific treaty obligations not to use methods and means of warfare that may be expected to have negative effects on the environment.

The first rule, in particular, has prompted many treaties banning specific weapons. The Hague formula prohibits weapons 'calculated to cause' unnecessary suffering, while its more modern counterpart in Protocol I uses the phrase, 'of a nature to cause' such injury or suffering. The latter is the better one in practice, as it relies less on the intention with

---

[77] See ICTY, *Final Report to the Prosecutor by the Committee Established to Review the NATO Bombing Campaign Against the Federal Republic of Yugoslavia* (2000) 39 ILM 1257, paras 71–79.

[78] HR Article 23(e), API Article 35(2).   [79] API Article 51(4).

which a weapon is used—any weapon can be used in such a way as to cause unnecessary suffering—and more on its intrinsic nature. This is the case with white phosphorus, which is not currently prohibited by LOAC but can certainly have very deleterious burning or asphyxiating effect if used directly against human beings; nevertheless, it is in the armoury of many States, including Russia, Israel, the USA and UK, for use against military objectives because of its obscurant or illuminating effect. Its use as an anti-personnel weapon, to flush out Iraqi insurgents in Fallujah in 2004, was therefore probably a violation of the rule.[80] It is important, however, to remember that suffering is an integral part of war, and therefore the concept of *unnecessary* suffering is inevitably both subjective and relative. The difficulties have been well expressed in the following terms:

The law does not specify the permissible level of disablement. In contemporary military operations, while the killing of enemy combatants is still contemplated, so is wounding them to put them out of action. This may cause them permanent injury. In either case suffering is implicit. But the law does not define unnecessary suffering, and views can differ markedly. Some are horrified by the prospect of blindness, others by the blast injuries caused by mines, and many regard burn injuries as particularly serious, but it is difficult to compare one type of injury with another and say that it necessarily signifies unnecessary suffering.... [T]herefore, all that can be done, in very general terms, is to try and balance the military utility of weapons with the wounding and incidental effects that they have.[81]

The ban on indiscriminate weapons is a corollary of the rules on protection of civilians, discussed above. It serves to prohibit such practices as area bombardment—treating an entire area as a military target, as was done by the German deployment of V1 and V2 rockets against southern England in World War II, and Iraq's use of Scud missiles against Saudi Arabia and Israel in 1991.

In addition to these general principles, treaty provisions exist to ban or restrict the use of the following specified weapons, *inter alia*:

1. explosive bullets or projectiles under 400 grammes weight;
2. Dum-dum bullets;
3. poison and poisoned weapons;
4. asphyxiating and poison gases, along with bacteriological and chemical weapons;
5. weapons causing injury by fragments in the human body undetectable by X-ray;
6. anti-personnel landmines and booby-traps;
7. incendiary weapons;
8. blinding laser weapons; and
9. cluster munitions (although the 2008 Dublin Convention is not yet in force).

The 1977 Environmental Modification Treaty also prohibits the deliberate manipulation of the environment as a method of warfare.

The one type of weapon that is conspicuous by its absence from explicit regulation in LOAC is nuclear weapons, the use of which is not forbidden by any treaty. Whether

---

[80] See *US Defends Use of White Phosphorus Munitions in Iraq* (2006) 100 AJIL 487; cf Israeli Ministry of Foreign Affairs, *The Operation in Gaza: Factual and Legal Aspects*, July 2009, paras 406–430.

[81] UK Ministry of Defence, 2004, para 6.1.2.

customary law prohibits the use of nuclear weapons is less obvious: their use has been condemned on many occasions by the UN General Assembly, which in 1994 requested an Advisory Opinion from the ICJ on the subject. The resulting Opinion,[82] which saw the Court split down the middle with seven votes in favour and seven against (one chair on the Court being vacant at the time the Opinion was rendered, due to the death of the previous incumbent), was widely derided as an exercise in evasiveness. The ICJ found that, while there was no specific prohibition or permissive rule in international law regarding the use of nuclear weapons, their use nevertheless would have to comply with 'the principles and rules' of IHL—in particular the rules relating to unnecessary suffering, in light of the injuries caused by radiation. In that context, the Court found that it would 'generally be contrary' to IHL to use nuclear weapons,[83] an opaque conclusion that has drawn considerable criticism. In fairness to the ICJ, it should be mentioned that its credibility would have suffered irreparable damage had it ruled conclusively either for or against legality: in the former case, non-nuclear States, which constitute a large majority in the world, would have condemned it as out of step with world opinion. But in the latter case, the nuclear weapons States would surely have simply ignored the Advisory Opinion. The UK's position, for instance, is that none of the rules of Additional Protocol I have any effect on, regulate, or prohibit, the use of nuclear weapons.[84] The ICRC, in its *Customary Law Study*, declined to express any position on the matter, ostensibly because it was *sub judice* the ICJ at the time of research for the *Study* (Henckaerts and Doswald-Beck, 2005, p 255).

In fact, it is difficult to see how the use of such tremendously destructive weapons could ever be IHL-compliant, although it is true that their sole use to date—by the US against Japan in 1945—averted the imaginably greater losses that a ground invasion of Japan would have incurred. However, it is conceivable that the use of a tactical nuclear weapon, deployed for instance by a submarine against an enemy surface fleet on the high seas, could be targeted against a purely military objective and be both necessary and proportionate in terms of IHL. Conversely, the use of a nuclear weapon against a civilian population would clearly be unlawful, not because of the nature of the weapon, but because of its deliberate use against a civilian object. Finally, the use of such weapons in a setting where their effects would be indiscriminate— for example, against military installations located near civilian population centres—would violate the ban on indiscriminate weapons generally, rather than any specific rule on nuclear weapons.

V. PROTECTION OF VICTIMS

For the purposes of legal protection, IHL defines three categories of person as 'victims' of armed conflicts, in the sense that they have specific rights as a consequence of their status. These categories are: the wounded and sick (including persons shipwrecked at sea), prisoners of war, and civilians. Each is subject to a detailed separate regime of legal protection; in the case of the wounded and sick on land, the treaty in question is the oldest in the canon of contemporary humanitarian law.

---

[82] *Legality of the Threat or Use of Nuclear Weapons, Advisory Opinion, ICJ Reports 1996*, p 226.
[83] Ibid, para 105(2)(E).   [84] Roberts and Guelff, 2000, p 510.

A. THE WOUNDED AND SICK

The Geneva Convention for the Amelioration of the Condition of the Wounded in Armies in the Field (1864), which famously resulted from Henri Dunant's experiences at the Battle of Solferino (1859) and the subsequent foundation of the ICRC (1863), was the first treaty to make specific provision for the protection of soldiers who had become *hors de combat* by virtue of wounds or sickness. The foundation principles of this area of the law, as laid down in the 1864 Convention and expanded in subsequent Geneva Conventions,[85] are:

1. relief must be provided for the wounded and sick without distinction as to status, allegiance or nationality;

2. the inviolability of medical personnel, establishments and units must be respected; and

3. the distinctive protective sign of a red cross on a white background must be recognised and respected.

Enemy wounded may not be attacked, but must be collected and cared for, with the same access to medical treatment as the State's own wounded.[86] The same protection from attack extends to enemy medical transports, units and hospitals, provided they do not forfeit this protection by being used to commit hostile acts; even then, they may be attacked only after due warning.[87] Medical personnel may carry weapons for their own defence and that of the wounded and sick in their care; neither they nor those in their care may be the object of reprisals. The Red Cross and its associated protective signs[88] may be used only for marking the personnel, transports, and establishments of the ICRC, military medical services, and other medical bodies (eg national Red Cross societies) specifically authorized to use the emblems. Misuse of any of the emblems will normally constitute a criminal offence under national law, and may additionally amount to the war crime of perfidy.

B. PRISONERS OF WAR

Since the advent of the Nation-State and regularly conscripted citizen-armies in the seventeenth century, it has been accepted that soldiers who surrender to the enemy are under the protection of the enemy State and not at the whim of the individual enemy commander. The sole reason for detaining them was that they should not be able to rejoin the enemy's forces and thereby negate the military advantage accrued by their removal from the field,

---

[85] GCI (1929); GCI (1949) (wounded and sick on land); GCII (1949) (wounded, sick, and shipwrecked at sea).

[86] Suggestions that wounded Taliban fighters captured in Afghanistan should not be treated in the same field hospitals as wounded British soldiers would, if implemented, have amounted to a violation of GCI Article 12 or the Conventions' Common Article 3: *The Guardian*, 23 January 2009.

[87] GCI Article 21. The same is true in respect of individual medical personnel.

[88] Since 1929 many (though not all) Islamic States have used the Red Crescent as a recognized alternative to the Red Cross—its use originated in the Russo-Turkish War (1877–1878), when Ottoman medical units adopted it for protection. Persia used its own (equally recognized) traditional emblem of the Red Lion and Sun from 1922, and reserves the right to use it still, although its use was discontinued after the 1979 Islamic Revolution because of its association with the former Shah's regime. Israel's unrecognized use of the Red Shield of David eventually led to the adoption of Additional Protocol III (2005), which provides for a third, universal protective emblem devoid of potential religious or national symbolism: the Red Crystal.

although it was common for prisoners to be 'paroled', whereby they were released on a promise not to re-enlist and resume fighting. The notion of reciprocity as a principle underpinning the law of war also provided an incentive for States to ensure that enemy soldiers taken prisoner should be well treated. Geneva Conventions II (1929) and III (1949) have since ensured that this aspect of IHL is particularly highly regulated, with many technical provisions deriving from the grant of POW status.

An essential aspect of the protection of POWs is that they are not in the hands of the individual units or commanders who have captured them, but in those of the State (the Detaining Power), which is then responsible in international law for their good treatment.[89] A POW is neither a criminal, although he may be prosecuted for crimes committed before capture,[90] nor a hostage. The Detaining State is under an absolute duty to ensure that POWs are not murdered, tortured, ill-treated,[91] or otherwise abused (eg by exposure to insults and public curiosity).[92] POWs cannot be the object of reprisals and no considerations of military necessity can justify their ill-treatment; thus, it would be unlawful to use them as human shields, 'to render certain points or areas immune from military operations'.[93] Equally, although the Detaining Power has a legitimate interest in questioning POWs in order to obtain intelligence, they are obliged only to provide their name, rank, date of birth, and military number, and it is illegal to coerce them to provide any other information.[94] They must be held in special camps located away from the combat zones; although the Detaining Power may transfer them to the custody of another State party to the Convention,[95] the State that originally captured them may remain responsible for their good treatment. POWs must be released and repatriated after the cessation of active hostilities,[96] although this requirement is not interpreted as authorizing forcible repatriation of POWs who do not wish to be repatriated: after the 1991 Gulf War many Iraqi POWs chose to remain in Saudi Arabia rather than return to Iraq.

C. CIVILIANS

The definition of civilians in IHL is essentially a negative one: a civilian is anyone who is not a combatant as defined by The Hague Regulations and Geneva Convention III and,

---

[89] GCIII Articles 12–13.

[90] Usually, though not invariably, for violations of IHL committed during the conflict in which he was captured. Cf the American trial of General Manuel Noriega for drug trafficking prior to the 1989 US invasion of Panama, *United States v Noriega* (1992) 808 F. Supp. 791 (S.D.Fla), and the British refusal to prosecute Lieutenant Commander Alfredo Astiz, captured on South Georgia during the Falklands War, for crimes committed during the 'Dirty War' in Argentina in the late 1970s: see Meyer, 1983.

[91] During the 2003 Gulf War there were instances of Iraqi POWs being beaten by American soldiers: *The Guardian*, 6 January 2004.

[92] In the 2003 Gulf War some Coalition POWs were shown being questioned on Iraqi television, while Western networks also carried footage of blindfolded Iraqi POWs: *The Christian Science Monitor*, 26 March 2003. See also Rogers, 2004, pp 52–53. British practice is not to broadcast such images if they enable any POW to be individually recognized. Broadcasting pictures of the captured Saddam Hussein undergoing medical and dental examination, however, was arguably justified as a factual demonstration of his capture.

[93] GCIII Article 23. Iraq clearly violated this provision in its treatment of Coalition POWs during the 1991 Gulf War: Rowe, 1993, pp 196–197.

[94] GCIII Article 17.

[95] See, eg, arrangements for transfer of British-captured POWs in the 1991 Gulf War to US custody, reprinted in Rowe, 1993, at pp 348–349.

[96] GCIII Article 118.

for those States that are party to it, Additional Protocol I. Part of the main emphasis of contemporary IHL is the protection of the civilian population and individual civilians: this is achieved both by safeguarding them in most circumstances from the direct effect of hostilities (as discussed above) and by providing for the specific protection of civilians who are in the power of a State of which they are not nationals. Unlike the sick and wounded or POWs, civilians were not previously covered by LOAC; while this was mainly because the nature of warfare prior to the early twentieth century was such that civilians were rarely subjected to direct attack and specific measures of protection were thus not thought necessary, the experience of 'total war' in the various conflicts of the 1930s and 1940s made it clear that development of the law in this direction was urgently required. The result was the entirely innovative Geneva Convention IV (1949).

The Convention protects nationals of one belligerent who find themselves in the power of another belligerent, either through being in the territory of an enemy State or in territory under belligerent occupation. It does not protect nationals of neutral States caught up in a conflict,[97] unless they are in occupied territory, in which case they benefit from the general protections accorded to all civilians in such territory. Thus, British citizens in Kuwait at the time of the Iraqi invasion in 1990 were covered by the Convention but those in Iraq itself were not, since the UK at that time was not a party to any conflict with Iraq and the UK still had diplomatic relations with that State. Only when Coalition military action started in 1991 did British citizens in Iraq come under the protections of the Convention. Civilians in the territory of an enemy State should normally be allowed to leave the State at any time during the conflict, although permission to leave may be refused if their departure would be contrary to the national interests of the State;[98] they may even be interned if absolutely necessary for security reasons,[99] although this would not authorize the mass internment of members of specific ethnic groups. If internment does occur, civilians are entitled to a standard of treatment effectively analogous to that accorded POWs. Civilians must not be subjected to reprisals or collective punishments,[100] held hostage,[101] or otherwise ill-treated.

D. BELLIGERENT OCCUPATION

Similar legal standards govern the treatment of civilians in occupied territory, who additionally must not be deported to any other State (including the Occupying Power).[102] The Occupying Power also has various detailed obligations concerning maintenance of the physical welfare of the civilian population, respect for private property and the administration of law and order (Benvenisti, 1993).[103] While these provisions of the Convention were adopted as a reaction to the systematic abuse of occupied territories by the Axis Powers in World War II, they built upon legal foundations already instituted by The Hague Regulations (1907). The greatest contemporary controversies surrounding their implementation have been in relation to the Israeli occupation of the Palestinian Territories since 1967, and the Coalition occupation of Iraq (2003–2004).

Although Israel denies the formal applicability of Convention IV to the West Bank on the grounds that it was not legally recognized as 'the territory of a High Contracting

---

[97] GCIV Article 4(2). [98] Ibid, Article 35. [99] Ibid, Article 42.
[100] Ibid, Article 33. [101] Ibid, Article 34. [102] Ibid, Article 49.
[103] Ibid, Articles 50–78.

Party' (ie Jordan) as required by Article 2 of the Convention, this argument has never been accepted by the international community; in any event, Israel claims to apply the provisions of the Convention on a *de facto* basis.[104] The principal criterion for the applicability of the law of belligerent occupation, as stated in Article 42 of The Hague Regulations, is that territory be 'actually placed under the authority of the hostile army... where such authority has been established and can be exercised'. The legal status of the territory prior to occupation is therefore irrelevant: the test for determining the existence of an occupation under customary international law is the factual one of effective control.[105] By the same token, *de facto* annexation or other changes to the legal status of the occupied territory—as were effected by Israel in East Jerusalem and the Golan Heights in 1967, by Argentina in the Falkland Islands in 1982 and by Iraq in Kuwait in 1990—cannot affect the *de jure* application of the law of belligerent occupation.[106] Those parts of the West Bank that are under the jurisdiction of the Palestinian Authority since the implementation of the Oslo Accords in 1993 are technically no longer under belligerent occupation; neither, since Israel's withdrawal in 2005, is the Gaza Strip, although uncertainty persists in relation to the latter, in light of Israel's continuing control over its borders, coast and airspace (Shany, 2005).

The comparatively brief occupation of Iraq gave rise to a different set of concerns under IHL. Although the US and UK, as the leading members of the Coalition Provisional Authority (CPA), formally accepted that they were *de jure* Occupying Powers within the meaning of Geneva Convention IV, the situation in Iraq from April 2003 was one of *debellatio*—the total defeat and extinction of authority in the occupied territory, a situation that had not occurred since the unconditional surrender of Germany in 1945. Occupying Powers are under an obligation to respect, 'unless absolutely prevented', the laws previously in force in the occupied territory,[107] because belligerent occupation in no way grants legal title to the Occupying Power and cannot affect the legal status of the territory under general international law: thus, Iraq continued to be a sovereign State in international law, although its powers of government were temporarily exercised by the CPA. The latter, however, substantively changed Iraqi law on a number of matters, most notably by the wholesale privatization of Iraq's previous centrally planned economy and opening it up to foreign investment, providing tax incentives for foreign corporations wishing to do business in the country and suspending all trade tariffs. The CPA also amended Iraqi criminal law by providing for the immunity of foreign contractors in Iraqi courts. The CPA's delegation to the Iraqi Governing Council of the power to create a special civilian court for the trial of officials of Saddam Hussein's regime was also problematic, as the Occupying Power may only create 'non-political military courts' for offences committed against the Occupying Power,[108] or for breaches of the laws and customs of war;[109] the CPA could not, therefore, have delegated a power which it did not itself possess.

The experience of occupation in Iraq also demonstrated the significance of involvement by the UN Security Council in mandating the occupation regime. The Council

---

[104] *Legal Consequences of the Construction of a Wall in the Occupied Palestine Territory, Advisory Opinion, ICJ Reports 2004*, p 136, paras 90–101.

[105] Cf *Armed Activities on the Territory of the Congo (Democratic Republic of the Congo v Uganda), ICJ Reports 2005*, p 168, paras 172–178.

[106] See, on Israel, SC Res 681 (20 December 1990); on Iraq, SC Res 670 (25 September 1990).

[107] HR Article 43.   [108] GCIV Article 66.   [109] Ibid, Article 70.

gave an *ex post facto* mandate to the CPA[110] which in some respects, as noted above, went further than the traditional law of belligerent occupation would permit (Scheffer, 2003; Kaikobad, 2005; Roberts, 2006); nevertheless, as binding obligations imposed by the Council under Chapter VII of the UN Charter, they have been judicially interpreted (in accordance with Article 103 of the Charter) as overriding restrictions derived from IHL.[111]

VI. THE LAW IN NON-INTERNATIONAL ARMED CONFLICTS

A substantial majority of the armed conflicts that have taken place since 1945 have been non-international in nature, yet none of the substantive LOAC applied to such conflicts before the adoption of Common Article 3 of the Geneva Conventions in 1949 and the concept of liability for war crimes committed in such conflicts was not enunciated until the ICTY's 1995 decision in *Tadić*. In that case, the Appeals Chamber opined that, 'What is inhumane, and consequently proscribed, in international wars, cannot but be inhumane and inadmissible in civil strife.'[112] Neither Common Article 3 nor the 1977 Additional Protocol II included any provision for individual criminal responsibility; nor did they purport to regulate methods and means of warfare, but focused exclusively on the protection of victims.

Common Article 3 has been described as 'a Convention in miniature' (Pictet, 1952, p 48) and 'a minimum yardstick' of humanitarian protection in all armed conflicts, whatever their characterization.[113] It requires that persons taking no part in hostilities, including those who have surrendered or are *hors de combat*, be treated humanely and without adverse discrimination; to that end, it prohibits 'violence to life and person', hostage-taking, humiliating and degrading treatment, and 'the passing of sentences and the carrying out of executions without previous judgment pronounced by a regularly constituted court…'. Within three decades recognition of the generality and vagueness of these provisions resulted in more detailed provision for fundamental guarantees, treatment of the wounded and sick, and protection of the civilian population in Additional Protocol II.

However, with a mere 15 substantive articles (compared to 84 in Protocol I), and no concept of grave breaches or compulsory enforcement, Protocol II is widely viewed as lacking teeth. It took a horrified Security Council's response to the Rwandan genocide to secure the Protocol's enforcement by criminal prosecutions, and even that was on a strictly ad hoc basis.[114] The *Tadić* decision played a seminal role in expanding, and providing some detail on, the rules of customary IHL applicable in non-international armed conflicts; a charge to which the ICRC returned with its 2005 *Study on Customary International*

---

[110] SC Res 1483 (22 May 2003), 1511 (16 October 2003) and 1546 (8 June 2004).

[111] *R (Al-Jedda) v Secretary of State for Defence* [2007] UKHL 58; [2008] 1 AC 332.

[112] *Prosecutor v Dusko Tadić*, Decision on the Defence Motion for Interlocutory Appeal on Jurisdiction (Interlocutory Appeal), Case No IT-94-1-AR72 (2 October 1995), para 516.

[113] *Military and Paramilitary Activities In and Against Nicaragua (Nicaragua v United States of America)*, *ICJ Reports 1986*, p 14, para 218.

[114] SC Res 955 (8 November 1994).

Humanitarian Law. Although these creative approaches have not been uncontroversial, largely due to methodological concerns surrounding the deduction of customary norms of international law (Wilmshurst and Breau, 2007), and the fact that certain States not party to the Protocols have seen the *Study* as an attempt to import various rules contained in those instruments 'by the back door' of custom,[115] they have served the valuable function of ensuring that the question of detailed legal regulation of conduct in non-international armed conflicts does not become a dead letter.

As noted in relation to the scope of application of IHL, there is a spectrum of conflict: apart from internal disturbances and tensions—including, in the British interpretation, acts of terrorism—which are not subject to LOAC at all, the lowest level is conflict 'not of an international character', which is governed by Common Article 3. If non-State forces have sufficient control of territory to satisfy the requirements of Protocol II, non-international conflicts are governed by the Protocol in addition to Common Article 3; finally, if other States intervene the conflict may become 'internationalized', leading to the application of the Geneva Conventions in full, plus Protocol I if the States concerned are parties thereto.

VII. IMPLEMENTATION AND ENFORCEMENT

Notwithstanding chronic weaknesses in the enforcement of international law generally, there are several methods by which compliance with IHL may be secured. In roughly ascending order of impact and effectiveness, these are:

1. recourse to belligerent reprisals;
2. States' responsibility for violations committed by their armed forces;
3. States' duty to disseminate IHL and provide for its instruction to their armed forces;
4. commanders' duty to supervise conduct and repress violations;
5. States' duty to implement IHL by providing criminal sanctions for its violation in their national legal systems;
6. criminal investigation and, where appropriate, prosecution of individuals accused of violations; and
7. external scrutiny and pressure by third parties.

A. REPRISALS

Belligerent reprisals—not to be confused with armed reprisals under the *jus ad bellum*—are violations of LOAC which may be permitted in response to prior violations by the enemy, as long as they are proportionate to those prior violations and have no other object than securing the cessation of illegal activity by the adverse party (Kalshoven, 1971). Historically they were seen as a not only legitimate, but often quite effective, method of

---

[115] See US Departments of State and Defense, *Letter to International Committee of the Red Cross Regarding Customary International Law Study* (2006) 46 ILM 514; also Parks, 2005.

forcing an enemy to comply with the law; however, the extent to which they have survived modern trends in both warfare and law since 1949 is doubtful. The Geneva Conventions prohibit reprisals against any persons protected by those instruments[116] and Protocol I additionally prohibits them against the civilian population and civilian objects generally.[117] Although these treaty provisions are clear, the extent to which reprisals are prohibited in customary law remains uncertain. Their last documented substantial use in an international armed conflict was during the Iran-Iraq War (1980–1988), when each belligerent attacked the other's cities and claimed that they were engaged in limited reprisals to stop similar attacks by the enemy (Henckaerts and Doswald-Beck, 2005, vol I, pp 521–522). The ICRC's *Customary Law Study* asserted that reprisals are also prohibited in non-international armed conflicts, a position which is arguably difficult to maintain in the light of State practice and *opinio juris* (Wilmshurst and Breau, 2007, pp 370–372).

The essential problem with reprisals is the risk that, 'far from enforcing the law, [they] can produce an escalating spiral of atrocities completely undermining respect for the law' (Greenwood, 1989, p 36), thereby achieving precisely the opposite effect to what was intended. The British use of poison gas on the Western Front in 1915, for instance, although intended as retaliation for the German use of the weapon, simply resulted in its adoption on all fronts and by all belligerents for the duration of World War I. Today, while many States expressly reserve the right to take belligerent reprisals, they generally do so with stringent conditions attached and subject to political approval at the highest level.[118]

B. STATE RESPONSIBILITY

As a general rule of public international law, States are legally responsible, and liable to pay compensation, for violations of LOAC committed by their armed forces. The rule is enunciated with reference to international armed conflicts in Article 3 of The Hague Convention IV (1907), and reparations have been required from defeated enemies in respect of their troops' depredations: for example, Part VIII of the Treaty of Versailles (1919), requiring Germany to pay compensation to the Allied Powers, was based upon the notion of German responsibility for the damage inflicted on Allied lives and property, especially in Belgium and France, during World War I. In 1991, the Security Council confirmed Iraq's legal responsibility for depredations of its troops during the occupation of Kuwait and established a UN Compensation Commission to process claims and allocate compensation for losses resulting therefrom.[119] Following the conclusion of their 1998–2000 conflict in the Horn of Africa, Ethiopia and Eritrea agreed the establishment of a joint Claims Commission to arbitrate all claims for loss or damage, including violations of IHL, which had occurred in the conflict.[120]

The weakness of the State responsibility doctrine in the armed conflict context is that it does not cover responsibility for violations committed by non-State actors: it is easy to hold States to account for their armed forces' actions in asymmetric conflicts, but their

---

[116] GCI Article 46, GCII Article 47, GCIII Article 13 and GCIV Article 33.

[117] API Articles 51(6), 52(1), 53(c), 54(4), 55(2) and 56(4).

[118] UK Ministry of Defence, 2004, paras 16.16–16.19.   [119] SC Res 687 (3 April 1991).

[120] See, eg, *Partial Awards on Prisoners of War (Ethiopia's Claim 4)* (2003) 42 ILM 1056; *Eritrea's Claim 17*, ibid, 1083.

irregular opponents fall outside the framework of State responsibility (unless a subsequent government adopts legal responsibility for their actions, as was done by the State of Israel in respect of the assassination of Count Folke Bernadotte by members of the Stern Gang in 1949 or their actions are actually imputable to another State).

C. DISSEMINATION AND SUPERVISION

In order to ensure that soldiers are aware of their rights and duties under international law, the Geneva Conventions and Protocol I impose obligations upon States parties to disseminate their provisions to their armed forces, and as widely as possible among the civilian population at large.[121] Most armed forces, therefore, have training programmes which include instruction in LOAC, both internally and by way of attendance at external (often academic) courses. Dissemination is usually undertaken by the military legal advisory services of the armed forces themselves,[122] but in the case of States that lack the relevant in-house military legal expertise, the ICRC plays a crucial and extensive role by providing seminars, training materials, consultancy, and other assistance.

Arguably the most crucial aspect of ensuring compliance in the armed forces is military discipline and the role of the commander in the supervision of conduct and repression of violations. Article 43(1) of Protocol I requires that armed forces 'shall be subject to an internal disciplinary system which, *inter alia*, shall enforce compliance with the rules of international law applicable in armed conflict'. The key component in such a system is the commander, who must ensure that the troops under his command comply with LOAC and must therefore himself be familiar with his rights and responsibilities. The contemporary law of command responsibility, which in modern terms is based on Article 86(2) of Protocol I, holds the commander liable if he:

1. personally himself sees or hears of illegal acts being committed;
2. receives reports of the illegal conduct of his troops through his officers (commissioned or not), staff and chain of command, yet fails to act to put a stop to their violations; or
3. is so negligent or reckless in the discharge of his command that he is unaware of the conduct of his troops.[123]

Article 87 then requires commanders to prevent and suppress violations of the law and report them to the appropriate authorities; it requires, however, that commanders be 'aware' of violations.

In a famous precedent in 1946, the former Commander-in-Chief of Japanese forces in the Philippines was executed as a war criminal despite his lack of knowledge, due to a breakdown in communications and the chain of command, of atrocities committed by troops under his overall command in Manila;[124] the modern doctrine, however, requires that a commander have actual effective control—not merely nominal or titular authority—over

---

[121] GCI Article 47, GCII Article 48, GCIII Article 127, GCIV Article 144 and API Article 83.

[122] The requirement to have such military legal advisory services is itself an obligation of API Article 82.

[123] A commander who gives an illegal order or himself commits a criminal act is of course equally liable, but not under the doctrine of command responsibility, which is concerned only with acts of omission.

[124] *Application of Yamashita* (1946) 327 US 1.

troops and actual knowledge of, or information concerning, crimes being committed,[125] a position which arguably gives rise to a concept of the 'reasonable commander'. Thus the standard of knowledge has shifted from a 'should have known' to a 'knew or had reason to know' test, a position which is undoubtedly fairer to the individual commander.

D. IMPLEMENTATION AND PROSECUTION

The most dramatic, although not the most effective, way of securing compliance with LOAC is to investigate and punish violations after they have occurred, through either international or national criminal courts. Acceptance of individual criminal responsibility for such crimes has been uncontroversial since the Nuremberg and Tokyo Trials after World War II. On the international level, the creation of the ICTY (1993) and International Criminal Tribunal for Rwanda (1994), followed by the establishment of other specialized criminal tribunals to deal with atrocities in Sierra Leone and Cambodia, among others, heralded a new age of activism in this respect. The first decade of the twenty-first century has seen the establishment of the world's first permanent International Criminal Court.

For centuries, States have asserted the right to prosecute both captured enemy nationals for violations of the laws and customs of war and their own soldiers for similar offences charged under national military or criminal law. Violations of the laws and customs of war, generically described as war crimes, are subject to universal criminal jurisdiction in customary international law; other types of offences specifically relevant, though not limited to, armed conflicts are crimes against humanity and genocide. States will usually have recourse to international war crimes law only when prosecuting foreign nationals; violations committed by its own troops will normally be treated as offences under the ordinary national criminal or military law. Thus, Lieutenant William Calley was charged with four counts of premeditated murder in violation of Article 118 of the US Uniform Code of Military Justice for his role in the massacre of Vietnamese civilians at My Lai in 1968. In respect of war crimes, the Geneva Conventions and Protocol I place all States parties under a duty to investigate and prosecute grave breaches of those instruments, or extradite suspects to another State; they must also enact legislation implementing these offences in their national criminal law.[126] In the UK, as in many other countries, there is special legislation in force to give effect to these obligations.[127] The degree of scrupulousness with which States investigate and prosecute violations committed by their own armed forces varies considerably, but it has certainly been a significant aspect of the response to violations committed by British forces in Iraq in 2003–2004.[128]

Liability for war crimes applies throughout the military hierarchy. As discussed above, commanders are responsible for the acts of their subordinates; conversely a soldier cannot plead, in defence to a war crimes charge, that he was following superior orders—in the UK as in many other States, soldiers are clearly forbidden to obey illegal orders. This represents

---

[125] *Prosecutor v Hadžihasanović & Kubura*, Judgment, Case No IT-01-47-T, Trial Chamber II, (15 March 2006).

[126] GCI Article 49, GCII Article 50, GCIII Article 129, GCIV Article 146, API Articles 85, 86(1), 88, and 89.

[127] Geneva Conventions Act 1957, Geneva Conventions (Amendment) Act 1995, International Criminal Court Act 2001, Geneva Conventions and United Nations Personnel (Protocols) Act 2009.

[128] See UK Ministry of Defence, *The Aitken Report—An Investigation into Cases of Deliberate Abuse and Unlawful Killing in Iraq in 2003 and 2004*, 25 January 2008.

a shift from the widely held pre-1944 position that superior orders were an absolute defence to a war crimes charge and a soldier would be liable to court-martial if he refused to obey an order,[129] and is clearly preferable in that otherwise, the vast majority of perpetrators would invariably be able to escape liability for their acts. It is equally no defence to claim that a war crime was committed for reasons of military necessity: allowance for the exigencies of military necessity is already made in many LOAC treaties, so that conduct that would otherwise constitute a violation may be permitted in certain circumstances. But if the rule is an absolute one, such as the prohibition of the wilful killing of protected persons, a plea of military necessity would be rejected.[130]

Prosecutions are an imperfect tool for enforcing LOAC: the difficulties of securing reliable evidence in respect of incidents occurring in combat conditions—leading many cases to be abandoned or dismissed—cannot be underestimated. It is also true that war crimes trials are often derided as 'victor's justice', in the sense that the defeated party does not have a chance to hold its enemies to account for ill-conduct. Nevertheless, they are often the prism through which consciousness of IHL is embedded in the general public.

E. EXTERNAL SCRUTINY

The proliferation of media reporting of abuses in armed conflicts since the early 1990s has had the effect of greatly increasing the importance of external scrutiny of States' forces' conduct and pressure for investigations. Sometimes this comes from public opinion, but more frequently it is prompted by reports from non-governmental organizations like Human Rights Watch or international organizations like the UN and its specialized agencies.[131] This sort of external pressure is not mandated by the law, but it can help to generate an independent process of internal scrutiny, which in turn can contribute to increased respect for the law. The Geneva Conventions and Protocol I, however, in any event make provision for monitoring compliance with IHL by the mechanisms of the Protecting Power system and the International Humanitarian Fact-Finding Commission.

The Protecting Power system pre-dates World War II and in its current form is contained in all four 1949 Conventions.[132] It was instituted to enable a belligerent in an international armed conflict to designate another State, the Protecting Power, to represent its interests and those of its nationals *vis-à-vis* enemy belligerents in matters relating to the conflict. The Protecting Power has rights of access to POW and detention camps, may attend trials of POWs and civilians held by the enemy belligerent, and may make representations to the enemy belligerent concerning compliance with LOAC generally. In the Falklands War the UK designated Switzerland and Argentina designated Brazil to act as their respective Protecting Powers; but on the whole the system has been underused in contemporary conflicts, usually because one side is reluctant to agree to the other side's nominee. Neither the Iran-Iraq, nor the Second Gulf, Wars saw the appointment of any

---

[129] Although this would not be the case if the order was manifestly illegal: see *The Llandovery Castle* (1921) 16 AJIL 708.

[130] *The Peleus Trial* [1945] I LRTWC 1.

[131] Eg UN Human Rights Council, *Report of the United Nations Fact-Finding Mission on the Gaza Conflict*, UN Doc A/HRC/12/48, 25 September 2009; Res A/HRC/RES/S-12/1.B, 16 October 2009.

[132] GCI, GCII, GCIII Article 10; GCIV Article 11.

Protecting Powers. Indeed, since 1949, only four international armed conflicts have seen Protecting Powers designated by both parties (Wylie, 2006, p 13).[133]

The International Humanitarian Fact-Finding Commission, which became operational in 1992, is mandated by Article 90 of Protocol I to investigate allegations of violations of the Protocol and the Conventions, but it may only act at the invitation of a State that has recognized its competence and only against a State that has indicated the same acceptance (to date seventy-one of the States parties to the Protocol have done so). Its reports are confidential to the parties concerned and it has no power of enforcement.

Finally, it is pertinent to mention the invaluable role of the ICRC, which not only seeks to provide humanitarian assistance to the victims of armed conflicts, but also is an indefatigable advocate of IHL and, in particular, of the Geneva Conventions and their Additional Protocols. The ICRC operates under very strict limitations as to publicity—its reports on unrestricted inspection visits to POW and detention camps are confidential, although one on ill-treatment of Iraqi detainees held by the Coalition in 2004 was famously leaked—and also depends on the consent of the parties to the conflict for their voluntary co-operation, although the latter must accept any offer by the ICRC to fulfil the humanitarian functions of a Protecting Power where none is appointed. It usually restricts itself to making private representations to the parties concerned, to urge them to comply with their obligations under IHL. Nevertheless, it does sometimes issue public reminders to all parties in a conflict to respect IHL and generally commands unrivalled respect and efficacy in improving compliance with the law in armed conflicts.

REFERENCES

BENVENISTI, E (1993), *The International Law of Occupation* (Princeton: Princeton University Press).

BYRON, C (2001), 'Armed Conflicts: International or Non-International?', 6 *JCSL* 63.

—— (2007), 'A Blurring of the Boundaries: The Application of International Humanitarian Law by Human Rights Bodies', 47 *Virginia JIL* 839.

DRAPER, GIAD (1965), 'The Interaction of Christianity and Chivalry in the Historical Development of the Law of War', 46 *Int Rev Red Cross* 3.

GREEN, LC (2008), *The Contemporary Law of Armed Conflict*, 3rd edn (Manchester: Manchester University Press).

GREENBERG, KJ and DATREL, JL (2005), *The Torture Papers* (Cambridge: Cambridge University Press).

GREENWOOD, C (1989), 'The Twilight of the Law of Belligerent Reprisals', 20 *Neth YBIL* 35.

HAPPOLD, M (2005), *Child Soldiers in International Law* (Manchester: Manchester University Press).

HENCKAERTS, J-M and DOSWALD-BECK, L (eds) (2005), *Customary International Humanitarian Law* (Cambridge: Cambridge University Press).

JESSUP, PC (1954), 'Should international law recognize an intermediate status between peace and war?', 48 *AJIL* 98.

---

[133] Since the 2008 conflict between Russia and Georgia, Switzerland has acted as Protecting Power for both States.

KAIKOBAD, KH (2005), 'Problems of Belligerent Occupation', 43 *ICLQ* 253.

KALSHOVEN, F (1971), *Belligerent Reprisals* (Leiden: Nijhoff).

LAUTERPACHT, H (1952), 'The Problem of Revision of the Law of War', 29 *BYIL* 382.

MAOZ, A (2005), 'War and Peace—an Israeli Perspective', 24 *Constitutional Forum* 35.

MEYER, MA (1983), 'Liability of Prisoners of War for Offences Committed Prior to Capture: The Astiz Affair', 32 *ICLQ* 948.

MOIR, L (2002), *The Law of Internal Armed Conflict* (Cambridge: Cambridge University Press).

PARKS, WH (2003), 'Special Forces' Wear of Non-Standard Uniforms', 4 *Chicago JIL* 493.

—— (2005), 'The ICRC Customary Law Study: a Preliminary Assessment', *ASIL Proceedings* 208.

PICTET, J (ed) (1952), *Commentary on the Geneva Convention (I) for the Amelioration of the Condition of the Wounded and Sick in Armed Forces in the Field* (Geneva: ICRC).

ROBERTS, A (2006), 'Transformative Military Occupation: Applying the Laws of War and Human Rights', 100 *AJIL* 580.

—— and GUELFF, R (2000), *Documents on the Laws of War*, 3rd edn (Oxford: Oxford University Press).

ROGERS, APV (2004), *Law on the Battlefield*, 2nd edn (Manchester: Manchester University Press).

ROWE, PJ (ed) (1993), *The Gulf War 1990–91 in International and English Law* (London: Routledge).

SCHEFFER, DJ (2003), 'Beyond Occupation Law', 97 *AJIL* 842.

SHANY, Y (2005), 'Faraway, So Close: The Legal Status of Gaza After Israel's Disengagement', 8 *YBIHL* 369.

SIVAKUMARAN, S (2006), 'Binding armed opposition groups', 55 *ICLQ* 369.

TURNS, D (2006), 'Weapons in the ICRC Study on Customary International Humanitarian Law', 11 *JCSL* 201.

UNITED KINGDOM MINISTRY OF DEFENCE (2004), *The Manual of the Law of Armed Conflict* (Oxford: Oxford University Press).

WALKER, CP (1984), 'Irish Republican Prisoners—Political Detainees, Prisoners of War or Common Criminals?', XIX *The Irish Jurist* 89.

WLMSHURST, E and BREAU, S (eds) (2007), *Perspectives on the ICRC Study on Customary International Humanitarian Law* (Cambridge: Cambridge University Press).

WYLIE, N (2006), 'Protecting powers in a changing world', 40 *Politorbis* 6.

FURTHER READING

The literature on this area of law has grown exponentially in the last 15 years. What follows is a necessarily selective list of suggestions for further reading in the area; all the works cited either provide insightful general commentary on international humanitarian law, or focus detailed analysis on specific topics within the area.

GENERAL

FLECK, D (ed) (2008), *The Handbook of International Humanitarian Law* (Oxford: Oxford University Press).

GREENWOOD, C (1987), 'The Concept of War in Modern International Law', 36 *ICLQ* 283.

—— (1996), 'International Humanitarian Law and the *Tadić Case*', 7 *EJIL* 265.

NEFF, S (2005), *War and the Law of Nations: A General History* (Cambridge: Cambridge University Press).

SCHMITT, MN (2007), '21st Century Conflict: Can the Law Survive?', 8 *Melb JIL* 443.

SCOPE OF APPLICATION

GREEN, LC (1951), 'The Nature of the "War" in Korea', 4 *ILQ* 462.

GREENWOOD, C (2003), 'War, Terrorism and International Law', 56 *Current Legal Problems* 505.

ROBERTS, A (2005), 'Counter-terrorism, armed force and the laws of war', 44 *Survival* 7.

STEWART, JG (2003), 'Towards a single definition of armed conflict in international humanitarian law: A critique of internationalized armed conflict', 850 *Int Rev Red Cross* 313.

TURNS, D (2007), 'The "War on Terror" Through British and International Humanitarian Law Eyes: Comparative Perspectives on Selected Legal Issues', 10 *NY City LR* 435.

CONDUCT OF HOSTILITIES

CORN, GS (2005), ' "Snipers in the Minaret— What is the Rule?" The Law of War and the Protection of Cultural Property: A Complex Equation', *The Army Lawyer* 28.

CRYER, R (2002), 'The Fine Art of Friendship: *Jus in Bello* in Afghanistan', 7 *JCSL* 37.

DINSTEIN, Y (2004), *The Conduct of Hostilities under the Law of International Armed Conflict* (Cambridge: Cambridge University Press).

GREENWOOD, C (1988), 'Belligerent Reprisals and the 1977 Protocols to the Geneva Conventions of 1949', 37 *ICLQ* 818.

SCHMITT, MN (2005), 'Precision attack and international humanitarian law', 859 *Int Rev Red Cross* 445.

PROTECTION OF VICTIMS

DÖRMANN, K (2003), 'The Legal Situation of "Unlawful/Unprivileged Combatants"', 850 *Int Rev Red Cross* 45.

HAMPSON, FJ (1991), 'The Geneva Conventions and the Detention of Civilians and Alleged Prisoners of War', *Public Law* 507.

ROBERTS, A (2005), 'The End of Occupation: Iraq 2004', 54 *ICLQ* 27.

IMPLEMENTATION AND ENFORCEMENT

BANTEKAS, I (1999), 'The Contemporary Law of Superior Responsibility', 93 *AJIL* 573.

GARRAWAY, C (1999), 'Superior Orders and the International Criminal Court: Justice Delivered or Justice Denied?', 836 *Int Rev Red Cross* 785.

ROGERS, APV (1990), 'War Crimes Trials under the Royal Warrant: British Practice 1945–1949', 39 *ICLQ* 780.

INDEX